THE LAWN TENNIS ASSOCIATION

Official Handbook
incorporating the LTA Club Manual
sponsored by The Prudential Assurance Company Limited

Patron: Her Majesty The Queen

Founded 1888

The heraldic description of the LTA Arms is as follows:
Azure, three escutcheons argent, that in the dexter chief charged with a rose gules leaved and slipped proper and enfiled with a ducal coronet or, that in the sinister chief charged with a thistle leaved and slipped proper and enfiled with a like coronet, and that in base charged with a daffodil leaved and slipped proper and also enfiled with a like coronet, all within a bordure checky argent and sable.

The Lawn Tennis Association
Barons Court, London W14 9EG
Telephone: 01-385 2366
Telex: 8956036

Designed and Published for the LTA by Dennis Fairey & Associates Ltd
Photography by Tommy Hindley
Articles commissioned and edited by David Irvine
Produced by the LTA Handbook Committee
Printed by Geerings of Ashford Ltd
ISBN 0-9510215-1-6
ISSN 0269-0454

CONTENTS

The views expressed in the articles published do not necessarily reflect the opinion of The Lawn Tennis Association and consequently must be treated as the sole opinion of the respective authors.

FOREWORD BY THE EDITOR

It was in 1980 that the Lawn Tennis Association introduced this, the first British tennis annual. In the foreword to that edition the belief was expressed that it would eventually become a 'must' for every follower of the game. It has taken time but now we feel that that prediction has been well justified.

We are able to present this, our seventh edition, confident in the knowledge that we now have a publication which forms an integral part of tennis literature. Confident — but not, we trust, complacent.

We sincerely hope that our readers, old as well as new, will find Tennis Great Britain 1986 even more comprehensive in its coverage than those which preceded it, an authoratative reference work embodying not only the relevant facts and figures but offering an insight into its future development.

Though essentially a work of record we could not resist the opportunity to look forward to a special landmark which falls due this summer — the 100th Wimbledon. And, in this, we could not have done more than enlist the help of Kitty Godfree, the oldest surviving champion, and Lance Tingay, the doyen of tennis writers.

There are special features too on County Week, one of the last great bastions of amateur tennis, and the extensive development work undertaken by the LTA to promote the junior game.

Finally my thanks to all who have contributed articles and photographs and helped in so many ways towards the book's preparation.

David Irvine
Editor

MESSAGE FROM THE PRESIDENT

1986 is a very important year for our Association. Following a further look at our administration structure, a new position has been created with the appointment of an Executive Director, Ian Peacock. He will head up a very strong team of executives at Headquarters. One of his tasks will be the marketing and development of our game in this country.

We wish all success to our Davis Cup team on their return to the World Group, and also to our national ladies' team who will compete in the annual Nabisco Wightman Cup match with the U.S.A. at the Royal Albert Hall, in the Federation Cup and in the new Ladies' European Cup.

Our National Training Centre and Tennis School at Bisham Abbey are a veritable hive of tennis activity and the exciting experiment of the school continues to expand. It is too early to say for sure whether the principle of an elite corps is the right one or not, but if effort and dedication are anything to go by we have every chance of success.

1985 has seen the first year of one of the largest and far-sighted projects ever undertaken by the L.T.A. A nationwide network of full-time regions, each with a National Coach/Development Officer working from what is in effect a branch office of the L.T.A., with the support of a secretary, part-time regional coaching staff and within a comprehensive committee structure, is now fully operational. Almost 1,000 boys and girls of all junior ages are currently receiving regional training.

Closely interwoven with the L.T.A.'s development plans is that of the Lawn Tennis Foundation. Originally set up to give the L.T.A. a smart kick in the pants for not paying enough attention to grass roots, it has through loss of sponsorship become increasingly funded by the L.T.A. Far now from being a separate critical element, it enjoys responsibility for looking after the expanding base of our pyramid. This is a vital part of the L.T.A.'s role.

Positive steps are now being taken to encourage youngsters to participate. Every endeavour is being made to link with Local Authorities and to solve the problem of the lack of encouragement and facilities for tennis in schools.

The very successful introduction of short tennis and the Prudential Junior Coaching Scheme are without doubt bringing into the game thousands who might not otherwise have picked up a racket. The spread of Junior Tennis Centres, which are junior clubs on public courts, is a pointer to the way forward, and the total of 124 established in 1985 will be doubled or even trebled this year. Few clubs have junior vacancies and this is a way of providing children alternative opportunities to play at times when they can.

This initiative has only been achieved through close co-operation with the Local Authorities, and negotiations for 1986 are now in hand with many Parks and Recreation Departments, encouraging them to set up their own development schemes, giving them help and expertise, and hoping therefore to create a climate where tennis can flourish.

There are distinct signs of growth at grass roots level and the widening of the base with the increase in the number of people playing tennis. My Association is well aware of its responsibilities for harnessing the growth and encouraging improvements in existing facilities at both club and public level. A priority will be to continue to encourage the building of more indoor courts throughout the country.

The aims of this annual publication are to promote tennis to the public in this country and to serve as a directory of information and statistics at national, county and club level.

Geoff Brown
President, The L.T.A.

MEET THE NEW 'SUPREMO'

BY MALCOLM FOLLEY

Ian Peacock knew the moment when he accepted the invitation to become the first director of the Lawn Tennis Association that he would be required to work under continual public scrutiny. People with the interests of British tennis at heart want results, not excuses. "Management in a goldfish bowl" is Peacock's description of the job he started at Baron's Court on January 2. "I recognise that, and it's an additional challenge," he says.

When the LTA Board of Management selected 51-year-old Peacock to fill the new, challenging post they chose a man steeped in commercial experience. "I am a marketing man at heart, and tennis has an extremely interesting marketing problem," he explains.

After a national service commission in the RAF, Peacock joined the sports goods firm Slazenger as a trainee salesman in 1955. His father, and uncle, were both golf professionals and the young Peacock had early designs on following their example. "In those days, it wasn't such a glamorous life as it is today and, besides. I didn't think I was good enough to make it," he says. "My father didn't encourage me to become a golf pro. He felt I'd be better off in the world of commerce."

Twenty-one years after joining Slazenger he became managing director of the company. In 1983 a radical company shake-up, involving the merger of the Dunlop and Slazenger brands, caused Peacock to rethink his future. "I had been with the company a long time, and had an enormous amount of pleasure, but it seemed a good opportunity to change the direction of my life."

He resigned to start his own sports market research company in a converted garage in Horley, Surrey where Malcolm Campbell built Bluebird. But the opportunity to play a major role in the future of British tennis proved an irresistable attraction. He had no hesitation in accepting the terms of reference offered. Peacock argues: "I wouldn't have taken the job, and given up a viable business, if I had not felt I would be able to make a personal contribution.

"Having said that, I've always believed, in business terms, evolution is better than revolution. I would see my role evolving and the level of influence I have expanding as time goes on. I think it would be naive, and impractical, to imagine that an organisation as well-structured as the LTA would change its style overnight. I would not expect that to happen. But I would hope that in time my ability to direct the resources of the Association would increase. That's what the Board of Management want, and I believe that's what will happen."

Wherever Peacock travels one question is repeatedly aimed at him: "When are you going to find Britain's Boris Becker?" Patiently, he replies: "It would have been very ingenious of me to take on the job given that the brief was to produce a Wimbledon champion in three years. That isn't the brief at all."

His objective, he says, is to broaden the base of the game in Britain, to create a climate suitable to breed a future champion. "I'm not in a position to say here is my masterplan to solve the problems of tennis," says Peacock, realistically. "So far we have the problems pretty well analysed. Identification of the correct solutions will take a little longer. I don't want to pontificate, suffice to say that I don't think the problems are insoluble."

Peacock is not a man easily flustered. That quality was never more evident than when he was trapped on the 19th floor of a blazing hotel in Toronto in January 1981. Only the efficiency of the Toronto Fire Department, and the vigilance of a Canadian medic saved his life. That, of course, and his own immense calm, and courage in a situation akin to a scene from the cinema epic 'Towering Inferno'.

Peacock made me promise not to overplay an incident he describes as "an adventure in my past". It's an easy pledge to keep. The facts do not need any journalistic embroidery. He awoke at 2.00 am on that fateful January morning — because his hotel room was smoke-filled. A telephone call to reception confirmed that the hotel was ablaze and he was instructed to escape down the emergency stairs. A quick glance out in the corridor brought little comfort. "The air was yellow and I couldn't see anything," he recalls.

He called reception again. There was nothing they could do. "I looked out of the window and down below I could see fire engines, crowds of people and the glow of the fire, which was coming up the building. At that moment I realised why people jump out of windows. You can see people who are safe, and you're in a bit of trouble. There's a tremendously strong desire to want to join the people who are safe."

Peacock resisted the temptation and, eventually, found the emergency stairs. Down and and down he ran. His last memory is reaching the bottom and seeing a fireman coming towards him. Then he collapsed.

What happened next is best illustrated by the label he keeps at his Surrey home. It reads: 'Unidentified male. Body No. 5'. Ian Peacock had been taken to a hospital mortuary and been assumed dead, along with seven other victims of the fire.

Fortunately some eagle-eyed medic spotted a flicker of movement — and so began the frantic efforts to resuscitate him. He spent five days in intensive care and another three weeks hospitalised before making a complete recovery from carbon monoxide poisoning.

"I am very, very lucky to be alive," he says. Peacock makes his brush with death sound no more harrowing than a visit to the dentist. "It's just a little bit of history, though I guess I do view things slightly differently now."

At the time, Peacock was busily engaged in contractual negotiations with John McEnroe senior, trying to lure McEnroe junior to sign with Slazenger. Mr McEnroe made several calls to the hospital to inquire about his recovery. Peacock, in concert with John Barrett, successfully 'wooed' the McEnroes and developed a product range for John."But when the contract landed at the Dunlop main board, they felt McEnroe ought to be with the company bearing the housename," explained Peacock. That is how McEnroe came to play with a Dunlop racket.

On a personal level, Peacock admires much about McEnroe. On a professional level, he has reservations. "McEnroe has put the game of tennis on the front pages," he says. "If you believe in the philosophy that as long as you spell the name right, any publicity is good publicity, then he has done a hell of a job for tennis. If you look a little deeper, he may have left a legacy that is now being reaped in the United States."

Yet Peacock detects the dawn of a new era in the game, and it is one that fills him with optimism. Hs argues: "People do take their attitudes from the players they look up to and golf, for example, has been incredibly lucky with its superstars. Almost without exception they have set an incredible example to players of all levels.

"Now, tennis has players at the top of the game that people genuinely admire. The climate of the game in Britain looks to be set fair, too."

He is anxious to build on that. "What tennis must do is make itself an attractive game that people want to play," he says. "It is disturbing, but there are barely 20 people in this country making a living from playing tennis. The game loses far too many players who played at school. Somewhere along the line, it fails to convert them into adult players.

"There can be no doubt that the game of tennis is an excellent product.

It's totally international, spans age barriers, can be enjoyed at a variety of skill levels, it's inexpensive and takes about the right length of time to play. But, clearly, something about the product in the post-war era has meant that it has not achieved its full potential in this country. So, it is a very interesting marketing challenge to find where it went wrong. How can you re-present and re-package this product to the public to achieve better results? It is a challenge I look forward to getting my teeth into."

The annual cash bonuses from Wimbledon provides a colossal one-off income for the LTA. But Peacock believes tennis, in cash terms, lags behind most of the other major sports in the country. "In total tennis is poor — but that's not its image," he says. "Much more money circulates in other sports, such as football, cricket and golf."

Peacock believes tennis players in Britain have a low expectation of club subscriptions. "It's a key problem," he insists. "Club members expect to pay around £20-£40. It doesn't generate cash to move around, doesn't encourage development of facilities (crucial, he feels, to prevent youngsters from deserting tennis in favour of another sport), so they can get revenue from bars and restaurants."

While West Germany has 2,500 covered courts, and Sweden boasts 1,200, Britain has just 180. "When we are talking about indoor tennis in this country, we are talking about a relatively new sport. To popularise and develop a new sport takes time. "The area we have to explore is how to create pay-as-you-play covered facilities at a price which is perceived to be acceptable. Until we have the right type of facilities that are readily available, almost any other plan that you put into practice has very little chance of succeeding."

Peacock estimates around one million people play tennis in Britain through the summer months. That figure is reduced, he says, to 50,000 by October. Therein lies the problem he must solve. He is hopeful that objective is not dependent on British team manager Paul Hutchins suddenly discovering a Becker in his midst.

Peacock reasons: "Any work we do in the future must be based on the broadest choice of people from all sections of the community. Our catchment area must be total. But there are objectives that we can set that don't rely on having a Briton playing on the last Sunday of Wimbledon. I think there is a lot we can do, and a lot of ways in which the game can expand in this country, without necessarily having a superstar player.'

As he sets about his task, Ian Peacock deserves our best wishes that he can succeed in his worthy ambition.

BRITISH RANKINGS

MEN

John Lloyd

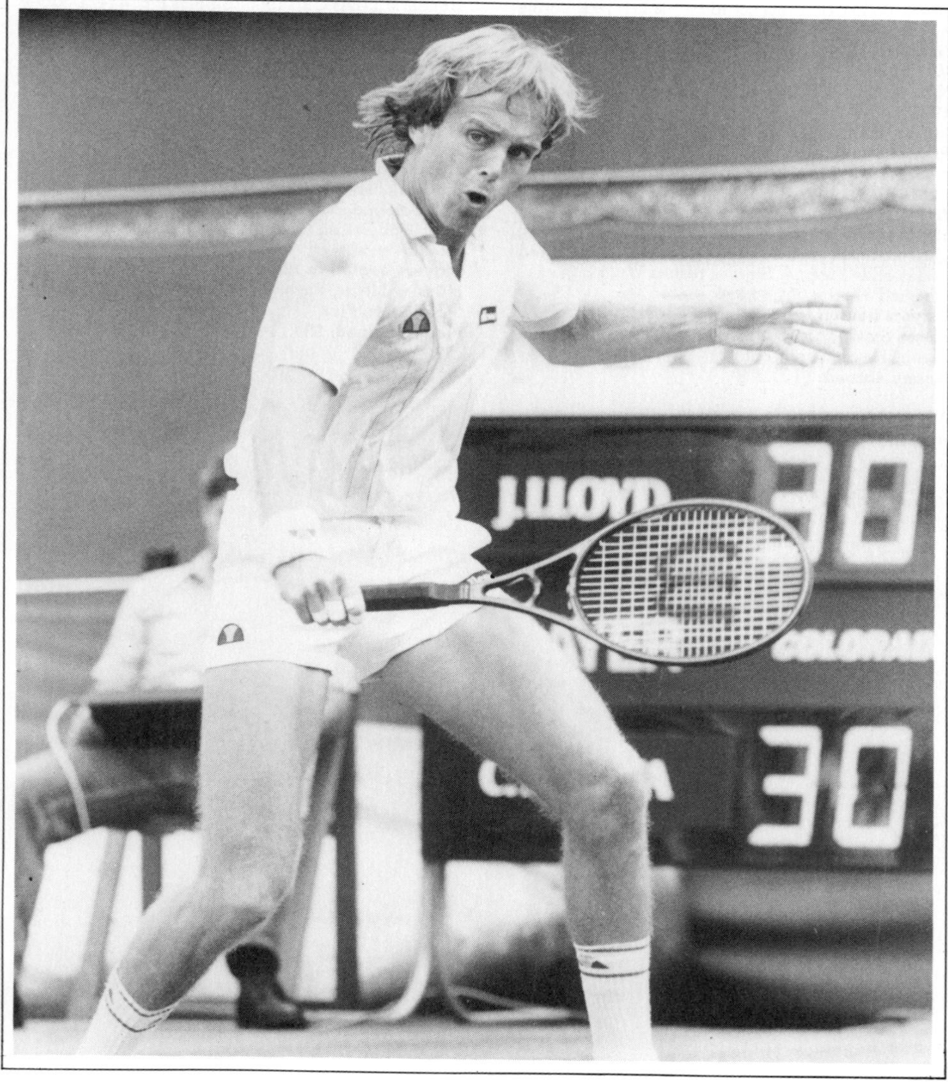

No. 1 JOHN LLOYD

Born: August 27, 1954 at Leigh-on-Sea
Lives: Amelia Island, Florida
Biography: Since Roger Taylor and Mark Cox retired, few players have done more to uphold British men's tennis than Lloyd. Apart from reaching the Australian Open final in 1977 and the US quarters in 1984 he has made more Davis Cup appearances than any other player in the Open era. Has also won two mixed doubles titles at Wimbledon with Wendy Turnbull. Married to the former Chris Evert, he has said this could be his last year on the circuit.
Honours: Davis Cup 1978-80, 83-85 (Singles P 34 W 15 Doubles P 15 W 10). King's Cup 1972-4-6-7-8. Nations Cup 1978-9. Galea Cup 1972-3. BP Cup 1973-4.
Junior titles: Under 16 (1970), Covered Court (1972)
Previous rankings: 1973 (8), 1974 (5), 1975 (4), 1976 (4), 1977 (3), 1978 (2), 1979 (2), 1980 (3), 1981 (-), 1982 (4), 1983 (4), 1984 (2), 1985 (1).
ATP Ranking at the end of 1985: 42
1985 Record: Played 21 Grand Prix tournaments, Quarter-finals at Australian Open, La Quinta, Las Vegas and Cologne. Singles results W 24 L 21. Finished 31st on Grand Prix.
Players beaten in 1985: include Joakim Nystrom, Tomas Smid, Scott Davis, Eliot Teltscher, Mike Leach, Heinz Gunthardt.
Money earned: $120,205

No. 2 JEREMY BATES

Born: June 19, 1962 at Solihull
Lives: Solihull
Biography: used the LTA's satellite circuit as a springboard to a highly successful first year on the Grand Prix, though his finest achievement was in helping Britain recover their position in the first division of the Davis Cup. Confirmed his newfound confidence by becoming national champion at 23. A stylish player with a powerful net game, he seems destined to take over Lloyd's mantle at No. 1.
Honours: Davis Cup 1985 (Singles P 6 W 4, Doubles P 1 W 1) King's Cup 1981-3-4-5. Galea Cup 1980-1-2.
Junior titles: Covered Court (1979). Grass Court (1979).
Previous rankings: 1981 (10), 1982 (6), 1983 (7), 1984 (4), 1985 (4).
ATP Ranking at end of 1985: 99
1985 Record: Played 11 Grand Prix tournaments. Semi-finalist at Tel Aviv, quarter-finalist at Bristol and Cologne. Retained his Manchester grass court title. Won British Closed Championship and several satellite events.
Players beaten in 1985: include Heinz Gunthardt, Miloslav Mecir, Pavel Slozil, Ben Testerman, Terry Moor, Marc Flur.
Money earned: $34,114

Jeremy Bates

No. 3 STEPHEN SHAW

Born: January 1, 1963 at Enfield
Lives: Middlesex
Biography: Failed to live up to early season promise after breaking into world's top 100 in May by reaching the semi-finals at Marbella and, after playing in the Davis Cup against Portugal, lost his place. An early interest in soccer (he had trials for Tottenham) turned to tennis and, from 1980 to 1982, studied at the University of Alabama.
Honours: Davis Cup 1984-5 (Singles P 3 W 1 Doubles P 1 W 1) King's Cup 1983-4-5.
Previous rankings: 1984 (12), 1985 (2).
ATP Ranking at end of 1985: 195
1985 Record: Played 12 Grand Prix events and was a semi-finalist at Marbella. Won doubles at Bordeaux with David Felgate.
Players beaten in 1985: Wally Masur, Marco Ostaja, Diego Perez and Eddie Edwards.
Money earned: $37,226

No. 4 STUART BALE

Born: January 21, 1964 in London
Lives: North London
Biography: Powerfully-built left-hander with aggressive serve-and-volley game who, like Lloyd, is coached by Bob Brett. Qualified against stiff opposition at Milan and Rotterdam in the spring and then spent much of the year competing in the United States, but without making hoped-for progress. Plans to use satellites to improve his ranking in 1986. Represented Britain in Los Angeles Olympics.
Honours: Galea Cup 1982-3-4. King's Cup 1985.
Junior tiles: Grass court (1983).
Previous rankings: 1984 (7), 1985 (6).
APT Ranking at end of 1985: 214
1985 Record: Played Seven Grand Prix tournaments, qualifying in four.
Players beaten in 1985: Guy Forget and John Frawley.
Money earned: $16,893

Stuart Bale

Stephen Shaw

No. 5 COLIN DOWDESWELL

Born: May 12, 1955 in London
Lives: Wimbledon
Biography: Since switching his allegiance to his native country — in the 'seventies he played Davis Cup for Rhodesia — he has proved an adept cup partner for Lloyd. His tournament career, after being ranked 34 in 1983, has slipped disastrously, though he remains a formidable doubles specialist. Plans to re-assess his future at the end of 1986.
Honours: Davis Cup 1984-5 (Singles P 2 W 0, Doubles P 4 W 4) King's Cup 1984.
Previous ranking: 1984 (1), 1985 (3).
APT Ranking at end of 1985: 256
1985 Record: Played 11 Grand Prix tournaments and reached the third round at Stratton Mountain. In doubles won Johannesburg with Christo van Rensburg and Palermo with Joakim Nystrom.
Players beaten in 1985: include Greg Holmes and Glen Layendecker.
Money earned: $36,517

No. 6 NICK FULWOOD

Born: October 2, 1963 at Risley
Lives: Risley
Biography: Under coach Chris Bradnam the 22-year-old Derbyshire player blossomed spectacularly at the Refuge national championships by reaching the men's singles finals and winning the doubles. Had earlier ambushed Dowdeswell in the Ilkley final. His powerful two-handed backhand is his main weapon. His efforts earned him a King's Cup place at the end of the year.
Junior titles: Covered court (1981). Under 16 grass (1979).
Previous rankings: 1983 (12), 1984 (-), 1985 (11).
ATP Ranking at end of 1985: 374
1985 Record: Finalist in British closed championships and a semi-finalist at Manchester. Played in three Grand Prix tournaments.
Players beaten in 1985: include Roberto Saad, Stephen Shaw and Colin Dowdeswell.
Money earned: $5,580

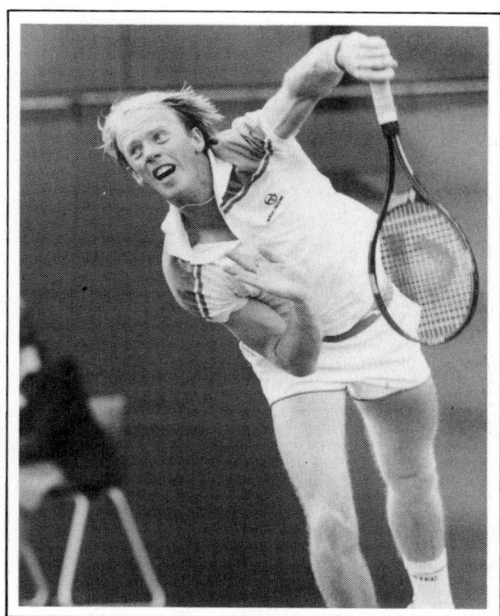

No. 7 JONATHAN SMITH

Born: January 29, 1955 at Exeter
Lives: London
Biography: Moved his base to Germany last season and devoted more time to coaching than playing. Never quite fulfilled his junior promise as champion on three different surfaces but made the last 32 at Wimbledon in 1977. Educated at Millfield and then University of Oregon, Smith's major successes have been in doubles, in which he represented Britain for two years.
Honours: Davis Cup 1981-2 (Doubles P 5 W 2) Galea Cup 1974-5. BP Cup 1975-6.
Junior titles: Covered Court (1973), Hard Court (1973), Grass Court (1973).
Previous rankings: 1975 (18), 1976 (14), 1977 (11), 1978 (10), 1979 (7), 1980 (8), 1981 (3), 1983 (3), 1984 (5), 1985 (5).
APT Ranking at end of 1985: 417
1985 singles record: Played only two Grand Prix events, qualifying for Vienna. A semi-finalist in the British closed championships.
Money earned: $7,101

No. 8 LEIGHTON ALFRED

Born: August 27, 1962 at Newport
Lives: Newport
Biography: Talented all-rounder who, as a schoolboy, played cricket and tennis for Wales before deciding on the latter for a sporting career. Three weeks before Wimbledon took Boris Becker to a third set tiebreak at Beckenham, earning himself a wild card for the Championships. Left-hander. Was awarded £500 Dewhurst prize as the most improved British player on the indoor satellite circuit.
Previous ranking: 1985 (9).
APT Ranking at end of 1985: 458

No. 9 JASON GOODALL

Born: January 23, 1967 in Yorkshire
Lives: Reading
Biography: Like most juniors found the transition to senior level a demanding change but succeeded in qualifying for the main draw at Auckland. Also took a set off Sweden's Joakim Nystrom on his initial appearance. Moved south two years ago to be nearer to Bisham Abbey and, within 12 months, became the youngest player to be ranked in Britain's top ten for more than 20 years.
Honours: Galea Cup 1984-5.
Previous rankings: 1985 (10).
ATP Rankings at end of 1985: 433

No. 10 ROBIN DRYSDALE

Born: September 18, 1952 at Denham
Lives: London
Biography: No longer a serious tournament player but still good enough, on a part-time basis, to compete with some success. As national co-ordinator of the Refuge championships was instrumental in making the new national event a success. Had his best years in the late 'seventies, reaching the quarter-finals of the Australian Open in 1977. Educated at Eton and Oxford and is now married with one son.
Honours: King's Cup 1979-80.
Junior titles: Grass court (1970).
Previous rankings: 1976 (11), 1977 (7), 1978 (6), 1979 (4), 1980 (6), 1981 (5), 1982 (-), 1983 (-), 1984 (15), 1985 (-).
ATP Rankings at the end of 1985: 556

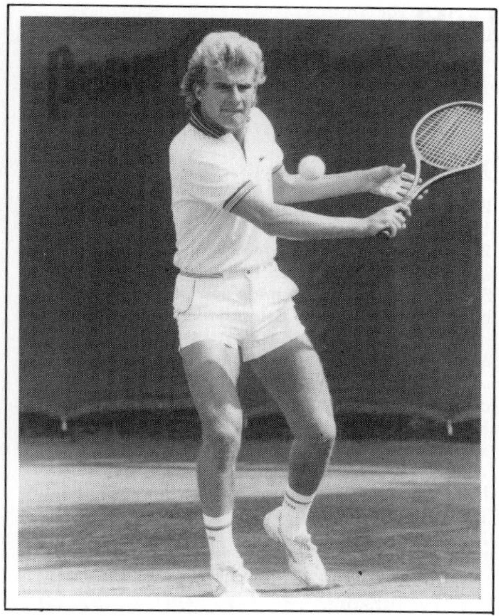

No. 11 DAVID FELGATE (Essex) **born 2.10.63**

No. 12 MICHAEL WALKER (North Wales) **born 21.4.65**

No. 13 RICHARD WHICHELLO (Kent) **born 27.5.67**

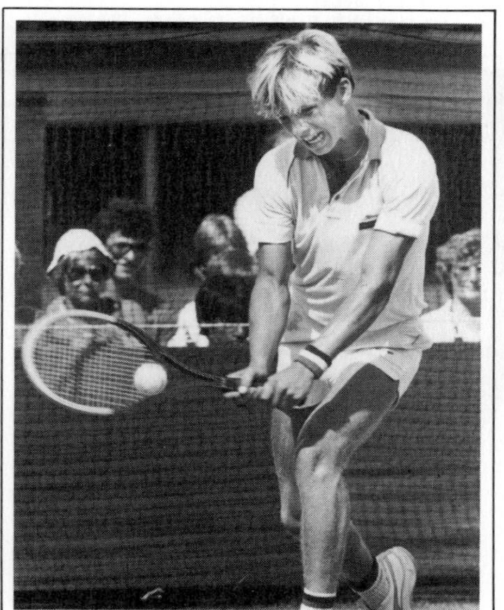

No. 14 MARK BLINCOW (Northants) **born 1.7.1961**

LADIES

No. 1 ANNABEL CROFT

Born: July 12, 1966 at Farnborough
Lives: Kent
Biography: Not since Christine Truman's emergence, some 25 years ago, has a teenager headed the British rankings. A deserved promotion, none the less, after a fine year which brought her first senior title at San Diego (ending a two-year drought) and notable victories over the ten players like Wendy Turnbull and Helena Sukova. Her progress owes much to coach Owen Davidson, who is confident 1986 will produce even better results.
Honours: Wightman Cup 1983-4-5. Federation Cup 1985. Maureen Connolly Cup 1983.
Junior titles: Under 12 Champion (1978), Under 14 (1979), Under 16 (1980), Wimbledon (1984) and Australian (1984).
Previous rankings: 1983 (8), 1984 (7), 1985 (4).
WTA Ranking at the end of 1985: 24
1985 Record: Played in 19 Virginia Slims tournaments. Won San Diego, semi-finalist at Melbourne and Brighton and quarters at Sydney and Tokyo. Also runner-up at Beckenham.
Players beaten in 1985: include Katerina Maleeva, Rosalyn Fairbank, Wendy Turnbull, Elizabeth Smylie, Catherine Tanvier, Helena Sukova, Pam Casale.
Money earned: $69,933

No. 2 JO DURIE

Born: July 27, 1960 at Bristol
Lives: London
Biography: Vastly improved form in the autumn arrested a decline which had taken her from fifth to 52nd in the world standings and promised much better things, despite losing her premier British ranking, in 1986. On her day the most impressive and dominant of our players, with a big serve and a sharp volley but too often lacks confidence, though coach Alan Jones remains confident it will come. Her best performances still her semi-final appearance at the French and US championships in 1983.
Honours: Wightman Cup 1979-85. Federation Cup 1981-85. Annie Soisbault Cup 1977-80. BP Cup 1977-80.
Junior titles: Hard court (1976), Grass court (1976) Covered Court (1976).
Previous rankings: 1977 (13), 1978 (12), 1979 (9), 1980 (4), 1981 (4), 1982 (3), 1983 (1), 1985 (1).
WTA Ranking at the end of 1985: 38
1985 Record: Semi-finalist at Brighton, quarters at New York and Fourth round at Wimbledon. Retained national doubles title with Anne Hobbs at Telford.
Players beaten in 1985: include Claudia Kohde-Kilsch, Steffi Graf (twice), Yvonne Vermaak, Peanut Louie, Anne Minter.
Money earned: $68,395

Jo Durie

Annabel Croft

Anne Hobbs

Sara Gomer

No. 3 ANNE HOBBS

Born: August 2, 1959 at Nottingham
Lives: London
Biography: Illness and injury prevented her playing seriously until the early summer but by the end of the year she had regained all the lost ground and had become British champion after a memorable final at Telford. Almost as important was her first tournament win (doubles as well as singles) on the world circuit at Auckland. Always a fine athlete, her form in 1985 suggested a growing maturity as a player.
Honours: Wightman Cup 1978-85. Federation Cup 1978-9-82-3-4-5. Anne Soisbault Cup 1977-9. Maureen Connolly Cup 1976-80.
Previous rankings: 1977 (14), 1978 (10), 1979 (4), 1980 (3), 1981 (3), 1982 (4), 1983 (4), 1984 (3), 1985 (2).
WTA Ranking at the end of 1985: 50
1985 Record: Played 14 Virginia Slims tournaments. Won singles and doubles at Auckland, was a quarter-finalist at Birmingham and New York Central and reached doubles final with Kathy Jordan at Melbourne.
Players beaten in 1985: include Rosaly Fairbank, Jo Durie, Hu Na, Barbara Potter, Barbara Gerken, Virginia Wade.
Money earned: $56,705

No. 4 SARA GOMER

Born: May 13, 1964 at Torquay
Lives: Devon
Biography: A tall, accomplished left-hander who, with Richard Lewis's help, made rapid strides in 1985 to move from 132nd to 72 in the world rankings and earn herself £1000 from Moet & Chandon for her efforts. Inevitably her serve and volley game was seen at its best on fast surfaces and after a successful run in the US she reached the quarters at Brisbane on grass in the autumn.
Honours: Maureen Connolly Cup 1983-5. Annie Soisbault Cup 1984.
Previous rankings: 1984 (9), 1985 (6).
WTA Ranking at the end of 1985: 72
1985 Record: Won San Antonio tournament, quarter-finalist at Brisbane.
Players beaten in 1985: include Betsy Nagelsen, Lea Antonopolis, Elena Eliseenko, Liz Smylie, Pascale Paradis, Annabel Croft.

No. 5 VIRGINIA WADE

Born: July 15, 1945 at Bournemouth
Lives: New York and London
Biography: By far Britain's most successful player of modern times she finally announced at the Australian Open, and at the age of 40, that her competitive days (singles anyway) were over. Even so her 1985 results were good enough to give her a world ranking of 89. In her heyday she won the US (1968), Australian (1972) and Wimbledon (1977) titles and some $1.5 million in prize money. Her Wightman Cup days spanned every tie from 1965 to 1985 and her Federation Cup matches totalled a record 100.
Honours: Wightman Cup 1965-85. Federation Cup 1967-83. Champion at Rome and British Hard Court title winner in 1967-8-73-4.
Previous rankings: 1968 (2), 1969 (1), 1970-1 (2), 1972-81 (1), 1982-4 (2), 1985 (3).
WTA Ranking at end of 1985: 89
1985 Record: Third round at Wimbledon and runner-up in Refuge at Telford.
Players beaten in 1985: include Wendy White, Lea Antonopolis, Sara Gomer, Molly Van Nostrand.

No. 6 AMANDA BROWN

Born: May 2, 1965 in Norfolk
Lives: Norwich
Biography: Few players worked harder, or travelled further, than Britain's former junior champion in 1985 and, if her results were not always as good as she might have hoped, she at least gained valuable experience. Her best effort was reaching the quarters at Melbourne. Fitting, perhaps, as that was where she won the Australian junior title in 1982 and 1983. Daughter of Norwich City manager Ken Brown.
Honours: Federation Cup 1984. Annie Soisbault Cup 1982-3. Maureen Connolly Cup 1982-5.
Junior titles: Covered Court (1981-2), Grass Court (1980-2), Australian (1982-3).
Previous rankings: 1983 (9), 1984 (5), 1985 (5).
WTA Ranking at the end of 1985: 114
1985 Record: Played in 13 Virginia Slims tournaments with a 5-13 record and lost to Annabel Croft in the quarters at Melbourne indoors.
Players beaten in 1985: include Sara Gomer, Beth Herr, Barbara Gerken.

Virginia Wade

Amanda Brown

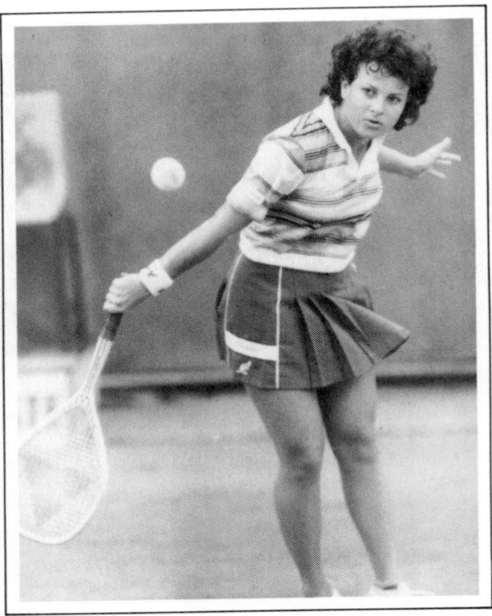

No. 7 SALLY REEVES

Born: July 8, 1964 in London
Lives: West Wickham
Biography: A tiny but tenacious player who proved her fighting qualities by qualifying for the Pretty Polly Classic at Brighton in October and justifying the award of a wild card at Wimbledon by being one of only five British players to survive the first round at Wimbledon.
Honours: Maureen Connolly Cup 1984-5.
Previous ranking: 1985 (11).
WTA Ranking at the end of 1985: 170

No. 8 RINA EINY

Born: March 29, 1965 at Calcutta
Lives: London
Biography: Winner of the national 16 and Under Grass court title in 1981. Represented Britain in the Los Angeles Olympics in 1984. Played only two major events last year, losing in the opening round at Paris and Wimbledon.
Honours: Annie Soisbault Cup 1983-4. Maureen Connolly Cup 1983-4.
Junior titles: 16 and Under Grass Court (1981).
Previous ranking: 1984 (8), 1985 (8).
WTA Ranking at the end of 1985: 174

No. 9 JO LOUIS

Born: April 27, 1967 at Hitchin
Lives: Devon
Biography: Though of quite different build to her famous boxing namesake she packed a big enough punch to knock Jo Durie, the holder, out of the national championships at Telford — the highlight of her career so far. Comes from a tennis playing family with her father, Bob, a former county player.
Honours: Maureen Connolly Cup 1985. Annie Soisbault Cup 1985.
Junior titles: 12 and Under Grass Court (1979), 14 and Under (1981), 16 and Under (1982).
No previous ranking.
WTA Ranking at the end of 1985: 217

No. 10 JULIE SALMON

Born: July 8, 1965
Lives: Brighton
Biography: Turned professional in 1981 after a fine junior career marked by two grass court titles in singles and one in doubles. So far her best effort in the senior game was her third round appearance at Wimbledon in 1984. Slipped 84 places in the world rankings after a disappointing year.
Honours: Maureen Connolly Cup 1983-4. Annie Soisbault Cup 1982-3-4.
Junior titles: Grass Court 1981-3.
Previous ranking: 1985 (7).
WTA Ranking at the end of 1985: 226

No. 11 LORRAYNE GRACIE (Lancs)

No. 12 LISA PENNINGTON (Lincs)

No. 13 JANE WOOD (Middlesex) **born 20.3.68**

No. 14 KATE BRASHER (Surrey) **born 2.8.62**

No. 15 CLARE WOOD (Sussex) **born 8.3.68**

No. 16 JOY TACON (Norfolk) **born 2.6.61**

No. 17 SUSIE MAIR (Scotland) **born 26.11.67**

No. 18 BELINDA BORNEO (Bedfordshire) **born 10.11.66**

FIRST NATIONAL SERIES

Men
Mike Appleton (Lancashire)
Stephen Botfield (Essex)
Chris Bradnam (Middlesex)
Austen Brice (Cheshire)
Nick Brown (Cheshire)
Chris Clarke (Buckinghamshire)
Ian Currie (Essex)
Willie Davies (Lancashire)
Jeremy Dier (Sussex)
John Feaver (Dorset)
Martin Guntrip (Kent)
Paul Hand (Berkshire)
Patrick Hughesman (Middlesex)
Simon Ickringill (Yorkshire)
David Ison (Leicestershire)
Nick Jones (North Wales)
Ben Knapp (Gloucestershire)
Richard Lewis (Middlesex)
Howard McGuiness (Essex)
Peter Moore (Surrey)
Brent Parker (Durham & Cleveland)
Chris Peet (Lancashire)
Paul Reekie (Essex)
Martin Robinson (Lancashire)
Nigel Sears (Sussex)
David Shaw (Lancashire)
James Turner (Avon)
John Whiteford (Sussex)

Women
Glynis Coles (Middlesex)
Lisa Gould (Essex)
Jo Griffiths (Wales)
Elizabeth Jones (Hampshire & I.O.W.)
Jane Langstaff (Surrey)
Nicola Lusty (Middlesex)
Sue McCarthy (Avon)
Denise Parnell (Cheshire)
Katie Rickett (Warwickshire)
Anne Simpkin (Leicestershire)
Sarah Sullivan (Essex)

LTA JUNIOR RANKINGS

Boys 18 & Under
1 Richard Whichello (Kent)
2 Jason Goodall (Yorkshire)
3 Austen Brice (Cheshire)
4 Christopher Peet (Lancashire)
5 Nick Jones (N. Wales)
6 Danny Sapsford (Surrey)
7 David Ison (Leicestershire)
8 Neale Pashley (Surrey)
9 Simon Booth (Warwickshire)
10 Laurence Matthews (Hants & I.O.W)
11 Stephen Heron (Yorkshire)
12 Mark Petchey (Essex)
13 Alex Rouse (Essex)
14 David Clarry (Surrey)
15 Darren Roberts (S. Wales)
16 Anthony Hunting (Leicestershire)
17 Jake Martyn (Sussex)
18 Colin Beecher (Kent)
19 Darren Kirk (Lincolnshire)
20 Vincent Ranson (Essex)

Girls 18 & Under
1 Jane Wood (Middlesex)
2 Jo Louis (Devon)
3 Clare Wood (Sussex)
4 Susie Mair (E. Scotland)
5 Anne Simpkin (Leicestershire)
6 Katie Rickett (Warwickshire)
7 Valda Lake (Devon)
8 Lisa Gould (Essex)
9 Teresa Catlin (Cambridgeshire)
10 Sue McCarthy (Avon)
11 Alison Fleming (Leicestershire)
12 Jenny Reeves (Kent)
13 Sally Timms (Essex)
14 Debbie Schauerman (Middlesex)
15 Alison Grant (Lincolnshire)
16 Kaye Hand (Berkshire)
17 Sally Godman (Surrey)
18 Claire Bateman (Essex)
19 Jane Phillips (Nottinghamshire)
20 Jackie Holden (Yorkshire)

Boys 16 & Under
1 Danny Sapsford (Surrey)
2 Neale Pashley (Surrey)
3 Simon Booth (Warwickshire)
4 Mark Petchey (Essex)
5 Colin Beecher (Kent)
6 Darren Kirk (Lincolnshire)
7 Andrew Fisher (N. Wales)
8 Nicholas Smith (Lancashire)
9 Ulrich Nganga (Norfolk)
10 Sean Wilkins (Hertfordshire&
11 Daniel Ahl (Devon)
12 Glenn Taylor (Gloucestershire)

13 Mark Loosemore (S. Wales)
14 Jeffrey Hunter (Surrey)
15 Dominic Coull (Essex)

Girls 16 & Under
1 Anne Simpkin (Leicestershire)
2 Teresa Catlin (Cambridgeshire)
3 Sue McCarthy (Avon)
4 Alison Fleming (Leicestershire)
5 Sally Timms (Essex)
6 Sally Godman (Surrey)
7 Claire Bateman (Essex)
8 Sarah Loosemore (S. Wales)
9 Amanda Gregory (Nottinghamshire)
10 Amanda Nall (Oxfordshire)
11 Alison Hill (Devon)
12 Nicola Entract (Dorset)
13 Julie Donovan (Warwickshire)
14 Alex Niepel (Lancashire)
15 Lynn Stern (Cornwall)

Boys 14 & Under
1 Nicholas Smith (Lancashire)
2 Simon Cornish (Somerset)
3 David Harris (Essex)
4 David Ireland (Leicestershire)
5 Kevin Cunningham (Lancashire)

Girls 14 & Under
1 Sarah Loosemore (S. Wales)
2 Julie Donovan (Warwickshire)
3 Samantha Smith (Essex)
4 Virginia Humphreys-Davis (Cambridgeshire)
5 Helena Walters (Essex)

PREVIOUS BRITISH RANKINGS

MEN

1968

1 Roger Taylor. 2 Mike Sangster. 3 Mark Cox and Bobby Wilson (equal). 5 Graham Stilwell. 6 Paul Hutchins. 7 Gerald Battrick and Peter Curtis (equal). 9 Stanley Matthews. 10 Keith Wooldridge and John Barratt (equal).

1969

1 Mark Cox. 2 Bobby Wilson. 3 Mike Sangster. 4 Gerald Battrick. 5 Peter Curtis. 6 Paul Hutchins. 7 Keith Wooldridge. 8 David Lloyd. 9 John Barratt. 10 Stanley Matthews.

1970

1 Mark Cox. 2 Graham Stilwell. 3 Gerald Battrick. 4 John Clifton. 5 Bobby Wilson. 6 David Lloyd. 7 Stanley Matthews. 8 Keith Wooldridge. 9 Paul Hutchins. 10 Peter Curtis.

1971

1 Roger Taylor. 2 Mark Cox. 3 Gerald Battrick. 4 Graham Stilwell. 5 Peter Curtis. 6 John Clifton and David Lloyd (equal). 8 John Paish. 9 Stanley Matthews. 10 Paul Hutchins. 11 John Barratt. 12 John de Mendoza. 13 Stephen Warboys.

1972

1 Mark Cox. 2 Roger Taylor. 3 Gerald Battrick. 4 John Paish. 5 David Lloyd. 6 Stanley Matthews. 7 Graham Stilwell. 8 John de Mendoza. 9 Ken Weatherley. 10 Stephen Warboys. 11 John Clifton. 12 Paul Hutchins.

1973

1 Roger Taylor. 2 Mark Cox. 3 Gerald Battrick. 4 John Paish. 5 Graham Stilwell. 6 David Lloyd. 7 John de Mendoza. 8 John Lloyd. 9 Stephen Warboys. 10 Ken Weatherley. 11 John Feaver. 12 John Clifton.

1974

1 Roger Taylor. 2 Mark Cox. 3 Gerald Battrick. 4 Christopher Mottram. 5 John Lloyd. 6 John Feaver. 7 Graham Stilwell. 8 Stephen Warboys. 9 David Lloyd. 10 John Paish. 11 John Clifton. 12 Mark Farrell. 13 Michael Collins. 14 Richard Lewis.

1975

1 Mark Cox. 2 Roger Taylor. 3 Christopher Mottram. 4 John Lloyd. 5 Mark Farrell. 6 Richard Lewis. 7 Martin Robinson. 8 Stephen Warboys. 9 Gerald Battrick. 10 Michael Collins. 11 John Paish. 12 John Feaver. 13 John Clifton. 14 David Lloyd. 15 Graham Stilwell. 16 Chris Wells. 17 Phil Siviter. 18 Jonathan Smith.

1976

1 Mark Cox and Christopher Mottram (equal). 3 Roger Taylor. 4 John Lloyd. 5 Graham Stilwell. 6 Martin Robinson. 7 John Feaver. 8 David Lloyd. 9 Richard Lewis. 10 Gerald Battrick. 11 Robin Drysdale. 12 Mark Farrell. 13 Stephen Warboys. 14 Jonathan Smith. 15 Chris Wells. 16 Michael Collins. 17 Mike Wayman. 18 Willie Davies. 19 Tony Lloyd. 20 John Cooper.

1977

1 Mark Cox. 2 Christopher Mottram. 3 John Lloyd. 4 Roger Taylor. 5 John Feaver. 6 David Lloyd. 7 Robin Drysdale. 8 Gerald Battrick. 9 Richard Lewis. 10 Martin Robinson. 11 Jonathon Smith. 12 Mike Wayman. 13 Andrew Jarrett. 14 Mark Farrell. 15 Stephen Warboys. 16 Tony Lloyd. 17 Rohun Beven. 18 John Whiteford. 19 Roger Webb. 20 Nigel Sears.

1978

1 Christopher Móttram. 2 John Lloyd. 3 Mark Cox. 4 Richard Lewis. 5 John Feaver. 6 Robin Drysdale. 7 Roger Taylor. 8 David Lloyd. 9 Mike Wayman. 10 Jonathan Smith. 11 Rohun Beven. 12 Andrew Jarrett. 13 Tony Lloyd. 14 Mike Appleton. 15 Chris Bradnam. 16 Chris Kaskow. 17 Neil Rayner. 18 Martin Robinson. 19 Jeremy Dier. 20 Nigel Sears.

1979

1 Christopher Mottram. 2 John Lloyd. 3 Mark Cox. 4 Robin Drysdale. 5 Andrew Jarrett. 6 John Feaver. 7 Jonathon Smith. 8 Richard Lewis. 9 Roger Taylor. 10 David Lloyd. 11 Rohun Beven. 12 John Paish. 13 Mark Farrell. 14 Willie Davies. 15 Chris Bradnam. 16 Mike Appleton. 17 John Whiteford. 18 Jeremy Dier. 19 Neil Rayner. 20 Tony Lloyd.

1980

1 Christopher Mottram. 2 Mark Cox. 3 John Lloyd. 4 Richard Lewis. 5 John Feaver. 6 Robin Drysdale. 7 Andrew Jarrett. 8 Jonathan Smith. 9 David Lloyd. 10 Chris Bradnam. 11 John Whiteford. 12 Rohun Beven. 13 Willie Davies. 14 Mike Appleton. 15 Jeremy Dier, 16 Robert Booth, 17 Nigel Sears. 18 Harvey Becker. 19 Kevin Harris. 20 Rayner.

1981

1 Christopher Mottram. 2 Mark Cox. 3 Jonathan Smith. 4 John Feaver. 5 Robin Drysdale. 6 Andrew Jarrett. 7 Richard Lewis. 8 Rohun Beven. 9 John Whiteford. 10 Jeremy Bates. 11 Jeremy Dier. 12 Keith Gilbert. 13 Harvey Becker. 14 Robert Booth. 15 Willie Davies. 16 Tony Lloyd. 17 Mike Appleton. 18 Kevin Harris. 19 Nigel Sears. 20 Nick Brown.

1982

1 Christopher Mottram. 2 Richard Lewis. 3 Jonathan Smith. 4 John Lloyd. 5 John Feaver. 6 Jeremy Bates. 7 Andrew Jarrett. 8 Jeremy Dier. 9 Nigel Sears. 10 John Whiteford. 11 Nick Brown. 12 Robert Booth. 13 Rohun Beven. 14 Mike Appleton. 15 Kevin Harris. 16 Willie Davies. 17 Harvey Becker. 18 Leighton Alfred. 19 Mark Holland. 20 David Shaw.

1983

1 Christopher Mottram. 2 Andrew Jarrett. 3 Jonathan Smith. 4 John Lloyd. 5 Richard Lewis. 6 John Feaver. 7 Jeremy Bates. 8 Jeremy Dier. 9 Martin Guntrip. 10 David Shaw and Tim Robson (equal). 12 Nick Fulwood. 13 Stuart Bale. 14 Mark Holland. 15 Nick Brown.

1984

1 Colin Dowdeswell. 2 John Lloyd. 3 Christopher Mottram. 4 Jeremy Bates. 5 Jonathan Smith. 6 Chris Bradnam. 7 Stuart Bale. 8 John Feaver. 9 Nick Brown. 10 Andrew Jarrett. 11 Richard Lewis. 12 Stephen Shaw. 13 Martin Guntrip. 14 David Felgate. 15 Jeremy Dier and Robin Drysdale (equal).

1985

1 John Lloyd. 2 Stephen Shaw. 3 Colin Dowdeswell. 4 Jeremy Bates. 5 Jonathan Smith. 6 Stuart Bale. 7 John Feaver. 8 Richard Lewis. 9 Leighton Alfred. 10 Jason Goodall. 11 Nick Fulwood. 12 David Felgate.

LADIES

1968

1 Ann Jones. 2 Virginia Wade. 3 Christine Truman and Joyce Williams (equal). 5 Winnie Shaw. 6 Robin Lloyd. 7 Nell Truman. 8 Frances MacLennan.

1969

1 Virginia Wade. 2 Winnie Shaw and Joyce Williams (equal). 4 Robin Lloyd. 5 Christine Janes. 6 Nell Truman. 7 Corinne Molesworth. 8 Frances MacLennan. 9 Janice Townsend. 10 Shirley Brasher.

1970

1 Ann Jones. 2 Virginia Wade. 3 Winnie Shaw. 4 Christine Janes. 5 Joyce Williams. 6 Corinne Molesworth. 7 Shirley Brasher. 8 Nell Truman. 9 Janice Townsend. 10 Jill Cooper.

1971

1 Ann Jones. 2 Virginia Wade. 3 Winnie Shaw. 4 Joyce Williams. 5 Corinne Molesworth. 6 Jill Cooper. 7 Nell Truman. 8 Shirley Brasher. 9 Lindsay Beavean. 10 Janice Townsend.

1972

1 Virginia Wade. 2 Joyce Williams. 3 Winnie Shaw. 4 Jill Cooper. 5 Christine Janes. 6 Nell Truman. 7 Shirley Brasher. 8 Janice Wainwright. 9 Jackie Fayter. 10 Veronica Burton and Corinne Molesworth (equal).

1973

1 Virginia Wade. 2 Joyce Williams. 3 Corinne Molesworth. 4 Winnie Wooldridge. 5 Jill Cooper. 6 Nell Robinson. 7 Glynis Coles. 8 Veronica Burton. 9 Lesley Charles. 10 Shirley Brasher. 11 Alex Cowie. 12 Jackie Fayter.

1974

1 Virginia Wade. 2 Glynis Coles. 3 Veronica Burton. 4 Lindsay Beavean. 5 Jackie Fayter. 6 Jill Cooper. 7 Lesley Charles. 8 Lindsay Blachford. 9 Corinne Molesworth. 10 Sue Mappin. 11 Penny Moor. 12 Sue Barker. 13 Annette Coe.

1975

1 Virginia Wade. 2 Sue Barker. 3 Glynis Coles. 4 Lesley Charles. 5 Sue Mappin. 6 Jackie Fayter. 7 Lindsay Beavean. 8 Veronica Burton. 9 Annette Coe. 10 Lindsay Blachford. 11 Linda Mottram. 12 Corinne Molesworth. 13 Belinda Thompson. 14.Michele Tyler.

1976

1 Virginia Wade. 2 Sue Barker. 3 Glynis Coles. 4 Linda Mottram. 5 Michele Tyler. 6 Lesley Charles. 7 Sue Mappin. 8 Lindsay Blachford. 9 Annette Coe. 10 Jackie Fayter. 11 Lindsay Blachford. 12 Belinda Thompson. 13 Veronica Burton. 14 Penny Moor. 15 Linda Geeves. 16 Corinne Molesworth.

1977

1 Virginia Wade. 2 Sue Barker. 3 Glynis Coles. 4 Michele Tyler. 5 Jackie Fayter. 6 Lindsay Beavean. 7 Linda Mottram. 8 Sue Mappin. 9 Lesley Charles. 10 Corinne Molesworth. 11 Belinda Thompson. 12 Veronica Burton. 13 Jo Durie. 14 Anne Hobbs. 15 Annette Coe. 16 Lindsay Blachford. 17 Jill Cottrell. 18 Anthea Cooper. 19 Julia Lloyd. 20 Clare Harrison.

1978

1 Virginia Wade. 2 Sue Barker. 3 Michele Tyler. 4 Glynis Coles. 5 Sue Mappin, 6 Lindsay Beavean. 7 Linda Mottram. 8 Jackie Fayter. 9 Lesley Charles. 10 Anne Hobbs. 11 Corinne Molesworth. 12 Jo Durie. 13 Belinda Thompson. 14 Cathy Drury. 15 Debbie Jevans. 16 Kate Glancy. 17 Annette Coe. 18 Linda Geeves. 19 Clare Harrison. 20 Kate Brasher.

1979

1 Virginia Wade. 2 Sue Barker. 3 Michele Tyler. 4 Anne Hobbs. 5 Glynis Coles. 6 Jackie Fayter. 7 Linda Mottram. 8 Sue Mappin. 9 Jo Durie. 10 Belinda Thompson. 11 Kate Glancy. 12 Corinne Molesworth. 13 Anthea Cooper. 14 Lesley Charles. 15 Lindsay Beavean. 16 Kate Brasher. 17 Veronica Burton. 18 Debbie Jevans. 19 Clare Harrison. 20 Cathy Drury.

1980

1 Virginia Wade. 2 Sue Barker. 3 Anne Hobbs. 4 Jo Durie. 5 Debbie Jevans. 6 Lesley Charles. 7 Glynis Coles. 8 Cathy Drury. 9 Corinne Molesworth. 10 Kate Brasher. 11 Belinda Thompson. 12 Anthea Cooper. 13 Jane Plackett. 14 Julie Walpole. 15 Debbie Packer. 16 Linda Geeves. 17 Michele Tyler. 18 Elizabeth Locke. 19 Sonia Davies. 20 Clare Harrison.

1981

1 Virginia Wade. 2 Sue Barker. 3 Anne Hobbs. 4 Jo Durie. 5 Debbie Jevans. 6 Kate Brasher. 7 Lesley Charles. 8 Anthea Cooper. 9 Glynis Coles. 10 Belinda Thompson. 11 Liza Pennington. 12 Linda Geeves. 13 Elizabeth Jones. 14 Debbie Stewart. 15 Cathy Drury.

1982

1 Sue Barker. 2 Virginia Wade. 3 Jo Durie. 4 Anne Hobbs. 5 Glynis Coles. 6 Debbie Jevans. 7 Kate Brasher. 8 Lesley Charles. 9 Anthea Cooper. 10 Elizabeth Jones.

1983

1 Jo Durie. 2 Virginia Wade. 3 Sue Barker. 4 Anne Hobbs. 5 Debbie Jarrett. 6 Glynis Coles. 7 Kate Brasher. 8 Annabel Croft. 9 Amanda Brown. 10 Elizabeth Jones.

1984

1 Jo Durie. 2 Virginia Wade. 3 Anne Hobbs. 4 Sue Barker. 5 Amanda Brown. 6 Shelley Wallpole. 7 Annabel Croft. 8 Rina Einy. 9 Sarah Gomer. 10 Kate Brasher.

1985

1 Jo Durie. 2 Anne Hobbs. 3 Virginia Wade. 4 Annabel Croft. 5 Amanda Brown. 6 Sara Gomez. 7 Julie Salmon. 8 Rina Einy. 9 Sue Barker. 10 Kate Brasher. 11 Sally Reeves. 12 Shelley Walpole.

TODAY AND 99 YESTERYEARS

BY LANCE TINGAY

If all Wimbledons are memorable, some are more memorable than others – and 1986 sees one that is very special. The Lawn Tennis Championships will be staged for the 100th time. The first was in 1877 but ten were missed because of the four years of the first World War and the six of the second. What difference between the cradle years and now?

Nearly 1,000 spectators paid one shilling each to see the first tournament, with its five playing days, in Worple Road where the All England Croquet Club had recently added "and Lawn Tennis" to its title. In 1985, over 13 sessions, the total attendance was 397,983.

A quiet social occasion (a break was ordained from the start to allow all to go to Lords for the socially *de rigueur* Eton and Harrow cricket match) had grown into a British institution and, arguably, the best known sporting event in the world. Except for a brief period in the 1890's the growth was uninterrupted – and fortuitous. It was not planned to become big. It just grew on its own success.

Yet if so different it is, remarkably, just the same. The game played in 1877 was identical, save for minor changes, with that of today. I refer to the rules, to the size and shape of the court, the scoring and all the basics we take for granted.

It was not like that in 1877, when, six weeks before the start, a committee comprising Dr Henry Jones, Julian Walsh and C G Heathcote, began to organise the novel tournament. Lawn tennis was not then codified. There were as many sets of rules as makers of bat and ball and nets. Big courts, small courts, wide ones, narrow ones, hour glass shaped ones – well, what best fitted the lawn on which the net was put? As for scoring, most borrowed the rackets method, with games consisting of 15 points up and won only by the server.

The trio of innovators decreed a court 78 by 27 feet, a service with one fault allowed from behind the baseline and scoring based on real tennis, with its familiar but curious 15, 30, deuce and so on. They laid down, in fact, the game of today. The length of the service court was to be shortened, the height of the net lowered but changes have been in minor detail only.

If we went back to a damp Thursday in July 1877 and watched the final in which Spencer Gore beat William Marshall 6-1, 6-2, 6-4 we would see no major difference. We might be surprised to see them change ends only at the end of the set but the speed with which they got on with the match might be welcome – the recent innovation of allowing a 90 seconds break on the change of ends was undreamt of.

They took the ball rather late but Gore, when he vollied, did so very early. He even reached across the net. But it was not very paceful. If there were bad bounces no one worried.

Lawn tennis it certainly was but there was a touch of the vicarage lawn about it. Indeed the winner in 1879 was a vicar, the Reverend John Hartley from a village in north Yorkshire. (This was the saint and sinner conflict, for Hartley won by beating V.St.Leger Goold who, nearly thirty years later, had the misfortune to be convicted of murder).

From 1881 it was different. That was the first year of the Renshaw twins, William and Ernest from Cheltenham, who hit upon the technique of serving hard, hitting hard and bustling the opposition to nowhere. The Renshaw twins created the modern game and turned a pastime into a sport.

These founding fathers of lawn tennis in its spectacular aspect brought the "Renshaw Boom". They were rich and charming and William went on winning with Ernest just behind him. The crowds began to flock to Wimbledon.

The London and South Western Railway rose to the opportunity. In those days access was only by horse cab from the Wimbledon Station or by foot along the path by the side of the railway. The L.S.W.R. erected a halt by the club giving access direct to the tournament.

There were ten courts at the old ground (which can still be seen as a playing field of Wimbledon Girls' High School) and the Centre Court was so called because it was just that. In 1884 permanent covered stands were built around it.

In the same year a men's doubles and women's singles event was inaugurated. The All England Club were a little laggardly with women for they had had events at Bath and Cheltenham and other provincial tournaments as well as from 1879 in the Irish meeting in Dublin. After Wimbledon's innovation in 1877 the game had boomed nation wide.

As for the men's doubles this had been an event held at Oxford since 1879. It languished somewhat and the two silver cups – still played for – passed to Wimbledon. At first both new events began only after the completion of the men's singles. They were not brought into a common timetable until 1887.

Women's and mixed doubles? These came later, as non-championship events with women's doubles from 1899 to 1907 and the mixed from 1900 to 1912. Both became championship events when in 1913 the newly formed International Federation granted Wimbledon the unwanted (and temporary) description as "The World Championships on Grass".

The method of making the draw changed in 1885 and all byes were given in the first round. Earlier the draw was

Final of the All-Commers Singles 1892 E W Lewis v J Pim

Photography: Le-Roye Productions Ltd.

made straight and any odd man after each round was given the bye. So it was that in 1877 Marshall had a bye in the semi-final!

When the Renshaws gave up there was something of a recession. In 1895, a year when Crown Princess Stephanie of Austria was the first royal visitor, there was a loss of £33. The entry for the women's singles was, in 1890, just four!

The charismatic personalities and skills of Reggie and Laurie Doherty at the turn of the century transformed Wimbledon. Its growth in prestige and popularity has never ceased, interrupted by the two world wars but picking up where it left off.

Even before 1914 it was obvious a move would have to be made. It came in 1922 and by that time the All England Club and the Lawn Tennis Association (founded in 1888) was jointly involved. The first formal association between the two bodies was in 1906. There was a renewed agreement in 1920 and the financing of the new ground was by the issue of £50 Debenture Shares, free of interest but with the right to a Centre Court seat. The original issue has long since been repaid but they are still issued and are to be had – at a price – by purchase on the Stock Exchange.

A joint Management Committee runs Wimbledon and by the agreement of 1934, with amendments in 1966, the AEC and the LTA are tied together.

The cost of the new Wimbledon, now so familiar, was £140,000. Boris Becker did not get much less than that as the champion in 1985. Stanley Peach was the architect and the Centre Court had a capacity of 9,989 seats with standing room for 4,000. This has grown to 12,433 seats with standing room restricted to about 2,000. With the stands and seats elsewhere the total seating is about 26,000.

Court One did not come into use until 1924. There were 13 courts used at the (very wet) 1922 meeting, 16 in 1937, later reduced to 15. With the acquisition of the sports ground to the north of the club and its subsequent addition to the 13½ acres of the original site 18 courts are now available – and the Centre Court back in the position from which its name was derived.

Not the least important clause in the 1934 agreement was that which gives the surplus to the LTA. Did any club anywhere give so much away? Prior to World War II the largest amount to be handed over was £13,868 in 1933. It reached £50,000 for the first time in 1953, £100,000 by 1975.

In 1981 it exceeded £1,000,000. Three years later it exceeded £4,000,000. Television fees and the discreet exploitation of Wimbledon's commercial value is the reason for the enormous increase. Yet it has been done without loss of the essential dignity of the All England Club and the prestige of the most highly regarded lawn tennis championship in the world.

The bench-mark of Wimbledon's transition from essentially amateur traditions was the change in 1968 from an amateur to open status for players. The story of how the change came about, a change which has brought new horizons, belongs to the game at large but it is a fact that the All England Club, for long held to be old fashioned and lost in the stuffiness of times past, brought it about.

The then Wimbledon Chairman, the late Herman David, a man of supreme integrity, found the state of "shamateurism" so morally offensive that he urged the LTA to change. His pressure eventually inspired the revolt of the LTA against the international rules at the end of 1967. The world game yielded to the British action.

In recent years millions have been spent in enlarging and improving Wimbledon's facilities. Some may ask if show business has not replaced a sporting event. I think not and it needs to be remembered that the greatest lawn tennis show on earth, with finances that put it in the class of big business, is managed and controlled by an amateur committee of 18 (including a woman, Virginia Wade) who do not receive, or want to receive, a penny for their pains.

If the money side of Wimbledon has changed drastically over its one hundred promotions so has the garb of its competitors. If you look at pictures from the early days it is obvious that the "all white" rule, which persisted for so long and still does to some degree, did not pertain. Skirts were ankle length, of course, but shoes and stockings (socks for men) were often black. This was not so much fashion as availability.

Women wore hats and when they did they had to serve under-arm. More did so than did not until after 1919. Women also wore corsets until the nineteen-twenties, though the ballerina like Suzanne Lenglen, the invincible French woman 1919-1926, clearly did not.

At Wimbledon, where women's

Maud Watson, first Lady Champion 1884

Photography: Le-Roye Productions Ltd.

fashion has always loomed large, there were landmarks. In 1929 the South African Billie Tapscott was bold enough to appear on the Centre Court with regulation white stockings. By 1939 shorts, for both men and women, were familar. The last male singles champion to play in long flannels was Yvon Petra of France in 1946.

There was another turning point in 1949 for it became possible to discuss what women wore underneath. That was the year when Gussie Moran made such a stir – heaven knows why – with her lace panties. Wimbledon has but reflected social change.

"Predominately white" is now the Wimbledon rule, with its discreet suggestions of compromise. The subject of women's dress still excites. Was there not the body stocking, in all white, of 1985? Wimbledon strives to keep its dignity without being fuddy-duddy.

The most traumatic Wimbledon was

Suzanne Lenglen

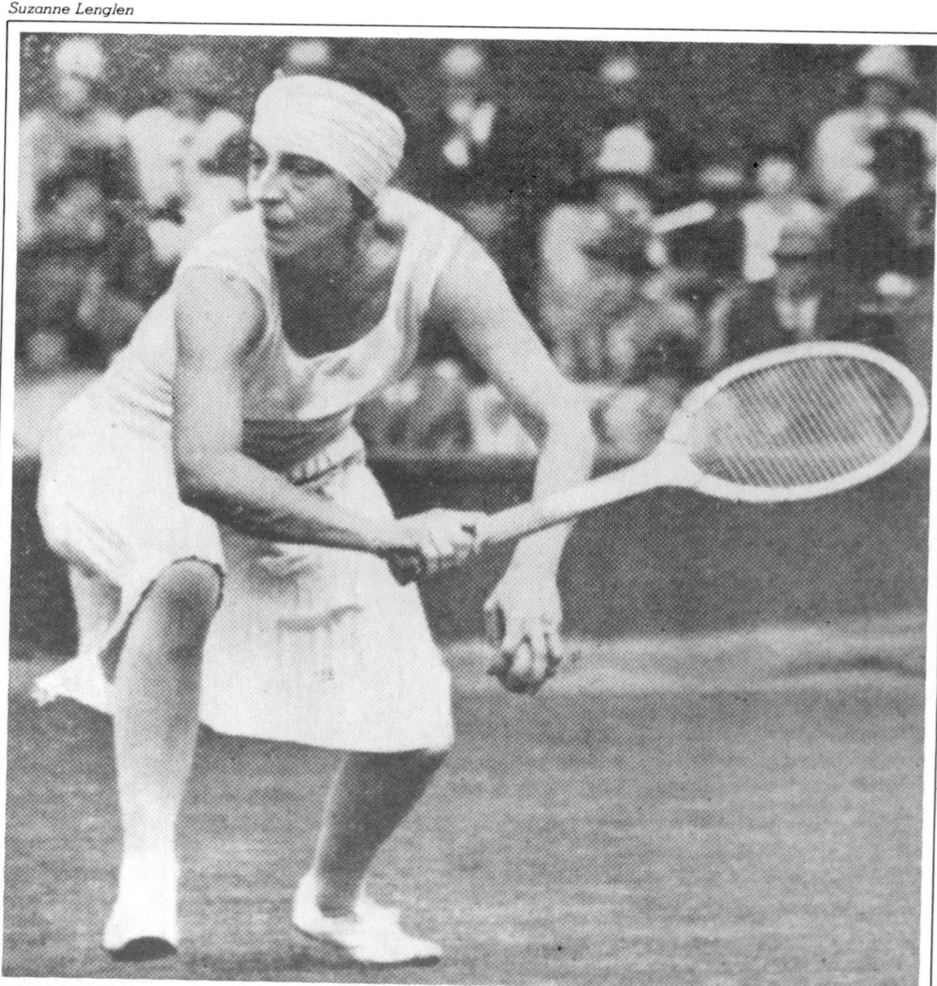

Photography: Le-Roye Productions Ltd.

the 87th in 1973. This was the year of the boycott by the newly formed Association of Tennis Professionals in protest against the suspension by the International Federation of the Yugoslav Nikki Pilic. It was not in any way Wimbledon's quarrel but the upshot was the withdrawal of 79 leading men players. The quality of the men's entry was diminished catastrophically. It was a front page story round the world.

Herman David said "There will be no recriminations" and the meeting went ahead. And as a tournament it seemed not one whit the worse! The attendance topped 300,000 for the first time. It indicated that Wimbledon was greater than the players. Not that anyone wanted the example to be repeated!

The year before, 1972, there had been a breakdown of administrative common sense – by the world authorities, not by Wimbledon – when some leading men players, including John Newcombe, the singles title holder, were not allowed entry because of their professional contracts.

It was also a landmark year because the men's singles final – a magnificent contest with Stan Smith beating Ilie Nastase – was held over by rain on the Saturday and staged on Sunday. It was done with some forboding since it was assumed that the law would not allow an entry charge and spectators went in free. But it was all quite orderly, with the Saturday ticket holders getting their places.

In 1982 the 12 scheduled days of Wimbledon, which had pertained since 1919, were extended to 13 with the finish on the Sunday. A year later the starting time, established as "precisely 2 p.m." in 1919 was put back to 12.30 a.m. except the Centre and Number One Courts. In 1877 it had been 4.30 p.m.!

There has been much change in 100 Wimbledons but much has remained the same. The basic rules for one. And, for another, the long shafted pony roller that stands at the north end of the Centre Court. The legend is that its need for repair prompted the staging of the first meeting in 1877. A £10 profit got it fixed.

And then, when they had used the roller to help lay the new turf of the new Centre Court in 1922, it was found that the stands built around it had no exit wide enough for it to pass through!

So, one or one hundred, what's the difference?

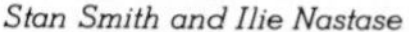

Stan Smith and Ilie Nastase

Photography: Le-Roye Productions Ltd.

WIMBLEDON

INTRODUCTION

BY DAVID IRVINE: THE GUARDIAN

There are times when fact surpasses fiction in the matter of providing ideal finishes. The 99th Wimbledon Championships, which began with lightning ripping a chunk off the outer wall of the Centre Court, ended inside the packed and sunlit stadium 14 days later where a human thunderbolt completed — and against all the odds — a savage and brilliant demolition of the men's field.

As Boris Becker walked across the court to accept the trophy, he received an ovation such has seldom been accorded to any champion in the past. That, though, was the only way the crowd could respond to what they knew was a unique moment in sporting history. At 17 the West German had become not only Wimbledon's youngest men's champion but the first to take the title unseeded.

Little over a year earlier Becker had left the grounds in a wheelchair and in tears, his left ankle torn and useless after falling awkwardly in his third round match with Billy Scanlon. He had suffered Wimbledon's agony; twelve months on and he was savouring its ecstacy.

One man, Johan Kriek, could be excused for thinking, "I told you so". At Queen's, where Becker had beaten him in the final of the Stella Artois tournament the previous months, he told the press: "If he plays this way he will win Wimbledon. Nobody will be able to beat him on grass."

In fact most thought if anyone could it would be his final opponent Kevin Curren, who like Kriek was born in South Africa but had taken US citizenship. After all he had demolished the holder, John McEnroe, and his immediate predecessor, Jimmy Connors, by the blazing accuracy of his serve.

But the 27-year-old Curren's touch deserted him when he needed it most. And far from being intimidated, as many had expected, Becker was inspired by the occasion. A mature and excitingly varied display that belied his tender years ended with the youngster winning the final 6-3, 6-7, 7-6, 6-4, after three hours and 18 minutes.

By a curious co-incidence the last unseeded European finalist had been another German, Wilhelm Bungert, now Becker's Davis Cup captain. But he lost in straight sets to John Newcombe. Only one other German had ever made the final: Baron Gottfried Von Cramm in the three successive years from 1935 to 1937, though without taking a single set.

If it was all change in the men's — and in each of the three doubles championships — it was a very familiar story in the ladies' singles, with Martina Navratilova defeating her great rival Chris Evert Lloyd for the fifth time in eight years.

A month earlier in Paris Mrs Lloyd had taken Miss Navratilova's French title in dramatic fashion and, when she won the opening set, the Centre Court buzzed with anticipation. Neither her hopes nor theirs were to be fulfilled. Gradually the defending Champion's powerful serve-and-volley game earned her command and, with it, victory by 4-6, 6-3, 6-2.

Apart from the finals, and a marvellous match between Henri Leconte and Ivan Lendl, the most

Boris Becker

memorable moments were provided by the weather; first the storm which accompanied the opening session, when only one match was completed, and then the deluge on men's semifinal day, when the Centre Court gangways became waterfalls, tents were blown over and trees demolished.

In the circumstances it was to the immense credit of the ground staff that the programme was completed on schedule. Indeed the men's semifinals were delayed by only 90 minutes thanks to the awning which protected the court. And despite everything attendances, well down the first week, broke all records — 396,007 passing through the gates with a remarkable 38,577 present on the second Tuesday.

John McEnroe

MENS SINGLES

Considering it was the first time for a decade that only one of the top four seeds — the exception, as in 1975, being Connors — succeeded in reaching the semifinals, it was somehow appropriate that it should be the least likely survivor who, at the end, outlasted the cream of the establishment.

Not that the daily carnage made it that much easier for Becker. Even after winning at Queen's he was still too low in the rankings to be seeded for the Championships and, apart from a handful of opportunities, he had neither played nor beaten most of those who were so favoured.

Admittedly the draw kept him clear of McEnroe and Connors, the two past champions, but he was still required to overcome four seeds — Joakim Mystrom (7), Tim Mayotte (16), Anders Jarryd (5) and Curren (8) — to take the title, which was no mean feat.

In fact he was to endure a bumpy ride throughout and one which was full of traumas. His opening match with Hank Pfister was delayed for a day by rain. He lost the first set and was just establishing his recovery when bad light forced a stoppage at 2-2 in the fourth. He then had to wait another night before making sure of going forward.

Against Nystrom only his remarkable instinct for survival saved him. Twice he had to break back in the fifth when the Swede served for the match. Then, facing Mayotte, he turned his left ankle — just as he had, though more seriously, the year before — considered but rejected the idea of conceding, and duly won another five-setter.

By the time he overcame the left-hander Leconte, who had again proved the bane of Ivan Lendl's career, the boy who had entered the tournament as a 14-1 outsider had become the favourite:

Anders Jarryd

even though Connors, who must have thought it was Christmas, was still in contention. But as the man from the bookie's observed: "We know King Midas when we see him!"

Others, though, were not so sure. In every year since 1977, when McEnroe had come roaring through from qualifying, there had been an unseeded semifinalist. But one by one — McEnroe, Tom Okker, Pat DuPre, Brian Gottfried, Rod Frawley, Chris Lewis (the only one to make the final) and Pat Cash — had failed in their quest for gold. Why should this teenager playing in what was, after all, only his 26th senior tournament, be the exception to the rule?

Perhaps the answer was that Becker understood no rules. It was as though, unlike those who had preceded him to the brink, he knew no fear nor felt any inhibitions. "I just try to think of it as another match, no more, and do my best," he kept saying. And to him the semifinal and final were no different.

With Becker crises came and crises went. It seemed that all he had to do was press a little harder on the accelerator. And he always had something in reserve. His approach to the 'big' points (those that decided sets and matches, those that slammed the door on his opponents' ambitions) was phenomenal.

Jarryd was to find that. He too had been through the mill — two sets down to Claudio Panatta in the first round, for instance — and when he led the German 6-2 and had two points for a two-set lead, his mind was clearly focussed on becoming the first Swede since Bjorn Borg to reach the final.

Unfortunately Becker had other ideas. On the first he produced an ace; on the second a forehand volley winner. Into a tiebreak it went and again Jarryd's hopes rose as he took a 3-1 lead. Yet that was as far as Becker allowed him. Sweeping the next six points the 17-year-old moved into top gear and, despite an overnight wait after more rain, ran away with the match 2-6, 7-6, 6-3, 6-3.

Curren, meanwhile, had attracted little or no attention until he beat Stefan Edberg in round four. Even then it was the consequence of his victory, not the result itself, that prompted speculation: for he was now lined up to meet McEnroe, the man who had set out as red-hot favourite.

Up to that point everything had seemed so easy for the defending champion. He had beaten Peter McNamara, Nduka Odizor, Christo Steyn and Andreas Maurer without dropping a set. Yet what did that add up to? A player ranked 632nd, another 119th and two qualifiers. Could anyone assess the American's real form on that sort of evidence?

When the confrontation came there was barely time for conjecture. Curren butchered the champion 6-2, 6-2, 6-4 in 109 minutes. "He just overpowered me," said the man who had done the same, and worse, to Connors in the 1984 final. "I felt really old out there."

Old and, by his standards, feeble. Just 12 months after dominating that great stage in a manner no other player has matched, he had succeeded in looking like an extra. It was the price he had had to pay, many felt, for missing Queen's.

Curren, meanwhile, had his sights trained on another left-hander — Connors, who he had gunned down with 33 aces in 1983. The American's excuse then was having to play on Court Two. But to Curren all courts are much of a muchness; and on Centre he roasted Connors again, 6-2, 6-2, 6-1.

Yet, by the final, the power of Hurricane Curren was dimishing. He was broken as early as the second game and that set the pattern. "I played a horrific game at that moment," he admitted, "and that sort of set me on the wrong path." The key game, both finalists agreed, was when Becker broke back at 3-4 in the third; after that he put Curren under ever more insistant pressure.

Kevin Curren

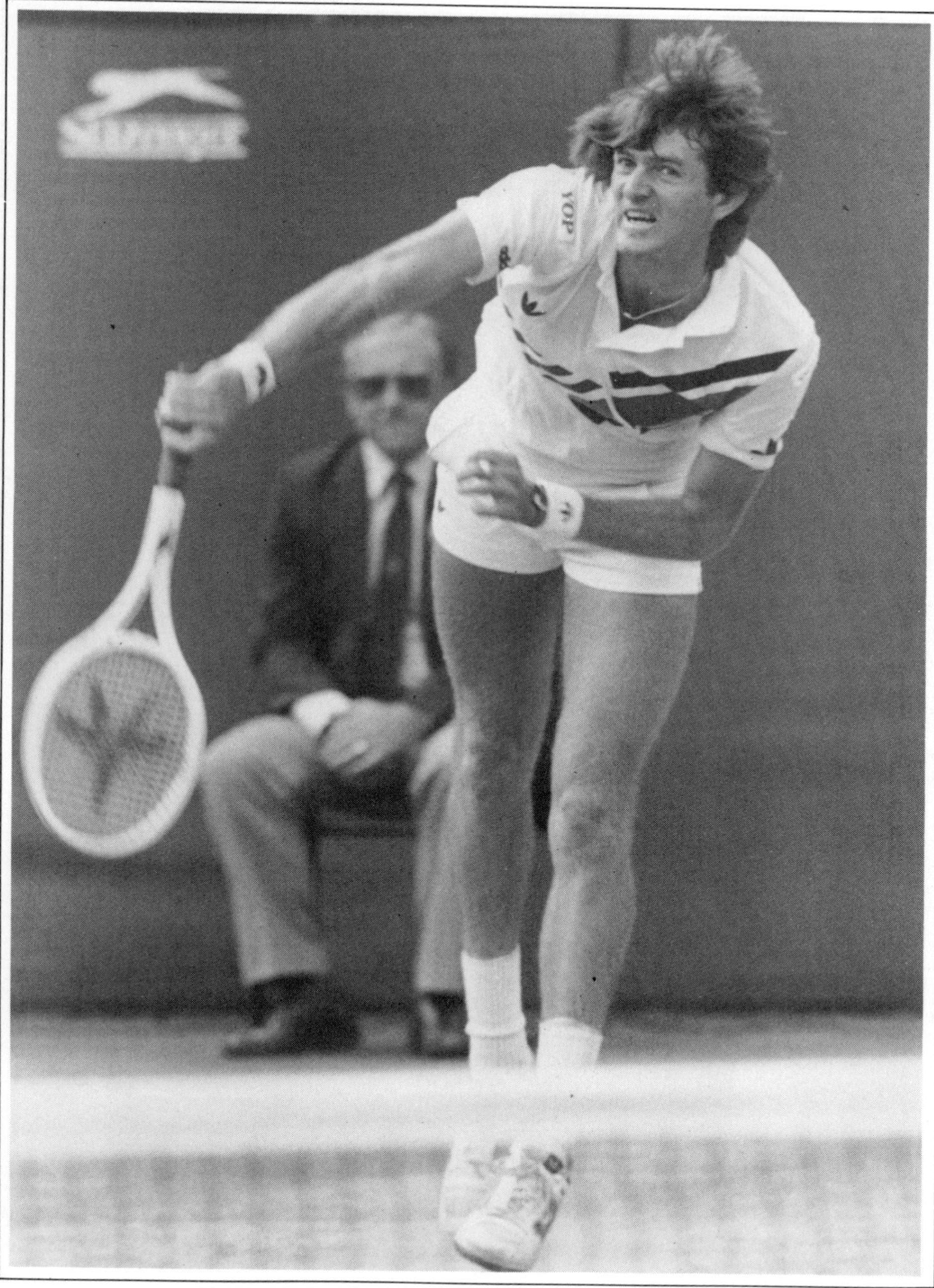

Jimmy Connors

"I've played harder servers," he said afterwards, "but none with greater placement." Not surprisingly it was a service winner — he had previously delivered 21 aces — that decided the match and the championship and, in the opinion of some, heralded the dawn of a new era in which power will predominate.

Becker, though, was not alone in enjoying Wimbledon. Slobodan Zivojinovic, the huge and cheerful Yugoslav, became an overnight sensation by beating Matts Wilander, the French champion, in round one. Ricardo Acuna,whose native Chile has no grass courts, played through qualifying and into the last eight. And John Lloyd, bringing a touch of British cheer to an often sodden landscape, had the satisfaction of knocking off the thirteenth seed, Eliot Teltscher.

One over-riding feeling remained, however. Something has to be done to restore some sense to the seedings. Of the 16 named only five justified their ranking and and only two — Curren and Jarryd — exceeded their predicted position. Once again the tournament had suffered from a ranking system determined, in the main, by clay court performances.

Suffered? Maybe one should say adversely affected. Can any championship be said to have suffered when it creates a new superstar? And that Becker is a superstar there is no doubt. More than that, though, he blew through Wimbledon like a breath of fresh air.

Matts Wilander defeated by Slobodan Zivojinovic

LADIES

Familiarity is said to breed contempt. But when two players are as dedicated, successful, competitive and familiar to one another as Miss Navratilova and Mrs Lloyd, it breeds something quite different — respect. Which is why neither complained when the seeding committee took their unprecedented step and made them joint favourites for the ladies' title.

At Roland Garros in June, Mrs Lloyd had redressed the shifting balance in their 12-year rivalry by winning a tense three-set decider for the French championship. That put her back at the top of the rankings. What the committee bore in mind, though, was the fact that in the four Wimbledon finals the two had played, Miss Navratilova had emerged the winner every time.

Not that anyone else was ever expected to make the final. And so it proved. Each waltzed through without losing a set — Mrs Lloyd at a cost of just 16 games — and it was not until the last possible set of the championship that Miss Navratilova edged ahead to take the crown for the sixth time in her career and equal the post-war record of Billie-Jean King.

Four of those titles had come in consecutive years, giving her a winning sequence of 27 matches since her loss to Hana Mandlikova in the 1981 semifinals. And though that still left her short of Suzanne Lenglen's five-in-a-row from 1919 to 1923, it marked a degree of domination which, considering the modern standard of opposition, must be regarded as being without parallel.

Martina Navratilova

Chris Lloyd

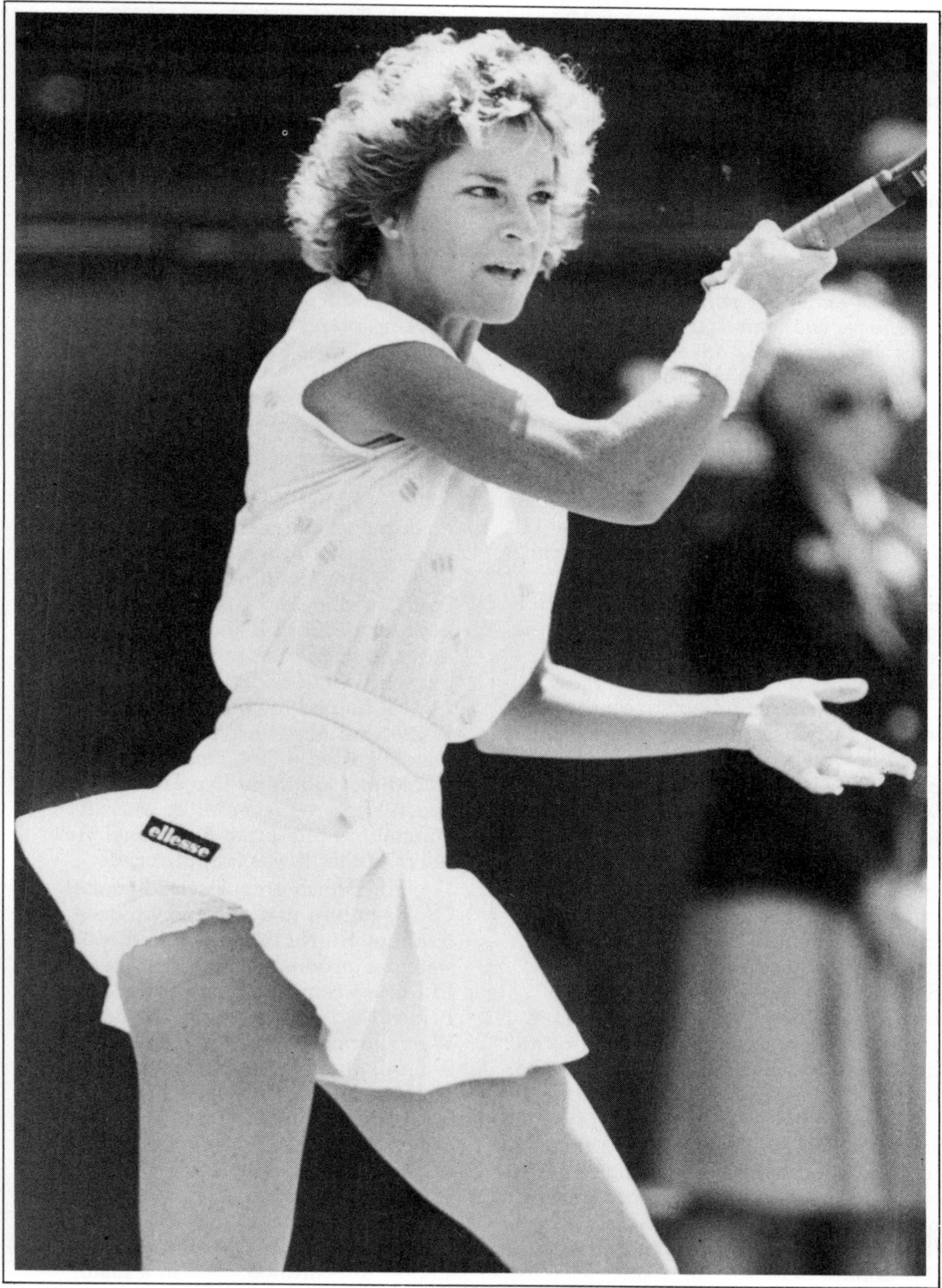

Of the five finals she and Mrs Lloyd had contested on Centre Court, Miss Navratilova felt the 1985 version was the most satisfying. "I was more of an underdog," she said, "maybe even more than the first time I won." And there was no hiding Mrs Lloyd's disappointment. "I had my chance and I couldn't take it," she said. "This is her court."

In fact it looked anything but in the first set when Mrs Lloyd, hitting the ball hard and deep, rattled the champion with the accuracy of her passing shots whenever she ventured to the net and exploited her early advantage to the full by breaking her in the third game.

But Miss Navratilova was not to be put off what she believed was her winning game. She insisted on pressing forward. And gradually, particularly as her serve picked up, the pressure began to tell. She couldn't save the first set but from the moment she broke in the fourth game of the second her confidence blossomed to a point where her triumph quickly looked an inevitability. The final score, 4-6, 6-3, 6-2, left no room for argument.

It was a sorry reflection on the women's game, nonetheless, to see the same two players dominating eight years after their first Wimbledon final. At 30 even Mrs Lloyd seemed mildly surprised to find how easily she had made the final.

Once again Miss Mandlikova, the girl most likely, failed to mount the sort of challenge that had been expected from her. She lost 6-1, 7-6 in round three to the Australian, Elizabeth Smylie. And Kathy Jordan, who had beaten Mrs Lloyd in the third round in 1983, fared even worse — falling to the little-known Russian, Larissa Savchenko, by 7-5, 3-6, 6-3 in round two.

For the first time the women's seeding sproved as unreliable a guide as the men's. Of the 16 players named, half had gone before the first round started: not only Miss Mandlikova (3) and Miss Jordan (10) but Claudia Kohde-Kilson (6), Bonnie Gadusek (9), Caterina Lindqvist (12), Carling Bassett (13), Wendy Turnbull (14) and the 15-year-old Argentine sensation, Gabriela Sabatini (15).

No-one was a less likely beneficiary than Molly Van Nostrand, who had entered at the qualifying stage against the advice of her doctor — she had undergone extensive foot surgery in March — but with the approval of her father. He had said: "You might as well. You won't be playing that much anyway!"

As it turned out the 20-year-old New Yorker sprang the biggest ambush of all by beating the fourth seed, the Bulgarian Manuela Maleeva, by 7-5, 6-2 for a quarter-final place and, though she subsequently lost to Zena Garrison, she was to return home almost £14,000 the richer.

Until Miss Van Nostrand's emergence, the main talking point had been the first round appearance of another American, Anne White, against Pam Shriver. And 'appearance' was the key word; because she took the court encased from neck to toe in a figure-hugging white bodysuit.

"It helped my tennis," claimed Miss White. But Miss Shriver, who won the match, called it "the most bizarre, stupid-looking thing I've seen on the court." Referee Alan Mills, without committing himself to a personal view, decreed that it was inappropriate.

For British enthusiasts, Annabel Croft's failure to overcome Chinese qualifier Hu Na in the opening round was to a large extent compensated for by Jo Durie's return to form. It was the British No 1 who removed the dangerous West German Miss Kohde-Kilsch 4-6, 6-1, 6-2 and she might have made the quarters had she converted either of the two first set points she had against her old rival Barbara Potter. But she didn't, and lost 7-6, 6-7, 6-1.

To many of the Wimbledon faithful, however, the championships will best be remembered for Virginia Wade's last singles appearance. And in a match

Miss Van Nosrand

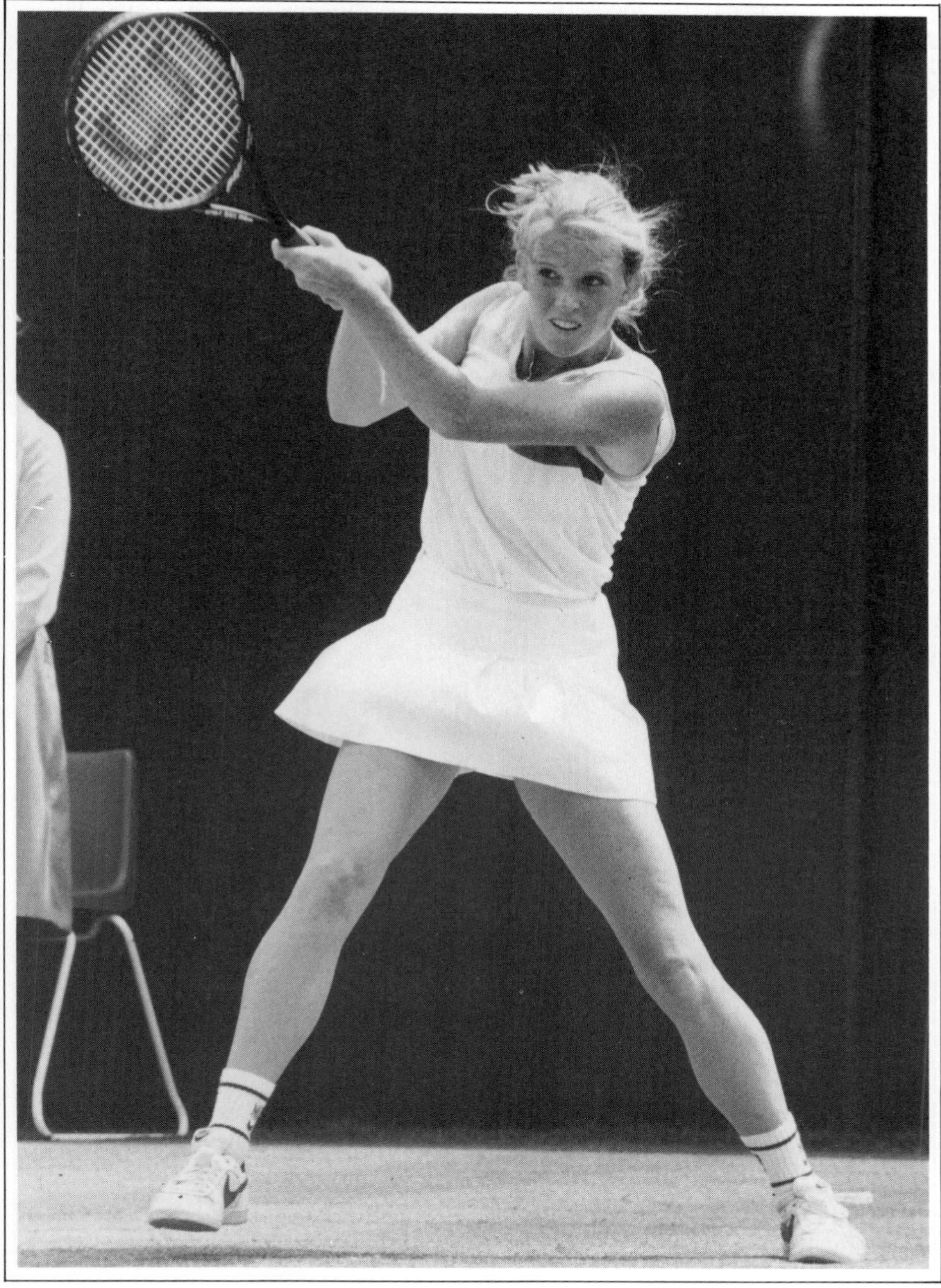

which was played, fittingly, on Centre Court just days before her 40th birthday. As ever she went down fighting, only losing to the fifth seeded Miss Shriver 6-2, 5-7, 6-2.

"To me," she said, "playing on the Centre Court is the most exciting thing in the world and I wanted to finish my career there against a good player. Everything worked out fine."

Pam Shriver

Jo Durie

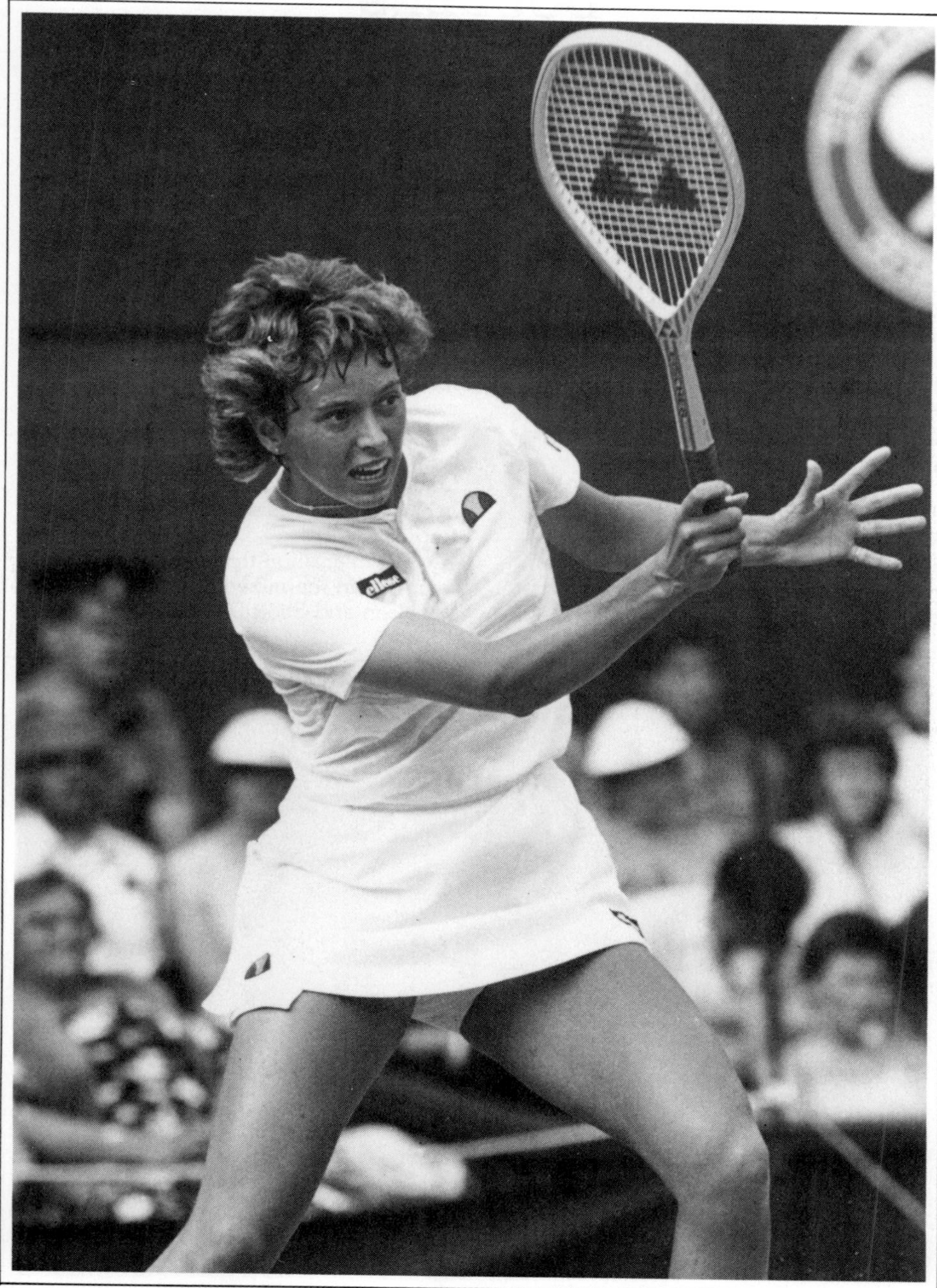

DOUBLES

It was a year of total change in the doubles. For the first time since 1958 a European partnership won the men's. In the women's Martina Navratilova and Pam Shriver fell one match short of equalling Suzanne Lenglen and Elizabeth Ryan's record of five successive titles. And in the mixed it was only after surviving a 23-21 final set in the semifinals that Miss Navratilova and Paul McNames succeeded to a crown held for two years by Wendy Turnbull and Britain's John Lloyd.

That represented some slight compensation for the disappointment Miss Navratilova must have felt. Forty-eight hours before the final curtain fell, she had been poised to become the first player since Billie Jean King in 1973 to hold three titles at once. That dream ended when she and her trusty lieutenant Pam Shriver, winner of their 110 previous matches together, were brought down 5-7, 6-3, 6-4 by third seeds Kathy Jordan and Elizabeth Smylie.

Having lost three previous finals to the holders with Anne Smith, Miss Jordan's revenge must have tasted all the sweeter. Her new-found Australian partner overcame early nervousness to play stunningly well at times although Miss Navratilova, it must be said, lacked her usual sharpness after her arduous singles final.

Her marathon three-and-a-half hour semifinal in the mixed, against Betsy Nagelsen and Scott Davis, may also have

Kathy Jordan and Elizabeth Smylie

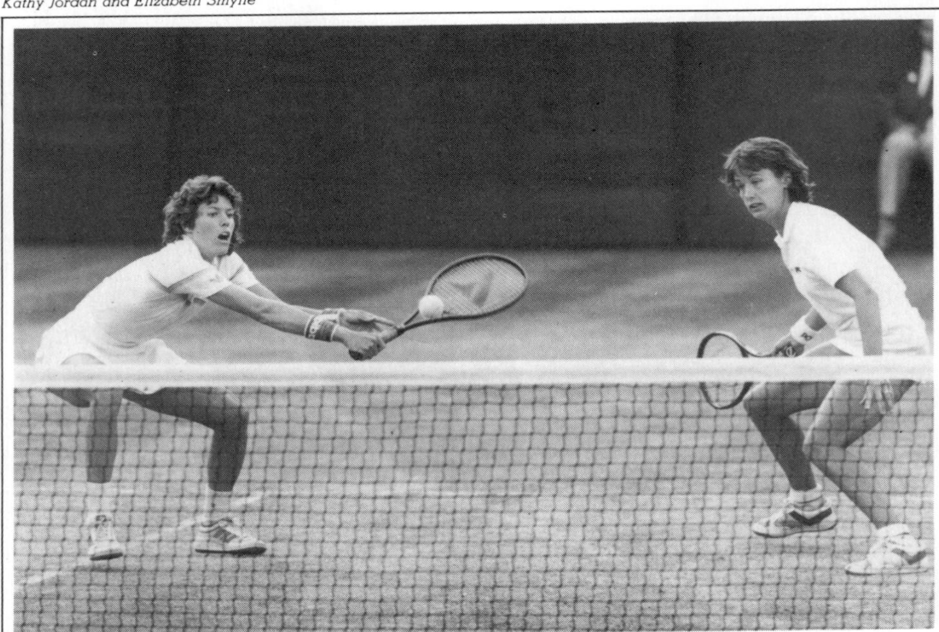

taken its toll. Played at the same time as the men's final, this proved an epic worthy of greater attention. Even Becker and Curren were at times distracted by the roars of excitement which washed over from No 1 Court.

The final was not short of tension and drama either. Australians John Fitzgerald and Mrs Smylie (again) showed great resilience in pushing the eventual champions, neither of whom had had a share of the title before, to 7-5, 4-6, 6-2.

For upsets and surprises, however, the men's event was unsurpassed. From round one, where Britain's Nick Brown and David Felgate ambushed America's third-seeded Ken Flach and Robert Seguso — who were to become US champions — by 8-6 in the fifth, to the final, in which Heinz Gunthardt and Balazs Taroczy overcame the Australians Pat Cash and Fitzgerald 6-4, 6-3, 4-6, 6-3, little or nothing went as expected.

It was a brilliant and well-deserved triumph for the Swiss and Hungarian team, who were also French champions in 1981. Using all their vast experience and guile they outwitted their younger opponents in a match of few rallies but aggressive and outstanding net play.

Yet the eighth seeds, the first European winners since Sweden's Sven Davidson and Ulf Schmidt 27 years before them, did remarkably well to survive the quarters. There they had to save five match points against Paul Annacone and Christo Van Rensburg in a 24-22 fifth set, the longest of the Championships.

As to Peter Fleming and John McEnroe, who had dominated for the two previous years, their interest as ended at the hands of Cash and Fitzgerald in the semifinals — leaving McEnroe without a Wimbledon title of any sort for the first time since his initial appearance in 1977.

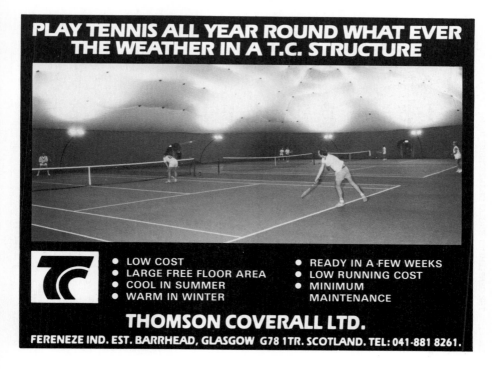

Event 1. — THE GENTLEMEN'S SINGLES CHAMPIONSHIP Holder: J P McEnroe

The Winner will become the holder, for the year only, of the CHALLENGE CUP presented to the Club by KING GEORGE V, and also of the CHALLENGE CUP presented by The All England Lawn Tennis and Croquet Club. The First Prize is a piece of silver, known as "The Renshaw Cup" annually presented to the Club by the surviving members of the family of the late ERNEST and WILLIAM RENSHAW. The Winner will receive silver replicas of the two Challenge Cups. A Silver Medal will be presented to the Runner-up and a Bronze Medal to each defeated Semi-finalist.

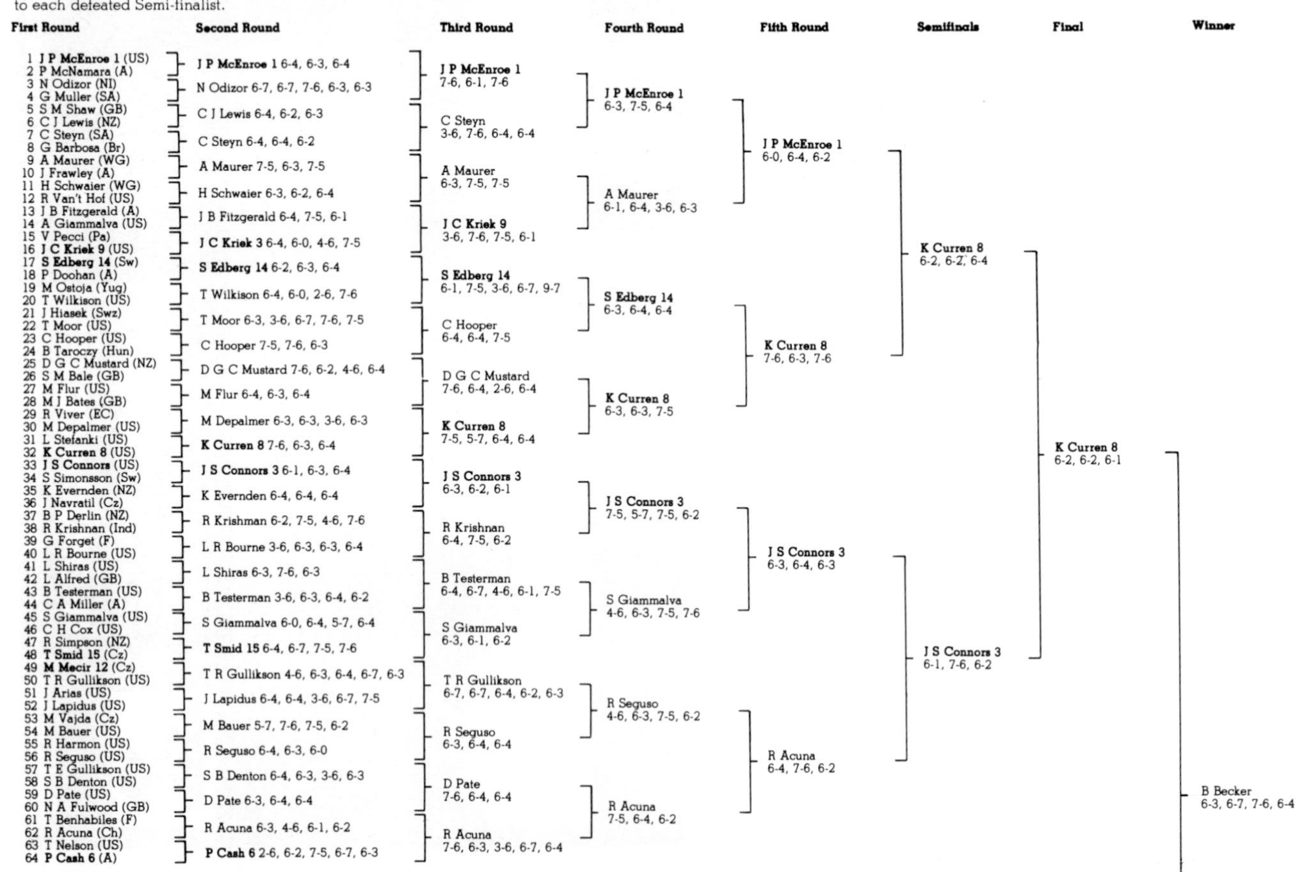

First Round

1 **J P McEnroe 1** (US)
2 P McNamara (A)
3 N Odizor (NI)
4 G Muller (SA)
5 S M Shaw (GB)
6 C J Lewis (NZ)
7 C Steyn (SA)
8 G Barbosa (Br)
9 A Maurer (WG)
10 J Frawley (A)
11 H Schwaier (WG)
12 R Van't Hof (US)
13 J B Fitzgerald (A)
14 A Giammalva (US)
15 V Pecci (Pa)
16 **J C Kriek 9** (US)
17 **S Edberg 14** (Sw)
18 P Doohan (A)
19 M Ostoja (Yug)
20 T Wilkison (US)
21 J Hiasek (Swz)
22 T Moor (US)
23 C Hooper (US)
24 B Taroczy (Hun)
25 D G C Mustard (NZ)
26 S M Bale (GB)
27 M Flur (US)
28 M J Bates (GB)
29 R Viver (EC)
30 M Depalmer (US)
31 L Stefanki (US)
32 **K Curren 8** (US)
33 **J S Connors** (US)
34 S Simonsson (Sw)
35 K Evernden (NZ)
36 J Navratil (Cz)
37 B P Derlin (NZ)
38 R Krishnan (Ind)
39 G Forget (F)
40 L R Bourne (US)
41 L Shiras (US)
42 L Alfred (GB)
43 B Testerman (US)
44 C A Miller (A)
45 S Giammalva (US)
46 C H Cox (US)
47 R Simpson (NZ)
48 **T Smid 15** (Cz)
49 **M Mecir 12** (Cz)
50 T R Gullikson (US)
51 J Arias (US)
52 J Lapidus (US)
53 M Vajda (Cz)
54 M Bauer (US)
55 R Harmon (US)
56 R Seguso (US)
57 T E Gullikson (US)
58 S B Denton (US)
59 D Pate (US)
60 N A Fulwood (GB)
61 T Benhabiles (F)
62 R Acuna (Ch)
63 T Nelson (US)
64 **P Cash 6** (A)

Second Round

J P McEnroe 1 6-4, 6-3, 6-4
N Odizor 6-7, 6-7, 7-6, 6-3, 6-3
C J Lewis 6-4, 6-2, 6-3
C Steyn 6-4, 6-4, 6-2
A Maurer 7-5, 6-3, 7-5
H Schwaier 6-3, 6-2, 6-4
J B Fitzgerald 6-4, 7-5, 6-1
J C Kriek 3 6-4, 6-0, 4-6, 7-5
S Edberg 14 6-2, 6-3, 6-4
T Wilkison 6-4, 6-0, 2-6, 7-6
T Moor 6-3, 3-6, 6-7, 7-6, 7-5
C Hooper 7-5, 7-6, 6-3
D G C Mustard 7-6, 6-2, 4-6, 6-4
M Flur 6-4, 6-3, 6-4
M Depalmer 6-3, 6-3, 3-6, 6-3
K Curren 8 7-6, 6-3, 6-4
J S Connors 3 6-1, 6-3, 6-4
K Evernden 6-4, 6-4, 6-4
R Krishman 6-2, 7-5, 4-6, 7-6
L R Bourne 3-6, 6-3, 6-3, 6-4
L Shiras 6-3, 7-6, 6-3
B Testerman 3-6, 6-3, 6-4, 6-2
S Giammalva 6-0, 6-4, 5-7, 6-4
T Smid 15 6-4, 6-7, 7-5, 7-6
T R Gullikson 4-6, 6-3, 6-4, 6-7, 6-3
J Lapidus 6-4, 6-4, 3-6, 6-7, 7-5
M Bauer 5-7, 7-6, 7-5, 6-2
R Seguso 6-4, 6-3, 6-0
S B Denton 6-4, 6-3, 3-6, 6-3
D Pate 6-3, 6-4, 6-4
R Acuna 6-3, 4-6, 6-1, 6-2
P Cash 6 2-6, 6-2, 7-5, 6-7, 6-3

Third Round

J P McEnroe 1 7-6, 6-1, 7-6
C Steyn 3-6, 7-6, 6-4, 6-4
A Maurer 6-3, 7-5, 7-5
J C Kriek 9 3-6, 7-6, 7-5, 6-1
S Edberg 14 6-1, 7-5, 3-6, 6-7, 9-7
C Hooper 6-4, 6-4, 7-5
D G C Mustard 7-6, 6-4, 2-6, 6-4
K Curren 8 7-5, 5-7, 6-4, 6-4
J S Connors 3 6-3, 6-2, 6-1
R Krishnan 6-4, 7-5, 6-2
B Testerman 6-4, 6-7, 4-6, 6-1, 7-5
S Giammalva 6-3, 6-1, 6-2
T R Gullikson 6-7, 6-7, 6-4, 6-2, 6-3
R Seguso 6-3, 6-4, 6-4
D Pate 7-6, 6-4, 6-4
R Acuna 7-6, 6-3, 3-6, 6-7, 6-4

Fourth Round

J P McEnroe 1 6-3, 7-5, 6-4
A Maurer 6-1, 6-4, 3-6, 6-3
S Edberg 14 6-3, 6-4, 6-4
K Curren 8 6-3, 6-3, 7-5
J S Connors 3 7-5, 5-7, 7-5, 6-2
S Giammalva 4-6, 6-3, 7-5, 7-6
R Seguso 4-6, 6-3, 7-5, 6-2
R Acuna 7-5, 6-4, 6-2

Fifth Round

J P McEnroe 1 6-0, 6-4, 6-2
K Curren 8 7-6, 6-3, 7-6
J S Connors 3 6-3, 6-4, 6-3
R Acuna 6-4, 7-6, 6-2

Semifinals

K Curren 8 6-2, 6-2, 6-4
J S Connors 3 6-1, 7-6, 6-2

Final

K Curren 8 6-2, 6-2, 6-1

Winner

B Becker 6-3, 6-7, 7-6, 6-4

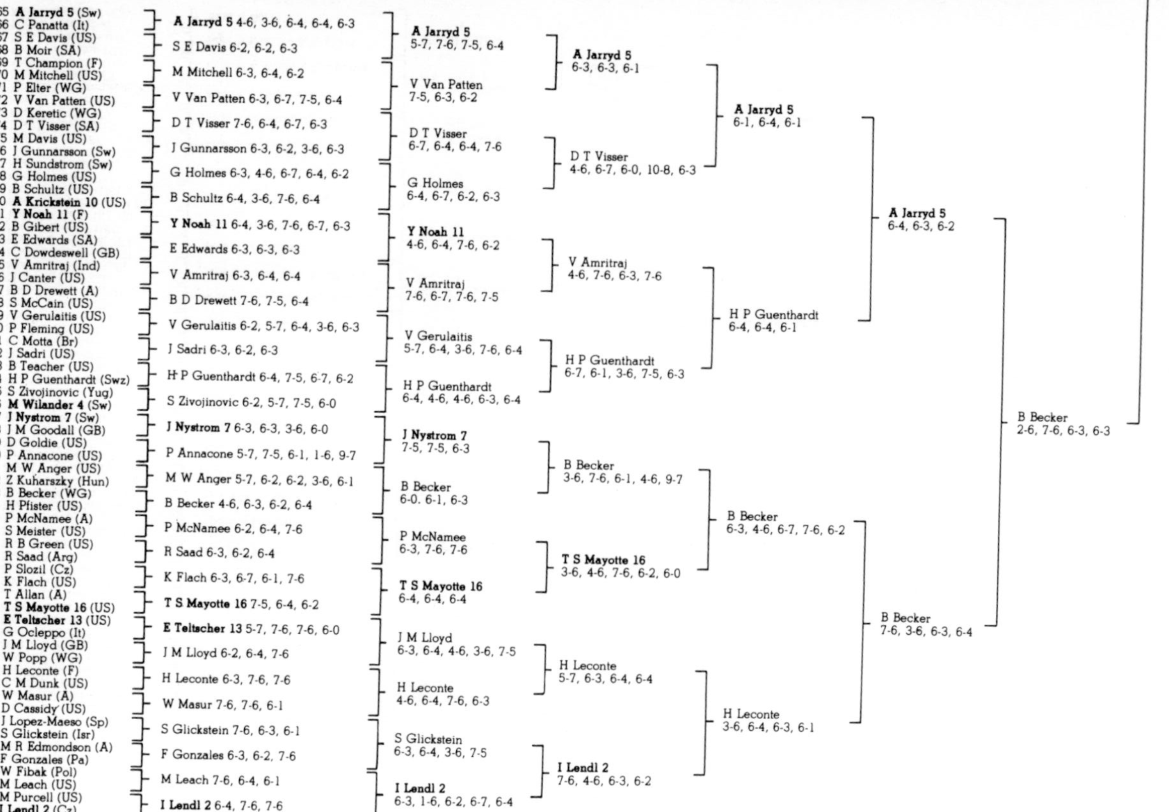

65 **A Jarryd 5** (Sw)
66 C Panatta (It)
67 S E Davis (US)
68 B Moir (SA)
69 T Champion (F)
70 M Mitchell (US)
71 P Elter (WG)
72 V Van Patten (US)
73 D Keretic (WG)
74 D T Visser (SA)
75 M Davis (US)
76 J Gunnarsson (Sw)
77 H Sundstrom (Sw)
78 G Holmes (US)
79 B Schultz (US)
80 **A Krickstein 10** (US)
81 **Y Noah 11** (F)
82 B Gibert (US)
83 E Edwards (SA)
84 C Dowdeswell (GB)
85 V Amritraj (Ind)
86 J Canter (US)
87 B D Drewett (A)
88 S McCain (US)
89 V Gerulaitis (US)
90 P Fleming (US)
91 C Motta (Br)
92 J Sadri (US)
93 B Teacher (US)
94 H P Guenthardt (Swz)
95 S Zivojinovic (Yug)
96 **M Wilander 4** (Sw)
97 **J Nystrom 7** (Sw)
98 J M Goodall (GB)
99 D Goldie (US)
100 P Annacone (US)
101 M W Anger (US)
102 Z Kuharszky (Hun)
103 B Becker (WG)
104 H Pfister (US)
105 P McNamee (A)
106 S Meister (US)
107 R B Green (US)
108 R Saad (Arg)
109 P Slozil (Cz)
110 K Flach (US)
111 T Allan (A)
112 **T S Mayotte 16** (US)
113 **E Teltscher 13** (US)
114 G Ocleppo (It)
115 J M Lloyd (GB)
116 W Popp (WG)
117 H Leconte (F)
118 C M Dunk (US)
119 W Masur (A)
120 D Cassidy (US)
121 J Lopez-Maeso (Sp)
122 S Glickstein (Isr)
123 M R Edmondson (A)
124 F Gonzales (Pa)
125 W Fibak (Pol)
126 M Leach (US)
127 M Purcell (US)
128 **I Lendl 2** (Cz)
A Jarryd 5 4-6, 3-6, 6-4, 6-4, 6-3
S E Davis 6-2, 6-2, 6-3
M Mitchell 6-3, 6-4, 6-2
V Van Patten 6-3, 6-7, 7-5, 6-4
D T Visser 7-6, 6-4, 6-7, 6-3
J Gunnarsson 6-3, 6-2, 3-6, 6-3
G Holmes 6-3, 4-6, 6-7, 6-4, 6-2
B Schultz 6-4, 3-6, 7-6, 6-4
Y Noah 11 6-4, 3-6, 7-6, 6-7, 6-3
E Edwards 6-3, 6-3, 6-3
V Amritraj 6-3, 6-4, 6-4
B D Drewett 7-6, 7-5, 6-4
V Gerulaitis 6-2, 5-7, 6-4, 3-6, 6-3
J Sadri 6-3, 6-2, 6-3
H P Guenthardt 6-4, 7-5, 6-7, 6-2
S Zivojinovic 6-2, 5-7, 7-5, 6-0
J Nystrom 7 6-3, 6-3, 3-6, 6-0
P Annacone 5-7, 7-5, 6-1, 1-6, 9-7
M W Anger 5-7, 6-2, 6-2, 3-6, 6-1
B Becker 4-6, 6-3, 6-2, 6-4
P McNamee 6-2, 6-4, 7-6
R Saad 6-3, 6-2, 6-4
K Flach 6-3, 6-7, 6-1, 7-6
T S Mayotte 16 7-5, 6-4, 6-2
E Teltscher 13 5-7, 7-6, 7-6, 6-0
J M Lloyd 6-2, 6-4, 7-6
H Leconte 6-3, 7-6, 7-6
W Masur 7-6, 7-6, 6-1
S Glickstein 7-6, 6-3, 6-1
F Gonzales 6-3, 6-2, 7-6
M Leach 7-6, 6-4, 6-1
I Lendl 2 6-4, 7-6, 7-6
A Jarryd 5 5-7, 7-6, 7-5, 6-4
V Van Patten 7-5, 6-3, 6-2
D T Visser 6-7, 6-4, 6-4, 7-6
G Holmes 6-4, 6-7, 6-2, 6-3
Y Noah 11 4-6, 6-4, 7-6, 6-2
V Amritraj 7-6, 6-7, 7-6, 7-5
V Gerulaitis 5-7, 6-4, 3-6, 7-6, 6-4
H P Guenthardt 6-4, 4-6, 4-6, 6-3, 6-4
J Nystrom 7 7-5, 7-5, 6-3
B Becker 6-0. 6-1, 6-3
P McNamee 6-3, 7-6, 7-6
T S Mayotte 16 6-4, 6-4, 6-4
J M Lloyd 6-3, 6-4, 4-6, 3-6, 7-5
H Leconte 4-6, 6-4, 7-6, 6-3
S Glickstein 6-3, 6-4, 3-6, 7-5
I Lendl 2 6-3, 1-6, 6-2, 6-7, 6-4
A Jarryd 5 6-3, 6-3, 6-1
D T Visser 4-6, 6-7, 6-0, 10-8, 6-3
V Amritraj 4-6, 7-6, 6-3, 7-6
H P Guenthardt 6-7, 6-1, 3-6, 7-5, 6-3
B Becker 3-6, 7-6, 6-1, 4-6, 9-7
T S Mayotte 16 3-6, 4-6, 7-6, 6-2, 6-0
H Leconte 5-7, 6-3, 6-4, 6-4
I Lendl 2 7-6, 4-6, 6-3, 6-2
A Jarryd 5 6-1, 6-4, 6-1
H P Guenthardt 6-4, 6-4, 6-1
B Becker 6-3, 4-6, 6-7, 7-6, 6-2
H Leconte 3-6, 6-4, 6-3, 6-1
A Jarryd 5 6-4, 6-3, 6-2
B Becker 7-6, 3-6, 6-3, 6-4
B Becker 2-6, 7-6, 6-3, 6-3

Heavy type denotes seeded players.
The figure against names denotes the order in which they have been seeded.

Event 2. — THE LADIES' SINGLES CHAMPIONSHIP Holder: Miss M Navratilova

The Winner will become the holder, for the year only, of the CHALLENGE TROPHY presented to The All England Lawn Tennis and Croquet Club. The Winner will receive a silver replica of the Trophy. A Silver Medal will be presented to the Runner-up and a Bronze Medal to each defeated Semi-finalist.

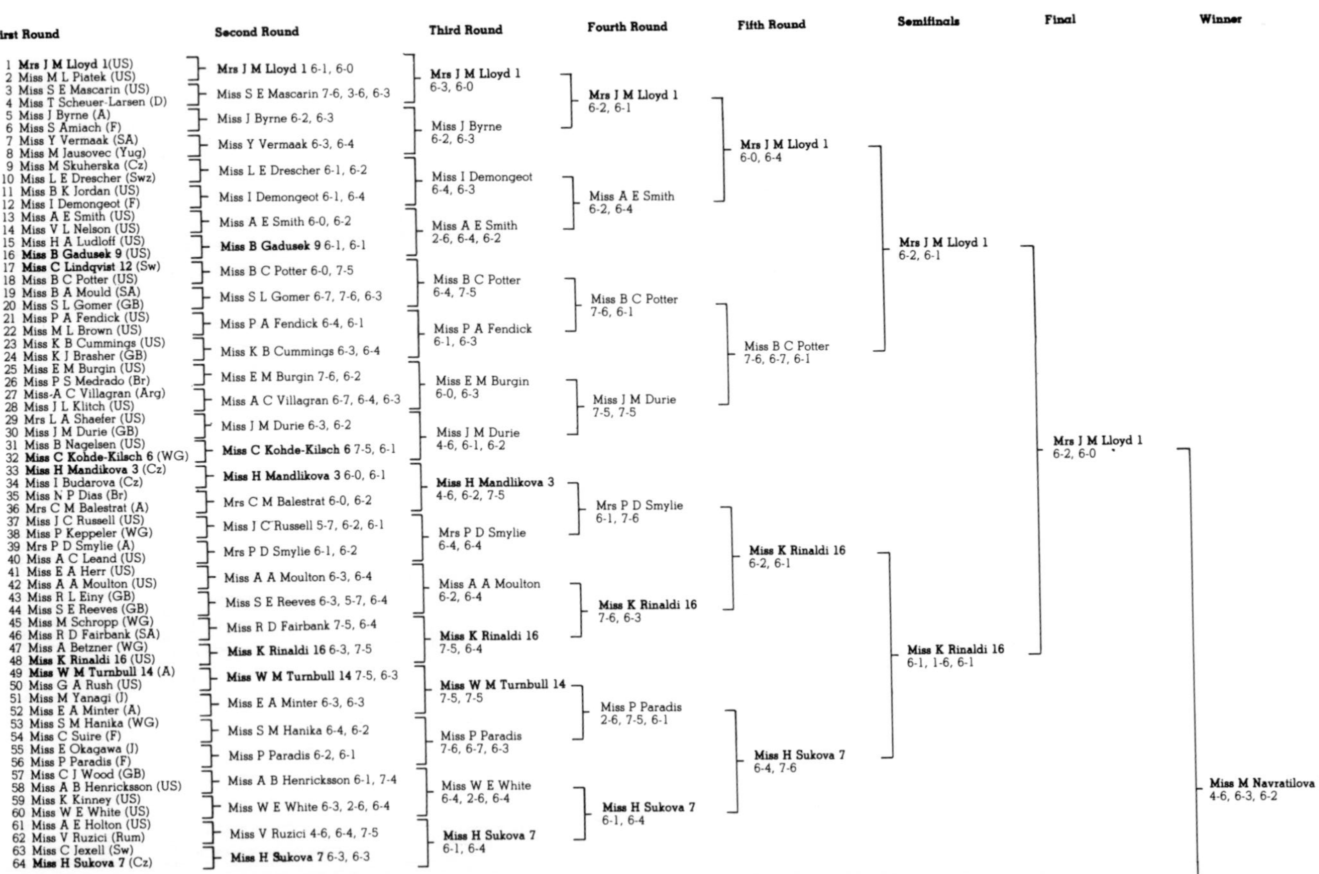

First Round

1 **Mrs J M Lloyd 1**(US)
2 Miss M L Piatek (US)
3 Miss S E Mascarin (US)
4 Miss T Scheuer-Larsen (D)
5 Miss J Byrne (A)
6 Miss S Amiach (F)
7 Miss Y Vermaak (SA)
8 Miss M Jausovec (Yug)
9 Miss M Skuherska (Cz)
10 Miss L E Drescher (Swz)
11 Miss B K Jordan (US)
12 Miss I Demongeot (F)
13 Miss A E Smith (US)
14 Miss V L Nelson (US)
15 Miss H A Ludloff (US)
16 **Miss B Gadusek 9** (US)
17 **Miss C Lindqvist 12** (Sw)
18 Miss B C Potter (US)
19 Miss B A Mould (SA)
20 Miss S L Gomer (GB)
21 Miss P A Fendick (US)
22 Miss M L Brown (US)
23 Miss K B Cummings (US)
24 Miss K J Brasher (GB)
25 Miss E M Burgin (US)
26 Miss P S Medrado (Br)
27 Miss-A C Villagran (Arg)
28 Miss J L Klitch (US)
29 Mrs L A Shaefer (US)
30 Miss J M Durie (GB)
31 Miss B Nagelsen (US)
32 **Miss C Kohde-Kilsch 6** (WG)
33 **Miss H Mandikova 3** (Cz)
34 Miss I Budarova (Cz)
35 Miss N P Dias (Br)
36 Mrs C M Balestrat (A)
37 Miss J C Russell (US)
38 Miss P Keppeler (WG)
39 Mrs P D Smylie (A)
40 Miss A C Leand (US)
41 Miss E A Herr (US)
42 Miss A A Moulton (US)
43 Miss R L Einy (GB)
44 Miss S E Reeves (GB)
45 Miss M Schropp (WG)
46 Miss R D Fairbank (SA)
47 Miss A Betzner (WG)
48 **Miss K Rinaldi 16** (US)
49 **Miss W M Turnbull 14** (A)
50 Miss G A Rush (US)
51 Miss M Yanagi (J)
52 Miss E A Minter (A)
53 Miss S M Hanika (WG)
54 Miss C Suire (F)
55 Miss E Okagawa (J)
56 Miss P Paradis (F)
57 Miss C J Wood (GB)
58 Miss A B Henricksson (US)
59 Miss K Kinney (US)
60 Miss W E White (US)
61 Miss A E Holton (US)
62 Miss V Ruzici (Rum)
63 Miss C Jexell (Sw)
64 **Miss H Sukova 7** (Cz)

Second Round

Mrs J M Lloyd 1 6-1, 6-0
Miss S E Mascarin 7-6, 3-6, 6-3
Miss J Byrne 6-2, 6-3
Miss Y Vermaak 6-3, 6-4
Miss L E Drescher 6-1, 6-2
Miss I Demongeot 6-1, 6-4
Miss A E Smith 6-0, 6-2
Miss B Gadusek 9 6-1, 6-1
Miss B C Potter 6-0, 7-5
Miss S L Gomer 6-7, 7-6, 6-3
Miss P A Fendick 6-4, 6-1
Miss K B Cummings 6-3, 6-4
Miss E M Burgin 7-6, 6-2
Miss A C Villagran 6-7, 6-4, 6-3
Miss J M Durie 6-3, 6-2
Miss C Kohde-Kilsch 6 7-5, 6-1
Miss H Mandlikova 3 6-0, 6-1
Mrs C M Balestrat 6-0, 6-2
Miss J C Russell 5-7, 6-2, 6-1
Mrs P D Smylie 6-1, 6-2
Miss A A Moulton 6-3, 6-4
Miss S E Reeves 6-3, 5-7, 6-4
Miss R D Fairbank 7-5, 6-4
Miss K Rinaldi 16 6-3, 7-5
Miss W M Turnbull 14 7-5, 6-3
Miss E A Minter 6-3, 6-3
Miss S M Hanika 6-4, 6-2
Miss P Paradis 6-2, 6-1
Miss A B Henricksson 6-1, 7-4
Miss W E White 6-3, 2-6, 6-4
Miss V Ruzici 4-6, 6-4, 7-5
Miss H Sukova 7 6-3, 6-3

Third Round

Mrs J M Lloyd 1 6-3, 6-0
Miss J Byrne 6-2, 6-3
Miss I Demongeot 6-4, 6-3
Miss A E Smith 2-6, 6-4, 6-2
Miss B C Potter 6-4, 7-5
Miss P A Fendick 6-1, 6-3
Miss E M Burgin 6-0, 6-3
Miss J M Durie 4-6, 6-1, 6-2
Miss H Mandlikova 3 4-6, 6-2, 7-5
Mrs P D Smylie 6-4, 6-4
Miss A A Moulton 6-2, 6-4
Miss K Rinaldi 16 7-5, 6-4
Miss W M Turnbull 14 7-5, 7-5
Miss P Paradis 7-6, 6-7, 6-3
Miss W E White 6-4, 2-6, 6-4
Miss H Sukova 7 6-1, 6-4

Fourth Round

Mrs J M Lloyd 1 6-2, 6-1
Miss A E Smith 6-2, 6-4
Miss B C Potter 7-6, 6-1
Miss J M Durie 7-5, 7-5
Mrs P D Smylie 6-1, 7-6
Miss K Rinaldi 16 7-6, 6-3
Miss P Paradis 2-6, 7-5, 6-1
Miss H Sukova 7 6-1, 6-4

Fifth Round

Mrs J M Lloyd 1 6-0, 6-4
Miss B C Potter 7-6, 6-7, 6-1
Miss K Rinaldi 16 6-2, 6-1
Miss H Sukova 7 6-4, 7-6

Semifinals

Mrs J M Lloyd 1 6-2, 6-1
Miss K Rinaldi 16 6-1, 1-6, 6-1

Final

Mrs J M Lloyd 1 6-2, 6-0

Winner

Miss M Navratilova 1 4-6, 6-3, 6-2

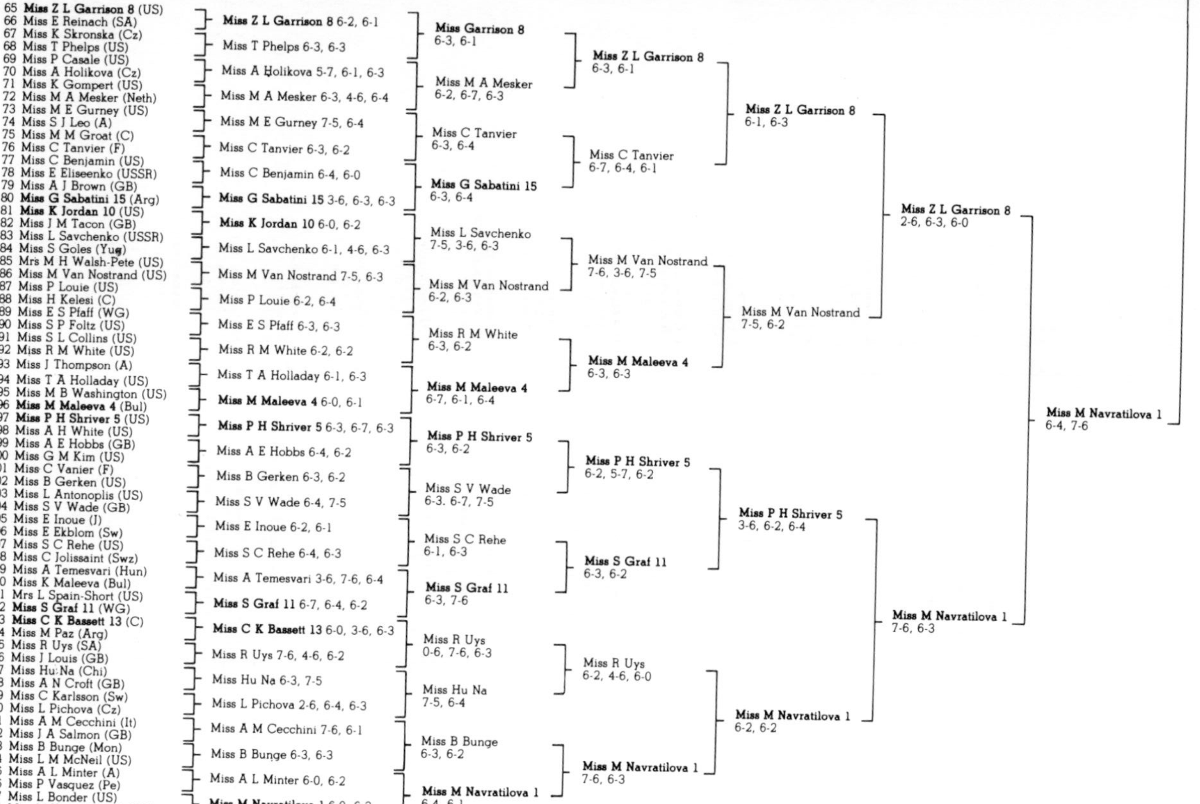

Heavy type denotes seeded players.
The figure against names denotes the order in which they have been seeded.

Event 3. — THE GENTLEMEN'S DOUBLES CHAMPIONSHIP Holder: P Fleming and J P McEnroe

The Winners will become the holders, for the year only, of the CHALLENGE CUP presented by the OXFORD UNIVERSITY LAWN TENNIS CLUB and the late SIR HERBERT WILBERFORCE respectively. The Winners will receive silver replicas of the Challenge Cup. A Silver Medal will be presented to each of the Runners-up, and a Bronze Medal to each defeated Semi-finalist.

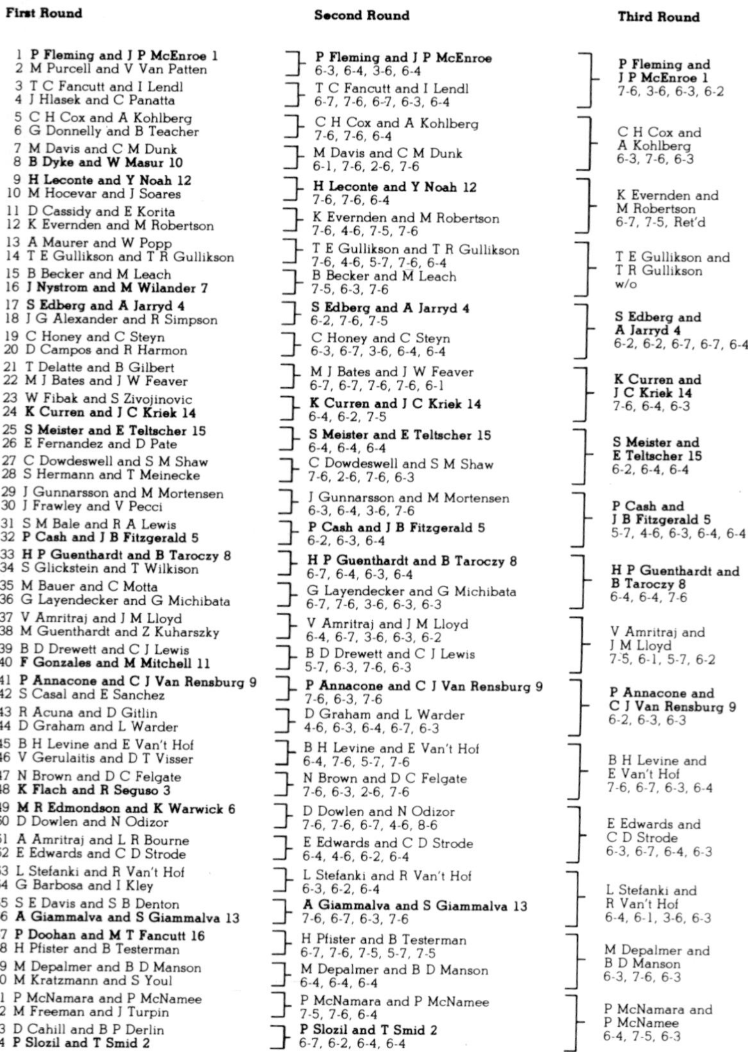

First Round	Second Round	Third Round
1 **P Fleming and J P McEnroe 1** 2 M Purcell and V Van Patten 3 T C Fancutt and I Lendl 4 J Hlasek and C Panatta	**P Fleming and J P McEnroe** 6-3, 6-4, 3-6, 6-4 T C Fancutt and I Lendl 6-7, 7-6, 6-7, 6-3, 6-4	**P Fleming and J P McEnroe 1** 7-6, 3-6, 6-3, 6-2
5 C H Cox and A Kohlberg 6 G Donnelly and B Teacher 7 M Davis and C M Dunk 8 **B Dyke and W Masur 10**	C H Cox and A Kohlberg 7-6, 7-6, 6-4 M Davis and C M Dunk 6-1, 7-6, 2-6, 7-6	C H Cox and A Kohlberg 6-3, 7-6, 6-3
9 **H Leconte and Y Noah 12** 10 M Hocevar and J Soares 11 D Cassidy and E Korita 12 K Evernden and M Robertson	**H Leconte and Y Noah 12** 7-6, 7-6, 6-4 K Evernden and M Robertson 7-6, 4-6, 7-5, 7-6	K Evernden and M Robertson 6-7, 7-5, Ret'd
13 A Maurer and W Popp 14 T E Gullikson and T R Gullikson 15 B Becker and M Leach 16 **J Nystrom and M Wilander 7**	T E Gullikson and T R Gullikson 7-6, 4-6, 5-7, 7-6, 6-4 B Becker and M Leach 7-5, 6-3, 7-6	T E Gullikson and T R Gullikson w/o
17 **S Edberg and A Jarryd 4** 18 J G Alexander and R Simpson 19 C Honey and C Steyn 20 D Campos and R Harmon	**S Edberg and A Jarryd 4** 6-2, 7-6, 7-5 C Honey and C Steyn 6-3, 6-7, 3-6, 6-4, 6-4	**S Edberg and A Jarryd 4** 6-2, 6-2, 6-7, 6-7, 6-4
21 T Delatte and B Gilbert 22 M J Bates and J W Feaver 23 W Fibak and S Zivojinovic 24 **K Curren and J C Kriek 14**	M J Bates and J W Feaver 6-7, 6-7, 7-6, 7-6, 6-1 **K Curren and J C Kriek 14** 6-4, 6-2, 7-5	**K Curren and J C Kriek 14** 7-6, 6-4, 6-3
25 **S Meister and E Teltscher 15** 26 E Fernandez and D Pate 27 C Dowdeswell and S M Shaw 28 S Hermann and T Meinecke	**S Meister and E Teltscher 15** 6-4, 6-4, 6-4 C Dowdeswell and S M Shaw 7-6, 2-6, 7-6, 6-3	**S Meister and E Teltscher 15** 6-2, 6-4, 6-4
29 J Gunnarsson and M Mortensen 30 J Frawley and V Pecci 31 S M Bale and R A Lewis 32 **P Cash and J B Fitzgerald 5**	J Gunnarsson and M Mortensen 6-3, 6-4, 3-6, 7-6 **P Cash and J B Fitzgerald 5** 6-2, 6-3, 6-4	**P Cash and J B Fitzgerald 5** 5-7, 4-6, 6-3, 6-4, 6-4
33 **H P Guenthardt and B Taroczy 8** 34 S Glickstein and T Wilkison 35 M Bauer and C Motta 36 G Layendecker and G Michibata	**H P Guenthardt and B Taroczy 8** 6-7, 6-4, 6-3, 6-4 G Layendecker and G Michibata 6-7, 7-6, 3-6, 6-3, 6-3	**H P Guenthardt and B Taroczy 8** 6-4, 6-4, 7-6
37 V Amritraj and J M Lloyd 38 M Guenthardt and Z Kuharszky 39 B D Drewett and C J Lewis 40 **F Gonzales and M Mitchell 11**	V Amritraj and J M Lloyd 6-4, 6-7, 3-6, 6-3, 6-2 B D Drewett and C J Lewis 5-7, 6-3, 7-6, 6-3	V Amritraj and J M Lloyd 7-5, 6-1, 5-7, 6-2
41 **P Annacone and C J Van Rensburg 9** 42 S Casal and E Sanchez 43 R Acuna and D Gitlin 44 D Graham and L Warder	**P Annacone and C J Van Rensburg 9** 7-6, 6-3, 7-6 D Graham and L Warder 4-6, 6-3, 6-4, 6-7, 6-3	**P Annacone and C J Van Rensburg 9** 6-2, 6-3, 6-3
45 B H Levine and E Van't Hof 46 V Gerulaitis and D T Visser 47 N Brown and D C Felgate 48 **K Flach and R Seguso 3**	B H Levine and E Van't Hof 6-4, 7-6, 5-7, 7-6 N Brown and D C Felgate 7-6, 6-3, 2-6, 7-6	B H Levine and E Van't Hof 7-6, 6-7, 6-3, 6-4
49 **M R Edmondson and K Warwick 6** 50 D Dowlen and N Odizor 51 A Amritraj and L R Bourne 52 E Edwards and C D Strode	D Dowlen and N Odizor 7-6, 7-6, 6-7, 4-6, 8-6 E Edwards and C D Strode 6-4, 4-6, 6-2, 6-4	E Edwards and C D Strode 6-3, 6-7, 6-4, 6-3
53 L Stefanki and R Van't Hof 54 G Barbosa and I Kley 55 S E Davis and S B Denton 56 **A Giammalva and S Giammalva 13**	L Stefanki and R Van't Hof 6-3, 6-2, 6-4 **A Giammalva and S Giammalva 13** 7-6, 6-7, 6-3, 7-6	L Stefanki and R Van't Hof 6-4, 6-1, 3-6, 6-3
57 **P Doohan and M T Fancutt 16** 58 H Pfister and B Testerman 59 M Depalmer and B D Manson 60 M Kratzmann and S Youl	H Pfister and B Testerman 6-7, 7-6, 7-5, 5-7, 7-5 M Depalmer and B D Manson 6-4, 6-4, 6-4	M Depalmer and B D Manson 6-3, 7-6, 6-3
61 P McNamara and P McNamee 62 M Freeman and J Turpin 63 D Cahill and B P Derlin 64 **P Slozil and T Smid 2**	P McNamara and P McNamee 7-5, 7-6, 6-4 **P Slozil and T Smid 2** 6-7, 6-2, 6-4, 6-4	P McNamara and P McNamee 6-4, 7-5, 6-3

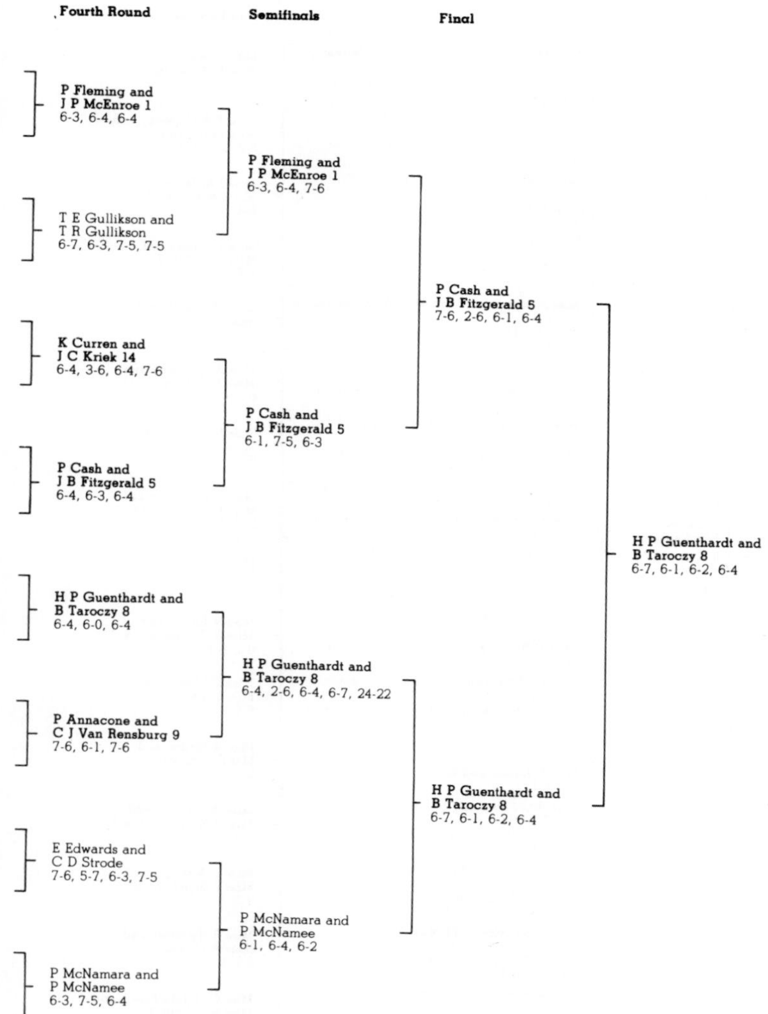

Fourth Round
Semifinals
Final
P Fleming and
J P McEnroe 1
6-3, 6-4, 6-4
T E Gullikson and
T R Gullikson
6-7, 6-3, 7-5, 7-5
K Curren and
J C Kriek 14
6-4, 3-6, 6-4, 7-6
P Cash and
J B Fitzgerald 5
6-4, 6-3, 6-4
H P Guenthardt and
B Taroczy 8
6-4, 6-0, 6-4
P Annacone and
C J Van Rensburg 9
7-6, 6-1, 7-6
E Edwards and
C D Strode
7-6, 5-7, 6-3, 7-5
P McNamara and
P McNamee
6-3, 7-5, 6-4
P Fleming and
J P McEnroe 1
6-3, 6-4, 7-6
P Cash and
J B Fitzgerald 5
6-1, 7-5, 6-3
H P Guenthardt and
B Taroczy 8
6-4, 2-6, 6-4, 6-7, 24-22
P McNamara and
P McNamee
6-1, 6-4, 6-2
P Cash and
J B Fitzgerald 5
7-6, 2-6, 6-1, 6-4
H P Guenthardt and
B Taroczy 8
6-7, 6-1, 6-2, 6-4
H P Guenthardt and
B Taroczy 8
6-7, 6-1, 6-2, 6-4

Heavy type denotes seeded players.
The figure against names denotes the order in which they have been seeded.

Event 4. — THE LADIES' DOUBLES CHAMPIONSHIP Holder: Miss M Navratilova and P H Shriver

The Winners will become the holders, for the year only, of the CHALLENGE CUP presented by H.R.H. PRINCESS MARINA, DUCHESS OF KENT, the late President of The All England Lawn Tennis and Croquet Club. The Winners will receive silver replicas of the Challenge Cup. A Silver Medal will be presented to each of the Runners-up and a Bronze Medal to each defeated Semi-finalist.

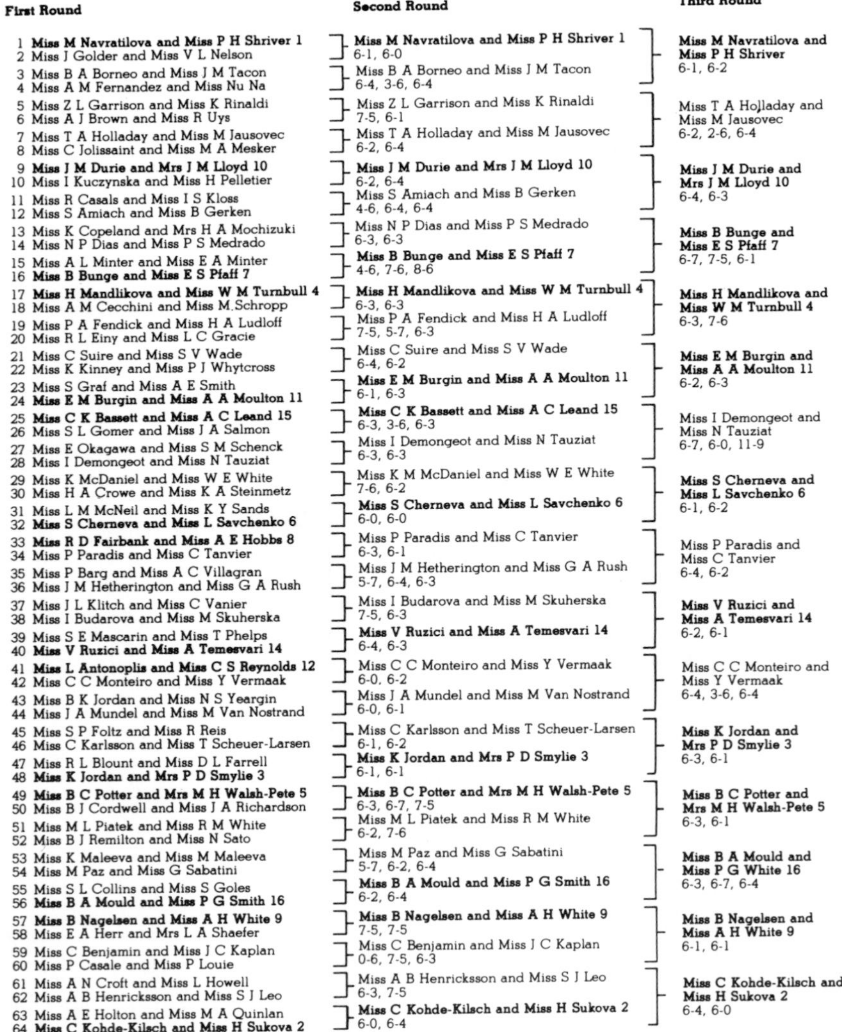

First Round	Second Round	Third Round
1 **Miss M Navratilova and Miss P H Shriver 1** 2 Miss J Golder and Miss V L Nelson	**Miss M Navratilova and Miss P H Shriver 1** 6-1, 6-0	**Miss M Navratilova and Miss P H Shriver** 6-1, 6-2
3 Miss B A Borneo and Miss J M Tacon 4 Miss A M Fernandez and Miss Nu Na	Miss B A Borneo and Miss J M Tacon 6-4, 3-6, 6-4	
5 Miss Z L Garrison and Miss K Rinaldi 6 Miss A J Brown and Miss R Uys	Miss Z L Garrison and Miss K Rinaldi 7-5, 6-1	Miss T A Holladay and Miss M Jausovec 6-2, 2-6, 6-4
7 Miss T A Holladay and Miss M Jausovec 8 Miss C Jolissaint and Miss M A Mesker	Miss T A Holladay and Miss M Jausovec 6-2, 6-4	
9 **Miss J M Durie and Mrs J M Lloyd 10** 10 Miss I Kuczynska and Miss H Pelletier	**Miss J M Durie and Mrs J M Lloyd 10** 6-2, 6-4	**Miss J M Durie and Mrs J M Lloyd 10** 6-4, 6-3
11 Miss R Casals and Miss I S Kloss 12 Miss S Amiach and Miss B Gerken	Miss S Amiach and Miss B Gerken 4-6, 6-4, 6-4	
13 Miss K Copeland and Mrs H A Mochizuki 14 Miss N P Dias and Miss P S Medrado	Miss N P Dias and Miss P S Medrado 6-3, 6-3	**Miss B Bunge and Miss E S Pfaff 7** 6-7, 7-5, 6-1
15 Miss A L Minter and Miss E A Minter 16 **Miss B Bunge and Miss E S Pfaff 7**	**Miss B Bunge and Miss E S Pfaff 7** 4-6, 7-6, 8-6	
17 **Miss H Mandlikova and Miss W M Turnbull 4** 18 Miss A M Cecchini and Miss M.Schropp	**Miss H Mandlikova and Miss W M Turnbull 4** 6-3, 6-3	**Miss H Mandlikova and Miss W M Turnbull 4** 6-3, 7-6
19 Miss P A Fendick and Miss H A Ludloff 20 Miss R L Einy and Miss L C Gracie	Miss P A Fendick and Miss H A Ludloff 7-5, 5-7, 6-3	
21 Miss C Suire and Miss S V Wade 22 Miss K Kinney and Miss P J Whytcross	Miss C Suire and Miss S V Wade 6-4, 6-2	**Miss E M Burgin and Miss A A Moulton 11** 6-2, 6-3
23 Miss S Graf and Miss A E Smith 24 **Miss E M Burgin and Miss A A Moulton 11**	**Miss E M Burgin and Miss A A Moulton 11** 6-1, 6-3	
25 **Miss C K Bassett and Miss A C Leand 15** 26 Miss S L Gomer and Miss J A Salmon	**Miss C K Bassett and Miss A C Leand 15** 6-3, 3-6, 6-3	Miss I Demongeot and Miss N Tauziat 6-7, 6-0, 11-9
27 Miss E Okagawa and Miss S M Schenck 28 Miss I Demongeot and Miss N Tauziat	Miss I Demongeot and Miss N Tauziat 6-3, 6-3	
29 Miss K McDaniel and Miss W E White 30 Miss H A Crowe and Miss K A Steinmetz	Miss K M McDaniel and Miss W E White 7-6, 6-2	**Miss S Cherneva and Miss L Savchenko 6** 6-1, 6-2
31 Miss L M McNeil and Miss K Y Sands 32 **Miss S Cherneva and Miss L Savchenko 6**	**Miss S Cherneva and Miss L Savchenko 6** 6-0, 6-0	
33 **Miss R D Fairbank and Miss A E Hobbs 8** 34 Miss P Paradis and Miss C Tanvier	Miss P Paradis and Miss C Tanvier 6-3, 6-1	Miss P Paradis and Miss C Tanvier 6-4, 6-2
35 Miss P Barg and Miss A C Villagran 36 Miss J M Hetherington and Miss G A Rush	Miss J M Hetherington and Miss G A Rush 5-7, 6-4, 6-3	
37 Miss J L Klitch and Miss C Vanier 38 Miss I Budarova and Miss M Skuherska	Miss I Budarova and Miss M Skuherska 7-5, 6-3	**Miss V Ruzici and Miss A Temesvari 14** 6-2, 6-1
39 Miss S E Mascarin and Miss T Phelps 40 **Miss V Ruzici and Miss A Temesvari 14**	**Miss V Ruzici and Miss A Temesvari 14** 6-4, 6-3	
41 **Miss L Antonoplis and Miss C S Reynolds 12** 42 Miss C C Monteiro and Miss Y Vermaak	Miss C C Monteiro and Miss Y Vermaak 6-0, 6-2	Miss C C Monteiro and Miss Y Vermaak 6-4, 3-6, 6-4
43 Miss B K Jordan and Miss N S Yeargin 44 Miss J A Mundel and Miss M Van Nostrand	Miss J A Mundel and Miss M Van Nostrand 6-0, 6-1	
45 Miss S P Foltz and Miss R Reis 46 Miss C Karlsson and Miss T Scheuer-Larsen	Miss C Karlsson and Miss T Scheuer-Larsen 6-1, 6-2	**Miss K Jordan and Mrs P D Smylie 3** 6-3, 6-1
47 Miss R L Blount and Miss D L Farrell 48 **Miss K Jordan and Mrs P D Smylie 3**	**Miss K Jordan and Mrs P D Smylie 3** 6-1, 6-1	
49 **Miss B C Potter and Mrs M H Walsh-Pete 5** 50 Miss B J Cordwell and Miss J A Richardson	**Miss B C Potter and Mrs M H Walsh-Pete 5** 6-3, 6-7, 7-5	**Miss B C Potter and Mrs M H Walsh-Pete 5** 6-3, 6-1
51 Miss M L Piatek and Miss R M White 52 Miss B J Remilton and Miss N Sato	Miss M L Piatek and Miss R M White 6-2, 7-6	
53 Miss K Maleeva and Miss M Maleeva 54 Miss M Paz and Miss G Sabatini	Miss M Paz and Miss G Sabatini 5-7, 6-2, 6-4	**Miss B A Mould and Miss P G White 16** 6-3, 6-7, 6-4
55 Miss S L Collins and Miss S Goles 56 **Miss B A Mould and Miss P G Smith 16**	**Miss B A Mould and Miss P G Smith 16** 6-2, 6-4	
57 **Miss B Nagelsen and Miss A H White 9** 58 Miss E A Herr and Mrs L A Shaefer	**Miss B Nagelsen and Miss A H White 9** 7-5, 7-5	**Miss B Nagelsen and Miss A H White 9** 6-1, 6-1
59 Miss C Benjamin and Miss J C Kaplan 60 Miss P Casale and Miss P Louie	Miss C Benjamin and Miss J C Kaplan 0-6, 7-5, 6-3	
61 Miss A N Croft and Miss L Howell 62 Miss A B Henricksson and Miss S J Leo	Miss A B Henricksson and Miss S J Leo 6-3, 7-5	**Miss C Kohde-Kilsch and Miss H Sukova 2** 6-4, 6-0
63 Miss A E Holton and Miss M A Quinlan 64 **Miss C Kohde-Kilsch and Miss H Sukova 2**	**Miss C Kohde-Kilsch and Miss H Sukova 2** 6-0, 6-4	

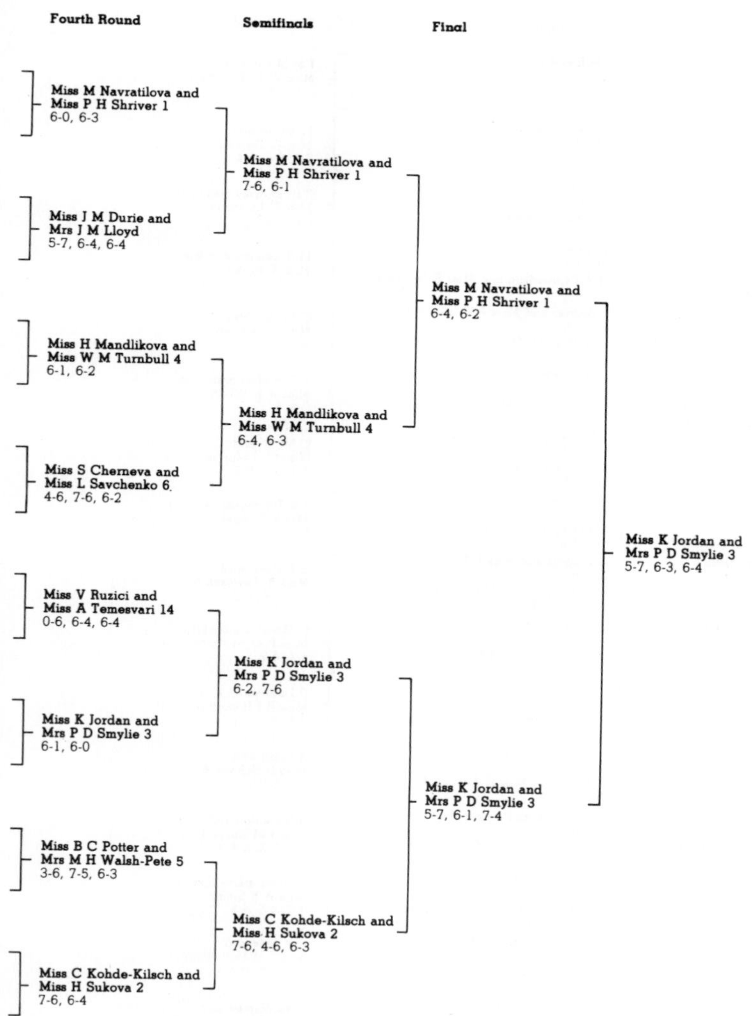

Heavy type denotes seeded players.
The figure against names denotes the order in which they have been seeded.

Event 5. — THE MIXED DOUBLES CHAMPIONSHIP Holder: J M Lloyd and Miss W M Turnbull

The Winners will become the holders, for the year, of the CHALLENGE CUP presented by the family of the late S H Smith. The Winners will receive silver replicas of the Challenge Cup. A Silver Medal will be presented to each of the Runners-up and a Bronze Medal to each defeated Semi-finalist.

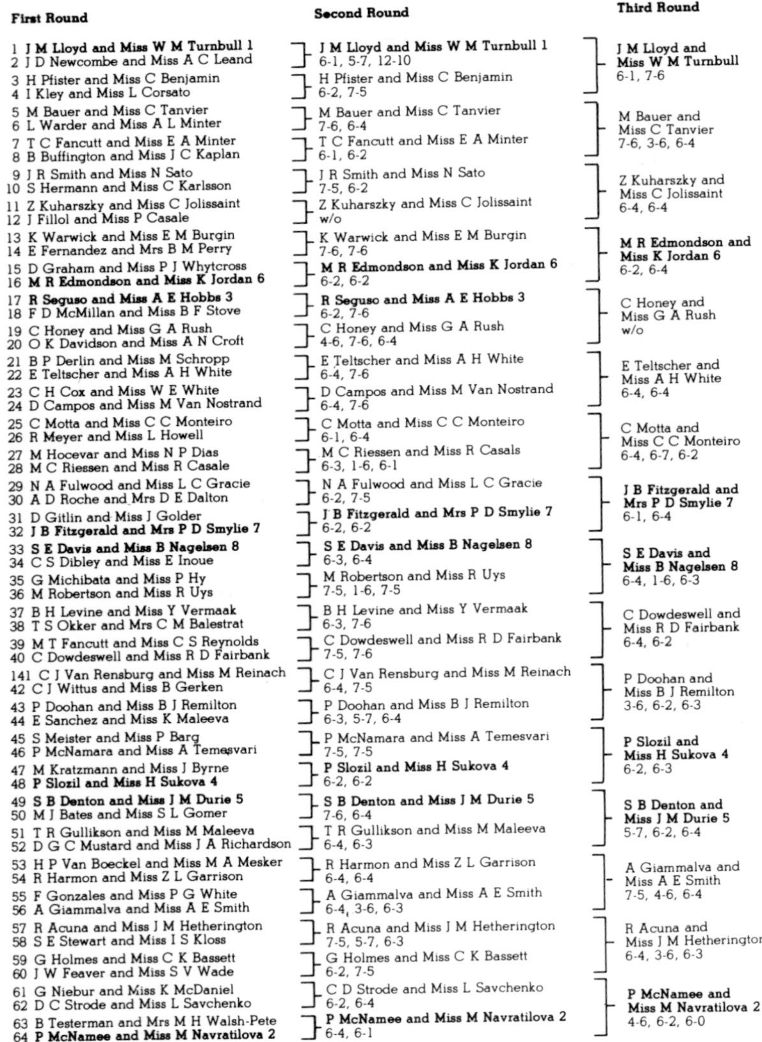

First Round	Second Round	Third Round
1 **J M Lloyd and Miss W M Turnbull 1**	**J M Lloyd and Miss W M Turnbull 1**	**J M Lloyd and Miss W M Turnbull**
2 J D Newcombe and Miss A C Leand	6-1, 5-7, 12-10	6-1, 7-6
3 H Pfister and Miss C Benjamin	H Pfister and Miss C Benjamin	
4 I Kley and Miss L Corsato	6-2, 7-5	
5 M Bauer and Miss C Tanvier	M Bauer and Miss C Tanvier	M Bauer and Miss C Tanvier
6 L Warder and Miss A L Minter	7-6, 6-4	7-6, 3-6, 6-4
7 T C Fancutt and Miss E A Minter	T C Fancutt and Miss E A Minter	
8 B Buffington and Miss J C Kaplan	6-1, 6-2	
9 J R Smith and Miss N Sato	J R Smith and Miss N Sato	Z Kuharszky and Miss C Jolissaint
10 S Hermann and Miss C Karlsson	7-5, 6-2	6-4, 6-4
11 Z Kuharszky and Miss C Jolissaint	Z Kuharszky and Miss C Jolissaint	
12 J Fillol and Miss P Casale	w/o	
13 K Warwick and Miss E M Burgin	K Warwick and Miss E M Burgin	**M R Edmondson and Miss K Jordan 6**
14 E Fernandez and Mrs B M Perry	7-6, 7-6	6-2, 6-4
15 D Graham and Miss P J Whytcross	**M R Edmondson and Miss K Jordan 6**	
16 **M R Edmondson and Miss K Jordan 6**	6-2, 6-2	
17 **R Seguso and Miss A E Hobbs 3**	**R Seguso and Miss A E Hobbs 3**	C Honey and Miss G A Rush
18 F D McMillan and Miss B F Stove	6-2, 7-6	w/o
19 C Honey and Miss G A Rush	C Honey and Miss G A Rush	
20 O K Davidson and Miss A N Croft	4-6, 7-6, 6-4	
21 B P Derlin and Miss M Schropp	E Teltscher and Miss A H White	E Teltscher and Miss A H White
22 E Teltscher and Miss A H White	6-4, 7-6	6-4, 6-4
23 C H Cox and Miss W E White	D Campos and Miss M Van Nostrand	
24 D Campos and Miss M Van Nostrand	6-4, 7-6	
25 C Motta and Miss C C Monteiro	C Motta and Miss C C Monteiro	C Motta and Miss C C Monteiro
26 R Meyer and Miss L Howell	6-1, 6-4	6-4, 6-7, 6-2
27 M Hocevar and Miss N P Dias	M C Riessen and Miss R Casals	
28 M C Riessen and Miss R Casale	6-3, 1-6, 6-1	
29 N A Fulwood and Miss L C Gracie	N A Fulwood and Miss L C Gracie	**J B Fitzgerald and Mrs P D Smylie 7**
30 A D Roche and Mrs D E Dalton	6-2, 7-5	6-1, 6-4
31 D Gitlin and Miss J Golder	**J B Fitzgerald and Mrs P D Smylie 7**	
32 **J B Fitzgerald and Mrs P D Smylie 7**	6-2, 6-2	
33 **S E Davis and Miss B Nagelsen 8**	**S E Davis and Miss B Nagelsen 8**	**S E Davis and Miss B Nagelsen 8**
34 C S Dibley and Miss E Inoue	6-3, 6-4	6-4, 1-6, 6-3
35 G Michibata and Miss P Hy	M Robertson and Miss R Uys	
36 M Robertson and Miss R Uys	7-5, 1-6, 7-5	
37 B H Levine and Miss Y Vermaak	B H Levine and Miss Y Vermaak	C Dowdeswell and Miss R D Fairbank
38 T S Okker and Mrs C M Balestrat	6-3, 7-6	6-4, 6-2
39 M T Fancutt and Miss C S Reynolds	C Dowdeswell and Miss R D Fairbank	
40 C Dowdeswell and Miss R D Fairbank	7-5, 7-6	
141 C J Van Rensburg and Miss M Reinach	C J Van Rensburg and Miss M Reinach	P Doohan and Miss B J Remilton
42 C J Wittus and Miss B Gerken	6-4, 7-5	3-6, 6-2, 6-3
43 P Doohan and Miss B J Remilton	P Doohan and Miss B J Remilton	
44 E Sanchez and Miss K Maleeva	6-3, 5-7, 6-4	
45 S Meister and Miss P Barg	P McNamara and Miss A Temesvari	**P Slozil and Miss H Sukova 4**
46 P McNamara and Miss A Temesvari	7-5, 7-5	6-2, 6-3
47 M Kratzmann and Miss J Byrne	**P Slozil and Miss H Sukova 4**	
48 **P Slozil and Miss H Sukova 4**	6-2, 6-2	
49 **S B Denton and Miss J M Durie 5**	**S B Denton and Miss J M Durie 5**	**S B Denton and Miss J M Durie 5**
50 M J Bates and Miss S L Gomer	7-6, 6-4	5-7, 6-2, 6-4
51 T R Gullikson and Miss M Maleeva	T R Gullikson and Miss M Maleeva	
52 D G C Mustard and Miss J A Richardson	6-4, 6-3	
53 H P Van Boeckel and Miss M A Mesker	R Harmon and Miss Z L Garrison	A Giammalva and Miss A E Smith
54 R Harmon and Miss Z L Garrison	6-4, 6-4	7-5, 4-6, 6-4
55 F Gonzales and Miss P G White	A Giammalva and Miss A E Smith	
56 A Giammalva and Miss A E Smith	6-4, 3-6, 6-3	
57 R Acuna and Miss J M Hetherington	R Acuna and Miss J M Hetherington	R Acuna and Miss J M Hetherington
58 S E Stewart and Miss I S Kloss	7-5, 5-7, 6-3	6-4, 3-6, 6-3
59 G Holmes and Miss C K Bassett	G Holmes and Miss C K Bassett	
60 J W Feaver and Miss S V Wade	6-2, 7-5	
61 G Niebur and Miss K McDaniel	C D Strode and Miss L Savchenko	**P McNamee and Miss M Navratilova 2**
62 D C Strode and Miss L Savchenko	6-2, 6-4	4-6, 6-2, 6-0
63 B Testerman and Mrs M H Walsh-Pete	**P McNamee and Miss M Navratilova 2**	
64 **P McNamee and Miss M Navratilova 2**	6-4, 6-1	

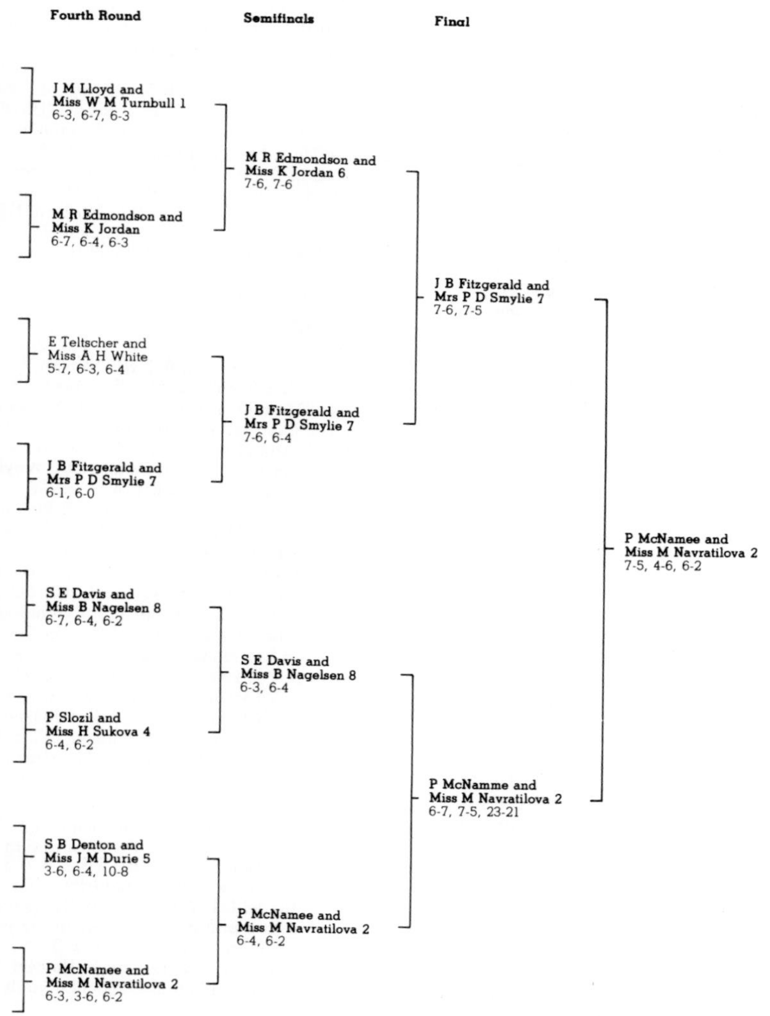

Heavy type denotes seeded players. The figure against names denotes the order in which they have been seeded.

WIMBLEDON QUALIFYING COMPETITION ROEHAMPTON

June 17th-22nd

MEN'S SINGLES

First round:

A Maurer bt G Saacks 7-6, 6-1. S Menon bt T Warnecke 7-6, 6-4. S Kruger bt E Winogradsky 6-4, 7-5. J A Rodriguez bt J R Smith 6-3, 6-0. M Hocevar bt M T Walker 7-6, 6-3. A J W Brice bt A Burrow 6-7, 6-1, 7-5. A Giammalva bt N Broad 6-4, 7-6. D Cahill bt L Dunlop 6-4, 6-4. A Mansdorf bt B Custer 6-4, 7-6. G Donnelly bt N Sears 6-2, 6-3. J Turner bt M Ueda 6-7, 7-6, 7-5. B Moir bt B Manson 3-6, 7-5, 6-3. R Agenor bt A Hocevar 5-7, 6-3, 6-3. M Robinson bt P Russell 6-4, 6-3. D Houston bt S Wood 7-6, 6-3. C Steyn beat C Kirmayr 6-7, 6-4, 6-3. C Mezzadri bt S Botfield 7-6, 4-6, 6-1. G Muller bt M Masencamp 6-4, 7-6. C Nunn bt P Parrini 7-5, 6-4. G Michibata bt A Boetsch 6-4, 6-2. R Saad bt R Kleege 6-4, 6-3. J Jones bt H S McGuinness 6-2, 4-6, 6-4. J Manset bt J Leytze 7-6, 7-6. J W Feaver bt L Lavalle 6-4, 1-6, 6-1. S Youl bt S Abadullah 6-2, 6-1. C M Dunk bt B Talbot 6-1, 6-4. D Howell bt K Van Der Merwe 6-1, 6-4. P Flynn bt E Korita 4-6, 7-6, 8-6. R Acuna bt M Baroch 6-7, 7-6, 6-3. C Stansbury bt F Errard 7-6, 6-4. D Gitlin bt O Rostagno 7-6, 6-3. M Freeman bt C Strode 6-4, 6-4. C Van Rensburg bt R Whichello 7-6, 4-6, 6-1. T Raal bt R Mani 6-0, 6-0. P Cano bt M Van Eekeren 6-3, 6-3. C Miller bt C Honey 7-6, 5-7, 9-7. K Evernden bt M Christensen 6-2, 6-1. M Kratzmann bt B Levine 6-2, 6-0. T Delatte bt P Hughesman 7-6, 6-7, 6-3. K Moir byt J Seveley 3-6, 7-5, 9-7. D Dowlen bt E Van't Hof 6-4, 6-4. B Cherry bt B Knapp 7-6, 7-6. A Amritraj bt C Kermode 6-2, 6-2. R Seguso bt D Stone 7-6, 6-4. M Anger bt C Emery 6-3, 6-4. M Robertson bt J Pugh 6-3, 6-4. M Groetsch bt S Medem 6-3, 6-3. J Clavet bt M Krippendorf 2-6, 6-4, 6-2. J Whiteford bt F Roese 7-5, 6-3. P L Reekie bt D Johnson 4-6, 6-3, 6-2. D G Mustard bt G Niebur 6-0, 6-0. D C Felgate bt A Andrews 6-4, 6-4. K Belcher bt J Soares 6-4, 6-4. C Cox bt T C Fancutt 6-1, 6-1. D Mansdorf bt M Mortensen 6-3, retd. A Kohlberg bt R Scott 3-6, 6-3, 6-1. R Van't Hof bt J Grabb 6-4, 6-4. L Warder bt A Moreno 6-3, 6-2. L Mattar bt D Utzinger 7-6, 4-6, 6-3. J Turpin bt R Meyer 6-4, 7-6. T Cain bt B. Dyke 6-2, 1-6, 6-3. T Champion bt M. Blincow 5-6, 7-5, 6-3. E Fernandez bt R Akel 3-6, 7-5, 6-2. L Palin bt K Warwick 7-5, 7-5.

Second round

Maurer bt Menon 6-3, 6-2. Kruger bt Rodriguez 6-2, 7-6. Hocevar bt Brice 6-2, 6-1. Giammalva bt Cahill 6-2, 6-4. Mansdorf bt Donnelly 2-6, 6-3, 12-10. B Moir bt Turner 6-4, 6-4. R. Agenor bt M Robinson 7-6, 6-4. Steyn bt Houston 6-4, 6-4. Muller bt Mezzadri 6-1, 6-3. Michibata bt Nunn 6-2, 6-2. Saad bt Jones 4-6, 6-3, 7-5. Manset bt Feaver 6-3, 6-7, 6-3. Dunk bt Youl 6-1, 4-6, 6-3. Howell bt Flynn 6-3, 3-6, 6-3. Acuna bt Stansbury 6-3, 6-4. Freeman bt Citlin 1-6, 6-1, 7-5. Van Rensburg bt Raal 6-1, 6-2. Miller bt Cane 2-6, 6-4, 6-3. Evernden bt Kratzmann 6-2, 7-6. K Moir bt Delatte 6-4, 6-3. Dowlen bt Cherry 3-6, 7-6, 6-2. Seguso bt Amritraj 7-6, 7-6. Anger bt Robertson 6-2, 6-4. Groetsch bt Clavet 3-6, 6-3, 6-4. Whiteford bt Reekie 7-6, 7-6. Mustard bt Felgate 6-2, 6-3. Cox bt Belcher 7-6, 3-6, 6-3. Kohlberg bt Maasdorp 6-2, 6-4. R Van't Hof bt Warder 6-2, 6-4. Mattar bt Turpin 6-7, 7-6, 6-2. Champion bt Cain 6-4, 6f4. Fernandez bt Palin 6-4, 7-6.

Qualifying round

A. Maurer (WG) bt Kruger (SA) 6-3, 6-4, 3-6, 7-5. A Giammalva (US) bt Hocevar (Br) 5-7, 6-3, 6-2, 7-6. B Moir (SA) bt A Mansdorf (Isr) 3-6, 6-1, 7-6, 6-4. C Steyn (SA) bt R Agenor (Hai). G. Muller (SA) bt C. Michibata (Can) 6-4, 7-6, 6-1. R Saad (Arg) bt J Manset (US) 7-6, 6-4, 7-6. C Dunk (US) bt D Howell (US) 6-2, 7-5, 7-5. R Acuna (Ch) bt M Freeman (US) 6-4, 6-4, 7-6. C Miller (Aus) bt C Van Rensburg (SA). K Evernden (NZ) bt K Moir (SA) 6-3, 7-6, 6-1. R Seguso (US) bt D Dowlen (US) 6-3, 6-4, 6-7, 6-3. M Anger (US) bt M Groetsch (US) 6-2, 6-4, 6-4. D G Mustard (NZ) bt J Whiteford (GB) 7-6, 6-2, 6-3. C Cox (US) bt A Kohlberg (US) 6-1, 4-6, 7-6, 6-3. R Van't Hof bt L Mattar (Br) 6-2, 6-0, 6-4. T Champion (Fra) bt E Fernandez (PR) 6-1, 7-6, 4-6, 4-6, 6-3.

WOMEN'S SINGLES

First round

M C Calleja bt C L Evert 6-1, 6-2. S T Mair bt V Remilton 7-5, 6-4. S Simmonds bt B Bramblett 6-3, 6-0. B K Jordan bt E Derly 6-1, 6-1. J Golder bt K Okamoto 6-3, 5-7, 6-3. B Cordwell bt M Hetherington 5-7, 7-5, 13-11. M Van Nostrand bt A Gulley 6-1, 6-2. N Herreman bt S Rimes 6-3, 6-3. N Tauziat bt P Whytcross 6-2, 6-4. L Gracie bt L Corsato 6-4, 4-1, retd. E Reinach bt J Forman 7-5, 6-4. C Bartos bt R Blount 6-7, 6-2, 6-2. J Griffiths bt M Quinlan 6-3, 4-6, 6-3. J Byrne bt M Turk 6-4, 6-4. H Crow by R Reis 4-6, 6-1, 7-5. J Mundel bt K Dreyer 6-0, 6-4. R Bryant bt K Steinmetz 3-6, 6-4, 6-1. S Cherneva bt K Dewis 6-4, 6-7, 6-2. B Borneo bt L Field 6-3, 6-2. P Fendick bt J Richardson 6-2, 6-2. Hun Na bt P Hy 6-1, 7-6. L O'Neil bt C Anderholm 6-1, 6-1. L Huebner bt C Jones 7-5, 2-6, 6-2. L Plchove bt V Lake 6-1, 6-4. K Kinney bt M Schillig 6-2, 6-1. A Fernandez bt H Pellitier 6-7, 7-5, 11-9. H Hulbert bt H Dahlstrom 6-3, 7-5. A Betzner bt C Carney 6-1, 6-4. L Howell by A Kijimuta 6-3, 6-4. A Ivan bt N Reva 6-3, 6-1. E Ekblom bt C Monteiro 2-6, 6-2, 11-9. K Sands bt L Geeves 6-3, 6-0.

Second round

Mair bt Calleja 6-3, 6-2. Jordan bt Simmonds 2-6, 7-6, 6-3. Cordwell bt Golder 6-2, 6-0. Van Nostrand bt Herreman 7-6, 6-3. Gracie bt Tauziat 5-7, 7-5, 6-3. Reinach bt Bartos 6-1, retd. Byrne bt Griffiths 6-1, 6-0. Crowe bt Mundel 6-1, 7-5. Bryant bt Cherneva 1-6, 6-3, 6-4. Fendick bt Borneo 6-1, 6-4. Hu Na bt O'Neil 6-4, 6-1. Plchova bt Huebner 7-6, 6-3. Kinney bt Fernandez 6-4, 6-4. Betzner bt Hulbert 6-3, 7-6. Howell bt Ivan 6-3, 6-3. Ekblom bt Sands 6-3, 6-3.

Qualifying round

Jordan (US) bt Mair 6-4, 6-2. Van Nostrand (US) bt Cordwell (NZ) 6-1, 6-0. Reinach (SA) bt Gracie 6-7, 6-0, 7-5. Byrne (Aus) bt Crowe (US) 6-3, 6-3. Fendick (US) bt Bryant (Aus) 6-4, 6-4. Hu Na (US) bt Plchova (Cz) 6-0, 6-3. Betzner (WG) bt Kinney (US) 6-4, 3-6, 6-3. Ekblom (Swe) bt Howell (US) 7-6, 6-2.

ROUNDS REACHED BY BRITISH MEN AT WIMBLEDON IN THE OPEN ERA

	68	69	70	71	72	73	74	75	76	77	78	79	80	81	82	83	84	85
R Taylor	2	2	S	2	—	S	1	1	1	1	1	1	1	—	—	—	—	—
M Cox	4	3	3	1	—	—	1	3	2	4	2	4	2	1	—	—	—	—
D A Lloyd	3	2	1	—	2	2	1	—	1	2	1	1	—	—	—	—	—	—
G Battrick	1	2	1	3	—	—	2	1	2	—	—	—	—	—	—	—	—	—
G Stilwell	2	3	1	2	—	—	1	4	—	—	—	—	—	—	—	—	—	—
S Warboys	—	—	1	—	1	1	1	—	2	—	—	—	—	—	—	—	—	—
J G Paish	—	1	1	1	3	1	1	1	—	—	1	—	1	—	—	—	—	—
P W Curtis	1	1	2	1	—	2	—	—	—	—	—	—	—	—	—	—	—	—
S J Matthews	1	2	1	1	1	1	—	—	—	—	—	—	—	—	—	—	—	—
R Becker	1	—	—	—	—	—	—	—	—	—	—	—	—	—	—	—	—	—
K Wooldridge	1	1	—	—	—	—	—	—	—	—	—	—	—	—	—	—	—	—
M J Sangster	2	1	—	—	—	—	—	—	—	—	—	—	—	—	—	—	—	—
G C Bluett	2	—	—	—	—	—	—	—	—	—	—	—	—	—	—	—	—	—
R K Wilson	1	4	1	—	—	—	—	—	—	—	—	—	—	—	—	—	—	—
J E Barrett	1	1	—	—	—	—	—	—	—	—	—	—	—	—	—	—	—	—
C Iles	2	—	—	—	—	2	—	—	—	—	—	—	—	—	—	—	—	—
M G Davies	1	—	—	—	—	—	—	—	—	—	—	—	—	—	—	—	—	—
P R Hutchins	1	1	—	—	1	—	—	—	—	—	—	—	—	—	—	—	—	—
A D Mills	1	1	—	—	—	—	—	—	—	—	—	—	—	—	—	—	—	—
J G Clifton	—	1	1	2	1	1	—	—	—	—	—	—	—	—	—	—	—	—
J de Mendoza	—	—	—	1	1	—	—	—	—	—	—	—	—	—	—	—	—	—
C McHugo	—	—	—	—	—	1	—	—	—	—	—	—	—	—	—	—	—	—
P Siviter	—	—	—	—	—	1	—	—	—	—	—	—	—	—	—	—	—	—
M W Collins	—	—	—	—	—	1	—	—	—	—	—	—	—	—	—	—	—	—
J Feaver	—	—	—	1	2	4	1	2	2	1	2	1	1	2	1	—	1	—
C J Mottram	—	—	—	—	2	—	3	—	1	3	2	2	2	2	4	1	—	—
R Drysdale	—	—	—	—	—	1	—	2	1	1	2	1	1	1	—	—	—	—
M Farrell	—	—	—	—	—	1	1	1	2	—	1	—	—	—	—	—	—	—
J M Lloyd	—	—	—	—	—	3	1	1	1	2	1	1	1	2	1	1	3	3
R A Lewis	—	—	—	—	—	1	—	1	3	1	1	1	1	1	1	1	1	—
M Robinson	—	—	—	—	—	—	—	1	1	—	—	—	—	—	—	—	—	—
J Smith	—	—	—	—	—	—	—	—	1	3	1	2	1	—	2	1	1	—
A H Lloyd	—	—	—	—	—	—	—	—	—	1	—	—	—	—	—	—	—	—
M Wayman	—	—	—	—	—	—	—	—	2	1	1	—	—	—	—	—	—	—
A Jarrett	—	—	—	—	—	—	—	—	—	1	1	1	2	1	1	2	—	—
R Beven	—	—	—	—	—	—	—	—	—	—	—	1	—	—	—	—	—	—
N Brown	—	—	—	—	—	—	—	—	—	—	—	—	—	—	1	—	—	—
M Bates	—	—	—	—	—	—	—	—	—	—	—	—	—	—	—	1	1	1
C Bradnam	—	—	—	—	—	—	—	—	—	—	—	—	—	—	—	1	—	—
S M Bale	—	—	—	—	—	—	—	—	—	—	—	—	—	—	—	2	2	1
C Dowdeswell	—	—	—	—	—	—	—	—	—	—	—	—	—	—	—	—	1	1
S Shaw	—	—	—	—	—	—	—	—	—	—	—	—	—	—	—	—	2	1
N Fulwood	—	—	—	—	—	—	—	—	—	—	—	—	—	—	—	—	1	1
L Alfred	—	—	—	—	—	—	—	—	—	—	—	—	—	—	—	—	—	1
J M Goodall	—	—	—	—	—	—	—	—	—	—	—	—	—	—	—	—	—	1
Total Played	*17*	*15*	*11*	*10*	*9*	*16*	*11*	*11*	*14*	*12*	*13*	*11*	*10*	*6*	*7*	*8*	*9*	*8*

ROUNDS REACHED BY BRITISH WOMEN AT WIMBLEDON IN THE OPEN ERA

	68	69	70	71	72	73	74	75	76	77	78	79	80	81	82	83	84	85
P F Jones	S	W	—	—	—	—	—	—	—	—	—	—	—	—	—	—	—	—
S V Wade	1	3	4	4	Q	Q	S	Q	S	W	S	Q	4	2	2	Q	3	3
W M Shaw	3	3	Q	Q	4	1	3	4	2	2	1	—	—	—	—	—	—	—
S Brasher	4	2	3	2	2	1	2	—	—	—	—	—	—	—	—	—	—	—
G T Janes	2	4	—	4	—	1	3	—	—	—	—	—	—	—	—	—	—	—
G M Williams	4	2	2	1	2	3	2	1	—	—	—	—	—	—	—	—	—	—
A Soady	2	1	—	—	—	—	—	—	—	—	—	—	—	—	—	—	—	—
J A Congdon	2	—	—	—	—	—	—	—	—	—	—	—	—	—	—	—	—	—
R Bentley	1	—	3	3	—	—	—	—	—	—	—	—	—	—	—	—	—	—
C Molesworth	2	1	—	1	1	1	1	2	3	2	—	—	—	—	—	—	—	—
J Townsend	2	1	1	—	—	—	—	—	—	—	—	—	—	—	—	—	—	—
F McLennan	2	1	—	—	—	—	—	—	—	—	—	—	—	—	—	—	—	—
M Lee	1	—	—	—	—	—	—	—	—	—	—	—	—	—	—	—	—	—
P Roberts	1	—	—	—	—	—	—	—	—	—	—	—	—	—	—	—	—	—
F E Truman	1	4	2	2	3	—	—	—	—	—	—	—	—	—	—	—	—	—
W V Hall	1	1	1	—	—	—	—	—	—	—	—	—	—	—	—	—	—	—
J A Lloyd	2	1	2	—	—	—	—	—	—	—	—	—	—	—	—	—	—	—
J P Cooper	—	2	3	2	3	2	—	—	—	—	—	—	—	—	—	—	—	—
J M Boundy	—	1	—	—	—	—	—	—	—	—	—	—	—	—	—	—	—	—
S M Tutt	—	2	—	—	—	—	—	—	—	—	—	—	—	—	—	—	—	—
S Holdsworth	—	1	1	2	—	—	—	—	—	—	—	—	—	—	—	—	—	—
E Ernest	—	1	2	—	—	—	—	—	—	—	—	—	—	—	—	—	—	—
M Greenwood	—	—	2	2	—	—	—	—	—	—	—	—	—	—	—	—	—	—
T Cowie	—	—	1	2	2	—	—	—	—	—	—	—	—	—	—	—	—	—
L E Beavan	—	—	1	4	1	2	1	4	1	1	—	—	—	—	—	—	—	—
J Fayter	—	—	1	2	1	1	1	2	2	2	1	—	—	—	—	—	—	—
V Burton	—	—	2	—	2	1	—	2	2	—	—	—	—	—	—	—	—	—
P Northern	—	—	2	—	—	—	—	—	—	—	—	—	—	—	—	—	—	—
G Coles	—	—	—	1	1	4	2	4	1	1	1	2	1	3	1	—	—	—
J Wainwright	—	—	—	1	—	—	—	—	—	—	—	—	—	—	—	—	—	—
K James	—	—	—	2	—	—	—	—	—	—	—	—	—	—	—	—	—	—
S Mappin	—	—	—	—	1	2	2	2	2	1	2	—	—	—	—	—	—	—
L Charles	—	—	—	—	2	2	4	3	1	3	2	1	2	1	—	—	—	—
S Barker	—	—	—	—	—	2	1	3	4	S	4	1	2	3	1	1	2	—
L Mottram	—	—	—	—	—	1	1	3	1	1	1	—	—	—	—	—	—	—
P Moor	—	—	—	—	—	2	1	—	—	—	—	—	—	—	—	—	—	—
L Blachford	—	—	—	—	—	3	1	1	1	—	—	—	—	—	—	—	—	—
A Coe	—	—	—	—	—	1	2	1	2	—	—	—	—	—	—	—	—	—
M Tyler	—	—	—	—	—	—	—	3	1	1	3	1	—	—	—	—	—	—
B Thompson	—	—	—	—	—	—	—	—	1	2	—	2	—	—	—	—	—	—
A Cooper	—	—	—	—	—	—	—	—	1	—	—	1	1	1	—	—	—	—
J Durie	—	—	—	—	—	—	—	—	—	1	1	2	1	4	1	3	2	4
A Hobbs	—	—	—	—	—	—	—	—	—	2	1	2	2	4	2	1	4	2
D Jevans	—	—	—	—	—	—	—	—	—	—	—	4	2	2	1	1	—	—
K Brasher	—	—	—	—	—	—	—	—	—	—	—	—	2	1	1	1	1	1
A Croft	—	—	—	—	—	—	—	—	—	—	—	—	—	—	1	1	3	1
E Jones	—	—	—	—	—	—	—	—	—	—	—	—	—	—	1	—	—	—
S Walpole	—	—	—	—	—	—	—	—	—	—	—	—	—	—	1	—	1	—
E Lightbody	—	—	—	—	—	—	—	—	—	—	—	—	—	—	1	—	—	—
C J Drury	—	—	—	—	—	—	—	—	—	—	—	—	—	—	—	1	—	—
R L Einy	—	—	—	—	—	—	—	—	—	—	—	—	—	—	—	1	1	1
S L Gomer	—	—	—	—	—	—	—	—	—	—	—	—	—	—	—	1	1	2
J A Salmon	—	—	—	—	—	—	—	—	—	—	—	—	—	—	—	1	3	1
A J Brown	—	—	—	—	—	—	—	—	—	—	—	—	—	—	—	2	2	1
S T Mair	—	—	—	—	—	—	—	—	—	—	—	—	—	—	—	—	1	—
J Louis	—	—	—	—	—	—	—	—	—	—	—	—	—	—	—	—	1	1
S Reeves	—	—	—	—	—	—	—	—	—	—	—	—	—	—	—	—	1	2
C Wood	—	—	—	—	—	—	—	—	—	—	—	—	—	—	—	—	—	1
J M Tacon	—	—	—	—	—	—	—	—	—	—	—	—	—	—	—	—	—	1
Total Played	*17*	*18*	*18*	*17*	*14*	*18*	*16*	*15*	*16*	*14*	*11*	*10*	*9*	*9*	*11*	*12*	*13*	*13*

WIMBLEDON SINGLES SEEDINGS SINCE 1968

MEN

1968
1 R G Laver. **2** K R Rosewall. **3** A Gimeno. **4** J D Newcombe. **5** R Emerson. **6** M Santana. **7** L A Hoad. **8** P Gonzales. **9** D Ralston. **10** B Bucholz. **11** F Stolle. **12** T S Okker. **13** A Ashe. **14** E C Drysdale. **15** A D Roche. **16** N Pilic.

1969:
1 R G Laver. **2** A D Roche. **3** T S Okker. **4** K R Rosewall. **5** A Ashe. **6** J D Newcombe. **7** C Graebner. **8** E C Drysdale. **9** R Emerson. **10** A Gimeno. **11** F Stolle. **12** P Gonzales. **13** R Moore. **14** R A J Hewitt. **15** D Ralston. **16** S R Smith.

1970
1 R G Laver. **2** J D Newcombe. **3** A Ashe. **4** A D Roche. **5** K R Rosewall. **6** Z Franulovic. **7** S R Smith. **8** I Nastase. **9** C Graebner. **10** R Emerson. **11** T S Okker. **12** E C Drysdale. **13** J Kodes. **14** A Gimeno. **15** C D Ralston. **16** R Taylor.

1971
1 R G Laver. **2** J D Newcombe. **3** K R Rosewall. **4** S R Smith. **5** A Ashe. **6** C Richey. **7** I Nastase. **8** E C Drysdale.

1972
1 S R Smith. **2** I Nastase. **3** M Orantes. **4** A Gimeno. **5** J Kodes. **6** P Barthes. **7** R A J Hewitt. **8** A Metreveli.

1973
1 I Nastase. **2** J Kodes. **3** R Taylor. **4** A Metreveli. **5** J S Connors. **6** B Borg. **7** O Davidson. **8** J Fassbender.

1974
1 J D Newcombe. **2** I Nastase. **3** J S Connors. **4** S Smith. **5** B Borg. **6** J Kodes. **7** T S Okker. **8** A Ashe. **9** K Rosewall. **10** A Metreveli. **11** T Gorman. **12** M Orantes.

1975
1 J S Connors. **2** K R Rosewall. **3** B Borg. **4** G Vilas. **5** I Nastase. **6** A Ashe. **7** S R Smith. **8** R Ramirez. **9** T S Okker. **10** J G Alexander. **11** R Tanner. **12** J Kodes. **13** M Riessen. **14** V Gerulaitis. **15** O Parun. **16** A D Roche.

1976
1 A Ashe. **2** J S Connors. **3** I Nastase. **4** B Borg. **5** A Panatta. **6** G Vilas. **7** R Tanner. **8** R Ramirez. **9** T S Okker. **10** J D Newcombe. **11** —. **12** A D Roche. **13** J Fillol. **14** B E Gottfried. **15** —. **16** S R Smith.

1977
1 J S Connors. **2** B Borg. **3** G Vilas. **4** R Tanner. **5** B E Gottfried. **6** I Nastase. **7** R Ramirez. **8** V Gerulaitis. **9** R Stockton. **10** A Panatta. **11** S R Smith. **12** W Fibak. **13** P Dent. **14** M Cox. **15** R Lutz. **16** H Solomon.

1978
1 B Borg. **2** J S Connors. **3** V Gerulaitis. **4** G Vilas. **5** B E Gottfried. **6** R Tanner. **7** R Ramirez. **8** A A Mayer. **9** I Nastase. **10** R Stockton. **11** J P McEnroe. **12** C J Mottram. **13** W Fibak. **14** J G Alexander. **15** A Ashe. **16** J D Newcombe.

1979
1 B Borg. **2** J P McEnroe. **3** J S Connors. **4** V Gerulaitis. **5** R Tanner. **6** G Vilas. **7** A Ashe. **8** V Pecci. **9** B E Gottfried. **10** W Fibak. **11** J G Alexander. **12** J Higueras. **13** M Orantes. **14** J L Clerc. **15** Tim Gullikson. **16** C Barrazzutti.

1980
1 B Borg. **2** J P McEnroe. **3** J S Connors. **4** V Gerulaitis. **5** R Tanner. **6** G Mayer. **7** P Fleming. **8** V Pecci. **9** P DuPre. **10** I Lendl. **11** —. **12** —. **13** W Fibak. **14** V Amaya. **15** S R Smith. **16** J L Clerc.

1981
1 B Borg. **2** J P McEnroe. **3** J S Connors. **4** I Lendl. **5** —. **6** B Teacher. **7** B E Gottfried. **8** R Tanner. **9** J L Clerc. **10** G Vilas. **11** V Pecci. **12** P McNamara. **13** Y Noah. **14** W Fibak. **15 B Taroczy. 16 V Gerulaitis.**

1982:
1 J P McEnroe. **2** J S Connors. **3** V Gerulaitis. **4** A A Mayer. **5** J C Kriek. **6** G Mayer. **7** M Wilander. **8** P McNamara. **9** A Gomez. **10** —. **11** B Teacher. **12** M Edmondson. **13** B E Gottfried. **14** R Tanner. **15** C J Mottram. **16** S Denton.

1983
1 J S Connors. **2** J P McEnroe. **3** I Lendl. **4** G Vilas. **5** M Wilander. **6** —. **7** J L Clerc. **8** V Gerulaitis. **9** S Denton. **10** —. **11** J C Kriek. **12** K Curren. **13** B E Gottfried. **14** W Scanlon. **15** H Pfister. **16** T S Mayotte.

1984
1 J P McEnroe. **2** I Lendl. **3** J S Connors. **4** M Wilander. **5** J Arias. **6** A Gomez. **7** —. **8** —. **9** H Sundstrom. **10** A Jarryd. **11** K Curren. **12** J C Kriek. **13** T Smid. **14** W Scanlon. **15** V Gerulaitis. **16** T S Mayotte.

1985
1 J P McEnroe. **2** I Lendl. **3** J S Connors. **4** M Wilander. **5** A Jarryd. **6** P Cash. **7** J Nystrom. **8** K Curren. **9** J C Kriek. **10** A Krickstein. **11** Y Noah. **12** M. Mecir. **13** E Teltscher. **14** S Edberg. **15** T Smid. **16 T S Mayotte.**

LADIES

1968
1 L W King. **2** B M Court. **3** N Richey. **4** P F Jones. **5** S V Wade. **6** M E Bueno. **7** J A M Tegart. **8** W W Bowrey.

1969
1 B M Court. **2** L W King. **3** S V Wade. **4** P F Jones. **5** N Richey. **6** K A Melville. **7** J M Heldman. **8** J M Tegart.

1970
1 B M Court. **2** L W King. **3** S V Wade. **4** K A Melville. **5** R Casals. **6** J M Heldman. **7** K Krantzcke. **8** H Niessen.

1971
1 B M Court. **2** L W King. **3** E Goolagong. **4** R Casals. **5** S V Wade. **6** K S Gunter. **7** F Durr. **8** H Masthoff.

1972
11 E Goolagong. **2** L W King. **3** K S Gunter. **4** C M Evert. **5** K A Melville. **6** R Casals. **7** S V Wade. **8** F Durr.

1973
1 B M Court. **2** L W King. **3** E Goolagong. **4** C M Evert. **5** R Casals. **6** S V Wade. **7** K A Melville. **8** O Morozova.

1974
1 L W King. **2** C M Evert. **3** E Goolagong. **4** R Casals. **5** S V Wade. **6** K A Melville. **7** — **8** O Morozova.

1975
1 C M Evert. **2** M Navratilova. **3** L W King. **4** E Cawley. **5** B M Court. **6** S V Wade. **7** O Morozova. **8** G E Reid.

1976
1 C M Evert. **2** E Cawley. **3** S V Wade. **4** M Navratilova. **5** O Morozova. **6** R Casals. **7** S Barker. **8** G E Reid.

1977
1 C M Evert. **2** M Navratilova. **3** S V Wade. **4** S Barker. **5** L W King. **6** R Casals. **7** B F Stove. **8** G E Reid. **9** D L Fromholtz. **10** M Jausovec. **11** F Durr. **12** K May.

1978
1 C M Evert. **2** M Navratilova. **3** E Cawley. **4** S V Wade. **5** L W King. **6** D L Fromholtz. **7** W M Turnbull. **8** B F Stove. **9** T Austin. **10** G E Reid. **11** M Kruger. **12** M Jausovec. **13** V Ruzici. **14** S Barker. **15** R Marsikova. **16** M Redondo.

1979
1 M Navratilova. **2** C Evert Lloyd. **3** E Cawley. **4** T Austin. **5** S V Wade. **6** D L Fromholtz. **7** L W King. **8** W M Turnbull. **9** G E Reid. **10** V Ruzici. **11** G R Stevens. **12** S Barker. **13** R Marsikova. **14** K Jordan. **15** B F Stove. **16** P Shriver.

1980
1 M Navratilova. **2** T Austin. **3** C Evert Lloyd. **4** E Cawley. **5** L W King. **6** W M Turnbull. **7** S V Wade. **8** D L Fromholtz. **9** H Mandlikova. **10** K Jordan. **11** G R Stevens. **12** V Ruzici. **13** S Barker. **14** A Jaeger. **15** R Marsikova. **16** S Hanika.

1981
1 C Evert Lloyd. **2** H Mandlikova. **3** T A Austin. **4** M Navratilova. **5** A Jaeger. **6** W M Turnbull. **7** P H Shriver. **8** V Ruzici. **9** S Hanika. **10** M Jausovec. **11** D L Fromholtz. **12** K Jordan. **13** B Bunge. **14** B C Potter. **15** R Marsikova. **16** J C Russell

1982
1 M Navratilova. **2** C Evert Lloyd. **3** T A Austin. **4** A Jaeger. **5** H Mandlikova. **6** W M Turnbull. **7** P H Shriver. **8** M Jausovec. **9** S Hanika. **10** B C Potter. **11** B Bunge. **12** L W King. **13** A E Smith. **14** A Leand. **15** V Ruzici. **16** E Cawley.

1983
1 M Navratilova. **2** C Evert Lloyd. **3** A Jaeger. **4** —. **5** P H Shriver. **6** B Bunge. **7** W M Turnbull. **8** H Mandlikova. **9** S Hanika. **10** L W King. **11** B C Potter. **12** V Ruzici. **13** J M Durie. **14** A Temesvari. **15** K Rinaldi. **16** C Kohde-Kilsch.

1984
1 M Navratilova. **2** C Evert Lloyd. **3** H Mandlikova. **4** P H Shriver. **5** Z L Garrison. **6** K Jordan. **7** M Maleeva. **8** E K Horvath. **9** W M Turnbull. **10** J M Durie. **11** L Bonder. **12** C Kohde-Kilsch. **13** B C Potter. **14** H Sukova. **15** A Temesvari. **16** C Bassett.

1985
1C Evert Lloyd. **2** M Navratilova. **3** H Mandlikova. **4** M Maleeva. **5** P H Shriver. **6** C Kohde-Kilsch. **7** H Sukova. **8** Z. L. Garrison. **9** B Gudusek. **10** K Jordan. **11** S Graf. **12** C Lindquist. **13** C Bassett. **14** W M Turnbull. **15** G Sabatini. **16** K Rinaldi.

MISCELLANY

YOUNGEST WINNERS

MEN

1985 B. Becker 17 yrs 228 days
1891 W Baddeley 19 yrs 174 days
1931 S B Wood 19 yrs 243 days
1976 B Borg 20 yrs 27 days
1881 W Renshaw 20 yrs 191 days
1932 H E Vines 20 yrs 278 days
1925 R Lacoste 21 yrs 2 days
1939 R L Riggs 21 yrs 132 days
1956 L A Hoad 21 yrs 225 days
1958 A Cooper 21 yrs 291 days

LADIES

1887 C Dod 15 yrs 285 days
1952 M Connolly 17 yrs 291 days
1905 M Sutton 18 yrs 286 days
1974 C M Evert 19 yrs 196 days
1962 K Susman 19 yrs 266 days
1884 M Watson 19 yrs 282 days
1971 E Goolagong 19 yrs 337 days
1919 S Lenglen 20 yrs 42 days
1963 M Smith 20 yrs 357 days

OLDEST WINNERS

MEN

1909 A W Gore 41 yrs 183 days
1930 W T Tilden 37 yrs 145 days
1914 N E Brookes 36 yrs 235 days
1887 H E Lawford 36 yrs 53 days
1954 J Drobny 32 yrs 263 days
1975 A Ashe 31 yrs 360 days
1880 J T Hartley 31 yrs 187 days
1969 R G Laver 30 yrs 331 days

LADIES

1908 C Sterry 37 yrs 281 days
1900 B Hillyard 36 yrs 242 days
1914 D Lambert-Chambers 35 yrs 304 days
1912 E W Larcombe 33 yrs 27 days
1938 H Wills-Moody 32 yrs 269 days
1955 A L Brough 32 yrs 113 days
1977 S V Wade 31 yrs 354 days
1975 B J King 31 yrs 224 days

ATTENDANCE RECORDS

1985 397,983
1984 391,673
1983 363,639
1981 358,152
1979 343,044
1975 338,591
1977 336,416
1978 335,501
1980 333,635
1982 320,283
1976 313,446
1974 306,161
1967 301,896
1971 298,896
1969 296,811
1972 296,761
1970 283,589
1966 277,215
1968 276,270

LONGEST AND SHORTEST FINALS

MEN

Shortest
20 games 1881 W Renshaw bt J Hartley
6-0, 6-1, 6-1
1936 F Perry bt G Von Cramm
6-1, 6-1, 6-0
Longest
58 games 1954 J Drobny bt K Rosewall
13-11, 4-6, 6-2, 9-7

LADIES

Shortest
12 games 1911 D Lambert-Chambers bt D Boothby
6-0, 6-0
Longest
46 games 1970 M Court bt B J King
14-12, 11-9

RECORD CHAMPIONSHIP MATCH

112 games 1969 (round one men's singles)
R A Gonzales bt C Pasarell
22-24, 1-6, 16-14, 6-3, 11-9
Time 5 hrs 12 mins

WINNERS OF THE MOST MEN'S SINGLES CHAMPIONSHIPS

7 W Renshaw (GB)
5 H L Doherty (GB), B Borg (Sweden)
4 R F Doherty (GB), A F Wilding (NZ), R Laver (Aus)

WINNERS OF MOST LADIES' SINGLES CHAMPIONSHIPS

8 Mrs F S Moody (nee Wills) (US)
7 Mrs R Chambers (GB)
6 Mrs G W Hillyard (GB), Mlle S Lenglen (Fr) Mrs L W King (US)

WINNERS OF MOST CHAMPIONSHIPS (SINGLES, DOUBLES AND MIXED DOUBLES)

MEN
H L Doherty (GB) with 13 (5 singles, 8 doubles)

LADIES
Mrs L W King (US) with 20
(6 singles, 10 doubles, 4 mixed)

WINNER'S PRIZE-MONEY SINCE 1968

	Men	Women	Total
1968	£2,000	£750	£26,150
1969	£3,000	£1,500	£33,370
1970	£3,000	£1,500	£41,650
1971	£5,000	£2,400	£50,470
1972	£5,000	£2,400	£50,330
1973	£5,000	£3,000	£52,400
1974	£10,000	£7,000	£97,100
1975	£10,000	£7,000	£108,875
1976	£12,500	£10,000	£157,740
1977	£15,000	£13,500	£204,340
1978	£19,000	£17,100	£259,772
1979	£20,000	£18,000	£277,066
1980	£20,000	£18,000	£293,464
1981	£21,600	£19,440	£332,136
1982	£41,667	£37,500	£593,366
1983	£66,600	£60,000	£978,211
1984	£100,000	£90,000	£1,458,280
1985	£130,000	£117,000	£1,934,760

A LIFETIME'S LOVE AFFAIR

BY LAURIE PIGNON

Kitty Godfree

There were times, especially in a stuffy classroom on a sunny afternoon, when I thought that Henry Ford hit the rivet on the head when he said: "History is bunk." I now know better.

History is the music of Mozart, the paintings of Rembrandt, the words and wisdom of Solomon. It is listening to the Earl of Stockton in the House of Lords; it is also meeting Kitty Godfree in the drawing room of The All England Club where she became a member in 1923.

This is a year when lawn tennis history is being made, a year when the hundredth Wimbledon Championships are taking place, and Mrs Godfree, either as a player or a spectator, has been involved in the last 67 of them.

On May 7th Kitty will celebrate, with family and friends, her 90th birthday, yet a couple of weeks before we met for our lunchtime drink she was playing a mixed doubles against Jean Borotra, a youngster of a mere 87, in a Centenary celebration match between the International Clubs of Great Britain and France.

Mrs Godfree plays fairly frequently but only doubles. "Naturally I am not as active as I was, and also because I had a hip operation eight years ago . . . but it was quite marvellous . . . it took all the pain away," she said, and her grey eyes sparkled, and the winter sunlight reflected in her white hair – her only concession to the passing years.

There have been several celebrations at Wimbledon, and Kitty Godfree has taken part in them all. I have a photograph of the Jubilee Championships in 1926 when she stood last in a line of Lady Champions to receive a commemorative medal from King George V, and then played an exhibition doubles against Suzanne Lenglen.

As with Virginia Wade half a century later, Kitty turned it into a truly British celebration when two weeks later she then won the title and received her prize from Queen Mary, and the adoration of a delighted crowd. In the Final she defeated the lovely and loved Spaniard Lili d'Alvarez, 6-2, 4-6, 6-3 after recovering in typical style from being within a point of 1-4 in the final set. "Lili was very attractive, and a very, very good half volleyer, even from a good length drive to the baseline. This saved her such a lot of running," remembered Kitty.

It had been two years earlier that the then Kathleen McKane – "The press called me 'Kitty McKane', I suppose it had a ring to it and it fitted the headlines better" – had won her first Championship, beating Helen Wills in the only Singles match the great American ever lost in her nine Wimbledons.

With so many yesterdays neatly stored in her mind's eye, Kitty recalls that July afternoon on the Centre Court, and the pain and the pleasure of fighting back from a losing position, as clearly as if the sweat on her brow was still damp from the effort.

To everyone's delight Kitty led 3-1, then the American, driving down both flanks, won nine of the next eleven games, and led by a set (6-4) and 4-1, and was four times within a point of making it 5-1.

"I remember that I was awfully nervous to start with, and frankly I don't know that I thought I could win. I knew that she was very good and having won the American championship at 17 the previous year she came over with a huge record. I was always a bad starter which didn't worry me awfully because I thought I would get into the match. At 1-2 in the second set I was still messing about and not doing much. I said to myself 'you must try and win some points.' I was getting her drives back but never really attacking, and I decided that wasn't any good at all. In the next game I felt I was getting the attack going and gradually my shots got better and better and I began to win a few points, then a few games, and like you know when a match changes the tension left me and went to Helen. Having been so near to winning the whole thing she must have felt like any other human being would . . . . 'Why am I not winning now . . . . what am I doing wrong . . . .' which is what we all do when we are well ahead and then begin to lose."

As with so many players, Kitty's career was over-shadowed by the incomparable Suzanne Lenglen, whom she defeated twice, but only in doubles. There was an international controversy when in 1926 the great French player withdrew from the Singles. Most historians put the cause down to a back-stage row with referee Frank Burrows, but Mrs Godfree is convinced that the root of the trouble was medical.

"She was never a really strong girl, she died of pernicious anaemia when she was quite young, and had suffered from that sort of illness all the time," she said.

"Suzanne was a marvellous player with a very delightful style which nobody else had ever had. She had every shot, and if she leapt in the air to hit the ball she still had her complete balance, and was never really made to look as if the stroke were difficult for her. I dont know what it was about her; perhaps it was her footwork for somehow she was always in position for her shot."

Mrs Godfree has no doubt that Suzanne Lenglen was the best player that she ever faced on court, but was she the greatest ever woman Champion?

"No I can't say that because it is to do with the times, and you have to be comparative, but what I sincerely believe is that if Suzanne were 20 today, and she had all the modern coaching and training, the new type of racket, the new type of balls, the change in the footfault rule and the huge incentive to become a millionaire in two or three year's time, I think that she would have done it.

"She didn't have any of that. We played the game for fun, and the biggest

Miss Helen Wills USA (1924) Ladies Singles Finalist

Suzanne Lenglen

incentive from my point of view was to get into an international team, and so get many trips abroad organised by the LTA . . . that was the fun side of it."

It was during one of those trips, to South Africa, that Kitty McKane married Lesley Godfree – in secret. "Our tour was four months in the winter of 1925-26, and all of us were in each other's company every day. We had visited the Victoria Falls and Lesley and I broke the journey to Cape Town by staying with friends for the week-end in Kimberley and we got married on the Saturday. We kept it secret because we wanted our parents to learn about it from us and not from the newspapers. We told the rest of the team on the boat home. They were surprised in a way, but I think they saw which way the wind was blowing during the tour."

That next summer when Kitty won her second Wimbledon she and Lesley became the only married couple to win the Mixed Doubles. "That really was fun and we had some awfully good wins (including beating Vincent Richards and Elizabeth Ryan in the semi-final). We did play jolly well; the following year we got to the Final, and my first son was born in 1929 and then I more or less dropped out."

Although she won other tournaments her last Wimbledon was in 1934 and during her 17 years of competition she won 46 Singles titles and 107 Doubles and Mixed Doubles.

Kitty's father, John – an importer and exporter of pianos – was, with regard to women and sport, ahead of his time and did everything to encourage his daughters Kathleen and Margaret. In 1909 Kitty played lawn tennis at school, and quickly developed an all court game which in those days was rare for women. She was also a pupil at England's first physical training college for women. For she was indeed an all-rounder, and at the age of ten was awarded the National Skating Association's bronze medal, and 'to keep fit and to keep my eye in during the winters, and because there was a shortage of indoor courts' took up Badminton and won the All England Championship (unofficial world championships) Singles four times.

Life was a wonderful adventure for Kitty, and still is. When she was nine she and her family, complete with governess, cycled to Berlin. "That was extraordinary. My father particularly enjoyed cycling for exercise and we had been doing so from the age of three or four. He had business in Berlin, and my mother agreed it would be fun. At that age you just go where Mummy and Daddy say, and Daddy said, 'Come on off we go . . ' and we went. We spent one week-end with an uncle in Cologne and stopped at Goslar, a famous and beautiful old town in the Harz mountains. We weren't rushing and it took us about three weeks."

It was in 1919 when Kitty played her first Wimbledon at Worple Road. "I started competing that April and I had played some of those biggish sort of tournaments around London like Roehampton, Beckenham and Queen's, but Wimbledon was the biggest, it had the biggest stand of all around the Centre Court. One of the drawbacks of the ground was that the main line trains from Waterloo to the West Country ran immediately alongside two courts – they were steam trains and they really made a terrific rattling noise as they passed." (The modern players have the same aggravation with the low flying jets over Flushing Meadow – the new home of the U.S. Open).

Some of the old timers were critical of the new Wimbledon in 1922 but not so the younger players like Kitty. "I thought it was wonderful, everything was very much bigger, there were more courts and wide spaces in between to walk along. We did not want more."

The first player to strike a ball on the Centre Court was Kity's future husband, and she remembers it as if it were yesterday. "Lesley had an agreement with Algie Kingscote that whoever won the toss would serve the first ball and after the point grab the ball and put it in his pocket. We had it for years, right up to the last war, then Lesley was in the Army and we were evacuated into the country, and when we came back home the poor little ball – which was wool covered in those days, had been eaten by the moths – instead of a souvenir it was a little bit of chewed up fluff."

At the top of Kitty's list of favourite players are Alice Marble and Louise Brough. "I admire people who play an all court game far more than those wonderful baseliners. I think that they have only learnt half the game. The attacker not only has to learn the ground strokes in order to get into the net, but has to learn to volley and smash."

Kitty says that if she were a young player today that she would have still wanted to reach the top, 'but if it meant working very hard as they do now, I would not be prepared to do that for nothing.' Kitty, as always a realist, added: "I think that if in the back of my mind I knew that if I worked very, very hard, and gave up everything else for the game I would earn a lot of money, I am not sure at that young age whether I could give my life a hundred per cent to lawn tennis. There are so many other things and sports I have enjoyed."

Louise Brough

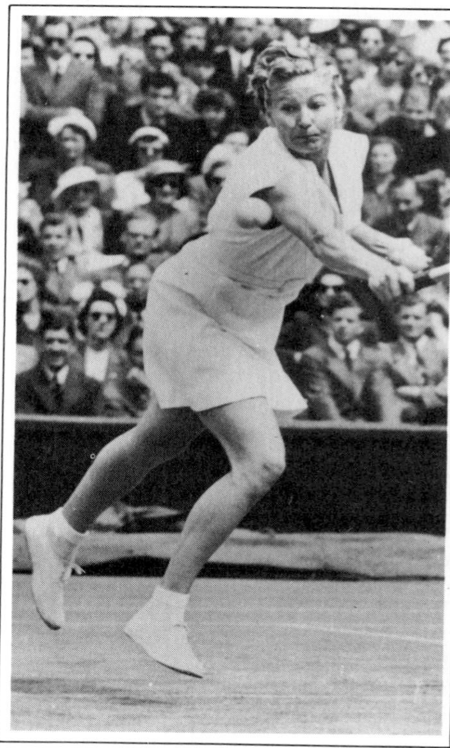

SENIOR TOURNAMENT LIST

JANUARY

7th-12th **European Women's Team Championship Qualifying Event** (In Two Sections) (Section A Inc. G.B.) Loano Sports Palace, Genoa, Italy.

7th-12th **W.C.T. World Doubles,** Royal Albert Hall, London SW7.

22nd-24th **The Lawn Tennis Association, British Men's Indoor Satellite Circuit Week 1** 'Pre-Qualifying', The Court Badminton & Tennis Centre, Peterborough, Cambridgeshire.

22nd-26th **B.A.S.F. European Cup** (European Men's Indoor Team Championship in four divisions) (Division 1, inc. G.B.), The Queen's Club, London W14.

25th-31st **The Lawn Tennis Association, British Men's Indoor Satellite Circuit Week 1** (Qualifying 25 & 26) The Court Badminton & Tennis Centre, Peterborough, Cambridgeshire.

29th-31st **The Lawn Tennis Association British Men's Indoor Satellite Circuit Week 2** 'Pre-Qualifying' Matchpoint Sports Club, Bramhall, Cheshire.

31st-2nd Feb **A.M.F. Head Alverstoke Winter Doubles** (Qualifying 24 to 26 Jan), Alverstoke L.T., S.R. & B.C., Gosport, Hampshire.

FEBRUARY

1st-7th **The Lawn Tennis Association British Men's Indoor Satellite Circuit Week 2** (Qualifying 1 & 2) Matchpoint Sports Club, Bramhall, Cheshire.

2nd **Prudential County Cup Winter Championships** Preliminary Stage (1st round of group Matches), (32 matches at venues across the county).

5th-7th **The Lawn Tennis Association British Men's Indoor Satellite Circuit Week 3** 'Pre-Qualifying' Telford Racquet & Fitness Centre, Telford, Shropshire.

8th-14th **The Lawn Tennis Association British Men's Indoor Satellite Circuit Week 3** (Qualifying 8 & 9) Telford Racquet & Fitness Centre, Telford, Shropshire.

12th-14th **The Lawn Tennis Association British Men's Indoor Satellite Circuit Week 4** 'Pre-Qualifying' London Indoor Centre, London W2.

13th-16th **Peart's North-East Spring Open,** North-East Tennis Centre, Tees-Side Airport, Darlington.

15th-21st **The Lawn Tennis Association British Men's Indoor Satellite Circuit Week 4** (Qualifying 15 & 16) The Queen's Club, London W14

16th **Prudential County Cup Winter Championships Preliminary Stage** (2nd round of group matches), (32 matches at venues across the country).

24th-28th **The Lawn Tennis Association British Men's Indoor Satellite Circuit Masters,** David Lloyd Sports Centre, Croydon, Surrey.

MARCH

2nd **Prudential County Cup Winter Championships Preliminary Stage** (3rd round of group matches), (32 matches at venues across the country).

7th-9th **Davis Cup by N.E.C.** (World Group First Round, 8 matches at venues to be arranged including Great Britain v Spain).

15th-26th ***Trustee Savings Bank South-West Regional Championships** (2nd) (County Postal Section) (venues to be arranged by the competitors).

16th **Prudential County Cup Winter Championships Preliminary Stage** (Men's and Ladies' Championships Group 1 Sectional play-offs), venues to be arranged.

23rd **Prudential County Cup Winter Championships Preliminary Stage** (Group winners play-offs) (8 matches at venues across the country).

24th-30th ***Wetherall North of England Hard Court Championships** (45th) (Senior events start on Wednesday 26) Southport Argyle L.T.C., Southport, Merseyside.

APRIL

1st-31st July **Refuge Assurance National Championships** (4th) (Postal Section) (venues to be arranged by the competitors).

5th-12th **Western Counties B.M.W.**
Horfield, Bristol (3rd)
(Qualifying 5 & 6),
Horfield Common Tennis Centre,
Bristol, Avon.

13th-19th **The Lawn Tennis Association International Spring Circuit Week 1,**
British Homes Stores Cumberland,
(Qualifying 13 & 14),
Cumberland L.T.C., London NW6.

14th-19th **The Lawn Tennis Association, Norwich**
(Qualifying 14) East Anglia L.T.C.
Norfolk L.T. & S.R.C.,
Norfolk, Norwich.

20th-26th **The Lawn Tennis Association International Spring Circuit Week 2**
(Qualifying 20 & 21),
The Queen's Club, London W14.

21st-26th **The Lawn Tennis Association, Telford**
Telford Raquet & Fitness Centre,
Telford, Shropshire.

26th ***London Parks (Postal) Winter Finals**
*(all postal matches are played within a
*25 mile radius of Charing Cross),
The All England L.T. & C.C.,
London SW19.

27th-3rd May **The Lawn Tennis Association International Spring Circuit Week 3**
(Qualifying 27 & 28)
Sutton L.T. & S.R.C.,
Sutton, Surrey.

28th-4th May **The Lawn Tennis Association West Worthing**
(Qualifying 28),
West Worthing L.T.C.,
Worthing, Sussex.

MAY

4th-10th **The Lawn Tennis Association International Spring Circuit Week 4**
(Qualifying 4 & 5),
West Hants L.T.C.,
Bournemouth, Dorset.

5th-10th **The Lawn Tennis Association Peterborough**
(Qualifying 25)
The Court Badminton & Tennis Centre,
Peterborough, Cambridgeshire.

11th **Prudential County Cup Winter Championships**
Intermediate Round,
(8 matches at venues across the country)

11th-16th **Stowford Press Cider North-East Summer Open**
(Qualifying 4),
North-East Tennis Centre,
Tees-Side Airport, Darlington.

11th-17th **The Lawn Tennis Association International Spring Circuit Week 5**
(including Men's Masters)
(Ladies' Qualifying 11 & 12),
Lee-on-Solent L.T. & S.R.C.,
Portsmouth, Hampshire.

17th-25th ***Prudential Paddington Senior**
(Qualifying 17 & 18),
Paddington Sports Club,
London W9.

26th-31st ***Grattan Heaton Bradford Senior**
Heaton T. & S.C.,
Heaton, Bradford, West Yorkshire.

29th-30th **Dow Chemical Classic**
'Pre-Qualifying',
(venue to be arranged).

JUNE

1st-7th ***North Wales Senior Open** (8th)
Prestatyn L.T.C.,
Clwyd, Wales.

2nd-7th **Holiday Inn — Midland Crown Plaza Manchester** (96th),
The Northern L.T.C.,
West Didsbury, Manchester.

2nd-8th **Direct Line Insurance Tennis at Beckenham** (100th), Beckenham L.T.C.,
Beckenham Cricket Club,
Beckenham, Kent.

7th-8th ***Trustee Savings Bank South-West Regional Championships** (2nd)
(County Finals)
(venues to be arranged in each of the six counties).

7th-18th **Dow Chemical Classic**
(Qualifying 7 & 8),
Edgbaston Priory Club,
Edgbaston, Birmingham.

7th-15th **Stella Artois Grass Court Championships,** (Qualifying 7 & 8),
The Queen's Club, London W14.

8th-14th ***Everton Park Novice,**
Everton Park Sports Centre,
Liverpool, Merseyside.

9th-13th **The Championships, Wimbledon, 'Pre-Qualifying'**
Surbiton L.T.C.
Surbiton, Surrey.

9th-14th ***Chapel Allerton,**
Chapel Allerton L.T & S.R.C.,
Leeds, Yorkshire.

14th-21st **The Bristol Trophy**
(Qualifying 14 & 15),
Bristol L.T. & S.C.,
Bristol, Avon.

14th-21st **Pikington Glass Ladies' Championships**
(Qualifying 14 & 15),
Devonshire Park,
Eastbourne, Sussex.

14th-7th Sept ***Trustee Savings Bank South-West Regional Championships** (2nd),
(Regional Postal Section),
(Venues to be arranged by the Competitors).

16th-20th **The Championships** Wimbledon
Qualifying Bank of England S.C.,
Roehampton, Surrey SW15.

16th-21st **South Northumberland Open**
South Northumberland L.T. & C.C.,
Gosforth, Newcastle-upon-Tyne.

23rd-6th July — ***THE CHAMPIONSHIPS,**
The All England L.T. & C.C.,
Wimbledon, London SW19.

JULY

6th-12th — ***Glenric, Huddersfield,**
Huddersfield L.T. & S.R.C.,
Huddersfield, Yorkshire.

7th-12th — ***Bedford Senior,**
Bedford L.T.C., Bedford.

7th-12th — **Durham & Cleveland Open,**
Ashbrooke L.T.C.,
Sunderland, Tyne & Wear.

7th-12th — ***East of England Championships**
(90th), Felixstowe L.T.C.,
Felixstowe, Suffolk.

14th-19th — ***Frinton-on-Sea** (73rd),
*Frinton-on-Sea L.T.C.,
*Frinton-on-Sea, Essex.

18th-20th — **Davis Cup by N.E.C.**
(World Group Quarter-Finals).

21st-25th — **Prudential County Cup Grass Court Championships** (80th),
(in 7 divisions),
(at venues across the country).

21st-26th — ***Discount Sleep Centre, Blackpool**
South Shore, South Shore L.T.C.,
Blackpool, Lancashire.

21st-27th — **Federation Cup by N.E.C.**
Praque, Czechoslovakia.

29th-2nd Aug — **Neston,**
Neston & District C.C.,
Parkgate, Cheshire.

28th-2nd Aug — ***Northamptonshire Open,**
Wellingborough School,
Wellingborough, Northamptonshire.

28th-2nd Aug — ***E.S.A.B. Welding Services,**
Northumberland Senior Open.
Northumberland County Tennis Ground,
Jesmond, Newcastle-upon-Tyne.

28th-2nd Aug — ***Tunbridge Wells Senior,**
Tunbridge Wells L.T.C.,
Tunbridge Wells, Kent.

28th-2nd Aug — ***Winchester,**
Winchester T. & S.C.,
Winchester, Hampshire.

AUGUST

2nd-9th — ***Stothert & Pitt Bath,**
Recreation Gound,
Bath, Avon.

2nd-9th — ***Charlie Brown Ilkley**
Ilkley L.T.C.,
Ilkley, Yorkshire.

4th-9th — ***Berkshire Open,**
*Reading University,
*Reading, Berkshire.

4th-9th — ***Charminster Insurance Bournemouth,**
West Hants L.T.C.,
Bournemouth, Dorset.

4th-9th — ***Stradey Park Hotel Carmarthenshire**
***Open,** (59th)
*Llanelli L.T. & S.R.C.,
Llanelli, Dyfed.

4th-9th — ***Framlingham**
*Framlingham College,
*Framlingham, Suffolk.

4th-9th — **Penzance,**
Penzance L.T.C.,
Penzance, Cornwall.

4th-9th — ***National & Provincial Building Society**
Torbay Torquay L.T.C.,
Torbay, Devon.

9th-15th — ***G.K.N. Sankey, Wrekin**
Telford Racquet & Fitness Centre,
Telford, Shropshire.

11th-16th — ***Wadham Stringer Alverstoke,**
Alverstoke L.T. & S.R. & B.C.,
Gosport, Hampshire.

11th-16th — ***Cubitt & West Cranleigh,**
Cranleigh C.C.,
Cranleigh, Surrey.

11th-16th — ***Cromer Senior** (67th),
Cromer L.T. & S.R.A.,
Cromer, Norfolk.

11th-16th — **Plymouth Senior,**
Mannamead L.T.C.,
Plymouth, Devon.

11th-16th — ***Prudential Sussex Open**
West Worthing L.T.C.,
Worthing, Sussex.

11th-17th — ***Burnham-on-Sea Senior**
*Avenue L.T.C.,
Burnham-on-Sea, Somerset.

11th-17th — ***Mogul Room and Beighton Motor Co. Sheffield.**
Hallamshire L.T. & S.R.C.,
Sheffield, Yorkshire.

13th-17th — **Wiltshire Senior Open** (77th),
Civil Service & N.A.L.G.O. Sports Ground,
Swindon, Wiltshire.

17th-24th — ***Rhuddlan Borough Rhyl** (2nd),
The Tennis Centre,
Rhyl, Clwyd, Wales.

18th-23rd — ***Pooles Audi, Havant** (67th),
*Avenue L.T. & S.R.C.,
*Havent, Hampshire.

18th-23rd — ***Mann Egerton and D.F.V.**
***Sports, Hunstanton,** Hunstanton
*Recreation Ground, Norfolk.

18th-30th (overseas players exempted to Sat 23 Aug) — ***Yugo Cars Jersey Senior Open,**
Caesarean C. & L.T.C.,
St. Helier, Jersey.

25th-30th — ***Yorkshire Building Society,**
*Dartmouth, Dartmouth L.T.C.,
Dartmouth, Devon.

SEPTEMBER

7th — **Prudential County Cup Winter Championships Quarter-Finals,**
(8 matches at venues across the country)

12th-14th — **Refuge Assurance National Championships** (4th),
(Area Finals),
(at 5 venues across the country).

13th-14th **Silk Cut Challenge Inter-Club Tournament** (Final Stages), The Queen's Club, London W14.

20th **Slazenger National Club Championships** (Final Stages), The All England L.T. & C.C., London SW19.

20th-21st ***Trustee Savings Bank South-West Regional Championships** (2nd), (Final Stages), Horfield Common Tennis Centre, Bristol, Avon.

20th-28th ***Weston Mercury Weston-super-Mare** *(weekends only), The Winter Gardens, *Weston-super-Mare, Avon.

27th ***London Parks (Postal) Summer Finals** *(all postal matches are played with a 25 mile radius of Charing Cross), The All England L.T. & C.C., London SW19.

OCTOBER

3rd-5th **Davis Cup by N.E.C.** (World Group Semi-Finals and relegation play-offs.)

6th-12th Sept **Refuge Assurance National Championships** (4th) (Finals), Telford Racquet & Fitness Centre, Telford, Shropshire.

18th-19th ***British Home Stores National Parks Championships** (2nd), (Postal Finals), Royal Victoria Park, Bath, Avon.

19th-26th **Pretty Polly Classic** (Qualifying 19 & 20), The Brighton Centre, Brighton, Sussex.

20th-24th **The Lawn Tennis Association Women's Authorised Series 'Pre-Qualifying'** The Queen's Club, London W14.

25th-26th **British Futures Doubles Trophy** (Postal) Finals, Telford Racquet & Fitness Centre, Telford, Shropshire.

30th-1st Nov **Nabisco Wightman Cup** (Great Britain v United States The Royal Albert Hall, London SW7.

NOVEMBER

1st-7th **The Lawn Tennis Association Women's Authorised Series Week 1** (Qualifying 1 & 2), (venue to be arranged).

4th-6th **Benson & Hedges Tennis Championships** 'Pre-Qualifying' The Queen's Club, London W14.

4th-7th **Remington Family Doubles National Championships** (2nd), (Final Stages), David Lloyd Racquet Centre, La Manga Club, Spain.

8th-9th **Prudential County Cup Winter Championships** Final Stages Telford Racquet & Fitness Centre, Telford, Shropshire.

8th-14th **The Lawn Tennis Association Women's Authorised Series Week 2** (Qualifying 8 & 9), (venue to be arranged.)

8th-16th **Benson & Hedges Tennis Championships,** (Qualifying 8 & 9) (no play on Monday 10), Wembley Arena, London NW10. (Qualifying at David Lloyd Slazenger Racquet Club, Hounslow, Middlesex.

15th-21st **The Lawn Tennis Association Women's Authorised Series Week 3** (Qualifying 15 & 16), Telford Racquet & Fitness Centre, Telford, Shropshire.

27th-30th **European Women's Team Championship** (In Three Divisions) (venue to be arranged).

29th-5th Dec **The Lawn Tennis Association Women's Authorised Series Week 4** (Qualifying 29 & 30), (venue to be arranged).

29th-30th ***British Futures Singles Tennis Trophy** *(Postal) Finals, *Telford Racquet & Fitness Centre, Telford, Shropshire.

DECEMBER

10th-14th **W.C.T. World Doubles** The Royal Albert Hall, London SW7.

19th-21st **Davis Cup by N.E.C.** (World Group Final).

* = Including Junior Event

JUNIOR TOURNAMENT LIST

JANUARY

Dec 30-Jan 4	**Prudential Junior Covered Court Championships of Great Britain.**
1st-4th	**The LTA South Region Closed Championships,** RAF Halton, Aylesbury, Buckinghamshire
2nd-3rd	**Derby City Winter Invitation** (1st) Moor Lane Sports Centre, Moor Lane, Derbyshire.
2nd-4th	**The LTA West Midlands Region,** Telford Racquet & Fitness Centre, Telford, Shropshire TF3 4JH.
10th-12th	**Prudential National Inter-Region Competition** Qualifying Round (three different venues).

FEBRUARY

10th-15th	**Clearview (1st),**Clearview Tennis Centre, Brentwood, Essex.
15th-22nd	**Ely's of Wimbledon Wilton,** Wilton L.T.C., London SW19
17th-21st	**Telford Winter (1st),** Telford Racquet & Fitness Centre, Telford, Shropshire.
17th-22nd	**Clearview (1st)** Clearview Tennis Centre, Brentwood, Essex.
18th-22nd	**Paddington Junior (2nd),** Paddington Sports Club, London W9.
28th-2nd Mar	**Prudential National Inter-Regional Competition,** Final Stages (three different venues)

MARCH

15th-26 May	***Trustee Savings Bank South-West Regional Closed Championships** (2nd) (County Postal Section), (venues to be arranged by the competitors).
24th-28th	**Staines & Co. Cooden Beach,** Cooden Beach Sports & Social Club, Bexhill-on-Sea, Sussex.
24th 28th	**Telford Easter** (1st), Telford Racquet & Fitness Centre, Telford, Shropshire.
24th-29th	**Park Hamper Birkenhead,** Birkenhead L.T.C., Birkenhead, Merseyside.
24th-29th	**Chelsea Building Society Grafton** (7th), Grafton L.T. & S.R.C., Streatham, London SW12.
24th-29th	**Pooles Volkswagen Lee-on-Solent,** Lee-on-Solent L.T. & S.R.C., Portsmouth, Hampshire.
24th-30th	***Wetherall North of England Hard Court Championships** (45th), Southport Argyle L.T.C., Southport, Merseyside.
29th-4th Apr	**Phoenix Assurance Bristol,** Horfield Common Tennis Centre, Bristol, Avon.
30th-4th Apr	**London & Manchester Assurance Exeter,** Exeter Golf & Country Club, Exeter, Devon.
31st-5th Apr	**Prudential Junior Hard Court Championships of Great Britain** (16 & Under), West Hants L.T.C., Bournemouth, Dorset.
31st-5th Apr	**Marshalls Garages, Chesham (1879),** Chesham L.T.C., (1879), Chesham, Buckinghamshire.
31st-5th Apr	**Ellesse Gunnersbury Triangle** (17th), Gunnersbury Triangle L.T.C., Acton, London W3.
31st-5th Apr	**McCarthy & Stone Hale Gardens,** Hale Gardens L.T.C., New Milton, Hampshire.
31st-5th Apr	**Alliance & Leicester Building Society Leicestershire Open** (1st), Leicester University Sports Ground, Leicestershire.
31st-5th Apr	**Mid-Sussex Open,** Comptons L.T.C., Horsham, Sussex.
31st-5th Apr	**Sherwoods North-East Easter Open,** North-East Tennis Centre, Tees-Side Airport, Durham & Cleveland.
31st-5th Apr	**Ormskirk,** Ormskirk L.T.C., Ormskirk, Lancashire.
31st-5th Apr	**Advantage International Sheen,** Sheen L.T. & S.R.C., London SW14.
31st-5th Apr	**Suffolk Open,** Fisons Sports Ground, Ipswich, Suffolk.
31st-5th Apr	**Wilson Whitehall & West Essex.** Whitehall L.T.C., Chingford, Essex.

APRIL

7th-11th	**Belmont Travel Cheam,** Cheam Sports Club, Sutton, Surrey.
7th-12th	**Prudential Junior Hard Court Championships of Great Britain.** (18 & Under), The All England L.T. & C.C., London SW19.
7th-12	**Mowlem Spectacor, Milton Keynes,** Stantonbury Leisure Centre, Milton Keynes, Buckinghamshire.
7th-12th	**Meridian Group Nottinghamshire Open,** Nottingham County Ground, Nottingham.
7th-12th	**Hartford Motors Oxford,** Norham Gardens L.T.C., Oxford.
7th-12th	**C.A.S.E. Communications Rickmansworth,** Rickmansworth L.T.C., Hertfordshire.
26th	***London Parks (Postal) Winter Finals** *(all postal matches are played within *a 25 mile radius of Charing Cross), The All England L.T. & C.C., London SW19.

MAY

2nd-5th **North Wales County Closed Junior Championships,** Brymbo Steel Works L.T.C., Clwyd, North Wales.

24th-27th **Luton Recreation Services, Luton** (13th), Putteridge Recreation Centre, Luton, Bedfordshire.

26th-30th **Lancaster (2nd),** Lancaster Cricket & Sports Club, Lancashire.

26th-30th **Wrexham** (4th), Brymbo Steel Works L.T.C., Clwyd, North Wales.

26th-31st **Prudential Junior Hard Court Champships of Great Britain** (14 & Under and 12 & Under), Craiglockart Sports Centre, Edinburgh, Scotland.

26th-31st **Laidlaw Brentwood,** Brentwood Hard Courts T.C., Essex.

26th-31st **Chesham Bois,** Chesham Bois L.T.C., Amersham, Buckinghamshire.

26th-31st **Andrews Air Conditioning Cleveland Open,** Yarm L.T.C., Yarm, Durham & Cleveland.

26th-31st **Derbyshire County Council Derbyshire Open,** Chesterfield L.T.C., Chesterfield, Derbyshire.

26th-31st **Dunlop Doncaster,** Doncaster L.T.C., Doncaster, Yorkshire.

26th-31st ***Grattan Heaton, Bradford Senior,** Heaton T. & S.C., Heaton, Bradford, West Yorkshire.

26th-31st **North Middlesex Open,** North Middlesex L.T.C., Hornsey, London N8.

26th-31st **Teignmouth,** The Den, Teignmouth, Devon.

27th-29th **St. Leonards-on-Sea,** The Green L.T.C., St. Leonards-on-Sea, Sussex.

27th-31st **Gibson Looe** (6th), Looe L.T.C., Looe, Cornwall.

28th-31st **Grimsby,** Wintringham School, Grimsby, South Humberside.

31st-1st June ***Hereford & Worcester County Closed *Senior Championships** (Preliminary *Rounds), Manor Park L.T.C., Great Malvern, Hereford & Worcester.

JUNE

7th-8th ***Hereford & Worcester County Closed *Senior Championships** (Final Stages), *Manor Park L.T.C., Great Malvern, Hereford & Worcester.

7th-8th ***Trustee Savings Bank South-West Regional Closed Championships** (2nd), (County Finals), (venues to be arranged in each of the counties).

8th **Daily Mail National Short Tennis Finals,** Telford Racquet & Fitness Centre, Telford, Shropshire.

8th-14th ***Everton Park Novice,** Everton Park Sports Centre, Liverpool, Merseyside.

9th-14th ***Chapel Allerton,** Chapel Allerton L.T. & S.R.C., Leeds, Yorkshire.

14th-21st ***Pilkington Glass Ladies Championships** Devonshire Park, Eastbourne, Sussex.

14th-7th Spt ***Trustee Savings Bank South-West Regional Closed Championships** (2nd) (Regional Postal Section) (venue to be arranged by competitors).

16th-21st ***South Northumberland Open,** South Northumberland L.T. & C.C. Gosforth, Newcastle-upon-Tyne.

16th-22nd **The LTA Grass Court Tournament** (I.T.F. Junior World Ranking Tournament, Group 2), Metropolitan Police Sports Ground, Esher, Surrey.

22nd-29th **The LTA International Junior Tournament Tournament** (I.T.F. Junior World Ranking Tournament, Group 1), Surbiton L.T.C., Surbiton, Surrey.

23rd-6th Jly ***THE CHAMPIONSHIPS,** The All England L.T. & C.C., London SW19.

JULY

3rd-12th ***Nottinghamshire County Closed Senior *Championships,** Nottingham County *Ground, Nottingham.

6th-12th ***Glenric Huddersfield,** Huddersfield L.T. & S.R.C., Huddersfield, Yorkshire.

7th-12th ***East of England Championships,** *(90th), Felixstowe L.T.C., *Felixstowe, Suffolk.

7th-12th ***Norfolk County Closed Senior *Championships,** East Anglia L.T.C., *Norfolk L.T. & S.R.C., Norwich, Norfolk.

12th-13th **Boodle & Dunthorne Cheshire County Closed Junior Championships** (Qualifying Rounds), Verdin Comprehensive School, Winsford, Cheshire.

14th-19th ***Frinton-on-Sea Senior** (73rd), Frinton-on-Sea L.T.C., Frinton-on-Sea, Essex.

14th-19th **Foster Menswear Solihull,** Solihull Arden Club, Solihull, Warwickshire.

20th-26th **Middlesbrough,** Linthorpe L.T.C., Middlesbrough, Durham & Cleveland.

21st-26th **Grattan Heaton, Bradford Junior,** Heaton T. & S.C., Heaton, Bradford, West Yorkshire.

21st-26th **Hoole,** Hoole L.T.C., Chester, Cheshire.

21st-26th **Leicestershire County Closed Junior Championships.** Leicester University Sports Ground, Leicestershire.

21st-26th **A.M.F. Head Pit Farm,** Pit Farm, (Guildford), Hard Courts T.C., Guildford, Surrey,

21st-26th ***Discount Sleep Centre South Shore,** South Shore L.T.C., Blackpool, Lancashire.

21st-26th **Surbiton** (19th), Surbiton L.T.C., Surbiton, Surrey.

21st-26th **Midshires Building Society Wolverhampton,** Wolverhampton L.T. & S.R.C., Wolverhampton, Staffordshire.

26th-1st Aug **Channel Islands Closed Junior Championships** (Jersey section), Grainville Sports Centre, St. Saviour, Jersey.

28th-1st Aug **North Yorkshire Open** (9th), Harrogate Sports Club, Harrogate, Yorkshire.

28th-1st Aug **Purley,** Purley C.C., Purley, Surrey.

28th-1st Aug **Queensgate Developments Windsor,** Windsor L.T.C., Windsor, Berkshire.

28th-2nd Aug **Cecil & Larter Bury & West Suffolk,** The Victory Ground, Bury St. Edmunds, Suffolk.

28th-2nd Aug **Mercantile & General Reinsurance Cheltenham,** The East Gloucestershire Club, Cheltenham, Gloucestershire.

28th-2nd Aug **Crawley,** Crawley L.T.C., Crawley, Sussex.

28th-2nd Aug **Fulwood,** Fulwood L.T.C., Drake's Sport & Leisure Club Preston, Lancashire.

28th-2nd Aug **Tudor Furnishings Great Missenden,** Great Missenden L.T.C., Great Missenden, Buckinghamshire.

28th-2nd Aug **Jersey Open** (2nd), Caesarean C. & L.T.C., St. Saviour, Jersey.

28th-2nd Aug **Boxmoor Home Improvements Leverstock Green,** Leverstock Green L.T.C., Hemel Hempstead.

28th-2nd Aug **Dunlop Lymm** (33rd), Lymm L.T. & C.C., Warrington, Cheshire.

28th-2nd Aug ***Northamptonshire Open,** Wellingborough School, Wellingborough, Northamptonshire.

28th-2nd Aug ***E.S.A.B. Welding Services Northumberland Senior Open,** Northumberland County Tennis Ground, Jesmond, Newcastle-upon-Tyne.

28th-2nd Aug **Broadway Sports Plymouth,** Carhullen L.T.C., Plymouth, Devon.

28th-2nd Aug ***Weekes, Tunbridge Wells Senior,** Tunbridge Wells L.T.C., Tunbridge Wells, Kent.

28th-2nd Aug ***Slazenger Winchester,** Winchester T. & S.C., Winchester, Hampshire.

28th-2nd Aug **Topsport Woking,** Woking L.T. & C.C., Woking, Surrey.

28th-3rd Aug **E & T Motors Connaught,** The Connaught Club, Chingford, Essex.

AUGUST

2nd-9th ***Stothert & Pitt Bath,** Recreation Ground, Bath, Avon.

2nd-9th ***Charlie Browns Ilkley,** Ilkley L.T. & S.C., Ilkley, Yorkshire.

4th-8th **Malvern,** Manor Park L.T.C., Great Malvern, Hereford & Worcester.

4th-8th **Observer The Green,** The Green L.T.C., St. Leonards-on-Sea, Sussex.

4th-9th **Aylesbury,** Aylesbury L.T. & S.R.C., Aylesbury, Buckinghamshire.

4th-9th ***Berkshire Open,** *Reading University, *Reading, Berkshire.

4th-9th ***Charminster Insurance Bournemouth,** West Hants L.T.C., Dorset, Bournemouth.

4th-9th **Cambridge Evening News Cambridgeshire Open,** Cambridge L.T.C., Gonville & Cauls College Ground, Cambridge.

4th-9th ***Stradey Park Hotel, Carmarthenshire Open** (59th), Llanelli L.T. & S.R.C., Llanelli, South Wales.

4th-9th **Cromer Junior** (31st), Cromer L.T. & S.R.A., Cromer, Norfolk.

4th-9th **Cumberland Open,** Bitts Park, Carlisle, Cumbria.

4th-9th **Thomas C. Adams, Estate Agents, Deeside,** Deeside Leisure Centre, Clwyd, North Wales.

4th-9th ***Framlingham,** *Framlingham College, *Woodbridge, Suffolk.

4th-9th **Hertford,** Hertford L.T.C., Hertfordshire.

4th-9th **Hightown,** The Hightown Club, Liverpool, Lancashire.

4th-9th **Redcoats and Champney Mid-Kent Open,** Y.M.C.A. Sports Centre, Maidstone, Kent.

4th-9th **Wise Speke & Company, Stockbrokers, Northumberland Junior Open** (51st), Northumberland County Tennis Ground, Newcastle-upon-Tyne, Northumberland.

4th-9th **Reigate,** Reigate and Surrey County L.T.C., Reigate, Surrey.

4th-9th **St. George's Hill,** St. George's Hill L.T.C., Weybridge, Surrey.

4th-9th ***National & Provincial Building Society Torbay,** Torquay L.T.C., Torquay, Devon.

4th-9th **Costmasters Construction West End,** West End (Pinner) L.T.C., Pinner, Middlesex.

9th-15th ***G.K.N. Sankey Wrekin,** Telford Racquet & Fitness Centre, Telford, Shropshire.

10th-14th **Wiltshire Junior Open,** Marlborough College, Marlborough, Wiltshire.

11th-15th **Phoenix Assurance, West of England Junior Championships,** Imperial Athletic Club, Bristol, Avon.

11th-16th **Prudential Junior Grass Court Championships of Great Britain** (16 & Under and 12 & Under), Devonshire Park, Eastbourne, Sussex.

11th-16th ***Wadham Stringer, Alverstoke Senior,** Alverstoke L.T., S.R. & B.C., Portsmouth, Hampshire.

11th-16th **Woolwich Building Society Bexley,** Bexley L.T. & S.R.C., Bexley, Kent.

11th-16th **Colwyn Bay,** Eirias Park, Clwyd, North Wales.

11th-16th **Coolhurst,** Coolhurst L.T. & S.R.C., Hornsey, London N8.

11th-16th ***Cubitt & West Cranleigh,** *Cranleigh C.C., *Guildford, Surrey.

11th-16th ***Cromer Senior** (67th), Cromer L.T. & S.R.A., Cromer, Norfolk.

11th-16th **National Westminster Bank Dorset Open,** East Dorset L.T. & C.C., Poole, Dorset.

11th-16th **Frinton-on-Sea Junior** (37th), Frinton-on-Sea L.T.C, Frinton-on-Sea, Essex.

11th-16th **Gerrards Cross,** Gerrards Cross L.T.C., Gerrards Cross, Buckinghamshire.

11th-16th **Kendal,** Kendal L.T.C., Kendal, Cumbria.

11th-16th **Milford-on-Sea,** Milford Country Club, Lymington, Hampshire.

11th-16th **New Malden,** New Malden T., S. & B.C., New Malden, Surrey.

11th-16th **Northern Novice,** The Northern L.T.C., Manchester, Lancashire.

11th-16th **Cobra Richmond,** Richmond L.T.C., Richmond, Surrey.

11th-16th **St. Albans,** St. Albans L.T. & C.C., St. Albans, Hertfordshire.

11th-16th **Arrow Plastics South Devon Novice Open,** King Edward VI College, Totnes, Devon.

11th-16th **Durham & Cleveland Open,** Ashbrooke L.T.C., Sunderland, Durham & Cleveland.

11th-16th **Swansea,** Langland Bay, Swansea, South Wales.

11th-16th **Cheshire Building Society, West Cheshire Open Junior,** The Upton Victory Hall L.T. & B.C., Wirral, Merseyside.

11th-16th ***Prudential Sussex Open** West Worthing L.T.C., West Worthing, Sussex.

11th-17th **Lowestoft & East Suffolk,** Normanston Park, Lowestoft, Suffolk.

11th-17th ***Mogul Room and Beighton Motor Co., Sheffield,** Hallamshire L.T. & S.R.C., Sheffield, Yorkshire.

17th-24th ***Rhuddlan Borough, Rhyl** (2nd), The Tennis Centre, Rhyl, Clwyd, Wales.

18th-22nd **Dawlish,** Dawlish L.T.C., Dawlish Playing Fields, Dawlish, Devon.

18th-22nd **Tosh Edgbaston Priory,** Edgbaston Priory Club, Birmingham, Warwickshire.

18th-22nd **Radlett,** Radlett L.T. & S.R.C., Watford, Hertfordshire.

18th-22nd **Belmont Travel Sutton Junior,** Sutton L.T. & S.R.C., Sutton, Surrey.

18th-23rd **Prudential Junior Grass Court Championships of Great Britain** (18 & Under and 14 & Under), Devonshire Park, Eastbourne, Sussex.

18th-23rd **Bedford Junior,** Bedford L.T.C., Bedfordshire.

18th-23rd **Broxbourne,** Broxbourne L.T.C., Hertford, Hertfordshire.

18th-23rd **Burham-on-Sea Junior,** Avenue L.T.C., Burnham-on-Sea, Somerset.

18th-23rd **East Grinstead,** East Grinstead L.T. & S.R.C., East Grinstead, Sussex.

18th-23rd **Esher** (14th), Esher L.T.C., Esher, Surrey.

18th-23rd **Felixstowe Junior,** Felixstowe L.T.C., Felixstowe, Suffolk.

18th-23rd ***Pooles Audi Havant,** *Avenue L.T. & S.R.C., Havant, Hampshire.

18th-23rd **Arco Sports & Leisure Hull,** Hull Young People's Institute, Hull, Humberside.

18th-23rd ***Mann Egerton & D.F.V. Sports *Hunstanton,** Hunstanton Recreation *Ground, Hunstanton, Norfolk.

18th-23rd **Marsden Building Society, St. Anne's-on-Sea,** St. Anne's-on-Sea L.T. & S.R.C., Lytham St. Anne's, Lancashire.

18th-23rd **Sportique Tunbridge Wells Junior,** Tunbridge Wells L.T.C., Tunbridge Wells, Kent.

18th-23rd **Westcliff-on-Sea,** Westcliff-on-Sea L.T.C., Southend, Essex.

24th-30th **Hampshire & Isle of Wight County Closed Junior Championships,** Alverstoke L.T., & S.R. & B.C., Portsmouth, Hampshire.

25th-28th **Wiltshire County Closed Championships,** Marlborough College, Marlborough, Wiltshire.

25th-29th **Devon County Closed Junior Championships,** Exeter Golf & Country Club, Exeter, Devon.

25th-29th **Durham & Cleveland County Closed Junior Championships,** Yarm L.T.C., Yarm, Durham & Cleveland.

25th-29th **Cheltenham and Gloucester Building Society Gloucestershire County Closed Junior Championships,** The East Gloucestershire Club, Cheltenham, Gloucestershire.

25th-29th **Somerset County Closed Junior Championships,** Millfield School, Street, Somerset.

25th-29th **Staffordshire County Closed Junior Championships,** Lichfield L.T.C., Lichfield, Staffordshire.

25th-29th **Warwickshire County Closed Junior Championships,** (venue to be arranged).

25th-30th **Bedfordshire County Closed Junior Championships,** Bedford L.T.C., Bedfordshire.

25th-30th **Windrush Garage Berkshire County Closed Junior Championships,** Eton College, Slough, Berkshire.

25th-30th **Amersham International Buckinghamshire County Closed Junior Championships,** Chesham Bois L.T.C., Amersham, Buckinghamshire.

25th-30th **Drivers Cambridgeshire County Closed Junior Championships,** Clare College, Cambridge.

25th-30th **Boodle & Dunthorne Cheshire County Closed Junior Championships,** Birkenhead L.T.C., Birkenhead, Cheshire.

25th-30th **Cumbria County Closed Junior Championships,** Penrith R.F.C., Penrith, Cumbria.

25th-30th **Paramount Motors Derbyshire County Closed Junior Championships,** Derbyshire L.T.C., Derby.

25th-30th **Midland Bank and Hi-Tec Essex County Closed Junior Championships,** Thorpe Bay L.T.C., Southend, Essex.

25th-30th **Jarvis Builders Hertfordshire County Closed Junior Championships,** Queenswood School, Hatfield, Hertfordshire.

25th-30th **National Westminster Bank Kent County Closed Junior Championships,** National Westminster Bank L.T.C., Beckenham, Kent.

25th-30th **Lancashire County Closed Junior Championships,** Southport Argyle L.T.C., Southport, Merseyside.

25th-30th **Middlesex County Closed Junior Championships,** Finchley Manor L.T.C., Finchley, London N3.

25th-30th **Norwich Union Insurance Norfolk County Closed Junior Championships,** East Anglia L.T.C., Norwich, Norfolk.

25th-30th **Walker, Walton & Hanson Nottinghamshire County Closed Junior Championships,** Nottingham County Ground, Nottingham.

25th-30th **National Westminster Bank Oxfordshire County Closed Junior Championships,** Norham Gardens, L.T.C., Oxford, Oxfordshire.

25th-30th **Shropshire County Closed Junior Championships,** Shrewsbury L.T.C., Shrewsbury, Shropshire.

25th-30th **Surrey County Closed Junior Championships,** Sheen L.T. & S.R.C., London SW14.

25th-30th **National Westminster Bank Sussex County Closed Junior Championships,** Southdown L.T.C., Lewes, Sussex.

25th-30th **Prudential Welsh National Closed Junior Championships,** Cardiff L.T.C., Cardiff, Wales.

25th-30th ***Arco Sports & Leisure Yorkshire *County Closed Championships,** *Hull Young People's Institute, Hull, Humberside.

26th-29th **Dorset County Closed Junior Championships,** Bournemouth School for Girls, Bournemouth, Dorset.

26th-29th **Hereford & Worcester County Closed Junior Championships,** Manor Park L.T.C., Great Malvern, Hereford & Worcester.

26th-29th **Northamptonshire County Closed Junior Championships,** Northampton County L.T.C., Northamptonshire.

26th-29th **Northumberland County Closed Junior Championships,** University of Newcastle, Newcastle-upon-Tyne, Northumberland.

26th-30th **Cornwall County Closed Junior Championships,** Bodmin School, Bodmin, Cornwall.

26th-30th **Lincolnshire County Closed Junior Championships,** Eastgate L.T.C., Lincoln, Lincolnshire.

26th-30th **Suffolk County Closed Junior Championships,** Stowupland School, Stowmarket, Suffolk.

27th-31st **Investment Bank of Ireland, Isle of Man Closed Junior Championships,** Queen Elizabeth II High School, Peel, Isle of Man.

31st *__Middlesex County Closed Senior__ *__Championships__ (final stages), *North Middlesex L.T.C., Hornsey, Middlesex.

SEPTEMBER

1st-3rd **Prudential Junior County Cup,** (22 groups at venues across the country).

12th-14th **Sport Goofy Trophy** (Postal) Finals (4th), Royal Victoria Park, Bath, Avon.

18th-20th **Nestlé Junior** (Postal) Finals (26th), (venue to be arranged).

20th-21st *__Trustee Savings Bank South-West Regional Closed Championships__ (2nd), (Final Stages), Horfield Common Tennis Centre, Bristol, Avon.

20th-28th *__Weston Mercury Weston-super-Mare,__ *The Winter Gardens, *Weston-super-Mare, Avon.

27th *__London Parks (Postal) Summer Finals,__ *(all postal matches are played within a *25 mile radius of Charing Cross). The All England L.T. & C.C., London SW19.

OCTOBER

18th-19th *__British Home Stores National Parks Championships (Postal) Finals,__ (2nd), Royal Victoria Park, Bath, Avon.

20th-24th **Telford Autumn** (1st), Telford Racquet & Fitness Centre, Telford, Shropshire.

20th-25th **Woodford Wells,** Woodford Wells L.T.C., Woodford Green, Essex.

25th-26th *__British Futures Doubles Trophy (Postal) Finals,__ Telford Racquet & Fitness Centre, Telford, Shropshire.

26th-1 Nov **Summit Stationery Hertfordshire Open,** Queenswood School, Hatfield, Hertfordshire.

27th-31st **Avon County Closed Junior Championships,** Royal Victoria Park, Bath, Avon.

27th-2nd Nov **National Westminster Bank Alverstoke Junior** (2nd), Alverstoke L.T., S.R. & B.C., Portsmouth, Hampshire.

NOVEMBER

29th-30th *__British Futures Singles Trophy__ *__(Postal) Finals,__ *Telford Racquet & Fitness Centre, Telford, Shropshire.

DECEMBER

15th-20th **The LTA South-West Region Open** The Palace Hotel, Torquay, Devon.

18th-21st **The LTA North Midlands Region Invitation** Coventry Racquet & Sport Centre, Coventry, Warwickshire.

27th-30th **Fenniturn Double Glazing North-East Christmas Open,** North-East Tennis Centre, Darlington, Durham & Cleveland.

29th-2 Jan 1987 **Berkhamsted,** Berkhamsted L.T. & S.R.C., Berkhamsted, Hertfordshire.

29th-3 Jan 1987 **Prudential Junior Covered Court Championships of Great Britain,** The Queen's Club, London W14.

JANUARY 1987

1st-2nd **Derby City Winter Invitation** (2nd), Moor Lane Sports Centre, Derby, Derbyshire.

1st-3rd **The LTA West Midlands Region, Invitation** Telford Racquet & Fitness Centre, Telford, Shropshire.

1st-4th **The LTA South Region Closed Championships,** R.A.F. Halton, Aylesbury, Buckingham.

9th-11th **Prudential National Inter-Regional Competition Qualifying Round,** (3 different venues).

FEBRUARY 1987

9th-14th **Clearview** (2nd), Clearview Tennis Centre, Brentwood, Essex.

14th-21st **Ely's of Wimbledon Wilton,** Wilton L.T.C., Wimbledon, London SW19.

16th-20th **Telford Winter** (2nd), Telford Racquet & Fitness Centre, Telford, Shropshire.

16th-21st **Clearview** (2nd), Clearview Tennis Centre, Brentwood, Essex.

17th-21st **Paddington Junior** (3rd), Paddington Sports Club, Maida Vale, London W9.

27th-1st Mar **Prudential National Inter-Regional Competition Final Stages,** (3 different venues).

SWEDES STILL IN COMMAND

BY JOHN OAKLEY: PRESS ASSOCIATION

DAVIS CUP

Few international team competitions have endured and enhanced their popularity like the Davis Cup. Now in its 86th year, it remains among the most sought-after trophies any sport has to offer and commands the support, loyalty and enthusiasm of 71 countries around the world.

This year, and for the first time, interest among emergent tennis nations is such that it has been possible to create an African zone; a far cry from the early days, at the turn of the century, when the competition was largely a private affair between the United States and Britain.

It was in 1899 that Dwight Filley Davis, a Harvard graduate, bought and put up for competition the solid silver and gold-lined punchbowl which is now, and for the second successive year, in Swedish hands.

Since then the Cup has seen periods of British, French, Australian and US domination (the Americans have so far won it 28 times); changes in the original format to broaden interest; sponsorship and, always, some of the most exciting and memorable matches the game has known.

Sweden's victory at the Munich Olympiahalle last December, their third, not only underlined the shift in the game's balance of power but proved to be the first since 1964 to be decided on the fifth and final rubber.

Not since the halycon days of the French Musketeers, more than 50 years ago, have a European country had such strength in depth in their Davis Cup squad as Sweden have today.

France could boast of Rene Lacoste, Henri Cochet and Jean Borotra, who each won Wimbledon twice, plus doubles specialist Jacques Brugnon. Sweden have Mats Wilander, Stefan Edberg, Anders Jarryd and Joakim Nystrom together with Henrik Sundstrom and Jan Gunnarsson, who both played in the first round tie in Chile, so it was no surprise that they carried off the Cup for the second successive year.

They did so by beating West Germany 3-2 in an enthralling final on a lightning fast court at the Olympiahalle in Munich from December 20 to 22 and despite having to play without Jarryd, a sore throat victim, in either singles or doubles.

Wimbledon champion Boris Becker, again rising to the big occasion, played superbly for the German team but Sweden's massive all-round strength proved the decisive factor. Becker beat both Edberg, on the first day, and Wilander, on the last, in four sets but in between the 18-year-old 1985 sensation lost the doubles in company with Andreas Maurer. The West German pair were crushed 6-4, 6-2, 6-1 by Wilander and Nystrom in 78 minutes and home hopes virtually disappeared with this result.

Michael Westphal, playing second singles for the Germans, must have felt a little out of his depth. At the time of the tie he was ranked only 51 in the world. Wilander, Edberg, Nystrom and Becker were all in the top eleven. But Westphal had Swedish nerves on edge in the fifth and deciding rubber when he won the opening set off Edberg and broke first in the third before the 19-year-old Swede managed to take control.

Certainly this was no ordinary final for it was the first that had seen five live rubbers since Australia beat the United States 3-2 in Cleveland in 1964. The final, however, began quietly enough with Wilander giving Westphal a lesson in baseline control. The young German can, at times, produce an awe-inspiring service as Wilander realised only too well as 19 aces flashed past his groping racket.

But Westphal had little else to offer save courage and determination and too often tried to outplay Wilander from the back of the court — a case of tennis suicide. So first blood to Sweden after two hours and 24 minutes 6-3, 6-4, 10-8.

Wilander was happy with the result but not with the spectators who had the irritating habit of clapping and stamping long and loud just as a player was about to serve. Such quaint behaviour did not disturb Edberg in the second rubber against Becker but the young Swede was palpably nervous in probably the most important match of his career.

Becker won 6-3, 3-6, 7-5, 8-6 because he served better than his rival and always had the courage to go for his shots on the important points. Exit Becker amid bedlam from an ecstatic German crowd.

The doubles were expected to be a close run affair but Wilander and Nystrom, playing together in the Davis Cup for the first time, simply romped home against Becker and Maurer 6-4, 6-2, 6-1 in 78 minutes and never dropped a serve. Poor Maurer lost his service five times in six attempts and admitted later he was "out of my class". Nystrom, in contrast, was the most dominating player on court and produced a stream of point-winning service returns.

Becker complained of a torn muscle in his left side following the doubles but he showed no sign of injury against Edberg nor against Wilander whom he beat 6-3, 2-6, 6-3, 6-3 to take the final into a deciding rubber.

Apart from a poor second set when he lost his service twice Becker was always in dominating form and Wilander was clearly exposed by the pace of the court. So to the last rubber and what a match it proved.

All Sweden and most of West Germany were convinced that Edberg would demolish Westphal but this was far from the case. Westphal hammered home another 22 aces, making 41 in his two singles rubbers, and not until Edberg had broken serve to lead 5-3 in the fourth set could the young Swede feel safe. Then, with confidence flowing back into his veins, Edberg served out to love to give Sweden the Cup for the second year running and the third time in all.

Sweden had deservedly retained the trophy so it seems odd to think that they might have lost in the opening round — by default. Having arrived in Chile for what appeared to be a comfortable tie the Swedish squad were both frightened and appalled when an earthquake, which took 145 lives, struck the South American country. Sweden refused to play on the scheduled dates, March 8 to 10, and Wilander was so upset that on the day after the first massive tremor he flew to safety to the United States.

Alejandro Peric, president of the Chilean Federation, insisted that Sweden should default the tie and said: "Nowhere in the rules does it say that a tie can be postponed or moved because the players are frightened". Henrik

Stefan Edberg

Sundstrom countered with a quote that will go down in tennis history. "It is very hard to practise your serve" he said, "while the earth is moving".

The Swedish party flew back to Europe while the officials were still arguing but the International Federation ruled that the tie should be replayed in Santiago from April 19 to 21.

Sweden had to play without Wilander and Jarryd, committed to a tournament in Houston, but Sundstrom won two singles and Gunnarsson helped Edberg to win the doubles as the holders triumphed 4-1 on a slow clay course. They also beat India 4-1 in Bangalore on grass and then crushed a weakened Australian team, missing both Pat Cash and Paul McNamee, 5-0 on an indoor clay court in Malmo in the semi-final.

West Germany's route to the final was via Spain, the United States and Czechoslovakia but they were considerably helped by having all home ties. Becker made his Cup debut against Spain in Sindelfingen and though he lost a dead rubber to Sergio Casal the Germans had already won the first three matches. The United States, without John McEnroe who had refused to sign a "good conduct" clause, were also beaten 3-2 in Hamburg where Hans-Joerg Schwaier surprisingly defeated Aaron Krickstein and Becker easily won his two singles.

Becker was again the dominating force in the 5-0 victory over Czechoslovakia in Frankfurt but it was Westphal who took the headlines with a six hour victory over Thomas Smid. World number one Ivan Lendl said he had a bad arm and played only in the doubles which did little for the Czech cause.

For Britain it was also a triumphant year though admittedly only in the 'Second Division' of the European Zone B. Relegated from the World Group for the first time the previous September, Britain began their climb back into the top flight by beating Portugal 5-0 in Nottingham where Stephen Shaw and new-boy Jeremy Bates played both singles and doubles in the absence of John Lloyd.

That tie was merely a preliminary skirmish for the difficult semi-final clash with Switzerland at Eastbourne where Heinz Gunthardt, a quarter-finalist at Wimbledon only the month before, was the big danger.

Lloyd was back in the team but he had to come back from two sets down before beating Jakob Hlasek 5-7, 2-6, 6-4, 7-5, 7-5 in the opening rubber. That was encouraging but the most heartening feature of the tie came in the second rubber when Bates, playing the match of his life, beat Gunthardt 6-0, 6-3, 2-6, 6-1.

That was virtually the end for Switzerland but Gunthardt and Hlasek maintained the excitement for a little longer by leading Lloyd and Colin Dowdeswell by two sets to one and 3-1 in the fourth before going down 7-5, 3-6, 4-6, 6-3, 6-2.

Heavy rain forced the last two rubbers to be abandoned but Paul Hutchins was a happy man with only Israel standing in the way of a return to the World Group. Hutchins again decided to gamble, as he had in the two previous years, of playing the Zone final on grass at Eastbourne despite the fact that it was not being played until October.

His plan almost back-fired because the tie was constantly hit by rain and the last two rubbers, one of them live, had to be switched to an indoor court at Herstmonceux ten miles from the original venue. The tie began badly for Britain with Shlomo Glickstein beating Bates 9-7, 3-6, 7-5, 3-6, 6-3 and Amos Mansforf, preferred to Shahar Perkiss in the singles, was locked at 6-6 in the first set with Lloyd when the first day's play was suspended.

Lloyd had to struggle manfully before winning 14-12, 6-3, 4-6, 6-3 when the match was resumed and it took so much out of the British player that the doubles was held over until the third

Paul Hutchins, John Lloyd and Colin Dowdsell

day. This was not to the liking of the spectators but under Davis Cup rules a player who has played in more than 30 games in one rubber can refuse to compete again that day.

From Britain's point of view it was a wise decision. A refreshed Lloyd and Dowdeswell beat Glickstein and Perkiss 6-4, 3-6, 7-5, 2-6, 6-3 and the reverse singles were put back to the following day. Israel should have been helped when heavy rain forced the tie indoors but Lloyd, playing at the top of his game, beat Glickstein 6-1, 6-1, 3-6, 6-3 to settle the issue. Bates then defeated Mansdorf in the dead rubber to make the score-line even more convincing.

So Britain, helped considerably by three successive home ties, were back in the World Group and when the draw was made in London for the 1986 campaign only nine days later they were again in luck. To the delight of Hutchins Britain will begin with a home tie with Spain.

In the four play-off matches to decide who goes down from the world Group the big shocks were the defeats of France and Argentina. France were beaten 4-1 by Yugoslavia in Belgrade and Argentina went down 3-2 to the USSR in Buenos Aires. Spain beat Japan 3-0 in Tokyo and Italy beat Chile 3-1 in Cagliari.

Denmark, like Britain, bounced straight back into the senior section by beating Rumania 3-2 in the European Zone A final in Bucharest while Mexico and New Zealand also gained promotion. Mexico did so by beating Brazil 4-1 in the American Zone final in Porto Alegre and New Zealand defeated Korea 4-0 in Christchurch on grass.

This year the Davis Cup has a record entry of 71 nations including newcomers Bangladesh, Ivory Coast, Libya, Malta, Saudi Arabia and Syria and the sponsors, the NEC Corporation of Japan, has increased the prize money to 1,210,000 US dollars.

DAVIS CUP 1985

World Group Competition

FIRST ROUND

USA **5** Japan **0** (Kyoto), India **3** Italy **2** (Calcutta), Czechoslovakia **3** USSR 2 (Tblisi), Paraguay **3** France **3** (Asuncion), West Germany **3** Spain **2** (Sindelfingen), Australia **3** Yugoslavia **2** (Split), Ecuador **4** Argentina **1** (Buenos Aires), Sweden **3** Chile **2** (Santigo).

QUARTER-FINALS

West Germany **3** USA **2** (Hamburg), Czechoslovakia **5** Ecuador **0** (Guayaguil), Australia **3** Paraguay **2** (Sydney), Sweden **4** India **1** (Bangalore).

SEMIFINALS

West Germany **5** Czechoslovakia **0** (Frankfurt), Sweden **5** Australia **0** (Malmo).

FINAL

Sweden **3** West Germany **2** (Munich).

World group play-off matches

Spain **3** Japan **2** (Tokyo), USSR **3** Argentina **2** (Buenos Aires), Yugoslavia **4** France **1** (Belgrade), Italy **3** Chile **1** (Cagliari).

Zoned Competition

EUROPEAN GROUP A

First round

Turkey bt Iran **w/o.** Hungary **4** Morocco **1.** Egypt **4** Algeria **1.** Monaco **4** Senegel **1.** Ireland **4** Cyprus **1.** Belgium **3** Bulgaria **1.** Second round: Romania **5** Turkey **0.** Egypt **3** Hungary **2.** Monaco **3** Ireland **2.** Denmark **5** Belgium **0.** Semifinals: Romania **4** Egypt **1.** Denmark **5** Monaco **0.** Final: Denmark **3** Romania **2.**

EUROPEAN GROUP A

First round

Netherlands **4** Finland **1.** Greece **4** Norway **1.** Zimbabwe 3 Poland **2.** Switzerland **3** Tunisia **0.** Portugal **5** Luxembourg **0.** Second round: Israel **4** Netherlands **1.** Austria **3** Greece **2.** Switzerland **5** Zimbabwe **0.** Great Britain **5** Portugal **0.** Semifinals: Israel **3** Austria **2.** Great Britain **3** Switzerland **0.** Final: Great Britain **4** Israel **1.**

BRITISH RESULTS

Portugal (at Nottingham)

S Shaw bt J Silva 6-3, 6-1, 6-1.
J M Bates bt P Cordeiro 6-4, 6-2, 6-0.
Bates & Shaw bt Cordeiro & Silva 6-3, 6-4, 6-2.
Shaw bt Cordeiro 6-4, 8-6.
Bates bt Silva 6-4, 6-4.

Switzerland (at Eastbourne)

J Lloyd bt J Hlasek 5-7, 2-6, 6-4, 7-5, 7-5.
J M Bates bt H Gunthardt 6-0, 6-3, 2-6, 6-1.
Lloyd & C Dowdeswell bt Gunthardt & Hlasek 7-5, 3-6, 4-6, 6-3, 6-2.

Israel (at Eastbourne)

J M Bates lost S Glickstein 9-7, 3-6, 7-5, 3-6, 6-3.
J Lloyd bt A Mansdorf 14-12, 6-3, 4-6, 6-3.
Lloyd & C Dowdeswell bt Glickstein & S Perkins 6-4, 3-6, 7-5, 2-6, 6-3.
Lloyd bt Glickstein 6-1, 6-1, 3-6, 6-3.
Bates bt Mansdorf 6-2, 1-6, 6-3.

EASTERN ZONE

First round

Taipei **5** Sri Lanka **0.** Hong Kong **4** Singapore **1.** Philippines **5** Malaysia **0.** Korea **5** Indonesia **0.** Second round: New Zealand **4** Tapei **1.** China **3** Hong Kong **2.** Phillipines **4** Thailand **1.** Korea **4** Pakistan **1.** Semifinals: New Zealand **5** China **0.** Korea **5** Philippines **0.**

Final

New Zealand **4** Korea **0.**

AMERICAN ZONE

First round

Brazil **5** Venezuela **0.** Colombia **3** Uruguay **2.** Canada **4** Commonwealth Carribean **0.** Mexico **3** Peru **2.** Semifinals: Brazil **4** Colombia **1** Mexico **3** Canada **2.** Final: Mexico **4** Brazil **1.**

WORLD GROUP DRAW FOR 1986

First round (March 7th-9th)

Mexico v West Germany; Ecuador v USA; New Zealand v Australia; Great Britain v Spain; Yugoslavia v USSR; India v Czechoslovakia; Italy v Paraguay; Denmark v Sweden.

British Davis Cup Record since 1946

1946 ROUND ONE

v France (Paris) lost 0-5.

Team

D W Barton, D McPhail, J S Olliff, H Billington.

1947 ROUND TWO

v Poland (Warsaw) won 3-2.

Quarterfinals

v South Africa (Scarborough) lost 1-4.

Team

A J Mottram, D W Barton, G L Paish, D W Butler.

1948 ROUND ONE

v India (Harrogate) won 3-2.

Round Two

v Norway (Oslo) won 4-1.

Quarterfinals

v Netherlands (Edgbaston) won 4-1.

Semifinals

v Sweden (Stockholm) lost 1-4.

Team

A J Mottram, H F Walton, G L Paish, H Billington.

1949 ROUND ONE

v Portugal (Lisbon) won 5-0.

Round Two

v Czechoslovakia (Wimbledon) lost 1-4.

Team

A J Mottram, G L Paish.

1950 ROUND ONE

v Italy (Eastbourne) lost 2-3.

Team

A J Mottram, G L Paish.

1951 ROUND TWO
v Finland (London) won 3-2.
Quarterfinals
v Sweden (Scarborough) lost 0-5.
Team
A J Mottram, G L Paish, A G Roberts.

1952 ROUND TWO
v Yugoslavia (Belgrade) won 3-2.
Quarterfinals
v Italy (Bologna) lost 1-4.
Team
A J Mottram, G L Paish, R Becker, J C Gregory.

1953 ROUND TWO
v Norway (Oslo) won 5-0.
Quarterfinals
v Belgium (Brussels) lost 1-4.
Team
A J Mottram, G L Paish, G D Oakley.

1954 ROUND TWO
v Brazil (Eastbourne) won 4-1.
Quarterfinals
v Belgium (Scarborough) lost 2-3.
Team
A J Mottram, G L Paish, G D Oakley.

1955 ROUND TWO
v Austria (Vienna) won 4-1.
Quarterfinals
v India (Manchester) won 3-2.
Semifinals
Italy (Eastbourne) lost 0-5.
Team
R Becker, A J Mottram, G L Paish, W A Knight, M G Davies, R K Wilson.

1956 ROUND TWO
v Yugoslavia (Belgrade) won 5-0.
Quarterfinals
v Chile (Bristol) won 3-2.
Semifinals
v Sweden (Stockholm) lost 1-4.
Team
R Becker, W Knight, M Davies, J E Barrett.

1957 ROUND TWO
v New Zealand (Eastbourne) won 5-0.
Quarterfinals
v France (Paris) won 3-2.
Semifinals
v Belgium (Brussels) lost 2-3.
Team
M Davies, R Wilson.

1958 ROUND TWO
v Brazil (Eastbourne) won 5-0.
Quarterfinals
v West Germany (Scarborough) won 5-0.
Semifinals
v France (Manchester) won 5-0.
European Zone Final
v Italy (Milan) lost 1-4.
Team
W Knight, M Davies, R Becker, R K Wilson.

1959 ROUND TWO
v Luxembourg (Morndorf Les Bains) won 5-0.
Quarterfinals
v Chile (Eastbourne) won 3-2.
Semifinals
v Spain (Barcelona) lost 2-3.
Team
W Knight, A R Mills, R K Wilson, M Davies.

1960 ROUND TWO
v Netherlands (Scheveningen) won 5-0.
Quarterfinals
v Belgium (Scarborough) won 5-0.
Semifinals
v Italy (Wimbledon) lost 1-4.
Team
W Knight, M Davies, M G Sangster, R Becker, R K Wilson.

1961 ROUND TWO
v Austria (Vienna) won 3-2.
Quarterfinals
v South Africa (Edgbaston) won 4-1.
Semifinals
v Sweden (Bastaad) lost 1-4.
Team
M Sangster, R K Wilson, A R Mills, A J Pickard.

1962 Round Two
v Austria (Vienna) won 4-1.
Quarterfinals
v Brazil (Eastbourne) won 4-1.
Semifinals
v Italy (Milan) lost 0-5.
Team
W Knight, M Sangster, A J Pickard.

1963 ROUND TWO
v Belgium (Brussels) won 5-0.
Quarterfinals
v USSR (Eastbourne) won 4-1.
Semifinals
v Spain (Bristol) won 4-1.
European Zone Final
v Sweden (Wimbledon) won 3-2.
Inter-Zone Final
v USA (Bournemouth) lost 0-5.
Team
W Knight, M Sangster, A J Pickard, R K Wilson.

1964 ROUND ONE
v Austria (Birmingham) won 5-0.
Round Two
v Ireland (Eastbourne) won 5-0.
Quarterfinals
v Yugoslavia (Manchester) won 3-2.
Semifinals
v France (Bristol) lost 2-3.
Team
W Knight, R Taylor, A R Mills, M Sangster, R K Wilson.

1965 ROUND ONE
v Israel (London) won 4-1.
Round Two
v Denmark (Copenhagen) won 3-1.
Quarterfinals
v South Africa (Eastbourne) lost 2-3.
Team
R Taylor, M Sangster, R K Wilson.

1966 ROUND ONE
v New Zealand (Queen's Club) won 4-1.
Round Two
v Hungary (Budapest) won 3-2.
Quarterfinals
v West Germany (Hanover) lost 2-3.
Team
R Taylor, M Sangster, R K Wilson.

1967 ROUND ONE
v Canada (Bournemouth) won 4-1.
Round Two
v Bulgaria (Sofia) won 5-0.
Quarterfinals
v Spain (Eastbourne) lost 2-3.
Team
M Sangster, R Taylor, R K Wilson, M Cox.

1968 ROUND ONE
v France (Bournemouth) won 3-0.
Round Two
v Finland (Queen's Club) won 5-0.
Quarterfinals
v Spain (Barcelona) lost 1-4.
Team
R K Wilson, M Cox, M Sangster, P R Hutchins.

1969 ROUND ONE
v Switzerland (Zurich) won 5-0.
Round Two
v Ireland (Eastbourne) won 5-0.
Semifinals
v West Germany (Edgbaston) won 3-2.
European Zone Final
v South Africa (Bristol) won 3-2.
Inter-Zone Semifinals
v Brazil (Wimbledon) won 3-2.
Inter-Zone Final
v Romania (Wimbledon) lost 2-3.
Team
M Cox, G Stilwell, P Curtis.

1970 ROUND ONE
v Austria (Edinburgh) lost 2-3.
Team
J Clifton, G Battrick, P W Curtis.

1971 ROUND ONE
v Yugoslavia (Zagreb) lost 0-3.
Team
G Battrick, S Matthews.

1972 ROUND ONE
v France (Paris) lost 1-4.
Team
D Lloyd, J G Paish.

1973 ROUND THREE
v West Germany (Munich) lost 1-4.
Team
M Cox, R Taylor, D A Lloyd.

1974 ROUND THREE
v United Arab Republic (Cairo) lost 0-5.
Team
D A Lloyd, J Lloyd.

1975 ROUND TWO
v Iran (Queen's Club) won 5-0.
Round Three
v Austria (Vienna) won 4-0.
Quarterfinals
v Spain (Barcelona) lost 2-3.
Team
R Taylor, J M Lloyd, J W Feaver, C J Mottram.

1976 ROUND THREE
v Switzerland (Zurich) won 4-1.
Quarterfinals
v Romania (Eastbourne) won 5-0.
Semifinals
v France (Eastbourne) won 4-1.
European Zone Final
v Italy (Wimbledon) lost 1-4.
Team
J W Feaver, R Taylor, J M Lloyd, D A Lloyd.

1977 SEMIFINALS
v Romania (Bucharest) lost 1-4.
Team
J W Feaver, J M Lloyd, D A Lloyd, R A Lewis.

1978 ROUND TWO
v Monaco (Monte Carlo) won 5-0.
Quarterfinals
v Austria (Bristol) won 5-0.
Semifinals
v France (Paris) won 3-2.
European Zone Final
v Czechoslovakia (Eastbourne) won 5-0.
Inter-Zone Final
v Australia (Crystal Palace) won 3-2.
Davis Cup Final
v USA (Palm Springs) lost 1-4.
Team
C J Mottram, J M Lloyd, D A Lloyd, M Cox, R A Lewis.

1979 SEMIFINALS
v Spain (Eastbourne) won 4-1.
European Zone Final
v Italy (Rome) lost 1-4.
Team
C J Mottram, J M Lloyd, M Cox, D A Lloyd.

1980 EUROPEAN ZONE SEMIFINALS
v Romania (Bristol) lost 2-3.
Team
C J Mottram, J W Feaver, D A Lloyd, J M Lloyd.

1981 ROUND ONE
v Italy (Brighton) won 3-2.
Round Two
v New Zealand (Christchurch) won 4-1.
Semi-finals
v Argentina (Buenos Aires) lost 0-5.
Team
C J Mottram, R A Lewis, J Smith, A Jarrett.

1982 ROUND ONE
v Italy (Rome) lost 2-3.
Non-Zonal play-off
v Spain (Barcelona) won 3-2.
Team
C J Mottram, R A Lewis, J Smith, A Jarrett.

1983 ROUND ONE
v Australia (Nth Adelaide) lost 1-4.
Non-Zonal play-off
v Chile (Eastbourne) won 4-1.
Team
J M Lloyd, C J Mottram, A Jarratt, J Bates.

1984 ROUND ONE
v Italy (Telford) lost 2-3
Non-Zonal play-off
v Yugoslavia (Eastbourne) lost 1-4
Team
J Lloyd, S Shaw, C Dowdeswell

BRITISH INTERNATIONAL HONOURS

DAVIS CUP

(Figures in brackets indicate number of rubbers played)
H W Austin 1929-37 (24)
J E Barrett 1956 (1)
D W Barton 1946-47 (2)
J Bates 1978 (3)
G Battrick 1970-71 (2)
A E Beamish 1911-19 (3)
R Becker 1952-60 (10)
H Billington 1946-48 (2)
E D Black 1900 (1)
D W Butler 1938-47 (4)
J G Clifton 1970 (1)
I G Collins 1929-30 (6)
M Cox 1967-79 (16)
C R O Cole-Rees 1925-29 (10)
W C Crawley 1909 (1)
P Curtis 1969-70 (6)
H F David 1932 (1)
M G Davies 1955-60 (16)
P M Dawson 1919 (1)
C P Dixon 1909-13 (5)
H L Doherty 1902-06 (5)
R F Doherty 1902-06 (5)
C Dowdeswell 1984-5 (4)
C G Eames 1928-29 (5)
M J Farrell 1975 (1)
J W Feaver 1977-80 (2)
J B Gilbert 1923-25 (6)
L A Godfree 1923-27 (11)
A W Gore 1900-12 (3)
J C Gregory 1926-52 (15)
C H Hare 1937-39 (4)
E Higgs 1927-28 (6)
G P Hughes 1929-36 (21)
P Hutchins 1968 (2)
A M Jarrett 1981-83 (7)
C M Jones 1938 (1)
A R F Kingscote 1919-24 (7)
C H Kingsley 1925-31 (9)
W A Knight 1955-60 (21)
H G N Lee 1930-34 (7)
H K Lester 1926 (1)
N R Lewis 1949 (1)
R A Lewis 1977-82 (7)
D A Lloyd 1971-80 (15)
J M Lloyd 1974-85 (22)
A H Lowe 1911-19 (3)
F G Lowe 1921-25 (4)
R Lycett 1921-23 (3)
S J Matthews 1971 (1)
T Mavrogordato 1914-19 (4)
D McPhail 1946 (1)
A R Mills 1959-64 (3)
A J Mottram 1947-55 (19)
C J Mottram 1975-83 (19)
G D Oakley 1953-54 (2)
J S Oliff 1946 (1)
G L Paish 1947-55 (19)
J G Paish 1972 (1)
J C Parke 1908-20 (8)
F J Perry 1931-36 (20)
J A Pickard 1961-63 (5)
J Pim 1902 (1)
F L Riseley 1904-22 (2)
M J G Ritchie 1908 (1)
A G Roberts 1951 (1)
H Roper Barrett 1900-19 (8)
M G Sangster 1960-68 (26)
L Shaffi 1939 (2)
N Sharpe 1930 (1)
S Shaw 1984-85 (2)
R A Shayes 1938-39 (5)
J Smith 1981-82 (5)
S H Smith 1905-06 (2)
G Stilwell 1969 (6)
R Taylor 1964-76 (18)
C R D Tuckey 1935-37 (3)
O G N Turnbull 1919-26 (6)
H F Walton 1948 (1)
J D P Wheatley 1923-26 (8)
F H D Wilde 1937-39 (6)
R K Wilson 1955-68 (34)
M Woosnam 1921-24 (6)

HANGING ON IN ESSEN

BY MALCOLM FOLLEY: THE DAILY MAIL

THE KING'S CUP

It was under the patronage of King Gustav V, a notable player himself, that the Swedish Tennis Association first launched a European indoor men's team championship half a century ago. Fittingly the competition came to be known as the King's Cup, though it is generally believed that the original trophy was lost in the Berlin blitz.

Designed on similar lines to the Davis Cup, with a challenge round operating, it became one of the most important Continental events in the late 'thirties but lapsed, after the war, until 1952. Britain's first appearance was not until 1962, with the trophy being won in the years from 1964 to 1967. With the advent of Open tennis, however, the event went into something of a decline.

In 1976 a league system was tried, with mixed success, and last year — on the Lawn Tennis Association's instigation — a divisional system at selected venues was introduced for the first time. To mark the British contribution the LTA were given the honour of staging the 1986 championship at Queen's Club with a new trophy, the European Cup, on offer.

Paul Hutchins knew the knives were out and being sharpened. A complete calamity in the King's Cup, at Essen, West Germany would be hard to explain in the face of escalating criticism, fuelled by relegation to the Second Division of the Davis Cup just a few months earlier.

Without Britain's number one John Lloyd at his disposal — and he played the last of his 54 singles and doubles King's Cup rubbers as far back as 1978 — Hutchins decided to give youth its chance, knowing such a policy was fraught with personal risk.

Yet Stuart Bale, Stephen Shaw and Jeremy Bates between them conjured a victory over Ireland that guaranteed Britain's existence in Division I of the King's Cup for another year. "I realised

Stuart Bale

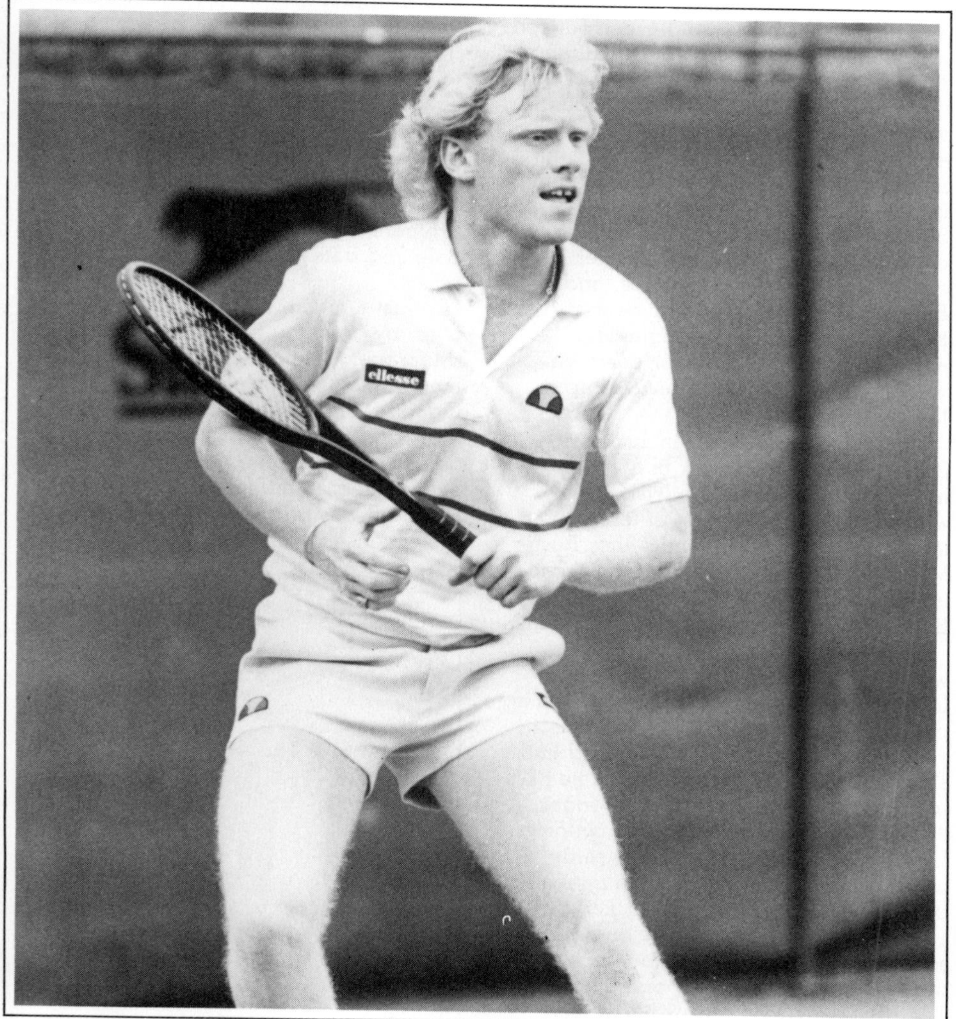

while sitting courtside against Ireland, probably even earlier, that I had put myself on the line with my selection here," Hutchins confessed.

"As Lloyd was unavailable, the easy way out was to pick our next two most experienced players, Colin Dowdeswell and Jonathon Smith. But I have enough confidence in my own ability, enough security in my private life to put myself on the line. When I do come to leave the LTA people can bitch, get the knives out and argue that I may not have produced a Wimbledon champion, but I will know I never compromised myself."

Bale, Shaw and Bates responded with commendable brio. Each one met and overcame a crisis in the critical first match with Ireland: Bale when he came from a set behind to beat Sean Sorensen; Shaw when he demonstrated considerable character in the later stages of the deciding doubles, and Bates swallowing disappointment at being omitted from the singles, for accepting the role of senior partner when Britain needed his leadership in the same match.

For the second year in succession, Britain were on the brink of a humiliating defeat by the Irish, who, with respect, are a nation of tennis leprechauns. Twelve months after Buster Mottram and Dowdeswell dug an escape tunnel against Doyle and Sorensen, Bates and Shaw repeated the achievement.

In the singles, Bale gave Britain a winning start, defeating Sorensen, no longer on the circuit full-time, yet still a player of cunning, 2-6, 7-6, 6-2. The young man from London's East End had ample opportunity to explode, as he had in the past, with frustration and anger. "Knowing I was playing for my country, I couldn't let people down," he said. "I could easily have behaved like a lunatic, but I knew that would have looked bad."

Doyle, who went to Yale on a golf scholarship, and switched to tennis, overcame Shaw, 6-3, 6-3, on raw power. The Irish-American serves like a man with no ambition to involve himself in rallies of any kind.

And so the tie, Britain's fate, and possibly Hutchins' future, went on the line in the doubles. The Irish pair won the first set, and on a day when a smog warning kept the traffic to a minimum in Essen, it looked as though Britain could have lost their way. Not so. Sorensen's brittle nerve cracked, and Doyle found the responsibility too great to burden, and dropped his own service twice in the final set as Shaw and Bates triumphed 2-6, 6-3, 6-2.

Not surprisingly, Sweden's accomplished team accounted for the young Britons 3-0 in their second group match. Bale was beaten by Stefan Simonsson, Shaw was beaten by Jan Gunnarsson, while the Simonsson brothers, Hans, joining Stefan, overcame Bale and Bates. The British did not win a set.

Just a month after winning the Davis Cup, by crushing the United States (McEnroe, Connors et al), the Swedes landed the King's Cup, the European indoor championships instigated by their own King Gustav V in 1936. They defeated Switzerland, the surprise team of the week, in the final, where Thomas Hogstedt was restored to the singles at the expense of Simonsson.

Stephen Shaw

Stefan Simonsson

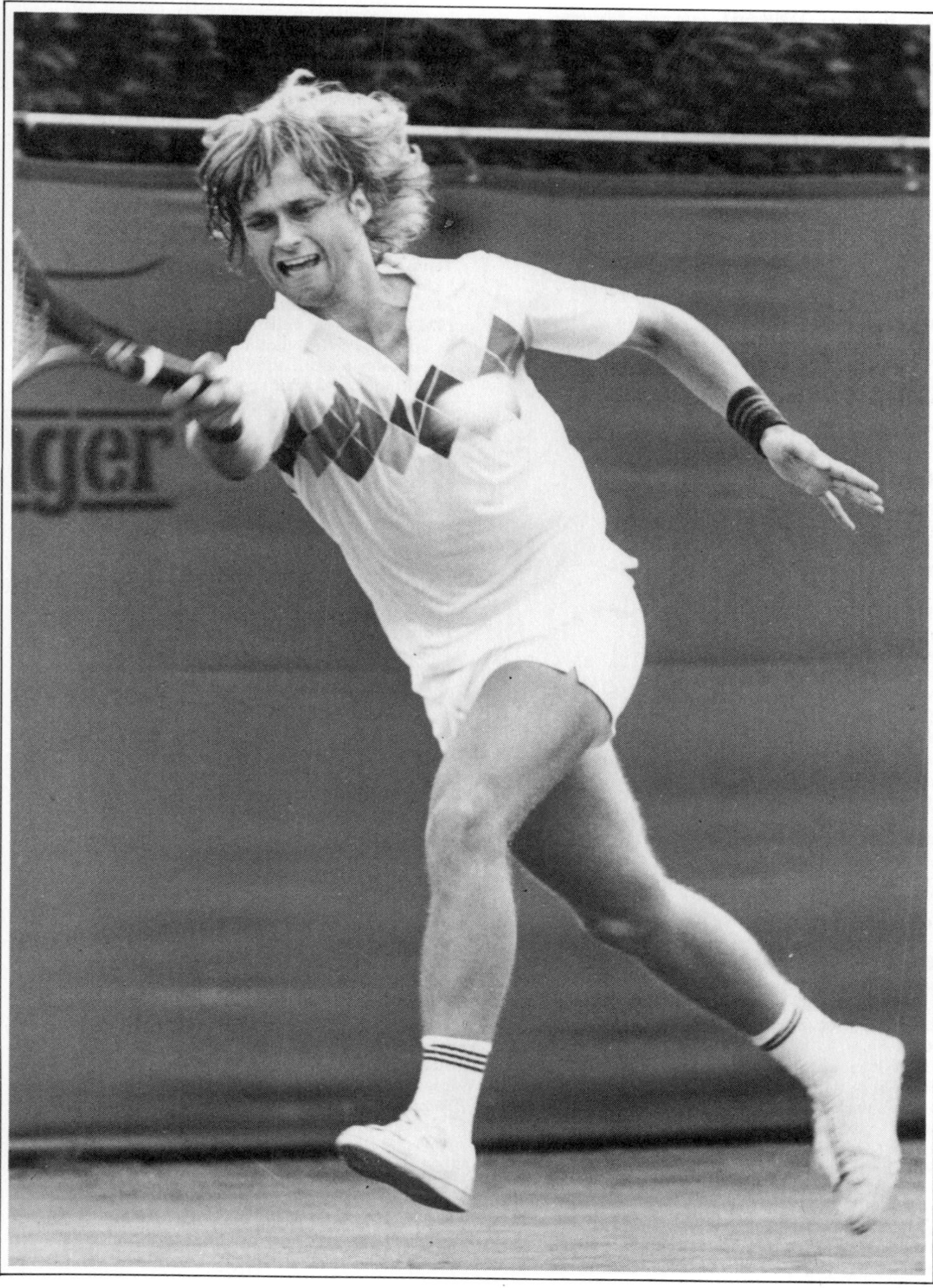

THE KING'S CUP

ESSEN, WEST GERMANY, January 15th-20th

DIVISION ONE – YELLOW GROUP
Sweden bt Ireland 2-1.
Great Britain bt Ireland 2-1.
British results:
S Bale bt S Sorenson 2-6, 7-6, 6-2.
S Shaw lost M Doyle 6-3, 6-3.
J Bates & Shaw bt Doyle & Sorensen 2-6, 6-3, 6-2.
Sweden bt Great Britain 3-0.
British results:
Bale lost S Simonsson 6-3, 6-4.
Shaw lost J Gunnarson 6-4, 7-6.
Bale & Bates lost S Simonsson & H Simmonsson 6-3, 6-4.

BLUE GROUP
Switzerland bt Czechoslovakia 2-1.
West Germany bt Czechoslovakia 2-1.
Switzerland bt West Germany 2-1.
Final
Sweden bt Switzerland 3-0.

British Performances

(First entered in 1962)
1962 GB bt Norway 4-1 (Oslo)
lost Yugoslavia 2-3 (Queen's Club).
1963 GB bt Poland 5-0 (Warsaw)
lost Sweden 2-3 (Stockholm).
1964 GB bt Sweden 3-0 (Stockholm) in final.
Also bt West Germany 4-1 (Bremen)
Denmark 3-2 (Copenhagen)
Belgium 3-0 (Stockholm).
Team
M Sangster (capt), R Taylor, R K Wilson.
1965 GB bt Denmark 2-1 (Torquay) in final.
Also bt Norway 5-0 (Oslo)
France 2-1 (Torquay).
Team
R K Wilson (capt), M Cox, G Stilwell, A R Mills.
1966 GB bt Italy 3-0 (Milan) in final.
Also bt Poland 5-0 (Warsaw)
Finland 5-0 (Helsinki)
Czechoslovakia 3-0 (Milan).
Team
R K Wilson (capt), R Taylor, M Sangster.
1967 GB bt Sweden 2-1 (Stockholm) in final.
Also bt West Germany 3-2 (Cologne)
Yugoslavia 4-1 (Ljubljana)
Spain 2-1 (Stockholm).
Team
R K Wilson (capt), M Cox, P Hutchins, R Taylor.
1968 GB bt Italy 5-0 (Padua)
lost Denmark 1-4 (Crystal Palace).
Team
M Cox (capt), G Battrick, P Curtis.
1969 GB bt Switzerland 4-1 (Bracknell)
bt Yugoslavia 5-1 (Ljubljana)
lost Czechoslovakia 1-2 (Cologne).
Team
M Cox, G Stilwell, P Curtis, J Clifton.
1970 GB lost Hungary 1-4.
1971 GB bt France 3-2 (Paris)
bt Finland 3-2 (Helsinki)
lost Czechoslovakia 1-4 (Basingstoke).
Team
G Battrick, J Paish, S Matthews, S Warboys.
1972 GB bt Netherlands (w/o)
lost West Germany 2-3 (Hanover).
Team
S Warboys, J M Lloyd.
1973 GB bt Switzerland (London) 3-2
lost Sweden (Stockholm) 2-3.
Team
S Warboys, C Mottram, D Lloyd, J Paish, M Cox.
1974 GB lost Czechoslovakia 1-4 (Plzen).
Team
J Lloyd, M Farrell.
1975 No Competition.
1976 GB Runners up to Hungary.
Bt Spain 2-1 (Washington)
bt Yugoslavia 2-1 (Zagreb)
lost Hungary 1-2 (Budapest)
lost W Germany 1-2 (Berlin)
bt Italy 2-1 (Bergamo)
bt France 2-1 (Edinburgh)
bt Sweden 3-0 (Edinburgh)
bt Spain 2-1 (Alicante)
bt Yugoslavia 3-0 (Nottingham)
bt Italy 3-0 (Nottingham)
lost Sweden 0-3 (Helsingborg)
bt Hungary 3-0 (Washington)
bt W Germany 3-0 (Washington)
lost France 1-2 (Bordeaux).
Team
J Lloyd, C Mottram, R Taylor, M Cox.
1977 GB Third behind winners Sweden.
Bt Yugoslavia 2-1 (Belgrade)
bt Yugoslavia 3-0 (Washington)
bt Spain 3-0 (Seville)
bt Spain 2-1 (Aberavon)
lost W Germany 1-2 (Washington)
lost W Germany 1-2 (Kiel)
bt Hungary 2-1 (Aberavon)
lost Hungary 1-2 (Budapest).
Team
J Lloyd, M Cox, D Lloyd.
1978 GB Seventh behind winners Sweden.
Lost Sweden 1-2 (Sunderland)
lost Austria 1-2 (Vienna)
bt Spain 3-0 (Sheffield)
lost Sweden 1-2 (Kalmar)
lost Austria 1-2 (Gloucester)
lost Spain 1-2 (Las Palmas).
Play-off
bt Yugoslavia 3-0 (Farnborough)
lost Yugoslavia 1-2 (Skopje).
Team
J Feaver, M Cox, J Lloyd, D Lloyd.
1979 GB Third behind winners Czechoslovakia.
Lost Hungary 0-3 (Sheffield)
bt Spain 2-1 (Sabadell)
bt West Germany 3-0 (Crawley)
lost Hungary 0-3 (Budapest)
bt Spain 3-0 (Cambridge)
bt West Germany 2-1 (Essex).

Play-off
bt Sweden 2-1 (Gloucester)
bt Sweden 2-1 (Norrkoping).
Team
R Drysdale, C J Mottram, C Bradnam, M Cox, D Lloyd.
1980 GB Seventh behind winners Czechoslovakia.
Lost Czechoslovakia 0-3 (Chrudin)
lost West Germany 0-3 (Kiel)
lost Sweden 0-3 (Sheffield)
lost Czechoslovakia 1-2 (Thurnaby)
bt West Germany 2-1 (Newcastle)
lost Sweden 0-3 (Motala).
Play-off
lost France 1-2 (Gloucester)
bt France 3-0 (Le Mans).
Team
A Jarrett, R Drysdale, R Beven, D Lloyd, C Mottram.
1981 GB Fifth behind winners West Germany.
Team
C J Mottram, R Lewis, D Lloyd, A Jarrett, J Bates, J Feaver, J Smith.
1982 GB Third in Group A.
Team
C J Mottram, J Feaver, J Whiteford, J Dier, R Lewis.
1983 GB Third behind winners West Germany.
Team
C Mottram, J Bates, R Lewis, A Jarratt, S Shaw.
British Results
Yellow Group
Bt Ireland 2-1
lost Czechoslovakia 3-0.
Team
C Mottram, C Dowdeswell, J Bates, S Shaw.
1984 GB retained Division One status. Beat Ireland 2-1, lost Czechoslovakia 0-3.
Team
J Bates, C Dowdeswell, S Shaw, C J Mottram.

A HAT-TRICK FOR CZECHS

BY DAVID IRVINE: THE GUARDIAN

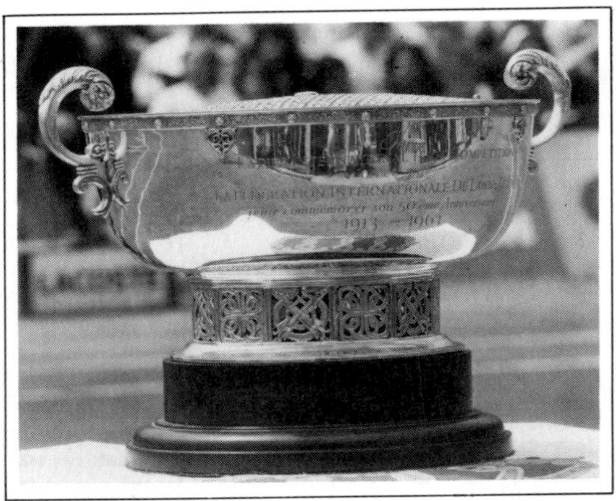

FEDERATION CUP

Though effectively the equivalent of the Davis Cup for men, the much newer Federation Cup for women — it was introduced by the ITF in 1963 — differs in that it is staged on a knockout basis at one venue with each tie being decided on two singles and one doubles match.

For more than half its life the most dominant country has been the United States, winners on 11 occasions. But more recently that role has been taken over by Czechoslovakia, who not only won for the third year running in October but, this July, have the distinction of becoming the first East European nation to host the event.

Only two other nations; Australia and South Africa, have held the trophy. Yet all indications are that, with more and more countries taking part each year, other nations will soon have their names inscribed on the trophy.

Manuela Maleena

Following their worst-ever performance at Sao Paolo the previous year, when they were beaten in the opening round, the British team had the satisfaction of justifying their seeding at the 23rd Federation Cup competition at Nagoya in October, reaching the quarter-finals before going out — as they did in Brazil — to the Bulgarian sisters Manuela and Katerina Maleeva.

A late re-draw, forced on the organisers by the withdrawal of the West Germans Steffi Graf and Claudia Kohde-Kilsch, worked to Britain's advantage. Originally Virginia Wade's team were expecting to face Argentina, who had the formidable teenager Gabriela Sabatini as their No. 1, but instead they began against a much-depleted German side and progressed by beating them and the host nation Japan to a place among the last eight.

As in Zurich and Sao Paolo the event was dominated by the Czechs, who won the trophy for the third time in succession and the fourth time in all. In the final they beat the United States 2-1 although it must be said that, once again, the Americans were without both Martina Navratilova and Chris Lloyd.

It is appropriate, in the light of the Czech team's consistency and support that this year's event will be held in Prague during July. And in accordance with tradition the 1985 event culminated with the Federation's flag being handed, for safe-keeping, to Josef Suk, president of the Czech Federation and father of Helena Sukova, whose contribution to the team's success since 1983 almost matches that of their No. 1, Hana Mandikova.

Everyone shares the hope that 1986, when the competition will be hosted for the first time by a East European nation, will see all the leading players involving themselves. For as Philippe Chatrier, the ITF president said: "Playing under the stress of team competition can often make a player better than he or she already is. I think the only losers this week were those who did not turn up".

As at the US Open, where she beat both Mrs Lloyd and Miss Navratilova, Miss Mandlikova proved herself an outstanding big-occasion player. Apart from the semi-final round, where she dropped the opening set to the elder Maleeva, she did not put a foot wrong in her seven matches.

Miss Sukova lost twice in singles competition, then redeemed herself in the doubles, and although Regina Marsikova and the Wimbledon junior champion Andrea Holikova were only called on for the 'dead' doubles rubbers they answered the call with an efficiency which suggested that Czechoslovakia's future is in good hands.

Round-by-round the Czechs disposed of Greece (2-1), Switzerland (2-1), Hungary (3-0), Bulgaria (2-1), and the USA (2-1), with Miss Mandlikova extending her winning singles sequence in the competition to 15 matches. Few were prepared to argue the point when she said that, had the Americans been at full-strength, the Czechs would still have won.

In the absence of Graf and Kohde-Kilsch, who both put personal considerations above national needs, the West Germans had no alternative but to summon up two relatively inexperienced youngsters in Petra Kepeler and Myriam Schropp. Britain were the beneficiaries, Jo Durie beating Keppeler 6-4 6-0 with Anne Hobbs defeating Schropp 6-8 6-4 before joining forces to overcome Keppeler and Andrea Betzner 6-4 3-6 6-4 in the doubles.

Against Japan Miss Wade decided to experiment with Miss Hobbs as No. 1 and Annabel Croft as No. 2. But while the former won a long match 5-7 6-3 6-2 against Masako Yanagi, the latter was well below her best in losing 7-6 6-7 6-3 to Etsuko Inouie. Thus it was left to the Durie-Hobbs combination to save the day by beating Inouie and Yanagi 6-7 6-8 6-2.

That put Britain into the quarter-finals against Bulgaria, against whom they had lost 3-0 twelve months earlier. There was some improvement — but not enough to earn the team a semi-final place. Miss Croft, opening the tie, was totally outclassed by Manuela and lost 6-2 6-2. Miss Durie battled spiritedly against the Bulgarian's 16-year-old sister Katerina but also had to concede 6-2 4-6 8-6. A victory in the doubles, on a default, was no real consolation.

Gabriela Sabatini

FEDERATION CUP
Nagoya, Japan
October 7th to 13th

Preliminary round
Belgium **3** Uruguay **0**, Ireland **3** Thailand **0**, Taipei **2** Finland **1**, Norway **2** Chile **1**, China **2** Indonesia **1**, Korea **2** Phillippines **1**.

First round
Czechoslovakia (1) **2** Greece **1**, Switzerland **2** Netherlands **1**, Hungary **3** Belgium **0**, Canada **2** Sweden (5) **1**, Bulgaria (4) **3** USSR **0**, Yugoslavia **3** Ireland **0**, Japan **3** Austria **0**, Great Britain (7) **4** Germany **0**, Italy (6) **3** Taipei **0**, Mexico **3** Norway **0**; Spain **2** Hong Kong **1**, Australia (3) **3** Denmark **0**, Argentina (8) **3** Peru **0**, New Zealand **2** France **1**, China **2** Brazil **1**, USA (2) **3** Korea **0**.

Sound round
Czechoslovakia **2** Switzerland **1**, Hungary **2** Canada **1**, Bulgaria **3** Yugoslavia **0**, Great Britain **2** Japan **1**, Italy **3** Mexico **0**, Australia **3** Spain **0**, Argentina **2** New Zealand **1**, USA **3** China **0**.

Quarter-finals
Czechoslovakia **3** Hungary **0**, Bulgaria **2** Great Britain **1**, Australia **3** Italy **0**, USA **2** Argentina **1**.

Semifinals
Czechoslovakia **2** Bulgaria **1**, USA **2** Australia **1**.

Final
Czechoslovakia **2** USA **1**.

DETAILED BRITISH RESULTS
Roune One (v West Germany)
A Croft bt M Schropp 6-3, 6-1
J Durie bt P Keppeler 6-4, 6-0
Durie & A Hobbs bt Keppeler & A Betzner 6-4, 3-6, 6-1

Round Two (v Japan)
Croft bt E Inoue 7-6, 6-7, 6-3
Hobbs lost M Yanagi 7-5, 3-6, 2-6
Durie & Hobbs bt Inoue & Yanagi 6-7, 6-3, 6-2

Quarter-final (v Bulgaria)
Croft lost M Maleeva 2-6, 2-6
Durie lost K Maleeva 2-6, 6-4, 6-8
Durie & Hobbs bt M Maleeva & K Maleeva 5-4 retd.

Previous Results

1963
Final (Queen's Club, London)
United States 2 Australia 1
Britain bt Canada 3-0
bt Austria 3-0
lost USA (Semifinals) 0-3
Team P F Jones, C Truman, D M Catt.

1964
Final (Germantown CC, USA)
Australia 2 United States 1
Britain bt Norway 3-0
bt South Africa 2-1
lost USA (Semifinals) 0-3
Team P F Jones, D M Catt.

1965
Final (Melbourne)
Australia 2 United States 1
Britain bt South Africa 2-1
lost USA (Semifinals) 0-3
Team P F Jones, C Truman, D M Catt.

1966
Final (Melbourne)
United States 3 West Germany 0
Britain bt Canada 3-0
bt Czechoslovakia 3-0
lost USA (Semifinals) 1-2
Team P F Jones, W M Shaw, E Starkie.

1967
Final (Berlin)
United States 2 Great Britain 0
Britain bt Sweden 3-0
bt Italy 2-1
bt Australia 3-0
Team S V Wade, P F Jones.

1968
Final (Paris)
Australia 3 Netherlands 0
Britain bt Sweden 3-0
bt Czechoslovakia 2-1
bt USSR 3-0
lost Australia (Semifinals) 0-2
Team S V Wade, G T Janes, W M Shaw.

1969
Final (Athens)
United States 2 Australia 1
Britain bt Belgium 3-0
bt West Germany 2-1
lost Australia (Semifinals) 0-3
Team W M Shaw, S V Wade, G M Williams.

1970
Final (Friedburg)
Australia 3 West Germany 0
Britain bt New Zealand 3-0
bt Netherlands 2-1
lost Australia (Semifinals) 0-3
Team W M Shaw, S V Wade, G M Williams.

1971
Final (Perth)
Australia 3 Great Britain 0
Britain bt New Zealand 3-0
bt United States 3-0
Team P F Jones, S V Wade, W M Shaw.

1972
Final (Johannesburg)
South Africa 2 Great Britain 1
Britain bt Japan 3-0
bt Argentina 2-1
bt West Germany 2-1
bt Australia 2-1
Team S V Wade, W M Shaw, G M Williams.

1973
Final (Bad Homburg)
Australia 3 South Africa 0
Britain bt Mexico 3-0
lost Romania (Quarter-finals) 1-2
Team S V Wade, G M Williams.

1974
Final (Naples)
Australia 2 United States 1
Britain bt Ireland 2-0
bt Norway 2-0
bt South Africa 2-1
lost Australia (Semifinals) 0-3
Team S V Wade, G L Coles, S Barker.

1975
Final (Aix-en-Provence)
Czechoslovakia 3 Australia 0
Britain bt Australia 3-0
bt Spain 2-0
lost France (Quarterfinals) 0-2
Team S V Wade, S Barker, G L Coles.

1976
Final (Philadelphia)
United States 2 Australia 1
Britain bt France 3-0
bt Hungary walkover
bt South Africa 2-1
lost Australia (Semifinals) 0-3
Team S V Wade, S Barker, M Tyler.

1977
Final (Eastbourne)
United States 2 Australia 1
Britain bt Denmark 3-0
bt South Korea 3-0
bt Sweden 3-0
lost Australia (Semifinals) 1-2
Team S V Wade, S Barker.

1978
Final (Melbourne)
United States 2 Australia 1
Britain bt Spain 3-0
bt West Germany 2-1
bt Czechoslovakia 2-1
lost United States (Semifinals) 0-3
Team S V Wade, S Barker, M Tyler, A E Hobbs.

1979
Final (Madrid)
United States 3 Australia 0
Britain bt New Zealand 3-0
bt Belgium 3-0
lost Czechoslovakia 0-3
Team S V Wade, S Barker, M Tyler, A E Hobbs.

1980
Final (Berlin)
United States 3 Australia 0
Britain bt Israel 3-0
bt Argentina 2-1
lost West Germany 0-3
Team S V Wade, S Barker, G Coles.

1981
Final (Tokyo)
United States 3 Great Britain 0
Britain bt Belgium 3-0
bt France 3-0
bt USSR 2-1 r/o
bt Australia 2-1
Team S Barker, S V Wade, J M Durie.

1982
Final (Santa Clara)
United States 3 West Germany 0
Britain bt Italy 2-1
bt Israel 3-0
lost Czechoslovakia 1-2
Team S V Wade, J M Durie, A E Hobbs, S Barker

1983
Final (Zurich)
Czechoslovakia 2 West Germany 1
Britain bt Luxembourg 3-0
bt Brazil 3-0
lost West Germany 1-2
Team S V Wade, J M Durie, A E Hobbs

1984
Final (Sao Paolo)
Czechoslovakia 2 Australia 1
Britain lost to Bulgaria 0-3
Team J M Durie, A E Hobbs, A Brown

British Federation Cup Players

(Figures in brackets indicate number of rubbers played)
S Barker 1974-82 (32)
A Brown 1984 (1)
D Catt 1963-65 (5)
G L Coles 1974-85 (17)
A Croft 1985 (3)
J M Durie 1981-84 (12)
A E Hobbs 1978-85 (15)
G T Janes 1963-68 (9)
P F Jones 1963-71 (18)
W M Shaw 1966-72 (19)
D E Starkie 1966 (3)
M Tyler 1976-79 (5)
S V Wade 1967-83 (100)
G M Williams 1969-73 (9)

WILLIAMSBURG WHITEWASH

BY JOHN PARSONS: DAILY TELEGRAPH

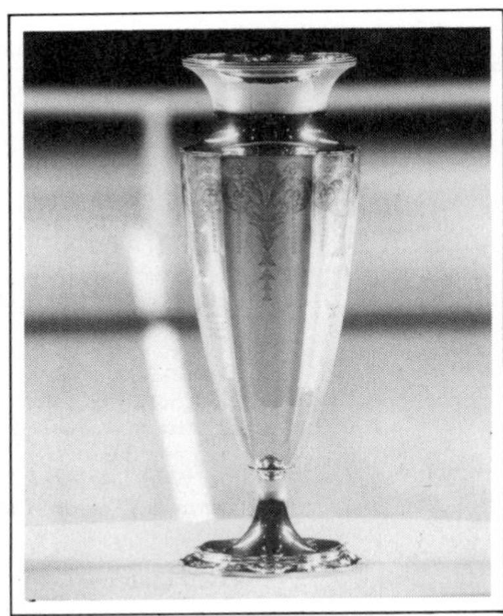

WIGHTMAN CUP

That special sporting relationship between Britain and the United States is never more clearly identified than in the Wightman Cup. Originally the brainchild of Mrs George W. Wightman — formerly Hazel Hotchkiss, four times US champion — and intended as a Davis Cup for women, it rapidly developed as a private rivalry which has gone on uninterrupted, except for the war years, since 1932.

For many years the lawns of Wimbledon and the West Side Club at Forest Hills provided alternate sites but, after experimenting with a series of varied venues, the event is now largely accepted as an indoor event; with Britain favouring London's Royal Albert Hall and the Americans the old colonial town of Williamsburg.

Last November, in front of their own supporters, the American team won for the 47th time in the 57-match series. This year, in London, Britain will be seeking their first success since 1978.

One of the recurring dilemmas surrounding the Nabisco Wightman Cup is that the event, especially when taking place in the United States, needs the support of at least some of the leading American players to have any public appeal. Yet when that happens it also means, more often than not, that the match itself will be too one-sided to enjoy universal credibility.

There was a classic illustration of that when the 1985 contest returned to Colonial Williamsburg, when there is certainly an enthusiastic enough, professional and voluntary response to make it sensible to designate this the permanent home for the competition in the United States.

With Chris Lloyd, Pam Shriver and Kathy Rinaldi all in the host team at a time when they were ranked respectively first, third and eleventh in the world, it was easier to sell the match on the attractive merits of its stars rather than the likely strength of the competition.

Indeed the eventual 7-0 defeat for Britain was almost inevitable. Despite the encouraging results some of the

Kathy Rinaldi

visiting players achieved at Brighton a week earlier they could expect little more mercy, even in this fiercely pro-British part of the United States, than offered to their invading forefathers more than 200 years earlier.

So it proved. At the end of a first day in which the Americans, in keeping with world rankings and individual reputations, took both of the opening singles but Anne Hobbs might easily have upset Kathy Rinaldi, national team manager Sue Mappin observed frankly, but with just a hint of understandable frustration, "Anything we had won today would have been a bonus. We didn't win anything."

It was a remark which remained apt throughout the three days of a match in which Britain, in losing for the seventh successive year and 7-0 for the third time in their last four visits to America, did not even achieve a set until the final rubber.

Then Miss Hobbs, renewing her partnership with Jo Durie which many feel should never have been broken after their splendid successes in 1983, at least stretched Mrs Lloyd and Miss Shriver to 6-3, 6-7, 6-2.

At the end of a rubber which had demonstrated beyond doubt how and why the Wightman Cup is so much more than just another tennis fixture, the 6,482 crowd, which had been caught up in the excitement of almost every point, even though there was only personal pride at stake, gave the players a standing ovation.

Those cheers were renewed, in even greater volume, during the closing ceremony. It was a remarkable scene. Over the three days attendances totalled 14,699 an increase of 2,800 on two years earlier.

The fact that the Americans had yet again scored a runaway victory was largely irrelevant in the eyes of the spectators or the Williamsburg organisers. "Give us another two or three Wightman Cup matches here and we'll fill this place" said one of the army of committee volunteers looking round the 10,000 seater sports arena at William and Mary Hall, where there is now even a special Wightman Cup reception lounge, complete with a huge carpet bearing the Wightman Cup logo.

One just hopes that such fervour is allowed — and encouraged — to continue. For as Mrs Lloyd, the American captain, commented at the end: "Everyone in our team is emotionally drained, despite the apparent ease of our win, because we get so excited about this event. There is so much more at stake when you play as a team, rather than just for yourself. At the back of your mind all the time is the knowledge that you are also playing for your country. We knew beforehand we should be able to win all seven matches. We were determined to so so — and we did."

Mrs Lloyd also joined in the chorus of voices calling for the American leg of an event which began in 1923, to stay in Williamsburg. "Over the years we've played in a lot of different American cities where the fans haven't really quite understood what the Wightman Cup is, it's prestige and the history behind it. Here in Williamsburg it has been different."

From the British point of view it was a case of having to grin and bear it. As an occasion, the Wightman Cup had once more been a resounding success but deep down it cannot have been much fun for the British players who, hard though they fought, were at times made to look little more than stooges for the stars to demonstrate their skills.

Miss Mappin, put a brave face on things by saying "I think it shows the respect they have for the event that the Americans always field a good team. We do have good players both in this team and among others below them who will be able to give a more creditable performance in the future. As it was we were up against the best in the world at a time when they were playing incredibly well."

Never was that more ruthlessly demonstrated than on the second day when Britain needed to win at least one of the rubbers to keep the match alive into day three. Instead it was a calamity. Annabel Croft, probably showing some reaction from her successes at Brighton a week earlier and undoubtedly feeling the pressure of so much responsibility as the British number one, achieved a place in Wightman Cup history for totally the wrong reason, when, in being overwhelmed by Pam Shriver, she became only the third player in 62 years to lose a singles 6-0, 6-0.

The match, such as it was, lasted 43 minutes and Miss Shriver hardly made an unforced error until netting a fore-hand volley when she stood at match point for the first time, on her way to joining Louise Brough in 1950 and Andrea Jaeger in 1981 as the only others to win a Wightman Cup singles rubber without the loss of a game.

"It was just one of those days when you do everything right, I don't know what she could have done differently" said the American. One answer to that might well have been "to win the first game." Strange though it may seem after a 6-0, 6-0 defeat, things might just have been totally transformed had Miss Croft,

Chris Lloyd

who opened aggressively on both flanks, been able to hold the break point she created in the tough, trend-forming opening game.

Miss Shriver saved it with a splendidly crisp volley, however, took the game with two more and from then on the Kent girl was too often either overpowered or outclassed or trying to force things too much on her own game, especially her vulnerable serve, that additional errors were all too predictable. It was both a grim lesson and a chastening experience, as evidenced by the sighs of resignation which emanated from Miss Croft during the closing stages.

After what happened it was hardly a surprise when, barely 30 minutes later, Miss Croft continued to struggle as she and Virginia Wade went down 6-4, 6-1 to Betsy Nagelsen and Anne White in the one rubber Britain thought they might win but which in the end merely clinched the American victory. The British pair battled well enough to 4-4 in the first set but from then on the trend was all too familiar.

It was a particularly disappointing 21st Wightman Cup match for Miss Wade, all the more so because the tall and elegant Miss White, who had created such a stir by her appearance in an all-white body stocking at Wimbledon a few months earlier, was one of her former protegés. She had learned well.

On the first day, Miss Durie had lost 6-2, 6-3 to Mrs Lloyd and Anne Hobbs 7-5, 7-5 to Kathy Rinaldi which, looking back, was probably the best British performance. In their previous meeting Miss Hobbs had managed only four games against the 1985 Wimbledon semi-finalist. On this occasion she won ten and it should have been more, because in both sets she broke back to 5-5 but then failed to take advantage of the fresh chance she had created.

Miss Durie did not play badly against Mrs Lloyd and certainly not against Miss Shriver when, despite serving problems, she pulled back from 1-5 to 4-5 in the second set, before losing 6-4 6-4, saving four match points in a thrilling eighth game of 13 deuces. Indeed this was another contest which drew rapt applause and appreciation from the crowd and a further example of why the Wightman Cup remains something special.

What would make it even more special from a British point of view, of course, would be if the time ever arrived when we could challenge the best the Americans have to offer on equal terms, instead of constantly living in hope but fearing the worst.

For the moment, providing the Americans continue to field a side which genuinely reflects their strength, they seem bound to add to their present 47-10 match lead, during which Mrs Lloyd has savoured 12 victories and one defeat. In singles she has a marvellous record of 26-0 to add to her 28-0 winning singles record in the Federation Cup, even though of late she, like Martina Navratilova has given this event a miss.

Jo Durie

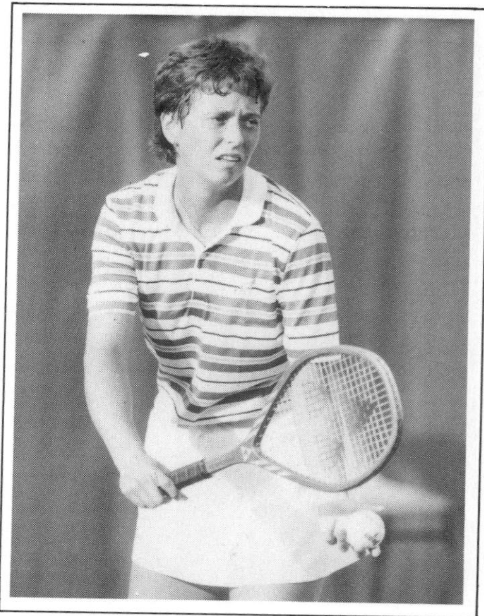

WIGHTMAN CUP

WILLIAMSBURG. October 31st - November 2nd

USA & Great Britain 0
C Evert Lloyd bt J Durie 6-2, 6-3
K Rinaldi bt A E Hobbs 7-5, 7-5
P Shriver bt A Croft 6-0, 6-0
A White & B Nagelsen bt V Wade & Croft 6-4, 6-1
Shriver bt Durie 6-4, 6-4
Evert Lloyd bt Croft 6-0, 6-3
Shriver & Lloyd bt Durie & Hobbs 6-3, 6-7, 6-2

Match Results Since 1980

1980 USA 5 Great Britain 2 (Albert Hall, London)
C Evert Lloyd (US) bt S Barker 6-1, 6-2 (GB)
A Hobbs (GB) bt K Jordan (US) 4-6, 6-4, 6-1
A Jaeger (US) bt S V Wade (GB) 3-6, 6-3, 6-2
R Casals & Lloyd bt G Coles & Hobbs 6-3, 6-3
Barker bt Jaeger 5-7, 6-3, 6-3
Lloyd bt Wade 7-5, 3-6, 7-5
Jordan & A Smith bt Wade & Barker 6-4, 7-5
1981 USA 7 Great Britain 0
(International Ampitheatre, Chicago)
T Austin (US) bt S Barker (GB) 7-5, 6-3
A Jaeger (US) bt A Hobbs (GB) 6-0, 6-0
C Lloyd (US) bt S V Wade (GB) 6-1, 6-3
Austin bt Wade 6-3, 6-1
Lloyd bt Barker 6-3, 6-0
Jaeger & P Shriver bt J Durie & Hobbs 6-1, 6-3
Lloyd & R Casals bt Wade & G Coles 6-3, 6-3
1982 USA 6 Great Britain 1 (Albert Hall, London)
B Potter (US) bt S Barker (GB) 6-2, 6-2
A Smith (US) bt S V Wade (GB) 3-6, 7-5, 6-3
C Lloyd (US) bt J Durie (GB) 6-2, 6-2
Durie & A Hobbs bt R Casals & Smith 6-3, 2-6, 6-2
Potter bt Durie 5-7, 7-6, 6-2
Lloyd bt Barker 6-4, 6-3
Potter & S Walsh bt Barker & Wade 2-6, 6-4, 6-4
1983 USA 6 Great Britain 1 (Williamsburg, USA)
M Navratilova (US) bt S Barker (GB) 6-2, 6-2
K Rinaldi (US) bt S V Wade (GB) 6-2, 6-2
P Shriver (US) bt J Durie (GB) 6-3, 6-2
Barker & Wade bt C Reynolds & P Smith 7-5, 3-6, 6-1
Navratilova bt Durie 6-3, 6-3
1984 USA 5 Great Britain 2 (London)
C Lloyd (US) bt A Hobbs (GB) 6-2, 6-2
A Croft (GB) bt A Moulton (US) 6-1, 5-7, 6-4
J Durie (GB) bt B Potter (US) 6-3, 7-6
Lloyd & Moulton bt S V Wade & A Brown 6-2, 6-2
Potter bt Hobbs 6-1, 6-3
Lloyd bt Durie 7-6, 6-1
Potter & S Walsh bt Durie & Hobbs 7-6, 4-6, 9-7

British Wightman Cup Players

(Figures in brackets indicate number of ties played)

S M Armstrong 1957 (1)
S Barker 1974-83 (10)
A E Beamish 1923-24 (2)
L Beavan 1973 (1)
R M Bentley 1966 (1)
N W Blair 1946-49 (3)
E W Bostock 1946-48 (3)
C M Brasher 1955-60 (6)
A Brown 1984 (1)
N B Brown 1939 (1)
V Burton 1973 (1)
A Buxton 1954-56 (3)
D M Catt 1961-64 (4)
L Charles 1973-77 (4)
A Clayton 1923-24 (2)
G L Coles 1973-81 (6)
E L Colyer 1924-26 (3)
B C Covell 1923-29 (3)
A Croft 1983-85 (3)
J Curry 1946-50 (2)
E M Dearman 1934-38 (5)
J Durie 1979-85 (6)
E Fearnley-Wittingsall 1928-32 (3)
H M Fletcher 1952-54 (3)
J Fry 1925-30 (4)
L A Godfree 1923-24 (7)
W C J Halford 1946 (1)
S Hammersley 1933-39 (6)
R M Hardwick 1936-39 (3)
E H Harvey 1925-30 (4)
M Heeley 1933 (1)
J Hill 1927 (1)
B E Hilton 1947-50 (4)
P A Hird 1954 (1)
A E Hobbs 1978-85 (8)
J Ingram 1937-38 (2)
G T Janes 1957-71 (11)
D Jevans 1979-80 (2)
P F Jones 1957-75 (13)
M B King 1930-35 (4)
R Lambert-Chambers 1925-26 (2)
M E Lumb 1937-38 (2)
N M Lyle 1934-36 (3)
S Mappin 1974-78 (4)
M Menzies 1935-48 (8)
L R C Michell 1928-32 (3)
C Molesworth 1972 (1)
A Mortimer 1953-64 (7)
A J Mottram 1947-52 (4)
B Nuthall 1927-39 (8)
I S V Partridge 1952 (1)
N Passingham 1946 (1)
R Rinkel-Quertier 1947-53 (6)
D E Round 1931-38 (6)
V E Scott 1939 (1)
M Scriven 1933-38 (3)
W M Shaw 1966-72 (7)
C C Shepherd Barron 1924-31 (4)
J A Shilcock 1953-58 (4)
D E Starkie 1962-66 (5)
G R Sterry 1927 (1)
F E Truman 1965-72 (5)
K J A Tuckey 1949-51 (3)
M Tyler 1977-78 (2)
S V Wade 1965-85 (21)
J Walker-Smith 1949-52 (4)
P E Ward 1951-58 (5)
P H Watson 1928-30 (3)
G M Williams 1967-72 (4)

A EUROPEAN TAKEOVER

BY RON ATKIN: THE OBSERVER

Ivan Lendl

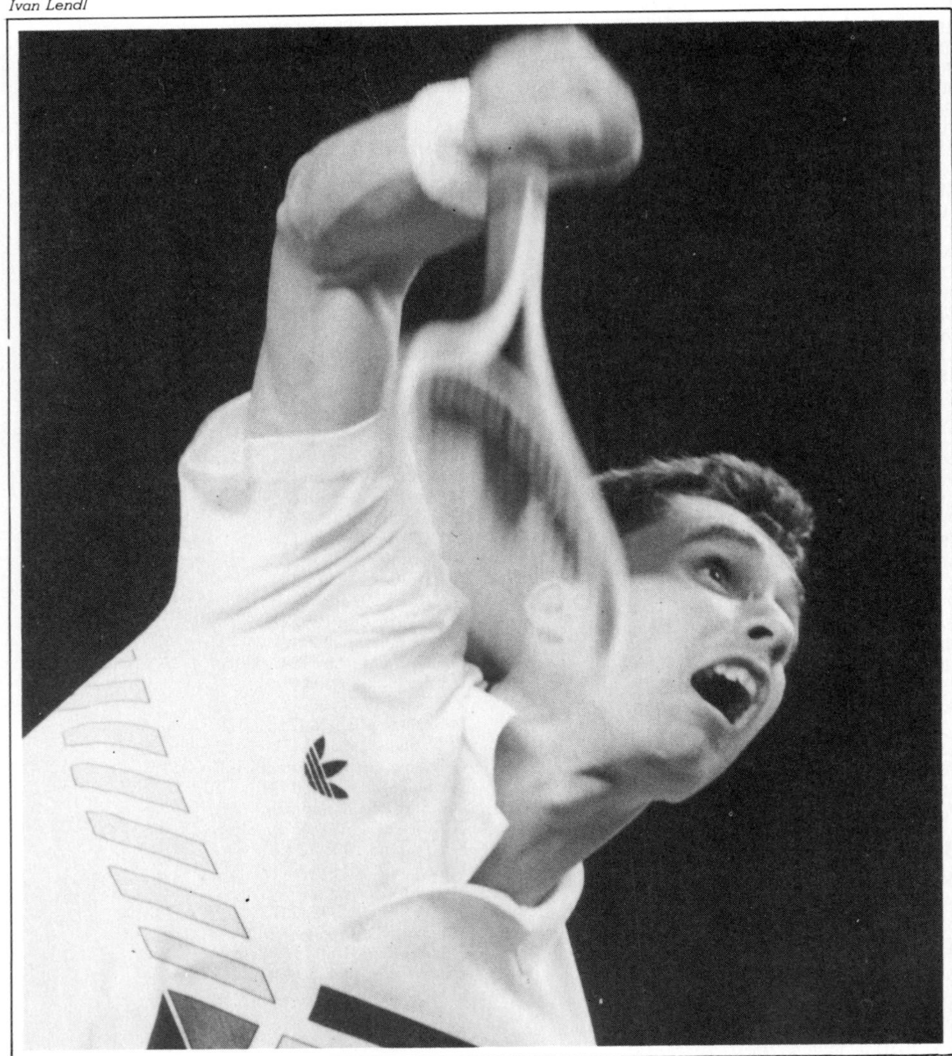

Victory over Boris Becker in the final of the Nabisco Masters at New York's Madison Square Garden in January confirmed Ivan Lendl's standing as number one in the world – a title he had officially collected six days earlier.

Winner of ten tournaments in 1985, including the US Open, a victor in 80 of his 87 matches, holder of a 31-match winning streak between August and December, Lendl amassed a formidable pile of statistics to underline his claim to replace John McEnroe as the best.

But if Lendl was without argument the top man, Becker was the brightest new name to emerge in a year which saw the United States suffer a series of blows to its tennis prestige.

The four Grand Slam titles were all annexed by Europeans. Mats Wilander won in Paris, Becker shook the sport with his victory at Wimbledon, Lendl triumphed at Flushing Meadow and Stefan Edberg made it a memorable year for Sweden by becoming champion of Australia.

Stefan Edberg

McEnroe lost his Wimbledon and US crowns, Jimmy Connors failed to collect a single title for the first time in 11 years and the Americans, riven by dissension, went down to a Becker-inspired West German side in the Davis Cup, a defeat which hastened Arthur Ashe's resignation as captain after five years in the job.

There was joy for Europe, too, in the Women's game where Hana Mandlikova disrupted the dominance of Martina Navratilova and Chris Evert Lloyd by beating both of them to win the US Open.

And in the Davis Cup final, an all-Europe affair, Sweden's talented squad overcame Becker and his supporting cast of many thousands in the Munich Olympic Hall to retain the trophy.

McEnroe ended the year under suspension following misbehaviour in the Australian Open and with question marks against his attitude, commitment and stamina. Connors, who also served a term of suspension in the autumn for misconduct, clung on to fourth place in the world rankings but at the age of 33 a slide from the peak is inevitable.

Discounting Kevin Curren and Johan Kriek, South Africans who fly an American 'flag of convenience' for political reasons, the United States had nobody else challenging for a spot in the top ten. Tim Mayotte, winner of the first Player's Championship at Delray Beach, and Paul Annacone were the only other Americans who could, with hand on heart, say they'd had a good year.

There were equally significant happenings off court. Within the space of 24 hours in early November the Men's International Professional Tennis Council unanimously approved a rule introducing the mandatory drug testing of players and then, at an historic press conference in London, declared war on the agents who it feels are dominating and undermining the professional game.

The MIPTC pulled no punches in its suit, filed in a US Federal District Court in New York. The agents, Mark McCormack, Donald Dell and Ray Benton, were accused of 'holding the game hostage and seeking to strangle it in an illegal web of pervasive conflicts, intimidation, fraud and corruption'. The agents were further charged, in a weighty 99-page document, with 'exerting extensive power over players from the cradle to the grave'.

Mike Davies, the Executive Director of the Association of Tennis Professionals, who had been elected chairman of the MIPTC in succession to Philippe Chatrier in September, said 'This suit says very plainly that the Council has gone to war with the agents.

'Their conflicts and entanglements now threaten our sport to the extent that we feel the agents must choose whether they will represent players or tournaments. They can't do both'. Or, as Chatrier added, 'The MIPTC has come to the conclusion that it must stand up and be counted'.

This bitter confrontation could become ruinously expensive if or when it comes to court but it is encouraging that the men's professional game is, however belatedly, attempting to impose some form of order on a situation which has grown steadily more chaotic since the arrival of Open tennis in 1968.

The year had opened with reverberations of that acrimonious Davis Cup final between Sweden and the United Sates and an embarrassed US Tennis Association attempting to extract written guarantees of future good conduct from Connors and McEnroe, who behaved so outrageously in Gothenburg.

Not surprisingly, they were spurned. The Americans took a team comprising Aaron Krickstein, Eliot Teltscher and the doubles team of Ken Flach and Robert Seguso to Hamburg in August for the quarter-final tie against West Germany and were beaten 3-2 when Becker swept past Krickstein 6-2, 6-2, 6-1 in the deciding rubber.

Germany had been in the grip of 'Beckermania' since that sensational Wimbledon and the nation could scarce contain its excitement as Czechoslovakia were crushed 5-0 in the Davis Cup semi-final. With Lendl competing only in the doubles because of a sore arm, the Czechs were hammered.

By now Becker was expected to win his singles rubbers – as he duly did – but the match which torpedoed Czech hopes was the six hour marathon in which the German number two, Michael Westphal, came back from a two-set deficit to overturn Tomas Smid 6-8, 1-6, 7-5, 11-9, 17-15 to give the Germans a 2-0 first-day lead and launch them towards their first appearance in the final for 15 years.

Sweden demolished an injury-hit Australian squad 5-0 in the other semi-final and with so many fine players to choose from (Henrik Sundstrom, hero of the win over the US the previous December, could not even find a place on the team this time) they are always strongly favoured to hold off the challenge of a German team which

Hana Mandlikova

possessed no one of real quality to support Becker.

Mats Wilander, who handed Becker a straight-sets thrashing in the second round of the French Open but subsequently lost to him in the Davis Cup and the Masters, won Paris in fine style by dismissing McEnroe in straight sets in the semi-finals and then taking Lendl's title away from him in a four-set final. It was Wilander's fourth Grand Slam title captured before he had reached his 21st birthday, a feat not matched even by Borg.

Wilander's Wimbledon hopes were blasted in the first round by the massive Yugoslav Slobodan Zivojinovic, who made his mark on the world scene elsewhere too, eliminating McEnroe in the Australian Open and beating Henri Leconte and Yannick Noah to help relegate France from the world zone of the Davis Cup.

But Wimbledon belonged to Boris – the first unseeded player to win the championship, the youngest ever and the first from Germany. Lendl and McEnroe, who had turned their backs on the pre-Wimbledon grass court tournaments in Britain in order to avoid harassment by the media, possibly paid the penalty. Lendl went out in the fourth round and McEnroe was put out in the quarter-finals.

These two contested the US Open final, however, and here again McEnroe was a loser as the 25-year-old Lendl ended three successive years as a beaten finalist.

Lendl must have nursed ambitions of adding the Australian title but was halted in the semi-finals by an on-song Edberg, who defeated fellow-Swede Wilander in the final.

Apart from the US championships, where Miss Mandlikova beat them both,

Michael Westphael

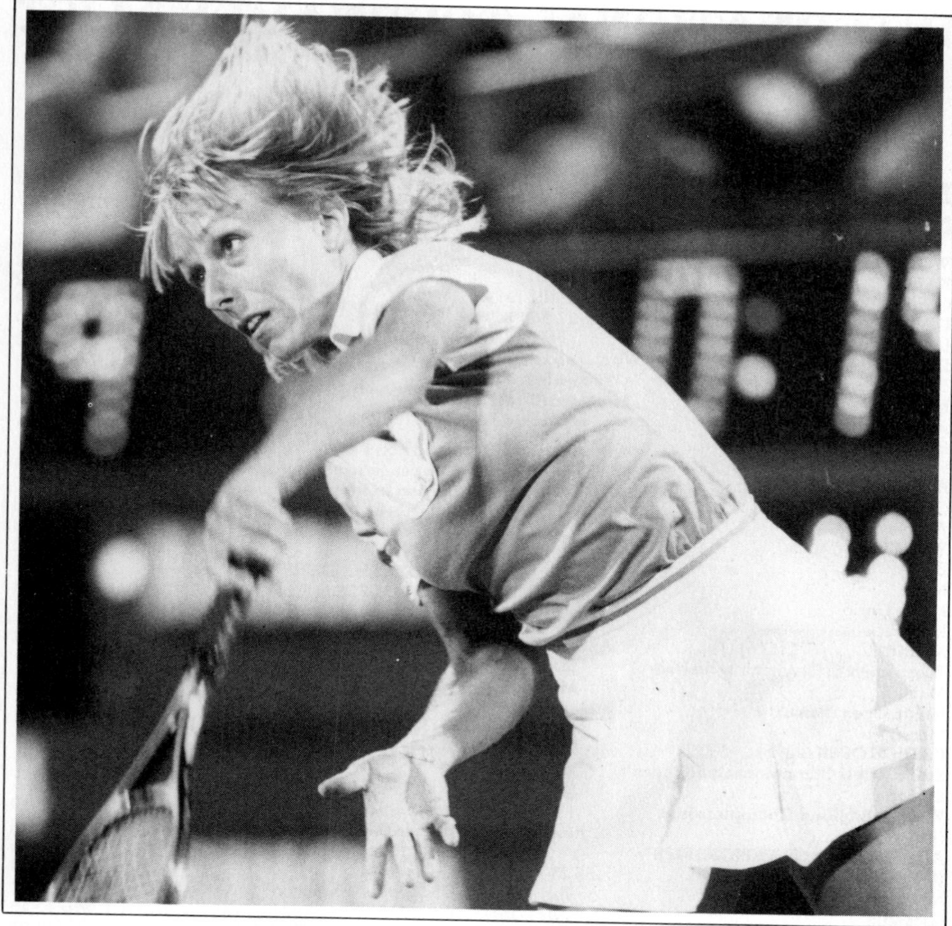

Martina Navratilova

Miss Navratilova and Mrs Lloyd continued to mop up the major titles. Mrs Lloyd won a three-set thriller in Paris but Martina had her revenge at Wimbledon and annexed the Australian title, too, pushing her career earnings to the brink of ten million dollars.

The women's game welcomed a bright new teenage star during the year in Gabriela Sabatini of Argentina and in Paris she made a fine impression. Nevertheless, the International Tennis Federation subsequently announced the imposition of age restrictions on youngsters turning professional to help prevent the sort of physical and mental stress which blighted the careers of such as Tracy Austin and Andrea Jaeger; a move which was as urgently needed as the action on agent domination of the sport.

Finally, tennis saw the appointment of professional umpires to help combat the growing criticism about 'amateurs' making decisions which could cost the players so dearly. Richard Kaufman of the United States and Jeremy Shales of Great Britain were the first two. Surely more will follow.

INTERNATIONAL TOURNAMENT LIST

MEN

NABISCO GRAND PRIX

WCT Doubles (Albert Hall, London)	Jan 6-12
NABISCO MASTERS (Madison Square Gardens)	Jan 13-19
US Professional Indoors (Philadephia)	Jan 27-Feb 2
US Indoors (Memphis)	Feb 3-9
Lipton Players Championships (Boca West)	Feb 10-23
La Quinta	Feb 24-Mar 2
Milan	Mar 10-16
Metz	Mar 10-16
Brussels	Mar 17-23
Fort Myers	Mar 17-23
Rotterdam	Mar 24-30
Chicago	Mar 31-Apr 6
Atlanta	Mar 31-Apr 6
WCT Finals (Dallas)	Apr 7-13
Bari	Apr 7-13
Nice	Apr 14-20
Monte Carlo	Apr 21-27
Indianapolis	Apr 28-May 4
Madrid	Apr 28-May 4
Tournament of Champions (New York)	May 5-11
Munich	May 5-11
Italian Open (Rome)	May 12-18
Florence	May 19-25
FRENCH OPEN (Paris)	May 26-June 8
Stella Artois Championships (Queen's)	June 9-16
Bologna	June 9-16
West of England Championships (Bristol)	June 16-22
ALL ENGLAND CHAMPIONSHIPS (Wimbledon)	June 23-July 6
Newport (Rhode Island)	July 7-13
Gstaad	July 7-13
Bordeaux	July 7-13
US PROFESSIONAL CHAMPIONSHIPS (Boston)	July 21-27
Swedish Open (Bastad)	July 21-27
Livingston (New Jersey)	July 21-27
Washington	July 28-Aug 3
Hilversum	July 28-Aug 3
Cleveland	July 28-Aug 3
Stratton Mountain	Aug 4-10
Kitzbuhel	Aug 4-10
Canadian Open (Toronto)	Aug 11-17
St. Vincent	Aug 11-17
Cincinnati	Aug 18-24
UNITED STATES OPEN (New York)	Aug 25-Sep 7
Stuttgart	Sept 8-14
Geneva	Sept 8-14
Los Angeles	Sept 15-21
German Open (Hamburg)	Sept 15-21
San Francisco	Sept 22-28
SPANISH OPEN (Barcelona)	Sept 22-28
Palmero	Sep 29-Oct 5
Pheonix	Oct 6-12
Brisbane	Oct 6-12
Toulouse	Oct 6-12
Tel Aviv	Oct 6-12
Australian Indoors (Sydney)	Oct 13-19
Tokyo Open	Oct 13-19
Basle	Oct 13-19
Tokyo Seiko	Oct 20-26
Melbourne Indoors	Oct 20-26
Vienna	Oct 20-26
Paris	Oct 27-Nov 2
Hong Kong	Oct 27-Nov 2
Swedish Indoors (Stockholm)	Nov 3-9
Benson & Hedges (London)	Nov 10-16
Houston	Nov 17-23
Johannesburg	Nov 17-23
Itaparica	Nov 24-30
NABISCO MASTERS (New York)	Dec 1-7
WCT DOUBLES (Albert Hall)	Dec 8-14

OTHER EVENTS

World Team Cup (Dusseldorf)	May 19-25

LADIES

VIRGINIA SLIMS WORLD CHAMPIONSHIP SERIES

Washington	Jan 6-12
New England (Worcester)	Jan 13-19
Florida (Key Biscayne)	Jan 27-Feb 2
Lipton Players' International	Feb 10-23
Oakland	Feb 24-Mar 2
US Indoors (Princeton)	Mar 3-9
Dallas	Mar 10-16
SLIMS CHAMPIONSHIP (New York)	Mar 17-23
Bridgestone Doubles	Mar 24-30
Tournament of Champions	Mar 31-Apr 6
Seabrook Island Classic	Mar 31-Apr 6
Family Circle Cup (Hilton Head)	Apr 7-13
WTA Championships (Amelia Is)	Apr 14-20
Australian Indoors (Sydney)	Apr 21-27
US Clay Court (Indianapolis)	Apr 28-May 4
Melbourne Indoors	Apr 28-May 4
Houston	May 5-11
German Open (Berlin)	May 12-18
Barcelona	May 19-25
European Open (Lugano)	May 19-25
FRENCH OPEN (Paris)	May 26-June 8
Edgbaston Cup (Birmingham)	June 9-15
Pilkington Glass Champs (Eastbourne)	June 16-22
ALL ENGLAND CHAMPIONSHIPS (Wimbledon)	June 23-July 6
Newport (Rhode Island)	July 14-20

Canadian Open (Toronto)	August 4-10
Los Angeles	August 11-17
United Bank Classic (Mahwah)	August 18-24
UNITED STATES OPEN (Flushing Meadow)	Aug 25-Sep 7
Pheonix	Sep 8-14
Florida Federal (Tampa)	Sep 15-21
Maybelline Classic (Ft. Lauderdale)	Sept 22-28
New Orleans	Sep 29-Oct 5
San Juan	Oct 6-12
Porsche Grand Prix (Filderstadt)	Oct 13-19
Pretty Polly Classic (Brighton)	Oct 20-26
New England	Nov 2-9
Chicago	Nov 10-16
VIRGINIA SLIMS CHAMPIONSHIP (New York)	Nov 17-23

OTHER EVENTS

FEDERATION CUP (Prague)	July 21-27
WIGHTMAN CUP (Albert Hall, London)	Oct 30-Nov 1

WORLD WIDE RESULTS

NABISCO GRAND PRIX

BENSON AND HEDGES OPEN $80,000

AUCKLAND, January 7th-13th

Semifinals
W Masur bt J Fitzgerald 5-7, 7-5, 7-5
C Lewis bt D Saltz 7-6, 7-6

Final
Lewis bt Masur 7-5, 6-0, 2-6, 6-4

British
J Lloyd bt B Levine 6-2, 6-2
lost G Layendecker 6-4, 7-6
J Smith lost B Dyke 6-7, 6-0, 6-3

Doubles Final
J Fitzgerald & C Lewis bt B Dyke & W Masur 7-6, 6-2

US PROFESSIONAL INDOOR CHAMPIONSHIPS $300,000

PHILADELPHIA, January 21st-27th

Semifinals
J McEnroe bt S Davis 6-2, 6-4
M Mecir bt J Connors 5-7, 6-4, 6-3

Final
McEnroe bt Mecir 6-3, 7-6, 6-1

Doubles Final
J Nystrom & M Wilander bt W Fibak & S Mayer 3-6, 6-2, 6-2

US NATIONAL INDOOR CHAMPIONSHIPS $250,000

MEMPHIS, January 28th-February 3rd

Semifinals
S Edberg bt J Connors 6-1, 6-4
Y Noah bt E Teltscher 3-6, 6-1, 7-5

Final
Edberg bt Noah 6-1, 6-0

British
J Lloyd bt Tom Gullikson 6-3, 6-3
lost Edberg 7-5, 6-3

Doubles Final
P Slozil & T Smid bt K Curren & S Denton 1-6, 6-3, 6-4

LIPTON PLAYERS' CHAMPIONSHIP $750,000

DELRAY, February 5th-17th

Semifinals
S Davis bt T Smid 7-6, 6-4, 4-6, 6-3
T Mayotte bt J Gunnarson 7-6, 6-2, 4-6, 6-1

Final
Mayotte bt Davis 4-6, 4-6, 6-3, 6-2, 6-4

British
S Shaw bt E Edwards 4-6, 7-6, 6-4
lost R Green 6-2, 3-6, 7-6
J Lloyd lost W Fibak 7-6, 7-6

Doubles Final
P Annacone & C Van Rensburg bt S Stewart & K Warwick 7-5, 7-5, 6-4

PILOT PEN CLASSIS $300,000

LA QUINTA, January 18th-24th

Semifinals
L Stefanki bt G Holmes 6-2, 4-6, 6-3
D Pate bt L Pimek 7-6, 6-4

Final
Stefanki bt Pate 6-1, 6-4, 3-6, 6-3

British
J Lloyd bt D Cassidy 6-1, 3-6, 7-6
bt R Seguso 4-6, 6-1, 7-6
bt B Testerman 6-4, 6-0
lost Pimek 6-1, 1-6, 6-4

Doubles Final
H Gunthardt & B Taroczy bt K Flach & R Seguso 3-6, 7-6, 6-3

MOLSON LIGHT CHALLENGE $125,000

TORONTO, February 18th-24th

Semifinals
A Jarryd bt W Fibak 4-6, 6-4, 6-3
K Curren bt E Teltscher 6-3, 6-3

Final
Curren bt Jarryd 7-6, 6-3

Doubles Final
P Fleming & A Jarryd bt G Layendecker & G Michibata 7-6, 6-2

HOUSTON SHOOTOUT $300,000

HOUSTON, February 25th-March 3rd

Semifinals
J McEnroe bt P Fleming 6-4, 6-0
K Curren bt S Perkiss 6-2, 6-2

Final
McEnroe bt Curren 7-5, 6-1, 7-6

Doubles Final
P Fleming & J McEnroe bt H Pfister & B Testerman 6-3, 6-2

BUENOS AIRES GRAND PRIX $75,000

BUENOS AIRES February 25th-March 3rd

Semifinals
D Perez bt J Brown 6-2, 6-4
M Jaite bt H De La Pena 7-5, 6-2

Final
Jaite bt Perez 6-4, 6-2

Doubles Final
Jaite & J Miniussi bt E Bengoechea & D Perez 6-4, 6-3

BELGIAN CHAMPIONSHIPS $200,000

BRUSSELS, March 11th-18th

Semifinals
W Wilander bt P Cash 6-3, 7-6
A Jarryd bt S Edberg 7-6, 3-6, 6-3

Final
Jarryd bt Wilander 6-4, 3-6, 7-5,

British
J Lloyd bt S Meister 6-1, 6-4
lost N Nystrom 4-6, 7-6, 6-4

Doubles Final
S Edberg & A Jarryd bt K Curren & W Fibak 6-3, 7-6

DUTCH CHAMPIONSHIPS $250,000

ROTTERDAM

Semifinals
M Mecir bt J Nystrom 6-3, 6-3
J Hlasek bt T Smid 6-3, 6-7, 6-3

Final
Mecir bt Hlasek 6-1, 6-2
British
S Bale bt G Forget 7-6, 6-2
lost T Smid 6-4, 6-2

Doubles Final
P Slozil & T Smid bt V Gerulaitis & P McNamee 6-4, 6-4

LORRAINE OPEN $80,000

NANCY, March 18th-25th

Semifinals
T Wilkison bt P Portes 6-1, 6-1
S Zivojinovic bt C Hooper 6-7, 7-6, 6-4

Final
Wilkison bt Zivojinovic 4-6, 7-6, 9-7

British
S Shaw bt W Masur 3-6, 6-2, 6-4
lost Portes 6-3, 6-2

Doubles Final
M Freeman & R Harmon bt J Navratil & J Svensson 6-4, 7-6

FILA TROPHY $300,000

MILAN, March 25th-31st

Semifinals
J McEnroe bt J Hlasek 6-3, 6-2
A Jarryd bt T Smid 6-3, 7-6

Final
McEnroe bt Jarryd 6-4, 6-1

British
S Bale bt J Frawley 3-6, 5-4, retd.
lost T Smid 6-4, 5-7, 6-4

Doubles Final
H Gunthardt & A Jarryd bt B Dyke & W Masur 6-2, 6-1

PAINE WEBBER CLASSIC $250,000

FORT MYERS, March 25th-31st

Semifinals
I Lendl bt S Giammalva 6-2, 6-1
J Connors bt A Gomez 3-6, 6-4, 6-3

Final
Lendl bt Connors 6-3, 6-2

British
J Lloyd lost Lendl 6-3, 6-3

Doubles Final
K Flach & R Seguson bt S Giammalva & D Pate 3-6, 6-3, 6-3

MONACO GRAND PRIX $325,000

MONTE CARLO, April 1st-7th

Semifinals
I Lendl bt H Sundstrom 4-6, 7-6, 7-6
M Wilander bt A Krickstein 6-2, 6-3

Final
Lendl bt Wilander 6-1, 6-3, 4-6, 6-4

Doubles Final
P Slozil & T Smid bt S Glickstein & S Perkiss 6-2, 6-3

PUENTO ROMANO OPEN $100,000

MARBELLA, April 22nd-28th

Semifinals
L Duncan bt E Bengechea 7-6, 6-3
H De La Pena bt S Shaw 6-4, 3-2 default

Final
De La Pena bt Duncan 6-0, 6-3

British
S Shaw bt M Ostaja 6-2, 6-2
bt D Perez 6-4, 6-7, 6-4
bt A Ganzabal 7-6, 6-4
lost De La Pena

Doubles Final
A Gomez & C Motta bt L Courteau & M Schapers 6-1, 6-1

EBEL GERMAN OPEN $250,000

HAMBURG, April 29th-May 5th

Semifinals
M Mecir bt M Wilander 6-1, 6-2
H Sundstrom bt J L Clerc 6-3, 6-4

Final
Mecir bt Sundstrom 6-4, 6-1, 6-4

Doubles Final
H Gildemeister & A Gomez bt H Gunthardt & B Taroczy 1-6, 7-6, 6-3

ALAN KING CLASSIC $400,000

LAS VEGAS, April 29th-May 5th

Semifinals
J Kriek bt T Smid 6-4, 6-3
J Arias bt K Flach 7-6, 7-5

Final
Kriek bt Arias 4-6, 6-3, 6-4, 6-2

British
J Lloyd bt M Leach 7-6, 7-5
bt S Davis 6-4, 7-6
lost Flach 6-4, 4-6, 6-4

Doubles Final
P Cash & J Fitzgerald bt P Annacone & C Van Rensburg 7-6, 6-7, 7-6

TOURNAMENT OF CHAMPIONS $80,000

FOREST HILL, May 6th-13th

Semifinals
I Lendl bt A Krickstein 6-1, 2-6, 6-1
J McEnroe bt H Sundstrom 6-2, 3-6, 6-2

Final
Lendl bt McEnroe 6-3, 6-3

British
S Shaw lost P Doohan 7-6, 6-4

Doubles Final
K Flach & R Seguson bt G Barbosa & I Kley 7-5, 6-2

BAVARIAN CHAMPIONSHIPS $100,000

MUNICH, May 6th-13th

Semifinals
J Nystrom bt J L Clerc 6-2, 6-4
H Schwaier bt D Perez 6-4, 6-4

Final
Nystrom bt Schwaier 6-1, 6-0

Doubles Final
M Edmondson & K Warwick bt S Casal & E Sanchez 4-6, 7-5, 7-5

ITALIAN CHAMPIONSHIPS $300,000

ROME, May 13th-20th

Semifinals
Y Noah bt B Becker 6-3, 6-3
M Mecir bt M Wilander 6-2, 6-4

Final
Noah bt Mecir 6-3, 3-6, 6-2, 7-6

Doubles Final
M Wilander & A Jarryd bt R Seguso & K Flach 4-6, 6-3, 6-2

GRAN PREMIO SPAIN $80,000

MADRID, May 13th-19th

Semifinals
A Maurer bt K Novacek 7-5, 6-3
L Duncan bt A Mansdorf 6-2, 6-3

Final
Maurer bt Duncan 7-5, 6-2

Doubles Final
K Barbosa & J Kley bt J Bardo & A Tous 7-6, 6-4

ROGER GALLET TOURNAMENT $80,000

FLORENCE, May 20th-27th

Semifinals
J Arias bt M DePalmer 6-2, 6-3
S Casal bt E Bengeochea 7-5, 7-5

Final
Casal bt Arias 3-6, 6-3, 6-2

British
S Shaw lost L Bottazi 6-1, 7-5

Doubles Final
D Graham & L Warder bt B Derlin & C Limberger 6-1, 6-1

FRENCH OPEN CHAMPIONSHIPS $1,000,000

PARIS, May 27th-June 9th

Semifinals
M Wilander bt J McEnroe 6-1, 7-5, 7-5
I Lendl bt J Connors 6-2, 6-3, 6-1

Final
Wilander bt Lendl 3-6, 6-4, 6-2, 6-2

British
J Lloyd bt G Ocleppo 6-3, 6-3, 6-1
lost T Benhabiles 6-3, 6-2, 7-6
S Shaw lost S Zivojinovic 4-6, 6-2, 2-6, 6-3, 8-6

Doubles Final
M Edmondson & K Warwick bt S Glickstein & H Simonsson 6-3, 6-4, 6-3

VOLVO CLASSIC $250,000

CHICAGO, April 1st-7th

Semifinals
J McEnroe bt S Davis 6-4, 6-1
J Connors bt A Gomez 6-4, 6-3

Final
McEnroe bt Connors default

Doubles Final
J Kriek & Y Noah bt K Flach & R Seguso 3-6, 4-6, 7-6, 6-1, 6-4

BUICK WCT FINALS $500,000

DALLAS, April 8th-14th

Semifinals
I Lendl bt J Connors 6-2, 2-1, retd.
T Mayotte bt J Nystrom 6-4, 4-6, 6-2, 7-5

Final
Lendl bt Mayotte 7-6, 6-4, 6-1

DONNAY INTERNATIONAL $80,000

NICE, April 8th-14th

Semifinals
H Leconte bt H Schwaier 7-5, 6-4
V Pecci bt D Perez 6-4, 6-2

Final
Leconte bt Pecci 6-4, 6-4

Doubles Final
C Panatta & P Slozil bt L Courteau & G Forget 3-6, 6-3, 8-6

KIM TOP LINE CLASSIC $80,000

BARI, April 15th-21st

Semifinals
C Panatta bt J Lopez-Maeso 6-0, 3-6, 6-4
L Duncan bt H Schwaier 6-3, 6-2

Final
Panatta bt Duncan 6-2, 1-6, 7-6

Doubles Final
M Ganzabal & C Panatta bt M Freeman & L Warder 6-4, 6-2

WCT ATLANTA OPEN $300,000

ATLANTA, April 22nd-28th

Semifinals
P Annacone bt K Curren default
J McEnroe bt M Leach 6-3, 6-3

Final
McEnroe bt Annacone 7-6, 7-6, 6-2

Doubles Final
P Annacone & C Van Rensburg bt S Denton & T Smid 6-4, 6-3

STELLA ARTOIS CHAMPIONSHIPS $200,000

QUEEN'S CLUB, LONDON, June 10th-16th

Final
B Becker bt J Kriek 6-2, 6-3

Doubles Final
K Flach & R Seguso bt P Cash & J Fitzgerald 3-6, 6-3, 16-14

GRAND PRIX CITTA $80,000

BOLOGNA, June 10th-16th

Semifinals
C Panatta bt A Tous 7-5, 6-3
T Tulasne bt D Keretic 6-0, 6-4

Final
Tulasne bt Panatta 6-2, 6-0

Doubles Final
P Cane & S Colombo bt J Arrese & A Tous 7-5, 6-4

WEST OF ENGLAND CHAMPIONSHIPS $100,000

BRISTOL, June 17th-22nd

Final
M Davis bt G Layendecker 4-6, 6-3, 7-5

Doubles Final
E Edwards & D Visser bt J Alexander & R Simpson 6-4, 7-6

THE CHAMPIONSHIPS $1,093,491

WIMBLEDON, June 24th-July 7th

Final
B Becker bt K Curren 6-3, 6-7, 7-6, 6-4

Doubles Final
H Gunthardt & B Taroczy bt P Cash & J Fitzgerald 6-4, 6-3, 4-6, 6-3

US PROFESSIONAL CHAMPIONSHIPS $210,000

BOSTON, July 8th-15th

Semifinals
M Wilander bt G Vilas 6-1, 6-3
M Jaite bt B Oresar 7-6, 6-1

Final
Wilander bt Jaite 6-2, 6-4

Doubles Final
L Pimek & S Zivojinovic bt P McNamara & P McNamee 2-6, 6-4, 7-6

SWISS OPEN $150,000

GSTAAD, July 8th-14th

Semifinals
J Nystrom bt G Forget 7-6, 6-7, 7-5
A Maurer bt M Edmondson 6-3, 3-6, 6-3

Final
Nystrom bt Maurer 6-4, 1-6, 7-5, 6-3

Doubles Final
W Fibak & T Smid bt B Drewett & M Edmondson 6-7, 6-4, 6-4

HALL OF FAME CHAMPIONSHIPS $80,000

NEWPORT, RHODE ISLAND, July 8th-14th

Semifinals
Tom Gullikson bt D Pate 7-6, 6-7, 7-5
J Sadri bt T Mayotte 6-4, 6-3

Final
Tom Gullikson bt Sadri 6-3, 7-6

Doubles Final
P Doohan & S Giammalva bt P Annacone & C Van Rensburg 6-1, 6-3

SWEDISH OPEN $80,000

BASTAD, July 15th-22nd

Semifinals
M Wilander bt D Keretic 6-3, 4-6, 6-4
S Edberg bt K Carlsson 6-4, 6-2

Final
Wilander bt Edberg 6-1, 6-0

Doubles Final
S Edberg & A Jarryd bt S Casal & E Sanchez 6-0, 7-6

NATIONAL BANK CLASSIC $210,000

WASHINGTON, July 15th-22nd

Semifinals
Y Noah bt J Connors 6-4, 3-6, 6-2
M Jaite bt C Ingaramo 6-4, 5-7, 6-2

Final
Noah bt Jaite 6-4, 6-3

British
S Shaw lost F Luna 6-2, 6-1

Doubles Final
H Gildemeister & V Pecci bt D Graham & B Taroczy 6-3, 1-6, 6-4

US CLAY COURT CHAMPIONSHIPS $375,00

INDIANAPOLIS July 23rd-30th

Semifinals
I Lendal bt B Becker 5-7, 6-2, 6-2
A Gomez bt Y Noah 6-0, 6-1

Final
Lendl bt Gomez 6-1, 6-3

Doubles Final
K Flach & R Seguso bt P Slozil & K Warwick 6.4, 6.4

NEW JERSEY OPEN $90,000

LIVINGSTONE, July 22nd-28th

Semifinals
B Teacher bt J Kriek 7-6, 6-4
B Gilbert bt J Grabb 6-3, 6-3

Final
Gilbert bt Teacher 4-6, 7-5, 6-0

British
J Lloyd lost Grabb 5-7, 6-1, 6-4

Doubles Final
M DePalmer & P Dochan bt E Edwards & D Visser 6-3, 6-4

DUTCH CHAMPIONSHIPS $90,000

HILVERSUM, July 22nd-28th

Semifinals
R Osterthun bt A Maurer 3-6, 7-6, 6-4
K Carlsson bt M Oosting 6-1, 6-4

Final
Osterthun bt Carlsson 4-6, 4-6, 6-4, 6-2, 6-3

Doubles Final
H Simonsson & S Simonsson bt C Limberger & K Woodforde 6-4, 5-7, 6-3

AUSTRIAN CHAMPIONSHIPS $150,000

KITZBUHEL, August 5th-11th

Semifinals
P Slozil bt S Casal 6-1, 6-4
M Westphal bt M Vajda 7-6, 6-3

Final
Slozil bt Westphal 7-5, 6-2

Doubles Final
S Casal & E Sanchez bt P Cano & C Panatta 6-3, 3-6, 6-2

VOLVO CLASSIC $250,000

STRATTON MOUNTAIN, August 5th-11th

Semifinals
J McEnroe bt R Seguso 6-2, 6-3
I Lendl bt J Connors 6-0, 4-6, 6-4

Final
McEnroe bt Lendl 7-6, 6-2

British
C Dowdeswell bt G Layendecker 7-6, 6-2
bt G Holmes 6-4, 7-5
lost Seguso 4-6, 6-2, 6-4
S Bale lost D Pate 7-5, 4-6, 6-2

Doubles Final
S Davis & D Pate bt K Flach & R Seguso 3-6, 7-6, 7-6

CANADIAN OPEN $300,000

MONTREAL, August 12th-19th

Semifinals
J McEnroe bt J Connors 6-2, 6-3
I Lendl bt J Arias 6-4, 6-2

Final
McEnroe bt Lendl 7-5, 6-3

Doubles Final
K Flach & R Seguso bt S Edberg & A Jarryd 7-6, 7-6

WESTERN OPEN $80,000

CLEVELAND, August 12th-19th

Semifinals
B Gilbert bt B Schultz 6-4, 6-4
B Drewett bt H Pfister 6-3, 7-5

Final
Gilbert bt Drewett 6-3, 6-2

British
C Dowdeswell lost M Bauer 7-6, 6-3

Doubles Final
L Palin & O Rahnasto bt H Pfister & B Testerman 6-3, 6-7, 7-6

ATP CHAMPIONSHIPS $300,000

MASON, OHIO, August 19th-25th

Semifinals
M Wilander bt T Wilkison 6-2, 6-1
B Becker bt J Nystrom 6-4, 7-5

Final
Becker bt Wilander 6-4, 6-2

British
J Lloyd lost Benhabiles 6-4, 6-3

Doubles Final
S Edberg & A Jarryd bt J Nystrom & M Wilander 4-6, 6-2, 6-3

US OPEN CHAMPIONSHIPS $1,250,000

FLUSHING MEADOW, August 26th-September 8th

Semifinals
J McEnroe bt M Wilander 3-6, 6-4, 4-6, 6-3, 6-3
I Lendl bt J Connors 6-2, 6-3, 7-5

Final
Lendl bt McEnroe 7-6, 6-3, 6-4

British
Lloyd bt V Pecci 7-5, 7-5, 7-5
lost T Mayotte 4-6, 6-1, 7-6, 7-5
J Bates lost Y Noah 6-3, 7-6, 6-3
C Dowdeswell lost E Bengeochea 4-6, 7-6, 7-5, 6-4

Doubles Final
K Flach & R Seguso bt H Leconte & Y Noah 6-7, 7-6, 7-6, 6-0

MERCEDES CUP $150,000

STUTTGART, September 9th-15th

Semifinals
I Lendl bt J L Clerc 6-2, 6-2
B Gilbert bt T Smid 6-4, 4-6, 7-5

Final
Lendl bt Gilbert 6-4, 6-0

Doubles Final
I Lendl & T Smid bt A Kohlberg & J Soares 4-6, 6-1, 6-3

SICILIAN CHAMPIONSHIPS $115,000

PALERMO, September 9th-16th

Semifinals
T Tulasne bt T Muster 6-0, 6-4
J Nystrom bt D Perez 7-6, 6-4

Final
Tulasne bt Nystrom 6-3, 6-1

British
C Dowdeswell lost S Casal 6-3, 6-3
J Bates lost C Pistolesi 7-5, 6-2

Doubles Final
C Dowdeswell & J Nystrom bt S Casal & E Sanchez 3-6, 7-5, 6-2

VOLVO CHAMPIONSHIPS $300,000

LOS ANGELES, September 16th-22nd

Semifinals
P Annacone bt J McEnroe w/o
S Edberg bt J Kriek 6-2, 6-3

Final
Annacone bt Edberg 7-6, 6-7, 7-6

British
J Lloyd bt T Moor 6-7, 6-4, 6-0
lost B Gilbert 7-5, 6-3

Doubles Final
S Davis & R Van't Hof bt P Annacone & C Van Rensburg 6-3, 7-6

MARTINI OPEN $115,000

GENEVA, September 16th-22nd

Semifinals
M Wilander bt H Leconte 3-6, 6-3, 6-1
T Smid bt J Aguilera 7-5, 6-4

Final
Smid bt Wilander 6-4, 6-4

Doubles Final
S Casal & E Sanchez bt C Kirmayr & C Motta 6-4, 4-6, 7-6

GRAND PRIX PASSING SHOT $90,000

BORDEAUX, September 16th-22nd

Semifinals
J Brown bt J L Clerc 6-7, 6-3, 6-1
D Perez bt T Tulasne 2-6, 6-3, 6-2

Final
Perez bt Brown 6-4, 7-6

British
S Shaw bt M Fleurian 6-3, 2-6, 6-1
lost J L Clerc 6-1, 7-5

Doubles Final
D Felgate & S Shaw bt L Pimek & B Willenborg 6-4, 5-7, 6-4

SPANISH OPEN $150,000

BARCELONA, September 23rd-29th

Semifinals
T Tulasne bt H Leconte 6-3, 6-2
M Wilander bt M Jaite 7-5, 6-3

Final
Tulasne bt Wilander 0-6, 6-2, 3-6, 6-4, 6-0

Doubles Final
S Casal & E Sanchez bt J Gunnarson & M Mortensen 6-3, 6-3

TRANSAMERICA OPEN $210,000

SAN FRANCISCO

Semifinals
S Edberg bt P Annacone 6-2, 3-6, 6-1
J Kriek bt R Green 6-2, 6-1

Final
Edberg bt Kriek 6-4, 6-4

British
J Lloyd bt B Testerman 7-6, 7-6
lost J McEnroe 6-1, 6-7, 7-6

Doubles Final
P Annacone & C Van Rensburg bt B Gilbert & S Mayer 3-6, 6-3, 6-4

SOUTH AFRICAN OPEN $300,000

JOHANNESBURG, October 7th-14th

Semifinals
M Anger bt J Arias 7-5, 4-6, 7-5
B Gilbert bt J Kriek 6-4, 6-4

Final
M Anger bt Gilbert 6-4, 3-6, 6-3

British
C Dowdeswell lost M Doyle 6-4, 6-1
S Shaw bt E Edwards 6-4, 6-4
lost R Wolstenholme 5-7, 7-5, 6-2
J Bates lost D Visser 6-3, 3-6, 6-4

Doubles Final
C Dowdeswell & C Van Rensburg bt A Mansdorf & S Perkiss 3-6, 7-6, 6-4

GWA MAZDA CLASSIC $80,000

BRISBANE, October 7th-14th

Semifinals
K Evernden bt G Layendecker 6-4, 6-7, 6-1
P Annacone bt S Youl 6-1, 7-6

Final
Annacone bt Evernden 6-3, 6-3

Doubles Final
M Davis & B Drewett bt B Schultz & B Testerman 6-2, 6-1

GRAND PRIX DE TOULOUSE $125,000

October 7th-14th

Semifinals
Y Noah bt G Forget 6-4, 6-2
T Smid bt R Krishnan 6-7, 6-3, 6-4

Final
Noah bt Smid 6-4, 6-4

Doubles Final
R Acuna & J Hlasek bt P Slozil & T Smid 3-6, 6-2, 9-7

CUSTOM CREDIT INDOOR CHAMPIONSHIPS $225,000

SYDNEY, October 14th-21st

Semifinals
I Lendl bt P Annacone 6-4, 6-5
H Leconte bt J Fitzgerald 6-3, 6-2

Final
Lendl bt Leconte 6-4, 6-4, 7-6

Doubles Final
J Fitzgerald & A Jarryd bt M Edmondson & K Warwick 6-3, 6-2

SWISS INDOOR CHAMPIONSHIPS $150,000

BASLE, October 14th-21st

Semifinals
Y Noah bt L Pimek 5-6, 6-2, 7-5
S Edberg bt W Fibak 6-3, 6-1

Final
Edberg bt Noah 6-7, 6-4, 7-6, 6-1

Doubles Final
Tim Gullikson & Tom Gullikson bt M Dickson & T Wilkinson 4-6, 6-4, 6-4

JAPAN & ASIAN CHAMPIONSHIPS $125,000

Semifinals
S Davis bt J Carlsson 6-4, 6-1
J Arias bt G Michibata 5-7, 6-3, 6-4

Final
S Davis bt Arias 6-0, 7-6

Doubles Final
S Davis & D Pate bt S Giammalva & G Holmes 7-6, 6-7, 6-3

ISRAELI CLASSIC $80,000

TEL AVIV, October 14th-21st

Semifinals
B Gilbert bt S Perkiss 6-2, 6-1
A Mansdorf bt J Bates 7-5, 3-6, 6-2

Final
Gilbert bt Mansdorf 6-3, 6-2

British
Bates bt M Flur 6-4, 6-4
bt I Bloom 2-6, 6-4, 6-4
bt P Carlsson 6-1, 6-4
lost Mansdorf
S Shaw lost Gilbert 6-3, 6-2

Doubles Final
B Gilbert & I Nastase bt D Robertson & F Segarceanu 6-7, 7-6, 7-5

SEIKO OPEN $350,000

TOKYO, October 21st-28th

Semifinals
I Lendl bt B Becker 6-3, 7-6
M Wilander bt J Connors def.

Final
Lendl bt Wilander 6-0, 6-4

Doubles Final
K Flach & R Seguso bt S Davis & D Pate 4-6, 6-3, 7-6

BLACK & DECKER CHAMPIONSHIPS $80,000

MELBOURNE, October 21st-28th

Semifinals
P Annacone bt C Van Rensburg 6-7, 6-4, 6-3
M Davis bt B Testerman 6-4, 6-7, 6-4

Final
M Davis bt Annacone 6-4, 6-4

Doubles Final
B Drewett & M Mitchell bt D Dowlen & N Odizor 4-6, 7-6, 6-4

COLOGNE CUP $80,000

October 21st-28th

Semifinals
R Krishnan bt M Dickson 2-6, 6-1, 7-5
P Lundgren bt T Wilkinson 6-4, 1-6, 7-6

Final
Lundgren bt Krishnan 6-3, 6-2

British
J Bates bt M Mecir 7-6, 1-6, 6-4
bt P Slozil 6-3, 6-3
lost Lundgren 6-4, 6-0
J Lloyd bt M Schapers 6-4, 4-6, 6-2
bt L Stafanki 7-6, 6-3
lost Krishnan 3-6, 6-3, 7-5

Doubles Final
A Antonitsch & M Schapers bt J Gunnarson & P Lundgren 6-4, 7-5

STOCKHOLM OPEN $300,000

November 4th-10th

Semifinals
J McEnroe bt S Edberg 6-3, 7-6
A Jarryd bt J Nystrom 6-3, 7-6

Final
McEnroe bt Jarryd 6-1, 6-2

Doubles Final
G Forget & A Gomez bt M DePalmer & M Donnelly 6-3, 6-4

BENSON AND HEDGES CHAMPIONSHIP $375,000

WEMBLEY, LONDON, November 11th-18th

Final
I Lendl bt B Becker 6-7, 6-3, 4-6, 6-4, 6-4

Doubles Final
A Jarryd & G Forget bt B Becker & S Zivojinovic 7-5, 4-6, 6-4

FISCHER CUP $100,000

VIENNA, November 18th-25th

Semifinals
J Gunnarson bt R Guntharot 7-6, 6-2
L Pimek bt A Maurer 6-3, 6-2

Final
Gunnarson bt Pimek 6-7, 6-2, 6-4, 1-6, 7-5

British
J Smith lost Casal 6-2, 6-7, 6-4

Doubles Final
M DePalmer & M Donnelly bt S Casal & E Sanchez 6-4, 6-3

SEIKO OPEN $200,000

HONG KONG, November 18th-25th

Semifinals
A Gomez bt J Hlasek 4-6, 6-3, 7-5
A Krickstein bt B Schultz 6-3, 6-2

Final
Gomez bt Krickstein 6-3, 6-3, 3-6, 6-4

British
C Dowdeswell lost R Krishnan 6-4, 4-6, 6-2

Doubles Final
B Drewett & K Warwick bt T Smid & J Hlasek 3-6, 6-4, 6-2

AUSTRALIAN OPEN $800,000

MELBOURNE, November 26th-December 9th

Semifinals
S Edberg bt I Lendl 6-7, 7-5, 6-1, 4-6, 9-7
M Wilander bt S Zivojinovic 7-5, 6-1, 6-3

Final
Edberg bt Wilander 6-4, 6-4, 6-3

British
J Lloyd bt T Smid 7-5, 6-7, 7-6, 6-5
bt J Hlasek 6-3, 6-4, 6-5
bt J Nystrom 6-2, 1-6, 6-4, 6-7, 6-4
lost Lendl 7-6, 6-2, 6-1

C Dowdeswell lost H Van Boeckel 7-5 retd
S Shaw lost F Keretic 6-2, 2-1 retd
J Bates lost M Flur 6-7, 6-7, 7-5, 6-4, 7-5
S Bale lost S Glickstein 6-5, 7-6, 7-6

Doubles Final
P Annacone & C Van Rensburg bt M Edmondsen & K Warwick 3-6, 7-6, 6-4, 6-4

NEW SOUTH WALES OPEN
$125,000

SYDNEY, December 9th-15th

Semifinals
H Leconte bt M Anger 6-4, 6-5
K Evernden bt M Dickson 6-4, 7-6

Final
Leconte bt Evernden 6-7, 6-2, 6-3

British
J Lloyd bt S Glickstein 6-4, 6-4
lost D Visser 6-3, 6-4
J Bates lost W Popp 3-6, 6-4, 6-1
C Dowdeswell lost L Shiras 6-1, 6-2
N Fulwood lost M Doyle 6-7, 6-4, 6-2

Doubles Final
D Dowlen & N Odizor bt B Dyke & W Masur 6-4, 7-6

SOUTH AUSTRALIAN OPEN
$80,000

ADELAIDE, December 16th-22nd

Semifinals
P Doohan bt W Masur 6-4, 2-0 retd
E Edwards bt C Steyn 7-6, 7-6

Final
Edwards bt Doohan 6-2, 6-4

British
J Bates lost R Saad 6-3, 7-6
C Dowdeswell lost T Benhabiles 6-3, 4-6, 7-6
N Fulwood lost W Scanlon 6-7, 6-4, 6-3

Doubles Final
M Edmondson & K Warwick bt W Aerts & T Warneke 6-4 6-4

VICTORIA OPEN $80,000

MELBOURNE, December 23rd-29th

Semifinals
J Canter bt M Edmondson 7-6, 7-6
P Doohan bt M Kratzmann 6-4, 6-3

Final
Canter bt Doohan 5-7, 6-3, 6-4

British
C Dowdeswell lost C Steyn 6-3, 6-1

Doubles Final
D Cahill & D Carter bt M Dickinson & R Saad 7-6, 6-1

1985 NABISCO PRIX FINAL POINTS STANDING

Singles		Points
1	Ivan Lendl (CZ)	4459
2	John McEnroe (US)	4103
3	Mats Wilander (SWE)	3308
4	Stefan Edberg (SWE)	2511
5	Boris Becker (WG)	2233
6	Jimmy Connors (USA)	2178
7	Yannick Noah (FRA)	1886
8	Anders Jarryd (SWE)	1860
9	Johan Kriek (US)	1497
10	Joakim Nystrom (SWE)	1482
11	Tim Mayotte (US)	1454
12	Tomas Smid (CZ)	1348
13	Miloslav Mecir (CZ)	1311
14	Henri Leconte (FRA)	1277
15	Brad Gilbert (US)	1271
16	Paul Annacone (US)	1205
17	Scott Davis (US)	1138
18	Kevin Curren (US)	1127
19	Martin Jaite (ARG)	981
20	Jimmy Arias (US)	959
21	Andrew Gomez (ECU)	879
22	Henrik Sundstrom (SWE)	842
23	David Pate (US)	794
24	Tim Wilkison (US)	758
25	Aaron Krickstein (US)	744
26	Jakob Hlasek (SWZ)	735
27	Thierry Tulasne (FRA)	704
28	Jan Gunnarsson (SWE)	691
29	Heinz Gunthardt (SWZ)	683
30	Slobodan Zivojinovic (YUG)	666
31	John Lloyd (GB)	596
32	John Sadri (US)	589
33	Matt Anger (US)	549
34	Greg Holmes (US)	546
35	Libor Pimek (CZ)	540
36	Eliot Teltscher (US)	529
37	Ramesh Krishnan (IND)	528
38	Jose-Luis Clerc (ARG)	479
38	Mike Leach (US)	479
40	Andreas Maurer (WG)	462
41	Sammy Giammalva (US)	442
42	Bud Schultz (US)	416
43	Lawson Duncan (US)	413
44	Larry Stefanki (US)	413
45	Diego Perez (URU)	408
46	Pavel Slozil (CZ)	393
47	Marty Davis (US)	376
48	Mark Dickson (US)	371
49	Francesco Cancellotti (ITA)	360
49	Guillermo Vilas (ARG)	360
51	Horacio de la Pena (ARG)	352
52	Wally Masur (AUS)	341
53	Hans Schwaier (WG)	352
54	Shahar Perkiss (ISR)	318

55	Jimmy Brown (US)	317
56	John Fitzgerald (US)	314
57	Ben Testerman (US)	312
57	Kelly Evernden (NZ)	312
57	Tom Gullikson (US)	312
60	Ken Flach (US)	304
61	Guy Forget (FRA)	303
62	Sergio Casal (SP)	296
63	Vitas Gerulaitis (US)	294
64	Robert Seguso (US)	293

DOUBLES		Points
1	Robert Seguso (US)	769
2	Ken Flach (US)	765
3	Christo van Rensburg (SA)	671
4	Kim Warwick (AUS)	587
5	Paul Annacone (US)	584
6	Anders Jarryd (SWE)	574
7	Tomas Smid (CZ)	513
8	Mats Wilander (SWE)	467
9	Pavel Slozil (CZ)	452
10	John Fitzgerald (AUS)	437
11	Heinz Gunthardt (SWZ)	423
12	Joakim Nystrom (SWE)	417
13	Mark Edmondson (AUS)	412
14	Balazs Taroczy (HUN)	379
15	Scott Davis (US)	302
16	Stefan Edberg (SWE)	296
17	Mike DePalmer (US)	290
18	Andres Gomez (EC)	271
19	Yannick Noah (FRA)	270
20	Gary Donelly (US)	249
21	Peter Fleming (US)	237
22	David Pate (US)	234
T23	Pat Cash (AUS)	225
T23	Emilio Sanchez (SP)	225

Doubles Teams		Points
1	Flach/Seguso	769
2	Annacone/Van Rensburg	575
3	Edmondson/Warwick	384
4	Slozil/Smid	366
5	Nystrom/Wilander	365
6	Gunthardt/Taroczy	366
7	Edberg/Jarryd	283
8	Casal/Sanchez	218
9	Cash/Fitzgerald	217
10	DePalmer/Donelly	173

NABISCO GRAND PRIX MASTERS Madison Square Garden, New York

January 14th-19th

SINGLES
First round
I Lendl (Cz) bt T. Smid (Cz) 6-1, 6-0.
T Mayotte (US) bt Y Noah (Fra) 6-4, 6-4.
A Gomez (Eucua) bt H Leconte (Fra) 7-6, 6-1.
I Kriek (US) bt S Edberg (Swe) 6-2, 4-6, 6-2.
B Becker (WG) bt P Annacone (US) 3-6, 6-3, 6-2.
M Wilander (Swe) bt S Davis (US) 6-3, 6-4.
A Jarryd (Swe) bt J Nystrom (Swe) 0-6, 6-1, 6-4.
B Gilbert (US) bt J McEnroe (US) 5-7, 6-4, 6-1.

Quarter Finals
Lendl bt Mayotte 6-3, 6-3. Gomez bt Kriek 6-3, 6-2. Becker bt Wilander 6-4, 4-6, 6-3. Jarryd bt Gilbert 6-1, 6-1.

Semifinals
Lendl bt Gomez 6-4, 7-5. Becker bt Jarryd 6-3, 6-4.

Final
Lendl bt Becker 6-2, 7-6, 6-4.

DOUBLES
First round
K Flach & R Seguso (US) bt S Casal & E Sanchez (Spa) 6-0, 7-6. J Nystrom & M Wilander (Swe) bt M Edmondson & K Warwick (Aus) 7-6, 4-6, 7-6. P Annacone (US) & C Van Rensburg (SA) bt H Gunthardt (Swz) & B Taroczy (Hun) 5-7, 6-3, 7-6. S Edberg & A Jarryd (Swe) bt P Slozil & T Smid (Cz) 7-6, 6-2.

Semifinals
Nystrom & Wilander bt Flach & Seguso 6-2, 6-1.
Edberg & Jarryd bt Annacone & Van Rensburg 6-4, 6-3.

Final
Edberg & Jarryd bt Nystrom & Wilander 6-1, 7-6.

FORMER WINNERS
1970 S R Smith (US) in Tokyo
1971 I Nastase (Rom) in Paris
1972 I Nastase (Rom) bt S R Smith (US) 6-3, 2-6, 3-6, 6-3, in Barcelona
1973 I Nastase (Rom) bt T Okker (Neth) 6-3, 7-5, 4-6, 6-3, in Boston
1974 G Vilos (Arg) bt I Nastase (Rom) 7-6, 6-2, 3-6, 6-4, in Barcelona
1975 I Nastase (Rom) bt B Borg (Swe) 6-2, 6-2, 6-1, in Stockholm
1976 M Orantes (Spa) bt W Fibak (Pol) 5-7, 6-2, 0-6, 7-6, 6-1, in Houston
1977 J Connors (US) bt B Borg (Swe) 6-1, 1-6, 6-4, in New York
1978-79 J McEnroe (US) bt A Ashe (US) 6-7, 6-3, 7-5, in New York
1979-80 B Borg (Swe) bt U Gerulaitis (US) 6-2, 6-2, 6-2, in New York
1980-81 B Borg (Swe) bt I Lendl (Cz) 6-4, 6-2, 6-2, in New York
1981-82 I Lendl (Cz) bt V Gerulaitis (US) 6-7, 2-6, 7-6, 6-2, 6-4, in New York
1982-83 I Lendl (Cz) bt J McEnroe (US) 6-4, 6-4, 6-2, in New York
1983-84 J McEnroe (US) bt I Lendl (Cz) 6-3, 6-4, 6-4, in New York
1985-85 J McEnroe (US) bt I Lendl (Cz) 7-5, 6-0, 6-4, in New York

VIRGINIA SLIMS SERIES

WASHINGTON $150,000

January 7th-14th

Semifinals
M Navratilova bt Z Garrison 6-1, 6-2
M Maleeva bt K Rinaldi 7-6, 6-1

Final
Navratilova bt Maleeva 6-3, 6-2

Doubles Final
G Fernandez & M Navratilova bt C Kohde-Kilsch & H Sukova 6-3, 3-6, 6-3

DENVER $75,000

January 14th-20th

Semifinals
Z Garrison bt L Savchenko 6-4, 6-4
P Louie bt G Sabatini 6-4, 4-6, 6-4

Final
Louie bt Garrison 6-4, 4-6, 6-4

British
S Gomer bt R Dreyer 6-4, 6-3
lost M L Piatek 6-3, 6-3

Doubles Final
M L Piatek & R White bt L Allen & S Walsh 1-6, 6-4, 7-5

KEY BISCAYNE $150,000

January 21st-27th

Semifinals
M Navratilova bt C Lindqvist 6-2, 6-3
C Evert-Lloyd bt P Louie 6-2, 6-1

Final
Evert-Lloyd bt Navratilova 6-2, 6-4

British
J Durie bt S Graf 2-6, 6-4, 7-5
lost Y Vermaak 6-1, 6-4
V Wade lost S Goles 2-6, 4-2 retd

Doubles Final
K Jordan & E Smylie bt S Cherneva & L Savchenko 6-4, 7-6

BMW CUP MARCO ISLAND $100,000

January 28th-February 3rd

Semifinals
P Casale bt K Jordan 7-5, 6-4
B Gadusek bt S Goles 6-4, 6-3

Final
Gadusek bt Casale 6-3, 6-4

British
V Wade bt W White 6-4, 6-4
bt M Torres 5-7, 6-3, 6-4
lost C Benjamin 6-2, 6-4
J Durie lost G Kim 2-6, 7-5, 6-3

Doubles Final
K Jordan & E Smylie bt C Benjamin & B Gadusek 6-3, 6-3

LIPTON PLAYERS CHAMPIONSHIPS $750,000

DELRAY BEACH. February 5th-7th

Semifinals
M Navratilova bt C Bassett 6-3, 6-3
C Evert-Lloyd bt S Graf 6-4, 6-2

Final
Navratilova bt Lloyd 6-2, 6-4

British
S Gomer bt K Skronska 7-6, 6-2
bt B Nagelsen 6-4, 6-2
lost C Lindgvist 6-4, 6-1
J Durie lost L Savchenko 6-3, 6-4
A Croft bt K Maleeva 6-2, 6-2
lost G Sabatini 6-1, 6-3
V Wade bt C Bartos 6-3, 4-6, 7-5
lost S Graf 6-2, 6-2
A Brown lost V Ruzici 1-6, 7-5, 6-3

Doubles Final
G Fernandez & M Navratilova bt K Jordan & H Mandlikova 7-6, 6-2

OAKLAND $150,000

February 18th-25th

Semifinals
C Evert-Lloyd bt Z Garrison 6-3, 6-2,
H Mandlikova bt H Sukova 6-4, 6-0

Final
Mandlikova bt Evert-Lloyd 6-2, 6-4

Doubles Final
H Mandlikova & W Turnbull bt R Fairbank & C Reynolds 4-6, 7-5, 6-1

US INDOOR CHAMPIONSHIPS
$150,000

March 4th-11th

Semifinals
H Mandlikova bt M Navratilova 7-6, 6-0
C Lindqvist bt C Tanvier 6-1, 6-4

Final
Mandlikova bt Lindqvist 6-3, 7-5

Doubles Final
M Navratilova & P Shriver bt M Mesker & E Smylie 7-5, 6-2

INDIANAPOLIS $75,000

March 4th-11th

Semifinals
H Mandlikova bt M Navratilova 7-6, 6-0
C Lindqvist bt C Tanvier 6-1, 6-4

Final
Mandlikova bt Lindqvist 6-3, 7-5

Doubles Final
M Navratilova & P Shriver bt M Mesker & E Smylie 7-5, 6-2

INDIANAPOLIS $75,000

March 4th-11th

Semifinals
E Burgin bt B Gadusek 6-1, 7-5
K Horvath bt B Nagelsen 6-2, 6-1

Final
Horvath bt Burgin 6-2, 6-4

British
A Brown lost K Horvath 6-3, 7-6

Doubles Final
E Burgin & K Horvath bt J Mundel & M Van Nostrand 6-4, 6-1

DALLAS $150,000

March 11th-17th

Semifinals
M Navratilova bt H Sukova 6-2, 7-5
C Evert-Lloyd bt C Lindqvist 6-1, 6-3

Final
Navratilova bt Evert-Lloyd 6-3, 6-4

British
J Durie lost M Navratilova 6-1, 6-3

Doubles Final
B Potter & S Walsh bt M Mesker & P Paradis 5-7, 6-4, 7-6

VIRGINIA SLIMS CHAMPIONSHIP
$500,000

MADISON SQUARE GARDEN, March 18th-24th

Semifinals
M Navratilova bt H Mandlikova 7-5, 7-6
H Sukova bt K Rinaldi 6-4, 6-2

Final
Navratilova bt Sukova 6-3, 7-5, 6-4

Doubles Final
M Navratilova & P Shriver bt C Kohde-Kilsch & H Sukova 6-7, 6-4, 7-6

WTA CHAMPIONSHIPS $50,000

PALM BEACH, March 25th-31st

Semifinals
K Horvath bt R Reggi 6-2, 6-3, P Delhees-Jauch bt T Phelps 6-2, 6-2

Final
Delhees-Jauch bt Horvath 3-6, 6-3, 6-3

British
A Croft lost G Sabatini 6-2, 1-6, 6-4

Doubles Final
J Russell & A Smith bt L Gildemeister & G Sabatini 1-6, 6-1, 7-6

SEABROOK ISLAND $75,000

April 1st-7th

Semifinals
K Maleeva bt S Goles 2-6, 6-4, 6-1
V Ruzici bt T Scheur-Larsen 6-1, 7-5

Final
Maleeva bt Ruzici 6-3, 6-3

British
A Croft lost P Delhees-Jauch 6-2, 6-4

Doubles Final
S Cherneva & L Savchenko bt E Burgin & L McNeil 6-1, 6-3

FAMILY CIRCLE CUP $750,000

HILTON HEAD, April 8th-14th

Final
C Evert-Lloyd bt G Sabatini 6-4, 6-0

WTA CHAMPIONSHIP $250,000

AMELIA ISLAND, April 15th-21st

Semifinals
Z Garrison bt H Mandlikova 7-5, 6-4, C Evert-Lloyd bt C Kohde-Kilach 5-7, 6-3, 6-2

Final
Garrison bt Evert-Lloyd 6-4, 6-3

British
A Croft lost L Bonder 6-4, 5-7, 6-1

Doubles Final
R Fairbank & H Mandlikova bt C Evert-Lloyd & C Bassett 6-1, 2-6, 6-2

SAN DIEGO $75,000

April 22nd-28th

Semifinals
A Croft bt M Gurney 5-7, 6-2, 6-3
W Turnbull bt M L Piatek 6-2, 6-1

Final
A Croft bt Turnbull 6-0, 7-6

British
A Croft bt L Thompson
bt B Jordan 6-4, 6-3
bt Fairbank 6-0, 6-3
bt Gurney 5-7, 6-2, 6-3
bt Turnbull 6-0, 7-6

TOURNAMENT OF CHAMPIONS

BUENA VISTA, April 22nd-28th

Semifinals
M Navratilova bt C Kohde-Kilsch 6-2, 6-1
K Maleeva bt B Gadusek 6-2, 6-1

Final
Navratilova bt K Maleeva 6-1, 6-0

Doubles Final
M Navratilova & P Shriver
bt E Burgin & K Horvath 6-3, 6-1

HOUSTON $150,000

April 28th-May 5th

Semifinals
M Navratilova bt H Sukova 6-3, 6-0
E Burgin bt M Maleeva 6-4, 7-6

Final
Navratilova bt Burgin 6-4, 6-1

British
J Durie lost D Spence 6-3, 6-2

Doubles Final
E Burgin & M Navratilova bt M Maleeva & H Sukova 6-1, 3-6, 6-3

AUSTRALIAN INDOOR CHAMPIONSHIPS $200,000

SYDNEY, March 11th-17th

Semifinals
P Shriver bt A Moulton 6-3, 6-2
D Balestrat bt G Fernandez 6-1, 6-3

Final
Shriver bt Balestrat 6-3, 6-3

British
A Croft bt E Croft 6-1, 3-6, 6-0
bt L Thompson 6-4, 6-1
lost A Moulton 6-2, 3-6, 6-1
S Gomer bt L Antonopolis 6-2, 6-3
lost B Potter 6-2, 6-0
A Hobbs lost D Balestrat 6-3, 6-4

Doubles Final
P Shriver & E Smylie bt B Potter & S Walsh 7-5, 7-5

GERMAN OPEN $150,000

BERLIN, May 14th-20th

Semifinals
C Evert-Lloyd bt K Rinaldi 6-1, 6-3
S Graf bt B Bunge 6-2, 6-3

Final
Evert-Lloyd bt Graf 6-4, 7-6

British
J Durie bt K Skuherska 6-2, 6-4
lost S Graf 3-6, 6-2, 6-3

Doubles Final
C Kohde-Kilsch & H Sukova bt S Graf & C Tanvier 6-4, 6-1

VICTORIAN INDOOR $75,000

MELBOURNE, May 14th-20th

Semifinals
P Shriver bt A Croft 7-6, 6-2
K Jordan bt B Potter 7-5, 6-3

Final
Shriver bt K Jordan 6-4, 6-1

British
A Croft bt M Schillig 6-2, 6-3
bt H Ludloff 5-7, 2-6, 6-2
bt A Brown 6-4, 6-3
lost Shriver 7-6, 6-2
Brown bt J Byrne 7-5, 6-3
bt S Gomer 6-2, 4-6, 6-3
lost Croft 6-4, 6-3
Gomer bt E Smylie 4-6, 7-5, 6-1
lost Brown 6-2, 4-6, 6-3
A Hobbs lost R White 3-6, 6-2, 6-0

EUROPEAN OPEN $100,000

LUGANO, May 20th-26th

Semifinals
B Gadusek bt H Sukova 6-4, 1-6, 6-4
M Maleeva bt S Hanika 6-1, 7-6

Final
Gadusek bt Maleeva 6-2, 6-2

Doubles Final
B Gadusek & H Sukova bt B Bunge & E Pfaff 6-2, 6-4

FRENCH OPEN $800,000

PARIS, May 23rd-June 8th

Semifinals
M Navratilova bt C Kohda-Kilsch 6-4, 6-4
C Evert-Lloyd bt G Sabatini 6-4, 6-1

Final
Evert-Lloyd bt Navratilova 6-3, 6-7, 7-5

British
V Wade bt S Gomer 7-6, 6-4
lost Navratilova 6-3, 6-0
A Croft lost M Jausovec 6-2, 6-0
R Einy lost A Villagran 6-2, 6-0
A Brown lost S Mascarin 6-3, 7-5
J Durie lost E Derly 7-6, 0-6, 6-4
A Hobbs lost R Fairbank 7-5, 6-2

Doubles Final
M Navratilova & P Shriver bt C Kohde-Kilsch & H Sukova 4-6, 6-2, 6-2

EDGBASTON CUP $125,000

BIRMINGHAM, June 9th-16th

Final
P Shriver bt B Nagelsen

Doubles Final
T Holladay & S Walsh bt E Burgin & A Moulton 6-4, 5-7, 6-3

PILKINGTON GLASS CHAMPIONSHIPS $150,000

EASTBOURNE, June 17th-23rd

Final
M Navratilova bt M Maleeva 6-4, 6-3

Doubles Final
M Navratilova & P Shriver bt K Jordan & E Smylie 7-5, 6-4

WIMBLEDON CHAMPIONSHIPS $900,000

June 24th-July 7th

Final
M Navratilova bt C Evert-Lloyd 4-6, 6-3, 6-2

Doubles Finals
K Jordan & E Smylie bt M Navratilova & P Shriver 5-7, 6-3, 6-4

NEWPORT, $150,000

RHODE-ISLAND, July 15th-21st

Semifinals
C Evert-Lloyd bt E Pfaff 7-5, 6-2
P Shriver bt W Turnbull 6-4, 7-6

Final
Evert-Lloyd bt Shriver 6-4, 6-1

Doubles Final
Evert-Lloyd & Turnbull bt P Shriver & E Smylie 6-4, 7-6

US CLAY COURT CHAMPIONSHIPS $200,000

INDIANAPOLIS, July 22nd-28th

Semifinals
A Temesvari bt K Gompert 6-3, 6-4
Z Garrison bt G Sabatini 6-4, 6-2

Final
Temesvari bt Garrison 7-6, 6-3

Doubles Final
M Maleeva & K Maleeva bt P Barg & P Smith 3-6, 6-3, 6-4

LOS ANGELES $250,000

July 29th-August 4th

Semifinals
C Kohde-Kilsch bt E Pfaff 6-4, 6-4
P Shriver bt Z Garrison 7-6, 6-4

Final
C Kohde-Kilsch bt Shriver 6-2, 6-4

British
A Croft lost E Pfaff 6-2, 7-6

Doubles Final
C Kohde-Kilsch & H Sukova bt H Mandlikova & W Turnbull 6-4, 6-2

CANADIAN OPEN $250,000

TORONTO, August 5th-11th

Semifinals
C Kohde-Kilsch bt H Sukova 6-4, 6-4
C Evert-Lloyd bt H Mandlikova 3-6, 6-2, 6-4

Final
Evert-Lloyd bt Kohde-Kilsch 6-2, 6-4

British
J Durie lost M Van Nostrand 6-4, 6-2
S Gomer lost T Phelps 6-4, 6-3

Doubles Final
G Fernandez & M Navratilova bt M Mesker & P Paradis 6-4, 6-0

MAHWAH CLASSIC $150,000

August 11th-18th

Semifinals
S Graf bt G Sabatini 4-6, 6-0, 6-3
K Rinaldi b t C Lindqvist 5-7, 6-2, 6-1

Final
Rinaldi bt Graf 6-4, 3-6, 6-4

British
J Durie bt P Louis 6-1, 6-1
lost A Jaeger 6-2 retd
A Croft bt S Cecchini 6-1, 4-6, 6-4
lost C Lindqvist 6-3, 6-4
A Brown bt M Longo 6-2, 4-6, 7-5
lost S Graf 6-1, 6-1
S Gomer lost H Kelesi 4-6, 7-5, 7-5

NEW YORK $75,000

August 19th-25th

Semifinals
H Kelesi bt H Sukova 7-6, 7-6
B Potter bt S Hanika 7-6, 2-1, retd

Final
Potter bt Kelesi 4-6, 6-3, 6-2

British
J Durie bt M Jausovec 6-2, 6-3
bt L Drescher 3-6, 6-1, 6-4
lost S Hanika 2-6, 7-5, 7-6
A Croft bt L Kannellopolou 3-6, 7-5, 6-2
lost B Potter 6-4, 7-6
S Gomer lost H Kelesi 7-6, 5-7, 6-4
A Hobbs lost K Maleeva 6-4, 6-2

US OPEN CHAMPIONSHIPS

August 27th-September 8th

Semifinals
H Mandlikova bt C Evert-Lloyd 4-6, 6-2, 6-3
M Navratilova bt S Graf 6-2, 6-3

Final
H Mandlikova bt Navratilova 7-6, 1-6, 7-5

British
A Hobbs bt J Durie 7-5, 6-1
bt R Casals 2-6, 6-3, 7-6
lost P Shriver 6-2, 6-3
Gomer lost M J Fernandez 6-1, 6-4
A Brown lost H Mandlikova 6-2, 6-1
Croft bt M Skuherska 6-1, 7-5
lost Mandlikova 6-2, 6-3

SALT LAKE CITY $75,000

Semifinals
C Benjamin bt L Gildemeister 6-4, 6-3

Final
Rehe bt Benjamin 6-2, 6-4

Doubles Final
S Cherneva & L Savchenko bt R Fairbank & B Mould 7-5, 6-2

CHICAGO $150,000

Semifinals
K Rinaldi bt K Jordan 6-0, 7-5
B Gadusek bt W Turnbull 7-6, 6-2

Final
Gadusek bt Rinaldi 6-1, 6-3

Doubles Finals
K Jordan & E Smylie bt E Burgin & J Russell 6-2, 6-2

NEW ORLEANS, $150,000

September 23rd-29th

Semifinals
C Evert-Lloyd bt L Bonder 6-3, 6-1
P Shriver bt A White 6-3, 6-2

Final
Evert-Lloyd bt Shriver 6-4, 7-5

Doubles Final
C Evert-Lloyd & W Turnbull bt M L Piatek & A White 6-1, 6-3

MAYBELLINE CLASSIC $150,000

September 27th-October 6th

Semifinals
M Navratilova bt P Louie 6-2, 6-1
S Graf bt B Gadusek 6-3, 7-6

Final
M Navratilova bt Graf 6-3, 6-1

Doubles Final
G Fernandez & R White bt R Fairbank & B Mould 6-2, 7-5

PORSCHE GRAND PRIX $175,000

STUTTGART, October 14th-20th

Semifinals
C Lindqvist bt C Kohde-Kilsch 2-6, 7-6, 6-4
P Shriver bt S Graf 6-4, 6-3

Final
Shriver bt Lindqvist 6-1, 7-5

British
A Brown lost Shriver 6-3, 6-4
J Durie lost L Bonder 1-6, 6-4, 6-3

Doubles Final
H Mandlikova & P Shriver bt C Karlsson & T Scheur-Larsen 6-2, 6-1

PRETTY POLLY CLASSIC $175,000

BRIGHTON, October 21st-28th

Final
C Evert-Lloyd bt M Maleeva 7-5, 6-3

Doubles Final
L McNeil & C Suire bt B Potter & H Sukova 4-6, 7-6, 6-4

EUROPEAN INDOOR CHAMPIONSHIPS $150,000

ZURICH, October 28th-November 3rd

Semifinals
H Mandlikova bt H Sukova 6-2, 7-6
Z Garrison bt C Kohde-Kilsch 6-3, 6-2

Final
Garrison bt Mandlikova 6-1, 6-3

Doubles Final
H Mandlikova & A Temesvari bt C Konde-Kilsch & H Sukova 6-4, 3-6, 7-5

FLORIDA FEDERAL OPEN $150,000

TARPON SPRINGS, November 4th-10th

Semifinals
G Sabatini bt A White 6-1 6-2
S Rehe bt C Bassett 4-6, 6-4, 6-4

Final
Rehe bt Sabatini 6-4, 6-7, 7-5

Doubles Final
C Bassett & G Sabatini bt L Boncer & L Gildemeister 6-0, 6-0

NATIONAL PANASONIC CLASSIC $150,000

BRISBANE, November 11th-18th

Semifinals
P Shriver bt H Sukova 7-6, 1-6, 6-2
M Navratilova bt C Kohde-Kilsch 6-1, 6-4

Final
Mandlikova bt Shriver 6-4, 7-5

British
S Gomer bt S Yanagi 6-2, 6-4
bt P Paradis 7-6, 6-4
bt A Croft 6-2, 7-5
lost M Navratilova 6-3, 6-1
J Durie bt M Jaggaru 7-5, 6-4
lost A Minter 6-3, 7-6
Croft bt E Inoue 4-6, 6-2, 6-3
lost Gomer
A Brown lost G Monteiro 6-2, 6-2
A Hobbs bt B Gerken 6-4, 6-4
lost W Turnbull 7-6, 6-1

Doubles Final
M Navratilova & P Shriver bt C Kohde-Kilsch & H Sukova 6-4, 6-7, 6-1

FAMILY CIRCLE NSW OPEN $150,000

SYDNEY, November 19th-25th

Semifinals
M Navratilova bt H Sukova 4-6, 6-3, 6-2
H Mandlikova bt C Kohde-Kilsch 6-0, 7-5

Final
Navratilova bt Mandlikova 3-6, 6-1, 6-2

British
S Gomer lost P Paradis 6-4, 6-2
A Brown lost E Incue 6-4, 5-7, 6-4
J Durie bt A Hobbs 3-6, 6-3, 6-3
lost S Cherneva 6-3, 6-3
A Croft bt M Schropp 63, 6-3
lost L Savchenko 7-5, 2-6, 6-4

AUSTRALIAN OPEN $750,000

MELBOURNE, November 25th-December 8th

Semifinals
C Lloyd bt C Kohde-Kilsch 6-1, 7-6
M Navratilova bt H Mandlikova 6-7, 6-1, 6-4

Final
Navratilova bt Lloyd 6-2, 4-6, 6-2

British
J Durie bt A Minter 6-4, 6-4
bt S Gomer 6-2, 6-3
lost C Kohde-Kilsch 3-6, 6-1, 6-2
V Wade bt M Van Nostrand 6-3, 5-7, 6-2
lost H Mandlikova 6-2, 7-6
A Hobbs bt Hu Na 6-2, 6-3
bt B Potter 6-4, 7-5
lost M Navratilova 6-3, 6-1
S Gomer bt L Spain-Short 6-2, 7-6
lost Durie, A Brown bt B Gerken 6-2, 1-6, 6-0,
lost D Balestrat 6-0, 7-5
A Croft lost C Kohde-Kilsch 7-5, 6-3

Doubles Final
M Navratilova & P Shriver bt K Kohde-Kilsch &
H Sukova 6-3, 6-4

NUTRIC METRICS OPEN $50,000

AUCKLAND, December 9th-15th

Semifinals
A Hobbs bt A Fernandez 6-7, 7-5, 7-6
L Field bt B Norton 6-1, 6-1

Final
Hobbs bt A Fernandez 6-7, 7-5, 7-6
L Field bt B Norton 6-1, 6-1

British
A Hobbs bt C Carney 3-6, 6-2, 6-3
bt J Richardson 6-0, 6-4
bt A M Feznandez 6-7, 7-5, 7-6
bt L Field 6-3, 6-1

Doubles Final
A Hobbs & C Reynolds bt A Villagran &
L Antonopolis 6-1, 6-3

PAN PACIFIC CHAMPIONSHIP $250,000

TOKYO, December 9th-15th

Semifinals
M Maleeva bt H Sukova 6-0, 6-2
B Gadusek bt C Kohde-Kilsch 6-4, 6-5

Final
Maleeva bt Gadusek 7-6, 3-6, 7-5

British
A Croit bt P Casale 6-3, 7-5
bt E Smylie 6-1, 6-1
lost M Maleeva 6-2, 6-2

Doubles Final
C Kohde-Kilsch & H Sukova bt M Mesker &
E Smylie 6-0, 6-4

A SCHOOL OF EXCELLENCE

BY JOHN PARSONS: DAILY TELEGRAPH

When Derek Bone, the LTA's National Junior Co-ordinator, was researching the practicality as well as the advisability of the specialist tennis school at Bisham Abbey, his travels took him to other centres of junior excellence, including those for ballet and music.

The message he kept being given, wherever he went, was that what tutors and coaches were dreaming of finding most of all, in any artistic or sporting vein, was an almost indefinable something extra — the quality which bridges the gap between impressive competence and sheer brilliance.

It was a salutory reminder, if one was needed, that however much help they may receive along the way, the greatest of champions, as personified by John McEnroe through most of 1983-4, are born and not made. There is a natural, inspirational talent within them which carries their performance into an altogether higher realm.

No-one, therefore, should expect the Bisham Abbey school, now in its third year, to be a guaranteed source of players who in the near future, will consign the name of Fred Perry to the record books, by taking his place, spanning half a century, as Britain's last men's singles champion at Wimbledon.

Yet far from being an argument against the need for a specialist tennis school, it tends to strengthen the case for one, inasmuch that if or when some exceptionally gifted, fully co-ordinated, physically ideal and mentally sound prospect comes along — such as a British Boris Becker — the facility for him to develop will already be there.

Geoff Brown, the LTA President, in his lively introduction to a not so lively Report of the Council, to last December's LTA annual meeting, said "It is far too early to say for sure whether the principle of an elite corps is the right one or not. But if effort and dedication are anything to go by, we have a good chance of success."

As someone who always regretted the lack of official support and confidence in the late 1960's for The Barrett Boys, a specialist travelling squad idea which the French then took on at all age groups with much obvious long term benefit, I believe elitism (which does not lead to mean protection) is just as necessary as the broadest possible bands of tennis strength all the way down to grass roots, with every opportunity, encouragement and incentive to reach that sort of peak.

That also is why Bone and National Team Manager Paul Hutchins, who has always been whole-hearted in his belief of such a scheme, stress that the School should be seen as an integral part of National Training and not something exclusive from it.

While carrying out his preparatory work before he and Hutchins had to "sell" the idea of the School, first to the relevant LTA committee and then to the Board of Management, Bone became increasingly convinced that Britain had to move in the same sort of direction as Czechoslovakia, France and West Germany etc, while at the same time working within our own educational set-up which has hardly been renowned for its enthusiasm in encouraging sport.

Fortunately Buckinghamshire not

only listened to Bone's plea but agreed that boys from Bisham could go to their schools even though, as they gently teased him, his geography was not quite right in that Bisham Abbey lies on the Berkshire, rather than the Buckinghamshire side of the River Thames.

John Clifton, whose wife Margy was also permanently involved until the arrival of Richard Brand, a physical education expert, as housemaster, needed little convincing about the potential value of the School when he was invited to return home from coaching in West Germany to take basic charge of the work to be done.

"The first thing which struck me when I came back, having seen what was on offer to a talented child in Germany in almost any City in terms of training programmes, was how relative little opportunity our youngsters had both in the time they were able to play and the time they saw their coaches" he says. "As such it was very simple to see why our juniors don't play so well as juniors abroad and I am firmly convinced that a centre of excellence, which is what we hope we are making Bisham Abbey, is one way of tackling the issue."

At the start of 1986 there were seven boys at the school, with their ages ranging from 12-16. Eventually, if the signs of progress continue to be encouraging, there could be several more, for there is the accommodation available. Under the policy laid down for use of the National Training Centre, there has to be equal opportunity for boys and girls although in fact there is no residential specialist training for girls at this stage because Sue Mappin, Britain's national womens team manager does not believe such a scheme would be suitable for them. The pressures and strains on boys and girls are often so different at that time of their lives.

Everyone, I suppose, in their mind's

eye has their vision of the ideal tennis player. Those such as Hutchins, Bone, Clifton and Clay Iles, who are principally responsible for choosing the boys they think will most benefit from being at Bisham, are no exception. Obviously they are looking for atheticism but more than that they want to see natural ball control, balance, a competitive enthusiasm and a willingness to think for themselves. After all you can only programme talent so far. Tennis players are human beings, not part of a production line and without self-induced initiative, they will not make much genuine headway.

Having the different age groups within the scheme is thought advisable, not only in terms of continuity but hopefully the older age group will constantly be an encouragement and inspiration to the next level down.

On a typical school day at Bisham, the boys will all be out for an early morning run around 7 a.m. This is done more as a form of discipline, rather than to wake them up but it is also of course, part of their fitness training, as are the physical exercises which Brand will put them through before they return for a shower and then breakfast at 7.50 a.m.

At 8.20 a.m. the mini-bus is waiting to take them to school — some to the Royal Grammar School, High Wycombe, others to Great Marlow. If their school timetable permits, some will be back on one or two days of the week for individual coaching or practice play, during the morning or afternoon. All are expected to be on court at Bisham between 4.45 p.m.-6.30 p.m., although on two evenings a week they will have fitness work with Bev Risman. Then it is time for homework.

Two of the factors uppermost in the minds of those running the Bisham scheme are that the boys must not neglect their scholastic work. Also, as Leif Dahlgren, the former director of coaching to the Swedish Tennis Association was at pains to point out to the 1985 seminar held by the Professional Tennis Coaches Association, everything possible must be done to see that tennis development remains fun.

On the majority of week-ends the Bisham boys will either have tournaments, international or other matches, or alternative tennis activities. From time to time they may even take part in other sports. Colin Beecher, for instance, is a useful school athlete and it is felt right that he and all the others, Danny Sapsford, Simon Booth, Nick Smith, Ulli Nganga, Simon Cornish and Andrew Foster, have the opportunity to broaden their horizons if they wish, for this too is part of developing their personality, which in turn can develop their tennis.

It is far from a protected or easy life. They are in effect serving an apprenticeship, at last able to hit as many tennis balls as their counterparts in the United States. Yet they are inevitably under a great deal of pressure from those who are quick to question the merits of the scheme if the boys do not win almost every match they play. They undoubtedly feel they have to win, which is sometimes the reason why they lapse, and it is noticeable how protective they have become about each other.

On the other hand it is excellent character-building if they can respond triumphantly to such pressures and good for those not involved in the scheme if they are inspired to raise their game to prove themselves just as talented on a particular day. It is, incidentally, accepted that some boys, because of their make-up will benefit just as much from not being at Bisham. The LTA, nevertheless, remains just as keen to help them.

Basically the job of the school is not, except possibly in the case of some of the youngest ones, to each basic stroke production and technique. By the time anyone goes to Bisham they really should have a solid and stable means of hitting the ball over the net in any given situation. The school's role is to try and guide them through the hard slog of learning how to play the game, at a time while they are still developing mentally and physically, by offering the best possible facilities, help and opportunities.

As John Clifton remarked: "Ambition has to be there. A lot of resentment from outside comes from an ignorance among the British public and some coaches of exactly what is happening in the tennis world. We're far too concerned about a player's technique when that should be regarded as only one of the attributes which goes into a tennis player. You have to learn how to cope with unexpected situations, how to shrug off a bad call or a crucial net cord, how to play the big points and how to win matches."

It will probably be ten years or more (the time it took the French to see any tangible results) before a wholly realistic assessment of the Bisham work can be made. By then we will be able to look back and see what improvements there have been in terms of international match results and individual performances by British players round the world.
the world.

What one can say at present is that anyone who visits Bisham Abbey to see for themselves what is being tried, will at least gain the impression that the priorities are right. From that stage on it is mainly down to the boys themselves. But do not expect miracles. Remember, champions, for the most part, are born — not made.

GREEN LIGHT FOR BRITAIN

BY IAN BARNES: DAILY EXPRESS

We may be short of winners, or even players in the world top 20, yet British tennis has never been short of ambition, optimism or even a conviction that better days are coming. Like British Rail, British tennis is fond of saying it is "getting there" and in 1985, if not exactly moving fast, there were signs that real progress was being made.

Nobody should rush to wave flags, open champagne or do anything else which might be construed as a celebration. The station marked "Promised Land" is still a long way off. But the signals are set fair if the encouraging things about the past year do, in fact, encourage British players and officials to stay the full journey.

Promotion back to the top flight of Davis Cup nations represents not only the major achievement of the year; it also provides the biggest challenge. Competition for team places has barely been more open and the only result of that must be the emergence of better players.

When Britain's appearance in the 1978 Davis Cup final failed to galvanise the nation's youngsters into wanting to become tennis stars, excuses were made about lack of opportunity or lack of facilities. Enthusiasts, it was argued, could not get the court time, at the right price, for them to indulge in tennis rather than soccer, cricket or swimming.

Not so in 1986. Considerable progress has been made — although there is still a long way to go — and it is up to the game's leaders to make sure that promising youngsters stay with tennis rather than find other diversions through sheer frustration. The opening of dozens of new indoor facilities around the country must be exploited by the authorities to give young players the court time that produces champions.

Jeremy Bates is a prime example of what a slow and patient process that can be. For years Bates was hailed as Britain's most promising young player without ever making the impact such an outstanding natural talent demanded. Without the support he had from the LTA he could easily have gone the way of so many of his contemporaries. But in 1985 all the complex parts of Jeremy Bates started to fall into place.

Success in the Spring Satellite Circuit was followed by a successful defence of his Manchester Grass Courts title. He played a crucial part in the Davis Cup wins over Portugal, Switzerland and Israel and crowned the year by taking the Refuge National championships.

A place in the world's top 100 for Bates shows what can be done, and will hopefully provide the incentive for young rivals like Nick Fulwood, Stuart Bale, Stephen Shaw, Richard Whichello and Jason Goodall to aim as high. If they need more convincing that hard work has its eventual reward they need look no further than Annabel Croft and Anne Hobbs.

Miss Croft used her first senior triumph, in the Virginia Slims of San Diego tournament, as a spring-board to a place in the world's top 30 and Miss Hobbs showed that determination and courage after injury and illness can pay off by winning the Refuge Women's title.

There was certainly no shortage during the year of patrons willing to

Jason Goodall

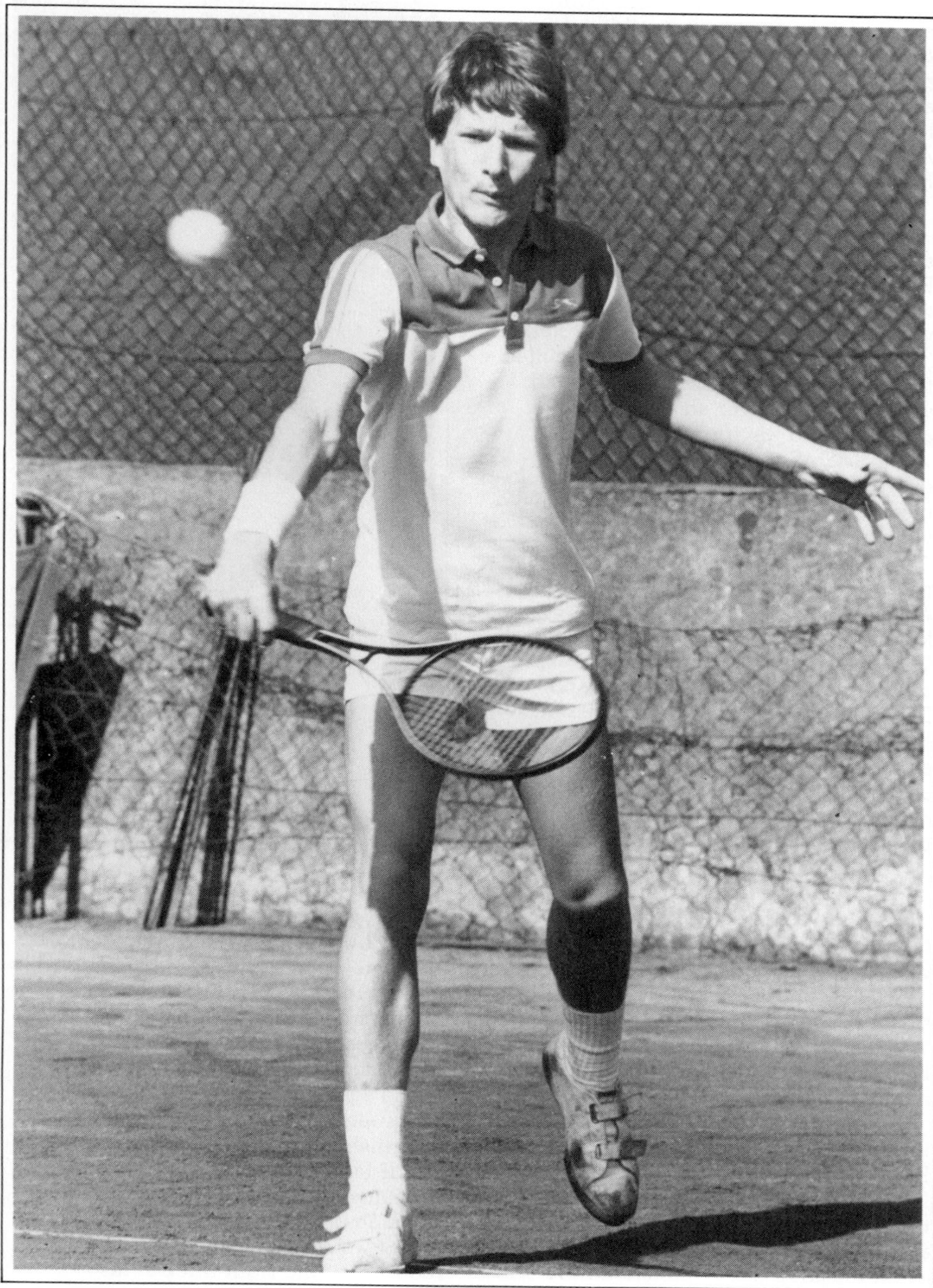

back those who show they are worthy of support. John Laing, the building contractors who had helped Miss Croft, put up another £30,000 to help the LTA send Whichello, Goodall and Chris Peet to tournaments and to train at Bisham Abbey with coaches Nigel Sears and Richard Lewis.

Jo Louis, Rina Einy, Belinda Borneo and Jane Wood were formed into a similar team with support from Pilkington Glass while Daihatsu returned to tennis and Cliff Richard stepped in with schemes to encourage future stars.

Charles Applewhaite was appointed to a new post as Director of Coaching, with a brief to cover all aspects of coaching and the training of coaches while Brian Blincoe was even more energetic than before in spreading the gospel of short tennis to attract ever-younger players playing the game.

It is with the younger set that the prosperity of the game lies and, for that reason alone, it was gratifying to see a fall in the average age of participants at County Week at least in the first division at Eastbourne where Essex men and Surrey women were again successful.

Club championships continued to expand on a national scale with Silk Cut and Slazenger-Blue Arrow competitions offering plenty of fun for thousands of players of all abilities. Edgbaston Priory — runners-up for two years — just edged out West Hants for the men's trophy and Queen's Club women beat the Grafton Club from Streatham for the Slazenger-Blue Arrow trophies.

Leicester's Carisbrook LTC lifted the Silk Cut Championships by beating Winchester, so taking the title out of London for the first time in its three year existence.

New sponsors were found for the important pre-Wimbledon event at Eastbourne — Pilkington Glass — and, late in the year, came the good news that the Dow Chemical Company is to sponsor the 1986 Edgbaston Cup, an event the LTA and Wimbledon have had to support financially for the past four years.

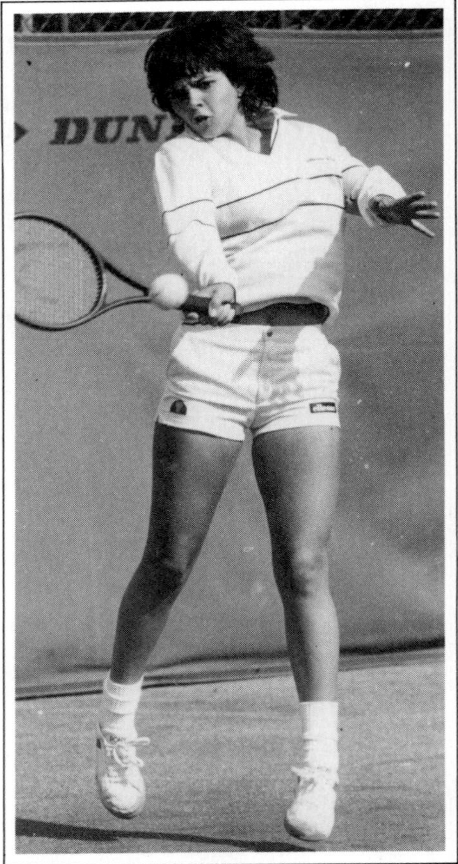

Belinda Borneo

A brand new event, the Remington-sponsored Father and Son championship made such a successful debut that it is to be extended, with LTA support to include a mothers and daughters championship in 1986 and the LTA rating scheme gained new backing from Volkswagen. Such international interest in British tennis must mean something.

If Ian Peacock, in his new role as executive director of the LTA can give as much good news in his first annual report we shall know that British tennis really is on the right track at last.

Rina Einey

MAYOTTE WINS 'REHEARSAL'

BY BRIAN CUTTRESS: EXCHANGE TELEGRAPH

Boris Becker's defeat of Tim Mayotte in the Kentish Times Tournament at Beckenham went almost unnoticed. He was just a very good junior beaten by a very good senior. Yet Beckenham will always be regarded as a milestone in the German's meteoric rise to fame and fortune.

It was to be the last time he would do anything or go anywhere unnoticed; the last time he could wander around the courts without being hounded by autograph hunters and the last time he would be happy to collect a £500 cheque for a week's work.

No-one could have imagined what was to come in the following few weeks as Becker struggled through his opening matches. He certainly caught the eye with his powerful serves and volleys but he had difficulty stringing more than a couple of winning shots together as he edged his way to the semi-final encounter with Mayotte.

It all began with an amazing first round match against Welsh left-hander Leighton Alfred, who ranked only eighth in Britain but managed to hold him until 6-6 in the final set. How could anyone have guessed then that Becker would go on to win the £30,000 first prize in the Stella Artois tournament at Queens Club, London the following week, then move on to his sensational Wimbledon?

Next in line was Stefan Kruger whom he defeated in straight sets and then came a triller with Larry Stefanki which he won 7-5 in the third. He beat Ricardo Acuna by much the same score so it seemed little more than a formality for Mayotte to slip by him and through to the final.

But Becker hammered down ace after ace to take the first set before the tall American, who was later to lose to the German at Wimbledon, snatched the second set and held on for his 3-6, 7-5, 6-4 victory.

Meanwhile, Kevin Curren, the top seed, gave a disappointing first round performance. He went down to Australia's Darren Cahill, who was about as little known to the Beckenham spectators as Becker, and then said how difficult he found it, after a long and enjoyable holiday, to come back to the tough tennis circuit. A few weeks later he looked even sadder as he lost to Becker in the Wimbledon final.

Leighton Alfred

Tim Mayotte

Curren was just the first of many seeds to fall in the early rounds of the men's singles. Scott Davis (3), Greg Holmes (5), Mike Leach (8), Ben Testerman (9), Tim Wilkison (10), John Fitzgerald (11), Vijay Amritraj (14), Brian Teacher (15) and Bob Green (16) all failed to reach the third round.

Yet unseeded Steve Denton, who beat Fitzgerald in the first round, came powering through to the final with the loss of just one set.

Mayotte made what threatened to be a disastrous start to the final when he cut his head on a shelf as he was leaving the dressing room and then lost three of the first four games. However he fought back bravely and forced the set to a tie breaker which he won 9-7 before rain caused a 55-minutes delay. When the players returned, Denton was unable to repeat his earlier form and Mayotte took six successive games for the title and a cheque for £2,000.

"This has been a perfect preparation for Wimbledon," said Mayotte without realising for whom he was actually speaking.

Barbara Potter ended a barren spell by taking the women's crown. She had not won a title for three years and there was not a lot Annabel Croft could do on the day to extend the run. Miss Potter was at her devastating best and pounded down 17 aces on her way through to an entralling 7-6, 4-6, 6-3 triumph.

Steffi Graf, the brilliant young German, was expected to contest the Saturday final but she had to withdraw earlier in the week because of an ankle injury. So it was left to another young German to make Beckenham, in retrospect, one of the most significant tournaments of the year.

KENTISH TIMES INTERNATIONAL

Beckenham, June 3rd-9th

MEN'S SINGLES

First round
D Cahill bt K Curren 7-5, 7-5. M Anger bt B Manson 6-3, 6-2. D Visser bt L Bourne 6-7, 6-4, 6-4. M De Palmer bt T Wilkison 6-3, 6-2. R Green bt M Robertson 6-4, 7-5. L Shiras bt C Honey 4-6, 6-1, 6-4. R Van't Hof bt M Groetsch 4-6, 6-3, 6-4. E Edwards bt G Holmes 7-6, 7-6. D Pate bt J Canter 6-4, 6-4. B Moir bt B Schultz 1-6, 6-3, 7-5. S Zivojinovic bt J Leytze 7-5, 6-4. V Amritraj bt J Sevelly 6-2, 6-3. S Denton bt J Fitzgerald 7-6, 7-6. M Kratzmann bt K van der Merwe 6-3, 6-1. C Steyn bt S Youl 6-4, 6-3. M Leach bt J Pugh 6-3, 6-2. B Becker bt L Alfred 6-2, 5-7, 7-6. S Kruger bt M Baroch 5-7, 7-6, 6-1. D Houston bt W Masur 6-4, 6-3. L Stefanki bt M Blincow 6-1, 2-6, 6-4. S Wood bt B Testerman 6-3, 1-6, 7-6. R Acuna bt S Gitlin 7-5, 6-4. M Freeman bt R Whichello 6-4, 7-5. S Davis bt B Dyke 6-4, 3-6, 6-4. R Krishnan bt T Cain 7-5, 6-1. P Reekie bt A Fillol 6-4, 6-4. N Odizor bt K Belcher 6-4, 7-6. P Fleming bt B Buffington 6-3, 6-2. B Teacher bt E Korita 6-3, 6-7, 7-5. C Hooper bt S Shaw 6-3, 7-5. C Stanbury bt S Bale 6-4, 6-7, 7-6. T Mayotte bt G Layendecker 6-1, 6-3.

Second round
Anger bt Cahill 7-6, 6-1. De Palmer bt Visser 6-4, 6-4. Shiras bt Green 6-7, 7-6, 6-4. Van't Hof bt Edwards 7-6, 6-4. Pate bt Moir 6-4, 5-7, 6-4. Zivojinovic bt Amritraj 6-7, 7-5, 6-1. Denton bt Kratzmann 6-4, 3-6, 6-3. Steyn bt Leach 6-3, 6-1. Becker bt Kruger 6-1, 7-6. Stefanki bt Houston 6-4, 6-3. Acuna bt Wood 6-2, 6-4. Freeman bt Davis 6-4, 6-3. Krishnan bt Reekie 6-3, 6-2. Fleming bt Odizor 7-6, 6-4. Hooper bt Teacher 7-6, 4-6, 6-3. Mayotte bt Stansbury 7-6, 7-6.

Third round
Anger bt De Palmer 6-3, 7-6. Shiras bt Van't Hof 7-5, 3-6, 6-0. Zivojinovic bt Pate 6-4, 6-4. Denton bt Steyn 6-4, 6-3. Becker bt Stefanki 6-7, 6-3, 7-5. Acuna bt Freeman 2-6, 6-0, 6-4. Krishnan bt Fleming 7-5, 6-4. Mayotte bt Hooper 6-4, 7-6.

Quarterfinals
Anger bt Shiras 1-6, 7-6, 6-4. Denton bt Zivojinovic 7-6, 6-4. Becker bt Acuna 5-7, 6-3, 7-5. Mayotte bt Krishnan 2-6, 6-2, 6-3.

Semifinals
Denton bt Anger 6-3, 7-6
Mayotte bt Becker 3-6, 7-5, 6-4

Final
Mayotte bt Denton 7-6, 6-0.

DOUBLES

Semifinals
G Layendecker & B Schultz bt J Sevelly & S Wood 4-6, 7-6, 6-4
C Hooper & T Wilkison bt B Manson & R Green 6-2, 6-3

Final
Hooper & Wilkison bt Layendecker & Schultz 8-6 (pro set)

LADIES' SINGLES

First round
A Hulbert bt S Schenk 6-2, 6-4. T Holladay bt V Binns 6-2, 6-3. B Borneo bt S Goodman 6-0, 6-1. M Brown bt J Reeves 6-3, 6-2. R Bryant bt M Reinach 6-3, 6-4. J Golder bt M Quinlan 6-4, 6-4. W White bt D Schauerman 6-0, 6-3. B Norton bt B Perry 6-4, 6-2. K McDaniel bt S Timms 6-1, 6-1. T Mochizuki bt S Nicholson 6-7, 6-4, 7-5. M Groat bt J Langstaff 7-6, 6-4. B Gerken bt B Welt 6-1, 6-0. G Kim bt J Salmon 6-3, 6-2. K Kinney bt M Parun 6-2, 6-1. S Rimes bt K Huebner 6-2, 6-0, A Brown bt R Seeman 6-1, 6-3. B Mould bt B Cordwell 6-4, 7-5. S Reeves bt J Tacon 6-4, 6-3. J Louis bt S Sullivan 6-2, 6-7, 7-5. R Uys bt K Brown 6-3, 6-1.

Second round
S Graf bt Hulbert 6-2, 0-6, 6-1. Holladay bt D Parnell 6-3, 6-2. Borneo bt S Amiach 6-1, 6-0. R White bt Brown w/o. A Croft bt Bryant 6-4, 6-3. White bt Goluer 6-0, 6-4. Norton bt McDaniel 6-2, 7-6. M Mesker bt Mochizuki 3-6, 7-5, 7-5. A Henricksson bt Groat 6-2, 6-1. L Jones bt Gerken 6-3, 6-4. Kim bt L Geeves 6-1, 4-6, 6-0. D Balestrat bt Kinney 6-2, 6-4. S Mascarin bt Rimes 7-5, 2-6, 6-4. Mould bt Brown 5-7, 6-4, 6-4. Reeves bt Louis 4-6, 6-4, 6-4. B Potter bt Uys 7-6, 6-2.

Third round
Graf bt Holladay 7-6, 7-5. R White bt Borneo 6-2, 7-5. Croft bt W White 7-6, 6-4. Mesker bt Norton 7-6, 7-5. Henricksson bt Jones 6-2, 7-6. Balestrat bt Kim 6-3, 6-0. Mould bt Mascarin 7-5, 6-2. Potter bt Reeves 6-1, 6-1.

Quarterfinals
R White bt Graf w/o. Croft bt Mesker 6-1, 6-0. Balestrat bt Henricksson 6-3, 6-0. Potter bt Mould 6-3, 6-2.

Semifinals
Croft bt R White 6-2, 6-2. Potter bt Balestrat 6-3, 6-3.

Final
Potter bt Croft 7-6, 4-6, 6-3.

DOUBLES

Semifinals
D Balestrat & T Holladay bt A Henricksson & M Mesker 2-6, 7-5, 6-2
T Phelps & S Mascarin bt B Mould & R White 7-5, 6-3

Final
Balestrat & Holladay bt Phelps & Mascarin 6-3, 6-3.

BATES KEEPS HIS TITLE

BY REGINALD BRACE: THE YORKSHIRE POST

It is fair to say that Jeremy Bates's rise to the august heights of being named the LTA's Player of the Year began at the GMC Northern tournament at Manchester. The event had a bit of everything: roasting sunshine, torrential rain, heroes of the Sixties and Seventies airing their mature skills in an over-35s event and today's aspirants for stardom warming up for Wimbledon.

But most of all it had Bates winning the men's title for the second consecutive year and clinching his Davis Cup debut against Portugal the following week. "I couldn't have done any more to get picked" he said — a sentiment with which Paul Hutchins, national team manager, agreed.

Bates did not waste his Davis Cup chance. He performed with distinction in the promotion run which brought victories over Portugal, Switzerland and Israel. In tournaments he did well at Bristol, and became the British closed champion at Telford.

Manchester's importance was that Jeremy maintained the impetus he built up in winning the British satellite circuit and showed the discipline to justify his Davis Cup breakthrough. He looked like a competitor who was at last beginning to believe in himself.

Despite the fact that he was the defending titleholder at the Northern, Bates was unseeded. All the seeding positions went to players higher than himself on the ATP computer, with Australia's Peter Doohan and the American Jay Lapidus occupying first and second places.

Bates had a world ranking of 258 when he went into the tournament but he defeated Russell Simpson of New Zealand (102), the New Yorker Marc Flur (97) and Florida's Dan Cassidy (86) in an impressive run which made him the first British player to win the tournament in successive years since the late Mike Sangster (1962-63).

Another young British prospect, Nick Fulwood, enjoyed a satisfactory tournament in which he defeated Tom Warneke, conqueror of the top seeded Doohan, and the volatile Argentinean Roberto Saad before falling victim to Bates — player of the week and ultimately Player of the Year.

The women's singles was relatively mundane although it produced a spirited final in which Yvonne Vermaak of South Africa beat Australia's Elizabeth Minter in three sets. Manchester, with its admirably progressive officials, needs to look at the declining appeal of its women's event which was once unequalled in the North.

Because of the infuriating weather it was difficult to pass judgement on the experiment of introducing a men's over-35 event as a tournament within a tournament. That the Northern received value for money from these golden oldies was indisputable.

Mark Cox, Roger Taylor, Nikki Pilic, Jan Kodes, Ray Moore, Colin Dibley, Owen Davidson and Tom Okker did their stuff both on court and off it in terms of mingling and co-operating with sponsors.

But it was fairly ironic that the over-35s prize money of £24,000 was £7,000 more than the combined total for the men's and women's singles, with the winner — Kodes after saving a match

Russell Simpson

point against Davidson in the final — receiving £5,000 as against Bates's first of £2,000.

Tour director David Whitehead had no qualms about the imbalance. "Don't forget that every member of our group must have won a Grand Slam title, been a national No. 1 or competed in the Davis Cup at the highest level," he said.

"They bring back to tennis all the things we used to appreciate: manners, style and enjoyment of the game. Quality. These guys are competitive but they have a camaraderie off court which is quite something."

Put these charismatic veterans into the main draw and they would not have survived for long against more youthful opponents. Pitched against each other they rekindled memories of days when tennis was not quite the hard-nosed business it is today.

It was a nostalgic facet of a GMC tournament which managed to succeed despite a week when too much was seen of duckboards, gloves and anoraks.

GMC MANCHESTER TOURNAMENT

Manchester,

June 3-8

MEN'S SINGLES

First round

T Warneke bt C Emery 6-2, 6-3. N Fulwood bt S Abdullahi 6-1, 6-3. C Clarke bt J Howarth 6-7, 7-6, 7-5. M Walker bt A Simcox 6-4, 6-4. C Fancutt bt S Botfield 6-2, 6-1. G Michibata D Ison 6-4, 6-2. D Maasdorp bt A Hellinger 6-2, 6-3. Heron bt P Moore 6-2, 6-1. E Akel bt D Shaw 6-3, 7-5. B Knapp bt P Russell 6-3, 6-3. D Johnson bt D Felgate 5-7, 6-3, 6-2. S Ickringill bt P Hugheman 7-6, 6-3. V Levine bt M Masencamp 3-6, 6-2, 6-3. M Robinson bt S Sammel 4-6, 6-3, 6-3. A Burrow bt S Tucker 6-2, 6-3. B Talbot bt C Kermode 6-0, 6-3.

Second round

Warneke bt P Doohan 7-6, 6-4. Fulwood bt Dunk 6-4, 6-0. J Turpin bt C Clarke 6-3, 7-5. R Saad bt Walker 6-3, 6-4. M Flur bt Fancutt 6-7, 6-3, 6-4. Michibata bt C Stroue 3-6, 7-6, 8-6. J Bates bt Massdorp 7-5, 6-2. R Simpson bt Heron 7-5, 6-3. J Frawley bt Akel 6-3, 6-7, 6-4. Knapp bt C Peet 6-2, 6-2. J Turner bt Johnson 6-3, 7-5. D Cassidy bt Ickringill 6-5, 6-2. S McCain bt Levine 6-4, 6-4. Fancutt bt Robinson 6-1, 6-1. D Stone bt Burrow 7-5, 7-6. J Lapidus 6-4, 6-4.

Third Round

Fulwood bt Warneke 6-4, 6-3. Saad bt Turpin 6-7, 6-3, 6-4. Flur bt Michibata 6-4, 6-3. Bates bt Simpson 4-6, 6-4, 6-2. Frawley bt Knapp 6-3, 6-2. Cassidy bt Turner 6-4, 7-6. McCain bt Fancutt 3-6, 6-1, 6-3. Lapidus bt Stone 6-4, 6-4.

Quarter-finals

Fulwood bt Saad 6-4, 5-7, 6-2. Bates bt Flur 6-4, 6-7, 6-2. Cassidy bt Frawley 6-2, 2-6, 6-2. Lapidus bt McCain 6-3, 6-2.

Semifinals

Bates bt Fulwood 6-4, 6-2.
Cassidy bt Lapidus 6-3, 6-1.

Final

Bates bt Cassidy 6-4, 6-2.

DOUBLES

Final

J Lapidus & B Levine bt J Nates & N Fulwood 6-3, 6-4.

LADIES SINGLES

First round

Y Vermaak bt L Gracie 6-1, 6-4. D Castillejo bt J Davis w/o. V Lake bt K Brown w/o. H Crowe bt B Niemeyer 7-5, 6-3. L Spain-Short bt L McConnell 6-0, 6-1. J Griffiths bt C Jones 6-2, 4-6, 6-4. J Went bt L Bakewell 6-2, 6-3. S Leo bt M Colville w/o. K Steinmetz bt L Pennington 6-1, 6-2. P Hy bt A Watson 6-1, 6-2. L Ristic bt J Paterson w/o. H Luscombe bt M Brown w/o. N Sato bt D Ladig 6-2, 6-1. M Redfearn bt R Bryant w/o. B Remilton bt S Bennett 6-2, 6-2. E Minter bt M Gracie 6-0, 6-0.

Second round

Vermaak bt Castillejo w/o. Crowe bt Lake 6-4, 6-7, 6-0. Spain-Short bt Griffiths 6-3, 6-4. Leo bt Went 6-0, 6-2. Steinmetz bt Hy 4-6, 6-3, 6-3. Luscombe bt Ristic 6-1, 6-0. Redfearn bt Sato 6-4, 4-6, 9-7. Minter bt R Remilton 6-2, 6-4.

Quarter-finals

Vermaak bt Crowe 6-4, 6-1. Spain-Short bt Leo 3-6, 6-1, 6-4. Steinmetz bt Luscombe 6-0, 6-4. Minter bt Redfearn 6-2, 6-4.

Semifinals

Vermaak bt Spain-Short 6-4, 7-5.
Minter bt Steinmetz 6-4, 6-3;

Final

Vermaak bt Minter 6-2, 5-7, 6-2.

DOUBLES

Final

B Remilton & K Sato led S Leo & E Minter 6-4, 1-0, abandoned.

BECKERMANIA IS BORN

BY BARRY NEWCOMBE: SUNDAY EXPRESS

Beckermania began at Queen's Club. So often the Stella Artois Championship has propelled its winners onwards to Wimbledon and further glory. It happened again with Boris Becker.

Prior to the Stella Artois, Becker had been beaten early at Beckenham. He was no higher than 11th seed at Queen's where Jimmy Connors, Kevin Curren, Pat Cash, and Johan Kriek led the rankings. But Becker came through the 64-strong field on a wave of confidence. He had to beat Cash and Kriek on the way to the title. And in a foretaste of Wimbledon he avoided men whose reputation might have overwhelmed him.

Becker blew white hot for a month. That is why he won at Queen's and why he was able to use that as a launch pad for Wimbledon. It was a month which turned his potential into fulfilment and if you were within listening distance of his opponents in the last days at Queen's Club you would have been convinced that Becker was the man for Wimbledon.

As Kriek observed after being beaten 6-2 6-3 in the final: "If he plays the way he did today, no one can beat him on grass. I have one of the best service returns in the game and I never had a chance to get to the ball. If he plays like that every day he can win Wimbledon."

Another much-travelled competitor, Paul McNamee, was flattened by Becker in the semi-finals and made similar observations on the Wimbledon prospects of the 17-year-old Becker. All this added to the evidence of our own eyes showed that a great champion was emerging.

At the start of the Stella Artois there was further evidence that a great champion was on the way down. Connors, who had been punching his way around the grass courts of England with distinction for 14 summers, found himself bundled out in the first round by a qualifier ranked 127th in the world.

Connors' come-uppance came at the hands of Mike DePalmer of Tennessee, an unsung tradesman of the circuit whose win over the three-time champion of Queen's Club could have hinged on two factors. First, DePalmer had learned that same day that he was a direct entry into Wimbledon. Second, Connors had been scraping around for adequate practice in London's bad weather and was out of trim.

Whatever, DePalmer came running hotter than Connors and beat him 7-5 6-3, giving Connors only his third first round beating in a three year period. Jimbo was so disconsolate afterwards that he talked of returning home to the U.S.A. and missing Wimbledon. In the end he did neither.

John McEnroe had decided not to play at Queen's Club. So had Ivan Lendl. This simply meant that the first prize of £25,437 was open to a wider field and Connors' departure stretched the options still further.

The crowds were larger than ever. But those expecting to see the British players make an impact were disappointed. Nick Fulwood lost in the first round to Slobodan Zivojinovic (and what a year on grass he was due to have) and John Lloyd fell in the second round to Wojtek Fibak. Britain's other leading players were absent on Davis Cup duty.

Mike DePalmer

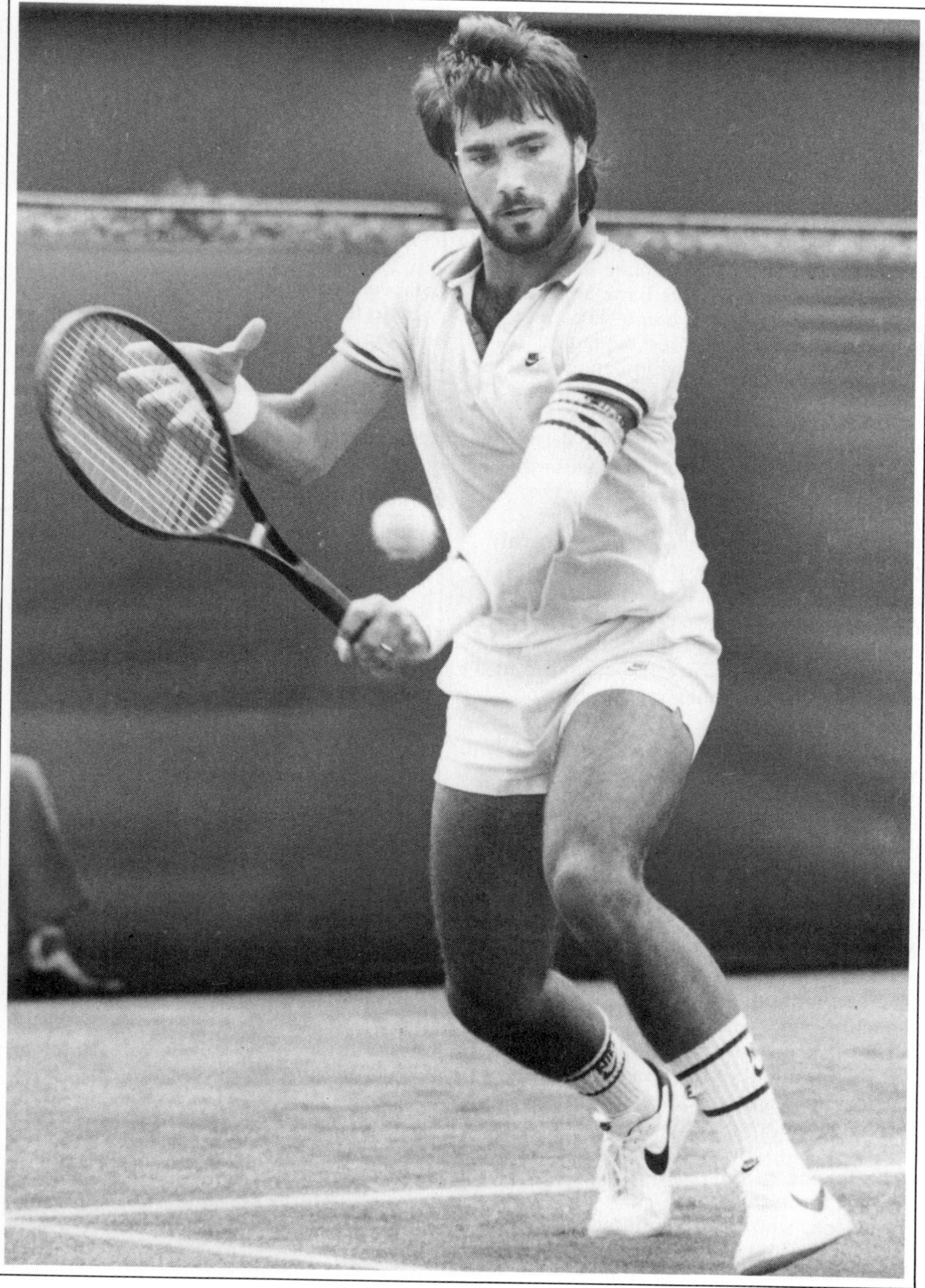

Fibak was the only player in the last 16 who did not have a natural grass court game. The other contenders all knew their way around on grass. Americans and Australians abounded. The Australians included the 20-year-old Pat Cash who had been suffering with a back injury for the previous three months.

In his first match at Queen's Club against Peter Doohan, another Australian, Cash hurt his back again. But in the last 16 Cash came through a long and demanding three set match with Mark Edmondson which suggested that his recovery was beginning. In the quarter finals he had to face Becker — and the West German won 6-4 6-4.

The other pairings in the last eight were: McNamee against Tim Mayotte; Russell Simpson v Kriek; Zivojinovic v Paul Annacone. Mayotte, who had rarely failed to play well on grass, looked a solid bet at this point and so did Annacone, who had played with resilience and concentration to defeat the second seeded Curren 6-7 7-6 8-6 in one of the tournament's most engaging contents.

But the quarter finals produced four straight sets victories. McNamee upstaged Mayotte, earning a match with Becker, Kriek had few difficulties with Simpson, and Zivojinovic came out of a first set tie break against Annacone to win the second set 6-1.

Becker needed 65 minutes to beat McNamee 6-1 6-4. Becker's cause was helped by the fact that McNamee served ten double faults — "The sun was upsetting me," said McNamee — but the West German was crisp and efficient.

"I think 'Bobo' (Zivojinovic) serves harder but Boris is right up there with them, he has tremendous potential," observed McNamee afterwards. "It's good for the game to see a guy like that coming through."

Kriek, who beat Zivojinovic 6-4 6-4, had the credentials to test Becker in the final. Twice champion of Australia, Kriek is one of the fastest movers in the game. He had taken a four week rest to prepare for Wimbledon. Against Becker he fancied his chances.

But Becker ran hot in the final. Watched by his parents, who had flown in without his knowledge to join the packed crowd which saw a star emerge, Becker hammered in 11 aces on the way to victory.

The aces were part of a comprehensive win. His court craft, his pace to the ball, his range of shot, his adaptability under fire all pointed out that Becker was of champion quality. The funny thing was that even this effort was not enough to win Becker a seeded place at Wimbledon. And look how he made everyone suffer for that.

Johan Kriek

Pat Cash

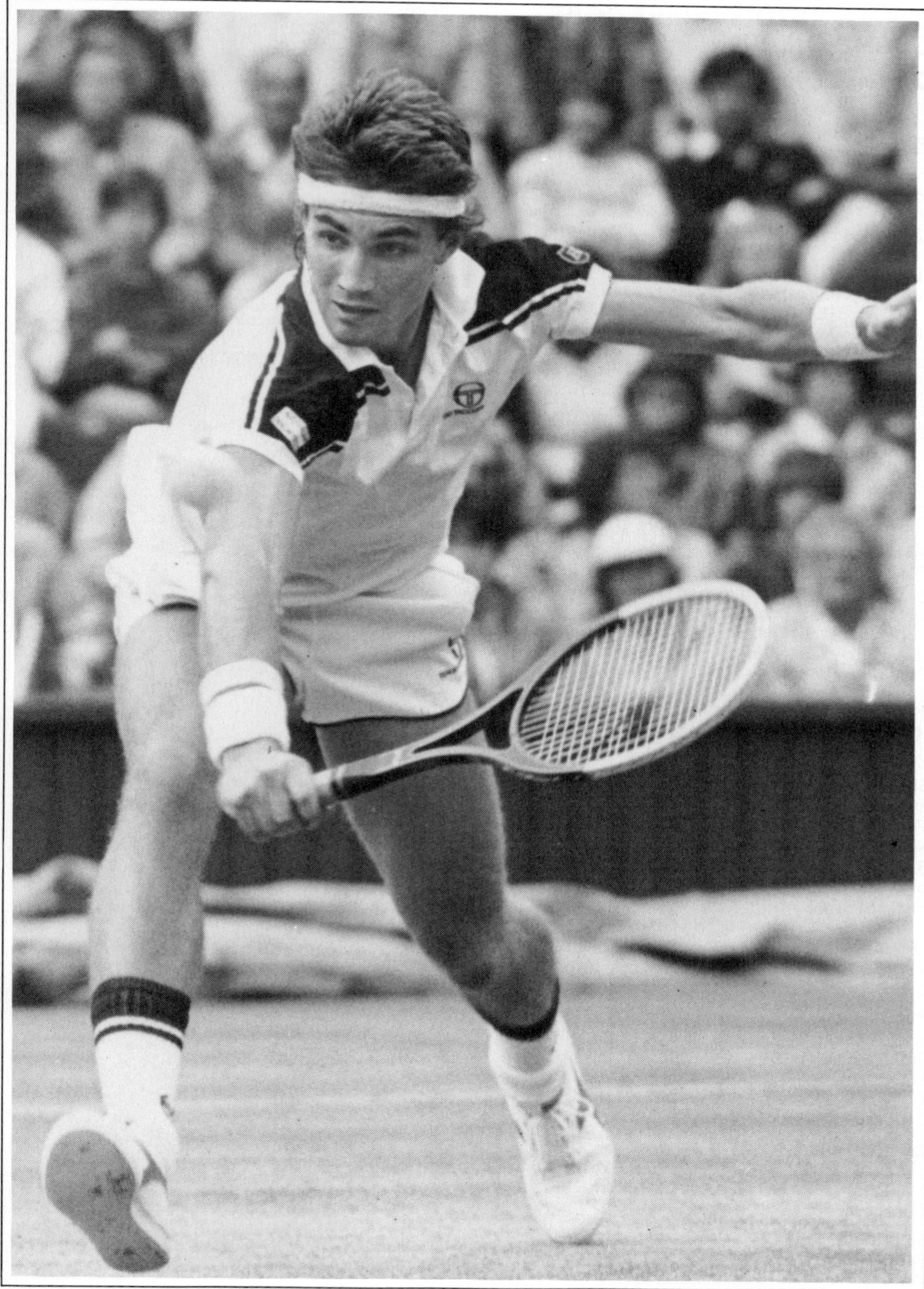

STELLA ARTOIS GRASS COURT CHAMPIONSHIPS

Queen's Club, London

June 10th-16th

SINGLES

First round

M DePalmer (US) bt J Conners (US) 7-7, 6-3. W Masur (Aus) bt M Davis (US) 7-6, 7-5. P McNamee (Aus) bt C Hooper (US) 6-1, 6-4. S Giammalva (US) bt S Meister (US) 6-1, 6-1. W Fibak (Pol) bt M Leach (US) 3-6, 7-6, 9-6. J Lloyd bt M Mitchell (US) 6-2, 6-3. Tom Gullikson (US) bt J Lapidus (US) 6-4, 7-6. T Mayotte (US) bt C Motta (Bzl) 4-6, 6-1, 6-1. P Cash (Aus) bt P Doohan (Aus) 6-3, 7-6. V Amritraj (Ind) bt L Bourne (US) 6-1, 6-4. M Edmondson (Aus) bt M Flur (US) 6-1, 6-1. C Lewis (NZ) bt G Holmes (US) 5-7, 6-2, 6-3. B Becker (WG) bt T Nelson (US) 7-6, 7-5. D Cassidy (US) bt D Visser (SA) 7-6, 4-6, 6-4. L Stefanki (US) bt S Denton (US) 6-1, 7-6. D Pate (US) bt C Van Rensburg (SA) 7-5, 6-7, 6-3. J Fitzgerald (Aus) bt S Davis (US) 7-5, 6-3. E Edwards (SA) bt P Fleming (US) 6-4, 3-6, 6-1. R Simpson (NZ) bt J Canter (US) 4-6, 6-3, 13-11. L Shiras (US) bt T Moor (US) 6-4, 7-5. R Krishnan (Ind) bt B Moir (SA) 6-1, 6-4. M Bauer (US) bt J Frawley (Aus) 7-5, 6-4. M Ostaja (Yug) bt R Harmon (US) 6-4, 7-6. J Kriek (US) bt T Cain (US) 4-6, 6-0, 6-1. H Leconte (Fra) bt J Turpin (US) 6-3, 6-2. S Zivojinovic (Yug) bt N Fulwood 6-1, 6-4. F Gonzales (Par) bt G Forget (Fra) 4-6, 6-3, 14-12. R Acuna (Chile) bt B Testerman (US) 5-7, 6-2. P Annacone (US) bt D Odizor (Nig) 6-1, 6-7, 6-4. T Wilkison (US) bt B Teacher (US) 7-6, 7-6. H Pfister (US) bt R Green (US) 6-3, 7-6. K Curren (US) bt J Sadri (US) 6-4, 6-4.

Second round

DePalmer bt Masur 7-6, 7-5. McNamee bt Giammalva 6-1, 6-2. Fibak bt Lloyd 7-6, 6-3. Mayotte bt Tom Gullikson 7-6, 7-6. Cash bt Amritraj 6-2, 6-3. Edmondson bt Lewis 6-7, 7-6, 6-4. Becker bt Cassidy 6-4, 7-6. Pate bt Stefanki 4-6, 6-1, 6-4. Fitzgerald bt Edwards 6-1, 7-6. Simpson bt Shiras 6-7, 6-1, 6-3. Krishnan bt Bauer 6-4, 6-4. Kriek bt Ostaja 6-4, 6-4. Zivojinovic bt Leconte 6-4, 6-4. Acuna bt Gonzales 6-4, 6-2. Annacone bt Wilkison 6-4, 5-7, 8-6. Curren bt Pfister 7-5, 7-6.

Third round

McNamee bt DePalmer 6-2, 7-6. Mayotte bt Fibak 6-0, 6-4. Cash bt Edmondson 7-6, 4-6, 10-8. Becker bt Pate 6-4, 6-7, 6-3. Simpson bt Fitzgerald 6-4, 7-6. Kriek bt Krishnan 6-3, 6-3. Zivojinovic bt Acuna 6-2, 6-4. Annacone bt Curren 6-7, 7-6, 8-6.

Quarterfinals

McNamee bt Mayotte 7-6, 7-5. Becker bt Cash 6-4, 6-4. Kriek bt Simpson 6-4, 7-6. Zivojinovic bt Annacone 7-6, 6-1.

Semifinals

Becker bt McNamee 6-1, 6-4.
Kriek bt Zivojinovic 6-4, 6-4.

Final

Becker bt Kriek 6-2, 6-3.

DOUBLES

Quarterfinals

Flach & Seguso bt Edmondson & Warwick 4-6, 6-4, 12-10. Donnelly & Wilkison bt Dowlen & Odizor 6-3, 6-7, 6-3. Amritraj & Lloyd bt Fernandez & Soares 6-7, 7-6, 6-4. Cash & Fitzgerald bt McNamara & McNamee 6-3, 6-4.

Semifinals

Flach & Seguso bt Donnelly & Wilkison 6-2, 7-6
Cash & Fitzgerald bt Amritraj & Lloyd 2-6, 6-2, 9-7.

Final

Flach & Seguso bt Cash & Fitzgerald 3-6, 6-3, 16-14.

SINGLES WINNERS SINCE 1977

1977 R Ramirez (Mexico)
1978 A D Roche (Australia)
1979 J P McEnroe (US)
1980 J P McEnroe (US)
1981 J P McEnroe (US)
1982 J S Connors (US)
1983 J S Connors (US)
1984 J P McEnroe (US)

HAPPY RETURN FOR SHRIVER

BY BILL EDWARDS

Pam Shriver

When Pam Shriver marked up a second notch on the Edgbaston Cup in the run-up to Wimbledon last June it had a special significance for the tall lass from Baltimore. It was the first time in a career, which saw her runner-up to Chris Lloyd in the US Open final of 1978 (at the age of 16), that she had successfully defended a title.

More than that, her victory worked out at a pound a second. That was the break-down of her £16,800 cheque for her five matches, which finished with a 6-1, 6-0 humiliation of Betsy Nagelsen in the final.

This is a tremendous rate of earning and it is to be hoped it will encourage her to come back and bid for the '''hat-trick.'' it was the third straight tournament win for Pam, the other two being in Australia from whence she came to Birmingham.

Although all the rounds were won in straight sets it was the final which was most devastating. Poor Betsy must have wondered what hit her as she was dismissed in a mere 43 minutes. It was all so disappointing for the crowd who had expected more from two attacking players.

Yet, there was no indication of such a walkover when Pam, who had experienced considerable trouble with her service throughout the week, double faulted to be 0-30.

Pam's serve suddenly clicked and out rolled the aces. She dropped only five more points on her service in the match, the last two being in the second set. The one consolation for Miss Nagelsen was that she had made the final unseeded and a cheque for £8,000 helped to soften the blow.

Anne Hobbs, once again last British representative, was the quarter final victim of Miss Shriver, beaten 6-4, 6-0. Anne had been well in contention until the tenth game when, taking a return, she struck her knee a heavy blow. She cried out sharply and never won another game as she hobbled through the rest of the match.

Anne refused to offer this as an excuse but did say: "I made a mistake of thinking about my opponent when I was 3-2 up. I guess I pressed too hard."

In the semi-finals, Pam beat an old school chum from Baltimore in Elise Burgin 6-4, 6-2. Not one to mince her words, Pam was fined in this match for an audible obscenity, then joked with the umpire that it was her description of a particular shot.

The British girls claimed five places in the draw and marked up three first round wins, but Miss Hobbs who beat Amanda Brown 6-2, 6-0 was the only one to progress further. Anne's best performance was in the third round with a 6-3, 7-5 win over the seeded Ros Fairbank, of South Africa.

Brown did well to win 6-3, 6-3 against Beth Herr (U.S.A.) before running into Miss Hobbs, while Jo Durie promised to get off that icy slide that was taking her down the rankings, with a 1-6, 6-2, 6-1 over that tough South African Yvonne Vermaak, who has upset so many higher ranked players in her career and was indeed runner-up to Billie Jean King in the inaugural Edgbaston Cup of 1982.

Most encouraging was the way Miss Durie fought back after losing that first set and trailing 0-2 in the second. Certainly it was a performance to lighten the gloom of the rain that interrupted the match in the second set and the cold which had the players in track suits.

The following day it all turned sour with Jo losing 6-4, 7-6 to Marcella Mesker of Holland. Jo tried hard to save that second set but was eventually beaten 11-9 in the tie break.

The appearance of Annabel Croft was short-lived as she succumbed 6-3, 7-5 to Susan Mascarin, while Sara Gomer lost 6-4, 3-6, 6-3 to Elizabeth Minter of Australia.

Seeding all went hay wire, Elizabeth Smylie and Sharon Walsh falling at the first hurdle. Alycia Moulton was the only seed from the bottom half to reach the last eight where she fell 7-6, 6-4 to Miss Mascarin who had already dismissed the 10th seed Anne Minter.

The tournament marked the introduction to grass for Gabriela Sabatini, the dazzling young Argentinian holder of the world junior title. She cried off from the singles after early practice then partnered her countrywoman Mercedes Paz in the doubles only to lose to Beverley Mould and Paula Smith in the first round.

The Edgbaston Priory Club provided a fine setting for a tournament of this type but it was a pity there was not greater support from local fans. Maybe they expect more of the bigger names but many were saving themselves for Eastbourne the following week.

The contract for the tournament comes up for renewal this year and although a new sponsor, Dow Chemical, has come in for 1986, the LTA will no doubt be giving serious thought to the future.

EDGBASTON CUP

Edgbaston Priory Club

June 10th-16th

SINGLES

First round

C Jolissaint (Swi) bt N Dias (Arg) 7-5, 6-2. M Mesker (Neth) bt E Inoue (Jap) 6-3, 7-5. J Durie bt Y Vermaak (SA) 1-6, 6-2, 6-1. A Brown bt B Herr (US) 6-3, 6-3. A Hobbs bt E Eliseenko (USSR) 6-2, 6-1. W White (US) bt H Ludloff (US) 7-5, 6-1. L Drescher (Swi) bt C Vanier (Fr). B Gerken (US) bt L McNeil (US) 6-3, 6-1. R White (US) bt L Savchenko (USSR) 4-6, 6-1, 6-4. C Benjamin (US) bt S Cherneva (USSR) 6-3, 7-6. R Uys (SA) bt M Brown (US) 3-6, 6-3, 6-4. E Minter (Aus) bt S Gomer 6-4, 3-6, 6-3. S Mascarin (US) bt H Kelesi (Can) 6-1, 7-5. K Skronska (Cz) bt J Mundel (SA) 6-2, 6-2. A Minter (Aus) bt G Kim (IS) 6-2, 5-7, 8-6. T Mochizuki (US) bt M Calleja (Arg) 7-6, 6-3. K Kinney (US) bt M Paz (Arg) 6-3, 6-4. M L Piatek (US) bt S Collins (US) 6-4, 6-3. A White (US) bt G Rush (US) 6-3, 6-4. A Henricksson (US) bt K Sands (US) 7-6, 6-7, 6-2. T Holladay (US) bt E Smylie (Aus) 6-1, 6-3. B Mould (SA) bt S Walsh-Pete 3-6, 6-0, 7-5. K Shaefer (US) bt S Amiach (Fr) 6-4, 3-6, 6-0. B Nagelsen (US) bt M Yanagi (Jap) 5-7 6-0, 6-4.

Second round

P Shriver (US) bt Jolissaint 6-3, 6-4. Mesker bt Durie 6-4, 7-6. Hobbs bt Brown 6-2, 6-0. R Fairbank (SA) bt W White 1-6, 6-3, 6-1. Drescher bt V Ruzici (Rom) 3-1, retd. White bt Gerken 6-4, 6-4. Benjamin bt Uys 6-4, 6-4. E Burgin (US) bt Minter 6-3, 7-6. Mascarin bt A Croft 6-3, 7-5. Minter bt Skronska 4-6, 6-4, 6-1. Kinney bt Mochizuki 7-5, 6-1. A Moulton (US) bt Piatek 6-2, 6-1. D Balestrat (Aus) bt A White 7-5, 6-3. Henricksson bt Holladay 6-4, 6-2. Shaefer bt Mould 6-2, 6-3. Nagelsen bt P Casale (US) 6-2, 6-2.

Third round

Shriver bt Mesker 6-1, 6-3. Hobbs bt Fairbank 6-3, 7-5. White bt Drescher 6-4, 6-0. Burgin bt Benjamin 6-3, 6-7. Mascarin bt Minter 6-2, 6-4. Moulton bt Kinney 6-2, 6-3. Henricksson bt Balestrat 7-6, 6-4. Nagelsen bt Shaefer 7-5, 6-3.

Quarterfinals

Shriver bt Hobbs 6-4, 6-0. Burgin bt White 6-7, 6-4, 6-4. Mascarin bt Moulton 7-6, 6-4. Nagelsen bt Henricksson 6-3, 6-3.

Semifinals

Shriver bt Burgin 6-4, 6-2
Nagelsen bt Mascarin 3-6, 7-5, 6-4

Final

Shriver bt Nagelsen 6-1, 6-0

DOUBLES

Quarterfinals

Hetherington & Rush bt Cherneva & Savchenko 4-6, 6-3, 7-5. Burgin & Moulton bt Casale & Mascarin 6-4, 3-6, 6-3. Holladay & Walsh-Pete bt Henricksson & Leo 5-7, 6-1, 6-3. Fairbank & Hobbs bt Mould & P Smith 3-6, 6-4, 6-2.

Semifinals

Burgin & Moulton bt Hetherington & Rush 7-6, 6-2
Holladay & Walsh-Pete bt Fairbank & Hobbs 6-4, 1-6, 6-3

Final

Holladay & Walsh-Pete bt Burgin & Moulton 6-4, 5-7, 6-3

SINGLES RECORD

1982 B J King (US)
1983 B J King (US)
1984 P Shriver (US)

DOUBLES RECORD

1982 J Durie & A Hobbs (GB)
1983 B J King & S Walsh (US)
1984 L Allen & W White (US)

THE OUTDOOR-INDOOR CHAMP

BY NEIL HARMAN: THE DAILY MAIL

The only audible applause to greet Marty Davis's first tennis championship success in Britain came from six of us perched on a wooden form. Several more people displayed their appreciation, but as they were standing behind windows separating the court from a lounge bar, it was noiseless.

If all of this seems a trifle peculiar, let me try to explain. Davis, a personable, cheerful Californian, became the LTA West of England grass court champion by playing the final on the Supreme surface of David Lloyd's Racket Club alongside Heathrow Airport.

Bristol, its courts waterlogged, its workmen exhausted, its patience almost at breaking point, had to be stripped of actually staging it's own final. The rains which fell constantly during the week before Wimbledon caused the shift of emphasis from the special techniques of grass, to the sweatier, more eerie confines of indoor tennis.

Davis, to his enormous credit, triumphed — although there could be no denying the enormous sense of anti-climax at the end of the tournament.

Four journalists and a couple of female spectators hardly constitutes an overwhelming reception for a champion. But Davis did not let such a lack of response detract from his delight at winning. In the final, hurriedly arranged with David Lloyd's good grace and facilities, Davis beat fellow American Glenn Layendecker 4-6, 6-3, 7-5 in a match notable for its immaculate spirit and behaviour.

Quite what John McEnroe might have made of a constantly humming fan, the lack of ball boys, appreciation and atmosphere, one is almost too petrified to imagine. Davis and Layendecker, accepting that there was nowhere else to go, played the game in an unfashionably sportsmanlike manner.

The winner, who has been playing the tournaments of the world since his 'teens without great success, acknowledged that it could prove a turning point. Almost as importantly, he enjoyed it. "I haven't played in many finals, and I didn't really care if it had to be switched here or to the Falkland Islands, I was just delighted to win it," he said.

"Of course we had to adapt to the surroundings and approach the game in a far different manner than had we been playing on grass. But I think Glenn was a great sport. A few calls were debatable but we decided to make a go of the final. It's the least we could do. The sportsmanship was of the very highest level."

If Bristol (or should I say Heston) was primarily the story of the Davis, Layendecker final, it did possess a warming British success story for the West Country tennis public. Jeremy Bates celebrated his 23rd birthday during the tournament by announcing his ability to stand tall in the very highest company.

He arrived in Bristol having triumphed in his Davis Cup debut singles against Portugal. On the Tuesday afternoon, he beat two Americans Scott McCain and Ken Flach with a touch of disdain which was glorious to see. Bates was eventually to succumb in a brilliant quarter final to the champion-elect, but

Marty Davis

that afternoon was one rich in promise and notable for the Englishman's ability to maintain tennis of an outstanding quality.

His serve, especially, was sure and he has that ability to turn a point with strokes utterly disguised but perfectly executed. In the end, against the more explosive Davis, his fatique mental and physical, was apparent.

If there was British triumph, there was a hint of sorrow for the prospects of the future of the tournament itself. The torrential rains, the meagre support of players from the highest echelons and the lack of a sponsorship all contrived to make the LTA look long and hard at the suitability of maintaining Bristol's place on the calendar.

They invested £170,000 into the tournament — only to see it messed around by appalling weather. "Players also want to be sure of grass court practice before Wimbledon," said tournament director Mike Sertin, "and can pick and choose what to do. That makes it extremely difficult to find sponsors. There must come a time when we will have to look seriously and ask if enough is enough?"

That will not come until after this years' championship which I, for one, hope will attract a sponsor willing to commit themselves to more than just a single week of expense. Bristol possesses excellent hospitality, surroundings and charm. It would be a shocking waste to lose those qualities from British tennis.

WEST OF ENGLAND CHAMPIONSHIPS

BRISTOL, June 17th-22nd

SINGLES

First round

H Leconte (Fra) bye G Ocleppo (It) bt C Hooper (US) 7-6, 6-2. R Knapp (US) bt D Visser (SA) 6-3, 7-6. M Bauer (US) bye P Doohan (Aus) bye L Bourne (US) bt B Derlin (NZ) 4-6, 6-4, 6-4. T O Gullikson (US) bt R Osterthun (WG) 7-5, 6-2. L Stefanki (US) bye T Wilkison (US) bye W Popp (WG) bt S Bale 6-2, 6-3. N Odizor (Nig) bt D Campos (Spa) 4-6, 6-3, 6-4. L Shiras (US) bye T Benhabiles (Fra) bye G Layendecker (US) bt E Edwards (SA) 7-6, 1-6, 9-7. B Schultz (US) bt M Edmondson (Aus) 4-6, 7-6, 6-4. R Green (US) bye B Teacher (US) bye T Nelson (US) bt R Simpson (NZ) 1-6, 6-4, 6-3. B Drewett (Aus) bt P Johnson (US). 6-4, 6-3. M Flur (US) bye J Lapidus (US) bye T Gullikson (US) bt S Zivojinovic (Yug) 2-6, 7-6, 6-4. S Meister (US) bt D Cassidy (US) 6-1, 61. C Forget (Fra) bye M Davis (US) bye W Masur (Aus) bt I Kley (US) 6-3, 3-6, 12-10. J Frawley (Aus) bt G Barbosa (Arg) 4-6, 7-5, 6-3. H Pfister (US) bye K Flach (US) bye J Bates bt S McCain (US) 6-3, 6-4. H Van Boeckel (Neth) bt S Shaw 6-3, 6-2. T Moor (US) bye.

Second round

Leconte bt Ocleppo 6-3, 6-2. Knapp bt Bauer 6-7, 6-3, 6-2. Doohan bt Bourne 6-1, 7-6. Stefanki bt Tom Gullikson 3-6, 7-6, 6-4. Wilkison bt Popp 6-4, 6-3. Odizor bt Shiras 6-2, 7-6. Layendecker bt Benhabiles 7-5, 3-6, 6-3. Schultz bt Green 6-7, 7-6, 6-4. Teacher bt Nelson 6-4, 3-6, 6-3. Flur bt Drewett 6-3, 7-5. Tim Gullikson bt Lapidus 7-5, 6-0. Forget bt Meister 7-6, 6-1. M Davis bt Masur 7-5, 5-7, 7-5. Frawley bt Pfister 1-6, 7-6, 6-3. Bates bt Flach 6-3, 6-2. Moor bt Van Boeckel 6-2, 7-6.

Third round

Knapp bt Leconte 6-4 6-2. Doohan bt Stefenki 7-6, 6-2. Odizor bt Wilkison 6-4, 6-4. Layendecker bt Schultz 6-3, 6-3. Teacher bt Flur 5-7, 7-6, 6-4. Forget bt Tim Gullikson 6-2, 6-3. M Davis bt Frawley 6-3, 6-4. Bates bt Moor 6-4, 5-7, 6-4.

Quarter-finals

Knapp bt Doohan 7-6, 3-6, 6-3. Layendecker bt Odizor 6-3, 6-4. Teacher bt Forget 2-6, 7-6, 6-4. M Davis bt Bates 4-6, 7-5, 9-7.

Semifinals

Layendecker bt Knapp 6-4, 6-3.
M Davis bt Teacher 6-3, 7-6.

Final

M Davis bt Layendecker 4-6, 6-3, 7-5.

DOUBLES

Quarter-finals

Gullikson & Gullikson bt Meister & Teacher 7-6, 3-6, 6-3. Edwards & Visser bt Cassidy & Layendecker 6-4, 6-7, 6-3. Alexander & Simpson bt Hlasek & Popp 7-6, 6-4. Drewett & Edmondson bt Bauer & Stefanki 6-1, 6-1.

Semifinals

Edwards & Visser bt Gullikson 6-3, 3-6, 7-5.
Alexander & Simpson bt Drewett & Edmondson 6-3, 1-6, 6-3.

Final

Edwards & Visser bt Alexander & Simpson 6-4, 7-6.

PREVIOUS SINGLES WINNERS

1981 M Edmondson (Aus)
1982 J Alexander (Aus)
1983 J Kriek (US)
1984 J Kriek (US)

STATEMENTS OF INTENT

BY HUGH JAMIESON: THE SUN

It began as a timely test of character for world champion Martina Navratilova and ended as a perfect omen for the player regarded as invincible yet suddenly under the microscope.

Martina's arrival at Devonshire Park, Eastbourne had been clouded with a dramatic defeat in the final of the French Open by arch-rival Chris Evert Lloyd that had threatened a new and exciting twist to the world of women's tennis.

Mrs Lloyd's marvellous Roland Garros triumph suddenly put her half-way towards a coveted Grand Slam following her Australian Open title and left Martina admitting: "It was the most emotional and exasperating match we had ever played against each other."

More to the point it suddenly had Chris, at 30, realising that Martina was not invincible after all — and that's where the Pilkington Ladies Championship came in on the doorstep of Wimbledon with all eyes on the "big two" still at each other's throats after 12 years world-wide rivalry.

The absence of Mrs Lloyd, who preferred to practise quietly in London, only added to the pressure especially as Martina found herself overtaken at the top of the rankings for the first time in three almost unbeatable years.

It meant a few days relaxation after Paris at the Women's Tennis Association headquarters on the Costa Del Sol at Marbella — and sure enough the smile and ring of confidence was back on Martina's face as she started the routine job of aiming for her sixth Eastbourne final.

She certainly had nothing to worry about — apart from Lori McNeill taking a set off her in the second round — until the talented Bettina Bunge suddenly handed out a quarter final fright that had Martina at odds with her game — and the umpire.

Bettina, fighting with tremendous spirit, matched her shot for shot in the best clash of the tournament, producing an exciting tie-break that could easily have gone either way in the tension that at one point was too much for Martina.

The worried world champion, saving three set points, finally triumphed on her fifth — but not before she had collected her first-ever recorded code violation for smashing a ball into the crowd in a mixture of anger and frustration at losing a vital point.

The shock of it all must have steadied her down because she was back in the groove to put stylish Bulgarian Manuela Maleeva in her place with a 6-1 6-2 semi-final win despite having break points against her in all her opening set service games!

That earned her a revenge tilt at fifth seeded Czech Helena Sukova, a tall rangy girl who had beaten her in the semi-finals of the Australian Open and had looked just as formidable at Eastbourne without dropping a set on the way to a semi-final confrontation with tough Aussie Wendy Turnbull.

Then the sparks began to fly. Turnbull let her experience take control, grabbing the first set and then holding three match points at 5-3 with Miss Sukova really nowhere to be seen.

But for once Miss Turnbull's aggressive instincts deserted her with Miss Sukova keeping her nerve and game intact to fight back and win a one hour 55 minute thriller 4-6 7-6, 6-4.

Yet with rain washing out the previous day's play both semi-finals and final had been scheduled for the same day with Martina ready to play four games after reaching the last four of the doubles in partnership with Pam Shriver.

And with Wimbledon just 48 hours away Martina looked on cue for one of the longest days of her glittering career as she retained her title in the shape of 6-3 6-4 win that always looked beyond the reach of Miss Sukova.

Martina, on the way back to her best, confirmed: "The way I played against Manuela earlier in the day gave me confidence because I was hitting the ball and concentrating well in the kind of windy conditions that made things difficult at times.

"Playing Eastbourne is just right as far as I'm concerned. It gives you matchplay on grass going into Wimbledon, confidence and for me — an omen.

"Every time I reach the final I win

Wendy Turnbull

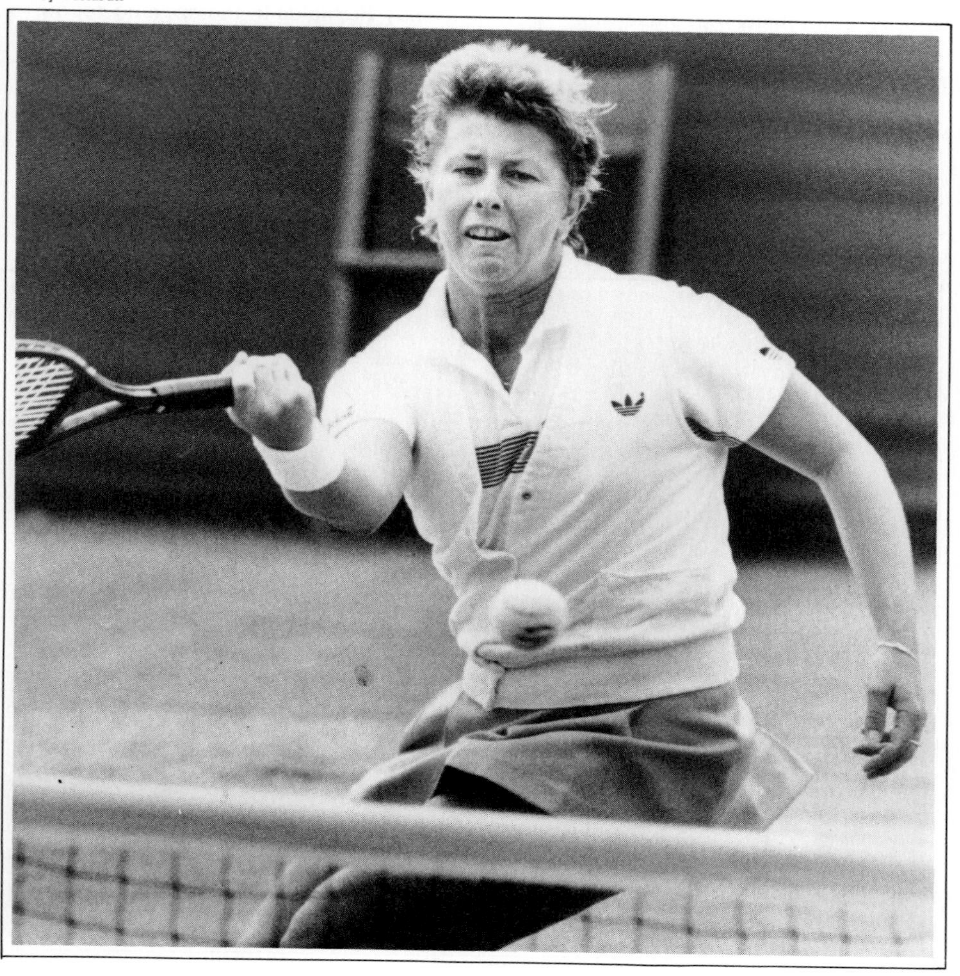

Wimbledon. But this place is special because a lot of fans come back every year sitting in the same seats and you get to recognise them after a while. You don't get that kind of thing anywhere else."

With rain intervening Martina and Pam, who earlier in the week had collected their 100th consecutive doubles victory, returned the following day to finish off a semi-final and then defeat Kathy Jordan and Elizabeth Smylie 7-5 6-4 in the final.

Elsewhere there had also been plenty to note including a number of shocks highlighted with Hana Mandlikova's 7-5 1-6 6-4 defeat by Swedish qualifier Carina Karlsson while Dianne Balestrat signalled her return to tennis conceding just three games to dump Carling Bassett on the sidelines.

Of the British girls only Jo Durie and Annabel Croft survived the opening round. That was it. Miss Durie suffered a nightmare experience against little sixth seeded American Zina Garrison losing 6-0 6-0 in a match she will want to forget while Miss Croft failed to make an impression on Alycia Moulton, the girl she beat in the Wightman Cup the previous year.

Sweet spot centred on the arrival of 15 year old doe-eyed Argentinian Gabriella Sabatini whose beauty created more space in the tabloids than her tennis. That was not surprising, especially as it was Gabby's first ever singles event on grass but after defeating Candy Reynolds in the opening round she was unlucky to run straight into another more experienced wondergirl Pascale Paradis.

Still it all added up to Pilkington getting value for sponsorship money — on and off court — with an event that to say the least has become such an attractive occasion.

Helena Sokova

Carina Karlsson

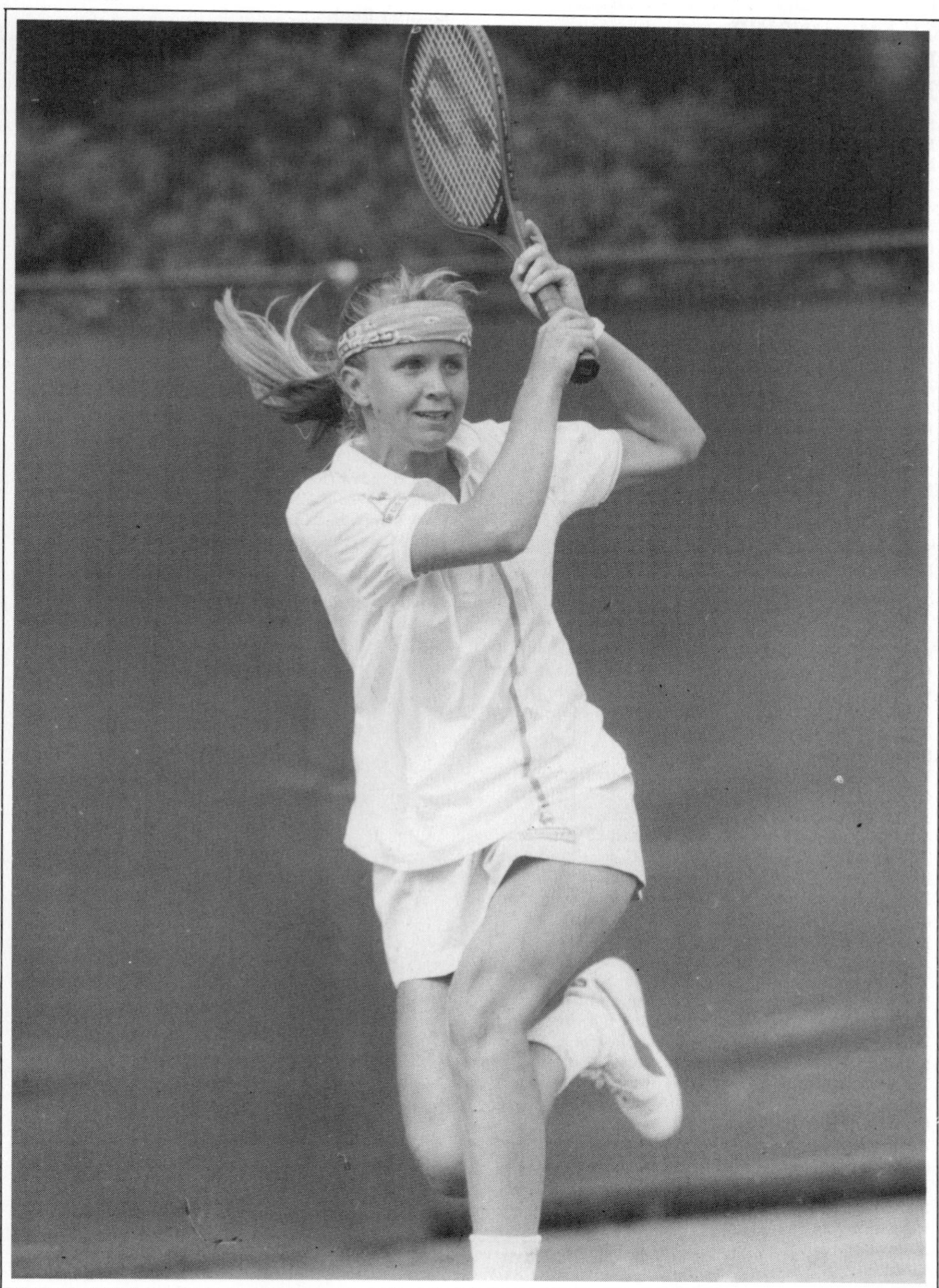

PILKINGTON GLASS LADIES CHAMPIONSHIP
Devonshire Park, Eastbourne
June 17th-23rd

SINGLES
First round
M Navratilova (US) bt B Nagelsen (US) 6-4, 6-4. L McNeil (US) bt Y Vermaak (SA) 2-6, 6-2, 6-1. A Croft bt C Tanvier (Fr) 7-6, 7-5. A Moulton (US) bt B Herr (US) 6-1, 6-1. B Bunge (WG) bt C Suire (Fr) 6-1, 6-0. K Shaefer (US) bt S Walsh-Pete (US) 6-1, 7-5. D Balestrat (Aus) bt A White (US) 6-3, 6-3. C Bassett (Can) bt C Vanier (Fr) 6-4, 6-3. M Maleeva (Bul) bt A Brown 6-3, 7-5. K Maleeva (Bul) bt M Gurney (US) 7-5, 4-6, 6-4. E Pfaff (WG) bt B Gerken (US) 6-4, 6-2. R Fairbank (SA) bt P Casale (US) 6-2, 6-2. K Rinaldi (US) bt A Hobbs 6-3, 6-3. C Jolissaint (Swi) bt E Burgin (US) 7-5, 7-5. B Mould (SA) bt A Leand (US) 6-1, 6-0. K Jordan (US) bt T Scheuer-Larsen (Den) 6-4, 6-1. C Lindqvist (Swe) bt G Fernandez (US) 6-4, 6-3. A Villagran (Arg) bt G Kim (US) 6-4, 1-6, 6-4. E Smylie (Aus) bt L Bonder (US) 6-3, 6-0. B Potter (US) bt R White (US) 6-2, 4-6, 6-2. P Louie (US) bt J Russell (US) 6-4, 6-4. A Henricksson (US) bt S Rehe (US) 7-6, 7-6. J Thompson (Aus) bt T Phelps (US) 6-4, 7-5. H Sukova (Cz) bt L Drescher (Swi) 6-3, 6-0. Z Garrison (US) bt A Minter (Aus) 6-3, 4-6, 6-2. J Durie bt C Benjamin (US) 2-6, 6-1, 6-4. W White (US) bt S Gomer 7-5, 6-4. W Turnbull (Aus) bt L Savchenko (USSR) 6-1, 7-6. G Sabatini (Arg) bt C Reynolds (US) 7-6, 6-0. P Paradis (Fr) bt H Ludloff (US) 6-7, 6-3, 6-3. M Mesker (Neth) bt V Wade 7-5, 6-4. C Karlsson (Swe) bt H Mandlikova (Cz) 7-5, 1-6, 6-4.

Second round
Navratilova bt McNeil 3-6, 6-2, 6-0. Moulton bt Croft 6-1, 6-2. Bunge bt Shaefer 6-4, 6-0. Balestrat bt Bassett 6-3, 6-0. M Maleeva bt K Maleeva 6-1, 6-3. Fairbank bt Pfaff 6-3, 6-2. Rinaldi bt Jolissaint 7-5, 6-1. K Jordan bt Mould 4-6, 7-6, 6-3. Lindqvist bt Villagran 6-2, 7-5. Potter bt Smylie 7-6, 6-2. Henricksson bt Louie 7-6, 6-2. Sukova bt Thompson 6-2, 6-3. Garrison bt Durie 6-0, 6-0. Turnbull bt W White 6-2, 6-1. Paradis bt Sabatini 6-7, 6-2, 6-3. Karlsson bt Mesker 7-6, 6-2.

Third round
Navratilova bt Moulton 6-1, 7-6. Bunge bt Balestrat 6-3, 2-6, 6-2. M Maleeva bt Fairbank 6-4, 6-4. Rinaldi bt K Jordan 7-5, 0-6, 6-4. Potter bt Lindqvist 5-7, 7-5, 6-3. Sukova bt Henricksson 6-4, 6-1. Turnbull bt Garrison 7-6, 6-4. Paradis bt Karlsson 7-6, 6-3.

Quarter-finals
Navratilova bt Bunge 7-6, 6-3. M Maleeva bt Rinaldi 6-1, 6-0. Sukova bt Potter 6-0, 7-6. Turnbull bt Paradis 3-6, 6-4, 7-5.

Semifinals
Navratilova bt M Maleeva 6-1, 6-2.
Sukova bt Turnbull 4-6, 7-6, 6-4.

Final
Navratilova bt Sukova 6-4, 6-3.

DOUBLES
Quarter-finals
Navratilova & Shriver bt Burgin & Moulton 6-3, 6-4. Potter & Walsh-Pete bt Cherneva & Savchenko 5-7, 6-4, 6-4. Mandlikova & Turnbull bt Bunge & Pfaff 6-1, 1-6, 6-3. K Jordan & Smylie bt Temesvari & Villagran 6-1, 6-3.

Semifinals
Navratilova & Shriver bt Potter & Walsh-Pete 6-2, 6-4. K Jordan & Smylie bt Mandlikova & Turnbull 6-2, 5-7, 6-1.

Final
Navratilova & Shriver bt K Jordan & Smylie 7-5, 6-4.

SINGLES RECORD
1978 M Navratilova (Cz)
1979 C Evert-Lloyd (US)
1980 T Austin (US)
1981 T Austin (US)
1982 M Navratilova (US)
1983 M Navratilova (US)
1984 M Navratilova (US)

DOUBLES
1978 B Stove (Neth) & C Evert-Lloyd (US)
1979 B Stove (Neth) & W Turnbull (Aus)
1980 K Jordon & A Smith (US)
1981 M Navratilova & P Shriver (US)
1982 M Navratilova & P Shriver (US)
1983 M Navratilova & P Shriver (US)
1984 M Navratilova & P Shriver (US)

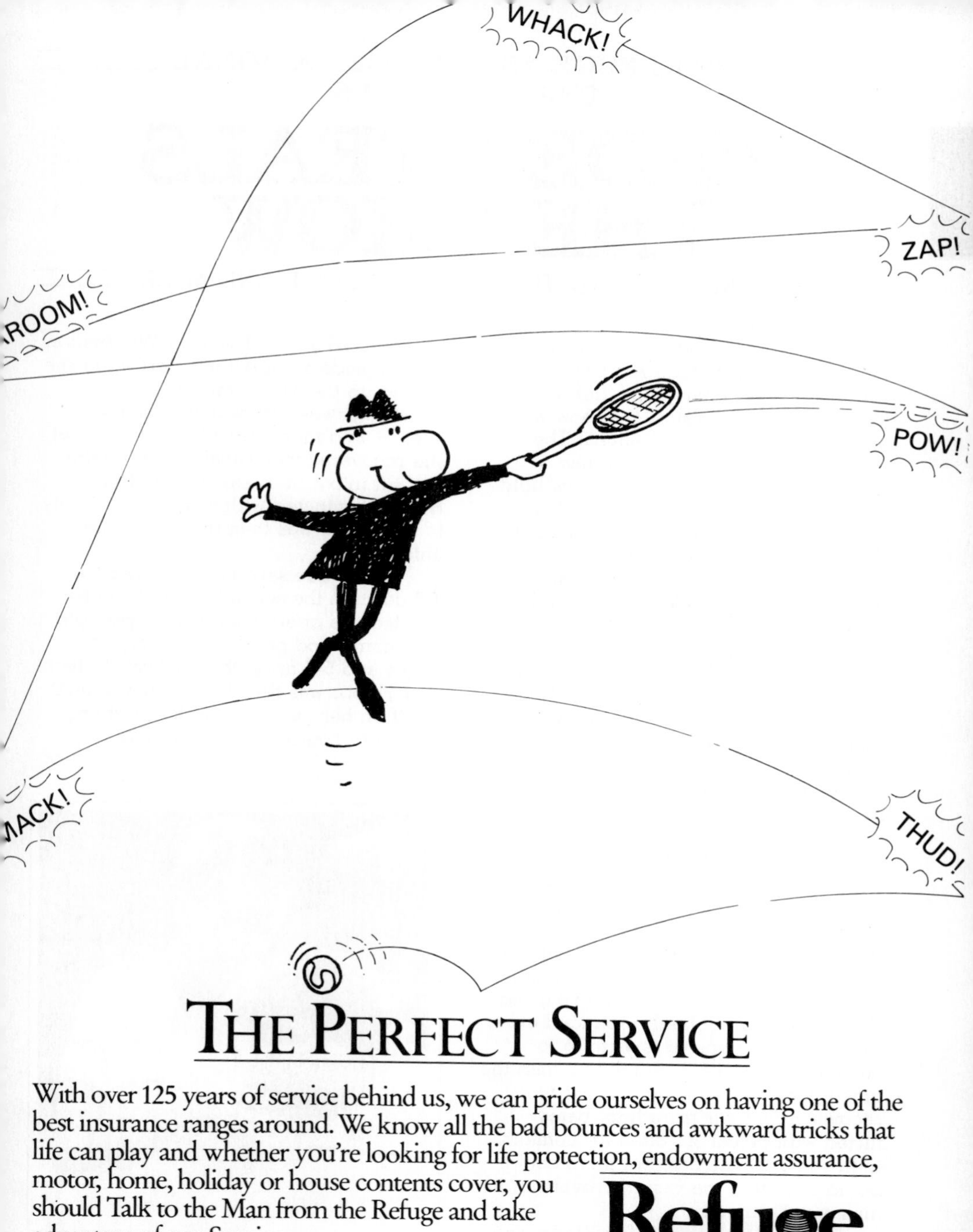
WHACK!
ZAP!
ROOM!
POW!
ACK!
THUD!
THE PERFECT SERVICE
With over 125 years of service behind us, we can pride ourselves on having one of the best insurance ranges around. We know all the bad bounces and awkward tricks that life can play and whether you're looking for life protection, endowment assurance, motor, home, holiday or house contents cover, you should Talk to the Man from the Refuge and take advantage of our Service.
Refuge
ASSURANCE PLC
Chief Office (& Registered Office) Oxford Street
Manchester M60 7HA. Telephone: 061-236 9432

WADE STEALS THE SHOW

BY MIKE WARD: BIRMINGHAM POST AND MAIL

Jeremy Bates and Anne Hobbs became the new Refuge Assurance National singles champions, but it was Virginia Wade who stole the show with a vintage performance at Telford. The former Wimbledon champion has illuminated many a stage in the twilight of her career, and she outshone Anne Hobbs even in defeat at the final hurdle.

Miss Hobbs was stretched to the limits of her considerable physical and mental endurance before scraping home in three sets. Bates had it much easier against Nick Fulwood.

Forget Miss Wade's insistence that she played tennis purely for fun. This was three hours, 16 minutes of painful, pulsating endeavour on the part of both Wightman Cup players. It was desperately sad that one of them had to lose. Neither deserved to. Miss Hobbs took the £7,500 first prize with a 7-6, 6-7, 9-7 victory, but this marvellous match so nearly went the other way.

Inevitably, the men's final paled by comparison. But take nothing away from Bates, who gave Britain's pre-Davis Cup aspirations a powerful boost in sweeping to his first Refuge title. The 23-year-old No. 2 seed from Solihull produced every stroke in his extensive repertoire to outclass Fulwood 6-3, 6-2 in less than the time it took for Hobbs and Wade to recover from their marathon. Bates flirted with defeat too often for comfort in the earlier matches, but there could be no disputing the vast improvement in his mental attitude.

As for the amazing Miss Wade, she gave her all and felt the anguish of defeat. Her effort ranked with so many of her epic performances in a career spanning 23 years. The 1977 Wimbledon Queen made an appalling start when she picked up the wrong racket – "one of the strings was almost gone", she said later – and found herself 3-0 adrift. Yet she recovered majestically to force the first set into a tie-break which Miss Hobbs dominated with renewed authority to win 7-4. It was then the real battle unfolded.

Miss Wade saved a match point at 4-5 down in the second set, but Hobbs, too, faced a crisis when her 40-year-old opponent stood poised for victory at deuce and 5-4 up in the final set. In fact Miss Hobbs was then 5-6 down and 0-30 adrift on her own serve before fighting back with courage to match Miss Wade's.

Anne Hobbs

Virginia Wade

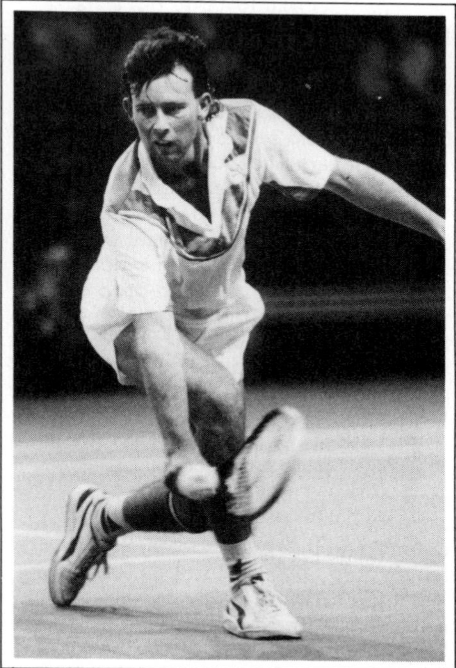
Jeremy Bates

The Refuge tournament has been rich with surprise and controversy since it was inaugurated in 1983, and the latest lived up to that reputation. Jonathan Smith launched a scathing attack on the establishment after routing Richard Whichello 6-2, 6-0 in the second round, while defending champions Colin Dowdeswell and Jo Durie were both removed prematurely.

Poor Miss Durie, whose depressing year hit rock bottom when she was bundled out in the third round by little Jo Louis of Devon, suffered a painful roasting later from her coach, Alan Jones.

If anybody had to work for his opening victory, it was Bates against the stubborn Yorkshire qualifier, Simon Ickringill. Bates saved six match points to contrive the greatest Houdini escape of his career. On a day when Dowdeswell ditched his contact lenses and nearly lost too, Bates came back to win from 1-5 down in the final set, surviving two hours and 47 minutes of compelling tennis.

Faced with an opponent who could do nothing wrong, Bates had given up the ghost in that sixth game, and it was in sheer desperation that he saved two of those match points with outrageous top-spin lobs, while Ickringill double-faulted on another at 5-3.

Dowdeswell's curious decision to remove his contact lenses in an indoor centre scarcely renowned for good lighting cost him the first set against Brent Parker, a 21-year-old qualifier from Gateshead. "It was an experiment which went wrong", admitted the defending champion. "I couldn't even read my name on the scoreboard". Dowdeswell, who was clearly seeing the ball very late and sometimes not at all, saved two break points at 4-4 in the second set, having dropped the first, before winning 3-6, 6-4, 6-2.

The next day brought the state of British tennis sharply into focus as the 30-year-old Smith beat the country's top-ranked junior out of sight in the second round. Destroying Richard Whichello 6-2, 6-0 was no satisfaction for Smith, who launched a scathing attack on national team manager, Paul Hutchins. "I don't think he's doing a very good job", said Smith. "It's sad that someone like me who has not played indoors for almost three months should drop only two games to a young guy reckoned to be one of Britain's best prospects. I don't think Whichello had the faintest idea."

It was Durie's turn to come under fire next day as she incurred the full wrath of coach Alan Jones after the latest disaster in her chequered career. In view of Miss Durie's plight and her apparent refusal to recognise it, the defending champion's defeat at the hands of Jo Louis was sadly predictable. What the diminutive 18-year-old Devonian lacked in height she made up for with an abundance of courage in a 7-5, 6-7, (1-7), 6-3 triumph which took her into the quarter-finals.

It just happens that the two girls shared the same coach. That was little consolation to Jones, who pulled no punches in a bitter condemnation of Miss Durie's performance. "She can sack me if she wants", he said. "But Jo has been kidding herself for far too long. Maybe this will do her good, because she seems to think there's some kind of fairy Godmother out there on court. Little Jo Louis was courageous. She deserved to win because she showed all the qualities that Jo Durie didn't. I'm furious, and fed up with her attitude."

Davis Cup squad members Bates, Dowdeswell and Stephen Shaw all eased into the quarter-finals with little fuss, but third-seeded Shaw came to grief the next day when he was beaten 1-6, 7-5, 8-6 by Nick Fulwood, the No. 5 seed from Derbyshire.

Dowdeswell made it into the semi-finals with an emphatic 6-4, 6-3 victory over former British No. 1 Buster Mottram, while Virginia Wade was an unwelcome intruder into Sue Mappin's plans for the 1985 Wightman Cup.

The last thing national team manager Mappin wanted to see was Wade ruthlessly brushing aside Amanda Brown 6-3, 6-4 to reach the semi-finals for the third year running. In short, Miss Wade played herself into a 21st successive Wightman Cup call-up against the United States, while 20-year-old Miss Brown played herself right out of the reckoning.

Nick Fulwood

There were more shocks on the way as top seeds Dowdeswell and Annabel Croft were unceremoniously despatched in the semi-finals by Fulwood and Hobbs respectively. Miss Croft showed promise in a match full of cultured rallies, but ran out of ideas in a 6-4, 6-3 defeat by her Wightman Cup team-mate. And Dowdeswell's hopes for retaining the title were buried without trace by 21-year-old Fulwood, who showed far more enterprise and aggression in his 6-4, 6-4 triumph.

Smith, who had surprised himself by making it all the way to the last four, succumbed to Bates, who was by now getting into his stride. Miss Wade reached the finals by beating the brave Middlesex girl Jane Wood, 6-2, 6-2, and the stage was set for the grand old lady to steal the spotlight in a memorable finish.

REFUGE ASSURANCE NATIONAL CLOSED CHAMPIONSHIPS

Telford

October 23rd-29th

MEN'S SINGLES

First round

B Parker (Durham & Cleveland) bt C Clarke (Bucks) 6-1, 6-2. D Sapsford (Surrey) bt A Douglas (Surrey) 6-3, 6-3. S King (Surrey) bt J Paish (Surrey) 6-4, 6-4. P French (Somerset) bt R Botfield (Essex) 6-7, 6-3, 6-4. R Booth (Dorset) bt S Booth (Warks) 6-1, 6-4. H McGuiness (Essex) bt M Curtis (Middx) 6-3, 6-2. B Knapp (Glos) bt T Robson (Oxon) 6-2, 6-4. J M Dier (Sussex) bt D Shaw (Lancs) 6-4, 3-6, 6-2. J Whiteford (Sussex) bt M Appleton (Lancs) 6-3, 6-2. J M Turner (Avon) bt P Hughesman (Middx) 6-7, 6-4, 6-4. S Heron (Yorks) bt H Becker (Midd) 6-4, 6-4. R Whichello (Kent) bt D Ison (Leics) 3-6, 7-6, 6-3. A Brice (Chesh) bt I Currie (Essex) 6-3, 6-4. C Peet (Lancs) bt N Sears (Sussex) 6-4, 4-6, 6-4. M Guntrip (Kent) bt E Davies (Lancs) 6-4, 3-6, 6-4. S Ickringill (Yorks) bt N Beedham (Derby) 6-4, 6-7, 6-2.

Second round

C Dowdeswell (Surrey) bt Parker 3-6, 6-4, 6-2. D Felgate (Essex) bt Sapsford 6-4, 5-7, 6-4. C J Mottram (Surrey) bt King 6-0, 6-1. J W Feaver (Dorset) bt French 6-1, 6-4. S M Shaw (Midd) bt Booth 5-7, 6-4, 6-3. C Bradnam (Midd) bt McGuiness 6-0, 6-2. Knapp bt M T Blincow (Northants) 6-1, 7-6. N A Fulwood (Derby) bt Dier 6-1, 1-6, 6-2. L G Alfred (S Wales) bt Whiteford 3-6, 7-6, 7-6. R W Drysdale (Essex) bt Turner 6-4, 6-3. M T Walker (N Wales) bt Heron 7-6, 6-4. J R Smith (Devon) bt Whichello 6-2, 6-0. Brice bt R A Lewis (Midd) 2-6, 6-3, 6-3. J M Goodall (Yorks) bt Peet 6-2, 6-1. N Brown (Cheshire) bt Guntrip 6-3, 6-2. M J Bates (Surrey) bt Ickringill 6-4, 6-7, 10-8.

Third round

Dowdeswell bt Felgate 6-2, 6-3. Mottram bt Feaver 6-2, 6-1. S Shaw bt Bradnam 6-2, 6-4. Fulwood bt Knapp 6-2, 6-1. Drysdale bt Alfred 4-6, 6-4, 8-6. Smith bt Walker 6-1, 6-1. Brice bt Goodall 7-6, 6-3. Bates bt Brown 6-3, 6-4.

Quarterfinals

Dowdeswell bt Mottram 6-4, 6-3. Fulwood bt S Shaw 1-6, 7-5, 8-6. Smith bt Drysdale 6-2, 6-4. Bates bt Brice 6-1, 6-3.

Semifinals

Fulwood bt Dowdeswell 6-4, 6-4.
Bates bt Smith 2-6, 6-4, 6-4.

Final

Bates bt Fulwood 6-3, 6-2.

LADIES' SINGLES

First round

S L Sullivan (Essex) bt N Barnabas (N Wales) 6-0, 6-3. S A Walpole (Surrey) bt C Billingham (Oxon) 7-5, 6-2. L Gould (Essex) bt T Catlin (Cambs) 6-4, 6-1. A Simpkin (Leics) bt S Timms (Essex) 7-6, 6-1. J Donovan (Warks) bt K Hunter (Surrey) 6-1, 5-7, 6-4. J C Rich (Norfolk) bt L Geeves (Midd) 6-3, 6-1. S Godman (Surrey) bt S Barker (Devon) 6-2, 6-3. K Brasher (Surrey) bt A Grunfeld (Lancs) 6-2, 6-1. G Coles (Midd) bt C Bhaguandas (Midd) 6-2, 6-0. J Langstaff (Surrey) bt A Niepal (Lancs) 6-1, 6-0. V Lake (Devon) bt S Byrne (Hants) 6-2, 2-6, 6-2. J Griffiths (N Wales) bt A Fleming (Leics) 5-7, 6-3, 8-6. J Caplen (Hants) bt C Bateman (Essex) 6-2, 6-4. S McCarthy (Avon) bt D Schauerman (Midd) 6-3, 6-2. E Jones (Hants) bt V Sims (Surrey) 6-3, 6-1. C Berry (Yorks) bt A Grant (Lincs) 6-2, 6-0.

Second round

A N Croft (Kent) bt Sullivan 6-0, 6-1. L C Gracie (Lancs) bt S Walpole 7-5, 6-1. S T G Mair (E of Scot) bt Gould 6-2, 6-3. Simpkin bt R L Einy (Midd) 6-7, 6-4, 10-8. A Hobbs bt Donovan 6-0, 6-0. Rich bt J A Salmon (Sussex) 6-4, 6-4. J M Tacon (Norf) bt Godman 4-6, 6-1, 6-1. S L Gomer (Devon) bt Brasher 6-1, 6-7, 6-3. A J Brown (Norfk) bt Coles 4-6, 6-2, 6-2. Langstaff bt C J Wood (Sussex) 7-6, 6-3. B A Borneo (Beds) bt Lake 6-1, 6-3. S V Wade (Kent) bt Griffiths 7-6, 7-5, S E Reeves (Kent) bt Caplen 4-6, 7-5, 6-2. J V Wood (Midd) bt McCarthy 6-4, 2-6, 7-5. J Louis (Devon) bt Jones 5-7, 6-4, 6-3. J M Durie (Avon) bt Berry 6-1, 6-3.

Third round

Croft bt Gracie 6-0, 6-2. Mair bt Simpkin 2-6, 6-3, 7-5. Hobbs bt Rich 6-1, 6-2. Gomer bt Tacon 6-3, 6-2. Brown bt Langstaff 6-4, 7-5. Wade bt Borneo 2-6, 6-1, 6-3. Wood bt Reeves 7-5, 7-6. Louis bt Durie 7-5, 6-7, 6-3

Quarterfinals

Croft bt Mair 6-3, 6-4. Hobbs bt Gomer 6-3, 4-6, 6-4. Wade bt Brown 6-3, 6-4. Wood bt Louis 7-6, 6-3.

Semifinals

Hobbs bt Croft 6-4, 6-3.
Wade bt Wood 6-2, 6-2.

Final

Hobbs bt Wade 7-6, 6-7, 9-7.

MEN'S DOUBLES

First round

Brice & Ison bt Pashley & Sapsford 6-1; 6-2. French & Turner bt Driver & Johnston 6-2, 6-4. Parker & Slater bt Boulton & Evans 6-1, 2-3, retd. Botfield & McGuiness bt Cooper & Stoakes 7-6, 6-3. Ickringill & D Shaw bt Robson & Weekes 6-4, 6-7, 6-4. Goodall & Whichello bt Beedham & Broomhead 6-2, 6-1. M Booth & R Booth bt Adamson & West 7-6, 6-4. Blincow & Smith bt Douglas & Mackie 6-4, 3-6, 6-2.

Second round

Bates & S Shaw bt Brice & Ison 6-3, 7-6. French & Turner bt Sears & Whiteford 6-2, 6-4. Bradnam & Fulwood bt Parker & Slater 6-4, 7-6. Drysdale & Mottram bt Botfield & McGuiness 6-3, 6-3. Alfred & Guntrip bt Ickringill & Shaw, Goodall & Whichello bt Dowdeswell & Feaver 6-4, 6-0. Dier & Lewis bt

Booth & Booth 6-2, 7-6. Blincow & Smith bt Brown & Felgate 6-4, 6-4.

Quarterfinals
Bates & Shaw bt French & Turner 6-2, 6-2. Bradnam & Fulwood bt Drysdale & Mottram 5-7, 6-2, 6-4. Goodall & Whichello bt Alfred & Guntrip 6-3, 4-6, 10-8. Dier & Lewis bt Blincow & Smith 5-7, 6-3, 9-7.

Semifinals
Bradnam & Fulwood bt Bates & Shaw 6-1, 6-3. Goodall & Whichello bt Dier & Lewis 6-2, 6-7, 6-2.

Final
Bradnam & Fulwood bt Goodall & Whichello 4-6, 6-4, 6-3.

LADIES' DOUBLES

First round
Brailsford & Lewis bt Whiteman & Russell 7-5, 1-6, 6-1. Fleming & Simpkin bt Billingham & Nall 6-2, 7-6. Bateman & Timms bt Atkin & Barnabas 6-1, 6-3. Reeves & Rich bt Gregory & Phillips 6-1, 6-0. Rickett & Wainwright bt Gradon & Wilson 6-3, 6-4. Gould & Grunfeld bt Ball & Siney 6-3, 6-3. Lake & McCarthy bt Bishop & Pearson 6-2, 6-2. Charles & Drury bt Parker & Plackett 6-3, 6-2.

Second round
Durie & Hobbs bt Brailsford & Lewis 6-1, 6-0. Mair & Wood bt Fleming & Simpkin 6-3, 7-6. Brown & Gracie bt Bateman & Timms 6-0, 6-0. Borneo & Tacon bt Reeves & Rich 6-1, 6-2. Louis & J Wood bt Rickett & Wainwright 6-0, 6-3. Gomer & Salmon bt Gould & Grunfeld 6-3, 7-5. Lake & McCarthy bt Coles & Parnell 7-6, 6-0. Croft & Wade bt Charles & Drury 6-1, 6-3.

Quarterfinals
Durie & Hobbs bt Mair & Wood 6-0, 3-6, 6-1. Brown & Gracie bt Borneo & Tacon 6-4, 6-1. Gomer & Salmon bt Louis & Wood 7-5, 6-4. Croft & Wade bt Lake & McCarthy 6-4, 7-6.

Semifinals
Durie & Hobbs bt Brown & Gracie 6-0, 6-2. Croft & Wade bt Gomer & Salmon 6-4, 7-5.

Final
Durie & Hobbs bt Croft & Wade 2-6, 7-6, 6-2.

DOUBLE BOOST AT BRIGHTON

BY DENNIS CUNNINGTON: PRESS ASSOCIATION

October in Brighton usually signifies the end of the busy holiday season. By then the seaside town has also said goodbye to its conference delegates. Then as the last of the deck-chairs are being stacked away, the tennis players begin to arrive — for October in Brighton is also synonymous with women's tournament time.

And what a marvellous week it was last October. For the second year Pretty Polly staged their Classic — and staged it with style too. Happily for the sponsors, the entry, with Chris Evert-Lloyd giving support once more, was a big improvement on 1984. Moreover the feeling of gloom had lifted from the town.

The Pretty Polly Classic of 1984 began within days of the bombing of the Grand Hotel, right next door to the Brighton Centre. No one was thinking straight, traffic was snarled up as it weaved its way through hastily prepared emergency one-way systems. Consequently, no one wanted to go out, and the crowds diminished.

But this time they were back again and, with two British players — Jo Durie and Annabel Croft — in the semi-finals on Saturday afternoon, there was a full house for that as well as the last day.

The cynics in the press room regard the Brighton women's tournament as the "Hendon's Benefit". The family of George, Eileen and Nola run it superbly. So, in reality, it is a benefit for the sponsors. And Pretty Polly freely admit that as a marketing exercise, it suits them down to the ground. They will be back this year, and, if they have any sense, take up their option of continuing into the future.

One look at the entries, and this particular tournament was always going to be Chris Lloyd versus the Young Ones. So it proved, for in the semi-finals and final, the American had to withstand the challenge of two enthusiastic teenagers, Miss Croft and Manuela Maleeva of Bulgaria, who had beaten her once in the final of a previous Italian open championship.

Miss Maleeva, 18 and, at the time, ranked No. 10 in the world was not easy to dispose of in the final. Mrs Lloyd won 7-5 6-3 in 97 minutes, and if the reader thinks that second set was easy — it wasn't. Miss Maleeva was within a point of going 4-1 in front. Had that happened, I believe the pace would have told on the 31-year-old American. As she admitted afterwards: "Winning tournaments gets harder and harder all the time."

But win she did. It was her third title at Brighton since 1980, and the 141st of her career. By the end of the week, she was back on top as the world No. 1.

If the week ended well for Mrs Lloyd, it bordered on the near-sensational for Miss Croft and Miss Durie. It had been seven years since Britain has had two players in the semi-finals of a major women's tournament. Then, the two Golden Girls were Virginia Wade and Sue Barker, and they met in the last four twice in successive weeks at tournaments in the United States. They won one each.

To reach the semi-finals at Brighton, Miss Croft and Miss Durie had each defeated a player ranked among the world's top ten. Both unseeded, their big moments had come in the second round. Miss Durie, who had been having a torrid time throughout the year, suddenly struck form and beat West Germany's Steffi Graf, 6-2 6-3. Miss Graf was the No. 2 seed and the world No. 7.

The next day, Miss Croft floundered throughout a first set, battled courageously in the second and played brilliantly in a third to defeat Helena Sukova of Czechoslovakia 2-6 7-5 6-4. The 20-year-old Miss Sukova was the tournament's third seed and stood No. 8 in the world.

These victories did wonders for our girls' morals and lifted them among the first 30 players in the world. Miss Croft was there for the first time in her life; for Miss Durie, it was a welcome return and, hopefully, the launching pad for even bigger improvement in her struggle to reach her former glory days when she had been as high as No. 5 at the end of 1983.

Still bouyant, both British players won their quarter-finals with some ease. Miss Croft beat the American, Terry Phelps 6-1 6-3 and Miss Durie took out Christiane Jolissaint of Switzerland 6-2 6-3. To be realistic, however, an all-British final was never likely, for always there was the formidable presence of Mrs Lloyd and the immensely talented Miss Maleeva standing in the way of that high hope.

So it proved, for the semi-finals went to the two overseas stars, Mrs Lloyd beating Miss Croft 6-3 6-2, and Miss Maleeva upsetting Miss Durie 6-3 7-6. Miss Croft never played badly and always as well as she was allowed by the vastly experienced American. Miss Durie, at 1-5 down in the second set looked as though she would be annihilated by Miss Maleeva until the British player struck a remarkable patch.

Miss Durie won five successive games to take the lead at 6-5, and that run cost her just seven points. It was a short, sharp devastating spell which, had it arrived earlier, might have produced a different result. Unhappily, the challenge could go no further, and the tie break whizzed by at 7-2.

Lloyd v Maleeva was, no doubt, the expected final. Perhaps not the best seen at Brighton, but a good one nonetheless.

Britain had Virginia Wade and Anne Hobbs wildcarded into the event, and Sally Reeves, fighting tigerishly as ever, battling a lone path through the qualifying competition. Miss Reeves is a gutsy little player I would have on my side anytime. After her three-day qualifying marathon, it was tough luck to come up against Miss Maleeva in the first round. The Bulgarian won 6-2 6-1, and even then Miss Reeves could still manage a smile. "She was shaking hands and I was still wondering when she was going to let me begin playing", she said.

Miss Hobbs, too, was the victim of an unkind draw. She caught Miss Sukova in ruthless first round mood and succumbed 6-1 6-2 without making the slightest impression.

At 40, Miss Wade could well have

Manuela Maleeva

been playing in her last tournament in Britain. Only time will tell if she really means to retire, but if so, her fans would have wished for a more fitting finale. It was poor reward for her dedication and contribution to bow out to a "lucky loser" from the qualifying — as she did 6-1 4-6 6-3 to Carina Karlsson of Sweden, the girl who had beaten her at Wimbledon in the summer of '84.

Terry Phelps

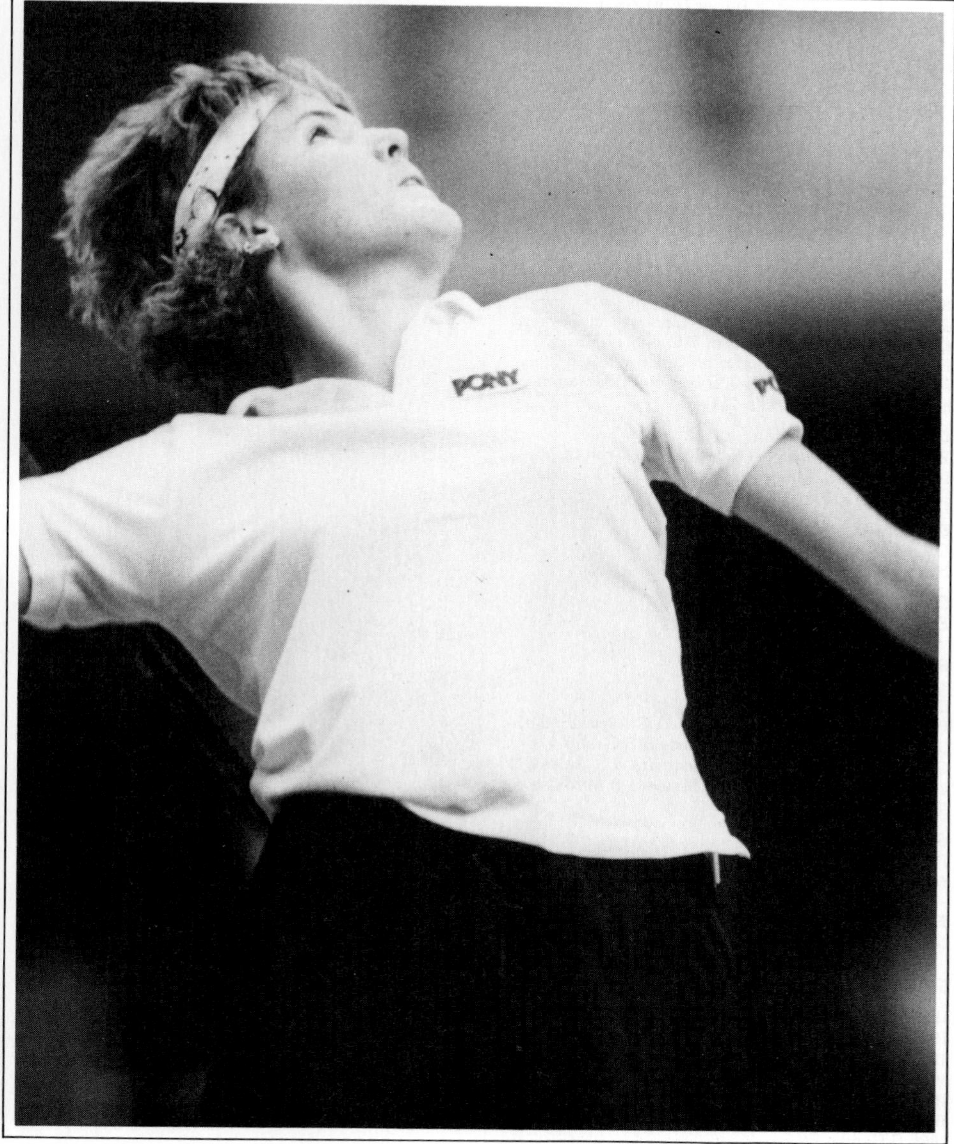

THE PRETTY POLLY CLASSIC

Brighton
October 22nd-27th

SINGLES

First round
C Evert Lloyd (US) bt P Huber (Aut) 7-6, 6-0. P Casale (US) bt M Van Nostrand (US) 6-4 6-1. B Gerken (US) bt A Cecchini (It) 6-3, 6-2. C Lindqvist (Swe) bt S Mascarin (US) 6-0 6-0. H Sukova (Cz) bt A Hobbs (GB) 6-1, 6-2. A Croft (GB) bt K Maleeva (Bul) 6-2, 7-6. P Paradis (Fr) bt R Reggi (It) 6-7, 6-3, 6-2. T Phelps (US) bt E Burgin (US) 6-0, 7-6. B Potter (US) bt S Goles (Yug) 6-3, 6-4. C Karlsson (Swe) bt V Wade (GB) 6-1, 4-6, 6-3. V Ruzici (Rom) bt J Russell (US) 6-2, 6-3. M Maleeva (Bul) bt S Reeves (GB) 6-2, 6-1. C Benjamin (US) bt S Hanika (WG), C Jolissaint (Swi) bt K Steinmetz (US) 6-3, 6-2. J Durie (GB) bt M Torres (US) 6-2, 4-6, 6-2. S Graf (WG) bt C Tanvier (Fr) 6-2 6-7, 6-2.

Second round
Evert Lloyd bt Casale 6-3, 6-1. Lindqvist bt Gerken 6-0, 6-0. Croft bt Sukova 2-6, 7-5, 6-4. Phelps bt Paradis 1-6, 6-4, 6-3. Potter bt Karlsson 6-2, 6-2. Maleeva bt Ruzici 6-2, 6-0. Jolissaint bt Benjamin 6-3, 6-4. Durie bt Graf 6-2, 6-3.

Quarterfinals
Evert Lloyd bt Lindqvist 6-2, 2-6, 7-6. Croft bt Phelps 6-1, 6-3. Maleeva bt Potter 6-2, 6-3. Durie bt Jolissaint 6-2, 6-3.

Semifinals
Evert Lloyd bt Croft 6-3, 6-2
Maleeva bt Durie 6-3, 7-6

Final
Evert Lloyd bt M Maleeva 7-5, 6-3

DOUBLES

Quarterfinals
B Potter & H Sukova bt E Burgin & C Jolissaint 6-4, 6-3. T Phelps & R Reggi bt J Durie & S Graf 6-4, 6-1. C Lindqvist & J Russell bt A Cecchini & S Goles 6-2, 7-6. L McNeil & C Suire bt K Maleeva & M Maleeva 3-6, 7-5, 6-4.

Semifinals
Potter & Sukova bt Phelps & Reggi 6-3, 7-6
McNeil & Suire bt Lindqvist & Russell 6-1, 6-2

Final
McNeil & Suire bt Potter & Sukova 4-6, 7-6, 6-4

SINGLES WINNERS

1978 V Ruzici (Rom)
1979 M Navratilova (Cz)
1980 C Evert Lloyd (US)
1981 S Barker (GB)
1982 M Navratilova (US)
1983 C Evert Lloyd (US)
1984 S Hanika (WG)

DOUBLES WINNERS

1978 V Wade (GB) & B Stove (Neth)
1979 A Kiyomura & A Smith (US)
1980 K Jordan & A Smith (US)
1981 B Potter & A Smith (US)
1982 M Navratilova & P Shriver (US)
1983 C Evert Lloyd & P Shriver (US)
1984 A Moulton & P Smith (US)

LENDL FIGHTS OFF BECKER

No-one missed John McEnroe or Jimmy Connors. Nor was there any reason to. With both the Wimbledon and US champions on parade, Wembley's afficionados wanted for nothing. As the seedings had predicted the Benson and Hedges Championship built to a tremendous climax with Ivan Lendl, the holder, being hustled to the brink of defeat before warding off Boris Becker's insistent challenge after three hours and 48 minutes of intense competition.

Serving at 3-4 in the fourth set — he had lost two of the first three — a weary-looking Lendl was in desperate trouble at 0-30. Suddenly, as if remembering it was he, and not his young German opponent, who was world No 1, the Czech counter-attacked. Incredibly he won 20 of the next 23 points. Though Becker continued to stalk him relentlessly, Lendl's confidence and consistency were, by then, high enough to carry him safely home 6-7, 6-3, 4-6, 6-4, 6-4.

None of his 26 previous victories, including that first US title win, had left Lendl so physically drained. But he survived the test and, in psychological terms, that was what mattered to him. He was not too proud, though, to admit it had been a close call. "Boris is improving day by day," he admitted. "I just hope he stops. I barely beat him this time and I'm getting a bit too old to improve now."

Above all it was this mutual respect — and Becker was equally generous in his assessment of Lendl — that stimulated the audience's sense of well being at seeing two superb athletes giving their all. How different, many must have thought, to that other, often disgraceful, five-set final at Wembley. between Connors and McEnroe in 1981.

In many ways it was a final which illustrated, quite perfectly, the way the balance of power in men's tennis had shifted from America to Europe; on one side of the net Lendl, the seasoned professional of 25, on the other Becker, the 17-year-old tyro. Of the old guard there was almost no sign.

Yet, as usual, and despite the late withdrawal of the Wimbledon runner-up Kevin Curren, Wembley had attracted a field which compared favourably with any other Super Series championship. Not only Lendl and Becker, one and seven respectively in the rankings, but four other players from the world's top ten.

Not that seedings counted for much. Stefan Edberg, who was later to beat Lendl for the Australian title, appeared to present a real threat to the Czech at the semifinal stage but, hampered by a heavy cold, failed to survive his second round match with David Pate.

Yannick Noah, who has never had much luck in Britain, went even sooner — having to retire at 1-4 in his first round match with John Sadri because of a shoulder injury — and Scott Davis followed him out at the same stage, beaten by fellow American Mike Leach.

This meant that there were three unseeded quarter-finalists: Pate, who confessed to a somewhat half-hearted commitment to the game; Ramesh Krishnan, that delightful Indian stylist with the soft centre; and Leach, a left-hander with a rocket-launching serve but not much else.

David Pate

Ramesh Krishnan

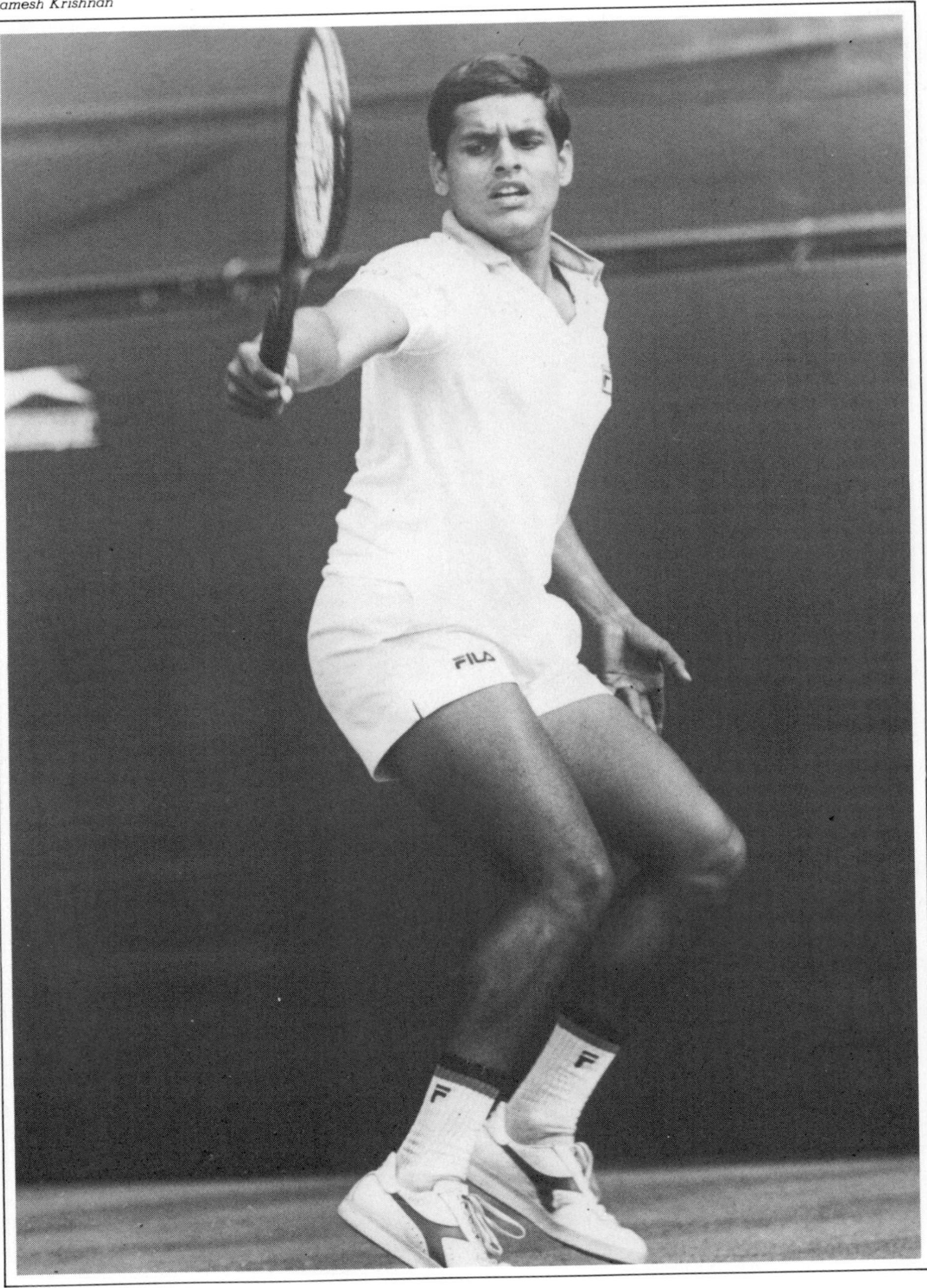

Hopes of British representation in the last eight seemed reasonable when the dismissal of Davis left a gap in John Lloyd's section of the draw (better still he had beaten Leach earlier in the year) but instead of taking advantage of the situation, he played poorly and lost 6-3, 6-3 to the Swede, Jan Gunnarson.

It was the other home-based wild card who so nearly came up trumps. After a splendid 6-4, 6-4 win over Ben Testerman in the opening round, Jeremy Bates gave Becker a real run for his money, only losing 7-5, 7-6 after proving himself the German's equal in all phases of the game bar the serve; a fact Becker underlined by delivering 16 aces.

Three of the quarters went as expected: Lendl and Anders Jarryd beating Johan Kriek and Krishnan respectively in straight sets and Becker getting the decision over Leach on a retirement when within one game of victory. It was in the fourth that the surprise came: Pate beating Joakim Nystrom 6-3, 3-6, 7-5. Clearly he had developed quite a taste for Swedes!

Kriek, who had suggested at Queen's that Becker could win Wimbledon, was even more forthright in tipping Lendl to take the Wembley title. "I never had a chance. He hits the ball so hard now, there's nothing you can do." Pate refused to be intimidated by Lendl's aggression in the semifinals, however, and pushed the Czech to 6-4, 6-7, 6-3 without really looking like winning while Becker saw off Jarryd in two tiebreak sets.

So it came down to the final everyone had wanted. And what a tremendous match it was. Becker, by his own reckoning, played better than in any of his Wimbledon matches and seemed to have Lendl at his mercy when he got to within six points of the £50,000 prize in the fourth set. Then came that stunning sequence of winners. "I'd never seen a guy play like that before," confessed Becker.

Forty minutes after receiving his runners-up prize Becker was back on court again to partner the Yugoslav Slobodan Zivojinovic in the doubles' final. That too ended in a near-miss disappointment, the pair losing 7-5, 4-6, 7-5 to Guy Forget and Anders Jarryd.

Johan Kriek

Ivan Llendl

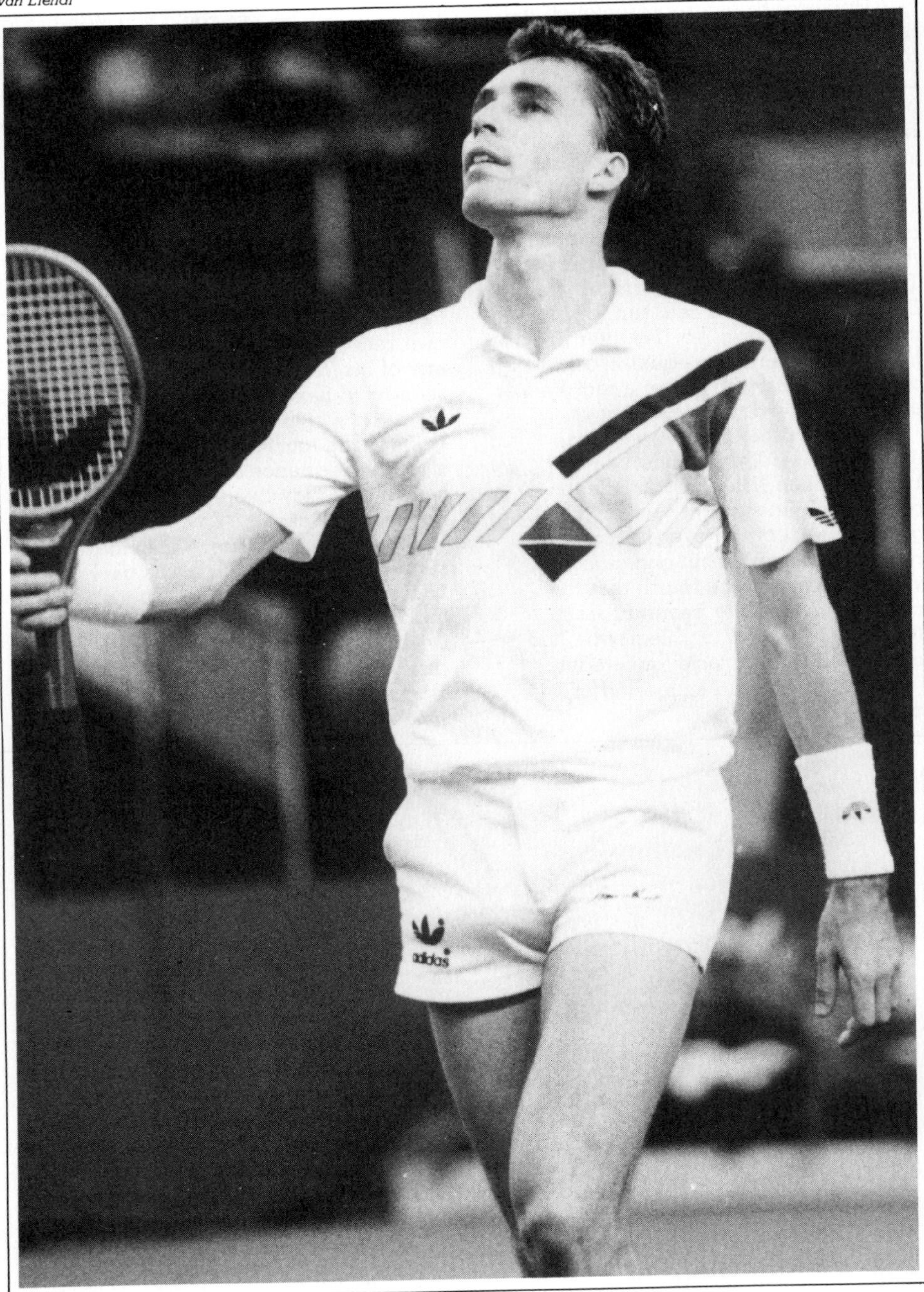

BENSON & HEDGES CHAMPIONSHIPS

Wembley, London

November 12th-17th

SINGLES

First round

I Lendl (Cz) bt L Stefanki (US) 3-6, 6-2, 6-0. T Smid (Cz) bt M Davis (US) 7-5, 7-5. T Nelson (US) bt A Gomez (Ec) 6-4, 6-2. J Kriek (US) bt L Pimek (Cz) 6-4, 5-2 retd. S Edberg (Sw) bt T Tulasne (Fr) 6-3, 7-6. D Pate (US) bt A Maurer (WG) 7-6, 6-4. G Forget (Fr) bt S Zivojinovic (Yug) 6-3, 6-4. J Nystrom (Sw) bt S Casal (Sp) 6-1, 6-0. A Jarryd (Sw) bt H Gunthardt (Swi) 6-3, 6-3. B Taroczy (Hun) bt M Jaite (Arg) 6-2, 6-0. R Krishnan (Ind) bt T Wilkison (US) 4-6, 6-4, 6-4. J Sadri (US) bt Y Noah (Fr) 4-1 retd. M Leach (US) bt S Davis (US) 6-0, 5-7, 6-1. J Gunnarson (Sw) bt J M Lloyd (GB) 6-3, 6-3. M J Bates (GB) bt B Testerman (US) 6-4, 6-4. B Becker (WG) bt S Glickstein (Isr) 6-2, 7-5.

Second round

Lendl bt Smid 6-2, 6-0. Kriek bt Nelson 6-2, 6-2. Pate bt Edberg 6-7, 6-4, 7-5. Nystrom bt Forget 6-4, 6-3. Jarryd bt Taroczy 6-4, 7-5. Krishnan bt Sadri 6-4, 3-6, 6-4. Leach bt Gunnarson 7-5, 6-3. Becker bt Bates 7-5, 7-6.

Quarterfinals

Lendl bt Kriek 6-2, 6-1, Pate bt Nystrom 6-2, 3-6, 7-5. Jarryd bt Krishnan 5-1, 7-5. Becker bt Leach 6-4, 5-3 retd.

Semifinals

Lendl bt Pate 6-4, 6-7, 6-3.
Becker bt Jarryd 7-6, 7-6.

Final

Lendl bt Becker 6-7, 6-3, 4-6, 6-4, 6-4.

DOUBLES

Quarterfinals

G Forget & A Jarryd bt H Gunthardt & B Taroczy 4-6, 6-2, 6-1. A Gomez & I Lendl bt S Casal & E Sanchez 7-6, 6-4. B Becker & S Zivojinovic bt M DePalmer & G Donnelly 3-6, 6-3, 6-2. P Fleming & C van Rensburg bt M Leach & T Wilkison 5-7, 7-6, 9-7.

Semifinals

Forget & Jarryd bt Gomez & Lendl 6-2, 6-3.
Becker & Zivojinovic bt Fleming & van Rensburg 6-3, 6-4.

Final

Jarryd & Forget bt Becker & Zivojinovic 7-5, 4-6, 6-4.

SINGLES WINNERS

1976 J S Connors (US)
1977 B Borg (Swe)
1978 J P McEnroe (US)
1979 J P McEnroe (US)
1980 J P McEnroe (US)
1981 J S Connors (US)
1982 J P McEnroe (US)
1983 J P McEnroe (US)
1984 I Lendl (Cz)

DOUBLES WINNERS

1976 S R Smith & R Tanner (US)
1977 A A Mayer (US) & F McMillan (SA)
1978 P Fleming & J P McEnroe (US)
1979 P Fleming & J P McEnroe (US)
1980 P Fleming & J P McEnroe (US)
1981 S Stewart & F Taygan (US)
1982 P Fleming & J P McEnroe (US)
1983 P Fleming & J P McEnroe (US)
1984 A Gomez (Ec) & I Lendl (Cz)

THE MAZDA CARS WORLD DOUBLES CHAMPIONSHIPS

EUROPEANS SET RECORD

BY PETER BLACKMAN: THE LONDON STANDARD

Christo Van Rensburg threatened to bring the house down and his partner Paul Annacone dealt more aces than Minnesota Fats, but finally they had to stand aside as Heinz Gunthardt and Balazs Taroczy won the World Doubles Championship for the third time. Van Rensburg's spectacular fall among the courtside ferns in the final at the Royal Albert Hall might have been serious enough to end it there and then if a photographer had not caught him in mid-flight.

As it was that spill by the South African caused a 20-minute delay while dinner-suited officials tried to repair the damage to woodwork and netting by using a hammer to secure two-inch long screws into the platform supports. This interlude brought some relief to a dour battle for the £50,000 first prize in the Mazda Cars event. Gunthardt from Switzerland and Taroczy from Hungary set their third time record with a 6-4, 1-6, 7-6 (7-2), 6-7 (6-8), 6-4 victory over the Australian Open champions as an encore to their fine success in mid-summer when they became the Wimbledon doubles champions,

The vital factor under the Albert Hall's cathedral-high dome was their greater experience. First they blunted the young American Annacone's laser-sharp service; then they set about slowing down the fast Van Rensburg. Ironically, after 36 games without a service break it was Annacone's serve that cracked in the fifth set when Gunthardt produced a whiplash service return to set up an easy volley for his partner. Thus, the first break point of the match against Annacone was match point for his opponent.

Gunthardt and Taroczy were the third seeds and the tall, articulate man from Zurich analysed their partnership this way: "I am fast and flashy and he is slow and steady. We smile a lot on court because that is the best way to stay calm and not up tight."

After beating the Australians Mark Edmondson and Kim Warwick at the start of the Red group action the defending champions, Ken Flach and Robert Seguso, admitted: "We both feel sluggish, We hope things improve or else we might lose the title." They then beat the Czech pair Pavel Slozil and Tomas Smid but then came unstuck against the late wild card entry of Britain's John Lloyd and the American Peter Fleming, who previously had found fame and fortune alongside John McEnroe.

In only their third match together they secured a semi-final place with a tactical master-stroke: serving to Flach they adopted a tandem formation (both players on the same side of the court) to restrict the Americans feared cross court return. Unfortunately calamity struck Lloyd and Fleming in the semi-final against Van Rensburg and Annacone. Fleming lost his temper and incurred a code violation for unsportsmanlike behavious – and the pair lost badly in three sets.

It was a good and exciting week for Lloyd and Fleming nonetheless. The British No. 1 relished his elevation alongside a proven world class doubles performer; while Fleming laced his game with some of the hardest serving of the week. "He really makes a tennis ball shift," observed Lloyd. Fleming on the other hand regretted his on-court

Heinz Gunthardt and Balazs Taroczy

outburst in which he claimed one of Van Rensburg's shots had been hit into the ground. "I totally lost my head and I am embarrassed by what happened," he said.

While Edmondson – he arrived in London in a low key mood after breaking his favourite racket in Adelaide – and Warwick were a disappointment, Slozil and Smid were a constant threat in the Red group. Annacone caught the eye in the Blue section. Van Rensburg of course played his part – he had to. The pair entered the Final on the back of a marathon operation – 10 hours 37 minutes spanning three matches over a 20 hour period. And in 14 sets, seven of them were tie breaks.

Taroczy was an endurance man of a sorts, too. He claimed on Day One that he had back trouble and he was unable to sit down for his first press conference. But once in the Final the trouble cleared. Was it gamesmanship? We shall never know!

Paul Annacone and Christo Van Rensburg

MAZDA CARS WORLD DOUBLES CHAMPIONSHIP

Royal Albert Hall, London

January 7-12

RED GROUP

K Flach & R Seguso (US) bt P Slozil & T Smid (Cz) 6-4, 3-6, 7-5, 3-6, 6-3.
P Fleming (US) & J Lloyd (GB) bt M Edmondson & K Warwick (Aus) 6-2, 7-5, 6-4.
Slozil & Smid bt Fleming & Lloyd 6-3, 6-2, 3-6, 7-6.
Flach & Seguso bt Edmondson & Warwick 6-4, 6-4, 7-6.
Slozil & Smid bt Edmondson & Warwick 6-7, 6-1, 7-6, 6-7, 7-5.
Fleming & Lloyd bt Flach & Seguso 2-6, 7-6, 7-5, 6-2.

BLUE GROUP

P Annacone (US) and C Van Rensburg (SA) bt S Casal & E Sanchez (Sp) 7-6, 6-7, 7-6, 7-5.
H Gunthardt (Swz) & B Taroczy (Hun) bt M DePalmer & G Donnelly (US) 6-3, 6-4, 7-6, 6-1.
DePalmer & Donnelly bt Casal & Sanchez 6-2, 7-6, 7-6.
Gunthardt & Taroczy bt Annacone & Van Rensburg 7-5, 4-6 7-6, 6-7, 6-3.
Annacone & Van Rensburg bt DePalmer & Donnelly 5-7, 6-3, 6-3, 7-6.
Casal & Sanchez bt Gunthardt & Taroczy 6-1, 6-1, 6-2.

Seventh Place Play-off

Edmondon & Warwick bt Casal & Sanchez 6-3, 6-4.

Fifth Place Play-off

DePalmer & Donnelly bt Slozil & Smid 6-2, 7-6.

Semifinals

Gunthardt & Taroczy bt Flach & Seguso 7-5, 3-6, 6-3, 7-6.
Annacone & Van Rensburg bt Fleming & Lloyd 6-1, 6-2, 6-2.

Final

Gunthardt & Taroczy bt Annacone & Van Rensburg 6-4, 1-6, 7-6, 6-7, 6-4.

RECORD

1979 P Fleming & J McEnroe (US)
1980 B Gottfried (US) & R Damirez (Mex)
1981 P McNamara & P McNamee (Aus)
1982 H Gunthardt (Swz) & B Taroczy (Hun)
1983 H Gunthardt (Swz) & B Taroczy (Hun)
1984 P Slozil & T Smid (Cz)
1985 K Flach & R Seguso (US)

JEREMY BATES COMES OF AGE

BY HEATHER DALLAS: PRESS OFFICER, THE LTA

In May last year Paul Hutchins described Jeremy Bates as "our best Satellite player for years." Perhaps it was an attempt to goad Bates into attaining greater heights. Whatever the reason, it seems to have been the turning point in Bates' career and he has since leapt up the world rankings and established himself as a force to be reckoned with on the international Circuit.

The fact remains, though, that Jeremy would not have reached his current world ranking — in the top 100 — without the help of the Satellite Circuits he has played during the last few years. They provided him with the all-important computer points to boost him up the ladder to international stardom.

That is what Satellite Circuits are all about — computer points. Forget about the prize money; it is meagre and just about covers the players' expenses during the Circuit. In fact, many of them probably make a loss. All they are really interested in is battling their way through each week in the hope of making the final 'Masters' week so that they can earn a few computer points which, in some cases, could boost them 100 or so places up the world rankings.

The LTA ran three such Circuits in 1985. The first was the Men's indoor Satellite Circuit, which ran for five weeks during January and February. Then came the Mixed Spring Circuit, which also ran for five weeks, during April and May and which, for the players, was probably the most fun and lastly a four week Women's indoor Circuit in November. This wasn't, strictly speaking, a satellite as each week was a separate tournament in it's own right but it was, nevertheless a circuit.

The point about a Satellite event is that a week-long 32 draw tournament is run during each of the first four weeks and players collect circuit points each week. The 16 players with the highest number of circuit points at the end of four weeks then go into the 'Masters' week which carries the highest number of world computer points.

The Men's indoor Satellite Circuit in January and February was, as in 1984, dominated by Jeremy Bates and Peter Lundgren from Sweden, although a third player, Stefan Ericksson, also of Sweden, pipped both of them at the final hurdle and won the 'Masters' and the circuit overall. All three players have since made their mark at top level and Lundgren and Ericksson, aged 22 and 21 respectively, stood at 27 and 117 in the world rankings by the end of 1985.

Five weeks spent on a Satellite Circuit can test even the strongest nerves and the third week of the event saw tempers erupt and a British player, Stuart Bale, was disqualified from the tournament at Telford. This was a shame as Bale had shown some excellent qualities in his King's Cup debut a few weeks earlier. On the whole, though, the circuit was played in extremely good spirit with few angry words.

The first week, played at The Court Tennis Centre, Peterborough was won by Lundgren who defeated Menno Oosting (Netherlands) in the final. Lundgren also won the second week, at Matchpoint in Bramhall, defeating Jeremy Bates in the final. Bates then went on to win the third week, played at Telford Racquet & Fitness Centre, by defeating Stefan Ericksson and Ericksson claimed the fourth week, back at Matchpoint, by gaining a revenge victory over Bates.

Those four players went into the 'Masters' event, at the David Lloyd Slazenger Racquet Club in Heston, as the top four seeds and they all justified their seedings by reaching the last four. Ericksson beat Bates, though, in a tough three set match and in the final he met Lundgren. Scarcely can such an exciting match have been watched by so few but Ericksson emerged as the winner after just over three hours on court 7-6 4-6 7-5.

The International Spring Circuit was for both men and women but, while the men's was a Satellite Circuit, the women played five separate week-long $10,000 tournaments. From the first week, which incorporated The British Home Stores tournament at the Cumberland Club, London, it was obvious that the mixing of the two sexes was going to be a bonus. To quote one of the players "We are more sociable on a mixed circuit. A bunch of us will go out on the town whereas it is not such fun to go with your own sex."

Whether many nights were spent "on the town" is not for these pages but the tennis didn't appear to suffer and even the fact that the prize money for the men was less than that for the women didn't seem to worry anybody.

It was this Circuit which sealed Jeremy Bates' future. He won one week, was runner-up twice and ended up by winning both the 'Masters' event and the circuit overall. He also took away with him around £3,000 and, as they say, never looked back.

One of his main rivals was the young Australian, Simon Youl. Youl beat Bates in the first two finals, at Cumberland Club and then the second week played at Queen's Club. The third week, staged at Sutton Tennis & Squash Club which they described as "their best ever event" was won by Bates who defeated Christer Allgardh of Sweden and the fourth week, at West Hants LTC in Bournemouth was won by Peter Lundgren who beat Peter Johnston of Australia. In the final of the 'Masters' played at the Lee-on-Solent LTC Bates, once again, defeated Christer Allgardh.

Simon Youl

The third week, at Matchpoint, was won by a 23 year old Dutch player, Carin Bakkum, who looked a class above many of the other players. She only played in that event and then in the qualifying for the final week at Telford but those two tournaments were enough to get her an official world ranking as they took her tally of tournaments played to six. In future, a WTA ranking will be obtained after only playing in three tournaments at this level.

The winner of the final week, Claudia Porwik, 17, from West Germany was one of the most delightful players on the circuit and she fulfilled her coach's promise at the beginning of the circuit when she said she would win at least one event. Always neatly turned out, Miss Porwik had a good circuit in both singles and doubles and she and her team-mates, most notably Christina Singer, demonstrated what depth of talent there is now in West Germany.

Jane Wood (Middlesex) and Clare Wood (Sussex), our top two 17 year olds, carried the banner for British tennis. Clare played in only two events but she reached the semi-final at Telford whereas Jane, who played in all four, reached two quarter-finals, at Peterborough and Telford. Liz Jones, 21 from Hampshire, who doesn't play much on the circuit now, also reached two quarter-finals at Queen's Club and Matchpoint and it was good to see Sarah Sullivan, 19 from Essex, displaying some of her undoubted talent in the earlier rounds.

Many British players will have benefited from the event, playing through the pre-qualifying rounds and then the qualifying events. They played against very tough foreign opposition on their home territory which will have given them invaluable experience in match-play and will have put them on the bottom rung of that all-important world tennis ladder.

The women's Circuit was dominated by the attractive, leggy South African, Elna Reinach. She won two events, the BHS at Cumberland Club and at Lee-on-Solent and was finalist at Sutton. An elegant Japanese player, Kumiko Okamoto won the titles at Queen's Club and Sutton and a hard-hitting Italian, Barbara Romano, playing only for one week, swept through the field at Bournemouth.

Running simultaneously with this circuit was a second-tier circuit for those players who failed to make the main event. This helped a lot of British players get the all-important tournament play and the venues were Norwich, where the tournament was sponsored by Anglian Windows; The Court Tennis Centre, Peterborough; West Worthing LTC; North East Regional Centre at Teesside Airport where the Stowferd Press Cider Tournament was held; and Telford Racquet & Fitness Centre where the Evian Tournament was played.

The women's indoor circuit in November, four $10,000 events, was dominated by our European neighbours with large contingents from West Germany, Czechoslovakia and France and, for the first time in this sort of event, a team from Russia.

The first two weeks, though, belonged to a 16 year old Swede, Cecilia Dahlman, who won both events, at Peterborough and at Queen's Club. More importantly, she had to qualify for both, because she was without a world ranking, and she played of total of 16 consecutive matches in 14 days. Tall and leggy, more should be heard of Miss Dahlman.

Elna Reinach with Cumberland Trophy

Peterborough

COURT TENNIS CENTRE, January 21st-25th

SINGLES
Semifinals
P Lundgren (Swe) bt B Derlin (NZ) 5-7, 6-3, 6-2
M Oosting (Neth) bt S Bale 3-6, 6-3, 6-4
Final
Lundgren bt Oosting 4-6, 7-5, 6-1
Doubles Final
Lundgren & S Eriksson (Swe) bt M Albert & G Vekemans (Neth) 6-4, 6-2

Bramhill

MATCHPOINT CLUB, January 28th-February 1st

SINGLES
Semifinals
S P Lundgren (Swe) bt S Eriksson (Swe) 6-4, 6-4.
J Bates bt M Christensen (Den) 6-2, 6-2.
Final
Lundgren bt Bates 6-2, 6-4.
Doubles Final
Eriksson & Lundgren bt I Werner (WG) & J Srenensky (Swz) 6-4, 6-4

Telford

RACQUET CENTRE, February 4th-8th

SINGLES
Semifinals
S Eriksson (Swe) bt M Albert (Neth) 6-0, 6-3
J Bates bt M Oosting (Neth) 6-4, 6-3
Doubles Final
Bates & B Derlin (NZ) bt M Albert & J Vekemans (Neth) 7-6, 6-4

Bramhall

MATCHPOINT CLUB, February 11th-15th

SINGLES
Semifinals
S Eriksson (Swe) bt P Lundgren (Swe) 6-1, 6-4
J Bates bt M Oosting (Neth) 6-4, 6-0
Final
Eriksson bt Bates 6-4, 6-2
Doubles Final
M Albert & J Vekemans (Neth) bt D Felgate & D Maasdorp (SA) 4-6, 6-3, 6-4

Heston

DAVID LLOYD CLUB, February 18th-22nd

SINGLES
Semifinals
P Lundgren (Swe) bt M Oosting (Neth) 6-1, 6-3
S Eriksson (Swe) bt J Bates 6-1, 6-7, 6-4
Final
Eriksson bt Lundgren 7-6, 4-6, 7-5
Doubles Final
S Ericksson & P Lundgren (Swe) bt J Bates & B Derlin (NZ) 6-4, 6-7, 6-3

British Home Stores Tournament

CUMBERLAND CLUB, April 16th-20th

MEN'S SINGLES
Semifinals
S Youl (Aus) bt N Fulwood 6-4, 6-4
J Bates bt P Lundgren (Swe) 7-6, 6-4
Final
Youl bt Bates 6-2, 6-4
Singles
Semifinals
C Cohen (Swz) bt P Etchemendy (Fra) 3-6, 6-3, 6-3
E Reinach (SA) bt J Louis 7-5, 6-3
Final
Reinach bt Cohen 7-5, 7-5

MEN'S DOUBLES
Final
J Bates & D Felgate bt M Kratzmann & Youl (Australia) 3-6, 7-6, 8-6

Queen's Club

April 23rd-27th

MEN'S SINGLES
Semifinals
S Youl (Aus) bt N Christensen (Den) 6-4, 6-3
J Bates bt P Johnston (Aus) 6-3, 3-6, 7-5
Final
Youl bt Bates 6-1, 6-4

LADIES SINGLES
Semifinals
K Okamoto (Jap) bt E Ekblom (Swe) 6-3, 5-7, 6-3
D Moise (Rom) bt J Tacon 6-3, 6-3
Final
Okamoto bt Moise 6-4, 6-2

MEN'S DOUBLES
Final
M Kratzmann & S Youl (Aus) bt L Alfred & P Lundgren (Swe) 6-3, 6-2

LADIES DOUBLES
Final
E Reinach & M Reinach (SA) bt X Li & N Zhong (China) 2-6, 6-2, 9-7

Sutton

April 30th - May 4th

MEN'S SINGLES
Semifinals
C Allgardh (Swe) bt P Flynn (Aus) 1-6, 7-6, 8-6
J Bates bt P Lundgren (Swe) 0-6, 6-1, 6-4
Final
Bates bt Allgardh 7-5, 6-4

LADIES SINGLES
Semifinals
K Okamoto (Jap) bt H Olsson (Swe) 6-3, 6-3
E Reinach (SA) bt X Li (China) 4-6 6-1, 6-0
Final
Okamoto bt Reinach 6-4, 6-7, 6-2

MEN'S DOUBLES
Final
M Kratzmann & S Youl (Aus) bt J Bates & D Felgate 6-4, 6-2

LADIES DOUBLES
Final
X Li & N Zhong (China) bt L Gracie & M Reinhardt (WG) 6-3, 6-3

West Hants Club

BOURNEMOUTH, May 6th-11th

MEN'S SINGLES
Semifinals
R Johnston (Aus) bt L Alfred 7-6, 4-6, 7-5
P Lundgren (Swe) bt S Youl (Aus) 7-5, 1-6, 7-5
Final
Lundgren bt Johnston 4-6, 6-2, 6-3

LADIES SINGLES
Semifinals
D Van Rensburg (SA) bt S Mair 6-1, 6-0
B Romano (It) bt E Reinach (SA) 7-6, 6-3
Final
Romano bt Van Rensburg 6-1, 6-4

MEN'S DOUBLES
Final
M Kratzmann & S Youi (Aus) bt J Bates & D Felgate 6-2, 7-5

LADIES DOUBLES
Final
X Li & N Zhong (China) bt E Renach & M Reinach (SA) 5-7, 7-5, 6-4

Lee-on-Solent

May 14th-18th

MEN'S MASTERS SINGLES
Semifinals
C Allgardh (Swe) bt S Youl (Aus) 6-1, 6-3
J Bates bt P Lundgren (Swe) 6-4, 4-6, 11-9
Final
Bates bt Allgardh 6-2, 6-3

LADIES SINGLES
Semifinals
E Reinach (SA) bt D Van Rensburg (SA) 6-4, 6-3
N Zhong (China) bt D Moise (Rom) 6-3, 6-1
Final
Reinach bt Zhong 6-3, 6-4

MEN'S DOUBLES
Final
M Kratzmann & S Youl (Aus) bt J Bates & D Felgate 6-3, 4-6, 10-8

LADIES DOUBLES
Final
E Reinach & M Reinach (SA) bt B Borneo & J Tacon 6-3, 6-3

Peterborough

November 4th-8th

Singles Final
C Dahlman (Swe) bt N Bajcikova (Cz) 7-5, 6-2
Doubles Final
J Novotna & R Rajchrtova (Cz) bt C Porwick & W Probat (WG) 5-7, 6-3, 6-4

Queen's Club

November 10th-11th

Singles Final
C Dahlman (Swe) bt N Jagerman (Neth) 2-6, 6-4, 6-1
Doubles Final
C Singer (WG) & P Tesarova (Cz) bt C Porwick & W Probst (WG) 5-7, 6-4, 6-3

Bramhall

November 18th-22nd

Singles Final
C Bakkum (Neth) bt J Novotna (Cz) 5-7, 6-3, 6-2
Doubles Final
B Borneo & J Tacon (GB) bt J Novotna & R Rajchrtova (Cz) 6-2, 6-3

Telford

November 25th-29th

Singles Semifinals
N. Jagerman (Neth) bt W Probst (WG) 6-2, 6-4
C Perwick (WG) bt C Wood (GB) 6-0, 6-3
Final
Porwick bt Jagerman 6-3, 6-4
Doubles Final
G Maso & S Pendo (US) bt B Borneo (GB) & N Jagerman (Neth) 4-6, 6-2, 6-3

PLAYING THE RATINGS GAME

BY MIKE APPLETON

The Rating snowball is rolling and growing at a rapid rate. Ten tournaments in 1984 and 750 rated players; 93 tournaments in 1985 and nearly 4,500 rated players. This year there are 189 tournaments in 22 counties and, with the massive sponsorship effort of Volkswagen, the new backers of the scheme, National co-ordinators Jeremy Dier and myself are hoping to top the 8,000 mark.

Let us examine for a moment why the LTA Volkswagen Ratings is so important to the future development of British tennis. The answer lies just across the water (or in time — a tunnel) in France, where a similar Ratings Scheme has been operating very successfully for the past 15 years or so. The French have developed their ratings tournament scene to nearly 5000, with over 1 million registered players.

A rating is now as important to a French tennis player as a handicap is to a British golfer — arguably the most talked-about aspect in the game. For the player, we finally have a method of measuring standard, and as soon as it becomes readily acceptable to all tennis players in the UK, as it has in France, then Britain will truly be able to quantify the depths of play in this country. Gone are the days when two players meet, when one describes his standard as "average" and the other "not bad". Not bad compared to who?

As a further illustration, in the very first ratings tournament at the Southdown club in Sussex in 1984, a ten year old boy played a man well into his fifties. Age wasn't important as they were both +40's (the lowest rating category) and were therefore equally matched when facing each other across the net. In another match at Crawley two weeks later, two ladies, again of +40 standard were drawn against each other. Although they often scored incorrectly and sometimes stopped to have a chat midway through a game or changeover, they thoroughly enjoyed themselves in a match that lasted over two hours. Indeed the referee was so taken back by the whole thing that he gave both ladies a can of new balls to take away with them!

The overall objective of the scheme, other than to provide players with a wonderful opportunity to play competitive singles, is to increase the standard at every level — or rating category — within the game. If the standard at the base of the game improves it will filter up through the levels to the very best players. A country has far more chance of producing a champion — the ultimate objective — if there are sufficient contenders available. France produced Yannick Noah, the 1984 French Champion, and they readily admit that he was a product of their 'classement sytem'. Since then other players have emerged, Leconte, Tulasne in the men; Tanvier, Paradis, and many more in the ladies.

The tournaments themselves are run over two weeks, usually Sunday to Sunday. Play is in the evenings during the week and throughout the day at weekends. All players are matched against opponents of similar ability, so whatever the standard, everybody enjoys a close match. Because of the attractive structure of the tournaments, the average life of a player is around two days (or evenings). If it turns out to be more than this, the player is either improving too quickly or has been allocated the wrong rating! Ratings are decided initially from information supplied by the player; they are subsequently reviewed by computer in the light of results gained during the year.

Tournaments consist of a series of draws. The draws are staggered so that the higher rated players start progressively later in the tournament and attractive prizes are offered at almost every level. Players reaching an advanced stage in their draw will qualify for a place in the next draw, already containing the higher rated players. The loser in each match keeps the balls, and as every match starts with new balls, the standard entry fee of £4.00 is practically refunded.

The clubs benefit as well; they are extremely unlikely to lose out financially and more often than not make a considerable profit. The entry fees, profits from gate money, programmes, catering etc. go directly to them. Club members don't lose out as the staggered draw format leaves ample courts free for friendly games and general use. Members also have the opportunity to play in the tournament.

It is somewhat surprising, therefore, that some clubs are sceptical about the scheme and do not participate. But anything new takes time to catch on, and when the consumer is the club and through the club, its members, the policy taken is to encourage the club as much as possible in the hope that they will participate in the scheme the following year.

Aside from the tournament scene, the scheme will have really 'made it' when it has managed to penetrate our rather antiquated club league system. The traditional 3 or 2 pair doubles structure has long been abandoned by our neighbouring countries where league matches are the highlight of the year. Matches always contain an element of singles and can often attract many hundreds of spectators; even the country's best players turn out to play.

Let us hope that, by the turn of the century, we will have gone some way to catching our competitors!

CARISBROOKE LIKE SILK

BY HENRY WANCKE

Having expressed a buoyant mood last year as regards sponsorship at club level, 1985 proved rather lean! Out of the four reported in 1984, only two were run this year — the Silk Cut Inter Club Championship and the Blue Arrow Slazenger National Club Championship. Pernod transferred all their tennis sponsorship support into the successful ratings scheme (which was not unexpected) whilst Sunbeam, surprisingly, withdrew completely.

Both remaining events held their finals during September, with Silk Cut on first at Queens. The event has been growing steadily in the three years it has been held. In 1983 only 255 clubs competed but 550 were involved on this occasion.

Played in eight areas during the preliminary stages, the resultant regional winners met on the weekend of September 14. Winchester and Carisbrooke were the favourites and ended up in the final — the first time a non-London club was to lift the title.

It was Carisbrooke from Leicester, who eventually became the Silk Cut champions, defeating the No 1 seeds. It was the third consecutive year that they had fought through to the National finals and it proved lucky. They had trouble in the first round, at which stage they could have lost to Torquay when they trailed 0-1 after losing the first rubber in the ladies. The men then levelled the score and the mixed combination of Neil Smith and Sally Kipping finally saw them through and set them on their successful run. In the semifinals, against Shirley Park, the same pairing again had to win the deciding rubber to ensure their progress to the title, after the Carisbrooke men had dropped their club's second rubber of the championship.

The final was forced into the new indoor courts at Queens and proved much faster than the outdoor shale surface used the preceding day. Carisbrooke missed no opportunities and won both the men's and ladies' doubles in three sets. Gill Thompson and Sally Kipping played safely, waiting for their opportunities and winning 5-7, 6-2, 6-3, after trailing 0-3 in the final set. Jon Ison and Neil Smith then adopted an aggressive mood and forced the pace of their match. Like the ladies, they dropped the first set but their positive outlook took the match and title 4-6, 6-4, 6-3. During the match though, Jon Ison received an official warning from the umpire for striking the ball into John Vinnell of Winchester.

Winchester Tennis & Squash Club, in reaching the final, only dropped one rubber en route to Gidea Park in the semis, having defeated Thorn Park in the first round or quarters. The Vagabonds and York also made their exits from the Championships, losing their first round matches to Gidea Park and Shirley Park respectively.

For their achievement, Carisbrooke's representatives won £1000 for their club, and cut glass whisky decanters for themselves. Plus a trip to the 1986 French Open. The losing finalists picked up £750 for their club coffers and a set of luggage for each of their team members.

The next club title to be resolved was the Slazenger Blue Arrow National

Championship the following weekend at Wimbledon. Having had its format changed from last year — there are now playing two divisions, which gives weaker clubs a better chance for honours — eight contesting clubs arrived on September 21st to compete for Division One and Two titles.

In the top Division, the usual contenders were present — Queens, Connaught, Edgbaston Priory, David Lloyd's, West Hants and Beckenham. In the ladies' section, Queens Club eventually beat Grafton 4-0 whilst Edgbaston Priory lifted the men's equivalent title by beating West Hants 2-2, 2-5, 5-5, 49-46! With rubbers and sets even, the title was decided on games and had Mike and Robert Booth (West Hants) managed to win their deciding set against Phil King and Phil Siviter (Edgbaston Priory) by 6-0 instead of 6-3, West Hants would have been champions.

Both clubs deserved a share of the honours. The Booths had been undefeated throughout the competition, a tremendous achievement, whilst Edgbaston Priory had put out the holders in the semifinal. At the end of the day Edgbaston Priory deserved their narrow win, their first title in the men's event.

The ladies' championship was also closely fought despite the 4-0 score. Grafton fought hard and their defeat was really a matter of missed chances. It was their first appearance in the final, having knocked out the title holders Edgbaston Priory in the semis. They are a young team and the signs indicate they will be back in future years. The winning team will be flying, courtesy of Blue Arrow, to Portugal for a holiday next year — which makes their efforts more than worthwhile.

In Division Two, St Serfs from Edinburgh won the men's title by beating Torquay 3-1 and Streetly Ladies defeated Clifton from Bristol, by the same margin.

Not a club event as such, but encompassing doubles play, the Remington Father and Son Championship was launched in March. Loosely based on the successful American competition, the event was decided on a postal-basis in 16 regions. with the champions being flown out to Southern Spain for a National final early in November.

The event proved very successful, with sponsorship being provided by Remington, Fila and Diadora and support from the La Manga Club, Peter Stuyvesant Travel, Dunlop and the Daily Express. The objectives of broadening the tennis-playing base in a family environment was quickly realised when 901 teams enrolled by the entry deadline in late May. Early October saw the regions completed and the standard was high with many ex-county players and their offspring still in the competition.

In brilliant sunshine, the National Final was hotly contested and the eventual innaugural champions were Ray and David Booth from Cheshire, who play at the Congleton Lawn Tennis Club — a Co-op manager and his joiner son. Unseeded, they came through a tough draw beating the favourites, Malcolm and Simon Booth in the semifinals. A steady pair, with lots of determination, they won their final by coming from behind and beating Robert and Graham Spalding from Nottingham, 5-7, 6-0, 6-2.

To reach the first British National Father and Son finals, regional champions played through six rounds. These were Ian and David McMillan (Ongar); David and Mark Tomlinson (Mill Hill); who went on to win the Plate; Robert and Russell Bruty (Bexleyheath); John and Andrew Walsh (Barnstaple); Gordon and Richard Proctor (Cheltenham); Jim and Tim Ferrier (Chandlers Ford, Hants); Paul and David Alexander (Banbury); James and Andrew Wishart (West Byfleet); Richard and Kevin Butcher (Sittingbourne); John and Stuart Tucker (Brentwood); Malcolm and Simon Booth (Sutton Coldfield); Ray and David Booth (Congleton); Robert and Graham Spalding (Wollaton, Nottingham); Graham and Ian Hodkinson (Worsley, Manchester); Brian and Paul Layfield (Pudsey); and James and James Wood (Bieldside, Aberdeen).

Their prize included products from the two co-sponsors and the trip to La Manga. For the players it proved an event they will not forget quickly and their thanks to all involved heartened all the sponsors. In view of the tournament's success, and in furtherance of the initial objectives of a family fun competition, a Mothers' and Daughter section is to be launched this year to complement this extremely worthwhile addition to the season's calendar.

Leicester: Silk Cut Inter-Club Champions

SILK CUT FINALS

QUEEN'S CLUB, September 14th-15th

Semifinals
Winchester bt Gidea Park (Romford) 2-1
Carisbrooke (Leicester) bt Shirley Park (Croydon) 2-1
Final
Carisbrooke bt Winchester 2-0
(Details — S Kipping & G Thompson bt P Birch & L Machin 5-7, 6-2, 6-3, I Ison & N Smith bt N Steventon & J Vinnell 4-6, 6-4, 6-3)

SLAZENGER BLUE ARROW NATIONAL CHAMPIONSHIPS

WIMBLEDON, September 21st

Men's Semifinals
Edgbaston Priory bt David Lloyd Slazenger Racquet Club 4-0
West Hants bt Beckenham 2-0
Final
Edgbaston Priory bt West Hants 2-2, 5-5, 4-9, 4-6
Ladies Semifinals
Queen's Club bt Connaught 3½-½, Grafton bt Edgbaston Priory 3-1
Final
Queen's Club bt Grafton 4-0

BRITISH TOURNAMENT SEASON

BWTA-TATE & LYLE INDOOR

BRAMHALL, March 16th-20th

Semifinals
C Wood bt A Hobbs 6-3, 6-2
S Gomer bt J Louis 6-2, 6-1
Final
Gomer bt Wood 6-4, 6-2

BWTA – SW FARMER GROUP INDOOR

QUEEN'S CLUB, March 26th-29th

Semifinals
K Brasher bt J Reeves 6-2, 6-3
J Louis bt J Wood 2-6, 6-3, 6-0
Final
Louis bt Brasner 6-1, 6-4

WETHERALL NORTH OF ENGLAND CHAMPIONSHIPS

SOUTHPORT, April 1st-7th

MEN'S SINGLES
Semifinals
R Lewis bt W Davies 6-3, 6-0
D Shaw bt B Parker 6-1, 6-2
Final
Lewis bt Shaw 6-4, 6-1

LADIES SINGLES
Semifinals
S Nicholson bt L Geeves 6-2, 4-6, 6-3
S Gomer bt J Griffiths w/o
Final
Gomer bt Nicholson 6-0, 6-1

MEN'S DOUBLES
Final
S Botfield & B Knapp bt W Davies & M Robinson 6-2, 6-3

LADIES DOUBLES
Final
S Gomer & L Gracie bt L Gould & C Wood 6-1, 6-1

BMW WESTERN COUNTIES

BRISTOL, April 8th-13th

MEN'S SINGLES
Semifinals
L Alfred bt P Moore 6-2, 6-3
B Knapp bt M Blincow 6-4, 4-6, 6-4
Final
Knapp bt Alfred 2-6, 6-3, 7-5

LADIES SINGLES
Semifinals
S Gomer bt S Sullivan 6-2, 6-1
S Nicholson bt M Dailey 6-3, 6-0
Final
Nicholson bt Gomer 5-7,6-4, 7-6

MEN'S DOUBLES
Final
P French & J Turner bt L Alfred & M Blincow 6-2, 6-2

LADIES DOUBLES
S Gomer & E Lightbody bt J Langstaff & S Nicholson 6-3, 6-3

ANGLIAN WINDOWS TOURNAMENT

NORWICH, April 16th-20th

MEN'S SINGLES
Semifinals
K Tomlin bt D Ison 6-2, 6-3
N Beedham bt I Currie 4-6, 6-3, 6-3
Final
Tomlin bt Beedham 6-3 4-4, retd

LADIES SINGLES
Semifinals
A Brown bt H Kluth 6-0, 6-0
D van Rensburg bt K Schimper 6-1, 6-1
Final
Brown bt Van Rensburg 6-2, 6-2

MEN'S DOUBLES
Final
S Botfield & P Hughesman bt S Heron & C Peet 6-3, 6-5

LADIES DOUBLES
Final
Schimper & Van Rensburg bt M Dailey & R Seeman 6-1, 7-5

LTA PETERBOROUGH TOURNAMENT

COURT TENNIS CENTRE, April 23rd-27th

MEN'S SINGLES
Semifinals
B Parker bt S Batchelor 6-1, 6-3
C Peet bt D Ison 6-4, 6-0
Final
Parker bt Peet 6-4, 6-4

LADIES SINGLES
Semifinals
S Nicholson bt L Geeves 6-1, 7-6
R Seeman bt J Reeves 6-3 6-1
Final
Nicholson bt Seemans 1-6, 6-4, 6-1

MEN'S DOUBLES
Final
S Heron & C Peet bt A Douglas & D Ison 6-1, 7-6

LADIES DOUBLES
J Langstaff & S Nicholson bt H Kluth & R Seeman 6-2, 7-5

LTA WORTHING TOURNAMENT

WEST WORTHING, April 30th-May 4th

MEN'S SINGLES
Semifinals
A Brice bt S Botfield 6-3, 7-6
M Reeves bt A Douglas 2-6, 7-5, 7-5
Final
Brice bt Reeves 6-4, 6-1

LADIES SINGLES
Semifinals
F Osawa bt P Sepulveda 1-6, 6-1, 7-6
L Geeves bt H Luscombe 4-6, 7-5, 6-1
Final
Geeves bt Osawa 6-3, 4-6, 6-4

MEN'S DOUBLES
Final
S Botfield & A Brice bt A Douglas & S Heron 6-0, 7-6

LADIES DOUBLES
Final
T Dubravcic & H Luscombe bt J Langstaff & S Nicholson 6-4, 6-4

STOWFORD PRESS CIDER TOURNAMENT

NORTH EAST REGIONAL CENTRE, May 7th-11th

MEN'S SINGLES
Semifinals
B Parker bt M Futcher 6-2, 6-3
H Slater bt P Pospisil 7-5, 6-1
Final
Parker bt Slater 7-6, 6-1

LADIES SINGLES
Semifinals
V Lake bt R Luscombe 5-7, 7-5, 6-4
J Holden bt J Phillips 4-5, 6-2, 6-0
Final
Holden bt Lake 6-4, 6-3

MEN'S DOUBLES
Final
M Futcher & M Harpin bt B Parker & H Slater 6-3, 6-4

LADIES DOUBLES
Final
H Luscombe & L Mansfield bt S Armitage & V Lake 6-3, 4-6, 6-2

MIXED DOUBLES
Final
F Bingham & J Holden bt A Higham & T Brazenhall 6-3, 1-6, 6-2

EVIAN TOURNAMENT

TELFORD, May 14th-17th

MEN'S SINGLES
Semifinals
B Parker bt R Ward 6-4, 6-1
L Davies bt I Mackinlay 7-5, 6-1
Final
Parker bt Davies 6-2, 6-2

LADIES SINGLES
Semifinals
J Griffiths bt D Schauerman 7-5, 6-1
J Phillips bt J Iddles 6-3, 6-4
Final
Griffiths bt Phillips 6-3, 4-6, 6-1

MEN'S DOUBLES
Final
L Davies & B Parker bt I Mackinlay & R Proctor 7-6, 3-6, 6-2

PRUDENTIAL PADDINGTON TOURNAMENT

LONDON, May 18th-26th

MEN'S SINGLES
Semifinals
R Drysdale bt D Maasdorb 7-5, 6-2
L Alfred bt B Knapp 6-4, 0-6, 6-4
Final
Alfred led Drysdale 2-0 (abandoned, rain)

LADIES SINGLES
Semifinals
K Brasher bt N Znong 6-4, 6-0
X Li bt L Pennington 6-3, 6-1
Final
Brasher led Li 2-1 (abandoned, rain)

MEN'S DOUBLES
Final
L Alfred & M Baroch bt R Carmichael & J Feaver 6-0, 6-4

LADIES DOUBLES
Final
X Li & N Zhong bt L Geeves & R Seeman 6-4, 6-4

GRATTAN HEATON TOURNAMENT

BRADFORD, May 27th-June 1st

MEN'S SINGLES
Semifinals
N Fulwood bt B Parker 6-3, 7-5
D Stone bt J Leytze 6-2, 6-1
Final
Stone bt Fulwood 1-6, 6-3, 6-4

LADIES SINGLES
Semifinals
H Luscombe bt M Redfearn 5-7, 6-4, 9-7
R Seeman bt L Ristic 7-5, 7-5
Final
Luscombe bt Seeman 6-4, 7-5

MEN'S DOUBLES
Final
N Fulwood & M Robinson bt V Bryan & P Reekie 6-3, 7-6

LADIES DOUBLES
Final
H Luscombe & M Redfearn bt L Ristic & R Seeman 6-1, 6-3

CHAPEL ALLERTON TOURNAMENT

LEEDS, June 10th-15th

MEN'S SINGLES
Semifinals
B Parker bt P Layfield 6-2, 6-0
C Strode bt T Hafique 6-3, 6-0
Final
Strode bt Parker 6-3, 3-6, 6-3

LADIES SINGLES
Semifinals
K McDaniel bt J Geiler 6-2 6-1
J Smith bt K Brown 5-7, 7-6, 6-1
Final
McDaniel bt Smith 6-4, 7-5

MEN'S DOUBLES
Final
G Neibur & C Strode bt N Garton & B Parker 6-4, 6-1

LADIES DOUBLES
Final
J Sculthorpe & J Smith bt J Geller & S Longbottom 6-3, 3-6, 8-6

MIXED DOUBLES
Final
D Sammel & S Longbottom bt G Neibur & K McDaniel 7-6, 2-6, 6-4

GUARDIAN ROYAL EXCHANGE EAST OF ENGLAND CHAMPIONSHIPS

FELIXSTOWE, July 8th-13th

MEN'S SINGLES
Semifinals
J Turner bt A Douglas 6-3, 3-6, 6-1
M Robinson bt P French 6-3, 6-4
Final
Turner bt Robinson 6-3, 4-6, 6-3

LADIES SINGLES
Semifinals
V Binns bt S Godman 6-1, 6-2
C Gillies bt S Longbottom 4-6, 6-1, 6-1
Final
Gillies bt Binns 2-6, 6-3, 6-2

MEN'S DOUBLES
Final
French & Turner bt Douglas & P Hand 7-6, 1-6, 6-3

LADIES DOUBLES
Final
Godman & A Nall bt Longbottom & C Petchey walkover

DURHAM AND CLEVELAND CHAMPIONSHIPS

SUNDERLAND, July 8th-13th

MEN'S SINGLES
Semifinals
M Baldridge bt F Bingham walkover
G Hinchcliffe bt M Slater 4-6, 7-5, 6-4
Final
Baldridge bt Hinchcliffe 6-1, 6-3

LADIES SINGLES
Semifinals
J Morton bt E Andrew 6-1, 5-7, 6-0
A Oliver bt J Ruffell 3-6, 7-6, 7-5
Final
Morton bt Oliver 3-6, 6-4, 6-1

MEN'S DOUBLES
Final
G Hinchliffe & M Lang bt M Slater & M Baldridge 6-1, 6-4

LADIES DOUBLES
Final
J Morton & A Oliver bt A Clayton & J Ruffell 6-2, 6-4

FRINTON-ON-SEA TOURNAMENT

FRINTON-ON-SEA, July 15th-20th

MEN'S SINGLES
Semifinals
M Robinson bt J Pugh walkover
R W Drysdale bt S Botfield 6-3, 7-6

Final
Drysdale bt Robinson 6-2, 6-2

LADIES SINGLES
Semifinals
C L Billingham bt J Muller 6-3, 5-7, 6-2
G Gillies bt L Ristic
Final
Gillies bt Billingham 4-6, 6-4, 6-2

MEN'S DOUBLES
Final
M Guntrip & S Matthews bt P J French & J Turner 7-6, 6-3

LADIES DOUBLES
Final
M P Collins & J L Muller bt C J Billingham & K Hand walkover

SLAZENGER WINCHESTER TOURNAMENT

July 29th-August 3rd

MEN'S SINGLES
Semifinals
L Scott bt D Ison 6-3, 4-6, 6-2
P Palandian bt D Roberts 6-1 6-2
Final
Palandian bt Scott 8-6 (pro set)

LADIES SINGLES
Semifinals
J Phillips bt S Armitage 7-6, 6-0
K Hand bt V Lake 6-3, 4-6, 7-5
Final
Phillips led Hand 6-2, 2-4, abandoned

DOUBLES
Abandoned

ESAB NORTHUMBERLAND OPEN

NEWCASTLE, July 29th-August 3rd

MEN'S SINGLES
Semifinals
P McNamara bt J Feaver 6-7, 7-6, 6-3
R A Lewis bt C M Robinson 7-6, 6-7, 6-2
Final
Lewis bt McNamara 2-6, 6-4, 7-6

LADIES SINGLES
Semifinals
S Barker bt S J McCarthy 6-3, 6-2
C H Berry bt J Griffiths 6-3, 1-6, 6-2
Final
Berry bt Barker 6-2, 2-6, 6-4

MEN'S DOUBLES
Final
P French & J Turner bt P McNamara & S Stewart 7-6, 1-6, 6-4

LADIES DOUBLES
Final
S McCarthy & T Price bt J Holden & S J Leach 4-6, 6-1, 7-6

NORTHAMPTONSHIRE CHAMPIONSHIPS

WELLINGBOROUGH, July 29th-August 3rd

MEN'S SINGLES
Semifinals
R Ward bt C Miller 6-3, 6-1
G Chester bt S Bone 3-6, 6-4, 6-0
Final
Chester bt Ward 6-4, 6-7, 6-2

LADIES SINGLES
Semifinals
K Brown bt V Waite 6-1 6-1
A Reichenbach bt I Wild 6-3, 6-1
Final
Brown bt Reichenbach 6-2, 7-6

MEN'S DOUBLES
Final
A Davies & M Dawson bt C Bertram & J Knight 6-4, 6-1

LADIES DOUBLES
Final
R Dickinson & K Brown bt A Reichenbach & I Wild 6-2, 6-2

TUNBRIDGE WELLS TOURNAMENT

July 29th-August 3rd

MEN'S SINGLES
Semifinals
N de Grunwald bt D Clarry 6-2, 6-2
A D Illingworth bt T W Godman 6-2, 6-4
Final
Illingworth bt De Grunwald 6-1, 7-6

LADIES SINGLES
Semifinals
H Narborough bt W D Compton 6-3, 6-3
S Gough bt J Blyth-Lewis 6-2, 6-0
Final
Narborough bt Gough 3-6, 6-3, 6-0

MEN'S DOUBLES
Final
De Grunwald & R Stoakes bt Godman & J W Watson 6-2, 6-2

LADIES DOUBLES
Final
Blyth-Lewis & Compton bt Narborough & J O'Farrell 7-6, 6-2

BATH TOURNAMENT

July 29th-August 3rd

MEN'S SINGLES
Semifinals
G Evans bt A Pearman 6-0, 6-2
S Partridge bt R Lenton 5-7, 6-2, 6-3
Final
Partridge bt Evans 6-1, 6-1

LADIES SINGLES
Semifinals
A Baldwin bt C Bowen 6-7, 6-3, 6-3
C Bateman bt S Mitchell 6-2, 6-1
Final
Bateman bt Baldwin 6-1 6-2

MEN'S DOUBLES
Final
J Startup & S Partridge bt N Geffaller & G Evans 6-3, 4-6, 6-2

LADIES DOUBLES
Final
A Baldwin & B Mitchell bt J Calley & W Worboys 6-3, 6-1

CHARLIE BROWN ILKLEY TOURNAMENT

August 3rd-10th

MEN'S SINGLES
Semifinals
N Fulwood bt S Botfield 5-7, 7-5, 6-2
S Ickringill bt S Shaw 7-6 retd
Final
Fulwood bt Ickringill 6-3, 7-6

LADIES SINGLES
Semifinals
C Berry bt S Barker 4-6, 6-3, 10-8
J Langstaff bt J Holden 6-4, 6-1
Final
Berry bt Langstaff 6-7, 6-1, 6-2

MEN'S DOUBLES
Final
J Feaver & N Fulwood bt M Guntrip & S Botfield 7-6, 6-2

LADIES DOUBLES
Final
S Longbottom & A Grant bt J Langstaff & C Berry 6-2, 6-3

BOURNEMOUTH OPEN

August 5th-10th

MEN'S SINGLES
Semifinals
A Douglas bt C Cutbill 6-3, 6-4
R Booth bt N Jones 5-7, 6-4, 6-3
Final
R Rooth bt Douglas 7-5, 6-3

LADIES SINGLES
Semifinals
A Fleming bt R Charlton 6-2, 6-1
K Brown bt F Couldridge 6-1, 7-6
Final
Fleming bt Brown 7-6, 6-2

LADIES DOUBLES
Final
A Fleming & A Gregory bt A Nall & N Entract 6-0, 7-6

FRAMLINGHAM

August 5th-10th

MEN'S SINGLES
Semifinals
A Isiorho bt K Mangum 6-2, 6-3
G Hempsall bt C Dimmock 7-6, 7-0
Final
Hempsall bt Isiorho 6-1, 6-7, 6-3

LADIES SINGLES
Semifinals
T O Durham bt S J Devereux 6-1 6-1
G Oakenfull bt S Pateman 4-6, 6-3, 6-1
Final
Durham bt Oakenfull 7-5, 7-5

MEN'S DOUBLES
Final
R A Smith & C Dimmock bt G Hempsall & G Hempsall 7-6, 6-7, 7-5

LADIES DOUBLES
Final
R E Dickinson & Y O Durham bt C M Sutton & S Pateman 6-2, 5-7, 6-4

LLANELLI OPEN

August 5th-10th

MEN'S SINGLES
Semifinals
N J Lee bt S Richards 3-6, 6-4, 6-3
S Matthews bt D H U James 7-5, 6-2
Final
Matthews bt Lee 7-5, 6-2

LADIES SINGLES
Semifinals
K Hand bt H L Taylor 6-0, 6-7, 6-1
D Schauerman bt R Griffiths 4-6, 6-4, 6-4
Final
Hand bt Schauerman 4-6, 7-5, 6-2

MEN'S DOUBLES
Final
D H U James & N J Lee bt D Reid & G Clark 6-3, 6-2

LADIES DOUBLES
Final
R L Griffiths & K Hand bt H L Taylor & S Mitchell 6-2, 6-3

TORBAY OPEN

August 5th-10th

MEN'S SINGLES
Semifinals
J Southcombe bt D Roberts 6-0, 6-2
S Tucker bt R Short 6-3, 6-4
Final
Southcombe bt Tucker 6-4, 6-1

LADIES SINGLES
Semifinals
J Smith bt L Stern 6-2, 5-7, 6-4
V Lake bt S Mitten 6-2, 7-5

Final
Lake bt Smith 6-1, 6-2

MEN'S DOUBLES
Final
Southcombe & Tucker bt S Allan & Short 6-1, 6-3

LADIES DOUBLES
Final
Lake & Stern bt J Caward & C Madge 6-0, 6-4

MIXED DOUBLES
Final
R Short & V Lake bt D Roberts & S Mitten 6-4, 6-3

ALVERSTOKE

August 12th-17th

MEN'S SINGLES
Semifinals
J Godfrey bt N Bray 6-1, 6-1
M Cook bt J Vinnell 6-4, 6-2
Final
Godfrey bt Cook 6-4, 6-0

WOMEN'S SINGLES
Semifinals
J Caplan bt K Brown 6-2, 6-4
S Byrbe bt M Allen 6-3, 6-3
Final
J Caplan bt Byrne 6-0, 6-2

MEN'S DOUBLES
Final
M Bray & J Vinnell bt M Cook & J Godfrey 3-6, 6-2, 6-2

LADIES DOUBLES
Final
J Caplan & K Brown bt S Byrne & M Allen 6-1, 6-2

BURNHAM-ON-SEA

August 12th-17th

MEN'S SINGLES
Semifinals
B G Lawrence bt A Pearman 6-4, 7-6
J Cambers bt G Tucker 6-4, 6-1
Final
Chambers bt Lawrence 6-0, 6-4

LADIES SINGLES
Semifinals
J Famous bt A Gwilliam 7-6, 3-6, 6-2
J Le Neve Foster bt H Cotton 6-1, 6-1
Final
Le Neve Foster bt Famous 6-1, 6-3

MEN'S DOUBLES
Final
R Knight & A Pearman bt J Chambers & J Horlor 6-4, 5-7, 6-2

LADIES DOUBLES
Final
J Cotton & H Cotton bt R Farthing & M Bell 7-6, 6-2

CRANLEIGH

August 12th-17th

MEN'S SINGLES
Semifinals
A Aldridge bt R Dwek 6-0, 6-3
M Wallace bt M Dawson 6-2, 6-3
Final
Wallace bt Aldridge 6-4, 6-1

LADIES SINGLES
Semifinals
J Langstaff bt A Blair 6-2, 6-1
V Sims bt L Solomon 6-1, 6-3
Final
Langstaff bt Sims 6-4, 6-1

LADIES DOUBLES
Final
Langstaff & Sims bt J Mundell & S Stott 6-4, 6-2

NORFOLK CHAMPIONSHIPS

August 12th-17th

MEN'S SINGLES
Semifinals
C Bailey bt A Dalton 6-2, 6-4
A Devaney bt I Thomas 6-4, 6-4
Final
Bailey bt Devaney 5-7, 7-6, 6-1

LADIES SINGLES
Semifinals
C Sutton bt S Baker 6-1, 6-4
J Smith bt J O'Farrell 6-3, 7-5
Final
Smith bt Sutton 6-4, 2-6, 6-4

MEN'S DOUBLES
Final
D Drake & J Ranson bt K Searby & C Warren 6-3, 5-7, 7-5

LADIES DOUBLES
Final
J O'Farrell & M Watson-Pegman bt V Bonham & J Sladden 6-3, 7-5

PLYMOUTH OPEN

August 12th-17th

MEN'S SINGLES
Semifinals
N Hand bt S Sherlock 6-2, 6-4
T Downing bt G Sullivan 6-3, 1-6, 7-5
Final
Hand bt Downing 7-5, 6-2

LADIES SINGLES
Semifinals
S Mitten bt R Toogood 6-0, 6-0
S Wherry bt A Spiers walkover

Final
Mitten bt Wherry 6-3, 6-0

MEN'S DOUBLES
Final
N Hand & G Sullivan bt M Coysh & E Morgan 7-6, 7-6

LADIES DOUBLES
Final
L McCloughlin & S Mitten bt H Sparks & J Weaver 6-2, 6-2

HALLAMSHIRE

SHEFFIELD, August 12th-18th

MEN'S SINGLES
Semifinals
C Peet bt M Walker 6-3, 6-1
J Turner bt M Robinson 6-4, 6-7, 6-3
Final
Turner bt Peet 7-6, 6-3

LADIES SINGLES
Semifinals
L Ristic bt S Longbottom 3-6, 6-4, 7-5
S Whiteman bt G Power 3-6, 6-3, 6-2
Final
Ristic bt Whiteman 6-2, 6-3

MEN'S DOUBLES
Final
D Sammel & J Turner bt R Drysdale & M Walker 7-6, 6-4

LADIES DOUBLES
Final
S Longbottom & C Power S Armitage & S Whiteman 6-4, 6-2

WEST WORTHING

August 12th-17th

MEN'S SINGLES
Semifinals
R Jeffreys bt D Ison w/o, A Broomhead bt L Matthews 6-4, 6-1
Final
Broomhead bt Jeffreys 6-2, 7-6

LADIES SINGLES
Semifinals
J Phillips bt J Reeves 6-4, 6-3
V Lake bt M Van Maarleveld 6-1, 7-5
Final
Lake bt Phillips 6-1, 6-1

MEN'S DOUBLES
Final
R Jeffreys & D Cutbill bt G Smith & K Holloeay 6-4, 6-3

LADIES DOUBLES
Final
K Hand & V Lake bt J Reeves & K Hunter 7-5, 3-6, 6-2

MIXED DOUBLES
Final
H Pringle & V Lake bt D James & D Schauerman 3-6, 6-1, 6-3

HAVANT

August 19th-24th

MEN'S SINGLES
Semifinals
J Turner bt P Hand 6-2, 7-6
J Howie bt A Douglas 7-6, 4-6, 6-2
Final
Turner bt Howie 7-6, 6-2

LADIES SINGLES
Semifinals
J Langstaff bt K Brown 6-4, 6-2
A Bishop bt W Compton 6-2, 7-6
Final
Langstaff bt Bishop 6-3, 6-3

MEN'S DOUBLES
Final
J Turner & P Hand bt M Cook & M Bray 6-2, 7-6

LADIES DOUBLES
Final
J Langstaff & A Bishop bt J Paterson & K Brown 6-2, 7-6

MIXED DOUBLES
Final
P Hand & J Langstaff bt G Smith & J Paterson 6-2, 6-4

HUNSTANTON

August 19th-24th

MEN'S SINGLES
Semifinals
C Warren bt R Smith 6-3, 6-1
K Searby A Higham 3-6, 6-3, 13-11
Final
Warren bt Searby 6-2, 4-6, 6-2

LADIES SINGLES
Semifinals
N Mackintosh bt S Devereux 6-2, 6-2
A Godfrey bt A Morrell 6-0, 6-3
Final
Mackintosh bt Godfrey 6-1, 6-4

MEN'S DOUBLES
Final
G Hempsall & G Hempsall bt I Bailey & N Parry 7-5, 6-3

LADIES DOUBLES
Final
N Mackintosh & A Morrell bt B Means & M Pretty 6-4, 6-2

DARTMOUTH

August 26th-31st

MEN'S SINGLES
Semifinals
J Turner bt B Ames 6-4, 6-2
P Hand bt P French 6-2, 6-1
Final
Turner bt Hand 6-4, 6-4

LADIES SINGLES
Semifinals
V Lake bt J Gradon 6-3, 7-6
K Hand bt K Rickett 6-4, 6-4
Final
Lake bt Hand 7-5, 6-3

MEN'S DOUBLES
Final
P French & J Turner bt S Allan & J Clunie 6-3, 6-2

LADIES DOUBLES
Final
K Hand & V Lake bt J Iddles & K Rickett 6-3, 4-6, 6-4

BRITISH HOME STORES NATIONAL PARKS CHAMPIONSHIP

ROYAL VICTORIA PARK, BATH, October 19th-20th

MEN'S SINGLES
Final
J Draper (Liverpool) bt P Bell (Exeter) 6-4, 6-3

MEN'S DOUBLES
Final
P Ranson & R Ranson (Sheffield) bt U Fielder & A Precious (Yorks) 5-7, 6-0, 7-5

LADIES SINGLES
Final
S Collinson (York) bt H Plumtree (Scunthorpe) 6-2, 6-1

LADIES DOUBLES
Final
S Imhof & M Meisi (Hammersmith) bt J Hutt & W Shepherd (York) 6-4, 6-4

MIXED DOUBLES
D Lazarus & E Andrews (Redbridge) bt A Savage & J Goulding (Sheffield) 6-4, 7-6

SCOTTISH LTA

SCOTTISH CHAMPIONSHIPS

Edinburgh July 7th - 13th

MEN'S SINGLES
Semifinals
C Dowdeswell bt L Alfred 6-4, 6-4. J Bates bt N Fulwood 6-1, 7-5.
Final
Bates bt Dowdeswell 6-2, 6-4.

MEN'S DOUBLES
Final
J Bates & N Fulwood bt B Buffington & J Pugh (US) 6-3, 7-5.

LADIES SINGLES
Semifinals
E Minter (Aus) bt S Gomer 3-6, 6-4, 8-6.
L Antoropolis (US) bt S T G Mair 6-4, 6-1.
Final
Antoropolis bt Minter 6-3, 6-0.

LADIES DOUBLES
Final
L Antoropolis & E Minter bt S Gomer & S T G Mair 6-1, 6-3.

MIXED DOUBLES
B Buffington (US) & Gomer bt R W Scott & T Price (US) 6-4, 7-6.

HARD COURT CHAMPIONSHIPS

Dundee, August 4th - 10th

MEN'S SINGLES
Semifinals
K R W Kordula (Dunfermline) bt P Rowlands (St Andrews) 6-2, 6-7, 6-1. I H Mackinlay (Barnton Park) bt I MacAnley (Craighelen) 6-2, 6-3.
Final
Mackinlay bt Kordula 6-4, 4-6, 6-4.

MEN'S DOUBLES
Final
K R W Kordula & R Terras (Queen's Park) bt J G Bell (Giffnock) & M S McGill (Colinton) 6-4, 4-6, 7-5.

LADIES SINGLES
Semifinals
S E L Moodie (Stepps) bt A Lavery (Cambuslang) 6-2, 5-7, 6-2. L J Reid (Waverley) bt A Wood (Dunfermline) 3-6, 6-2, 6-4.
Final
Reid bt Moodie 6-2, 6-3.

LADIES DOUBLES
Final
E Armstrong (Kilmacolm) & G Armstrong (Kilmacolm) bt J M Erskine (Broomhill) & L J Reid (Waverley) 6-3, 6-7, 6-3.

MIXED DOUBLES
Final
I H MacKinlay & L J Reid bt A B Galbraith (Bridge of Weir) & K Christie (Broomhill) 6-1, 6-1.

COVERED COURT CHAMPIONSHIPS

Nov 29th - December 1st

MEN'S SINGLES
Final
S Curtis bt A Broomhead 7-6, 1-6, 6-3.

MEN'S DOUBLES
Final
M T Coyne & C M Robinson bt S Curtis & P Hand 7-6, 6-4.

LADIES SINGLES
Semifinals
P Palmer bt A Lavery 7-5, 6-7, 6-3. A Bishop bt A Morrell 6-1, 6-2.
Final
Bishop bt Palmer 6-1, 6-2.

LADIES DOUBLES
Final
S Fletcher & K McLoughlin winners in Round-Robin event.

NEW LOOK FOR COUNTY CUP

BY REGINALD BRACE: THE YORKSHIRE POST

Devonshire Park

County Week, alias the Prudential County Cup, has been the backbone of British tennis for so long that to suggest it is suffering from the equivalent of a slipped disc is tantamount to heresy. But there is a groundswell of opinion which would like to change this splendid competition where players perform for the good of their county not their bank balances, and the atmosphere recalls the days when skill, sportsmanship and enjoyment were the measure of success, not points on the ATP computer.

County Week is a defiant amateur outpost in an increasingly professional game. There are no tetchy umpiring rows because there are no court officials. Players make their own calls. If there are disputes — and one is not suggesting this is a week of tennis tranquillity where tempers never fray — the magic words "Play two" usually settle the argument.

It is an exhausting contest in which players run themselves to a standstill for the good of a county it often costs them money, and a week's holiday, to represent. But however ferocious the match, rival sides invariably unwind in the bar. While fitness is a necessity on County Week, it is a handicap to be tee-total!

The bizarre tends to become commonplace in County Week. I know of no other event where a match was restarted because both pairs thought they were a set and a service break up. One year the Essex youngster David Felgate was charged with contempt of court in the sense that he was scarring the Devonshire Park turf with his service action. Eastbourne Corporation took a serious view of this but a ripping yarn had a happy ending when David agreed to change his action from a foot drag to a jump.

That was the year when Kent women lost a key player — Anthea Stewart — after part of a greenhouse collapsed on her. The stories are endless — like Yorkshire men winning promotion from Group Two in 1978 by 0.416 over Hampshire on a percentage of sets won to sets played. And who could forget Richard Whichello's sensational dash across the decorative mushrooms in the Grand Hotel's pool at Eastbourne last July? A breathtaking performance, that.

Are we not in danger of destroying something precious in talking of tampering with this venerable tennis institution? I would say we were if two leading advocates of change were not only men whose opinions I respect, but County Week stalwarts themselves: Charles Applewhaite and Mark Cox.

Although they adopt slightly different stances, Applewhaite and Cox would like to see the County Week format adjusted to include singles. They feel it is impeding the development of British tennis for these inter-county grass court championships to be decided on doubles alone.

Singles is played in the Prudential hard court championships held during the winter but in terms of county tennis the summer is dominated by doubles — a situation which is reflected in inter-club leagues and club play generally.

Charles Applewhaite, a Lancashire loyalist who is now the LTA's Director of Coaching, is worth quoting at length on the issue. "There is no doubt that County Week is a super event — no doubt at all," he said. "But in terms of tennis development in this country there is a lack of opportunity for the competitive player to play singles.

"The situation has changed slightly in the last two years with the welcome advent of the ratings tournaments — but the fact remains that it is difficult for a senior player to play singles on a regular basis. The majority of county matches and club leagues are doubles.

"We are left with a situation where we are training youngsters to become good at singles only to move into a singles vaccum when they go out into the senior world. I would like to see counties and clubs playing some singles in their matches. Most teams are made up of three pairs playing three doubles each, a total of nine rubbers. If each person played a singles and a doubles you would get the same amount of matches and strike a more realistic balance.

"This is the system used effectively on the Continent including Germany where I played club league tennis. It works there, I feel it would work here — and County Week would be an ideal catalyst. If County Week, and the fixtures leading to it were changed to singles and doubles then clubs would be tempted to experiment.

"I realise there are traditionalists who would fight shy of altering the format. Perhaps some of the older players might see it as a threat to involvement in county competition. But I visualise a seven man team where you could include a player who would only play singles with a seventh player coming in for the doubles. County women players already play singles and doubles in their winter competition.

"We have to remember that one of the big problems of British tennis is a

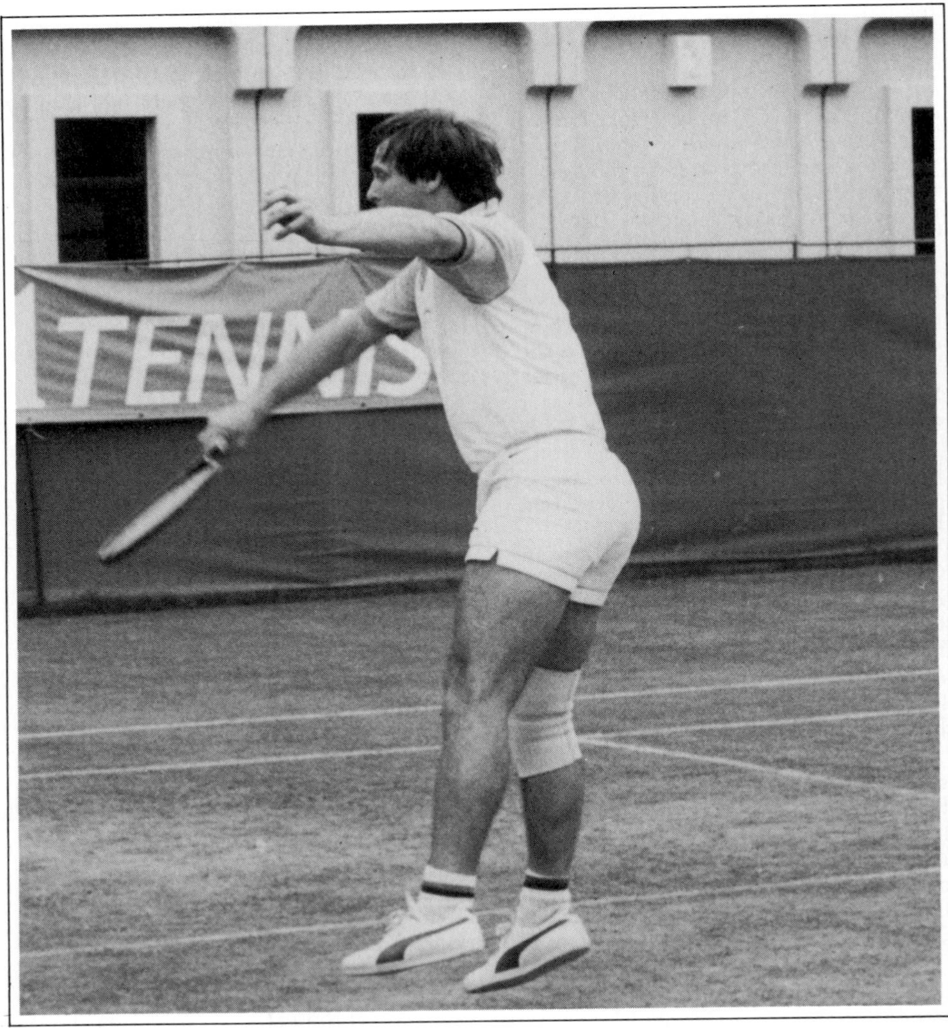

David Lloyd hitting out for Essex

lack of competitive opportunity. It's not too bad for the juniors, who have lots of tournaments. But many of the events where seniors used to play are no longer there — and I think anything which encourages singles play at county and club level should be welcomed."

Over to Mark Cox, TV pundit, Davis Cup coach and former British No. 1, who plays for Leicestershire. He is a firm supporter of the County Week concept, but, like Applewhaite, believes that the absence of singles is detrimental to a player's progress. Taking the argument a stage further, Mark feels that County Week should be moved from its traditional slot, three weeks after Wimbledon, to clear the way for a tournament circuit.

"First of all, I think County Week

should incorporate some singles. My county spend the entire summer playing friendly doubles matches in preparation for County Week. This has got to be inhibiting in the context of the British game.

"It would be better if players had more opportunities to compete in singles — and, taking a broader look, the position of County Week in the calendar makes it difficult to create a series of tournaments on grass after Wimbledon.

"If County Week was moved to the end of August you could organise a viable circuit which would maintain the momentum of Wimbledon. When I was a kid we had the Exmouths, Torquays and Eastbournes and a number of international players stayed on. Now, many of these tournaments have disappeared, although it is nice to see Edinburgh, Newcastle and Ilkley flourishing.

"So yes — I'm in favour of singles on County Week for the ultimate benefit of the game in Britain, and shifting it to a date in the summer when it would not break up a possible circuit which would be attractive for the better players."

Should County Week be adapted to accommodate singles? Should it be moved to make way for the circuit Mark Cox advocates? The topic will doubtless be debated at length by the Grand Hotel mandarins in Group One at Eastbourne in July. Last year it was Whichello's Walk — and he did it entirely on doubles. Tennis doubles, of course . . .

The Spirit of County Week

COUNTY CHAMPIONSHIPS

THE PRUDENTIAL COUNTY CUP GRASS COURT CHAMPIONSHIPS

(Inter-County Week) July 22-26

MEN'S CHAMPIONSHIP

County	Matches	Rubbers	Sets	Games
GROUP 1				
EASTBOURNE				
1. Essex	5-0	36- 9	77-30	597-465
2. Kent	4-1	23-22	54-51	541-517
3. Middlesex	3-2	22-23	50-56	488-544
4. Somerset	2-3	17-28	42-63	479-536
5. Lancashire	1-4	21-24	53-55	544-546
6. Derbyshire	0-5	16-29	43-64	504-545
GROUP 2				
SOUTHSEA				
1. Buckinghamshire	5-0	33-12	71-36	559-460
2. Yorkshire	4-1	30-15	66-35	510-414
3. Surrey	2-3	22-23	48-56	488-509
4. Berkshire	2-3	19-26	49-58	501-529
5. Warwickshire	2-3	19-26	48-59	530-554
6. Hertfordshire	0-5	12-33	33-71	438-560
GROUP 3				
CAMBRIDGE				
1. West of Scotland	4-1	28-17	61-43	527-463
2. Leicestershire	3-2	25-20	57-47	531-485
3. East of Scotland	3-2	25-20	58-50	520-506
4. North Wales	3-2	21-24	51-54	520-535
5. Oxfordshire	2-3	20-25	45-59	481-517
6. Nottinghamshire	0-5	16-29	44-63	485-558
GROUP 4				
CROMER				
1. Avon	5-0	28-17	60-43	529-481
2. Cheshire	3-2	27-18	64-43	553-455
3. Sussex	3-2	21-24	48-54	478-506
4. Hereford & Worcester	2-3	23-22	54-53	528-519
5. Gloucestershire	1-4	19-26	45-56	444-479
6. Northamptonshire	1-4	17-28	39-61	429-521
GROUP 5				
EALING				
1. South Wales	5-0	33-12	71-39	594-529
2. Hampshire & I.O.W.	4-1	27-18	63-47	552-518
3. Dorset	3-2	24-21	55-51	522-522
4. Norfolk	2-3	16-29	43-65	508-566
5. Northumberland	1-4	22-23	54-54	525-485
6. Staffordshire	0-5	13-32	38-68	489-570
GROUP 6				
MALVERN				
1. Devon	4-1	28-17	60-46	553-508
2. Lincolnshire	3-2	26-19	64-49	596-542
3. Wiltshire	3-2	24-21	64-54	524-536
4. Bedfordshire	3-2	23-22	53-63	520-505
5. Cambridgeshire	2-3	20-25	50-54	504-512
6. Durham & Cleveland	0-5	14-31	39-64	444-538
GROUP 7				
FELIXSTOWE				
1. Suffolk	5-0	31-14	68-38	544-465
2. Cornwall	3-2	26-19	59-46	539-488
3. North of Scotland	3-2	24-21	55-49	497-488
4. South of Scotland	2-3	23-22	58-52	552-525
5. Shropshire	2-3	18-27	40-58	437-485
6. Cumbria	0-5	13-32	32-69	436-554

LADIES CHAMPIONSHIP

County	Matches	Rubbers	Sets	Games
GROUP 1				
EASTBOURNE				
1. Surrey	5-0	37- 8	78-25	566-354
2. Essex	3-2	24-21	54-50	481-457
3. Yorkshire	3-2	23-22	53-52	484-499
4. Kent	2-3	18-27	44-57	420-484
5. Lancashire	2-3	17-28	44-61	460-499
6. Warwickshire	0-5	16-29	39-67	441-559
GROUP 2				
CHELTENHAM				
1. Sussex	4-1	31-14	66-37	521-424
2. Devon	4-1	30-15	64-32	496-363
3. Norfolk	4-1	28-17	60-40	492-399
4. Lincolnshire	2-3	18-27	40-61	390-484
5. Hampshire & I.O.W.	1-4	13-32	35-67	410-515
6. Middlesex	0-5	15-30	37-65	396-520
GROUP 3				
WORTHING				
1. Avon	5-0	30-15	65-38	524-423
2. Cheshire	4-1	25-20	57-48	508-464
3. Nottinghamshire	3-2	24-21	58-51	523-452
4. Buckinghamshire	1-4	22-23	54-52	470-467
5. Berkshire	1-4	20-25	44-56	419-474
6. Hereford & Worcester	1-4	14-31	33-66	330-494
GROUP 4				
EXMOUTH				
1. Derbyshire	4-1	28-17	63-43	512-442
2. Leicestershire	3-2	26-19	58-43	470-420
3. West of Scotland	3-2	23-22	48-51	440-476
4. Bedfordshire	3-2	22-23	47-50	430-443
5. Cambridgeshire	2-3	26-19	56-42	482-407
6. Oxfordshire	0-5	10-35	32-75	423-569
GROUP 5				
POOLE				
1. Hertfordshire	5-0	36- 9	77-31	585-452
2. North Wales	4-1	28-17	61-39	508-425
3. Somerset	3-2	27-18	59-42	505-412
4. Staffordshire	2-3	18-27	43-61	452-520
5. Durham & Cleveland	1-4	15-30	41-66	434-544
6. North of Scotland	0-5	11-34	31-73	406-537

GROUP 6
HUNSTANTON

1. Cornwall	5-0	29-16	66-46	566-496
2. Gloucestershire	4-1	29-16	63-42	516-421
3. Suffolk	3-2	29-16	65-39	540-417
4. East of Scotland	2-3	21-24	52-54	492-514
5. Shropshire	1-4	15-30	37-67	415-521
6. South Wales	0-5	12-33	35-70	385-545

GROUP 7
CAMBRIDGE

1. Dorset	5-0	34-11	73-28	527-341
2. Northumberland	4-1	32-13	66-34	492-361
3. Northamptonshire	3-2	26-19	56-41	441-433
4. Wiltshire	2-3	20-25	46-56	457-468
5. South of Scotland	1-4	16-29	40-61	444-509
6. Cumbria	0-5	7-38	19-80	296-545

PRUDENTIAL COUNTY CUP WINTER CHAMPIONSHIPS

MEN

Quarter-finals
Essex bt Yorkshire 8-4
Surrey bt Derbyshire 7-5
Middlesex bt Leicestershire 7-5
Lancashire bt Buckinghamshire 8-4

Semifinals
Essex bt Surrey 8-4
Lancashire bt Midlesex 11-1

Final
Essex bt Lancashire 6-6, 13-13, 126-123 (on games)

WOMEN

Quarter-finals
Surrey bt Essex 6-3
Norfolk bt Lancashire 6-3
Lincolnshire bt Sussex 5-4
Middlesex bt Warwickshire 5-4

Semifinals
Surrey bt Norfolk 6-3
Middlesex bt Lincolnshire 5-4

Final
Middlesex bt Surrey 5-4

VETERAN GAME IS BOOMING

BY CLARENCE JONES

Once again, Veteran tennis boomed for Britain during the year 1985. It began with 140 clubs and 6,000 affiliated players. By the end of the LTA's year the figures had risen to around 150 clubs and 6,500 members. National championships and various forms of tournaments and one day competitive cum social events brought considerable pleasure to those who entered and attended.

Internationally, the veterans game became ever more integrated. The list of veteran competitions compiled and circulated by the ITF reached a staggering 161 of which 37 were graded "VIP", thus donning them with computer points status. If there is one sorry factor in British veterans' tennis, it is the inability to provide competitors who collect sufficient points to find their names among the world's high flying enthusiasts.

In step with the increasing number of players, the 11th National Championships reached new record heights, 380 entering the overall draw of 13 events; that compared with 271 in 1983 and 350 in 1984.

Sponsored by the newly formed company, Doe Sports Ltd, the bigger entry occupied increased court time which was supplied by the Queens and All England Clubs. The two new events — men's singles, 70 and over, women's singles, 60 and over — produced an extra work load but Norman Seabright, as always indefatigable, and backed by willing helpers, got through and the £1,400 prize money was duly handed out.

Not too often to the holders of events however, as only Roger Becker, Eric Bulmer, and doubles pair C. R. Lacy-Thompson and R. J. C. Reardon held on to their titles. K. G. Jones and J. A. Starling lost the final of the over 65 final for the second year in succession, and to the same pair. Mrs P. George and Lady Swynnerton also finished runners-up in the 50 and over ladies' doubles, this time to Mrs H. Cheadle and Mrs J. J. Walker-Smith, the one-time Wightman Cup player and quarter-finalist in the Wimbledon singles.

Internationally, the gigantic effort made by the Australians lured fifteen nations "down under" where the British contingent of 12 men and seven women contested the prestigious World Veterans Championships. None of the events ended with British players going up to the rostrum for the first prize. Alan and Jill Mills almost made it in the new I.T.F. mixed doubles, Ann Tullog and Alan Basford beating them 7-5 in the third set of the final after winning four earlier rounds.

Lorna Cawthorn reached the final of the over 50 ladies, then lost to the number one seed Celia Massoneli of Italy. In other events the winners were: Ian Bailey, 45s and over; Hugh Stewart, over 55s; R. Sorlein, over 60s; J. Gilchrist, over 65s; F. Klien, over 70s; J. Fassbender, over 30s. Women's singles: Heidi Orth, over 40s.

No fewer than 22 British players represented Great Britain in the seven international team championships; 14 of them having competed in the 1984 series. Without question, and as in the many international events for those below veteran tennis, the nation desperately needs more talented players to take on the ever strengthening, opposing teams. There is an important rider; they must be equally exemplary ambassadors.

Roger Becker

DOE SPORT LTD NATIONAL VETERANS' CHAMPIONSHIPS

WIMBLEDON AND QUEEN'S CLUB, August 12th-17th

MEN'S FINALS

Over 45 Singles
R Becker bt D Shears 6-3, 7-5
Over 45 Doubles
D Shears & B Storr bt R Becker & A Mills walkover
Over 55 Singles
P Field bt G Sacerdote 6-3, 6-2
Over 55 Doubles
F C Bowles & G Foster bt J Draper & W Osterburg 7-6, 6-1
Over 60 Singles
A Kalman bt J E Rudd 6-1, 6-4
Over 60 Doubles
C R Lacy-Thompson & R J C Reardon bt K G Jones & J A Starling 6-3, 7-6
Over 65 Singles
E R Bulmer bt G Hesz 6-2, 6-3
Over 65 Doubles
R E Carter & E L Frith bt A E Murray & T A Rowney 6-1, 6-2
Over 70 Singles
R A F Reynolds bt A E Murray 6-3, 6-4

LADIES FINALS

Over 40 Singles
S Brasher bt J V A Bathman 6-1, 6-1
Over 40 Doubles
R Illingworth & R H Lauder bt J V A Boothman & A Buxton 6-4, 7-6
Over 50 Singles
S Brasher bt R Illingworth 6-2, 6-2
Over 50 Doubles
H Cheadle & J J Walker-Smith bt P George & Lady Swynnerton 6-1, 6-1

PRUDENTIAL VETERANS' COUNTY CUP

BRAMHALL

Semifinals
Warwickshire bt Hertfordshire 4-1
Surrey bt Scotland 3-2

Final
Warwickshire bt Surrey 3½-1½

LOOKING TO THE FUTURE

BY JIM COATES

The major part of this publication's review of tennis is devoted to a record of high sporting achievement. It records the success of names, both famous and lesser known, in senior and junior competitions. Inevitably, this is where the greatest interest will always lie. Yet we should never forget that once upon a time these famous names were mere beginners. The spadework for a country's tennis success is prepared years in advance.

The concept of developing the grass roots, broadening the base, widening the pyramid, whichever cliché happens to be fashionable at a particular moment, is one that receives media recognition from time to time, usually when there has been a catastrophic international result. Yet there seems little positive interest in scrutinising how the game is being popularised in this country. If we have any real concern in the future of British tennis, we should look seriously at the efforts that are being made to establish a strong foundation.

There are two main targets in the development of British tennis. One is to produce a climate wherein youngsters with high athletic potential are encouraged to play tennis rather than to throw javelins, kick footballs, perfect double somersaults. The other is to encourage the general public, no matter what the age or standard, to take up the game. The more people who play, the more chance there is of unearthing a Borg or a Navratilova. 1985 saw a positive leap forward by the LTA to achieve these aims.

We are bringing literally thousands of new faces into the game. Until very recently, with a few exceptions, those who played tennis had some family connection with the game and this inevitably meant a narrow catchment area. All that is changing fast. Short Tennis (mini-tennis with a sponge ball and a plastic bat) has been a means of introducing children as young as 5 or 6 to the skills and pleasures of racket games. Closely linked with this has been the LTA/PRUDENTIAL JUNIOR COACHING SCHEME whereby, in 1300 Coaching Centres stretching from Aberdeen to Falmouth, youngsters have been given basic tennis lessons at a very modest cost.

Clubs in many areas will not be able to cope with this new influx of would-be members. Indeed, one suspects that some will not even wish to. There is thus a need to establish places where boys and girls can play regularly and this problem is being tackled by the setting up of LTA/PRUDENTIAL JUNIOR TENNIS CENTRES, mainly in the parks, some of them on school courts.

Already these Tennis Centres have appeared in 21 English counties and a few in Scotland and Wales. Many more are planned for 1986. The debt that British tennis owes Prudential Assurance Company should never be underestimated. Their sponsorship of National and County events is well known, but their input into the primary stages of the game is considerable.

The development of Junior Tennis Centres represents a significant move by the LTA in that it is based on liaison with local authorities. Most towns of any size have tennis courts in their parks; most courts in the parks are underused. The

The four Winning Captains from the Midland Bank/LTA Schools Tennis Championships

forging of bonds between the two organisations is a logical step, and the links now go way beyond the provision of Tennis Centres. The LTA is seeking ways of promoting joint development schemes. The possibilities were successfully explored in 1985 in Leicester, Sheffield and Newcastle-upon-Tyne, where hundreds of youngsters were attracted by a comprehensive coaching and playing programme.

The problems of school tennis are now being faced also. They are more complex than is usually realised. The BRITISH SCHOOLS LTA has been reorganised, given an input of funding and encouraged to go on the initiative. County Schools Tennis Associations are being set up with a wide-ranging competitive programme, coaching opportunities for both pupil and teacher, and a development programme similar to that of the USTA, with peripatetic coaches visiting schools.

THE MIDLAND BANK/LTA SCHOOLS CHAMPIONSHIPS have been one of the great success stories of grass roots tennis. League play is followed by a knock-out competition, leading to Regional and National Finals. Despite union difficulties, there were 550 leagues in 1985 for 15 and Under and 13 and Under players. Next year will see the addition of 11 and Under and 9 and

Under (Short Tennis) leagues.

The Lawn Tennis Foundation has been at the heart of this grass roots work. "Originally set up to give the LTA a smart kick in the pants for not paying enough attention to grass roots, the Foundation is now increasingly funded by the LTA. Far from now being a separate critical element, it enjoys responsibility for looking after the expanding base of our pyramid". This was Geoff Brown, LTA President, at the Annual General Meeting.

Two other highly significant events were associated with the Foundation's work. The famous NESTLE JUNIOR TOURNAMENT reached its Silver Jubilee Year and HRH the Duchess of Kent graced the finals won by Daniel Ahl (Devon) and Alison Fleming (Leics). Nestle are the longest serving sponsors of British tennis, and few, if any, tournaments can claim to have catered for between half and three quarters of a million youngsters. The first NATIONAL PARKS CHAMPIONSHIPS, sponsored by BHS, with 2,500 competitors, came to a successful conclusion at Bath in October.

There seems no doubt that 1985 was a significant year for the foundations of the game.

Jim Coates, Manager of the Lawn Tennis Foundation, serves as LTA National Grass Roots Co-ordinator and Executive Officer of the British Schools LTA

Daniel Ahl and Alison Fleming, winners of the Nestlé English and International Titles

GIRLS AGAIN SET THE PACE

BY BILL EDWARDS

Once again it was the girls, rather than the boys, who set the pace in junior tennis during 1985. There were no Australian or Junior Wimbledon titles, unfortunately, but it was a season of hope for the future.

An interesting rivalry built up between Jane Wood and Clare Wood (they are not related) and pushing them along were Anne Simpkin, Teresa Catlin, Sue McCarthy and Sarah Loosemore.

All this indicated growing strength in depth with several fine youngsters such as Nicole Entract, Julie Donovan, Virginia Humphrey Davies, Victoria Graeme-Barber and Colette Hall emerging in the 16,14 and12 age groups.

The biggest success internationally was achieved by Anne Simpkin, Teresa Catlin and Sue McCarthy when they went to Japan for the World Youth Championships (under 16) in November, knocked out West Germany, beat the host country, and reached the semifinal before falling to Australia, who had already beaten the United States. Apart from this, Britain's form in the various internationals and winter training internationals were disappointing.

Teresa Catlin

Top junior of the year was Jane Wood, who collected her accolade at the LTA Awards dinner in December. The 17 years old North Londoner won two Prudential British junior titles; the covered courts at the beginning of the year and the hard courts at Wimbledon in the Spring. However she was denied the opportunity of a junior Grand Slam when she was sent to the United States during the grass court championships.

Jane did return to reach the semifinal of the Refuge British Closed championships, where she lost to Virginia Wade. That was a magnificent performance and she would appear to have her feet firmly planted on the ladder to success.

The clash of the Prudential grass courts and overseas commitments is disturbing and leaves the impression that junior championships are not held in sufficient regard by the powers that be. We have had this same thorny question before and two or three years ago the championships dates were altered to avoid this. Now they are back in the same swing.

Many men feel that national championships should have priority. It is all very well to argue that the international field is where the game should be learned, but it can also help to break the confidence of youngsters before they are ready. We have seen it happen several times. Let the young players win the national title AND DEFEND IT before sending them away.

In the absence of Jane Wood, the grass court title went to Anne Simpkin, 16, from Leicester, who had the rare distinction of winning the under 16 and under 18 titles within a week of each other. Sue Barker (1972) and Kate Brasher (1978) are the only players to have held both titles at the same time.

The winning of those two titles by Miss Simpkin was one of the best performances of 1985, but, possibly because of her age, Anne was not among the nominations for Junior of the Year.

The under 16 girls look the more exciting group and it is significant that in both the under 16 and under 18 finals, the runner-up to Anne was another 16 year old, Teresa Catlin, of Cambridge, with whom she is developing a very healthy rivalry that could take them both to the top. It is reminiscent of that rivalry between Christine Truman (now Mrs Janes) and Ann Haydon (now Mrs Jones) in the 1950's.

Into this category comes Nicole Entract, 15, of Dorset, who is perhaps more at home on hard courts than grass. She followed the winning of the under 12's in 1982 and the under 14's in 1984, by adding the under 16's grass. That is nice steady progress, with the stamp of a future world rank.

Julie Donovan, 14, from Warwickshire, added the under 14's hard courts to the under 12's she had won the previous year, but later in the year found herself giving way to Sarah Loosemore, 14, of South Wales, who defeated Julie in the under 14's grass court final, and repeated the victory in the Sport Goofy final.

Out on her own in the under 12's was Colette Hall, 12, of Dorset. She dominated her group by winning both the hard courts and the grass courts as well as the Sport Goofy titles.

Switching to the boys, Richard Whichello, making every effort to keep that volatile temperament under control, won both the under 18's covered and hard court titles, but like Jane Wood, had to miss the grass courts. In his absence this title went to Nick Jones, of North Wales, who upset the strongly fancied Austen Brice in the semi-final and Chris Peet, the top seed, in the final.

Danny Sapsford dominated the earlier part of the season among the under 16's but it was his Surrey colleagues Neale Pashley, who, regaining his old form, came out top in the grass courts. Danny was left with the hard courts title.

Anne Simpkin

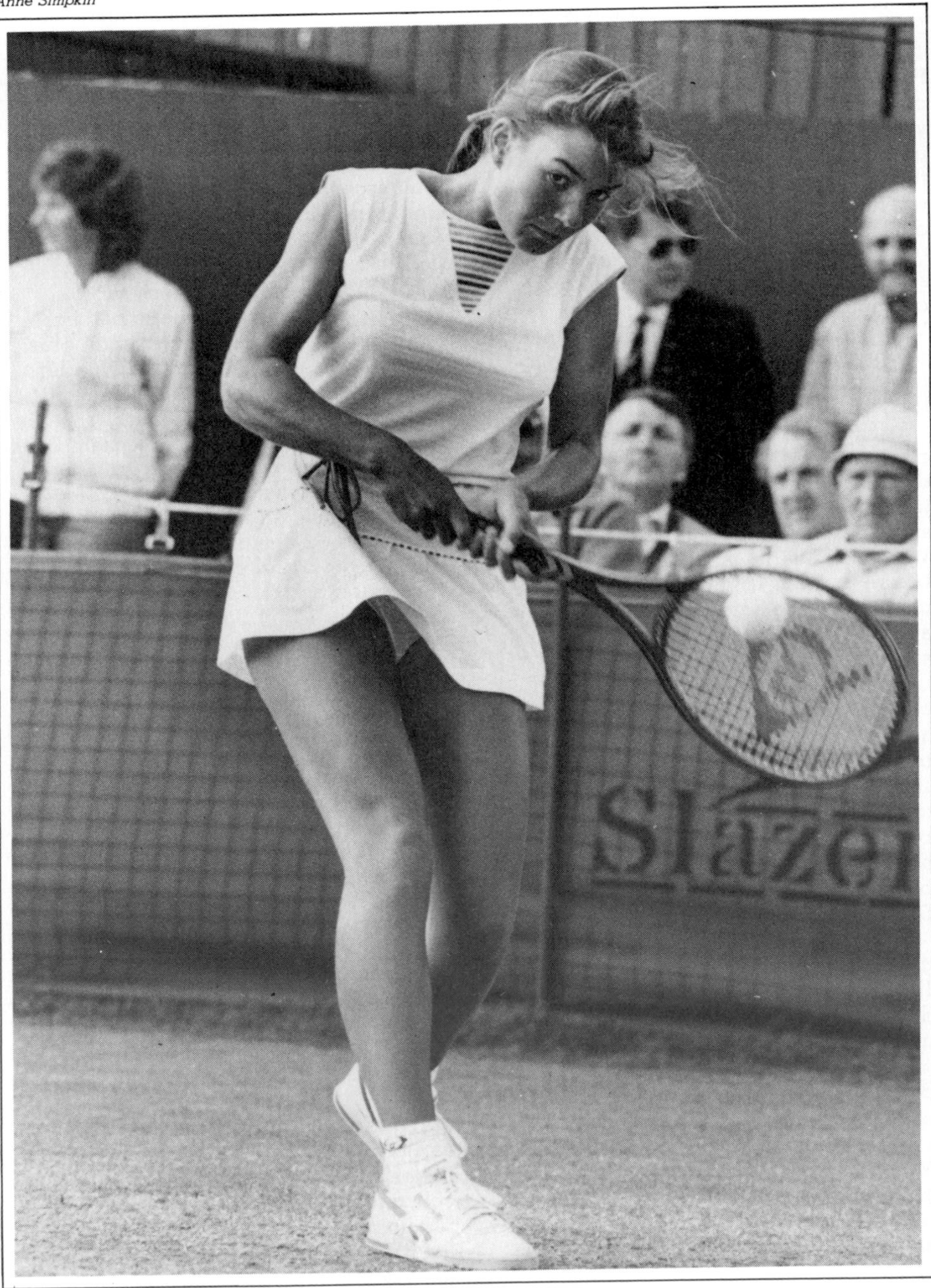

Simon Cornish, 14, from Somerset, took the under 14's hard courts, while Nick Smith, 14, of Lancashire, who many still consider the best bet for the future, won the grass.

Another keen rivalry sprung up between Giles Gibson, 12, from Dorset, who won the under 12 hard courts, and Stuart Silvester, 12, of Norfolk, who turned the tables in the grass courts final.

The LTA did not let the loss of Saab sponsorship interrupt the Winter Training Series. They funded it themselves, with Nick Smith and Sarah Loosemore winning the under 14's, and Simon Booth and Alison Fleming winning the under 12's. The year of waiting has been rewarded with a new sponsorship from the Royal Bank of Scotland plus a new sponsorship for the under 18's from Dewhurst, the butchers.

Schooling interrupted the activities of Jo Louis, Clare Wood, and Suzie Mair in 1985, but all three showed they must not be written off. Miss Louis had the outstanding junior performance of the year when she beat Jo Durie, Britain's No 1 and defending champion, in the Refuge British Closed championships. Miss Mair and Miss Wood joined forces to win the Prudential British junior hard court doubles. Performances have been encouraging. May they continue.

Danny Sapsford

1985 BRITISH JUNIOR CHAMPIONSHIPS

PRUDENTIAL JUNIOR COVERED COURT CHAMPIONSHIPS OF GREAT BRITAIN

TELFORD, December 31st-January 5th

BOYS' SINGLES

First round

R Every bt C B Bailey 2-6, 6-4, 6-3. T J Maylam bt A Fisher 6-3, 4-6, 6-1. J M Dawson bt M A Nuttall 4-6, 6-2, 6-4. D J Roberts bt D S Joelson 6-3, 6-3. C Beecher bt M R J Petchey 7-6, 6-4. S G Heritage bt J Hill 3-6, 6-4, 6-3. V G Ranson bt J R Martyn 7-6, 6-3. N R Jones bt K P Fraser 6-1, 6-2. A J Rouse bt S F L Turnsek 6-2, 6-1. S H Booth bt M J Syms 6-3, 6-4. M Coombes bt U J Nganga 6-4, 6-3. J H Mackinlay bt L M Ahmed 7-5, 6-1. A Davies bt D E Kirk 7-5, 6-1. D Clarry bt C M D Weekes 6-4, 6-4. A St J Hunting bt G N Drake 0-6, 6-2, 6-1.

Second round

R A W Whichello bt T W Godman 6-3, 6-0. Maylam bt Every 6-1, 0-6, 9-7. H A Pringle bt Dawson 6-3, 6-3. D Sapsford bt Roberts 6-1, 6-2. D P Ison bt Beecher 6-2, 6-0. S W Wilkins bt Heritage 7-5, 3-6, 6-2. Jones bt Ranson 6-2, 6-3. S M Heron bt J M Lenton 6-1, 7-6. C J Peet bt C H Miller 6-2, 6-2. Rouse bt Booth 7-5, 4-6, retd. C Brown bt Coombes 5-7, 6-2, 6-4. A J W Brice bt Mackinlay 6-3, 6-4. L G Matthews bt Davies 7-5, 6-4. Clarry bt S Bennett 7-6, 6-4. Hunting bt D R Smith 6-2, 6-3. J M Goodall bt J M Green 6-1, 6-2.

Third round

Wichello bt Maylam 6-2, 6-0. Sapsford bt Pringle 6-4, 6-4. Ison bt Wilkins 6-1, 6-4. Heron bt Jones 6-4, 6-3. Peet bt Rouse 6-1, 6-1. Brice bt Brown 6-3, 6-4. Matthews bt Clarry 6-3, 4-6, 6-3. Goodall bt Hunting 6-3, 6-2.

Quarter-finals

Whichello bt Sapsford 6-0, 5-7, 6-1. Heron bt Ison 6-4, 2-6, 6-4. Peet bt Brice 6-1, 7-5. Goodall bt Matthews 7-6, 6-2.

Semifinals

Wichello bt Heron 4-6, 6-2, 6-4.
Goodall bt Peet 6-4, 6-3.

Final

Whichello (Kent) bt Goodall (Yorks) 3-6, 6-2, 10-8.

DOUBLES

Quarter-finals

J M Goodall & R Whichello bt N R Jones & J M Wallace 6-3, 6-3. A J W Brice & D P Ison bt D M Ahmed & D Clarry 6-3, 6-1. A St J Hunting & L G Matthews bt C B Bailey & D J Roberts 4-6, 6-2, 6-4. S M Heron & C J Peet bt D Sapsford & D R Smith 3-6, 6-2, 6-1.

Semifinals

Goodall & Whichello bt Brice & Ison 6-1, 6-4.
Heron & Peet bt Hunting & Matthews 4-6, 6-3, 6-3.

Final

Goodall & Whichello bt Heron & Peet 6-4, 6-3.

GIRLS' SINGLES

First round

S J McCarthy bt F A Couldridge 6-1, 6-4. R E Charlton bt A Simpkins 0-6, 7-5, 11-9. D Schauerman bt S Byrne 7-6, 6-3. K Howden bt A Fitzgibbon 6-3, 6-1. S L Timms bt S J Armitage 6-1, 6-2. R L Kendall bt K S Patel 5-7, 7-6, 6-4. J M Reeves bt K D Hand 6-3, 6-1. A S Hill bt K S Russell 6-7, 6-4, 6-1. T A Catlin bt P Cantrell 6-0, 6-2. V Lake bt A C Nall 6-3, 6-3. A S Fleming bt C L Bateman 6-0, 7-5. J M Gracie bt S J Ambrose 6-3, 6-4. K J Charlton bt A E Root 6-4, 2-6, 6-3. K F Hunter bt B McCormick 6-2, 7-6. C L Billingham bt C L Tee 6-2, 6-0. S Godman bt A Mills 6-1, 6-3.

Second round

McCarthy bt J Louis 4-6, 7-6, 6-3. Charlton bt B Suzin 6-2, 6-1. Schauerman bt J Iddles 3-6, 6-4, 6-4. S J Whiteman bt Howden 6-2, 6-1. L C Gould bt Timms 2-6, 6-4, 6-4. Kendall bt S L Mitten 6-4, 6-4. J M Reeves bt B L Welt 6-2, 6-2. K A Rickett bt Hill 6-1, 6-0. A M Grant bt Catlin 6-4, 3-6, 6-3. Lake bt R J Galassini 6-2, 6-4. Fleming bt L T Stern 7-6, 6-3. A L Grunfeld bt Gracie 6-2, 6-2. J R Holden bt Charlton 6-1, 6-0. L Phillips bt Hunter 6-3, 6-0. Billingham bt I J Wild 7-5, 6-2. J V Wood bt Godman 6-3, 6-4.

Third round

Charlton bt McCarthy 6-3, 6-1. Schauerman bt Whiteman 6-2, 6-4. Gould bt Kendall 6-4, 6-4. Reeves bt Rickett 6-4, 6-4. Grant bt Lake 4-6, 7-6, 7-5. Grunfeld bt Fleming 7-5, 6-4. Holden bt Phillips 6-0, 7-6. Wood bt Billingham 6-3, 6-3.

Quarter-finals

Charlton bt Schauerman 7-6, 1-6, 6-3. Reeves bt Gould 6-4, 6-2. Grunfeld bt Grant 7-5, 7-5. Wood bt Holden 7-6, 7-5.

Semifinals

Charlton bt Reeves 6-4, 6-3.
Wood bt Grunfeld 6-0, 6-2.

Final

Wood (Middlesex) bt Charlton (Berks) 6-2, 6-1.

DOUBLES

Quarter-finals

A M Grant & J Louis bt S Godman & A C Nall 6-1 6-2. S J McCarthy & A Simpkin bt K F Hunter & J M Reeves 6-3, 6-2. C L Billingham & J L Phillips bt A S Fleming & L T Stern 6-3, 2-6, 6-4. L C Gould & A L Grunfeld bt K D Hand & V Lake 6-3, 4-6, 6-2.

Semifinals

Grant & Louis bt McCarthy & Simpkins 3-6, 6-0, 6-3.
Gould & Grunfeld bt Billingham & Phillips 7-5, 7-6.

Final

Grant & Louis bt Gould & Grunfeld 6-4, 6-3.

PRUDENTIAL JUNIOR HARD COURT CHAMPIONSHIPS OF GREAT BRITAIN

18 and Under

WIMBLEDON, April 8th-13th

BOYS' SINGLES

First round

D J Roberts bt V G Ranson 6-3, 6-4. A St J Hunting bt O R Jackson 6-1, 6-2. N C Pashley bt M J Syms 6-4, 6-3. C Beecher bt D Clarry 6-0, 6-4. T W Godman bt J M Dawson 5-7, 7-5, 6-3. C M D Weekes bt C H Miller 6-4, 6-3. K P Fraser bt M Coombes 6-3, 6-3. A J Rouse bt S F Turnsek 6-2, 6-4. T J Maylam bt M A Nuttall 6-1, 6-1. S H Booth bt S E Wilkins 6-1, 6-3. A Fisher bt D Kirk 6-1, 6-1. S Heritage bt A Davies 7-6, 2-6, 7-5. J M Lenton bt U J Nganga 6-1, 6-1. M R Petchey bt J P Ranson 7-6, 6-4. D M Drake bt N P Smith 6-0, 6-3. D J Rigby bt D R Smith 6-0, 6-3.

Second round

R A W Whichello bt Roberts 3-6, 6-2, 6-1. Hunting bt S Bennett 7-6, 6-3. Pashley bt J J Hunter 7-5, 7-6. Beecher bt D P Ison 6-2, 6-3. C J Peet bt Godman 6-3, 6-1. Weekes bt J M Hill 6-4, 6-3. Fraser bt J R Martyn 6-1, 6-0. L G Matthews bt Rouse 7-5, 7-5. D Sapsford bt Maylam 6-3, 6-2. Booth bt H A Pringle 6-1, 6-4. G J Spalding bt Fisher 6-3, 6-3. S M Heron bt Heritage 6-1, 3-6, 6-1. A J W Brice bt L H Ahmed w/o, Petchey bt Lenton 6-3, 6-3. Drake bt Rigby 6-3, 6-2. J M Goodall bt P J Wright 6-0, 6-0.

Third round

Whichello bt Hunting 6-0, 6-2. Pashley bt Beecher 6-1 6-3. Peet bt Weekes 6-3, 7-5. Fraser bt Matthews 7-6, 6-2. Sapsford bt Booth 6-7, 6-1, 6-2. Heron bt Spalding 7-6, 6-4. Brice bt Petchey 6-1, 6-2. Drake bt Goodall w/o.

Quarter-finals

Whichello bt Pashley 6-4, 6-3. Peet bt Fraser 6-4, 6-2. Sapsford bt Heron 2-6, 6-4, 6-4. Brice bt Drake 6-3, 6-2.

Semifinals

Whichello bt Peet 4-6, 7-6, 7-5.
Brice bt Sapsford 6-1, 6-3.

Final

Whichello (Kent) bt Brice (Cheshire) 2-6, 7-5, 6-3.

BOYS' DOUBLES

Quarter-finals

A Davies & J M Dawson bt J M Goodall & R A W Whichello w/o, A J W Brice & D P Ison bt D Alexander & S G Heritage 6-4, 6-1. A St J Hunting & L G Matthews bt R C Lowther & S Wilkins 7-6, 7-5. S M Heron & S J Peet bt V G Ranson & A J Rouse 6-3, 6-3.

Semifinals

Brice & Ison bt Davies & Dawson 6-4, 6-1.
Heron & Peet bt Hunting & Matthews 6-2, 6-4.

Final

Brice & Ison bt Heron & Peet 6-7, 6-3, 6-4.

GIRLS' SINGLES

First round

R L Kendall bt K S Russell 6-1 6-4. L G Gould & L T Stern 7-5, 6-0. A C Nall bt I J Wild 6-0, 6-4. S L Timms bt C L Billingham 7-5, 6-2. K D Hand bt F A Couldridge 6-3, 6-4. K A Rickett bt S L Makepeace 6-2, 6-0. N R Mackintosh bt J Pearson 7-5, 6-1. S L Mitten bt G G Bhaguandas 3-6, 6-2, 7-5. A S Fleming bt A E Root 6-2, 6-2. S J Loosemore bt S J Armitage 6-0, 1-6, 6-0. V Lake bt D Schauerman 6-1, 6-4. A M Grant bt C L Bateman 4-6, 7-5, 6-1. C R Petchey bt K A Howden 6-5, 6-2. S Godman bt B L Welt 6-2, 7-6. L K Hartley bt R J Galassini 6-4, 6-2. K F Hunter bt A M Niepel 6-1, 6-0.

Second round

S T G Mair bt Kendall 6-1, 6-1. Gould bt N J Entract 6-1, 4-6, 6-1. Nail bt J Iddles 6-4, 6-4. Timms bt J M Reeves 6-1, 6-3. C J Wood bt Hand 6-4, 2-6, 6-3. Rickett bt C L Tee 6-1, 6-2. S J Byrne bt Mackintosh 6-7, 6-3, 9-7. S J Whiteman bt Mitten 5-7, 6-1, 6-4. Fleming bt A Grunfeld 6-3, 6-2. Loosemore bt J M Gracie 6-2, 6-2. Lake bt S J McCarthy 6-3, 3-6, 6-4. J V Wood bt Grant 6-1, 6-1. J R Holden bt Petchey 6-1, 6-1. Godman bt A Randall 7-6, 6-1. A L Gregory bt Harley 7-6, 6-4. J Louis bt Hunter 6-3, 6-2.

Third round

Gould bt Mair 3-6, 6-2, 6-4. Nall bt Timms 6-2, 7-5. C J Wood bt Rickett 6-1, 7-5. Whiteman bt Byrne 6-2, 6-3. Fleming bt Loosemore 6-4, 6-3. J V Wood bt Lake 6-1, 6-3. Holden bt Godman 6-2, 6-0. Louis bt Gregory 6-1, 6-1.

Quarter-finals

Gould bt Nall 7-5, 6-3. C J Wood bt Whiteman 6-1, 6-1. J V Wood bt Fleming 6-3, 6-1. Louis bt Holden 6-4, 3-6, 6-4.

Semifinals

Gould bt C J Wood
J V Wood bt Louis 6-0, 6-3.

Final

J V Wood (Middlesex) bt Gould (Essex) 2-6, 6-4, 6-2.

GIRLS' DOUBLES

Quarter-finals

J Lucis & J V Wood bt K D Hand & V Lake 5-7, 6-2, 6-2. J R Holden & R L Kendall bt A C Fitzgibbon & D Schauerman 7-5, 7-5. A S Fleming & L T Stern bt L C Gould & A L Grunfeld 6-0, 6-4. S T G Mair & C J Wood bt K F Hunter & J M Reeves 6-3, 6-0.

Semifinals

Louis & Wood bt Holden & Kendall 7-5, 7-5.
Mair & Wood bt Fleming & Stern 6-1, 6-3.

Final

Mair & C Wood bt Louise & J Wood 6-3, 1-6, 6-2.

18 and Under

WEST HANTS CLUB, BOURNEMOUTH, April 1st- 6th

BOYS' SINGLES

Quarter-finals

D Sapsford bt M R J Petchey 6-2, 7-6. N P Smith bt N C Pashley 7-6, 5-7, 6-4. C Beecher bt S E Wilkins 6-3, 6-2. S H Booth bt A Fisher 6-4, 6-7, 6-2.

Semifinals
Sapsford bt Smith 6-0, 6-4.
Beecher bt Booth 6-2, 3-6, 6-3.
Final
Sapsford (Surrey) bt Beecher (Kent) 6-2, 6-0.

BOYS' DOUBLES
Semifinals
N C Pashley & D Sapsford bt S H Booth & A Fisher 7-5, 2-6, 6-4.
J J Hunter & M R J Petchey bt N J Dean & D E Kirk 7-5, 4-6, 8-6.
Final
Pashley & Sapsford bt Hunter & Petchey 6-3, 6-4.

GIRLS' SINGLES
Quarter-finals
N J Entract bt A M Niepel 6-1, 6-3. S Godman bt A L Gregory 6-3, 6-1. S L Timms bt A S Fleming 6-4, 6-1. S J McCarthy bt A C Nall 6-1, 6-1.
Semifinals
Entract bt Godman 3-6, 6-4, 6-1.
Timms bt McCarthy 7-5, 6-3.
Final
Entract (Dorset) bt Timms (Essex) 6-3, 1-6, 6-4.

GIRLS' DOUBLES
Semifinals
A S Fleming & A T Stern bt S J Ambrose & T A Catlin 6-4, 7-5.
C L Bateman & S L Timms bt S Godman & A C Nail 6-3, 7-5.
Final
Fleming & Stern bt Bateman & Timms 6-1, 6-7, 6-4.

14 and Under

CRAIGLOCKHART SPORTS CENTRE, EDINBURGH, May 27th-June 1st

BOYS' SINGLES
Quarter-finals
N P Smith bt T J Rowe 6-2, 6-3. D P Harris bt J A Jones 7-5, 6-4. D R Ireland bt K P Cunningham 6-4, 7-5. S J Cornish bt J A Haycock 6-3, 6-2.
Semifinals
Smith be Harris 6-1, 6-2.
Cornish bt Ireland 6-1, 6-3.
Final
Cornish (Somerset) bt Smith (Lancs) 6-2, 6-4.

DOUBLES
Semifinals
D P Harris & N Smith bt D R Ireland & L T Shasby 6-3, 6-1.
S J Cornish & A L Foster bt S R Jackson & J A Jones 6-3, 7-5.
Final
Cornish & Foster bt Harris & Smith 3-6, 7-6, 6-2.

GIRLS' SINGLES
Quarter-finals
S J Loosemore bt S E Jenkins 2-6, 7-6, 6-1. S Gulati bt V S Humphreys-Davies 3-6, 6-3, 7-5. J H Dobovan bt S L Smith 6-4, 6-0. H Walters bt H R Lockhart 6-0, 6-2.

Semifinals
Loosemore bt Gulati 6-4, 7-5.
Donovan bt Walters 6-0, 6-4.
Final
Donovan (Warks) bt Loosemore (S Wales) 6-3, 6-1.

DOUBLES
Semifinals
J H Donovan & S J Loosemore bt C Smith & T Smith 6-2, 6-1.
S Smith & H Walters bt L A Jeffries & H C Worboys 6-1, 6-0.
Final
Donovan & Loosemore bt Smith & Walters 3-6, 6-3, 6-4.

12 and Under

EDINBURGH, May 27-June 1

BOYS' SINGLES
Semifinals
G B G Gibson bt S A Bonham 6-0, 6-1.
S M Silvester bt O Backhouse 6-0, 6-0.
Final
Gibson (Dorset) bt Silvester (Norfolk) 6-1, 6-3.

DOUBLES
Final
G B G Gibson & S M Silvester bt A J Blackman & R A Booth 6-1, 6-3.

GIRLS' SINGLES
Semifinals
S L Bentley bt E L Bond 6-3, 6-3.
C Hall bt V Graeme-Barber 6-3, 4-6, 6-2.
Final
Hall (Dorset) bt Bentley (Lincs) 6-4, 6-3.

DOUBLES
Final
S L Bentley & C Hall bt K Clatworthy & J C Crees 6-2, 6-0.

PRUDENTIAL JUNIOR GRASS COURT CHAMPIONSHIPS OF GREAT BRITAIN
18 and Under

DEVONSHIRE PARK, EASTBOURNE, August 19th-24th

BOYS' SINGLES
First round
C Bailey bt J M Jill 3-6, 6-2, 6-2. V Ranson bt S F Turnsek 6-2, 1-6, 6-1. D E Kirk bt J J Hunter 6-4, 7-5. J R Martyn bt C H Miller 6-3, 6-2. S H Booth bt J M Lenton 3-6, 6-3, 6-4. A St J Hunt bt S G Heritage 6-0, 6-1. D D Clarry bt C Beecher 6-1, 6-4. A J Rouse bt G N Drake 6-0, 6-4. A E Fisher bt M J Alridge 7-5, 6-0. M A Nuttall bt D M Drake 6-4, 6-1. T Godman bt S E Wilkins 4-6, 6-3, 6-3. R S Hutchinson bt D J Rigby 6-4, 5-7, 6-0. M R Petchey

bt T J Maylam 6-0, 6-2. C Brown bt G Spalding 7-6, 6-4. C J Nganga bt A Davies 6-4, 0-6, 6-4. R Every bt S Bennett 3-6, 6-4, 6-4.

Second round

C J Peet bt Bailey 6-1, 7-6. J H Mackinlay bt Ranson 6-1, 6-2. Kirk bt D R Roberts 7-5, 4-6, 6-3. D P Ison bt Martyn 6-1, 6-3. S M Heron bt P Wright 2-6, 6-4, 7-5. Booth bt Hunting 4-7, 6-4, 6-4. H A Pringle bt Clarry 1-6, 6-4, 6-3. L G Matthews bt Rouse 2-6, 6-5, 6-3. N R Jones bt Fisher 6-3, 6-4. Nuttall bt M Coombes 6-1, 7-5. N C Pashley bt Godman 6-4, 7-5. D Sapsford bt Hutchinson 7-6, 6-3. Petchey bt O Jackson 6-0, 6-1. Brown bt G M Weeks 7-5, 2-6, 6-4. Nganga bt J M Lawson 7-5, 6-2. A J W Brice bt Every 6-4, 6-1.

Third round

Peet bt Mackinlay 6-3, 6-0. Ison bt Kirk 6-3, 6-4. Booth bt Heron 3-6, 7-5, 6-2. Matthews bt Pringle 7-5, 5-7, 6-0. Jones bt Nuttall 6-2, 6-2. Pashley bt Sapsford 6-3, 6-3. Petchey bt Brown 6-0, 6-2. Brice bt Nganga 6-1, 6-0.

Quarter-finals

Peet bt Ison 4-6, 6-4, 7-5. Matthews bt Booth 6-3, 7-5. Jones bt Pashley 6-3, 6-3. Brice bt Petchey 6-4, 7-6.

Semifinals

Peet bt Matthews 6-3, 6-4.
Jones bt Brice 7-6, 1-6, 6-2.

Final

Jones (N Wales) bt Peet (Lancs) 6-1, 6-2.

BOYS' DOUBLES

Quarter-finals

A J W Brice & D P Ison bt R S Hutchinson & J Malabar 6-3, 6-4. S H Booth & A Fisher bt C Bailey & C M D Weekes 6-1, 3-6, 6-1. J Martyn & H Pringle bt D J Rigby & D J Roberts 6-3, 4-6, 6-5. S M Heron & C J Peet bt J J Hunter & M R Petchey 6-4, 6-2.

Semifinals

Brice & Ison bt Booth & Fisher 6-2, 6-3.
Heron & Peet bt Martyn & Pringle 6-3, 7-5.

Final

Brice & Ison bt Heron & Peet 4-6, 6-2, 7-5.

GIRLS' SINGLES

First round

S J McCarthy bt A Reichenbach 6-0, 6-3. J L Phillips bt V Heath 6-0, 6-4. A L Gregory bt F A Couldridge 6-3, 2-6, 6-3. A M Grant bt K D Hand 7-6, 2-6, 6-4. T Catlin bt R Stokes 6-1, 6-1. A C Nall bt L T Stern 6-4, 6-3. S J Ambrose bt L Hare 6-2, 6-2. K S Russell bt D Walker 7-5, 6-1. A M Niepel bt S J Byrne 7-6, 6-7, 6-1. L K Harley bt B L Welt 6-1, 6-4. A S Fleming bt B Suzin 6-0, 6-4. S J Hancock bt J M Gracie 7-5, 6-3. A Simpkin bt C R Petchey 6-2, 6-2. A E Randall bt S Makepeace 6-4, 6-2. C J Bateman bt I J Wild 6-0, 6-2.

Second round

McCarthy bt C J Wood 7-6, 6-7, 6-2. Phillips bt A Root 6-1, 6-2. Gregory bt R J Galassini 6-3, 6-2. Grant bt S J Whiteman 6-3, 6-3. Catlin bt A L Grunfeld 6-1, 6-3. Nail bt J E Iddles 6-4, 6-0. A S Hill bt Ambrose 6-1, 6-2. K Patel bt Russell 6-4, 1-6, 6-2. J M Reeve bt Niepel 6-2, 6-4. D Soheurman bt Harley 6-4, 6-4. Fleming bt Hanock 6-4, 6-1. V Lake bt N J Entract 6-3, 6-2. K Rickett bt K F Hunter 6-2, 6-2. Simpkin bt J Pearson 6-0, 6-1. C Bhaguandas bt Randall 7-6, 7-6. Bateman bt L C Gould 3-6, 6-2, 6-3.

Third round

McCarthy bt Phillips 6-2, 6-1. Grant bt Gregory 5-7, 6-2, 6-2. Catlin bt Nail 6-4, 6-2. Hill bt Patel 6-0, 7-5. Reeves bt Schauerman 6-4, 6-1. Lake bt Fleming 7-6, 6-1. Simpkin bt Rickett 6-1, 5-7, 6-3. Bateman bt Bhaguandas 4-6, 6-3, 6-3.

Quarter-finals

Grant bt McCarthy 6-1, 6-3. Catlin bt Hill 6-1, 6-7, 6-3. Lake bt Reeves 7-5, 6-4. Simpkin bt Bateman 6-2, 5-7, 6-2.

Semifinals

Catlin bt Grant 6-4, 7-6.
Simpkin bt Lake 6-3, 7-6.

Final

Simpkin (Leics) bt Catlin (Cambs) 6-2, 7-5.

GIRLS' DOUBLES

Quarter-finals

A S Fleming & L T Stern bt S Hancock & C Petchey 7-5, 6-4. R Dickinson & S Ford bt A C Reichanbach & K Russell 6-3, 6-7, 6-3. S J McCarthy & A Simpkin bt K S Patel & J J Wild 6-0, 3-6, 6-1. J E Iddles & K A Rickett bt A Root & S J Whiteman 7-6, 6-0.

Semifinals

Fleming & Stern bt Dickinson & Ford 7-6, 5-7, 6-1.
McCarthy & Simpkin bt Iddles & Rickett 6-2, 6-0.

Final

McCarthy & Simpkin bt Fleming & Stern 6-1, 6-4.

16 and Under

DEVONSHIRE PARK, EASTBOURNE, August 12th-17th

BOYS' SINGLES

First round

L F Bannister bt N A Green 7-5, 6-4. J W Routledge bt T J Paton 6-1, 6-4. J J Hunter bt S Holloway 6-2, 6-3. M J Aldridge bt D R Ireland 7-5, 6-2. G A Rae bt J M Lenton 4-6, 6-3, 6-2. K G Harris bt R Scarfe 6-1, 6-0. T W McKone bt N J Dean 6-3, 4-6, 6-3. D E Kirk bt U J Nganga 6-4, 6-3. D B Coull bt M C Edmeston 6-1, 1-6, 6-2. D Bishop bt S A Byrne 6-3, 7-6. J J Mercer bt G R Reayer 6-2, 6-0. N H Mansell bt P Ware 6-0, 6-2. C R Craig bt R C Lowther 7-5, 6-4. G N Drake bt M J Long 7-5, 6-0. A R Woods bt I A Nicholas 6-3, 6-1. D W Ahl bt D P Harris 6-2, 2-6, 6-1.

Second round

D Sapsford bt Bannister 6-2, 6-1. Routledge bt C Wilkinson 2-6, 6-1, 6-3. C Taylor bt Hunter 6-4, 6-7, 6-3. N P Smith bt Aldridge 7-5, 6-2. M R Petchey bt Rae 6-4, 6-2. M E Loosemore bt Harris 6-1, 6-3. S J Cornish bt McKone 6-1, 6-3. Kirk bt S E Wilkins 6-4, 6-4. N C Pashley bt Coull 7-5, 6-1. M P Brannelly bt Bishop 6-4, 3-6, 6-4. G N Engleman bt Mercer 7-6, 6-3. Mansell bt C Beecher 6-3, 5-7, 6-2. E A Fisher bt Craig 6-3, 6-1. Drake bt P J Tague 7-6, 2-6, 6-1. Woods bt K L Dykes 6-2, 7-6. S H Booth bt Ahl 6-3, 6-1.

Third round
Sapsford bt Routledge 6-0, 6-3. Taylor bt Smith 6-4, 6-0. Petchey bt Loosemore 6-1, 3-6, 8-6. Kirk bt Cornish 6-2, 6-1. Pashley bt Brannelly 6-0, 6-1. Engleman bt Mansell 4-6, 6-2, 6-2. Fisher bt Drake 3-6, 7-5, 6-2. Booth bt Woods 6-7, 7-5, 6-3.
Quarter-finals
Sapsford bt Taylor 6-4, 6-2. Kirk bt Petchey 6-1, 3-6, 6-0. Pashley bt Engleman 6-0, 6-1. Booth bt Fisher 6-3, 3-6, 6-3.
Semifinals
Sapsford bt Kirk 7-5, 3-6, 6-2.
Pashley bt Booth 6-4, 6-1.
Final
Pashley (Surrey) bt Sapsford (Surrey) 3-6, 6-3, 6-2.
BOYS' DOUBLES
Quarter-finals
N J Dean & G N Drake bt N C Pashley & D E Sapsford 2-0 retd, S H Booth & A E Fisher bt C Beecher & C J Nganga 6-1, 6-1. D E Kirk & S Wilkins bt M J Long & J W Routledge 6-3, 2-6, 7-5. J J Hunter & M R Petchey bt G Engleman & A R Woods 6-2, 6-0.
Semifinals
Booth & Fisher bt Dean & Drake 6-5, 6-2.
Hunter & Petchey bt Kirk & Wilkins 4-6, 6-1, 6-3.
Final
Hunter & Petchey bt Boots & Fisher 6-2, 6-4.
GIRLS' SINGLES
First round
D Sptingall bt S Masterson 6-4, 6-3.
C L Tee bt K L Fisher 6-3, 6-4. C L Bateman bt C L See 6-4, 6-4. H J Gracie bt A E Randall 4-1 retd. J H Donovan bt J M Turnbull 6-1, 6-1. S Smith bt A K Palmer 4-6, 6-3, 6-4. S Loosemore bt H Evans 6-1, 6-1. A M Niepel bt M. A. Milford 6-1, 6-4. V J Heath bt A C Nall 6-4, 6-1. S Makepeace bt M T G Mair 6-4, 6-3. V L Wait bt J K Jenkins 5-7, 6-4, 6-0. N C Topper bt S Jenkins 6-4, 6-3. L T Stern bt N J Livingstone 7-5, 6-4. S J Peach bt M Loughton 6-3, 6-3. R J Stokes bt A R T Tate 6-3, 6-4. S J Ambrose bt R A Atkin 6-3, 6-2.
Second round
A Simpkin bt Springall 6-0, 6-2. Tee bt H Walters 6-3, 6-3. Bateman bt R F Violett 6-2, 7-5. A S Fleming bt Gracie 6-1, 6-1. S J McCarthy bt Donovan 6-4, 6-0. Smith bt J Pearson 6-3, 4-6, 6-2. Loosemore bt B L Welt 6-0, 6-1. A L Gregory bt Niepel 6-2, 6-3. S Godman bt Heath 6-2, 6-0. Makepeace bt L A Jeffries 6-0, 7-5. I J Wild bt Wait 1-6, 6-0, 6-3. Topper bt N J Entract 4-6, 6-4, 6-3. Stern bt K Turner 6-4, 6-0. A S Hill bt Peach 4-6, 6-3, 6-2. Stokes bt S C M Eve 6-3, 6-4. T A Catlin bt Ambrose 6-2, 6-4.
Third round
Simpkin bt Tee 5-2 retd. Bateman bt Fleming 6-1, 7-6. McCarthy bt Smith 6-1, 6-1. Gregory bt Loosemore 6-7, 6-3, 6-3. Godman bt Makepeace 6-2, 6-1. Wild bt Topper 6-0, 3-6, 6-3. Stern bt Hill 2-6, 6-2, 6-2. Catlin bt Stokes 6-3, 6-1.
Quarter-finals
Simpkin bt Bateman 6-2, 6-1. Gregory bt McCarthy 6-3, 6-3. Godman bt Wild 6-3, 6-1. Catlin bt Stern 6-3, 7-5.
Semifinals
Simpkin bt Gregory 6-2, 6-4.
Catlin bt Godman 6-1, 6-4.
Final
Simpkin (Leics) bt Catlin (Cambs) 1-6, 6-3, 6-2.

GIRLS' DOUBLES
Quarter-finals
A S Fleming & L T Stern bt S Ambrose & J Pearson 6-4, 6-3. C Bateman & S Jenkins bt T Catlin & B L Welt 7-6, 7-6. S Godman & A C Nall bt S Masterton & P J Tilin 6-3, 6-2. S J McCarthy & A Simpkin bt S J Peach & C L Tee w/o.
Semifinals
Fleming & Stern bt Bateman & Jenkins 6-2, 6-1.
McCarthy & Simpkin bt Godman & Nall 6-1, 2-0, retd.
Final
McCarthy & Simpkin bt Fleming & Stern 6-2, 6-3.

14 and Under

DEVONSHIRE PARK, EASTBOURNE, August 19th-24th

BOYS' SINGLES
Quarter-finals
N P Smith bt N Simmonds 6-4, 6-1. S J Bell bt J A Haycock 6-1, 6-3. D P Harris bt D Draper 6-3, 6-2. S J Cornish bt K P Cunningham 6-4, 7-6.
Semifinals
Smith bt Bell 6-2, 6-4.
Cornish bt Harris 6-4, 7-6.
Final
Smith (Lancs) bt Cornish (Somerset) 6-4, 6-0.

DOUBLES
Semifinals
D P Harris & N P Smith bt D C Hinds & I T Shasby 2-6, 6-2, 8-6.
S J Cornish & A L Foster bt S H Jackson & J A Jones 6-2 6-4.
Final
Harris & Smith bt Cornish & Foster 6-3, 6-4.

GIRLS' SINGLES
Quarter-finals
S J Loosemore bt L A Jefferies 5-7, 6-3, 6-1. S L Smith bt R F Violett 6-1, 2-6, 6-2. V S Humphreys-Davies bt H Walters 6-2, 6-1. J H Donovan bt S Gulati 6-2, 6-2.
Semifinals
Loosemore bt Smith 6-4, 4-6, 6-3.
Donovan bt Humphreys-Davies 7-6, 6-3.
Final
S Loosemore (S Wales) bt Donovan (Warks) 4-6, 6-4, 6-2.

GIRLS' DOUBLES
Semifinals
J H Donovan & S Loosemore bt K L Fisher & K S Williams 6-2, 6-2.
G E Hiley & L J Nimmo bt S L Smith & H Walters 1-6, 6-1, 9-7.
Final
Donovan & Loosemore bt Hiley & Nimmo 4-6, 6-1, 6-3.

12 and under

DEVONSHIRE PARK, EASTBOURNE, August 12th-17th

BOYS' SINGLES

Quarter-finals

G B G Gibson bt B R Amies 6-1, 6-0. M C Moreso bt N Weal 6-1, 6-3. S J Bonham bt M A George 3-6, 6-3, 6-0. S M Silvester bt S P Breese 7-5, 6-1.

Semifinals

Gibson bt Moreso 6-4, 6-3.
Silvester bt Bonham 6-3, 7-6.

Final

Silvester (Norfolk) bt Gibson (Dorset) 6-2, 6-0.

DOUBLES

Semifinals

G B G Gibson & S M Silvester bt M A George & I J Pearson 6-2, 5-7, 6-2.
S A Bonham & M C Moreso bt S J Gray & P C Robinson 6-0, 5-7, 6-2.

Final

Gibson & Silvester bt Bonham & Moreso 6-4, 7-5.

GIRLS' SINGLES

Quarter-finals

C Hall bt C Ashworth 6-3, 3-6, 8-6. N J Matthews bt E S Woodhouse 4-6, 6-4, 5-1. V Graeme-Barber bt C E A White 6-3, 6-3. S L Bentley bt S A Lewis 6-2, 6-3.

Semifinals

Hall bt Matthews 6-0, 6-2.
Graeme-Barber bt Bentley 6-3, 4-6, 6-0.

Final

Hall (Dorset) bt Graeme-Barber (Cambs) 6-7, 6-4, 6-3.

DOUBLES

Semifinals

S L Bentley & C Hall bt J M Alexander & C E J Athow 6-1, 6-2.
L K Jackson & S A Lewis bt V Graeme-Barber & J F Tucker 6-3, 6-3.

Final

Bentley & Hall bt Jackson & Lewis 6-2, 4-6 6-4.

PRUDENTIAL JUNIOR COUNTY CUP 1985

September 2nd-4th

BOYS

Group 1, Queen's Club
Champions — Essex
Runners-up — Surrey
Relegated — Yorkshire

Group 2, Edgbaston Priory
Promoted — Lancashire
Relegated — Kent

Group 3, West Warwickshire
Promoted — South Wales
Relegated — Norfolk

Group 4, Leicester
Promoted — Hampshire & I.O.W.
Relegated — Nottinghamshire

Group 5, Peterborough
Promoted — Sussex
Relegated — Durham & Cleveland

Group 6, Bristol
Promoted — Staffordshire
Relegated — Cornwall

Group 7, Nottingham
Promoted — Leicestershire
Relegated — Derbyshire

Group 8, Stourbridge
Promoted — West of Scotland
Relegated — Somerset

Group 9, Tring
Promoted — Cambridgeshire
Relegated — Wiltshire

Group 10, Edinburgh
Promoted — North of Scotland
Relegated — Northumberland

Group 11, Shrewsbury
Promoted — Northamptonshire

GIRLS

Group 1, Queen's Club
Champions — Essex
Runners-up — Surrey
Relegated — Middlesex

Group 2, Winchester
Promoted — Avon
Relegated — Kent

Group 3, Northampton
Promoted — Nottinghamshire
Relegated — Lancashire

Group 4, Chesham Bois
Promoted — Berkshire
Relegated — Cheshire

Group 5, Berkhamsted
Promoted — Lincolnshire
Relegated — Buckinghamshire

Group 6, Cheltenham
Promoted — Hertfordshire
Relegated — Hereford & Worcester

Group 7, Edgbaston Priory
Promoted — Dorset
Relegated — South Wales

Group 8, Exeter
Promoted — Gloucestershire
Relegated — West of Scotland

Group 9, Banbury
Promoted — North of Scotland
Relegated — Bedfordshire

Group 10, Solihull
Promoted — Northumberland
Relegated — South of Scotland

Group 11, Lytham St Annes
Promoted — Shropshire

JUNIOR WINTER SERIES RESULTS

WINTER SERIES – Grand Finals

TELFORD, March 28th-30th
Boys 16 and Under
S Booth (Warks) bt C Beecher (Kent) 7-5, 6-0
Girls 16 and Under
A Fleming (Leics) bt T Catlin (Cambs) 6-3, 6-5
Boys 14 and Under
N Smith (Lancs) bt S Cornish (Somerset) 7-6, 6-3
Girls 14 and Under
S Loosemore (Wales) bt H Walters (Essex) 6-0, 6-4

SPORT GOOFY TROPHY FINALS

BATH, September 13th-15th
Boys 14 and Under
N Smith (Lancs) bt S Cornish (Som) 7-5, 6-2
Girls 14 and Under
S Loosemore (Wales) bt J Donovan (Warks) 6-2, 6-3
Boys 12 and Under
C Gibson (Dorset) bt S Silvester (Norfolk) 6-1, 6-1
Girls 12 and Under
C Hall (Dorset) bt V Graeme-Barber (Cambs) 7-6, 5-7, 6-2

NESTLE INTERNATIONAL FINALS

QUEEN'S CLUB, September 1st
Boys' Final
D Ahl (England) bt A Fisner (Wales) 6-4, 6-4
Girls' Final
A Fleming (England) bt S Loosemoor (Wales)

WALL'S JUNIOR CIRCUIT FINALS

QUEEN'S CLUB, October 23rd-26th
Boys
M Aldridge bt G Fanning 6-3, 6-1

INTERNATIONAL JUNIOR COMPETITIONS WITH BRITISH ENTRY

WIMBLEDON JUNIOR CHAMPIONSHIPS

BOYS' SINGLES

First round

L Lavalle (Mex) bt R Tsujino (Jap) 6-2, 6-2. T Srichapan (Thai) bt L Pang (Hong Kong) 6-2, 6-1. D Ison (GB) bt E Collins (Ire) 6-3, 6-4. S Matsuoa (Jap) bt F Anda (Sp) 7-6, 6-4. T Trigueiro (US) bt C Pistolesi (It) 7-6, 6-5. M Nastase (Rom) bt N Jones (GB) 6-3, 6-3. H Whichello (GB) bt I Saric (Yug) 4-6, 6-3, 6-0. F Davin (Arg) bt M Kaplan (SA) 6-2, 4-6, 6-4. J Yzaga (Per) bt C Peet (GB) 6-1, 6-1. M Van Eekeren (Nth) bt C Suk (Cz) 6-3, 6-1. P Korda (Cz) bt V Thongkumchu (Thai) 6-2, 6-4. J Blake (US) bt A Solano (Col) 6-0, 6-3. G Roldan (Arg) bt R Harriso (Hong Kong) 6-4, 6-3. G Saacks (SA) bt N Silveira (Ven) 6-4, 7-5. J Kim (Kor) bt K Ng (Hong Kong) 4-6, 6-2, 6-4. W Kowlaski (Pol) bt A Moreno (M) 6-4, 6-4. V Paloheimo (Fin) bt P Flynn (Aus) 3-6, 7-6, 6-2. S Grenier (Fr) bt M Filippini (Ur) 6-3, 7-5. C Garner (US) bt R Gajarco (Ch) 6-4, 6-0. Barrientos (Ph) bt B Haygarth (SA) 1-6, 6-3, 6-4. B Custer (Aus) D Shapiro (SA) 4-6, 7-6, 7-5. K Braasch (WG) bt N Bendtsen (Den) 6-7, 6-2, 6-2. J Sanchez (Sp) bt G Cohen (Zim) 6-2, 6-3. D Engel (Sw) bt J Goodall (GB) 1-6, 7-5, 6-1. J Silva (Por) bt A J W Brice (GB) 6-1, 6-4. R Hertzog (Swz) bt Z Ali (In) 6-3, 6-1. E Furusho (Br) bt J Lizardo (Phi) 6-1, 6-2. J Boytim (US) bt B Farrow (US) 7-6, 7-6. F Errard (Fra) bt S Cortes (Chi) 6-4, 6-4. U Colombini (It) bt H Aiyar (In) 6-4, 6-2. A Meeus (B) bt Z Irani (In) 3-6, 6-4, 10-8. E Velez (M) bt C Allgardh (Sw) 5-7, 6-4, 6-3.

Second round

Lavalle bt Srichapan 6-4 6-0. Matsuoka bt Ison 6-3, 6-3. Trigueiro bt Nastase 6-4, 6-4. Davin bt Whichello 3-6, 6-2, 6-1. Yzag bt Van Eekeren 6-3, 6-3. Korda bt Blake 6-4, 1-6, 6-1. Saacks bt Roldan 7-6, 3-6, 6-2. Kim bt Kowalski 6-2, 3-6, 6-3. Paloheimo bt Grenier 6-3, 6-4. Barrientos bt Garner 7-5, 4-6, 6-0. Custer bt Braasch 6-2, 6-3. Sanchez bt Engel 4-6, 7-5, 6-3. Silva bt Hertzog 6-2, 6-7, 6-1. Boytim bt Furusho 6-3, 6-4. Colombini bt Errard 4-6, 7-6 12-10. Velez bt Meeus 6-2, 6-3.

Third round

Lavalle bt Matsuoka 6-3, 6-2. Trigueiro bt Davin 6-1, 6-4. Yzaga bt Korda 6-7, 7-5, 6-2. Saacks bt Kim 6-1, 6-3. Barrientos bt Paloheimo 6-2, 6-4. Sanchez bt Custer 6-7, 6-3, 7-5. Silva bt Boytim 6-2, 7-6. Velez bt Colombini 6-4, 6-4.

Quarter-finals

Lavalle bt Trigueiro 5-7, 6-3, 6-1. Yzaga bt Saacks 4-6, 6-1, 7-5. Barrientos bt Sanchez 4-6, 6-4, 6-3. Velez bt Silva 7-5, 6-3.

Semifinals

Lavalle bt Yzaga 2-6, 6-2, 6-3. Velez bt Barrientos 7-6, 6-0.

Final

Lavalle bt Velez 6-4, 6-4.

GIRLS' SINGLES

First round

K Schimper (SA) bt H Witvoet (Neth) 6-4, 6-7, 8-6. J Louis (GB) bt L Field (Aus) 6-3, 6-4. J Wood (GB) bt I Dreihuis (Nth) 1-6, 7-6, 6-2. M Roldan (Arg) bt N Missana (Ven) 6-1, 6-0. S Wasserman (B) bt P Moreno (Hong Kong) 6-4, 7-6. E Derly (Fra) bt S London (US) 6-2, 6-4. S Noix Chateau (Fr) bt R Basuki (Indon) 5-7, 6-4, 6-4. M Lundqvist (Sw) bt S Mair (GB) 5-7, 6-1, 6-2. M Turk (Aus) bt L Tedjomukti (Indo) 6-0, 6-0. A Kijimuta (Jap) bt J Saberon (Phi) 6-4, 6-4. D Van Rensburg (SA) bt N Sodupe (US) 6-2, 6-2. J Richardson (NZ) bt N Tauziat (Fr) 6-4, 7-5. R Wiser (WG) bt A Isaza (Col) 6-3, 6-3. R Zrubakova (Cz) bt P Tarabini (Arg) 6-2, 6-4. G Miro (Br) bt P Sepulveda (Ch) 6-2, 6-2. D Ketelaar (Nth) bt S Meier (WG) 6-1, 6-1.

Second round

H Kelesi (Can) bt Schimper 6-1, 2-6, 6-4. Louis bt E Kajitani (Jap) 6-4, 6-3. Wood bt E Hirose (Jap) 6-3, 7-6. H Dahlstrom (Sw) bt Roldan 6-3, 6-0. A Holikova (Cz) bt Wasserman 6-1, 7-5. Derly bt M Raimo (Br) 6-0, 6-1. A Devries (R) bt Noix Chateau 5-7, 6-4, 6-4. E Reinach (SA) bt Lundqvist 6-4, 6-4. M J Fernandez (US) bt Turk 1-6, 6-4, 6-0. Keimuta bt A Dechaume (Fr) 2-6, 6-4, 7-5. Van Rensburg bt C Wood (GB) 6-4, 7-5. Richardson bt J Thompson (Aus) 6-3, 4-6, 6-2. J Byrne (Aus) bt Wieser 6-2, 6-0. E Rossides (US) bt Zrubakova 3-6, 7-6, 6-2. Miro bt T Summa (Thai) 6-2, 6-2. Ketelaar bt L Garrone (It) 3-6, 6-3, 9-7.

Third round

Kelesi bt Louis 6-1, 6-0. Dahlstrom bt Wood 6-4, 6-4. Holikova bt Derby 6-1, 6-3. Reinach bt Devries 6-3, 6-2. Fernandez bt Kijimuta 6-3, 6-2. Richardson bt Van Rensburg 6-1, 7-5. Byrne bt Rossides 7-6, 6-7, 10-8. Ketelaar bt Miro 6-4, 6-4.

Quarter-finals

Kelesi bt Dahlstrom 6-1, 6-2. Holikova bt Reinach 6-2, 7-5. Fernandez bt Richardson 6-4, 6-3. Byrne bt Ketelaar 6-1, 6-2.

Semifinals
Holikova bt Kelesi 6-3, 6-3.
Byrne bt Fernandez 6-5, 6-3.
Final
Holikova bt Byrne 7-5, 6-1.

FRENCH JUNIOR CHAMPIONSHIPS

PARIS, June 2nd-9th

BOYS' SINGLES
Final
J Yzaga (Peru) bt T Muster (Austria)

GIRLS' SINGLES
Final
L Garrone (Italy) bt D Van Rensburg (SA)

UNITED STATES JUNIOR CHAMPIONSHIPS

FLUSHING MEADOW, September 2nd-8th

BOYS' SINGLES
Final
T Trigueiro (US) bt J Blake (US) 6-2, 6-3

GIRLS' SINGLES
Final
D Garrone (Italy) bt A Holikova (Czech) 6-2, 7-6

AUSTRALIAN OPEN JUNIOR CHAMPIONSHIPS

MELBOURNE, December 2nd-9th

BOYS' SINGLES
Final
S Barr (Aus) bt S Furlong (Aus)

GIRLS' SINGLES
Final
J Byrne (Aus) bt L Field (Aus)

WORLD YOUTH CUP
(Boys and Girls 16 and Under)

KOBE, JAPAN, November 13th-17th

BOYS
Semifinals
Australia 2 USSR 1, USA 3 Venezuela 0
Final
Australia 2 USA 1

GIRLS
Quarter-finals
France 3 Hong Kong 0
Czechoslovakia 3 Peru 0
Great Britain 3 Japan 0
Australia 2 USA 1
Semifinals
Czechoslovakia 2 France 1
Australia 3 Great Britain 0
Final
Czechoslovakia 3 Australia 0
Britain beat West Germany 2-1 and Japan 3-0 before losing to Australia. Team: T Catlin, A Simpkin, S McCarthy.

ORANGE BOWL

MIAMI BEACH, December 18th-24th

BOYS' SINGLES
Final
C Pistolesi (It) bt B Oresar (Yug)

GIRLS' SINGLES
Final
A M Fernandez (US) bt P Tarabini (Arg)

MAUREEN CONNOLLY TEAM COMPETITION
Great Britain v USA
Ladies 21 and Under

QUEEN'S CLUB, LONDON, December 12th-14th

Great Britain **5** USA **6**
(Results, British first: S Reeves lost A Hulbert 5-7, 7-5, 6-4. J Louis lost R Reis 4-6, 7-5, 6-0. S Gomer bt J Holdren 6-0, 6-1. Louis & J Wood lost Hulbert & Reis 4-6, 7-5, 6-2. J Wood lost W Wood 7-6, 6-3. A Brown lost T Phelps 6-2, 6-2. Louis bt Hulbert 6-2, 6-2. Reeves bt Reis 6-3, 4-6, 6-2. Brown bt Holdren 3-6, 6-4, 6-3. Gomer lost Phelps 6-4, 5-7, 6-3. Gomer & Brown bt Phelps & Wood 6-4, 7-6).

Previous Winners
1973 USA 6, Great Britain 0 (La Jolla)
1974 USA 6, Great Britain 0 (Little Rock)
1975 Great Britain 6, USA 4 (Torquay)
1976 USA 6, Great Britain 5 (Naples, Fla)
1977 USA 10, Great Britain 1 (Torquay)
1978 USA 10, Great Britain 1 (Deer Creek, Fla)
1979 USA 8, Great Britain 3 (Bradford)
1980 USA 9, Great Britain 2 (Houston)
1981 USA 8, Great Britain 3 (Cambridge)
1982 USA 6, Great Britain 5 (Dallas)
1983 USA 8, Great Britain 3 (Cambridge)
1984 USA 10, Great Britain 1 (Delray Beach)

GALEA CUP
Men 20 and Under

In the qualifying zone, played at Stalowa Wola, Poland in July, Great Britain was represented by J M Goodall, B J Knapp, T M Walker and R A W Whichello with N C Sears as non-playing captain. They beat Morocco 4-1 but lost to Poland 2-3. Final: Italy 3 USA 2.

Previous winners
1950 Italy
1951 France
1952 Italy
1953 France
1954 Italy

1955 Italy
1956 Spain
1957 Spain
1958 Spain
1959 West Germany
1960 France
1961 France
1962 France
1963 Czechoslovakia
1964 USSR
1965 Czechoslovakia
1966 Czechoslovakia
1967 France
1968 Spain
1969 Spain 3, Czechoslovakia 2
1970 Czechoslovakia 3, Spain 2
1971 Sweden 5, France 0
1972 Great Britain 4, Spain 1
1973 Spain 4, Great Britain 1
1974 Czechoslovakia 4, Spain 1
1975 Czechoslovakia 3, Spain 2
1976 West Germany 3, Italy 2
1977 Argentina 3, France 2
1978 France 3, Czechoslovakia 2
1979 France 3, Czechoslovakia 2
1980 France 3, Spain 2
1981 West Germany 5, Australia 0
1982 Australia 3, Spain 2
1983 France 5, Spain 0
1984 Czechoslovakia 4, Argentina 1

COUPE ANNIE SOISBAULT

Ladies 20 and Under

This was played at Le Touquet in July. Great Britain, represented by B A Borneo, J Louis and J V Wood with L J Charles as non-playing captain, beat Italy 2-1 but lost to the USSR 0-3.

Final

Czechoslovakia 3 Argentina 0

Previous winners

Played at Le Touquet
1965 Netherlands
1966 France
1967 Netherlands
1968 USSR
1969 USSR
1970 USSR 3, France 0
1971 France 2, Czechoslovakia 1
1972 USSR 2, Great Britain 1
1973 Great Britain 2, USSR 1
1974 Czechoslovakia 2, Great Britain 1
1975 Great Britain 2, Romania 1
1976 Czechoslovakia 2, Great Britain 1
1977 Czechoslovakia 3, Switzerland 0
1978 USSR 3, Switzerland 0
1979 Great Britain 2, Czechoslovakia 0
1980 Czechoslovakia 2, Australia 1
1981 Netherlands 2, USSR 0
1982 USSR 2, Great Britain 1
1983 France 2, Czechoslovakia 1
1984 USA 3, Czechoslovakia 0

VALERIO CUP

Boys 18 and Under

In the qualifying competition at Mons in August, Great Britain, represented by A J W Brice, J M Goodall, D P Ison, C J Peet and R A W Whichello and with N C Sears as non-playing captain, beat Austria 3-2 but lost to Czechoslovakia 0-5.

Final

Italy 3 Sweden 2

Previous winners

1970 Sweden 4, France 1
1971 Italy 4, West Germany 0
1972 Czechoslovakia 3, USSR 2
1973 Czechoslovakia 4, USSR 2
1974 Spain 3, Italy 2
1975 Italy 3, USSR 2
1976 West Germany 4, France 1
1977 Italy 5, Romania 0
1978 Sweden 3, Italy 2
1979 Sweden 4, West Germany 1
1980 Spain 4, France 1
1981 Sweden 3, Italy 2
1982 Italy 3, Spain 2
1983 Sweden 4, Spain 1
1984 Italy 3, France 1

COUPE JEAN BOROTRA

Boys 16 and Under

The qualifying zone was played at Lee-on-Solent in July. Great Britain, represented by C Beecher, S H Booth, N C Pashley, M R J Petchey and D E Sapsford (with J G Clifton non-playing captain) lost 1-4 to Czechoslovakia and 0-5 to France.

Final

Sweden 3 France 2

Previous winners

1980 Sweden 3 Czechoslovakia 0
1981 Italy 3 USSR 2
1982 Sweden 4 Spain 1
1983 USSR 3 Sweden 2
1984 Italy 4 Sweden 1

COUPE HELVETIE

Girls 16 and Under

The qualifying zone was played at Estoril in July. Great Britain, represented by T A Catlin, N J Entract, A S Fleming, S J McCarthy and A Simpkin (with A P Stewart as non-playing captain) beat Portugal 5-0 but lost to Sweden 0-5.

Final

West Germany 4 Sweden 1

Previous winners

1977 Italy 3, Switzerland 2
1978 Bulgaria 5, West Germany 0
1979 Sweden 5, France 0
1980 Sweden 2, West Germany 2
1981 Sweden 3, Italy 2
1982 USSR 3, France 2
1983 USSR 3, Sweden 2
1984 Czechoslovakia 4, West Germany 1

COPA DEL SOL
Boys 14 and Under
The eliminating zone was played at La Jarrie, France in July. Great Britain, represented by S J Cornish, K P Cunningham, A L Foster, D R Ireland and N P Smith (D J Bone was non-playing captain) beat Norway 5-0 but lost to France 2-3.

Final

Austria 5 Italy 0

Previous winners

1979 Italy 3, France 2
1980 Sweden 4, Italy 1
1981 Sweden 3, Israel 2
1982 Sweden 4, West Germany 1
1983 Sweden 5, Holland 0
1984 West Germany 4, Spain 1

COUPE EUROPA
Girls 14 and Under
The eliminating zone was held at Genk, Belgium, in July. Great Britain, represented by J H Donovan, S Gulati, S J Loosemore, R F Viollet and H Walters (with J M Dier as non-playing captain) lost to Belgium 1-4 and to Austria 0-3.

Final

USSR 3 Italy 2

Previous winners

1982 Sweden 3, West Germany 2
1983 West Germany 3, France 2
1984 France 4, Sweden 1

THE QUEEN CLUB
Girls 18 and Under
No team entered in 1985.

Final

Italy 4, Sweden 1

Previous winners

1972 Romania 3, West Germany 2
1973 Great Britain 3, Spain 2
1974 Czechoslovakia 3, France 2
1975 Great Britain 4, Czechoslovakia 1
1976 Great Britain 3, Switzerland 1
1977 Czechoslovakia 5, Sweden 0
1978 Czechoslovakia 5, Sweden 0
1979 Czechoslovakia 3, Switzerland 1
1980 Switzerland 3, USSR 2
1981 Sweden 3, Czechoslovakia 2
1982 Italy 4, Czechoslovakia 1
1983 Italy 4, Czechoslovakia 1
1984 Sweden 3, Czechoslovakia 1

ROLEX INTERNATIONAL
Port Washington, December

Boys' Singles Final

U Stenluno (Swe) bt S Ohta (Jap) 6-2, 6-1

Girls' Singles Final

P O'Reilly (US) bt J Pospisilora (Cz) 7-6, 6-3

ESTABLISHING FOUNDATIONS

BY HEATHER DALLAS: PRESS OFFICER, THE LTA

Only three years ago the regional network in Britain was given a new lease of life with the appointment of Brian Blincoe as the Director of National Development. In those three years a quite radical change in British tennis has taken place, not only in regional development but at the base of the tennis pyramid which has quite dramatically expanded, especially with the highly successful introduction of short tennis.

This change is mainly due to Blincoe and his largely unsung but select team of National Coach/ Development Officers (NCDOs) who are paving the way towards the production of many more players in the future.

At the time of his appointment, in October 1982, there were only two full-time regional officers in England (Blincoe himself had pioneered the first full-time region in the East from 1977). Now there are eight, with similar appointments in Scotland and Wales. Each region is an official 'arm' of the LTA with a fully deployed NCDO working with the support of a full-time secretary and part-time regional training staff.

Choosing the right man for the job was no easy task. As Blincoe says: 'They needed to be proven coaches, have experience as administrators as well as a general tennis background and have the sort of personality that would attract the respect and goodwill of all those whose paths they would cross.'

The right men were found, however, and within only two and a half years. Although 1985 was only the first year when regional development could truthfully be said to embrace the entire country the results are already encouraging.

But what do the NCDOs do? 'Certainly they are striving to provide the national scene with many more, younger and better prepared players' said Blincoe. 'But that target is inseperably interwoven with many other aspects such as early introduction and encouragement, competitions, liaison with countries, coaches and coaching standards, public relations and so on. In fact, the NCDOs' responsibilities embrace the whole spectrum of junior tennis development. It is, without doubt, a tough and demanding job.'

The creation of this nationwide framework of Regional development, one of the biggest steps ever taken by the LTA, has attracted relatively little publicity. Yet some 1,000 boys and girls aged between eight and 18 are currently receiving regional training and standards are already showing positive signs of improvement in the lower age national championships. Blincoe is philosophical about not hitting the headlines, 'In many ways it is a compliment. However vital and however well done, the laying of sound foundations will never attract the type of spotlight that will ultimately focus on the end result. It would only be if things went wrong that everyone would read about our efforts at this stage.

'The hard work being put in by the regions isn't going to produce champions overnight', he added, 'But, if you like, we are sowing the seeds for tomorrow's headlines. I would expect the fruits of the regional labour to blossom increasingly over the next 10 years although I appreciate that other countries are not going to stand still to let us catch them up.'

To back up this statement, Paul Hutchins was quoted last year in The Daily Telegraph as saying 'Certainly I'm much more optisimtic now about our own coaching and development. If those two areas under the direction of Charles Applewhaite (the LTA Director of Coaching) and Brian Blincoe could have been operating over the last ten years with me we'd have a much better overall system.'

Blincoe, who constantly acknowledges the value of the Prudential sponsorship and the efforts of the Lawn Tennis Foundation in bringing on junior and grass roots development is only too well aware of how dependent the regional programmes are upon the work of the counties. 'However well the regions do their job they can only help and encourage those who emerge from the counties', he said. 'It is really only within the counties that youngsters (especially those from non-tennis playing backgrounds) can be encouraged to take up the game and then be spotted if they have outstanding talent.

'Some counties are doing an excellent job' he added, quoting the success of Cambridgeshire which has a population of less than 600,000 but has many top juniors. 'But I am only too aware of just how much pressure this involves for honorary officials – especially since the advent of short tennis. This has added to their workload but does provide a perfect additional opportunity of attracting so many more children into the game.' This can be proved by the fact that although the national launch of short tennis was only three and a half years ago there are now around 100,000 children playing the game, thousands of whom might not otherwise have been attracted into tennis.

'Among these children must be many with exceptional athletic talent which makes them potential champions of the future' said Blincoe. 'If, and it is a very crucial if, they are spotted and initially helped and encouraged at local level, the region will certainly play its part. In fact, some of the original short tennis recruits are already beginning to appear in the national 12 & Under championships.'

Short Tennis at Telford.

Short tennis, though, is only one part of Blincoe's overall responsibilities. He and his NCDOs are also committed to the development of overall standards of play and the general popularity of the game at all levels.

Much of the future of British tennis lies in the hands of this dedicated band of men. Blincoe is the sort of person who inspires confidence in others. He is a charasmatic yet thorough and methodical man who, judging by his record at county and regional level certainly does produce results. On his office wall are the statistics which are already beginning to confirm this.

'I see British tennis as being rather like a jig-saw' he said. 'Certainly the Development Department and the regions have a vital role to play in putting together several very important pieces. But to get the whole picture we need all the pieces in place. Here, at the LTA, I feel that I am part of a still relatively new and yet excellent and hardworking team, all of whom are striving to get their parts of the jig-saw in place. I am in no way complacent but I am confident that the picture is starting to take shape and our record of success will definitely improve in the years ahead.'

SHORT TENNIS

Most of the following Short Tennis items are available by post from the Lawn Tennis Association.

1. VIDEO
A 15 minute video entitled 'Short Tennis – A Teachers' Guide'. The film, available on VHS only, is aimed at primary and middle school teachers to help them in the introduction of Short Tennis into their schools. It demonstrates a progressive series of exercises to enable the child to master the different aspects of the game, and shows how to keep the maximum number of children involved within the area of a single court. Copies of the video may be borrowed from your County Short Tennis Action Group Organiser, or purchased direct from the LTA. The video is also available on loan from the LTA Information Department/Regional Offices.
Price: £15.00 incl. postage.

2. TEACHERS NOTES
This illustrated booklet, entitled 'A Guide to the Introduction of Short Tennis for Teachers' sets out a detailed programme for the introduction of Short Tennis to groups of children. Ideal for teachers or sports organisers. it is designed to compliment the videa. It also contains the complete rules of Short Tennis.
Price: £1.00 incl. postage.

3. RULES OF SHORT TENNIS
The complete rules of Short Tennis accompanied by an abbreviated guide for parents or teachers are included in the booklet entitled 'Short Tennis – Rules & Teachers' Guide'.
Price: 50p incl. postage.

4. SCORE PADS
30 sheets on cardboard backing, the reverse of which contains a sample completed sheet.
Price: 50p incl. postage.

5. VIDEO
A 45-minute video of the 1985 Daily Mail Short Tennis Championships. This film, which focuses upon the National Finals played at the Telford Racquet & Fitness Centre on 9th June 1985, includes interviews with parents and officials, a brief background to the game and full coverage of both Finals with commentary by the LTA's Womens Team Manager, Sue Mappin. Copies of this video may be loaned (postage charge only) from your regional office (see LTA Regional Officers/Offices page).
Price: £19.95 incl. postage.

But to purchase this item only please write direct (with cheque) to Screen Sport Ltd, P.O. Box 29, Parkgate Estate, Knutsford, Cheshire.

6. STICKERS
Official LTA stickers 4" in diameter. White with green boy or girl figure jumping over a net and yellow wording 'Short Tennis The Search for a Champion'.
Price: 25p incl. p&p.

7. TEE-SHIRTS
Official LTA short tennis tee-shirts. Yellow with green boy or girl figures jumping over a net back and front and with the wording 'Short Tennis The Search for a Champion'.
Price: Sizes 26, 28, 30, 32 £3.50
Size 34 £4.00.

8. BADGES
An official woven LTA 'I Can Play Short Tennis' badge 3" in diameter (boy or girl versions) may be purchased by any youngster able to play a game of short tennis. This purchase can, however, only be through the County Short Tennis Organiser.
Price: 50p incl. p&p.

(These badges are mainly used for end of course type awards. Entitlement – being simply able to play a game of short tennis).

SHORT TENNIS RULES

1. COURT

The game should be played on a Short Tennis court 13.4m × 6.1m (44′ × 20′), or a Badminton court, which is exactly the same size.

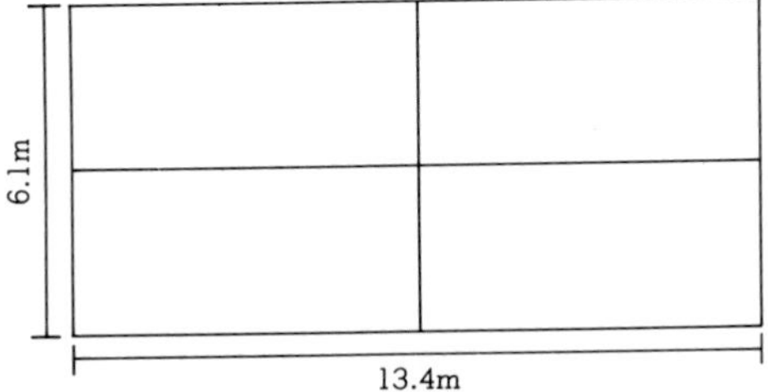

2. COURT BOUNDARIES

The following are guidelines only. Short Tennis can certainly be played and enjoyed within more restricted boundaries. In fact if (when using a Badminton court) the side or baselines are particularly close to a wall, the inner side and/or base 'tramlines' can become the court limits.

	General Play	Competition
Minimum run-back	1.8m (6′)	2.6m (8′6″)
Minimum side-run	1.5m (5′)	2.1m (7′)
Minimum side-run between courts	1.8m (6′)	2.7m (9′)
Minimum unobstructed height over court	4.0m (13′)	5.2m (17′)

N.B. When playing short tennis with the livelier **outdoor** ball the **'competition'** run-back and side runs above becomes the **minimum** practical boundaries.

3. NET

The net should be 0.8m (2′7″) in height at the centre, and 0.85m (2′9″) at the posts.

N.B. The Slazenger equipment is ideal but any net (e.g. a Badminton net) suspended at the regulation height on Badminton, or other posts, is quite suitable.

4. SCORING

Matches should be on a 'First to 11 points' basis.
In the event of the score reaching 10-10, the match should continue until one player has a lead of 2 points (e.g. 13-11).
Apart from the use of the word 'love' for 'nil', scores should be called numerically, 1, 2, 3, etc.

N.B. While 11 points are suggested, this figure can be amended (e.g. 9) to suit individual circumstances.

5. SERVICE

(a) The service must fall within the diagonal half of the opponent's court.

(b) In the event of a service not falling within the appropriate area, a second attempt may be made but if this also fails the point is lost by the server.

(c) The service shall be delivered from behind the baseline, alternate points from the right then left hand sides.

(d) The service may be delivered over or under arm but the ball may not bounce before being struck.

(e) The service must be allowed to bounce. If the receiver strikes the service before it bounces he loses the point.

(f) Service should alternate between players every two points.

(g) Should the serve strike the top of the net and fall 'in', this delivery shall be replayed.

6. PLAY

(a) During play (except when receiving service) players may strike the ball either before or after the bounce.

(b) Players should change ends every eight points.

(c) In the event of the ball striking the ceiling, walls, or other obstructions, the striker loses the point.

7. DOUBLES

In the event of doubles being played, all rules are the same except the four players serve two points in rotation; i.e. the partner of the player who serves the first two points shall serve for the fifth and sixth points, etc.

8. GENERAL NOTES

(a) Short Tennis is played in exactly the same way as Lawn Tennis and therefore for any amplification of the above rules those applying to Lawn Tennis apply.

(b) The scoring system suggested above
 (i) makes it easier to introduce very young children to a competitive situation.
 (ii) allows games to be played and a competitive situation to be structured when there are time constraints.

(c) Although the simplified scoring system is recommended for Short Tennis matches, it is nonetheless recognised that Short Tennis does also provide an ideal opportunity to introduce young children to the full tennis scoring system.

RECORDS

INTERNATIONAL

THE DAVIS CUP

1900 USA 3 British Isles 0 (Boston)
1901 No Competition
1902 USA 3 British Isles 2 (New York)
1903 British Isles 4 USA 1 (Boston)
1904 British Isles 5 Belgium 0 (Wimbledon)
1905 British Isles 5 USA 0 (Wimbledon)
1906 British Isles 5 USA 0 (Wimbledon)
1907 Australasia 3 Great Britain 2 (Wimbledon)
1908 Australasia 3 USA 2 (Melbourne)
1909 Australasia 5 USA 0 (Sydney)
1910 No Competition
1911 Australasia 5 USA 0 (Christchurch)
1912 British Isles 3 Australasia 2 (Melbourne)
1913 USA 3 British Isles 2 (Wimbledon)
1914 Australasia 3 USA 2 (New York)
Competition Suspended
1919 Australasia 4 British Isles 1 (Sydney)
1920 USA 5 Australasia 0 (Auckland)
1921 USA 5 Japan 0 (New York)
1922 USA 4 Australasia 1 (New York)
1923 USA 4 Australasia 1 (New York)
1924 USA 5 Australasia 0 (Philadelphia)
1925 USA 5 France 0 (Philadelphia)
1926 USA 4 France 1 (Philadelphia)
1927 France 3 USA 2 (Philadelphia)
1928 France 4 USA 1 (Paris)
1929 France 3 USA 2 (Paris)
1930 France 4 USA 1 (Paris)
1931 France 3 Great Britain 2 (Paris)
1932 France 3 USA 2 (Paris)
1933 Great Britain 3 France 2 (Paris)
1934 Great Britain 4 USA 1 (Wimbledon)
1935 Great Britain 5 USA 0 (Wimbledon)
1936 Great Britain 3 Australia 2 (Wimbledon)
1937 USA 4 Great Britain 1 (Wimbledon)
1938 USA 3 Australia 2 (Philadelphia)
1939 Australia 3 USA 2 (Haverford)
Competition Suspended
1946 USA 5 Australia 0 (Melbourne)
1947 USA 4 Australia 1 (Forest Hills)
1948 USA 5 Australia 0 (Forest Hills)
1949 USA 4 Australia 1 (Forest Hills)
1950 Australia 4 USA 1 (Forest Hills)
1951 Australia 3 USA 2 (Sydney)
1952 Australia 4 USA 1 (Adelaide)
1953 Australia 3 USA 1 (Melbourne)
1954 USA 3 Australia 2 (Sydney)
1955 Australia 5 USA 0 (Forest Hills)
1956 Australia 5 USA 0 (Adelaide)
1957 Australia 3 USA 2 (Melbourne)
1958 USA 3 Australia 2 (Brisbane)
1959 Australia 3 USA 2 (Forest Hills)
1960 Australia 4 Italy 1 (Sydney)
1961 Australia 5 Italy 0 (Melbourne)
1962 Australia 5 Mexico 0 (Brisbane)
1963 USA 3 Australia 2 (Adelaide)
1964 Australia 3 USA 2 (Cleveland)
1965 Australia 4 Spain 1 (Sydney)
1966 Australia 4 India 1 (Melbourne)
1967 Australia 4 Spain 1 (Brisbane)
1968 USA 4 Australia 1 (Adelaide)
1969 USA 5 Romania 0 (Cleveland)
1970 USA 5 West Germany 0 (Cleveland)
1971 USA 3 Romania 2 (Charlotte)
1972 USA 3 Romania 2 (Bucharest)
1973 Australia 5 USA 0 (Cleveland)
1974 South Africa beat India walkover
1975 Sweden 3 Czechoslovakia 2 (Stockholm)
1976 Italy 4 Chile 1 (Santiago)
1977 Australia 3 Italy 1 (Sydney)
1978 USA 4 Great Britain 1 (Palm Springs)
1979 USA 5 Italy 0 (San Francisco)
1980 Czechoslovakia 4 Italy 1 (Prague)
1981 USA 3 Argentina 1 (Cincinatti)
1982 USA 4 France 1 (Grenoble)
1983 Australia 3 Sweden 2 (Melbourne)
1984 Sweden 4 USA 1 (Gothenberg)
1985 Sweden 3 West Germany 2 (Munich)

THE KING'S CUP

1936 France
1937 France
1938 Germany
1952 Denmark
1953 Denmark
1954 Denmark
1955 Sweden
1956 Sweden
1957 Sweden
1958 Sweden
1959 Denmark
1960 Denmark
1961 Sweden
1962 Denmark
1963 Yugoslavia
1964 Great Britain
1965 Great Britain
1966 Great Britain
1967 Great Britain
1968 Sweden

1969 Czechoslovakia
1970 France
1971 Italy
1972 Spain
1973 Sweden
1974 Italy
1975 No Competition
1976 Hungary
1977 Sweden
1978 Sweden
1979 Czechoslovakia
1980 Czechoslovakia
1981 West Germany
1982 West Germany
1983 West Germany
1984 Czechoslovakia
1985 Sweden

THE WIGHTMAN CUP

1923 USA 7 Great Britain 0 (Forest Hills)
1924 Great Britain 6 USA 1 (Wimbledon)
1925 Great Britain 4 USA 3 (Forest Hills)
1926 USA 4 Great Britain 3 (Wimbledon)
1927 USA 5 Great Britain 2 (Forest Hills)
1928 Great Britain 3 USA 3 (Wimbledon)
1929 USA 4 Great Britain 3 (Forest Hills)
1930 Great Britain 4 USA 3 (Wimbledon)
1931 USA 5 Great Britain 2 (Forest Hills)
1932 USA 4 Great Britain 3 (Wimbledon)
1933 USA 4 Great Britain 3 (Forest Hills)
1934 USA 5 Great Britain 2 (Wimbledon)
1935 USA 4 Great Britain 3 (Forest Hills)
1936 USA 4 Great Britain 3 (Wimbledon)
1937 USA 6 Great Britain 1 (Forest Hills)
1938 USA 5 Great Britain 2 (Wimbledon)
1939 USA 5 Great Britain 2 (Forest Hills)
1940-45 Competition Suspended
1946 USA 7 Great Britain 0 (Wimbledon)
1947 USA 7 Great Britain 0 (Forest Hills)
1948 USA 6 Great Britain 1 (Wimbledon)
1949 USA 7 Great Britain 0 (Forest Hills)
1950 USA 7 Great Britain 0 (Wimbledon)
1951 USA 6 Great Britain 1 (Brookline)
1952 USA 7 Great Britain 0 (Wimbledon)
1953 USA 7 Great Britain 0 (Forest Hills)
1954 USA 6 Great Britain 0 (Wimbledon)
1955 USA 6 Great Britain 1 (Rye)
1956 USA 5 Great Britain 2 (Wimbledon)
1957 USA 6 Great Britain 1 (Pittsburgh)
1958 Great Britain 4 USA 3 (Wimbledon)
1959 USA 4 Great Britain 3 (Pittsburgh)
1960 Great Britain 4 USA 3 (Wimbledon)
1961 USA 6 Great Britain 1 (Chicago)
1962 USA 4 Great Britain 3 (Wimbledon)
1963 USA 6 Great Britain 1 (Cleveland)
1964 USA 5 Great Britain 2 (Wimbledon)
1965 USA 5 Great Britain 2 (Cleveland)
1966 USA 4 Great Britain 3 (Wimbledon)
1967 USA 6 Great Britain 1 (Cleveland)
1968 Great Britain 4 USA 3 (Wimbledon)
1969 USA 4 Great Britain 3 (Cleveland)
1970 USA 4 Great Britain 3 (Wimbledon)
1971 USA 4 Great Britain 3 (Cleveland)
1972 USA 5 Great Britain 2 (Wimbledon)
1973 USA 5 Great Britain 2 (Brookline)
1974 Great Britain 6 USA 1 (Deeside)
1975 Great Britain 5 USA 2 (Cleveland)
1976 USA 5 Great Britain 2 (Crystal Palace)
1977 USA 7 Great Britain 0 (Oakland)
1978 Great Britain 4 USA 3 (Albert Hall, London)
1979 USA 7 Great Britain 0 (West Palm Beach, Florida)
1980 USA 5 Great Britain 2 (Albert Hall, London)
1981 USA 7 Great Britain 0 (International Amphitheater, Chicago)
1982 USA 6 Great Britain 1 (Albert Hall, London)
1983 USA 6 Great Britain 1 (Williamsburg)
1984 USA 5 Great Britain 2 (Albert Hall, London)
1985 USA 7 Great Britain 0 (Williamsburg)

THE FEDERATION CUP

1963 United States 2 Australia 1
1964 Australia 2 United States 1
1965 Australia 2 United States 1
1966 United States 3 West Germany 0
1967 United States 2 Great Britain 0
1968 Australia 3 Netherlands 0
1969 United States 2 Australia 1
1970 Australia 3 West Germany 0
1971 Australia 3 Great Britain 0
1972 South Africa 2 Great Britain 1
1973 Australia 3 South Africa 0
1974 Australia 2 United States 1
1975 Czechoslovakia 3 Australia 0
1976 United States 2 Australia 1
1977 United States 2 Australia 1
1978 United States 2 Australia 1
1979 United States 3 Australia 0
1980 United States 3 Australia 0
1981 United States 3 Great Britain 0
1982 United States 3 West Germany 0
1983 Czechoslovakia 2 West Germany 1
1984 Czechoslovakia 2 Australia 1
1985 Czechoslovakia 2 United States 1

THE CHAMPIONSHIPS

These records include:
In the Men's and Ladies' Singles and Men's Doubles Events: The Championships belonging to the A.E.L.T.C. from their inception to the present time.
In all five events: The Championships belonging to the L.T.A., namely, the World's Championships on Grass Courts for the years 1913, 1914 and 1919 to 1923 inclusive (after which date the title was abolished) and the Championships on Grass Courts recognised by the International Tennis Federation for the years 1924 to the present time.

**Holders did not defend.*
§Challenge Round abolished in 1922; holders played through.

MEN'S SINGLES FINALS

1877 Spencer W Gore bt W Marshall 6-1, 6-2, 6-4
1878 P F Hadow bt Spencer W Gore 7-5, 6-1, 9-7
*1879 J Hartley bt V St Leger Goold 6-2, 6-4, 6-2
1880 J Hartley bt H F Lawford 6-3, 6-2, 2-6, 6-3
1881 W Renshaw bt J T Hartley 6-0. 6-1, 6-1
1882 W Renshaw bt E Renshaw 6-1, 2-6, 4-6, 6-2, 6-2
1883 W Renshaw bt E Renshaw 2-6, 6-3, 6-3, 4-6, 6-3
1884 W Renshaw bt H F Lawford 6-0, 6-4, 9-7
1885 W Renshaw bt H F Lawford 7-5, 6-2, 4-6, 7-5
1886 W Renshaw bt H F Lawford 6-0, 5-7, 6-3, 6-4
*1887 H F Lawford bt E Renshaw 1-6, 6-3, 3-6, 6-4, 6-4
1888 E Renshaw bt H F Lawford 6-3, 7-5, 6-0
1889 W Renshaw bt E Renshaw 6-4, 6-1, 3-6, 6-0
1890 W J Hamilton bt W Renshaw 6-8, 6-2, 3-6, 6-1, 6-1
*1891 W Baddeley bt J Pim 6-4, 1-6, 7-5, 6-0
1892 W Baddeley bt J Pim 4-6, 6-3, 6-3, 6-2
1893 J Pim bt W Baddeley 3-6, 6-1, 6-3, 6-2
1894 J Pim bt W Baddeley 10-8, 6-2, 8-6
*1895 W Baddeley bt W V Eaves 4-6, 2-6, 8-6, 6-2, 6-3
1896 H S Mahony bt W Baddeley 6-2, 6-8, 5-7, 8-6, 6-3
1897 R F Doherty bt H S Mahony 6-4, 6-4, 6-3
1898 R F Doherty by H L Doherty 6-3, 6-3, 2-6, 5-7, 6-1
1899 R F Doherty bt A W Gore 1-6, 4-6, 6-2, 6-3, 6-3
1900 R F Doherty bt S H Smith 6-8, 6-3, 6-1, 6-2
1901 A W Gore bt R F Doherty 4-6, 7-5, 6-4, 6-4
1902 H L Doherty bt A W Gore 6-4, 6-3, 3-6, 6-0
1903 H L Doherty bt F L Riseley 7-5, 6-3, 6-0
1904 H L Doherty bt F L Riseley 6-1, 7-5, 8-6
1905 H L Doherty bt N E Brookes (Aus) 8-6, 6-2, 6-4
1906 H L Doherty bt F L Riseley 6-4, 4-6, 6-2, 6-4
*1907 N E Brookes (Aus) bt A W Gore 6-4, 6-2, 6-2
*1908 A W Gore bt H Roper Barrett 6-3, 6-2, 4-6, 3-6, 6-4
1909 A W Gore bt M J G Ritchie 6-8, 1-6, 6-2, 6-2, 6-2
1910 A F Wilding (NZ) bt A W Gore 6-4, 7-5, 4-6, 6-2
1911 A F Wilding (NZ) bt H Roper Barrett 6-4, 4-6, 2-6, 6-2, retd
1912 A F Wilding (NZ) bt A W Gore 6-4, 6-4, 4-6, 6-4
1913 A F Wilding (NZ) bt M E McLoughlin (US) 8-6, 6-3, 10-8
1914 N E Brookes (Aus) bt A F Wilding (NZ) 6-4, 6-4, 7-5
1915-18 Competition suspended
1919 G L Patterson (Aus) bt N E Brookes (Aus) 6-3, 7-5, 6-2
1920 W T Tilden (US) bt G L Patterson (Aus) 2-6, 6-3, 6-2, 6-4
1921 W T Tilden (US) bt B I C Norton (SA) 4-6, 2-6, 6-1, 6-0, 7-5
Challenge round abolished
*1922 G L Patterson (Aus) bt R Lycett 6-3, 6-4, 6-2
1923 W M Johnston (US) bt F T Hunter (US) 6-0, 6-3, 6-1
1924 J Borotra (Fra) bt R Lacoste (Fra) 6-1, 3-6, 6-2, 3-6, 6-4
1925 J R Lacoste (Fra) bt J Borotra (Fra) 6-3, 6-3, 4-6, 8-6
1926 J Borotra (Fra) bt H Kinsey (US) 8-6, 6-1, 6-3
1927 H Cochet (Fra) bt J Borotra (Fra) 4-6, 4-6, 6-3, 6-4, 7-5
1928 J R Lacoste (Fra) bt H Cochet (Fra) 6-1, 4-6, 6-4, 6-2
1929 H Cochet (Fra) bt J Borotra (Fra) 6-4, 6-3, 6-4
1930 W T Tilden (US) bt W L Allison (US) 6-3, 9-7, 6-4
*1931 S B Wood (US) bt F X Shields (US) walkover
1932 H E Vines (US) bt H W Austin 6-4, 6-2, 6-0
1933 J Crawford (Aus) bt E Vines (US) 4-6, 11-9, 6-2, 2-6, 6-4
1934 F J Perry bt J Crawford (Aus) 6-3, 6-0, 7-5
1935 F J Perry bt G Von Cramm (Ger) 6-2, 6-4, 6-4
1936 F J Perry bt G Von Cramm (Ger) 6-1, 6-1, 6-0
*1937 J D Budge (US) bt G Von Cramm (Ger) 6-3, 6-4, 6-2
1938 J D Budge (US) bt H W Austin 6-1, 6-0, 6-3
*1939 R L Riggs (US) bt E T Cooke (US) 2-6, 8-6, 3-6, 6-3, 6-2
1940-45 Competition suspended
*1946 Y Petra (Fra) bt G E Brown (Aus) 6-2, 6-4, 7-9, 5-7, 6-4
1947 J A Kramer (US) bt T P Brown (US) 6-1, 6-3, 6-2
*1948 R Falkenburg (US) bt J E Bromwich (Aus) 7-5, 0-6, 6-2, 3-6, 7-5
1949 F R Schroeder (US) bt J Drobny (Egypt) 3-6, 6-0, 6-3, 4-6, 6-4
*1950 J E Patty (US) bt F A Sedgman (Aus) 6-1, 8-10, 6-2, 6-3
1951 R Savitt (US) bt K McGregor (Aus) 6-4, 6-4, 6-4
1952 F Sedgman (Aus) bt J Drobny (Egypt) 4-6, 6-2, 6-3, 6-2
*1953 E V Seixas (US) bt K Neilsen (Den) 9-7, 6-3, 6-4
1954 J Drobny (Egypt) bt K R Rosewall (Aus) 13-11, 4-6, 6-2, 9-7
1955 M A Trabert (US) bt K Nielsen (Den) 6-3, 7-5, 6-1

*1956 L A Hoad (Aus) bt K R Rosewall (Aus) 6-2, 4-6, 7-5, 6-4
1957 L A Hoad (Aus) bt J A Cooper (Aus) 6-2, 6-1, 6-2
*1958 A J Cooper (Aus) bt N A Fraser (Aus) 3-6, 6-3, 6-4, 13-11
*1959 A Olmedo (US) bt R G Laver (Aus) 6-4, 6-3, 6-4
*1960 N A Fraser (Aus) bt R G Laver (Aus) 6-4, 3-6, 9-7, 7-5
1961 R G Laver (Aus) bt C R McKinley (US) 6-3, 6-1, 6-4
1962 R G Laver (Aus) bt M F Mulligan (Aus) 6-2, 6-2, 6-1
*1963 C R McKinley (US) bt F S Stolle (Aus) 9-7, 6-1, 6-4
1964 R S Emerson (Aus) bt F S Stolle (Aus) 6-4, 12-10, 4-6, 6-3
1965 R S Emerson (Aus) bt F S Stolle (Aus) 6-2, 6-4, 6-4
1966 M Santana (Sp) bt R D Ralston (US) 6-4, 11-9, 6-4
1967 J D Newcombe (Aus) bt W P Bungert (WG) 6-3, 6-1, 6-1
1968 R G Laver (Aus) bt A D Roche (Aus) 6-3, 6-4, 6-2
1969 R G Laver (Aus) bt J D Newcombe (Aus) 6-4, 5-7, 6-4, 6-4
1970 J D Newcombe (Aus) bt K R Rosewall (Aus) 5-7, 6-3, 6-2, 3-6, 6-1
1971 J D Newcombe (Aus) bt S R Smith (US) 6-3, 5-7, 2-6, 6-4, 6-4
*1972 S R Smith (US) bt I Nastase (Rom) 4-6, 6-3, 6-3, 4-6, 7-5
*1973 J Kodes (Cz) bt A Metreveli (USSR) 6-1, 9-8, 6-3
1974 J S Connors (US) bt K R Rosewall (Aus) 6-1, 6-1, 6-4
1975 A R Ashe (US) bt J S Connors (US) 6-1, 6-1, 5-7, 6-4
1976 B Borg (Swe) bt I Nastase (Rom) 6-4, 6-2, 9-7
1977 B Borg (Swe) bt J S Connors (US) 3-6, 6-2, 6-1, 5-7, 6-4
1978 B Borg (Swe) bt J S Connors (US) 6-2, 6-2, 6-3
1979 B Borg (Swe) bt R Tanner (US) 6-7, 6-1, 3-6, 6-3, 6-4
1980 B Borg (Swe) bt J P McEnroe (US) 1-6, 7-5, 6-3, 6-7, 8-6
1981 J P McEnroe (US) bt B Borg (Swe) 4-6, 7-6, 7-6, 6-4
1982 J S Connors (US) bt J P McEnroe (US) 3-6, 6-3, 6-7, 7-6, 6-4
1983 J P McEnroe (US) bt C J Lewis (NZ) 6-2, 6-2, 6-2
1984 J P McEnroe (US) bt J S Connors (US) 6-1, 6-1, 6-2
1985 B Becker (WG) bt K Curren (US) 6-3, 6-7, 7-6, 6-4

LADIES' SINGLES FINALS

1884 M Watson bt L Watson 6-8, 6-3, 6-3
1885 M Watson bt B Bingley 6-1, 7-5
1886 B Bingley bt M Watson 6-3, 6-3
1887 C Dod bt B Bingley 6-2, 6-0
1888 C Dod bt G W Hillyard 6-3, 6-3
*1889 G W Hillyard bt L Rice 4-6, 8-6, 6-4
*1890 L Rice bt M Jacks 6-4, 6-1
*1891 C Dod bt G W Hillyard 6-2, 6-1
1892 C Dod bt G W Hillyard 6-1, 6-1
1893 C Dod bt G W Hillyard 6-8, 6-1, 6-4
*1894 G W Hillyard bt L Austin 6-1, 6-1
*1895 C Cooper bt H Jackson 7-5, 8-6
1896 C Cooper bt W H Pickering 6-2, 6-3
1897 G W Hillyard bt C Cooper 5-7, 7-5, 6-2
*1898 C Cooper bt L Martin 6-4, 6-4
1899 G W Hillyard bt C Cooper 6-2, 6-3
1900 G W Hillyard bt C Cooper 4-6, 6-4, 6-4
1901 A Sterry bt G W Hillyard 6-2, 6-2
1902 M E Robb bt A Sterry 7-5, 6-1
*1903 D K Douglass bt E W Thomson 4-6, 6-4, 6-2
1904 D K Douglass bt A Sterry 6-0, 6-3
1905 M Sutton (US) bt D K Douglass 6-3, 6-4
1906 D K Douglass bt M Sutton (US) 6-3, 9-7
1907 M Sutton (US) bt R Lambett Chambers (nee Douglass) 6-1, 6-4
*1908 A Sterry bt A M Morton 6-4, 6-4
*1909 D P Boothby bt A M Morton 6-4, 4-6, 8-6
1910 R Lambert Chambers bt D P Boothby 6-2, 6-2
1911 R Lambert Chambers bt D P Boothby 6-0, 6-0
*1912 D R Larcombe bt A Sterry 6-3, 6-1
*1913 R Lambert Chambers bt R J McNair 6-0, 6-4
1914 R Lambert Chambers bt D R Larcombe 7-5, 6-4
1915-18 No Competition
1919 S Lenglen (Fra) bt R Lambert Chambers 10.8, 4-6, 9-7
1920 S Lenglen (Fra) bt R Lambert Chambers 6-3, 6-0
1921 S Lenglen (Fra) bt E Ryan 6-2, 6-0
Challenge Round abolished
1922 S Lenglen (Fra) bt F I Mallory (US) 6-2, 6-0
1923 S Lenglen (Fra) bt K McKane 6-2, 6-2
1924 K McKane bt H N Wills (US) 4-6, 6-4, 6-4
1925 S Lenglen (Fra) bt J Fry 6-2, 6-0
1926 L A Godfree bt Sta de Alvarez (Sp) 6-2, 4-6, 6-3
1927 H N Wills (US) bt Sta de Alvarez (Sp) 6-2, 6-4
1928 H N Wills (US) bt Sta de Alvarez (Sp) 6-2, 6-3
1929 H N Wills (US) bt H H Jacobs (US) 6-1, 6-2
1930 F S Moody (US) bt E Ryan (US) 6-2, 6-2
*1931 C Aussem (Ger) bt H Krahwinkel (Ger) 6-2, 7-5
*1932 F S Moody (US) bt H H Jacobs (US) 6-3, 6-1
1933 F S Moody (US) bt D E Round 6-4, 6-8, 6-3
*1934 D E Round bt H H Jacobs (US) 6-2, 5-7, 6-3
1935 F S Moody (US) bt H H Jacobs (US) 6-3, 3-6, 7-5
*1936 H H Jacobs (US) bt S Sperling (Den) 6-2, 4-6, 7-5
1937 D E Round bt J Jedrzejowska (Pol) 6-2, 2-6, 7-5
*1938 F S Moody (US) bt H H Jacobs (US) 6-4, 6-0
*1939 A Marble (US) bt K E Stammers 6-2, 6-0
1940-45 No Competition
*1946 P M Betz (US) bt A L Brough (US) 6-2, 6-4
*1947 M E Osborne (US) bt D J Hart (US) 6-2, 6-4
1948 A L Brough (US) bt D J Hart (US) 6-3, 8-6
1949 A L Brough (US) bt W D du Pont (US) 10-8, 1-6, 10.8
1950 A L Brough (US) bt W D du Pont (US) 6-1, 3-6, 6-1
1951 D J Hart (US) bt S J Fry (US) 6-1, 6-0
1952 M Connolly (US) bt A L Brough (US) 7-5, 6-3
1953 M Connolly (US) bt D J Hart (US) 8-6, 7-5
1954 M Connolly (US) bt A L Brough (US) 6-2, 7-5
*1955 A L Brough (US) bt J Fleitz (US) 7-5, 8-6
1956 S J Fry (US) bt A Buxton 6-3, 6-1

*1957 A Gibson (US) bt D R Hard (US) 6-3, 6-2
1958 A Gibson (US) bt A Mortimer 8-6, 6-2
*1959 M E Bueno (Braz) bt D R Hard (US) 6-4, 6-3
1960 M E Bueno (Braz) bt S Reynolds (SA) 8-6, 6-0
*1961 A Mortimer bt C C Truman 4-6, 6-4, 7-5
1962 J R Susman (US) bt V Sukova (Cz) 6-4, 6-4
*1963 M Smith (Aus) bt B J Moffitt (US) 6-3, 6-4
1964 M E Bueno (Braz) bt M Smith (Aus) 6-4, 7-9, 6-3
1965 M Smith (Aus) bt M E Bueno (Braz) 6-4, 7-5
1966 L W King (US) bt M E Bueno (Braz) 6-3, 3-6, 6-1
1967 L W King (US) bt P F Jones 6-3, 6-4
1968 L W King (US) bt J M Tegart (US) 9-7, 7-5
1969 P F Jones bt L W King (US) 3-6, 6-3, 6-2
1970 B M Court (Aus) bt L W King (US) 14-12, 11-9
1971 E F Goolagong (Aus) bt B M Court (Aus) 6-4, 6-1
1972 L W King (US) bt E Goolagong (Aus) 6-3, 6-3
1973 L W King (US) bt C M Evert (US) 6-0 7-5
1974 C M Evert (US) bt O Morozova (USSR) 6-0, 6-4
1975 L W King (US) bt R Cawley (Aus) 6-0, 6-1
1976 C M Evert (US) bt R Cawley (Aus) 6-3, 4-6, 8-6
1977 S V Wade bt B F Stove (Nth) 4-6, 6-3, 6-1
1978 M Navratilova (Cz) bt C M Evert (US) 2-6, 6-4, 7-5
1979 M Navratilova (Cz) bt C Evert Lloyd (US) 6-4, 6-4
1980 E F Cawley (Aus) bt C Evert Lloyd (US) 6-1, 7-6
1981 C Evert-Lloyd (US) bt H Mandlikova (Cz) 6-2, 6-2
1982 M Navratilova (US) bt C Evert Lloyd (US) 6-1, 3-6, 6-2
1983 M Navratilova (US) bt A Jaeger (US) 6-0, 6-3
1984 M Navratilova (US) bt C Evert Lloyd (US) 7-6, 6-2
1985 M Navratilova (US) bt C Evert Lloyd (US) 4-6, 6-3, 6-2

MEN'S DOUBLES FINALS

1884 E Renshaw & W Renshaw bt E W Lewis & E L Williams 6-3, 6-1, 1-6, 6-4
1885 E Renshaw & W Renshaw bt C E Farrer & A J Stanley 6-3, 6-3, 10-8
1886 E Renshaw & W Renshaw bt C E Farrer & A J Stanley 6-3, 6-3, 4-6, 7-5
1887 H Wilberforce & P B Lyon bt J H Crispe & E Barrett Smith 7-5, 6-3, 6-2
1888 E Renshaw & W Renshaw bt H Wilberforce & P B Lyon 2-6, 1-6, 6-3, 6-4, 6-3
1889 E Renshaw & W Renshaw bt E W Lewis & G Hillyard 6-4, 6-4, 3-6, 0-6, 6-1
1890 J Pim & F Stoker bt E Lewis & G Hillyard 6-0, 7-5, 6-4
1891 W Baddeley & H Baddeley bt J Pim & F Stoker 6-1, 6-3, 1-6, 6-2
1892 E Lewis & H Barlow bt W Baddeley & H Baddeley 4-6, 6-2, 8-6, 6-4
1893 J Pim & F Stoker bt E Lewis & H Barlow 4-6, 6-3, 6-1, 2-6, 6-0
1894 W Baddeley & H Baddeley bt H Barlow & C Martin 5-7, 7-5, 4-6, 6-3, 8-6
1895 W Baddeley & H Baddeley bt W Eaves & E Lewis 8-6, 5-7, 6-4, 6-3
1896 W Baddeley & H Baddeley bt R Doherty & H Nisbet 1-6, 3-6, 6-4, 6-2, 6-1
1897 R Doherty & H Doherty bt W Baddeley & H Baddeley 6-4, 4-6, 8-6, 6-4
1898 R Doherty & H Doherty bt H Nisbet & C Hobart 6-4, 6-4, 6-2
1899 R Doherty & H Doherty bt H Nisbet & C Hobart 7-5, 6-0, 6-2
1900 R Doherty & H Doherty bt H Nisbet & H Roper Barrett 9-7, 7-5, 4-6, 3-6, 6-3
1901 R Doherty & H Doherty bt D Davis & H Ward 4-6, 6-2, 6-3, 9-7
1902 S Smith & F L Riseley bt R Doherty & H Doherty 4-6, 8-6, 6-3, 4-6, 11-9
1903 R Doherty & H Doherty bt S Smith & F Riseley 6-4, 6-4, 6-4
1904 R Doherty & H Doherty bt S Smith & F Riseley 6-1, 6-2, 6-4
1905 R Doherty & H Doherty bt S Smith & F Riseley 6-2, 6-4, 6-8, 6-3
1906 S Smith & F Riseley bt R Doherty & H Doherty 6-8, 6-4, 5-7, 6-3, 6-3
1907 N Brookes & A Wilding bt B Wright & K Behr 6-4, 6-4, 6-2
1908 A Wilding & M Ritchie bt A W Gore & H Roper Barrett 6-1, 6-2, 1-6, 1-6, 9-7
1909 A Gore & H Roper Barrett bt S Doust & H Parker 6-2, 6-1, 6-4
1910 A Wilding & M Ritchie bt A Gore & H Roper Barrett 6-1, 6-1, 6-2
1911 A Gobert & M Decugis bt M Ritchie & A Wilding 9-7, 5-7, 6-3, 2-6, 6-2
1912 H Roper Barrett & C Dixon bt A Gobert & M Decugis 3-6, 6-3, 6-4, 7-5
1913 H Roper Barrett & C Dixon bt F W Rahe & H Kleinschroth 6-2, 6-4, 4-6, 6-2
1914 N Brookes & A Wilding bt H Roper Barrett & C Dixon 6-1, 6-1, 5-7, 8-6
1915-18 Competition suspended
1919 R Thomas & P O Wood bt R Lycett & R W Heath 6-4, 6-2, 4-6, 6-2
1920 R N Williams & C Garland bt A Kingscote & J C Parke 4-6, 6-4, 7-5, 6-2
1921 R Lycett & M Woosnam bt F Lowe & A Lowe 6-3, 6-0, 7-5
1922 J Anderson & R Lycett bt G Patterson & P O Wood 3-6, 7-9, 6-4, 6-3, 11-9
1923 R Lycett & L Godfree bt Count de Gomar & E Flaquer 6-3, 6-3, 3-6, 6-3, 6-3
1924 V Richards and F Hunter bt R Williams & W Washburn 6-3, 3-6, 8-10, 8-6, 6-3
1925 R Lacoste & J Borotra bt H Hennesey & R Casey 6-4, 11-9, 4-6, 1-6, 6-3
1926 H Cochet & J Brugnon bt V Richards & H Kinsey 7-5, 4-6, 6-3, 6-2
1927 F Hunter & W Tilden bt K Brugnon & H Cochet 1-6, 4-6, 8-6, 6-3, 6-4
1928 H Cochet & J Brugnon bt G L Patterson & J B Hawkes 13-11, 6-4, 6-4
1929 W Allison & J Van Ryan bt J C Gregory & I Collins 6-4, 5-7, 6-3, 10-12, 6-4
1930 W Allison & J Van Ryan bt J H Doeg & G M Lott 6-3, 6-3, 6-2
1931 G M Lott & J Van Ryan bt H Cochet & J Brugnon 6-2, 10-8, 9-11, 3-6, 6-3
1932 J Borotra & J Brugnon bt G P Hughes & F Perry 6-0, 4-6, 3-6, 7-5, 7-5

1933 J Borotra & J Brugnon bt R Nunoi & J Satoh 4-6, 6-3, 6-3, 7-5
1934 G Lott & L Stefen bt J Borotra & J Brugnon 6-2, 6-3, 6-4
1935 J H Crawford & A K Quist bt W Allison & J Van Ryan 6-3, 5-7, 6-2, 5-7, 7-5
1936 G P Hughes & C R Tuckey bt C E Hare & F H Wilde 6-4, 3-6, 7-9, 6-1, 6-4
1937 J D Budge & C Mako bt G P Hughes & C R Tuckey 6-0, 6-4, 6-8, 6-1
1938 J D Budge & C Mako bt H Henkel & G von Metaxa 6-4, 3-6, 6-3, 8-6
1939 E Cooke & R L Riggs bt C Hare & F H Wilde 6-3, 3-6, 6-3, 9-7
1940-45 Competition suspended
1946 T Brown & J A Kramer bt G Brown & D E Pails 6-4, 6-4, 6-2
1947 R Falkenburg & J Kramer bt A J Mottram & O W Sidwell 8-6, 6-3, 6-3
1948 J E Bromwich & F A Sedgman bt T Brown & G Mulloy 5-7, 7-5, 7-5, 9-7
1949 R Gonzales & F Parker bt G Mulloy & F Schroeder 6-4, 6-4, 6-2
1950 J Bromwich & A K Quist bt G Brown & O Sidwell 7-5, 3-6, 6-3, 3-6, 6-2
1951 K McGregor & F Sedgman bt J Drobny & E Sturgess 3-6, 6-2, 6-3, 3-6, 6-3
1952 K McGregor & F Sedgman bt E V Seixas & E Sturgess 6-3, 7-5, 6-4
1953 L A Hoad & K Rosewall bt R N Hartwig & M G Rose 6-4, 7-5, 4-6, 7-5
1954 R N Hartwig & M G Rose bt E V Seixas & M A Trabert 6-4, 6-4, 3-6, 6-4
1955 R N Hartwig & L Hoad bt N A Fraser & K Rosewall 7-5, 6-4, 6-3
1956 L A Hoad & K Rosewall bt N Pietrangeli & O Sirola 7-5, 6-2, 6-1
1957 G Mulloy & J E Patty bt N A Fraser & L A Hoad 8-10, 6-4, 6-4, 6-4
1958 S Davidson & U Schmidt bt A Cooper & N Fraser 6-4, 6-4, 8-6
1959 R S Emerson & N Fraser bt R G Laver & R Mark 8-6, 6-3, 14-16, 9-7
1960 R Osuna & R D Ralston bt M G Davies & R K Wilson 7-5, 6-3, 10-8
1961 R E Emerson & N Fraser bt R A Hewitt & F S Stolle 6-4, 6-8, 6-4, 6-8, 8-6
1962 R A Hewitt & F S Stolle bt B Jovanovic & N Pilic 6-2, 5-7, 6-2, 6-4
1963 R Osuna & A Palafox bt J C Barclay & P Darmon 4-6, 6-2, 6-2, 6-2
1964 R A Hewitt & F S Stolle bt R S Emerson & K Fletcher 7-5, 11-9, 6-4
1965 J D Newcombe & A D Roche bt K Fletcher & R A Hewitt 7-5, 6-3, 6-4
1966 K Fletcher & J Newcombe bt W W Bowrey & O K Davidson 6-3, 6-4, 3-6, 6-3
1967 R A Hewitt & F McMillan bt R S Emerson & K Fletcher 6-2, 6-3, 6-4
1968 J Newcombe & A Roche bt K Rosewall & F S Stolle 3-6, 8-6, 5-7, 14-12, 6-3
1969 J Newcombe & A Roche bt T S Okker & M Riessen 7-5, 11-9, 6-3
1970 J Newcombe & A Roche bt K Rosewall & F S Stolle 10-8, 6-3, 6-1
1971 R S Emerson & R G Laver bt A R Ashe & R D Ralston 4-6, 9-7, 6-8, 6-4, 6-4
1972 R A Hewitt & F McMillan bt S R Smith & E Van Dillen 6-2, 6-2, 9-7
1973 J S Connors & I Nastase bt J R Cooper & N Fraser 3-6, 6-3, 6-4, 8-9, 6-1
1974 J Newcombe & A Roche bt R C Lutz & S Smith 8-6, 6-4, 6-4
1975 V Gerulaitis & A Mayer bt C Dowdeswell & A Stone 7-5, 8-6, 6-4
1976 B E Gottfried & R Ramirez bt R Case & G Masters 3-6, 6-3, 8-6, 2-6, 7-5
1977 R Case & G Masters bt J Alexander & P C Dent 6-3, 6-4, 3-6, 8-10, 6-4
1978 R A Hewitt & F McMillan bt P Fleming & J P McEnroe 6-1, 6-4, 6-2
1979 P Fleming & J P McEnroe bt B E Gottfied & R Ramirez 4-6, 6-4, 6-2, 6-2
1980 P McNamara & P McNamee bt R Lutz & S Smith 7-6, 6-3, 6-7, 6-4
1981 P Fleming & J P McEnroe bt R Lutz & S Smith 6-4, 6-4, 6-4
1982 P McNamara & P McNamee bt P Fleming & J P McEnroe 6-3, 6-2
1983 P Fleming & J P McEnroe bt T E Gullikson & T R Gullikson 6-4, 6-3, 6-4
1984 P Fleming & J P McEnroe bt P Cash & P McNamee 6-2, 5-7, 6-2, 3-6, 6-3
1985 H Gunthard & B Taroczy bt P Cash & J Fitzgerald 6-4, 6-3, 4-6, 6-3

LADIES' DOUBLES FINALS

1913 R McNair & D P Boothby bt A Sterry & R Lambert Chambers 6-4, 2-4 retd
1914 E Ryan & M Morton bt D R Larcombe & F Hannam 6-1, 6-3
1915-18 Competition suspended
1919 S Lenglen & E Ryan bt R Lambert Chambers & D R Larcombe 4-6, 7-5, 6-3
1920 S Lenglen & E Ryan bt R Lambert Chambers & D R Larcombe 6-4, 6-0
1921 S Lenglen & E Ryan bt A E Beamish & I Peacock 6-1, 6-2
1922 S Lenglen & E Ryan bt A D Stocks & K McKane 6-0, 6-4
1923 S Lenglen & E Ryan bt J Austin & L Colyer 6-3, 6-1
1924 G Wightman & H Wills bt B C Covell & K McKane 6-4, 6-4
1925 S Lenglen & E Ryan bt A V Bridge & C G McIlquham 6-2, 6-2
1926 E Ryan & M Browne bt L S Godfree & L Colyer 6-1, 6-1
1927 H Wills & E Ryan bt E L Heine & I Peacock 6-3, 6-2
1928 M Holcroft Watson & P Saunders bt E Harvey & E Bennett 6-2, 6-3
1929 M Holcroft Watson & L Mitchell bt B Covell & D Shepherd-Barron 6-4, 8-6
1930 F S Moody & E Ryan bt E Cross & S Palfrey 6-2, 9-7
1931 D Shepherd-Barron & P Mudford bt D Metaxa & J Sigart 3-6, 6-3, 6-4

1932 D Metaxa & J Sigart bt E Ryan & H H Jacobs 6-4, 6-3
1933 R Mathieu & E Ryan bt F James & A Yorke 6-2, 9-11, 6-4
1934 R Mathieu & E Ryan bt D Andrus & S Henrotin 6-3, 6-3
1935 F James & K E Stammers bt R Mathieu & S Sperling 6-1, 6-4
1936 F James & K E Stammers bt S P Fabyan & H H Jacobs 6-2, 6-1
1937 R Mathieu & A M Yorke bt M R King & J B Pitman 6-3, 6-3
1938 S P Fabyan & A Marble bt R Mathieu & A Yorke 6-2, 6-3
1939 S P Fabyan & A Marble bt H H Jacobs & A M Yorke 6-1, 6-0
1940-45 Competition suspended
1946 A L Brough & M Osborne bt P M Betz & D J Hart 6-3, 2-6, 6-3
1947 D J Hart & P C Todd bt A Brough & M Osborne 3-6, 6-4, 7-5
1948 A L Brough & W du Pont bt D J Hart & P C Todd 6-3, 3-6, 6-3
1949 A L Brough & W du Pont bt G Moran & P C Todd 8-6, 7-5
1950 A L Brough & W du Pont bt S J Fry & D J Hart 6-4, 5-7, 6-1
1951 S J Fry & D J Hart bt A L Brough & W du Pont 6-3, 13-11
1952 S J Fry & D J Hart bt A L Brough & M Connolly 8-6, 6-3
1953 S J Fry & D J Hart bt M Connolly & J Sampson 6-0, 6-0
1954 A L Brough & W du Pont bt S J Fry & D J Hart 4-6, 9-7, 6-3
1955 A Mortimer & J A Shilcock bt S J Bloomer & P Ward 6-3, 9-7
1956 A Buxton & A Gibson bt F Muller & D G Seeney 6-1, 8-6
1957 A Gibson & D R Hard bt K Hawton & T D Long 6-1, 6-2
1958 M Bueno & A Gibson bt W du Pont & M Varner 6-3, 7-5
1959 J Arth & D R Hard bt J G Fleitz & C C Truman 2-6, 6-2, 6-3
1960 M Bueno & D R Hard bt S Reynolds & R Schuurman 6-4, 6-0
1961 K Hantz & B J Moffitt bt J Lehane & M Smith 6-3, 6-4
1962 B J Moffitt & J R Susman bt L E G Price & R Schuurman 5-7, 6-3, 7-5
1963 M E Bueno & D R Hard bt R A Ebbern & M Smith 8-6, 9-7
1964 M Smith & L R Turner bt B J Moffitt & J R Susman 7-5, 6-2
1965 M E Bueno & B J Moffitt bt F Durr & J Lieffrig 6-2, 7-5
1966 M E Bueno & N Richey bt M Smith & J M Tegart 6-3, 4-6, 6-4
1967 R Casals & L W King bt M Bueno & N Richey 9-11, 6-4, 6-2
1968 R Casals & L W King bt F Durr & P F Jones 3-6, 6-4, 7-5
1969 B M Court & J M Tegart bt P S Hogan & M Michel 9-7, 6-2
1970 R Casals & L W King bt F Durr & S V Wade 6-2, 6-3
1971 R Casals & L W King bt B M Court & E Goolagong 6-3, 6-2
1972 L W King & B F Stove bt D E Dalton & F Durr 6-2, 4-6, 6-3
1973 R Casals & L W King bt F Durr & B Stove 6-1, 4-6, 7-5
1974 E Goolagong & M Michel bt H F Gourlay & K M Krantzcke 2-6, 6-4, 6-3
1975 A Kiyomura & K Sawamatusu bt F Durr & B Stove 7-5, 1-6, 7-5
1976 C Evert & M Navratilova bt L W King & B Stove 6-1, 3-6, 7-5
1977 E Cawley & J C Russell bt M Navratilova & B Stove 6-3, 6-3
1978 G E Reid & W Turnbull bt M Jausovec & Ruzici 4-6, 9-8, 6-3
1979 L W King & M Navratilova bt B Stove & W Turnbull 5-7, 6-3, 6-2
1980 K Jordan & A Smith bt R Casals & W Turnbull 4-6, 7-5, 6-1
1981 M Navratilova & P Shriver bt K Jordan & A Smith 6-3, 7-6
1982 M Navratilova & P Shriver bt K Jordan & A Smith 6-4, 6-1
1983 M Navratilova & P Shriver bt R Casals & W M Turnbull 6-2, 6-2
1984 M Navratilova & P Shriver bt K Jordan & A Smith 6-3, 6-4
1985 K Jordan & E Smylie bt M Navratilova & P Shriver 5-7, 6-3, 6-4

MIXED DOUBLES FINALS

1913 H Crisp & Mrs C Tuckey bt J C Parke & Mrs D Larcombe 3-6, 5-3 retd
1914 J C Parke & Mrs D Larcombe bt A F Wilding & Miss M Broquedis 4-6, 6-4, 6-2
1915-18 Competition suspended
1919 R Lycett & Miss E Ryan bt A Prebble & Mrs Lambert Chambers 6-0, 6-0
1920 G Patterson & Miss S Lenglen bt R Lycett & Miss E Ryan 7-5, 6-3
1921 R Lycett & Miss E Ryan bt M Woosnam & Miss P Hawkins 6-3, 6-1
1922 P O Wood & Miss S Lenglen bt R Lycett & Miss E Ryan 6-4, 6-3
1923 R Lycett & Miss E Ryan bt L Deane & Mrs D Shepherd-Barron 6-4, 7-5
1924 J Gilbert & Miss K McKane bt L Godfree & Mrs Shepherd-Barron 6-3, 3-6, 6-3
1925 J Borotra & Miss S Lenglen bt H de Morpurgo & Miss E Ryan 6-3, 6-3
1926 L A Godfree & Mrs Godfree bt H Kinsey & Miss M Browne 6-3, 6-4
1927 F Hunter & Miss E Ryan bt L A Godfree & Mrs Godfree 8-6, 6-0
1928 P Spence & Miss E Ryan bt J Crawford & Miss D Akhurst 7-5, 6-4
1929 F T Hunter & Miss H Wills bt I G Collins & Miss J Fry 6-1, 6-4
1930 J Crawford & Miss E Ryan bt D Prenn & Miss H Krahwinkel 6-1, 6-3

1931 G M Lott & Mrs L Harper bt I G Collins & Miss J C Ridley 6-3, 1-6, 6-1
1932 E Maier & Miss E Ryan bt H C Hopman & Miss J Sigart 7-5, 6-2
1933 G von Cramm & Miss H Krahwinkel bt B Farquarson & Miss M Heeley 7-5, 8-6
1934 R Miki & Miss D Round bt H W Austin & Mrs Shepherd-Barron 3-6, 6-4, 6-0
1935 F Perry & Miss D Round bt H C Hopman & Mrs Hopman 6-4, 6-4
1936 F Perry & Miss D Round bt J D Budge & Miss S P Fabyan 7-9, 7-5, 6-4
1937 J D Budge & Miss A Marble bt Y Petra & Mrs R Mathieu 6-4, 6-1
1938 J D Budge & Miss A Marble bt H Henkel & Miss S P Fabyan 6-1, 6-4
1939 R L Riggs & Miss A Marble bt F H D Wilde & Miss N B Brown 9-7, 6-1
1940-45 Competition Suspended
1946 T Brown & Miss A L Brough bt G Brown & Miss D Bundy 6-4, 6-4
1947 J E Bromwich & Miss A L Brough bt C Long & Mrs N Bolton 1-6, 6-4, 6-2
1948 J E Bromwich & Miss A L Brough bt F A Sedgman & Miss D Hart 6-2, 3-6, 6-3
1949 E W Sturgess & Mrs S Summers bt J E Bromwich & Miss A Brough 9-7, 9-11, 7-5
1950 E W Sturgess & Miss A Brough bt G Brown & Mrs P Todd 11-9, 1-6, 6-4
1951 F Sedgman & Miss D J Hart bt M Rose & Mrs N Bolton 7-5, 6-2
1952 F Sedgman & Miss D J Hart bt E Morea & Mrs T D Long 4-6, 6-3, 6-4
1953 E V Seixas & Miss D J Hart bt E Morea & Miss S Fry 9-7, 7-5
1954 E V Seixas & Miss D J Hart bt K Rosewall & Mrs W du Pont 5-7, 6-4, 6-3
1955 E V Seixas & Miss D J Hart bt E Morea & Miss A Brough 8-6, 2-6, 6-3
1956 E V Seixas & Miss S J Fry bt G Mulloy & Miss A Gibson 2-6, 6-2, 7-5
1957 M G Rose & Miss D R Hard bt N Fraser & Miss A Gibson 6-4, 7-5
1958 R N Howe & Miss L Coughlan bt K Nielsen & Miss A Gibson 6-3, 13-11
1959 R Laver & Miss D R Hard bt N A Fraser & Miss M Bueno 6-4, 6-3
1960 R Laver & Miss D R Hard bt R N Howe & Miss M Bueno 13-11, 3-6, 8-6
1961 F Stolle & Miss L R Turner bt R N Howe & Miss E Buding 11-9, 6-2
1962 N A Fraser & Mrs W du Pont bt R D Ralston & Miss A Haydon 2-6, 6-3, 13-11
1963 K Fletcher & Miss M Smith bt R A Hewitt & Miss D R Hard 11-9, 6-4
1964 F Stolle & Miss L R Turner bt K Fletcher & Miss M Smith 6-4, 6-4
1965 K Fletcher & Miss M Smith bt A D Roche & Miss J M Tegart 12-10, 6-3
1966 K Fletcher & Miss M Smith bt R Ralston & Mrs L W King 4-6, 6-3, 6-3
1967 O K Davidson & Mrs L W King bt K Fletcher & Miss M Bueno 7-5, 6-2
1968 K Fletcher & Mrs M Court bt A Metreveli & Miss O Morozova 6-1, 14-12
1969 F S Stolle & Mrs P F Jones bt A Roche & Miss J Tegart 6-2, 6-3
1970 I Nastase & Miss R Casals bt A Metreveli & Miss O Morozova 6-3, 4-6, 9-7
1971 O K Davidson & Mrs L W King bt M C Riessen & Mrs M Court 3-6, 6-2, 15-13
1972 I Nastase & Miss R Casals bt K Warwick & Miss E Goolagong 6-4, 6-4
1973 O K Davidson & Mrs L W King bt R Ramirez & Miss J Newberry 6-3, 6-2
1974 O K Davidson & Mrs L W King bt M J Farrell & Miss L Charles 6-3, 9-7
1975 M C Riessen & Mrs M Court bt A J Stone & Miss B Stove 6-4, 6-3
1976 A D Roche & Miss F Durr bt R Stockton & Miss R Casals 6-3, 2-6, 7-5
1977 R A Hewitt & Miss G R Stevens bt F McMillan & Miss B Stove 3-6, 7-5, 6-4
1978 F McMillan & Miss B Stove bt R Ruffels & Mrs L W King 6-2, 6-2
1979 R A Hewitt & Miss G R Stevens bt F McMillan & Miss B Stove 7-5, 7-6
1980 J Austin & Miss T Austin bt R Edmonds & Miss D Fromholtz 4-6, 7-6, 6-3
1981 F McMillan & Miss B F Stove bt J Austin & Miss T Austin 4-6, 7-6, 6-3
1982 K Curren & Miss A E Smith bt J M Lloyd & Miss W Turnbull 2-6, 6-3, 7-5
1983 J M Lloyd & Miss W M Turnbull bt S Denton & Mrs L W King 6-7, 7-6, 7-8
1984 J M Lloyd & Miss W M Turnbull bt S Denton & Miss K Jordan 6-3, 6-3
1985 P McNamee & Miss M Navratilova bt J Fitzgerald & E Smylie 7-5, 4-6, 6-2

PLATE COMPETITION

MEN'S SINGLES

1896 A W Gore
1897 H Baddeley
1898 G W Hillyard
1899 W V Eaves
1900 G Greville
1901 P G Pearson
1902 B Hillyard
1903 A W Gore
1904 G Greville
1905 W V Eaves
1906 G W Hillyard
1907 A F Wilding (NZ)
1908 O Kreuzer (Ger)
1909 R B Powell (Can)
1910 A H Gobert (Fra)
1911 A H Lowe
1912 F M Pearson
1913 F G Lowe
1914 C P Dixon
1915-18 No Competition
1919 F R L Crawford
1920 F G Lowe
1921 J B Gilbert
1922 B I Norton (SA)
1923 J Washer (Bel)
1924 J Condon (SA)
1925 B von Kehrling (Hun)
1926 J B Gilbert
1927 A Gentien (Fra)
1928 M Sleem (Ind)
1929 E G Chandler (US)
1930 E du Plaix (Fra)
1931 V G Kirby (SA)
1932 H Cochet (Fra)
1933 F H D Wilde
1934 H W Artens
1935 J Yamagishi (Jap)
1936 D N Jones (US)
1937 W Sabin (US)
1938 D W Butler
1939 D McNeill (US)
1940-45 No Competition
1946 R Abdesselam (Fra)
1947 E W Sturgess (SA)
1948 F Ampon (Phi)
1949 E H Cochell (US)
1950 G L Paish
1951 N M Cockburn (US)

1952 L Ayala (Chi)
1953 G L Paish
1954 H W Stewart (US)
1955 N A Fraser (Aus)
1956 H W Stewart (US)
1957 G L Forbes (SA)
1958 P Remy (Fra)
1959 J Javorsky (Cz)
1960 T Ulrich (Den)
1961 J Ulrich (Den)
1962 J A Douglas (US)
1963 E L Scott (US)
1964 R K Wilson
1965 O K Davidson (Aus)
1966 R Taylor
1967 J H McManus (US)
1968 G Battrick
1969 T Koch (Braz)
1970 R R Maud (SA)
1971 R D Crealey (Aus)
1972 K G Warwick (Aus)
1973 J G Clifton
1974 T I Kakulia (USSR)
1975 T Koch (Braz)
1976 B E Fairlie (NZ)
1977 M C Riessen (US)
1978 D H Collings (Aus)
1979 P C Kronk (Aus)
1980 S Glickstein (Isr)
1981 D Carter (Aus)
1982 Not Contested
1983-85 Not Contested

LADIES' SINGLES

1933 C Rosambert (Fra)
1934 L Valerio (It)
1935 L Valerio (It)
1936 F S Ford
1937 F James
1938 D Stevenson (Aus)
1939 R D McKelvie
1940-45 No Competition
1946 J Jedrzejowska (Pol)
1947 J Jedrzejowska (Pol)
1948 H Weiss (Arg)
1949 A Bossi (It)
1950 K L A Tuckey
1951 F Bartlett (SA)
1952 B Abbas (Egypt)
1953 M P Harrison
1954 R Walsh
1955 F Muller (Aus)
1956 T D Long (Aus)
1957 M B Hellyer (Aus)
1958 S Reynolds (SA)
1959 C Brasher
1960 D M Catt
1961 R H Bentley
1962 M L Gerson (SA)
1963 F Durr (Fra)
1964 V Sukova (Cz)
1965 A Dmitrieva (USSR)
1966 P M Walkden (Rho)
1967 P S A Hogan (US)
1968 S V Wade
1969 B A Grubb (US)
1970 E F Goolagong (Aus)
1971 M R Wainwright
1972 K M Krantzcke (US)
1973 H F Gourlay (Aus)
1974 M V Korschina (USSR)
1975 D L Fromholtz (Aus)
1976 M Wikstedt (Swe)
1977 Y Vermaak (SA)
1978 T E Guerrant (US)
1979 S Barker
1980 R Fairbank (SA)
1981 S Saliba (Aus)
1982 C C Monteiro (Braz)
1983 A J Brown
1984 M L Brown (US)
1985 E Reinach (SA)

INVITATION JUNIOR TOURNAMENT

BOYS' SINGLES

1947 K Nielsen (Den)
1948 S Stockenberg (Swe)
1949 S Stockenberg (Swe)
1950 J A T Horn
1951 J Kupferburger (SA)
1952 R K Wilson
1953 W A Knight
1954 R Krishnan (Ind)
1955 M P Hann
1956 R Holmberg (US)
1957 J I Tattersall
1958 E Buchholz (US)
1959 T Lejus (USSR)
1960 A R Mandestam (SA)
1961 C E Graebner (US)
1962 S J Matthews
1963 N Kalogeropoulos (Gr)
1964 I El Shafei (Egypt)
1965 V Korotkov (USSR)
1966 V Korotkov (USSR)
1967 M Orantes (Sp)
1968 J G Alexander (Aus)
1969 B Bertram (SA)
1970 B Bertram (SA)
1971 R Kriess (US)
1972 B Borg (Swe)
1973 W Martin (US)
1974 W Martin (US)
1975 C J Lewis (NZ)
1976 H Gunthardt (Swe)
1977 W Winitski (US)
1978 I Lendl (Cz)
1979 R Krishnan (Ind)
1980 T Tulasne (Fr)
1981 M Anger (US)
1982 P Cash (Aus)
1983 S Edberg (Swe)
1984 M Kratzmann (Aus)
1985 L Lavalle (Mex)

GIRLS' SINGLES

1948 O Miskova (Cz)
1949 C Mercellis (Bel)
1950 L Cornell
1951 L Cornell
1952 F ten Bosch (Neth)
1953 D Kilian (SA)
1954 V A Pitt
1955 S M Armstrong
1956 A S Haydon
1957 M Arnold (US)
1958 S M Moore (US)
1959 J Cross (SA)
1960 K Hantze (US)
1961 G Baksheeva (USSR)
1962 G Baksheeva (USSR)
1963 D M Salfati (Fra)
1964 J Bartkowicz (US)
1965 O Morozova (USSR)
1966 B Lindstrom (Fin)
1967 J Salome (Neth)
1968 K Pigeon (US)
1969 K Sawamatsu (Jap)
1970 S Walsh (US)
1971 M Kroshina (USSR)
1972 I Kloss (SA)
1973 A Kiyomura (US)
1974 M Jausovec (Yug)
1975 N Chmyreva (USSR)
1976 N Chmyreva (USSR)
1977 L Antonopolis (US)
1978 T Austin (US)
1979 M L Piatek (US)
1980 D Freeman (Aus)
1981 Z Garrison (US)
1982 C Tanvier (Fra)
1983 P Paradis (Fra)
1984 A N Croft
1985 A Holikova (Cz)

CHAMPIONSHIPS OF GREAT BRITAIN

REFUGE ASSURANCE NATIONAL CHAMPIONSHIPS

These Championships first held in 1983, are the British National Closed Championships.

MEN'S SINGLES

1983 C Bradnam
1984 C Dowdeswell
1985 J Bates

MEN'S DOUBLES

1983 C Dowdeswell and J Feaver
1984 N Brown and D Felgate
1985 C Bradnam and N Fulwood

LADIES' SINGLES

1983 J Durie
1984 J Durie
1985 A Hobbs

LADIES' DOUBLES

1983 J Durie and A Hobbs
1984 J Durie and A Hobbs
1985 J Durie and A Hobbs

THE HARD COURT CHAMPIONSHIPS OF GREAT BRITAIN

MEN'S SINGLES

1924 R Lycett
1925 P D B Spence (SA)
1926 J Brugnon (Fra)
1927 R Lacoste (Fra)
1928 R Lacoste (Fra)
1929 H W Austin
1930 H G N Lee
1931 C Boussus (Fra)
1932 F J Perry
1933 F J Perry
1934 F J Perry
1935 F J Perry
1936 F J Perry
1937 H W Austin
1938 Kho Sin Kie (China)
1939 Kho Sin kie (China)
1940-45 No Competition
1946 J E Harper (Aus)
1947 E W Sturgess (SA)
1948 E W Sturgess (SA)
1949 P Masip
1950 J Drobny (Cz)
1951 J Drobny (Cz)
1952 J Drobny (Cz)
1953 E Morea (Arg)
1954 A J Mottram
1955 S Davidson (Swe)
1956 J E Patty (US)
1957 J Drobny (Cz)
1958 W A Knight
1959 L A Gerrard (NZ)
1960 M G Davies
1961 R Emerson (Aus)
1962 R G Laver (Aus)
1963 W A Knight
1964 W A Knight
1965 J E Lundquist (Swe)
1966 K N Fletcher (Aus)
1967 J E Lundquist (Swe)
1968 K R Rosewall (Aus)
1969 J D Newcombe (Aus)
1970 M Cox
1971 G Battrick
1972 R A J Hewitt (SA)
1973 A Panatta (It)
1974 I Nastase (Rom)
1975 M Orantes (Sp)
1976 W Fibak (Pol)
1977 No Competition
1978 J Higueras (Sp)
1979 No Competition
1980 A Gimenez (Sp)
1981 V Pecci (Par)
1982 M Orantes (Sp)
1983 J Higueras (Sp)
1984 No Competition
1985 No Competition

LADIES' SINGLES

1924 E Ryan (US)
1925 E Ryan (US)
1926 J D Fry
1927 B Nuthall
1928 E A Goldsack
1929 E L Heine (SA)
1930 J Fry
1931 R Mathieu (Fra)
1932 R Mathieu (Fra)
1933 D E Round
1934 D E Round
1935 K E Stammers
1936 K E Stammers
1937 A Lizana (Chile)
1938 M C Scriven
1939 K E Stammers
1940-45 No Competition
1946 E W A Bostock
1947 N Bolton (Aus)
1948 B E Hilton
1949 P J Curry
1950 P J Curry
1951 D J Hart (US)
1952 D J Hart (US)
1953 D J Hart (US)
1954 D J Hart (US)
1955 A Mortimer
1956 A Mortimer
1957 S J Bloomer
1958 S J Bloomer
1959 A Mortimer
1960 C C Truman
1961 A Mortimer
1962 R Schuurman (SA)
1963 P F Jones
1964 P F Jones
1965 P F Jones
1966 P F Jones
1967 S V Wade
1968 S V Wade
1969 B M Court (Aus)
1970 B M Court (Aus)
1971 B M Court (Aus)
1972 E F Goolagong (Aus)
1973 S V Wade
1974 S V Wade
1975 J Newberry (US)
1976 H Masthoff (WG)
1977 No Competition
1978 I Riedel (WG)
1979 No Competition
1980 No Competition
1981 J Durie
1982 No Competition
1983 No Competition
1984-85 No Competition

MEN'S DOUBLES

1924 F L Riseley and J D P Wheatley
1925 Capt H S Lewis-Barclay and C H Kingsley
1926 G R O Crole-Rees and C G Eames
1927 J Brugnon and R Lacoste
1928 P D B Spence and C H Kingsley
1929 G R O Crôle-Rees and C G Eames
1930 H W Austin and J S Olliff
1931 H W Austin and C H Kingsley
1932 J S Olliff and F J Perry
1933 J H Crawford and D P Turnbull
1934 J H Crawford and V B McGrath
1935 C E Malfroy and A C Stedman
1936 G P Hughes and C R D Tuckey
1937 C E Hare and F H D Wilde
1938 Kho Sin Kie and G Lyttleton Rogers
1939 H Billington and J S Olliff
1940-45 No Competition
1946 J E Harper and C E Malfroy
1947 E Fannin and E W Sturgess
1948 E W Sturgess and R van Meegeren
1949 J Bartroli and P Masip
1950 V Cernik and J Drobny
1951 L Norgarb and E W Sturgess
1952 J Drobny and F Sedgman
1953 F Ampon and R Deyro
1954 K Nielsen and T Ulrich
1955 A J Mottram and G L Paish

1956 R N Howe and U Schmidt
1957 G L Forbes and A Segal
1958 M G Davies and R K Wilson
1959 G L Forbes and A Segal
1960 M G Davies and W A Knight
1961 R Emerson and R Laver
1962 J Drobny and R Laver
1963 R Hewitt and F Stolle
1964 K E Diepraam and E C Drysdale
1965 A R Mills and I Buding
1966 R Taylor and R K Wilson
1967 R A J Hewitt and F D McMillan
1968 R Emerson and R Laver
1969 R A J Hewitt and F D McMillan
1970 T S Okker and A D Roche
1971 W W Bowrey and O K Davidson
1972 R A J Hewitt and F D McMillan
1973 J Gisbert and I Nastase
1974 J Gisbert and I Nastase
1975 J Gisbert and M Orantes
1976 W Fibak and F V McNair
1977 No Competition
1978 L Saunders and R Thung
1979 No Competition
1980 C Edwards and E Edwards
1981 R Cano and V Pecci
1982 P McNamee and C Mottram
1983 T Smid and S Stewart
1984-85 No Competition

LADIES' DOUBLES
1924 E Ryan and D Shepherd-Barron
1925 E Ryan and E Colyer
1926 B Nuthall and G R Sterry
1927 V Chamberlain and C Tuckey
1928 M Watson and B Nuthall
1929 E Goldsack and J Ridley
1930 J Fry and E Harvey
1931 B Nuthall and E Ryan
1932 P Whittingstall and B Nuthall
1933 D Round and M Heeley
1934 L Godfree and S Noel
1935 J Pittman and A Yorke
1936 F James and K Stammers
1937 E Dearman and J Ingram
1938 E Dearman and J Ingram
1939 J Nicoll and B Nuthall
1940-45 No Competition
1946 E Bostock and M Menzies
1947 N Bolton and H Hopman
1948 B Hilton and M Menzies
1949 B Hilton and W Halford
1950 B Hilton and K Tuckey
1951 S Fry and D Hart
1952 S Fry and D Hart
1953 S Fry and D Hart
1954 D Hart and A Mottram
1955 S Bloomer and P Ward
1956 A Buxton and D Hard
1957 S Bloomer and D Hard
1958 J Shilcock and P Ward
1959 A Mortimer and P Ward
1960 A Haydon and A Mortimer
1961 A Haydon and Y Ramirez
1962 R Schuurman and E Starkie
1963 P Jones and D Starkie
1964 J Lehane and H Schulze
1965 E Starkie and A van Zyl
1966 P Jones and D Starkie
1967 P Jones and V Wade
1968 G Janes and F Truman
1969 B Court and J Tegart
1970 B Court and D Dalton
1971 P Curtis and F Durr
1972 E F Goolagong and H F Gourley
1973 P Coleman and W Turnbull
1974 K Heldman and V Wade
1975 L Charles and S Mappin
1976 D Boshoff and I Kloss
1977 No Competition
1978 J Durie and A Hobbs
1979 No Competition
1980 J Erskine and E Lightbody
1981 J Durie and D Jevans
1982-85 No Competition

MIXED DOUBLES
1924 R Lycett and Miss E Ryan
1925 P D B Spence and Miss E L Colyer
1926 D A Hodges and Miss J Fry
1927 P D B Spence and Miss B Nuthall
1928 H Cochet and Miss E Bennett
1929 G P Hughes and Miss J Fry
1930 C H Kingsley and Miss J Fry
1931 F J Perry and M Heeley
1932 A Martin-Legeay and Mme R Mathieu
1933 H G N Lee and Miss F James
1934 R Miki and Miss D E Round
1935 C R D Tuckey and Miss M C Scriven
1936 F J Perry and Miss D E Round
1937 F H D Wilde and Miss M Whitmarsh
1938 C Boussus and Miss N Wynne
1939 C F Malfroy and Miss B Nuthall
1940-45 No Competition
1946 D W Butler and Mrs W A Bostock
1947 E W Sturgess and Mrs S P Summers
1948 E W Sturgess and Miss J Quertier
1949 P Masip and Miss J Gannon
1950 G E Brown and Mrs B E Hilton
1951 E W Sturgess and Miss D Hart
1952 G L Paish and Mrs J Rinkel-Quertier
1953 G L Paish and Mrs J Rinkel-Quertier
1954 K Nielsen and Miss D Hart
1955 R N Howe and Miss J A Shilcock
1956 R N Howe and Miss P E Ward
1957 R N Howe and Miss D R Hard
1958 W A Knight and Miss S J Bloomer
1959 W A Knight and Miss S J Bloomer
1960 W A Knight and Mrs C W Brasher
1961 A R Mills and Mrs A R Mills
1962 M P Hann and Miss C Yates-Bell
1963 A R Mills and Mrs A R Mills
1964 R N Howe and Miss J P Lehane
1965 R R Maud and G S Swan
1966 P van Lingen and Miss F Urban
1967 R R Maud and Miss S V Wade
1968 R N Howe and Miss S V Wade
1969 R R Maud and Miss S V Wade

1970 R A J Hewitt and Mrs L W King
1971 F D McMillan and Mrs D E Dalton
1972 F D McMillan and Mrs J B Chanfreau
1973 F D McMillan and Miss S V Wade
1974 M J Farrell and Miss J L Charles
1975 D A Lloyd and Miss S A Walsh
1976 C Dowdeswell and Miss D A Boshoff
1977 No Competition
1978 R A Lewis and Miss L J Charles and J W Feaver and Miss K Wooldridge — Divided
1979-85 No Competition

21 AND UNDER CHAMPIONSHIPS OF GREAT BRITAIN

MEN'S SINGLES
1962 W W Bowrey (Aus)
1963 M Cox
1964 K Wooldridge
1965 G R Stilwell
1966 P W Curtis
1967 G Battrick
1968 J G Paish
1969 J de Mendoza
1970 J de Mendoza
1971 C J Mottram
1972 C J Mottram
1973 M J Farrell
1974 C S Wells
1975 C J Lewis (NZ)
1976 J Whiteford
1977 K M Revie
1978 M R E Appleton
1979 M R E Appleton
1980 N Brown
1981 D Watt
1982-85 No Competition

MEN'S DOUBLES
1962 S J Matthews and G R Stilwell
1963 M Cox and K Wooldridge
1964 S J Matthews and D A R Russell
1965 G Battrick and D A Lloyd
1966 P R Hutchins and G H Woodward
1967 J G Clifton and J de Mendoza
1968 J de Mendoza and K F Weatherley
1969 J de Mendoza and J P R Williams
1970 J de Mendoza and J P R Williams
1971 R W Drysdale and G M Newton
1972 R A Leslie and R A Lewis
1973 M J Farrell and R J Frost
1974 C M Robinson and C S Wells
1975 A H Lloyd and J R Smith
1976 P Bradnam and G J Slater
1977 N D Gooden and W J Gowans
1978 T Heath and M R West
1979 T Heath and D J Watt
1980 M J Bates and D J Watt
1981 M T Fancutt and P S Farrell
1982-85 No Competition

LADIES' SINGLES
1962 M R Cooper
1963 J A G Lloyd
1964 F E Truman
1965 W M Shaw
1966 S Mappin
1967 J H Townsend
1968 C Molesworth
1969 W Gilchrist (Aus)
1970 J P Cooper
1971 G Coles
1972 G Coles
1973 L Blanchford
1974 A Coe
1975 B R Thompson
1976 D Evers (Aus)
1977 C J Drury
1978 S G Davies
1979 C J Drury
1980 D Parnell
1981 C Drury
1982-85 No Competition

LADIES' DOUBLES
1962 F V M Maclennan and Miss F E Walton
1963 M M Lee and A L Owen
1964 N Truman and G M Williams
1965 A Soady and J H Townsend
1966 E M Ernest and M McAnally
1967 A Soady and J H Townsend
1968 A Soady and J H Townsend
1969 W A Gilchrist and J A Congdon
1970 J P Cooper and J A Fayter
1971 L J Charles and W G Slaughter
1972 L J Charles and J A Fayter
1973 L D Blachford and A M Coe
1974 A M Coe and L C Robinson
1975 D Evers and D A Jevans
1976 J Cottrell and J P Wilson
1977 C Harrison and D A Jevans
1978 J Cottrell and J P Wilson
1979 C J Drury and E D Lightbody
1980 E D Lightbody and J L Weighly
1981 L Stewart and D Taylor
1982-85 No Competition

MIXED DOUBLES
1962 M Cox and Miss F E Walton
1963 M Cox and H W Allen and P R Breed and Miss M R Cooper — Divided
1964 K Wooldridge and Mrs G M Williams
1965 G R Stilwell and Miss J H Townsend
1966 Cancelled owing to rain
1967 H Rahim and Miss J H Townsend and J G Clifton and Miss S Mappin — Divided
1968 K F Weatherley and Miss J H Townsend
1969 J G Paish and Miss J A Congdon
1970 P W Sussams and Miss V A Burton
1971 M J Farrell and Miss L J Charles
1972 R A Lewis and Miss G L Coles
1973 R A Lewis and Miss L D Blachford
1974 J C Cooper and Miss A M Coe
1975 Divided at the semi-final stage
1976 P A Bourdon and Miss D Evers
1977 W J Gowans and Miss C Harrison
1978-80 No Competition
1981 M T Blincow and Miss L Stewart
1982-85 No Competition

THE COVERED COURT CHAMPIONSHIPS OF GREAT BRITAIN

MEN'S SINGLES

1935 J Borotra
1936 K Schroeder
1937 H W Austin
1938 J Borotra
1939-47 No Competition
1948 J Borotra
1949 J Borotra
1950 J Drobny
1951 G L Paish
1952 J Drobny
1953 J Drobny
1954 J Drobny
1955 V Skonecki
1956 A Huber
1957-58 M G Davies
1959 R K Wilson
1960 W A Knight
1961 J A Pickard
1962 R K Wilson
1963 R K Wilson
1964 M J Sangster
1965 R K Wilson
1966-67 No Competition
1968 R A J Hewitt
1969 R Laver
1970 R Laver
1971 I Nastase
1972-85 No Competition

MEN'S DOUBLES

1935 D N Jones and D Prenn
1936 C E Hare and F H D Wilde
1937 D W Butler and F H D Wilde
1938 H Billington and J S Olliff
1939-47 No Competition
1948 C J Hovell and C M Jones
1949 H Billington and G L Paish
1950 H Cochet and J Drobny
1951 A J Mottram and G L Paish
1952 A J Mottram and G L Paish
1953 J E Barrett and D L M Black
1954 J Drobny and R K Wilson
1955 R N Howe and V Skonecki
1956 G L Paish and J A Pickford
1957-58 M G Davies and R K Wilson
1959 G L Paish and A R Mills
1960 M J Sangster and R K Wilson
1961 L P Coni and M A Otway
1962 A R Mills and R K Wilson
1963 B Jovnovic and N Pilic
1964 R Taylor and R K Wilson
1965 A R Mills and R K Wilson
1966-67 No Competition
1968 R C Lutz and S R Smith
1969 R Emerson and R Laver
1970 K R Rosewall and S R Smith
1971 R A J Hewitt and F D McMillan
1972-85 No Competition

LADIES' SINGLES

1935 M C Scriven
1936 A Lizana
1937 M C Scriven
1938 M C Scriven
1939-47 No Competition
1948 G Hoahling
1949 P J Curry
1950 J Quertier
1951 J S V Partridge
1952 A Mortimer
1953 A Mortimer
1954 A Mortimer
1955 J A Shilcock
1956 A Buxton
1957-58 J A Shilcock
1959 A Mortimer
1960 A Mortimer
1961 A Mortimer
1962 A S Haydon
1963 D M Catt
1964 P F Jones
1965 P F Jones
1966-67 No Competition
1968 B M Court
1969 P F Jones
1970 L W King
1971 L W King
1972-85 No Competition

LADIES' DOUBLES

1935 J B Pittman and A M Yorke
1936 M Whitmarsh and A M Yorke
1937 J Saunders and V E Scott
1938 E M Dearman and J Ingram
1939-47 No Competition
1948 P J Curry and J Quertier
1949 W C J Halford and P A O'Connell
1950 R Anderson and P J Curry
1951 E W Dawson-Scott and E M Wilford
1952 H M Fletcher and J Rinkel-Quertier
1953 P Chatrier and J A Shilcock
1954 R J R Bullied and A Mortimer
1955 J A Shilcock and P E Ward
1956 J A Shilcock and P E Ward
1957-58 J A Shilcock and P E Ward
1959 A Mortimer and P E Ward
1960 S M Armstrong and Mrs C W Brasher
1961 D M Catt and A Mortimer
1962 A S Haydon and C C Truman
1963 P F Jones and R Schuurman
1964 P F McClenaughan and F M E Toyne
1965 P F Jones and S V Wade
1966-67 No Competition
1968 M A Eisel and W M Shaw
1969 P F Jones and S V Wade
1970 R Casals and L W King
1971 F Durr and S V Wade
1972-85 No Competition

MIXED DOUBLES

1935 J Borotra and Miss M C Scriven
1936 J S Olliff and Miss F James
1937 K Schroeder and Miss J Saunders
1938 C M Jones and Miss E H Harvey
1939-47 No Competition
1948 J Borotra and Mrs G Walter
1949 G L Paish and Miss J Quertier
1950 G L Paish and Miss J Quertier
1951 G L Paish and Miss J Quertier
1952 G L Paish and Miss J Quertier
1953 G D Oakley and Mrs P Chatrier
1954 M G Davies and Miss D Spiers
1955 W A Knight and Miss J A Shilcock
1956 G L Paish and Miss J A Shilcock
1957-58 M G Davies and Miss P E Ward
1959 No Competition
1960 W A Knight and Mrs C W Brasher
1961 J R McDonald and Miss D M Catt
1962 P Darmon and Mrs P Darmon
1963 G D Oakley and Miss C C Truman
1964 R N Howe and Miss P R McClenaughan
1965 R Carmichael and Mrs P F Jones
1966-67 No Competition
1968 S R Smith and Mrs B M Court
1969-85 No Competition

JUNIOR CHAMPIONSHIPS OF GREAT BRITAIN

JUNIOR HARD COURT CHAMPIONSHIPS

§Prudential sponsorship instituted for Junior Championships in 1978.

BOYS' SINGLES

1908 C G Eames
1909 C A Caslon
1910 P W James
1911 H L de Morphurgo
1912 V Burr
1913 B Martyr
1914-18 No Competition
1919 C H Weinberg
1920 C H Weinberg
1921 J Weakley
1922 H W Austin
1923 N H Latchford
1924 J S Olliff
1925 J S Olliff
1926 E R Avory
1927 R A Court
1928 F H D Wilde
1929 J W Nuthall
1930 D G Freshwater
1931 C E Hare
1932 H D B Faber
1933 M D Deloford
1934 R E Mulliken
1935 H T Baxter
1936 H T Baxter
1937 G L Emmett
1938 D G Snart
1939-45 No Competition
1946 A G Roberts
1947 A G Roberts
1948 J A T Horn
1949 J A T Horn
1950 J Prouse
1951 R K Wilson
1952 W A Knight
1953 W A Knight
1954 G E Mudge
1955 O S Prenn
1956 J I Tattersall
1957 J I Tattersall
1958 H M Harvey
1959 J Baker
1960 S J Matthews
1961 S J Matthews
1962 S J Matthews
1963 G R Stilwell
1964 G Battrick
1965 D A Lloyd
1966 J P R Williams
1967 J de Mendoza
1968 A F C Whittaker
1969 M W Collins
1970 M W Collins
1971 C J Mottram
1972 C J Mottram
1973 J R Smith
1974 K M Revie
1975 P A Bourdon
1976 A M Jarrett
1977 A N Paton
§1978 H B Becker
1979 K Gilbert
1980 D Crichton-Miller
1981 D Shaw
1982 D Felgate
1983 P Moore
1984 S Cole
1985 R Whichello

GIRLS' SINGLES

1908 L E Bull
1909 E M Hirst
1910 V Fison
1911 V M Speer
1912 V M Speer
1913 G B Palmer
1914-18 No Competition
1919 D Bouette
1920 J W Austin
1921 J W Austin
1922 G R Sterry
1923 B Corbin
1924 B Nuthall
1925 B Nuthall
1926 B Nuthall
1927 N Mackintosh
1928 M Heeley
1929 M C Scriven
1930 P G Brazier
1931 K S W Hewitt
1932 J R Harman
1933 E N S Dickin
1934 D Rowe
1935 V E Scott
1936 G C Hoahing
1937 R Thomas
1938 J Nicholl
1939-45 No Competition
1946 P Rodgers
1947 N T Seacy
1948 S Partridge
1949 L M Cornell
1950 L M Cornell
1951 E M Watson
1952 V A Pitt
1953 V A Pitt
1954 A S Haydon
1955 A S Haydon
1956 C C Truman
1957 C C Truman
1958 C Webb
1959 R A Blakelock
1960 R A Blakelock
1961 F E Walton
1962 J French
1963 M Greenwood
1964 W M Shaw
1965 J A Congdon
1966 J A Congdon
1967 D Bridger
1968 D P Oakley
1969 V A Burton
1970 N A Dwyer
1971 G L Coles
1972 G L Coles
1973 S Barker
1974 L Mottram
1975 M Tyler
1976 J M Durie
1977 D A Jevans
§1978 K J Brasher
1979 E Jones
1980 L Pennington
1981 S Walpole
1982 S Walpole
1983 S Walpole
1984 S Mair
1985 J Wood

BOYS' DOUBLES

1921 C E J Evers and J Weakley
1922 H G N Cooper and D S Milford
1923 H W Austin and M V Callendar
1924 R D N Pryce-Jones and M V Callendar
1925 J S Olliff and C S Higgins
1926 J S Olliff and M McL Symington
1927 J W Nuthall and R K Tinkler
1928 F H D Wilde and J W Nuthall
1929 J W Nuthall and Hon P Aitken
1930 M E Angel and W I Nicoll
1931 H D B Faber and G L Mytton
1932 M K J A Dewar and C E Hare
1933 D M Bull and J S Nuthall
1934 J D Eggar and C J Hovell
1935 D R Bocquet and J B H Daniel
1936 H T Baxter and G L Emmett
1937 G L Emmett and R C Nicoll
1938 D N Hardwick and P E Hare
1939-45 No Competition
1946 C W Fox and T R Manderson
1947 B G Hawkings and A G Roberts
1948 J A T Horn and C V Baxter
1949 J A T Horn and G T Lewis
1950 J M Gracie and R J Lee
1951 W A Knight and R K Wilson
1952 W A Knight and R K Wilson
1953 W A Knight and R K Wilson
1954 R D Bennett and M P Hann
1955 M L Booth and D P Gordon
1956 C R Applewhaite and J I Tattersall
1957 C R Applewhaite and J I Tattersall
1958 W J King and R Taylor
1959 J Baker and T J Reynolds
1960 M Cox and R D Jones
1961 S J Matthews and G R Stilwell
1962 S J Matthews and G R Stilwell
1963 S J Matthews and G R Stilwell
1964 G Battrick and J Sung
1965 D A Lloyd and K F Weatherley

1966 J G Paish and J P R Williams
1967 J de Mendoza and J P R Williams
1968 S J Creed and P W Etheridge
1969 G M Newton and I A Thompson
1970 M J Farrell and J M Lloyd
1971 M J Farrell and J M Lloyd
1972 J M Lloyd and C F Mabbitt
1973 J Jones and A H Lloyd
1974 A M Jarrett and C J Kaskow
1975 R C Beven and C J Kaskow
1976 C Bradnam and A M Jarrett
1977 M R E Appleton and J M Dier
§1978 M J Bates and P S Farrell
1979 M J Bates and K E G Gilbert
1980 L Alfred and S Taylor
1981 N A Fulwood and D A Shaw
1982 D C Felgate and T Mitchell
1983 B J Knapp and R A W Whichello
1984 B J Knapp and R A W Whichello
1985 A J W Brice and D Ison

GIRLS' DOUBLES

1921 Miss D Soames and Miss G R Sterry
1922 Miss B Corbin and Miss M Lambert
1923 Miss B Corbin and Miss M Lambert
1924 Miss B Nuthall and Miss S Hartley
1925 Miss M T Lamb and Miss B Nuthall
1926 Miss E M Dearman and Miss B Nuthall
1927 Miss N Mackintosh and Miss J Marshall
1928 Miss B M Kendle and Miss A M Yorke
1929 Miss J Cunningham and Miss F K Scott
1930 Miss Y J Allnatt and Miss P Craske
1931 Miss J Saunders and Miss K E Stammers
1932 Miss E N S Dickin and Miss M Whitmarsh
1933 Miss E N S Dickin and Miss M Whitmarsh
1934 Miss P W Hewitt and Miss E M Vavasour
1935 Miss P W Hewitt and Miss B M Johnson
1936 Miss A P Cardinall and Miss B M Johnson
1937 Miss P L MacCorkindale and Miss B M Crosoer
1938 Miss M L Harris and Miss J Nicoll
1939-45 No Competition
1946 Miss P Rogers and Miss P E Ward
1947 Miss N T Seacy and Miss I S Vallence
1948 Miss J P Mead and Miss S P Thain
1949 Miss R J R Bulleid and Miss A Mortimer
1950 Miss J M Petchell and Miss D Spiers
1951 Miss V M Lewis and Miss M L Morgan
1952 Miss P Della-Porta and Miss D Midgley
1953 Miss P Della-Porta and Miss D Midgley
1954 Miss A S Haydon and Miss G I M Hurdman
1955 Miss S M Armstrong and Miss A S Haydon
1956 Miss S M Armstrong and Miss A S Haydon
1957 Miss D M Catt and Miss C C Truman
1958 Miss C Webb and Miss M G White
1959 Miss R A Blakelock and Miss A E O'Neil
1960 Miss F E Walton and Miss J M Wilson
1961 Miss J V Gilkerson and Miss J E Scoble
1962 Miss M B H McAnally and Miss S V Wade
1963 Miss M Greenwood and Miss S Percivall
1964 Miss S L Cullen-Smith and Miss S Mappin
1965 Miss J A Congdon and Miss B L Davies
1966 Miss J A Congdon and Miss B L Davies
1967 Miss J P Cooper and Miss C Molesworth
1968 Miss V A Burton and Miss D P Oakley
1969 Miss J A Fayter and Miss H E Retter
1970 Miss L J Charles and Miss C S Colman
1971 Miss S Barker and Miss N Salter
1972 Miss L Geeves and Miss L J Mottram
1973 Miss S Barker and Miss N A Dwyer
1974 Miss S Barker and Miss L J Mottram
1975 Miss C A Leatham and Miss M Tyler
1976 Miss C J Drury and Miss A E Hobbs
1977 Miss C Harrison and Miss D Jevans
§1978 Miss K J Brasher and Miss D S Parker
1979 Miss T Heath and Miss D K A Taylor
1980 Miss C Gaskin and Miss S L Gomer
1981 Miss C Gaskin and Miss S L Gomer
1982 Miss A J Brown and Miss J Louis
1983
1984 Miss B Borneo and Miss S Mair
1985 S Mair and C Wood

MIXED DOUBLES

1921 H W Austin and Miss J W Austin
1922 H W Austin and Miss E M Dearman
1923 H W Austin and Miss E M Dearman
1924 C G Fletcher and Miss B Nuthall / J S Olliff and Miss S Hartley — Divided
1925 No Competition
1926 J W Nuthall and Miss B Nuthall
1927 R J Ritchie and Miss J M Ingram
1928 F H D Wilde and Miss E V Elder
1929 D G Freshwater and Miss P G Brazier
1930 M E Angel and Miss Y J Allnatt
1931 H D B Faber and Miss K E Stammers
1932 G L Mytton and Miss M Whitmarsh
1933 N E Hooper and Miss E N S Dickin
1934 No Competition
1935 Not held as a Championship Event
1936 D R Bocquet and Miss P M Seaton
1937 P E Hare and Miss R Thomas
1938 R C Nicoll and Miss J Nicoll
1939-45 No Competition
1946 A G Roberts and Miss P Rodgers
1947 A G Roberts and Miss R J R Bulleid
1948 C V Baxter and Miss N T Seacy
1949 J A T Horn and Miss P A Lewis
1950 D S Timms and Miss M Harris
1951 R Becker and Miss M Watson
1952 W A Knight and Miss V A Pitt
1953 W A Knight and Miss V A Pitt
1954 M P Hann and Miss J A Fulton
1955 O S Prenn and Miss J A Fulton
1956 J I Tattersall and Miss H J M Durose
1957 C R Applewhaite and Miss C C Truman
1958 G C Bluett and Miss C A Silver
1959 T D Phillips and Miss C Webb
1960 M Cox and Miss F E Watson
1961 S J Matthews and Miss R A Blakelock
1962 S J Matthews and Miss S V Wade
1963 M R Lewinsohn and Miss S M Veale
1964 J Sung and Miss W M Shaw
1965 K F Weatherley and Miss J A Congdon
1966 J G Paish and Miss S Edgecombe
1967 J P R Williams and Miss D P Oakley
1968 S J Creed and Miss D P Oakley
1969 G M Newton and Miss W G Slaughter

1970 M W Collins and Miss C S Colman
1971 R A Leslie and Miss C M Panton
1972 C J Mottram and Miss S Barker
1973 C J Kaskow and Miss D Barker
1974 Cancelled owing to rain
1975 R C Bevan and Miss M Tyler
1976 A M Jarrett and Miss D A Jevans
1977 N A Rayner and Miss C Harrison
1978-84 No Competition

BOYS' SINGLES UNDER 16
1982 P Moore (Surrey)
1983 J Goodall (Yorks)
1984 A Brice (Cheshire)
1985 D Sapsford (Surrey)

BOYS' SINGLES UNDER 14
1982 A Brice (Cheshire)
1983 D Sapsford (Surrey)
1984 M Petchey (Essex)
1985 S J Cornish (Somerset)

BOYS' SINGLES UNDER 12
1982 J J Hunter (Surrey)
1983 D Harris (Essex)
1984 S Jackson (Cheshire)
1985 C B G Gibson (Dorset)

GIRLS' SINGLES UNDER 16
1982 J Louis (Devon)
1983 A Grant (Lincs)
1984 A Simpkin (Leicester)
1985 N Entract (Dorset)

GIRLS' SINGLES UNDER 14
1982 A Simpkin (Leicester)
1983 T Catlin (Cambs)
1984 N Entract (Dorset)
1985 J Donovan (Warks)

GIRLS' SINGLES UNDER 12
1982 N Entract (Dorset)
1983 J Donovan (Warks)
1984 V Humphreys-Davies (Cambs)
1985 C Hall (Dorset)

JUNIOR GRASS COURT CHAMPIONSHIPS

§*Prudential sponsorship instituted.*

BOYS' SINGLES
1970 R Drysdale
1971 S Warboys
1972 R A Lewis
1973 J Smith
1974 A Jarrett
1975 P Bourdon
1976 C Bradnam
1977 M Appleton
§1978 J Dier
1979 J Bates
1980 D Crichton-Miller
1981 R Coull
1982 S M Bale
1983 A Lakatos
1984 R A W Whichello
1985 N Jones

BOYS' DOUBLES
1970 K B McCollum and R A V Walker
1971 R A Leslie and R A Lewis
1972 R A Leslie and R A Lewis
1973 P Bradnam and J Trafford
1974 R J Haak and A M Jarrett
1975 W J Gowans and N C Sears
1976 M D Grive and N A Rayner
1977 M R E Appleton and J M Dier
§1978 J M Dier and C F Emery
1979 M J Bates and K E G Gilbert
1980 A Galbraith and D Nicholson
1981 P Heath and J D Poxon
1982 C M Haworth and K Hodges
1983 B Knapp and R A W Whichello
1984 J Goodall and M Walker
1985 A J W Brice and D Ison

MIXED DOUBLES
1978 No Competition
1979 M J Bates and Miss D K A Taylor
1980 S Taylor and Miss K Turton
1981 N A Fulwood and Miss N J Lusty
1982 J D Poxon and Miss C Gaskin
1983 R A W Whichello and Miss L C Gould
1984 M Walker and Miss C Wood
1985 D E Kiek and Miss A Simpkin

GIRLS' SINGLES
1970 L Charles
1971 G Coles
1972 S Barker
1973 S Barker
1974 S Barker
1975 L Mottram
1976 J Durie
1977 C Drury
§1978 K Brasher
1979 K Brasher
1980 A Brown
1981 J Salmon
1982 A Brown
1983 J Salmon
1984 S Mair
1985 A Simpkin

GIRLS' DOUBLES
1970 C S Coleman and L J Charles
1971 L D Blachford and F J Candy
1972 A M Coe and N A Dwyer
1973 S Barker and N A Dwyer
1974 S Barker and L J Mottram
1975 A P Cooper and C Harrison
1976 J M Durie and C Harrison
1977 J M Durie and A E Hobbs
§1978 C J Drury and D S Parker
1979 J C Reardon and J C Walpole
1980 J Harris and L Pennington
1981 C M Berry and N J Lusty
1982 A J Brown and J A Salmon
1983 S Mair and S Sullivan
1984 B Borneo and S Mair
1985 S J McCarthy and A Simpkin

BOYS' SINGLES UNDER 16
1965 J de Mendoza (Surrey)
1966 A Whitaker (Surrey)
1967 G Newton (Yorks)
1968 I Thomson (Middx)
1969 M Wayman (Surrey)
1970 J Lloyd (Essex)
1971 C Mottram (Surrey)

1972 S Donald (Scotland)
1973 C Roger-Vasselin (Surrey)
1974 A Paton (Lancs)
1975 A Paton (Lancs)
1976 J Dier (Sussex)
1977 P Farrell (Lancs)
§1978 J Key (Surrey)
1979 N Fulwood (Derby)
1980 P Heath (Yorks)
1981 T Mitchell (Yorks)
1982 P Moore (Surrey)
1983 R A W Whichello (Kent)
1984 D Sapsford (Surrey)
1985 N Pashley (Surrey)

BOYS' SINGLES UNDER 14
1965 S Warboys (Essex)
1966 R Walker (Bucks)
1967 P Siviter (Warks)
1968 C Mottram (Surrey)
1969 C Wells (Kent)
1970 A Lloyd (Essex)
1971 A Jarrett (Derby
1972 C Bradnam (Middx)
1973 N Rayner (Essex)
1974 M Taylor
1975 S Taylor (Bucks)
1976 P Farrell (Lancs)
1977 D Crichton-Miller (Surrey)
1978 P Heath (Yorks)
1979 M Collins (Essex)
1980 D Shann (Herts)
1981 R A W Whichello (Kent)
1982 A Brice (Cheshire)
1983 N Pashley (Surrey)
1984 M Petchey (Essex)
1985 N P Smith (Lancs)

BOYS' SINGLES UNDER 12
1972 D Atkinson (Som)
1973 N Gerrard (Derby)
1974 J Bates (Surrey
1975 A Castle (Som)
1976 P Heath (Yorks)
1977 D Petrie (Bucks)
1978 B Knapp (Glos)
1979 R A W Whichello (Kent)
1980 C Bailey (Norfolk)
1981 D Sapsford (Surrey)
1982 J Hunter (Surrey)
1983 N Smith (Cheshire)
1984 J Haycock (Surrey)
1985 M Silvester (Norfolk)

GIRLS' SINGLES UNDER 16
1965 S Morgan (Kent)
1966 D Bridger (Devon)
1967 J Fayter (Devon)
1968 L Charles (Worcs)
1969 D Staniszewski (Surrey)
1970 D Staniszewski (Surrey)
1971 N Dwyer (Devon)
1972 S Barker (Devon)
1973 J Wilson (Surrey)
1974 M Tyler (Kent)
1975 C Harrison (Surrey)
1976 D Jevans (Essex)
1977 K Brasher (Surrey)
§1978 K Brasher (Surrey)
1979 L Pennington (Lincs)
1980 R Einy (Middx)
1981 A Croft (Kent)
1982 J Louis (Devon)
1983 S Mair (E of Scot)
1984 C Wood (Sussex)
1985 A Simpkin (Leics)

GIRLS' SINGLES UNDER 14
1965 D Oakley (Essex)
1966 A Coe (Devon)
1967 L Blachford (Essex)
1968 N Phelan (Surrey)
1969 N Dwyer (Devon)
1970 L Mottram (Surrey)
1971 M Tyler (Kent)
1972 L Robinson (Yorks)
1973 J M Durie (Glos)
1974 D Jevans (Essex)
1975 S Davies (Middx)
1976 K Brasher (Surrey)
1977 J Champion (Som)
1978 E Jones (Hants)
1979 A Brown (Norfolk)
1980 A Croft (Kent)
1981 J Louis (Devon)
1982 A Simpkin (Leicester)
1983 S McCarthy (Avon)
1984 N Entract (Dorset)
1985 S J Loosemorr (S Wales)

GIRLS' SINGLES UNDER 12
1972 J M Durie (Glos)
1973 S Davies (Middx)
1974 S Grace (Hants)
1975 J Champion (Som)
1976 C Gaskin (Surrey)
1977 V Binns (Devon)
1978 A Croft (Kent)
1979 J Louis (Devon)
1980 C Bhaguandas (Middx)
1981 A Simpkin (Leicester)
1982 N Entract (Dorset)
1983 J Donovan (Warks)
1984 R Viollet (Lancs)
1985 C Hall (Dorset)

JUNIOR COVERED COURT CHAMPIONSHIPS

§Prudential sponsorship instituted.

BOYS' SINGLES
1956 M J Sangster
1957 M J Sangster
1958 J I Tattersall
1959 J Baker
1960 T J Reynolds
1961 M Cox
1962 S J Matthews
1963 P W Curtis
1964 M E Ratcliff
1965 G Battrick
1966 D A Lloyd
1967 J de Mendoza
1968 S A Warboys

1969 M W Collins
1970 R A V Walker
1971 C J Mottram
1972 J M Lloyd
1973 J R Smith
1974 P Bradnam
1975 W J Gowans
1976 A N Paton
1977 N A Rayner
§1978 D Atkinson
1979 M J Bates
1980 P Farrell
1981 N Fulwood
1982 P Heath
1983 J Clunie
1984 R Whichello
1985 R Whichello
1986 D Sapsford

GIRLS' SINGLES

1956 C C Truman
1957 S M Armstrong
1958 C C Truman
1959 C Webb
1960 R A Blakelock
1961 F Walton
1962 S J Holdsworth
1963 M B H McAnally
1964 M Veale
1965 W M Shaw
1966 J A Congdon
1967 C Molesworth
1968 V A Burton
1969 V A Burton
1970 L D Blanchford
1971 G L Coles
1972 S Barker
1973 L J Mottram
1974 L J Mottram
1975 M Tyler
1976 J M Durie
1977 C J Drury
§1978 K Brasher
1979 K Brasher
1980 E Jones
1981 A Brown
1982 A Brown
1983 B Borneo
1984 A Grunfeld
1985 J Wood
1986 S McCarthy

BOYS' DOUBLES

1956 R W Dixon and M J Sangster
1957 M J Sangster and M J Woolven
1958 H M Harvey and M J Sangster
1959 R B B Avory and J Baker
1960 D K Martin and T D Phillips
1961 S J Matthews and G R Stilwell
1962 S J Matthews and G R Stilwell
1963 P R Hutchins and M E Ratcliff
1964 D A Lloyd and K F Weatherley
1965 G Battrick and J M M Cooper
1966 J G Paish and J P R Williams
1967 J de Mendoza and J P R Williams
1968 S J Creed and P W Etheridge
1969 G M Newton and I A Thomson
1970 M J Farrell and J M Lloyd
1971 C J Mottram and P Siviter
1972 R A Leslie and R A Lewis
1973 P Bradnam and J Trafford
1974 C Bradnam and P Bradnam
1975 P A Bourdon and R G Haak
1976 M D Grive and N A Rayner
1977 M R E Appleton and J M Dier
§1978 H B Becker and A A Simcox
1979 R P Boulton and N Gerrard
1980 J Bates and P Farrell
1981 S Bale and D Shaw
1982 P A Heath and J D Poxon
1983 B Knapp and R A W Whichello
1984 B Knapp and R A W Whichello
1985 J Goodall and R A W Whichello
1986 S Booth and D Sapsford

GIRLS' DOUBLES

1956 D M Catt and C C Truman
1957 S M Armstrong and M R O'Donnell
1958 D M Catt and J M Trewby
1959 J E Kemp and J M Tee
1960 M M Lee and A L Owen
1961 F T A Anstey and F E Walton
1962 M B H McAnally and S V Wade
1963 M B H McAnally and S V Wade
1964 A F Morris and S M Veale
1965 A F Morris and W M Shaw
1966 J A Congdon and B L Davies
1967 J P Cooper and C Molesworth
1968 S M Langdale and W G Slaughter
1969 L J Charles and W G Slaughter
1970 L D Blachford and A Lloyd
1971 A M Coe and N A Dwyer
1972 S Barker and N Salter
1973 S Barker and N A Dwyer
1974 L J Mottram and B R Thompson
1975 C A Leatham and M Tyler
1976 A P Cooper and D A Jevans
1977 A P Cooper and D A Jevans
§1978 K M Glancy and D L Morgan
1979 K J Brasher and D K A Taylor
1980 C Gaskin and E Jones
1981 A Brown and E Jones
1982 C Gaskin and S L Gomer
1983 C Gillies and A Grant
1984 S Longbottom and J Smith
1985 A Grant and J Louis
1986 K Hand and U Lake

INTER COUNTY CHAMPIONSHIPS

INTER-COUNTY CHAMPIONSHIP ON GRASS

§*Prudential sponsorship instituted.*

MEN

1895 Gloucestershire
1896 Surrey
1897 Middlesex
1898 Gloucestershire
1899 Gloucestershire
1900 Gloucestershire
1901 Gloucestershire
1902 Middlesex
1903 Gloucestershire
1904 Gloucestershire
1905 Gloucestershire
1906 Gloucestershire
1907 Yorkshire
1908 Middlesex
1909 Warwickshire
1910 Middlesex
1911 Surrey
1912 Middlesex
1913 Middlesex
1914 Staffordshire
1915-19 No Competition
1920 Middlesex
1921 Middlesex
1922 Middlesex
1923 Lancashire
1924 Middlesex
1925 Middlesex
1926 Middlesex
1927 Middlesex
1928 Middlesex
1929 Middlesex
1930 Middlesex
1931 Middlesex
1932 Middlesex
1933 Warwickshire
1934 Middlesex
1935 Middlesex
1936 Middlesex
1937 Middlesex
1938 Middlesex
1939 Warwickshire
1940-46 No Competition
1947 Middlesex
1948 Warwickshire
1949 Surrey
1950 Surrey
1951 Surrey
1952 Warwickshire
1953 Surrey
1954 Middlesex
1955 Surrey
1956 Middlesex
1957 Middlesex
1958 Surrey
1959 Lancashire
1960 Middlesex
1961 Lancashire
1962 Middlesex
1963 Middlesex
1964 Middlesex
1965 Lancashire
1966 Essex
1967 Yorkshire
1968 Middlesex
1969 Surrey
1970 Surrey
1971 Surrey
1972 Surrey
§1973 Surrey
1974 Surrey
1975 Middlesex
1976 Essex
1977 Essex
1978 Essex
1979 Essex
1980 Middlesex
1981 Middlesex
1982 Essex
1983 Middlesex
1984 Middlesex
1985 Essex

LADIES

1899 Surrey
1900 Surrey
1901 Yorkshire
1902 Kent
1903 Middlesex
1904 Surrey
1905 Cheshire
1906 Middlesex
1907 Durham
1908 Surrey
1909 Surrey
1910 Surrey
1911 Middlesex
1912 Surrey
1913 Middlesex
1914 Surrey
1915-19 No Competition
1920 Surrey
1921 Middlesex
1922 Middlesex
1923 Surrey
1924 Middlesex
1925 Sussex
1926 Middlesex
1927 Surrey
1928 Surrey
1929 Surrey
1930 Middlesex
1931 Surrey
1932 Surrey
1933 Surrey
1934 Middlesex
1935 Middlesex
1936 Surrey
1937 Surrey
1938 Middlesex
1939 Middlesex
1940-46 No Competition
1947 Surrey
1948 Middlesex
1949 Middlesex
1950 Surrey
1951 Middlesex
1952 Middlesex
1953 Middlesex
1954 Surrey
1955 Warwickshire
1956 Middlesex
1957 Warwickshire
1958 Warwickshire
1959 Surrey
1960 Surrey
1961 Surrey
1962 Surrey
1963 Yorkshire
1964 Surrey
1965 Surrey
1966 Surrey
1967 Warwickshire
1968 Surrey
1969 Surrey
1970 Surrey
1971 Surrey
1972 Devon
§1973 Middlesex
1974 Devon
1975 Devon
1976 Surrey
1977 Surrey
1978 Surrey
1979 Middlesex
1980 Surrey
1981 Kent
1982 Middlesex
1983 Kent
1984 Kent
1985 Surrey

INTER-COUNTY WINTER CHAMPIONSHIPS

§*Prudential sponsorship instituted.*

MEN

1920-21 Surrey
1921-22 Surrey
1922-23 Lancashire
1923-24 Middlesex
1924-25 Middlesex
1925-26 Middlesex
1926-27 Surrey
1927-28 Surrey
1928-29 Surrey
1929-30 Surrey
1930-31 Middlesex
1931-32 Middlesex
1932-33 Surrey
1933-34 Middlesex
1934-35 Surrey
1935-36 Middlesex
1936-37 Middlesex
1937-38 Middlesex
1938-39 Middlesex
1939-45 No Competition
1946-47 Warwickshire
1947-48 Warwickshire
1948-49 Warwickshire
1949-50 Warwickshire
1950-51 Warwickshire
1951-52 Surrey
1952-53 Surrey
1953-54 Surrey
1954-55 Warwickshire
1955-56 Middlesex
1956-57 Middlesex
1957-58 Middlesex
1958-59 Middlesex
1959-60 Middlesex
1960-61 Middlesex
1961-62 Middlesex
1962-63 Surrey
1963-64 Middlesex
1964-65 Middlesex
1965-66 Essex
1966-67 Yorkshire
1967-68 Essex
1968-69 Surrey
1969-70 Surrey
1970-71 Surrey
1971-72 Surrey

1972-73 Lancashire
1973-74 Essex
1974-75 Essex
1975-76 Essex
§1976-77 Middlesex
1977-78 Lancashire
1978-79 Essex
1979-80 Surrey
1980-81 Essex
1981-82 Surrey
1982-83 Lancashire
1983-84 Essex

LADIES'

1920-21 Surrey
1921-22 Middlesex
1922-23 Middlesex
1923-24 Surrey
1924-25 Middlesex
1925-26 Middlesex
1926-27 Surrey
1927-28 Surrey
1928-29 Surrey
1929-30 Middlesex
1930-31 Surrey
1931-32 Surrey
1932-33 Surrey
1933-34 Surrey
1934-35 Middlesex
1935-36 Middlesex
1936-37 Surrey
1937-38 Surrey
1938-39 Middlesex
1939-45 No Competition
1946-47 Middlesex
1947-48 Middlesex
1948-49 Surrey
1949-50 Warwickshire
1950-51 Kent
1951-52 Middlesex
1952-53 Middlesex
1953-54 Middlesex
1954-55 Middlesex
1955-56 Middlesex
1956-57 Middlesex
1957-58 Surrey
1958-59 Warwickshire
1959-60 Surrey
1960-61 Middlesex
1961-62 Surrey
1962-63 Surrey
1963-64 Yorkshire
1964-65 Surrey
1965-66 Surrey
1966-67 Surrey
1967-68 Surrey
1968-69 Surrey
1969-70 Surrey
1970-71 Middlesex
1971-72 Surrey
1972-73 Middlesex
1973-74 Devon
1974-75 Surrey
1975-76 Surrey
§1976-77 Yorkshire
1977-78 Middlesex
1978-79 Middlesex
1979-80 Surrey
1980-81 Yorkshire
1981-82 Middlesex
1982-83 Surrey
1983-84 Surrey

JUNIOR INTER-COUNTY CHAMPIONSHIPS

§Prudential sponsorship instituted.

BOYS

1967 Warwickshire
1968 Surrey
1969 Essex
1970 Surrey
1971 Middlesex
1972 Middlesex
1973 Middlesex
1974 Sussex
1975 Sussex
1976 Middlesex
1977 Essex
§1978 Buckinghamshire
1979 Buckinghamshire
1980 Lancashire
1981 Essex
1982 Essex
1983 Essex
1984 Essex
1985 Essex

GIRLS

1967 Devon
1968 Devon
1969 Devon
1970 Surrey
1971 Devon
1972 Devon
1973 Surrey
1974 Surrey
1975 Essex
1976 Kent
1977 Yorkshire
§1978 Sussex
1979 Surrey
1980 Surrey
1981 Essex
1982 Surrey
1983 Yorkshire
1984 Middlesex
1985 Essex

LTA SCHOOLS COMPETITIONS

THE ABERDARE CUP

For teams of three girls' pairs who play doubles only. A Knockout Competition, arranged on an area basis, leads to area and national finals.

ABERDARE CUP WINNERS

1944 St Paul's Girls' School (Middlesex)
1945 Malvern Girls' College (Worcester)
1946 Queenswood (Herts)
1947 Sherborne School for Girls (Dorset)
1948 Benenden School (Kent)
1949 Sutton High School (Surrey)
1950 Chelmsford CHS (Essex)
1951 Sherborne School for Girls (Dorset)
1952 Putney High School (Surrey)
1953 Benenden School (Kent)
1954 Putney High School (Surrey)
1955 Benenden School (Kent)
1956 Queen Anne's School (Berkshire)
1957 Queenswood (Herts)
1958 Roedean (Sussex)
1959 Queenswood (Herts)
1960 Queen Anne's, Reading
1961 St Helena School
1962 Tunbridge Wells GS (Kent)
1963 Queen Anne's, Reading
1964 Millfield School (Somerset)
1965 Queen Anne's, Reading
1966 St Margaret's, Exeter
1967 Millfield School (Somerset)
1968 Talbot Heath (Hants)
1969 Marist Convent
1970 Marist Convent
1971 Marist Convent
1972 Marist Convent
1973 Millfield School (Somerset)
1974 Millfield School (Somerset)
1975 Millfield School (Somerset)
1976 Millfield School (Somerset)
1977 Ilford CHS (Essex)
1978 Millfield School (Somerset)
1979 Perse School (Cambridgeshire)
1980 Millfield School (Somerset)
1981 Millfield School (Somerset)
1982 Banbury Comprehensive (Oxon)
1983 Banbury Comprehensive (Oxon)
1984 Repton (Derbyshire)
1985 Repton (Derbyshire)

THE GLANVILL CUP

For teams of three boys' pairs, who play doubles only. A Knockout Competition, arranged on an area basis, leads to area and national finals.

GLANVILL CUP WINNERS

1945 King's College School (Surrey)
1946 Stowe School (Bucks)
1947 King's College School (Surrey)
1948 Stowe School (Bucks)
1949 King's College School (Surrey)
1950 Stowe School (Bucks)
1951 King's College School (Surrey)
1952 University College School (Middlesex)
1953 University College School (Middlesex)
1954 Westminster School (Middlesex)
1955 King's College School (Surrey)
1956 Eltham College (Kent)
1957 Millfield School (Somerset)
1958 St Paul's School (Middlesex)
1959 Millfield School (Somerset)
1960 St Paul's School (Middlesex)
1961 Millfield School (Somerset)
1962 Millfield School (Somerset)
1963 Millfield School (Somerset)
1964 Millfield School (Somerset)
1965 Millfield School (Somerset)
1966 Millfield School (Somerset)
1967 University College School (Warwicks)
1968 Rugby
1969 Millfield School (Somerset)
1970 Millfield School (Somerset)
1971 Millfield School (Somerset)
1972 Millfield School (Somerset)
1973 Millfield School (Somerset)
1974 Millfield School (Somerset)
1975 Millfield School (Somerset)
1976 Millfield School (Somerset)
1977 Millfield School (Somerset)
1978 Millfield School (Somerset)
1979 St George's, Weybridge (Surrey)
1980 Millfield School (Somerset)
1981 Millfield School (Somerset)
1982 Repton School (Derbyshire)
1983 Millfield School (Somerset)
1984 Repton School (Derbyshire)
1985 Millfield School (Somerset)

MIDLAND BANK – LTA SCHOOLS CHAMPIONSHIPS

Boys 15 and Under:
Bournemouth School bt Head of England
Girls 15 and Under:
Haberdashers Aske's bt Maiden Erlegh Reading
Boys 13 and Under:
King Edward's School bt Fuffeyn H.S.
Girls 13 and Under:
St. Joseph's, Lincoln bt Banbury.

BRITISH SCHOOLS LTA CHAMPIONSHIPS

Boys 19 and Under (Clark Cup) — Repton School;
Boys 15 and Under (Melbourne Cup) — Repton
Boys 13 and Under (Curtis Cup) — Bristol G.S.
Girls 19 and Under — Marist Convent
Girls 15 and Under — Church H.S. Newcastle,
Girls 13 and Under — St. Michael's, Petworth

LTA COLOURS, BADGES AND AWARDS

1. The entitlement to colours, badges and awards has been granted to players who have been nominated to represent Great Britain or England in international matches.
2. Colours were awarded only to those who were nominated to represent Great Britain in the Davis Cup, Federation Cup and Wightman Cup team championships. The British badge, LTA badge and England badge were awarded to playes nominated for other international matches, certain championships and international tours.
3. The chronology of the institution and award of colours and badges is as follows:
   (a) **Prior to 1st January 1937.** Colours were awarded for the Davis Cup and Wightman Cup. The British badge and the LTA badge were awarded for other events.
   (b) **From 1st January 1937.** New colours were adopted. These were awarded for the Davis Cup, Wightman Cup and (from 1963) for the Federation Cup. The British badge and the England badge — which superseded the LTA badge — were awarded for other events. No new colours or badges were awarded after 1974.
   (c) **From 1st January 1984.** The award of colours and badges was discontinued. The new LTA International Award was instituted. Players nominated to represent Great Britain in the International Team Championships (Davis Cup, King's Cup, Federation Cup and Wightman Cup) may qualify for this new award.
   (d) **Championship Badges.** Champions in singles, doubles and mixed doubles are entitled to wear a championship badge in addition to the colours.
4. The description and the regulations for the award and wearing of colours and badges may be found in the LTA Official Handbooks of the relevant period.
5. The new LTA International Award is a plate bearing the arms of the LTA and the words "The Lawn Tennis Association International Award".

The following are entitled to wear the Old Colours and the Championship Badges stated.

J O Anderson (1922) 1 silver
Lt-Col H S Lewis-Barclay (1925)
R S Barnes (1909)
Colonel A Berger (1925)
C H L Cazalet 1 green
M Decugis (1911) 1 silver
C S Garland (1920) 1 silver
J C Masterman
R D Poland (1924)
R N Williams (1920) 1 silver
P O'Hara Wood 1 silver (1919) 1 green
Mrs Atkins 2 silver, 1 green
Mrs F R Chiesman (1925)
Mrs Neville Durlacher (1899) 1 silver
Mrs Douglas 2 silver, 1 green
Mrs Hannam (1912)
Miss E D Holman (1920)
Mrs Huddleston (1910) 1 silver
Mrs J L Leosk (1909) 1 silver
Mrs Luard 1 silver (1910) 1 green
Miss W A Longhurst (1911) 3 silver
Mrs R J McNair (1913) 1 silver
Mrs T M Mavrogordato (1911) 1 green
Mrs C G McIlquham (1925)
Mrs Peacock (1922)
Mrs Pickering (1897) 4 silver
Lady Stewart (1908) 1 silver
Mrs Winch

The following are entitled to wear either the New Colours adopted on January 1st, 1937, or the Old Colours and the Championship Badges stated:—

P M Davson (1919)
C G Eames (1925)
C H Kingsley (1926)
J D P Wheatley (1923)
Mrs R C Clayton (1923)
Mrs B C Covell (1923)
Mrs L A Godfree 2 gold (1923) 2 green
Miss E H Harvey (1925)
Mrs T A Lakeman (1925)

The following are entitled to wear the New Colours adopted on January 1st, 1937, and the Championship Badges stated:—

MEN

H W Austin (1929)
J E Barrett (1957)
D W Barton (1946)
G Battrick (1969)
H Baxter (1948)
R Becker (1955)
D W Butler (1938)
J G Clifton (1970)
M Cox (1967)
P W Curtis (1969)
M G Davies (1957)
C E Hare (1937)
G P Hughes (1928) 1 silver
P R Hutchins (1968)
C M Jones (1938)
W A Wright (1956)
H G N Lee (1930)
N R Lewis (1949)

D A Lloyd (1972)
D MacPhail (1946)
S J Matthews (1971)
A R Mills (1959)
A J Mottram (1947)
G D Oakley (1954)
G L Paish (1947)
J G Paish (1972)
F J Perry 3 gold (1931) 2 green
J A Pickard (1959)
M J Sangster (1961)
G R Stilwell (1966)
R Taylor (1963)
C R D Tuckey (1935) 1 silver
H F Walton (1948)
R J Wilson (1957)
F H D Wilde (1937)

LADIES'
Mrs G Ackroyd (1928)
Mrs D A Bank (1928)
Mrs M Barker (1952)
Miss S Barker (1974)
Mrs J E Barrett 1 gold (1953) 1 silver
Mrs N W Blair (1946)
Mrs C W Brasher (1955)
Mrs A Buxton 1 silver (1955)
Mrs D F Cartwright (1933)
Miss L J Charles (1974)
Mrs P Chatrier (1952)
Mrs E M Cleverly (1934)
Miss G L Coles (1974)
Hon Mrs P F Glover (1934)
Mrs W H L Gordon (1937)
Mrs A Hales (1952)
Mrs W C J Halford (1946)
Mrs S H Hammersley (1933) 2 silver
Mrs C E Hare (1936)
Mrs C Harrison (1947)
Mrs E Hughesman (1946)
Mrs I Hume (1967)
Mrs G T Janes (1958)
Mrs P F Jones 1 gold (1958) 1 green
Mrs J Keller (1962)
Mrs M R King (1936)
Mrs D L Little 2 gold (1931) 1 silver, 3 green
Miss S Mappin (1974)
Mrs F Martin-Davies (1946)
Mrs J Maule (1949)
Mrs M Menzies (1935) 2 silver
Mrs A J Mottram (1947)
Mrs J Rinkel-Quertier (1947)
Mrs C Robinson (1968)
Mrs F C Shoemaker (1928)
Mrs W M Simmers (1928)
Mrs J K Spann (1953) 1 silver
Mrs F H Vivian (1933)
Miss S V Wade (1966) 1 gold
Mrs D E Wagstaffe (1963)
Mrs J J Walker Smith (1949)
Mrs K Wooldridge (1966)
(Note:—Badges awarded to winners of Championship events: Gold—Singles; Silver—Men's and Ladies' Doubles; Green—Mixed Doubles).

The following are entitled to wear the Old British Badge:—

MEN
H W Austin 1928
E R Avory 1933
C G Eames 1928
G P Hughes 1929
H G N Lee 1930
F J Perry 1931
C R D Tuckey 1935
F H D Wilde 1934

LADIES'
Mrs G Ackroyd 1928
Mrs D A Bank 1929
Mrs W I Blakstad 1928
Mrs D F Cartwight 1932
Mrs E M Cleverly 1934
Hon Mrs P F Glover 1934
Mrs S H Hammersley 1933
Mrs M R King 1930
Mrs D L Little 1931
Mrs M Menzies 1934
Mrs E A Rowbottom 1929
Mrs F C Shoemaker 1928
Mrs W M Simmers 1928
Mrs F H Vivian 1933

The following are entitled to wear the British Badge and Blazer adopted on January 1st, 1937:—

MEN
J E Barrett 1952
D W Barton 1946
G Battrick 1968
H Baxter 1946
R Becker 1953
D W Butler 1937
M Cox 1964
P W Curtis 1968
M G Davies 1955
M J Farrell 1974
J W Feaver 1974
E J Filby 1946
M P Hann 1961
C E Hare 1937
J A T Horn 1953
C M Jones 1938
W A Knight 1953
N R Lewis 1949
D A Lloyd 1971
J M Lloyd 1973
D MacPhail 1946
J de Mendoza 1972
A R Mills 1958
A J Mottram 1946
C J Mottram 1973
G D Oakley 1949
J G Paish 1971
G L Paish 1946
J A Pickard 1953

LADIES'
M Barker 1953
Mrs J E Barrell 1952
Miss L J Beaven 1973
Mrs N W Blair 1946
Mrs C W Brasher 1955
Miss V A Burton 1973
Miss A Buxton 1955
Miss L J Charles 1973
Mrs P Chatrier 1952
Miss G L Coles 1973
Mrs J Drobny 1946
Mrs W H L Gordon 1938
Mrs A Hales 1951
Mrs W C J Halford 1948
Mrs Hamilton 1946
Mrs C Harrison 1946
Miss P A Hird 1956
Mrs E Hughesman 1946
Mrs G J Jones 1957
Mrs P F Jones 1957
Mrs J Keller 1960
Mrs R H Lauder 1965
Mrs F Martin-Davies 1946
Mrs J Maule 1949
Miss C Molesworth 1972
Mrs Morris 1949
Mrs A J Mottram 1947
Mrs D J Poynder 1946
Mrs G Primrose 1968

A G Roberts 1949
M J Sangster 1960
L Shaffi 1946
G R Stilwell 1964
S A Warboys 1973
F H D Wilde 1937
R K Wilson 1953
K Wooldridge 1969

Mrs J Rinkel-Quertier 1947
Mrs C Robinson 1965
Miss V E Scott 1938
Mrs J K Spann 1953
Miss S V Wade 1964
Mrs D E Wagstaffe 1962
Mrs J J Walker-Smith 1950

The following are entitled to wear the L.T.A. Badge and by decision of the Council in September, 1948, are also entitled to wear the England Badge adopted on January 1st, 1937:—

MEN

H W Austin 1928
E R Avory 1932
J L Chamberlain 1935
G R O Crole-Rees 1928
C G Eames 1928
D G Freshwater 1935
C E Hare 1934
G P Hughes 1929
H G N Lee 1929
F J Perry 1931
E C Peters 1930
F J Ritchie 1932
R W Standring 1928
H K Tinkler 1933
R R D Tuckey 1933
C H D Wilde 1933

LADIES'

Mrs G Ackroyd 1928
Mrs D F Cartwright
Mrs F R Chiesman 1928
Mrs E M Cleverly 1933
Mrs B C Covell 1929
Mrs D E C Eyres 1933
Mrs R Gladstone 1931
Hon Mrs P F Glover 1933
Mrs S H Hammersley 1932
Mrs C E Hare 1934
Miss E H Harvey 1928
Mrs R E Haylock 1930
Mrs M R King 1930
Mrs T A Lakeman 1929
Mrs D L Little 1930
Mrs C G McIlquham 1928
Mrs M Menzies 1933
Mrs D J P O'Meara 1928
Mrs G F Powell 1935
Mrs E A Rowbottom 1928
Mrs F C Shoemaker 1928
Mrs W M Simmers 1931
Mrs F H Vivian 1933

The following are entitled to wear the England Badge adopted on January 1st, 1937:—

MEN

J E Barrett 1951
D W Barton 1946
H Baxter 1946
E A Beads 1965
R Becker 1952
R D Bennett 1957
G C Bluett 1967
D W Butler 1938
R E Carter 1947
M W Collins 1973
M Cox 1962
J D C Crump 1963
P W Curtis 1967
E J David 1946
R W Dixon 1962
M D Deloford 1938
J W Feaver 1973
E J Filby 1938
G S W Fitt 1948
J M Gracie 1963
M P Hann 1955
C E Hare 1937
J A T Horn 1951
C J Hovell 1950
P R Hutchins 1967
C Illes 1964
C M Jones 1937
W A Knight 1952
R J Lee 1952
R A Lewis 1974
C F O Lister 1950
D A Lloyd 1968
S J Matthews 1962
J de Mendoza 1970
G R B Meredith 1937
A R Mills 1956
W J Moss 1949
A J Mottram 1946
P Moys 1956
R E Mulliken 1938
G D Oakley 1949
G L Paish 1946
J G Paish 1968
F J Piercy 1947
A G Roberts 1947
L Shaffi 1946
D H Slack 1947
D G Snart 1949
A J N Starte 1951
G R Stilwell 1963
J I Tattersall 1962
R Taylor 1961
H E Truman 1961
H F Walton 1948
S A Warboys 1972
K F Weatherley 1971
G L Ward 1955
J M Ward 1961
I J Warwick 1955
F H D Wilde 1937
R K Wilson 1952
K Wooldridge 1964

LADIES'

Mrs M Barker 1951
Miss S Barker 1973
Mrs J E Barrett 1952
Miss L J Beaven 1971
Miss L D Blachford 1973
Mrs D R Bocquet 1948
Mrs C W Brasher 1954
Mrs J H Brown 1952
Mrs R J R Bulleid 1953
Miss A Buton 1954
Mrs L Cawthorn 1963
Mrs P Chatrier 1951
Mrs C Clark 1956
Miss J P Cooper 1911
Mrs D L Coutts 1949
Mrs T W Cowie 1969
Mrs G R Cox 1960
Mrs M H Cox 1951
Mrs A Dawes 1949
Mrs E W Dawson-Scott 1947

Mrs J L Deloford 1958
Mrs E C Ford 1949
Miss J A Fulton 1964
Mrs A Hales 1951
Mrs W C J Halford 1937
Mrs I Hamilton 1960
Mrs C Harrison 1950
Mrs E Hughesman 1950
Mrs J Kennedy 1964
Mrs R H Lauder 1961
Mrs M S Macgregor 1958
Mrs P Maclean 1954
Mrs H Matheson 1963
Mrs J Maule 1950
Miss E A Middleton 1948
Mrs A R Mills 1961
Mrs A J Mottram 1950
Miss L J Mottram 1974
Miss P O'Connell 1946
Mrs L J Osborne 1947
Miss J M Petchell 1954
Mrs D J Poynder 1937
Mrs G Primrose 1964
Mrs J Rinkel-Quertier 1950
Mrs D W Roberts 1960
Miss V E Scott 1937
Mrs B I Shenton 1955
Mrs J K Spann 1953
Miss S Tutt 1967
Mrs M R Wainwright 1968
Mrs J J Walker-Smith 1950

The following are the holders of the LTA International Awards

MEN

J. W. Feaver
A. J. Jarrett
R. A. Lewis
J. M. Lloyd
C. J. Mottram
J. R. Smith

LADIES

Miss J. M. Durie
Miss A. E. Hobbs
Miss M. Tyler

THE LTA NATIONAL AWARDS

SENIOR PLAYER OF THE YEAR:
Male
1982 C J Mottram
1983 J M Lloyd

Female
1982 Miss J M Durie
1983 Miss J M Durie

1984 J M Lloyd
1985 J Bates

JUNIOR PLAYER OF THE YEAR
Male
1982 S Bale
1983 D Sapsford

Female
1982 Miss S Mair
1983 Miss A Croft

1984 Miss A Croft
1985 Miss J Wood

OFFICIAL OF THE YEAR:
1982 F W Hoyles
1983 Cmdr. C D Lane
1984 A R Mills
1985 C J Gorringe

NATIONAL TEAM AWARD:
1982 None given
1983 None given
1984 None given
1985 Davis Cup Team GB

COUNTY TEAM OF THE YEAR:
Male
1982 Essex Boys
1983 Middlesex Men

Female
1982 Norfolk Ladies
1983 Kent Ladies

1984 Kent Ladies
1985 Essex Men

GRAND PRIX/VIRGINIA SLIMS TOURNAMENT OF THE YEAR (exc. Wimbledon)
1982 Hard Court Championships, Bournemouth
1983 B.M.W. Championships, Eastbourne
1984 Stella Artois Championships, Queens
1985 Pilkington Glass Ladies Championships, Eastbourne

NATIONAL TOURNAMENT OF THE YEAR:
1982 G.M.C. Tournament, Manchester
1983 Kentish Times Tournament, Beckenham
1984 British Home Stores, Cumberland
1985 ESAB Northumberland Tennis Tournament

MEDIA PERSON OF THE YEAR:
1985 J Parsons

MERITORIOUS SERVICE AWARD:
1982 C Spychala
1983 D Maskell, OBE
1984 Miss O Newson
1985 Mrs J Pryce

CARL AARVOLD AWARD FOR INTERNATIONAL ACHIEVEMENT:
1982 Sir B Burnett
1983 P Chatrier
1984 T Tinling
1985 D N Hardwick

SPECIAL AWARD
1985 Nestlé Company Limited

THE LAWN TENNIS ASSOCIATION 1986

COUNCIL FOR 1986

PRESIDENT

G B Brown (1972), 85 Watford Way, Hendon London NW4 (01-202 9118 pri, 01-278 8144 bus).

DEPUTY PRESIDENT

R J Presley (1975), 2 Vale Lodge, Downs Lane, Leatherhead, Surrey KT22 8JQ (0372 372049 pri, 01-629 8191 bus).

HONORARY LIFE VICE-PRESIDENTS

Sir Carl Aarvold OBE, TD, DL (1962), The Coach House, Crabtree Lane, Westhumble, Dorking, Surrey RH5 6BQ (0306 882771).
E R Avory (1937), Littleton Farm, Shepperton-on-Thames, Middlesex (093 28 62342).
C H E Betts (1945), 20 Hanger Lane, Ealing, London W5 3HH (01-992 2468).
B Howard-Baker (1932-36, 1945), c/o Glascoed Hall, Llansilin, nr Oswestry, Shropshire.
J S Harrison (1948), East View, Aldborough, Boroughbridge, York YO5 9ES (09012 2759).
D V Penman OBE, TD (1949), Pantiles, Langham Road, Robertsbridge, East Sussex TN32 5EP (0580 880377).
W T Pool (1969), 1 Treetops, Martello Park, Canford Cliffs, Poole, Dorset BH13 7BA (0202 709838).
E C Robbins (1958), Robin Lodge, 43 The Crescent, Belmont, Surrey SM2 6BP (01-643 2891).
H J Sargeant JP (1950), Stone Grange, Coniscliffe Road, Hartlepool, Cleveland (0429 75025).
J R White (1952), Little Orchard, Otmoor Lane, Beckley, Oxfordshire (086 735 284).

VICE-PRESIDENTS

D D Carmichael (1960), 1 Royal Terrace, Edinburgh EH7 5AD (031 557 4455).
J R Cochrane, CBE, JP (1972), Filia Regis, Cheltenham Place, Parkgate, South Wirral, Cheshire L64 6QJ (051 336 7503 pri, 051 236 1637 bus).
D N Hardwick (1948), 'Eastfield,' Cheselbourne, Dorchester, Dorset DT2 7NP (025 887 251).
Group Capt P G Hill RAF (retd) (1973), The Orchard, Claygate Lane, Shipbourne, Tonbridge, Kent TN11 9RN (0732 810587).
G L Paish MBE (1970), 35 Elmpark Gardens, South Croydon, Surrey CR2 8RW (01-657 1277).
J B Pinnock (1965), The Berries, 7 Main Road, Biddenham, Bedford, Bedfordshire MK40 4BB (0234 61356).
R G Robinson (1954), Long View, Limes Lane, Buxted, nr Uckfield, East Sussex TN22 4PB (082 581 2551).

HONORARY TREASURER

D D Carmichael (1960), 1 Royal Terrace, Edinburgh EH7 5AD (031-557 4455).

HONORARY LIFE COUNCILLORS

S E Andrew MBE (1958), 25 Matmore Gate, Spalding, Lincolnshire PE11 2PN (0775 2763).
R O Baillon (1956), Orchard House, Adlands Lane, Church Brampton, Northampton (0604 844485).
H F Dauncey (1955), One Acre, Whiteleaf, Aylesbury, Buckinghamshire HP17 0LG (084 44 3357).
R V Fontes (1954-1978, 1981), Walmer Cottage, Greenacre Close, Knutsford, Cheshire WA16 8NL.
F A Jarvis MC (1954), 212 Station Road, Harpenden, Hertfordshire AL5 4EH (05827 2534).
P M Lindner (1952-1980, 1985), Clock House, Springfield Lane, Broadway, Hereford & Worcester WR12 7BT (0386 853358).
Dr E J Mann (1955), 11 Coppice Close, 42 Dove Lane, Solihull, West Midlands.
C G Moeller (1960), 92 Hawkesworth Lane, Guiseley, Nr. Leeds, Yorkshire (0943 75495).
Mrs C Z Morse (1947), Mendham Priory, Harleston, Diss, Norfolk IP20 0JH (0379 86236).
W E Palmer (1962), 86 Eastbrook Road, Lincoln, Lincolnshire LN6 7EP (0522 695202).
E M Pitts (1960), 61 Hayes Road, Bromley, Kent BR2 9AE (01-460 4273).
J G Rae (1967-69, 1971), 91 Buncer Lane, Blackburn, Lancashire BB2 6SN (0254 51026).
A P Wakeley (1958-1978, 1980), 27 Hazebrouck Road, Faversham, Kent ME13 7PU (0795 531519).

COUNCILLORS

T A Adamson (1983), 4 Eastmoor Court, Eastmoor Park, Harpenden, Hertfordshire (05827 2189 pri, 0923 21149 bus). HERTFORDSHIRE.
Mrs B W Barber JP (1978), Parkside Farm, Ipstones, Stoke-on-Trent, Staffordshire ST10 2NG (053871 373). STAFFORDSHIRE.
F C Bowles (1984), The Post Office Stores, West Pennard, Glastonbury, Somerset BA6 8NL (0458 32955). SOMERSET.
Mrs O Brown (1985), 10 Cavendish Road, Bristol, Avon BS9 4DZ (0272 623473). AVON.
W F G Brunsdon (1980) 65 Heol-y-Gors, Whitchurch, Cardiff, South Glamorgan CF4 1HG (0222 628241 pri, 0222 371838 and 0222 397571 ext 236 bus). WALES.
R E Carter (1975), 4 Hazeldene, Seaford, Sussex BN25 5NQ (0323 890083). VETERANS' LTA.

G A Cass (1976), Middlefield, Huntingdon Road, Cambridge CB3 0LH (0223 276234 pri, 0223 312393 bus). CAMBRIDGE UNIVERSITY.
F J Collins (1982), 16 Bowes Drive, Ongar, Essex CM5 9AU (0277 362763 pri, 0920 5973 bus). ESSEX.
Mrs T M Collins (1980), 28 Meadow Way, Chigwell, Essex IG7 6LR (01-500 5782). YORKSHIRE.
G T Collinson (1986), 14 Woodlands Road, Shotley Bridge, Consett, Co. Durham DH8 0DE (0207 503247 pri, 0207 502551 bus). DURHAM & CLEVELAND.
K C Cook OBE, (1981), 8 Hill Road, Birkenhead, Merseyside L43 8TL (051 652 1252 pri, 051 652 4943 bus). CHESHIRE.
B G Coombs (1977), 'Wyvern,' Woollard, Pensford, Avon BS18 4HY (076 18 562 pri, 0272 294901 bus). AVON.
R J Cruse (1984), Croft Cottage, Abbotskerswell, Newton Abbot, Devon TQ12 5NS (0626 66026). DEVON.
W E Curtis (1975), 22 Longfield Road, Capel St Mary, Ipswich, Suffolk IP9 2XG (0473 311526). BRITISH SCHOOLS' LTA.
R Cushing JP (1976), 31 Balcombe Court, West Parade, Worthing, Sussex BN11 3QP (0903 206557 pri, 0903 38273 bus). SUSSEX.
K L Dewick (1977), 55 Chessfield Park, Little Chalfont, Amersham, Buckinghamshire HP6 6RU (024 04 3818). BUCKINGHAMSHIRE.
E R Dry (1982), Compass House, 14 Queens Road, Ferndown, Wimborne, Dorset BH22 9RT (0202 875985 pri, 0202 677423 bus). DORSET.
R H M Ellis (1985), 'Wych Gate,' Broughton Road, Adlington, Macclesfield, Cheshire SK10 4ND (0625 829273 pri, 0538 382451 bus). CHESHIRE.
W Enoch (1983), 13 Lathbury Road, Oxford OX1 7AT (0865 58134 pri, 0865 52031 bus). OXFORDSHIRE.
R K Foster (1986), 39 Coombe Drive, Dunstable, Beds LU6 2AE (0582 62532 pri, 0582 603166 bus). BEDFORDSHIRE.
Mrs J I Fyfe (1986), 33 Princes Avenue, London W3 8LX (01-992 6508). MIDDLESEX.
Dr R P H Gasser (1984), Brasenose College, Oxford OX1 4AJ (0865 248641). OXFORD UNIVERSITY.
Sqn Ldr E I G Geddes (1986), RAF Sports Board, Ministry of Defence, Adastral House, Theobalds Road, London WC1X 8RU (0462 813627 pri, 01-430 7295 bus). ROYAL AIR FORCE.
Miss M E Gill (1983), 236 West Parade, Lincoln LN1 1LY (0522 23983 pri, 0522 33561 bus). LINCOLNSHIRE.
C J Gorringe (1980), The All England Club, Church Road, Wimbledon, London SW19 5AE (01-946 2244). ALL ENGLAND CLUB.
J M Gracie (1982), Chantry Dane, Legh Road, Knutsford, Cheshire WA16 8LP (0565 3605 pri, 061 440 9000 bus). LANCASHIRE.
J W D Greatrex (1979), 'Crantock,' 81 Cardiff Road, Dinas Powis, South Glamorgan CF6 4JT (0222 512320 pri, 0222 371838 bus). WALES.
A G Grosset (1980), Alex Morison & Co, WS, 33 Queen Street, Edinburgh EH2 1LE (031 447 6460 pri, 031 226 6541 bus). SCOTLAND.
E R Hammer (1971), 22 Manor Way, Beckenham, Kent BR3 3LJ (01-650 3833). KENT.
B J Harriss (1985), 66 Church Avenue, Pinner, Middlesex HA5 5JF (01-866 3468 pri, 01-831 2877 bus). MIDDLESEX.
J H Harris JP (1971), Cavell House, Swardeston, Norwich, Norfolk NR14 8DZ (0508 78195 pri, 0603 610271 bus). NORFOLK.
J Harrop (1977), 27 Cumnor Hill, Oxford OX2 9EY (0865 863470 pri, 0865 240827 bus). OXFORDSHIRE.
R F Hartle (1968), 'Rushmere,' Mugginton Lane End, Weston Underwood, Derbyshire DE6 4PP (077 389 306 pri). DERBYSHIRE.
B R Hatton (1984), 51 Village Way, Pinner, Middlesex HA5 5AB (01-868 7607 pri, 65 20402 bus). INTERNATIONAL CLUB.
Lt Col H W Heath (1978), Ministry of Defence, DAR 2, Room 1108, Empress State Building, Lillie Road, London SW6 1TR (71 53167 pri, 01-385 1244 ext 2716 bus). ARMY.
J C Henshaw (1984), 15 Abbotsfield Drive, Shrewsbury, Shropshire SY2 6OJ (0743 4835 pri, 0743 63344 bus). SHROPSHIRE.
J Hunting (1986), 21 Roundhill Road, Leicester LE5 5RJ (0533 737260 pri, 0533 551551 ext 2293 and 2331 bus). LEICESTERSHIRE.
B C Hyde (1985), Pear Tree Cottage, Valley Lane, Chessetts Wood, Lapworth, West Midlands B94 6HB (05643 2318 pri, 021 705 7987/7988 bus). WARWICKSHIRE.
R A James (1984), 45 Lemon Street, Truro, Cornwall TR1 2NS (0872 79330 pri, 0872 76166 bus). CORNWALL.
A R W Jones JP (1976), 6 Ribblesdale Place, Preston, Lancashire PR1 3NA (0772 719052 pri, 0772 59824 bus). LANCASHIRE.
K G Jones (1976), 27 Sutherland Road, Goldthorn Park, Wolverhampton, Staffordshire WV4 5AR (0902 342858 pri, 0902 41635 bus). STAFFORDSHIRE.
I A King (1981), The Mount, Stoke Prior, Bromsgrove, Worcestershire B60 4JU (0527 31281 pri, 021 233 2468 bus). HEREFORD & WORCESTER.
R Kingsley Mills (1981), 614 Stratford Road, Birmingham B11 4BE (05645 77878 pri, 021 777 6762 bus). WARWICKSHIRE.
Mrs H S Lee (1974-76, 1978), The Grange, Newmans Green, Acton, Sudbury, Suffolk CO10 0AB (0787 310094). SUFFOLK.
S D Lester (1977), 2 Leigh Court, Harrow-on-the-Hill, Middlesex HA2 0HZ (01-864 8822). MIDDLESEX.
Miss S J Livingston (1984), The Beaconsfield School of Lawn Tennis, Beaconsfield, Buckinghamshire HP9 2BY (04946 4744). BWTA.
D L McAdam JP (1975), 44-46 Shields Road, Newcastle-upon-Tyne NE6 1DR (091 2860361 pri, 091 2651350 bus). NORTHUMBERLAND.

M C McAfee (1976), Dormie House School, 15 Riversdale Road, West Kirby, Wirral, Merseyside L48 4EY (051 625 8348). CHESHIRE.
I C McCulloch TD (1985), Glen Fruin, Brickyard Lane, Farnsfield, Newark, Nottinghamshire NG22 8JS (0623 882443 pri, 0602 470032 bus). NOTTINGHAMSHIRE.
I W McDiarmid (1982), Heatherdale, 12 Greenbank Crescent, Southampton SO1 7FQ (0703 766302). HAMPSHIRE & IOW.
Mrs J M Maher (1985), 12 Oakley Road, Wimborne, Dorset BH21 1QJ (0202 883979 pri, 09295 6301 bus). BRITISH SCHOOLS' LTA.
M C Martin (1974), The Paddocks, Hungarton, Leicester LE7 9JY (053 750 230 pri, 0533 773399 bus). SLTR.
B C Mead (1983), Wickham Barn, 12 College Lane, Hurstpierpoint, Sussex BN6 9AG (0273 833161 pri, 01-480 4105 bus). SUSSEX.
P J A Mornard (1985), Slip Cottage, School Hill, Nacton, nr Ipswich, Suffolk IP10 OEH (0473 88640 pri, 0473 88225 bus). SUFFOLK.
D W Moseley (1986), 48 Lynmouth Road, Hucclecote, Gloucester, Glos. GL3 3JD (0452 60592). GLOUCESTERSHIRE.
P C Nicolson (1985), 11 Kirk Park, Edinburgh EH16 6HZ (031 664 6747 pri, 031 655 6105 bus). SCOTLAND.
J R Nixon (1973), Pottleford, Hayton, Carlisle, Cumbria CA4 9JD (022 870 454). CUMBRIA.
Mrs S J Papé (1984), Ravensden Farm, Bedford Road, Rushden, Northamptonshire NN10 0SQ (0933 56221). NORTHAMPTONSHIRE.
Capt R H Parsons RN (Retd) (1979), 1 York Crescent, Lee-on-Solent, Hampshire PO13 9AX (0705 550688 pri, 0705 822351 ext 23868/9 bus). ROYAL NAVY.
R S Paterson (1984), 40 Cedarwood Avenue, Newton Mearns, Glasgow G77 5LP (041 639 5323 pri, 041 429 4994 bus). SCOTLAND.
Miss D L M Portway TD (1980), 33 Millington Road, Cambridge CB3 9HW (0223 350183). CAMBRIDGESHIRE.
M A E Powell (1983), Lower Hardenhuish Farmhouse, Chippenham, Wiltshire SN14 6HN (0249 652338 pri, 0249 653361 bus). WILTSHIRE.
Miss J C L Poynder (1986), 1 South Grove, 69 Abbey Road, Malvern, Worcs WR14 3HH (06845 4435). PTCA.
J R Ramsbottom (1986), Woodlands, 26 Falcon Road, Bingley, West Yorkshire BD16 4DW (0274 565218 pri, 0274 818271/2 bus). YORKSHIRE
P A Richardson (1982), Fir Grange, 130 Wetherby Road, Harrogate, North Yorkshire HG2 7AB (0423 883927 pri, 0532 694244 bus). YORKSHIRE.
J C Robbins (1973), 52 Fairfax Avenue, Epsom, Surrey KT17 2QP (01-393 3836 pri, 01-623 6622 bus). SURREY.
L Robinson (1976), 6 Grange Avenue, Rotherfield Peppard, nr Henley-on-Thames, Oxon RG9 5JP (049 17 406). BERKSHIRE.
M S Robottom (1985), Les Fougères, St John, Jersey, CI (0534 61608 pri, 0534 44806 bus). CHANNEL ISLANDS.
Mrs N Rushton (1984), 9 Stone Edge Road, Higherford, Nelson, Lancs BB9 6BB (0282 64123). LANCASHIRE.
A R Scarlett (1981), 16 Martindale, London SW14 7AL (01-876 9593 pri, 01-385 3421 bus). SURREY.
K Sefton (1986), "The Barn", Bakers Lane, Thorpe Satchville, Leics LE14 2DE (0664 840589 pri, 0533 769151 bus). LEICESTERSHIRE.
J C Sherwood-Smith (1980), 40 Pinewood Green, Iver Heath, Buckinghamshire SL0 0QG (0753 653822). BUCKINGHAMSHIRE.
A Smith (1981), 6 Warren Avenue, Chelsfield, Orpington, Kent BR6 6HX (66 51802). KENT.
Mrs T Snow (1984), Arncroft, Breinton, Hereford HR4 7PD (0432 273640 pri, 0432 56292 bus). HEREFORD & WORCESTER.
Mrs F D Teubler (1986), 38 Boyne Park, Tunbridge Wells, Kent TN4 8ET (0892 24009). KENT
C M Thomson (1983), 10 Kirkdene Bank, Newton Mearns, Glasgow, Scotland G77 5RG (041 639 6822 pri, 041 332 8791 bus). SCOTLAND.
H E Truman (1974), Flat 2, 48 St. Martin's Lane, London WC2N 4EJ (01-836 3209). ALL ENGLAND CLUB.
J E Tucker (1977), Clearview Tennis Centre, Warley Hall Lane, Little Warley, nr Brentwood, Essex CM13 3EN (0277 811569 pri, 04024 43462 bus). ESSEX.
Mrs V Walley (1984), 3 Gainsborough Road, London W4 1NJ (01-994 3890 pri, 01-219 6301 bus). CIVIL SERVICE.
Mrs S M Ward (1984), 5 Lady Jane Court, Caversham, Reading, Berkshire RG4 0JH (0734 472659 pri, 0734 27337 bus). BERKSHIRE.
K St J Wiseman (1984), 5 Abbotts Way, Highfield, Southampton, Hants SO2 1QU (0703 556377 pri, 0703 227681 bus). HAMPSHIRE & IOW.
Miss S E Wolstenholme (1981), Corner House, 54 Kitsbury Road, Berkhamsted, Hertfordshire HP4 3EA (04427 3952 pri). HERTFORDSHIRE.

Notes
(i) The year of election or re-election is given in brackets. Service has been continuous since the last or only date mentioned.
(ii) All correspondence should be sent to the first address shown.

LTA MANAGEMENT COMMITTEE AND COMMITTEES FOR 1986

MANAGEMENT COMMITTEE 1986

President G B Brown
Deputy President R J Presley
Honorary Treasurer D D Carmichael
Executive Director I D Peacock
Secretary J C U James
Men's National Team Manager P R Hutchins
Women's National Team Manager Miss S Mappin

CHAIRMAN OF THE FIVE OPERATING COMMITTEES

Competitions and Tournaments J H Harris
County and Club I A King
Marketing and Sponsorship J R Cochrane
National Development, Coaching and Schools Miss S E Wolstenholme
National Training and International Match G A Cass

The Council have elected the following additional members:

G L Paish
J E Tucker

OPERATING COMMITTEES

COMPETITIONS & TOURNAMENTS

J H Harris (Chairman), Mrs O Brown, R Cushing, K L Dewick, Group Capt P G Hill, S D Lester, Miss S J Livingston, D G Lock.

COUNTY & CLUB

I A King (Chairman), Miss M E Gill, E R Hammer, J Harrop, J C Henshaw, B C Mead, Mrs N Rushton, Mrs T Snow.

*G C Bluett

MARKETING & SPONSORSHIP

J R Cochrane (Chairman), B G Coombs, M C Martin, J C Robbins, M S Robottom, A Smith, C M Thomson.

NATIONAL DEVELOPMENT, COACHING & SCHOOLS

Miss S E Wolstenholme (Chairman), Mrs B W Barber, W E Curtis, A G Grosset, Mrs J M Maher, Miss J C L Poynder, J C Sherwood-Smith, J E Tucker.

*J R Coates

NATIONAL TRAINING & INTERNATIONAL MATCH

G A Cass (Chairman), T A Adamson, F J Collins, J M Gracie, J H Harris, I C McCulloch, G L Paish. H E Truman.

Men's and Women's National Team Managers—ex-officio.

STEERING COMMITTEES

ASSOCIATE MEMBERSHIP

A Smith (Chairman), R J Cruse, Miss M E Gill, B C Hyde, D G Lock, Mrs S J Papé, P A Richardson, J C Robbins.

FINANCE

D D Carmichael (Chairman), R J Cruse, Dr R P H Gasser, I A King, R Kingsley Mills, M C Martin, J B Pinnock.

RULES

G L Paish (Chairman), J W D Greatrex, Lt Col H W Heath, P J A Mornard, R G Robinson, Mrs V Walley, K St J Wiseman.

TECHNICAL & RESEARCH

A R Scarlett (Chairman), J M Gracie, B J Harriss, B R Hatton, J C Henshaw, Group Capt P G Hill, I C McCulloch, R G Robinson.

*A A Townsend

*Non-Council Member

JOINT COMMITTEES & REPRESENTATIVES ON OTHER BODIES

COMMITTEE OF MANAGEMENT OF THE CHAMPIONSHIPS

The President, D D Carmichael, J R Cochrane, Group Capt P G Hill, G L Paish, R J Presley, R G Robinson.

JOINT FINANCE BOARD

The President, D D Carmichael, J H Harris, J B Pinnock, R J Presley, R G Robinson.

ALL ENGLAND LT GROUND LTD

D D Carmichael, D N Hardwick, R G Robinson.

ALL ENGLAND LTC (WIMBLEDON) LTD

G B Brown, D D Carmichael, D N Hardwick.

INTERNATIONAL TENNIS FEDERATION

D N Hardwick (Committee of Management), The President, J R Cochrane, G L Paish, (Delegates to AGM), R E Carter (Veterans' Committee), P A Sandilands (Technical Committee).

EUROPEAN TENNIS ASSOCIATION

G L Paish (Committee of Management and Chairman, European Cup), R J Presley, The Secretary (Delegates to AGM), Miss S J Livingston (Women's Tournament Administrator), D G Lock (Men's Tournament Committee).

THE BRITISH SCHOOLS' LTA

Mrs B W Barber, Miss S E Wolstenholme, The Secretary.

THE LAWN TENNIS FOUNDATION LTD

J R Cochrane , J E Tucker, The Secretary.

BRITISH OLYMPIC ASSOCIATION

The Secretary

REGISTERED PROFESSIONAL COACHES' BENEVOLENT FUND

S E Andrew, D D Carmichael, J C Sherwood-Smith.

SPORTS COUNCIL

J R Cochrane, R G Robinson (representing CCPR).

IAKS

P A Sandilands

LOANS SUB-COMMITTEE

J B Pinnock (Chairman), E R Hammer, J Harrop, J C Henshaw, B C Hyde, I A King, J C Robbins.

YOUNG PLAYERS' FUND

D D Carmichael (Honorary Treasurer), G A Cass (Chairman, Training & International Match Committee).

QUEEN'S CLUB BOARD

G B Brown (Chairman), R E Carter, Lt Col H W Heath, J B Pinnock, R J Presley, J E Tucker.

WEST HANTS CLUB BOARD

D G Lock

BISHAM ABBEY COMMITTEE

The Secretary

CCPR

R G Robinson (Executive Committee and Major Spectator Sports Division), The Secretary (Games and Sports Division).

PTCA EXECUTIVE COMMITTEE

C R Applewhaite.

* * * * * *

AUDITORS

Messrs Deloitte Haskins & Sells, Box 207, 128 Queen Victoria Street, London EC4P 4JX (01-248 3913, telex 887880).

BANKERS

Coutts & Co., 15 Lombard Street, London EC3V 9AU (01-623 1010).

CUSTODIAN TRUSTEES

Coutts & Co, 440 Strand, London WC2R 0QS (01-379 6262).

SOLICITORS

Messrs Warren Murton & Co, 19 Harley Street, London W1 (01-637 3861).

SOLICITORS (LOANS)

Messrs Taylor, Willcocks, Zabell & Co, 110 Church Hill Road, Cheam, Surrey (01-644 9612).

LTA HEADQUARTERS AND REGIONAL STAFF

LTA MANAGEMENT COMMITTEE

G B Brown
R J Presley
D D Carmichael
I D Peacock
J C U James
P R Hutchins
Miss S Mappin
G A Cass Chairman – National Training & International Match
J R Cochrane – Marketing & Sponsorship
J H Harris Chairman – Competitions & Tournaments
I A King Chairman – County & Club
Miss S E Wolstenholme Chairman – National Development, Coaching & Schools
G L Paish
J E Tucker

HEADQUARTERS EXECUTIVE STAFF

Paul Hutchins National Men's Team Manager
Sue Mappin National Women's Team Manager
Charles Applewhaite Director of Coaching
Brian Blincoe Director of National Development
Heather Dallas Press Officer
Ian Hume Marketing & Promotions Officer
John James Secretary
Ian Peacock Executive Director
Oliver Rogger, FCCA Accountant
Phillip Sandilands Technical Officer
Mike Sertin Events & Tournaments Manager

LTA MEDICAL OFFICER

Dr Jim McCollum, MB, ChB.

REGIONAL STAFF

All correspondence to be addressed to the following:

ENGLAND

EAST (Bedfordshire, Cambridgeshire, Essex, Hertfordshire, Norfolk, Suffolk)
C W Dunkley (National Coach/Development Officer)
The LTA East Region, Regional Office, Clearview Tennis Centre, Warley Hall Lane, Little Warley, nr Brentwood, Essex CM13 3EN (0277 811323).

SOUTH EAST (Kent, Middlesex, Surrey, Sussex)
G R Bone (National Coach/Development Officer)
The LTA South East Region, Regional Office, Lamerton House, 23a High Street, Ealing, London W5 5DF (01-840 4060).

SOUTH (Berkshire, Buckinghamshire, Hampshire & IOW, Oxfordshire, Channel Islands)
M J Sanderson (National Coach/Development Officer)
The LTA South Region, Regional Office, Slough Tennis Centre, PO Box 501, Salt Hill Park, Bath Road, Slough SL1 3TP (0753 38983).

SOUTH WEST (Avon, Cornwall, Devon, Dorset, Somerset, Wiltshire)
R D Jones (National Coach/Development Officer)
The LTA South West Region, Regional Office, Cheltenham House, 22-24 Clare Street, Bristol BS1 1YA (0272 272787).

WEST MIDLANDS (Hereford & Worcester, Gloucestershire, Staffordshire, Shropshire, Warwickshire)
D J Roberts (National Coach/Development Officer)
The LTA West Midlands Region, Regional Office, Telford Racquet & Fitness Centre, St Quentin Gate, Telford Town Centre, Telford, Shropshire TF3 4JH (0952 506997).

NORTH WEST (Cheshire, Cumbria, Lancashire, Isle of Man)
R Cowell (National Coach/Development Officer)
The LTA North West Region, Regional Office, LTA Regional Centre, Dairyhouse Lane, Bramhall, Cheshire SK7 1RW (061 439 9096).

NORTH EAST (Durham & Cleveland, Northumberland, Yorkshire)
I A Smith (National Coach/Development Officer)
The LTA North East Region, Regional Office, Hull YPI, Chanterlands Avenue, Hull HU5 3EF (0482 448430).

NORTH MIDLANDS (Derbyshire, Leicestershire, Lincolnshire, Northamptonshire, Nottinghamshire)
K S Reynolds (National Coach/Development Officer)
The LTA North Midlands Region, Regional Office, Watchorn Tennis Club, Ewart Lane, Alfreton, Derby DE5 7AU (0773 836717).

WALES

P J Warren (National Development Officer/Coach)
WLTA, The National Sports Centre for Wales, Sophia Gardens, Cardiff (Cardiff 371838).

SCOTLAND

I G Woodcraft (Development/Coaching Officer)
SLTA, 12 Melville Crescent, Edinburgh EH3 7LU (031-225 1284).

NATIONAL TRAINING CENTRE

Bisham Abbey, Marlow, Bucks (06284 2818/6119).
Management—**John and Margy Clifton.**
National Tennis School—**Derek Bone.**

The President, Geoff Brown

Deputy President, Ron Presley

Executive Director, Ian Peacock

The Secretary, John James

Mike Sertin, Events & Tournaments Manager

Paul Hutchins, National Men's Team Manager

Sue Mappin, National Women's Team Manager

Brian Blincoe, Director of National Development

Charles Applewhaite, Director of Coaching

Ian Hume, Marketing & Promotions Officer

Heather Dallas, Press Officer

Philip Sandilands, Technical Officer

Oliver Rogger, FCCA, Accountant

PAST PRESIDENTS, CHAIRMEN AND HONORARY TREASURERS

PRESIDENTS

1888-1896	W Renshaw
1896-1897	The Rt Hon The Earl of Cavan
1897-1906	W H Collins
1907-1926	The Rt Hon Lord Desborough, KG, GCVO
1927-1932	The Rt Hon The Viscount d'Abernon, PC, GCB, GCMO
1932-1956	The Rt Hon Viscount Templewood, GCSI, GBE, CMG
1957-1962	His Grace the Duke of Devonshire, MC
1963-1981	Sir Carl Aarvold, OBE, TD, DL
1982-1984	J R Cochrane, CBE, JP
1985	G B Brown

CHAIRMEN OF THE COUNCIL

1907-1908	S A E Hickson
1909-1910	A W Gore
1911	H H Monckton
1912-1913	R J McNair
1914-1920	S A E Hickson
1920-1921	A Sterry
1922	Brig Gen A L, Macfie, CB, VD, DL
1923, 1924	A E M Taylor, MBE
1925	F L Riseley
1926	H H Monckton
1927	R J McNair
1928	C Pflaum
1929	P W Jewson, JP
1930	T M Mavrogordato
1931	A C Griffiths
1932	Sir Leonard Lyle, Bart, JP
1933	F C Lohden, OBE
1934	H Roper Barrett
1935	G F Goodman
1936	A D Prebble
1937	A Herschell
1938	P H Stevens
1939-1945	C R Glanvill
1946	J H King
1947	F T Stowe
1948	A H Wilson
1949	V R Penman
1950	S E Charlton
1951	J Crawford, JP
1952	H W Thomas
1953	H A Buckler
1954	J Eaton Griffith, CMG, OBE
1955	W H Mellor
1956-1957	T W Ranson
1958	Sir Robert Fraser, KCB, KBE
1959	W J Greener, JP
1960	W E Ramsden
1961	C W Banks
1962-1963	E R Avory
1964	G W Bell
1965	W L P Woolley
1966	J S Harrison
1967	W E Attewell
1968	D N Hardwick
1969	S H Hawkins
1970	D V Penman, OBE, TD
1971	R H Buxton
1972	Group Capt F W Judge, RAF (Retd)
1973	R G Robinson
1974	C H E Betts
1975	J R White
1976	Major E C Fraser
1977	C C Bullock, TD, JP
1978	D D Carmichael
1979	G L Paish, MBE
1980	J B Pinnock
1981	J R Cochrane, CBE, JP

From 1982 the Offices of Chairman of the Council and President were combined.

HONORARY TREASURERS

1888-1921	S A E Hickson
1922-1933	G H Musgrave
1934-1947	Sir Clarence Sadd, CBE, DL, JP
1948-1961	H Garton Ash, OBE, MC
1962-1970	Sir Robert Fraser, KCB, KBE
1971-1980	H J Sargeant, JP
1981-1984	D D Carmichael and J B Pinnock
1985	D D Carmichael

ASSOCIATIONS AFFILIATED TO THE LAWN TENNIS ASSOCIATION

THE SCOTTISH LAWN TENNIS ASSOCIATION

Secretary—**D Lynd MBE,** 12 Melville Crescent, Edinburgh EH3 7LU (031 225 1284).
Representatives on the LTA Council—**A G Grosset, C M Thomson, R S Paterson, P C Nicholson.**
Number of Affiliated Clubs 198

EAST OF SCOTLAND COUNTY

Hon Secretary—**Mrs J O Stewart,** 18 Meadowbank Terrace, Edinburgh EH8 7AS (031 661 6770).

NORTH OF SCOTLAND COUNTY

Hon Secretary—**W B McGregor,** Ferndale, Station Terrace, Invergowrie, Dundee (08267 475).

SOUTH OF SCOTLAND COUNTY

Hon Secretary—**Mrs E M Clark,** 37a Monument Road, Ayr (0292 64249).

WEST OF SCOTLAND COUNTY

Hon Secretary and Treasurer—**J Y Crawford,** 14 Kirkburn Road, Strathblane (0360 70747).

NORTH OF SCOTLAND LAWN TENNIS ASSOCIATION

Hon Secretary and Treasurer—**Mrs A Jamieson,** The Linn, Inshes, Inverness (31260).
Aberlour—Queens Road, Aberlour. Courts: H2. *Secretary:* D McPherson, 21 Sellar Place, Aberlour (401).
Dingwall—*Secretary:* Mrs M McKenzie, Inch Vaney Court, Dingwall (64615).
Elgin—Courts: H4. *Secretary:* Mrs M Crombie, 3 Deanshaugh, The Bishopmill, Elgin.
Forres—Albert Street, Forres. Courts: H4. *Secretary:* Mrs M Patnch, 1 Chapleton Place, Forres (72505).
Gordounstoun—*Secretary:* G Broad, Gordonstoun School, Elgin (0343 830603/830250).
Grantown-on-Spey—Courts: H8. *Secretary:* Mrs R Farquhair, 5 Strathspey Road, Grantown-on-Spey (0479 2218).
Inverness—Bishops Road, Inverness (30751). Courts: AW3. *Secretary:* J Chisholm, 24 Rangemoor Road, Inverness (230175).
Keith—Courts: H4. *Secretary:* Mrs P Lumsden, Annwood, Seafield Avenue, Keith (2035).
Kingussie—*Secretary:* S Hamlet, 30 High Street, Kingussie (212).
Kinloss—*Secretary:* Mr B Deniss, 1 Douglas Crescent, Kinloss CIDTT Unit, RAF Kinloss. Kinloss (72161 day only).
Nairn—Albert Street, Nairn. Courts: H6. *Secretary:* A Murdoch, 9 Mill Terrace, Nairn (52657).
Rothes—*Secretary:* H McBain, 9 Green Street, Rothes (03403 432).

NORTH EAST OF SCOTLAND LAWN TENNIS ASSOCIATION

Hon Secretary and Treasurer—**Mrs M Ramsey,** Littleways, Bieldside, Aberdeen (0224 867633).
Hon Junior Secretary—**J Smith,** 99 North Deeside Road, Peterculter, Aberdeen (0224 734473).
Hon Men's Match Secretary—**D McDermid,** 51 Baker Street, Abderdeen.
Hon Ladies' Match Secretary—**Mrs C Robertson,** 25 Rosemount Park, Blair Gowrie (0250 3009).

Aboyne—*Secretary:* Mrs F Smith, Bank House, Tarland.
Banchory—Scotstoun Gardens, Bridge of Don, Aberdeen. Courts: AW3. *Secretary:* J K Tierney, "Munia", Woodside Road, Banchory.
Cults—32 Abbotshall Place, Cults, Aberdeen. Courts: AW6. *Secretary:* M Garden, 14 Albyn Place, Aberdeen (0224 644481).
Garioch—Harland Road, Inverurie, Aberdeenshire. Courts: H2. *Secretary:* J. Wilson, 3 Maryfield West, Inverurie.
Kemnay—Courts: H3. *Secretary:* M Wallace, 30 The Glebe, Kemnay.
Kings College Staff—Courts: H2. *Secretary:* Dr Loula Dalgarno, 16 College Bounds, Old Aberdeen.
Longside—Cairngall, Longside, Aberdeenshire. Courts: H2. *Secretary:* Mrs M Stephen, 9 Church Lane, Longside (077 982 514).
Osborne—Eday Road, Aberdeen. Courts: H3. *Secretary:* A Perrott, 22 Camperdown Road, Aberdeen.
Pecten—Courts: H3. *Secretary:* Mrs M Everitt, Shell Exploration, 1 Altens Farm Road, Nigg, Aberdeen.
Rubislaw—Cromwell Road, Aberdeen. Courts: AW3. *Secretary:* Mrs D Doney, 73 Woodend Place, Aberdeen.
Stonehaven—Courts: AW3. *Secretary:* Miss C McWilliam, 8 Fetteresso Terrace, Stonehaven.
Turriff—Bowling Green Road, Turriff. Courts: AW3. *Secretary:* Mrs J Cruickshank, Kirton, Fyvie, Turriff.
Westburn—Courts: G4. *Secretary:* Wm Grant, 67 Westburn Drive, Aberdeen.

MIDLAND COUNTIES OF SCOTLAND LAWN TENNIS ASSOCIATION

Hon Secretary and Treasurer—**Mrs M E McFarlane,** 9 Seacraig Court, Newport on Tay (543106).
Hon Treasurer—**W R M King,** "Annandale", 1 Hillcrest Road, Dundee (0382 29751 bus, 0382 69096 pri).
Hon Match Secretary—**M R F Clark,** Old Bank House, Bank Street, Alyth, Perthshire (0382 22785 bus, Alyth 2337 pri).

Arbroath—Arbircot Road, Arbroath. Courts: H3. *Secretary:* M Milne, Jungfrau, 45 Marymusk Road, Arbroath DD11 2BZ.
Broughty Ferry—Holly Crescent, Broughty Ferry, Dundee (78613). *Secretary:* A Baillie, 14 Bellefield Avenue, Dundee (67266).
Carnoustie—(Maulesbank). *Secretary:* Mrs M Watson, "Claremont", 8 Holyrood Street, Carnoustie.
Craigielea—*Secretary:* R Doig, 37 Nesbitt Street, Dundee (41089).
Darnhall—*Secretary:* Miss M Shirley, 15 Balmanno Park, Kintillo, Bridge of Earn (Perth 312096).
Duffus—Duffus Park, Cupar. Courts: H4. *Secretary:* Miss H Walker, St Thomas's, Skinner Steps, Cupar (52562).
Dundee High School FP—*Secretary:* Linda Forrest, 13 Nesbitt Street, Dundee (43639).
Forfar—Courts: H4. *Secretary:* I Gordon, 23 Inchgarth Avenue, Forfar (64062 pri, 62551 ext 52 bus).
Games Club—c/o Forthill Sports Club, Fintry Place, Broughty Ferry, Dundee DD5 3DN (75550). Courts: G3, H6. *Secretary:* Miss H Main, 52 Fintry Place, Broughty, Ferry, Dundee.
Glenrothes—*Secretary:* Mrs D Maclean, 2 Annadale Gardens, Glenrothes (752521).
Harris Academy FP—*Sseretary:* G Angus, 18 Oxford Street, Dundee (60334).
Invergowrie—Errol Road, Invergowrie By Dundee. Courts: H3. *Secretary:* Miss G Couttie, 30 Morris Place, Invergowrie (350).
Kinnoull—Muirhall terrace, Perth (24071). Courts: H4. *Secretary:* A S Henderson, 32 Pitcullen Terrace, Perth (25544).
Kinross—Courts: H2. *Secretary:* Mrs A Milburn, Katrine Place, Kinross (63121).
Lochee—*Secretary:* R Smith, 22 Wellgrove Street, Lochee, Dundee.
Lundin Sports—Courts: H3. *Secretary:* T J Macaskill, Bank of Scotland Buildings, Forth St Leven (Lundin Links 320210).
Montrose—Dorwood Place, Montrose. Courts: H6. *Secretary:* G R V Baxter, Whitehouse, Warrack Terrace, Montrose (73960).
NCR—National Cash register (Mfg) Co Ltd, Camperdown, Dundee. Courts: AW3. *Secretary:* F Binnie, 10 Cardriss Street, Dundee (89594 pri, 60151 bus).
Newport—Cupar Road, Newport-on-Tay, Fife. Courts: H3. *Secretary:* R Logie, 2 Tayview Terrace, Newport-on-Tay (542252).
Perth—Balmousie Street, Perth. Courts: AW4. Secretary: Mrs C Sinclair, 23 Florence Place, Perth (21964).
Pittenweem—Courts: H3. *Secretary:* Mrs M Wilson., Crawhill, Anstruther (310356).
St Andrews—*Secretary:* Mrs L E Leith, 25 Canongate, St Andrews (74309).
St Andrew's University—Courts: H5. *Secretary:* Miss C Gray, Knockhill of Nydie House, St Andrews (Anstruther).
Scone—Courts: H3. *Secretary:* D D Gibson, 27 Douglas Road, Scone, Perth.
Stobsmuir—*Secretary:* D Duncan, 34 Baldovan Terrace, Dundee (451198).
Tayport—Courts: AW3. *Secretary:* Miss S Donald, 8 Greenside Place, Tayport (552398).
West End—*Secretary:* N Stewart, 15 Victoria Road, West Ferry (Dundee 79566).
Wormit—Bay Road, Wormit, Fife. Courts: AW3. *Secretary:* Miss W Irons, 6 Craigshannoch Road, Wormit, Newport-on-Tay (541646).

CENTRAL DISTRICTS LAWN TENNIS ASSOCIATION

Hon Secretary—**J Nicol,** 17 Wellside Place, Falkirk (25210/21520 bus, 24842 pri).
Hon Treasurer—**C Smith,** Westwood, 7 Randolph Terrace, Stirling (61147).
Hon Match Secretary—**P Kelly,** 17 Halberts Crescent, St Ninians, Stirling (811594 pri, 3141 bus).

Auchterarder—Mrs S McDougall, 'Lynburn,' Ruthven Street, Auchterarder (2189).
Bridge of Allan—Minewood Pavilion, Mine Road, Bridge of Allan (3456). Courts: H6. *Secretary:* Mr N Chell, 2 Stanley Drive, Bridge of Allan (832799).
British Petroleum—Little Kerse, Grange Road, Grangemouth (483147). Courts: H3. *Secretary: J Scott, 211 Bo'ness Road, Grangemouth (485047 pri, 483422 ext 6506 bus).*
Castings—Glynwed Social & Sports Club, Etna Road, Falkirk (23738). Courts: H3. *Secretary:* J Mitchell, 182 Windsor Road, Falkirk (21647 pri, Larbert 554221 bus).
DCL—Courts: H2. *Secretary:* Mrs J Collier, 26 Middleton.
Dollar—Courts: H3. *Secretary:* Mrs E Houston, Old West Manse, Dollar (2904).
Dunblane—Courts: H4. *Secretary:* J Lees, McLean & Stewart, Solicitors, 51 High Street, Dunblane (823217 bus, 822928 bus).
Falkirk—Hamilton Drive, Falkirk. Courts: H3. *Secretary:* R D Webster, 6 Rennie Street, Falkirk (21349 pri, 22922 bus).
High Valleyfield—Courts: H2. *Secretary:* R Philp, 85 Dunimarle Street, High Valleyfield, Fife (Newmills 880935).
Killearn—Courts: AW3. *Secretary:* Mrs A Lockhead, 33 Lampson Road, Killearn (50873 pri, 041 221 4621 bus).

Linlithgow—Leatore Youth Hostel, Boghall, Linlithgow. Courts: H3. *Secretary:* I Wilkie, 131 Baronshill Avenue, Linlithgow (844431 pri, 031 229 9292 ext 3401 bus).
Livilands—Randolph Road, Stirling. Courts: H3. *Secretary:* P Kelly, 17 Halberts Crescent, Stirling (822594 pri, 73141 bus).
Patons and Baldwins—*Secretary:* A Cousins, 7 Alexandra Drive, Alloa (212352 pri, 214331 bus).
Stirling (Laurelhill)—Laurelhall Place, Stirling. Courts: H3. *Secretary:* L Taggart, 30 Snowdon Place, Stirling (72151).
Strathblane—*Secretary:* Miss F Maclean, 12 Southview Drive, Blanefield (70919 pri, 041 776 5141 ext 46 bus).
University of Stirling—Courts: H4. *Secretary:* R. Witherington, c/o The Gannochy, University of Stirling (61029).

EAST OF SCOTLAND LAWN TENNIS ASSOCIATION

Hon Secretary—**Mrs J O Stewart,** 18 Meadowbank Terrace, Edinburgh EH8 (031 661 3776).
Hon Treasurer—**I E Hastie,** 37 Comiston Drive, Edinburgh EH10 5QS (031 447 4533).
Hon Match Secretary—**J C Paterson,** 22 Buckstone Loan, Edinburgh EH10 6UE (031 445 3362).

Abercorn—Abercorn Crescent, Edinburgh (031 661 1952). Courts: H5. *Secretary:* J W Kerr, 8 Fettes Row, Edinburgh (031 557 3128).
Aberdour—Courts: AW3. *Secretary:* Mrs S Travers, 10 McLauchlan Rise, Aberdour (0383 860044).
Barnton Park—12 Barnton Park, Edinburgh. Courts: H4. *Secretary:* Mrs C Sinclair, 5 Barnton Gardens, Edinburgh EH4 6AF (031 336 2309).
Blackhall—Keith Terrace, Edinburgh. Courts: AW3. *Secretary:* Mrs M Smith, 16f Silverknowes View, Edinburgh (031 336 5005).
Bonnyrigg & Lasswade—Flindean Place, Bonnyrigg. Courts: H3. *Secretary:* G Scott, 1 Broomieknowe Park, Bonnyrigg (031 663 7477).
Braid—Cluny Gardens, Edinburgh. Courts: H3. *Secretary:* I Hastie, 37 Comiston Drive, Edinburgh (031 447 4533).
Brucehaven—Dunfermline Road, Limekilns, Fife. Courts: H2. *Secretary:* Margaret Arnott, 18 North Loanhead, Limekilns, Fife (872785).
Colinton—Westgarth Avenue, Colinton (031441 1051). Courts: H6. *Secretary:* N Mair, 15 Dreghorn Loan, Edinburgh (031 441 2061).
Corstorphine—Belgrave Road, Edinburgh. Courts: H3. *Secretary:* Mrs B Norrish, 3 Glebe Grove, Edinburgh EH12 7SH (031 334 1640).
Craigmillar Park—Courts: AW4. *Secretary:* Mrs A Thomson, 12 Esslemont Road, Edinburgh (031 667 6714).
Dean—Lennox Street, Edinburgh 4. Courts: H4. *Secretary:* B Thomson, 36 Inverleith Place, Edinburgh EH3 5QB (031 552 2949).
Drummond—Scotland Street Lane, Edinburgh 7. Courts: H2. *Secretary:* G S Bailey, 36 Beresford Gardens, Edinburgh EH4 (031 552 9452 pri, 031 333 3341 bus).
Dunfermline—Courts: H4. *Secretary:* Miss E Davison, 4 Old Kirk Place, Dunfermline.
Dunfermline College of Physcial Education—Crammond Road North, Crammond, Edinburgh EH4 6JD (031 336 5018). Courts: H12, AW4, Indoor 1. *Secretary:* Miss A Irvine, DCPE, Cramond Road North, Edinburgh EH4 6JD (031 836 5041 room 163).
Dyvours—Portgower Place, Edinburgh. Courts: H2, G3. *Secretary:* D M Smith, 21 Corbiehill Road, Edinburgh EH4 5EB (031 336 4086 pri, 031 655 6279 bus).
Gullane—*Secretary:* Mrs E Burley, Mayfield, East Links Road, Gullane (0620 84227).
Hatton—Courts: H3. *Secretary:* Miss P Saddler, 28 Baberton Mains Row, Edinburgh (031 442 1625).
Kirkcaldy—Bogily Road, Kirkcaldy. Courts: H5. *Secretary:* Mrs M B Hall, 2 East Fergus Place, Kirkcaldy (0592 260297).
Kirton Park—Bathgate. Courts: H3. *Secretary:* Mrs J Cosgrove, 11 Linefield Crescent, Bathgate (51 56153).
Lomond Park—Lennox Row, Trinity, Edinburgh 5. Courts: H5. *Secretary:* Miss S Anderson, 9 Bonnington Grove, Edinburgh (031 554 3058).
Merchiston—Polworth Terrace, Edinburgh. Courts: H3. *Secretary:* Mrs A Cockburn, 42 Craiglockhart Terrace, Edinburgh (031 443 8962).
Middleton Hall—Uphall, West Lothian. Courts: H2. *Secretary:* Mrs E Thomson, 33 Tippet Knowes Road, Winchburgh (890177).
Mortonhall—Pentland Terrace, Edinburgh. Courts: AW5. *Secretary:* Mrs J Short, 27 Lygon Road, Edinburgh (031 667 8907).
Murrayfield—Courts: H4. *Secretary:* Mrs K Robertson, 87 Corstorphine Road, Edinburgh 12 5QE (031 337 3772 pri, 031 225 2552 ext 3556 bus).
St Leonards—St Leonards Playing Fields, Dunfermline. Courts: H2. *Secretary:* J Sumpter, 23 Linburn Road, Dunfermline KY11 4LJ (0383 722119).
St Serf's—Clark Road, Edinburgh. Courts: AW3. *Secretary:* Miss A E Beattie, 11 Bonnington Grove, Edinburgh (031 553 4976 pri, 031 225 6311 bus).
Thistle—Craiglockhart Centre, Colinton Road, Edinburgh. Courts: H7. *Secretary:* Miss S M McNeil, 18 Woodhall Terrace, Juniper Green, Edinburgh (031 453 4129).
University of Edinburgh King's Buildings, West Mains Road. Courts: H4. *Secretary:* —C Stewart, 32 Stafford Street, Edinburgh (031 225 7965).
Waverley—Suffolk Road, Edinburgh (031 667 9517). Courts: H4. *Secretary:* MrsK Tulloch, 3 Seaview Terrace, Edinburgh (031 669 6926).

BORDERS LAWN TENNIS ASSOCIATION

Hon Secretary—**D Hodgson,** The Old School House, Tilmouth, Cornhill-on-Tweed (0890 2463).
Hon Treasurer—**J Henderson,** The Bield, Crailing, Jedburgh (0835 5212).
Hon Ladies' Match Secretary—**Mrs E Beeby,**

Ingleside, Buccleuch Road, Hawick (72078).
Hon Men's Match Secretary—**M Anderson,** 24b Damdale, Peebles (21745).
Junior Match Secretary—**W Gordon,** 2 Channel Street, Galashiels.

Duns—Courts: AW2. *Secretary:* Mrs N Young, 50 Berrywell Drive, Duns (83542).
Earlston—Courts: AW2, H1. *Secretary:* Mrs S Whiteford, 3 Westfield Street, Earlston (301).
Galashiels—Courts: H4. *Secretary:* Mrs T Renwick, Mill Cottage, Annay Road, Melrose (2557).
Hawick—Buccleuch Park, Hawick. Courts: AW3. *Secretary:* Mrs E Beeby, Ingleside, Buccleuch Road, Hawick (72078).
Innerleithen—Courts: AW2. *Secretary:* Mrs D Welsh, 6 Hall Street, Innerleithen (830412).
Jedburgh—Courts: H2. *Secretary:* Mrs G Hall, 4 Main Street, Meiton (Roxburgh 205).
Kelso Orchard—Poynder Place, Kelso. Courts: H2. *Secretary:* A Anderson, Maxwellheugh Cottage, Kelso (24753).
Lauder—Courts: H2. *Secretary:* Mrs L Runciman, Upperboon, Lauder (337).
Lennel—Swinton Road, Coldstream. Courts: AW2. *Secretary:* T Hodgson, The Old School House, Tillmouth, Cornhill-on-Tweed, Northumberland (0890 2463).
Peebles—Glen Road, Peebles. Courts: H3, AW2. *Secretary:* I Tait, Dunderave, Innerleithen Road, Peebles (20763).
St Boswells—Courts: H2. *Secretary:* Mrs J McNab, Invercraig, Springfield Terrace, St Boswells (22274).
Selkirk—Back Row, Selkirk. Courts: H2, AW2. *Secretary:* T Welsh, 29 Hillside Terrace, Selkirk (20401).
Wilton Park—Wilton Lodge Park, Hawick. Courts: H6. *Secretary:* Mrs M Elliot, 4 Crumhaugh Hill Road, Hawick TD9 0BX (73433).

WEST OF SCOTLAND LAWN TENNIS ASSOCIATION

Hon Secretary and Treasurer—**J Y Crawford,** 14 Kirkburn Road, Strathblane, Stirling (0360 70747).
Hon Ladies Match Secretary—**Miss C A Lindsay,** 66 Webster Road, Mount Vernon, Glasgow (041 778 3075).
Hon Men's Match Secretary—**R S Paterson,** 40 Cedarwood Avenue, Newton Mearns, Renfrewshire (041 639 5323 pri, 041 639 5323 pri, 041 424 4040 bus).

Anchor Linton—Linwood Sports Centre, Brediland Road, Linwood (Johnstone 31233). Courts: H4. *Secretary:* Miss M Yorkston, 97 Tannadice Avenue, Glasgow G52 3OS (041 883 9626).
Anniesland—101 Helensburgh Drive, Glasgow (041 959 6564). Courts: H4. *Secretary:* D Y Simpson, 9 Northland Drive, Glasgow G14 (041 959 4574).
Ardgowan—Ardgowan Square, Greenock (0475 23418). Courts: H4. *Secretary:* D R George, 15 Robertson Street, Greenock (0475 83821 pri, 041 445 2351 bus).
Arthurlie—Courts: H3. *Secretary:* Mrs J K Walton, 79 Levern Crescent, Barrhead (041 881 1877).
Bardowie—Station Road, Bardowie By Milgavie. Courts: H2. *Secretary:* A White, 1a Boclair Crescent, Bearsden, Glasgow (041 943 0325).
Bearsden—Jubilee Gardens, Bearsden, Glasgow. Courts: H4. *Secretary:* Mrs M Laird, 21 Morven Road, Bearsden, Glasgow (041 942 0322).
Bishopbriggs—Balmuidy Road, Bishopriggs, Glasgow. Courts: H3. *Secretary:* Miss J Irvine, 71 Balmuidy Road, Bishopriggs (041 772 37607).
Bishopton—Poplar Avenue, Bishopton. Courts: H3. *Secretary:* Mrs M Nichol, 66 Stuart Road, Bishopton (863272).
Bridge of Weir—Gryfe Road, Bridge of Weir. Courts: H3. *Secretary:* L J Jolliffe, 15 Earl Place, Bridge of Weir (613357).
Brookfield—Brookfield Village Hall, Brookfield. Courts: H2. *Secretary:* J Ferguson, Stanley Drive, Brookfield (Johnstone 20428 pri, 041 221 3107 bus).
Broomhill—2 Mitre Road, Glasgow (041 334 2519). Courts: AW4. *Secretary:* R Whitesmith, 24 Cloan Crescent, Bishopbriggs (041 772 7316 pri, 041 558 0111 ext 222 bus).
Burnside—Burnside Road, Burnside, Rutherglen. Courts: AW3. *Secretary:* D Leonard, 1 Douglas Avenue, Burnside, Rutherglen (041 634 4800).
Busby—Carmunnock Road, Busby, Clarkston, Glasgow. Courts: H3. *Secretary:* Mrs C H Wills, 81 Beechlands Drive, Clarkston, Glasgow (041 639 4428).
Cambuslang—Courts: H4. *Secretary:* Mrs D Chesters, 49 Buchanan Drive, Cambuslang (041 641 2567).
Cardross—Church Avenue, Cardross. Courts: AW3. *Secretary:* Sandra Brown, 8 Barrs Road, Cardross (536).
Clarkston—East Woodmains Road, Clarkston (041 638 1155). Courts: H6. *Secretary:* Miss L McGhee, 4 Fereneze Avenue, Clarkston, Glasgow (041 638 4883).
CPC (UK) Ltd—Falside Road, Paisley (041 884 5111). Courts: H2. *Secretary:* R S Jackson, 20 Church Street, Lochwinnoch, Renfrewshire (Lochwinnoch 842851 pri, 041 884 5111 bus).
Craighelen—215 East Clyde Street, Helensburgh (5403). Courts: AW5. *Secretary:* Mrs T McDonald, 1 Mossend Avenue, Helensburgh (5605).
Mrs C Greensted, 10 East Argyle Street, Helensburgh.
Dowanhill—27 Dowandside Road, Glasgow G12 9DW. Courts: H1, AW3. *Secretary:* J Gilroy, 1/1, 61 Ferry Road, Glasgow (041 334 6411 pri, East Kilbride 43328 bus).
Drumchapel—1 Garscadden Road, Glasgow. Courts: H4. *Secretary:* G Connor, 75 Stanmore Road, Glasgow (041 632 3647 pri, 041 641 2071 bus).
Eaglesham—Cheapside Street, Eaglesham. Courts: H3. *Secretary:* A Gordon, 106 Alexander Avenue, Eaglesham, Renfrewshire (Eaglesham 2738).
East Kilbride—Strathaven Road, East Kilbride (36002). Courts: AW4. *Secretary:* E McMurtie, 14

Tulliallan Place, East Kilbride (32892).
Elderslie—Newton Drive, Elderslie. Courts: H4. *Secretary:* Mrs G Drury, 17 Lantine Road, Paisley (889 4512).
Ferguslie—Corsebar Road, Meikleriggs, Paisley. Courts: H7. *Secretary:* Mrs G Copeland, 12 Stanley Drive, Paisley (041 884 2666).
Fort Matilda—Newark Street, Greenock. Courts: H6. *Secretary:* I A Paterson, 46 Lyle Road, Greenock (0475 31940 pri, 041 221 6991 bus).
Giffnock—Percy Drive, Giffnock, Glasgow (041 638 7268). Courts: AW6. *Secretary:* Mrs J Carruthers, 8 Strathview Grove, Netherlee, Glasgow (041 637 6300).
Hamilton—Blacksburn Lane, Motherwell Road, Hamilton. Courts: AW4. *Secretary:* V Young, 2 Valance Tower, Regent Gate, Bothwell (Uddingston 817661 pri, 041 248 2700 bus).
Helensburgh—Courts: H6. *Secretary:* Mrs G Black, Letrault Farm, Aros Road, Rhu, Helensburgh (Rhu 820289).
Hillhead—Hughenden Road, Glasgow G12. Courts: H6. *Secretary:* P J Sommerville, 2 Queen Square, Glasgow G4 (041 423 0167 pri, 041 248 7070 ext 2307 bus).
Hillpark—Tinto Road, Glasgow G43 (041 637 8512). Courts: H4. *Secretary:* Mrs E C Dow, 55 Lambie Crescent, Glasgow G77 (639 5330 pri, Prestwick 77815 bus).
Hillington—Montrose Avenue, Hillington Estate, Glasgow. Courts: H4. *Secretary:* Mrs R Macrae, 1 Shiel Court, Barrhead (041 881 4308).
Jordanhill College of Education—Courts: H3. *Secretary:* D Morrison, Southbrae Drive, Glasgow (041 959 1232).
Kelvindale—90a Baronald Drive Glasgow G12 (041 334 2366). Courts: H3. *Secretary:* G Wollard, 28 Beaconsfield Road, Glasgow G12 (041 357 1172 pri, 041 0392 bus).
Kilmalcolm—Courts: H3. *Secretary:* Mrs N Adams, Ard Goil, Kilmalcolm, Renfrewshire (2691).
Kirkhill—32 Whitefield Avenue, Cambuslang, Glasgow. Courts: H4. *Secretary:* Mrs J Cumming, 6 Stewarton Drive, Cambuslang (641 3965).
Kirktonhill—Dixon Avenue, Dumbarton. Courts: H3. *Secretary:* Mrs S C Galbraith, 358 Main Street, Burnbrae, Alexandria (53563).
Lanark—Chapland Road, Lanark. Courts: H2. *Secretary:* I Hunter, 32 Carneuk Avenue, Carluke (0555 71930 pri, 0563 23105 bus).
Lenzie—Lindseybeg Road, Lenzie. Courts: H4. *Secretary:* Mrs L E Thompson, 3 Crawford Avenue, Lenzie (776 4379).
Milngavie & Bearsden—Auchenhowie Road, Milngavie, Glasgow (041 956 3817). Courts: H3, AW + . *Secretary:* R Reid, 9 Douglastown Gardens North, Milngavie, Glasgow.
Mount Vernon—Bowling Green Road, Mount Vernon, Glasgow G32. Courts: H3. *Secretary:* A Buchanan, 115 Wilton Street, Glasgow G20 (041 204 1051).
Newlands—Monreith Road, Newlands, Glasgow (041 632 1742). Courts: AW6. *Secretary:* C Kerr, c/o Newlands LTC (041 633 1286 pri, 041 649 2836 bus).
Oban—Courts: H5. *Secretary:* H McLean, Kildalton, Longsdale Road, Oban, Argyll (0631 63516 pri, 0631 72291 bus).
Paisley—South Avenue, Thornley Park, Paisley (041 884 2812). Courts: H4. *Secretary:* A C Morrison, 30 Stonefield Avenue, Paisley (041 884 2605).
Partickhill—Partickhill Road, Glasgow G11. Courts: H3. *Secretary:* P Dewar, 74 Chancellor Street, Glasgow G11. (041 334 6086 pri, 041 221 2516 bus).
Poloc—"Shawholm", 2026 Pollokshaws Road, Glasgow G43 1AT (041 632 0730). Courts: H6. *Secretary:* S Coom, c/o Poloc Tennis Club (041 429 3319 pri, 041 221 2731 bus).
Queen's Park—381 Langside Road, Glasgow G42 (041 423 0152). Courts: G3. *Secretary:* P de Cecco, 205 Ashcroft Drive, Glasgow (041 637 4746).
Rutherglen—Viewpark drive, Rutherglen, Glasgow. Courts: H4. *Secretary:* Mrs E Crawford, 32 Highburgh Drive, Rutherglen (647 3475).
Springwells—Motherwell Street, Airdrie. Courts: H2. *Secretary:* Mrs M Scobie, 14 Springwells Crescent, Airdrie (69518).
Stepps—Lenzie Road, Stepps, Glasgow G33 6BN. Courts: H3. *Secretary:* Mrs J Blue, 25 Lenzie Road, Stepps, Glasgow (041 779 2123).
Stamperland—Courts: H3. *Secretary:* Miss A Findley, 90 Nethervale Avenue, Netherlee, Glasgow (041 637 9198).
Stonehouse—Courts: H2. *Secretary:* Miss F McBain, 43 Brankston Avenue, Stonehouse (791879).
Strathaven—1 Crosshill Road, Strathaven, ML10 6EF. Courts: H2. *Secretary:* A Steele, 5 Ryeland Street, Strathaven (20559).
Strathclyde Police—Courts: H3. *Secretary:* R McDonald, 162 Fergus Drive, Glasgow (041 946 9684 pri, 041 445 1113 bus).
Thorn Park—Thorn Road, Bearsden, Glasgow (041 942 6645). Courts: H3. *Secretary:* Mrs C Beattie, 95 Allander Road, Bearsden (041 942 7625).
Titwood—Glencairn Gardens, Glasgow G41. Courts: H5. *Secretary:* Mrs S Armour, 59 Dixon Avenue, Glasgow (041 423 4161).
Uddingston—Old Glasgow Road, Uddington (814278). Courts: H4. *Secretary:* Miss S I Henry, 11 Clydebrae Drive, Bothwell (Uddington 852122).
Uplawmoor—Behind Mure Hall, Tannoch Road, Uplawmoor. Courts: H3. *Secretary:* J Scott, The Braes, Glen Lane, Uplawmoor (458).
Weir Recreation—Albert Park, Kintore Road, Glasgow G44. Courts: H4. *Secretary:* Mrs J Armour, 82 The Oval, Stamperland, Glasgow (041 637 9290 pri, 041 637 7141 ext 2818 bus).
Westermains—Woodland Avenue, Kirkintilloch. Courts: H3. *Secretary:* Miss G Siddons (041 776 3379 pri, 041 772 3210 bus).
Western—30 Hyndland Road, Glasgow (041 339 0065). Courts: 6. *Secretary:* E McGregor, 11 Campsie Drive, Bearsden (041 942 4243).
Westerton—Westerton, Bearsden, Glasgow. Courts: H3. *Secretary:* Mrs V Robertson, 63 Maxwell Avenue, Westerton, Bearsden, Glasgow (041 942 3294).

Whitecraigs—22 Roddinghead Road, Whitcraigs, Giffnock, Glasgow (041 639 2744). Courts: H3. *Secretary:* J B G Harvey, 12 Greenhill Avenue, Giffnock (041 638 6119 pri, 041 221 6876 bus).
Wishaw—Courts: H4. *Secretary:* Mrs J M Brown, 16 Coronation Street, Wishaw (0698 384391 pri, 0698 832195 bus).
Woodend—10 Chamberlain Road, Glasgow G13 1QE (041 959 1428). Courts: H3, AW4. *Secretary:* G S Ross, 199 Westland Drive, Glasgow G14 (041 959 6469).
Yarrow—Courts: H2. *Secretary:* N McIver, 182 Sunnyside Drive, Glasgow G15.

SOUTH WEST OF SCOTLAND LAWN TENNIS ASSOCIATION

Hon Secretary—**G Legg,** Kirkbank, Glenlochar, Castle Douglas (Crossmichael 218).
Hon Treasurer—**D Williamson,** 18 Queen Elizabeth Drive, Castle Douglas (3149).
Hon Match Secretary—**W Kirkwood,** 14 Charles Street, Annan (Annan 2762).

Beechgrove—Beechgrove Grounds, Beechgrove, Moffat. Courts: H6. *Secretary:* Mrs M Little, Laurel Bank, Beechgrove, Moffat (20855).
Castle Douglas—Club Pavilion, Lochside Park, Castle Douglas. Courts: AW2. *Secretary:* G Laing, 33 St Andrew Drive, Castle Douglas (3149).
Crichton Royal—Campbell House, Crichton Royal, Dumfries. Courts: AW4. *Secretary:* Miss N Gibson, Rosedale Kennels, Racks Road, Dumfries (Collin 678).
Dalbeattie—Courts: AW3. *Secretary:* Miss E Taylor, Edenholme Farm, Dalbeattie (610397).
Dumfries College of Technology—Heathhall, Dumfries. Courts: H4. *Secretary:* Miss B Lochhead, 4 Montague Street, Dumfries.
Garlieston—Courts: AW2. *Secretary:* Mrs E M McCreath, Garlieston Home Farm, Garlieston (267).
Lockerbie—Courts: AW2. *Secretary:* R S Varrie, 19 Lambhill Terrace, Lockerbie (3738).
Nunholm, Dumfries—Courts: H4. *Secretary:* Mrs B Tingley, "Overoon", Dunscore (9782 308).
Seaforth—*Secretary:* Mrs M Macrae, "Shawhill", Annan (2638).
Thornhill—Courts: H2. *Secretary:* Mrs E Irving, Ventuno, 21 West Morton Street, Thornhill (30567).

AYRSHIRE LAWN TENNIS ASSOCIATION

Hon Secretary—**Mrs J B Kennedy,** 27 Forehill Road, Ayr (0292 266553).
Hon Treasurer—**J B Clark,** 12 Ronaldshaw Park, Ayr (0292 264249).
Ladies Match Secretary—**Mrs E M Clark,** 12 Ronaldshaw Park, Ayr (0292 264249).
Men's Match Secretary—**A J Todd,** 17 Corsehill Park, Ayr (0292 267366 pri, Girvan 2591).

Ayr—Southpark Road, Ayr. Courts: H3. *Secretary:* Mrs N McCrossin, 1 Baird Road, Alloway, Ayr (0292 41422).
Beith—Public Park, Beith. Courts: AW3. *Secretary:* Miss S McKerracher, 76 Eginton Street, Beith (4237).
Carrick—Ballantyne Drive, Ayr. Courts: H4. *Secretary:* Mrs S Anderson, 12 Ballantyne Drive, Ayr (0292 265220).
Coylton—Hole Road, Coylton. Courts: AW2. *Secretary:* J Turner, 17b Hillhead, Coylton (Joppa 507).
Darvel—Gowanbank, Darvel. Courts: H2. *Secretary:* B Luna, 18 Brown Street, Newmilns.
Fairlie—Recreation Ground, Fairlie. Courts: H2, AW1. *Secretary:* Mrs A Ellor, 'Coironan', Main Road, Fairlie.
Kilmarnock—London Road, Kilmarnock. Courts: H4. *Secretary:* Mrs M Donn, 4 Howard Street, Kilmarnock.
Kilmaurs—The School, Kilmaurs. Courts: AW2. *Secretary:* Mrs S Lightbody, Garden Cottage, Tour Estate, Kilmaurs.
Skelmorlie—*Secretary:* The Crescent, Skelmorlie. Courts: H2. *Secretary:* Wm Shepherd, 34 Annetyard Drive, Skelmorlie.
Symington—The Park, Symington. Cours: AW3. *Secretary:* Mrs J Russell, Brewlands Farm, Symington.
Troon—5 Victoria Drive, Troon. Courts: AW6. *Secretary:* Mrs J McDonald, 55 Gailes Road, Troon (311541).
West Kilbride—Nethermiln, West Kilbride. Courts: H4. *Secretary:* R Mottram, 14a Meadowfoot Road, West Kilbride.

WELSH LAWN TENNIS ASSOCIATION

Hon Secretary—**W F G Brunsdon,** 65 Heol-y-Gors, Whitchurch, Cardiff (Cardiff 628241).
Hon Treasurer—**E Garth Jones,** MA, c/o Lloyds Bank Ltd, Windsor Road, Penarth, South Glamorgan (Penarth 705621).
Hon Men's Match Secretary—**J W D Greatrex,** 81 Cardiff Road, Dinas Powis, South Glamorgan (Dinas Powis 512320).
Hon Ladies' Match Secretary—**Mrs A N Beames,** Penylan Cottage, Ty Gwyn Avenue, Penylan, Cardiff (486485).
Junior Match Secretary—**W F G Brunsdon,** WLTA Office, National Sports Centre for Wales, Sophia Gardens, Cardiff (371838).
Representatives on the Council—**W F G Brunsdon, J W D Greatrex.**
Number of Affiliated Clubs 101
Number of Affiliated Schools 149

SOUTH WALES LAWN TENNIS ASSOCIATION

Hon Secretary—**D F Ward,** 32 Chargot Road, Llandaff, Cardiff, S Glam. (Cardiff 564998).
Hon Treasurer—**A G J Jones,** 19 Maesygwernen Close, Morriston, Swansea, West Glamorgan (Swansea 72099).
Hon Men's Match Secretary—**Commander G M Lloyd RM (Retd),** "Greystones", 2 Lan Park Road, Pontypridd, M. Glamorgan CF37 2DH (0443 402904).
Hon Ladies' Match Secretary—**Mrs A N Beames,** Penylan Cottage, Ty Gwyn Avenue, Penylan, Cardiff (486485).
Junior Match Secretary—**R West,** 44 Clydach Road, Craig Cefn Parc, Swansea, West Glamorgan (Swansea 843667).

AFFILIATED CLUBS

Aberaeron—Courts: H2. Secretary: W J A Bowen, Rhydaeron, Aberaeron SA46 0DP (Aberaeron 570272).
Abergavenny LTC—Courts: AW2, S2. *Secretary:* D C B Bissett, 25 Belgrave Road, Abergavenny, Gwent (Abergavenny 6858).
Aberystwyth—Courts: AW2, H1. *Secretary:* Mrs C Hughes, 3 Caemawr, Penrhyncoch, Aberystwyth (828401).
Allt-yr-yn LTC—Courts: AW3, S3, G8. Mrs M Evans, 'Glanant,' 17 Caerphilly Close, Rhiwderin, Newport, Gwent (Newport 893070).
Barry Athletic—Courts: AW4, G2. *Secretary:* A Smith, 4 Joseph Parry Close, Llandough Pannard CF6 1PL.
Beddau—Secretary: L Sims, 15 The Parade, Church Village, Pontypridd.
BP (Llandarcy) Club (Tennis Section)—Courts: H3. *Secretary:* W Thomas, 14 Ridgwood Gardens, Afan Valley Road, Cimla, Neath, West Glamorgan (Briton Ferry 812341 ext 6227 bus).
Bridgend—Merthymawr Road, Bridgend. Courts: AW6, G4 (2 floodlit). *Secretary:* P Caddy, 50 Quarella Road, Bridgend CF31 1JN (58284).
British Airways Speedbird Club Tennis Section—Courts: AW2. *Secretary:* Malcolm Jones, 17 The Paddocks, Upper Church Village, nr Pontypridd (Newtown Llantwit 204000).
British Steel Corporation Margam Works—Courts: H4. *Secretary:* Mrs M Davies, 1 Beechwood Road, Margam, Port Talbot (Port Talbot 884429).
Caerphilly—Courts: AW3. *Secretary:* Mrs V Emment, 22 Narberth Court, Hendredenny, Caerphilly, Mid Glamorgan (Cardiff 861309).
Cardiff AC—Courts: AW4, G3. *Secretary:* Julian Greenwood, 14 Clos Mabon, Ribiwbina, Cardiff, S Glam (Cardiff 692378 pri, Pontypridd 408331 bus).
Cardiff—Courts: AW8, G3 (2 floodlit). Castle Grounds, North Road, Cardiff. *Secretary:* Mrs G Richards, 109 Penlan Road, Llandough, Penarth (707951).
Cardigan Tennis Club—Courts: H4. *Secretary:* B J Lee, Highlands, Sarnau, Llandysul, Dyfed (Llangranog 445).
Carmarthen LTC—Courts: AW3. *Secretary:* J Davies, 2 Cwmoernant, Carmarthen, Dyfed SA31 1EG.
Chepstow Athletic—Courts: H3. *Secretary:* I Wood, 3 Meadow Lane, Mounton Road, Chepstow, Gwent.
Cowbridge & District—Courts: AW3. *Secretary:* J Legg, 12 Geraints Close, Cowbridge CF7 7BT (3797).
Creigiau—Courts: AW3. *Secretary:* H Drake, "Blue Cedars", 29 Pen-y-Groes, Groespaen, Pontyclun, M. Glamorgan CF7 8PA (Pentyrch 891275).
Cwmtawe—Courts: H3. *Secretary:* R West, 44 Clydach Road, Craig Cefn Parc, Swansea (Llanelli 757031 bus, Swansea 843667 pri).
Dinas Powis—The Common, St Andrews Road, Dinas Powis, South Glamorgan. *Fixture Secretary:* Mrs A Rankin, 22 Windy Ridge, Dinas Powis, S Glam (0222-513435). Courts: AW3, S6, G3 (2 floodlit). Secretary: Mrs J Bransfield, 7 Tenby Close, Dinas Powis (514501).
Firbank Dale LTC—Heather Road, Newport. Courts: G4. *Secretary:* M Singleton, "Niruana", Pentre Lane, Llantrisant, Cwmbran, Gwent (06333 2236).
Garw Valley—Courts: H3. *Secretary:* Elfyn George, 1 Treharne Drive, Penyfai, Bridgend (Aberkenfig 721196).
Gilfach Welfare—Courts: H3. *Secretary:* M Fortune, 68 West Street, Bargoed CF8 8SA (Pontypridd 405171 ext 55).
Glamorgan LT & Croquet Club—Courts: H3, G3. *Secretary:* M. Dudley-Jones, Keepers Cottage, Merthyr Mawr, Bridgend, Mid Glamorgan.
Glyn Neath LTC—*Secretary:* Mrs M Morgan, Hendrewyddil Farm, Glynneath, West Glamorgan (Glynneath 720431).
Haverfordwest—Courts: AW4, S2. *Secretary:* Mrs M R Carter, 74 Waterloo Road, Hakin, Milford Haven, Dyfed (4703 pri, 3272 bus).

ICI Fibres Ltd—Courts: S6. *Secretary:* Mrs I Dodd, 23 Five Oaks Lane, Croesyceiliog, Cwmbran, Gwent NP4 2LS.
Kenfig Hill LTC—R Williams, 61a Cefn Road, Cefn Cribwr, nr Bridgend, Mid Glamorgan (740339).
Lisvane TC—*Secretary:* D D Lermon, Beech House, Cotswold Avenue, Lisvane, Cardiff (751017).
Llancarfan LTC—Courts: AW1. *Secretary:* Mrs P S Dodwell, Chapel House, Llancarfan, South Glamorgan.
Llandybie—Courts: AW3. *Secretary:* B L Thomas, 53 Ammanford Road, Llandybie, Ammanford, Dyfed (Amman Valley 2172 bus).
Llanelli—Courts: AW4, G9 (2 floodlit). *Secretary:* Miss J Barker, 'Greylands,' Pen-y-Bryn, Llanelli, Dyfed (Llangennech 820366).
Llanfrechfa Grange LTC—Courts: H2. *Secretary:* A D Clement, 9 Millbrook Court, Littlemill, Pontypool (543).
Llantrisant LTC—Courts: H2. *Secretary:* D Pitman, 5 Heol Mwyrdy, Yorkdale, Beddau, Mid Glamorgan.
Llantwit Major—Courts: AW3. *Secretary:* Mrs Joyce Morris, 6 Anglesey Close, Llantwit Major, South Glamorgan CF6 9GF (3807).
Mackintosh—Courts: AW1, H4. *Secretary:* Miss L Stephens, 226 Newport Road, Cardiff (486984).
Merthyr Tydfil Tennis Club—Courts: H3. *Secretary:* D V Baker, 248 Twyng Arael, Swansea Road, Merthyr Tydfil, M. Glamorgan CF48 (0685 6043).
Monmouthshire Croquet and Lawn Tennis—Courts: AW2, G6. *Secretary:* D Vaughan, 32 Monk Street, Abergavenny, Gwent (Raglan 690253).
Morriston—Courts: AW4, S2. *Secretary:* A L Windsor, 236 Birchgrove Road, Birchgrove, Swansea SA7 9JV (0792 815458).
Neath Borough—Courts: AW6. *Secretary:* D Evans, 20 Heol Glynderwen, Caewern, Neath, West Glamorgan (Neath 3385).
Newport Athletic—Rodney Road, Newport, Gwent. Courts: AW1, S3, G8. *Secretary:* K G Phillips, 39 Penylan Close, Bassaleg, Newport (894172).
Newport (Pembs) LTC—Courts: H2. *Secretary:* R W Atkinson, 'Llysmeddg,' Newport, Pembs SA42 0SY.
Panteg House LTC—*Secretary:* S B Morgan, 18 Wainfelin Avenue, Wainfelin, Pontypool, Gwent.
Park (Whitchurch)—Courts: AW3, G3. *Secretary:* Parry Evans, 19 St Francis Road, Whitchurch, Cardiff (616644).
Penarth—Rectory Road, Penarth, South Glamorgan. Courts: AW3, G6. *Secretary:* Mrs Margaret Price, 17 Britten Road, Penarth CF6 2QJ (Penarth 707648).
Penarth-Windsor—Courts: S3, G3. *Secretary:* Mrs S V Seymour, 164 Westbourne Road, Penarth, S. Glam. CF6 2BQ (0222 703960).
Penclawdd T.C.—*Secretry:* P Hughes, 2 Tabernacle Terrace, West End, Penclawdd, Swansea, W. Glam. SA4 3YN.
Penllyne LTC—*Secretary:* Mrs W Dobson, 1 rear of Village Post Office, Penllyne, nr Cowbridge, South Glamorgan CF7 7RT.
Pentyrch Tennis Club—*Secretary:* I Batchelor, 39 Brynhaul, Pentyrch, nr Cardiff (891304).
Pontypridd LTC—Courts: H6, G3. *Secretary:* M Nicholls, 11 Glas Cwm, Coed-y-cwm, Pontypridd.
Penylan LTC—Courts: S3. *Secretary:* M G Jones, 32 North Rise, Uanishen, Cardiff (Cardiff 891304).
Peterston-s-Ely LTC—Courts: AW3. *Secretary:* Miss P Newman, 16 Hamilton Street, Cardiff CF1 9BP (383831).
Polytechnic of Wales—*Secretary:* Miss R Arrowsmith, Polytechnic of Wales, Buttrills Road, Barry (733101).
Radyr—Courts: AW2 H3, G3. *Secretary:* Mrs Dorothy Walker, Carreg Melin, 5 Bryn Derwen, Radyr, South Glamorgan (Radyr 842198).
Rhiwbina—Courts: AW7. *Secretary:* B Lien, 1 Brooklyn Close, Rhiwbina Hill, Cardiff CF4 6UT (617515).
Rhondda TC—Courts: H5. K Gillard, 'Sarin,' Maindy Crescent, Ton Pentre, M Glam (Tony Pandy 422587).
Risca TC—Courts: H10. Miss Gaynor Adams, Risca Leisure Centre, Pontymason Lane, Risca, Newport, Gwent (Newport 613983).
St Fagans—Courts: AW1, H2 (2 floodlit). *Secretary:* R Wallace, 26 Radnor Road, Canton, Cardiff, S Glam (43527).
St Pierre (Chepstow) TC—Courts: H2 (2 floodlit). *Secretary:* E Potter, Ridgeway, Llanfair Discoed, Chepstow, Gwent.
Six Bells—Courts: H2. *Secretary:* C Hill, 65 Gladstone Street, Abertillery, Gwent (Abertillery 212073).
South Gower Sports Club (Tennis Section)—Courts: H4. *Secretary:* Mrs D H Rosser, Highmead, Rhossili, nr Swansea (Rhossili 571).
South Glamorgan Institute of Higher Education TC—Courts: H8. Mr R Moore, SGIHE, Cyncoed Road, Cyncoed, Cardiff (755755).
South Pembs LTC—*Secretary:* G N Smith, Burnside, Morgans Hill, Pembroke, Dyfed.
Stow Park LTC—Courts: H3, S3 (2 floodlit). *Secretary:* S Smith, Stow Park LTC, Woodville Road, Newport, Gwent (Newport 62370).
Swansea Lawn Tennis and Squash Rackets Club—Courts: S6. *Secretary:* R Ambrose, 44 Caswell Road, Newton, Swansea.
Tredegar LTC—Courts: AW1. *Secretary:* M J Coakley, 31 Mafeking Terrace, Georgetown, Tredegar NP2 3LG (Tredgar 3301).
University of Wales, Aberystwyth—Courts: H3, S3, G3. The Hon Secretary: University College of Wales, Aberystwyth.
University of Wales Institute of Science and Technology (UWST)—*Secretary:* Ian Gerstein, 19 Penylan Road, Cardiff.
Usk LT & ATH Club—Courts: H2. M Bowles, 5 Church Street, Usk, Gwent.
Whitehead Sports—Courts: H1, G3. *Secretary:* K Arnold, 14 Queens Gardens, Magor, Gwent (Magor 880371).
Ystradgynlais LTC—Courts: H3. *Secretary:* R Gould, 8 Richmond Park, Ystradgwyn, Swansea SA9 1SG.

Ynystawe—Mrs M Jones, 43 Bwllfa Road, Ynystawe, nr Swansea, West Glamorgan.
Whitland LTC—Dion Jones, 'Powys,' Gilfach Hill, Lampeter Velfrey, Narberth, Dyfed (0834 83345).

SCHOOL ASSOCIATIONS

Glamorgan Schools Association—*Secretary:* Miss M Coghlan, Radyr Comprehensive School, Heol Isaf, Radyr, Cardiff (Cardiff 842059).
Pemrokeshire Secondary School LTA—*Secretary:* Mrs N E Hearn, The Scantlings, Thornton, Milford Haven, Dyfed.

SCHOOL CLUBS

Girls

Afon Taf High — Yew Street, Troedyrhiw. **Bedwellty Comprehensive Lower School** — New Tredegar. **Bettws Comprehensive School** — Bettws, Newport, Gwent. **Bishopston School** — Bishopston, Swansea. **Bryn Hafren** — Merthyr Dyfan Road, Barry. **Caerphilly Girls'** — Grammar School. **Cefn Hengoed** — Bonymaen, Swansea. **Cefn Saeson Comprehensive School** Neath. **Cowbridge High School. Dwr-y-Felin** — Cadoxton Road, Neath. **Dumbarton School** —Bryn-y-Nor Road, Swansea. **Emmanuel School** — Derwen Fawr, Swansea. **Ffynone High School** — 36 St James Crescent, Swansea. **Fitzalan High School** — Lawrenny Avenue, Leckwith, Cardiff. **Gowerton School** — Cecil Road, Gowerton, Swansea. **Greenhill Comprehensive** — Tenby, Dyfed. **Howells School** — Llandaff, Cardiff. **Lewis Girls' Comprehenive School** —Oakfield Street, Ystrad Mynach. **Llangatwg School** — Llangatwg, Neath. **Llanishen High School** — Heol Hir, Llanishen, Cardiff. **Monmouth School for Girls. Morriston School** — Morriston, Swansea. **Neath Girls' Grammar School. Newcastle Emlyn Secondary School** — Newcastle Emlyn. **Newport High School for Girls. Pen-y-Dre High School** — Gurnos Estate, Merthyr Tydfil. **Pen-yr-Heol School** Pen-yr-Heol, Gorseinon, Swansea. **Pontypool Grammar School for Girls** — Pontypool, Gwent. **Pontypridd Grammar School for Girls** — Treforest, Pontypridd. **Sandfields School** — Sandfield, Port Talbot. **St. Clare's Convent School** — Porthcawl. **St. Joseph's RC Comprehensive School** — Port Talbot. **Whitchurch Comprehensive** — Whitchurch, Cardiff. **Ystal-y-Fera School** — Ystal-y-Fera, Swansea.

Boys

Barry Boys Comprehensive School — Port Road West, Barry. **Crickhowell High School** — Crickhowell. **Jones West Monmouth School** — Pontypool. **Llandovery College** — Llandovery. **Lewis Boys' Comprehensive School** — Pengam, Blackwood. **Milford Central School** — North Road, Milford Haven. **Monmouth School** — Monmouth. **Neath Grammar School** — Neath. **St. Illtyd's College** — Rumney, Cardiff. **YsgolGyfun,** Llanhari. **Pontyclun,** Nr Bridgend.

CO-EDUCATIONAL

Aberaeron Comprehensive School Aberaeron. **Bassaleg School** — Newport, Gwent. **Bettws Comprehensive School** — Newport. **Bishop Hannon School** — Beechley Drive, Pentrebane, Cardiff. **Bishop of Llandaff Church in Wales School** — Llandaff, Cardiff. **Bishop Gore Comprehensive School** — Swansea. **Bishop Vaughan Comprehensive School** — Mynydd Garnlwyd Road, Morriston, Swansea. **Brynmawr Comprehensive School** — Brynmawr, Gwent. **Bryncelynnog Comprehensive School** — Beddau. **Brynteg Comprehensive School** — Ewenny Road, Bridgend. **Cantonian High School** — Fairwater Road, Cardiff. **Cardiff High School** — Llandennis Road, Cardiff. **Cardigan Comprehensive School** — Cardigan. **Chepstow Comprehensive School** — Chepstow, Gwent. **Coed-y-Lan Comprehensive School** — Pontypridd. **Croesyceiliog Comprehensive School** — Croesyceiliog, Gwent. **Cwmtawe Comprehensive School** — Pontardawe, Swansea. **Duffryn High School** — Newport. **Dwr-y-Felin Comprehensive School** — Neath. **Ferndale Comprehensive School** — rear Excelsior Terrace, Maerdy. **Hawthorn Comprehensive School** — School Lane, Hawthorn. **Howardian High School** — Hampton Court Road, Penylan, Cardiff. **Jones West Monmouth School** — Pontypool. **King Henry VIII Comprehensive School** — Abergavenny. **Lampeter Comprehensive School** — Lampeter. **Lady Mary High School** — Cyncoed Road, Cyncoed, Cardiff. **Lliswerry Comprehensive School** — Lliswerry, Newport. **Llandyssul Grammar School** — Llandyssul. **Maesteg Comprehensive School** — School Road, Maesteg. **Milford Grammar School** — Steynton Road, Milford Haven. **Mostyn RC High School** — Caerau Lane, Wenvoe, South Glam. **Mid-Rhondda Comprehensive School** — Tonypandy. **Ogmore Comprehensive School** — Fairy Glen, Ogmore Vale. **Olchfa Comprehensive School** — Swansea. **Pencoed Comprehensive School** — Coychurch Road, Pencoed. **Pembroke Comprehensive School** — Pembroke. **Porth Comprehensive School** — Cemetery Road, Porth. **Pontllanfraith Comprehensive School** — Pontllanfraith, Gwent. **Penglais Comprehensive School** — Aberystwyth. **Penweddig Comprehensive School** — Aberystwyth. **Queen's Comprehensive School** — Queen's Hill, Newport, Gwent. **Radyr Comprehensive School** — Radyr, South Glam. **Reformed Presbyterian Church School** — Cardiff. **Risca Comprehensive School** — Risca, Gwent. **Rumney High School** — Newport Road, Cardiff. **Rhyd-y-Felin Comprehensive School** — Ynys Terrace, Rhyd-y-Felin, Pontypridd. **Stanwell Comprehensive School** — Archer Road, Penarth. **St. Cyres High School** — St Cyres Road, Penarth. **St Ilan Comprehensive School** — Pontygwandy Road, Caerphilly. **Sir Thomas Picton School** — Prendergast, Haverfordwest. **St. Martin's Comprehensive School** — Hillside, Caerphilly. **Tasker Milward School** — Portfield,

Haverfordwest. **Tonyrefail Comprehensive School** — Tonyrefail. **Tregaron Comprehensive School** — Tregaron. **Upper Rhondda Comprehensive School** — Treorchy. **Vaynor and Penderyn School** — Cefn Coed, Merthyr Tydfil. **Willows High School** — Willows Avenue, Tremorfa, Cardiff. **Ynysawdre Comprehensive School** — Tondu, Bridgend. **Ysgol Cyfun Penweddig** — St David's Road, Aberstwyth. **Y Pant Comprehensive School** — Pontyclun, Llantrisant.

All correspondence to School Clubs should be addressed to the Master or Mistress in charge of Lawn Tennis.

MID-WALES LAWN TENNIS ASSOCIATION

Hon Secretary—**P. Rowe,** Kenday House, Church Street, Rhayader, Powys (Llandrindod Wells 4178).
Hon Treasurer—**J A H Humphreys,** Plasy-yn-Dre, Church Street, Rhayader, Powys (0597 810502).

AFFILIATED CLUBS

Llandrindod Wells LTC—*Secretary:* H W Hutchins, 23 Oaklands, Builth Wells, Powys (553033).
Llanidloes LTC—*Secretary:* Mrs G Jones, Sunningdale, Bryndu Road, Llanidloes, Powys (3127).
Newtown LTC—*Secretary:* Mrs C Badger, 7 Dysart Terrace, Newtown, Powys (25221).
Rhayader LTC—*Secretary: Miss J Bates, Nantgwyn, East Street, Rhayader, Powys (810396).*

SCHOOL CLUBS

Boys

Christ College — Brecon.

Co-Educational

Maesydderwen CS — Ystradgynlais, Powys. **Brecon High School** — Brecon, Powys. **Builth High School** — Builth Wells, Powys. **Llandrindod Wells High School** — Llandrindod Wells, Powys. **John Beddoes** — Presteigne, Powys. **Newtown High School** — Newtown, Powys. **Welshpool High School** — Welshpool, Powys. **Llanfyllin High School** — Llanfyllin, Powys. **Llanfair High School** — Llanfair, Caereinion, Powys.

NORTH WALES LAWN TENNIS ASSOCIATION

Hon Secretary—**C J Rudkin,** 19 Ffordd Derwyn, Penyffordd, Chester CH4 0JT (Buckley 544258).
Hon Treasurer—**A A Goodall,** 29 Bryntirion Drive, Prestatyn, Clwyd (7010).
Hon Men's Match Secretary—**G C Roberts,** Tamworth House, Garden Court, Garden Village, Wrexham, Clwyd (262662 pri, 265383 bus).
Hon Ladies' Match Secretary—**Miss I Wakefield,** Winston, 404 Abergele Road, Old Colwyn, Clwyd (Colwyn Bay 515705/515880).
Junior Match Secretary—**L Aby,** 6 Heol Dinas, Wrexham, Clwyd.
Hon Junior Girls Match Secretary—**G Jones,** Perdaylan, Black Lane, Pentic, Broughton, Wrexham, Clwyd (Wrexham 755953).
Hon Junior County Secretary—**I D Jones,** 25 Glyn Avenue, Wrexham, Clwyd (Wrexham 262202).

AFFILIATED ASSOCIATIONS

Gwynedd LTA—*Secretary:* G Cowell, 85 Gladstone Terrace, Bangor, Gwynedd (Bangor 362655).
(Anglesey, Caernarvonshire and Merionethshire). (Affiliated Clubs marked*)
Clwyd LTA—*Secretary:* R D Moore, 13 Roseway, Burton, Rossett, Wrexham (Rossett 570839). (Affiliated clubs marked**)

AFFILIATED CLUBS

****Bangor**—*Secretary:* Mrs C Cox, 1 Maes Awel, Llandegfan, Menai Bridge, Anglesey, Gwynedd (Menai Bridge 712818).
Bangor Normal College—*Secretary Tennis:* George Site, Menai Bridge Road, Bangor.
****Brymbo Steel Works**—*Secretary:* T Capper, Bryncelyn, Wrexham Road, Brynteg, Wrexham (Wrexham 756423).
Caernarfon—Courts: H4. *Secretary:* R W Jones, 9 Segontium Terrace, Caernarfon.
Corwen LTC—Courts: AW2. *Secretary:* Mrs C Roberts, Arwelfa, The Crescent, Corwen, Clwyd.
Criccieth—Courts: AW2, G4. *Secretary:* Mrs L Keane, 'Wern Ddu,' Criccieth Terrace, Gwynedd (Criccieth 2050).
****Deeside Leisure Centre**—Courts: AW2. *Secretary:* Mrs J Coppack, 49 Aston Park Road, Queensferry, Deeside, Clwyd (818373).
****Denbigh**—Courts: G4. *Secretary:* Miss M Williams, 85 Vale Street, Denbigh.
Holyhead—Courts: AW3, H3. *Secretary:* J E Boylin, 76 Market Street, Holyhead, Gwynedd (Holyhead 2229).
Hope & Penyffordd—Courts: S3. *Secretary:* Mrs D Wright, Somerset Cottage, Chester Road, Pennyffordd, Chester.
****Llangefni**—Courts: H2. *Secretary:* Mrs P Philimore, Bodrwyn Bach, Cerrigeinwen, Bodorgan, Anglesey, Gwynedd (0407 613067).
Llangollen LTC—*Secretary:* Mrs E Davie, White Mart, Pentre Dwr, Llangollen, Clwyd (860003).
****Llanrwst**—*Secretary:* J P Howarth, Westwood, Llanddoget Road, Llanwrst, Gwynedd.
****Mold**—Courts: H4. *Secretary:* R Atherton, 87 Moorcroft, New Brighton, Mold, Clwyd (57850).
****Penrhyn Bay**—Courts: S2. *Secretary:* G K Williams, 'Beech Mount,' Penrhynisaf Road, Penrhyn Bay, Gwynedd (Llandudno 49436).
****Prestatyn**—Courts: AW1, S4. *Secretary:* J Lodwick, 111 Meliden Road, Prestatyn, Clwyd.
****Pwllheli**—Courts: S6. *Secretary:* H Evans, 2 Cae Llyr, Efail Newydd, Pwllheli, Gwynedd (613067).
****Rhos-on-Sea**—*Secretary:* Mrs J Bentley,

'Whitegates,' 40 Lansdowne Road, Colywn Bay, Clwyd (Colwyn Bay 30634).
****Rhyl**—*Secretary:* Miss I Wright, 41 Bryntirion Drive, Prestatyn, Clwyd LL19 9NT (3402).
****Ruthin**—Courts: H1. *Secretary:* Mrs B Ross, Nant Ucha Farm, Cyffylliog, nr Ruthin, Clwyd.
****St Asaph and Vale of Clywd**—Courts: AW1. *Secretary:* Mrs S M Thomas, 27 Bishop's Walk, St Asaph, Clwyd (St Asaph 583100).
Trearddur Bay LTC—Courts: H2. *Secretary:* G A Davies, 6 The Rise, Trearddur Bay, Gywnedd (860910).
****University College of North Wales**—Courts: AW1. *Secretary:* Hon Secretary University College LTC, Students Union, Deiniol Road, Bangor.
****Wrexham (Garden Village)**—*Secretary:* Mrs D Longson, Pen-y-Garn, Top Road, Gwynfryn, Wrexham, Clwyd LL11 5UN (Wrexham 758682).

SCHOOL CLUBS

Boys

****Rhydal** — Colwyn Bay. ****St Chads** — Prestatyn.

Girls

Lowther College — Bodelwyddan, Abergele. ****Penrhos College for Girls** — Colwyn Bay, Clwyd. **Howell's School** — Denbigh. **Bryn Offa School** — Wrexham, Clwyd. **Glan Clwyd** — St Asaph, Clwyd. **Rhyl High School** — Rhyl, Clwyd.

Co-Educational

****Grove Park School** — Wrexham. ****Colwyn Bay High School.** ****Yale Sixth Form College** — Wrexham. ****Ysgol Dyffryn Conwy** — Llanrwst. ****Ysgol Emrys Ap Iwan** — Abergele. ****Broomfield School** — Wrexham. ****Darland School** — Rossett. ****Bryn Alyn School** — Gwersyllt. **Kelsterton College of Technology.** ****Connah's Quay HS.** ****Ysgol Glan Clwyd** — St Asaph. ****St Richard Gwyn HS** — Flint. ****Edward Jones HS** — Rhyl. **Deeside Senior HS** — Queensferry. ****Brynhyfryd School** — Ruthin. ****Denbighshire Technical College** — Wrexham. ****Denbigh High School** — Denbigh. ****Dinas Bran School** — Llangollen. ****Maelor High School** — Penly-Wrexham. ***Ysgol John Bright** — Llandudno. **Ysgol y Creuddyn** — Penrhyn Bay, Llandudno, Gwynedd. **Ysgol Morgan** — Wrexham, Clwyd. **Castell Alun** — Hope, nr Wrexham, Clwyd. **Prestatyn High School** — Prestatyn, Clwyd. **Eirias High School** — Colwyn Bay, Clwyd. **St Davids School** — Wrexham, Clwyd. **Flint High School** — Flint, Clwyd. **Buckley Olfed High** — Buckley, Clwyd. **Mold Alun** — Mold, Clwyd. **Ysgol Maes Garman** — Mold, Clwyd.

*Affiliated to Gwynedd LTA
**Affiliated to Clwyd LTA

All correspondence to School Clubs should be addressed to the Master or Mistress in charge of lawn tennis.

OTHER AFFILIATED ORGANISATIONS (15)

Brymbo Open Junior Tournament—I D Jones, 25 Glyn Avenue, Clwyd, Wrexham (Wrexham 262202).
Pembrokeshire Lawn Tennis Committee—B Hearne, 26 Merlins Hill, Merlin Bridge, Haverfordwest, Pembs (Haverfordwest 66205).
Swansea Tennis Tournament Committee—*Secretary:* G W Fursland, 146 Swansea Road, Waunarlwydd, Swansea, W Glam SA5 4SS (Swansea 874094).
Colwyn Bay Lawn Tennis Tournament Committee—*Secretary:* Mrs W A Hughes, 22 Pentre Avenue, Abergele, Clwyd (Abergele 823953).
Deeside Recreations Sports Centre Tournament Committee—*Secretary:* c/o Deeside Leisure Centre, Queensferry.
M Bevan North Wales Hard Court Tournament—*Secretary:* Miss M Williams, 85 Vale Street, Denbigh, Clwyd.
Prestatyn Tennis Committee—*Secretary:* Mr A A Goodall, Holmlea, 29 Bryntirion Drive, Prestatyn (7010).
Rhuddlan Borough Open Tennis Tournament—Director of Tourism and Amenities, Borough of Rhuddlan, Rhyl.
Welsh Championship Lawn Tennis Tournament Committee—*Secretary:* J M Locke, Coniston, Parkfield Place, Newport (66199).
Welsh LTA Covered Courts Committee—*Secretary:* W F G Brunsdon, 65 Heol-y-Gors, Whitchurch, Cardiff (Cardiff 68241).
Welsh LTA Hard Court Championships—*Secretary:* Mr J Lightbody, 42 Fairy Grove, Killay, Swansea, W Glam (Swansea 202580).
Wrexham Garden Village Tournament Committee—*Secretary:* R D Moore, 13 Roseway, Burton, Rossett, Wrexham, Clwyd (Rossett 570839).
Carmarthen Championships—J N P Brown, Broom Cottage, 5 Lando Road, Pembrey, Dyfed (Burry Prt 2589).
Clwyd Junior Tennis Tournament—Mrs G Scott, Bellendene, Llanbedr DC, Ruthin, Clwyd (Ruthin 2989).
Penn/Mackintosh Tournament—J Hartland, Mackintosh LTC, Keppoc Street, Roath, Cardiff (42380).
Prudential Welsh Junior Champs—W F G Brunsdon, Welsh LTA Office, National Sports Centre for Wales, Cardiff (371838).

COUNTY ASSOCIATIONS OF ENGLAND

(see also Appendix to Rules of The Lawn Tennis Association)

1. **Avon**
2. **Bedfordshire**
3. **Berkshire**
4. **Buckinghamshire**
5. **Cambridgeshire**
6. **Cheshire (including parts of Greater Manchester and Merseyside)**
7. **Cornwall**
8. **Cumbria**
9. **Derbyshire**
10. **Devon**
11. **Dorset**
12. **Durham and Cleveland (including part of Tyne and Wear south of the River Tyne)**
13. **Essex (including part of Greater London)**
14. **Gloucestershire**
15. **Hampshire and Isle of Wight**
16. **Hereford and Worcester**
17. **Hertfordshire**
18. **Kent (including part of Greater London)**
19. **Lancashire (including part of Greater Manchester and Merseyside)**
20. **Leicestershire**
21. **Lincolnshire (including part of Humberside)**
22. **Middlesex (see Appendix to Rules)**
23. **Norfolk**
24. **Northamptonshire**
25. **Northumberland (including part of Tyne and Wear north of the River Tyne)**
26. **Nottinghamshire**
27. **Oxfordshire**
28. **Shropshire**
29. **Somerset**
30. **Staffordshire (including part of West Midlands)**
31. **Suffolk**
32. **Surrey (including part of Greater London)**
33. **Sussex**
34. **Warwickshire (including part of West Midlands)**
35. **Wiltshire**
36. **Yorkshire (including part of Humberside**

AVON COUNTY LAWN TENNIS ASSOCIATION

Hon Secretary—**Mrs J A Schollar,** 357 North Road, Yate, Bristol BS17 5LJ (Rangeworthy 593).
Hon Treasurer—**Mr P Harrowell,** 36 Oakleigh Close, West Town, Backwell, Bristol BS19 3JU.
Men's Match Secretary—**Mr A G Barker,** 165 Southmead Road, Westbury-on-Trym, Bristol BS10 5DW (624016).
Ladies' Match Secretary—**Mrs R C Steed,** 'Green Gables,' Moorend, Hambrook, Bristol (561193).
Representatives on the Council—**B G Coombs, Mrs O Brown.**

AFFILIATED CLUBS (44)

Almondsbury—M4/M5 Junction (Almondsbury 61334). Courts: H4. *Secretary:* 13 East Shrubbery, Redland, Bristol BS6 6SX (731688).
Backwell—Backwell Playing Fields. Courts: H3. *Secretary:* Mrs D Sellick, 24 Dark Lane, Backwell, Bristol BS19 3NS (Flax Bouton 3753).
Bath—1 Tennyson Road. Courts: G4, H2. (Bath 25625). *Secretary:* Mrs J Gregory, 28 Meadow Park, Bathford, Bath (859322).
Bloomfield—Wellsway, Bath. Courts: H4. (Bath 25825). *Secretary:* R Appleyard, 53 Longfellow Avenue, Bath (Bath 313906).
Bristol Lawn Tennis & Squash Centre—Redland Green, Bristol BS6 7HF (731139). Courts: G7, H4. *Secretary:* c/o Club.
Bristol Aerospace—Southmead Road, Filton. Courts: G2, H4. (692507). *Secretary:* N Workman, 48 Robertson Road, Bristol BS5 6JT.
Bristol Central—Derby Road, St Andrews. Courts: H3. *Secretary:* Mrs M Groves, 22 High Street, Staple Hill, Bristol BS16 5HW (569072).
Bristol Waterworks—Tennessee Green off Kellaway Avenue. Courts: H2. *Secretary:* P Baumbach, Bristol Waterworks Co, Bridgwater Road, Bristol BS99 7AU (665881).
Carnarvon—Redland Road (between Cotham Brow and South Road). Courts: H3. *Secretary:* Mrs N Agar, Furness House, 13 Freeland Place, Hotwells, Bristol BS8 4NP (28666).
Cleeve—King George IV Recreation Field. Courts: H2. *Secretary:* Mrs G Gould, Corners, 48 Bishops Road, Cleeve, Bristol (Yatton 832827).
Cleeve Hill—Cleeve Hill Downend. Courts: H2. *Secretary:* Mrs F A Williams, 43 Cleeve Park Road, Downend, Bristol (561429).
Clevedon—Princes Road, Clevedon (Clevedon 871737). *Secretary:* Mr L Pasquill, 10 Irving Close, Clevedon, Bristol BS21 6YS (877675).
Clifton—Beaufort Road, Clifton (734350). Courts: G2, H5. *Secretary:* H Mitchell, 4 Avon Grove, Sneyd Park, Bristol (683788).
Congresbury—Recreation Club, Stonewell Drive, Congresbury. Courts: H3. Secretary: Mrs A Whittaker, 24 Park Road, Congresbury, Avon (Yatton 833277).
Crescent—Kensington Park Road and Lodway Road, Brislington. Courts: H2. *Secretary:* Mrs S

George, 74 Queensdown Gardens, Bristol BS4 3JF (774519).
Crossbow—The Park, School Road, Frampton Cotterell. Courts: H2. *Secretary:* Mrs P Tanner, 36 Lower Chapel Lane, Frampton Cotterell, Avon BS17 2RL (Winterbourne 778660).
Downend & Fishponds—Cleeve Hill, Downend. Courts: H2. *Secretary:* Mrs L Hynam, 23 Hampton Park, Redland, Bristol (739929).
Dyrham—rear of 17 Laurie Crescent, Henleaze. Courts: H2. *Secretary:* Mrs S Allingham, 31 Wadham Drive, Frenchay, Bristol (568461).
Henleaze—Tennessee Green off Springfield Green, Westbury Park. Courts: H2. *Secretary:* Miss D Freeman, 4 Stadium Road, Westbury Park, Bristol BS6 7YE (41939).
Herbert Gardens—Clevedon. Courts: G3. *Secretary:* C M Bushby, 93, North Street, Nailsea, Bristol (852921).
Imperial—West Town Lane, Knowle. Courts: G16, H6. *Secretary:* Mrs S M Allen, c/o Mardon Son & Hall Ltd, Tower Road North, Warmley, Bristol (667161).
King's Club—Bottom of Kings Drive (427667). Courts: H7. *Secretary:* Miss M Salisbury, 32 Woodstock Road, Bristol BS6 7EP (424842).
Knowle—Wells Road, Knowle. Courts: H4. *Secretary:* Mrs J Lane, 'Claremont,' Church Road, Whitchurch, Bristol BS14 0PR (836934).
Lansdown LT & Squash Rackets Club—Northfields, Lansdown (Bath 25763). Courts: G6, H5. *Secretary:* c/o Club.
Long Ashton—Recreation Ground, Keedwell Hill. Courts: H2. *Secretary:* M Preston, 7 Rayens Cross Road, Long Ashton, Bristol BS18 9EA (LA 2825).
Long Ashton Research Station—Research Station, Long Ashton (Long Ashton 2181). Courts: H2. *Secretary:* Mrs A Belcher, Research Station, Long Ashton BS18 9AF.
Nailsea—Mizzymead Recreation Centre, Nailsea (Nailsea 854181). Courts: H3. *Secretary:* Mrs S Irens, Double House, Backwell Common, Backwell, Bristol (Nailsea 852786).
Phoenix Club—Gloucester Amenity Co, Nevil Road. Courts: H3. *Secretary:* R Barrow, 7 Hambledon House, 18-20 Cotham Road, Cotham, Bristol BS6 6DR (738657).
Portishead—Lake Grounds. Courts: H3.
Purnells—Purnell & Sons, Paulton. Courts: H2. *Secretary:* Mrs P Jones, 13 South View Place, Midsomer Norton, Bath (Midsomer Norton 414158).
RAF Locking—Weston-super-Mare. Courts: H5. *Secretary:* Officer i/c Tennis, RAF Locking, Weston-super-Mare BS24 7AA.
Redland—Redland Road (between Cotham Brow and South Road). Courts: H4. *Secretary:* D Hughes, 173 Badminton Road, Downend, Bristol (570116).
Redwood Lodge—Beggar Bush Lane, Failand (LA 2771). Courts: H4. *Secretary:* Mrs B Watson, 10 Wincombe Close, Nailsea, Bristol BS19 2TF (851481).
Saltford—Wedmore Road. Courts: H3. *Secretary:* D Brumskill, 85 Manor Road, Keynsham, Bristol (Keynsham 4921).
Sodbury—Wickwar Road, Chipping Sodbury. Courts: H4. *Secretary:* M V Polley, The Brambles, Synwell Lane, Wotton-under-Edge, Glos (Dursley 842896).
Somerdale—Fry's Keynsham (61789). Courts: H4. *Secretary:* R Hollister, 34 Lytes Cary Road, Keynsham BS18 1XD (Keynsham 5897).
Stothert & Pitt—Newton Fields, Lower Bristol Road (Bath 314400). Courts: H2. *Secretary:* P Witty, 125 Englishcombe Lane, Bath (Bath 29243).
Sun Life Tennis Club—Sun Life Sports Ground, Cribbs Causeway, Henbury (502303). Courts: H4. *Secretary:* S Robson, 18 Gilroy Close, Longwell Green, Bristol BS15 6YT (Bitton 6275).
Thornbury—Mundy Playing Fields. Courts: H3. *Secretary:* Mrs D Moffat, Grove House, The Street, Alveston BS12 2SX (Thornbury 412273).
University of Bristol—Coombe Lane, Stoke Bishop. Courts: H8, G8. *Secretary:* S P Savage, Men's Tennis Club, University of Bristol Union, Queen's Road, Clifton, Bristol.
Westbury Park—Russell Green, Westbury Park. Courts: H2. *Secretary:* M Burridge, 58 The Crescent, Henleaze, Bristol BS9 4RR (624314).
Winterbourne—Recreation Ground off Parkside Avenue. Courts: H2. *Secretary:* Mrs P Strong, 15 Crossman Avenue, Winterbourne, Bristol (774040).
Woodborough—rear of Winscombe Hotel. Courts: H3. *Secretary:* Mrs C Patterson, Winthill House, Banwell, Avon (Banwell 822040).
Woodlands—Bibury Crescent,Hanham, Bristol. Courts: H2. *Secretary:* M Morrison, 18 Ravendale Drive, Longwell Green, Bristol (888 3316).

OTHER AFFILIATED ORGANISATIONS (4)

Avon County Tennis Coaches Ass—*Secretary:* John A Doe, 186 Stoke Lane, Stoke Bishop, Bristol BS9 3RS (0272 681161).
Avon County Veterans LTC—*Secretary:* Mrs S Savage, 8 Oswald's Court, Redland, Bristol BS6 7HX.
City of Bristol Parks Dept—Colston House, Colston Street, Bristol 1.
The Atlantic Tennis Club—c/o Grand Atlantic Hotel, Weston-Super-Mare, Avon. *Secretary:* J Tucker.

AFFILIATED SCHOOL CLUBS (51)

Badminton School — Westbury-on-Trym, Bristol. **Bath High School** — Lansdown, Bath. **Sir Bernard Lovell School** — Oldland Common, Bristol. **Clifton High School** — Clifton, Bristol. **Colston's Girls' School** — Cheltenham Road, Bristol. **Diocesan School** — Baytree Road, Bath BA1 6ND. **La Retraite** — Clifton, Bristol. **Redland High School** — Redland, Bristol. **Red Maids' School** — Westbury-on-Trym, Bristol. **St Brandon's School** — Clevedon BS21 7SD. **St Ursula's School** — Westbury-on-Trym, Bristol. **Merrywood School** — Downton Road, Bristol. **Nailsea School** —

Mizzymead Road, Nailsea. **Bristol Grammar School** — Tyndalls Park Road, Bristol. **The Cathedral School** — College Green, Bristol 2. **Colston's Boys' School** — Stapleton, Bristol. **The Downs School** — Wraxall, Bristol BS19 1PF. **Merrywood School** — Downton Road, Bristol. **Tockington Manor Prep School** — Tockington Manor, Tockington, nr Bristol BS12 4NY. **Monkton Combe School** — nr Bath BA2 7HG. **Ashton Park** — Blackmoors Lane, Bower Ashton, Bristol. **Broadlands School** — Keynsham, Bristol. **Broadoaks School** — Broadoak Road, Weston-super-Mare, Avon. **Castle School** — Park Road, Thornbury, Bristol 12. **Chipping Sodbury** — Chipping Sodbury, nr Bristol. **Clevedon Comprehensive School** — Clevedon, Avon. **Cotham Grammar School** — Cotham Lawn Road, Bristol. **Fairfield Grammar School** — Montpelier, Bristol. **Filton High School** — New Road, Stoke Gifford, Bristol. **Gordano School** — Portishead, nr Bristol. **Gordano School** — Portishead, nr Bristol. **Hanham High School** — Hanham, Bristol. **Henbury School** — Marissal Road, Henbury, Bristol. **Norton Hill School** — Midsomer Norton, Bath. **Patchway High School** — Hempton Lane, Almondsbury, Bristol 12. **Ridings High School** — Winterbourne, Bristol. **St Mary Redcliffe & Temple** — Somerset Square, Bristol. **St Bede's School** — Long Cross, Lawrence Weston, Bristol. **Somervale Comprehensive School** — Midsomer Norton, Bath. **Whitefield School** — Alexander Park, Fishponds, Bristol. **Worle School** — Weston-super-Mare, Avon. **Writhlington School** — Radstock, Bath. **Wyvern School** — Sandringham Road, Weston-super-Mare, Avon. **Portway School** — Shirehampton, Bristol. **Backwell School** — Backwell, Bristol 19. **Marlwood School** — Vattingstone Lane, Alveston, nr Bristol. **Grange School** — Tower Road North, Warmley, nr Bristol. **Sidcot School** — Winscombe, Bristol BS25 1PD. **Mangotsfield School** — Mangotsfield, Bristol. **Downend School** — Westerleigh Road, Downend, Bristol. **Kingsfield School** — Kingswood, Bristol. **Lockleaze School** — Hogarth Walk, Lockleaze, Bristol. **Pen Park School** — Pen Park Road, Southmead, Bristol. **St George** — Russell Town Avenue, Bristol. **Clifton College** — College Road, Clifton, Bristol 8. **Queen Elizabeths Hospital** — Berkeley Place, Clifton, Bristol 8. **Wellsway School** — Chandag Road, Keynsham, Bristol. **St Brendons Schools** — Broomhill Road, Brislington, Bristol 4. **Kingswood School** — Special Unit, Britannia Road, Kingswood, Bristol. **Ralph Edward's School** — North Road, Bath BA2 6HO.

BEDFORDSHIRE COUNTY LAWN TENNIS ASSOCIATION

Hon Secretary—**R J Elam,** 57 Village Road, Bromham (Oakley 2492).
Hon Coaching & Junior Secretary—**Mrs E Davies,** 42 Steppingley Road, Flitwick, Bedfordshire (0525 713221).
Hon Treasurer—**L H Omerod,** 14 Sharnbrook Road, Souldrop (Bedford 781664).
Hon Men's Match Secretary—**G Saunders,** 70 Flitwick Road, Ampthill (403803).
Hon Ladies' Match Secretary—**Mrs K Jones,** 9 Rowley Road, St Neots, Cambs (Huntingdon 216073).
Representative on the Council—**MrR K Foster.**

AFFILIATED CLUBS (22)

Bedford—Bradgate Road, Bedford (Bedford 52837). Courts: G14, H4. *Secretary:* J Edwards, 21 Buckfast Avenue, Bedford (43111).
Biggleswade Conservatives—St Andrew's Street, Biggleswade (2225). Courts: H2. *Secretary:* Mrs M Ward, 3 West View, Beeston Green, Sandy (81920).
Colworth House LTC (Unilever Ltd)—Colworth House, Sharnbrook. Courts: H4. *Secretary:* M Hale, 34 Grange Gardens, Sharnbrook (Bedford 781247/781281).
Dunstable—Downs Road, Dunstable (696360). Courts: H3. *Secretary:* C McDougall, 4 First Avenue, Dunstable (69949).
Electrolux Recreation—Oakley Road, Luton (51788). Courts: H3. *Secretary:* R Holt, 90 Pembroke Avenue, Luton (582357).
Flint LTC—Lancaster Avenue, Luton. Courts: H2. *Secretary:* Mrs J Lowden, 2 Hillcrest Bungalow, Dunstable Road, Caddington, Luton (Luton 458800).
Flitwick & Ampthill LTC—Windmill Road, Flitwick. Courts: G3, H3. *Secretary:* J. Gardner, 5 Warwick Close, Flitwick, Bedford (Flitwick 715958).
Harlington—Harlington Upper School, Harlington. Courts: H6. *Secretary:* Mrs P King, 19 Brian Road, Harlington (Toddington 3283).
Henlow LTC—Henlow Middle School, Henlow. Courts: H4. *Secretary:* Mrs J Jordan, 16 Church Street, Henlow, Beds (Hitchin 811977).
Langford—Langford Memorial Playing Field, Langford. Courts: H2. Secretary: R Huxtable, 38 Newis Crescent, Clifton, Beds (Hitchin 811601).
Leighton Buzzard Town Cricket and Tennis Club—Bell Close, Lake Street, Leighton Buzzard (371529). Courts: G2, H2. *Secretary:* Mrs S. R Channon, 10 Copper Beech Way, Leighton Buzzard (376983).
Linslade—Mentmore Road, Linslade. Courts: H2. *Secretary:* Mrs C Pinchin, 3 Malvern Drive, Linslade (0525 384860).
Lower Gravenhurst LTC—Barton Road, Lower Gravenhurst. Courts: H1. *Secretary:* J C Parrish, Brookend Green Farm, Barton Le Cley, Beds (0582 881286).
Luton Co-op Sports Club—Stockingstone Road, Luton. Courts: H2. *Secretary:* R Mallett, 46 Wardown Crescent, Luton (34929).
Luton & Vauxhall LTC—Brache Sports Ground, Park Street, Luton (454785). Courts: G3, H6. *Secretary:* B Turner, 32 Ringwood Road, Luton (599036).

Riverside—Goldington Road, Bedford (52726). Courts: G9, H7. *Secretary:* Mrs K Fletcher, 16 Oak Close, Wootton, Bedford (766160).
Sharnbrook—Lodge Road, Sharnbrook. Courts: G1, H2. *Secretary:* Mrs Harrison, Avonlea, Odell Road, Sharnbrook (Bedford 781315).
Silsoe LTC—Courts: H3. *Secretary:* Mrs B Baldwin, 15 High Street, Silsoe, Beds (Silsoe 60445).
Toddington LTC—Recreation Ground, Luton Road, Toddington. Courts: H3. *Secretary:* M McDonald, 15 Broughton Avenue, Toddington (3326).
Westoning—Recreation Ground, Greenfield Road, Westoning. Courts: H2. *Secretary:* A Clarke, 7 Tyburn Lane, Westoning (Flitwick 713207).
Woburn Sands—off High Street, Woburn Sands. Courts: H2. *Secretary:* Mrs A Harris, 5 Phoebe Lane, Wavendon, Milton Keynes (582186).
Woodlands LTC—Courts: G2. *Secretary:* P G Smith, Woodlands, Thurleigh Road, Milton Ernest, Bedford (Milton Ernest 2914).

OTHER AFFILIATED ORGANISATIONS (3)

Bedford College of Physical Education—37 Lansdowne Road, Bedford (51966).
Bedfordshire Schools LTA—42 Steppingley Road, Flitwick.
Luton Junior Tournament Committee—*Secretary:* H G Hann, Wardown Park, Old Bedford Road, Luton.

SCHOOL CLUBS (47)

Boys
Bedford School — Bedford. **Bedford Modern School** — Manton Lane, Bedford.

Girls
Bedford High School — Bedford. **Clarendon School** — Hayes. **Challney Girls High School** — Luton. **Dame Alice Harpur School** — Bedford. **Denbigh High School** — Luton. **Queensbury School** — Dunstable. **St Andrew's School** — Bedford. **Stopsley High School** — St Thomas' Road, Stopsley, Luton.

Mixed
Alban Middle School — Great Borford, Beds. **Ashcroft High School** — Luton. **Dunstable College of FE** — Dunstable. **Fulbrook Middle School** — Woburn Sands. **Gilbert Inglefield School** — Leighton Buzzard. **Goldington Middle School** — Bedford. **Harlington Upper School** — Harlington. **Hastingsbury Upper School** — Kempston. **Holmead School** — Biggleswade. **John Donne Lower School** — Blunham. **John Howard Upper School** — Bedford. **Lealands High School** — Luton. **Lea Manor High School** — Luton. **Leighton Middle School** — Leighton. **Lincroft Middle School** — Oakley. **Lower Stondon Lower School** — Henlow. **Luton Sixth Form College** — Luton. **Manshead School** — Dunstable. **Mill Vale Middle School** — Dunstable. **Newnham Middle School** — Bedford. **Northfields Upper School** — Dunstable. **Parkfields School** — Toddington. **Pilgrim Upper School** — Bedford. **Polam School** — Bedford. **Rice Trevor Lower School** — Bromham. **Rushmoor School** — Bedford. **Sandye Place School** — Sandy. **Sharnbrook Upper** — Sharnbrook. **Springfield Lower School** — Hempston. **Stopsley Junior School** — Luton. **St Bede's School** — Bedford. **St George School** — Toddington. **St Gregory's Middle School** — Bedford. **Vandyke Upper** — Leighton Buzzard. **Woodlands Middle School** — Flitwick. **Woodside Middle School** — Bedford.

All correspondence to School Clubs should be addressed to the Master or Mistress in charge of lawn tennis.

BERKSHIRE LAWN TENNIS ASSOCIATION

Hon Secretary—**Mrs S Ward,** 5 Lady Jane Court, Caversham, Reading (Reading 472659).
Hon Junior Secretary—**Mrs B M Warren,** 70 Eastfield Road, Burnham, Slough, Berkshire (062 86 2238).
Hon Treasurer—**P Manners,** 16 Sheridan Avenue, Caversham, Reading (Reading 479162).
Hon Men's Match Secretary—**A R Lucas,** 'Ostlers,' Kybes Lane, Pound Green, Grazeley, nr Reading, Berks (Reading 883490).
Hon Ladies' Match Secretary—**Mrs J Woodward,** 43 Rochester Way, Woodley, Reading, Berkshire (Reading 695749).
Hon Veterans' Match Secretary—**J S Dunningham,** 'Harvest Moon,' Bradcutts Lane, Cookham Dean, Maidenhead, Berks (Bourne End 24625).
Representatives on the Council—**L Robinson, Mrs S Ward.**

AFFILIATED CLUBS (40)

Atomic Weapons Research Establishment—AWRE, Aldermaston. Courts: G4, H3. *Secretary:* T. Maish, Building A88, Awre, Aldermaston, Berks (Tadley 4111 ext 7910).
Basildon—Recreation Ground, Bethesda Street, Upper Basildon, Berks. Courts: H2. *Secretary:* Mrs A Morrison, The Vicarage, Upper Basildon (Upper Basildon 223).
Berkshire County Sports Club—Sonning Lane, Sonning, nr Reading. Courts: H4. *Secretary:* Miss M Brooks, 25 The Grove, Reading (588092).
Bisham Abbey—Bisham Abbey National Sports Centre, nr Marlow, Bucks. Courts: H3. *Secretary:* Mr A Ferris, c/o Bisham Abbey, nr Marlow, Bucks (Marlow 2818).
Bracknell—Holly Bank, Bracknell. Courts: H5. *Secretary:* Mrs J Adamson, 109 Sutherland Chase, Ascot (28346).
Caversham—Conisboro Avenue, Caversham, Reading (474566 ground). Courts: G3, H6. *Secretary:* Mrs L Logi, The Grey House, New Road, Shiplake, Oxon (Wargrave 2120).
Caversham Park—Clayfield Corpse, Caversham Park Road, Caversham Park Village, Reading.

Courts: H3. *Secretary:* A Patrick, 1 Pendennis Avenue, Caversham Park, Reading (472954).
Chieveley—Recreation Centre, Chieveley. Courts: H2. *Secretary:* Mrs E Abbott, Hazel Hanger Farm, Chieveley, Berks (Chieveley 250).
Courage (Central) Sports and Social Club—Berkeley Avenue, Reading. Courts: G3, H2. *Secretary:* Mrs M Bone, Courage (Central) Ltd, Bridge Street, Reading (55931 ext 302).
Crescent—Home Park, Windsor. Courts: G5. *Secretary:* P Cawthorne, 17 Meadow Close, Old Windsor, Berks (Windsor 52925).
Crowthorne—Morgan Recreation Ground, Crowthorne. Courts: H2. *Secretary:* Mrs B Dixon, 5 Hangerfield Close, Yateley, Hants (Yateley 871938).
Foster Wheeler—Shiplake College, Shiplake, Oxon. Courts: H3. *Secretary:* D Linton, 3 Briars Close, Pangbourne, Berkshire (Pangbourne 2337).
Greenacre Squash & Tennis Club—Greenham Road, Newbury, Berks. Courts: H3. *Secretary:* Mrs P Chissell, 81 Goreslands, Wash Common, Newbury, Berks.
Hungerford—The Croft, Hungerford, Berks. Courts: H1, G3. *Secretary:* Mrs S Keefe, 40 Coldharbour Road, Hungerford, Berks (Hungerford 2935).
Ibis—Scours Lane, Reading. Courts: G3, H4. *Secretary:* P R Grantham, 29 Sharwood Drive, Reading (Reading 414644).
Kintbury—Recreation Grounds, Kintbury, Berks. Courts: G2, H1. *Secretary:* Mrs J Stock, Bramble Cottage, 18 Blandys Hill, Kintbury (58548).
Latika Junior Tennis Club—Holly Bank, Bracknell. Courts: H6. *Secretary:* Mrs Down, Winlad, Forest Road, Ascot (Winkfield Row 885400).
Madison Lang LTC—Charters, Charters Road, Sunningdale. Courts: H5. *Secretary:* Jennifer Leninton (Ascot 27331). c/o The Club.
Maidenhead—79 All Saints Avenue, Maidenhead (23785 club). Courts: H9. *Secretary:* J Voisey, 1 Castle Drive, Maidenhead (Maidenhead 26642).
Newbury—Almond Avenue, Shaw, Newbury. Courts: H4. *Secretary:* Mrs C Baxter, 19 Sutherlands, Newbury, Berks (Newbury 45125).
Odney—Cookham. Courts: H6. *Secretary:* Mr B Rees, 2 Mynchen Road, Knotty Green, Beaconsfield.
Pangbourne & District—Recretation Ground, Pangbourne. Courts: H3. *Secretary:* Mrs J Cook, 19 Briars Close, Pangbourne, Berks (Pangbourne 4209).
Purley—Recreation Ground, Beech Road, Purley, Berks. Courts: G3. *Secretary:* S K Wilkinson, 32 Beech Road, Purley, Berks (Pangbourne 3189).
Royal Ascot—Ascot Wood, High Street, Ascot. Courts: H3. *Secretary:* R Ratcliffe, 20 Llanvair Drive, South Ascot (Ascot 21739).
Salt Hill—Salt Hill Playing Fields, Slough. Courts: G3. *Secretary:* Mr K Glynn, 158 High Street, Langley, Slough (46861).
Shinfield—Millworth Lane, Shinfield, Reading. Courts: G2, H2. *Secretary:* Mrs Dale, 38 Clares Green Road, Spencers Wood, Reading.
Slough NALGO—Salt Hill Park, Bath Road, Slough, Berks. Courts: H4. *Secretary:* H B Bellairs, Dept of Technical Services, Town Hall, Slough, Berks (Slough 23881 ext 336).
Sonning—Recreation Ground, Sonning. Courts: H2. *Secretary:* M J Loudwell, Cotswold, Bath Road, Sonning (Reading 693602).
Southern Electricity House Sports and Social Club—Southern Electricity House, Littlewick Green, Maidenhead. Courts: G1, H2. *Secretary:* D J Meeten, Southern Electricty House, Littlewick Green (2166 ext 357).
Transport & Road Research Laboratory—Old Wokingham Road, Crowthorne, Berks. Courts: H3. *Secretary:* Mrs M C Semmens, 20 Wild Briar, Wokingham (Everley 732967),
Twenty—Alexander Gardens, Barry Avenue, Windsor. Courts: H3. *Secretary:* Mrs K Oliver, 13 Englefield Close, St Judes Road, Englefield Green, Egham, Surrey.
Twyford—Recreation Ground, Twyford. Courts: H3. *Secretary:* Mrs E Northcott, Rushmoor, 464 Reading Road, Winnersh, Wokingham, Berks (Wokingham 786276).
University of Reading—Elmhurst Road, Reading. Courts: G12, H14. *Secretary:* H Archer, Wells Hall, Upper Redland Road, Reading.
Wargrave—Woodclyffe Recreation Ground, Wargrave. Courts: G2, H4. *Secretary:* N Goodchild, 20 Silverdale Road, Wargrave, Berks (Wargrave 3405).
Wellington College Enterprises—Wellington College, Crowthorne, Berks. Courts: H8. *Secretary:* P R Smethurst, 3 Alderbrook Close, Crowthorne, Berks (Crowthorne 6767).
Windsor—Maidenhead Road, Windsor. Courts: G4, H6. *Secretary:* Mrs M Allbless, 9a Woodland Avenue, Windsor (59714).
Wokingham—Wellington Road, Wokingham, Berks. Courts: H3. *Secretary:* M J Harper, 50 Holmes Crescent, Wokingham, Berks (Wokingham 785500).
Woodlands Lawn Tennis and Social Club—Wendover Way, Woodlands Drive, Tilehurst, Reading. Courts: G1, H2. *Secretary:* Miss C J Trendall, 12 Chapel Hill, Tilehurst, Berks (R 23488).
Woodley—Silver Fox Crescent, Woodley, Reading. Courts: H3. *Secretary:* Miss L Jones, 23 Selcourt Close, Woodley, Reading (693092).
Yattendon and Frilsham—Village Hall, Yattendon. Courts: H2. *Secretary:* Mrs C Petter, 'Crastons,' Yattendon (Hermitage 201337).

OTHER AFFILIATED ORGANISATION (1)

Tournament Committee

Newbury & District LTA—*Secretary:* Mrs S Griffith, Speen Manor, Bath Road, Newbury, Berks (Newbury 43028).

AFFILIATED SCHOOLS (60)

Boys

Ashmead — Northumberland Avenue, Reading. **Bradfield College** — Bradfield. **Brockhurst** —

Marlston House, Hermitage. **Crosfields School** — Shinfield, Reading. **Desborough Comprehensive** — Shoppenhangers Road, Maidenhead. **Douai Abbey** — Upper Woolhampton, Reading. **Eton College** — Eton. **Leighton Park** — Shinfield, Reading. **Princess Marina College** — Arborfield Garrison, nr Reading. **Reading** — Erleigh Road, Reading. **Slough Grammar School** — Lascelles Road, Slough. **Stoneham School** — Cockney Hill, Reading. **The Forest School** — Robin Hood Lane, Winnersh. **Windsor Country Grammar School for Boys** — Maidenhead Road, Windsor.

Girls

Abbey — Kendrick Road, Reading. **Downe House** — Cold Ash, Newbury. **Garth Hill School** — Sandy Lane, Bracknell. **Heathfield** — Ascot. Holt School — Wokingham. **Kendrick** — Kendrick School, Reading. **Luckley** — Oakfield School, Wokingham. **Maidenhead College** — 1 College Avenue, Maidenhead. **Marist Convent** — Sunninghill. **Newlands School** — Farm Road, Maidenhead. **Queen Anne's** — Caversham, Reading. **Slough High School** — Twinches Lane, Slough. **St Bartholomews School Newbury** — Andover Road, Newbury. **St Bernard's Convent** — 1 Langley Road, Slough. **St Joseph's Convent** — Upper Redlands Road, Reading. **St Mary's Girls School** — St Mary's Road, South Ascot. **St George's** — Ascot. **Windsor High School** — Imperial Road, Windsor.

Mixed

Bulmershe School — Cheques Way, Woodley, Reading. **Cox Green Comprehensive** — Cox, Green, Maidenhead. **Denefield School** — Long Lane, Tilehurst. **Downs School** — Compton, Newbury. **Easthamstead Park** — Wokingham, Berks. **Emmbrook School** — Emmbrook Road, Wokingham. **Furze Platt Junior School** — Oaken Grove, Maidenhead. **Furze Platt Comprehensive** — Marlow Road, Maidenhead. **Highdown School** — Surley Road, Emmer Green, Reading. **Hugh Faringdon School** — Fawley Road, Southcote, Reading. **John O'Gaunt Comprehensive** — Priory Road, Hungerford. **Kennet Comprehensive** — Stoney Lane, Thatcham, Berks. **Langley Grammar** — Reddington Drive, Langley, Slough. **Maidenerlegh School** — Earley, Reading. **Meadway School** — Tilehurst, Reading. **Priors Court** — Priors Court Road, Chieveley. **Ranelagh School** — Bracknell. **St Andrew's School** — Buckhold, Pangbourne. **Sandhurst School** — Awlsmoor Road, Sandhurst. **Theale Green School** — Bath Road, Theale. **The Herschel High School** — Northampton Avenue, Slough. **Turnpike School** — Avon Way, Newbury. **Upton Grammar School** — Lascelles Road, Slough. **Waingels Copse School** — Denmark Avenue, Woodley. **Wellington College** — Crowthorne, Berks. **Willink School** — Burghfield Common.

BUCKINGHAMSHIRE COUNTY LAWN TENNIS ASSOCIATION

Hon Secretary—**K L Dewick,** 55 Chessfield Park, Little Chalfont, Amersham, Bucks (Little Chalfont 3818).
Hon Junior Secretary—**Mrs G Petter,** 2 Brownswood Road, Beaconsfield (3805).
Hon Treasurer—**D Oldcorn,** Clocktower House, The Willows, Maidenhead Road, Windsor (Windsor 55744).
Hon Men's Match Sectretary—**A Jones,** 34 Trinity Avenue, Marlow (4645).
Hon Ladies' Match Secretary—**Mrs J Thomas,** 17 Howards Wood Drive, Gerrards Cross (884912).
Representatives on the Council—**K L Dewick, J Sherwood-Smith.**

AFFILIATED CLUBS (52)

Aylesbury (Wendover Road)—Courts: H12. *Secretary:* P Bell, 17 Kynaston Avenue, Aylesbury (Ayl 5787).
Beaconsfield LTC—BUDC Courts, Wilton Crescent, Beaconsfield. Courts: H4. *Secretary:* Mrs S Cornish, 1 Clauds Close, Hazlemere (0494 711519).
Broomwade Tennis Club—Courts: H3. *Secretary:* A Worley, 18 Green Road, Terriers, High Wycombe (40515).
Buckingham—Chandos Road, Buckingham. Courts: G2, H2. *Secretary:* Mrs M Buckingham, 7 Chandos Road, Buckingham (815334).
Bucks County Council Staff Sports & Social—Mandeville Road, Aylesbury. Courts: G2, H3. *Secretary:* J Harcourt, 192 Ingram Avenue, Aylesbury (84861).
Burnham Tennis Association—Courts: H3. *Secretary:* Mrs D Marsh, 115 Hag Hill Rise, Taplow, Maidenhead, Berks (Burnham 4805).
Chalfont St Giles Tennis Club—Playing Fields, Chalfont St Giles, Courts: H4. *Secretary:* Mrs D Colman, Orchard End, Ashwells Way, Chalfont St Giles (4508).
Chalfont St Peter—Playing Fields, Chalfont St Peter. Courts: H3. *Secretary:* P Clarke, 24 Ashlea Road, Chalfont St Peter (Gerrards Cross 882027).
Cheddington—Courts: H2. *Secretary:* Mrs N Hagan, 6 High Street, Cheddington, Beds (Ched 668584).
Chesham LTC (1879)—Pednor Mead End, Pednor Road, Chesham. Courts: H4. *Secretary:* Mrs K Weber, 5 Stanley Avenue, Chesham HP5 2JF (773359).
Chesham Bois—Woodfield Park, Amersham. Courts: H10. *Secretary:* J W Savidge, Malmsmead, Holloway Lane, Chesham Bois (Amersham 7047).
Dorney—*Secretary:* Mrs J A Paton, 25 Harcourt Road, Dorney Reach, Maidenhead, Berks (Maidenhead 23723).
Edlesborough—Courts: H2. *Secretary:* D Tansley, 18 The Pastures, Edlesborough, Beds (Eaton Bray 221559).
Equity, Law & Life LTC—Amersham Road. Courts: H5. *Secretary:* Mrs P Taylor, Marketing

Department, Equity Law and Life Assurance Soc Ltd, Amersham Road, High Wycombe (33377 ext 464).

Farnham Common Sports Club (Tennis Section)—One Pin Lane, Farnham Common. Courts: H6. *Secretary:* D Chapman, Northfields, Templewood Lane, Farnham Common (2742).

Flackwell Heath—*Secretary:* A Shea, 3 Fairfield Close, Bourne End (27397).

Gerrards Cross—Bull Lane. Courts: H8, G9. *Secretary:* M Stephenson, 17 North Park, Gerrards Cross (882481).

Gerrards Cross (Dukeswood) LTC—Dukes Wood. Courts: H6. *Secretary:* Mrs C Cayton, Highview, 2 The Queensway, Gerrards Cross (885209).

Gilpin LTC—Mrs M Swallow, 100 High Street, Olney, Bucks MK46 4BE (Bedford 711895).

Great Missenden—London Road, Great Missenden. Courts: G7, H7. *Secretary:* M Lloyd, Outwoods, Marriotts Avenue, South Heath, Great Missenden.

Haddenham LTC—*Secretary:* Mrs J Houghton, 21 Slave Hill, Haddenham (291238).

Halton Village LTC—RAF Tennis Centre, Halton. Courts: G3, H3. Secretary: Mrs J O'Connor, 46 Cubb Field, Aylesbury (33407).

Hambledon—*Secretary:* Mrs J Sanderson, 233 Greys Road, Henley on Thames (575833).

Hazells—Victoria Park. Courts: G3, H2. *Secretary:* C M Plumb, Hazell Watson & Viney Ltd, The Printing Works, Aylesbury (82345).

Hazelmere—Hazelmere Recreation Ground, High Wycombe. Courts: H4. *Secretary:* M E Atkins, 147 Gordon Road, High Wycombe HP13 6EP.

High Wycombe—Bassetbury Lane, High Wycombe (High Wycombe 23253). Courts: H6. *Secretary:* Miss G Humphreys, 2 Daws Hill Lane, High Wycombe (30820).

Holmer Green—Courts: H3. *Secretary:* Mrs R Patterson, 44 Hogg Lane, Holmer Green (High Wycombe 713189).

Horsenden (Risboro') LTC—Horsenden Lane, Princes Risborough. Courts: H4. *Secretary:* Mrs A M Adlam, 6 Salisbury Close, Princes Risborough (Princes Risborough 5423).

ICI Paints Division Recreation—Fir Tree Avenue, Stoke Green. Courts: G6, H4. *Secretary:* Miss R Crook, ICI Ltd, Paints Division, Wexham Road, Slough (31151, ext 2016).

Iver Heath LTC—Church Road, Iver Heath. Courts: H2. *Secretary:* D A Bosson, 2 Bangors Road North, Iver Heath, SL0 0BG (Iver 651172).

Lacey Green LTC—Courts: H3. *Secretary:* Miss S Munday, Byways, Goodacre Lane, Lacey Green (Princes Risboro 6261).

Little Chalfont Sports Club—Elizabeth Avenue. Courts: H6. *Secretary:* Mrs P Wood, 2 Buckingham Court, Chestnut Lane, Amersham (28075).

Long Crendon LTC—Chearsley Road, Long Crendon. Courts: H2. *Secretary:* Miss A Dudley-Smith, Braken Cottages, Chearsley Road, Long Crendon, Aylesbury (201034).

Marlow Sports (NT Section)—Pound Lane, Marlow. Courts: H3. *Secretary:* Mrs P Langford, Woodside, Riverwoods, Marlow (4127).

Milton Keynes LTC—Central Gardens, Bletchley. Courts: H6. *Secretary:* T Sumpter, 146 Water Eaton Road, Bletchley (Milton Keynes 70482).

Naphill—Naphill Playing Fields. Courts: H2. *Secretary:* Miss D Strange, 3 Woodlands Drive, Naphill (3553).

Newport Pagnell LTC—Courts: H4. *Secretary:* T Stratton, 78 Holland Way, Newport Pagnell (610588).

Penn and Tylers Green LTC—Elm Road, Penn. Courts: H2. *Secretary:* Mrs M Stevens, 6 Pimms Close, Cock Lane, High Wycombe (Penn 4338).

Perme LTC (Tennis Section)—Courts: H2. *Secretary:* K Ledbury, RPE, Westcott, Aylesbury.

Princes Risborough—Back Lane, Princes Risborough. Courts: G4, H2. *Secretary:* Mrs R Englemann, 20 Jasmine Crescent, Princes Risborough (6494).

Richings Park—Wellesley Avenue, Iver. Courts: H4. *Secretary:* I Cook, 3 Syke Cluan, Richings Park, Iver (652439).

Rio, High Wycombe—Fryers Lane, High Wycombe. Courts: H3. *Secretary:* all correspondence to Mrs M Wallen, Silver Birches, Hughenden Valley, High Wycombe.

Stewkley—Courts: H2. *Secretary:* C Gardiner, Clarendon House, High Street, South Stewkley (052 524 706).

Stoke Poges—Bell's Hill, Windsor Road, Stoke Poges. Courts: H3. *Secretary:* Ms R O Facer, 6 Hawtrey Close, Slough, Berks (Slough 79451).

Stony Stratford—Ancell Trust Sports Ground, Vicarage Road. Courts: G4, H5. *Secretary:* Mrs J Taylor, Leamingham Farm, Castlethorpe, Milton Keynes (510235).

Wendover & Chiltern Hills Lawn Tennis & Squash Club—Dobbins Lane, Wendover. Courts: H4. *Secretary:* Mrs A Oudot, 4 Chiltern Road, Wendover (624990).

Widmer End—Widmer End Recreation Ground. Courts: H3. *Secretary:* R Humphreys, 63 Straight Bit, Flackwell Heath (Bourne End 22770).

Winslow—Dene Hill, Sheep Street, Winslow. Courts: G3. *Secretary:* Mrs S Roebuck, 6 Lydiard Close, Aylesbury (84490).

Wolverton Sports (Tennis Section)—Osborne Street, Wolverton. Courts: H5. *Secretary:* Miss A Lloyd, 5 Atherstone Court, Two Mile Ash, Milton Keynes (567961).

Woburn Golf and Country Club—Courts: H3. *Secretary:* Mrs J Spier, Bow Brickhill, Milton Keynes (70756).

Wooburn Park Tennis Club—Wooburn Green, Bucks. Courts: H3. *Secretary:* Mrs S Milhofer, 40 Green Lane, Burnham (Burnham 5195).

Wraysbury—The Green. Courts: H3. *Secretary:* Mrs H Wordham, Hamilton, 11 Welley Road, Wraysbury (2648).

OTHER AFFILIATED ORGANISATIONS

Aylesbury & District Tennis League—*Secretary:* Mrs M R Felgate, Lindisfarne, Hog Lane, Ashley Green (3274).

Milton Keynes Tennis League—*Secretary:* Mrs A Harris, 5 Phoebe Lane, Wavenden, Milton Keynes (582186).
Aylesbury College—*Secretary:* P B Lapham, Aylesbury College of Further Education, Oxford Road, Aylesbury (4571).
Amersham College—*Secretary:* G R Link, Tennis Section, Stanley Hill, Amersham.
Open University—*Secretary:* Mrs J Kemp, 3 Marshworth, Tinkers Bridge, Milton Keynes (660354).

AFFILIATED SCHOOLS

Aylesbury High School — Girls. **Beaconsfield High School** — Girls. **Beconsfield Secondary School** — Mixed. **Brudenell School** — Amersham (Girls). **Burnham Grammar School** — Mixed. **Convent of Jesus and Mary** — Thornton (Girls). **Heatherton House** — Chesham Bois (Girls). **High March** — Beaconsfield (Mixed). **Holy Cross Convent** — Chalfont St Peter (Girls). **Dr. Challoners High School** — Little Chalfont (Girls). **Chesham High School** — Mixed. **John Colet School** — Wendover (Mixed). **Lowndes School**— Chesham (Girls). **Lady Verney High School** — High Wycombe (Girls). **Pipers Corner School** — Great Kinghill (Girls). **Radcliffe School** — Wolverton. **Sir Henry Floyd School** — Aylesbury (Mixed). **St Mary's School** — Gerrards Cross (Girls). **Oakdene School** — Beaconsfield (Girls). **Thornton College** — Bletchley. **Waddesdon Church of England School** — Mixed. **Wycombe Abbey School** — High Wycombe (Girls). **Wycombe High School for Girls** — High Wycombe.

CAMBRIDGESHIRE LAWN TENNIS ASSOCIATION

Hon Secretary—**B Poulter,** 5 Hinton Road, Fulbourn, Cambridge (880648).
Hon Junior Secretary—**Mrs L Davison,** 53 Gilbert Road, Cambridge (354300).
Hon Treasurer—**J E Allsop,** 21 Beaumont Road, Cambridge CB1 4PU (Cambridge 248495).
Hon Men's Match Secretary—**R Chapman,** 24a Fordham Road, Soham, Ely CB7 5AQ (Ely 721150 or 722154).
Representative on the Council—**Miss D L M Portway.**

AFFILIATED CLUBS (38)

Buckden—*Secretary:* M J Pepper, 50 Manor Gardens, Buckden, St Neots, Huntingdon PE18 9TN (Huntingdon 811502).
Burwell—*Secretary:* Mrs S Senior, 10 Silver Street, Burwell (Newmarket 741686).
Cambridge—Caius College Ground, Coton Footpath, Cambridge. Courts: G8, H4. *Secretary:* Mrs L Watt, 142 Hinton Way, Great Shelford, Cambridge (843235).
Cocks & Hens—Madingley Road. Courts: G8, H2. *Secretary:* Mrs V Parkes, 7 Shepreth Road, Barrington, Cambridge CB2 5SB (870397).
Cambridge University Press—Shaftesbury Road, Cambridge. Courts: G4. *Secretary:* D M Ash, 13 Ward Road, Cambridge CB1 3SY (243833).
Chesterton Former Pupils—*Secretary:* J McRobbie, 33 Enniskillen Road, Cambridge CB4 1SQ (314153).
Comberton—Recreation Ground. Courts: H2, G2. *Secretary:* Mrs P Coe, 30 Westlands, Comberton (3105).
Cottenham SSC—*Secretary:* Mrs P Seely, 33 Dunstal Field, Cottenham, Cambridge CB4 4UH (Cottenham 50751).
D Abo—*Secretary:* M Dobell, c/o Weston Colville Hall, Cambridge CB1 5PE (West Wratting 461).
Eastways—Eastholm School. Courts: H5. *Secretary:* J L Rudd, 7 Priors Gate, Werrington, Peterborough (77361).
Ely Beet Sport & Social Club—Courts: G3. *Secretary:* Mr B Taylor, 37 Lynton Drive, Ely (Ely 3142).
FBC Ltd—Harston. Courts: H2. *Secretary:* N J De'ath, 11 Church Road, Hauxton, Cambridge (870121).
Foxton Village—Courts: H2. *Secretary:* Mrs H Neill, 4 Fowlmere Road, Foxton, Cambridge CB2 6RS (Cambridge 871085).
Girton—Courts: H2. *Secretary:* Mr B Spencer, 23 Redgate Road, Girton, Cambridge (276428).
Great Shelford—Courts: H2. *Secretary:* Mrs S Morton, Steading, 10c Church Street, Great Shelford, Cambs (Cambridge 843671).
Great Staughton—*Secretary:* Mrs H Darby, 22 Beachampstead Road, Great Staughton, Hunts (Huntingdon 861253).
Haslingfield—*Secretary:* Mr V Ayres, 1 Pates Close, Haslingfield, Cambs.
Hemingfords—Manor Road, Hemingford Grey. Courts: H2. *Secretary:* Mrs J Headley, 6 Langley Way, Hemingford Grey, Huntingdon, Cambs (64511).
Histon—Recreation Ground, Bridge Road. Courts: G4. *Secretary:* M Hubbard, 4 Garry Drive, Cambridge (314443).
Homerton College—Hills Road. *Secretary:* Miss C Sheray, Homeaton College, Hills Road, Cambridge.
Huntingdon and Godmanchester—County Buildings, High Street, Huntingdon. Courts: G6. *Secretary:* Ms C Siddall, 2 Beech Avenue, Great Stukeley, Hunts (Huntingdon 51399).
Longstanton—*Secretary:* Mr B Harrison, 31 Ladywalk, Longstanton, Cambridge (Crafts Hill 81250).
Longthorpe—*Secretary:* Mrs M Taylor, 42 Apsley Way, Longthorpe, Peterborough (Peterborough 265739).
Sir M MacDonald & Partners—*Secretary:* Miss A Stuck, Sir M MacDonald & Partners, Station Road, Cambridge (66455).
Meldreth—Courts: H1. *Secretary:* G Clayton, 66 North End, Meldreth, Royston (60571).
NALGO—*Secretary:* S J Mudge, 2 Maple Close, Linton, Cambridge (892737 or 317634).

Peterborough City—*Secretary:* Miss J Mead, 63 Adderley, Bretton, Peterborough PE3 8RB.
Plant Breeding Institute—Courts: G3, H2. *Secretary:* Miss A M Squire, Plant Breeding Institute, Maris Lane, Trumpington, Cambridge CB2 2LQ (840411).
Pye Sports Club (Tennis Section)—St Andrew's Road, Cambridge. Courts: H2. *Secretary:* Mr T Silk, Pye Telecommunications Ltd, St Andrews Road, Cambridge (61222).
RAF Alconbury—J B Briley, RAF Alconbury, Box 234, Huntingdon (Huntingdon 64857).
RAF Hospital Ely—Lynn Road, Ely. Courts: H3. *Secretary:* Squadron Leader K Nulliah (Ely 5781).
Ramsey—Cricket Field Lane, Ramsey. Courts: G3. *Secretary:* Miss E Halden, Common Farm, Upwood, Hunts (Ramsey 812246).
Soham—*Secretary:* Mrs M Bysouth, 82 Paddock Street, Soham, Ely CB7 5JA (Ely 721750).
St Neots—*Secretary:* Mrs S Cook, The Old Vicarage, 19 Bushmead Road, Eaton Socon, St Neots (Huntingdon 73074).
Stapleford—Haverhill Road. Courts: H2. *Secretary:* D J Outram, 150 Hinton Way, Great Shelford (Cambridge 842776).
Thomas Cook S & STC—Thorpewood, Peterborough. Courts: H4. *Secretary: A R Williams, 7 Glamis Gardens, Peterborough (264454).*
West Hill Park Foxton—Courts: H1. *Secretary:* Mr I O'Reilly, 21 West Hill Road, Foxton (Cambridge 871356).
Wisbech Town—Harecroft Road, Wisbech. Courts: G5. *Secretary:* P J Peukert, Oakleigh, 27 Queens Road, Wisbech.

OTHER AFFILIATED ORGANISATIONS (3)

Cambridgeshire LTA Junior Committee—*Secretary:* Mrs L Davison, 53 Gilbert Road, Cambridge CB4 3NX (Cambridge 354300).
Cambridgeshire Tennis Coaches' Association—Miss S Rich, Cambridge University LTA, Gresham Road, Cambridge (357185).
Cambridge Boys—Mrs J Ambler, 91 High Street, Little Wilbraham, Cambs.

AFFILIATED SCHOOLS (33)

Boys
St Faith's School — 6 Trumpington Road. **Perse School for Boys** — Hills Road, Cambridge CB2 2QE.

Girls
Perse School for Girls — Union Road, Cambridge CB2 1HF. **St Marys Convent** — Bateman Street, Cambridge CB2 1LY.

Mixed
Barton CE School — Burwell House. **Bushfield Community School. Cambridge College of Arts & Tech. Caldecote Community Primary School. Duxford CE. Community School. Eastholm School. Elton CE Primary School. Fawcett Infants School. Gamlingay Village College. Godmanchester CP School. Highless Junior School. Hills Road Sixth Form College. Hinchingbrooke School. Ken Stimpson Community School. Longsands Community College. Melbourn Village College. Neale-Wade Community College. Oakdale CP School. Papworth Everard Community Primary School. Park Lane CP School. Ravensthorpe Infants School. Sawston Village College. Long Road Sixth Form College. St Mary's RC School.** Royston. **Sir Harry Smith Community College. Thorpe Junior School. Walton Comprehensive School. Welland CP School** — Junior School. **Walton Comprehensive School. Welland CP School. Witchford Village College.**

CHESHIRE COUNTY LAWN TENNIS ASSOCIATION

Hon Secretary—**G R D Porteous,** 'Kinross,' 8 Church Meadow Lane, Heswall, Wirral, Merseyside L60 4SB (051-342 1713).
Hon Treasurer—**R W Hughes,** 81 Dale Street, Liverpool L2 2HT (051 236 1002 bus, 051 342 3766 pri).
Hon Men's Match Secretary—**N de Wit,** Hamilton House, School Lane, Ness Holt, South Wirral L64 4DG (051 709 3677 bus, 051 336 5537 pri).
Hon Ladies' Match Secretary—**Mrs M Penn,** 'Hatherlow,' Alan Drive, Hale, Altrincham (061-980 2814).
Representatives on the Council—**M C McAfee, K C Cook OBE, R H M Ellis.**

AFFILIATED CLUBS (82)

Alderley—Ethelbert Road, Meols, Wirral, Merseyside L47 5AD (051-632 2913). Courts: H4. *Secretary:* M J O'Connell, 47 Queens Avenue, Meols, Wirral, Merseyside (051-632 1216).
Alderley Edge Cricket & LTC—Moss Lane, Alderley Edge. Courts: G8. *Secretary:* G F Littler, 14 Torkington Road, Wilmslow SK9 2AE (Wilmslow 525661 pri, 061-832 7413 bus).
Alsager—Sandbach Road, North Alsager, Stoke-on-Trent. Courts: H4. *Secretary:* Mrs J Ross, 24 Milton Crescent, Talke, Stoke-on-Trent ST7 1PF (Kidgrove 4059).
Bertram—Bertram Drive, Meols, Wirral, Merseyside (051-632 1982). Courts: H5. *Secretary:* C Roberts, 10 Garden Hey Road, Meols, Wirral, Merseyside (051-632 2936).
BICC Tennis Club—BICC, Chester Road, Helsby, via Warrington. Courts: H4. *Secretary:* Miss H Marshall, 18 Rydal Grove, Helsby, WA6 0ET (Helsby 3436).
Birkenhead—70/72 Shrewsbury Road, Oxton, Birkenhead L43 2HY (051-652 2163). Courts: H9. *Secretary:* Mrs G Konrad, "Inscot", Budworth Road, Noctorum, Birkenhead, Merseyside (051-652 5343).
Bowdon—Elcho Road, Bowdon WA14 (061-928 5015). Courts: G8, H3. *Secretary:* D N Odling, 2 Laurel Bank, Stamford Road, Bowdon WA14 (061-928 3957).

Bowdon Bowling & LTC—Stamford Road (entrance Winton Road), (061-928 3905). Courts: G3, H3. *Secretary:* Mrs J Crosby, 10 Highgate Road, Altrincham, Cheshire WA14 4QZ (061-928 3849).
Brabyns—Brabyns Bow, Marple, Cheshire (061-427 3726). Courts: H7. *Secretary:* M K Miller, 5 Burnside Cottage, Hollins Lane, Marple Bridge, nr Stockport SK7 1EN (061-427 7537).
Bramhall Lane—Ramsdale Road, Bramhall, Stockport (061-439 5560). Courts: H8. *Secretary:* Mrs A Collier, 'Tann Pitts,' 18 Moss Lane, Bramhall, Stockport SK7 1EH (061-439 4650).
Bramhall Park—Bramhall Park Road, Bramhall, Stockport (061-439 5514). Courts: H6. *Secretary:* N G Shepherd, 49 Albany Road, Bramhall, Stockport SK7 1NE (061-439 5341).
Bramhall Queensgate Sports Club—Queensgate, Bramhall (061-439 4672). Courts: H6. *Secretary:* D Berry, 5 Victoria Close, Bramhall, Stockport SK7 2BZ (061-439 2831).
Broadway (Cheadle)—Barcheston Road, Cheadle SK8 1LL. Courts: H3. *Secretary:* Mrs P J Baker, 1 Old Broadway, Withington, Manchester M20 9DH.
Brooklands Sports Club—The Pavilion, George's Road, Sale M33 3NL (061-973 3899). Courts: G10, H5. *Secretary:* J Davies, 75 Hamnett Court, Ainscough Road, Birchwood, Warrington, WA3 7PN (Warrington 51102 bus).
Cheadle—Cheadle (Kingsway) Sports Club Ltd (061-428 5881). Courts: G2, H4. *Secretary:* Mrs W I Jones, 10 Donnington Avenue, Cheadle, Stockport (061-428 4455).
Chester (Hough Green)—Wrexham Road, Chester. Courts: G3, H5. *Secretary:* J Hoyle, 18 Oaklands Crescent, Tattenhall, Nr Chester (Tattenhall 70951).
Claremont—Claremont Drive, W Timperley. Courts: G1, H3. *Secretary:* J I Roberts, Ger-y-Coed, Claremont Drive, West Timperley, Altrincham.
Congleton—Crescent Road, Congleton, Cheshire (373). Courts: G3, H5. *Secretary:* Mrs. M. Doe, 31 Somerset Close, Congleton (Congleton 277624).
Croftside—Courts: H3. *Secretary:* Mrs P Walsh, "Woodland", Meadow Close, Wilmslow SK9 6JN.
Daten Sports & Social Club (Tennis Section)—Charnock Road, Culcheth, Warrington WA3 4ES (Culcheth 3096). Courts: H4. *Secretary:* Mrs M Dowson, 26 Lodge Drive, Culcheth, Warrington WA3 4ES (Culcheth 3635).
Davenport—Flowery Field, Woodsmoor, Stockport (061-483 3950). Courts: H4. *Secretary:* Mrs D S Elliott, 2 Carrfield Avenue, Woodsmoor, Stockport SK3 8TN (061-483 3917).
Delamere Park—Delamere Parkway, West Cuddington, Northwich. Courts: H2. *Secretary:* G Burrows, 1 Ravensfield, Delamere Park Estate (0606 883883).
Disley Amalgamated Club—Jacksons Edge, Disley, Stockport SK12 2JR (Disley 3092). Courts: H3. *Secretary:* Mrs M Jones, 1 Wybersley Road, High Lane, Stockport (Disley 2496).
Gatley—Belmont Road, Gatley, Cheadle. Courts: H6. *Secretary:* Mrs I Pullar, 47 Gleneagles Road, Heald Green, Cheadle.
Glan Aber—Glan Aber Park, Hough Green. Courts: H4. *Secretary:* c/o R Mayorcas, 5 Lache Lane, Chester CH4 7LP (0244 675240).
Grappenhall Village—Bradshaw Lane, Grappenhall, Warrington. Courts: H5. *Secretary:* Mr J D Dixon, 4 Barrymore Court, Grappenhall, Warrington WA4 2QZ (0925 67588).
Greave—Hillcourt Road, Romiley. Courts: H3. *Secretary:* P Tysoe, 32 Werneth Road, Woodley, nr Stockport (061-430 2568).
Hale—Park Avenue, off Park Drive, Hale (061-981 3855). Courts: G4, H4. *Secretary:* J Johnston, 35 Valley Way, Knutsford WA16 9AY (Knutsford 4048).
Hale Barns—Chapel Lane, Hale Barns. Courts: H4. *Secretary:* A Sykes, 4 Sandown Drive, Hale Barns WA15 0BA (061-980 6756).
Handforth Hall—Woodlands Road, Handforth SK9 3AP. Courts: H4. *Secretary:* Miss S Wood, 25 Ullswater Road, Handforth, Wilmslow.
Heswall—Quarry Road East, Heswall (051-342 1775). Courts: G2, H6. *Secretary:* Mrs C Irving, "Zetland", Oldfield Road, Heswall, Wirral, Merseyside (051 342 2641).
Heyes Lane—Courts: H2. *Secretary:* Mrs J Bowers, 104 Manchester Road, Wilmslow SK9 2JX (0625 524324).
High Legh—Coopers Square, High Leigh, nr Knutsford. Courts: H3. *Secretary:* Miss C Royle, 7 Linden Close, Lymm WA13 9PH (Lymm 5509).
Hoole—Fairfield Road, Hoole, Chester. Courts: H5. *Secretary:* J N Cadman, 66 Hoole Road, Chester CH2 3NL (0244 25937).
Hooton & District—Berwick Road, Little Sutton, Wirral L66 4PR. Courts: H4. *Secretary:* T Barton, 6 Debra Road, Great Sutton, South Wirral L66 4LW (051-339 5909).
Hoylake—Eddisbury Road, off Meols Drive, Hoylake, Wirral (051-632 3491). Courts: G5, H3. *Secretary:* N J Carlile, 27 Lennox Lane, Bidston, Birkenhead L43 7RD (051 652 8097).
ICI (Alderley Park)—Icicals Social Club, ICI Pharmaceuticals Division, Alderley Park, Macclesfield SK10 4TF (0625 582828). Courts: H3. *Secretary:* Mrs G Brown, 42 Beatty Drive, Congleton CW12 2ER (Congleton 79039).
ICI (Widnes) Recreation Club—Liverpool Road, Widnes WA8 7EY (051-424 2350 staff) (members 051-424 2355). Courts: H4. *Secretary:* D Scott, 11 Kirkwall Drive, Penketh, Warrington (Penketh 7416).
Knutsford—Mereheath Lane, Knutsford (Knutsford 2721). Courts: G2, H7. *Secretary:* F P Delaunay, 49 Beggarmans Lane, Knutsford WA16 9BA (0565 51706).
Lane—Coroners' Lane, Widnes. Courts: H3. *Secretary:* A C Harmer, 8 Clarence Avenue, Widnes WA8 9EL (051-424 1509 pri, 051-423 1391 ext 69 bus).
Lymm LT & Croquet Club—Brookfield Road, Lymm (Lymm 4855). Courts: G9, H4. *Secretary:* B R Bealing, 20 Wychwood Avenue, Lymm WA13 0NE (Lymm 3721).
Macclesfield—Victoria Road, Macclesfield

(24249). Courts: H4. *Secretary:* Miss S Toole, 113 Bond Street, Macclesfield SK11 6RE.
Malpas & District Sports Club—Oxheyes, Wrexham Road, Malpas SY14 (0948 860 662). Courts: H4. *Secretary:* P Chamberlain, 16 Springfield Avenue, Malpas SY14 8QD (0948 860 529).
Mottram and District—Courts: H3. *Secretary:* N Higginbottom, 12 Woodbrooke Avenue, Hyde SK14 2SQ (061-368 1440).
Mountwood—Cecil Road, Prenton, Birkenhead, Wirral. Courts: H3. *Secretary:* Mrs E Kermode, 42 Prenton Farm Road, Prenton, Birkenhead (051-608 9550).
Nantwich—Mount Drive, Nantwich. Courts: G3, H2. *Secretary:* Mrs C M Farrall, 19 Mount Drive, Nantwich CW5 6JF (0270 624335).
Neston & District Cricket (LT Section)—Parkgate Road, Parkgate, South Wirral (051-336 4199). Courts: G8, H3. *Secretary:* Mrs C Bates, Sandstone Ridge, Gorstons Lane, Little Neston, South Wirral L64 4EF (051-336 3156).
North Cheshire—Gerard Avenue, Wallasey. Courts: H4. *Secretary:* Mrs B Towers, 17a Hoseside Road, Wallasey L45 0LA (051 639 1068).
Oxton Cricket & LTC—Townfield Lane, off Talbot Road, Birkenhead (051-652 1331). Courts: G5, H2. *Secretary:* Mrs T C Hodges, 40 Parkbridge Road, Prenton, Birkenhead, Merseyside L42 9JT.
Padgate Tennis & Bowling Club—Green Lane, Padgate, Warrington. Courts: H6. *Secretary:* N Deakin, 601 Warrington Road, Risley, Warrington (Culcheth 4242).
Pinewood—Napps Way, Heswall (051-342 1611). Courts: H4. *Secretary:* D S Banks, 291 Telegraph Road, Heswall, Wirral L60 6RN (051-342 5276).
Port Sunlight—Leverhulme Sports Field, Green Lane, Bromborough, Wirral (051-334 3677). Courts: H8. *Secretary:* Mrs H Wood, 61 Chorley Way, Bebington, Wirral L63 9LS (051-334 5434).
Pownall Park—Carrwood Road, Pownall Park, Wilmslow. Courts: H3. *Secretary:* Mrs S M Kaye, 47 Hawthorn Lane, Wilmslow SK9 5DG (Wilmslow 525433).
Poynton Sports Club (Tennis Section)—London Road, North Poynton SK12 (Poynton 873765). Courts: G2, H3. *Secretary:* R A Mason, 17 Brookfield Avenue, Poynton SK12 1HZ (0625 875966).
Prenton—Storeton Road, Prenton, Birkenhead (051-608 1915). Courts: G2, H3. *Secretary:* Mrs A Ritson, 33 Westminster Drive, Bromborough, Wirral, Merseyside L62 6AN (051 334 2461).
Prestbury Village—off Bollin Grove, Prestbury (Prestbury 828343). Courts: H6. *Secretary:* Mrs S G Youatt, 5 Elm Rise, Castleford Park, Prestbury (Prestbury 829446 pri, 061-928 6333 ext 210 bus).
Rolls Royce Motors Sports and Social Club—Minshull New Road, Crewe (Crewe 214911). Courts: H6. *Secretary:* P J Bridge, 165 Gainsborough Road, Crewe CW2 7PL (Crewe 661046 pri, 0270 255155 ext 3385 bus).
Ryecroft Park Sports Club—Park Avenue, Cheadle Hulme SK8 6EU (061-485 2998). Courts: H5. *Secretary:* Mrs J B Sheard, 18 Furness Road, Cheadle Hulme, Stockport SK8 7PX (061 439 8256).
Sale Cricket, Tennis & Hockey and Old Salians RUFC—Rockwood, Clarendon Road, Sale (061-973 7250). Courts: H5. *Secretary:* P J Robinson, 65 St. John's Road, Lostock, Bolton, Lancs BL6 4HB.
St Lukes—Charles Road, Hoylake. Courts: H2. *Secretary:* Mrs E Stott, 23 Thorns Drive, Greasby, Wirral L49 3PU (051-677 8477).
Shell Club—Shell Tennis Section, Shell Sports Club, Whitby, Ellesmere Port, South Wirral (051-355 3125). Courts: H4. *Secretary:* C Rogers, Farthings, Well Lane, Mouldsworth, Cheshire CH3 8AU (Manley 445).
Stockton Heath—Delphfields Road. Courts: H6. *Secretary:* Mr A Tylor, Rose Cottage, Knutsford Road, Budworth Heath, Northwich (Comberbach 891042 pri, 061-228-2211 bus).
Styal—Altrincham Road, Styal. Courts: H3. *Secretary:* K A Davis, The Coach House, Kennerleys Lane, Wilmslow SK9 5EQ (0625 526147).
Tame Valley—Greenbridge Lane, Greenfield, nr Oldham, Lancs (Saddleworth 2679). Courts: H3. *Secretary:* F J T Tanner, Flat 4, The Nook, Greenfield, nr Oldham, Lancs (Saddleworth 70912 pri, Saddleworth 2273 ext 1 bus).
Tarporley—High Street, Tarporley. Courts: H2. *Secretary:* Mrs B Bebington, Brook House Farm, Stapleford, Tarvin, Chester CH3 8HL (0829 40358).
Tarvin—King George VI Playing Field, Tarvin, Chester. Courts: H3. *Secretary:* Mrs M Hearndon, 4 Deans Way, Tarvin, Chester CH3 8L (Tarvin 41374).
Tattenhall—Flacca Field, Tattenhall. Courts: G3, H2. *Secretary: Tennis Section,* Mrs R Gilbert, The Roost, Higher Burwardsley, Tattenhall, nr Chester (Tattenhall 70428).
Temple Lawn Tennis & Social Club—15 Winstanley Road, Sale M33. Courts: H5. *Secretary:* R Bilsborrow, 65 Park Road, Sale (061-973 6452).
Thorndale—Thorndale Lane, off Wallasey Road, Wallasey, Wirral (051-638 1231). Courts: H6. *Secretary:* Miss J Owen, 24 Lea Road, Wallasey, Wirral.
Thornton Hough—Courts: H2. *Secretary:* Mrs M Bernard, 5 Mere Avenue, Raby Mere, Wirral L63 0NE (051-334-4661).
Timperley Cricket Hockey LT and Lacrosse Club—Stockport Road, Timperley, Altrincham (061-980 4397). Courts: G4, H6. *Secretary:* E Brookes, 1 Hall Lane, Baguley, Manchester M23 8AQ (061 998 9185).
Upton Victory Hall Lawn Tennis & Badminton Club—The Victory Hall, Salacre Lane, Upton, Wirral (051-677 3861). Courts: G5, H4. *Secretary:* Miss M W H Jones, 11 Wroxham Drive, Upton, Wirral L49 0TS (051-677 5864).
Wallasey Manor—Kingsway, Wallasey, Wirral (051-630 5905). Courts: H5. *Secretary:* D Hill, 14 Warren Drive, Wallasey (051-639-4688).
Warren—The Warren Club, Grove Road, Wallasey, Wirral L45 0JD (051-639 4527). Courts:

G3. *Secretary:* G Thomas, "Greystones", 21a Warren Drive, Wallasey, Merseyside (051 639 3624).
Warrington Sports Club—Walton Lea Road, Walton (Warrington 63210). Courts: H4. *Secretary:* K Everett, 119 Ellesmere Road, Lower Walton, Warrington WA4 3EE (0925-64658).
Whitby—Castle Drive, Whitby, Ellesmere Port, South Wirral. Courts: H3. *Secretary:* Mrs C A Cable, 14 Whitebeam Avenue, Great Sutton, South Wirral L66 2UR (051-356 3027).
Wilmslow—Cumber Lane, Wilmslow, Cheshire. Courts: H5. *Secretary:* Mrs H A Reeman, Wood Hill, Mottram Road, Alderley Edge SK9 7DR (0625 583321).
Winnington Hall—Northwich CW8 4DU (Northwich 74444) (Manager 705300). Courts: G7, H3. *Secretary:* Dr I B Parker, 9 Park Lane, Hartford, Northwich (74024).
Winsford—Knights Grange Sports Complex, Winsford. Courts: H2. *Secretary:* Mrs B Shone, 2 West View, Church Minshull, Nantwich. (0270-071 388).
Woodside—Brookside Lane, High Lane, Stockport (Disley 4218). Courts: H6. *Secretary:* Mrs A P Joynson, 1 Derwent Road, High Lane, Stockport SK6 8AT (Disley 2458).
Wrenbury District—c/o East View, Top O'th Town, Broomhall, Nantwich (Crewe 780460). Courts: H2. *Secretary:* Mrs P Scott, 28 Oakfield Avenue, Wrenbury, Nantwich (0270 780 018).

AFFILIATED SCHOOLS (55)

Boys

Altrincham Grammar School — Altrincham. **Birkenhead School** — Oxton, Birkenhead. **Calday Grange Grammar School** — West Kirby. **Holmes Chapel Comprehensive School** — Holmes Chapel. **The King's School** — Chester. **Mosslands School** — Wallasey. **Moseley School** — Cheadle. **Mostyn House School** — Parkgate, Wirral. **Offerton High School** — Offerton, Stockport. **Sandbach School** — Sandbach.

Girls

All Hallows Catholic High School — Macclesfield. **Altrincham County Grammar School** — Altrincham. **Bebington Secondary School for Girls** — Bebington, Wirral. **Birkenhead High School GPDST** — Claughton, Birkenhead. **Cheadle Hulme School for Girls** — Cheadle Hulme. **Cransley School** — Great Budworth, nr Northwich. **Clucheth Hall School** — Altrincham. **Fairfield High School** — Widnes. **Goudhurst College** — Nantwich. **Hammond School** — Chester. **Hartford High School for Girls** — Hartford. **Helsby High School for Girls** — Helsby. **Highfield School** — Oxton, Birkenhead. **Leftwich County High School** — Northwich. **Loreto Convent Grammar School** — Altrincham. **Malpas Heber County High School** — Malpas. **Malbank School** — Nantwich. **Mount Carmel School** — Alderley Edge. **Queen's School** — Chester. **St Hilary's School** — Alderley Edge. **Sale County Grammar School for Girls** — Sale. **Shavington School for Girls** — Shavington. **Sir John Dean's College** — Northwich. **Upton Hall School** — Upton, Wirral. **Weatherhead High School** — Wallasey. **Wirral County Grammar School for Girls** — Bebington.

Mixed

Alsager Comprehensive School — Alsager. **Congleton Heathfield County High School** — Congleton. **Crewe Kings Grove County High School** — Crewe. **Dormie House School** — West Kirby. **Ellesmere Port Catholic High School** — Whitby, Ellesmere Port. **Ellesmere Port Stanney County Comprehensive School** — Ellesmere Port. **Frodsham High School** — Frodsham. **Lymm Grammar School** — Lymm. **Macclesfield County High School** — Macclesfield. **Marple Hall High School** — Marple. **Overleigh St Mary's CE Primary School** — Chester. **Padgate County High School** — Padgate, Warrington. **Stockton Heath County High School** — Appleton, Warrington. **Plessington High School** — Rock Ferry, Birkenhead. **Stockport Grammar School** — Stockport. **Tarporley County High School** — Tarporley. **Whitby County Comprehensive School** — Whitby, Ellesmere Port. **Widnes Sixth Form College** — Widnes. **Wilmslow County High School** — Wilmslow. **Winsford Verdin County Comprehensive School** — Winsford.

OTHER AFFILIATED ORGANISATIONS

Birkenhead Junior Tournament Committee—*Secretary:* M E D Hare, 12 Prenton Farm Road, Prenton, Birkenhead, Merseyside (051-608 2247).
Cheshire Girls' Schools Association—*Secretary:* Miss L Barrett, Ellesmere Port Grammar School, Sycamore Drive, Whitby, Ellesmere Port.
Chester & District Tennis League—*Secretary:* M C Snelson, 'Radley,' Wittering Lane, Lower Heswall, Wirral L60 9JL (051-342 2774).
Heswall Camp & Activity Centre—Manager: Mrs J M Biddulph, Heswall Camp House, Broad Lane, Heswall, Wirral, Merseyside L60 9JY (051 342 2359).
Hoylake Tournament Committee—*Secretary:* J Palmer, Malden, Low Wood Grove, Barnston, Wirral, Merseyside (051-648 2031).
Junior North East Cheshire Lawn Tennis League—*Secretary:* Mrs S G Youatt, 5 Elm Rise, Castleford Park, Prestbury (Prestbury 82944 pri, 061 928 6333 ext 210 bus).
Merseyside Youth Association—Barnston Dale, Storeton Lane, Barnston, Wirral L61 1BX. *Secretary:* E R Shaw, Dale House, Storeton Lane, Barnston, Wirral (051-648-1412).
Midland Bank/LTA Schools League (Wirral)—*Secretary:* M E D Hare, 12 Prenton Farm Road, Prenton, Birkenhead, Merseyside (051-608 2247).
Slazenger Chester Junior League—*Secretary:* Dr D Hart, 71 Upton Lane, Upton-by-Chester (0244 381483).
West Cheshire Veterans' Tournament Committee—*Secretary:* M E D Hare, 12 Prenton Farm Road, Prenton, Birkenhead, Merseyside (051-608 2247).

West Cheshire Winter League—*Secretary:* N Nelson, 35 Tudorville Road, Bebington, Wirral, Merseyside (051-645 5783).
Wirral Tennis League—*Secretary:* Miss B Cain, 42 Chiltern Road, Prenton, Birkenhead, Merseyside (051-608 1307).
Wirral Floodlit League—*Secretary:* Mrs V Blythe, 49 Queens Drive, Prenton, Birkenhead, Merseyside (051-608 7049).
Wirral Junior Summer League—*Secretary:* M E D Hare, 12 Prenton Farm Road, Prenton, Birkenhead, Merseyside (051-608 2247).

CORNWALL LAWN TENNIS ASSOCIATION

Hon Secretary—**Mrs A Nicholson,** 93 Sea Road, Carlyon Bay, St Austell (Par 3767).
Hon Junior Secretary—**J Bird,** Lowerton Farm, Camelford (3280).
Hon Treasurer—**H Fletcher,** 4 Grove Park Terrace, Liskeard (44842).
Hon Men's Match Secretaries—**D R Williams,** Lower Treforest, 66 Westerlands Road, Wadebridge (3597). **J M Webster,** Sunnybanks Farm, Fletchers Bridge, Bodmin (5048).
Hon Ladies' Match Secretaries—**Mrs N A Watkins,** 'Hazel Mead,' Priory Road, Easton-in-Gordano, nr Bristol BS20 0PR (027581-2474). **Mrs E Jenkin,** St Erbyn's School, Clarence Street, Penzance (3567).
Representative on the Council—**R A James,** 35 Bosvean Gardens, Truro (79330).

AFFILIATED CLUBS (32)

Bodmin—The Priory. Courts: H3. *Secretary:* D Gramaldi, 12 Old Market Place, Bodmin PL31 1NA.
Boscawen Park—Boscawen Park, Truro. Courts: H4. *Secretary:* Mrs P James, 35 Bosvean Gardens, Truro (79330).
Bude Haven—Bude Haven Recreation Grounds. Courts: H4. *Secretary:* Mrs R A Pearce, Kings Hill House, 63 Kings Hill, Bude (4540).
Callington—George Place, Callington. Courts: H1. *Secretary:* Miss L Trebilcock, East Harrowbarrow, St Dominic, Callington (St Dominic 50156).
Cambourne Mount Pleasant—The Grammar School, Camborne. Courts: H2. *Secretary:* S Boyle, 21 Bassett Road, Camborne (712421).
Falmouth—Western Terrace, Falmouth. Courts: G3, H4. *Secretary:* Mrs N Banks, 32 Dracaena Avenue, Falmouth (313416).
Hayle—Courts: H2. *Secretary:* Mrs K Lindsay, 34 Reawla Lane, Gwinear, Hayle (Leedstown 516).
Helston—Coronation Park. Courts: H2. *Secretary:* R Grime, 6 Cross Street, Helston (2984).
Holman Sports Club (Tennis Section)—Camborne. Courts: H2. *Secretary:* Mrs M Davies, 'Rosebank,' 7 Penware Parc, Camborne.
Launceston—Courts: H2. *Secretary:* Mrs D Allen, 16 Hawks Tor Drive, Lewannick, Launceston (542).
Liskeard—Courts: H2. *Secretary:* Mrs S Hess, Little Fursdon Farm, Liskeard (43896).
Looe and Hannafore—Hannafore. Courts: G1, H4. *Secretary:* W Richardson, 54 Portbyan Road, The Downs, West Looe (Looe 3212).
Newlyn—*Secretary:* W Harvey, 6 Lyn Terrace, Newlyn, Penzance.
Newquay—The Golf Club, Tower Road. Courts: H3. *Secretary:* B Dell, 53 Parklands Close, Newquay (3969).
Padstow—*Secretary:* Miss S Thomas, 31 Dennis Road, Padstow (532337).
Penryn—*Secretary:* Mrs J Nicholls, St Anthony, 97 Trescoben Road, Falmouth.
Penwith—Courts: H2. *Secretary:* Mrs A Webb, 42 Fore Street, St Just.
Penzance—Penlee Memorial Park. Courts: H6 (2 all weather). *Secretary:* Mrs K Simpson, Thornleigh, Potiou, Zennor, St. Ives.
Perranporth—Courts: G6, H3. *Secretary:* A E Adams, 4 Higher Bolenna (Perranporth 3025).
Porthleven—Courts: H4. *Secretary:* Mrs S McKenney, 'Shilo,' West View, Porthleven.
Redruth—Trevingey Terrace. Courts: H6. *Secretary:* C Goate, Heather Stone, Alexandra Road, Illogan, Redruth (Portreth 842628).
RAF St Mawgan—Station. Courts: H3. *Secretary:* Officer i/c Tennis, RAF St Mawgan, Newquay (Newquay 2201 ext 356 Flt Lt M Rodgers).
Royal Naval Air Station Culdrose—Culdrose. Courts: H6. *Secretary:* LPT Paul Lucas, Seahawk Tennis Club, RNAS Culdrose, Helston (4121 ext 2404/2255).
St Agnes—Goonvrea Road leading to Chapelporth. Courts: H2. *Secretary:* Mrs D Taylor, 'Pennymoon,' Mithian, St Agnes (3259).
St Austell—Poltair. Courts: H4. *Secretary:* G Duane, 14 Fairway, Carlyon Bay, St Austell (Par 4749).
St Ives—Primrose Valley. Courts: H3. *Secretary:* Miss J Fisher, Lower Stennack, Beckbury Cottage, St Ives.
St Stephen—St Austell. Courts: H2. *Secretary:* K Polmounter, 25 Gwindra Road, St Stephen (823329).
Saltash—Longstone. Courts: G2, H2. *Secretary:* J Singleton, 37 Lower Port View, Saltash.
Stithians—Playing Field. Courts: H1. *Secretary:* Mrs S Nicholas, 2 Glen Dor, New Road, Stithians (860142).
Torpoint—Thanckes Park. Courts: G1, H2. *Secretary:* Miss S Pollock, Chapeldown Road, Torpoint.
Truro, City of (Hard Courts)—Boscawen Park. Courts: H2. *Secretary:* Mrs C Roxborough, 1 Prospect Cottage, Bodmin Road, Truro (73051).
Wadebridge—Playing Fields, Egloshayle. Courts: H5. *Secretary:* Mrs A Williams, Lower Treforest, 66 Westerlands Road, Wadebridge (3597).

OTHER AFFILIATED ORGANISATIONS (4)

Cornwall Technical College—Trevenson. Courts: H3 (indoor 1). *Secretary:* Mrs P Holland, CTC, 11 Wall Road, Reawla, Hayle, Leedstown (442).
Penzance Open Tournament Committee—Penlee Park. Courts: G2, H4. *Secretary:* Mrs P Venn, 9 Park Corner, Penzance (65643).

St Austell Restricted Tournament Committee—Poltair Playing Ground. Courts: H4. *Secretary:* Mrs A Nicholson, 93 Sea Road, Carlyon Bay, Par (3767).
Treganna Castle Hotel—St Ives. Courts: G3, H3. *Secretary:* The Resident Manager, St Ives (Penzance 795254).

SCHOOL CLUBS (35)

Humphry Davy Grammar School for Boys' — Penzance. **Cape Cornwall School** — St Just. **Penwith VI Form College** — Penzance. **Mounts Bay School** — Penzance. **Hayle School. St Ives School. Redruth School. Camborne School. Cornwall Technical College** — Camborne and Falmouth. **Helston School. Mullion School. Pool School. Falmouth School. Penryn School. Penair School** — Truro. **Richard Lander School** — Truro. **The Roseland School** — Tregony. **Mid-Cornwall College of Further Education** — St Austell. **Fowey School. Newquay Treviglas School. Penrice School** — St Austell. **Poltair School** — St Austell. **St Austell VI Form College. St Stephen-in-Brannel School. Bodmin School. Budehaven School. Camelford Sir James Smith's. Launceston College. Wadebridge School, Callington School. Liskeard School. Looe School. Saltash School. Torpoint School.**

CUMBRIA LAWN TENNIS ASSOCIATION

Hon Secretary—**R A Bedgar,** ACIS, 71 Strathnaver Avenue, Barrow-in-Furness, Cumbria LA14 3DQ (Barrow 41300 pri, Barrow 25500 bus).
Hon Treasurer—**J W Bell,** 16 Westover Avenue, Warton, Carnforth, Lancs (Carnforth 3116 pri, Milnthorpe 3363 bus).
Hon Men's Match Secretary—**F R McCade,** 38 The Green, Houghton, Carlisle (35467).
Hon Ladies' Match Secretary—**Mrs C Davis,** 14 Hill Close, Sedgewick, Kendal LA8 0JR (Kendal 61076).
County Coach and Junior Coaching Organiser—**A C Palmer,** Reading Room House, Hallbankgate, nr Brampton, Carlisle (Hallbankgate 524).
Hon Boys Match Secretary—**M W Robinson,** Pastorale, Linstock, Carlisle (33595).
Hon Girls' Match Secretary—**Mrs P Henderson,** 3 Forge Pond, Dalston, Carlisle (Dalston 711533).
Representative on the Council—**J R Nixon,** Pottleford, Hayton, Carlisle (Hayton 454).

AFFILIATED CLUBS (24)

Arnside—Courts: H2. *Secretary:* Mrs J Ellison, Greystones, Borwick Avenue, Warton, nr Carnforth, Lancs (732559).
Cavendish—Edenside. Courts: H3. *Secretary:* R A Ridley, 49 Beech Grove, Stanwix, Carlisle (35084).
Chatsworth—St Aidans Road, Courts: G4, H2. *Secretary:* Mrs D Henderson, 31 Mayson Street, Currock, Carlisle (43795).
Cockermouth—Courts: H3. *Secretary:* Mrs J V Geater, Foxwold, Wythop Mill, nr Cockermouth, CA13 9YP.
Dalston—Courts: G2, H2. *Secretary:* S A Sinclair, Gambling Croft, Hawksdale, Carlisle CA5 7BJ (Dalston 710664).
Dalton Cricket Club—Courts: G3. *Secretary:* K Barnes, East View, Pennington, Lindal (Ulverston 53188).
Eden—Brampton Road, Carlisle. Courts: G4, H2. *Secretary:* D Rowell, 28 Teasdale Road, Lowry Hill, Carlisle CA3 0HF (Carlisle 31783)
Endmoor—Courts: H2. *Secretary:* Mrs L Sinfield, 40 Greenways Drive, Low Park, Endmoor, Kendal (Sedgwick 60394)
Harrington—Courts: G1, H1. *Secretary:* G E Corrie, 'Carnarvon,' 34 Moorclose Road, Harrington, Workington (830823).
Kendal—Mintbridge. Courts: H4. *Secretary:* Mr G C Whitwham, 11 Greengate, Levens, Kendal (Sedgwick 60679).
Keswick & District—Fitz Park. Courts: G7, H6. *Secretary:* Miss N Chew, Pinfold Close, Wordsworth Street, Keswick CA12 4HU (Keswick 73387).
Maryport Athletic—Memorial Gardens, Netherton Road, Courts: G2, H3. *Secretary:* Mr N D Illman, 34 Queens Avenue, Seaton, Workington (3147).
Milnthorpe—Courts: H2. *Secretary:* Miss L Wright, Greenacres, Heathwaite Close, Storth, Milnthorpe (Arnside 761660).
NALGO Barrow—West Mount, Barrow. Courts: H1, G6. *Secretary:* R Rogers, 245 Abbey Road, Barrow-in-Furness (37270).
Netherfield—Parkside Road, Courts: H2. *Secretary:* P Creer, 11 Whinfell Drive, Kendal.
North Lonsdale—Berners Close, Grange-over-Sands. Courts: H2. *Secretary:* Mrs D Davies, 'Fox Rock,' Allithwaite Road, Grange-over-Sands, Cumbria (Grange 2241).
Patterdale—Ullswater, Cumbria. Courts: H2. *Secretary;* M C Tonkin, Patterdale Hotel, Penrith CA11 0NN (Glenridding 08532 231).
Penrith—Castle Park. Courts: H4. *Secretary:* Mrs V M Mossop, Thorn Tree, Lazonby, Penrith CA10 1BL (Lazonby 204).
Ulverston—Dragley Beck. Courts: G4. *Secretary:* Mrs J. Rogers, 1 Lyndhurst Road, Ulverston (Ulverston 52492).
Vickers Sports Club—Hawcoat Park, Barrow. Courts: G5, H6. *Secretary:* A G Parker, 30 Hill Road, Barrow-in-Furness (Barrow 21261)
Whitehaven—Whitehaven Playground. Courts: G3, H3. *Secretary:* R B Hellier, 19 Ruskin Drive, Hillcrest, Whitehaven CA28 6TB (Whitehaven 4283).
Wigton—Courts: H3. *Secretary:* Mrs H Varty, 7 Deer Park, Wigton (42905).
Windermere—*Secretary:* Mrs C Hornby, 8 Brantfell House, Bowness-on-Windermere.
Workington (Ashfield)—Newlands Lane, Workington. Courts: G2, H3. *Secretary:* Mr P Cram, 14 Ashfield Gardens, Workington (Workington 65236).

OTHER AFFILIATED ORGANISATIONS (9)

Barrow & District Tennis League—*Secretary:* R A Bedgar, 71 Strathnaver Avenue, Barrow-in-Furness (Barrow 41300).

Barrow & District Junior Tennis League—*Secretary:* G Weatherburn, 34 Thwaite Street, Barrow-on-Furness (Barrow 38431).

Carlisle & District Tennis League—*Secretary:* J E Messenger, 23 Croft Road, Carlisle (36123).

Carlisle Corporation Municipal Tournament Committee—Bitts Park. Courts: G6, H4 and St James Park Courts: H3. *Secretary:* Hon Secretary, Municipal Tournament, c/o Parks Dept, Civic Centre, Carlisle (23411 ext 312).

Cumberland (Carlisle) Lawn Tennis Tournament Committee—Edenside. *Secretary:* D. Rowell, 28 Teasdale Road, Carlisle (Carlisle 31783).

Cumbria Schools LTA—*Secretary:* Mrs J Smith, Stile End, Dovenby, Cockermouth CA13 0PN (0900 824366).

Kendal & District Tennis League—*Secretary:* P Cook, 'Kirn', 52 Kentsford Road, Grange-over-Sands LA11 7BB (Grange-over-Sands 2615).

West Cumberland Junior Lawn Tennis Tournament—*Secretary:* Mrs M Bradshaw, 11 Sunnyside, Seaton, Workington.

West Cumbria Tennis League—*Secretary:* R Hannah, Mountain View Cottage, High Lorton, Cockermouth CA13 9TX (Lorton 321).

AFFILIATED SCHOOLS (25)

Boys

Park View Comprehensive School — Barrow-in-Furness. **Sedbergh School.**

Girls

Park View Comprehensive School — Barrow-in-Furness. **Casterton School** — Kirkby Lonsdale. **Cockermouth Grammar School** — Lorton Road, Cockermouth. **Kendal High School. Keswick School. Queen Elizabeth Grammar School** — Penrith. **St Anne's School** — Windermere. **Victoria High School** — Ulverston.

Mixed

Austin Friars School — St Anns Hill, Carlisle. **Caldew School** — Carlisle. **Eden Secondary School** — Carlisle. **Harraby Secondary School** — Carlisle. **Heversham Grammar School** — Milnthorpe. **John Ruskin Secondary School** — Coniston. **Milnthorpe Secondary School. Morton Secondary School** — Carlisle. **Nelson Thomlinson School** — Wigton. **Thorncliffe School** — Thorncliffe Road, Barrow-in-Furness. **Queen Elizabeth Grammar School** — Kirkby Lonsdale. **Samuel Kings Secondary School** — Alston. **Trinity Secondary School** — Carlisle. **Ullswater Secondary School** — Penrith. **White House School** — Brampton. **Workington Grammar School.**

DERBYSHIRE LAWN TENNIS ASSOCIATION

Hon Secretary—**Margaret Robinson,** 36 Broadway, Duffield, Derby DE6 4BU (841260).

Hon Treasurer—**Mrs S Cotton,** 51 Chain Lane, Mickleover, Derby (513505).

Hon Men's Match Secretary—**J S Fletcher,** Littleacres, St Johns Road, Smalley, Derby (880620 pri, Langley Mill 712317 bus).

Hon Junior Match Secretary (Boys)—**C Booth,** 17 Field Close, Hilton, Derbys (Etwall 4278 pri).

Hon Ladies' Match Secretary—**Miss B Allsopp,** Eweford Edge, Unthank Lane, Holmesfield, Sheffield (890358 pri).

Hon Junior Match Secretary (Girls)—**Miss B Allsopp,** Eweford Edge, Unthank Lane, Holmesfield, Sheffield (890358 pri).

Representative on the Council—**R F Hartle.**

AFFILIATED CLUBS (43)

Alfreton Palmer Morewood—Welfare Ground, Grange Road, Alfreton. Courts: G1, H5. *Secretary:* D Perkins, 'Carn Brae', 74 Grange Street, Alfreton, Derby, (Alfreton 833372 pri, Matlock 3411 ext 7820 bus).

Allestree South View—Recreation Ground, Allestree. Courts: H2. *Secretary:* G Marshall, 60 Ferrers Way, Darley Abbey, Derby (Derby 550106 pri).

Ashbourne—Ashbourne Lower School, Old Derby Road, Ashbourne. Courts: H5. *Secretary:* D Cater, West Firs, Waterhouses, Staffs (Waterhouses 560 pri).

Bamford—Off Station Road, Bamford. Courts: H3, G3. *Secretary:* N G Whitelaw, Hurlingham, Hope Road, Bamford, Sheffield (Hope Valley 51500 pri).

Belper Meadows—nr Christ Church, Belper. Courts: G3, H1. *Secretary:* M Davies, 6 Albert Street, Belper, Derbys (Belper 4339).

Belper Sports Centre Tennis Club—Belper Sports Centre. Courts: H4. Secretary: P W Allsopp, 2 Swiss Cottages, The Chevin, Belper (Belper 4539 pri).

Breadsall—Brookside Road, Breadsall, Derby. Courts: H2. *Secretary:* Mrs N Clifford, 28 Rectory Lane, Breadsall, Derby (Derby 833487 pri).

Buxton Cricket, Bowls & Tennis Club—The Park, Buxton. Courts: H3. *Secretary:* J D Rushton, 21 Devonshire Road, Buxton (Buxton 4540 pri, Buxton 71111 bus).

Carlton—Carlton Road, Derby. Courts: G2, H1. *Secretary:* F W Rowley, 3 Onslow Road, Mickleover, Derby (Derby 514807 pri).

Carlton Meadows—*Secretary:* R F Hartle, 'Rushmere', Mugginton Lane End, Weston Underwood, Derby (Cowers Lane 306 pri)

Central United Reformed Church Tennis Club—Brayfield Road, Littleover, Derby. Courts: G4. *Secretary:* Mrs A Shaw, 108 Whitaker Road, Derby (43743 pri).

Chesterfield—Hawkesley Avenue, Chesterfield. Courts: H9. *Secretary:* Thalsall, 37 Mansfeldt Road, Newbold, Chesterfield (Chesterfield 76478 pri).

Chesterfield Queens Park—Queens Park, Chesterfield. Courts: H2. *Secretary:* M Donohoe, 39 Raven Avenue, Tibshelf, Derbys (Ripley 875367 pri).

Church Broughton—Village Green, Church Broughton. Courts: H1. —*Secretary:* J G Kerslake, Copsewood, Church Broughton, Derbys DE6 5AR (Sudbury 245 pri, Leek 385731 bus).

County Officers(NALGO)—Matlock College of Education, Matlock. *Secretary:* P Goodwin, c/o County Analyst's Dept, County Offices, Matlock.
Derbyshire—Crewe Street, Derby. Courts: G5, H3. *Secretary:* P A Collier, 91 Palmerston Street, Derby (Derby 760442 pri Derby 31111 ext 768 bus).
Duffield—Town Street, Duffield. Courts: H7. *Secretary:* I H Acford, The Smithy, Mugginton, Weston Underwood, Derby (Ashbourne 60677 pri, Derby 72241 bus).
Edale LTC—Courts: H1. *Secretary:* Mrs P Murray-Leslie, The Vicarage, Edale, Sheffield S30 2ZA (Hope Valley 70254 pri).
Erratics—rear Rowditch Recreation Ground, Uttoxter Old Road, Derby. Courts: G3. *Secretary:* L V Smith, 111 Station Road, Mickleover, Derby (Derby 514291 pri, Derby 31384 bus).
Etwall—John Port School, Etwall, Derby. Courts: H9. *Secretary:* W M Wade, 44 Willington Road, Etwall, Derby, DE6 6NR (Etwall 3117 pri, Derby 42424 ext 335 bus).
Holymoorside—off Holymoor Road (adjacent to Bowling Green), Holymoorside, Chesterfield. Courts: H3. *Secretary:* Mrs P E Jackson, 135 Whitecotes Lane, Chesterfield, Derbys (Chesterfield 38419 pri).
Ilkeston Juniors LTC—Ilkeston Community Centre, Godfrey Drive Ilkeston. Courts: H6. *Secretary:* R K Pearson, 35 May Street, Cotmanhay, Ilkeston (Ilkeston 324263 pri).
Ilkeston Rutland—King George Avenue, Ilkeston. Courts: H4. *Secretary:* J P Mainwaring, 18 Summerfields Way, Ilkeston, Derbys DE7 9HF (Ilkeston 309662 pri).
International Combustion—Sinfin Lane, Derby. Courts: H3. *Secretary:* B Simpson, Rockbank, 35 Wordsworth Avenue, Sinfin, Derby DE2 9HQ (Derby 769722 pri, Derby 760223 ext 2544 bus).
Lakeside—Friesland Sports Centre, Sandiacre, Notts. Courts: H5. *Secretary:* B Howells, 125 Greenhills Road, Eastwood, Notts (Langley Mill 763795 pri, Langley Mill 763141 bus).
Littleacres—31 St Johns Road, Smalley, Derby. Courts: H1, G1. *Secretary: J S Fletcher, Littleacres, 31 St Johns Road, Smalley, DerbyDE7 6EG (Derby 880620 pri, Langley Mill 712317 bus).*
Little Eaton—St Peter's Park, Little Eaton, Derby. Courts: H3. *Secretary:* P B Mason, 428 Kedleston Road, Allestree, Derby (Derby 551713 pri, Derby 841791 ext 226 bus).
Littleover—40 Eastwood Drive, Littleover, Derby. Courts: H3. *Secretary:* A Peyton, 172 Stenson Road, Derby DE3 7JG (767556 pri).
Long Eaton—Manor Farm Recreation Ground, Toton. Courts: H3. *Secretary:* Mrs J Osaman, 99 Douglas Road, Long Eaton (721148 pri).
Melbourne—Penn Lane, Melbourne. Courts: H2. *Secretary:* P Fox, 10 Windsor Avenue, Melbourne, Derby (Derby 48562 bus, Melbourne 3119 pri).
Netherseale—at rear of School. Courts: G2, H3. *Secretary:* N D Smith, 4 Clifton Road, Netherseale, Burton-on-Trent (Burton-on-Trent 214468 bus, 760647 pri).
Ockbrook & Borrowash—Nottingham Road, Borrowash. Courts: H5. *Secretary:* Mrs J H Lee, 112 Sandringham Road, Sandiacre, Nottingham NG10 5LE (Long Eaton 724478 pri).
Ridgeway—*Secretary:* Mrs K M Mason, 17a High Lane, Ridgeway, Sheffield S12 3XF.
Ripley—Heage Road, Ripley. Courts: G2, H3. *Secretary:* J S Taylor, 143 Heage Road, Ripley, Derby DE5 3GG (Ripley 42284 pri).
Rolls-Royce Welfare—Rolls-Royce Sports Ground, off Osmanston Park Road, Derby. Courts: G6, H4. *Secretary:* Mrs B A Fleetwood, 41 Murray Road, Mickleover, Derby (Derby 514942 pri).
Rose Hill Methodist Tennis Club—Littleover Lane, Derby. Courts: G3, H2. *Secretary:* Miss K Trelfa, 4 Hamilton Road, Derby DE3 6RT (49254 pri).
Shipley Hall—Shipley Hall. Courts: G1, H4. *Secretary:* A S Last, The Poplars, Shipley, Derby (Langley Mill 714988 pri).
Somercotes—Recreation Ground, High Street, Somercotes. Courts: H4. *Secretary:* A V Walker, 171 Birchwood Lane, Somercotes, Derby (Leabrooks 605448 pri, Derby 45431 bus).
Spondon Tennis Club—Asterdale Club, Borrowash Road, Spondon, Derby. Courts: H6. *Secretary:* C Brisbourne, 22 Max Road, Chaddesden DE2 4GX (Derby 674865 pri, Derby 661422, ext 2088 bus).
Stanton—Hallam Fields, Ilkeston. Courts: H5. *Secretary:* T P Hodson, 16 St Andrews Drive, Ilkeston (322974 pri).
Watchorn—Ewart Lane, Alfreton. Courts: H2 (covered), G3. *Secretary:* Ms Y Scott, 8 Ewart Lane, Alfreton, Derby DE5 7AY (835916 pri).
Whitworth—Whitworth Institute, Darley Dale, Matlock. Courts: H3. *Secretary:* A Turner, 19 Painters Way, Two Dales, Derbyshire DE4 2SB (Matlock 3456 ext 303 bus).
Woodlands—Kedleston Road, Allestree, Derby. Courts: G4, H2. *Secretary:* Mrs J Rose, 'Overbrook,' Kniveton, Ashbourne, Derby (Ashbourne 42214 pri).

OTHER AFFILIATED ORGANISATIONS (3)

Chesterfield Tournament & League Committee—*Secretary:* Mrs C Race, The Old Reading Room, Heath, Nr Chesterfield (851880).
Derby Area League—*Secretary:* Mrs B A Fleetwood, 41 Murray Road, Mickleover, Derby (Derby 514942 pri).
Derbyshire Association of Tennis Coaches and Teachers.

AFFILIATED SCHOOLS (12)

Girls
Buxton School— Buxton. **Derby High School for Girls** — Derby. **Ockbrook School for Girls** — Ockbrook, nr Derby. **Presentation Convent School** — Matlock. **St Elphin's School for Girls** — Darley Dale, Matlock.
Mixed
Ecclesbourne School — Duffield. **Homelands School** — Derby. **Lady Manners School** — Bakewell. **Repton School** — Repton, Derbys. **Swanwick Hall School** — Swanwick. **Trent College** — Long Eaton, Derbys. **Tupton Hall School** — Nr. Chesterfield.

DEVON COUNTY LAWN TENNIS ASSOCIATION

Joint Hon Secretaries—**S C Melville,** 31 Old Abbey Court, Salmon Pool Lane, Exeter (76976). **A M Westmorland,** 6 Duchy Avenue, Preston, Paignton (554576).
Hon Treasurer—**R J Cruse,** Croft Cottage, Abbotskerswell, Newton Abbott (66026).
Hon Men's Match Secretary—**J M Barter,** 76 Chard Road, Heavitree, Exeter (75719).
Hon Ladies' Match Secretary—**Mrs S F C Rowe,** 3 Church Lane, Exeter (50805).
Juniors' Hon Secretary—**Mrs J Rowsell,** Red-A-Ven, Topsham Road, Exeter (Topsham 3184).
Representative on the Council—**R J Cruse.**

AFFILIATED CLUBS (48)

Barnstaple Bowling, Croquet and Tennis—Ashleigh Road, Barnstaple. Courts: H3. *Secretary:* G R Symons, 16 Rumsam Gardens, Barnstaple (71756).
Bovey Tracey—Courts: H2. *Secretary:* Mrs S Poustie, 31 Ashburton Road, Bovey Tracey (832620).
Bradninch—*Secretary:* J H Emerton, 63 Westfield, Bradninch, Exeter (881384).
Britannia Royal Naval College—Dartmouth. Courts: G2, H5. Fixtures *Secretary:* Sports Office at the College (Dartmouth 2141 ext 498).
Budleigh Salterton Games—Cricket Field Lane, Budleigh Salterton. Courts: G4, H2. *Secretary:* Mrs R Ager, 28 Queens Road, Budleigh Salterton (5892).
Carhullen—Lockington Avenue, Hartley, Plymouth (Plymouth 71692). Courts: H4. *Secretary:* H A Rowe, 18 Weston Park Road, Peverell, Plymouth.
Chagford—*Secretary:* M Weeden, 47 New Street, Chagford, Newton Abbot (Chagford 2256).
Chudleigh—*Secretary:* Mrs A Brown, Waddon House, Chudleigh, Newton Abbot.
Churston—Churston Road, Churston Ferrers, Brixham. Courts: H2. *Secretary:* T G Morgan, 3 Higher Rydons, Brixham (6145).
Civil Service Sports Association—Beacon Down, Plymouth. Courts: G2, H2. *Secretary:* J A Vincent, 21 Dorset Avenue, Exeter.
Cowley—Cowley Road, Exeter. Courts: G2. *Secretary:* C Johnson, 8 Moorland Way, Exwick, Exeter EX4 2ET (34689).
Cranford—Cranford Club, 42 Salterton Road, Exmouth. Courts: G12, H5. *Secretary:* J Bradford at the Club (Exmouth 5771).
Dartmouth—Courts: H4. *Secretary:* Mrs C A Webb, 10 Northford Road, Dartmouth TQ6 9EP (2368).
Dawlish—Dawlish Playing Fields, Exeter Road, Dawlish (Dawlish 2218). Courts: G4, H2. *Secretary:* Mrs R Rowley, 18 High Holcombe Road, Teignmouth (5427).
Exeter Golf and Country—Exeter Golf Club, Countess Wear. Courts: H6. *Secretary:* c/o The Club, Countess Wear, Exeter (Topsham 4139).
Exmouth LTC—Maer Ground, Sea Front, Exmouth. Courts: G4, H1. *Secretary:* D M Ellis, 39 Foxholes Hill, Exmouth (6415).
Feniton—Feniton Cricket Ground. *Secretary:* Mrs C A Cousens, 4 Bridge Cottages, Feniton, Honiton (850102).
Ilfracombe—Bicclescombe Park, Ilfracombe. Courts: H4. *Secretary:* Mrs P Spink, Muddiford House, Higher Muddiford, Barnstaple EX31 4EZ.
Ivybridge Tennis Club—Erme Valley Playing Fields, Ivybridge. Courts: H4. *Secretary:* Mrs S M Robertson, 55 Trehill Road, Ivychurch PL21 0AZ (Plymouth 892082).
Kingsbridge—Courts: H3. *Secretary:* D Tucker, 6 Alvington Terrace, Westville, Kingsbridge.
London & Manchester Assurance Company LTC—*Secretary:* Ms T Northcott, London & Manchester Assurance Company Ltd, PO Box 44, Exeter EX5 1DS.
Lympstone—Courts: H2. *Secretary:* Ms J Scarfe, The Cottage, Quay Lane, Lympstone, Exmouth (74625).
Mannamead—Collings Park, Eggbuckland, Plymouth. Courts: G4, H4. *Secretary:* J Hickley, 83 Salisbury Road, St Judes, Plymouth.
Newton Abbot—Courts: G4, H1. *Secretary:* J H Vincent, 15 Moorsend, Newton Abbot.
Okehampton—Simmons Park. Courts: H2. *Secretary:* S A Reddaway, Cherrywell, Sampford Courtenay, Okehampton (North Tawton 417).
Ottery St Mary—Courts: H4. *Secretary* Mrs J E Rolf, 6 Moorlands, West Hill, Ottery St Mary (3038).
Paignton—Oldway, Paignton. Courts: G3, H3. *Secretary:* Mrs J Vickery, 3 West Hill Road, Paignton.
Plymouth—Peverell Park. Courts: G5, H2. *Secretary:* M P Gill, 4 Pilgrim Close, Milehouse, Plymouth.
Plympton—Courts: H2. *Secretary:* Mrs I Buckler, 5 Wolverwood Lane, Plympton St Maurice, Plymouth.
Plymstock—Dean Cross Playing Field, Plymstock. Courts: H2. *Secretary:* D J Tolkien, 26 Under Lane, Plymstock, Plymouth (42015).
Russell Avenue—Russell Avenue, Hartley, Plymouth. Courts: H3. *Secretary:* Mrs Joan Kelcey, 6 Little Ash Gardens, St Budeaux, Plymouth, Devon PL5 1JZ (Plymouth 361570).
St Budeaux—Verna Road, St Budeaux, Plymouth. Courts: H2. *Secretary:* W F Old, 170 Victoria Road, St Budeaux, Plymouth (366355).
St Thomas—Courts: G3. *Secretary:* R Toterdell, April Cottage, 4 The Gardens, Newton Poppleford, Sidmouth (Colaton Raleigh 68392).
Salcombe—*Secretary:* Mrs J Pedley, 2 Waterloo Place, Kingsbridge.
Sampford Peverell—*Secretary:* A F Weller, 'Rocas,' Boobery, Sampford, Peverell, Tiverton.
Sidmouth Cricket, Lawn Tennis, Croquet & Hockey Club—Fortfield Terrace, Sidmouth. Courts: G6. *Secretary:* B Fitzgerald, Belmont Hotel, Sidmouth (2555).
Thurlestone Golf Club—Tennis Section. *Secretary:*

P J Norton, 14 Town Close, Dartmouth (2048).
Tiverton—Bolham Road, Tiverton. Courts: H4. *Secretary:* G W Wilson, 27 Gold Street, Tiverton.
Torquay—Belgrave Road, Torquay. Courts: G7, H6. *Secretary:* Mrs J Heale, at the Club.
Tunnels—Rivermead Road, Exeter. Courts: H2. *Secretary:* Mrs S Holding, 29 Rivermead Road, Exeter (73423).
University of Exeter—*Secretary:* J L Tink, Athletic Union, Cornwall House, St Germans Road, Exeter (79852).
Victoria Park Exeter—Lyndhurst Road, Exeter. Courts: H4. *Secretary:* At the Club.
Westward Ho—Avon Lane, Westward Ho. Courts: H4. *Secretary:* S P Colwill, 3 Leonards Road, Northiam, Bideford.
Whitchurch Tennis Club—*Secretary:* C W Smyly, Pathways, Grenofen, Tavistock, Devon PL19 9EW.
Whiteford Road—Mannamead, Plymouth. Courts: H3. *Secretary:* Mrs B C Wilkins, 39 Shute Park Road, Plymstock, Plymouth (44395).
Willand—Willand Village Hall Grounds, Willand. Courts: H3. *Secretary:* Miss E J Levett, 40 Somerlea, Willand, Cullompton (Tiverton 820662).
Wingfield Park LTC—Heavitree Social Club, East Wonford Hill, Heavitree, Exeter. Courts: H2. *Secretary:* Mrs M Frost, 'Marrondale,' Sand Down Lane, Newton St Cyres, Exeter (Newton St Cyres 331).
Witheridge—Courts: H1. *Secretary:* Mrs A Alleyne, 17 Fore Street, Witheridge, Tiverton EX16 8AH.

OTHER AFFILIATED ORGANISATIONS (15)

Barnstaple Junior Lawn Tennis School—*Secretary:* Mrs K M Cheetham, Stonefield, South Park, Barnstaple (2384).
Bridge Club Junior Tennis Club—St Thomas' High School, Cowick Lane, Exeter EX2 9JL. *Secretary:* Mrs E Jarvis at the Club.
Dartmouth Royal Regatta Tennis Tournament—*Secretary:* N E Bradley, Rock Hill, Warfleet, Dartmouth.
Exeter Nomads—*Secretary:* Ms H C Bull, 63 Rosebarn Lane, Exeter (54808).
Exeter Tennis Week—*Secretary:* R F Davies, 83 Hill Barton Road, Exeter.
Fox Hill Playing Field—Axminster. *Secretary:* Mrs N Weller, 52 Fox Hill, Axminster (32879).
Hill Lane Junior LTC—Hartley, Plymouth. *Secretary:* Mrs M Page, 10 Minses Close, Elburton, Plymouth.
North Devon and District—*Secretary:* P G Clarke, Southfield, Barbican Lane, Barnstaple EX32 8LB.
Park Lane Junior LTC—Barnstaple. The Hon Secretary at the club.
Plymouth and District LT Clubs—*Secretary:* C Worley, 24 Buena Vista Drive, Glenholt, Plymouth (775955).
Summerway Junior—Exeter. *Secretary:* C Ray, 2 The Mede, Whipton, Exeter (66884).
Teignmouth Junior Tennis School—*Secretary:* Mrs K Sutherland, 3 Heywoods Road, Teignmouth.
Torbay Junior LTC—*Secretary:* Mrs T Kanuick, 47 Winsu Avenue, Paignton.
Torquay Junior Tennis Tournament—*Secretary:* The Parks Superintendent, Torbay Corporation, Castle Circus, Torquay.
Whimple—*Secretary:* Mrs S Stott, Kerswell Coach House, Broadclyst, Exeter EX5 3AF (Broadclyst 771).

AFFILIATED SCHOOLS (60)

Boys
Ashburton and Buckfastleigh Secondary School — Ashburton. **Blundells School** — Tiverton. **Braunton School** — Braunton. **Devonport High School for Boys** — Plymouth. **Exeter School** — Exeter. **Exmouth School** — Exmouth. **Ilfracombe School** — Ilfracombe. **Kellys College** — Tavistock. **King Edward VI School** — Totnes. **Okehampton School** — Okehampton. **Plymouth College** — Plymouth. **Shebbear College** — Beaworthy. **St Boniface College** — Plymouth. **Torquay Grammar School** — Torquay. **West Buckland School** — Filleigh, Barnstaple.

Girls
Barnstaple Grammar School — Barnstaple. **Bishop Blackall School** — Exeter. **Broadclyst SM School** — Broadclyst. **Convent of Notre-Dame** — Teignmouth. **Chulmleigh County Secondary School** — Chulmleigh. **Colyton Grammar School** — Colyton. **Churston Ferrers Grammar School** — Brixham. **Croft Lodge School** — Torquay. **Edgehill College** — Bideford. **Exmouth Grammar School** — Exmouth. **Queen Elizabeth School** — Crediton. **Ilfracombe School** — Ilfracombe. **Great Torrington School** — Torrington. **Kings School** — Ottery St Mary. **Marist Convent** — Paignton. **Maynard School** — Exeter. **Mount St Mary Convent School** — Exeter. **Newton Abbot Grammar School** — Newton Abbot. **Newton Abbot Junior School** — Newton Abbott. **Newton Ferrers Grammar School** — nr Plymouth. **North Devon College** — Barnstaple. **Okehampton School** — Okehampton. **Paignton County Secondary** — Paignton. **Plympton Grammar School** — Plympton. **Plympton Secondary Modern School** — Plympton. **Plymouth High School** — Plymouth. **St Dunstan's Abbey** — Plymouth. **Sidmouth School** — Sidmouth. **Stoodleigh Knowle Convent School** — Torquay. **St Margaret's School** — Exeter. **Stover School** — Newton Abbot. **Stoke Damerell High School** — Plymouth. **Tavistock School** — Tavistock. **Teignmouth Grammar School** — Teignmouth. **Technical College** — Exeter. **The Convent of Assumption** — Sidmouth. **Stella Marist Convent School** — Bideford. **The Convent School** — Exmouth. **Tiverton Grammar School** — Tiverton. **Tiverton Heathcote Secondary School** — Tiverton. **Torquay Grammar School** — Torquay. **Torrington Secondary Modern School** — Torrington. **King Edward VI School** — Totnes.

All correspondence to School Clubs should be addressed to the Master or Mistress in charge of lawn tennis.

DORSET COUNTY LAWN TENNIS ASSOCIATION

Hon Secretary—**E R Dry,** 14 Queens Road, Ferndown BH22 9RT (875985).
Hon Treasurer—**J A Howitt,** Swanston, Russell Avenue, Swanage (423497).
Hon Men's Match Secretary—**R Burns,** 23 Lissenden, 1 Burton Road, Poole (Bournemouth 768613).
Hon Ladies' Match Secretary—**Mrs J Maher,** 12 Oakley Road, Wimborne (883979).
Junior Organizer—**L Couldridge,** 2 Chapel Close, Corfe Mullen, Dorset (0202 693652).
Representative on the Council—**E R Dry.**

AFFILIATED CLUBS (28)

Abbey Life—*Secretary:* 30 Shelley Road, Boscombe, Bournemouth, Dorset BH1 4HY. (Bournemouth 292373).
Blandford—Blandford Sports Centre, Milldown Road, Blandford Forum. Courts: H3. *Secretary:* Mrs S Gibson, 9a Havelins Road, Stour Paine, Blandford (53924).
Boscombe—Boscombe Gardens, Bournemouth. Courts: G1, H2. *Secretary:* Miss A Luckham, 101 Maxwell Road, Winton, Bournemouth (528710).
Bournemouth Civil Service—Manor Farm Road, Kinson, Bournemouth (Northbourne 2723). Courts: H3 (2 floodlit). *Secretary:* Mrs C Vinnicombe, 89 King John Avenue, Bearwood, Bournemouth BH11 9RZ (572530).
Bradford Abbas—Courts: H3. *Secretary:* C J Gillham, 39 Queens Road, Bradford Abbas, Sherborne.
Bridport—Courts: H3. *Secretary:* Miss A Prior, Aysgarth, 62 Crock Lane, Bridport (22927).
Christchurch—Cedar Courts, Iford Bridge. Courts: H4. *Secretary:* Miss P Watts, 19 Cedar Avenue, Christchurch BH33 2PS.
Caundle—Courts: H2. *Secretary:* Mrs M Cooper, 109 Acremon Street, Sherborne DT9 3PH (4516).
Dorchester—Weymouth Avenue, Dorchester. Courts: H3. *Secretary:* S Mascarenas, 6 Hillfort Close, Dorchester (65736).
East Dorset—Salterns Road, Parkstone (Parkstone 740219). Courts: G11, H8. *Secretary:* Mrs J Phillips, 'Quoins,' Jenny's Lane, Matravers, Poole (Morden 340).
Ferndown—King George VI Playing Fields. Courts: H4. *Secretary:* Mrs B Bunce, 'Danmill', Woolsbridge Road, St Leonards, Ringwood.
Gillingham—Courts: H2. *Secretary:* Mrs Williams, Kimberley Cottage, Milton on Stour, Gillingham (3826).
Lytchett Matravers—County Primary School, Lytchett, Minster. *Secretary:* Mrs L Knox, 20 Charborough Close, Lytchett Matravers, Poole BH16 5ED.
Melcombe Regis—Fernhill Avenue, Weymouth. Courts: H2. *Secretary:* Mrs J Esquilant, 40 Cleveland Avenue, Weymouth (775409).
Poole Teachers Club—Courts: H3. *Secretary:* Mrs P Finlay, 36 Highfield Road, Corfe Mullen (Broadstone 693293).
St Leonards & St Ives—Courts: H3. *Secretary:* Mrs M Taylor, 34 Lions Lane, Ashley Heath, Ringwood (78110).
Sherborne—Courts: H4. *Secretary:* Mrs S Andrews, Walton, Bristol Road, Sherborne (813656).
Southbourne—Iford Lane, Tuckton, Bournemouth. Courts: H5. *Secretary:* Mrs White, 3 Squirrel Close, Stour Way, Christchurch (486628).
Stalbridge—Courts: H1. *Secretary:* R R Dendy, Middle Farm, Stalbridge Weston, Sturminster Newton (Stalbridge 62698).
Swanage—Beach Gardens. Courts: H6. *Secretary:* Mrs J Garnsworthy, 20 Anglebury Avenue, Swanage (424650).
Swanmore—Swanmore Gardens, Swanmore Road, Boscombe East. *Secretary:* Mrs M Cooke, 172 Victoria Road, Ferndown (876844).
Verwood—Moorland Road, Verwood. Courts: H2. *Secretary:* Mrs S Rea, 21 Edmondsham Road, Verwood (822454).
Victoria Avenue—Victoria Avenue, Winton, Bournemouth. Courts: G4, H2. *Secretary:* D Lloyd, 13 Castle Gate Close, Bournemouth (514881).
West Hants—Roslin Road South, Bournemouth (519455). Courts: G6, H10, artificial turf 4, 3 Playde (floodlit), indoor 2. *Secretary:* The Secretary, The Club House, Melville Park, Roslin Road, South, Bournemouth (519455).
West Moors—Memorial Hall, West Moors. Courts: G3, H2. *Secretary:* Mrs A Lamb, 'Marandor', Woodland Walk, Ferndown.
Weymouth Civil Service—Courts: H2. *Secretary:* Mr K Skilling, 15 Clarendon Avenue, Redlands, Weymouth.
Weymouth—Radipole Park Drive, Weymouth. Courts: H4. *Secretary:* P Boyce, 99 Clearmount Road, Weymouth (786463).

AFFILIATED SCHOOLS (114)

Boys
Bournemouth School — Bournemouth. **Dumpton School** — Wimborne. **Foster's School** — Sherborne. **Hardy's School** — Dorchester. **Homefield School** — Christchurch. **Hurn Court School** — Bournemouth. **Milton Abbey School** — Milton Abbas. **Poole Grammar School** — Poole. **Portchester Boys' School** — Bournemouth. **Seldown School** — Poole. **Sherbourne School** — Sherborne. **Winton Boys' School** — Bournemouth.

Girls
Ashley Cross School — Poole. **Avonbourne School** — Bournemouth. **Bournemouth School for Girls** — Bournemouth. **Castlefield School** — Dorchester. **Convent of the Sacred Hearts** — Weymouth. **Croft House School** — Shillingstone. **Glenmoor School for Girls** — Bournemouth. **Hanford School** — Child Okeford. **Lord Digby's School** — Sherborne. **Parkstone Grammar School** — Poole. **Queensmount School** — Bournemouth. **St Anthony's-Lewston School** — Sherbourne. **St**

Mary's Convent — Shaftesbury. **St. Mary's Gate School** — Bournemouth. **St. Monica's School** — Poole. **Sherbourne School for Girls** — Sherborne. **Talbot Heath School** — Bournemouth. **Wentworth Milton Mount School** — Bournemouth

Mixed
Alderney Middle School — Poole. **Allenbourn Middle School** — Wimborne. **All Saints CE School** — Weymouth. **All Saints Primary School** — Bishop's Caundle. **Baden Powell Middle School** — Poole. **Beaminster Comprehensive School** — Beaminster. **Beaufort School** — Bournemouth. **Blandford Upper School** — Blandford. **Branksome Heath Middle School** — Poole. **Broadstone Middle School** — Broadstone. **Broadwey School** — Weymouth. **Budmouth School** — Weymouth. **Burton Bradstock CE Primary School** — Burton Bradstock. **Bryanston School** — Blandford. **Canford School** — Wimborne. **Castle Court School** — Corfe Mullen. **Christ The King RC School** — Bournemouth. **Clayesmore School** — Iwerne Minster. **Colfox School** — Bridport. **Corfe Hills Upper School** — Corfe Mullen. **Cranborne Middle School** — Cranborne. **Dorchester Middle School** — Dorchester. **Enmore Green CE First School** — Shaftesbury. **Ferndown Middle School** — Ferndown. **Ferndown Upper School** — Ferndown. **Forres School** — Swanage. **Gillingham School** — Gillingham. **Grange School** — Christchurch. **Hamworthy First School** — Poole. **Hamworthy Middle School** — Poole. **Hayeswood First School** — Wimborne. **Henry Harbin School** — Poole. **Herbert Carter Secondary School** — Poole. **Highcliffe Comprehensive School** — Christchurch. **Highcliffe Junior School** — Christchurch. **Hillbourne Middle School** — Poole. **Hillside First School** — Verwood. **Hill View Junior School** — Bournemouth. **Kemp Welch School**— Poole. **King Alfred's Middle School** — Shaftesbury. **Kingsleigh Junior School** — Bournemouth. **Kingsleigh School** — Bournemouth. **Kinson Primary School** — Bournemouth. **Lady St Mary First School** — Wareham. **Lockyer's Middle School** — Corfe Mullen. **Lytchett Minster Upper School** — Lytchett Minster. **Milldown CE Middle School** — Blandford. **Moordown St John's CE Primary School** — Bournemouth. **Motcombe Grange School** — Shaftesbury. **Oakdale Middle School** — Poole. **Oakmead Secondary School** — Bournemouth. **Purbeck School** — Wareham. **Royal Manor Comprehensive School** — Portland. **Queen Elizabeth's School** — Wimbourne. **St Aldhelm's School** — Sherborne. **St Antony's Convent School** — Sherborne. **St. Catherine's RC Primary School** — Bridport. **St Edward's RC Secondary School** — Poole. **St Leonard's Middle School** — Blandford. **St Mary's CE Middle School** — Puddletown. **St Mary's CE Primary School** — Beaminster. **St Mary's CE Primary School** — Bradford Abbas. **St. Mary's CE Primary School** — Stalbridge. **St. Michael's CE Middle School** — Colehill. **St Osmund's CE Middle School** — Dorchester. **St Peter's RC School** — Bournemouth. **Sandford Middle School** — Wareham. **Shaftesbury CE First School** — Shaftesbury. **Shaftesbury School** — Shaftesbury. **Sherborne Abbey CE Primary School** — Sherborne. **Somerford Junior School** — Christchurch. **Sturminster Newton High School** — Sturminster Newton. **Summerbee School** — Bournemouth. **Swanage First School** — Swanage. **Swanage Middle School** — Swanage. **Symondsbury CE Primary School** — Bridport. **Turlin Moor First School** — Poole. **Turlin Moor Middle School** — Poole. **Talbot Combined School** — Poole. **Twynham Comprehensive School** — Christchurch. **Uplands School** — Poole. **Verwood CE First School** — Verwood. **Westham Junior School** — Weymouth. **West Moors Middle School** — West Moors. **William Barnes Primary School** — Sturminster Newton. **Woodroffe School** — Lyme Regis. **Wyke Regis CE Junior School** — Weymouth.

Any Dorset school not included in the above list and wishing to receive information about tennis or short tennis events in Dorset schools should inform the DSTA Secretary – Mrs J M Copland, 19 Paddock Close, Lytchett Matravers, Poole (Lytchett Minster 624281).

DURHAM AND CLEVELAND LAWN TENNIS ASSOCIATION

Hon Secretary—**J C Marshall,** 23 Victoria Terrace, Catchgate, Stanley, Co Durham (Stanley 234685).
Hon Junior Secretary—**G T Collinson Esq,** 14 Woodlands Road, Shotley Bridge, Consett, Co Durham (0207 503247).
Hon Treasurer—**J M Peart,** 4 Sherwood Close, Shotley Bridge, Consett, Co Durham (Consett 505791).
Hon Men's Match Secretary—**A Foreman,** 10 Page Avenue, South Shields, Tyne & Wear (South Shields 562117).
Hon Ladies' Match Secretary—**Mrs R Whyte,** 'Windways,' 21 Woodlands Road, Shotley Bridge, Consett, Co Durham (Consett 503047).
Representative on the Council—**G T Collinson.**

AFFILIATED CLUBS (33)

Acklam Sixth Form College—Hall Drive, Middlesbrough. Courts: H6. Mrs M King, c/o Acklam Sixth Form College, Hall Drive, Middlesbrough.
Barnard Castle—Bowes Museum, Barnard Castle. Courts: H3. *Secretary:* Mr D Hunter, 34 Newgate Road, Barnard Castle, Co Durham DL12 8NG.
Belford House—Belford Road, Sunderland. Courts: H6. *Secretary:* Miss S Clark, 57 Fletcher Crescent, New Herrington. Sunderland.
Blaydon Methodist—Axwell Park, Blaydon on Tyne. Courts: H4. *Secretary:* Mrs D Rochester, 75 Nun's Moor Road, Newcastle NE4 9AY.
Boldon—Dipe Lane, South Boldon. Courts: H6. *Secretary:* P W Golightly, 96 Beckenham Avenue, East Boldon.
Brookside—Orchard Street, Birtley. Courts: H2.

Secretary: C Magee, 31 Danelaw, Lumley, Chester-le-Street.
Burnmoor Cricket, Tennis & Football Club—Burnmoor. Courts: H1. *Secretary:* J Stavers, 24 Grange Avenue, Fences Houses, Co Durham.
Burnopfield & Dipton—Cenotaph, Burnopfield. Courts: H3. *Secretary:* Miss B Airey, 25 Oakfields, Burnopfield, Newcastle upon Tyne.
Chilton—Courts: H2. *Secretary:* I W Watson, 22 Byerley Road, Shildon.
Durham Archery—Margery Lane, Durham City. Courts: G3, H6. *Secretary:* Mrs J Cotton, 123 Devonshire Road, Belmont, Durham DH1 2BL.
Durham Moor—Dryburn Road, Durham Moor. Courts: H2. *Secretary:* A Wardle, 6 Dryburn Road, Durham Moor, Durham City DH1 5AJ.
Hartlepool—Graville Avenue. Courts: H5. *Secretary:* G E Shepherd, 139 Mowbray Road, Hartlepool TS25 2ND.
Heathfield Senior High LTC—Durham Road, Low Fell, Gateshead. Courts: H3. *Secretary:* Mr J Lambert, 15 Benwell Grange Avenue, Newcastle NE15 6RP.
Lanchester—Ford Road, Lanchester. Courts: G3. *Secretary:* Mrs G A Reeve, Old Police House, Dipton Stanley, Co Durham DH9 9EB.
Linthorpe—Prissick Base, Marton Road, Middlesbrough. Courts; SG9. *Secretary:* Dr K N Clark, 2 Grey Towers Drive, Nunthorpe, Middlesbrough.
Marske—Mount Pleasant, Redcar. Courts: H5. *Secretary:* Mrs J Gaskill, 55 High Street, Marske-by-the-Sea TS1 6TQ.
Middlesbrough Tennis and Badminton—Highfield Road, The Longlands, Middlesbrough. Courts: H4. *Secretary:* S Beckton, 14 Lansdowne Road, Yarn TS15 9NX.
Murton Welfare—Murton Colliery Welfare Ground, Murton. Courts: H3. *Secretary:* Mr G Gilroy, 32 William Road, Murton, Co Durham.
New Blackwell—Carmel Road, Darlington. Courts: H6. *Secretary:* D. Reeve, 5 West View, Darlington DL3 8BP.
New Silksworth Colliery Welfare—Sunderland Recreation Area. Courts: SG3. *Secretary:* W E Lumley, 46 Summerhill, East Herrington, Sunderland SR3 3TW.
North East Regional Tennis Centre—Teeside Airport. Courts: H12. *Secretary:* Mrs M Todd, 'Rosendale,' Manfield, Darlington.
Norton Hall—The Green, Norton. Courts: G1, H2. *Secretary:* Lawn Tennis Section, Norton Hall, The Green, Norton, Stockton-on-Tees.
Pyrex Social Club—South Hylton, Sunderland. Courts: H3. *Secretary:* J Lane, 205 Whitefield Crescent, Whitfield Estate, Penshaw, Houghton-le-Spring, Tyne & Wear DM4 7QY.
Reyrolles—South Drive, Hebburn, Newcastle-Upon-Tyne. Courts: H3. *Secretary: Lawn Tennis Section, Reyrolles.*
Shildon—Welfare Ground, Shildon. *Secretary:* D. Wearmouth, 49 Byerley Road, Shildon, Co Durham DL4 1SM.
Shotley & Benfieldside Spa Ground, Shotley Bridge & Benfield Close. Courts: H9. *Secretary:* Mrs J Wake, 10 Victoria Terrace, Hamsterley, Colliery, Newcastle NE17 7SJ.
Sunderland—Ashbrook, Sunderland. Courts: G3, H3. *Secretary:* Miss P A Ross, 9 Arden Square, Farringdon, Sunderland (289286).
Thorney Close—Thornley Close School, Telford Road, Sunderland. Courts: H8. *Secretary:* P Humble, 223 Cleveland Road, Sunderland SR4 7QR.
Westoe—Oban Road, South Shields. Courts: G4, H3. *Secretary:* Miss E Balfour, 72 Warwick Road, South Shields.
Whickham—Broom Lane, Southfield View, Whickham. Courts: H3. *Secretary:* Mrs V Eltringham, 11 Carrsyde Close, Fellside Park, Whickham, Newcastle NE16 5UE.
Wolviston—Billingham. Courts: H2. *Secretary:* R Littlewood, 11 Grange View, Wolviston, Cleveland.
Yarm—Leven Road, Yarm. Courts: H9. *Secretary:* J Lakinski, 9 Seymour Drive, Eaglescliffe, Cleveland, TS16 0LG.

OTHER AFFILIATED ORGANISATIONS (6)

Billingham Organising Committee—*Secretary:* Hon Secretary, Billingham Forum, Billingham on Tees.
Durham University—The Racecourse. Courts: G3, H4. *Secretary:* Hon Secretary, Durham University LTC, The Union, Durham.
Grey College, Durham University—*Secretary:* Hon Secretary, Grey College LTC Durham.
Sedgefield Community Centre—*Secretary:* Mrs F M Redpath, 5 The Leas, Sedgefield, Co Durham.
St Cuthbert's Society—*Secretary:* Hon Secretary, Lawn Tennis, St Cuthbert's Society, 12 South Bailey, Durham.
Sir William Tunrers Sixth Form College —*Secretary:* Mrs V Parnell, c/o Sir William Turners Sixth Form College, Redcar Lane, Redcar, Cleveland.

AFFILIATED SCHOOLS (44)

St Aidan's Comprehensive School — Sunderland. **Briertonhill Technical** — Hartlepool. **Grangefield Comprehensive School** — Stockton on Tees. **Queen Elizabeth Sixth Form College** — Darlington. **South Shields Comprehensive Technical** — South Shields. **Usworth School** — Washington. **St Annes School** — Wolsingham, Co Durham. Church High School. **Durham Girls High School** — Durham. **Dyke House Girls School** — Hartlepool. **Hummers Knott Comprehensive School** — Darlington. **Polam Hall School** — Darlington. **St. Anthony's** — Sunderland. **Sunderland Church High School** — Sunderland.
Bede Hall Campus — Billingham, Teeside. **Bede School** — Sunderland. **Blackfyne Comprehensive School** — Consett. **Blaydon Comprehensive School** — Blaydon. **A J Dawson School** — Wingate. **Deanery Comprehensive School** — Chester le Street. **Dryden Senior High School** — Gateshead.

Durham Johnston Comprehensive School — Durham. **Durham Wearside Secondary School** — Durham. **Ferryhill Comprehensive School. Greencroft Comprehensive School** — Annfield Plain. **Hartlepool Grammar School** — Hartlepool. **Hookergate Comprehensive School** — Rowlands Gill. **Houghton le Spring Comprehensive School** — Sunderland. **King James I School** — Bishop Auckland. **Seaham Comprehensive School** — Seaham, Co Durham. **Monkwearmouth Comprehensive School** — Sunderland. **Newton Aycliffe Greenfield Comprehensive** — Greenfield Way, Newton Aycliffe. **Penny Well Comprehensive School** — Sunderland. **Red House Prep School** — Stockton-on-Tees. **Ryhope Comprehensive School** — Sunderland. **Spennymoor Comprehensive School** — Spennymoor. **Springfield Comprehensive School** — Jarrow. **Tanfield Comprehensive School** — Stanley. **Thornhill Comprehensive School** — Sunderland. **Washington Comprehensive School** — Washington. **Wolsingham Comprehensive School** — Wolsingham.

All correspondence to School Clubs should be addressed to the Games Master or Mistress in charge of lawn tennis.

ESSEX COUNTY LAWN TENNIS ASSOCIATION

Hon Secretary—**C Rippon,** 95 High Street, Chelmsford (262481).
Hon Treasurer—**H G Whittle,** Killicks End, Rectory Meadow, Alexandra Road, Sible Hedingham, Halstead (0787 61391).
Hon Men's Match Secretary—**M Vine,** 23 Cranston Park Avenue, Upminster (01-621 1110).
Hon Ladies Match Secretary—**Mrs V L Pratt,** 40 Monkhams Avenue, Woodford Green (01-504 9565).
Hon Junior Secretary—**G Abbott,** 56 Lambourne Gardens, Chingford E4 (01-529 3864).
Representatives on the Council—**J Tucker, F Collins.**

AFFILIATED CLUBS (87)

Aldersbrook—Blakehall Crescent, Wanstead, London E11 (01-989 6072). Courts: H6 (2 floodlit). *Secretary:* N Rafis, 29 Ewellhurst Road, Clayhill, Ilford (01-550 5048).
Athenaeum—383a Aldborough Road, Seven Kings (590 5171). Courts: H3. *Secretary:* Mrs J Hughes, 27 Aberdour Road, Goodmayes (01-590 3025).
Avenue—Lower Park Road, Loughton (01-508 4803). Courts: H4. *Secretary:* Mrs M Kind, 14 Algers Close, Loughton (01-508 5055).
Basildon—Mopsies Park, Basildon. Courts: H3 (floodlit). *Secretary:* Mrs M Crook, 344 Falstones, Basildon (42478).
Belchamp & District—Community House, Eagles Road, Belchamp St. Pauls. Courts: H2. *Secretary:* Mrs B A Stewart, Gunners, Bakers Road, Belchamp St Paul, Sudbury, Suffolk (Clare 277198).
Bentley and District—Bentley Village Club, Ongar Road, Brentwood. Courts: H3 (floodlit). *Secretary:* Mrs J M Ansell, 60 Stour Way, Upminster (25567).
Billericay—Mountessing Road, Billericay. Courts: H5 (floodlit). *Secretary:* Mrs M Drewery, Kessley, Margaretting Road, Galleywood, Chelmsford CM2 8TS (83265).
Braintree—Clockhouse Way, Cressing Road, Braintree. Courts: H1, G4. *Secretary:* Mrs J Gray, 14 Roman Court, Chelmer Road, Braintree (43715).
Brentwood—Old County Cricket Ground, Shenfield Road, Brentwood (217407). Courts: G2, H7. *Secretary:* W Low, 4 Tudor Close, Shenfield (Brentwood 223559).
Brentwood Hard Courts—Childerditch Lane, Brentwood (210489). Courts: H7 (3 floodlit). *Secretary:* L H F Bass, The Bungalow, 4 South Weald Road, Brentwood (227160).
Britannia—Langston Road, Loughton (01-508 6221). Courts: H6. *Secretary:* P Deadman, B of E Printing Works, Langston Road, Loughton.
Buckhurst Hill—Epping New Road, Buckhurst Hill (01-504 0780). Courts: H4. *Secretary:* S. Higgs, 21 Long Deacon Road, Chingford E4 (5240304).
Castle Hedingham—St. James Street. Courts: H3. *Secretary:* P C Drury, Magnolia Cottage, Audley End, Gestingthorpe, Halstead (Hedingham 60683).
Chadwell Heath—Hainault Road, Little Heath, Romford (01-590 1298). Courts: H6 (3 floodlit). *Secretary:* P Tyrell, 40 Ilfracombe Gardens, Chadwell Heath, Romford (01-599 7044).
Chigwell—Grange Crescent, Chigwell. Courts: H3. *Secretary:* K Lakey, 31 Chigwell Park Drive, Chigwell (500 5242).
Chigwell Sports Club Ltd—High Road, Chigwell (01-500 1111). Courts: H6 (2 floodlit). *Secretary:* Miss E Andrews, 1 Denner Road, Chingford, London E4 (01-529 0523).
Colchester Garrison Officers—St John's Green, Colchester (Colchester 72031). Courts: H4, G9. *Secretary:* The Tennis Secretary, Arley Grange, Ipswich Road, Dedham.
Connaught—Barn Hoppett Rangers Road, London E4 (01-529 2341). Courts: G3, H6 (2 floodlit) (2 covered). *Secretary:* Mrs A R Petchey, 11 Tycehurst Hill, Loughton (508 2648).
Countryman Club—Marine Parade, Dovercourt (Harwich 502041). Courts: H3. *Secretary:* Mrs S Hourihane, 256 High Street, Dovercourt (Harwich 503456).
Cranbrook Castle—St George's Road, Ilford (01-554 6685). Courts: H5. *Secretary:* M A Jones, 34 Vista Drive, Redbridge (550 3301).
Cranston Park—Coniston Avenue, Upminster. Courts: H7. *Secretary:* Mrs D H Tanner, 32 Sims Close, Romford (25840).
Dagenham Cables—Exeter Road, Dagenham (01-592 0515). *Secretary:* J H Hamlin, 43 Beamway, Dagenham (01-595 1572).
Danbury—The Playing Fields, Danbury. Courts: H3. *Secretary:* W E White, Twin Trees, White Elm Road, Danbury (3249).

Dedham—*Secretary:* H Green, Meadowcroft, Bargate Lane, Dedham, Colchester (323357).
Dunmow—Foakes Hall, Stortford Road, Dunmow. Courts: H2. *Secretary:* Mrs S Amos, 32 Brookfields, Stebbing, Dunmow (Stebbing 656).
Earls Colne Green Farm Meadow, Halstead Road, Earls Colne. Courts: H4. *Secretary:* T. Beart, 5 Oxford Court, Earls Colne, Colchester (Earls Colne 2977).
Elm Park—Woburn Avenue, Elm Park (Hornchurch 42689). Courts: H2. *Secretary:* At Club.
Elsenham—Courts: H2. *Secretary:* Mrs L M Segar, Crossways, Elsenham (Bishops Stortford 813289).
Epping—Lower Bury Lane, Epping. Courts: H2. *Secretary:* Mrs A Holland, 56 Stewards Green Road, Epping (74069).
Ford Sports—Ford Sports Club, Aldborough Road, Newbury Park, Ilford (01-592 6869). Courts: H6.
Forest—Fyfield Road, London E17 (01-520 0019). Courts: H4. *Secretary:* Mrs M Lewis, 63 Fladgate Road, Leytonstone, London E11 (989 6479).
Frinton-on-Sea—Holland Road, Frinton-on-Sea (4055). Courts: G22, H4. *Secretary:* Mrs K Denholm.
Gidea Park—Gidea Close, Gidea Park (Romford 41012). Courts: H3 Alphagrass 4. *Secretary:* Miss J A Hill, 35 Cranham Road, Hornchurch (50617).
Great Baddow—Ladywell Lane, Sandon (Chelmsford 72304). Courts: H6 (floodlit). *Secretary:* J Perks, 656 Galleywood Road, Chelmsford (81538).
Grosvenor—23 Grosvenor Gardens, Upminster. Courts: H4. *Secretary:* A C Clarke, 6 Masefield Drive, Upminster (23269).
Grove (Chelmsford)—between 177 and 179 Moulsham Drive, Chelmsford. Courts: H6. *Secretary:* A Smith, 73 Crocus Way, Springfield, Chelmsford (465472).
Grove (Saffron Walden)—East Street, Saffron Walden. Courts: H5 (1 floodlit). *Secretary:* G H Peake, 36 Wheatsheaf Way, Linton, Cambridge (892516).
Hadleigh Park—Elm Road, Castle Lane, Hadleigh. Courts: H3. *Secretary:* F Dowson, 30 Glenmere Park Avenue, Thundersley, Benfleet (Southend 555274).
Harlow—Harlow Sports Centre, Hammarskjold Road, Harlow (26313). Courts: H3 (2 floodlit). *Secretary:* W Calvert, 53 The Chantry, Harlow (417895).
Henham—Carters Lane, Henham. Courts: H2. *Secretary:* Mrs F Copping, Petri Lodge, The Chase, Churst Street, Henham (Bishops Stortford 850552).
Hockley—Folley Lane, Hockley (Southend 201030). Courts: H3 (floodlit). *Secretary:* Mrs B P Fraser, 16 St James Gardens, Westcliff-on-Sea, Hockley (Southend 42992).
Hornchurch—Station Lane, Hornchurch. Courts: H3. *Secretary:* Mrs J E Smith, 70 Moray Way, Rise Park, Romford (63353).
Hutton & Shenfield Union Church—Brockley Grove, Hutton. Courts: H4. *Secretary:* A Ennals, Little Traps, Shenfield Green, Shenfield (Brentwood 220334).
Hylands—Hylands Park, Osborne Road, Hornchurch. *Secretary:* D J Wood, 40 Hall Lane, Upminster (20672).
Ingatestone & Fryerning—rear 9 High Street, Ingatestone. Courts: H2. *Secretary:* Mrs J Lewis, Bramwood Farm, Highwood Road, Highwood, Chelmsford CM1 3QD.
Kelvedon Hatch—School Road, Kelvedon Hatch. Courts: H2. *Secretary:* Mrs P Fearnley, Benodet, Beehive Chase, Wyatts Green, Brentwood (822145).
Laun House—Laun House, Laundry Lane, Nazeing. Courts: H1. *Secretary:* Mrs J A Lawton (Nazeing 2234).
Leigh-on-Sea—Adalia Crescent, Highlands Estate, Leigh-on-Sea (Southend 710104). Courts: H3. *Secretary:* D Wright, 131 Highland Boulevard, Leigh-on-Sea (Southend 72619).
Lexden Hill—West End Sports Ground, Shrub End, Colchester (74535). Courts: G6. *Secretary:* A Harper, 4 Brougham Glades, Stanway, Colchester.
Linkside—Overton Drive, Wanstead, London E11 (01-989 5773). Courts: H7. *Secretary:* Mrs M Owen, 17 Ashby Close, Hornchurch (51012).
Little Baddow—The Rodney, Little Baddow. Courts: H2. *Secretary:* Mrs M Carnell, 'Chelmer,' Woodham Walter, nr Maldon (Danbury 2641).
Marconi—Beehive Lane, Chelmsford (69422). Courts: G6, H4 (floodlit). *Secretary:* R Floyd, 1 Plough Cottages, Tye Common Road, Billericay.
Meadville—Mitcham Road, off Meads Lane, Seven Kings. Courts: H3. *Secretary:* A Oblitey, 133 St Albans Road, Seven Kings, Ilford (01 590 3937).
Mountnessing—Roman Road, Mountnessing. Courts: H3 (2 floodlit). *Secretary:* Mrs B Lewin, 11 Thorncroft, Hornchurch (46634).
North Ilford—Redbridge Sports Centre, Barkingside (01-501 0019 ext 7). Courts: H5 (Omniturf-floodlit). *Secretary:* Miss C V Feetham, 348 Henley Road, Ilford (478 6582).
Old Chelmsfordians—Lawford Lane, Sports Field. Courts: H3. *Secretary:* N L Grant, 26 Rainsford Avenue, Chelmsford (267806).
Old Chigwellians—Chigwell School, Chigwell. Courts: H2, G2. *Secretary:* J Robinson, 26 Weald Way, Romford (47404).
Old Southendians—15-17 Crowstone Road, Westcliff-on-Sea (Southend 351553). Courts: G6, H3. *Secretary:* I Currie, 10 Imperial Avenue, Westcliff on Sea S50 8NE (0702 345083).
Ongar—Love Lane, Ongar. Courts: H4. *Secretary:* Miss A Ponsonby, The Coach House, Chivers Road, Stonoon Massey, Brentwood (823173).
Paths (Rise Park)—Beauly Way, Rise Park, Romford. Courts: H2. *Secretary:* Mrs Y D Bruce, 7 Maidstone Avenue, Romford (40959).
Rayleigh—rear of 71-73 High Road, Rayleigh (775245). Courts: H5. *Secretary:* Mrs K Middleton, 15 Oak Road South, Hadleigh (Southend 556958).
Rochford—Church Walk, Rochford. Courts: H3 (floodlit). *Secretary:* N McCouat, The Venture, 20c Central Avenue, Rochford (Southend 549103).

Roydon—The Playing Fields, Roydon. Courts: H2. *Secretary:* Mrs M White, Bardwells, Epping Road, Roydon (2227).
Southend—Vaughan Avenue, Hamstel Road, Southend-on-Sea. Courts: G3, H5. *Secretary:* Mrs D Sorrell, 18 Fortescue Chase, Thorpe Bay (Southend 586946).
Springlane—Technical College Playing Fields, Spring Lane, Colchester. Courts: H13. *Secretary:* Mrs J Harman, Drakensberg, Church Lane, Colchester (53746).
Standard (Harlow) A & SC—c/o STL, London Road, Harlow (29531 ext 2580). Courts: H3. *Secretary:* P G Tomlinson, 51 The Lawn, Harlow.
Stansted—Cambridge Road, Stansted. Courts: H2. *Secretary:* c/o Mrs J E Hollis, Little Fosters, 105 Cambridge Road, Stansted (B Stortford 812073).
Stock—Willowbrook, Stock Road, Ingatestone. Courts: H3 (floodlit). *Secretary:* Mrs A Bill, Brookfield, Ingatestone Road, Stock.
Theydon Bois—Sidney Road, Theydon Bois. Courts: H5. *Secretary:* Mrs P Walter, 20 The Weind, Theydon Bois (3485).
Peter Thompson Squad—Raphael Park, Parkway, Gidea Park. Courts: H4. *Secretary:* H G Whittle, Killicks End, Rectory Meadow, Alexandra Road, Sible Hedingham, Halstead (0787 61391).
Thorpe Bay—Thorpe Bay Gardens, Thorpe Bay (Southend 585245). Courts: G8, H8. *Secretary:* D Fine, 40 Lodwick, Shoeburyness (5656).
Thurrock—Montgomery Close, Gloucester Avenue, Grays. Courts: H3. *Secretary:* Mrs C Pittick, 57 Chadwell Road, Grays Thurrock (32138).
Tucker Bros—Clearview Tennis Centre, Warley Hall Lane, Little Warley, Brentwood (811569). Courts: H6, G1 (floodlit). *Secretary:* J E Tucker.
University of Essex—Wivenhoe Park, Colchester. Courts: H3.(floodlit). *Secretary:* R Passey, Sports Federation, University of Essex, Wivenhoe Park, Colchester (863211 ext 29).
Valentines—9-11 Castleview Gardens, Ilford. Courts: H6. *Secretary:* J Green, 41 Norwood Avenue, Rush Green, Romford (61515).
Walthamstow—48a Greenway Avenue, London E17 (01-520 5042). Courts: H3 (floodlit). *Secretary:* D Hayes, 43 Cherrydown Avenue, Chingford, London E4 (529 5983).
Westcliff Hard Court—8 The Ridgeway, Westcliff-on-Sea (Southend 78385). Courts: H3, Omnicourt 4 (floodlit). *Secretary:* Mrs L Pitt, 14 Rosary Gardens, Westcliff-on-Sea (Southend 344151).
Westcliff-on-Sea—626 London Road, Westcliff-on-Sea (Southend 41589). Courts: G7, H4. *Secretary:* Mrs J Pearce, 47c Imperial Avenue, Westcliff-on-Sea (Southend 339320).
West Essex—'The Rolls,' Larkshall Road, Higham's Park, London E4 (01-527 3889). Courts: H3. *Secretary:* Mrs S Edler, 42e Chingford Avenue, E4 (01-524 2135).
West Horndon—West Horndon, Brentwood. Courts: H2. *Secretary:* Mrs B Finding, 12 Dunmow Gardens, West Horndon, Brentwood.
Westphelians—Eudo Road, Colchester. Courts: H3. *Secretary:* G W Pool, 11 Forsythia Close, Springfield, Chelmsford (469505).
Whitegates—London Road, Clacton-on-Sea. Courts: G3. *Secretary:* J Russel, 206 Thorpe Road, Clacton-on-Sea (428532).
Whitehall—Larkshall Road, Chingford, London E4. Courts: H4. *Secretary:* Mrs F A Hurford, 11 Balliol Avenue, South Chingford, London E4 (01-529 8986).
Wickford—Patmore Memorial Sports Ground, Runwell Road. Courts: H3 (2 floodlit). *Secretary:* Mrs S E Ellis, 10 First Avenue, Wickford (Wickford 4901).
Wingletye—Fielder Sports Ground, Cromer Road, Hornchurch. Courts: H2. *Secretary:* Miss M Offord, 1 Marlborough Gardens, Upminster (29252).
Woodford Wells—Monkham's Lane, Woodford Green (504 1954). Courts: G5, H7 (3 floodlit). *Secretary:* Mrs G Holford, 6 Norman Court, 78 Monkhams Avenue, Woodford Green (01-505 9019).
Writtle—Paradise Road, Writtle. Courts: H4 (floodlit). *Secretary:* P J Smith, 2 Totnes Walk, Chelmsford (355523).

OTHER AFFILIATED ORGANISATIONS (7)

Bradfords Tennis & Swimming Academy—M G Matthews, 239 Buckhurst Way, Buckhurst Hill (01-504 4354).
Chingford School of Tennis—British Legion Road, Whitehall Road, Chingford E4 (01-527 3142).
Paths Tennis Coaching Association—Raphael Park, Main Road, Romford & Central Park, East Ham, E6. *Secretary:* Mrs P E Bruce, 7 Maidstone Avenue, Romford (40959).
Redbridge Sports Centre—Forest Road, Barkingside, Ilford.
Southend and District LTA—*Secretary:* F A Pike, 6 Rubens Close, Shoeburyness (3874).
Valentines Junior Tennis Squad—2 Morland Road, Ilford.
The Steve Luck Squad—The Plume School, Fambridge Road, Maldon. *Secretary:* S Luck, 4 Keats Close, Maldon (57858).

AFFILIATED SCHOOLS (70)

Boys

Beal School — Ilford. **Brentwood School** — Brentwood. **Epping Forest High** — Loughton. **Sir George Monoux** — London E17. **Colchester Royal Grammar School** — Colchester. **Davenant Grammar** — Loughton. **Westcliff High** — Westcliff. **Chigwell School** — Chigwell. **Eton House School** — Thorpe Bay. **Southend High School** — Southend.

Girls

Braeside — Buckhurst Hill. **Frances Bardsley School** — Romford. **Chelmsford County High** — Chelmsford. **Epping Forest High** — Loughton. **Glenarm College** — Ilford. **Loughton County High** — Loughton. **New Hall** — Boreham. **Southend**

High School — Southend. **Ursuline High School** — Brentwood. **Walthamstow High School** — London E17. **Woodford County High School** — Woodford Green. **Westcliff High** — Westcliff. **Colchester County High** — Colchester. **Valentines High School** — Ilford. **St Johns School** — Epping. **St Nicholas School** — Harlow.

Mixed
Abbscross Technical — Hornchurch. **Bancrofts School** — Woodford Green. **Buckhurst Hill High School** — Buckhurst Hill. **Clacton County High School** — Clacton. **Deanes School** — Benfleet. **Emerson Park** — Hornchurch. **Felsted School** — Felsted. **Forest School** — Snaresbrook. **Gaynes School** — Brackendale Gardens, Upminster. **Hassenbrook County** — Stanford-le-Hope. **Highams Park Senior High** — Highams Park. **King Harold Comprehensive** — Broomstick Hall Road, Waltham Abbey. **Loughton School** — High Road, Loughton. **Mark Hall Secondary** — Harlow. **Mayflower School** — Stock Road, Billericay. **Moulsham Comprehensive** — The Hides, Harlow. **Ongar Comprehensive** — Ongar. **Passmores Comprehensive** — Tendring Road, Harlow. **St Martins** — Hutton. **St Mark's Comprehensive** — Tripton Road, Harlow. **Stewards Comprehensive** — Harlow. **Gilberd School** — Colchester. **Coopers Company & Coborn School** — Upminster. **Burnt Mill School** — Harlow. **Marshall Park School** — Romford. **Brays Grove School** — Harlow. **Latton Bush School** — Harlow. **West Hatch Technical** — Chigwell. **William Edwards Secondary** — Grays. **Beauchamps Secondary** — Wickford. **Brentwood County High** — Brentwood. **Hedley Walter Comprehensive** — Brentwood. **Hockerill School** — Bishops Stortford. **Palmers College** — Little Thurrock. **Ramsey School** — Halstead. **Chingford Senior** — Chingford. **Shoeburyness** — Shoeburyness. **Sweyne School** — Rayleigh. **St Edwards School** — Romford.

All correspondence to School Clubs should be addressed to the Master or Mistress in charge of lawn tennis.

GLOUCESTERSHIRE COUNTY LAWN TENNIS ASSOCIATION

Hon Secretary—**D Moseley,** 48 Lynmouth Road, Hucclecote, Gloucester (610592).
Hon Men's Match Secretary—**M G Angell,** 33 Whitethorn Drive, West Winds, Prestbury, Cheltenham (581648).
Hon Ladies' Match Secretary—**Mrs P J Kerr,** Bentham Manor, Bentham, nr Cheltenham (Glos 862580).
Hon Treasurer—**Mr Adrian Montague-Smith,** "Gowanlea", Blacklains, Birdlip GL4 8LH (0452 863652).
Hon Junior Secretary—**D E Rockett,** 4 King Arthur Close, Charlton Park, Cheltenham (529809).
Representative on the Council—**D Moseley.**

AFFILIATED CLUBS (43)

Beckford—Beckford Sports Field. Courts: H2. *Secretary:* Mrs J Alexander, Old Police Station, Beckford, Tewkesbury, Glos (Evesham 881814).
Berkeley Nuclear Sports & Social Club—Berkeley Power Station main entrance (413). Courts: H2. *Secretary:* Mrs H Harwood, 11 Torch Acre Rise, Dursley (Dursley 46146).
Bourton Vale—Rissington Road, Bourton-on-the-Water. Courts: H2. *Secretary:* R H Dix, Parklands House, Park Street, Stow-on-the-Wold (Stow-on-the-Wold 31725).
Bredon—centre of Bredon Village. Courts: H2. *Secretary:* J McKay, Long Farthing, Bredon (72581).
Cam—Cam Recreation Ground. Courts: H2. *Secretary:* Mrs A Smart, 2 Beechwood Grove, Wotton-under-Edge (842553).
Central Electricity Generating Board—access Barnwood Bypass (652222). Courts: H3. *Secretary:* T H Boyd, 9 Salterley Grange, Leckhampton Hill, Cheltenham (Gloucester 653253 bus, Chel 518541 pri).
Chalford—Highfield, Franch Lynch (Brimscombe 884214). Courts: H2, G2. *Secretary:* Mrs J H Page, 64 Lypiatt View Bussage, Stroud, Glos (Brimscombe 882984).
Chipping Campden—NPFA Ground, Chipping Campden. Courts: H2. *Secretary:* C E E Fleming, Arles House, Broadway, Worcester (0386 853217).
Churchdown—Church Road, Churchdown (713122). Courts: H2. *Secretary:* Mrs S Stait, 32 Winston Road, Churchdown, Gloucester (Churchdown 713714).
Cirencester—Cheltenham Road, Stratton, Cirencester (3204). Courts: H5. *Secretary:* N Reynolds, c/o Cirencester Squash & Tennis Club, Cheltenham Road, Cirencester (Swindon 644572).
Civil Service (Cheltenham)—Tewkesbury Road, Uckington, Cheltenham (Coombe Hill 424). Courts: H4. *Secretary:* N M Blencowe, 33 Upper Park Street, Cheltenham (Cheltenham 576457).
Civil Service (Gloucester)—Estcourt Road, Gloucester (28317). Courts: H3. *Secretary:* G B Osborne, 15 Skylark Way, Gloucester (422548).
College of St Paul & St Mary—The Park, Cheltenham (513836). Courts: H10, G2. *Secretary:* R J Shelmerdine, 42 The Lawns, Gotherington, nr Cheltenham (Bishops Cleeve 3535).
Cranham—Playing Fields. Courts: H1. *Secretary:* Mrs F D Hough, Greystones, Cranham (Painswick 812170).
De La Bere—Southam, Cheltenham (512556). Courts: H4. *Secretary:* R E Griffin, De La Bere Country Club, Southam, Cheltenham (521556).
Dolphins (Tetbury)—Hare & Hounds Hotel, Westonbirt. Courts: H2. *Secretary:* M Marchington, The Folly, Didmarton, Badminton (Didmarton 618).
Dowty (Arle Court) (Tennis Section)—Arle Court, Cheltenham (525515). H2. *Secretary:* T Parker, 16 Barton Way, Up Hatherly, Cheltenham (Cheltenham 511589 pri, Cheltenham 21411 ext 257 bus).

Dowty (Ashchurch)—Dowty Sports Ground, Ashchurch, Tewkesbury (0684 272440). Courts: H2. *Secretary:* S C Travis, 7 Willis Walk, Ashchurch, Tewkesbury (295465).
Dursley—Dursley Recreation Ground. Courts: H2. *Secretary:* Mrs S M Trafford, Sunnyside, Dursley Road, Cambridge, Glos (532).
Eagle Star—Quatgoose Lane, Swindon Village, Cheltenham. Courts: H3. *Secretary:* D A Grainger, Eagle Star Group, Bath Road, Cheltenham (521311 ext 2412).
East Gloucestershire—Old Bath Road, Cheltenham (Cheltenham 522780/30562). Courts: G15, H10. *Secretary:* Mrs P M Bocquet, 21 Glencairn Court, Lansdowne Road, Cheltenham (30562).
Gloucester—St Oswolds Rad, Gloucester. Courts H4. *Secretary:* Mr P Kell, 11 Goddard Way, Tuffley, Gloucester (503012).
Gloucester Wotton—Denmark Road, Gloucester. Courts: G4, H2. *Secretary:* D L Cook, 35 Colerne Drive, Hucclecote, Gloucester (60644).
Gotherington—Gotherington Playing Field. Courts: H2. *Secretary:* Mrs D Freeman, Rhossli, Malleson Road, Gotherington, nr Cheltenham, (Bishops Cleeve 2393).
Innsworth RAF—Innsworth Lane. Courts: H2. *Secretary:* R G Parker, RAF PMC, P Man 7, RAF Innsworth (Churchdown 712612 ext 2235/2478).
Lechlade—Lechlade Playing Field, Burford Road. Courts: H2. *Secretary:* Mrs S A Jenkins, 44 Roman Way, Lechlade, Glos (Farringdon 52623).
Longhope—Recreation Ground. Courts: H2. *Secretary:* Mrs R Clutterbuck, Pentire Church Road, Longhope, Glos (Glos 830933).
Lydney Trust—Lydney Trust Recreation Ground, entrance by Bus Station. Courts: H4. *Secretary:* K F Everett, 16 Ashway, Woolaston, Lydney (Netherend 210).
Mackenzie Hall TC—Brockweir, Hewelsfield. Courts: H1. *Secretary:* Mrs B D Linford, Rose Cottage, St Briavels Common, Lydney (0594 530386).
Mercantile & General—Coldpool Lane, Up Hatherley, Cheltenham (529894). Courts: H2. *Secretary:* S Weston, M & G Reinsurance Plc, St James Square, Cheltenham (36111 ext 122).
Minchinhampton—Stuart Playing Field, Minchinhampton. Courts: H3. *Secretary:* Mrs E A Hoskin, 18 Besbury Park, Minchinhampton (Brimscombe 882597).
Nomads—King George V Playing Fields, Nailsworth. Courts: H2. *Secretary:* Mrs M Lee, 7 Orchard Mead, Nailsworth (Nailsworth 3558).
Northleach—King George Playing Fields. Courts: H2. *Secretary:* Mrs J Stevens, 43 North Home Road, Cirencester (Cirencester 3647).
Old Centechs—Moorend Grove, Leckhampton. Courts: G2. *Secretary:* M Burdge, 191 Leckhampton Road, Cheltenham (527383).
Painswick—Recreation Grounds and Broadham Field, Painswick (813250). Courts: H4. *Secretary:* D L Hudson, Hillcrest, Gloucester Street, Painswick (813250).
Pineholt—Hucclecote, Gloucester (66282). Courts: H2. *Secretary:* Mrs J Griffiths, Chandos, Cranham (Gloucester 812804).
Redmarley—(D'Abitot). Village Hall Playing Fields. Courts: H2. *Secretary:* Mrs P Nelmes, Yew Tree House, Tirley, Glos (Tirley 622).
Royal Agricultural College—Cirencester. Courts: H3. All contacts: Administration Office (Cirencester 2531).
Smiths Club—Newlands Corner, Bishops Cleeve (2752). Courts: H3. *Secretary:* W R Richards, 2 Ashmead Drive, Gotherington, Nr Cheltenham (Bishops Cleeve 2330).
South Cotswold—St Michaels Field, King Street, Cirencester. Courts: H2. *Secretary:* Mrs V Bowley, Church Farm, Ashton Keynes, Swindon, Wilts (Cirencester 861288).
Stroud—Courts: H4. *Secretary:* Mrs A Taylor, 4 Briar Close, The Woodlands, Slad Road, Stroud (79515).
Stonehouse—Oldends Lane, Stonehouse. Courts: H2. *Secretary:* Mrs P Dunster, Fern Cottage, Shute Street, Kings Stanley, Glos (Stonehouse 3107).
Upton St Leonards—Recreation Ground. Courts: H2. *Secretary:* Mrs L A Leithead, 29 Bondend Road, Upton St Leonards, Gloucester (66921).

AFFILIATED SCHOOLS (37)

Boys

Cheltenham College — Cheltenham. **Cheltenham Grammar School** — Cheltenham. **Crypt School** — Gloucester. **King's School** — Gloucester. **Marling School** — Stroud. **Saintbridge School** — Gloucester. **Sir Thomas Rich's School** — Gloucester. **Whitefriars School** — Cheltenham.

Girls

Charlton Park School — Cheltenham. **Cheltenham Ladies' College** — Cheltenham. **Gloucester High School** — Gloucester. **Ribston Hall School** — Gloucester. **The Convent of Clothilde** — Lechlade. **Pates Grammar School** — Cheltenham. **Stroud High School** — Stroud. **Westonbirt School** — Tetbury.

Mixed

Arle Comprehensive School — Cheltenham. **Berkhampstead School** — Cheltenham. **Berry Hill School** — Coleford. **Beaufort School** — Gloucester. **Bourneside School** — Cheltenham. **Brockworth Comprehensive School** — Brockworth. **Charlton Kings Secondary School** — Cheltenham **Chipping Campden Grammar School** — Chipping Campden. **Chosen Hill School** — Churchdown. **Churchdown Comprehensive School** — Churchdown. **Cirencester Comprehensive School** — Cirencester. **Cleeve School** — Bishops Cleeve. **Dean Close School** — Cheltenham. **Kingshill School** — Cirencester. **Manor School** — Eastcombe. **Monkscroft School** — Cheltenham. **Naunton Park Secondary School** — Cheltenham. **Newent School** — Newent. **Oakley Secondary School** — Cheltenham. **Rednock School** — Dursley. **St Benedict's School** — Cheltenham. **Sir William Romney's School** — Tetbury. **Tewkesbury**

School — Tewkesbury. **Westwoods Grammar School** — Northleach. **Winchcombe Secondary School** — Winchcombe. **Wycliffe College** — Stonehouse. **Wynstones Whaddon** — Gloucester.

HAMPSHIRE AND ISLE OF WIGHT LAWN TENNIS ASSOCIATION

Hon Secretary—**I W McDiarmid,** Heatherdale, 12 Greenbrank Crescent, Southampton SO1 7FQ (0703 766302).
Hon Treasurer—**C R Trippe,** 'Summerfield,' Park Road, Winchester SO22 6AA (63239).
Hon Men's Match Secretary—**K St J Wiseman,** 5 Abbotts Way, Southampton SO2 1QU (0703 556377).
Hon Ladies' Match Secretary—**Dr J Pell, 102 Napier Road, Southsea PO5 2RB (0705 817618).**
Junior Organiser (Boys)—**M St G Gross,** Flat 3, Exeter Grange, Exeter Park Road, Bournemouth BH2 5AZ (0202 21341).
Junior Organiser (Girls)—**Mrs B Pell,** West Winds, Hampton Lane, Winchester (52467).
Representatives on the Council—**I W McDiarmid, K St J Wiseman.**

AFFILIATED CLUBS (72)

Arlesford—Arlebury Park, The Avenue. Courts: H3. *Secretary:* Miss P Taylor, 38 The Dean, Arlesford, Hants SO24 9AZ (4191).
Alverstoke LT Squash & Badminton Club—Green Lane, Alverstoke (Gosport 83726). Courts: H3, G6 (indoor). *Secretary:* Mrs M Hunter, 8 Russell Place, Southampton SO2 1NU (550485).
Andover—The Drove, Andover. Courts: H3. *Secretary:* Mrs A Kelly, 4 St Hubert Road, Andover SP10 3QA (54309).
Avenue Havant—Southleigh Road, Havant (482750). Courts: G10, H7. *Secretary:* C Manvell, 16 Hallett Road, Havant PO9 2PJ (471127).
Avondale—Ewshott Lane, Church Crookham, Fleet. *Secretary:* W Clewes, 4 Annandale Drive, Lower Bourne, Farnham, Surrey GU10 3JD (Farnham 724948).
Basingstoke Waverley—Fairfields Road, Basingstoke. Courts: G3. *Secretary:* Mrs P Elliott, 2 Boonway, Oakley, Basingstoke RG23 7BS (781386).
Bass—Anstey Road, Alton (83506) *Secretary:* Mrs M Hart, The Spinney, Shalden, Alton GU34 4DT (83239).
Bassett—Wilton Road, Southampton (774694). Courts: H4 (2 floodlit). *Secretary:* Mrs A Crews, 20 Bassett Green Close, Southampton SO2 3QS (766546).
Bitterne Church—Whites Road, Bitterne, Southampton. Courts: H2. *Secretary:* E R Davison, The Retreat, Cranbury Gardens, Bursledon SO3 8FB.
Brighstone—Brighstone Recreation Ground, Isle of Wight. Courts: H2. *Secretary:* Mrs J Smith, 14 Wilberforce Road, Brighstone, Isle of Wight PO30 4BD (740054).
British Hovercraft Corporation—Church Path, East Cowes, Isle of Wight. Courts: H3. *Secretary:* D Peters, Panorama, East Cowes Road, Whippingham, Isle of Wight PO32 6NH (Wootton Bridge 882595).
Broken Lance, Portsmouth—Alexandra Park Sports Complex. *Secretary:* M Le Poidevin, 40 Beach Road, Southsea PO5 2JH (0705 735473).
Broughton TC—Buckholt Road, *Secretary:* Mrs K Henderson, 1 Paynes Lane, Broughton, Hants SO20 8AH (9330 321).
Buckland—Knowsley Road, Cosham. Courts: G4. *Secretary:* B K Sibley, 388 Havant Road, Farlington, Portsmouth PO6 1NF (0705 388304).
***Buriton**—Petersfield. *Secretary:* Mr R T Morehen, 12 The High Street, Buriton, Petersfield GU31 5RX.
Denmead—King George V Playing Fields, Ashling Park Road. Courts: H3. *Secretary:* Dr P McErlean, Maple Lodge, Southwick Road, Denmead PO7 6LA (Waterlooville 255947).
Esso (Fawley) Recreation Club—Esso Club, Holbury (Blackfield 2350). Courts: H6. *Secretary:* N Marsh, 38 Southbourne Avenue, Holbury, Hants SO4 1NT (Fawley 892606).
***Farnborough**—Tilebarn Close. Courts: H3. *Secretary:* Mrs S Cissell, 13 Chalfont Drive, Farnborough GU14 6SJ.
Folland Aircraft & S Club—King's Avenue, off Hamble Lane, Hamble, Southampton SO3 5NF (Hamble 3371). Courts: G2, H2. *Secretary:* G Windle, 26 Sellwood Road, Netley Abbey, Southampton SO3 5BB (Hamble 3024).
Four Marks—Lymington Bottom Road. Courts: H2. *Secretary:* Mrs G Icough, 87 Winchester Road, Four Marks GU34 5HS (0420 63710).
Free Lance—Canoe Lake, Southsea. Courts: G3. *Secretary:* C H Hall, 10 Cavendish Drive, Waterlooville PO7 7JP (Waterlooville 2762).
Glebian—Westend Road, Southampton. Courts: H3. *Secretary:* R Tribbeck, 7 Downside Avenue, Southampton SO2 7BU (449925).
Goodworth Clatpord—Courts: H2. *Secretary:* Mrs J Stephens, Redroof, Barrow Hill, Goodworth, Clatford, Andover SP11 7RF (0264 52942).
Grayshott—Beechanger Road. Courts: H2. *Secretary:* Mrs J Worth, 'Charnwood,' Portsmouth Road, Hindhead, Surrey GU26 6AQ (5665).
Hale Gardens—Hale Gardens, New Milton. Courts: G3, H3. *Secretary:* H Townsend, Nylai, Kings Lane, Sway, Lymington SO4 9GS (0590 682436).
Hampshire Constabulary Ltd—*Secretary:* P/Sgt J Hazlett, Eastleigh Police Station, Leigh Road, Eastleigh, Hants (612291 ext 143).
Headley—Headley Playing Fields. Courts: H2. *Secretary:* Mrs E Chamberlain, 2 Victoria Cottages, Mount Pleasant Road, Lindford, Bordon GU35 0PR (04203 3943).
Hedge End TC—Northam Road, Hedge End. Courts: H2. *Secretary:* Mrs L Blake, 4 Marvin Close, Hedge End, Hants SO3 2EW (Botley 4120).
Hook & Newnham—King George V Playing Field, Hook Common. Courts: H2. *Secretary:* L

Whitehouse, 3 Nightingale Gardens, Hook RG29 9DS (2139).
Horndean Community Centre—Merchistoun Road, Horndean. Courts: H3. *Secretary:* Mrs P Lockwood, 7 Goodwood Close, Cowplain, Hants (Waterlooville 264062).
Kingsgate—Norman Road, Winchester. Courts: H2 (1 floodlit). *Secretary:* Mrs J Covill, 4 Fordington Road, Winchester SO22 5AL (0962 52975).
Lee-on-Solent LT & Squash Rackets Club—Manor Way, Lee-on-Solent (79381). *Secretary:* Mrs J Holt, 6 Manor Way, Lee-on-Solent PO12 9JU (550381).
Liphook—Haslemere Road, Liphook. Courts: G3. *Secretary:* Mrs J Hill, Lane House, Kingsley Green, Haslemere GU27 3LU (2155).
Littleton LTC—Littleton Recreation Ground, The Hallway, Littleton. Courts: G2, H4. *Secretary:* Mrs J Gill, 46 Main Road, Littleton, Winchester SO22 6QQ (880597).
Lymington—Avenue Road, Lymington. Courts: H2. *Secretary:* M Lambert, 35 Carrisbrooke Court, Stem Lane, New Milton BH25 5US (619951).
Lyndhurst—Sandy Lane, Lyndhurst. Courts: H2. *Secretary:* Mrs D Callow, 'Moonriver,' Broadlands Road, Brockenhurst SO4 7SX (Lymington 22381).
Manydown Tennis Centre—Wooton St Lawrence. Courts: 2 (indoor). *Secretary: Miss C Abbott, Little Lodge, Peasemore, Newbury RG26 0JH (248398).*
Meon Valley Golf & Country TC—Sandy Lane, Shedfield (Wickham 833455). Courts: H3. *Secretary:* Mrs J Hibbert, 6 Chestnut Rise, Droxford, Hants SO3 1NY (0489 878564).
Milford Country Club—Lucerne Road (Milford 475). Courts: G4, H7. *Secretary:* Mrs J Shellard, 17 Rothesay Drive, Highcliffe BH23 4LB (72463).
Newman Collard—Hillbrow Road, Liss. Courts: H2. *Secretary:* Mrs R Cock, 10 Longmead, Liss GU33 7JX (895386).
Newport Victoria Sports—Mountbatten Centre, Fairlee Road, Newport, Isle of Wight. Courts: G3. *Secretary:* Miss V Leigh, 10 Cypress Road, Newport, Isle of Wight PO30 1EY (552976).
Oakley—Andover Road, Church Oakley, Basingstoke. Courts: G2, H2. *Secretary:* Mrs M Spaight, 1 Wither Rise, Oakley, Basingstoke RG23 7BP (781300).
Odiham—Chamberlain Gardens, Odiham. Courts: H2. *Secretary:* Mrs L Wood, Hilden, Kings Street, Odiham.
Old Basing—Old Basing Recreational Ground. Courts: H2. *Secretary:* Mrs C Mitchell, 45 London Road, Basing, Basingstoke RG24 0GS (52225).
Pirelli General—Pasfield Avenue, Eastleigh. Courts: H4. *Secretary:* D Yeandle, 13 Wooderson Close, Bishopstoke, Eastleigh SO5 6QB (0703 600474).
Portals Sports & Social Club—Laverstoke Lane, Whitchurch (316). Co: H.2. *Secretary:* Mrs L Pearce, 7 St Marys Road, Kingsclere, Newbury, Berks RG15 8NF (0635 298737).
Portchester—Westlands Green, Portchester. Courts: H4. *Secretary:* Miss B Frost, 103 Mill Road, Fareham PO16 0UA.
Portsmouth Civil Service—Copnor Road, Hilsea, Portsmouth (62538). *Secretary:* Mrs S Harvey, 78 Crofton Road, Portsmouth PO4 8NY (738200).
Portswood—Abbotts Way, Southampton. Courts: H2, G4. *Secretary:* D J Allerton, 36 Church Lane, Southampton SO2 1SZ (0703 555257).
Preston Candover—Village Hall. Courts: G2, H1. *Secretary:* D S Lindop, 8 Coombehurst Drive, Basingstoke RG21 3HE.
Romsey—Sports Centre, Romsey. Courts: H2. *Secretary:* Mrs R Donovan, 20 The Thicket, Romsey SO5 8SZ (517310).
Ropley—Recreation Ground. Courts: H2. *Secretary:* Mrs S E Brown, Exeter House, Church Street, Ropley, Hants SO24 9AA (3435).
Rowlands Castle TC—Recreation Ground, Rowlands Castle. *Secretary:* Mrs F Fawcett, 'Swallows', Prinsted, Emsworth, Hants PO10 8HS (0243 375505).
Royal Aircraft Establishment, Farnborough—RAE Road, Farnborough. Courts: H4. *Secretary:* Mrs J Rayner, 9 Haywood Drive, Fleet GU13 9SZ (5331).
Ryde LT & Croquet Club—Playstreet Lane, Pattlands, Ryde. Courts: G6, H2. *Secretary:* Mrs M L Young, 35 Ashey Road, Ryde, Isle of Wight (62706).
Ryde Mead—Church Lane, Ryde. Courts: H5. *Secretary:* Miss J S Eades, Little Whitefield Orchard, Ashey Road, Ryde, Isle of Wight PO33 4BB (0983 62249).
Sandleheath—Fordingbridge. Courts: H2. *Secretary:* P. Cairnes, 16 Ashford Road, Fordingbridge (52229).
Sarisbury Green—Sarisbury Green Community Centre (Locks Heath 3114). Courts: H2. *Secretary:* Mrs B Glasspool, 9 Cranbury Gardens, Old Netley, Southampton SO3 8FB (Bursledon 3302).
Southampton School of Lawn Tennis Coaching—Courts: G1, H2. *Secretary:* Miss S Holt, No 5, 157 Bassett Avenue, Southampton SO1 7EP. (769507).
Southern Electricity—Lower Drayton Lane, Cosham (79444). *Secretary:* C Weatherill, 62 Freshfield Gardens, Waterlooville PO7 7TL (379444).
South Hants—Northlands Road, Southampton (22136). Courts: G4. *Secretary:* Mrs J Brooker, 12 Ingersley Rise, Southampton SO3 3DN (West End 2547).
Steep—Church Steep. Courts: H4. *Secretary:* D Brooks, 2 The Avenue, Petersfield GU31 4JQ (68331).
Swanmore—Mayhill Lane, Swanmore. Courts: H2. *Secretary:* D Wallace, 52 High Street, Fareham PO16 7BG (286211).
Sway—Adjoining St Lukes School, Sway. Courts: H2. *Secretary:* Mrs M McEwan, 36 Oakenbrow, Sway, Hants SO4 0DY (0590 683214).
Thornden—Thornden School, Chandlers Ford (69722). *Secretary:* D M Thomas, 17 Saxon Walk, Chandlers Ford SO5 2HZ (Chandlers Ford 3096).
Twyford—Roman Road, Twyford. Courts: G2. *Secretary:* Mrs S Skiba, Holly House, Roman Road, Twyford, Soton SO21 1QW (Twyford 712087).
Ventnor—St Boniface Road, Ventnor, IOW.

Courts: H2. *Secretary:* Mrs G Grimshaw, 'Underwood,' Sandrock Road, Niton Undercliff, Ventnor, IOW PO38 2NQ (731042).
Warsash—Osborne Road, Warash. Courts: H2. *Secretary:* Mrs J Fisher, 16 Crofton Way, Warsash SO3 6FP (Locks Heath 3581).
West End—Church Hill, West End. Courts: H3. *Secretary:* Mrs L Alma, 26 Glen Eyre Road, Southampton SO2 3GG (769605).
West Meon—Courts: H1. *Secretary:* Miss M T Edwards, Garretts Farm, West Meon, Hants GU32 1LZ (274).
Winchester Tennis & Squash Club—Bereweeke Road. Courts: G11, H9 (4 floodlit). *Secretary:* B Mussell, Winchester LT & SR Club, Bereweeke Road, Winchester SO22 6AP (54028).
Woolton Hill Sports—Woolton Hill, nr Newbury (Highclere 253380). Courts: H3. *Secretary:* A Davis, 'Woodfern', Broadlayings, Woolton Hill, Newbury RG15 9TT (0635 253458).

OTHER AFFILIATED ORGANISATIONS (9)

Aldershot & District LTA—*Secretary:* Mrs G V Aspinall, 35 Jubilee Lane, Boundstone, Farnham GU10 4JA (Fresham 4272).
Basingstoke & District League—*Secretary:* Mrs M Collins, Southview, Freefolk, Whitchurch RG23 7QS (2971).
East Hants League—*Secretary:* Mrs M Hart, The Spinney, Shalden, Alton GU34 4DT (83239).
Isle of Wight & District LTA—*Secretary:* D C Fothergill, 2 Arno Villa, Newport Road, Niton, Ventnor, Isle of Wight (09837 30979).
Portsmouth & District LTA—*Secretary:* N Adnitt, 31 Kennedy Crescent, Alverstroke, Gosport PO12 2ND (0705 523336).
Southampton LTA—*Secretary:* Mrs A Carcas, Dunfield Copse, Exbury Road, Blackfield, Southampton SO4 1XE (Fawley 893270).
Southampton Junior Tennis Coaching Club—*Secretary:* G J Ferrier, 26 Pine Crescent, Chandlers Ford, Southampton SO5 1LL (04215 2863).
Southampton Schools LTA—*Secretary:* Mrs S Field, Sholing Girls' School, Middle Road, Southampton SO2 8PH (448861).
South East Hant School LTA—*Secretary:* J E Wright, Havant College, New Road, Havant PO9 1QL.

AFFILIATED SCHOOLS (59)

Boys
Churchers College — Petersfield GU31 4AS. **Embly Park School** — Romsey SO5 0ZE. **King Edward VI School** — Southampton SO9 3FP. **St John's College** — Southsea PO5 3QW. **Winchester College** — Winchester.

Girls
Atherley School — Southampton. **Farnborough Hill Convent College** — Farnborough. **Ferhill Manor School** — New Milton. **Harriett Costello School** — Basingstoke. **North Foreland Lodge** — Sherfield-on-Loddon, nr Basingstoke. **Portsmouth High School** — Portsmouth. **Regent's Park Girls School** — Southampton SO9 4LT. **St Anne's School** — Southampton. **St Swithun's School** — Winchester. **Upper Chine School** — Shanklin, Isle of Wight.

Mixed
Alton College — Alton. **Barton Peveril Grammar School** — Eastleigh. **Bedales School** — Petersfield. **Bohunt School** — Liphook GU30 7NY. **Brighton Hill** — Basingstoke RG22 4DH. **Brockenhurst College** — Brockenhurst. **Burgate School** — Fordingbridge. **Calthorpe Park Bi-Lateral School** — Fleet. **Cams Hill School** — Fareham. **Carisbrooke High** — Newport, Isle of Wight. **Cranborune School** — Basingstoke. **Ditcham Park School** — Ditcham Park, Petersfield GU31 5RN. **Farnborough College** — Farnborough. **Glen Eyre School** — Southampton. **Hampton Park School** — Southampton SO2 3SZ. **Hardley School** — Fawley, Southampton SO4 1PA. **Harrow Way School** — Andover SP10 3RH. **Henry Beaufort School** — Harestock, Winchester. **Itchen College** — Southampton SO9 3AX. **John Hanson School** — Andover. **Kings School** — Romsey Road, Winchester. **Millbrook School** — Southampton SO9 3SB. **Moyles Court School** — Ringwood BH24 3NF. **Noadswood School** — Dibden, Purlieu SO4 5ZF. **Oak Farm School** — Farnborough GU14 8SS. **Oaklands School** — Waterlooville, Hants. **Peter Symond's College** — Winchester. **Porchester Comprehensive School** — Porchester, Fareham. **Prices College** — Fareham. **Priory School** — Southsea. **Richard Taunton College** — Southampton SO9 5GF. **Sandown High School** — Sandown, Isle of Wight. **St Edmunds School** — Portsmouth PO1 1RX. **Stanbridge Earl's School** — Romsey. **Tent Valley School** — Stockbridge SO20 6HA. **Testwood Comprehensive School** — Totton SO4 3ZW. **The Mountbatten School** — Romsey SO5 8SY. **The Vyne School** — Basingstoke. **The Wavell School** — Farnborough GU14 6BH. **Thornden School** — Chandlers Ford. **Totton College** — Totton. **Westgate County Secondary School** — Fair Oak, nr Eastleigh. **Wilden School** — Hedge End SO3 4EJ. **Yately School** — Yately, Hants.

All correspondence to School Clubs should be addressed to the Master or Mistress in charge of lawn tennis.

HEREFORD AND WORCESTER COUNTY LAWN TENNIS ASSOCIATION

Hon Secretary—**Mrs T Snow,** Arncroft, Breinton, Hereford (273640 or 56292 bus).
Hon Junior Secretary—**Mrs C Siviter,** Tyrol, Merricks Close, Bewdley, Worcester (0299 400396).
Hon Treasurer—**Mrs E Barker,** Glebe Lodge, Leigh, Worcester (0886 32438).

Hon Men's Match Secretary—**W Devitt,** 9 The Ridgeway, Stourport on Severn, Worcs (02993 2339).
Hon Ladies' Match Secretary—**Mrs J Robinson,** Oldborough Barn, Loxley, Warwick (0789 841760).
Representatives on the Council—**I A King, Mrs T Snow.**

AFFILIATED CLUBS (47)

Abbey Stadium LTC—Birmingham Road, Redditch. Courts: H6, G3. *Secretary:* S Davies, Abbey Stadium, Redditch (60206/44460).
Ashton Under Hill LTC—Recreation Ground, Elmley Road, Ashton Under Hill, Evesham. Courts: H2. *Secretary:* Mrs L Somerset, Coppice Cottage, Cottons Lane, Ashton Under Hill, Evesham, Worcs (Evesham 881911).
Barnt Green Sports—Margesson Drive, Bittel Road, Barnt Green. Courts: G4, H4. *Secretary:* Mrs C Partridge, 31 Duxford Close, Headless Cross, Redditch (Redditch 44952).
Bewdley—Stourport Road, Bewdley. Courts: G3, H5 (2 floodlit). *Secretary:* Mrs S Venables, 23 Forest Close, Bewdley (402800).
Blakedown & Churchill—Sports Centre, Blakedown. Courts: H3 (2 floodlit). *Secretary:* Mrs S R Hewitt, 12 Greyhound Lane, Stourbridge, West Midlands DY8 3AA (Stourbridge 395912).
Bodenham & District—Parish Hall, Bodenham, Herefordshire. Courts: H2. *Secretary:* A P Tomlinson, Old Post Office, Peas Green, Bodenham (056884 640).
Brintons TC—Brintons Sports Ground, Stourport Road, Oldington, Kidderminster. Courts: H3. *Secretary:* C Carter, c/o Brintons Social Club, Exchange Street, Kidderminster (3444).
Bromsgrove Cricket, Hockey and Tennis Club—St Godwalds Road, Bromsgrove. Courts: H6 (2 floodlight). *Secretary:* Miss S Fox, 44 Cottage Lane, Marlbrook, Bromsgrove (021 445 34993).
Bromwich Lane (Worcester)—Bromwich Lane, St Johns, Worcester. Courts: G3, H2. *Secretary:* Mrs C J Powell, 6 Old Forge, Whitbourne, Worcs WR6 5SB (Knightwick 21655).
Bromyard—Queen Elizabeth High School, Bromyard, Herefordshire. Courts: H4. *Secretary:* Mrs E Powell, The Elms, Buckenhill, Bromyard, Herefordshire (Bromyard 83265).
Civil Service (Worcester Area)—Whittington Road. Courts: H3. *Secretary:* K J Beard, Friston, Coxwell Drive, Malvern, Worcester (Malvern 4037).
CMC (formerly Gilt Edge)—CMC Leisure Centre, Stourport Road, Oldington, Kidderminster. Courts: H3. *Secretary:* D V Sadler, 40 Whitegate Drive, Kidderminster (754783).
Cookley—Lea Lane, Cookley. Courts: H3. *Secretary:* Ms S Parkes, 2 Lea Lane, Cookley, Nr Kidderminster, Worcs DY10 3TX (Kidderminster 850989).
County Council Sports—Claines Lane. Courts: H3. *Secretary:* R H Warner, Udine, Church Lane, Whittington, Worcester WR5 3RQ (Worcester 353771 pri, Worcester 353366 ext 2500 bus).
Cutnall Green Tennis & Social Club—The Sports Ground, Cutnall Green. Courts: H2. *Secretary:* Mrs E M Nicholl, The Grange, Elmbridge, nr Droitwich, Worcester (052786 264).
Droitwich—St Peter's Fields, Droitwich. Courts: H6 (4 floodlit). *Secretary:* Mrs A Dutton, 20 The Oaklands, Droitwich, Worcester (Droitwich 773657).
Evesham Rowing—The Boat House, Abbey Park. Courts: G4, H3. *Secretary:* Mrs G Burton, 3 Manor Gardens, Aldington, Evesham, Worcester (Evesham 830153).
Fladbury—Station Road, Fladbury. Courts: H3. *Secretary:* Mrs J Portergill, Brooklands, Fladbury, Pershore, Worcester (Evesham 860302).
Goodrich—Goodrich, Ross-on-Wye. Courts: G2. *Secretary:* Mrs M Phillips, Shoppe Cottage, Llangrove, Nr Ross on Wye (098984 265).
Hagley—Hagley RC High School, Brake Lane, Hagley. Courts: H5. *Secretary:* J Kyte, 12 Station Road, Hagley, Stowbridge (0562 885923).
Hallow—Hallow, nr Worcester. Courts: G2, H3 (1 floodlit). *Secretary:* Mrs P Homer, Old Pastures, Worlds End, Hallow (0905 640659).
Hartlebury—The Green, Waresley, Hartlebury. Courts: H2 (2 floodlit). *Secretary:* R Litchfield, 39a Nursery Grove, Franche, Kidderminster (Kidderminster 68636).
Hereford City Sports—Grandstand Road, Hereford. Courts: G9, H3. *Secretary:* Mrs M Louis, 8 Farr Close, Tupsley, Hereford (268451).
Hereford Lads Club—Wildemarsh Common, Hereford. Courts: H3 (3 floodlit). *Secretary:* Mrs J Williams, Hereford Lads Club, Widemarsh Common, Hereford (0432 273468).
Hereford Whitecross—Sollars Close, Whitecross Road, Hereford HR4 0LX. Courts: G4, H3. *Secretary:* Mrs M Hastie, 48 Three Elms Road, Hereford (267251).
High Duty Alloys—Cherry Tree Walk, Blatchley, Redditch. Courts: H2 (2 floodlit). *Secretary:* Ms J Birkett, 93 Oakenshaw Road, Redditch, Worcs (Redditch 23794).
Inkberrow—Sands Lane. Courts: H3. *Secretary:* Mrs M Cowie, 6 Himbleton Close, Lodge Park, Redditch (28588).
Kay's Sports & Social Club—Cinderella Ground, Bransford Road, Worcester. Courts: G3. *Secretary:* G Lawrence, 26 Clevedon Green, South Littleton, Evesham, Worcester (0386 831024).
Lady Hawkins Association Club—Lady Hawkins School, Kington. Courts: H4. *Secretary:* Mrs O Morgan, Bridge Farm, Almeley, Herefordshire (Eardisley 446).
Ledbury—Underdown, Ledbury. Courts: H3. *Secretary:* Mrs B Onions, Sevenoes, Bank Crescent, Ledbury, Herefordshire (Ledbury 2028).
Leominster—Sports Club, Leominster. Courts: H3. *Secretary: D J Milner, 21 Silwian Close, Leominster, Herefordshire (Leominster 3798).*
Madley—New Hard Courts, Brampton Road, Madley. Courts: H3. *Secretary:* Mrs G C Andrews, Webton Court, Madley (Golden Valley 250220).

Manor Park—Albert Road, Malvern. Courts: G9, H8 (2 floodlit). *Secretary:* Mrs J Paget, 123 Meadow Road, Malvern, Worcs (06845 65466).
Marden—Playing Field, Marden, Hereford. Courts: H2. *Secretary:* Mrs L Turbett, 48 St Peters Close, Moreton on Lugg, Hereford (265906).
Mathon Cradley & Storridge Sports Club—Courts: H2. *Secretary:* Mrs P Pugh, Cherrywood, Cradley, Malvern (Ridgeway Cross 482).
Pershore & District Sports—The Bottoms, Defford Road, Pershore. Courts: H3. *Secretary:* Mrs A Barrett, 18 Worcester Road, Pershore (553159).
RAF Hereford—Credenhill, Hereford. Courts: H6. *Secretary:* Sqn Ldr D B Armstrong, S Dent Off, RAF Hereford, Credenhill (Hereford 761555 ext 349).
Royal Signals Radar Establishment—Pickersleigh Avenue, Malvern Link. Courts: H2 (1 floodlit). *Secretary:* Mrs J H Atkinson, 11 North End Lane, Malvern (06845 61175).
South Herefordshire—Wilton Road, Ross-on-Wye. Courts: G8, H2. *Secretary:* Mrs J Mellor, The Homestead, Anton Street, Ross-on-Wye (0989 63864).
Stourport—Tan Lane, Stourport. Courts: G6, H4 (floodlit 2). *Secretary:* T Morgan, The Heath, Wilden Top, Stourport (Stourport 3458).
Tenbury—The Burgage, Teme Street, Tenbury Wells. Courts: G2, H2. *Secretary:* S Gripton, 16 Holly Road, Burford, Tenbury Wells, Worcs.
Three Counties—Hereford. *Secretary:* Mrs M J Edwards, Felton Court, Felton, Herefordshire (Burley Gate 203).
Wolverley—Memorial Hall, Wolverley, nr Kidderminster. Courts: H2 (1 floodlit). *Secretary:* J D Neale, 44 Pineridge Drive, Blakebrook, Kidderminster (69150).
Woolhope—Berryfield, Woolhope. Courts: H2. *Secretary:* Mrs K M Watkins, Rudge End, Woolhope (Fownhope 371).
Worcester Golf & Country—Boughton Park, Bransford Road, Worcester. Courts: G3, H4 (2 floodlit). *Secretary:* Mrs E Barker, Glebe Lodge, Leigh, Worcester (0886 32438).
Worcester—Northwick Close, Worcester (51092). Courts: G3, H7 (4 floodlit). *Secretary:* J V Blake, 5 Beech Avenue, Worcester (52552).
Wythall—Silver Street, Hollywood, Birmingham. Courts: H3. *Secretary:* Mrs P Bryant, 35 Truemans, Heath Lane, Hollywood B47 5QE (021 430 7946).

OTHER AFFILIATED ORGANISATIONS (13)

Albright and Wilson (Winter League)—*Secretary:* P Swingler, 4 Yewhurst Road, Solihull (021 705 5991).
Alveley (Winter League)—*Secretary:* Mrs D Constable, 3 Bridge Road, Alveley, Shropshire (Quatt 780434).
Halesowen (Winter League)—*Secretary:* Mrs J Buckle, 2 Kidderminster Road, Hagley.
Hereford & Worcester County Tennis Parents Association—*Secretary:* Mrs A Jones, 10 Hennels Avenue, Webheath, Redditch, Worcester (Redditch 41762).
Kidderminster & District Tennis League—*Secretary:* D Wood, 142 Kidderminster Road, Hagley (885045).
Ludlow Castle (Winter League)—*Secretary:* Mrs C White, Saanen, 73 Downton View, Ludlow, Shropshire (Ludlow 3939).
Ludlow & South Shropshire (Winter League)—*Secretary:* Mrs S Sherbourne, 48 Old Street, Ludlow, Shropshire (Ludlow 4430).
Malvern Junior Tournament—*Secretary:* B Marks, 44 Hastings Road, Malvern, Worcester (64027).
Old Hill Cricket & Tennis Club—Miss R D Case, 22 Timbertree Road, Cradley Heath, Warley, West Midlands (Cradley Heath 69985).
Stourbridge—Sugar Loaf Lane, Iverley, Stourbridge (3613). Courts: G6, H10 (2 floodlit). *Secretary:* J Lorbert, 1 Elm Drive, Blakedown, Kidderminster (Kidderminster 700563).
Wall Heath—Enville Road Recreation Ground. Courts: H4. *Secretary:* Miss E. Harris, 46 Ridge Road, Kingswinford (0384 274712).
Wollaston (Winter League)—Prestwood Drive, Stourton, Stourbridge. Courts: H4 (2 floodlit). *Secretary:* R S Pike, Wychway, 126a Ham Lane, Pedmore, Stourbridge, West Midlands (Hagley 883115).
Worcester College of Education—Henwick Fr. Courts: H7. *Secretary:* Miss M Green, Worcester College of Higher Education, Worcester (Worcester 424788 or 427672).

SCHOOL CLUBS (62)

Boys (4)

Belmont Abbey — Hereford. **King's School** — Worcester. **Royal Grammar School** — Worcester. **The College** — Malvern.

Girls (10)

Alice Otley School — Worcester. **Blessed Edward Oldcorne School** — Worcester. **Christopher Whitehead School** — Worcester. **Dodderhill School** — Droitwich. **Ellerslie** — Malvern. **Holy Trinity Convent** — Kidderminster. **Lawnside** — Malvern. **Malvern Girls College** — Malvern. **St James and the Abbey** — West Malvern. **St Mary's Convent** — Worcester.

Mixed (48)

Abbey High School — Redditch. **Arrow Vale** — Redditch. **Aylestone School** — Hereford. **Bewdley High School** — Bewdley. **Bishop of Hereford Bluecoat School** — Hereford. **Bridley Moor High School** — Redditch. **Bromsgrove School** — Bromsgrove. **Burlish Middle School** — Stourport. **Chase High School** — Malvern. **Droitwich High School** — Droitwich. **Dyson Perrins CE School — Malvern. Elgar High School** — Worcester. **Evesham High School** — Evesham. **Franche Middle School** — Kidderminster. **Hagley RC High School** — Hagley. **Hanley Castle High School** — Hanley Castle. **Harry Cheshire High School** — Kidderminster. **Haybridge High School** — Hagley.

Hereford Cathedral School — Hereford. **Hereford Sixth Form College** — Hereford. **John Kyrle High School** — Ross on Wye. **John Masefield High School** — Ledbury. **King Charles I School** — Kidderminster. **King Edward Sixth Form College** — Stourbridge. **Kingstone School** — Kingstone, Hereford. **Lady Hawkins School** — Kington. **Leys High School** — Redditch. **Lodge Farm Middle School** — Redditch. **North Bromsgrove High School** — Bromsgrove. **Nunnery Wood Secondary School** — Worcester. **Pershore High School** — Pershore. **Prince Henry's High School** — Worcester. **Reaside Middle School** — Frankley. **Ridgeway Middle School** — Redditch. **St John's Middle School** — Blakebrook, Worcester. **St Mary's School** — Lugwardine, Hereford. **St Peter's Middle School** — West Redditch. **South Bromsgrove High School** — Bromsgrove. **Stourport County Secondary School** — Stourport. **The Haywood School** — Hereford. **The Hill Junior High School** — Upton on Severn. **The Minster School** — Leominster. **Waseley Hill High School** — Rubery. **Weobley School** — Weobley, Herefordshire. **Whitecross School** — Hereford. **Wigmore High School** — Wigmore. **Woodrush High School** — Hollywood, Birmingham. **Worcester VI Form College** — Worcester.

HERTFORDSHIRE LAWN TENNIS ASSOCIATION

Hon Secretary—**Miss S E Wolstenholme,** Corner House, 54 Kitsbury Road, Berkhamsted HP4 3EA (04427 3952).
Hon Junior Secretary—**Mrs S Howgego,** 'Woodfield', Woodfield Lane, Brookmans Park, Hatfield AL9 6JJ (Potters Bar 52809).
Hon Treasurer—**P Angus,** 50 Bloomfield Road, Harpenden (5735).
Hon Men's Match Secretary—**M P Hudson,** 106 Gravel Lane, Boxmoor, Hemel Hempstead (Hemel Hempstead 54098).
Hon Ladies' Match Secretary—**Mrs A J Allnutt,** 2 Cowper Road, Berkhamsted, Herts (73075).
Representatives on the Council—**T A Adamson, Miss S E Wolstenholme.**

AFFILIATED CLUBS (58)

Allenburys Sports & Social—Harris Lane, Ware. Courts: H7. *Secretary:* Tennis Section, Dr L Carey, 3 The Lawns Close, Melbourn, Royston (61461 pri, 0920 3993 ext 2309 bus).
Berkhamsted Lawn Tennis & Squash Rackets Club—Lower Kings Road, Berkhamsted (3095). Courts: G3, H6, AG3 (6 floodlit). *Secretary:* Mrs V Perris, Hay House, Westbrook Hay, Hemel Hempstead (59761).
Bishop's Stortford—Cricketfield Lane, Bishop's Stortford (54463). Courts: G6, H5 (3 floodlit). *Secretary:* Mrs S Fuller, The Briars, Ardley End, Hatfield Heath, Bishop's Stortford CM22 7AJ (730765 pri, 55191 X-ray Dept bus).
Brookman's Park—Golf Course Road, Brookman's Park, Hatfield. Courts: H6. *Secretary:* Mrs S Howgego, 'Woodfield', Woodfield Lane, Hatfield AL9 6JJ (0707 52809).
Broxbourne—Mill Lane, Broxbourne (Hoddesdon 466901). Courts: G8, H3 (3 floodlit). *Secretary:* J W Felton, 'Badgers', Middle Street, Nazeing, Essex EN9 2LB (Nazeing 3570 pri, 01 283 1412 bus).
Cassiobury—The Gardens, Cassiobury Estate, Watford. Courts: H6. *Secretary:* Miss S Woodward, 46 The Avenue, Watford WD1 3NS (21621 pri, 21221 bus).
Cheshunt Cricket, Lawn Tennis & Bowls—Albury Ride, Cheshunt (Waltham Cross 23920). Courts: G3, H3. *Secretary:* Mrs R Hyde, 12 Highwood Road, Hoddesdon (460891 pri, Potters Bar 42311 bus).
Chorleywood—Walled Garden, Chorleywood House (4199). Courts: H6, F3. *Secretary:* Mrs Sally Packard, 40 Blacketts Wood Drive, Chorleywood (3000 pri, 0494 451938 bus).
County Hall LTC—Leahoe, Hertford. Courts: H4. *Secretary:* E S Saint, 101 Forresters Drive, Welwyn Garden City AL7 2JA (326446 pri, Hertford 555326 bus).
Datchworth Sports Club—Datchworth Green. Courts: H2. *Secretary:* Mrs A Wightman, Tudor Lodge, Datchworth Green, Datchworth, Knebworth (Stevenage 812692).
Digswell—Digswell Playing Field, Hertford Road, Digswell. Courts: H3 (2 floodlit). *Secretary:* D Watts, 97 Warren Way, Digswell, Welwyn (4634).
Dyrham Park Country Club—Galley Lane, Barnet (440 3361). Courts: H2. *Secretary:* D V Prentice, Dyrham Park Country Club. All correspondence address to The Secretary.
Elliswick—Browning Road, Harpenden (68685). Courts: G4, H4. *Secretary:* Mrs A Fox, 20 The Deerings, Harpenden (67670).
Elstree & Borehamwood—Meadow Park, Borehamwood. Courts: H3. *Secretary:* Mr H G Stevens, 9 Cardinal Avenue, Borehamwood (953 1428 pri).
Elstree Lawn Tennis Club—Aldenham Road, Elstree. Courts: H3. *Secretary:* Ms J Longbourne, Palmers Lodge, Allum Lane, Elstree (01-953 5511 pri).
Gable End—Gable End. *Secretary:* Mrs G Goldberg, Gable End, Arkley Lane, Barnet.
Greenwood Park—Tippendell Lane, Chiswell Green, St Albans. Courts: H4. *Secretary:* Mrs P Baker, 17 The Croft, Chiswell Green, St Albans AL2 3AR (57206).
Harpenden—Amenbury Lane, Harpenden (3961). Courts: G8, H8 (3 floodlit). *Secretary:* Dr Darryl Tant, Algonquin, 30 Roundwood Park, Harpenden AL5 3AF (63362 pri, 0582 26123 bus).
Hatfield—1 College Lane, Hatfield (64199). Courts: G4, H5. *Secretary:* Mrs Sheila Miller, 83 Bushey Lee, Welwyn Garden City (330133).
Hertford—Hartham Common, Hertford (56481). Courts: H6 (3 floodlit). *Secretary:* Mr A Heath, 4 Aldwyke Rise, Ware (2612).
Hitchin—Bancroft Recreation Ground, Hitchin. Courts: H3 (3 floodlit). *Secretary:* Mrs Betty Norman, 13 Ruskin Lane, Hitchin SG4 0PN (34005).

Hoddesdon—Beech Walk, Hoddesdon (469783). Courts: H7, G3. K C Alderman, 33 Sadlers Way, Hertford SG14 2DZ (558040).
ICI Lawn Tennis Club—ICI Site, Bessemer Road, Welwyn Garden City. Courts: H5 (3 floodlit). *Secretary:* D L Mitchell, 52 William Way, Letchworth.
ICL Sports & Social Club—Whitethorn Lane, Letchworth (73789). Courts: G4, H2. *Secretary:* Mrs Zena Diamandis, 16 Blackmore, Letchworth (673546 pri, 678266 bus).
Kendal Hall Country Club (Tennis Section)—Radlett. Courts: H6. *Secretary:* Mr M Lane, 20 Gordon Avenue, Stanmore, Middx, HA7 3QD (01 954 2189 pri, 01 637 7397 bus).
Kimpton—Parkfield East, Park Lane, Kimpton. Courts: H2. *Secretary:* Mrs Helen Colliss, 22 Parkfield Crescent, Kimpton, Hitchin (Kimpton 832079).
Kodak (Hemel Hempstead)—Wood Lane End, Hemel Hempstead. Courts: H3. *Secretary:* R Smith, 24 Park Hill Road, Hemel Hempstead (55268 pri, 61122 ext 44243 bus).
Laing Sports (Tennis Section)—Rowley Lane, Arkley (449 8485). Courts: G3, H3 (1 floodlit). *Secretary:* Mrs M Mountford, 63 Hillside Gardens, Barnet, EN5 2NQ (01-440 2283 pri, 01-906 5483 bus).
Letchworth—Paddock Close, Letchworth (684797). Courts: H6 (2 floodlit). *Secretary:* W Sandy, 19 Stotfold Road, Hitchin SG4 0QN (32370).
Leverstock Green—Grasmere Close, Leverstock Green. Courts: G4, H8 (2 floodlit). *Secretary:* J Bruley, 71 Cherry Orchard, Hemel Hempstead HP1 3NH (42091 pri, Dunstable 64155 bus).
Little Gaddesden—The Pavillion, Church Road, Little Gaddesden, Berkhamsted. Courts: H3. *Secretary:* Michael Rennie, Dennison House, Little Gaddesden, Nr Berkhamsted.
Long Marston Club—Emma's Orchard, Cheddington Lane, Long Marston, nr Tring. Courts: H2. *Secretary:* Mrs S J Dean, Aspens Farm, Marsworth, nr Tring HP23 4NE (Cheddington 661427).
Marshalswick—Sherwood Avenue, St Albans. Courts: H4. *Secretary:* Mrs R Walton, 87 Windmill Avenue, St Albans (63159).
Moor Park—Moor Park, Rickmansworth (773146). Courts: G9, H6. *Secretary:* Mrs W Hillman, 43 Dene Road, Northwood, Middx (23467).
Northaw & Cuffley—Northaw Road, Cuffley 875996. Courts: H4. *Secretary:* Mrs L Bridges, 34 Burleigh Way, Cuffley, EN6 4LG (875859 pri, 01 801 6044 bus).
Northwood & Oxhey—Carew Road, Northwood (22767). Courts: AG4 (3 floodlit). *Secretary:* G Bohrn, 103 Green Lane, Northwood (28266 pri, 0865 250440 bus).
Orchard—Blakemere Road, Welwyn Garden City. Courts: H3. *Secretary:* Mrs Gill Yandall, 137 Oakdale, Welwyn Garden City AL8 7QS (323794).
Oxhey Hall LTC—Oxhey Hall Community Centre, Broadfield Lane, Oxhey (Watford 21991). Courts: H3. *Secretary:* Mr K Godfrey, 6 Raglan Gardens, Oxhey, Watford WD1 4LL (49693 pri, 44444 bus).
Parkway—Turmore Dale, Welwyn Garden City. Courts: H4. *Secretary:* Mrs J Weiss, Chiswell House, Potters Heath, Welwyn (Stevenage 812443 pri).
Potters Bar—The Walk, Potters Bar (44180). Courts: H6. *Secretary:* A H Lambley, 77 Baker Street, Potters Bar EN6 2EX (51736 pri).
Radlett Lawn Tennis & Squash Club—Watling Street, Radlett (4523). Courts: H6, AG6 (6 floodlit AG). *Secretary:* F J Lyons, 7 Summerhouse Lane, Aldenham, Watford WD2 8DL (Radlett 6346 pri, Potters Bar 50912 bus).
Rickmansworth—Meadow Way, Rickmansworth (774033). Courts: H10 (2 floodlit). *Secretary:* B Brehout, 35 Sherfield Avenue, Rickmansworth WD3 1NN (778526).
Rosedale Sports Club—Andrews Lane, Cheshunt (Waltham Cross 23983). Courts: G2, H2. Secretary: Mr M S Winfield, 13 Claremont, Cheshunt EN7 5QR (Waltham Cross 30515 pri, Hatfield 60965 bus).
Rothamsted—Rothamsted Experimental Station, Harpenden (2999). Courts: H4. *Secretary:* Mrs J M Bailey, 65 Springfield Crescent, Harpenden (61307 home, 5241 bus ext 2180).
Royston—Therfield Heath, Baldock Road, Royston (43613). Courts: H3. *Secretary:* Mr T Pitt, 34 Icknield Walk, Royston SG8 7JX (46685).
St Albans—Jersey Lane, St Albans (65252). Courts: G6, H7 (2 floodlit). *Secretary:* R M Graham, 53 Woodstock Road North, St Albans (61169 home, 01-486 5555 ext 4209 bus).
Salisbury—Salisbury Avenue, St Albans. Courts: G2, H1. Secretary: Mrs D Minto, 23 Hedley Road, St Albans AL1 5JL (62110).
Sawbridgeworth—Townfields, Springhall Road. Courts: G3, H4. *Secretary:* Mrs J Mulvany, 'Fair Green Place,' Fairgreen, Sawbridgeworth (Bishops Stortford 723126).
Standon and Puckeridge—Station Road, Standon. Courts: H3. *Secretary:* Mrs A Sapsed, Newsells Farm, Barkway, nr Royston SG8 8DG (Royston 43122 pri, 41571 bus).
STC (A & SC)—Tennis Section, STC Sports Ground, Denham Road, New Southgate N11 1HB (01 368 1234). Courts: H4 (4 floodlit). *Secretary:* D P Bowler, STC (Telecommunications) Ltd, Dept 32761, Oakleigh Road South, New Southgate N11 1HB (01 361 1606 pri, 01 368 1234 ext 2932 bus).
Stevenage—Knebworth Sports & Social Club, Old Knebworth Lane, Stevenage (313320). Courts: H6 (3 floodlit). *Secretary:* Ms C Stewart, 45 Shephall Green, Stevenage (68651).
Sun Sports—Bellmount Wood Avenue, Watford (27453). Courts: H6. Secretary: Mrs E A Brook, 344 Hempstead Road, Watford WD1 3NA (32548).
Tewin—Upper Green, Tewin. Courts: H2. *Secretary:* Mrs M J Kitchen, 49 Burnham Green Road, Welwyn (Bulls Green 267).
Townsend—Waverley Road, St Albans (53306). Courts: G5, H6 (3 floodlit). *Secretary:* Mrs Clare Wallace, 43a Lansdowne Road, Biscot, Luton, Beds LU1 3ES (0582 29935).
Tring—Tring Park Cricket Club, Tring. Courts:

H6. Secretary: Mrs E Northcott, Green Edge, 5 Fox Close, Wigginton, Tring, HP23 6ED (3155).
Wellcome Sports & Social Club (Tennis Section)—Kitcheners Field, Berkhamsted (4937). Courts: H3. *Secretary:* Miss A Parker, Wellcome Foundation Ltd, Ravens Lane, Berkhamsted (6421 pri, 3333 ext 209 bus).
Welwyn Tennis Club—The Playing Fields, off London Road, Welwyn (7180). Courts: H5 (3 floodlit). *Secretary:* R B S Walker, Bonds Cottage, 8 Elmoor Avenue, Welwyn (5932).
West Herts & Watford—Park Avenue, Watford (29239). Courts: G3, H6 (3 floodlit). *Secretary:* Peter Ellwood, 35 Bembridge Place, Linden Lea, Leavesden, Watford (0923 675349 pri, 01 450 8911 bus).
Wymondley—Recreation Ground, Little Wymondley, Hitchin. Courts: H2. *Secretary:* Mrs E Turney, 12 Uplands Avenue, Hitchin SG4 9NH (51050).

OTHER AFFILIATED ORGANISATIONS (2)

Hertfordshire Schools' Tennis Association—*Secretary:* Mrs Iris Luckett, 51 Toms Lane, Kings Langley (63969).
Hertfordshire Tennis Coaches Association—*Secretary:* Mrs P Hall, 67 Billy Lows Lane, Potters Bar (58661).
Watford & District League—*Secretary:* Mrs L Moxon, 86 Holywell Road, Studham, Dunstable, Beds (Whipsnade 373106 pri, St Albans 60423 ext 43 bus).
Hertfordshire Schools Tennis Association

AFFILIATED SCHOOLS (82)

Boys

Aldenham School — Elstree. **Aldwickbury School** — Wheathampstead Road, Harpenden. **Berkhamsted School** — Berkhamsted. ***Edgegrove School** — Aldenham, Watford. **Grange Park School** — London Road, Bushey, Watford. **Haberdashers' Askes' School** — Elstree. **Heath Mount School** — Woodhall Park, Hertford. **Hitchin Boys' School** — Hitchin. ***Lockers Park School** — Lockers Park Lane, Hemel Hempstead. **Richard Hale School** — Hale Road, Hertford. **St Albans School** — Abbey Gateway, St. Albans. **Verulam School — Brampton Road, St Albans. Watford Boys' Grammar School** — Rickmansworth Road, Watford.

Girls

Abbott's Hill — Bunkers Lane, Hemel Hempstead. **Berkhamsted School for Girls** — Berkhamsted. **Bishops' Hatfield Girls' School** — Woods Avenue, Hatfield. **Broxbourne School** — High Road, Broxbourne. **Haberdasher Aske's School for Girls** — Elstree. **Hertfordshire and Essex High School** — Warwick Road, Bishops' Stortford. **Hitchin Girls' School** — Highbury Road, Hitchin. **Loreto College** — Hatfield Road, St Albans. **Northfield School** — Watford. **Princess Helena College** — Preston, Hitchin. **Queenswood School** — Brookmans Park, Hatfield. **Rickmansworth Masonic School** — Rickmansworth Park. **St Albans Girls' School** — Sandridgebury Lane, St Albans. **St Albans High School** — Townsend Avenue, St Albans. **St Angela** — Hitchin. **St Francis College** — Letchworth. **St Margaret's** — Merryhill Road, Bushey. ***Stormont School** — Potters Bar. **Watford Girls Grammar School** — The Crescent, Watford.

Mixed

Adeyfield School — Longlands, Hemel Hempstead. ****Augustus Smith School** — Berkhamsted. **Barclay School** — Walkern Road, Stevenage. **Beaumont School** — Oakwood Drive, St Albans. **Bishop's Stortford College** — Maze Green Road, Bishops Stortford. **Chancellors School** — Pine Grove, Brookmans Park, Hatfield. **Chauncey School** — Park Road, Ware. **Dame Alice Owen's School** — Dugdale Hill, Potters Bar. ***Duncombe School** — Bengeo, Hertford. **Francis Bacon School** — Drakes Drive, St Albans. **Francis Combe School** — Horseshoe Lane, Watford. **Goffs School** — Goffs Lane, Cheshunt. **Haileybury College** — Hertford. **Hatfield Polytechnic** — PO Box 109, Hatfield. **Heathcote School** — Shepall Green, Stevenage. **Hemel Hempstead School** — Heath Lane, Hemel Hempstead. **Hertfordshire College of Higher Education** — Wall Hall, Aldenham, Watford. **John Warner School** — Stanstead Road, Hoddesdon. **King's Langley School** — !ove Lane, Kings Langley. ***Ladbrooke JMI School** — High Street, Potters Bar. **Leventhorpe School** — Cambridge Road, Sawbridgeworth. **Longdean** — Hemel Hempstead. **Mountbatten School** — St Albans Road, Hemel Hempstead. **Mount Grace School** — Upper School, Church Road, Potters Bar. ***Newberries JMI School** — Newberries Avenue, Radlett. **Nicholas Breakspear School** — Colney Heath Lane, St Albans. **Nobel School** — Mobbsbury Way, Chells, Stevenage. **Onslow School** — Old Rectory Drive, Hatfield. **Parmiters School** — New High Elms, Watford. **Queen's School** — Aldenham Road, Bushey. **Rickmansworth School** — Rickmansworth. ***Sacred Heart School** — King Harry Lane, St Albans. St Audreys School — Travellers Lane, Hatfield. **St Clement Danes School** — Chenies Road, Chorleywood. St Dominics School — Southdown Road, Harpenden. **St Edmunds College** — Old Hall Green, Ware. **St George's School** — Sun Lane, Harpenden. **St Joan of Arc's Convent** — Rickmansworth. **Sele School** — Welwyn Road, Hertford. **Sheredes School** — Cock Lane, Hoddesdon. **Sherrardswood School** — Welwyn Garden City. **Simon Balle School** — Mangrove Road, Hertford. **Sir Frederick Osborn School** — Herns Lane, Welwyn Garden City. **Sir John Lawes School** — Manland Way, Harpenden. **Stanborough School** — Lemsford Lane, Welwyn Garden City. ****Thomas Bourne School** — Durrants Lane, Berkhamsted. **Townsend C of E School** — St Albans. **Tring School** — Mortimer Hill. **Wheathampstead School** — Butterfield Road, Wheathampstead. **William Penn School** — Shepherds Lane, Rickmansworth.

*Primary/Prep Schools. **Middle Schools.

KENT COUNTY LAWN TENNIS ASSOCIATION

Joint Hon Secretaries—**G J K Darby,** Kirkstone, Beckenham Place Park, Beckenham BR3 2BN (01 658 7050). **Austin Smith,** 6 Warren Avenue, Chelsfield, Orpington BR6 6HX (Farnborough 51802).
Hon Juniors Secretary—**Mrs J Wightman JP,** 102 Watling Street, Dartford DA2 6AF (23586).
Hon Treasurer—**G J Povey,** Tresanton, Oldfield Road, Bromley BR1 2LF (01 467 2138).
Hon Men's Match Secretary—**P A Bourdon,** 32 Gastein Road, London W6 8LU (01385 5929).
Hon Ladies' Match Secretary—**Miss J A Blyth-Lewis,** 1b Henwood Green Road, Pembury, Tunbridge Wells TN2 4LB (Pembury 3813).
County Ground—Green Street Green Road, Dartford. Courts: H3 (2 floodlit).
Representatives on the Council—**E R Hammer, Austin Smith, Mrs F D Teubler.**

AFFILIATED CLUBS (153)

Ashford—Little Gill Farm, Mersham (Ashford 72222). Courts: H1. *Secretary:* M C Collins, 30 Cherry Glebe, Mersham, Ashford TN25 6NL (26667).
Askean—60a Broad Walk, Kidbrooke, London SE3 8NB (01-856 1025). Courts: H3. *Secretary:* Miss J A McEwan, 29 Hurst Road, Erith DA8 3EW (Dartford 340945).
Balfour Beatty—Beaverwood Road, Chislehurst (01-300 1385). Courts: H3 (floodlit). *Secretary:* W Head-Rapson, Balfour Beatty Engineering Ltd, Marlowe House, 109 Station Road, Sidcup DA15 7AU (01-300 3355).
Barham—Recreation Ground, Barham. Courts: H2. *Secretary:* Mrs B E Webb, 80 Whitstable Road, Canterbury CY2 8EB (451223).
Bearsted & Thurnham—Church Lane, Bearsted (Maidstone 30065). Courts: H5. *Secretary:* Mrs J M Bowrage, 11b Yeoman Lane, Bearsted, Maidstone ME14 4BX (39185).
Beckenham—Foxgrove Road, Beckenham BR3 2AS (01-650 0266). Courts: G9, H7 (2 floodlit). *Secretary:* Mrs J J Jenkins, 29 Hayes Way, Beckenham BR3 2RJ (01-658 2481).
Bellingham—183 Bellingham Road, Catford, London SE6 1EQ (01-698 1643). Courts: H5. *Secretary:* Mrs S Paton, 189 Sangley Road, London SE6 2DY (01 698 8593).
Belvedere—Woolwich Road, Abbey Wood, London SE2 0DY (Erith 36724). Courts: G4, H2. *Secretary:* C M Ellis, 16 Westergate Road, London SE2 0DR (01 310 4499).
Bethersden—Mill Lane, Bethersden. Courts: H2. *Secretary:* K W Brannan, Monkery Cottage, Wissenden, Bethersden, Ashford TN26 3EL (Bethersden 536).
Bexley—Parkhurst Road, Bexley DA5 1AX (Crayford 524544). Courts: G3, H6 (2 floodlit). *Secretary:* W Antoun, 35 Eardley Road, Belvedere, DA17 6EX (Erith 435174).
Bexleyheath—Parkview Road, Welling DA16 1SY (01-303 4755). Courts: H4. Miss E Howard, 64 Granville Road, Welling DA16 1SQ (01 303 1785).
BICC (Erith)—Church Manorway, Erith (01-311 2222). Courts: G1. *Secretary:* J H D Bryan, 39 Nurstead Road, Erith DA8 1LS (31979).
Biddenden—Sports Field, Biddenden. Courts: H2 (floodlit). *Secretary:* Mrs J A Higgins, 1 Buckhurst Cottage, Biddenden, Ashford TN27 8HF (Biddenden 291634).
Biggin Hill—Church Road, Biggin Hill. Courts: H3. *Secretary:* Mrs G Chappell, 3 Orchard Drive, Edenbridge TN8 5ES (863517).
Blackheath—Charlton Road, Blackheath, London SE3 7EY (01-858 1578). Courts: G7, H4 (2 floodlit). *Secretary:* Miss K E Willmott, Flat F, 28 Kidbrooke Park Road, London SE3 0LW (01-856 5985).
Blackheath Wanderers—rear of 63 Eltham Road, Lee, London SE12 8UF (01-852 5901). Courts: G4, H1. *Secretary:* P Bevis, 35 Leysdown Road, London SE9 3LY (01-857 1961).
Bowaters (Kemsley & Sittingbourne)—Gore Court Road, Sittingbourne (24411). Courts: G3, H2. *Secretary:* Mrs M A Boorman, 48 Roseleigh Road, Sittingbourne ME10 1RS (23740).
Bowaters (Northfleet)—Nelson Road, Northfleet DA11 7EE (Gravesend 352474). Courts: G3, H2. *Secretary:* A Cappleman, 224 Beaumont Drive, Northfleet, Gravesend DA11 9NZ (358893).
Bowring—31 Eltham Road, Lee, London SE12 8EX (01-852 6622). Courts: H3. *Secretary:* D B Wheeler, 18 Coopers Close, Burgess Hill, West Sussex RH15 8AN (47742).
BP (Britannic House)—Kangley Bridge Road, Sydenham, London SE26 5AQ (01-778 7158). Courts: G4, H8 (2 floodlit). *Secretary:* J M Buckman, 23 Eddington Close, Loose, Maidstone ME15 9XG (41618).
Brenchley and Matfield—Memorial Hall, Brenchley. Courts: H2. *Secretary:* C D Wheeler, Weirleigh, Gedges Hill, Matfield, Tonbridge TN12 7DU (Brenchley 2822).
Bridge—Patrixbourne Road, Bridge. Courts: H2. *Secretary:* Mrs H J Whiting, 20 Conyngham Lane, Bridge, Canterbury CT4 5JX (830506).
Broadstairs & St Peters—Callis Court Road, Broadstairs. Courts: G9. *Secretary:* Mrs M M Bate, Sunburst Lodge, First Avenue, Kingsgate, Broadstairs CT10 3LP. (Thanet 62394).
Broadwater—Nevill Gate, Tunbridge Wells. Courts: G3. *Secretary:* Mrs L M Sage, 71 Frant Road, Tunbridge Wells TN2 5LH (40924).
Bromley—Sandford Road, Bromley BR2 9AN (01-460 0936). Courts: G9, H6 (2 floodlit). *Secretary:* I J Glen, 9 Sandford Road, Bromley BR2 9AL (01 460 8360).
Bromley Cricket—98 Plaistow Lane, Bromley BR1 3AS (01-460 0281). Courts: G8, H4 (2 floodlit). *Secretary:* Mrs J E Wright, 25 West Way, Petts Wood, Orpington BR5 1LN (26885).
Canterbury—Pilgrims Way, Canterbury. Courts: H5. *Secretary:* Miss I M Hills, 40 St Stephen's Hill, Canterbury CT2 7AX (463446).
Catford Wanderers—Southend Lane, Catford,

London SE6 3AB (01-698 1259). Courts: G8, H3. *Secretary:* T P Mulvaney, 46 Meadowview Road, London SE6 3NN (01-461 0231).
Central Church—Shipman Road, Forest Hill, London SE23 2DR. Courts: H4. *Secretary:* P Smith, 62 Windermere Road, London SW16 5MG (01-679 1981).
Charing—Arthur Baker Field, Charing. Courts: H2. *Secretary:* Mrs S Hotchkiss, Periton Court, Westwell, Ashford TN25 4JX (Charing 2680).
Chatham—Maidstone Road, Chatham. Courts: G4. *Secretary:* Mrs J M Cochran, 5 Gerrard Avenue, Rochester ME1 2RN.
Chelsfield Park—Oxenden Wood Road, Chelsfield. Courts: H2. *Secretary:* Mrs I E Silvester, 184 World's End Lane, Chelsfield, Orpington BR6 7SS (Farnborough 56298).
Chilham—Branch Road, Chilham. Courts: H2. *Secretary:* Mrs A M R Boardman, Paddock Old House, Canterbury Road, Challock, Ashford TN25 4DL (Challock 341).
Chipstead Place—Nursery Pace, Chipstead. Courts: H4. *Secretary:* M G Roffey, Hernewood Cottage, Gracious Lane, Sevenoaks TN13 1TJ (454862).
Chislehurst—Empress Drive, Chislehurst. Courts: H4. *Secretary:* Mrs C J Hunt, 81 Brownspring Drive, London SE9 3JY (01-857 8270).
Civil Service (Gillingham)— Watling Street, Gillingham (Medway 31786). Courts: G3. *Secretary:* J F A Hollands, 6 Russell Court, Chatham ME4 5LE (Medway 409904).
Civil Service (Maidstone)—Recreation Close, Maidstone (676881). Courts: H2. *Secretary:* B Moody, 35 Victoria Street, Maidstone ME16 8JA (682586).
Cobham Hall—Cobham DA12 3BL (Shorne 3376). Courts: H7. *Secretary:* Mrs S P Ferrers, 2 Lake Drive, Higham, Rochester ME3 7LZ (Shorne 2784).
Corkscrew Hill—Corkscrew Hill, West Wickham. Courts: H3. *Secretary:* Mrs N Croxford, 12 Greenway Gardens, Shirley, Croydon CR0 8QG.
Courage—West Common Road, Hayes, BR2 7BY (01-462 2324). Courts: G3, H3. *Secretary:* L J Quarendon, 26 Merlin Grove, Beckenham BR3 3HU (01-650 3765).
Crescent—Sydney Road, Sidcup DA14 6RA (01-300 2336). Courts: G6, H4. *Secretary:* M J Newman, 9 Kirkham Road, London E6 4RY (01-474 7558).
Crockham Hill—Dairy Lane, Crockham Hill. Courts: H2. *Secretary:* Mrs J F Webb, Corner Cottage, 1 Birdwood Cottages, Main Road, Edenbridge TN8 6SP (866304).
Cuaco—Copers Cope Road, Beckenham BR3 1RJ (01-650 1708). Courts: G3, H3. *Secretary:* J C Haslam, Commercial Union Properties Ltd, 80 Pall Mall, London SW1Y 5HF (01-283 7500 ext 3560).
Dover—Lower Road, River. Courts: G3. *Secretary:* J Morgan, 97 Barton Road, Dover CT16 2LX (213214).
East Malling—Mill Street, East Malling. Courts: H2. *Secretary:* Mrs S Fallon, 90 Mill Street, East Malling, Maidstone ME19 6BU (West Malling 843091).
East Malling Research Station—Bradbourne, East Malling ME19 6BJ (West Malling 843833). Courts: H2. *Secretary:* J H Carder, 49 Elm Crescent, East Malling, Maidstone ME19 6DF (West Malling 843852).
Edenbridge—Mill Hill, Edenbridge. Courts: H2. *Secretary:* T J Amey, 12 Croft Court, Edenbridge TN8 5BZ (864638).
Evington—Evington Lees, Hastingleigh. Courts: G2. *Secretary:* C J J Pell, Little Coombe, Hastingleigh, Ashford TN25 5JB (Elmsted 296).
Farnborough—Starts Hill Road, Farnborough. Courts: H2. *Secretary:* C P Shakspeare, 12 Masefield View, Orpington BR6 8PH (Farnborough 52648).
Faversham—Recreation Ground, Faversham. Courts: H3. *Secretary:* A P Wakeley, 27 Hazebrouck Road, Faversham ME13 7PU (531519).
Fleetway Printers—Parrock Road, Gravesend (65503). Courts: G4. *Secretary:* A K Tuffee, 1 Leith Park Road, Gravesend DA12 1LN (66618).
Folkestone—Coolinge Lane, Folkestone. Courts: G3, H3. *Secretary:* J H Lane, Cuckoo Lodge, Acrise, Folkestone CT18 8LH (Hawkinge 3141).
Folkestone Harbour—Wear Bay Road, Folkestone. Courts: G4. *Secretary:* C G Pack, Courtlands, St Andrews Road, Littlestone, New Romney TN28 8RB (63460).
Folkestone Sports Centre—Radnor Park Avenue, Folkestone CT19 5HX (58222). Courts: H6 (Indoor 2). *Secretary:* D S Bagnall, 56a Capel Street, Capel-Le-Ferne, Folkestone CT18 7LY (56315).
Frindsbury—Frindsbury Road, Frindsbury. Courts: G6. *Secretary:* Mrs E Denman, 48 Ladywood Road, Cuxton, Rochester ME2 1EP (Medway 722414).
Glenhurst—Glenhurst Avenue, Bexley DA5 3QW (Crayford 522613). Courts: H4. *Secretary:* Miss J A Compton, 76 Hearns Rise, St Mary Cray, Orpington BR5 3NB (74767).
Gore Court—Key Street, Sittingbourne ME10 1YT (23813). Courts: G6. *Secretary:* Mrs J I Goodwin, 115 Bell Road, Sittingbourne ME10 4HG (25855).
Gravesend—Wrotham Road, Gravesend DA11 0QP (52592). Courts: G5, H2. *Secretary:* Mrs R Bickley, Woodhay, Copthall Road, Ightham, Sevenoaks TN15 9DU (Borough Green 882402).
Gravesham—Milton Road, Gravesend. Courts: G5, H3 (floodlit). *Secretary:* Mrs Y I Goodwin, 174 Livingstone Road, Gravesend DA12 5DP (359203).
Hadlow—Williams Field, Hadlow. Courts: H3. *Secretary:* B A Goldsmith, 10 Victoria Road, Golden Green, Tonbridge TN11 0LP (Hadlow 850265).
J & E Hall—Darenth Road, Dartford DA1 1LZ (27222). Courts: G6, H5. *Secretary:* K R Halford, 133 Northview, Swanley BR8 7TB (65781).
Hartley Country Club—Culvey Close, Hartley DA3 8BS (Longfield 2176). Courts: H4 (2 floodlit). *Secretary:* Mrs J Philpott, 9 Round Ash Way, Hartley, Dartford DA3 8BT (Longfield 2601).
Hayes (Kent)—Barnet Wood Road, Hayes BR2 7AA (01-462 3430). Courts: H5 (2 floodlit). *Secretary:* Mrs K Steer, Barnet Mead, Barnet Wood Road, Bromley BR2 8HJ (01-462 1060).

Headcorn—Lenham Road, Headcorn. Courts: G2, H1 (floodlit). *Secretary:* D Sawyer, Fifth Quarter Cottage, Lenham Road, Headcorn, Ashford TN27 9LE (Maidstone 890737).
Herne Bay—Beacon Road, Herne Bay (374574). Courts: H3 (2 floodlit). *Secretary:* Mrs J M White, 100 Pear Tree Road, Herne Bay CT6 7XN (363183).
Hildenborough—Riding Lane, Hildenborough, and Sports Ground, Tonbridge. Courts: G6, H2. *Secretary:* Mrs P Balcombe, Hillbrow, London Road, Hildenborough, Tonbridge TN11 8NQ (Hildenborough 832041).
Hollingbourne—Lance Memorial Ground, Hollingbourne. Courts: H2. *Secretary:* Mrs K S Brice, Limekiln House, Hollingbourne Hill, Hollingbourne, Maidstone ME17 1QH (Hollingbourne 520).
Hongkong Bank Group—Lennard Road, Beckenham BR3 1QW (01-778 7434). Courts: G2, H3. *Secretary:* G Farncombe, Hongkong Bank Group, 99 Bishopsgate, London EC2P 2LA (01-638 2366).
Horsmonden—Maidstone Road, Horsmonden. Courts: H2. *Secretary:* K J Mills, 8 Orchard Way, Horsmonden, Tonbridge TN12 8JX (Brenchley 2569).
Howdon—Stanhope Grove, Beckenham BR3 3HL (01 650 0388). Courts: H7. *Secretary:* B Wadley, 92 De Frene Road, SE26 4AG (01 699 2847).
Hythe—The Grove, Hythe. Courts: G6, H2. *Secretary:* Mrs A E Brame, 13 Herdson Road, Folkestone CT20 2PB (54109).
Kemsing—Heverham Road, Kemsing. Courts: H4. *Secretary:* Mrs P A Wilkinson, Brindle House, Mount Harry Road, Sevenoaks TN13 3JL (450552).
Kent County Constabulary—Sutton Road, Maidstone. Courts: G3. *Secretary:* Lawn Tennis Secretary, Kent County Constabulary Sports Club, Police Headquarters, Sutton Road, Maidstone ME15 9BZ (65432).
Kingsnorth—Jemmett Road, Ashford. Courts: H2. *Secretary:* Major C Lewis, 54 Albert Road, Ashford TN24 8NU.
Knockholt Village—Main Road, Knockholt. Courts: H2. *Secretary:* Mrs J Decoine, 3 Parkside, Halstead, Sevenoaks TN14 7HA (Knockholt 33145).
Knoll (Orpington)—Mayfield Avenue (via footpath), Orpington (24797). Courts: H5. *Secretary:* Miss C Pembro, 130 Spur Road, Orpington BR6 0QW (31381).
Knoll (Willesborough)—Canterbury Road, Kennington. Courts: H2. *Secretary:* P C F Hill, 93 Harvey Road, Willesborough, Ashford TN24 0AR (24388).
Leigh—Lealands Avenue, Leigh. Courts: H2. *Secretary:* Mrs A de Saulles, 4 Cinder Hill Cottages, Panshurst Road, Leigh, Tonbridge TN11 8HX (Penshurst 870137).
Lessa (South East)—135 Footscray Road, Eltham, London SE9 2SY (01-850 4816). Courts: H5. *Secretary:* P S Gore, 36 Fernheath Way, Dartford DA2 7PF (54301).
Leybourne Grange—Leybourne (West Malling 841385). Courts: G2, H2. *Secretary:* J D Seal, 97 Keats Road, Larkfield, Maidstone ME20 6TR (West Malling 845031).
Livesey Memorial Hall—Perry Hill, Catford, London SE6 4HD. Courts: H3. *Secretary:* B J Murkin, 16 Blakes Green, West Wickham BR4 0RA (01-777 6245).
Lloyds Bank—Copers Cope Road, Beckenham BR3 1RJ (01-658 3818). Courts: G8, H6. *Secretary:* C L Prince, 137 Wickham Way, Beckenham, BR3 3AP (01-658 6496).
London Borough of Greenwich—Eltham Green Road, Eltham, London SE9 6BA (01-850 3098). Courts: G3. *Secretary:* M R Jaques, 66 Woodside Road, Sidcup DA15 7JQ (01-309 7398).
London Transport (CRS)—Hawksbrook Lane, Beckenham BR3 3SR (01-650 2406). Courts: H4. *Secretary:* W R Campbell, 24 Harecourt Road, London N1 2LW (01-226 8252).
Lydd—Dennes Lane, Lydd. Courts: H3. *Secretary:* D J Brown, 29 Poplar Lane, Lydd, Romney Marsh TN29 9LA (Lydd 20116).
Maidstone—Giddyhorn Lane, Maidstone. Courts: H3. *Secretary:* Miss J M Morgan, 11 Coverdale Avenue, Maidstone ME15 9DR (681674).
Maidstone Oakwood Park—Oakwood Park, Maidstone. Courts: H2. *Secretary:* Mrs D L Letchford, 15 Mote Avenue, Maidstone ME15 7SU (57377).
Marconi Avionics/BP Kent—Bells Lane, Hoo ME3 9JD (Medway 250402). Courts: H4. *Secretary:* J E Rowland, 229 City Way, Rochester ME1 2TL (Medway 43337).
Marden—Stanley Road, Marden. Courts: G1, H2. *Secretary:* Mrs G H D Tarry, Desillian, Pattenden Lane, Marden, Tonbridge TN12 9QS (Maidstone 831716).
Margate—Tivoli Park Avenue, Margate CT9 5TH (Thanet 220892). Courts: H6 (2 floodlit). *Secretary:* C R Whittingham, 26 Bowes Avenue, Margate CT9 5EP (Thanet 32165).
Martin Dene—Martin Dene, Bexleyheath. Courts: H3. *Secretary:* K Dobbs, 5 Shinglewell Road, Erith DA8 1NF (435879).
Meopham—Wrotham Road, Meopham. Courts: H3. *Secretary:* Mrs E A Hryniewicz, Fircroft, Wrotham Road, Meopham, Gravesend DA13 0HT (Meopham 813725).
Metrogas—Horn Lane, Greenwich, London SE10 0RT (01-858 5824). Courts: H3 (1 floodlit). *Secretary:* E A Finch, 30 Dunwich Road, Bexleyheath DA7 5EW (Erith 439613).
Midland Bank—Lennard Road, Beckenham BR3 1QW (01-778 6885). Courts: G12, H4. *Secretary:* Mrs W Stewart, 15 Den Road, Bromley BR2 0NH (01 460 8364).
Mount Pleasant (PO)—Blackheath Park, Blackheath, London SE3 0HB (01-852 9001). Courts: H4. *Secretary:* D P Costelloe, 23 Arcus Road, Bromley BR1 4NN (01-697 3305).
National Westminster Bank—Copers Cope Road, Beckenham BR3 1NZ (01-650 4559). Courts: G15, H6, Indoor 1. *Secretary:* B F A Murphy, 107 The Drive, Beckenham BR3 1EF (01-658 1579).
New Ash Green—North Ash Road, New Ash

Green. Courts: H3. *Secretary:* Mrs A U Wilson, 6 Capelands, New Ash Green, Dartford DA3 8LG (Ash Green 873078).
New Romney—Dymchurch Road, New Romney. Courts: H3. *Secretary:* Miss P Amos, 63 Rolfe Lane, New Romney TN28 8JL (2188).
Northfleet & District—College Road, Northfleet. Courts: G4. *Secretary:* Mrs S P Rush, 64 Gravesend Road, Strood, Rochester ME2 3PN (Medway 718220).
Offham—Church Road, Offham. Courts: H2. *Secretary:* Mrs R Tanner, 23 Offham Road, West Malling, Maidstone ME19 6RB (West Malling 845970).
Old Dunstonian—St Dunstan's Lane, Beckenham BR3 3SS (01-650 1779). Courts: G3, H3. *Secretary:* M Ennals, 26 Lime Tree Walk, West Wickham BR4 9ED (01 462 2460).
Old Wilsonians—Hayes Hill, Hayes BR2 7HN (01-462 2600). Courts: G3, H4. *Secretary:* Mrs M F Badcock, Montagu, Keston Avenue, Keston BR2 6BH (Farnborough 51531).
Orpington—Goddington Lane, Orpington BR6 9SH (34902). Courts: H6 (1 floodlit). *Secretary:* Mrs E Radford, 112 Tubbenden Lane, Orpington BR6 9PR (53084).
Otford—High Street, Otford. Courts: H3. *Secretary:* Miss J R Nielson, 29 Westerham Road, Sevenoaks TN13 2PX (452970).
Paddock Wood—Maidstone Road, Paddock Wood. Courts: H3. *Secretary:* G A Mitchell, The Old Bakery, Queen Street, Paddock Wood, Tonbridge TN12 6PH (Paddock Wood 2571).
Parklangley—44-46 Wickham Way, Beckenham BR3 3AH (01-650 0827). Courts: G8, H6 (4 floodlit). *Secretary:* Mrs M Tout, 71 Village Way, Beckenham BR3 3NJ (01-650 3138).
Peek Frean—Sidcup Road, Lee, London SE12 9AJ (01-850 1357). Courts: G5. *Secretary:* G P H Stephens, 121 The Drive, Bexley DA5 3BY (01-303 3546).
Pembury—Lower Green Road, Pembury. Courts: G2. *Secretary:* Mrs J P Prosser, 13 Ridgeway, Pembury, Tunbridge Wells TN2 4ER (Pembury 2682).
Pfizer—Ramsgate Road, Richborough. Courts: H3, Indoor 1. *Secretary:* A J Gibbings, 6 Sandown Lees, Sandwich CT13 9NZ (612685).
Private Banks—Catford Road, London SE6 4SW (01 690 1931). Courts: G6, H2. *Secretary:* E E Harris.
RACS—177 Footscray Road, Eltham, London SE9 2SZ (01-850 1641). Courts: H7. *Secretary:* G Lewis, 27 Yester Road, Chislehurst BR7 5HN (01 467 0718).
Reed (Aylesford)—Station Road, Ditton (Maidstone 76824). Courts: G3, H3. *Secretary:* A M Rigby, 56 Georgian Way, Wigmore, Gillingham ME8 0QZ (Medway 362835).
River Originals—Lewisham Road, River. Courts: G4. *Secretary:* D A Leach, 24 Riverdale, River, Dover CT17 0QX (823926).
Rolvenden—Bull Field, Rolvenden. Courts: H1. *Secretary:* B W Wright, 19 High Strret, Rolvenden, Cranbrook TN17 4LP (240398).
Royal Arsenal—Church Manorway, Abbey Wood, London SE2 9HP (01-310 4170). Courts: H4. *Secretary:* Mrs M A Mansfield, 20 Benares Road, London SE18 1HY (01-854 5350).
St John's—Masonic Hall, St John's Road, Tunbridge Wells TN4 9UY (43852). Courts: G3, H2. *Secretary:* S P Maclean, 5 The Meads, Camden Park, Tunbridge Wells TN2 5BX (35287).
St Margarets—Glebe Close, St Margarets-at-Cliffe. Courts: H2. *Secretary:* L Watkins, The Pines, St Margarets Road, St Margarets Bay, Dover CT15 6EF (853229).
Sandhurst—Horns Road, Hawkhurst. Courts: G1, H6. *Secretary:* E H Nichols, Lynwood, Horns Road, Hawkhurst TN18 4QU (3213).
SCB (Petts Wood)—Crossway, Petts Wood. Courts: H3. *Secretary:* T F Wrafter, 34 Great Thrift, Petts Wood, Orpington BR5 1NG (21129).
Sellindge—Swan Lane, Sellindge (2437). Courts: H2 (floodlit). *Secretary:* J W Seeley, 49 Prospect Way, Brabourne Leas, Ashford TN25 6RL (Sellindge 3497).
Sevenoaks Clarendon—Plymouth Drive, Sevenoaks. Courts: H6. *Secretary:* Miss S Julius, 3 Plymouth Park, Sevenoaks TN13 3RR (455449).
Shooters Hill—Eaglesfield Road, Shooters Hill, London SE18 3DA. Courts: H4 (2 floodlit). *Secretary:* D A Wise, 3 Craigholm, Shooters Hill, London SE18 3RR (01 856 1087).
Sissinghurst—Jubilee Field, Sissinghurst. Courts: H1. *Secretary:* Mrs J M Churton, The Old Vicarage, Biddenham Road, Sissinghurst, Cranbrook TN17 2JP (712964).
Springfield—Sandling Road, Maidstone (671411). Courts: H2. *Secretary:* Mrs J Paterson, 190 Boxley Road, Maidstone ME14 2HG (53404).
Standard Telephones (Greenwhich)—Ivor Grove, New Eltham, London SE9 2AJ (01-850 2057). Courts: H4. *Secretary:* J A Livermore, 160 Charlton Lane, London SE7 8AA (01-858 3683).
Staplehurst—Frittenden Road, Staplehurst (892503). Courts: G3, H2. *Secretary:* J Forbes-Buckingham, 53 Surrenden Road, Staplehurst, Tonbridge TN12 0LY (Staplehurst 892865).
Stargram—Radnor Park Avenue, Folkestone CT19 5HX (58222). Courts: H2. *Secretary:* Mrs E A Doy, Orion Insurance Co Ltd, Orion House, Bouverie Road West, Folkestone CT20 2RW (57481).
Stour Centre—Tannery Lane, Ashford TN23 1PL (39966). Courts: H4 (floodlit). *Secretary:* Dr L M S Williams, 86 Manorfields, Singleton, Ashford TN23 2YP (21569).
Sundridge Park—Lawn Close, Bromley BR1 3NA (01-460 2588). Courts: G12, H4 (2 floodlit). *Secretary:* B J John, 31 Broadheath Drive, Chislehurst BR7 6EU (01-467 7549).
Surrenden—Recreation Ground, Pluckley. Courts: H3. *Secretary:* Mrs J Gwillim, The Bungalow, Rushbrooke Farm, Pluckley, Ashford TN27 0SD (Pluckey 203).
Sutton Valence—Maidstone Road, Sutton Valence. Courts: H3. *Secretary:* Mrs W E Payne, Shirley House, Tumblers Hill, Sutton Valence, Maidstone ME17 3AF (842277).

Sutton & Wilmington—Oakfield Park, Wilmington (Dartford 21149). Courts: G3. *Secretary:* K H Saunderson, Appledore, Rays Hill, Horton Kirby, Dartford DA4 9DB (Farningham 862056).
Swanley—St Mary's Road, Swanley. Courts: G3. *Secretary:* J Thorpe, 63 Swanley Lane, Swanley BR8 7JF (64635).
Sydenham—Lawrie Park Road, Sydenham London SE26 6ET (01-778 4217). Courts: G5, H3 (2 floodlit). *Secretary:* T A Stent, 64a Dacres Road, London SE23 2NR (01-699 0529).
Tankerton—St Anne's Road, Tankerton. Courts: H4. *Secretary:* M Harman, 146 Cromwell Road, Whitstable CT5 1NF (261604).
Tonbridge—Sports Ground, Tonbridge (353241). Courts: G8, H3. *Secretary:* A C Nicholl, Appledene, Higham Lane, Tonbridge TN11 9QR (850 894).
Tunbridge Wells—Nevill Gate, Tunbridge Wells TN2 5ES (25625). Courts: G13, H7. *Secretary:* R F Bandy, 38 Pennine Walk, Tunbridge Wells TN2 3NW (31811).
United—Rye Road, Hawkhurst. Courts: H3 (2 floodlit). *Secretary:* Mrs J H Moss, 1 Course Horn Barn, Course Horn Lane, Cranbrook TN17 3NR (712957).
University of Kent—Courts: H8, Indoor 1. *Secretary:* Lawn Tennis Secretary, University Sports Federation, Sports Centre, The University, Canterbury CT2 7NL (68027).
VCD—Old Road, Crayford DA1 4DN (524262). Courts: G11, H2. *Secretary:* Mrs C M H Brennan, 106 Martens Avenue, Bexleyheath DA7 6AN (Crayford 524669).
Walmer—Archery Square, Walmer (Deal 372502). Courts: G8. *Secretary:* K G Wilson, Oast House, Kennel Hill, Waldershare, Dover CT15 5AX (825407).
Wardens—Cheriton Road, Folkestone. Courts: H4. *Secretary:* K R Finch, 1 Southmead Close, Folkestone CT19 5LH (76180).
Wellcome (Beckenham)—Langley Court, South Eden Park Road, Beckenham BR3 3BS (01-658 2211). Courts: G2, H4 (2 floodlit), Indoor 1. *Secretary:* M T E Orr, 18 Hurst Road, Sidcup DA15 9AA (01-300 0543).
Wellcome (Dartford)—High Street, Dartford DA1 1DJ (23743). Courts: G5, H4 (2 floodlit). *Secretary:* P W Taylor, 7 Wharncliffe, Bean Road, Greenhithe DA9 9JD (844365).
Wendover—Glanville Road, Bromley BR2 9LW (01-460 4052). Courts: H5. *Secretary:* Miss M E Walkley, 55 Godwin Road, Bromley BR2 9LG (01-464 4796).
Westbury—Westbury Road, Beckenham. Courts: G2. *Secretary:* D C Farmer, 42 Groveland Road, Beckenham BR3 3QA (01-650 4111).
Wickham Park—228-230 Pickhurst Rise, West Wickham (01-777 2550). Courts: G6, H3. *Secretary:* R Pechey, 34 Bramerton Road, Beckenham BR3 3PB (01 650 5198).
Winget—Watling Street, Strood. Courts: G3, H2. *Secretary:* R E Savage, 2 Cross Street, Strood, Rochester ME2 3AE.
Wingham—Goodnestone Road, Wingham. Courts: H2. *Secretary:* Mrs E J Hulburd, Canon Place, School Lane, Wingham, Canterbury CT3 1BD (720463).
Woodchurch—Recreation Ground, Tenterden or Victoria Park, Ashford. Courts: H2. *Secretary:* Mrs J F Beadle, 26 Lower Road, Woodchurch, Ashford TN26 3SQ (Woodchurch 313).
Woodstock—Research Centre, Sittingbourne (24444). Courts: H3. *Secretary:* Mrs S F Speight, 76 The Street, Newnham, Sittingbourne ME9 0LL (Eastling 635).
Wye—Bridge Street, Wye. Courts: H2. *Secretary:* Mrs J O Gilbert, 11 Chequers Park, Wye, Ashford TN25 5BA (Wye 812467).
Y Sportscentre—Melrose Close, Maidstone ME15 6BD (43317). Courts: H5 (floodlit). *Secretary:* R S Knight, 118 College Road, Maidstone ME15 6SU (682219).

OTHER AFFILIATED ORGANISATIONS (15)

Ashford & District League—D B Cue, 55 Church Road, Willesborough, Ashford TN24 0JZ (31674).
Christ Church College—North Holmes Road, Canterbury CT1 1QU (65548). Courts: H4. *Secretary:* Lawn Tennis Secretary.
Dartford Faculty of Education & Movement Studies—Thames Polytechnic, Oakfield Lane, Dartford DA1 2SZ (26151). Courts: H9 (floodlit). *Secretary:* Head of Movement Study & Recreation.
Dover & District League—A Bartley, 34 Beresford Road, Dover CT17 0QR.
East Kent Association—Mrs B M Hales, 37 Castle Road, Hythe CT21 5HL (66207).
Goldsmiths College—4 Water Lane, Sidcup (01-300 8712). Courts: H6. *Secretary:* M P Runnicles, 124c Drakefell Road, London SE14 5SQ (01 732 1560).
Gravesham Association—J Douglas, 48 Hillingdon Road, Gravesend DA11 7LG (67279).
Guy's Hospital—Brockley Rise, Forest Hill, London SE23 1NW (01-690 1612). Courts: G7, H2. *Secretary:* R Jennings, 103 Leicester Road, Hinckley, Leics LE10 1LR.
Kent County Tennis Coaches Association—D B Haines, 59 Westwood Lane, Welling DA16 2HJ (01-303 3258).
Kent Messenger Tournament—*Secretary:* A E Mole, Messenger House, New Hythe Lane, Larkfield, Maidstone ME20 6SG (77880).
Maidstone & District Association—Mrs E Bond, 229 Willington Street, Maidstone ME15 8EW (61257).
North Kent Association—D A Wise, 3 Craigholm, Shooters Hill, London SE18 3RR (01-856 1087).
St Bartholomew's Hospital—Perry Street, Chislehurst BR7 6HA (01-467 3543). Courts: G6, H2. *Secretary:* G F Bristow, St Bartholomew's Hospital Medical College, West Smithfield, London EC1A 7BE (01-606 7404).
Samuel Montagu Boys' Club—122 Broad Walk, Kidbrooke, London SE3 8ND (01-856 1126). Courts: H3 (floodlit). *Secretary:* Club Leader.

Tunbridge Wells Tournament—*Secretary:* Group Capt P G Hill, The Orchard, Claygate Lane, Shipbourne, Tonbridge TN11 9RN (Plaxtol 810587). Junior Tournament Secretary: D A Myles, 21 Quarry Rise, Tonbridge TN9 2PQ (353627).

AFFILIATED SCHOOLS (117)

Boys (24)
Bethany — Cranbrook TN17 1LB. **Bexley & Erith Technical High** — Bexley DA5 1NE. **Bickley Park** — Bromley BR1 2DY. ***Chatham Grammar** — Chatham ME4 6JB. ***Eltham College** — London SE9 4QF. **Foxbush** — Tonbridge TN11 9HN. ***John Roan** — London SE3 7UD. ***Judd** — Tonbridge TN9 2PN. **Langley Park Boys** — Beckenham BR3 3BP. **New Beacon** — Sevenoaks TN13 2PB. ***Norton Knatchbull** — Ashford TN24 0QJ. **Ravens Wood** — Bromley BR2 8HP. **Ravensbourne** — Bromley BR2 9EH. ***St Augustine's College** — Westgate CT8 8NL. ***St Dunstan's College** — London SE6 4TY. **St Joseph's Academy** — London SE3 9TY. ***St Lawrence College** — Ramsgate CT11 7AE. ***St Olaves** — Orpington BR6 9SH. ***Simon Langton** — Canterbury CT4 7AS. ***Sir Joseph Williamson's Mathematical** — Rochester ME1 3EL. **Skinners** — Tunbridge Wells TN4 9PG. ***Tonbridge — Tonbridge TN9 1JP. Wellesley House** — Broadstairs CT10 2DG. ***Wildernesse** — Sevenoaks TN13 3SN.

Girls (52)
***Ashford** — Ashford TN24 8PB. ***Baston** — Bromley BR2 7AB. ***Beaverwood** — Chislehurst BR7 6HE. **Beckenham Convent** — Beckenham BR3 2BH. ***Bedgebury Park** — Cranbrook TN17 2SH. ***Benenden** — Cranbrook TN17 4AA. **Blackheath High** — London SE3 0TF. ***Bromley High** — Bromley BR1 2TW. ***Bullers Wood** — Chislehurst BR7 5LJ. ***Cator Park** — Beckenham BR3 1QR. ***Cobham Hall** — Gravesend DA12 3BL. ***Combe Bank Educational Trust** — Sevenoaks TN14 6AE. ***Convent of the Nativity** — Sittingbourne ME10 1AE. **Dartford Grammar** — Dartford DA1 2NT. ***Dover Grammar** — Dover CT16 2PZ. ***Eltham Hill** — London SE9 5EE. **Farringtons** — Chislehurst BR7 6LR. **Folkestone** — Folkestone CT20 3QX. **Fort Pitt Grammar** — Chatham ME4 6TJ. ***Fosse Bank** — Tonbridge TN9 2NT. ***Gravesend Grammar** — Gravesend DA11 0JE. ***Haberdashers' Aske's** — London SE14 5NY. ***Highworth** — Ashford TN24 8UD. ***Holy Trinity Convent** — Bromley BR1 3LL. ***Invicta Grammar** — Maidstone ME14 5DS. **Kent College** — Tunbridge Wells TN2 4AX. **Langley Park Girls** — Beckenham BR3 3BE. ***Maidstone Grammar** — Maidstone ME16 0SF. **Marden Grange** — Tonbridge TN12 9AG. ***Newstead Wood** — Orpington BR6 9SA. ***Northfleet** — Gravesend DA11 8AQ. ***Prendergast** — London SE6 4JQ. **Rainham** — Gillingham ME8 0BX. **Ramsden** — Orpington BR5 4LG. ***Ravensbourne** — Bromley BR1 2SQ. ***Rochester Grammar** — Rochester ME1 3BY. ***St Catherine's** — Bexleyheath DA6 7QJ. ***St Hilary's** — Sevenoaks TN13 3LD. **St Mary's Convent** — Folkestone CT20 2JU. ***St Stephen's College** — Broadstairs CT10 3NP. ***St Ursula's Convent** — London SE10 8HN. ***Simon Langton** — Canterbury CT1 3EW. ***Stratford House** — Bromley BR1 2DZ. ***Sydenham** — London SE26 4RD. ***Sydenham High** — London SE26 6BL. ***Tonbridge Grammar** — Tonbridge TN9 2JR. ***Tunbridge Wells Grammar** — Tunbridge Wells TN4 9UJ. ***Ursuline Convent** — Westgate CT8 8LX. ***Walthamstow Hall** — Sevenoaks TN13 3UL. **Weald of Kent Grammar** — Tonbridge TN9 2JP. ***West Heath** — Sevenoaks TN13 1SR. ***Wilmington Grammar** — Dartford DA2 7BB.

Mixed (41)
***Abbey Wood** — London SE2 9AJ. **Addey & Stanhope** — London SE14 6TJ. **Bexley Grammar** — Welling DA16 2BL. **Bexleyheath** — Bexleyheath DA6 7DA. **Chatham South Secondary** — Chatham ME4 6NT. **Chislehurst & Sidcup Grammar** — Sidcup DA15 9AG. **Cliffe Woods Middle** — Rochester ME3 8UJ. ***Colfe's** — London SE12 8AW. ***Coopers** — Chislehurst BR7 5PS. **Cranbrook** — Cranbrook TN17 3JD. **Downs** — Dartford DA1 1QE. ***Dulwich College Preparatory** — Cranbrook TN17 3NP. ***Erith** — Erith DA8 3BN. **Gordon** — Gravesend DA12 2LZ. **Hartsdown** — Margate CT9 5RE. **Homewood Comprehensive** — Tenterden TN30 6LT. ***Kent College** — Canterbury CT2 9DT. ***King's** — Canterbury CT1 2ES. ***King's** — Rochester ME1 1TD. ***Malory** — Bromley BR1 5EB. **New Ash Green Middle** — Dartford DA3 8JZ. **Northfleet Grammar** — Gravesend DA11 8AG. **Rainham Mark Grammar** — Gillingham ME8 7AJ. ***Riverside** — Erith DA18 4DW. **Riverston** — London SE12 8UF. **Rothelawe** — Ashford TN23 2QE. **St Anne's Preparatory Convent** — Canterbury CT2 0EW. ***St Christopher's** — Beckenham BR3 2PA. ***St Edmund's** — Canterbury CT2 8HU. **St George's** — Broadstairs CT10 2LH. **St George's** — Gravesend DA11 7LS. **St Gregory's** — Tunbridge Wells TN4 9XL. **St John Fisher** — Chatham ME4 6SG. ***St John Rigby** — West Wickham BR4 9HN. **St John's RC Comprehensive** — Gravesend DA12 2JW. ***St Mary's & St Joseph's** — Sidcup DA14 6BP. **St Thomas More Secondary** — London SE9 2SU. ***Sedgehill** — London SE6 3QW. ***Sevenoaks** — Sevenoaks TN13 1HU. ***Sir William Nottidge** — Whitstable CT5 1PX. ***Sutton Valence** — Maidstone ME17 3 HN.

All correspondence to school clubs should be addressed to the staff in charge of lawn tennis.
*Affiliated to British Schools LTA.

LANCASHIRE COUNTY LAWN TENNIS ASSOCIATION

Hon General Secretary—**E E Hindle,** 12 Sawley Drive, Great Harwood, Blackburn (0254 887286).
Hon Junior Secretary—**J G Hodgkinson,** 8 Bedford Avenue, Worsley, nr Manchester (061 790 2795).
Hon Treasurer—**I E Shaw,** 10 Rydal Avenue, Poulton-le-Fylde (0253 891246 pri, 810221 bus).

Hon Men's Match Secretary—**A Wilson,** 2 Dundonnell Road, Nelson (0282 67698).
Hon Ladies' Match Secretary—**Miss G M Carney,** 30 Dalston Drive, Didsbury, Manchester 20 (061 434 6921 bus).
Representatives on the Council—**J M Gracie, A R W Jones JP, Mrs N Rushton.**

AFFILIATED CLUBS (136)

AFFILIATED SCHOOLS (55)

OTHER AFFILIATED ORGANISATIONS (15)

EASTERN AREA

AFFILIATED CLUBS (37)

Albert Bowling & Tennis—39-41 Old Lansdowne Road, West Didsbury, Manchester 20 (061 445 1056). Courts: G3, H3. *Secretary:* B McConnell, 34 Ferndene Road, Manchester 20 (061-445 2737).
Albion—Ambleside Avenue, Ashton-under-Lyne. Courts: H3. *Secretary:* Miss H Robinson, 88 Waterloo Road, Ashton Under Lyne (061 339 2331).
Alkrington Tennis & Social—Uplands, Alkrington, Middleton, Manchester. Courts: H4. *Secretary:* P Manchester, 190 Baguley Crescent, Rhodes, Middleton, Manchester.
Bamford—War Office, Bamford, Rochdale. Courts: H4. *Secretary:* Mrs M Burrows, 31 Pear Tree Avenue, Coppull, Chorley.
Bank Top—Ashworth Lane, Bank Top, Bolton. Courts: H4. *Secretary:* W R Nowell, 227 Cox Green Road, Egerton, Bolton (50024).
Bellingham—Wigan Lane, Wigan. Courts: H4. *Secretary:* Mrs M Hughes, 12 Clifton Crescent, Wigan (35900).
Bolton C & T—Green Lane, Bolton. Courts: H4. *Secretary:* M. Williamson, 36 Bolton Fold Crescent, Little Hulton, Worsley, Manchester (061 790 4248).
Bradshaw—The Rigbys, Bradshaw, Bolton. Courts: H3. *Secretary:* Mrs J Axford, 81 Lea Gate Close, Harwood, Bolton (52148).
Bury Sports (Tennis)—Radcliffe Road, Bury (061-764 1528). Courts: G4, H4. *Secretary:* B D Shaw, 22 Newton Drive, Greenmount, Bury (Tottington 4227).
Cheetham Hill—Catherine Road, Manchester 8 (061-740 1728). Courts: H3. *Secretary:* Miss I T Ritchie, 8 Heywood Court, Baguley Crescent, Rhodes, Middleton (061 653 9763).
Chorlton-Cum-Hardy Cricket (Tennis)—Hardy Lane, Manchester 21 (061-881 2883). Courts: G2, H3. *Secretary:* Mrs S Kendrick, 58 Clyde Road, West Didsbury, Manchester 20 (061 445 4505).
Didsbury—509 Parrs Wood Road, Didsbury, Manchester 20 (061-445 1838). Courts: H4. *Secretary:* Mr R P Kumar, 20 Granville Gardens, Didsbury, Manchester (061 445 8980).
Eagley—off Blackburn Road, Dunscar, Bolton. Courts: H4. *Secretary:* Mrs A Roscoe, 101 Hardy Mill Road, Harwood, Bolton (20710).
Fallowfield Bowling & Lawn Tennis—81 Wellington Road, Fallowfield, Manchester 14 (061-224 4617). Courts: H3. *Secretary:* A J Perry, 30 Manchester Road West, Withington, Manchester (061 434 9766).
Fernlea—off Burnley Lane, Chadderton, Oldham. Courts: H4. *Secretary:* Mrs B M Lloyd, 10 Tern Close, Meadowcroft Park, Bamford, Rochdale (353510).
Hawkshaw—Two Brooks Lane, Hawkshaw, Bury. Courts: H2. *Secretary:* Mr N Billinge, 382 Bolton Road, Hawkshaw, Bury (Tottington 6511).
Heaton Mersey Cricket, Tennis & Lacrosse—Oakley Villas, Heaton Moor, Stockport (061-432 1757). Courts: G2, H3. *Secretary:* J Davies, 1 Flowery Field, Wordsmoor, Stockport (061 483 2230).
Holcombe Brook Sports (Tennis)—Longsight Road, Holcombe Brook, Bury. Courts: H5. *Secretary:* J D Waddington, Lower Fowl Cotes Farm, Summerseat Lane, Holcombe Brook, Bury, BL0 9TW (020488 3367).
Hollinwood C T & B—Lime Lane, Roman Road, Hollinwood, Oldham (061 681 3385). Courts: H3. *Secretary:* M H A Fink, 1 Croft Brow, Garden Suburb, Oldham (061 624 2763),
ICI (Blackley) Recreation—Hazelbottom Road, Crumpsall, Manchester. Courts: H4. *Secretary:* D J Milner, Process Technology Dept, Research Dept, Hexagon House, Blackley, Manchester (061 796 7649 pri, 061 740 1460 ext 1240 bus).
Leigh Cricket Club—Beech Walk, Leigh (671818). Courts: H6. *Secretary:* Mrs A Coleman, 30 Lightburn Avenue, Leigh (601468).
Lostock—Regent Road, Lostock, Bolton (41834). Courts: H5. *Secretary:* E J Lord, 79 Brazley Avenue, Horwich, Bolton (0204 692173).
Manchester University Men's—The University Union, Oxford Road, Manchester 13 (061-273 5111). Courts: H15. *Secretary:* Hon Sec, Lawn Tennis Club, c/o Athletic Union, 333 Oxford Road, Manchester 13.
Manor—Cobden Street, Waterhead, Oldham. Courts: H2. *Secretary:* N Daniels, 2 Haugh Hill Road, Moorside, Oldham (061 626 4118 or 633 3711).
Markland Hill—Victoria Road, Heaton, Bolton (40000). Courts: H6 (1 covered). *Secretary:* The Tennis Secretary, c/o The Club.
Middleton—Towncroft Avenue, Middleton, Manchester. Courts: H3. *Secretary:* Miss S Butterworth, 255 Manchester New Road, Alkrington, Middleton (061-643 2593).
Monton Sports (Tennis)—Welbeck Road, Ellesmere Park, Eccles. (061-789 3699). Courts: H3. *Secretary:* K Brookes, c/o The Club.
Moss Side—St Werburgh's Road, Chorlton-cum-Hardy, Manchester 21. Courts: H4. *Secretary:* H Sudlow, 17 Egerton Road South, Manchester 21 (061-881 5380).
Northern—Palatine Road, West Didsbury, Manchester 20 (061-445 3093/5738). Courts: G15, H7 (1 covered). *Secretary:* I A Stewart, c/o The Club.

Prestwich Cricket, Tennis & Bowling—The Heys, Prestwich, Manchester (061-773 2524). Courts: H7. *Secretary:* Miss S Keshishian, 7 Simister Green, Prestwich (061 773 7584).
Rochdale—Beechwood, Manchester Road, Rochdale. Courts: G3, H3. *Secretary:* Mrs E Mitchell, 42 Tandle Hill Road, Royton, Oldham (061 624 3520).
Stand—Hamilton Road, Whitefield, Manchester (061-766 6793). Courts: H3. *Secretary:* Mrs L H Fogg, 12 Cranford Close, Whitefield (061 766 6793).
Werneth Cricket, Bowling & Tennis—Chamber Road, Oldham (061 624 4967). Courts: H4. *Secretary:* D F Ashford, c/o The Club.
West Heaton Bowling & Tennis—Prince's Road, Heaton Moor, Stockport (061-432 2313). Courts: H6. *Secretary:* Mrs E V Moores, c/o The Club.
Whalley Range Cricket & Lawn Tennis—Kingsbrook Road, Manchester 16 (061-881 1414). Courts: H3. *Secretary:* S K Pullin, 119 Kingsbrook Road, Manchester 16 (061 861 9692).
Whitegate Taverns—Royal Toby, Castleton, Rochdale. Courts: H3. *Secretary:* M Brierley, Parkway House, 24 Longwood Road, Trafford Park, Manchester (061 872 5346).
Winstanley Park—Winstanley Park Estate, Winstanley, Wigan. Courts: H3. *Secretary:* Mrs J Walker, 11 Conway Drive, Billinge, Wigan (Billinge 893100).

OTHER AFFILIATED ORGANISATIONS (4)

Bolton Sports Federation Tennis League—*Secretary:* Mrs R Platt, The Willows, 72 Chorley New Road, Lostock, Bolton (40750).
Manchester & District Lawn Tennis League—*Secretary:* Mrs S Tasker, 62 Ashbourne Grove, Whitefield, Manchester (061 766 6387).
South-West Manchester Lawn Tennis League—*Secretary:* J L Rendall, 22 Woodbourne Road, Brooklands, Sale.
Walkden & District Tennis League—*Secretary:* A Simms, 51 Glen Avenue, Roe Green, Worsley Penn, Salford.

SCHOOL CLUBS (18)

Boys

Bolton School (Boys Division)—Bolton. **Manchester Grammar School**—Rushholme, Manchester. **North Manchester High School for Boys**—Charlestown Road, Manchester. **William Hulme's Grammar School**—Chorlton, Manchester.

Girls

Bolton School (Girls' Division) Brookway High School—Wythenshawe. **Canon Slade Grammar School**—Bolton. **Holy Cross College**—Bury. **Manchester High School for Girls. Withington Girls' School** — Manchester 14.

Mixed

Hayward School—Bolton. **Mount St Joseph Grammar School**—Bolton. **St Patrick's Catholic High School**—Eccles, Manchester. **St Augustine's RC Secondary School**—Farnworth, Bolton. **Selwyn Jones High School** — Newton-le-Willows, Merseyside. **South Bolton Sixth Form College. Whitley High School**—Wigan. **Winstanley College**—Orrell, Wigan.

All correspondence to school clubs should be addressed to the Master or Mistress in charge of lawn tennis.

NORTHERN AREA

AFFILIATED CLUBS (50)

Accrington Cricket & Tennis—Thorneyholme Road, Accrington (33495). Courts: H3. *Secretary:* A S Dobson, 129 Avenue Parade, Accrington (36460).
Barton & Myerscough—adj Village Hall, Garstang Road, Barton, Preston. Courts: H2. *Secretary:* Mrs K Harris, 26 Holmeswood Crescent, Barton, Preston (Broughton 864427).
Bispham—Cavendish Road, Bispham, Blackpool. Courts: G4. *Secretary:* K L Gaunt, 34 Sandicroft Avenue, Hambleton.
Blackburn Northern Cricket & Tennis—Pleckgate Road, Blackburn (47969). Courts: H5. *Secretary:* Mrs K Best, Jersey Farm, Knowsley Road, Ramsgreave, Blackburn (49960).
Blackpool Marton Institute—Sedbergh Avenue, Marton, Blackpool. Courts: H4. *Secretary:* I Rushton, 4 Rosary Avenue, Marton, Blackpool.
Bolton-Le-Sands—The Playing Field, Bolton-Le-Sands, Carnforth. Courts: H2. *Secretary:* G H M Forrest, 30 Broadlands Drive, Bolton-le-Sands, Carnforth (West Bank 824346).
Bowerham—Barton Road, Lancaster (66534). Courts: H4. *Secretary:* Mrs A Riley, 4 Riverside Close, Halton, Lancaster (0524 811513).
Brierfield—Heyhead Park, Brierfield, Nelson. Courts: H3. *Secretary:* G Hill, 32 Livingstone Street, Brierfield, Nelson.
Broughton & District—Whittingham Lane, Broughton, Preston (863006). Courts: H3. *Secretary:* T Threadgold, 125 Conway Drive, Fulwood, Preston (718677).
Burnley—Belvedere Road, Burnley (22048). Courts: H6. *Secretary:* J R Pickup, Abbotsford, Fence, nr Burnley.
Cherry Tree—Preston Old Road, Cherry Tree, Blackburn. Courts: H4. *Secretary:* Mrs R Cooper, 16 Wilworth Crescent, Blackburn (48224).
Cleveleys Park—West Drive, Cleveleys, Blackpool (Cleveleys 2132). Courts: G4, H1. *Secretary:* Mrs J Fisher, 40 Winchcombe Road, Thornton Cleveleys, Blackpool (853686).
Clitheroe—Chatburn Road, Clitheroe (22896). Courts: H3. *Secretary:* R W Driver, 9 Rydal Place, Chatburn, Clitheroe (0200 41492).
Craven—Bent Lane, Colne. Courts: H2. *Secretary:* Mrs S M Lupton, The Boat House, Slipper Mill, Foulridge, Colne (862470).

Darwen—Sunnyhurst Lane, Darwen. Courts: H2. *Secretary:* Mrs M Bibby, Rocklea, 40 Sunnyhurst Lane, Darwen (71741).

East Lancashire Crosshill—Alexandra Meadows, Dukes Brow, Blackburn (51742), and Crosshill Road, Blackburn (51894). Courts: G6, H5. *Secretary:* J L Greenwood, 19 Gorse Road, Blackburn (698706).

Fairhaven—Ashton Marine Park, Fairhaven, Lytham St Annes. Courts: G7. *Secretary:* G W Coles, 9 Folkstone Road, Lytham St Annes (725356).

Feniscowles & Pleasington—Memorial Ground., Feniscowles, Blackburn. Courts: H3. *Secretary:* Mrs M Hunt, Blue Garth, Preston New Road, Mellor Brook, Blackburn (Mellor 2767).

Freckleton—Rawstrone Sports Centre, Bush Lane, Freckleton, Preston. Courts: H2. *Secretary:* Mrs M Smith, 12 Eastway, Freckleton, Preston (632078).

Fulwood—Watling Street Road, Fulwood, Preston (717045). Courts: H4. *Secretary:* R J Baron, 31 Fulwood Hall Lane, Fulwood, Preston (700738).

Garstang & District—Community Centre Playing Field, Garstang, Preston. Courts: H2. *Secretary:* Mrs P Pearson, 'Tarnbrook', 6 York Grove, Garstang, nr Preston (Garstang 3536).

Guardian Royal Exchange Sports & Social—Mythrop Road, Lytham St Annes. Courts: H3. *Secretary:* A Buxton, 168 Forest Drive, Lytham St Annes (733 433 pri, 733 151 ext 192 bus).

Hambleton—Church Lane, Hambleton, Blackpool. Courts: H2. *Secretary:* Mrs J M Nuttall, 37 Royal Road, Hambleton, Blackpool (700803).

ICI (Thornton) Recreation—off Gamble Road, Thornton, Blackpool. Courts: H2. *Secretary:* K M Galloway, 15 Rossendale Avenue, South, Thornton, Blackpool (Cleveleys 76135 pri, Cleveleys 6144 bus).

Lancaster Cricket Bowling & Lawn Tennis—Lune Road, Lancaster. Courts: H4. *Secretary:* Mr J C Prosser, 16 Ashford Close, Lancaster (0524 62811).

Leyland Fox Lane Sports & Social—Fox Lane, Leyland (22733). Courts: H3. *Secretary:* Miss K Thornber, 6 Highfield Avenue, Farington, Preston (Leyland 34385 pri, Preston 633333 ext 142 bus).

Lunesdale—Ball Lane, Caton, Lancaster. Courts: G3, H1. *Secretary:* Mrs Brenda Worthington, Regent House, 4 Regent Street, Lancaster LA1 1SG.

Lytham—Church Road, Lytham St Annes (734137). Courts: G10, H2. *Secretary:* Mrs J Crosby, 14 Willows Avenue, Lytham (736280).

Norcross—DHSS Central Office, Norcross, Blackpool. Courts: H2. *Secretary:* Mrs P Leftley, 3 Pennine View, Great Eccleston, Preston (Great Eccleston 70878 pri, Cleveleys 856123 ext 6368 bus).

Moorland—Breck Road, Poulton-le-Fylde, Blackpool (883277). Courts: H5. *Secretary:* Miss T Armour, 1 Willow Tree Gardens, Thornton Cleveleys (Cleveleys 824507 pri, 882233 bus).

Norbreck—Clovelly Avenue, Norbreck, Blackpool. Courts: H2. *Secretary:* Mrs G Rolley, c/o The Club.

Parkwood—Parkwood Drive, Rawtenstall, Rossendale. Courts: H3. *Secretary:* Mrs G Harris, The Holme, Holme Road, Clayton-le-Moors, Accrington (33163).

Penwortham—Manor Lane, Penwortham, Preston (742583). Courts: H4. *Secretary:* Miss C M Lever, 40 Danesway, Walton-Le-Dale, Preston (39947).

Penwortham St Mary's—Mornington Road, Penwortham, Preston. Courts: H2. *Secretary:* P Treacher, 5 Langholme Road, Penwortham, Preston (742782).

Queens—Skye Crescent, Shadsworth Road, Blackburn. Courts: H3. *Secretary:* M R Haworth, The Old Barn, Hurst Lane, Rawtenstall (Rossendale 228391).

Reedley—Lucas Sports Ground, Reedley Drive, Burnley. Courts: H4. *Secretary:* I Woolstencroft, 34 Thursby Road, Burnley (26786).

St Annes Tennis & Squash—Avondale Road, Lytham St Annes (722637). Courts: G3, H6. *Secretary:* D A Lees, 30 Glen Eldon Road, Lytham St Annes (727193).

St Chad's Church—Vicarage Road, Poulton-le-Fylde, Blackpool. Courts: H3. *Secretary:* Mrs J Coulton, 53 Westby Way, Poulton-Le-Fylde (885637).

St Margaret's, Ingol—Tag Lane, Ingol, Preston. Courts: H3. *Secretary:* J Sheldon, 19 Banksfield Avenue, Fulwood, Preston (728104).

St Michael's-on-Wyre—Hall Lane, St Michael's, Preston. Courts: H2. *Secretary:* Mrs P Lee, Longfield, Garstang Road, St. Michaels (678).

St Teresa's—Queensway, Penwortham, Preston. Courts: H2. *Secretary:* Mrs C A Robertson, 74 Kensington Avenue, Penwortham (Preston 748742).

Slyne-with-Hest—Hanging Green Lane, Slyne-with-Hest, Lancaster. Courts: H2. *Secretary:* Mrs J Theobold, Parkfield, Slyne, Lancaster.

South Shore—Midgeland Road, Blackpool (67753). Courts: G11, H6 (1 covered). *Secretary:* E N Senior, 147 Highfield Road, Blackpool (41876).

Springfields Social & Recreational Association—Dodney Drive, Lea, Preston (729351 ext 7458). Courts: H3 (1 covered). *Secretary:* S M Fensom, 4 Langport Close, Fulwood, Preston (717424).

Thornton—Lime Grove, Thornton, Blackpool. Courts: H2. *Secretary:* Miss S Wildridge, 71 Adelaide Street, Fleetwood (77843).

Trimpell Sports & Social—Out Moss Lane, Morecambe (412984). Courts: H2. *Secretary:* Mrs J Coxhill, 13 Clifton Drive, Bare, Morecambe.

Whalley—Mitton Road, Whalley, Blackburn. Courts: G1, H2. *Secretary:* A D Taylor, High Lawn, 12 Mitton Road, Whalley (2260).

Windsor—Windsor Park, Walgarth Drive, Chorley. Courts: H5. *Secretary:* A A Brotherton, 4 Cherry Tree Grove, Chorley (64566).

Withnell Fold Sports & Social—Withnell Fold, Chorley. Courts: H2. *Secretary:* Mrs S Drinkall, Brinscall Hall Farm, Dick Lane, Brinscall, nr Chorley (Brinscall 831650).

Wrea Green—Mill Lane, Wrea Green, Preston. Courts: H2. *Secretary:* Mrs W Webster, Skelrigg, 50 Bryning Lane, Wrea Green, Preston (Kirkham 685337).

OTHER AFFILIATED ORGANISATIONS (6)

Burnley Evening Tennis League—*Secretary:* C Riley, 22 Brennand Street, Burnley (20312).
East Lancashire Lawn Tennis League—*Secretary:* J Cox, 7 Meadow Close, Billington, Whalley, Blackburn (Whalley 3107).
Fylde Tennis League—*Secretary:* Mrs A E Mann, 26 Myra Road, Fairhaven, Lytham St Anne's (736631).
Lancashire Polytechnic—*Secretary:* B. Hepworth, Students' Union, Lancashire Polytechnic, Fylde Road, Preston.
Preston Tennis Tournament—*Secretary:* D Dean, 290 Sharoe Green Lane North, Fulwood, Preston (719376).
Ribble Tennis League—*Secretary:* Mrs E M Halsall, 31 Ribbledale Place, Preston (54489).

AFFILIATED SCHOOLS (21)

Boys
Arnold School—Blackpool. **King Edward VII School**—Lytham St Annes. **Rossall School**—Fleetwood. **Stonyhurst College**—Stonyhurst, Blackburn.

Girls
Elmslie Girls' School—Blackpool. **Lancaster Girls' Grammar School. Newman College**—Preston. **Notre Dame Grammar School**—Blackburn. **Our Lady's High School**—Lancaster. **Queen Mary School**—Lytham St Annes. **Royal Grammar School for Girls**—Clitheroe. **Westholme School**—Blackburn.

Mixed
Blackpool Collegiate Grammar. Darwen Vale High School. Hutton Grammar School—Preston. **Lytham St Annes High School. Moorhead High School**—Accrington. **Morecambe High School. Rhyddings County High School**—Accrington. **Southlands High School**—Chorley. **W R Tuson College**—Preston.

All correspondence to school clubs should be addressed to the Master or Mistress in charge of lawn tennis.

WESTERN AREA

AFFILIATED CLUBS (49)

Ainsdale—772a Liverpool Road, Ainsdale, Southport (78534). Courts: G1, H6. *Secretary:* R Anderson, 13 Crosby Road, Birkdale, Southport (65994).
Aughton—Granville Park, Aughton, Ormskirk. Courts: G4, H3. *Secretary:* M G Forth, 14 Croft Heys, Aughton, Ormskirk (Aughton Green 422604).
Birkdale—Victoria Park, Rotten Row, Southport. Courts: G6. *Secretary:* C F Kingsford, 114 Park Road, Formby, Merseyside (76325).
Blundellsands—Warren Road, Blundellsands, Liverpool 23 (051-924 4624). Courts: G8, H4. *Secretary:* G Evans, Avalon, 13 Richard Road, Blundellsands, Liverpool 23.
Bohemians—Sandforth Park, Queens Drive, Liverpool 13 (051-228 7132). Courts: H5. *Secretary:* Miss M Smith, 18 Agincourt Road, Liverpool 12 (051 220 7795).
Brownmoor Park—Brownmoor Park, Crosby, Liverpool 23. Courts: H4. *Secretary:* Mrs J Price, 14 College Road, Crosby, Liverpool 23.
Campion—St Anthony's Road, Blundellsands, Liverpool 23. Courts: H4. *Secretary:* C H Taggart, 28 Ashlar Road, Waterloo, Liverpool (051 924 3265).
Carlton—Dunkirk Road, Birkdale, Southport. Courts: H4. *Secretary:* Mrs S J Coulthard, c/o 16 Northam Close, Southport (231526).
Cheshire Lines Recreation & Welfare Association—Southmead Road, Liverpool 19 (051-427 7176). Courts: H2. *Secretary:* J A Grayson, 7 Roskell Road, Woolton, Liverpool 25 (051 486 2104).
Clair Gardens—Woolton Road, nr Queens Drive, Liverpool 15. Courts: H2. *Secretary:* C D Lee, 10 Roedean Close, Woolton, Liverpool 25 (051 428 3693).
Cressington—Salisbury Road, Liverpool 19. Courts: H3. *Secretary:* A G Mandy, 291 Brodie Avenue, Liverpool 19 (051-427 4657).
East Wavertree & Childwall Owners' & Residents Association—129a Dunbabin Road, Liverpool 16 (051-772 3455). Courts: H6. *Secretary:* Mrs J L Coleman, 17 Church Road, Woolton, Liverpool 25 (051 428 9502 pri, 051 236 7862 bus).
Eccleston Park—Forest Green, Eccleston Park, Prescot, Merseyside. Courts: G1, H5. *Secretary:* A N Murray, 7 Grange Drive, Eccleston Hill, St Helens (52087).
Formby—90 Gores Lane, Formby, Merseyside. Courts: G5, H4. *Secretary:* Miss A E Thirlwell, 19 Birch Green, Formby L37 1NG (75259).
Formby Holy Trinity—Rosemary Lane, Formby, Merseyside. Courts: G1, H3. *Secretary:* Mrs M A Richards, 24 Tarn Road, Formby (Formby 71948).
Hightown (Tennis)—Sandy Lane, Hightown, Merseyside (051-929 2769). Courts: G7, H3. *Secretary:* Mrs M Barber, Altmouth, Alt Road, Hightown, Liverpool 38 (051 929 2705).
Hillside—Clive Lodge, Clive Road, Southport. Courts: G2, H6. *Secretary:* Miss A B Howard, 7 Grinstead Close, Birkdale, Southport (68434).
Littlewoods—The Pavilion, Park Lane, Netherton, Liverpool 10 (051-523 2365). Courts: H4. *Secretary:* R Tyms, 3 Midlothian Drive, Crosby, Liverpool 23 (051 928 6611 ext 28 bus).
Liverpool Cricket Club (Tennis)—Aigburth Road, Grassendale, Liverpool 19 (051-427 2930). Courts: G6, H5. *Secretary:* D Smith, 15 Middlefield Road, Liverpool 18 (051 428 1150).
Liverpool Electric Supply—Thingwall Road, Wavertree, Liverpool 15 (051-722 3838). Courts: H5. *Secretary:* J H Nelson, 20 Wilberforce Road, Liverpool 4 (051-525 9012 pri, 051-236 6933 bus).
Liverpool Jewish—16a Dunbabin Road, Childwall, Liverpool 16. Courts: H4. *Secretary:* R Morron, 54 Acres Court Road, Grange Lane, Liverpool 25 (051 428 3293).

Liverpool University—Sports Ground, Wyncote, Mather Avenue, Liverpool 18 (051-724 4948). Courts: G4, H4. (1 covered). *Secretary:* M C Carter, Students' Union, Brownlow Hill, Liverpool.
Lucas/Rowan—Bootle Tennis Centre, Maguire Avenue, Bootle (051 428 3293). Courts: H4. *Secretary:* P McCabe, 176 Hawthorne Road, Bootle, Liverpool 20 (051-922 0678).
Lydiate—Sandy Lane, Lydiate, Merseyside. Courts: H3. *Secretary:* Mrs M Adamson, 21 Merrilox Avenue, Lydiate, Merseyside (051 526 2111).
Maghull—King George V Playing Field, Hall Lane, Maghull, Merseyside. Courts: H4. *Secretary:* Miss L Marshall, Quarry House, 109 Hall Lane, Maghull, Merseyside (051 526 1693 pri, 051 227 5234 ext 2360 bus).
Mawdesley—Hurst Green, Mawdesley, Ormskirk. Courts: H3. *Secretary:* Mrs C Brodie, 4 Sycamore Close, Mawdesley, Liverpool L40 2QR (0704 822647).
Mersey Bowmen—Sefton Park, Liverpool 17 (051-727 4064). Courts: G9, H4. *Secretary:* Miss A Husband, 18 Ivydale Road, Liverpool 18 (051 734 0925).
Moor Park—Moor Lane, Thornton, Liverpool 23. Courts: H5. *Secretary:* D J Nelson, 12 Woodland View, Thornton, Liverpool 23.
Mossley Hill Athletic Club (Tennis)—Mossley Hill Road, Liverpool 18 (051-724 4377). Courts: H6. *Secretary:* Mrs J McMonagle, 664 Mather Avenue, Liverpool 19 (051-427 5469).
NALGO—Alder Road, West Derby, Liverpool 12 (051-228 5250). Courts: H6. *Secretary:* Mrs J Quayle, 24 Bellefield Avenue, Liverpool 12 (051-228 1733).
North Meols—Mill Lane Crescent, Southport (27149). Courts: G5, H3. *Secretary:* Miss C E Ratcliffe, 44 Sandown Court, Albert Road, Southport (32069).
Ormskirk—County Road, Ormskirk. Courts: H5. *Secretary:* Mrs J C Spurr, 61 County Road, Ormskirk (75391).
Palmerston—Elm Hall Drive, Liverpool 18 (051 733 7063). Courts: H6. *Secretary:* D Blowes, 72 Linkside Road, Woolton, Liverpool 25 (051 428 4018).
Pilkington Recreation Club (Tennis)—Ruskin Drive, St Helens, Merseyside (St Helens 23764). Courts: H6. *Secretary:* R M Thompson, 33 Hollin Hey Close, Billinge, Wigan (893302).
Rainford—Rainford, nr St Helens, Merseyside. *Secretary:* R Spensley, 3 Spring Vale, Reeds Brow, Rainford (5209).
Rainhill—Victoria Terrace, Rainhall, Prescot, Merseyside. Courts: H4. *Secretary:* Mrs M Furner, 14 Hilary Close, Eccleston Park, Prescot, Merseyside (051 426 5952 pri, 051 709 7272 ext 267 bus).
Rookery—Roe Lane, Southport (25841). Courts: G7, H2. *Secretary:* N Shallcross, 118 Churchgate, Southport.
St Helens—Windleshaw Road, St Helens, Merseyside. Courts: H6. *Secretary:* Mrs S Aspden, 96 Holly Road, Haydock, St Helens (56721).
Salisbury—Salisbury Gardens, Montclair Drive, Liverpool 18. Courts: H2. *Secretary:* Miss A Lockhart, 18 Tullimore Road, Liverpool 18.
Sandheys—Brooke Road West, Waterloo, Liverpool 22. Courts: H2. *Secretary:* Mrs J Hope, 40 Mariners Road, Blundellsands, Liverpool 23 (051 924 0718).
Southbank—138-140 Scarisbrick New Road, Southport. Courts: H3. *Secretary:* Miss C Livesley, 79 Segars Lane, Ainsdale, Southport (77054).
Southport Argyle—Argyle Road, Southport (301132). Courts: H7. *Secretary:* Mrs B Bond, 16 Threlfalls Lane, Southport (20942).
Sphynx—Everard Road, Southport. Courts: G4, H4. *Secretary:* J A Preston, 7 Wyresdale Avenue, Southport (0704 37098).
Thingwall—Garden Suburb, Thingwall Road, Liverpool 15. Courts: H3. *Secretary:* Mrs J M Fearns, 7 Belfield Crescent, Huyton, Liverpool 36 (051 489 1841).
Trinity—25a Lynwood Road, Rice Lane, Liverpool 9. Courts: H3. *Secretary:* Mrs P D'Arcy, 22 Delph Park Avenue, Arghton, West Lancs (Aughton Green 422170).
Vagabonds—Sandfield Park, Queens Drive, Liverpool 12 (051-228 2568). Courts: G4, H4. *Secretary:* D Rooney, 15 Corwen Crescent, Liverpool 14.
Waterloo—Park Road, Waterloo, Liverpool 22. Courts: H6. *Secretary:* Mrs C Nelson, 12 The Crescent, Waterloo Park, Liverpool 22 (051 928 5140).
Weld—73b York Road, Birkdale, Southport (65063). Courts: H4. *Secretary:* Miss J Smedley, 61 Dunbar Crescent, Southport (78896).
Woodlands—Dundonald Road, Aigburth, Liverpool 17. Courts: H4. *Secretary:* Miss M Kelbrick, 18 Rosemont Road, Liverpool 17 (051 724 1875).

OTHER AFFILIATED ORGANISATIONS (8)

Edge Hill College—St Helen's Road, Ormskirk. Courts: H4. *Secretary:* c/o The College.
Everton Park—Edinburgh Street, Liverpool 4 (051 207 1921). *Secretary:* M E D Hare, 12 Prenton Farm Road, Prenton, Birkenhead, Wirral.
ICI (Widnes) Recreation—Liverpool Road, Widnes, Cheshire (051 486 3255). Courts: H4. *Secretary:* D Scott, 11 Kirkwell Drive, Penketh, Warrington (Penketh 7416).
I M Marsh College of Physical Education—Barkhill Road, Liverpool 17 (051-724 2321). Courts: H9 (2 covered). *Secretary:* Miss S Skinner, 17 Bessbrook Road, Aigburth, Liverpool 17.
Slazenger Liverpool & District Group League—*Secretary:* H V Davies, 16 Melbreck Road, Mossley Hill, Liverpool 18 (051-427 7880).
Liverpool Institute St Katherine College—Standpark Road, Childwall, Liverpool 16.
Liverpool Polytechnic—Byrom Street, Liverpool 3 (051 207 3581). *Secretary:* M E D Hare, 12 Prenton Farm Road, Prenton, Birkenhead, Wirral.
Southport & District League—*Secretary:* H Bond, 3 Fylde Road, Southport (27781).

AFFILIATED SCHOOLS (15)

Boys
Birkdale High School — Southport. **Liverpool College** — Liverpool 18. **Merchant Taylors School for Boys** — Crosby, Liverpool 23.

Girls
Aigburth Vale Comprehensive School — Liverpool 17. **Belvedere School** — Liverpool 8. **Convent of Mercy Broughton Hall High School** — Liverpool 12. **Greenbank High School for Girls** — Hillside, Southport. **Huyton College for Girls** — Liverpool. **Liverpool Institute High School for Girls** — Liverpool 8. **Merchant Taylors School for Girls** — Crosby, Liverpool 23. **Notre Dame High School** — St Helens. **Prescot Girls Grammar School.**

Mixed
Formby Range High School — Stapleton Road, Formby. **Old Hall High School** — Maghull, Merseyside. **Ormskirk Grammar School.**

All correspondence to school clubs should be addressed to the Master or Mistress in charge of lawn tennis.

LEICESTERSHIRE COUNTY LAWN TENNIS ASSOCIATION

Hon Secretary—**Mr J Hunting,** 21 Roundhill Road, Leicester (0533 737260).
Hon Treasurer—**Mr R Wright,** 11a Holbrook Road, Leicester (0533 706354).
Hon Men's Match Secretary—**K W Chambers,** 35 Elms Road, Leicester (707287).
Hon Ladies' Match Secretary—**Mrs J Gartshore,** 64 Knighton Drive, Leicester (709431).
Hon Junior Organiser—**Mrs J Butterfield,** 8 Southernhay Road, Leicester (703416).
Representatives on the Council—**K Sefton, J Hunting.**

AFFILIATED CLUBS (61)

Arts & Recreation Department—Mowmacre Community and Sports Centre, Thurcaston Road, Leicester. Courts: H3. *Secretary:* M J Hobbs, 171 Knighton Road, Knighton, Leicester (705516 pri, 5522644 bus).
Ashby Castle—South Street, Ashby-de-la-Zouch. Courts: H6. *Secretary:* J E Stanley, 1 Alton Way, Ashby-De-La-Zouch (Ashby 412550).
Barrow-on-Soar—Cotes Road, Barrow-on-Soar. Courts: H3. *Secretary:* B Bullock, 10 Derwent Road, Barrow-in-Soar, Loughborough, Leics (Quorn 413680).
Beacon—Main Street, Woodhouse Eaves. Courts: H2. *Secretary:* J Rollinson, 5 Hastings Road, Woodhouse Eaves (Woodhouse Eaves 890005).
Belvoir Vale Tennis Club—Main Street, Hose, Leics. Courts: H2. *Secretary:* Mrs J Brown, The Old Vicarge, Hose, Melton Mowbray, Leics (Harby 61326).
Blaby Victoria—Blaby & District Social Centre, Lutterworth Road, Blaby. Courts: H3. *Secretary:* Mrs S Clayton, 16 Kingsmead Road, Knighton, Leicester (888812 pri, 555051 bus).
British Shoe Corp—Works, Sunningdale Road, Braunstone, Leicester. Courts: H3. *Secretary:* S Sellars, 55 Bradgate Road, Anstey, Leicester (364876 pri, 871355 ext 2816 bus).
Carisbrooke—Carisbrooke Road, Leicester (705316). Courts: H10 (3 floodlit). *Secretary:* Mrs C Jagger, 17 Southernhay Close, Leicester (704934).
Cavendish—Glenville Avenue, Glen Hills, Blaby. Courts: H3 (1 floodlit). *Secretary:* Mrs R Hecks, Wealdway, Lutterworth Road, Gilmorton (Lutterworth 4945).
Charnwood— Nanpantan Sports Ground, Nanpantan Road, Loughborough. Courts: G4, H4 (2 floodlit). *Secretary:* A J Morris, 28 King Edward Road, Loughborough (236439).
County Hall—County Hall, Glenfield. Courts: H3. *Secretary:* T A Iliffe, 11 Gladstone Street, Kibworth, Beauchamp (Kibworth 3410 pri, 871313 bus).
Croft—Recreation Ground, Croft. Courts: H2. *Secretary:* P Smith, 1 The Beeches, Hill Top, Earl Shilton, Leics (48913).
Dunlop—Groby Commercial College, Ratby Road, Groby. Courts: H4. *Secretary:* R. Blencoe, 77 Nansen Road, Leicester (736471 pri, 730281 bus).
Earl Shilton Kingscroft—King's Walk (off Wood Street), Earl Shilton. Courts: H2. *Secretary:* Mrs J Orton, 76 Equity Road East, Earl Shilton (Earl Shilton 46525).
Electricity Sports—Electricity Sports Ground, Aylestone Road, opp Cattle Market. Courts: H2. *Secretary:* Mrs V M Marshall, 86 Alan Moss Road, Loughborough (Loughborough 261701 bus).
Enderby—Mill Lane, Enderby (nr Brockington High School). Courts: H3. *Secretary:* Mrs A Poli, 11 Laurel Road, Blaby, Leicester (779960).
English Electric—Cambridge Road, Whetstone. Courts: H4. *Secretary:* J Farmer, 22 Goodwood Road, Leicester (414526).
Fisons—Holt Drive, Loughborough. Courts: H3. *Secretary:* Miss J D Smith, 11 Shepherd's Close, Shepshed, Leicester (Shepshed 504320 pri).
Foxton—Foxton Recreation Ground. Courts: H2. *Secretary:* C Lees, Cogan House, Swingbridge Street, Foxton, Market Harborough (East Langton 331 pri).
GEC (Leicester)—Marconi Ground and Control Systems/GEC Measurements, Scudamore Road, New Parks, Leicester. Courts: H3. *Secretary:* M D Juett, 134 Carisbrooke Road, Leicester (708345 pri, 871481 bus).
Gynsill—corner Gynsill Lane and Gorse Lane, Anstey. Courts: H4 (1 floodlit). *Secretary:* Mrs D English, 18 All Saints Road, Thurcaston, Leicester (362669 pri).
Hamilton—Tennis Avenue, off Sandy Lane, Melton Mowbray. Courts: H5. *Secretary:* Miss P J Blowers, 45 Edendale Road, Melton Mowbray (Melton Mowbray 67897 pri).
3M Health Care—Leicester Road, Loughborough, Leics. Courts: H3. *Secretary:* K A Smelt, 25

School Lane, Quorn, Loughborough, Leics (Quorn 415006 pri, Loughborough 268181 bus).
Highfields—Moat Comm College, Maidstone Road. Courts: H4. *Secretary:* R Kotak, 28 Sheringham Road, Leicester (365652 pri, 761481 bus).
Hillside—14 Stanley Drive, Humberstone. Courts: H3. *Secretary:* Mrs P M Holyoak, 90 Downing Drive, Evington, Leicester (415926 pri).
Hinckley Central—Leicester Road, Hinckley. Courts: H4. *Secretary:* P Moore, 10 Holly Lane, Barwell (Hinckley 43476 pri, Hinckley 635294 bus).
Hinckley Town—Hinckley Sports Club Ground, Leicester Road, Hinckley. Courts: H4. *Secretary:* N Smith, Crabtree Cottage, Trevor Road, Hinckley, Leics (Hinckley 636486).
Holwell Works—Asfordby Hill, Melton Mowbray. Courts: H2. *Secretary:* J Spiby, 10 Gladstone Avenue, Melton Mowbray (Melton Mowbray 64907).
Houghton—Houghton Playing Field, Weir Lane. Courts: H2. *Secretary:* Mrs V Greasley, 20 Deane Gate Drive, Houghton-on-the-Hill, Leics (432993).
Huncote—Sportsfield Lane, Huncote. Courts: H2. *Secretary:* P Mills, 7 Ringwood Close, Desford, Leicester (Desford 3134 pri, 669331 bus).
Husbands Bosworth—Playing Fields, Killworth Road, Husbands Bosworth. Courts: H1. *Secretary:* Mrs J Murdock, 8 Highcroft, Husbands Bosworth, Lutterworth (Market Harborough 880159).
Kegworth—King George V Playing Fields, Nottingham Road, Kegworth, nr Derby. Courts: H3. *Secretary:* Mrs B Bradwell, 26 Langley Drive, Kegworth, Derby (Kegworth 3969 pri, Loughborough 263151 bus).
Ketton—Pit Lane. Courts: H2. *Secretary:* Mrs C Bearne, Baxter Lodge, Main Road, Collyweston, Stamford, Lincs (0780 83362 pri).
Kibworth—Smeeton Road, Kibworth Beauchamp Courts: H4. *Secretary:* Mrs E Reynolds, 11a Links Road, Kibworth Beauchamp, Leicester (Kibworth 3195 pri).
Leicester Banks Sports Club—Banks Road, Aylestone (Leicester 832000). Courts: H5. *Secretary:* Mrs J M Croft, 37 Malling Avenue, Broughton Astley (Sutton Elms 283727).
Leicester Building Society—adjacent to Offices, Glen Road, Oadby. Courts: H3. *Secretary:* R J Coyle, 16 St James Close, Oadby, Leicester (710325 pri, 717272 bus).
Leicester Forest East—King's Walk, Leicester Forest East. Courts: H3 (1 floodlit). *Secretary:* Mrs J Wright, 20 Glenfield Lane, Kirby, Muxloe (393735).
Leicester Polytechnic—Scraptoft Campus of Polytech, Scraptoft. Courts: H3. Western Boulevard. Courts: H2 (1 indoor). *Secretary:* c/o J Hunting, School of Physical Education, Leicester Polytechnic, Leicester (551551 Poly, 737260 pri).
Leicestershire—Westernhay Road, Leicester (705279). Courts: G9, H9 (1 floodlit). *Secretary:* Mrs D E Longmore, Leicestershire LTC, Westernhay Road, Leicester (705279).
Leicestershire Constabulary—rear 390 Hinckley Road, Leicester. Courts: H2. *Secretary:* J P Warner, 88 Main Street, Thornton, Leicester (20845 bus).
Loughborough Town—Forest Road, Loughborough (side of Emmanuel Church). Courts: G2, H6 (2 floodlit). *Secretary:* Dr S Stevens, 101 Valley Road, Loughborough, Leics. (Loughborough 215139 pri, Loughborough 263171, ext 243 bus).
Loughborough University—University Grounds, Ashby Road, Loughborough. Courts: H4. *Secretary:* Tennis Section Secretary, c/o Athletic Union, Loughborough University, Ashby Road, Loughborough (217766 ext 40).
Lutterworth—Coventry Road, Lutterworth. Courts: H3. *Secretary:* Mrs J Campbell-Barker, 11 Willowtree Crescent, Lutterworth (Lutterworth 3277 pri).
Market Bosworth—School Field, Station Road, Market Bosworth. Courts: H3. *Secretary:* Mrs H Buckingham, 20 York Close, Market Bosworth, Leics (Market Bosworth 291159 pri).
Market Harborough—Great Bowden Recreation Ground, Great Bowden. Courts: H3. *Secretary:* Mrs J Barrett, Laburnum Cottage, Old, nr Northampton (0604 781402).
Medbourne—Village Playing Field, Medbourne. Courts: H2. *Secretary:* A E Coon, Thatched Cottage, Nevill Holt, Market Harborough (Medbourne Green 243 pri, Medbourne Green 234 bus).
Northfields—Melton Road, Syston. Courts: H4 (1 floodlit). *Secretary:* Mrs J J Parker, Connaught House, Howe Lane, Rothley (303560).
Oadby—Leicester Road, Oadby (712889). Courts: H6. *Secretary:* P K Clark, 36 The Yews, Oadby, Leics (719605 pri, 546221 bus).
Oakham—The Vale, Cricket Lawns, Oakham. Courts: H3. *Secretary:* G Holt, 10 Chater Road, Oakham, Leics (Oakham 55168 pri).
Oaks & District—Oaks Road, Oaks in Charnwood, Shepshed. Courts: H3. *Secretary:* Mrs B Webster, 40 Conway Drive, Shepshed (Shepshed 504451 pri).
Quorn—rear Manor House Hotel, Woodhouse Road, Quorn. Courts: H4. *Secretary:* Mrs J Curd, 5 Brookside Road, Loughborough (Loughborough 236645 pri).
Ravenstone—Ravenslea Estate, Ravenstone. Courts: H2. *Secretary:* Mrs E Ritchie, 3 St Michael's Drive, Ravenstone (Coal 35187).
Rolls-Royce (Mountsorrel)—South Factory on A6 road, Mountsorrel Lane, Rothley. Courts: H2. *Secretary:* G M Cowley, 23 Oakfield Avenue, Birstall, Leicester (673633 pri, 302311 bus).
Rothley Ivanhoe—Mountsorrel Lane, Rothley. Courts: H6. *Secretary:* Mrs E J Aspell, 8 Hoby Road, Thurssington, Leics (Rearsby 638 pri).
Roundhill—24 and 26 Homeway Road, Leicester. Courts: H4 (1 floodlit). *Secretary:* J Hall, 30 Hatherleigh Road, Evington, Leicester (739407 pri, 25705 school).
Shakespeare—Shakespeare Park, Avon Road, Braunstone. Courts: H2. *Secretary:* Mrs A Gardner, 26 Gilberts Drive, Newbold Verdon, Leics (Desford 3593 pri).

Shepshed—Hind Leys College, Forest Street, Shepshed. Courts: H4. *Secretary:* Mr D Everett, 20 Belvoir Way, Shepshed (53005 pri).
Sileby—Seagrave Road, Sileby (opp Greedon Rise). Courts: H3. *Secretary:* Mr D Thompson, 119 Heathcote Drive, Sileby, Leics (Sileby 2993 pri, 664456, ext 2893 bus).
Stoney Stanton—Playing Fields (off Carey Hill Road), Stoney Stanton. Courts: H3 (1 floodlit). *Secretary:* B C Law, 38 Tansey Crescent, Stoney Stanton (Sapcote 3689).
Thorn/EMI Lighting Ltd—adjacent to Works, Melton Road. Courts: H2. *Secretary:* M T Durston, Thorn EMI Lighting Ltd, Melton Road, Leicester (Melton Mowbray 84069 pri, 661531 ext 405 bus).
Victoria—Holmfield Avenue, Leicester. Courts: H5 (1 floodlit). *Secretary:* G Coltman, 74 Oakfield Avenue, Birstall, Leicester (671050 pri, 664456 bus).
Watermead—Leicester Co-op Society Social Club Playing Fields, Birstall Road, Leicester. Courts: H3. *Secretary:* Mr D Cartwright, 32 Kingsgate Avenue, Birstall, Leicester (675398 pri, 352011 bus).
Westfields—20 Eastfield Road, Leicester. Courts: H4. *Secretary:* Mrs C Moore, 409 Ratby Lane, Kirby Moxloe, Leicester (392566 pri).
Wigston—Horsewell Lane (Little Hill) Wigston (opp Ecobs Garden Centre). Courts: H4. *Secretary:* A Wallace, 75 Newton Lane, Wigston, Leicester (887441).

AFFILIATED SCHOOLS (19)

Boys
Lancaster School — Leicester. **Oakham School** — Oakham. **City of Leicester School** — Evington, Leicester. **Wyggeston and Queen Elizabeth I College** — Leicester. **Uppingham** — Uppingham.

Girls
Sir Jonathan North School — Leicester. **Wyggeston Collegiate** — Leicester.

Mixed
Hastings High — Burbage. **John Cleveland College** — Hinckley. **Kibworth High School** — Kibworth. **Leicester Grammar School** — Leicester. **Loughborough Grammar School** — Loughborough. **Loughborough High School** — Loughborough. **Lutterworth Grammar School** — Lutterworth. **Manor High School** — Oadby, Leicester. **Portland House School** — Leicester. **Stoneygate** — Leicester.

All correspondence to School Clubs should be addressed to the Master or Mistress in charge of lawn tennis.

LINCOLNSHIRE LAWN TENNIS ASSOCIATION

Hon Secretary—**Miss M Gill,** 236 West Parade, Lincoln (0522 23983 pri, 0522 33561 bus).
Hon Junior Secretary—**Mrs J C Davis,** 42 Langworthgate, Lincoln (0522 27294).
Hon Treasurer—**W E Palmer,** 86 Eastbrook Road, Lincoln (0522 695202).
Hon Men's Match Secretary—**P J Bentley,** 21 Mainwaring Road, Lincoln (0522 25050 pri, 0522 32123 bus).
Hon Ladies' Match Secretary—**Mrs J Dickinson,** The Mill House, Atterby, Lincoln (067-381 327).
Representative on the Council—**Miss M Gill.**

AFFILIATED CLUBS (48)

Bardney (Lincsgran Sports & Welfare)—Club Sports Field, Bardney. Courts: H2. *Secretary:* D Papworth, 3 Manor Close, Bardney, Lincoln.
Boston—125 Sleaford Road. Courts: G5, H4 (1 floodlit). *Secretary:* F Cammack, 8a Pilgrim Road, Boston.
Boston Health Services—*Secretary:* D Mellor, 10 Windmill Drive, Heckington, Sleaford, Lincs.
Boston Norprint—*Secretary:* S A Hill, Norprint Ltd, Horncastle Road, Boston.
Boston, Rochford Tower Hall—Hawthorne Tree Corner, Fishtoft. Courts: H2. *Secretary:* Mr R J Nash, 89 Tower Road, Boston, Lincs.
Bottesford—*Secretary:* D Sowerby, 2 Malling Walk, Bottesford, Scunthorpe.
Bourne & District—Abbey Lawn, Bourne. Courts: G5, H2. *Secretary:* P J Walton, 14 Fir Avenue, Bourne.
Caistor—Courts: H1. *Secretary:* S Wilson, 16 The Meadow, Caistor, Lincs.
RAF Cranwell—The Officer i/c Tennis, RAF Cranwell.
Deeping—Towngate East. Courts: G2. *Secretary:* A D Jones, 54 Church Street, Market Deeping, Peterborough.
Gainsborough Rose Sports & Social—North Warren Road. Courts: G9, H1. *Secretary:* A Scott, 87 Beckett Avenue, Gainsborough.
Gainsborough Town—Corringham Road. Courts: G5. *Secretary:* Mrs G V Burgin, The Old Vicarage, Morton, Gainsborough.
Grantham—Manthorpe Road. Courts: G5. *Secretary:* Mrs B Cooper, 26 Longcliffe Road, Grantham.
Grantham Aveling-Barford—'Arnold,' North Parade, Grantham. Courts: G5, H4. *Secretary:* The Tennis Secretary, Aveling-Barford, Grantham.
Grantham, Playmore—*Secretary:* J Hernaman, The Old Cottage, Hawthorpe, Bourne.
Great Gonerby—*Secretary:* R S Stahel, 10 Lime Grove, Caythorpe, Grantham.
Grimsby—College Street, Bargate. Courts: G7, H3. *Secretary:* W Chapman, 9 Hainton Avenue, Grimsby.
Grimsby NALGO—*Secretary:* E R Holden, Jenue, Campions Lane, North Thoresby, Grimsby, South Humberside.
Grimsby Ross Group—Weelsby Road. Courts: G3, H4. *Secretary:* The Secretary, Tennis Section, Ross Group, Weelsby Road, Grimsby.
Grimsby, St James'—Hereford Avenue. Courts: G5, H3. *Secretary:* Miss L Blackburn, 14 Franklin House, Beechwood Avenue, Grimsby.

Grimsby, Welholme—Weelsby Avenue. Courts: G6, H2. *Secretary:* Mrs A Preston, 32 Gloucester Avenue, Grimsby.
Helpringham—Station Road. Courts: G2. *Secretary:* C W Richardson, Grove Farm, Swaton, Sleaford.
Horncastle & District—Stanhope Road. Courts: G3. *Secretary:* Mrs J Tinkler, Greenacres, Rowgate Hill, Scramblesby LN11 9KU.
Kirton & District—Church Lane. Courts: G4. *Secretary:* A Spinks, Wilmere, Littleside Lane, Kirton Holme, Boston.
Kirton Lindsey Blue Circle—*Secretary:* B A Chudley, Stonegarth, 15 Spa Hill, Kirton-in-Lindsey.
Lincoln, Claytons—Lee Road. Courts: G4, H2. *Secretary:* Mr N Barrett, 21 Spa Street, Lincoln LN2 5NQ.
Lincoln College of Technology—*Secretary:* Secretary i/c Tennis, College of Technology, Lincoln.
Lincoln, Eastgate—Langworthgate. Courts: G5, H3. *Secretary:* P Smallwood, 7a Greetwell Road, Lincoln.
Lincoln, Longdales—*Secretary:* Mrs J Wilson, 12 Thonock Close, Lincoln.
Lincoln, Ruston Marconi—Newark Road. Courts: G6, H3. *Secretary:* R E Taylor, 107 Holywell Road, Lincoln.
Louth—Westgate. Courts: G2. *Secretary:* N A N Sharpley, 10 Mercer Row, Louth.
Market Rasen, Willoughby—Walesby Road. Courts: G2, H1. *Secretary:* A J Padley, Hambledon Cottage, Walesby Road, Market Rasen.
Nettleham—Courts: H2. *Secretary:* Mrs V Morris, 18 Kingsway, Nettleham, Lincoln.
North Hykeham—*Secretary:* R Smith, 8 Cresta Close, North Hykeham, Lincoln.
North Scarle—*Secretary:* Mrs R M Griffin, The Old Wheelwrights, High Street, North Scarle, Lincoln.
Ruskington—Courts: H2. *Secretary:* Mrs J M Pow, 20 London Road, Silk Willoughby, Sleaford, Lincs.
Saxilby—*Secretary:* Mrs J Wright, 66 Manor Road, Saxilby, Lincoln LN1 2HP.
Scotter—*Secretary:* Mrs J Bilton, 24 North Moor Road, Scotter, Gawsborough, Lincs.
Scunthorpe, Appleby, Frodingham Steel Co Ltd—Brumby Hall. Courts: G8, H4. *Secretary:* K Wadd, 20 Hawarth Close, Scunthorpe.
Scunthorpe LTC—*Secretary:* P Hutchinson, 34 Lakeside Drive, Scunthorpe.
Sleaford—*Secretary:* Mrs S Owens, 10 Park Crescent, Sleaford.
Spalding, Leverton & Co—Albion Street. Courts: H2. *Secretary:* D J G Hall, c/o Leverton & Co, Westlode Street, Spalding.
Spalding, Parkside—Pinchbleck Road. Courts: G3. *Secretary:* Miss J Peach, Peartree Farm, Glenside South, West Pinchbeck, Spalding.
Spalding Town—Holyrood Walk, off Clay Lane. Courts: G5 (2 floodlit). *Secretary:* Mrs L Williams, 36 Market Place, Folkingham, Sleaford, Lincs.
Spilsby & District—Hundleby Road. Courts: G8. *Secretary:* Mrs M E Dawson, Dalby House, Dalby, Spilsby (2237).
Stamford Rock—Empingham Road. Courts: G2. *Secretary:* L V Shaw, 100 Queen's Walk, Stamford.
Washingborough—*Secretary:* Mrs J M Preston, 15 Sutton Close, Washingborough, Lincoln.
Woodhall Spa—Jubilee Park. Courts: H2. *Secretary:* Mrs P M Chapman, Tiki, Woodland Drive, Woodhall Spa.
Wragby—Courts: H2. *Secretary:* Mrs H Anstile, Highfield, Louth Road, Wragby, Lincoln.

OTHER AFFILIATED ORGANISATION (1)

North Kelsey League—*Secretary:* C E Bennett, Grange Lane, North Kelsey, Lincoln.

AFFILIATED SCHOOLS (35)

Boys
Boston Grammar. Carre's Grammar — Sleaford. **Stamford School. The King's School** — Grantham.

Girls
Gleed Girls Secondary School — Spalding. **Grantham Girls High School. Spalding Girls High School. Stamford Girls High School. St Josephs** — Lincoln.

Mixed
Alford Grammar. Ancaster High School — Lincoln. **Banovallum School** — Horncastle. **Baysgarth School** — Barton-on-Humber. **Bourne Grammar. Caistor Grammar. De Aston School** — Market Rasen. **Foxhills School** — Scunthorpe. **Gartree School** — Tattershall. **Gough Comprehensive School** — Bottesford, Scunthorpe. **Havelock School** — Grimsby. **John Leggott College** — Scunthorpe. **King Edward VI School** — Louth. **Lincoln Christ's Hosptial School. Lumley Secondary School** — Skegness. **Monks Dyke School** — Louth. **North Kesteven School** — North Hykeham, Lincoln. **Queen Elizabeth Grammar School**—Gainsborough. **Robert Pattison School** — North Hykeham, Lincoln. **South Park High School** — Lincoln. **St Bede's School** — Scunthorpe. **St James's School** — Grimsby. **The City School** — Lincoln. **The Grammar School** — Horncastle. **The Sir John Nelthrope School** — Brigg. **Waltham Toll Bar School** — Grimsby. **William Farr School** — Welton-by-Lincoln. **Wintringham School** — Grimsby.

MIDDLESEX COUNTY LAWN TENNIS ASSOCIATION

Hon Secretary—**B J Harriss,** 66 Church Avenue, Pinner, Middx HA5 5JF (01-866 3468).
Hon Treasurer—**R Shipton,** 171 Oldfield Lane North, Greenford, Middlesex (578 5465).
Hon Men's Match Secretary—**A G Farrant,** 15 Colne Road, London N21 (360 4646).
Hon Ladies' Match Secretary—**Mrs F J Wardley,** Aldeburg, 3 Park Close, Ellesmere Road, Chiswick, London W4 (994 4759).
Hon Juniors Secretary—**D Tomlinson,** 8 Copthall Drive, London NW7 (959 3535).
Representatives on the Council—**B J Harriss, S D Lester, Mrs J Fyfe.**

AFFILIATED CLUBS (169)

Abbey National Building Society—Preston Hill, Harrow (204 4906). Courts: H3. *Secretary:* Mrs C A Edsall, Abbey National Building Society, Abbey House, Baker Street, London NW1 6XL (01-486 5555).

Acorn—Whitchurch School Playing Fields, Marsh Lane, Stanmore (952 2766). Courts: H6. *Secretary:* A A G Morris, 66 Dene Gardens, Marsh Lane, Stanmore HA7 4TD (954 8473).

Acton Cricket and Tennis Club—Manor Park Grounds, East Acton Lane W3 (743 3869). Courts: G4. *Secretary:* Mrs V A Harvey, 28 Beaumont Road, Acton Green, W4 5AP.

Angela Buxton Centre—Northway Gardens, London N2. Courts: H2, ART G2. *Secretary:* Ms A Buxton, Angela Buxton Centre, 16 Winnington Road, London N2 (455 6216).

Avenue—The Avenue, Sylvan Avenue, London N3. Courts: H3. *Secretary:* H A Allwood, 112 Long Lane, Church End, Finchley, London N3 (346 6328).

Bankes—Donnefield Avenue, Canons Park, Edgware (952 1564). Courts: H4. *Secretary:* Mrs J Mole, 17 Vernon Drive, Stanmore (863 6005).

Barclays Bank Sports Club—Park View Road, Ealing, W5 (998 4904). Courts: H4, G10. *Secretary:* A G Evans, 13 Beacon Close, Uxbridge, Middx (0895 38744 pri, 979 8331 bus).

Bar Lawn Tennis Society—*Secretary:* L Pilkington, Flat C, Regency Court, 37 Albert Square, London SW8 1BY (582 3196).

Barn Hill—Barn Hill, adjacent open space, Wembley Park. Courts: H5. *Secretary:* N Felton, 14 Sudbury Hill Close, Wembley (904 3746).

Bounds Green Bowling & LTC—entrance side of 66 Brownlow Road, London N11 (888 4721). *Secretary:* D A Collingwood, Tennis Secretary, c/o The Club.

Bourneside Sports Club—Grovelands Hospital Grounds, The Bourne, Southgate, London N14 (8865179). Courts: H3. *Secretary:* S. Bishop, 13 Hawthorn Grove, Enfield EH2 0DS (367 6661).

Brampton—67 Brampton Grove, The Burroughs, Hendon, London NW4 (202 0617). Courts: H4. *Secretary:* A Orchard, 28a Cavendish Avenue, N3 (346 6005).

Brentham—Meadvale Road, Ealing (997 2624). Courts: G7, H3. *Secretary:* K Butcher, 20 Brentham Way, Ealing, W5 (997 0154).

Britannia TC—Britannia Leisure Centre. Courts: H6. *Secretary:* G Fulford, 11 Rosendale Way, Elm Village, St Pancras Way, Camden NW1 (388 9030).

British Airways—Crane Lodge Road off High Street (Cranford), Heston. Courts: G6, H6. *Secretary:* Miss L Arculus, 7 Imperial House, Station Parade, Virginia Water, Surrey GU25 4AA (Wentworth 2048 pri, 562 3653 bus).

British Gas (Western Tennis Section)—Twyford Avenue, Acton (992 1400). Courts: G3, H10. *Secretary:* Mr W F Bradley, British Gas Corporation, 59 Bryanston Street, London W1 (723 7030 ext 2475).

Brondesbury—Harman Drive, Farm Avenue, Cricklewood, London NW2 (452 2983). Courts: H7 (3 all weather). *Secretary:* P Hodes, 8 Lyme Terrace, NW1 (267 8728).

Brookside (Crouch End)—Crouch End Playing Fields, Park Road, Crouch End, London N8 (340 9960). Courts: H3. *Secretary:* Miss S V Ellam, 88 Victoria Road, Wood Green, N22 4XF (889 8554).

Broomfield—85a Hedge Lane, London N9 (886 9999). Courts: H2. *Secretary:* Mrs Z Hubbard, 91 Bush Hill Road, Winchmore Hill, N21 2DC (360 0017).

BRSA (Enfield)—Holtwhite's Hill, Gordon Hill, Enfield (363 4449). Courts: H5. *Secretary:* F T Gallagher, 31 Manor Road, Enfield, Middx EN2 0AN.

Bush Hill Park—Abbey Road, Bush Hill Park, Enfield (363 0997). Courts: G5, H5. *Secretary:* Miss J Hinson, 10 Myddelton Close, Enfield, EN1 4AJ (363 5735 pri, 366 9328 bus).

Calthorpe Cricket & LTC—Crouch End Playing Fields, Park Road, London N8. Courts: H6. *Secretary:* L Gough, 20 St James' Avenue, London N20 (368 7059).

Campden Hill—9 Aubrey Walk, London W8 (727 4050). Courts: H12. *Secretary:* The Secretary, c/o The Club.

Carlton Century—Preston Park, Carlton Avenue East, Wembley. Courts: H3. *Secretary:* B Shelley, 21 The Ridgeway, Kenton, Harrow HA3 0LN.

CAV—West End Road, Northolt (Pavilion: Wax 1796). Courts: H6. *Secretary:* D Platford, 26 Kenton Avenue, Sunbury on Thames (76 86458).

Chandos—Wellgarth Road, Golders Green, London NW11 (455 3012). Courts: H2, AG6. *Secretary:* Mrs S Warshaw, 3 London Road, Stanmore, Middx (958 9333).

City Livery Club (Tennis Section)—(353 2431). *Secretary:* J Langstaffe, 16 Sunny Bank, Epsom, Surrey (78 21604).

Civil Service—Duke's Meadows, Chiswick, London W4. Courts: G11, H6. *Secretary:* J D Nicholson, Morningside, 18 Errol Gardens, Motspur Park, New Malden, Surrey KT3 6QF (949 1970).

Cloisters Wood LTC—Wood Lane, Stanmore, Middlesex (954 4846). Courts: 3 Art Grass. *Secretary:* c/o The Club.

Coles Green—Coles Green Road, Cricklewood, London NW2. Courts: H3. *Secretary:* B Bagchi, 8 Fairways, Stanmore, Middx (204 3768).

Conquest Club—Wood Lane, Osterley (560 2892). Courts: H3. *Secretary:* M N Pearson, Cashiers Dept, Pyrene House, Sunbury Cross, Sunbury on Thames (76 85588).

Conway—Conway Road, Southgate, London N14. Courts: H5. *Secretary:* Ms C Whetstone, 38 Durants Park Avenue, Ponders End, Enfield, Middx EN3 7EA.

Coolhurst LT & Squash Rackets Club—Courtside, Coolhurst Road, Crouch End, N8 (340 4272). Courts: G5, 2 Art G, H5 (All Weather, 1 covered, 2 floodlit). *Secretary:* R M Beckley, c/o Club, (340 6611 club office).

Cumberland—25 Alvanley Gardens, London NW6 (435 6022). Courts: G4, SG3, H5. *Secretary:* J R Smethurst, 96 Agar Grove, London NW1 9TL.

David Lloyd Slazenger Racquet Club—Southall Lane, Hounslow TW5 9PE (573 0143). Courts: 12 Covered, 8 Art Grass. *Secretary:* c/o The Club.
Drive—59a The Drive, Edgware (958 3651). Courts: H6. *Secretary:* Mrs P Emanuel, 23 Snaresbrook Drive, Stanmore, Middx (958 7846).
Durnsford Sports Centre TC—Rhodes Avenue, Wood Green, N22 (881 3610). Courts: H3. *Secretary:* B Gravis, c/o The Club (803 6958 pri).
Ealing—Creffield Road, Ealing, London W5 (992 0370). Courts: G12, H6. *Secretary:* A M Rowland, 42 Western Gardens, Ealing, W5 3RU (992 1052 pri, 242 0861 ext 263 bus).
Eastcote—Kaduna Close, off Joel Street, Eastcote (866 7072, 868 8835). Courts: H5. *Secretary:* Mrs E Crockford, 21 Middleton Drive, Pinner, HA5 2PQ (866 8461).
Edmonton Sports (Lawn Tennis Section)—Hyde Side, Church Street, Edmonton, London N9 (807 5341). Courts: G6, H3. *Secretary:* Miss A Billett, 28 Heaton Court, High Street, Cheshunt, Herts (97 32877).
Elms (Stanmore)—Pynnacles Close, Church Road, Stanmore (954 3852). Courts: H4. *Secretary:* R Benge, 12 Winscombe Way, Stanmore, Middx (954 0876).
Elmwood—All Souls Avenue and Holland Road, Willesden, London NW10 (965 3425). Courts: H6. *Secretary:* T Black, Flat C, 169 Finborough Road, SW10 (373 5213).
Enfield—71 The Ridgeway, Enfield (363 4666). Courts: G2, H4. *Secretary:* C L Hoath FCII, 46 Sheringham Avenue, Southgate, N14 4UG (360 5990).
Enfield Chase (Village Road) Tennis Club Ltd—Croft Mews, Park Avenue, Enfield (360 5939). H6 (4 floodlit). *Secretary:* Mrs S Peachey, 147 Kenilworth Crescent, Enfield, Middlesex (366 4730).
Enfield Cricket—Wellington Road, Enfield. Courts: G3. *Secretary:* R D Bowerman, 65 Princes Avenue, Finchley, N3 2DA (349 0791).
Exiles—Meadowbank, 27 Cambridge Park, Twickenham (892 1787). Courts: H3. *Secretary:* Miss J Chapple, Meadowbank, 27 Cambridge Park, Twickenham (01-892 4602).
Farm Walk—Farm Walk, Temple Fortune, London NW11. Courts: H3. *Secretary:* A Harris, 10 Cholmley Gardens, Aldred Road, NW6 1AE (435 6562 pri, 629 0811 bus).
Finchley—rear of 47-51 Brent Way, London N3 (346 2291). Courts: H5. *Secretary:* H Spencer, 11 Hamilton Way, Finchley, N3 (346 1520).
Finchley Manor—Lyndhurst Gardens, London N3 (346 1327). Courts: H9. *Secretary:* Mrs H Rance, 21 Wickliffe Avenue, Finchley, London N3 (346 6835).
Forty-Five Club—c/o The Queens Club, W Kensington, W14. *Secretary:* E Wittman, c/o Queens Club (937 2767 pri).
Friern Hospital Sports & Social Club—Friern Hospital. Courts: H1. *Secretary:* G Corry, Hon Gen Secretary, Friern Hospital, New Southgate, London N11 3BP (368 1288).
GEC (London)—Preston Road, Wembley (904 1980). Courts: H6. *Secretary:* Miss B Brown, Hirst Research Centre, GEC Co Ltd, East Lane, Wembley (904 1262 ext 406).
Georgians LTC—Crouch End Playing Fields, Park Road, London N8. Courts: H3. *Secretary:* Mrs D Frith, 12 Clarendon Road, Cheshunt, Herts (97 27592).
Glaxo Sports & Social—Glaxo Operations UK, Greenford Road, Greenford. Courts: H3. *Secretary:* Miss A Gale, Glaxo Export Ltd, Graham Street, N18 8JZ (253 3060).
Globe—210a Haverstock Hill, London NW3 (435 0248). Courts: H10. *Secretary:* S Haller, 16 Ingram Road, N2 9QA (883 4169).
Gloucester—Gloucester Road, New Barnet, Herts (449 4434). Courts: G4, H4. *Secretary:* Mrs G Oza, 214 Church Hill Road, East Barnet, Herts (361 8123).
Great Western Railway—Castle Bar Park, Vallis Way, Argyle Road, Ealing, London W13 (723 7000 ext 2959). Courts: G4, H6. *Secretary:* F A Roser, 31 Blackmore Avenue, Southall (574 4939).
Greenford—76 Ravenor Park Road, Greenford (578 4678). Courts: H3. *Secretary:* Miss J L Gregory, 202 Boston Road, Hanwell W7 2AD (579 0646).
Guinness—Coronation Road, Park Royal Brewery, London NW10 (965 7700). Courts: G5, H3. *Secretary:* J Harding, Hon Secretary Tennis Section, c/o Arthur Guinness Son & Co (Park Royal) Ltd, Park Royal Brewery, London NW10 7RR (965 7700).
Gunnersbury Triangle—rear of Princes Avenue, Gunnersbury Park, Acton, London W3 (992 4755). Courts: H6. *Secretary:* Mrs J Fyfe, 33 Princes Avenue, London W3 (992 6508).
Hadley Wood LTC—adjoining Hadley Wood Station BR. Courts: H4. *Secretary:* Lady J Harris, 4 Walmar Close, Hadley Wood, Barnet, Herts EN4 0NU (449 6212).
Hampstead Cricket—Lymington Road, London NW6 (435 0631). Courts: H5. *Secretary:* Miss B E Tredre, 19 West Drive, Harrow Weald, Middx HA3 6TX (954 1225 pri).
Hampstead Garden Suburb—Lyttleton Road, Playing Fields, London N2. Courts: H2. *Secretary:* H Gross, 11 Valley Avenue, N12 (445 9602).
Hanley—Crouch End Playing Fields, Park Road, London N8 (340 7442). Courts: H4. *Secretary:* K R Franklin, 82 Cavendish Road, London N4 1RS (634 5364).
Harefield Tennis Club—Moorhall Green, South Harefield. Courts: H3. *Secretary:* Mrs B Baker, 21 Hawksworth Close, Northwood HA6 2FT.
Harrow LTC—Harrow School Courts, Football Lane, Peterborough Road, Harrow-on-the-Hill. Courts: H3. *Secretary:* B Simpson, 7 Byron Hill Road, Harrow-on-the-Hill (422 7657).
Harrow Baptist—44-46 Bonnersfield Lane, Harrow. Courts: H4. *Secretary:* E A Fillmore, 34 Northwick Park Road, Harrow (427 3925).
Harrow Town Cricket & LTC—Rayners Lane, Harrow, Middx HA2 9TY (866 8733). Courts: H4. *Secretary:* M F Lowrie, 52 Greystoke Avenue, Pinner HA5 5SL (863 1379).

Harrow Weald—49-51 College Road, Harrow Weald (427 0301). Courts: H5. *Secretary:* Mrs C Wood, 15 Bellfield Avenue, Harrow Weald (428 4956).

Harrow & Wembley Postal Districts Sports Club—Swakeleys Sports Ground, Swakeleys Drive, Ickenham. Courts: H2. *Secretary:* M J Pullinger, c/o Head Post Office, 51 College Road, Harrow (427 5121 ext 47).

Hartswood—31-33 Hartswood Road, Stamford Brook, London W12 (743 8529). Courts: G4, H2. *Secretary:* Miss S Watson, 34 Percy Road, W12 9QA (740 8070).

Harvard Park—619 London Road, Isleworth. Courts: H5. *Secretary:* Mrs H J Wiggett, 14 Clement Gardens, Hayes, Middx UB3 4AR (848 9208).

Hatch End Hard Courts—20 Clonard Way, Hatch End (428 2563). Courts: H7 (3 all weather). *Secretary:* Mrs J Kerridge, 73 Rowlands Avenue, Hatch End HA5 4BX (428 3084).

Hayes North TC—Rosedale Park, Uxbridge Road, Hayes. Courts: H1. *Secretary:* Mrs L Smith, 8 St Stephens Road, Yiewsley, Middx UB7 7RL.

Hazelwood—Ridge Avenue, London N21 (360 1384). Courts: G4, H6 (1 covered). *Secretary:* P N Harrold, 17 Sherbrook Gardens, Winchmore Hill, N21 (360 8036).

Headstone—Hillfield Close, Woodberry Avenue (off Pinner View), Harrow (427 8473). Courts: 3 red, 2 all weather. *Secretary:* Mrs J Ginger, 52 Links Way, Croxley Green, Rickmansworth, Herts (92 36431).

Highgate—Twyford Avenue, Fortis Green, East Finchley, London N2 (883 6917). Courts: G3, H3 (all weather). *Secretary:* D Liebeck, 19 Danvers Road, N8 7HH (348 0457 pri, 629 6434 bus).

Highgate Cricket & LTC—Crouch End Playing Fields, Park Road, Hornsey, London N8 (340 6534). Courts: H5. *Secretary:* S Pounds, 65 Redstone Road, N8 (340 2730).

Holland Park—1 Addison Road, London W14 (603 3928). Courts: G4, H4. *Secretary:* Miss D Wilbraham, 44 Knowsley Road, SW11 (228 5571).

Hornsey—Tivoli Road, Crouch End, London N8 (340 5546). Courts: Art G 6. *Secretary:* Mrs C Nash, 40 Creighton Avenue, Muswell Hill, N10 1NU (883 6285).

Hurlingham—Fulham, London SW6 (736 2662 tennis pavilion). Courts: G20, H20. *Secretary:* Miss J Gasser (Games Assistant), The Hurlingham Club, Ranelagh Gardens, London SW6 (736 8411 ext 47).

Ibis—Ibis Sports Ground, Duke's Meadows, Chiswick Bridge (994 3314). Courts: G12, H3. *Secretary:* M Wiseman, Dept GPST1, Prudential Assurance Co Ltd, 142 Holborn Bars, London EC1 (405 9222 ext 2167).

Imperial College LTC—Imperial College Athletic Ground, Sipson Lane, Harlington (759 9649). Courts: G6. *Secretary:* S Cain, c/o IC Union, Prince Consort Road, South Kensington, London SW7 (589 2963 bus).

KCA LTC—Woodcock Park, Kenton. Courts: H1. *Secretary:* D G Catlin, 128 Shaftesbury Avenue, Kenton, Harrow, Middx (907 0323).

Kenlyn—Croftdown Road, London NW5. Courts: H2. *Secretary:* Mrs V L Day, 38 Bramshill Gardens, London NW5 1JH (272 4579 pri, 485 3048 bus).

Kenton Cricket & LTC—Kenton Park Road, Kenton (907 7538). Courts: H6. *Secretary:* Mrs P Littlejohns, 46 Kenton Lane, Kenton, Middx (907 4164).

Kodak Recreation Society—Harrow View, Wealdstone. Courts: H9. *Secretary:* Mr Huggins, 41 Tenby Avenue, Kenton, Middx (907 7465).

Lammas & Walpole Parks LTA—Lammas Enclosure, Culmington Road, Ealing, London W5. Courts: H6. *Secretary:* J Chandler, 16 Kerrison Road, Ealing, W5 (567 0325 pri, 583 7635 bus).

Langdon Park TC—Langdon Park Sports Centre, Byron Street, E14. Courts: H6. *Secretary:* S Jobanputra, 448 Katherine Road, Forest Gate E7 8NP.

Lensbury—Lensbury Club, Broom Road, Teddington (977 8821). Courts: G5, H14. *Secretary:* Miss J R Martin, PN/O, Shell International Petroleum Co Ltd, Shell Centre, London SE1 7NA (934 5147).

Little Venice TC—Little Venice Gardens, Paddington W9. Courts: H1. *Secretary:* J Waddington, 5 Connaught, Clifton Road W9 (286 1689).

London Indoor TC—1 Alfred Road, W2. Courts: C3. *Secretary:* T W Carling, as above (286 1985 pri, 727 4641 bus).

London Transport (Met Railway) Athletic—Forty Avenue, Wembley Park (904 4126). Courts: H4. *Secretary:* D M Austin, 24 Glenalmond Road, Kenton HA3 9JY (204 1216).

Lords & Commons TC—Westminster School, Vincent Square, London SW1 (219 3000). Courts: H3. *Secretary:* J Hannam MP, House of Commons, London SW1 (219 4486).

Lowlands—Lowlands Road, Eastcote, Pinner (866 6579). Courts: H6. *Secretary:* Mrs P Salisbury, 74 Cuckoo Hill Road, Pinner, Middx.

Marks & Spencer Social Centre—*Secretary:* Miss J Faithfull, Michael House, 47 Baker Street, London W1 (935 4422).

Mayfield—Clubhouse, Kenmare Gardens, Palmers Green, N13 5DR (807 5798). Courts: H4. *Secretary:* R Ripsher, 39 The Orchard, Winchmore Hill, London N21 2DJ (360 9180).

Meadhurst—Meadhurst. (Sunbury-on-Thames 762315). Courts: H4. *Secretary:* Mrs M K Moseley, BP Research Centre, Chertsey Road, Sunbury-on-Thames TW16 7LN (762140 bus).

Mercury—138 Willifield Way, London NW11 (458 6599) behind Fellowship House. *Secretary:* G Ruben, Geraldine Cottage, Pine Grove, N20 8LD (445 5004).

Middlesex Polytechnic—Trent Park, Cockfosters, Barnet, Herts (449 9691). *Secretary:* J Watson, 28 Moorhurst Avenue, Goffs Oak, Cheshunt, Waltham Cross, Herts EN7 5LE.

Mill Hill—Sylvan Avenue, Mill Hill. Courts: H3. *Secretary:* Mrs Coulter, 25 Fairview Way, Edgware (958 8356).

Muswell Hill Methodist—North Bank Estate (behind Methodist Church), Pages Lane, Muswell Hill, London N10. Courts: H4. *Secretary:* S Brooks, 21 Lynmouth Road, Fortis Green N2 9LR (883 4181).
Muswell Hill URC LTC—Southern Road, London N2. Courts: H4. *Secretary:* Mrs M Stacy, 31 Fordington Road, London N6 (883 3131).
Myddleton—1,060 High Road, Whetstone (entrance next to 1,054) (445 6684). Courts: H3. *Secretary:* P Eisenegger, 67 Hillside Gardens, Barnet, Herts EN5 2NQ (449 6979).
National Physical Laboratory—NPL, Teddington. Courts: G5, H3. *Secretary:* Dr E A Nichol, Electrical Science Div, Queens Road, Teddington, Middx (977 3222 ext 3843).
Neeld—Graham Road, Hendon Central, London NW4 (202 9274). Courts: H3. *Secretary:* Mrs I R Jenkins, 23a Manor Road, Barnet, Herts EN5 2LE (440 9748).
Nimrod—The Ridgeway, Mill Hill NW7. *Secretary:* Dr P Field, Lab of Neurobiology, c/o National Inst Medical Res, Mill Hill, London NW7 (959 3666).
North Harrow—Cumberland Road. Courts: H3. *Secretary:* Mrs A Squire, 22 Hallam Gardens, Hatch End HA5 4PR.
North Middlesex—Park Road, Crouch End, London N8 (883 6674/883 1374). Courts: G3, H7 (2 all weather). *Secretary:* R Harvey, 56 Marlborough Road, Bowes Park, N22 4NN (448 1127, 881 4127).
Northumberland Park—Northumberland Park Sports Centre, Worcester Avenue, N17. Courts: H7. *Secretary:* J Morris, c/o The Club (520 5465 pri, 801 9964 bus).
Oakleigh Park LT & Squash Club—100 Oakleigh Road North, Whetstone, London N20 (445 6422). Courts: H10, (7 AW floodlit). *Secretary:* Miss C Earle, 13 Beech Avenue, Oakleigh Park South, N20 (445 6295).
Old Actonians Association—Sports Club, Gunnersbury Drive, London W5 (567 4556). Courts: H4 (Art Grass). *Secretary:* M Nicholls, 16 Blackthorne Court, Dormer Wells Lane, Southall, Middx (571 0713 pri, 841 4511 bus).
Old Gaytonians—South Vale, Sudbury Hill, Harrow (423 4133). Courts: H3. *Secretary:* Mrs J B Thompson, 151 Joel Street, Eastcote, Pinner, Middx HA5 2PD (868 1780).
Old Latymerians—190 Wills Crescent, Hounslow (894 2848). *Secretary:* Miss S Miller, 30 Fearnley Crescent, Oak Avenue, Hampton, Middx (953 1688 bus).
Our Lady of Muswell—Rhodes Avenue, London N22 (888 9672). Courts: H4. *Secretary:* Mrs B J Hazelwood, 4 Old Park Ridings, Grange Park, N21 (360 1230).
Paddington—Castellain Road, London W9 (286 1234). Courts: H10. *Secretary:* Mr Carter c/o Club.
Palmers Green URC—Oakfield Road, Southgate, London N14. Courts: H4. *Secretary:* Mrs L Atkinson, "Clovelly", 85 Old Park Ridings, Grange Park, London N21 2ER (360 4926).
Parkside—Vale Farm Sports Ground, Watford Road, Wembley. Courts: G3, H2. *Secretary:* D Abbott, 4 Woodhall Gate, Pinner, Middx HA5 4TL (866 9358).
Parkside (Southall)—Southall Park, Southall. Courts: H2. *Secretary:* T B Highton, 33 Church Road, Heston, Middx (577 3479).
Parkside (Southgate)—Bourneside Sports Ground, Queen Elizabeth's Drive, Southgate, London N14 (886 5404). Courts: H4. *Secretary:* S J W Milns, 2 Queen Anne's Grove, Enfield, Middlesex (360 5675).
Parsons Green—Broomhouse Lane, Fulham, London SW6 (736 1401). Courts: H5. *Secretary:* Mrs J Kirk, 20 Birbeck Road SW19 (540 3413).
Pembroke—Pembroke Square, Kensington, London W8. Courts: H1. *Secretary:* J B McVittie/Jane McVittie, 72 Scarsdale Villas, London W8 6PP (937 8926).
Pinner—Little Moss Lane, Pinner (866 8846). Courts: H6. *Secretary:* Mrs D Manchester, 12 Cecil Park, Pinner HA5 5HH (866 5719).
Polytechnic LTC—The Polytechnic Sports Ground, Cavendish Road, Chiswick W4. Courts: G10, H6. *Secretary:* A Colmer, 77 Elton Avenue, Greenford UB6 0PP (422 8306 pri, 576 7712 bus).
Polytechnic of North London LTC—Honeypot Lane, Stanmore (952 1893). Courts: G5, H4. *Secretary:* C Cope, 21 Wood End, Park Street, St Albans, Herts (0727 73066).
Queens—West Kensington (385 3421). Courts: G12, H14 (8 covered). *Secretary:* J Edwardes, The Queen's Club, West Kensington, London W14.
Ravens—Friary Road, London N12 (445 4711). Courts: H4. *Secretary:* Mrs G Salisbury, 2 Gloucester Road, New Barnet, Herts (440 5549).
Ravenscroft—Blenheim Road, Wood Street, Barnet. Courts: G2, H2. *Secretary:* Miss G East, 9 Elizabeth Close, Barnet EN5 4DP (440 1936).
Riverside—Burlington Lane, London W4 (984 0645). Courts: H4. *Secretary:* Miss J Bard, 122 Pears Road, Hounslow (572 3526).
St Columba—30/32 Carbery Avenue, Acton, W3. Courts: H4. *Secretary:* Mrs W B Nicol, 213 Deeds Grove, High Wycombe, Bucks HP12 3PD (0494 446138).
St George's Church (Headstone)—Pinner View, Harrow. Courts: G4, H3. *Secretary:* Mrs M Jackson, 33 Grasmere Gardens, Harrow Weald (427 1984).
St Mary's—Musgrave Road, Isleworth. Courts: H3. *Secretary:* R Tweddle, Flat 1, 13 Fabian Road, Fulham SW6 7TY.
Shepherd's Bush—East Acton Lane, London W3 7HB (743 1686). Courts: H5. *Secretary:* K Whellor, c/o Shepherds Bush LTC, East Acton Lane, W3 7HB.
Southgate County Old Scholars—Brackendale Sports Ground, Winchmore Hill, London N21 (886 8746). Courts: H5. *Secretary:* Mrs S A Whyman, 20 Oaklands, Winchmore Hill, London N21 3DD.
South Hampstead—Milverton Road, Brondesbury Park, London NW6 (459 2801). Courts: H5. *Secretary:* Mrs B Sargeant, 185 Chevening Road, NW6 6DT (960 1237).
Stock Exchange LTC—The Stock Exchange, London EC2. *Secretary:* P N Harrold, 17 Sherbrook Gardens, Winchmore Hill, London N21 2NX (360 8036).

Stormont LT and Squash Racquets Club—11 Lanchester Road, Highgate, London N6 (883 3106). Courts: H2. *Secretary:* Mrs P Banks, 67 Fordington Road, London N6 (883 0295).
Taywood—Taywood Sports and Social Club, Willow Tree Lane, Ruislip Road, Greenford (845 4783). Courts: H3. *Secretary:* A J Lindford, Taywood Sports & Social Club, Broadmead Road, Northolt, Middx.
Teddington—Vicarage Road, Teddington (977 3648). Courts: H5. *Secretary:* Miss J Thurlow, 145 Fairfax Road, Teddington, Middx (977 3665).
Templars—Portsdown Avenue, Golders Green, London NW11 (455 9097). Courts: H5 (5 floodlit). *Secretary:* Miss J Mills, 13 Hogarth Hill, Golders Green, London NW11 (455 8364).
Temple Fortune—122 Bridge Lane, London NW11 (455 2184). Courts: H6. *Secretary:* S Bennet, 145 Cranbourne Gardens, NW11 (455 3649).
Thistleworth—The Pavilion, Ridgeway Road North, Isleworth (560 1412). Courts: G2, H7. *Secretary:* A Darragh, 44 Somerset Waye, Heston, Hownslow TW5 9HG (570 3479).
Tithe Farm—The Pavilion, Lucas Avenue, Harrow (866 9659). Courts: H4. *Secretary:* N J Kariya, 46 Lakeview, Edgware, Middx (958 6108).
Totteridge TC—Great Bushey Drive, Totteridge Lane, London N20. Courts: H8 (7 AW, 3 floodlit). *Secretary:* D Fuchs, 11 Elton Avenue, High Barnet, Herts EN5 2EB (440 3880).
Tower Hamlets TC—St Georges Fields, Copperfield Road E1 (790 5965). Courts: H2. *Secretary:* The Secretary, Langdon Park Sports Centre, Byron Street, E14.
Trevelyan—326 Preston Road, Harrow. *Secretary:* I Jacoby, 6 West Close, Wembley Park HA9 9PJ (904 6478).
Twickenham—Lebanon Park. Courts: H5. *Secretary:* M Kerslake, 336 Nelson Road, Whitton Twickenham (898 2852).
UCS Old Boys' (Old Gowers)—University College School, Hampstead. Courts: H6. *Secretary:* K Ellis, 46 Midholm, London NW11 6LN (455 4372).
Uxbridge—Uxbridge Cricket Club, Park Road, Uxbridge. Courts: G3, H5. *Secretary:* Mrs P Childs, 17 Stowe Crescent, Ruislip (0895 51133 ext 3431).
Vagabond Club—Holwell Place, Pinner (866 9003). Courts: H2. *Secretary:* Mrs J M Thorn, 45 Lankers Drive, N Harrow (868 0069 pri, 427 0692 bus).
Vanderbilt Racquet Club—31 Sterne Street W2. Courts: C5 (Covered). *Secretary:* C J Swallow, c/o The Club.
Veterans LTC of Great Britain—*Secretary:* Group Captain P Ridsdale, 40 Grove Way, Esher, Surrey (398 4412).
Vicars Moor—Sherbrook Gardens, London N21 (360 7497). Courts: H6. *Secretary:* A J Maitland-Clark, 23 Shrubbery Gardens, Winchmore Hill, N21 2QU (360 9718).
Waterfall Sports—Pymmes Green Road, London N11 (368 5025). Courts: H4. *Secretary:* Mrs M Chipperfield, 12 Woodfield Drive, East Barnet, Herts (361 9891).
Wayfarers—Swakeleys Drive, Ickenham. Courts: H5. *Secretary:* Mrs L Hall, 11 The Avenue, Ickenham UB10 8NR (71 33979).
Weld LTC—The Walker Cricket Ground,, Waterfall Road, London N14. Courts: AW4. *Secretary:* Mrs A C Peel, 5 Winchmore Villas, Winchmore Hill Road, N14 1QB (822 1070).
Wembley Sports Association—Vale Farm, Sudbury, Wembley (904 2644). Courts: G3, H3. *Secretary:* Mrs K J Roberts, 11 Stanley Park Drive, Wembley (902 5272).
Wembley Hill LT & Social—rear 222 Harrow Road and 35 Vivian Avenue, Wembley Hill. Courts: H2. *Secretary:* Mrs B Temblett, 499 Watford Way, Mill Hill, NW7.
Wembley & Sudbury LT & Squash Club—Sylvester Road, Wembley (902 2942). Courts: H5 (2 floodlit). *Secretary:* H King, 20b Elms Lane, Wembly, Middx.
West End (Pinner) Ltd—Cuckoo Hill Road, Pinner (866 9600). Courts: H6. *Secretary:* Miss J Finnemore, 15 Eastfields, Eastcote, Pinner HA5 2SR (866 4223).
West Heath—Croftway, Ferncroft Avenue, London NW3 (435 7707). Courts: G3, H2. *Secretary:* Miss M Stevens, 27 St Peter's Way, Monpelier Road, W5 2QR (991 1921).
West Middlesex LT & Croquet—Drayton Bridge Road, West Ealing, London W13 (998 3297). Courts: G8, H3. *Secretary:* Mrs G Miller, 88 Argyl Road, Ealing, W5 (998 5354).
Whitton—Kneller Gardens, Isleworth. Courts: H4. *Secretary:* G S Stubbs, 23 Norman Avenue, St Margaret, Twickenham (892 0700).
Winchmore Hill—The Paulin Ground, Fords Ground, London N21 (360 1271). Courts: G5, H4. *Secretary:* Mrs J Pryke, 5 Windsor Road N13 (886 2393).
Woodlands—Bournside Sports Ground, The Bourne, Southgate, London N14 (886 3344). Courts: H5. *Secretary:* P Shanks, 26 Sterling Road, Enfield EN2 0LN (367 2712).
Woodside Park Club (Tennis Section)—Southover, Woodside Park, London N12 (445 3510). Courts: H4. *Secretary:* P McNamara, 7 Singleton Scarp, Woodside Park, N12 (446 0629).
Wood Vale—11/13 Wood Vale, Muswell Hill, London N10 (883 1947). Courts: H5 (2 all weather). *Secretary:* Mrs E M E Greer, 19 Allison Road, N8 (340 8126).
Wycombe House Cricket & Tennis Club—Wood Lane, Osterley (560 8124). Courts: H4. *Secretary:* Mrs M Coffin, 368 Jersey Road, Isleworth (560 3825).

OTHER AFFILIATED ORGANISATIONS (1)

Stella Artois International Tournament—Queens Club.

AFFILIATED SCHOOLS (73)

Boys
Belmont — Mill Hill, NW7. **City of London** — EC4. ***Harrow** — Harrow. **Henry Compton** — SW6.

***Highgate** — N6. **Holloway** — N7. ***Latymer Upper** — W6. ***Mill Hill** — NW7. **Queen Elizabeth Grammar** — Barnet. **St Benedicts** — W5. ***University College** — NW3. ***Westminster** — SW1. **William Ellis** — NW5.

Also affiliated to Public Schools LTA.

Girls
Brentford — Brentford. **Channing House** — N6. **City of London** — EC2. **Convent of the Sacred Heart** — W6. **Copthall County Grammar** — NW7. **Ellen Wilkinson High** — W3. **Francis Holland** — W1. **Francis Holland** — SW1. **Glendowner Prep** — SW7. **Glendower Senior** — SW7. **Godolphin & Latymer** — W6. **Harvington** — W5. **Hasmonean Grammar** — NW7. **Heathfield** — Harrow. **Henrietta Barnet** — NW11. **Highbury Hill High** — N5. **Ladbroke** — W10. **La Sainte Union Convent** — NW5. **Lady Eleanor Hollies** — Hampton. **Lady Margaret** — SW6. **North London Collegiate** — Edgware. **Northwood College** — Northwood. **Notting Hill & Ealing High** — W13. **Parliament Hill** — NW5. **Peterborough & St Margaret's High** — Harrow. **Queen's College** — W1. **Queen Elizabeth Grammar** — Barnet. **Queen's Gate** — SW7. **Southbourne** — Ruislip. **South Hampstead High** — NW3. **St Anne's Convent** — W5. **St Helen's** — Northwood. **St Michael's Convent Grammar** — N12. **St Paul's** — W6. **Starcross** — N1. **The Green School** — Isleworth. **The Mount** — NW7. **Waldegrave School** — Twickenham TW2 5LH.

Mixed
Acland Burghley — NW5. **Cardinal Wiseman** — Greenford. **Chiswick Comprehensive** — W4. **Drayton Manor Grammar** — W7. **Faraday Sec Comp** — Acton W3. **Featherstone High** — Southall. **Greenford High** — Greenford. **Harrow Weald Jnr College** — Harrow Weald. **Hayes County Grammar** — Hayes. **Lampton** — Hounslow. **Latymer** — N9. **Moat Mount Bilateral** — NW7. **Orange Hill Senior** — Edgware. **Orange Hill Jnr** — Edgware. **Preston Manor High** — Wembley Park. **Rectory Comprehensive** — Hampton. **Richmond/Thames College** — Twickenham. **St Mary's CE** — NW4. **The International School of London** — NW1. **Twyford High** — W3. **Villiers High** — Southall. **Vyners School** — Ickenham.

All correspondence to School Clubs should be addressed to the Master or Mistress in charge of Lawn Tennis.

NORFOLK LAWN TENNIS ASSOCIATION

Hon Secretary—**Mrs P M Butcher,** 200 Unthank Road, Norwich (53896).
Hon Treasurer—**A G G Payne,** 22 St Walstan's Close, Costessey, Norwich (Norwich 743359).
Hon Men's Match Secretary—**J P. Cameron,** The Old Vicarage, East Walton, King's Lynn, (Narborough 337407, weekdays 01-534 2483).
Hon Ladies' Match Secretary—**Mrs H Kerrison,** The White House, Haddiscoe, Norwich (Aldeby 246).
Hon Junior Match Secretary—**Mrs B Blincoe,** Lime Kiln Barn, Stoke Holy Cross, Norwich (Framingham Earl 3603).
Hon Veterans Match Secretary—**Mr R J Newman,** Koon-a-Warra, Coltishall Lane, Horsham St Faiths, Norwich (897991).
Representative on the Council—**J H Harris JP.**

AFFILIATED CLUBS (42)

Acle TC—Courts: H3. *Secretary:* Lynne Madge, 10 Rosetta Road, Spixworth, Norwich (890252(.
Aylsham—Recreation Ground, Aylsham. Courts: G2, H3. *Secretary:* G M R Grimes, 7 Pound Lane, Aylsham (733027).
Barclays Bank Sports—*Secretary:* R. Littlewood, 22 Amderley Drive, Eaton, Norwich.
Blenheim—The Avenues, Norwich. Courts: G2. *Secretary:* M R Kett, 186 Spixworth Road, Old Catton, Norwich (26978 bus, 43708 pri).
Blofield—Margaret Harker Hall, Blofield. Courts: G4, H1. *Secretary:* Mrs S Clarke, Red Gables, Blofield, Norwich (712175).
British Sugar Corporation—Poplar Avenue, Saddlebow, Kings Lynn. Courts: G2, H2. *Secretary:* D Simpson BSc, 17 Spenser Road, Gaywood, King's Lynn (673579).
Bungay TC—Courts: H2. *Secretary:* Mrs S McClean, 14 Ditchingham Way, Bungay (Bungay 74848).
Carrow—Lakenham Sports Centre, Norwich. Courts: G3, H3. *Secretary:* Miss M Smith, 2 Woodside Court, Bracondale, Norwich (660166 bus, 626789 pri).
Cringleford—Playingfields, Oakfields Road, Cringleford. Courts: G2, H2. *Secretary:* Mrs G L Coiley, Pond Farm, Cringleford, Norwich (54895).
Cromer—Norwich Road, Cromer. Courts: G12, H2. *Secretary:* Mrs A North-Graves, Cromer Lawn Tennis & Squash Association, Norwich Road, Cromer (Cromer 513741).
Dereham—Cherry Drive, Dereham. Courts: H2. *Secretary:* Mrs C J Powles, 102 Norwich Road, Dereham (5906).
Diss—Walcott Road, Diss. Courts: G3. H3. *Secretary:* Mrs S Arnold, 1 Riverside, Denmarit Bridge, Diss (Diss 4452).
Earlham—Courts: G3. Secretary: Mrs S Bell, 62 College Road, Norwich (53664).
East Anglia—Lime Tree Road, Norwich. Courts: G4, H7. *Secretary:* Mrs I M Wain-Heapy, 45 Keswick Road, Cringleford, Norwich NR4 6UG (54463).
East Harling—Courts: G3. *Secretary:* Mrs C Hustler, Town Farm, East Harling, Norwich (718263).
Gorleston LTC—Courts: H4. *Secretary:* Mrs H Kerrison, The White House, Haddiscoe, Norwich (Aldeby 246).
Gothic—Heartsease Lane, Norwich. Courts: G3. *Secretary:* W G Harvey, 22 Stanmore Road,

Thorpe St Andrew, Norwich (34236 pri, 28333 ext 267 bus).
Harleston—The Playingfields, Harleston. Courts: H2, G3. *Secretary:* Mr C Hudson, 9 Shortford Road, Harleston (853284).
Heigham—The Avenues, Norwich. *Secretary:* A Payne, 22 St Walstan's Close, Costessey, Norwich (Norwich 743359).
Mann Egerton—Courts: G2. *Secretary:* T J Breed, 598 Dereham Road, Norwich (743248).
Norfolk County Council—Courts: H4. *Secretary:* Mrs G F Walpole, 1 Gilbert Close, Alpington, Norwich (4870).
North Elmham—East Dereham. *Secretary:* Mrs G Digby, 41 Hall Road, East Dereham.
North Walsham—Tungate Farm, N Walsham. Courts: H3. *Secretary:* Mrs B D Rossie, Tungate Farm, North Walsham (404966/403303).
Norwich City College—Ipswich Road, Norwich. Courts: H2. *Secretary:* Mr B Ryan, PE Unit, Norwich City College, Ipswich Road, Norwich (660011 ext 310).
Norwich Union—Pinebanks, Thorpe, Norwich. Courts: G4. *Secretary:* G C Hardman, 50 Proctor Road, Sprowston, Norwich (410179 pri, 22200 bus).
Oasis TC—Plumstead Road, East, Thorpe. Courts: H2. *Secretary:* Mrs L K Cooper, 34 Prince Andrew's Road, Hellesdon (411101).
Old Catton—Church Street, Old Catton, Norwich. Courts: H2. *Secretary:* Mrs J Newman, 50 Oak Lane, Old Catton, Norwich (Norwich 46493).
Ravine—Marine Parade, Gorleston. Courts: H2. *Secretary:* 14 Wadham Road, Gorleston (604742).
Reepham—Reepham Playingfields, Reepham, Norwich. Courts: H2. *Secretary:* P J Aitchinson, 43 Ollands Road, Reepham, Norwich (870782).
Scarning—East Dereham, Norfolk. Courts: H2. *Secretary:* Mrs S Eagle, Podmore Farm, Scarning, Norfolk (Wendling 283).
Sedgwick—Victoria House, Queens Road, Norwich. Courts: G3. *Secretary:* B B Davis, Sedgwick Place, Queens Road, Norwich (60202 ext 5314 bus).
Sprowston—Recreation Ground Road, Sprowston. Courts: H2. *Secretary:* Mrs S Murrell, 217 Thunder Lane, Thorpe, Norwich (32070).
Stanley—Woodrow Pilling Park, Thorpe. Courts: G. *Secretary:* D A Ellis, 12 Kedleston Drive, Cringleford, Norwich (52663 pri, 29628 bus).
Stanmore—Stanmore Road, Thorpe St Andrew, Norwich. Courts: H2. *Secretary:* W G Harvey, 22 Stanmore Road, Thorpe St Andrew, Norwich (34236 pri, 28333 bus).
Taverham—Sandy Lane, Taverham. Courts: H2. *Secretary:* Mrs D Perry, 10 Herrick Road, Taveham, Norwich (867033).
Terrington St Clement—Courts: H2. *Secretary:* Mrs J M Price, 35 Lynn Road, Terrington St Clement, King's Lynn, Norfolk (828605).
Thetford—Courts: H2. *Secretary:* Mrs B Smith, 4 Byron Walk, Thetford, Norfolk (63231).
University of East Anglia—Earlham Park, Norwich. Courts: H12. *Secretary:* Mr A Baxter, Sports Centre, UEA, Norwich (56161 ext 2507).
Watton—Courts: H4. *Secretary:* Mrs B Leech, Little Hockham Hall, Great Hockham, Thetford, Norfolk (Great Hookham 252).
West Norfolk Kings Lynn. Courts: H1, G4. —*Secretary:* Miss N Finnigan, 15 Ryelands Road, Wootton, Kings Lynn.
Wymondham—Browick Road, Wymondham. Courts: H3. *Secretary:* Mr R Greengrass, 15 Sycamore Avenue, Wymondham NR18 0HE (Wymondham 605240).

OTHER AFFILIATED ORGANISATIONS (5)

Norfolk Tennis Coaches Association—*Secretary:* Mrs P Smith, 18 Mill Gardens, Horsfold, Norwich (Norwich 897377).
Norwich Winter Tennis Association—*Secretary:* Mrs S Arnold, 1 Riverside, Denmarit Bridge, Diss (Diss 4452).

AFFILIATED SCHOOLS (74)

Boys

Bracondale School — Norwich. **Burebank College** — Aylsham. **Duncan Hall School** — Scratby, Great Yarmouth. **Greshams School** — Holt. **Langley School** — Norwich. **Norwich School** — Norwich. **Paston School** — North Walsham. **Town Close School** — Norwich.

Girls

All Hallows School — Ditchingham. **Norwich High School** — Norwich. **Notre Dame High School** — Norwich. **North Walsham C Girls** — Market Place, North Walsham. **Old Hall School** — Hethersett, Norwich. **Runton Hill School** — West Runton, Cromer. **Thorpe House School** — Norwich. **West Norfolk and King's Lynn Girls' High School** — King's Lynn.

Mixed

Acle Secondary School — Acle. **Attleborough Secondary School** — Attleborough. **Aylsham Secondary School** — Aylsham. **Blyth-Jex School** — Norwich. **Bowthorpe School** — Norwich. **Caister Secondary School** — Great Yarmouth. **Claydon C Secondary** — Gorleston. **Cliffe Park C Secondary** — Gorleston. **Costessey Secondary School** — Norwich. **Cromer Secondary School** — Cromer. **Dereham Neatherd High** — Norwich Road, Dereham. **Dereham Church Middle School** — Dereham. **Dereham Northgate High** — Cemetery Road, Dereham. **Diss County High** — Walcot Road, Diss. **Downham Market Grammar School** — Downham Market. **Earlham C Comp** — Earlham Road, Norwich. **Eaton CNS Comp** — Eaton Road, Norwich. **Fakenham High** — Field Lane, Fakenham. **Framingham Earl Secondary School** — Norwich. **Gaywood Park C High** — Queensway Road, Kings Lynn. **Gorleston St Edmunds VA** — Gorleston. **Gorleston VC High** — Lynn Grove. **Great Yarmouth Grammar School** — Great Yarmouth. **Harleston Archbishop Sawcroft CE VA High** — Harleston. **Hearthsease C Comp** — Marryat Road, Norwich. **Hellesdon High** — Middletons Lane, Hellesdon. **Hethersett C High** — Hethersett. **Hewett Comp** — Cecil Road, Norwich.

Hoveton Broadlands C High — Hoveton. **Hunstanton Smithdon** — Hunstanton. **King Edward C High** — Gaywood Road, King's Lynn. **Litcham C High** — Litcham. **Loddon The Hobart High** — Loddon. **Long Stratton C High** — Long Stratton. **Martham Flegg C High** — Martham. **Melton Constable, The Astley School** — Briston, Melton Constable. **Methwold C High** — Methwold. **North Walsham C High** — Spenser Avenue, North Walsham. **Old Buckenham C High** — Old Buckenham. **Oriel Grammar** — Gorleston. **Reepham C High** — Reepham. **Sheringham C High** — Holt Road, Sheringham. **Springwood C High** — Queensway, King's Lynn. **Sprowston C High** — Cannerby Lane, Sprowston. **Stalham C High** — Stalham. **Swaffhan Hamonds High** — Swaffham. **St Clements High** — Terrington St Clement. **Taverham C High** — Taverham. **Thetford Charles Burrell School. Thetford, Lady Musker School. Thorpe St Andrew C High** — Thorpe, Norwich. **Upwell CS** — Upwell. **Watton, Wayland High** — Merton Road, Watton. **West Walton Marshland High** — West Walton, King's Lynn. **Wells Alderman Peel High** — Wells-next-the-Sea. **Wymondham C High** — Folly Lane, Wymondham. **Wymondham College** — Morley, Wymondham. **Yarmouth, Alderman Leach CS** — Great Yarmouth.

All correspondence to School Clubs should be addressed to the Master or Mistress in charge of lawn tennis.

School Tournament Organiser/Secretary: Miss P Fuller, 35 Yesmere, Mulbarton, Norwich, Norfolk (Mulbarton 70442).

NORTHAMPTONSHIRE LAWN TENNIS ASSOCIATION

Hon Secretary—**Mrs S J Papé,** Ravensden Farm, Bedford Road, Rushden NN10 0SQ (0933 56221).
Hon Treasurer—**J A Cooper FCA,** Croft House, Vyse Road, Boughton, Northampton NN2 8RR (0604 842393).
Hon Men's Match Secretary—**Mr R Fowler,** Home Farm, Ravensthorpe, Northampton (0604 770415).
Hon Ladies' Match Secretary—**Mrs M Taylor,** Langdene, Overstone Lane, Overstone, Northampton NN6 6AA (43814).
Hon Juniors Secretary—**Mrs M Young,** Lauderdale, Sandy Lane, Church Brampton, Northampton NN6 8AX (Northampton 844029).
Representative on the Council—**Mrs S J Papé.**

AFFILIATED CLUBS (42)

Abington—Park Avenue South. Courts: G3. *Secretary:* Mrs M McFarlane, 8 Park Avenue South, Northampton (35707).
Anglia Building Society—Rushmere Road, Northampton. Courts: H3. *Secretary:* P Salt, c/o Anglia BS, Moulton Park, Northampton NN3 1NL (495353).
Brackley—Buckingham Road, Brackley. Courts: H4. *Secretary:* Mrs C M Skermer, 'Kenton,' Marston St Lawrence, Banbury (Banbury 710597).
British Timken Social & Athletic—British Timken, Dunton. Courts: H3. *Secretary:* S Marsh,Sports Office, British Timken, Duston, Northampton (52311 ext 128).
Burton Latimer—Regent Road, Burton Latimer. Courts: H2. *Secretary:* Miss J Bryan, 46 Park Road, Burton, Latimer (Burton Latimer 3881).
Byfield—The Green, Byfield. Courts: H2. *Secretary:* Mrs M C Bull, Kings Farthing, 28 Banbury Lane, Byfield (Byfield 60845).
Corby Sports & Leisure Club—Occupation Road, Corby. Courts: H6. *Secretary:* P Montgomery, 7 The Ridings, Desborough (Kettering 761674).
Dallington—Dallington. Courts: A6 (2 floodlit). *Secretary:* P H Bateman, 17 Glassthorpe Lane, Harpole (831601).
Daventry—Stefen Hill, London Road, Daventry. Courts: H3. *Secretary:* Mrs J Edge, 1 Daventry Road, Norton, Daventry (72445).
Deanshanger—Little London, Deanshanger. Courts: H2. *Secretary:* Mrs D Harvey, 12 Calverton Road, Stony Stratford (Milton Keynes 563177).
Desborough—Desborough Leisure Centre, The Hawthorns, Desborough. Courts: G2, H2. *Secretary:* Mr G Crowther, 58 Queen Street, Desborough (Kettering 760443).
Earls Barton—The Piece, Earls Barton. Courts: H3. *Secretary:* Mrs M Runnicles, 4 Lytham Court, Wellingborough (677193).
Express Lifts Sports—Weedon Road, St James's, Northampton. Courts: H3. *Secretary:* Tennis Section, Express Lifts, Mr C Dunmore, 4 Hunsbury Green, Hunsbury Hill, Northampton (0604 64974).
Ferrers & Rushden—Sports Ground, Vine Hill Drive, Higham Ferrers. Courts: H4. *Secretary:* D Stevenson, 22 Philip Way, Higham Ferrers (Rushden 311383).
Geddington Lawn Tennis Club—Village Hall, Queen Street, Geddington. Courts: H2. *Secretary:* G Hopkins, Ingarsby, 19 New Road, Geddington, Nr Kettering (Great Oakley 742324).
Guilsborough Hall—Church Mount, Guilsborough. Courts: H1. *Secretary:* Mr A Simkins, 14 Church Mount, Guilsborough, Northampton NN6 8QA (Northampton 740421).
Harpole—Larkhall Lane, Harpole. Courts: H3. *Secretary:* Mr P Hartgrove, 62 Carrs Way Harpole, Northants (0604 830804).
Ise Valley LTC—Ise Lodge Estate, Kettering. Courts: H3. *Secretary:* Mr K Singh, 151 Stamford Road, Kettering, Northants (0536 516903).
Islip LTC—High Street, Islip. Courts: G2. *Secretary:* Mr R Wright, 33 Midland Road, Thrapston, Northants (9942 2697).
Kettering North Lodge—North Park, Bath Road, Kettering. Courts: H2. *Secretary:* Ms Janet Page, 15 Shakespeare Road, Kettering NN16 9QZ (Kettering 512239).

Kettering Park—Wickstead Park, Kettering. Courts: H2. *Secretary:* Mrs P M Lee, 36 Ise Road, Kettering (513105).
Kettering Post Office LTC—George Street, Kettering. Courts: H2. *Secretary:* B D Ashby, 25 Windermere Road, Kettering (82749).
Kilsby LTC—Kilsby Village Hall, Rugby Road, Kilsby, nr Rugby. Courts: H2. *Secretary:* Mrs L Loader, White House, Chapel Street, Kilsby, Rugby, Warwickshire.
Kingsthorpe (Imperial)—Moulton Park Upper School, Boughton Green Road, Northampton. Courts: H3. *Secretary:* R N Alibone, 8 Partridge Close, Kingsthorpe, Northampton (Northampton 845328).
Kingsthorpe Middle School Tennis Club—Kingsthorpe Middle School, Welford Road, Northampton. Courts: H5. *Secretary:* Mrs M E Duley, 153 Sherwood Avenue, Spring Park, Northampton NN2 8TA (844580).
Middleton Cheney—Playing Fields, Main Road, Middleton Cheney. Courts: H2. *Secretary:* Miss B Carrick, 23 Church Lane, Middleton Cheney (Banbury 710588).
Northampton LTC—Cherry Orchard School, Wellingborough Road, Weston Favell, Northampton (407571). Courts: H6 (2 floodlit). *Secretary:* Mr G Carson, 11 Manor Road, Hanging Houghton (Northampton 880861).
Northampton County—Church Way, Weston Favell, Northampton. Courts: H8. *Secretary:* Mr T R Linnell, 124 Park Avenue North, Northampton (714608).
Northampton Mascot—Berrywood Road, Duston, Northampton. Courts: H6. *Secretary:* Mr B Wooding, 74 Broadmead Avenue, Northampton (0604 404669).
Northants Electricity—Wellingborough Road, Weston Favell, Northampton. Courts: H3. *Secretary:* Miss D Beesley, 63 Sywell Road, Overstone, Northampton NN6 0AE.
Old Northamptonians—Billing Road. Courts: G3. *Secretary:* G J Billingham, 119 Booth Lane South, Northampton NN3 3EY (Northampton 406917).
Overstone—Overstone Solarium, Overstone, Northampton (Northampton 47709). Courts: H3. *Secretary:* J Blowers, 33 St Peters Way, Cogenhoe, Northants (0604 891549).
Old Grammarians Tennis Club—Unit 39, Industrial Estate, Finedon Road, Wellingborough. *Secretary:* H Garrod, 2 Whytewell Road, Wellingborough (224525).
St Andrews Hospital—Billing Road, Northampton. Courts: H2. *Secretary:* E Condon, 25 Maclean Close, Abington Vale, Northampton (37502).
Skew Bridge Country Club—Northampton Road, Rushden, Northants (Rushden 53808). Courts: H2 (floodlit). *Secretary:* Mrs A Haskins, Beulah Cottage, 57 East Street, Stanwick , Wellingborough (Wellingborough 622911).
Spinney Tennis Club—Northampton Road, Recreation Ground, Kettering. Courts: H2. *Secretary:* Mr T Chapman, 20 Slade Crescent, Kettering, Northants (Kettering 520530).
Towcestrians LTC—Greens Norton Road, Towcester. Courts: G2, H2. *Secretary:* Mrs J Sawbridge, The Homestead, Watling Street, Paulerspury, Towcester (032 733 213).
United—Mendip Road, Northampton. Courts: G2, H3 (2 floodlit). *Secretary:* C A Yuill, 26 Beechwood Drive, Westone, Northampton (404311).
Welford—Welford. Courts: H2. *Secretary:* Mrs P Bircher, The Vicarage, Northampton Road, Welford, Northants (Welford 676).
Wellingborough—Hatton Avenue, Wellingborough. Courts: H3. *Secretary:* Miss P Kemp, 16 The Headlands, Wellingborough.

AFFILIATED SCHOOLS (47)

Boys
Northampton School for Boys — Northampton.
Pope John School — Tower Hill Road, Corby.

Girls
Chichele School — Spencer Road, Rushden.
Northampton School for Girls — Northampton. **Our Lady School** — Occupation Road, Corby.
Southfield School for Girls — Kettering.

Mixed
Abington Vale Middle School — Bridgewater Drive, Northampton. **Beanfield School** — Corby. **Blackthorn Middle School** — Northampton. **Boothville Middle School** — Northampton. **Campion School** — Bugbrooke, Northampton. **Cherdent School** — Middleton Cheney. **Cherry Orchard Middle School** — Northampton. **Daventry School** — Daventry. **Daventry Grange School** — Daventry, Northampton. **Daventry Southbrook Comprehensive** — Daventry, Northampton. **King John School** — Thrapston, nr Kettering. **Kingsbrook School** — Deanshanger. **Kingsley Park Middle School** — Northampton. **Kingsthorpe Middle School** — Northampton. **Kingswood School** — Corby. **Latimer School** — Burton Latimer, nr Kettering. **John Lea School** — Wellingborough. **Lings Upper School** — Northampton. **Lodge Park Comprehensive** — Corby. **Magdalen College** — Brackley. **Millway Middle School** — Duston, Northampton. **Montagu School** — Kettering. **Montsaye School** — Rothwell, nr Kettering. **Moulton Secondary School** — Moulton, Northampton. **Oundle Middle School** — Oundle, nr Peterborough, Cambs. **Prince William School** — Oundle, nr Peterborough, Cambs. **Raunds Manor School** — Raunds, Wellingborough. **Roade School** — Roade. **St Georges Middle School** — Northampton. **Sir Chris Hatton School** — Wellingborough. **Sponne School** — Towcester. **The Ferrers School** — Queens Way, Higham Ferrers, Rushden. **Thomas Becket RC Upper School** — Northampton. **Weavers School** — Wellingborough. **Weston Favell Upper School** — Booth Lane, Weston Favell, Northampton. **Wollaston School** — Wollaston.

INDEPENDENT SCHOOLS

Girls
Northampton High School — Northampton. **St Peters School** — Kettering.

Mixed
Quinton House School — Upton Hall, Upton, Northampton. **Wellingborough School** — Wellingborough.

All correspondence to School Clubs should be addressed to the Master or Mistress in charge of lawn tennis.

NORTHUMBERLAND LAWN TENNIS ASSOCIATION

Hon Secretary—**J M W Grainger,** 55 Linden Way, Darras Hall, Newcastle-upon-Tyne NE20 9JF (0661 23996).
Hon Treasurer—**P Mickler,** 13 Wilson Gardens, Gosforth, Newcastle-upon-Tyne.
Hon Men's Match Secretary—**Robin Robinson,** Eagle Star Group, Eagle Star House, 2-8 Fenkle Street, Newcastle-upon-Tyne (612421).
Hon Ladies' Match Secretary—**Miss A Appleby,** 4 Grove House, Moor Road North, Gosforth, Newcastle-upon-Tyne (091 285 8140).
Junior Match Secretary—**G F Brady,** 9 Launceston Close, Kingston Park, Newcastle Upon Tyne (091 286 6068).
Representative on the Council—**D L McAdam.**

AFFILIATED CLUBS (28)

Alnwick Tennis Club—Duchess School, Alnwick. Courts: H8. *Secretary:* Mrs J Short, 3 Low Row, Stamford, Alnwick.
Amble Tennis Club—Courts: H4. *Secretary:* Mr M J Lawrence, 61a High Street, Amble.
Ashington Welfare—Welfare Recreation Ground, Ellington Road, Ashington. Courts: G8, H3. *Secretary:* Mr C Allington, 45 Coronation Terrace, Ashington.
Bath Terrace—Bath Terrace, Blyth. Courts: H2. *Secretary:* Mr J Brown, 62 Thompson Street, Blyth.
Benwell Hill—Denton Bank, West Road, Newcastle 5. Courts: H4. *Secretary:* J R Armstrong, 25 Bracknell Gardens, West Denton, Newcastle-upon-Tyne 5.
Beverley Park—Beverley Park, Monkseaton, Whitley Bay. Courts: H4. *Secretary:* Mrs P Blackah, 9 Ashfield Grove, Whitley Bay, Tyne & Wear.
Bohemian TC—Courts: H3. *Secretary:* Mrs J Long, 48 South Bend, Brunton Park, Gosforth, Newcastle-upon-Tyne.
Collingwood—Priors Park, Tynemouth. Courts: H3. *Secretary:* A S Carmichael, 65 Millview Drive, Tynemouth, Tyne & Wear.
Cullercoats—Beverley Gardens, Cullercoats. Courts: H3. *Secretary:* Mrs J Arkley, 62 Farringdon Road, Cullercoats, Northumberland.
Department of Health and Social Security—Old Whitley Road, Longbenton, Newcastle-upon-Tyne 12. Courts: H4. *Secretary:* Mr J Ingram, 17 Worthing Close, Redesdale Park, Wallsend, Tyne & Wear.
Forest Hall LTC—adjoining Springfield Institute, Forest Hall, Newcastle-upon-Tyne 12. Courts: H3. *Secretary:* Mr J M Storey, 26 Moor Road North, Gosforth, Newcastle-upon-Tyne.
Gosforth—West Avenue, Gosforth, Newcastle-upon-Tyne 3. Courts: H5. *Secretary:* Mr G Snowdon, 21 Beechcroft Avenue, Kenton Park, Newcastle-upon-Tyne.
Gosforth Garden Village—Rosewood Avenue, Gosforth. Courts: H2. *Secretary:* Mrs S Hall, 7 Lodge Close, Hamsterly Mill, Rowlands Gill, Co Durham.
Jesmond—Osborne Road, Newcastle-upon-Tyne 2. Courts: G3, H2. *Secretary:* Mrs J Allan, 32 Wyncote Court, Newcastle-upon-Tyne 7.
Morpeth Cricket (Tennis Section)—Stobhill, Morpeth. Courts: H4. *Secretary:* Mr. R Coates, 4 Wansdyke, Lancaster Park, Morpeth, Northumberland.
Newcastle Maccabi—Courts: H3. *Secretary:* A H Ingram, 1 Kingsley Avenue, Melton Park, Newcastle 3.
Newcastle Polytechnic TC—Bullocksland Sports Grounds, Kerton Bank Foot. Courts: H6.
North Eastern Electricity Recreation (Tennis Section)—Kings Road, Wallensend. Courts: G3, H6. *Secretary:* Mr R Burnett, 9 Forster Avenue, South Shields, Tyne & Wear.
Northumberland Lawn Tennis and Squash Rackets Club—County Tennis Ground, Osborne Road, Newcastle-upon-Tyne. Courts: G11, H12 (1 indoor). *Secretary:* c/o Mr I Wood, County Tennis Ground, Osborne Road, Jesmond, Newcastle-upon-Tyne.
Ponteland TC—Memorial Hall, Darras Road, Ponteland, Newcastle-upon-Tyne. Courts: H3. *Secretary:* Mrs L Ellis, 41 Runnymede Road, Ponteland.
Riding Mill TC—Millfield Road, Riding Mill. Courts: H3. *Secretary:* Mrs P Forster, 'Westwood', March Burn Lane, Riding Mill.
South Northumberland—Roseworth Terrace, Gosforth, Newcastle 3. Courts: G11, H4. *Secretary:* Mr L Wilde, 8 Dawlish Gardens, Low Fell, Gateshead.
Stocksfield—Guessburn, Stocksfield. Courts: H3. *Secretary:* Miss F E Chappell, 'Broomsticks', Meadowfield Park South, Stocksfield.
Tynedale—Priors Flat, Hexham. Courts: G6, H3. *Secretary:* Mrs D E Sowerby, 14 Cresent Avenue, Hexham.
University of Newcastle Medical Men's LTC—Medical School Sports Ground, Heaton Road, Newcastle 6. Courts: H5. *Secretary:* The Tennis Secretary, Medical School, University of Newcastle, Newcastle-upon-Tyne 1 (Newcastle 328511 ext 3035).
Wylam—Elmbank Road, South Wylam. Courts: H3. *Secretary:* Mrs M Mitcham, 'Meadowfield', Wylam, Wood Road, Wylam.

OTHER AFFILIATED ORGANISATIONS (6)

Northumberland Association of Youth Clubs—*Secretary:* J Clavering, Fawdon Youth Club and Social Centre, Fawdon Park Road, Newcastle-upon-Tyne NE3 2PJ.
Northumberland Lawn Tennis Coaching Association —*County Organiser:* Judith Whitfield, 61 Newminster Road, Fenham, Newcastle-upon-Tyne NE4 9LL.
Esab Northumberland Open Tournament—*Secretary:* A S Carmichael, 65 Millview Drive, Tynemouth NE30 2QD.
Northumberland Open Junior Tournament—*Secretary:* Mr T Lang, 4 Ladyrigg, Darras Hall, Newcastle-upon-Tyne.
Northumberland and Durham Tennis League—*Secretary:* K E Whitfield, 61 Newminster Road, Fenham, Newcastle-upon-Tyne NE4 9LL.
South Northumberland Open Tennis Tournament—*Secretary:* Mr M Clark, 35 Lonsdale Court, West Lesmond Avenue, Lesmond, Newcastle NE2 3HF.
Newcastle Park Tennis Association—*Chairman:* Mr Bruce Lawson, 7 Saville Place, Newcastle-upon-Tyne.

AFFILIATED SCHOOLS (22)

Boys
Dame Allan's Boys' School — Newcastle 4. **Grammar School of King Edward VI** — Morpeth. **Royal Grammar School** — Newcastle 2. **King's School** — Tynemouth.

Girls
Central Newcastle High School — Newcastle 2. **Newcastle Upon Tyne Church High School** — Newcastle 2. **Dame Allan's Girls' School** — Newcastle 4. **La Sagesse Convent High School** — Newcastle 2. **Duchess School** — Alnwick. **Westfield School** — Newcastle 3. **Sacred Heart Comprehensive School** — Newcastle.

Mixed
Astley High School — Seaton, Delaval. **Bedlington Grammar School. Blyth Grammar School** — Blyth. **Gosforth County High School** — Gosforth. **Queen Elizabeth School** — Hexham. **Whitley Bay High School** — Whitley Bay. **Walbottle School** — Newcastle 5. **Preston High School** — North Shields. **Ponteland High School** — Ponteland. **Benfield School** — Newcastle 6.

All correspondence to School Clubs should be addressed to the Master or Mistress in charge of lawn tennis.

NOTTINGHAMSHIRE LAWN TENNIS ASSOCIATION

Hon Secretary—**I C McCulloch TD,** Glen Fruin, Brickyard Lane, Farnsfield, Newark (Mansfield 882443 pri, Nottingham 470032 bus).
Hon Treasurer—**P R Coope,** 9 Clarendon Street, Nottingham (417408 bus).
Hon Men's Match Secretary—**J S Campbell,** 5 Alford Grove, Beeston, Nottingham (253680).
Hon Ladies' Match Secretary—**Miss S A Cook,** 56 Windsor Road, Mansfield, Notts (0623 645497 pri).
Hon Junior Secretary—**Mrs A Spalding,** 32 Redwood Avenue, Wollaton, Nottingham (284553).
County Ground—Tattershall Drive, The Park, Nottingham (473702).
Representative on the Council—**I C McCulloch.**

AFFILIATED CLUBS (41)

Attenborough—Attenborough Village, beyond level crossing. Courts: G1, H3. *Secretary:* Mrs S R Baldock, 1a Thorneywood Road, Long Eaton (Long Eaton 69275).
Bingham—Station Road, Bingham. Courts: G2, H2. *Secretary:* Mr D Richards, 129 Hoe View Road, Chopwell Bishop, Notts (892788).
Boots Athletic—Lady Bay, West Bridgford. Courts: G8, H4. *Secretary:* D Gilbert, 27 May Avenue, Wollaton, Nottingham (283414).
Burton-Joyce—Cragmoor Road, Burton-Joyce. Courts: H3. *Secretary:* Mrs E Wright, 8 Carnarvon Drive, Burton-Joyce (3718).
Calverton Miners' Welfare—Park Road, Calverton, Nottingham. Courts: H3. *Secretary:* Mrs L Smithurst, 42 Flatts Lane, Calverton (Nottingham 653254).
Caunton—Playing Field, Manor Road, Caunton, Notts. Courts: H2. *Secretary:* Mrs A Macintyre, "Dalj", Mill Lane, Caunton, Newark, Notts (Caunton 562).
Chilwell Garrison—Courts: G3, H2. *Secretary:* Officer i/c Tennis, COD Chilwell, Nottingham (Nottingham 254811).
Collingham—Dale Field, South Collingham, nr Newark. Courts: G4, H1. *Secretary:* Mr P D Hambly, Lenton House, Swinderby Road, Collingham, Newark (892639).
Eastwood—Church Walk, off Alexandra Street, Eastwood. Courts: H4. *Secretary:* Mrs W Atherton, 44 Carmen Close, Watnall, Notts (Nottingham 383801).
Fairview—Hills Road, Woodthorpe, Nottingham. Courts: H3. *Secretary:* M Penfold, 52 Weaverthorpe Road, Woodthorpe (260578).
Farnsfield—New Hill, Farnsfield. Courts: H2. *Secretary:* Mrs P Newman, 4 Gregory Gardens, Tippings Lane, Farnsfield, NG22 8EQ (Mansfield 882381).
Gedling—Conway Road, Carlton. Courts: H4. *Secretary:* Mr B Savidge, 35 Freda Avenue, Gedling (877728).
Keyworth & District—Elm Avenue, Keyworth. *Secretary:* Mrs J Godber, 15 Violet Road, W Bridgford, Notts (814281).
Magdala—Corner Woodborough Road and Mapperley Road. Courts: G3, H2. *Secretary:* Mrs J M Wheelhouse, 64 Breckhill Road, Woodthorpe, Nottingham (262754 pri).
Mansfield—Pheasant Hill, Chesterfield Road, Mansfield. Courts: G9, H3. *Secretary:* P Allsopp, 26 Highland Road, Mansfield (27552).

Mansfield Colliery Welfare TC—Forest Town, Mansfield (650347). Courts: G2, H1. *Secretary:* Mr G Hartley, 21 Longdale, Mansfield Woodhouse, Notts.
Mapperley Park—Carisbrooke Drive, Mapperley Park, Nottingham. Courts: G1, H3. *Secretary:* Mr M A Smith, 12 Esher Grove, Mapperley Park, Notts (621736).
Musters—Musters Road, West Bridgford. Courts: H4. *Secretary:* Mrs G E A Fyles, 30 Repton Road, West Bridgford, Nottingham (Nottingham 233901).
Newark—behind Girls' High School, London Road, Newark. Courts: G10. *Secretary:* W Wright, Daunt House, 13 Church Street, Long Bennington, Newark (Lovedon 81357).
Nottingham—Tattershall Drive, The Park, Nottingham. Courts: G3, H5. *Secretary:* Miss J Ledger, 369 Coppice Road, Arnold, Nottingham (Nottingham 262965 pri, Nottingham 202131 bus).
Nottinghamshire Combined Constabulary —John Player & Son Sports Ground, Aspley Lane, Nottingham. Courts: H3. *Secretary:* R Checkley (PC 1929), Station Street Police Station, Meadows, Notts (Radcliffe-on-Trent 3647 pri, Radcliffe-on-Trent 581721 bus).
Nottingham University—Highfields, University Boulevard, Nottingham. Courts: G4, H7 (2 indoors). *Secretary:* Tennis Secretary, Athletics Union, Portland Building, The University, Nottingham.
Notts College of Education—Clifton. Courts: H12. *Secretary:* Tennis Secretary, Staff Room, Notts College of Education, Clifton, Notts.
Old Nottinghamians—Valley Road, Nottingham. Courts: H3. *Secretary:* J Britton, 5 Middlebeck Drive, Mapperley Plains, Nottingham (267255 pri, Long Eaton 4317 bus).
Players—Aspley Lane, Nottingham. Courts: G5, H11. *Secretary:* R D Holland, 155 Main Street, Newthorpe, Nottingham (Langley Mill 4950).
Plessey—Courts: H3. *Secretary:* Mr R Marshall, c/o Sports Office, Plessey, trent Road, Beeston (254831 ext 3669).
RAF Newton—RAF Station, Newton. Courts: H2. *Secretary:* Sqn Ldr P E Charlton, Officers Mess, RAF Newton, Notts (East Bridgeford 20771 ext 350).
Raleigh Athletic Club—Coach Road, Wollaton, Nottingham. Courts: H4. *Secretary:* Mr R Herrod, 17 Stanstead Avenue, Rise Park, Nottingham (273217).
Ransome, Hoffman, Pollard (Neward)—Elm Avenue, Newark. Courts: G6, H4. *Secretary:* K E Clavering, 67 Boundary Road, Newark (72302).
Retford—Hospital Road, Retford. Courts: G5, H3. *Secretary:* Mrs P M Pearson, 66 Broad Gores, Clarborough, Retford (Retford 706207).
Ruddington—Recreation Ground, Loughborough Road. Courts: H3. *Secretary:* Mrs N Sayers, 33 Elms Close, Ruddington, Nottingham (213322).
Southwell—Memorial Ground, Bishops Drive, Southwell. Courts: H3. *Secretary:* Mrs B Calthrop, Honing House, Westage, Southwell, Notts NG25 0LT (Southwell 812282).
Stapleford, Wotan—Toton Lane, Stapleford, Nottingham. Courts: H4. *Secretary:* K Oxley, 222 Bye Pass Road, Chilwell, Nottingham (258490).
Sutton-in-Ashfield—Lawn Pleasure Grounds, Station Road, Sutton in Ashfield. Courts: H6. *Secretary:* Mrs B A Wass, 14 Lawn Avenue, Sutton-in-Ashfield (Mansfield 553870 pri).
Sutton Bonington & District—Landcroft Lane, Sutton Bonington. Courts: H2. *Secretary:* Mr D Brown, 54 Main Street, Costock, Loughborough (E Leake 2629).
Trent Polytechnic TC—'The Dome', Trent Polytechnic, Clifton Main Site, Clifton, Notts (213316 ext Tennis Club). Courts: H3 (2 indoor). *Secretary:* Mr N Jones, Student Union (Tennis), Trent Polytechnic.
West Bridgford—Wilford Lane, West Bridgford. Courts: G5, H5. *Secretary:* Mr P Crowther, 89 Bransdale Road, Clifton, Nottingham NG11 9JB (212590).
West Bridgford Royal British Legion—Gertrude Road, West Bridgford. Courts: G3, H4. *Secretary:* Mrs C Richards, 37 Valley Road, West Bridgford, Nottingham (232428).
Wheatley—North Wheatley Playing Fields, nr Retford, Notts. Courts: G1, H1. *Secretary:* B D Shead, The Cottage, Low Street, North Wheatley, Retford (Gainsborough 880327 pri, Wickersley 547222 bus).
Wollaton Village—Cricket Ground, Wollaton. Courts: H3. *Secretary:* Mrs B Hawksworth, 105 Grangewood Road, Wollaton, Nottingham (283439).
Woodthorpe—Albemarle Road, Woodthorpe, Nottingham. Courts: H6. *Secretary:* Mrs M Morley, 13 Albermarle Road, Woodthorpe, Nottingham (607582).

AFFILIATED SCHOOLS (34)

Boys

Nottingham Boys' High School — Nottingham. **Trinity Comprehensive** — Nottingham. **Welback College** — Worksop, Notts. **Worksop College** — Worksop, Notts.

Girls

Hollygirt School — Nottingham. **Nottingham Girls High School** — Nottingham.

Mixed (29)

Alderman Derbyshire — Hucknall Lane, Bulwell, Nottingham. **Arnold Hill Comprehensive** — Arnold, Nottingham. **Beckett** — Ruddington Lane, Wilford, Nottingham. **Bilborough College** — Nottingham. **Bramcote Hills** — Moor Lane, Bramcote, Beeston, Nottingham. **Carlton-le-Willows** — Wood Lane, Gedling, Nottingham. **Chilwell Comprehensive** — Queen's Road West, Chilwell, Beeston, Nottingham. **Christ the King School** — Darlton Drive, Arnold, Nottingham. **Col Frank Seely** — Flatts Lane, Calverton, Nottingham. **Dagfa House** — Broadgate, Beeston, Nottingham. **Farnborough Comprehensive** — Clifton, Nottingham. **Forest Fields College** — Nottingham. **Gedling** — Wollaton Avenue, Gedling, Nottingham. **Greenholme School** — 392 Derby Road, Nottingham. **Greenwood Dale** — Sneinton

Boulevard, Nottingham. **Haywood** — Edwards Lane, Sherwood, Nottingham. **Henry Mellish** — Highbury Vale, Bulwell. **Hartland Comprehensive** — Worksop. **Lilley & Stone School** — Newark, Nottinghamshire. **Manning School** — Gregory Boulevard, Nottingham. **Magdalene** — Barnby Road, Newark . **Mansfield Woodhouse** — Manor Parkhall Road, Mansfield. **Meden School** — Warsop, Mansfield. **Nottingham Bluecoat School** — Aspley Lane, Nottingham. **Rushcliffe Comprehensive** — Boundary Road, West Bridgford, Nottingham. **South Wolds Comprehensive** — Keyworth, Nottingham. **The West Bridgford School** — Loughborough Road, West Bridgford, Nottingham. **Thos Magnus** — Earp Avenue, Newark. **Wm Sharpe** — Bramhall Road, Bilborough, Nottingham.

All correspondence to School Clubs should be addressed to the Master or Mistress in charge of lawn tennis.

OXFORDSHIRE LAWN TENNIS ASSOCIATION

Hon Secretary—**W Enoch,** 13 Lathbury Road, Oxford OX2 7AT (58134 pri, 52031 bus).
Hon Treasurer—**B Wyatt,** 15 Blenheim Drive, Oxford (58005).
Hon Men's Match Secretary—**H Blackler,** 5 Oakthorpe Mansions, Banbury Road, Oxford (58893).
Hon Ladies' Match Secretary—**Mrs P Mortimer,** 75 Staunton Road, Headington, Oxford (0865 61171).
Hon Junior Secretary—**Mrs M Webb,** Mallory, Black Bourton, Oxfordshire (0993 841943).
Representatives on the Council—**W Enoch, J Harrop.**

AFFILIATED CLUBS (43)

Abingdon—Albert Park, Abingdon. Courts: G4. *Secretary:* Mrs J McWhirter, 13 Park Crescent, Abingdon OX14 1DF (Abingdon 20232).
AERE Harwell—Courts: G3, H4 (1 indoor). *Secretary:* Dr T G Pett, 20 St Amand Drive, Abingdon OX14 5RQ (0235 26033).
Banbury—Horton View, Banbury. Courts: G1, H5. *Secretary:* Mrs M Andrew, 43 Main Road, Middleton Cheney, Banbury (Banbury 710769).
Banbury West End—Chapel Lane, Adderbury. Courts: H7. *Secretary:* Mrs J Edwards, 46 Grange Road, Banbury, Oxon (0295 57313).
Benson—Sunnyside Bensort. Courts: G2, H2. *Secretary:* Miss P Brown, 24 The Moorlands, Benson, Oxford (Wallingford 38773).
Bicester—Garth Park, Launton Road, Bicester. Courts: H3. *Secretary:* Mrs J Kelly, 26 Rectory Close, Marsh Gibbon, Bicester, Oxon OX6 0HT (Stratton Audley 466).
Chinnor—Station Road, Chinnor. Courts: H3. *Secretary:* Mrs A Neighbour, 15 High Street, Chinnor, Oxford OX9 4DJ (Kingston Blount 52495).
Cholsey—Recreation Ground, Cholsey. Courts: H3. *Secretary:* Mrs E Watts, 7 Pound Lane, Cholsey, Wallingford OX10 9NR (0491 651761).
Colston—Broadwell, Kencot, nr Lechlade, Glos. Courts: G4, H3. *Secretary:* Mrs C Foreshaw, 12 Busby's Close, Clanfield, Witney (Clanfield 367).
Didcot—Edmonds Park, Park Road, Didcot. Courts: H3. *Secretary:* G R Breag, 32 Edwin Road, Didcot OX11 8LE (Didcot 814082).
Dorchester-on-Thames—Recreation Ground. Courts: H2. *Secretary:* Mrs P Smith, 11 Martins Lane, Dorchester on Thames, Oxford OX9 5PJ (Oxford 340768).
Faringdon—Southampton Street, Faringdon. Courts: H3. *Secretary:* Mrs P M Perkins, 5 Leamington Drive, Faringdon, Oxon SN7 7JZ (Faringdon 21077).
Goring—Sheepcote Field, Gatehampton Road, Goring. Courts: H3. *Secretary:* Mrs B Berwick, Townsend House, Streatley, Henley-on-Thames, (Goring 874166).
Hanborough District—Long Hanborough Playing Fields. Courts: H2. *Secretary:* Mrs C S White, Hilbury View, Hill Farm Lane, Duns Tew, Oxford OX5 4JH.
Headington—Lincoln College Ground, Bartelmas Close, Oxford. Courts: G2. *Secretary:* M D Ray, 43 Feilden Close, Ducklington, Witney (Witney 3591).
Kings Sutton—Charlton Road, Kings Sutton, nr Banbury, Oxon. Courts: H3. *Secretary:* Mrs B Lascelles, 2 Old Vicarage Gardens, Cropredy, Banbury, Oxon (029575 353).
Mapledurham LTC—Playing Fields, Upper Woodcote Road, Reading. Courts: H3. *Secretary:* Mrs M Jones, 41 Galsworthy Drive, Caversham Park, Reading, Berks RG4 0PR.
Morris Motors—Crescent Road, Cowley. Courts: H3. *Secretary:* C P Roberts, 29 Glymeway, Long Hanborough, Witney, Oxon (Freeland 882971).
Norham Gardens—Benson Place, Oxford (54136). Courts: H6. *Secretary:* W Snyder, 3 Elms Drive, Old Marston, Oxford (63279).
North Oxford—Banbury Road North, Oxford. Courts: G10, H4. *Secretary:* Mrs R Kenning, 63 Linkside Avenue, Oxford (54316).
North Court Junior Club—Filzharry's School, Abingdon. Courts: H6. *Secretary:* Mrs G Hashman, 20 Sandleigh Road, Wootton, Abingdon OX13 6DP (Oxford 735105).
Oxford City—Holywell Ford, Oxford. Courts: G4, H3. *Secretary:* Mrs J A Tucker, Glebe Barn, Little Tew Road, Church Enstone, Oxford OX7 4LM (Enstone 505).
Oxford Sports—North Hinksey, Village End, Oxford. Courts: H9. *Secretary:* Mrs J L Barrett, 28 Leys Road, Cumnor, Oxford OX2 9QF (863581).
Oxford University Press—Jordan Hill, Banbury Road, Oxford. Courts: G4. *Secretary:* Mrs C Nicholl, 20a Blewbury Road, East Hagbourne, Oxon OX11 9LF (Blewbury 813826).
Peppard—Peppard Common, Oxon. Courts: G4, H6. *Secretary:* Mrs P Needham, 58 Harpsden Road, Henley-on-Thames (576961).

Phyllis Court Members Club Ltd—Phyllis Court Club, Marlow Road, Henley-on-Thames. Courts: H3. *Secretary:* R I Bulloch, Phyllis Court Club, Marlow Road, Henley-on-Thames (0491 574366).
Portcullis Wallingford Sports Trust—Hithercroft, Wallingford. Courts: H4. *Secretary:* Miss K Jestico, 84 St Nicholas Road, Wallingford, Oxford OX10 8JA (0491 38837).
Royal Military College of Science—Wellington Hall, RMCS Shrivenham. Courts: H5. *Secretary:* Lt P Frostick, 390 Degree Course, RMCS, Shrivenham, Swindon, Wilts SN6 8LA (78551ext2411).
Shiplake—Memorial Avenue, Shiplake, Henley-on-Thames. Courts: H2. *Secretary:* Mrs F Ahara, 15 Brocks Way, Shiplake, Oxon RG9 3JG (Wargrave 2467).
Southfield—Lincoln College Ground, Bartlemas Close, Cowley, Oxford. Courts: G5, H1. *Secretary:* Miss K Hunnisett, 29 Lyne Road, Kidlington, Oxford OX5 1AE (Kidlington 79457).
The Sportsman—*Secretary:* J Rolfe, 13 Stanton Harcourt Road, Witney, Oxon (73991).
Thame Sports—Queen's Road, Thame. Courts: G4, H2. *Secretary:* Mrs E Kaminski, 15 Dunbar Drive, Thame OX9 3YD (Thame 4921).
Upper Heyford—RAF Upper Heyford, Oxford. Courts: H2. *Secretary:* Mrs P Benkel, 1 Barnfield Close, Bicester, Oxon (Bicester 249238).
Wantage—Foliat Drive, Wantage. Courts: H3. *Secretary:* Mrs H Thomason, 33 Harlington Avenue, Grove, Wantage OX12 7NG (4265).
Watlington—War Memorial Club, Shirburn Street. Courts: H3. *Secretary:* Mrs C Hollesley, April Cottage, Russells Water, Oxon RG9 6ER (Nettlebed 641385).
West Witney—West Witney Sports Ground. Courts: G2, H2. *Secretary:* B F Hill, 32 Vanner Road, Witney OX8 6PF (72422).
Wheatley—Lady Spencer Churchill College, Holton, Nr Oxford. Courts: H3. *Secretary:* A Morrice, 34 Beech Road, Wheatley, Oxford OX9 1UR (Wheatley 3125).
Woodcote Tennis Club—Langtree School, Woodcote. Courts: H4. *Secretary:* Mrs A M Sims, 39 West Chiltern, Woodcote, Reading, Berks (0491 681472).
Woodstock Bowls & Tennis Club—Cadogan Park, Woodstock. Courts: H4. *Secretary:* Mrs S K Thompson, 15 Plane Tree Way, Woodstock, Oxford OX7 1PE (Woodstock 812004).

AFFILIATED SCHOOLS (30)

Boys
Magdalen College School — Oxford. **Oxford School** — Oxford. **St Edward's School** — Oxford. **St Birinus** — Didcot.

Girls
Milhamford — Oxford. **Langtree School** — Woodcote. **Rye St Anthony School** — Oxford. **Tudor Hall School** — Banbury. **Wychwood** — Oxford. **St Helen & St Katherine** — Abingdon. **Didcot** — Didcot. **Convent of Our Lady** — Abingdon. **St Mary's Convent** — Wantage.

Mixed
Banbury School — Banbury. **Bicester School** — Bicester. **Blessed George Napier School** — Banbury. **Cheney School** — Oxford. **Chiltern Edge School** — Sonning Common. **Gillott's School** — Henley-on-Thames. **Gosford Hill School** — Kidlington. **Henry Box School** — Witney. **Icknield School** — Watlington. **Lord Williams School** — Thame. **Marlborough School** — Woodstock. **Matthew Arnold School** — Oxford. **Peers School** — Oxford. **Spendlove School** — Charlbury. **Appleton Primary** — Appleton. **Abbey** — Berinsfield. **Bishop Carpenter Primary** — North Newington. **Blake CE Primary** — Cogges. **Bletchington Parochical** — Bletchington. **Carterton** — Carterton. **Chalgrove CP** — Chalgrove. **Chipping Norton** — Chipping Norton. **Cowley St John Upper** — Oxford. **Cranford** — Oxford. **Cropley CE Primary** — Banbury. **Cumnor CE Primary** — Oxford. **Cooper** — Bicester. **Drayton — Drayton. Faringdon** — Faringdon. **Finmere Primary** — Finnere. **Garsington Primary** — Oxford. **Goring Primary** — Goring. **King Alfred** — Wantage. **Larkmead** — Abingdon. **Launton Primary** — Bicester. **Longfields CP** — Bicester. **Manor** — Long Hanborough. **Manor Junior** — Didcot. **North Kidlington CP** — Kidlington. **Rush Common CP** — Agingdon. **Segsbury** — Wantage. **Stephen Freeman** — Didcot. **St Edmund Campion** — Oxford. **Temple Cowley Middle** — Oxford. **Warriner** — Bloxham. **Wheatley Park** — Wheatley. **Wheatley Park Lower** — Wheatley. **Wallingford** — Wallingford. **Wantage CE** — Wantage. **Watlington Primary** — Watlington. **Woodstock Primary** — Woodstock. **Woodcote Primary** — Woodcote.

All correspondence to School Clubs should be addressed to the Master or Mistress in charge of lawn tennis.

SHROPSHIRE COUNTY LAWN TENNIS ASSOCIATION

Hon Secretary—**J C Henshaw,** 15 Abbotsfield Drive, Shrewsbury (4835).
Hon Treasurer—**A K Corbett,** Fens, 19 Leegomery Road, Wellington (42907).
Hon Junior Secretary—**Miss E Boyle,** 14 Hadley Gardens, Leegomery, Telford (55556).
Hon Men's Match Secretary—**A Papier,** 16 Mill Street, Ludlow (4840).
Hon Ladies' Match Secretary—**Miss E. Boyle,** 14 Hadley Gardens, Leegomery, Telford (55556).
Representative on the Council—**J C Henshaw.**

AFFILIATED CLUBS (44)

Albrighton—Cross Road, Albrighton. Courts: G1, H4. *Secretary:* Mrs J B Smith, 15 Barclay Close, Albrighton, nr Wolverhampton, Staffs.
Alveley—Recreation Association Playing Fields, Alveley. Courts: G1, H2. *Secretary:* P A Morgan, 7 Cedar Close, Alveley, nr Bridgnorth W15 6JY (Quatt 780449).

Bishops Castle—Love Lane, Bishops Castle. Courts: G3. *Secretary:* Mrs M Jackson, 1 Lavender Bank, Bishops Castle SY9 5BD.
Bomere Heath—Bomere Heath. Courts: H2. *Secretary:* Mrs S Shellswell, Home Farm, Berwick Estate, Berwick, Shrewsbury.
Boughey Gardens—Newport. Courts: H4. *Secretary:* K G Smith, 10 Oak Avenue, Newport (Telford 811781).
Bridgnorth—off Cricket Meadow, off Victoria Road, Bridgnorth (4951). Courts: H4 (all floodlit). *Secretary:* L J Winwood, 93 Sydney Cottage Drive, Bridgnorth (4678).
Brookside Country Club—Bronygarth, Oswestry (773288). Courts: H3. *Secretary:* Mrs P Welti, Brookside Country Club, Bronygarth, Oswestry (773288).
Broseley—King Street, Broseley. Courts: H2. *Secretary:* Mr A Giltine, 17 Quarry Road, Broseley Wood.
Churchstoke—Churchstoke. Courts: G2. *Secretary:* Mrs T Kinsey, The Green, Churchstoke.
Church Stretton—Recreation Ground, Church Stretton. Courts: H2. *Secretary:* C Mansell, Watling Street, Church Stretton (723058).
Claverley—High Street, Claverley. Courts: H2 (both floodlit). *Secretary:* Miss B A Pearson-Fenn, 10 High Street, Claverley, Wolverhampton, Staffs.
Cound—Cound Village. Courts: H2. *Secretary:* D Rawlings, 35 Severn Way, Cressage, Shrewsbury SY5 6DS (Cressage 475).
Criftins—Criftins, nr Ellesmere. Courts: H2. *Secretary:* C Knight, Dudleston Grange, Dudleston Heath, nr Ellesmere (Dudleston Heath 361).
Dawley—Dawley Park, Doseley Road, Dawley. Courts: H3. *Secretary:* Mrs C Heighway, 'Gorwaine', off Fielding Close, Broseley (Telford 882743).
Ellesmere—Cremorne Gardens. Courts: H2. *Secretary:* Miss R Woollam, Escob Farm, St Martins, nr Oswestry (Chirk 772441).
Garrison—COD Donnington, Telford. *Secretary:* Officer i/c Tennis, Central Ordnance Depot, Donnington, Telford.
Grove—Market Drayton. Courts: H2. *Secretary:* Mrs S Richards, 9 Westland Road, Market Drayton.
High Ercall—High Ercall. Courts: H4. *Secretary:* Miss S Shepherdson, 19 Forest Close, Shawbirch, Telford (52647).
Highley—Highley, Bridgnorth. Courts: H2. *Secretary:* Mrs M A Phillips, Woodhill Stores Garden Village, Highley, Bridgnorth.
Hollies—Tarporley Road, Whitchurch. Courts: H3 (2 floodlit). *Secretary:* R Shrimplin, 7 The Grove, Tarporley Road, Whitchurch (3600).
Lilleshall Hall—Lilleshall Hall, Newport (603003). Courts: H4 (all floodlit). *Secretary:* Mrs D Goulson, Beaufort Lodge, Lilleshall (Telford 607652).
Lilleshall Village—by Monument, Lilleshall, nr Newport. Courts: H2. *Secretary:* Mrs M Tomkinson, Oulton Farm, Norbury, Stafford (Woodseaves 223).
Longden—Douglas Swire Memorial Hall, Longden. Courts: H2 (both floodlit). *Secretary:* Mrs R Pagett, 24 Chestnut Close, Hanwood, nr Shrewsbury (Shrewsbury 860635).
Ludlow Castle—The Linney, Ludlow. Courts: H4. *Secretary:* Mrs C White, Saanen, Downton View, Ludlow SY8 1JE (Ludlow 3939).
Ludlow & South Shropshire—Burway Lane, Ludlow. Courts: G4, H2 (both floodlit). *Secretary:* Miss F Beaumont, 6 Upper Raven Lane, Ludlow (4430).
Midlands Electricity Sports & Social Club—Sundorne Road, Shrewsbury. Courts: H2. *Secretary:* S Glennie, MEB, Spring Gardens, Shrewsbury (53911 ext 378).
Minsterley—Courts: H2. *Secretary:* Mrs C A Harvey, The Bungalow, Blackmore, Westbury SY5 9RL (Halfway House 512).
Much Wenlock—Much Wenlock. Courts: H4. *Secretary:* J A Harding, Laurences Cottage, Much Wenlock.
Oswestry—Welsh Walls, Oswestry. Courts: H3. *Secretary:* Miss H Dale, 12 Hampton Close, Oswestry (653523).
Postal—Abbey Foregate, Shrewsbury. Courts: H2 (1 floodlit). *Secretary:* R Hotchkiss, 66 Mary Webb Road, Meole Estate, Shrewsbury SY3 9NT (61908).
Priory—Priory School, Longden Road, Shrewsbury. Courts: H4. *Secretary:* D Kilby, 7 Grangefields Road, Shrewsbury (53081).
RAF Cosford—P Ed Wing, RAF Cosford, Albrighton, W Midlands. Courts: 4 indoor, H6, G6. *Secretary:* Fl Lt P Jaques, BS Sqn, RAF Cosford, Albrighton, W Midlands (Albrighton 2393 ext 536).
RAF Shawbury—Shawbury, Shropshire. *Secretary:* Officer i/c Tennis, RAF Shawbury, Shrewsbury.
Shifnal—Shifnal Cricket, Bowls & Tennis Club, nr War Memorial Club, Shifnal. Courts: H3. *Secretary:* P Broderick, 40 Aston Road, Shifnal TF11 8DU (462092).
Shifnal Sports Centre—Aston Street, Shifnal. Courts: H3 (all floodlit).
Shrewsbury—Crescent Lane, Town Walls, Shrewsbury (3575). Courts: G6, H5 (2 floodlit). *Secretary:* A Cross, 28 Kennedy Road, Shrewsbury (64679).
Telford—Wellington, Telford (3355). Courts: H2. *Secretary:* Mrs C Thomas, 12 Slaney Street, Oakengates, Telford (617609 pri, 505051 ext 580 bus).
Town Walls—Crescent Lane, Town Walls, Shrewsbury. Courts: H3 (all floodlit). *Secretary:* Mrs B Cheetham, 73 Grange Road South, Shrewsbury (51791).
Wem—Recreation Ground, Park Road, Wem. Courts: H4. *Secretary:* Mrs D Strong, 6 Tilley Road, Wem (32061).
Wollerton—Wollerton, Hodnet, nr Market Drayton. Courts: G2, H2. *Secretary:* Mrs M Hopkins, 3 The Eastlands, Marchamley, Shrewsbury (Hodnet 732).
Woodfield—Woodfield Road, Shrewsbury. Courts: H5. *Secretary:* Mrs J Speake, 15 Bewdley Avenue, Shrewsbury SY2 5UQ (57405).

Worfield—Recreation Ground, Worfield, Bridgnorth. Courts: H2. *Secretary:* Mrs Thomas, 3 Dingle Drive, Beckbury, Shifnal (Ryton 285).
Worthen—Worthen. Courts: G2. *Secretary:* R Wootton, Goodwins, Worthen.

OTHER AFFILIATED ORGANISATIONS (2)

Shropshire Inter-Club League.
Telford Racquet & Fitness Centre—St Quentins Gate, Telford Town Centre, Telford TF3 4JH (507070). Courts: 8 indoor Savannah, 6 outdoor. *Director:* B Gray.

AFFILIATED SCHOOLS (13)

Boys
Adams Grammar School for Boys — Newport. **Wrekin College** — Wellington. **Shrewsbury School** — Kingsland. **Ellesmere College** — Ellesmere. **The Manor School** — Crescent Road, Hadley.

Girls
Adcote Girls' School — Shrewsbury. **Bridgnorth Endowed School** — Bridgnorth. **Manor School** — Crescent Road, Hadley, Telford. **Shrewsbury High School. The Grammar High School** — Moreton Hall Girls School, Weston Rhyn, nr Oswestry.

Comprehensive
Abraham Darby Comprehensive School — Coalbrookdale, Telford. **Priory School** — Longden Road, Shrewsbury.

Sixth Form College
Shrewsbury Sixth Form College.

All correspondence to School Clubs should be addressed to the Master or Mistress in charge of lawn tennis.

SOMERSET COUNTY LAWN TENNIS ASSOCIATION

Hon Secretary—**L F Stephens,** 19 Burley Gardens, Street, Somerset (Street 42030).
Men's Match Secretary & Captain—**A G Pearman,** Greystones, Stoughton, Wedmore, Somerset (Wedmore 712430).
Hon Ladies' Match Secretary—**Mrs V Flicker,** 17 Wood Close, Portway, Wells (Wells 74777).
Hon Juniors Match Secretary—**Mrs M Holder,** The South Plantation, West Monkton, Taunton (West Monkton 412314)
Hon Treasurer—**H A Warren,** 55 Church Road, West Huntspill, Highbridge (Burnham-on-Sea 785859).
Representative on the Council—**F C Bowles.**

AFFILIATED CLUBS (26)

Avalon—Courts: 1 all weather. *Secretary:* D W Kemp, Burleigh Cottage, Burleigh Lane, Street (43439).
Avenue—The Grove, Burnham-on-Sea. Courts: H5 (2 floodlit), G4. *Secretary:* Mrs P Rich, Quantock View, Hill Lane, Brent Knoll, Highbridge (Brent Knoll 760523).
Brent Knoll & Mark—Brent Street. Courts: H2. *Secretary:* Mrs S Holley, Ferndale, Wick Lane, Brent Knoll, Highbridge (760611).
Bridgwater—Taunton Road, Bridgwater. Courts: H5. *Secretary:* Mrs C Sedgwick, 65 Sedgemoor Road, Bridgwater (451822).
British Cellophane—Courts: H3. *Secretary:* Miss H Chave, British Cellophane Ltd, Bath Road, Bridgwater TA6 4PA (424321 ext 622).
Castle Cary Constitutional—Station Road. Courts: H2. *Secretary:* Mrs B P Joslin, Henton House, South Cary, Castle Cary (50823).
Chard Town—Dening Fields, Chard. Courts: H2, G2. *Secretary:* Miss P M Bellsham, Hillcot, Combe Hill, Combe Street, Nicholas, Chard TA20 3NW (Chard 2024).
Cheddar—Barrows Road, Cheddar. Courts: H2. *Secretary:* Mrs J May, 4 New Road, Cheddar (742815).
Dulverton—The Sportsfield. Courts: H2. *Secretary:* Mrs J Archer, Quarry Cottage, Exbridge, Dulverton (23766).
Elms—Elm Grove, Taunton. Courts: G4. *Secretary:* Mrs J Jeremiah, 1 Richmond Road, Taunton (82924).
Frome Selwood—Somerset Road, Frome. Courts: H3. *Secretary:* Mrs R Blacklidge, Park Hill Grange, Bath Road, Frome BA11 2HL (63436).
Glastonbury & Street LTC—c/o The Victoria Club, Leigh Road, Street BA16 0HB. Courts: H4 (floodlit) G2. *Secretary:* Timothy Bowles, The PO Stores, West Pennard, Glastonbury (32955).
Ilminster—Shruddick Lane. Courts: H2. *Secretary:* D B Harper, Park House, Park Lane, Donyatt, Ilminster TA19 0RN (Ilminster 2994).
Langport & Huish Episcopi—The Recreation Field, Langport. Courts: H2. *Secretary:* Mrs J Budd, 'Greenways', Westmoor Lane, Hambridge, Longport, Rivel, Somerset (Isle Brewers 461).
Long Sutton LTC—Courts: H3. *Secretary:* Mrs S E Woodley, 'Lonicera', Picts Hill, Langport TA10 9AA (Langport 252315).
Minehead—Alexandra Road. Courts: G2, H2. *Secretary:* Mrs M Brown, "Clarevaux", 1 Lower Park, Minehead, Somerset TA24 8AX.
Somerton—Gassons Lane. Courts: H2. *Secretary:* Mrs J Phippen, Batu Cottage, Kingsdon, Yeovil (Ilchester 840162).
South Petherton—Recreation Field. Courts: H2. *Secretary:* Miss E B Ponder, Newlyn, 6 Lightgate Road, South Petherton TA13 5AJ (40586).
Templars LTC—Recreation Ground. Courts: H2. *Secretary:* Mrs N Gilman, 42 Bowden Road, Templecombe (70352).
Tor—Benedict Street, Glastonbury. Courts: H3. *Secretary:* Mrs C Smith, 32 Chalice Way, Glastonbury (32452).
Wedmore—Recreation Ground. Courts: H2 (floodlit). *Secretary:* Mrs J Pope, Providence House, Blackford, Wedmore (712986).
Wellington—Courtland Road, Wellington. Courts: H2. *Secretary:* Mrs C S Moore, 11 Pyles Thorne Road, Wellington (2782).

Wells—Athletic Field, Rowdens Road, Wells. Courts: G3, H3. *Secretary:* Mrs H Willmott, 12 North Road, Wells (Wells 73722).
Williton—Mansey Lane, Williton. Courts: G2. *Secretary:* Dr W Kingsbury, Inkberrow, West Quantoxhead, Taunton (Williton 32376 and 32701).
Woodstock—Richmond Road, Taunton. Courts: H3. *Secretary:* P J Deal, 22 Westleigh Road, Taunton, Somerset (78385).

OTHER AFFILIATED ORGANISATIONS (2)

Cote School of Tennis—*Secretary:* Mrs B Blackburn, Rose Cottage, Burtle Road, East Huntspill, nr Highbridge, Somerset (Burnham-on-Sea 785974).
Somerset Tennis Coaches Association—*Secretary:*

AFFILIATED SCHOOLS (31)

All Hallows — Cranmore. **Bishop Fox** — Taunton. **Bruton School for Girls** — Bruton. **Cathedral School** — Wells. **Chilton Cantelo** — Yeovil. **Downside School** — Stratton-on-the-Fosse. **Frome College** — Frome. **Huish Episcopi School** — Langport. **King Alfred School** — Burnham-on-Sea. **Kings College** — Taunton. **Kings School** — Bruton. **Millfield School** — Street. **Millfield Junior School** — Glastonbury. **Minehead School** — Alcombe, Minehead. **Preston Comp** — Yeovil. **Priorswood School** — Taunton. **Queens College** — Taunton. **Rossholme School** — East Brent. **St Audries School** — West Quantoxhead, Taunton. **St Dunstan's School** — Burnham-on-Sea. **St Margaret's School** — Bridgwater. **St Martin's Prep School** — Crewkerne. **Sexey's School** — Bruton. **Taunton School** — Taunton. **The Hall School** — Wincanton. **The Park School** — Yeovil. **Tor School** — High Ham. **Wadham School** — Crewkerne. **Wellington School** Wellington. **Westfield School** — Yeovil. **Whitstone School** — Shepton Mallet.

STAFFORDSHIRE LAWN TENNIS ASSOCIATION

Hon Secretary—**B Fairclough,** 112 Park Hall Road, Walsall WS5 3LZ (021 357 4972).
Hon Junior Secretary—**B Boughey,** 41 Chadsfield Road, Rugeley (088 94 3484).
Hon Treasurer—**L Hanby,** 343 Hagley Road, Stowbridge (Stourbridge 0562 883417 pri).
Hon Men's Match Secretary—**B Greatrex,** Inglewood, Hargreaves Lane, Rowley Avenue, Stafford (Stafford 42676 pri, 45518 bus).
Hon Ladies' Match Secretary—**Mrs C J Rossiter,** 5 Salisbury Grove, Off Penns Lane, Wylde Green, Sutton Coldfield, W Midlands B72 1XY (021 373 2157).
Representatives on the Council—**K G Jones, Mrs B W Barber.**

AFFILIATED CLUBS (63)

Abbots Bromley—The Village Institute, Abbots Bromley. Courts: H2. *Secretary:* Mrs S Knight, 2 Bagots View, Abbots Bromley, Rugeley (Burton-on-Trent 840485).
Accles & Pollock—Brades Rise, Oldbury. Courts: H3. *Secretary:* R Lycett, Accles & Pollock, Oldbury, Warley, West Midlands (021 557 1130 pri, 021 552 1500 bus).
Albert—Aldersley Road, Lower Tettenhall, Wolverhampton. Courts: H6. *Secretary:* P A Jennings, 61 Cranmere Avenue, The Wergs, Tettenhall (W'Ton. 758586 pri, W'ton 52251 bus).
Allied Breweries TC—Belvedere Road, Burton-on-Trent. Courts: H3. *Secretary:* M A Holmes, 57 Henhurst Ridge, Burton-on-Trent DE13 9TH (Burton 66739 pri, Burton 66322 ext 2117 bus).
Allied Breweries—Belvedere Road, Burton-on-Trent. *Secretary:* G Arkesden, 357 Anglesey Road, Burton-on-Trent (0283 43320 bus).
Ashby Road Lawn Tennis & Squash Rackets Club—Ashby Road, Burton (5043). Courts: H4. *Secretary:* Miss P Dale, 34 Dalebrook Road, Burton (Burton 38845 pri, Burton 45320 ext 2915 bus).
Basford—West Avenue, Basford. Courts: H4. *Secretary:* Mrs N Emery, 100 Hassam Parade, Wolstanton, Newcastle-under-Lyme (Newcastle 6227719).
Barton—Eflinch Lane, Barton under Needwood. Courts: H4. *Secretary:* Mrs Z Montgomer, High Croft, Hanbury, Burton-on-Trent (B-on-T 813448 pm).
Bass Burton—The Meadow Road, Trent Bridge, Burton. Courts: G3, H3. *Secretary:* R P Greenfield, c/o Employee Relations Dept, Bass Brewing Ltd, High Street, Burton-on-Trent (Burton-on-Trent 45301 ext 2246 bus).
Bilston—Villiers Avenue, off Wellington Road. Courts: H4. *Secretary:* M A Watson, Alma House, 15 Regent Street, Bilston (Bilston 404347 pri, Walsall 32511 bus).
Birmingham Road (Walsall)—rear Crest Motel, Birmingham Road. Courts: H5. *Secretary:* A G Mammatt, 42 Jesson Road, Walsall (24471 pri, 27521 bus).
BTR Silvertown—Horninglow Road, Burton-on-Trent. Courts: H2. *Secretary:* H. Godfrey, 1 Balmoral Road, Borrowash, Derby (Derby 670955 pri, Burton 61611 bus).
Bloxwich—Stafford Road, Bloxwich, Walsall. Courts: H3. *Secretary:* R Przybyiko, 12 Albert Clarke Drive, Willenhall, West Midlands (Bloxwich 407534).
Brewood TC—Engleton Lane, Brewood. Courts: H2. *Secretary:* Mrs G R Foster, 6 Deansfield Road, Brewood (Brewood 850710).
Burton Manor Sports Ass—Burton Manor Road, Hyde Lea, Stafford. Courts: H3. *Secretary:* D Harding, Thaxted Hyde Lea, Stafford (Stafford 45499).
Burton-on-Trent Technical College—Meadow Lane, Burton-on-Trent. Courts: H2. *Secretary:* K E Sherrad, 136 Newton Road, Burton-on-Trent (Burton 61096 pri, 45401 bus).
Cannock LTC—The Stadium, Pye Green Road, Cannock, Staffs. Courts: H4. *Secretary:* I Williams, 3 Arthur Street, Chadsmoor, Cannock (Cannock 71865 pri, 6261 bus).
Cheslyn Hay—Sports Centre, Saredon Road, Cheslyn Hay, Staffs. Courts: H4. *Secretary:* J. Devey, 8 St James Road, Cannock (Cannock 5264).

Codsall Ex Service Sports Club—Wood Road, Cosdall, West Midlands. Courts: H3. *Secretary:* D R Manning, 112 Coniston Road, Tettenhall, W'ton. (W'ton 753393 pri, W'ton 23179 bus).
Conder Sports—Shobnall Playing Fields, B-o-T. Courts: H2. *Secretary:* Mr B Tye, Couder Midlands, Wellington Road, Burton-on-Trent, (Derby 514423 pri, Burton 45377 bus).
Crabtree LTC—*Secretary:*
Dowty Boulton Paul—Wobaston Road, Fordhouses, Wolverhampton (Wolverhampton 787103). Courts: H2. *Secretary:* E A Penny, c/o Dowty Boulton Paul Ltd (Codsall 4486 pri, Wolverhampton 783191 bus).
Draycott—Cresswell Lane, Draycott. Courts: H6 (2 floodlit). *Secretary:* S M Wardle, 8 Birchdale Close, Lower Tean, Tean (0538 7220).
ECC Tennis Club—Showell Road, Bushbury. Courts: H3. *Secretary:* T Riley, 79 Brenton Road, Wolverhampton (32457 pri, 27831 bus).
Endon LTC—Station Road, Endon, S-o-T. Courts: H5. *Secretary:* D Carlidge, 103 Courtway Drive, Sneyd Green, Stoke-on-Trent (281088).
Etching Hill—East Butts Road (off Chaseley Road). Courts: H3. *Secretary:* A J Birch, 306 Huntington Terrace Road, Hednesford WS11 2MX (Hednesford 5808 pri, Lichfield 414881 bus).
Florence—Cemetery Road, Longton (Stoke 39440). Courts: H4. *Secretary:* A Webb, 50 Lyneside Road, Knypersley, Stoke-on-Trent (515718 pri, 372005 bus).
GEC—Stychfields, Wolverhampton Road, Stafford. Courts: H3. *Secretary:* Mrs B Horton, 3 Sabine Street, Stafford (Stafford 5583280).
Glebelands TC—High Street, Church Eaton, Stafford. Courts: H3. *Secretary:* Ms C Edwards, 5 Oak Close, Church Eaton, Stafford (823067).
Goodyear—Wingfoot Park, Stafford Road, Wolverhampton. Courts: H3. *Secretary:* W A Farnell, 68 Clockmill Road, Pelsall, Walsall (Pel 691714 pri, 90 22321 bus).
Grange (Burton-on-Trent)—St Paul's Square. Courts: G4, H2. *Secretary:* Mrs K Warren, Garden Cottage, Bladon, Newton Solney, Burton-on-Trent. (B-o-T 61721 pri, B-o-T 66333 ext 128 bus).
Halesowen—Manor Way, Halesowen. Courts: H3. *Secretary:* Mrs J Buckle, 2 Kidderminster Road, Hagley, Worcs (886085).
Hanbury LTC—Hanbury Crescent, Penn W'ton. Courts: H2. *Secretary:* J H Lewis, 9 Scott Avenue, Penn, W'ton (339821).
John Taylor High School Dunstall Road, Barton-under-Needwood, Burton-on-Trent. Courts: H8. *Secretary:* R A Gray, 4 The Green, Barton-under-Needwood (2340 pri, Burton-on-Trent 31111 ext 2343 bus).
Lea Hall—Sandy Lane, Rugeley. Courts: H2. *Secretary:* G C Dubey, 5 Hawthorn Way, Rugeley (Rug 6237).
Litchfield—Birmingham Road. Courts: G4, H2. *Secretary:* I Phipps, The Lodge, Hoarcross Hall, Burton-on-Trent (0283 361011).
Lichfield Friary—The Dell, Lichfield. Courts: H3. *Secretary:* Mrs P H Evans, 71 Ferndale Road, Lichfield (Lichfield 51793 pri, Heath Hayes 79004 bus).
Linden Lea—Linden Lea, Finchfield, off Finchfield Road West. Courts: H3. *Secretary:* Mrs J Lewis, 3 The Dingle, Finchfield, Wolverhampton (762557 pri, Telford 460427).
Little Aston Tennis Club—Little Aston Lane, Little Aston, Sutton Coldfield. Courts: H3. *Secretary:* Mrs R Dennis, 62a Streety Lane, Sutton Coldfield, West Midlands (021 353 5679).
Marston LTC—Wobaston Road, Stafford. Courts: H3. *Secretary:* G York, 25 St Chad's Close, Brewood (Brewood 850757).
Midshires Building Society—IMI Marston Sports Ground, Wobaston Road, W'ton. Courts: H3. *Secretary:* T J Holbrook, Midshires Building Society, PO Box 81, Wolverhampton (Walsall 23182 pri, Wolverhampton 710710 bus).
Norton Cricket and Tennis Club—Community Drive, Smallthorne, Stoke. Courts: H3. *Secretary:* R J Clarke, 38 Magdalen Road, Blurton, Stoke-on-Trent (S-o-T 310270).
Old Hill TC—Barrs Road, Cradley Heath, WM. Courts: H4. *Secretary:* Miss S A Newman, 86 Lodge Field Road, Halesowen, W Midlands B62 8BA (021 559 2509 pri, 0384 65787 bus).
Penkridge—Pinfold Lane, Penkridge. Courts: H2. *Secretary:* Mrs L Benning, Three Hammers House, Stafford Road, Coven Heath (Standeford 791230).
Pirelli—Derby Road, Burton (opposite BTR Factory). Courts: H2. *Secretary:* D Tilley, 27 Hawks Drive, Winshill, Burton-on-Trent (Burton-on-Trent 32386 pri, Burton 216161 ext 194 bus).
Quarry Bank—Merry Hill, Quarry Bank. Courts: H3. *Secretary:* M J Pearson, 50 Meriden Avenue, Wollaston, Stourbridge, West Midlands (Stourbridge 5689 pri, 021 559 1511 bus).
Reedswood—Bentley Lane, Walsall. Courts: H2. *Secretary:* G Nicholls, 61 Greenfields Road, Shelfield, Walsall WS4 1RT (Pelsall 685 755 pri, 021 4020 ext 295 bus).
Spital Bowling & Tennis Club—Wiggington Road, Tamworth. Courts: H3. *Secretary:* G Penny, 152 Gillway Lane, Tamworth (Tamworth 62540).
St Edwards—*Secretary:* S Cope, Ash House, Cheadle Road, Blythe Bridge, Stoke-on-Trent (Blythe Bridge 5025).
Stone—Newcastle Road, Stone. *Secretary:* Miss V Inskip, 29 Crestwood Drive, Walton, Stone (Stone 815120).
Stourbridge—Sugar Loaf Lane, Iverley, Stourbridge. Courts: G6, H10 (2 floodlit). *Secretary:* Mr J Lorbett, 1 Elm Drive, Blakedown, Kidderminster (0562 700563 pri, Stourport 4689 bus).
Streetly Cricket & Sports Club—Briar Avenue, Streetly. Courts: H2. *Secretary:* Mrs J P Williams, 115 Chester Road, Streetly, Sutton Coldfield B74 2HE.
T P Riley—T P Riley School, Lichfield Road, Walsall. *Secretary:* M Rees, 70 Persehouse Street, Walsall (20218 pri, Bloxwich 76463 bus).
Wall Heath—Enville Road, Recreation Ground, Wall Heath. Courts: H4. *Secretary:* Miss E J Harris, 46 Ridge Road (Kingswinford 274712).
Walsall Arboretum—Arboretum, Walsall. Courts: H3. *Secretary:* Mr R D Taylor, 44 Argyle Road, Walsall (Walsall 32069 pri, W'ton 712551).

Walsall Wood (Oak Park)—Oak Park, Lichfield Road, Walsall Wood. Courts: H2. *Secretary:* Mr J Carter, 50 Gilpin Crescent, Pelsall, Walsall (Pelsall 691144 pri, 021 743 2446 bus).
Walton Lawn Tennis Club—Village Hall, Walton, Stafford. Courts: H4. *Secretary:* Mrs C Burnett, 90 Cannock Road, Stafford (660801 pri).
Wednesbury TC—Wood Green Road, Walsall. Courts: H5. *Secretary:* M Keen, 24 Hydes Road, Wednesbury, West Midlands (021 556 4037).
West Midlands College—Gorway Road. Courts: H12. *Secretary:* West Midlands College, Gorway Road, Walsall WS1 3BD (Walsall 29141).
Wollaston—Prestwood Drive, Stourton, nr Stourbridge, Worcs. Courts: H6. *Secretary:* R S Pike, 126a Ham Lane, Stourbridge, West Midlands (Hagley 883115).
Wolverhampton—Newbridge Crescent. Courts: H7, G7. *Secretary:* Tennis Secretary, Neville Lodge, Newbridge Crescent, Tettenhall, Wolverhampton (755265).
Woodfield Sports & Social (Tennis Section)—Penn Road, Courts: H4. *Secretary:* F Butler, 27 Coton Road, Goldthorn Hill, W'ton (W'ton 330238 pri, W'ton 42289 bus).
Wombourne—Church Road, Wombourne, W'ton. Courts: H3. *Secretary:* Mrs J Owens, 104 Wombourne Park, Wombourne (893646).

OTHER AFFILIATED ORGANISATIONS (3)

Burton Area Lawn Tennis Association—*Secretary:* R A Gray, 4 The Green, Barton-under-Needwood, Burton-on-Trent (Barton-under-Needwood 2340).
Action Youth International—*Secretary:* Mr J Close, Knowle Bank House, Knowle Bank Road, Audley, Staffs ST7 8DT (0782 720736 pri, 0782 722888 bus).
Staffordshire League—Mr G Carter, 25 Coalway Road, Penn, W'ton (Wollaston 5342069).

AFFILIATED SCHOOLS (42)

Boys
Queen Mary Grammar School — Sutton Road, Walsall. **The Wulfric School** — St Mary's Drive, Burton-on-Trent.

Girls
Blythe Bridge High School — Cheadle Road, Stoke-on-Trent. **Clayton High School** — Clayton Hall, Newcastle. **Queen Mary's High School** — Upper Forster Street, Walsall. **St Mary & St Anne** — Abbots Bromley, Rugeley. **The Orme Girls' School** — Victoria Road, Newcastle.

Mixed
Aelfgar School — Taylor's Lane, Rugeley. **Aldridge School** — Tynings Lane, Aldridge, Walsall. **Barr Beacon School** — Old Hall Lane, Aldridge, Walsall. **Blessed William Howard** — Rowley Avenue, Stafford. **Blurton High School** — Beaconsfield Drive, Blurton, Stoke-on-Trent. **Blythe Bridge High School** — Cheadle Road, Blythe Bridge, Stoke-on-Trent. **Chase Town High School** — Pool Road, Chasetown, Walsall. **Darlaston Comprehensive** — Herbert's Park Road, Walsall. **Dartmouth High School** — Wilderness Lane, Great Barr, Birmingham. **Denstone College** — Uttoxeter. **Endon High School** — Leek New Road, Endon, Stoke-on-Trent. **Forest of Needwood** — Station Road, Rolleston, Burton-on-Trent. **Friary Grange** — Eastern Avenue, Lichfield. **Great Wyrley High School** — Hall Lane, Great Wyrley, Walsall. **Hagley Park School** — Rugeley. **Highfields School** — Boundary Way, Penn, Wolverhampton. **Holden Lane High School** — Milton Road, Sneyd Green, Stoke-on-Trent. **King Edward VI High School** — Upper Street, Johns Street, Lichfield. **King Edward VI High School** — West Way, Stafford. **Leek High School** — Springfield Road, Leek. **Longton High School** — Box Lane, Stoke-on-Trent. **Marshlands High School** — Mile House Lane, Newcastle, Staffs. **Newcastle-under-Lyme School** — Victoria Road, Newcastle, Staffs. **Royal Wolverhampton School** — Penn Road, Wolverhampton. **St Dominics Priory School** — Station Road, Stone. **St Thomes More Comprehensive** — Bilston Road, Willenhall. **Stoke-on-Trent Rith Form College** — Victoria Road, Fenton, Stoke-on-Trent. **T P Riley Comprehensive School** — Lichfield Road, Bloxwich, nr Walsall. **Trentham High School** — Allerton Road, Trentham, Stoke-on-Trent. **Walton High School** — The Rise, Walton-on-the Hill, Stafford. **The Westwood High School** — Westwood Park, Leek, Staffs. **Willfield High School** Lander Place, North Ubberley, Stoke-on-Trent. **Wolgarton High School** — Cannock Road, Staffordshire.

All correspondence to School Clubs should be addressed to the Master or Mistress in charge of lawn tennis.

SUFFOLK COUNTY LAWN TENNIS ASSOCIATION

Hon Secretary—**C B Hall,** 10 Anita Close, West, Ipswich IP2 0JJ (Ipswich 51289).
Hon Treasurer—**B C Driscoll,** 38 Kingsfield Avenue, Ipswich (58722).
Hon Men's Match Secretary—**I Moore,** 31 Victoria Close, Thurston IP31 5LX (0359 30100).
Hon Ladies' Match Secretary—**Mrs H S Lee,** The Grange, Newmans Green, Acton, Sudbury CO10 0AB (953 310094).
Hon Secretary—Juniors Committee, **Mrs E Griffiths,** 55 Looe Road, Felixstowe (0394 2746).
Junior Fixtures—**Mrs P Brown,** 'Cranborne', The Street, Whitnesham, Ipswich (985696).
Representatives on the Council—**P J Mornard, Mrs H S Lee.**

AFFILIATED CLUBS (58)

Bramford Tennis Club—The Playing Field. Courts: H3. *Secretary:* W Betts, 60 Leggatt Drive, Bramford, Ipswich (41544).

Brettenham Park LTC—Brettenham Park, Ipswich. Courts: H3. *Secretary:* A Colling, Old Buckenham Hall School (0473-74075).
Bredfield & Dist—Bredfield Playing Field. Courts: H2. *Secretary:* Mrs Y Schofield, 22 Lime Kiln Quay Road, Woodbridge IP12 1BB, Bury St Edmunds (6221).
British Sugar Sports & Social Club—PO Box 15, Bury St Edmunds IP32 7BB. Courts: H2. *Secretary:* G H Battle, BS Corp Ltd, Hollow Road, Bury St Edmunds IP32 7BB (0284 63291).
British Telecom Research—Courts: H2. *Secretary:* R Hunter, 18 Warren Close, Elmswell, Bury St Edmunds IP30 9DS (0359 40818).
Brown, William & Co—Humber Doucy Lane, Ipswich. Courts: H2. Secretary: R C Clover, Wm Brown & Co (IPS) Ltd, Greyfriars Road, Ipswich IP4 5JE (73463 pri, 56761 ext 130 bus).
Copdock & Washbrook—Courts: H2. *Secretary:* Mrs M Southgate, 38 Charlottes, Washbrook, Ipswich (86 409).
Cowell's Athletic—Turners Bramford Road, Ipswich. Courts: H2. *Secretary:* J W Ling, W S Cowells Ltd, Wharfdale Road, Ipswich.
Cranes—Nacton Road. Courts: H3. *Secretary:* A Seals, Cranes Ltd, Nacton Road, Ipswich IP3 0QW (75212).
Deben Junior Club—Kingston Field, Woodbridge. Courts: H7, G9. *Secretary:* Mrs J Parlett, 11 Upper Moorfield Road, Woodbridge IP12 4JW (993 2757).
Eastern Coachworks—Norfolk Street, Lowestoft (0502 69224). Courts: H2, G1. *Secretary:* K S Whatling, 164 Carlton Road, Lowestoft.
Eastern Electricity Wherstead House—Wherstead. Courts: G1, H2. *Secretary:* Miss S Atkins, Planning Programming Dept, EEB, Russell Road, Ipswich IP1 2DQ (221331).
Exning—Glanelly Road. Courts: H2. *Secretary:* Miss E Wall, 9 Wickham House Cottages, Wickhambrook, Newmarket (870 279).
Felixstowe—Bath Road, Felixstowe (2940). Courts: G13, H6. *Secretary:* R P Davis, 26 Gosford Way, Felixstowe IP12 4RT (0394 270630).
Fisons (Ipswich)—Harvest House, Felixstowe. Courts: G1, H3 Playford Road, Ipswich. *Secretary:* L S Hosken, 31 Milnrow, Ipswich IP2 0SN (681250).
Framlingham—Badingham Road. Courts: H3. *Secretary:* Mrs V Volz, Cear Charsfield, Woodbridge (047337-430).
Greene King LTC—Victory Ground, Newton Road, Bury St Edmunds. Courts: H2. *Secretary:* G M Cooper, Westgate Brewery (0284 63222).
Grundisburgh LTC—Playing Field. Courts: H3. *Secretary:* Mrs S Mercer, The Gate House, Witnesham (85689).
Guardian Royal Exchange—Tuddenham Road, Ipswich. Courts: G6, H3. *Secretary:* P J Wood, 99 Bridgewater Road, Ipswich IP2 9QH (684498).
Gunton Park—Corton Long Lane, Courts: H2. *Secretary:* G H. Drake, 157 Corton Road NR32 4PR (0502 66804).
Hadleigh—Meadows Way, Calais Street, Hadleigh. Courts: H4. *Secretary:* Miss J Lay, 10 Laburnam Way, Nayland, Colchester (262541).
Halesworth—Dairy Hill. Courts: H2. *Secretary:* D E Gardam, 6 Highfield Road, Halesworth IP19 8SJ (09867 2656).
Haverhill—Sports Centre. Courts: G4, H3. *Secretary:* Mrs M McGregor, 32 Arrendene, Haverhill CB9 9JQ (0440 703828).
Hoxne LTC—Courts: H2. *Secretary:* Mrs A Feaveryear, Trenchard, Cross Street, Hoxne IP21 5AH (0379 360).
ICI (Paints Division), Stowmarket—Needham Road (3161). Courts: H4. *Secretary:* S Hawes, 23 Meadowvale Close, Ipswich.
Ipswich & Dist NALGO—*Secretary:* Mrs N S Hine, 4 Corder Road, Ipswich (51722). Courts: H2 Park Road.
Ipswich Sports Club—Henley Road (51143). Courts: H9 (3 floodlit). *Secretary:* Mrs M Hawes, 147 Henley Road, Ipswich IP1 4NL (215333).
Ipswich YMCA—Bourne End, Wherstead Road, Ipswich (57008). Courts: H4. *Secretary:* Mrs M Darling, 18 Leggatt Close, Needham Market.
Kesgrave—Bell Lane. Courts: H2. *Secretary:* Mrs M E Moss, 1a Cambridge Road, Kesgrave, Ipswich IP5 7GN.
Kirkley LTC—Kensington Gardens. Courts: H2. *Secretary:* B Robinson, 9 Viburnum Green, Lowestoft (0502 88610).
Lavenham LTC—Comm Council Ground. Courts: H3. *Secretary:* Mrs V Morley, Loose Hall, Hitcham, Ipswich IP7 7LY (740322).
Lower Layham—Courts:H 2. *Secretary:* R D Young, Ashbrook House, Layham Road, Layham, Ipswich IP7 5NB.
Maidenhall Junior Club—Sports Centre, Halifax Road (214469). Courts: H2. *Secretary:* Mrs C M Teevan, 26 Martin Road, Ipswich IP2 8BJ (211578).
Newmarket—Hamilton Road, Newmarket (0638 663291). Courts: G4, H5. *Secretary:* W E Stuart, 2 Princess Way, Newmarket CB8 0NX (0638 3291).
Nomads—Bramford Road. Courts: H2. *Secretary:* M R Bull, 32 Blackwater Avenue, Colchester CO4 3UT (864459).
Northgate Junior Club—Northgate Sports Centre. Courts: H4. *Secretary:* Mrs A Allard, 74 Brunswick Road, Ipswich IP4 4BP (78487).
North Lowestoft—Denes Oval. Courts: H2. *Secretary:* J M Walford, 6 Beverley Close, Oulton Broad NR33 8QQ (0502 61383).
Orwell Park—Orwell Park School, Nacton, Ipswich IP10 0EH . Court: H3. *Secretary:* P J Mornard (Nacton 225).
Oulton Broad—Denes Oval. Courts: H2. *Secretary:* Mrs M Hollby, 27 Daffodil Walk, Lowestoft NR33 8NR (0502 85440).
Ransomes/Reavells—Sidegate Avenue, Ipswich (76141). Courts: G3, H3. *Secretary:* A C Jennings, 26 Longfield Road, Capel St Mary, Ipswich IP9 2XG (0473 311 291).
Risbygate Bowls & Lawn Tennis—Westley Road, Bury St Edmunds (0284 5143). Courts: H4. *Secretary:* K Morton, 11 Woodland Place, Great Barton, Bury St Edmunds IP31 2TG (028487 318 pri, 039 870 723 bus).

Roundwood—Stone Lodge Lane, Ipswich. Courts: H4. *Secretary:* P Andreasen, 21 Warwick Road, Ipswich (212977).
Royal Hospital School Old Boys—Courts: H3. *Secretary:* D Marsh, c/o RH School, Ipswich ID2 2RT.
St John's—Westbury Road, Ipswich. Courts: H4. *Secretary:* B S Croucher, 44 Chatsworth Drive, Rushmere Park, Ipswich IP4 5XD (73488).
Saxmundham Dist Sports & Social Club—Courts: H2. *Secretary:* Mrs F Foreman, 6 Rendham Road, Saxmundham (922194).
Southwold—Hotson Road. Courts: H3. *Secretary:* Mrs J Bird, "Rosscarberry", Reydon, Southwold (723903).
Sproughton—Church Lane. Courts: H3. *Secretary:* Mrs M Sillett, Bramford Hall, Ipswich IP8 4JP (42340).
Stephen Walters & Sons Ltd—Cornard Road, Sudbury (0787 72266). Courts: H1. *Secretary:* R Lynton, Stephen Walters & Sons Ltd, Sudbury (0787 72510).
Stowmarket—Courts: H4. *Secretary:* A E Winchester, 24 Church Walk, Stowmarket IP14 1ET (612105 pri, 612060 bus).
Stradbroke Tennis Club—Wilby Road, Stradbroke (037 984 438). Courts: H3. *Secretary:* Mrs M Ellis, Queen Street, Stradbroke IP21 5HG(438).
Sudbury—Sports Centre, Tudor Road. Courts: H3. *Secretary:* Mrs B Francis, Goodwin, Sudbury Road, Newton Green, Sudbury CO10 0QH (75127).
Tattingstone—Green Lane. Courts: G3, H1. *Secretary:* Mrs A J Pearce, Wythesdone, Church Lane, Tattingstone IP9 2NA (328466).
Thurston—Thurston Upper School. Courts: H6. *Secretary:* Miss J S Troll, 5 Bunbury Avenue, Great Barton, Bury St Edmunds (0284 64415).
Willis Faber & Dumas—Rushmere (215789). Courts: H3 (1 indoor). *Secretary:* T Johnson, 182 Cauldwell, Hall Road, Ipswich IP4 5DB (217911 bus).
Woodbridge—The Avenue, Woodbridge. Courts: H4. *Secretary:* Mrs B Sutton, 6 Norman Close, Woodbridge IP12 1JT.
Woolpit—*Hon Secretary:* J Levatis, Piper Green Road, Woolpit, Bury St Edmunds (0359 40708).
Wrentham—Long Green, Wrentham. Courts: H2. *Secretary:* Mrs M Smith, 23 Mill Lane, Wrentham, Beccles NR34 7JQ (050 275 364).

OTHER AFFILIATED ORGANISATIONS (7)

Bury & West Suffolk Tennis Tournament—Victory Ground, Bury St Edmunds. *Secretary:* R V Wilson, 12 Diomed Drive, Gt Barton, Bury St Edmunds IP31 2TD (028 487 455).
Framlingham Tournament Committee—Framlingham College. Courts: G15. *Secretary:* Mrs B Martin, 10 Pembroke Road, Framlingham IP13 9HA (723442).
Lowestoft & East Suffolk Junior Tournament Committee,—B W Soloman, Recreation & Amenities Dept, Esplanade, Lowestoft (0502 65989 ext 104). **Ipswich & District League**—*Secretary:* P Goodman, 14 Mayfield Road, Ipswich.
Lowestoft & District League—*Secretary:* F G Moore, 12 High Beech, Lowestoft (4677).
Sudbury & District League—*Secretary:* Mrs B Mauldon, Stambourne, Melford Road, Sudbury.
Suffolk LTA Junior Tournament Committee—Mrs S Watts, 16 Grange Road, Kesgrave, Ipswich (622288).
Suffolk Tennis Coaches Association—*Secretary:* S Woodgett, 6 Belmont Court, Newmarket (0638 662712).

AFFILIATED SCHOOLS (101)

Northern Area

Beccles Middle School — Beccles. **Sir John Leman School. Benjamin Britten High School. Bungay High School. Bungay Middle School. Debenham C of E School. Denes High School** — Lowestoft. **Elm Tree Middle School** — Lowestoft. **Eye School. Framlingham School. Framlingham Mills School. Gisleham Middle School** — Lowestoft. **Halesworth Middle School. Harris Middle School** — Lowestoft. **Kirkley High School** — Lowestoft. **Kirkley Middle School** — Lowestoft. **Leiston High School. Leiston Middle School. Lothingland Middle School** — Lowestoft. **Pakefield Middle School** — Lowestoft. **Reydon School. Roman Hill Middle School** — Lowestoft. **Saxmundham Middle School. Stradbroke School. Worlingham Middle School** — Beccles.

Southern Area

Butley C of E Middle School — Woodbridge. **Chantry School** — Ipswich. **Claydon High School** — Ipswich. **Copleston School** — Ipswich. **Deben High School** — Felixstowe. **East Bergholt Modern** — Colchester. **Farlingaye High School** — Woodbridge. **Hadleigh High School. Holbrook Modern School** — Ipswich. **Kesgrave High School** — Ipswich. **Kingston Middle School** — Woodbridge. **Nacton Heath** — Ipswich. **Northgate High School** — Ipswich. **Orwell High School** — Felixstowe. **St Albans RC Aided School** — Ipswich. **Stoke High. Thurleston High School** — Ipswich. **Westbourne High School** — Ipswich.

Western Area

All Saints C of E Middle School — Sudbury. **Bacton School** — Stowmarket. **Beyton Middle School. Breckland Middle School** — Brandon. **Castle Hill Middle School** — Haverhill. **Chalkstone Middle School** — Haverhill. **Clare Middle School. College Heath Middle School. Combs Middle School** — Stowmarket. **County Upper School** — Bury St Edmunds. **Gt Cornard Middle School** — Bury St Edmunds. **Gt Cornard Upper School** — Sudbury. **Hardwick Middle School** — Bury St Edmunds. **Haverhill Castle Manor Upper School. Horringer Court Middle School** — Bury St Edmunds. **Howard Middle School** — Bury St Edmunds. **Ixworth Middle School** — Ixworth. **King Edward VI Upper School** — Bury St Edmunds. **Mildenhall Riverside Middle School. Mildenhall Upper School. Needham Market Middle School** — Haverhill. **Newmarket High School. Newmarket**

Upper School. Parkway Middle School — Haverhill. **St Benedict's RC Aided Upper School** — Bury St Edmunds. **St Felix C of E Middle School** — Newmarket. **St James C of E Aided Middle School** — Bury St Edmunds. **St Louis RC Middle School** — Bury St Edmunds. **Scaltback Middle School** — Newmarket. **Stanton Blackbourne C of E Middle School. Stoke-by-Nayland Middle School. Stowmarket High School. Stowmarket Middle School. Sudbury Upper School. Thurston Upper School** — Bury St Edmunds. **Uplands Middle School** — Sudbury. **Westley Middle School** — Bury St Edmunds.

Other Schools
Amberfield School — Ipswich. **Brandeston Hall School** — Woodbridge. **Convent of Jesus & Mary School** — Ipswich. **Culford School** — Bury St Edmunds. **Felixstowe College. Framlingham College. Chadacre** — Bury St Edmunds. **Ipswich High School. Ipswich School. Morton Hall** — Bury St Edmunds. **Old Buckenham Hall School** — Brettenham. **Orwell Park School** — Ipswich. **Royal Hospital School** — Ipswich. **St Felix** — Southwold. **St Georges** — Gt Finborough. **St Joseph's College** — Ipswich. **Salter's Hall School** — Sudbury. **Stoke College Prep. Stoke College** — Stoke-by-Clare. **Suffolk College. Woodbridge School. Wolverstone Hall School** — Ipswich.

All correspondence to School Clubs should be addressed to the Master or Mistress in charge of lawn tennis.

SURREY COUNTY LAWN TENNIS ASSOCIATION

Hon Secretary—**J C Robbins,** 52 Fairfax Avenue, Epsom KT17 2QP (01-393 3836).
Hon Treasurer—**L F Guillem FCA,** 35-37 Grosvenor Gardens, London SW1 (01-828 3156 bus).
Hon Men's Match Secretary—**C B Hutchings,** 30 Pennington Drive, Weybridge (Walton-on-Thames 29887).
Hon Boys' Match Secretary—**B Johnston,** 25 Mount Pleasant, Ewell (01 393 7799).
Hon. Ladies' Match Secretary—**Mrs S Burditt,** 20 Orchards Way, Hurst Green, Oxted (Oxted 3572).
Hon Girls' Match Secretary—**Mrs P C Willson,** 33 Gatesden Road, Fetcham, Leatherhead (Leatherhead 374543).
Hon Men's Veterans Match Secretary—**D C Page,** "Brockman", St Catherines, Hook Heath, Woking GU22 0HW (72326).
Hon Ladies' Veterans Match Secretary: **Mrs S Hill,** 16 Coombe Wood Hill, Purley (01-660 7898).
Representatives on the Council—**R J Presley, J C Robbins, A R Scarlett.**

AFFILIATED CLUBS (140)

Alfold—Recreation Ground, Crossways, Alfold. Courts: H2. *Secretary:* J Boyse, 103 Cranleigh Mead, Cranleigh (274069).

All England Lawn Tennis & Croquet—Church Road, Wimbledon, London SW19 (01-946 2244). Courts: G18, H11. *Secretary;* R D Ambrose, All England LT & Croquet Club, Church Road, Wimbledon, London SW19 (01-946 2244).

Ash—Coronation Gardens, Ash. Courts: H3. *Secretary:* R P Simpson, Jaspers, 50 Tudor Way, Church Crookham, Aldershot, Hants GU13 0LX (Fleet 28340).

Ashford—Woodthorpe Road, Ashford, Middlesex. Courts: H6. *Secretary:* P Blundell, 10 Ford Road, Ashford, Middx TW15 2RD.

Ashtead Tennis Players—Ashtead Recreation Ground, Ashtead. Courts: H4. *Secretary:* R J Beveridge, 139 Craddocks Avenue, Ashtead KT21 1NR (03722 73675).

Atkins Sports & Social Club—Woodcotegrove, Ashley Road, Epsom (26140). Courts: H2. *Secretary:* C H P Bass, Atkins Sports & Social Club, Woodcote Grove, Ashley Road, Epsom (26140).

Avorian Nomads—*Secretary:* P V Stiles, 15 Stringham Copse, Seemarsh, Ripley GU23 6JE.

Bagshot & Crawley Rise—Portsmouth Road, Camberley. Courts: H1. *Secretary:* T Gibson, The Orchard, 9 Kings Ride, Camberley (23539).

Bank of England Sports (Lawn Tennis Section)—(01-876 8417). Priory Lane, Roehampton, London SW15 (01-876 2830). Courts: G19, H7. *Secretary:* N C Hughes, Maths GP4/2 FSD HO4, Bank of England, Threadneedle Street, EC2R.

Banstead Downs—Bolters Lane, Banstead. Courts: H4. *Secretary:* C J Barrett, 38 Tangier Way, Tadworth (Burgh Heath 53109).

Barclays Bank Sports—1212 London Road, Norbury, London SW16. Courts: G5, H2. *Secretary:* T Shotten,

Barnes—Lonsdale Road, Barnes, London SW13 (01-748 6220). Courts: H3. *Secretary:* J W Anderson, 8 Lowther Road, Barnes SW13 9ND (01-748 8415).

BBC—Motspur Park, New Malden (01-942 1255). Courts: H8. *Secretary:* P F Gorringe, 23 Audley Firs, Walton on Thames KT12 5NW (01 567 6655 ext 264).

Birtley—Bramley. Courts: H3. *Secretary:* T L Williams, 'Conifers,' Upfold Lane, Cranleigh (Cranleigh 4867).

Bourne—12 Frensham Road, Farnham (Farnham 716144). Courts: H6. *Secretary:* Mrs A Buckingham, Bourne Club, 12 Frensham Road, Farnham (Farnham 716144).

Brightwell—Brightwell Gardens, Farnham (back of Regal Cinema). Courts: H3. *Secretary:* Mrs K M Keith, 39 Alma Way, Heath End, Farnham (Aldershot 23982).

Byfleet—Dartnell Park, West Byfleet (Byfleet 42849). Courts: G6, H6. *Secretary:* M L Barratt, 3 Oakcroft Close, West Byfleet (Byfleet 46924).

Camber—Dulwich Common, London SE21 (01-693 2459). Courts: H3. *Secretary:* Miss E Sherwood, 46 Vale Lodge, Perry Vale, Forest Hill SE23.

Camberley—Southcote Park, Portsmouth Road, Camberley. Courts: H4. *Secretary:* Miss M Harley, 13 Park Road, Camberley (0276 22416).
Carshalton—Beeches Avenue, Carshalton. Courts: H5. *Secretary:* G G Way, 14 Upland Road, Sutton (01-643 2514).
Cassac—Lloyd Park, Coombe Road, Croydon. Courts: H3. *Secretary:* J R P Henton, Lloyd Park Avenue, Coombe Road, Croydon CR0 5SA (01 688 5783).
Cedars—6 Melrose Road, Southfields, London SW18. Courts: H3. *Secretary:* N L Webb, The Lodge, 65 Parkside, London SW19 (01-947 0021).
Central Electricity Laboratories—Cleeve Road, Leatherhead (Leatherhead 4488). Courts: H3. *Secretary:* Mrs A E Ely, Kelvin Avenue, Leatherhead KT22 7SE.
Cheam—Peaches Close (01-642 1817). Courts: G7, H6. *Secretary:* Mrs L Ward, 17 Wolsey Close, Worcester Park KT4 7EF (01 337 8993).
Cheam Fields—Devon Road, Cheam (01-642 1319). Courts: G3, H3. *Secretary:* A Prizant, 6 Regents Close, Whyteleafe RR3 0AH (01 668 3996).
Chipstead Hard Court—High Road, Chipstead. Courts: H5. *Secretary:* Mrs R Holmes, 5 Peaks Hill, Purley CR2 3JG (01-660 5412).
Chobham and District—Recreation Ground, Chobham. Courts: H3. *Secretary:* Mrs V Griffiths, 10, Morton Close, Horsell, Woking (Woking 65707).
Claygate—rear of Torrington Close, Claygate. Courts: H4. *Secretary:* B J Whitney, Rosebank, 29 Beaconsfield Road, Claygate (Esher 62762).
Coombe Wood—Galsworthy Road, Kingston Hill. Courts: G5, H2. *Secretary:* D J Gibbons, Brook Orchard, High Drive, New Malden.
Coopers Hill Recreational Trust—Coopers Hill, Englefield Green. *Secretary:* Mrs P S Latimer, 'Lamorna,' 5 Lodge Close, Middle Hill, Englefield Green TW20 0JN (Egham 37017).
Coulsdon Court—Coulsdon Court Road, Coulsdon. Courts: H4. *Secretary:* N J Lamble, Coulsdon Court LTC.
Cranleigh (Merton Park)—Cranleigh Road, Merton Park, London SW19 (Liberty 7565). Courts: H5. *Secretary:* G R Stephenson, 9 North Close, Morden SM4 4HG (01 540 2003).
Dorking Lawn Tennis and Squash—Roman Road, Dorking. Courts: H8. *Hon Secretary:* c/o Dorking LTC, Roman Road, Dorking.
Dormansland—High Street, Dormansland, nr Lingfield. Courts: H2. *Secretary:* N A Snell, 12 Ladbroke Hurst, Dormansland RH7 6QB (Lingfield 834579).
Downs (Cheam)—Holland Avenue, Cheam (01-642 3019). Courts: H4. *Secretary:* Mr S J Street, 15 Sommerville Gardens, Cheam SM1 2BU.
Downswood—Tattenham Corner, Epsom. Courts: H3. *Secretary:* Mrs B Webb, 40 Tangier Way, Burgh Heath (Burgh Heath 53842).
Dulwich—Turney Road, London SE21(main entrance in Burbage Road) 01-274 1242. Courts: G6, H5. *Secretary:* Mrs D M Fenner, 8 Dulwich Village SE21 7IL (01 693 2983).
Dunsfold—King George's Field, Dunsfold, Godalming. Courts: H2. *Secretary:* Mrs P A Skates, Hawthorn, Avenue Road, Cranleigh.
Ebbisham Sports—Eastway, Pound Lane, Epsom. Courts: H4. *Secretary:* Miss M Clarke, c/o The Club.
Effingham Golf Club (Lawn Tennis Section)—Effingham. Courts: G2, H2. *Secretary:* A J B Norman, Effingham Golf Club, Effingham.
Elmsway—Elmsway, Ashford, Middlesex. Courts: G3, H1. *Secretary:* J W Langmead, 135 The Avenue, Sunbury on Thames, Middx.
Elmwood—337 Tamworth Lane, Mitcham (1262). Courts: H3. *Secretary:* Mrs L I Connell, 19 Brockenhurst Way, London SW16 (01-764 6437).
Ember—between 21 and 23 The Drive, Esher (Emberbrook 2145). *Secretary:* Mrs J Condon, 21 Grove Way, Esher.
Epsom—Woodcote Road, Epsom. Courts: G7, H5. *Secretary:* Mrs P Cadge, Leaside, Dene Road, Ashtead (Ashtead 75233).
Esher—Milbourne Lane, Esher. Courts: G6, H3. *Secretary:* Mrs J Nelson-Smith, Brandywine, Orchard Way, Esher KT10 9DY (Esher 65447).
Ewell—West Street, Ewell (01-393 1815). Courts: H3. *Secretary:* R Behrend, 126 Stoneleigh Park Road, Ewell (01-393 2272).
Ewell Downs—Ewell Downs Road, Ewell. Courts: H3. *Secretary:* Mrs B Lorkin, 7 Wimborne Close, Epsom.
EwhurstEwhurst Recreation Ground, Ewhurst. Courts: H2. *Secretary:* Dr R B Dean, Ashcroft, Ockley Road, Ewhurst GU6 7QF (Cranleigh 277561).
Felbridge—Crawley Down Road, opposite Warrent Close, Felbridge. Courts: H2. *Secretary:* Mrs S Kilian, 25 Tiltwood Drive, Crawley Down, Crawley RH10 4AD (0342 713946).
Foxhills—Stonehill Road, Ottershaw (Ottershaw 2050). Courts: H6. *Secretary:* Hon Sec Tennis Section (as above).
Gardens—343 Wimbledon Park Road, London SW19 (01-788 3807). Courts: H6. *Hon Secretary:* Mrs B Robins, 25 Blincoe Close, Thursley Gardens SW19.
Godalming—Broadwater Recreation Ground, Farncombe, Godalming. Courts: H3. *Secretary:* Mrs M Wilson, Firbank, Portsmouth Road, Milford, Godalming.
Godstone—Godstone Green, Godstone. Courts: G2, H2. *Secretary:* Mrs P M Bellchambers, 43 Markfield Road, Caterham CR3 6RQ (43595).
Grafton Lawn Tennis & Squash Racquets—70a Thornton Road, Clapham Park, London SW12 (01-673 2891). Courts: H8 (1 floodlit). *Secretary:* Mrs R Lewis, Grafton LTC, 70a Thornton Road, Clapham Park, London SW12 (01-673 2891).
Hindhead—Beacon Hill Road, Hindhead. Courts: H2. *Secretary:* Mrs S Goddard, 1 Downside, Clovelly Road, Hindhead.
Honor Oak Cricket & Lawn Tennis—Dulwich Common, London SE21 (Gipsy Hill 2122). Courts: H4. *Secretary:* Miss D Haydon, 121 Westwood Park, Forest Hill, London SE23 (699 7309).

Horley—Vicarage Lane, Horley. Courts: G4, H5. *Secretary:* Mrs A C Davies, 10 Westleas, Horley RM6 8AF.
Horsley Sports (Lawn Tennis Section)—East Horsley. Courts: H6. *Secretary:* I Stemson, Whistlers, Little Cranmore Lane, West Horsley, Leatherhead.
Horton Hospital Staff Sports & Social (Lawn Tennis Section)—Horton Hospital, Epsom (Epsom 2343). Courts: H2. *Secretary:* M R Junaideen, Villa 3, Horton Hospital Epsom (Epsom 29696 ext 242).
Hurst Green—The Pavillion, Mill Lane, Hurst Green, Oxted. Courts: H2. *Secretary:* Mrs F Dick, Kilnfield, Itchingwood Common, Limpsfield.
Inner City—Brixton. *Secretary:* S Antwi, 159 Stebbing House, Queensdale Crescent, Hollands Park W11.
Kingswood—The Glade Kingswood. Courts: H4. *Secretary:* E Lovis, Wood Grange, Lilley Drive, Kingswood RT20 6JA.
Leatherhead—Cannon Grove, Fetcham. Courts: H4. *Secretary:* Mrs J Loose, 11 Sheridans Road, Great Brookham (Brookham 57882).
Lightwater—Lightwater Country Park, The Avenue, Lightwater. Courts: H3. *Secretary:* Mrs A Pritchett, 2 Birchwood Drive, Lightwater GU18 5RX.
Limpsfield—Detillens Lane, Limpsfield. Courts: G6, H7. *Secretary:* W H Mather, Limpsfield LTC, Detillens Lane, Limpsfield (01-988 4079).
Magdelen Park—Magdalen Road, Wandsworth Common, London SW18 (01-874 8313). Courts: H8. *Secretary:* H E Emes, 60 Lyford Road, Wandsworth Common, London SW18 (01-874 8257).
Malden Wanderers Cricket & Lawn Tennis—Cambridge Avenue, New Malden (01-942 0685). *Secretary:* The Secretary, Malden Wanderers LTC, Cambridge Avenue, New Malden.
Maori—Ivydene, Old Malden Lane, Worcester Park (01-337 1072). Courts: H4. *Secretary:* G W Weston, Canberra House, 47 Middlesex Street, London E1 7AL (01-383 8000).
Merrow—Epsom Road, Merrow, Guildford. Courts: G3, H3. *Secretary:* Mrs M Vallis, Ingatestone, Westward House, Abbotswood, Guildford (0483 502716).
Metropolitan Police Athletic Association (Lawn Tennis Section)—Imber Court, Thames Ditton (Emberbrook 1267). Courts: G15, H6. *Secretary:* Insp D Alldridge MBE, Room G11, Wellington House, Buckingham Gate, London SW1.
Milk Marketing Board Sports & Social (Lawn Tennis Section)—Thames Ditton (01-398 4101). Courts: H3. *Secretary:* Miss B M Coley, Milk Marketing Board, Thames Ditton (01-398 4101 ext 359).
Mytchett—Mytchett Recreation Ground, Hamsmoor Road, Hytchett. Courts: H2. *Secretary:* Mrs G Carter, 29 Bramble Bank, Frimley Green, Camberley GU16 6PN (0252 836129).
National Westminster Bank—Stanford Road, Norbury, London SW16. Courts: G10, H9. *Secretary:* K Eagle, The Eyrie, 316 Avery Hill Road, Eltham (01-850 4496).
New Malden Tennis, Squash & Badminton Club—Courtlands, Somerset Close, Kingston Bypass, New Malden (Malden 0539). Courts: H9. *Secretary:* K A Davies, New Malden LTC, Somerset Close, New Malden.
Norbury Park—Ederline Avenue, Norbury, London SW16 (Pollards 2531). Courts: G4, H4. *Secretary:* J Saunders, 16 Ederline Avenue, Norbury SW16.
North Dulwich—152a East Dulwich Green, London SE22 (01-693 4554). Courts: H4. *Secretary:* Mrs C Bruggermeyer, 38 Beckwith Road, London SE24 (01-274 8047).
Old College Lawn Tennis & Croquet—Gallery Road, Dulwich, London SE21 (01-693 3511). Courts: G4, H4. *Secretary:* Miss L Maccabe, 113 Dulwich Village, SE21 (01 693 2127).
Old Cranleighan—Cranleigh School, Cranleigh. Courts: G3, H7. *Secretary:* T Abbott, 19 Glenville Gardens, Hindhead.
Old Surbitonians—Fairmile Lane, Cobham (3245). Courts: H2. *Secretary:* Virginia Chappell, Ashdown, Surrey Gardens, Effingham (04865 3449).
Onslow Village—Onslow Village, Guildford. Courts: H4. *Secretary:* R P Scurfield, Thatchers, 5 Abbots Close, Onslow Village, Guildford (Guildford 38264).
Oxted Lawn Tennis Club—Master Park, Oxted. Courts: G2, H1. *Secretary:* Mrs J Smith, 5 Quarry Close, Oxted.
Oxshott Village Sports (Lawn Tennis Section)—Steels Lane, Oxshott. Courts: G4, H4. *Secretary:* Mrs L Mackenzie, 98 Tilt Road, Cobham KT11 3HQ (Cobham 67947).
Petersham Sports & Social—River Lane, Petersham. Courts: G6. *Secretary:* C Carmody, 15 St James Avenue, Eastcote, Hampton Hill, Middlesex.
Phoenix—Duke's Avenue, New Malden. Courts: H3. *Secretary:* N R Moseley, 189 Elm Road, New Malden.
Pit Farm (Guildford)—Hillier Road, Guildford. Courts: H7. *Secretary:* Mrs S Williams, 7 Clarence Close, Walton-on-Thames (Walton 229727).
Priory Park—Riverside, Kew (junction of Bushwood Road and Forest Road, Kew). Courts: H3. *Secretary:* Miss J Chiä, 3 Kendrey Gardens, Whitton, Middx TW2 7PA.
Public Schools Old Boys—*Secretary:* W M A Carroll, Beech Cottage, Trodds Lane, Merrow, Guildford (Guildford 72479).
Purley—The Ridge, Purley (Uplands 0608). Courts: G9, H7. *Secretary:* Mrs E Murdoch, 52 Queenswood Avenue, Wallington SM6 8HS (01 647 2455).
Purley Bury Social & Sports—53 Purley Bury Avenue, Purley. *Secretary:* Mrs J Hayden, 20 Grasmere Road, Purley (01 660 4630).
Putney—Balmuir Gardens, Putney, London SW15 (01-788 0618). Courts: G5, H5. *Secretary:* Club Secretary: Balmuir Gardens, Putney, London SW15.
Queen Mary's Hospital—Carshalton (01-643 3300). Courts: G2, H2. *Secretary:* J F Brown, 'Cornerways,' Grange Close, Leatherhead (01-643 3300 ext 351 bus).

RAC Country—Woodcote Park, Epsom (Ashtead 6311/2/3/4). Courts: G2, H4. *Secretary:* Club Secretary, Royal Automobile Club, 89 Pall Mall, London SW1.
Raynes Park Residents—rear of 131 Grand Drive, Raynes Park, London SW20. Courts: H3. *Secretary:* Miss S M Lambkin, 75 Grand Drive, SW20 9DW.
Redhill—Linkfield Lane, Redhill (66705). Courts: G6, H4. *Secretary:* R Chapman, Everest, 15 Weald Way, Reigate RH2 7RC (Reigate 44350).
Reedham Park—Old Lodge Lane, Purley. Courts: G4, H4. *Secretary:* Mrs G Ross, 2 Bradmore Green, Coulsdon.
Reigate and Surrey County—Manor Road, Reigate (42652). Courts: G8, H6. *Secretary:* Mr B Justice, Three Gables, Beech Road, Reigate (42075).
Reigate Priory—Park Lane, Reigate (Reigate 21282). Courts: G5, H4. *Secretary:* Mrs T Gray, 94 Park Lane East, Reigate RH2 8LW.
Richmond—Old Deer Park, Kew Road, Richmond (01-940 2520). Courts: G9, H4. *Secretary:* N B Pinnington, 17 Ailsa Road, St Margarets, Twickenham TW1 1QJ.
Riddlesdown—Lower Barn Road, Purley. Courts: H3. *Secretary:* M G Piper, 86 Foxon Lane, Caterham CR3 5SD (Caterham 43843).
Roehampton—Roehampton Lane, London SW15 (876 1621). Courts: G15, H13. Secretary: Games *Secretary,* Roehampton Club, Roehampton Lane, London SW15 (01-876 1621).
St Andrew's (Cheam)—Sandy Lane, Cheam. Courts: H3. *Secretary:* Mrs B M Hunnisett, 104a Burdon Lane, Cheam, Sutton (642 5776).
St George's Hill—East Road, St George's Hill, Weybridge (Bar 42624). Courts: G17, H12. *Secretary:* J G W Davidson, St Georges Hill LTC, East Road, St Georges Hill (Weybridge 43541).
St Pauls LTC—*Secretary:* Mrs D Topp, 30 Britton Crescent, Sanderstead CR2 0JP.
Sanderstead—Penwortham Road, Sandersted (01-660 2130). Courts: H5. *Secretary:* J R Baxter FCIS, 5 Kendall Avenue, South Sanderstead (01660 0465).
Sanderstead United Reformed Church—Farm Fields, Sanderstead Hill. Courts: H2. *Secretary:* Miss G J Martin, 24a Campden Road, South Croydon.
Sanderstead Village—26a Sanderstead Court Avenue. Courts: H4. *Secretary:* Miss A M Grieve, 28 Royston Avenue, Wallington SM6 8HY.
Selsdon—21a Queenhill Road, Selsdon. Courts: H4. *Secretary:* A Holton, 42 Ladygrove, Pixton Way, Forestdale, Croydon CR0 9LS.
Shalford—Kings Road, Shalford. Courts: H2. *Secretary:* Mrs D Lowe, 43 Kings Road, Shalford, Guildford GU4 8JX (Guildford 557586).
Sheen Lawn Tennis and Squash—9 Fife Road, East Sheen, London SW14 (01-876 4756). Courts: H8 (1 floodlit). *Secretary:* C Northey, Paynesfield Avenue, East Sheen SW14 8DW (01 876 4050).
Shirley—Spring Park Road, Shirley, Croydon. Courts: H4. *Secretary:* Mrs V G Penered, 88 Shirley Avenue, Shirley, Croydon (01-654 4928).
Shirley Park—Sandilands, Addiscombe Road, Croydon (Addiscombe 5449). Courts: G6, H6. *Secretary:* J R Sewell, 120 Addiscombe Road, Croydon CR0 5PQ (01-656 4046).
Sigi Cornish Tennis Centre—Canbury Gardens, Kingston. Courts: H4. *Secretary:* Mrs S Cornish, 52 Woodville Road, Ham.
South Croydon—Beech Copse, South Croydon (01-688 1782). Courts: H5. *Secretary:* Mrs G M Dickson, 136 Foresters Drive, Wallington (01-647 8944).
Southfields—Gressenhall Road, London SW18. *Secretary:* Mrs M Bailey, 7 Gressenhall Road SW18 (01-874 6853).
Spencer—Fieldview, Burntwood Lane, Wandsworth Common, London SW18 (01-874 2717). Courts: G6, H5. *Secretary:* J Conway, 83 Trevelyan Road, Tooting, SW17 (01-672 5483).
Standard Chartered Bank—The Wilderness, Molesey Park Road, East Molesey (01-979 4346). Courts: H3. *Secretary:* K J Williams, c/o Standard Chartered Bank Plc, 2 Regent Street, London SW1Y.
Surbiton—Berrylands, Surbiton (01-399 1594). Courts: G13, H7. *Hon. Secretary:* Surbiton LTC, Berrylands, Surbiton.
Sutton Cricket Club (Tennis Section)—Gander Green Lane, Sutton (01-642 6888). Courts: G4. *Secretary:* D S Parker, 7 Gander Green Lane, Cheam (01-643 7151, 01-228 4008 bus).
Sutton Tennis & Squash Club—Devonshire Road, Sutton (01-642 0209). Courts: H9. *Secretary:* R JHamlin, c/o Sutton Tennis and Squash Club.
Sutton Highfields—Mayfield Road, Sutton. Courts: G6. *Secretary:* Mrs L Donovan, 65 The Ridgeway, Sutton.
Telford Park—35a Killieser Avenue, Streatham Hill, London SW2 (01-674 3061). Courts: G4, H5. *Secretary:* Mrs B Wallower, 4 Palfrey Place SW8 1PA.
Thames Ditton—Weston Green Road, Thames Ditton. Courts: G7, H3. *Secretary:* M Barter, 59a Barnfield Avenue, Kingston KT2 5RD.
University of Surrey—Manor Farm, Guildford. Courts: H9. *Secretary:* Secretary of the Lawn Tennis Club, Students Union, University of Surrey, Guildford.
Wallington Sports (Lawn Tennis Section)—Hillside Gardens, Sandy Lane, Wallington (01-647 3583). Courts: G3, H4. *Hon Secretary:* c/o The Club.
Walton Court Sports and Social (Tennis Section)—Elmgrove Recreation Ground, Walton-on-Thames (28888). Courts: H2. *Hon Secretary:* Birds Eye Walls Ltd, Station Avenue, Walton-on-Thames (98 2888).
Walton-on-Thames—Stompond Lane, Walton-on-Thames (220677). Courts: H7. *Secretary:* Mrs Z J Ashforth, 67 Stoke Road, Walton Kt12 3DD.
Warlingham Sports (Lawn Tennis Section)—Church Lane, Warlingham. Courts: H5. *Secretary:* Mr E J Buck, 9 Harrow Road, Warlingham CR3 9EY.
Wentworth—Wentworth Drive, Wentworth, Virginia Water (Wentworth 22013). Courts: G4, H9. *Secretary:* Col D Beard, Wentworth Club Ltd, Virginia Water GU25 4LF.

West Norwood—Knights Hill, West Norwood, London SE27 (01-670 Hill 4592). Courts: H4. *Secretary:* W Bolton, 97 Northwood Road, Thornton Heath (01 771 1590).
Westside—Woodhayes Road, West Wimbledon, London SW20 (01-946 1254). Courts: G7, H7. *Secretary:* Mrs J Forrester, 17 McKay Road, Wimbledon SW20 (01-946 1487).
West Surrey—Enton Green, nr Godalming. Courts: H3. *Secretary:* Mrs A Vine, Merrions, off Tuesley Lane, Godalming (Godalming 22200).
Weybridge—Walton Lane, Weybridge (46876). Courts: H5 (1 floodlit). *Secretary:* Miss A Grossmith, 2 Greenlands Road, Weybridge KT13 8PP.
Wigmore—43 Becmead Avenue, Streatham, London SW16 (01-769 3671). Courts: H8 (1 floodlit). *Secretary:* N G Calverley, 135 Wavertree Road, SW2.
Wilton—Wilton Grove, Wimbledon, London SW19 (01 542 0293). Courts: H4. *Hon Secretary:* Miss L Morgan, 41 Westcoombe Avenue, London SW20.
Wimbledon Club—Church Road, Wimbledon Park, London SW19 (01-946 7403). Courts: G9, H6. *Secretary:* Mrs P Staniszewski, Flat 1, 9 Inner Park Road, Wimbledon SW19 (01-788 9053).
Wishel—Fircroft Close, Woking. Courts: H2. *Secretary:* Miss M J Turner, Tejeda, Wych Hill Way, Woking (Woking 60496).
Woking Lawn Tennis & Croquet—Pine Road, Hook Heath, Woking (Woking 60574). Courts: G10, H9. *Secretary:* Mrs M J Jones, Woking LTC, Pine Road, Hook Heath, Woking (Woking 60574).
Woldingham—Craigmyle Glebe, Woldingham (2265). Courts: H5. *Secretary:* Mrs J Parsons, Bramley Down, Long Hill, Woldingham (Woldingham 2025).
Woodfield Grove Hard Courts Club—Woodfield Grove, Streatham, London SW16. Courts: H4. *Secretary:* Mrs L Machin, Boundary Corner, 2 Ullathorne Road, Streatham SW16 1SN (01 769 6530).
Worcester Park Athletic—Green Lane, Worcester Park (01-337 4995). Courts: G3, H3. *Secretary:* Mrs P J Jones, 31 Windsor Avenue, New Malden KT3 5EY (01-942 8509).
Wrecclesham—Wrecclesham Recreation Ground, The Street, Wrecclesham, Farnham. Courts: H3. *Secretary:* Mrs M J Rowdon, Harwen, Shortheath Road, Farnham GU9 8SE (710442).

OTHER AFFILIATED ORGANISATIONS (9)

Cranleigh Tournament Committee—Cranleigh Cricket Ground, Cranleigh. Courts: G17. *Secretary:* Miss M E Parker, Cobblers, East Shalford Lane, Shalford, Guildford (62122).
Dorking & Leatherhead District League—*Secretary:* T. Wilkinson, 17 Sanger Drive, Horley.
Eugene Bann Tennis Centre—Crabhill Lane, South Nutfield. Courts: H5. *Secretary:* E Bann, Eugene Bann Tennis Centre.
Prince Georges Tennis Training Club—Prince George's Playing Fields, Grand Drive, London SW20. Courts: G2, H2. *Secretary:* Mrs M Hayward, 155 Westway, London SW20 (01-542 0820).
Streatham Cup—*Secretary:* N Foreman, 2 Glade Gardens, Shirley, Croydon CR0 7UA.
Surrey Schools LTA—*Secretary:* D A F Shaw, Esher County. Courts: G5. Weston Green, Thames Ditton.
Surrey Tennis Coaches Association—*Secretary:* J P Guillonnet, 17 Devon Avenue, Twickenham, Middx (898 7456).
The Chaucer League—*Secretary:* T L Williams, Conifers, Upfold Lane, Cranleigh GU6 8PD.
The Mark Cox Indoor Tennis Club—The Club House, North Road SW19 (01 542 9913).

AFFILIATED SCHOOLS (115)

Boys (42)

Aberdour — Burgh Heath. ***Alleyn's School** — SE22. ***Barrowhill** — Godalming. **Bec School** — SW17. **Beverley Boys School** — New Malden. **Cranleigh School** — Cranleigh. **Charterhouse** — Godalming. **Cranmore School** — West Horsley. **Downsend School** — Leatherhead. **Dulwich College** — Dulwich SE21. **Dulwich College Prep School** — SE21. **East Fields High School** — Mitcham. ***Emanuel School** — SW11. **Epsom College** — Epsom. **Ernest Bevin School** — SW17 **Esher County Grammar School** — Thames Ditton. **Ewell Castle School** — Ewell. **Gordon Boys School** — Woking. ***Glyn County Grammar School** — Ewell. **Hampton Boys School** — Hampton. **Hall Grove Preparatory School** — Bagshot. **Hazelwood Preparatory School** — Oxted. **Kings College School** — Wimbledon. **Parkside School** — Stoke D'Abernon. **Priory School** — Banstead. ***Purley County Grammar School for Boys** — Old Coulsdon. **Reeds School** — Cobham. **Richard Challoner School** — Epsom. **Reigate Grammar School** — Reigate. **Rokeby School** — Kingston. **Rutlish School** — SW20. **St George's College** — Weybridge. **St John's School** — Leatherhead. ***St Joseph's College** — SE19. **St Paul's School** — SW13. **Sondes Place County Secondary School** — Dorking. **Spencer Park School** — SW18. ***Tiffins Boys School** — Kingston-upon-Thames. **Trinity School** — Croydon. **Tudor School** — Kingston-upon-Thames. **Woburn Hill School** — Weybridge. **Woodcote House School** — Windlesham.

*Affiliated to British Schools LTA

Girls (53)

City of London Freemen's School — Ashtead Park. ***Claremont School** — Esher. ***Coloma Convent Grammar School** — Croydon. **Commonweal Lodge School** — Purley. ***Convent of the Sacred Heart** — Woldingham. **Coombs Girls Schools** — New Malden. **Croham Hurst School** — South Croydon. ***Croydon High School for Girls** — Croydon. **Dunnottor School** — Reigate. **Ensham School** — Morden. ***Eothens School** — Caterham. **Garratt Green School** — SW17. ***Greenacre School** — Banstead. **Guildford County School** — Guildford. ***Guildford High School** — Guildford. ***James Allen's Girls' School** — SE22. **King Edward's School** — Godalming. **Kingsdale School** — SE21.

La Retraite High School — SW12. **Laverock School** — Oxted. ***Manor House School** — Little Bookham. ***Marymount School** — Kingston. ***Nonsuch County School for Girls** — Cheam. **Notre Dame Senior School** — Cobham. **Notre Dame Convent School** — Lingfield. **Old Palace School** — Croydon. ***Parsons Mead School** — Ashstead. **Priors Field** — Godalming. **Purley High School for Girls** — Coulsdon. ***Putney High School** — SW15. ***Rosebery Grammar School** — Epsom. **Rowan High School** — SW16. **Royal Naval School** — Haslemere. ***St Catherine's School** — Bramley. ***St Martin's-in-the-Fields High School** — SW2. ***St Maur's Convent** — Weybridge. ***St Michael's School** — Limpsfield. ***St Philomena's School** — Carshalton. **St Teresas Convent School** — Dorking. ***Sir William Perkins School** — Chertsey. **Spelthorne College** — Ashford. ***Streatham Hill & Clapham High School** — SW2. ***Surbiton High School** — Kingston-upon-Thames. **Sutton High School** — Sutton. ***The Tiffins Girls' School** — Kingston-upon-Thames. **Tolworth Girls School** — Tolworth. **Tormead School** — Guildford. **Trinity Secondary School** — SE1. **Virgo Fidelis Convent** — SE19. ***Wallington High Girls' School** — Carshalton. **Walsingham School** — SW4. **Welsh Girl's School** — Ashford, Middlesex. ***Wimbledon High School** — SW19.

*Affiliated to British Schools LTA

Mixed (20)
American Community School — Cobham. **Archbishop Tenisons School** — Croydon. **Ashcombe School** — Dorking. **Box Hill School** — Dorking. **Broadwater County Secondary School** — Godalming. **Caterham School** — Caterham. **De Burgh County Secondary School** — Tadworth. **Farnham College** — Farnham. **George Abbott School** — Burpham. ***Godalming County Grammar School** — Godalming. **Liberty Middle School** — Mitcham. **Milbourne Lodge School** — Esher. **Nork Park County Secondary School** — Banstead. **Oxted County School** — Oxted. **Putney Park School** — Putney. **Reigate College** — Reigate. **Richmond-upon-Thames Colleges** — Twickenham. **Riversdale Primary School** — SW18. **Ronald Ross School** — SW19. **Royal Alexander & Albert Secondary School** — Reigate. **Sutton West County Secondary School** — Surbiton. **Tasis England School** — Thorpe. ***Waynflete County Secondary School** — Esher. **Western Middle School** — Mitcham.

*Affiliated to British Schools LTA

All correspondence to School Clubs should be addressed to the Master or Mistress in charge of lawn tennis.

SUSSEX COUNTY LAWN TENNIS ASSOCIATION

Hon Secretary—**D W H Tripp,** 80 Shirley Drive, Hove BN3 6UL (Brighton 501379).
Hon Secretary (Junior Committee)—**A W J Rogers, MBE,** 16 Mayo Lane, Bexhill-on-Sea TN39 5EA (0424 210964).
Hon Treasurer—**Mrs B K Kedge,** 10 Doubledays, Burgess Hill, RH15 0HT (3474).
Hon Men's Match Secretary—**P H J Maurice,** 11 Lansdowne Close, Worthing (47294 pri, 31217 bus).
Hon Ladies' Match Secretary—**Mrs N Jewers,** 76 Limmer Lane, Felpham, Bognor Regis (822133).
Hon Girls' Match Secretary—**Miss P McNamara,** 2 Vale Walk, Findon Valley, Worthing (0903 62537).
Representatives on the Council—**R Cushing JP, B C Mead.**

AFFILIATED CLUBS (69)

Amherst—Amherst Road, Hastings (Hastings 439063). Courts: G3, H4. Secretary: Mrs A Gilbey, 33 Amherst Road, Hastings TN34 1TT (0424 421 318).
Angmering-on-Sea—Homelands Avenue, East Preston, Littlehampton BN16 1PS (Rustington 770173). Courts: H5 (2 floodlit). *Secretary:* Mrs J M Rosbrook, c/o Wyke House, 35 Willowhayne Avenue, Angmering-on-Sea BN16 1PE (Rustington 775004).
Arundel—Mill Road, Arundel. Courts: H3. *Secretary:* Mrs S Hawkesfield, 45 King Street, Arundel BN18 9BN (883280).
Balcombe—Oldlands Avenue, Balcombe. Courts: H2. *Secretary:* Mrs A Parry, Rocks Lane Cottage, Rowhill Lane, Balcombe RH17 6JG (0444 811245).
Barclays Bank Sports (Brighton & Lewes) (Lawn Tennis Section)—*Secretary:* M G Redfern, Barclays Bank Plc, 84 High Street, Billingshurst RM14 9QT (04038 4771).
Barcombe—Recreation Ground, Barcombe. Courts: H3. *Secretary:* Ms J Searle, 4 Streatfield Road, Uckfield TN22 2BQ (5428).
Beecham Research Laboratories Sports & Social Club—Courts: H3. *Secretary:* Miss J C Greenstreet, Employee Relations, Beecham Pharmaceuticals, Clarendon Road, Worthing (39900 ext 229).
Billingshurst—Recreation Ground, Lower Station Road, Billingshurst. Courts: H3. *Secretary:* Mrs V C Crabb, Tarbet Croft, Marringdean Road, Billingshurst RH14 9HD (2057).
Blackboys LTA—Gun Farm Sports Centre, Blackboys TN22 5JZ (Framfield 240). Courts: H2. *Secretary:* H S Uberoi, c/o Club.
Bognor—Nyewood Lane, Bognor Regis (865091). Courts: G4, H5 (2 floodlit). *Secretary:* Mrs S Briggs, Ley Cottage, 31 Ley Road, Felpham PO22 7HU (Bognor Regis 863695).
Brighton TC—Brighton Rackets Club, Withdean Sportsman, Tongdean Lane, Brighton BN1 5JD (553159). Courts: H4 (floodlit), covered 3. *Secretary:* F T Brennan, at the Club (557658 pri, Worthing 3999 ext 137 bus).
Brighton & Hove Parks LTA—various Parks Clubs, Brighton & Hove. Courts: H40. *Secretary:* J Denman, 34 Bramber Avenue, Hove BN3 8GW (Brighton 734511).

Buckingham Tennis Club—Buckingham Park, Shoreham (3013). Courts: H3. *Secretary:* Mrs P Channon, 310 Upper Shoreham Road, Shoreham-by-Sea BN4 6BA (2777).
Carmel—St Helier's Avenue, Hove 3 (Brighton 37205). Courts: H2. *Secretary:* S Bloch, 68 Berriedale Avenue, Hove BN3 4JJ (Brighton 730650).
Chelsea College Brighton Polytechnic—Trevin Towers, Gaudick Road. Eastbourne (21400). Courts: H12. *Secretary:* Miss W Burrows, 53 Priory Heights, Eastbourne BN20 8SP (34522).
Chichester LT & Squash Club—Oaklands Park, Chichester (785664 and 787269). Courts: G3, H6 (3 floodlit). *Manager:* Mrs V Trotman, 14 Conduit Mead, Chichester PO19 4UP (Chichester 773957).
Comptons—Leechpond Hill, Lower Beeding (419). Courts: H3, Shales. *Secretary:* Miss D A Silver, 9 Hernbrook Drive, Horsham RH13 6EW (65801).
Cooden Beach Sports & Social Club—Withyham Road, Cooden, Bexhill (Cooden 4810). Courts: H5. *Secretary:* I C Coutts, 79 Cooden Drive, Bexhill-on-Sea TN39 3AN (210533).
Crablands Bowling & LTC—Crablands, Selsey. Courts: G2, H3. *Secretary:* C H French, 16 Warner Road, Selsey PO20 9DE (604947).
Crawley—The Pavilion, Hazelwick Avenue, Three Bridges (Crawley 33388). Courts: H8. *Secretary:* Mrs M C M Gibbs, Chalky Pits House, Grattons Drive, Pound Hill, Crawley RH10 (513463).
Crawley Down—King George V Recreation Ground, Sandy Lane, Crawley Down. Courts: H3. *Chairman:* C R Hicks, 'Ingleside', Copthorne Common Road, Copthorne RH10 3JX (713777).
Cross-in-Hand—Hardy Roberts Playing Fields, Cross-in-Hand. H4. *Secretary:* Mrs J Eldridge, 'Shalimar', Ghyll Road, Heathfield TN21 0XL (3740).
Crowborough Lawn Tennis & Squash Club—Church Road, Crowborough TN6 1BN (2618). Courts: H9 (2 floodlit). *The Secretary:* PO Box 8, Church Road, Crowborough TN6 1BN (2618).
Crowhurst LTC—Crowhurst Playing Field, Crowhurst. Courts: H1. *Secretary:* Mrs P A Roberts, 19 Craig Close, Crowhurst, Battle TN33 9DE (Crowhurst 498).
Cuckfield—Recreation Ground, Cuckfield. Courts: H3. *Secretary:* Mrs C Burgoyne, 28 Mytten Close, Cuckfield, Haywards Heath RH17 5LN (459717).
Danehill—The Villages LTC, Recreation Ground, Danehill. Courts: H2. *Secretary:* Mrs J Virtue, Grindfield Farm, Furners Green, Uckfield TN22 3RE (Chelwood Gate 284).
Dental Estimates Board Sports & Social (Lawn Tennis Section)—Dental Estimates Board, Compton Place Road, Eastbourne BN20 8AD (641133). Courts: H2. *Secretary:* B Miller (ext 440 c/o Dental Estimates Board 641133).
Ditchling—Recreation Ground, Ditchling. Courts: H1. *Secretary:* R H Borradaile, 36 Beacon Road, Ditchling BN6 8UL (Hassocks 2311).
Eastbourne (Devonshire Park)—Devonshire Park, Eastbourne (29942). Courts: G6, H2. *Secretary:* Mrs S Weldon, 13 Ashburnham Road, Eastbourne BN21 2HX (639390).
East Grinstead LT & Squash Club—Ship Street, East Grinstead (21160). Courts: G4, H4. *Secretary:* R A Blenkinsop, 9 Austen Close, East Grinstead RH12 1RZ (21868).
East Hoathly & Halland—War Memorial Playing Fields, East Hoathly. Courts: H3 (2 floodlit). *Secretary:* Mrs J Townsley, 9 Godfrey Close, Lewes BN7 2ED (471327).
Estcots (formerly Grenestede LTC)—East Court, East Grinstead. Courts: H2. *Secretary:* Mrs M Weeks, 3 Blenheim Close, East Grinstead RH19 3XN (24531).
Fishbourne LTC—Blackboy Lane, Fishbourne, Chichester. Courts: G2. *Secretary:* D Annals, Chaldock, Salthill Road, Fishbourne, Chichester PO19 3PZ (783133).
Forest Row—Chapel Lane, Forest Row. Courts: H2. *Secretary:* K J Wood, 27 Farm Close, Worsted Farm, East Grinstead RH19 3QQ (0342 22771).
Goffs—Gildredge Park, Eastbourne. Courts: H3. *Secretary:* Mrs V Roberts, 81 Pashley Road, Eastbourne BN20 8EA (21212).
Grasshoppers—The Drive, Hove (Brighton 771934). Courts: H3. *Secretary:* Mrs S Cullen JP, 6 Orpen Road, Hove, Brighton BN3 6NN (505718).
Hailsham—Recreation Ground, Western Road, Hailsham. Courts: G3, H2. *Secretary:* B Rogers, 20 Oxendean Gardens, Lower Willingdon, Eastbourne BN22 0RR (509529).
Hampden Park—Hampden Park, Eastbourne (off Decoy Drive). Courts: H5. *Secretary:* Mrs S Puttock, 13 Westfield Close, Polegate BN26 6EJ (2423).
Haywards Heath & District—Victoria Park, Haywards Heath. Courts: H3. *Secretary:* Mrs G Wood, 'Birchlands', 19 Lewes Road, Haywards Heath RH17 7SP (455567).
Horsham—Cricketfield Road, Horsham. Courts: G6, H3 (2 floodlit). *Secretary:* A H Sharp, 23 Blunts Way, Horsham RH12 2BJ (0463 60461 pri, 01 928 8989 ext 2096 bus).
Howard—The Sports Field, St Fora's Road, Littlehampton (Littlehampton 3944). Courts: G4. *Secretary:* Miss H Manners, 22 Greenacres Ring, Angmering Village BN16 4BU (Worthing 770693).
Hurstpierpoint LTC—Recreation Ground, South Avenue, Hurstpierpoint. Courts: H3. *Secretary:* Mrs J Woodham, The Hyde, West Furlong Lane, Hurstpierpoint BN6 9RH (832050).
Ifield—Ifield Drive, Ifield, Crawley. Courts: H2. *Secretary:* W G Brinkley, 1 Oulton Walk, Furnace Green, Crawley RH10 6RH (22563).
Lindfield—Lindfield Common, Lindfield. Courts: H4. *Secretary:* Mrs P C Turner, 135 America Lane, Haywards Heath (0444 412666).
Mayfield—Station Road, Mayfield. Courts: H5. *Secretary:* Dr G G Shackel, Spinneys, Five Ashes, Mayfield TN20 6HH (873113).
Middleton Sports Club—Sea Lane, Middleton-on-Sea (3157). Courts: G4, H2. *Secretary:* Mrs C L Hudson, 5 Denham Close, Shrubbs Field, Middleton, Bognor Regis PO22 5SJ (3994).

Midhurst & District—June Lane, Midhurst. Courts: H5. *Secretary:* C W Saunders, 9 Elmleigh, Midhurst GU29 9HA (4176).
Newhaven—Court Farm Road. Courts: H2. *Secretary:* R K Jackson, 53 Western Road, Newhaven BN9 9JW (512162).
Newick—Blind Lane. Courts: H3. *Secretary:* Mrs H Bryan, 37 Leveller Road, Newick BN8 4PL (3608).
Pavilion & Avenue—Wilbury Avenue, Hove (734266). Courts: H6. *Secretary:* Mrs A Foreman, 15 Hogarth Road, Hove BN3 5RG (Brighton 730288).
Peacehaven TC—Playing Fields, Piddinghoe Avenue, Peacehaven. Courts: H3. *Secretary:* Ms P L Wilson, 68 Lincoln Avenue, Peacehaven, Brighton BN9 7JU (Peacehaven 3404).
Petworth—Angel Street, Petworth. Courts: G4. *Secretary:* B C Harding, Westbury, Sheepdown Drive, Petworth GU28 0BW (420044).
Plumpton LTC—King George V Playing Field, Plumpton Green. Courts: G1. *Secretary:* Mrs J M Holmes, 'Downleigh', Station Road, Plumpton BN7 3BS (Plumpton 890191).
Preston LT & Croquet Club—Preston Drive, Brighton (505731). Courts: G5, H5 (2 floodlit). *Secretary:* J Brewins, 155 Waldegrave Road, Brighton BN1 6GJ (556624).
Rogate TC—Recreation Ground, Rogate, Petersfield, Hants. Courts: H2. *Secretary:* Mrs S Outram, 'Rotherside', Durford Hill, Petersfield, Hants GU31 5AZ (Rogate 305).
Rudgwick—King George V Playing Field, Bucks Green. Courts: H4 (2 floodlit). *Secretary:* Mrs N Harrison, Pallinghurst Farm, Rudgwick RH12 1NF (2203).
Rye—Military Road, Rye. Courts: G8, H2. *Secretary:* C H N Moy, Tollgates, Playden, Rye TN31 7PS (223394).
Seaford & Blatchington—Belgrave Road, Seaford (892232). Courts: G5, H4. *Secretary:* M P Howard, 15 Fitzgerald Avenue, Seaford BN25 1AU (897150).
Sedlescombe—Sedlescombe Playing Fields, Sedlescombe. Courts: H2. *Secretary:* J K Chittenden, 16 High Street, Battle TN33 0AJ (0424 62334).
Southdown—Cockshut Road, Southover, Lewes (477387). Courts: G8, H5 (5 floodlit). *Secretary:* G M Nichols, 39 Houndean Rise, Lewes BN7 1EQ (474530).
Steyning—Memorial Playing Field, Charlton Street. Courts: H2. *Secretary:* Mrs E Homeyard, 11 Ingram Road, Steyning BN4 3PF (814826).
Storrington—Greyfriars Lane, Storrington. Courts: H5 (2 floodlit). *Secretary:* Miss S Haslett, Old House Farm Cottage, West Chiltington, Pulborough RH20 2LG (West Chiltington 2456).
Sunallon—Meadowlands, North Heath Lane, Horsham (53814). Courts: H7. *Secretary:* Mrs D J Harding, c/o Sun Alliance & London Insurance Group, North Street, Horsham RH12 1BT (64141 ext 3662).
Sussex Constabulary—Sports Ground, Police HQ, Kingsham Road, Chichester. Courts: G2. *Secretary:* PC A C Gilbert, c/o Police Station (West), Crawley RH10 1XQ (24242).
Sussex County LTC—Kingston Lane, Southwick (Brighton 591874). Courts: G2, H5 (2 floodlit). *Chairman:* C Morris, 132 St Andrews Road, Worthing BN13 1HH (65077).
The Green—Tower Road West, St Leonards-on-Sea (430221). Courts: G6, H3. *Secretary:* Miss S King, 5 Gilbert Road, St Leonards-on-Sea TN38 0RH (0424 428057).
Weald LT & Squash Club—South Bank, Hassocks (4283). Courts: G6, H5. *Secretary:* J Stubbs, 44 Hurst Road, Hassocks BN6 9NL (3076).
West Hoathly—Secretary: H1. *Secretary:* Mrs J Johnson, 'Midgehurst', Sharpthorne, East Grinstead RH19 4TH (Sharpthorne 810660).
West Worthing—Titnore Way, Titnore Lane, Goring, Worthing BN12 6NY (47270). Courts: G12, H8 (8 floodlit). *The Secretary,* c/o Club (Worthing 47270).

OTHER AFFILIATED ORGANISATIONS (4)

Beauport Sports Club—The Ridge West, St Leonards-on-Sea TN37 7PP (Hastings 51020).
Devonshire Park—Eastbourne (24252). Courts: G21, H4. *Secretary:* Entertainments Manager, Devonshire Park, Eastbourne (25252).
The Brighton Centre—King's Road, Brighton (203131). Correspondence to: Director of Resort & Conference Services, Brighton Borough Council, Marlborough House, 54 Old Steine, Brighton BN1 1EQ (Brighton 29801 ext 340).
The Weald Lawn Tennis League—*Secretary:* F H Askew, Club Cottage, The Green, Godstone RH9 8DY (842866).

AFFILIATED SCHOOLS (51)

Public Schools

Ardingly College. Brighton College. Christ's Hospital — Horsham. **Eastbourne College. Hurstpierpoint College. Lancing College. Seaford College** — Petworth.

Boys

Cottesmore — Crawley. **High School for Boys** — Chichester. **Newlands Prep School** — Seaford. **St Andrew's School** — Worthing. **Worth Abbey** — Crawley.

Girls

Beresford House — Eastbourne. **Brighton & Hove High School** — Brighton. **Burgess Hill School for Girls. Charters Towers School** — Bexhill. **Convent of the Holy Family** — Littlehampton. **Farlington School** — Horsham. **Gaisford High School** — Worthing. **Lavant House School** — Chichester. **Margaret Hardy High School** — Patcham, Brighton. **Micklefield School** — Seaford. **Millais School** — Horsham. **Moira House** — Eastbourne. **Roedean** — Brighton. **Rosemead** — Littlehampton. **St Leonards Mayfield Convent** — Mayfield. **St Margarets Convent of Mercy** — Midhurst. **St Mary's Hall** — Brighton. **St Michaels** — Petworth.

Sion Senior School — Worthing. **Southover Manor** — Lewes. **Springfield Park** — Horsham. **Tanbridge House School** — Horsham. **Towers Convent** — Upper Beeding. **Wadhurst College.**

Mixed
Beacon School — Crowborough. **Blatchington Mill Comprehensive** — Hove. **Brighton, Hove and Sussex 6th Form College** — Hove. **Collyers 6th Form College** — Horsham. **Dorothy Stringer High School** — Brighton. **Haywards Heath College. Hove Park Comprehensive** — Hove. **Longhill Secondary** — Rottingdean. **Midhurst Grammar School. Priory School** — Lewes. **St Bede's** — Upper Dicker. **Steyning Grammar School** — Steyning. **Temple Grove** — Herons Ghyll. **Windlesham House School** — Washington. **Worthing 6th Form College** — Worthing.

WARWICKSHIRE LAWN TENNIS ASSOCIATION

Hon Secretary—**B C Hyde,** Pear Tree Cottage, Valley Lane, Lapworth, Solihull (Lapworth 2318 pri, 021 705 7987/8, bus).
Hon Treasurer—**M G H Spencer,** 1 Hazeley Close, Birmingham B17 (021 429 5587).
Hon Men's Match Secretary—**R Cull,** 160 Oak Farm Road, Bournville, Birmingham B30 1EU (021 458 4037).
Hon Ladies' Match Secretary—**Mrs D Pepper,** 38 Walsall Road, Sutton Coldfield, West Midlands B74 4QR (021 308 4367).
Hon Junior Match Secretary—**S Beale,** 31 Roman Lane, Sutton Coldfield, West Midlands (021 353 0761).
Representatives on the Council—**R Kingsley-Mills, B C Hyde.**

AFFILIATED CLUBS (104)

BIRMINGHAM AREA

Ansells Brewery Tennis Club—Aldridge Road, Perry Barr, Birmingham B42 2TP (356 4296). Courts: G2, H2. *Secretary:* E J Farmer, 31 Carter Road, Great Barr, Birmingham B43 6JR (021 358 6560).
Avery—Sandon Road, Edgbaston, Birmingham (021-429 1143). Courts: G1, H4. *Secretary:* R F Remedios, Soho Foundry, Smethwick, Warley, West Midlands (021 558 1112 ext 147).
Beechcroft—Beechcroft Avenue, Hall Green, Birmingham 28. Courts: H3. *Secretary:* Mrs G Alder, 90 Cropthorn Road, Shirley, Solihull (021 745 7221).
Birmingham Municipal Tennis Club—Sedgemere Road, Yardley, Birmingham 25 (783 2694). Courts: H5. *Secretary:* Carol J Davison, 46 Farnol Road, Yardley, Birmingham (021 783 2694).
Bournville—Girls Grounds, Bournville Lane, Bournville, Birmingham (021 458 2209). Courts: G4. *Secretary:* D L Woolsgrove (021 458 2000 ext 2131 bus). 140 St Denis Road, Selly Oak, Birmingham B29 4LY.
Britannic Assurance Co Ltd Sports & Social Club (Tennis Section)—Moor Green Lane, Moseley, Birmingham B13 8QF (021449 4444). Courts: H4. *Secretary:* R W Evans, c/o Britannic Assurance Co Ltd, Moor Green, Moseley, Birmingham 13 (021 449 444 ext 2288, 021 430 3169 pri).
CEGB—Haslucks Green Road, Shirley, Solihull (021 744 8511 ext 374). *Secretary:* Mrs J Berry, 677f Stratford Road, Shirley (021 745 7670).
Chantry—Moseley Private Park. Courts: H5. *Secretary:* S M Frazier, 70 Prospect Lane, Solihull B91 1MS (021 744 4928).
Civil Service Sports Association—Civil Service Sports Ground, Old Damson Lane, Elmdon, Solihull (021 779 2136). Courts: H2. *Secretary:* Mrs P Haines, 295 Baldwins Lane, Hall Green, Birmingham B28 0RG (021 744 7417).
Edgbaston Priory Club—Sir Harry's Road, Edgbaston, Birmingham B15 2UZ (021 440 2492). Courts: G12, H4 (1 covered), AW7. Secretary: P Huxley, Sir Harry's Road, Birmingham B15 2UZ (021 440 2492).
Edgbaston Archery & Lawn Tennis Society—14 Westbourne Road, Edgbaston B15 3TR (021-454 2846). Courts: G6, H6. *Secretary:* M Groucott, 31 Banbury Road, Northfield, Birmingham 31 (021 477 2102).
Entaco Tennis Club 1948—Eldorado Close (off High Street), Studley (Studley 2671). Courts: G3, H2. *Secretary:* Mrs J Knowles, 32 Stapleton Road, Studley (Studley 2127).
Fort Dunlop Lawn Tennis Section—Wood Lane Erdington, Birmingham (021 373 8101 ext 2656 bus). Courts: G10, H3. *Secretary:* K T Griffiths, 39 Swallowfield, Tamworth (86 50168 pri, 021 384 4444 ext 2458 bus).
Grange Hill Lawn Tennis Club—Grange Hill Road, Kings Norton, Birmingham (021 458 2351). Courts: H3. *Secretary:* Mrs J Hooper, 16 Beaks Hill Road, Kings Norton, Birmingham (021 458 3258).
Hamstead LTC—Butlers Road, Handsworth Wood, Birmingham 20 (021 554 5092). Courts: G3, H5. *Secretary:* P Davies, 49 Leopold Avenue, Birmingham B20 1EU (021 357 2027).
Handsworth Victoria Bowling & Tennis Club (Tennis Section)—Hamstead Road, Handsworth, Birmingham (021 554 7790). Courts: H3. *Secretary:* N E Pilnick, 4 Cherry Orchard Road, Handsworth Wood, Birmingham 20 (021 554 7755).
Holly Quinton—rear 14 Clive Road, Birmingham 32 (021 422 3202). *Secretary:* Mrs J Law, 53 White Road, Quinton, Birmingham (021 422 7765).
IMI (Kynoch) Ltd Tennis Club—off Wellhead Lane, Perry Barr. *Secretary:* R Young, IMI (Kynoch) Ltd, Witton Emp Relations Dept, Witton, Birmingham B6 7BA (021 356 4848).
Inco Alloy Products—c/o Tally Ho LTC, Edgbaston Road, Birmingham B5 7QS (440 2115). Courts: G2, H2. *Secretary:* V A Tracey, Inco Products Ltd, Wiggin Street, Birmingham (021 454 4871).
Kalamazoo—Hawkesley Mill Lane, Northfield, Birmingham (021 475 2191). Courts: H2.

Secretary: J A Goodman, Kalamazoo Ltd, Northfield, Birmingham B31 2RW (021 475 2191).

King's Heath Cricket & Football Club (Tennis Section)—Alcester Road South, King's Heath (entrance opposite Livingstone Road) (021 444 4680). Courts: G3, H3. *Secretary:* P Bennett, 68 Smirrels Road, Hall Green, Birmingham 28 (021 777 6780).

Lucas (North)—Edgbaston Road, (old Tally Ho Ground) Birmingham B5 7QS. *Secretary:* R Edwards, 32 Torridon Croft, Russell Road, Birmingham B13 8RG (021 449 1829).

Marston Green Tennis Club—Elmdon Road, Marston Green, Birmingham (021 779 4330). Courts: H4. *Secretary:* Mrs R E Smyth, 59 Highwood Avenue, Solihull, West Midlands B92 8QZ (743 3553).

Midlands Electricity Board Sports (Tennis) (1972)—c/o Haslucks Green Road, Shirley, Solihull (021-744 8511). *Secretary:* D R Hartland, 117 Velsheda Road, Shirley, Solihull (021-744 5696).

Mitchells & Butlers—Portland Road, Edgbaston, Birmingham B17 (021 558 1481 ext 2236). Courts: G7, H3. *Secretary:* Mrs P Clutterbuck, 166 Broadway Avenue, Hasbury, Halesowen (021 550 6038 pri, Wolverhampton 54551 ext 275 bus).

Moorpool—corner Moorpool Avenue and Margaret Grove, Harborne, Birmingham 17. Courts: H2. *Secretary:* Mrs E Gilbert, 55 Moorpool Avenue, Harborne, Birmingham B17 9DS (021 427 7140).

Moseley Lawn Tennis Club—Billesley Lane, Moseley, Birmingham. *Secretary:* Mrs E Griffiths, 19 Robert Court, Wake Green Park, Moseley B13 9XH (021 449 7432).

RAFA (Harborne)—Tennal Grove, Harborne, Birmingham 17. Courts: H2. *Secretary:* R Colaba, 20 Hartford Close, Harborne, Birmingham 17 (021 429 3816).

Sparkhill Tennis Club—(Hall Green Ltd), Petersfield Road, Hall Green, Birmingham B28 (021 777 5509). Courts: H6. *Secretary:* D J March, 76 Peterfield Road, Hall Green, Birmingham B28 7JF (021 777 6464).

Springfield (Handsworth) Lawn Tennis Club Ltd—Church Lane, Handsworth Wood, Birmingham B20 (021 523 7703). Courts: H6. *Secretary:* P Voake, 18 Railway Road, Perry Barr, Birmingham B20 3HT.

Weoley Hill—Weoley Hill, Selly Oak, Birmingham 29. Courts: H6. *Secretary:* L G Earwaker, 16 Linden Road, Bournville, Birmingham B30 1JS (021 472 3201).

West Midlands Police Social & Athletic Club—Pershore Road, Edgbaston, Birmingham (021 472 2944). Courts: G1, H3. *Secretary:* WPC G Crowe, 37 Regis Heath Road, Rowley Regis B65 0PA (021 559 3282).

Woodlands (Northfield)—Northfield, Birmingham 31. Courts: H2. *Secretary:* J Boardman, 44 Wychall Lane, Birmingham B38 8TA (021 458 1962).

Yardley—Queens Road, Yardley, Birmingham. Courts: H4. *Secretary:* G Capener, 123 Jayshaw Avenue, Great Ban B43 5RX (021 358 4508).

SOLIHULL AREA

Blossomfield—The Wardens, Widney Lane, Solihull, West Midlands (021 705 3254). Courts: H7. *Secretary:* Mrs J Gittins, 1 Reservoir Road, Solihull (021 707 0641).

Knowle & Dorridge—Grove Road, Knowle, Solihull, West Midlands B93 0PJ (560 2342). Courts: G4, H4. *Secretary:* C W Sansom, 18 Warren Drive, Dorridge, Solihull, West Midlands (Knowle 3572).

Solihull Arden Club—Sharmans Cross Road, Solihull, West Midlands (705 1680). Courts: G7, H8. *Secretary:* Mike Hull, 26 Manor Road, Solihull (021 704 4544).

Solihull Cricket & Tennis—Tippetts Field, Marsh Lane, Solihull (705 5271). Courts: H6. *Secretary:* Mrs E M Morris, Southways, 15 Oakley Wood Drive, Solihull B91 2PH (021 705 4767).

Tanworth-in-Arden Tennis Club—Muntzfield, Bates Lane, Tanworth-in-Arden, Warwickshire. Courts: H3. *Secretary:* Mrs A Dawes, Metchley Cottage, Vicarage Hill, Tanworth-in-Arden, Solihull (Tanworth-in-Arden 2198).

West Warwickshire Club Ltd (Tennis Section)—Grange Road, Olton, Solihull, West Midlands B91 1DA (021 706 2192). Courts: G8, H10. *Secretary:* Miss A Tollett, 70 Stoneleigh Road, Solihull B91 1DJ (021 704 1955).

COVENTRY, RUGBY & NUNEATON AREA

Coventry & District Lawn Tennis League—*Secretary:* A F Taylor, 22 Salisbury Avenue, Coventry (0203 414065).

AEI/GEC Sports & Social Club, Rugby—Hillmorton Road, Rugby. Courts: G4, H6. *Secretary:* B M Beech, 166 Lower Hillmorton Road, Rugby (0788 75502 pri, 0788 2121 bus).

Alvis LTC—Alvis Sports Ground, Holyhead Road off Four Pounds Avenue, Coventry, West Midlands CV5 8JH (0203 25501). Courts: G2, H2. *Secretary:* P Farrelly, 32 Ferndale Road, Binley Woods, Coventry, West Midlands (0203 353249).

Beechwood Lawn Tennis Club (Coventry)—Beechwood Avenue, Earlsdon, Coventry CV5 6FQ (Coventry 70438). Courts: G3, H4. *Secretary:* Mrs P Halsey, 41 Okehampton Road, Styvechale, Coventry (Coventry 415576).

Berkswell-Balsall Common—Meeting House Lane, Balsall Common. Courts: H5. *Secretary:* P H Nurse, 45 Sunnyside Lane, Balsall Common, West Midlands (Berkswell 34038).

Courtaulds Sports & Social (Tennis Section)—Lockhurst Lane, Coventry (88441 ext 94). Courts: G2, H4. *Secretary:* T Varnon, 5 Crossley Court, Cross Road, Coventry.

Coventry & North Warwickshire Cricket Club—Binley Road, Coventry (451426). Courts: G6, H5. *Secretary:* Mrs M Stringer, 40 Park Paling, Cheylesmore, Coventry CV3 5LJ (Coventry 501719).

GEC (Coventry)—Allard Avenue, Binley, Coventry. Courts: G1, H4. *Secretary:* R Mason, 1 Marlborough Road, Ball Hill, Coventry (Coventry 456873).

GEC (Willans)—Essex Street off Newbold Road, Rugby. *Secretary:* A Hipwell, 47 Portland Road, Rugby CV21 3RX (Rugby 61233 bus).
Grove—18a Tile Lane, Coventry. Courts: H3.
Alfred Herbert LTC (Tennis Section)—Cross Road, Edgwick, Coventry CV6 6GU (0203 88386). Courts: G2, H4. *Secretary:* N C Reynolds, 9 Reynolds Road, Village on the Green, Bedworth.
Jaguar Daimler (Climax)—Middlemarch Road, Radford, Coventry. Courts: H4. *Secretary:* Miss P Brooks, 117 Grangemouth Road, Radgford, Coventry (51831).
Nuneaton LTC—Caldwell Road, Nuneaton. *Secretary:* Mrs J D Simcock, 211 St Nicolas Park Drive, Nuneaton CU11 6EL (381524).
Rugby Lawn Tennis Club (1876)—Webb Ellis Road, Rugby, West Midlands CV22 7AU. Courts: G6, H2. *Secretary:* Mrs Stokhuyzen, The Cottage, 8 Moultrie Road, Rugby (815348).
Sphinx—Siddeley Avenue, Coventry (458890). *Secretary:* Dr S Wong, 4 Calder Close, Bulkington (Bedworth 317098).
Talbot Tennis Club—Memorial Park, Coventry. Courts: H2. *Secretary:* J D Scott, 5 Chancellors Close, Coventry (Coventry 412675 pri, Coventry 303505 ext 730 bus).
Telecom Tennis Club—Ash Green High School, Ash Green Lane, Exhall, nr Coventry. Courts: H2. *Secretary:* Ashok Thakrar, 32 Holmcroft, Walsgrave Manor, Coventry CU22 NI1 (Coventry 616622 pri, Coventry 22572 bus).
University of Warwick-Students—Kirby Corner Road, Coventry. Courts: H18. *Secretary:* Debbie Cook/Liz Shackleton, 39 Astill Grove, Cheylesmore.

WARWICK, LEAMINGTON AND STRATFORD AREA

Automative Products—Tachbrook Road, Leamington Spa. *Secretary:* B L Reason, 69 Dunblane Drive, New Cubbington, Leamington Spa (Leamington Spa 29866).
Claverdon—Station Road, Claverdon. Courts: H2. *Secretary:* E A Covington, Polperro, Langley Road, Claverdon (Claverdon 2168).
Hampton-in-Arden Sports Club (Tennis Section)—Shadow Brook Lane, Hampton-in-Arden, Solihull. *Secretary:* E Whitfield, 285 Warwick Road, Solihull (021 706 0943).
Henley-in-Arden—Memorial Playing Fields, Henley-in-Arden (3430). Courts: H4. *Secretary: Mrs G Cunningham, Brook Furlong, Birmingham Road, Henley-in-Arden (Henley 2702).*
Kenilworth Lawn Tennis & Squash Club—Crackley Lane, Kenilworth, West Midlands CV8 2JS (52673). Courts: G5, H8. *Secretary:* Mrs J Vincent, 34 Sunningdale Avenue, Kenilworth (0926 54640).
Leamington—Guy's Cliffe Avenue, Leamington Spa (25845). Courts: G6, H6. *Secretary:* R Wainhouse, 29 Hill Street, Leamington (Leamington Spa 20816).
Rowington—Rowington Village Hall. Courts: H2. *Secretary:* Mrs J Smith, Kingswood Cottage, Dicks Lane, Rowington.
Stratford-on-Avon LTC—Southern Lane, Stratford-on-Avon, Warwickshire CV37 6BH (Stratford-on-Avon 204179). Courts: G5, H3. *Secretary:* Mrs J Shearing, 'Willowmere', The Close, Clifford Chambers, Stratford-upon-Avon (0789 204718).
Warwick Boat Club Ltd—33 Mill Street, Warwick (492043). Courts: G7, H4. *Secretary:* W L Plant, 25 Acacia Road, Leamington Spa (20225).
Warwickshire Constabulary—*Secretary:* P Freeman, 13 Kirton Close, Whitnash, Leamington Spa (29512).
Warwickshire County Council Staff LTC (1954)—WCC Sports Ground, Mynton Road, Warwick. Courts: H2. *Secretary:* Mrs M Curtis, 25 Alcester Road, Wooton Wawen, Warwicks (Henley in Arden 2280).
Whitnash Lawn Tennis Club—Heathcote Road, Whitnash (Leamington 36577). Courts: H2. *Secretary:* Mr G M Grimes, 20 Green Close, Whitnash, Leamington Spa (Leamington Spa 20428).

SUTTON COLDFIELD AREA

Boldmere Tennis Club—138 Jockey Road, Sutton Coldfield. Courts: H4. *Secretary:* P Yardley, 9 Blakeland Road, Perry Barr, Birmingham (021 356 8257).
Castle Bromwich Ltd—Erdington Playing Fields, Grange Road, Erdington, Birmingham B24 (021 350 4000). Courts: H2. *Secretary:* R Worley, 22 West Rise, Lichfield Park, Sutton Coldfield (021 329 3460).
Coleshill Lawn Tennis Club 1884—200 yards due east of Coleshill Parish Church (rear of cemetery), entrance from Maxstoke Lane or through cemetery. Courts: G2, H3. *Secretary:* M A Bramley, 108 Chester Road, Castle Bromwich, Birmingham (021 747 3588).
Curdsworth Tennis Club—King George V Playing Fields, Kingsbury Road, Curdsworth. Courts: H2. *Secretary:* J Teal, 51 Far Highfield, Sutton Coldfield BT6 8BP (0675 70167).
Four Oaks—Hartopp Road, Four Oaks, Sutton Coldfield (308 0672). Courts: G4, H3 (3AW). *Secretary:* P W Humpidge, 2 Beaconsfield Road, Sutton Coldfield (021 354 4984).
Goldieslie Club Ltd—Goldieslie Road, Sutton Coldfield (021 354 1231). Courts: H2. *Secretary:* G Stewart, 40 Clarry Drive, Four Oaks, Sutton Coldfield (021 308 5781).
Streetly Lane Tennis Club Ltd—Park View Road, Streetly, Sutton Coldfield (021-353 3004)! Courts: G3, H4 (3AW). *Secretary:* E R Ham, 55 Inglewood Road, Streetly (021 353 3300).
Sutton Coldfield Hard Courts—Highbridge Road, Wylde Green, Sutton Coldfield (021 354 1125). Courts: G7, H5 (1 covered). *Secretary:* Mrs J O Dingley, 24 Beech Hill Road, Wylde Green, Sutton Coldfield (021 373 2051).
Sutton Coldfield United Reform Church Tennis Club (1925)—Tamworth Road, Sutton Coldfield. *Secretary:* Mrs A Perry, 82 Dower Road, Four Oaks, Sutton Coldfield (021 308 5364).

Water Orton—Vicarage Lane, Water Orton. Courts: H2. *Secretary:* A J Mowett, 29 Mercer Avenue, Water Orton, Birmingham (021 747 6732).
Wylde Green Church Tennis Club—Britwell Road, Sutton Coldfield. Courts: H2. *Secretary:* J Stones, 9 Sunnybank Road, Sutton Coldfield (021 373 7482).

COVENTRY, RUGBY AND NUNEATON AREA

Atherstone Miners Welfare Tennis Club (1961)—Atherstone Miners Welfare Club, South Street, Atherstone. Courts: H2. *Secretary:* N J Pumfrey, 40 Greendale Close, Atherstone, Warwickshire (Atherstone 4350).
Griff & Cotton—Heath End Road, Nuneaton (2656). Courts: G2, H3. *Secretary:* D Dougill, 79 Fairisle Drive, Glendale Estate, Nuneaton CV10 7LL (Nuneaton 370002).
Nuneaton—Caldwell Road, Nuneaton. Courts: G3, H4. *Secretary:* Mrs J D Simcock, 211 St Nicholas Park Drive, Nuneaton CV11 6EL (Nuneaton 381524).

OTHER AFFILIATED ORGANISATIONS

Birmingham Area Lawn Tennis League—17 Mens Divisions, 12 Ladies Divisions. Stone Mixed Doubles Cup. *Secretary:* R Worley, 22 West Drive, Sutton Coldfield (021 329 3460).
Coventry Area Lawn Tennis League.
LJTF—*Chairman:* L Mare, Oakdene, Rushbrook Lane, Tanworth-In-Arden (2596).
Warwickshire Schools League—*Secretary:* R Worsley, 22 West Rise, Sutton Coldfield (021 329 3460).

AFFILIATED SCHOOLS (47)

Boys
Ash Green High School—Coventry. **Bishop Vesey Grammar School**—Sutton Coldfield. **King Edward's School (1552)**—Birmingham. **King Henry VIII School**—Coventry. **Rugby School**—Rugby. **Solihull School**—Solihull. **Warwick School Tennis Club (1949)**—Warwick.

Girls
Edgbaston Church of England College—Birmingham. **Edgbaston High School**—Edgbaston. **Hodge Hill Girls School. Convent of The Holy Child Jesus Edgbaston**—Edgbaston. **King Edward VI High School**—Birmingham. **King Edward's Camp Hill School for Girls**—Birmingham. **Kings High School for Girls**—Warwick. **The Kingsley School**—Leamington. **Kings Norton Mixed School. St Joseph's Convent**—Kenilworth. **St Martin's School**—Solihull. **St Paul's Grammar School**—Birmingham. **Selly Park Girls School**—Birmingham. **Stratford-upon-Avon Girls' Grammar School**—Stratford-upon-Avon. **Wroxall Abbey School (1872)**—Haseley Knob.

Mixed
Alderman Callow School and Community College. Bablake School—Coventry. **Bluecoat School**—Coventry. **Coleshill School**—Coleshill. **John Eillmott School (1958)**—Sutton Coldfield. **Lyng Hall Comprehensive School**—Coventry. **Saltey School**—Birmingham. Swanshurst Girls School—Birmingham. **Waverly School.**

All correspondence to School Clubs should be addressed to the Master or Mistress in charge of lawn tennis.

WILTSHIRE LAWN TENNIS ASSOCIATION

Hon Secretary—**Miss P J Clanchy,** 16 Westrop, Highworth, Wilts (762252).
Hon Treasurer—**M A E Powell,** Lower Hardenhuish Farmhouse, Chippenham SN14 6HN (652338).
Hon Men's Match Secretary—**A Davidson,** 55 Highbury Park, Warminster (213540).
Hon Ladies' Match Secretary—**Miss N Gardner,** 1a New Road, Purton, Swindon (770681).
Representative on the Council—**M A E Powell.**

AFFILIATED CLUBS (30)

Aldbourne—Castle Street. Courts: H2, G1. *Secretary:* R Harding, The Beeches, Liddington Warren Farm, Swindon (790233).
Allied Dunbar—Wills. Courts: H2. *Secretary:* J Cleeves, 37 Goldsborough Close, Eastleaze, Swindon (872599).
Avon Rubber Sports & Social—Melksham House, Market Place. Courts: G4, H2. *Secretary:* Miss M Wiltshire, 54 Granville Road, Melksham (Melksham 704573).
Bradford-on-Avon—Culver Close. Courts: H2. *Secretary:* Mrs B C Anderson, 21 Meadowfield, Bradford-on-Avon (5281).
British Rail—Shrivenham Road, Swindon. Courts: H6, G3. *Secretary:* Mrs E E Haller, 19 Thorne Road, Eldene, Swindon (641965).
Burmah House TC—Headlands School, Cricklade Road, Swindon. Courts: H4. *Secretary:* J Roche, Public Affairs, Burmah House, Pipers Way, Swindon (3015 ext 2284).
Chippenham—Bristol Road. Courts: G3, H3. *Secretary:* Mrs M Gear, Folly Cottage, Great Somerford, Chippenham (Seagry 720081).
Chippenham Park—John Coles Park, Chippenham. Courts: H3. *Secretary:* N Smith, 58 Stonelea Close, Chippenham (657237).
Civil Service & NALGO (Swindon)—Penhill Farmhouse, Penhill, Swindon. Courts: H4. *Secretary:* D A Codd, 6 Ellingdon Road, Wroughton (812664).
Corsham—Courts: H1. Secretary: Mrs M Phippard, 13 Kirby Road, Corsham (713507).
Corsley—Courts: H2, G1. *Secretary:* Mrs B Fouracres, 7 Brimhill Rise, Chapmanslade (529).
Devizes—London Road. Courts: H3, G3. *Secretary:* Mrs S Hockley, Highclere, The Breach, Devizes (5310).
Downton—Courts: H3. *Secretary:* Mrs D Shaw, 26 Twynham Close, Downton, Salisbury (20462).

Durnford—The Barn Great, Durnford, Salisbury. Courts: H1. *Secretary:* Mrs H Bruce, The Barn, Great Durnford, Salisbury (Middle Woodford 309).
Highworth—Highworth Recreation Ground. Courts: H3. *Secretary:* K White, Couage Field, Hampton, Highworth, Swindon (762387).
Malmesbury—Tetbury Hill. Courts: H3. *Secretary:* Mrs A Taylor, Kennel Field Cottage, Foxley Green, Malmesbury (3769).
Minety—Recreation Ground. Courts: H2. *Secretary:* Mrs P Hooley, 5 Oakleaze, Minety, Malmes (860585).
Pewsey—Pewsey Recreation Ground. G3, H3. *Secretary:* Miss A Higgins, 7 High Street, Manton, Marlborough (53038).
Purton—The Red House, Purton. Courts: H5. *Secretary:* Mrs J Neate, 57 Ringsbury Close, Purton (770117).
Ramsbury LTC—Courts: H2. *Secretary:* Mrs D Inward, 9 Orchard Close, Ramsbury (Marlboro 20300).
Riverside LTC—New Bridge Road, Salisbury. Courts: G4. *Secretary:* Mrs B Bruce, 17 Highlands Road, Salisbury (335748).
Salisbury—Harnham (27197). Courts: G7, H4. *Secretary:* Mrs G Scott, 14 Radnor Road, Salisbury (0722 25117).
Swindon Hard Courts—Cumberland Road, Swindon. Courts: H3. *Secretary:* Mrs G Hardy, 13Selby Crescent, Freshbrook (872249).
The White Horse—Matravers School, Westbury. Courts: H4. *Secretary:* J V Ford, Silver Birches, Wellhead Lane, Westbury, Wilts (822546).
Trowbridge Westbourne—Westbourne Gardens, Trowbridge. Courts: G2, H2. *Secretary:* Mrs Y Gabb, 77 Bradford Road, Trowbridge (2460 bus).
Westbury & Warminster—Warminster Park. Courts: H3. *Secretary:* J M Royds, 7 Norton Bavant, Warminster (40491).
Wills—Colbourne Street, Swindon. Courts: H2, G5. *Secretary:* Mrs C King, 34 Trajan Road, Stratton, Swindon (823325).
Wiltshire Farmers—Public Courts Devizes. Courts: H2. *Secretary:* D Scott, Nursteed House, Nursteed, Devizes (6121).
Wootton Bassett TC—Gerard Buxton Sports Ground, Rylands Way. Courts: H3. *Secretary:* Miss L Nash, 13 Gainsborough Avenue, Wootton Bassett (850525).

OTHER AFFILIATED ORGANISATIONS (3)

Wiltshire Archers—*Secretary:* Mrs Goldborough, Combery Mills, Littleton Panell, Devizes (Lavington 3253).
Wilts County Tournament Committee—Penhill Farmhouse, Swindon. *Secretary:* Mrs S Mundy, 4 Brecon Close, Lawn, Swindon (26624).
Wilco—Cumberland Road, Swindon. Courts: H2. *Secretary:* D Ward, 61 Chestnut Springs, Lydiard Millicent, Purton (770759).

AFFILIATED SCHOOLS (25)

Boys
Bishop Wordsworth — 11 The Close, Salisbury (3851). **The Old Ride** — Bradford on Avon.

Girls
Grittleton House School — Chippenham. **La Retraite Convent** — Campbell Road, Salisbury (Salisbury 3094). **Sheldon School** — Hardenhuish Lane, Chippenham (51216). **St Mary's School** — Calne (815899). **South Wilts Grammar School** — Salisbury (23326). **Stonar** — Cottles Park, Atworth, Melksham (702309).

Mixed
Castledown School — Ludgershall, nr Andover, Hants (778). **Churchfields** — Swindon (28451). **Corsham Comprehensive. Dauntsey School** — West Lavington, Devizes. **Drove School. Godolphin School** — Salisbury (2577). Courts: G3, H3. **Highworth Comprehensive** — Shrivenham Road, Highworth, Swindon (762426). **John Bentley** — Calne. **Kingdown School** — Warminster. **Lavington School** — West Lavington, Devizes. **Marlborough College** — Marlborough (54173). **Oakfield School** — Marlowe Avenue, Swindon (5043). **Ridgeway Comprehensive** — Inverary Road, Wroughton (812824). **Salisbury Technical College** — Southampton Road, Salisbury (23711). **The Headlands Senior School School** — Cricklade Road, Swindon (28030). **St Joseph's** — Swindon (825999). **Trowbridge Technical College** — Trowbridge. **Wootton Bassett School** — Lime Kiln, Wootton Bassett (852121).

YORKSHIRE COUNTY LAWN TENNIS ASSOCIATION

Hon Secretary—**R Whitaker,** 15 Lynton Drive, Heaton, Bradford BD9 5JH (46242 pri, 493533 bus).
Hon Treasurer—**B J Austin,** Flat 2, Carr Croft, Parish Ghyll Road, Ilkley LS29 9NE (Ilkley 607448 pri).
Joint Hon Men's Match Secretaries—**S Ickringill,** The Laurels, 28 Station Road, Steeton (Keighley 52287). **R A Armytage,** Pine Grove Country Club, Myers Grove Lane, Sheffield S6 5JG (342830).
Hon Ladies' Match Secretary—**Mrs T Collins,** 28 Meadow Way, Chigwell, Essex IG7 6LR (01-500 5782).
Juniors Secretary—**J R Coates,** 163 Church Lane, Cantley, Doncaster DN4 6RY (Doncaster 538342 pri, 01-385 4233 bus).
Representatives on the Council—**Mrs T Collins, P A Richardson.**

AFFILIATED CLUBS (108)

Adel War Memorial Association—Tennis Section, Adel Memorial Hall, Church Lane, Adel. Courts: H4. *Secretary:* C C Pearson, 12 Kingsley Avenue, leeds LS16 7NY (679692).
Austwick Playing Field LTC—Austwick Village. Courts: H2. *Secretary:* Alison Wood, Town End Cottage, Austwick, Nr Lancaster LA2 8BQ (Clapham 539).
Bailey Hills TC—Bingley. Courts: G1, H2. *Secretary:* Arthur Baxter, 18 Grange Park Road, Cottingley, Bingley (562668).

Barnsley—Wilthorpe Road. Courts: H4. *Secretary:* E Macdonald, 4 Pennine Way, Pogmoor, Barnsley (205671).
Barwick in Elmet—Welfare Avenue. Courts: H3. *Secretary:* Mrs B Darnell, 18 Gascoigne Road, Barwick in Elmet, Leeds LS15 4LR (812437).
Beauchief TC—46 Old Park Road, Sheffield (745098). Courts: H5. *Secretary:* Mrs J S Fox, Fox Hall, Fox Lane, Bradway, Sheffield S17 4RL (362653).
Beckfoot—Beckfoot Lane, Bingley. Courts: H4. *Secretary:* Mrs E Turner, 27 St Aidans Road, Baildon, Shipley BD17 (585328).
Bedale—Leyburn Road (22085). Courts: H3. *Secretary:* Mrs A K Stockdale, Green Pastures, Hunton, Bedale (Bedale 50241).
Beverley & East Riding—York Road, Beverley. Courts: G4, H3. *Secretary:* R K Gaydon, 4 Molescroft Road, Beverley, North Humberside (0482 868407).
Birstwith Tennis Club—Courts: H2. *Secretary:* Mrs M Brown, South View, Clint, Harrogate (770512).
Bishopsthorpe Tennis Club—Courts: H3. *Secretary:* R Pears, 4 Myrtle Avenue, Bishopthorpe, York (705843).
Brentwood LTC—Courts: H6. *Secretary:* Miss V Hill, 6 Cherry Tree Court, Sheffield (581776).
British Railways Staff Association (Hull)—Courts: G4, H4. *Secretary:* A Fulstow, 8 Paterson House, Rain Hill Road, Hull (446549).
British Steel Corporation—Sheffield. Courts: H4. *Secretary:* G C Freeston, 65 Hareward Road, Firth Park, Sheffield S5 9UB (385569).
Bubwith LTC—Courts: H2. *Secretary:* Mrs K Lund, 1 Honeypot, Bubwith, Selby, North Yorks (Bubwith 757).
Castleford TC—Saville Park, Hightown. Courts: H3. *Secretary:* M Artis, 273 Lower Mickletown, Methley, Leeds (Castleford 515871).
Castle Garth—Courts: H4. *Secretary:* Mrs A Ellison, 18 Cedar Court, Partridge Wood Hill, Wetherby (65702).
Chapel Allerton LT & Squash—Stainbeck Lane, Leeds 7. Courts: G9, H5 (3 covered). *Secretary:* Bill Lumsden, Sports Manager, Chapel Allerton LT & Squash Club, Wensley Avenue, Stainbeck Lane, Chapel Allerton, Leeds 7 (682862).
City of Leeds YMCA TC—Courts: H6. *Secretary:* D M Strachan, 3 Oakdene Court, Shadwell Lane, Leeds LS17 8XS (685284).
Collingham—Collingham, nr Leeds. Courts: H2. *Secretary:* J Henson, 'Beliche,' Harewood Road, Collingham (72497).
Cottingham—Hull Road, Cottingham. Courts: G7, H5. *Secretary:* J C Topper, 30 Hull Road, Cottingham (Hull 847747).
Craven—Gargrave, nr Skipton. Courts: G5, H2. *Secretary:* C M D Roberts, 16 North Street, Gargrave (614).
Cross Hills LTC—Keighley Road, Cross Hills, Keighley. Courts: H3. *Secretary:* C Powell, Skipton Road, Silsden, Keighley (Steeton 53288).
Doncaster—Saxton Avenue, Bessacarr, Doncaster. Courts: G3, H9. *Secretary:* Mrs B J Rainey, 62 Arklow Road, Doncaster DN2 5LD (49907).
Driffield LTC—Courts: G6. *Secretary:* Mrs A Farnsworth, Driffield YO25 (0377 44224).
Driffield—Recreation Club, Bridlington Road. Courts: G4, H2. *Secretary:* Mrs G Bell, New Bungalow, Church Lane, Fridaythorpe YO25 9RU (0377 88220).
Ecclesall—Ecclesall, Sheffield 11. Courts: H7. *Secretary:* G B Addison, 2 Duncombe Street, Walkley, Sheffield S6 3RJ (338213).
Elland Athletic Bowling Club (Tennis Section)—Hullan Edge. Courts: H2. *Secretary:* P W Townend, Carandon, Victoria Road, Elland (73339).
Forgemasters Sports & Social Club—Atlas Ground, Shirecliffe Road. Courts: H4. *Secretary:* F Senior, Gen Sec Forgemasters S & SC, Don Valley House, Brightside Lane, Sheffield S9 2PZ (449071 ext 3201).
Fulford TC—Courts: H3. *Secretary:* Mrs J Haw, 6 Heslington Croft, Fulford, York (27899).
Fulwood—Chorley Road, Fulwood, Sheffield. Courts: G3, H4. *Secretary:* J R Westaway, 28c Queen Victoria Road, Totley Rise, Sheffield (365179).
The Georgian TC—Courts: H2. *Secretary:* Ms J Oakes, 28 Stanmore Place, Leeds 4 (742945).
Glaisdale TC—Carr Lane, Glaisdale, Whitby. Courts: H1. *Secretary:* Mrs M Hutchinson, 5 Arncliffe Terrace, Glaisdale, Whitby YO21 2QJ.
Grove LTC—Millhouse Lane, Sheffield. Courts: H4. *Secretary:* M Dunstan, 21 Harley Road, Sheffield (351385).
Grove Hill—Grove Hill, Ilkley Road, Otley. Courts: H4. *Secretary:* Mrs P A Hunt, 18 Milner Bank, Otley LS21 3NE (463510).
Hallamshire Tennis & Squash Club—Hunters Bar, Sheffield. Courts: G7, H6 (covered 2). *Secretary:* Mr M Newton, Flat 1, Oakburn Court, Broomhall Road, Sheffield S10 2DR.
Hangingwater—Hangingwater Road, Sheffield. Courts: H3. *Secretary:* T D Nowlin, 5 Mylor Road, Sheffield S11 7PF (663970).
Harlow Tennis Club—Harlow Hill, Otley Road. Courts: H3. *Secretary:* K H Smith, Mount Pleasant, Sleights Lane, Kettlesing, Harrogate (771126).
Harrogate Civil Service—St George's Road, Harrogate. Courts: H3. *Secretary:* S Ramplin, 64 Hookstone Avenue, Harrogate (870407).
Harrogate Sports—Leeds Road, Harrogate. Courts: H6. *Secretary:* D Fildes, 2 Ennerdale Road, Leeds LS12 5EN (Leeds 791064).
Heaton Lawn Tennis and Squash—Emm Lane, Bradford 9. Courts: H9 (1 covered). *Secretary:* D Hanson, c/o Club, Crofton Road, Heaton, Bradford 9 (41508).
Hessle—Boothferry Road, Hessle. Courts: G5, H3. *Secretary:* Jean Twigger, 11 Marlborough Avenue, Hessle, East Yorks (647919).
Hillside LTC—off Spen Lane, Cleckheaton. Courts: H3. *Secretary:* K Womersley, 7 Rosedale Avenue, Hartstead, Liversedge (0274 872251).
Holmes Ladder TC—Hexthorpe Flats, Doncaster. Courts: H3. *Secretary:* J B Sculthorpe, 77 St Anne's Road, Bellevue, Doncaster DN4 5DZ (25461).

Horsforth (Throstle Nest)—New Road Side, Horsforth. Courts: H4. *Secretary:* Miss C A Smethurst, 42 Back Lane, Horsforth, Leeds LS18 4RF (Horsforth 582526).
Huddersfield—Cemetery Road, Edgerton, Huddersfield. Courts: G5, H5 (1 covered). *Secretary:* Dr N Varey, 6 Heaton Road, Gledholt, Huddersfield (546722).
Hull Young People's Institute—Ferens Avenue, Cottingham Road. Courts: G20, H1 (1 covered). *Secretary:* P Jefferson, 15 Willow Court, Carr Lane, Willerby, Hull HU10 6JL (0482 650801 pri, 41445 bus).
ICI Huddersfield Ltd—Leeds Road, Huddersfield, Yorks. On A62 Huddersfield to Leeds Road 1½ miles out. Courts: H5. *Secretary:* T Taylor, ICI Recreation Club, Leeds Road, Huddersfield (514367).
Ilkley—Stourton Road, Ilkley. Courts: G15, H5 (2 covered). *Secretary:* C D Jones, Birch Garth, Rose Bank, Burley-in-Wharfdale, Ilkley (B-I-W 863760).
Keighley—Woodville Road, Keighley. Courts: H4. *Secretary:* Mrs H Ogden, 13 Westview Grove, Keighley (604025).
Kirbymoorside TC—Courts: H2. *Secretary:* D Bloore, Low Park Farm, Kirbymoorside, York YO6 6HR (31463).
Knaresborough TC—Courts: 3. *Secretary:* Mrs P Stevenson, 47 Wetherby Road, Knaresborough (863874).
Leeds Permanent Building Soc—Courts: H3. *Secretary:* D Haigh, 24 Hunger Hills Drive, Horsforth, Leeds (586419).
Linton—Linton, Wetherby. Courts: H2. *Secretary:* Mrs S M Stewart, The Croft, Sicklingham, nr Wetherby LS22 4BD (62134).
Liversedge—Hudd Road, Liversedge. Courts: G4, H4. *Secretary:* S Brooke, 17 Farrar Avenue, Mirfield (494513).
Longley Tennis & Bowling Club—Longley Road, Almondbury, Huddersfield. Courts: H5. *Secretary:* G Durrans, 64 Southfields Road, Waterloo, Huddersfield HD5 5RJ (20009).
Low Harrogate—Victoria Road, Harrogate. Courts: H4. *Secretary:* Miss C Ellison, Flat 10, Majestic Court, Springfield Avenue, Harrogate (66616).
Malton Squash & Bowls LTC—Old Maltongate. Courts: G7, H2. *Secretary:* P Asquith, White House Farm, Kirby Misperton, Malton (Kirby Misperton 218).
Mexborough Athletic Club—Adwick Road, Mexborough. Courts: H5. *Secretary:* R A Lamb, 25 Chatsworth Avenue, Mexborough (584382).
Mirfield—Huddersfield Road, Mirfield. Courts: H3. *Secretary:* S Sharpe, 2 Springfield Park, Mirfield (495032).
Moor Allerton Golf Club (Tennis Section)—Coal Road, Blackmoor, nr Scarcroft. Courts: H7. *Secretary:* Rhona Rappaport, c/o Moor Allerton Golf Club, Coal Road, Wike, Leeds (661154).
Moor Allerton Memorial Hall TC—Stonegate Road, Leeds. Courts: H3. *Secretary:* Mrs A Voss, 590 Stonegate Road, Leeds LS17 6EL (693295).
Park TC—Bute Avenue. Courts: H2. *Secretary:* Mr P McLoughlin, 4 Coach Road, Hove Edge, Brighouse (0484 712711).
Pine Grove Country Club—Courts: H1. *Secretary:* R E Armytage, c/o Pinegrove Country Club, Myers Grove Lane, Sheffield S6 5JG (342830).
Poole in Wharfedale TC—Poole in Wharfedale. Courts: H2. *Secretary:* R H Drake, 2 Arthington Lane, Pool in Wharfedale, Yorks LS21 1LG (842340).
Poppleton Sports & Social Club—Nether Poppleton, York. Courts: H3. *Secretary:* Mrs S Swift, Long Ridge Lane, Upper Poppleton, York (795410).
Queens (Halifax)—Moorlands View, Savile Park. Courts: G4, H4. *Secretary:* Mrs B R Dolan, Linden Royde, Linden Road, Halifax (53413).
Rastrick (Private Tennis Club)—Courts: H4 (1 covered). *Secretary:* Mrs K Thornton, Oaks Green Farm, 89 Crowtrees Lane, Rastrick, Brighouse (78125).
Rawdon Golf & LTC—Buckstone Drive, Rawdon. Courts: G4, H3. *Secretary:* Mrs M Taylor, 5 Borrins Way, Baildon, Shipley (Bradford 585235).
Ripon—Mallorie Park Drive. Courts: H3. *Secretary:* Mrs K Hart, 32 Hillshaw Park Way, Ripon (5262).
Roundhay—Shaftesbury Avenue, Street Lane, Leeds 8. Courts: G2, H4. *Secretary:* B Marshall, 39 Chandos Avenue, Leeds LS8 1QX (663957).
Rustlings—Collegate Crescent, Sheffield 10. Courts: G3, H3. *Secretary:* G S Hellowell, 45 Swaledale Road, Sheffield 7 (57482).
Ryedale Sports Club—Thornton Road. Courts: H2. *Secretary:* Mrs A Rudd, 19 Castle Close, Thornton Dale, Pickering (0751 72484).
St Chads TC—Courts: H2. *Secretary:* Miss E Boothman, 4 Church Hill, Bramhope, Leeds (843411).
St Peters (Shipley)—Fernhill Road off Moorhead Lane. Courts: H3. *Secretary:* Miss D Moore, 22 Fernhill Road, Shipley (Bradford 585606).
Salts TC—Courts: H3. *Secretary:* Mrs B Beaumont, 23 Villa Road, Bingley, West Yorkshire BD16 4ER (Bradford 562533).
Sandal LTC—Walton Lane, Sandal. Courts: H6. *Secretary:* Mrs J M Read, 12 Beechfield, Sandal, Wakefield (250609).
Scarborough—Courts: G5. *Secretary:* M White, 44 Fountayne Road, Hunmanby, nr Filey YO14 0LU (890178).
Scholes—Belle Vue Avenue, Scholes. Courts: H3. *Secretary:* R Hawley, 97 Swinnon Lane, Leeds 13 (555054).
Sheffield Amateur Sports—Abbeydale Park, Dore. Courts: H8. *Secretary:* G C Scott, 65 Furniss Avenue, Dore, Sheffield S17 3QJ (364302).
Sheffield & District Parks & Associate Clubs—Public Parks Courts. Courts: H3. *Secretary:* D W Smith, 90 Ecclesfield Road, Chapeltown, Sheffield S30 4TE (469481).
Sheriff Hutton TC—Bulmer Road. Courts: H2. *Secretary:* Mrs J M Johnstone, Cherry Tree Cottage, West End, Sheriff Hutton, York (626).
Slazenger Sports—School Lane, High Street. Courts: H2. *Secretary:* Mrs M E Killey, 32 Manor Lane, Ossett WF5 0LJ (Wakefield 279019).

Spa LTC—Old Swan Hotel, Harrogate. Courts: H3. *Secretary:* Miss H Walton, 2 Coppice Close, Harrogate (521851).
Starbeck—Bogs Lane, Starbeck. Courts: H3. *Secretary:* Miss V J Gooch, 54 Fairways Avenue, Harrogate (886756).
Stillington TC—Courts: H3. *Secretary:* Mrs E Richards, The Green, Stillington, York YO6 1JX (Easingwold 810085).
Stokesley TC—Courts: H3. *Secretary:* Mrs M Altringham, 1 The Bakery, Newby, Middlesbrough (312888).
Sutton-on-Derwent—Courts: G2, H1. *Secretary:* R S Twining, 2 Woldcroft, Sutton, York (0904 85432).
Swanland TC—Playing Fields, Memorial Hall, Swanland. Courts: G3, H2. *Secretary:* Mrs D A Parker, 7 Tranby Ride, Anlaby, Hull HU10 7ED (654292).
Temple Newsam—Whitkirk, nr Leeds. Courts: G2, H5. *Secretary:* D S Oates Esq, 33 Hollyshaw Crescent, Leeds LS15 7AN (643112).
Thirsk Athletic—Thirsk Racecourse. Courts: G6, H2. *Secretary:* Mrs V A White, Stalysides, Worlds End, Sowerby, Thirsk-In-Yorks (0845 23016).
Thongsbridge—Huddersfield Road, Thongsbridge. Courts: H5. *Secretary:* Mrs P Barton, 39 Grove Cottages, Bolster Moor, Glocar, Huddersfield (651513).
Towers—Stonegate Road, Leeds 6. Courts: H2. *Secretary:* Mrs S Welch, 5 Thorn Lane, Leeds (668751).
Undercliffe—Pollard Lane, Bradford. Courts: H3. *Secretary:* Mrs S McGhie, 11 Westminster Terrace, Bradford BD3 0HG (633900).
Upper Armley—Stanningley Road, Armley, Leeds. Courts: H2 (1 covered). *Secretary:* Miss M B Smith, 9 Rossefield Place, Leeds LS13 3RJ (Pudsey 564444).
Wakefield—College Ground, Pinderfields Road. Courts: H6. *Secretary:* A Barclay, 54 Mountbatten Avenue, Sandal, Wakefield WF2 6HD (257249).
Walkington TC—Back View, Walkington, Beverley. Courts: H3. *Secretary:* Mrs A Smith, 18 Middlehowe Green, Walkington, Beverley, N Humberside HU17 8TG (Hull 869239).
Walton—Barnsley Road. Courts: H3. *Secretary:* Mrs M W Charlesworth, 17 Thornhill Close, Walton, Wakefield (255034).
Westfields TC—Richmond. Courts: H2. *Secretary:* Mrs I Vollborth, 42 Laburnum Grove, Richmond (5099).
West Yorks Metropolitan Council Sports SC—116 Walton Lane, Sandal, Wakefield. Courts: H6. *Secretary:* C Darnley, 371 Milnthorpe Lane, Sandal, Wakefield (255358).
Wheatley Hills TC—Greenhouse Road, Wheatley Hills. Courts: H3. *Secretary:* Miss F Merriman, 51 Cecil Avenue, Warmswoth, Doncaster (851767).
Whitby TC—Courts: H2. *Secretary:* Miss E May, 13 Hermitage Way, Eskdaleside, Sleights Whitby YO22 5HG (810989).
Wigginton TC—Y. Courts: H3. *Secretary:* Mrs V Butler, 39 Towthorpe Road, Haxby, York (768869).
York LTC—Clifton Park, Skipton Road, York. Courts: H5. *Secretary:* M Prime, 8 Flavian Grove, Clifton, York (30217).
York Civil Service TC—Y. Courts: H3. *Secretary:* Mrs S Walters, 36 Thornhills, Haxby, York (763010).
York Railway Inst—Courts: H4. *Secretary:* I Ryder, 28 Gladstone Street, Acomb, York Y02 4NG (783154).

OTHER AFFILIATED ORGANISATIONS (5)

Doncaster Metropolitan College of HE—Doncaster. Courts: H8. *Secretary:* D G Lyne.
Doncaster Junior Tennis Association—Danum Road School, Danum Road, Doncaster. Courts: H6. *Secretary:* B Robinson, 21 Sandrock Drive, Bessacarr, Doncaster (531544).
Harrogate & District Tennis League—*Secretary:* I G Hargreaves, 11 Hookstone Wood Road, Harrogate HG2 8PN (0423 887964).
Sheffield & District LTA—*Secretary:* D B Webb, 471 Halifax Road, Greenside, Sheffield 55O 3PB (0742 467328).
South Yorkshire Lawn Tennis Association—*Secretary:* R Lamb, 25 Chatsworth Avenue, Mexborough S30 3PB (0742 467328).

AFFILIATED SCHOOLS (93)

Boys (13)

Ampleforth College — York. **Archbishop Holgate's** — York. **Ashville College** — Harrogate. **Belle Vue Boys School** — Bradford. **Bootham School** — York. **Giggleswick School** — Settle. **Hymers College** — Hull. **Leeds Grammar School** — Leeds. **Malsis School** — Keighley. **Pocklington School** — Pocklington. **Queen Elizabeth Grammar School** — Wakefield. **St Peters School** — York. **Woodhouse Grove School** — Bradford.

Girls (22)

Bar Grammar School — York. **Beverley High School for Girls** — Beverley. **Bradford Girls Grammar School** — Bradford. **Brighouse Girls Grammar School** — Brighouse. **Crossley and Porter** — Halifax. **Fulneck Girls' School** — Pudsey. **Gateways High School** — Leeds. **Harrogate College** — Harrogate. **Howden Clough High School** — Batley. **Hull High School** — Hull. **Hunmanby Hall School** — Yorks. **Leeds Girls High School** — Leeds. **The Mount School** — York. **Notre Dame Grammar School** — Leeds. **Queen Ethelburga's School** — Harrogate. **Queen Margaret's School** — York. **St Hilda's School** — Whitby. **St Philomena's Convent** — North Humberside. **Sheffield High School for Girls** — Sheffield. **Skipton Girls High School** — Skipton. **Wakefield Girls High School** — Wakefield. **York College for Girls** — York.

Mixed Schools (53)

Abbeydale Grange School — Sheffield. **Aston Comprehensive** — Sheffield. **Balby Carr School** — Doncaster. **Bingley Grammar School** — Bingley. **Bridlington School** — Bridlington. **Brinsworth Comp School** — Rotherham. **Bruntcliffe High**

School — Leeds. **Buttershaw Upper School** — Bradford. **Campsmount High School** — Doncaster. **Clare Hall County Sec School** — Halifax. **Colne Valley High School** — Huddersfield. **Danum Grammar School** — Doncaster. **Don Valley High School** — Doncaster. **Driffield School** — Driffield. **Ellers High School** — Doncaster. **Edlington Comp School** — Doncaster. **Fairfax School** — Bradford. **Friends School** — Great Ayton. **Greenhand College** — Huddersfield. **Grange School** — Bradford. **Greenhead Grammar School** — Keighley. **Hall Cross Comprehensive** — Doncaster. **Heckmondwike Grammar School** — Heckmondwike. **Huddersfield New College** — Huddersfield. **Hurlfield School** — Sheffield. **Ilkley Grammar School** — Ilkley. **Guiseley School** — Leeds. **Jordanthorpe Comp School** — Sheffield. **Kettlethorpe High School** — Wakefield. **Kimberworth Comp School** — Rotherham. **King Edward VII School** — Sheffield. **Lady Lumley's School** — Pickering. **Lawnswood School** — Leeds. **Mexborough Mixed Sec School** — Mexborough. **Mirfield School** — Mirfield. **Myers Grove School** — Sheffield. **Newfield School** — Sheffield. **Rotherham School Sports Assoc** — Rotherham. **Outwood Grange School** — Wakefield. **Rodillian School** — Wakefield. **Rhodesway School** — Bradford. **Ripon Grammar School** — Ripon. **St Andrew's School** — Malton. **St Francis Xavier Sec School** — Richmond. **Scarborough College** — Scarborough. **Sherburn High School** — Leeds. **Silverdale School** — Sheffield. **Tapton Secondary School** — Sheffield. **Thornton School** — Bradford. **Wath Comp School** — Rotherham. **Stainbeck High School** — Leeds. **Wyke Manor School** — Bradford. **Wolfreton School** — Hull.

ISLAND ASSOCIATIONS

CHANNEL ISLANDS LAWN TENNIS ASSOCIATION

Hon Secretary—**Miss J Le Boutillier,** Vilcanota, Rue de Maupertuis, Mont-a-l'abbe, St Helier, Jersey, CI (Jersey 64126).
Hon Treasurer—**Mjr M Lees,** Lynton, Rue des Marettes, St Martin, Jersey (Jersey 53867).
Men's Match Secretary—**A D Crichton,** Whitton Grange, Route Des Issues, St John, Jersey (61659).
Ladies's Match Secretary—**Miss C A Alford ,** Michael Voisin & Co, St Helier, Jersey, CI (Jersey 77511).
Junior Secretary—**A Cross,** Athena, Mont des Croix, St Brelade, Jersey, CI (Jersey 45827).
Representative on the Council—**M S Robottom.**

AFFILIATED CLUBS (6)

The Caesarean Croquet and Lawn Tennis Club—Grands Vaux, St Helier, CI. Courts: H11 (2 floodlit). *Secretary:* A T Le Quesne, Lower Flat, Fairview, St Aubins Road, St Helier, Jersey, CI (Jersey 79755).
The '76 Club—Grainville, St Saviour, Jersey, CI. Courts: H6. *Secretary:* C Osgood, 20 Clos de la Bataille, Grouville, Jersey, CI (Jersey 52850).
St John's Sports and Recreation Centre—St John, Jersey, CI. Courts: H2, Indoor 1. *Chairman Tennis Section:* I Campbell, Le Fleurion, St John, Jersey, CI (Jersey 61660).
St Martin's Lawn Tennis Club—La Rue du Hurel, St Martin, Guernsey, CI. Courts: H5. *Secretary:* M Wilton, Rue des Reines, Forest, Guernsey, CI (Guernsey 64001).
La Mare de Carteret Tennis Club—La Mare de Carteret School, Cobo, Guernsey, CI. Courts: H7. *Secretary:* D Stagg, Moorlands, La Vasselerie, St Andrews, Guernsey, CI (Guernsey 38034).
Alderney Tennis Club—Operates on Private Courts H2. *Secretary:* Mrs C Atkinson, Val Stables, La Val, Alderney, CI (Alderney 2900).

AFFILIATED SCHOOLS (16)

Boys
Victoria College—St Helier, Jersey, CI.**De La Salle College**St Saviour, Jersey, CI.
Elizabeth College—St Peter Port, Guernsey, CI.

Girls
Jersey College for Girls—St Helier, Jersey, CI.
Beaulieu Convent—St Saviour, Jersey, CI.
The Ladies College—St Peter Port, Guernsey, CI.
Blanchelande—St Martin, Guernsey, CI.

Mixed
D'Hautrée—St Saviour, Jersey, CI.
Grainville—St Saviour, Jersey, CI.
Hautlieu Grammar—St Saviour, Jersey, CI.
Le Rocquier—St Clement, Jersey, CI.
Les Quennevais School and Community Centre—St Brelade, Jersey, CI.
St Michael's Preparatory School—St Saviour, Jersey, CI.
La Mare de Carteret Secondary—Cobo, Guernsey, CI.
The Grammar School—St Andrews, Guernsey, CI.
St Anne School—Braye Road, Alderney, CI.

Correspondence should be addressed to The Head of PE at each school.
For Primary Schools Please contact A Cross, The PE Adviser, States of Jersey Education Department, or P Sherbourne, The Teachers' Centre, Guernsey Education Council.

ISLE OF MAN LAWN TENNIS ASSOCIATION

Hon Secretary—**B C Leahy,** Kapsigeri, Croite Quill Road, Lonan (0624 781 525).
Hon Treasurer—**B Walton,** 17 Mount View Close, Ballachurry, Douglas.

AFFILIATED CLUBS (7)

Albany—Ballaughton, Spring Valley, Douglas. Courts: H3. *Hon Secretary:* Mrs J Clague, 7 Mount View Road, Onchan (0624 24359).
Castletown—Malew Street, Castletown. Courts: H3. *Hon Secretary:* D Wilkinson, 40 The Crofts, Castletown.
Douglas—Kensington Road, Douglas. Courts: G4. *Hon Secretary:* Mrs S Thompson, 2 Glen View Road, Onchan (0624 23472).
Mooragh—Mooragh Park, Ramsey. Courts: H2. *Hon Secretary:* J G Corlett, 4 Lheaney Grove, Ramsey (0624 814244).
Peel—Marine Parade, Peel. Courts: H4. Hon *Secretary* Mrs B Baxter, Melbourne House, Peveril Road, Peel (0624 842722).
Ramsey—Grammar School, Lezayre Road, Ramsey. Courts: H6. *Hon Secretary:* Miss P Manson, Cronk Mayn Beg, Jurby Road, Ramsey.
Southern—Breagle Glen, Port Erin. Courts: H3. *Hon Secretary:* R Henry, Millcroft, Ballafesson, Port Erin (0624 833744).

NON-TERRITORIAL ASSOCIATIONS

ARMY LAWN TENNIS ASSOCIATION

Hon Secretary—**Lt Col H W Heath,** Ministry of Defence, DAR 2, Room 1108, Empress State Building, Lillie Road, London SW6 1TR (01-385 1244 ext 2716). 2 Stagbury House, Outwood Lane, Chipstead, Surrey CR3 3NF (Downland 53167).
Hon Treasurer—**Major A S Moore,** RAPC, Guards Depot, Alexander Barracks, Pirbright, Brookwood, Surrey GU24 0DT (04867 4511 ext 342).
Hon Match Secretary—**Col B Reeves,** HQ South East District, Steele's Road, Aldershot, Hants GU11 2DP (0252 24431 ext 3238).
Representative on the Council—**Lt Col H W Heath.**

ROYAL AIR FORCE LAWN TENNIS ASSOCIATION

Hon Secretary—**Wg Cdr M R Yule,** HQ RAF Support Command, RAF Brampton, Huntingdon, Cambs PE18 8QL (0480 52151 ext 2515).
Hon Treasurer—**Flt Lt R C Smith,** RAF, Boscombe Down, Salisbury, Wiltshire SP4 0JF (Amesbury 23331 ext 2714 or 2667).
Hon Match Secretary—**Sq Ldr M T Leatt,** RAF Honington, Bury St Edmunds, Suffolk IP31 1EE. (03596 561 ext 2291).
Representative on the Council—**Group Capt P G Hill.**

ROYAL NAVY LAWN TENNIS ASSOCIATION

Hon Secretary—**Cmdr A J Spruce,** RN, HMS Daedalus, Lee-on-Solent, Hampshire (0705 550143 ext 4181).
Hon Treasurer—**Lt Cmdr B L J Maddock,** HMS Centurion, Grange Road, Gosport, Hants (Portsmouth 822351ext 2525).
Representative on the Council—**Captain R H Parsons, RN.**

OXFORD UNIVERSITY LAWN TENNIS CLUB

Hon Secretaries—**J Simon** (New College), **M Young** (St Edmunds Hall).
Representative on the Council—**Dr R P H Gasser** (Brasenose College).

CAMBRIDGE UNIVERSITY LAWN TENNIS CLUB

Joint Hon Secretaries
Men's—**P B Kleidman** (Trinity College).
Ladies'—**Miss S E Swift** (Emmanuel College).
Chairman—**G A Cass,** Cambridge University Press, The Edinburgh Building, Shaftesbury Road, Cambridge CB2 2RU.
Senior Treasurer—**A P Styan,** University Printing House, Shaftesbury Road, Cambridge CB2 2BS.
Representative on the Council—**G A Cass.**

THE ALL ENGLAND LAWN TENNIS AND CROQUET CLUB

Chief Executive—**C J Gorringe.**
Championships Director—**A R M Grier.**
Financial Director—**J A Hughes.**
Marketing Director—**R E McCowen.**
Club Secretary—**R D Ambrose,** The All England Lawn Tennis and Croquet Club, Church Road, Wimbledon, London SW19 5AE (01-946 2244).
Representatives on the Council—**C J Gorringe, H E Truman.**

CIVIL SERVICE LAWN TENNIS ASSOCIATION

Chairman—**Mrs V Walley,** 3 Gainsborough Road, London W4 1NJ (01 994 3890 pri).
Hon Secretary—**Mrs P Jenkins,** 37 March Court, Warwick Drive, Putney, London SW15 6LE (01 789 3396 pri, 01 382 7574 bus).
Hon Treasurer—**Mrs S Hamilton,** 6 Wayside, East Sheen, London SW14 (01-876 2623 home).
Hon Men's Match Secretary—**F A Hacking,** 59 Malvern Gardens, Kenton, Middlesex (01-204 4897).
Hon Ladies' Match Secretary—**Miss E Robinson,** 20 Coleport Close, Cheadle Hulme, Cheadle, Cheshire (061 485 3305 pri).
Headquarters Ground—Duke's Meadows, Chiswick (01-994 1202).
Representative on the Council—**Mrs V Walley.**

THE BRITISH SCHOOLS LAWN TENNIS ASSOCIATION

Chairman—**J R Cochrane,** CBE, JP.
Executive Officer—**J Coates.**
Office—c/o The Lawn Tennis Foundation, The Queen's Club, West Kensington, London W14 9EQ (01-385 4233).
Representatives on the LTA Council—**Mrs J M Maher, W E Curtis.**

INTERNATIONAL LAWN TENNIS CLUB OF GREAT BRITAIN

Hon Secretary—**B R Hatton,** 51 Village Way, Pinner, Middlesex HA5 5AB (01-868 7607).
Hon Treasurer—**J A H Curry,** New Place, The Ridges, Finchamstead, Berks.
Representative on the Council—**B R Hatton.**

VETERANS' LAWN TENNIS ASSOCIATION OF GREAT BRITAIN

Chairman—**R E Carter,** 4 Hazeldene, Seaford, Sussex BN25 5NQ (Seaford 890083).
Hon Secretary—**Mrs V Walley,** 3 Gainsborough Road, London W4 1NJ 601 994 3890).
Hon Treasurer—**G S Carter,** 141 Castellain Mansions, Castellain Road, London W9 1HG (01 286 8448).
Representative on the Council—**R E Carter.**

THE BRITISH TENNIS UMPIRES ASSOCIATION

Officers and Committee for 1986

Acting Chairman—**P Harffey.**
Hon Secretary—**Mrs J R Jones,** 11 Ruden Way, Epsom, Surrey KT17 3LL (Burgh Heath 55809).
Hon Treasurer—**P J Lane,** 51 Greenhayes Avenue, Banstead, Surrey SM7 2JJ (Burgh Heath 53541).

BRITISH WOMEN'S TENNIS ASSOCIATION

Beaconsfield School of Lawn Tennis, Beaconsfield, Bucks HP9 2BY (049 46 4744).
President—**Miss S Livingston.**
Director—**Miss S Okin.**
Representative on the Council—**Miss S J Livingston.**

PROFESSIONAL TENNIS COACHES' ASSOCIATION

President—**W J Moss.**
Chairman—**Major F M S D Brancker,** Marks Barn Cottage, Crewkerne, Somerset (0460 72389).
Treasurer—**F L Harbour,** 16 Aylesford Avenue, Beckenham, Kent BR3 3SD (01-650 0900).
Secretary—**Mrs P M Bocquet,** 21 Glencairn Court, Lansdown Road, Cheltenham, Gloucestershire GL50 2NB (Cheltenham 524701).
Representative on the Council—**Miss J C L Poynder.**

BRITISH UNIVERSITIES SPORTS FEDERATION

General Secretary—**J C Siddall,** 28 Woburn Square, London WC1H 0AD (01-580 3618).

INSURANCE LAWN TENNIS ASSOCIATION

Hon Secretary—**W H Evans,** Friends Provident Life Office, Pixham End, Dorking, Surrey (885055).
Hon Treasurer—**J W Glyn,** Royal Reinsurance Co Ltd, Home Foreign Dept, 34-36 Lime Street, London EC3M 7JE (01 623 2345 ext 4390).
Hon Match Secretary—**I Hird,** Equity & Law Life Assurance Society Plc, Amersham Road, High Wycombe, Bucks (0494 33377).

THE UNITED BANKS LAWN TENNIS ASSOCIATION

Hon Secretary—**C J Mowforth,** 68 High Firs Crescent, Harpenden, Herts AL5 1NA.
Hon Match Secretary—**R Spindler,** 43 Ancastle Green, Henley-on-Thames, Oxon, RG9 1TS (Henley 577578 pri, 01-588 6464 bus).

THE SOCIETY OF LAWN TENNIS REFEREES

Chairman—**D G Lock.**
Hon Secretary/Treasurer—**M C Martin,** The Paddocks, Hungarton, Leicester, LE7 9JY.
Representative on the Council—**M C Martin.**

THE LAWN TENNIS FOUNDATION

Chairman—**C H T Brown.**
Manager—**Jim Coates,** The Lawn Tennis Foundation, Queen's Club, Barons Court, West Kensington W14 9EQ (01-385 4233).

INTERNATIONAL TENNIS FEDERATION

President — Mr P Chatrier.

Hon Life Vice-Presidents — Mr J Borotra, Dr G de Stefani, Mr A Heyman.

Hon Life Counsellors — Mr L E Ashenheim, Mr J E Carrico, Mr L Gorodi, Mr J S Harrison, Padma Bhushan R K Khanna, Mr S Malless, Mr S B Reay, Mr W H Woods.

Committee of Management

Mr P Chatrier, Federation Francaise de Tennis, Stade Roland Garros, 2 Avenue Gordon Bennett, 75016 Paris, France. Tel: (1) 47 43 96 81.
Mr H L Delatour Jr, 120 Fawn Lane, Portola Valley, California, 94025, USA. Tel: 415-851-2082.
Dr H Grimm, Thiersteinerrain 97, 4059 Basle, Switzerland. Tel: (61) 50 76 74.
Mr D N Hardwick, Eastfield, Cheselbourne, Dorchester, Dorset DT2 7NP, Great Britain. Tel: (025 887) 251.
Mr G D Jorgensen, 1507 First Federal Savings Bldg, 3003 No. Central Avenue, Phoenix, A2 850 12, USA. Tel: (602) 263 9771.
Mr E Kawatei, 7-2 Chayana-Cho, Ashiya 659, Japan. Tel: (0797) 31 6027/28.
Mr P Llorens, Balmes 470, 2°2a, Barcelona 08022, Spain. Tel: (3) 247 0641.
Mr A Metreveli, Sportkomitet, Leselidze Street, Tbilisi, USSR. Tel: 722442.
Mr R Nikolic, Prote Mateje 44, 11,000 Belgrade, Yugolsavia. Tel: (11) 430 728.
Mr A Pena, Apartado Aereo No. 90325, Bogota, Colombia. Tel: Bogota 255 8579.
Mr B R Tobin, LTA of Australia, Box 343, South Yarra, Victoria 3141, Australia. Tel: (3) 2674277.

Vice-Presidents — Mr H L Delatour Jr, Mr P Llorens, Mr B R Tobin.

Hon Treasurer — Mr D Jude.

Secretariat — Miss S Woodhead - General Secretary, Mr T Hallberg - Director of Men's Tennis, Mr D MacCurdy - Director of Development, Miss B Wancke - Director of Women's Tennis, Mr C S Stokes - Davis Cup Sponsorship Administrator, Mrs N Simmons - Junior Programmes Co-ordinator.

Sponsorship & Business Consultant — Dr P Angeli.

ADDRESSES OF AFFILIATED ASSOCIATIONS

(a) MEMBERS WITH VOTING RIGHTS (82)

Algeria—Federation Algerienne de Tennis, Centre des Federations Sportives, Cite Olympique B.P. 88 El Biar, Algers. Tel: (213) 79/39/39, Telex: ALGERS 61379 CFS DZ. President: Mr L Benazzi, Secretary: Mr R Bouakkaz.
Argentina—Asociacion Argentina de Tenis, Av. San Juan 1315/17, (1148) Capital Federal, Buenos Aires. Cable: Argtennis, Buenos Aires, Tel: (1) 26-1569/27-0101264696, Telex: 17336 ARGTEN AR. President: Mr J J Vasquez, Secretaries: Mr F Turno, Mr L J Rival.
Australia—L.T.A. of Australia Ltd., Box 343, South Yarra, Victoria 3141. Cable: Tencourt, Melbourne, Tel: (3) 267 4277, Telex: 36893 TENCRT. President: Mr B R Tobin, Executive Director: Mr C McDonald.
Austria—Osterreichischer Tennisverband, Hainburgerstrasse 36, A 1030 Vienna. Cable: Austriatennis, Vienna, Tel: (222) 753345/733352, Telex: 131652 OETEN A. President: Dr T Zeh, Secretary: Mr P Nader.
Bahrain—Bahrain Lawn Tennis Federation, P.O. Box 26985, Bahrain. Cable: Tennis, Bahrain, Tel: (973) 687236, Telex: 8292 GPIC BN. President: Dr T Al-Moayed, Secretary: Mr A Fakhro.
Bangladesh—Bangladesh Tennis Federation, Tennis Complex, Ramna Green, Dacca 2. Cable: Tennisfed, Dacca. Tel: (2) 506650, Telex: 642401 SHER BJ (mark: for tennis). Acting Secretary: Mr M H Jamaly.
Belgium—Royal Belgian Tennis Federation, Passage International Rogier 6, BTE 522, 1210 Brussels. Cable: Tennisfeder, Brussels, Tel: (2) 217 2365, Telex: 24023 TENFED B. President: Mr P P de Keghel, Secretaries: Mr W Goethals, Mr F Lemaire.
Bolivia—Federacion Boliviana de Tenis, Calle Mexico 1638, Casilla 20887, La Paz. Cable: Fedboltenis, La Paz, Tel: 378769. President: Sr T Sagarnaga P, Secretary: Sr M Adriazola.
Brazil—Confederacao Brasileira de Tenis, Rua Anfilofio de Carvalho No. 29, Grupo 407/8-ZC-20.030 Centro, Rio de Janeiro. Cable. Cebetenis, Rio de Janeiro, Tel: (21) 251 3920. President: Mr E Saller, Secretary: Mr C Alberto Martelotti.
Bulgaria—Bulgarian Tennis Federation, 18 Tolbuchin Blvd, 1040 Sofia. Cable: Besefese Tennis, Sofia, Tel: 80-3710 or 8651, Telex: 22723 or 22724 BSFS BG. President: Mr S Ganev, Secretary: Mr T Tzvetkov.
Cameroon—Federation Camerounaise de Lawn Tennis, B.P. 1121, Yaoundé. Cable: Fecatennis-MJS. Yaounde, Tel: 233860/1310 or 224329, Telex: 8568 KN or MNFA 8261 KN. President: Brig. Gen. J Tataw, Secretary: Dr N Mboulet.
Canada—Canadian Tennis Association, 3111 Steeles Avenue West, Downsview, Ontario,

Canada M3J 3H2. Cable: Sportrec, Ottawa. Tel: (416) 665-9777, Telex: 053 3660 SPORTREC OTT. President: Mr F Godbout. Executive Director: Mr D Steele. Director High Performance: Ms D Wilson.

Chile—Federacion de Tenis de Chile, Almirante Simpson No. 36, Casilla 1149, Santiago. Tel: (2) 2227279, Telex: 241328 COCH CL. President: Mr A Peric, Secretary: Mr A Alvarez.

China, People's Republic of—Tennis Association of the People's Republic of China, 9, Tiyuguan Road, Beijing. Cable: Sportschine, Beijing, Tel: 751313, Telex: 22323 CHOC CN. President: Mr L Zhengcao, Secretary: Mr Liu Huaitang.

Chinese Taipei Tennis Association—Chinese Taipei Tennis Association, 10th Fl. 53 Ren-Aird, Sec 3, Taipei, Taiwan. Cable: Sinovision, Taipei, Tel: 7716190, Telex: 25080 CHINA TV. President: Mr H P Chung, Secretary: Mr E S C Wang.

Colombia—Federación Colombiana de Tenis, Apartado Aereo No. 1, Bogota, 10.917. Cable: Fedetenis, Bogota, Tel: (2) 81 8330, Telex: 41275 ICJD. President: Mr G Obando, Executive Secretary: Mr K Wodak.

Cuba—Federacion Cubana de Tenis de Campo, Calle 13 NR 601 ESQ AC, Vedado Habana 4. Cable: Olimpicuba, Habana, Tel: (7) 418883/402921/ 415394, Telex: 0511332 INDER CU. President: Mr R Martinez, Secretary: Mr M Osorio.

Cyprus—Cyprus Tennis Federation, Nikitara Str 19, P.O. Box 3931, Nicosia. Cable: Tennis, Nicosia. Tel: (02) 450875, Telex: 5300 OLYMPIC CY. President: Mr P Christodoulou, Secretary: Mr D Solomonides.

Czechoslovakia—Ceskoslovenska Tenisova Asociace, Na Porici 12, 115 30 Prague 1. Cable: Sportsvaz, Prague, Tel: (2) 249451-5/245167, Telex: CSTVC 122650. President: Mr C Suk, Secretary: Mr M Polak.

Denmark—Dansk Tennis Forbund, Idraettens Hus, Broendby Stadion 20, 2605 Broendby, Denmark. Cable: Tennisforbund, Copenhagen, Tel: (2) 455555 Ext. 276, Telex: 33111 IDRAET DK (mark: Att. Tennis). President: Mr J Bertelsen, Secretary: Mr J Ahlstrand.

Ecuador—Federacion Ecuatoriana de Tenis, P.O. Box 4587, Guayaquil, Ecuador, Tel: 512123/524060, Telex: 3862 EMPRES ED, Cable: FEDETENNIS, QUITO. President: Mr N Macchiavello, Secretary: Mr C Carbo.

Egypt—Egyptian Lawn Tennis Federation, 13 Kasr el Nil Street, Cairo. Cable: Gyplawnten, Cairo, Tel: (2) 753235, Telex: 93697 SAFLM UN (mark: Att. Tennis). President: Mr G El Nazer, Secretary: Dr A Tewfik.

Finland—Suomen Tennisliitto, Radiokatu 12, Box 27, 00250 Helsinki 25. Cable: Tennisliitto, Helsinki. Tel: (0) 4737255, Telex: 121797 SVUL SF. President: Mr A Narakka, Secretary: Mr E Kiuttu.

France—Federation Francaise de Tennis, Stade Roland Garros, 2 Avenue Gordon Bennett, 75016 Paris. Cable: Tenisfedet, Paris, Tel: (1) 47 43 96 81, Telex: TENFED 611871F. President: Mr P Chatrier, Secretary: Mr J C Collinot.

German Democratic Republic—Deutscher Tennis-Verband der DDR, Storkower Strasse 118, 1055 Berlin. Tel: (2) 54 98 533, Telex: 114919 DTSB DD. President: Mr K H Sturm, Secretary: Mr W Joch.

Germany, Federal Republic of—Deutscher Tennis Bund e.V., Leisewitzstr. 26, 3000 Hannover 1. Cable: Tennisbund, Hannover, Tel: (511) 281067, Telex: 921378 DTB D. President: Dr C Stauder, Executive Director: Mr G Sanders.

Great Britain—The Lawn Tennis Association, Barons Court, West Kensington, London W14 9EG. Cable: LAWNTENNA, LONDON, W14, Tel: 01-385 2366, Telex 8956036 THELTA G. President: Mr G B Brown, Secretary, Mr J C U James.

Greece—Hellenic Tennis Federation, 89 Patission Str., 104 34 Athens. Cable: Efotennis, Athens, Tel: (1) 8210478/8815804, Telex: 222415 EFOA GR. President: Mr D Stefanides, Secretary: Mr D Gangas.

Hong Kong—Hong Kong Tennis Association Ltd, Room 911, Queen Elizabeth Stadium, Oi Kwan Road, Hong Kong. Cable: Tennis, Hong Kong, Tel: (5) 741546, Telex: 73411 RYODEN HX. President: Dr P Kwok, Secretary: Dr E W Hardisty.

Hungary—Magyar Tenisz Szovetseg, Dozsa Gyorgy ut 1-3, H-1143 Budapest. Cable: Comsport Tennis, Budapest, Tel: (1) 630-852, Telex: 225105 OTSH HV. President: Mr I Gulyas, Secretary: Mr F Zentai.

India—All India Lawn Tennis Association, Power Centre Private Ltd., 755 Mount Road, Madras 600 002. Cable: Powerpack, Madras, Tel: (44) 812725, Telex: 41 7869 GSET IN. President: Mr R Mpstural, Hon Secretary: Mr L Reddy.

Indonesia—Indonesian Tennis Association, Jln. Olahraga V/3 Kemanggisan, Slipi, Jakarta 11.480. Cable: Tennis Indonesia, Jakarta, Tel: (0646) 5482488, Telex: 45214 KONI IA. President: Major Gen. H Jonosewojo, Secretary: Mr S Nartomo.

Iran—Tennis Federation of Islamic Republic of Iran, Department of International Affairs, P.O. Box 11, 1642, Tehran. Cable: Olympic, Tehran, Tel: (21) 826999, Telex: 212691 VARZ IR. President: Mr G H Noorian, Secretary: Mr M Sefatti.

Iraq—Iraqi Tennis Federation, c/o Iraqi National Olympic Committee, P.O. Box No 441, Baghdad. Cable: Iroq, Baghdad, Tel: (1) 97390 (a.m.) 98879 (p.m.) 98874, Telex: 2824. President: Mr N Shaker, Secretary: Mr G Bakose.

Ireland—Irish Lawn Tennis Association, 22, Upper Fitzwilliam Street, Dublin 2. Cable: Irishtennis, Dublin, Tel: (01) 606332, Telex: 31295 ILTAEI. President: Mrs Mr C J Brennan, Secretary: Mrs M Hogg.

Israel—Israel Tennis Association, P.O. Box 20073, Tel Aviv 61 200. Cable: ILTA, Tel Aviv, Tel: (3) 613911/625864 Ext. 5348. Telex: 341118 BXTVIL . Chairman: Mr D Harnik, Secretary: Mr Z Meyer.

Italy—Federazione Italiana Tennis, Viale Tiziano 70, 00196 Rome. Cable: Italtennis, Rome, Tel: (6)

36858 213/210 or 3960092, Telex: 613330 FIT I. President: Avv. P Galgani, Secretary: Dott. G. Annibali.

Ivory Coast—Federation Ivoirienne de Tennis, 08 BP 300 08, Abidjan 01.Tel: 414057, Telex: 23555 IHCHOT CI. President: Mr J C Delafosse, Secretary: Mr K Kouadjo.

Jamaica—Jamaica Lawn Tennis Association, 2A Piccadilly Road, P.O. Box 175, Kingston 5. Cable: Lawntenna, Kingston, Tel: New Kingston 2441/2442, Telex: 2442. President: Mr W A Scholefield, Secretary: Mrs Y K Walsh.

Japan—Japan Tennis Association, c/o Kishi Memorial Hall, 1-1-1 Jinnan, Shibuya-ku, Tokyo 150. Cable: Niplotenis, Tokyo, Tel: (3) 481 2321, Telex: JAAAJ 27697 (mark: Att. Japan Tennis), Telecopier: 03-467-5192. President: Mr T Kosaka, Secretary: Mr S Shimizu.

Kenya—Kenya Lawn Tennis Association, P.O. Box 43184, Nairobi. Cable: Tennis, Nairobi, Tel: 567256, Telex: 22575 KATE NBO. Chairman: Mr J Carneiro, Hon. Secretary: Mrs M E Walker.

Korea, Republic of—Korea Tennis Association, Room 505, Sports Building, 19 Mukyo-Dong, Chung-Ku, Seoul. Cable: Kortennis, Seoul, Tel: 777-4028 or 777-6081-9, Ext. 52, Telex: KOCSEL K24989. President: Mr C K Cho, Secretary: Mr Y M Huh.

Kuwait—Kuwait Tennis, Table Tennis & Squash Federation, P.O. Box 1462, Hawalli, Kuwait, Cable: TENNIS, Kuwait, Tel: 424948, Telex: COMITE 23192 KT (mark: Att. Tennis Assn.). President: Mr K A Al-Bannai, Secretary: Mr A Alrifae.

Lebanon—Federation Libanaise de Tennis, P.O. Box 113-5591, Hamra, Beyrouth. Cable: Tennispong, Beyrouth, Tel: (961) 34 22 82, Telex: 20653 GESPA LE (mark: for E A Yazbeck). President: Mr A K Matar, Hon Secretary: Mr E A Yazbeck.

Libya—Jamahiriya Tennis Federation, P.O. Box 879, Tripoli. Cable: Almadrab, Tripoli. Tel: (21) 39156. Telex: 20710 RIADAH LY or 20420 LY LIBOLYMPIC. President: Mr A N Oweit, Secretary: Mr M Krewi.

Luxembourg—Federation Luxembourgeoise de Tennis, 7, Avenue Victor Hugo, Luxembourg 1750. Cable: Federation Luxembourgeoise de Tennis, Luxemburg, Tel: 47 31 57, Telex: 3556 COSL LU. President: Mr G Logelin, General Secretary: Mrs A Berger.

Malaysia—Lawn Tennis Association of Malaysia, Dept of Education Studies, Faculty of Education Studies, UPM Serdang, Selangor. Cable: Tennis Kuala Lumpur, Tel: (03) 586101 ext 471, Telex: UNIPER MA 37454. President: Hon Mr Abdul Ghafar Baba, Secretary: Mr A A Zakaria.

Malta—Malta Lawn Tennis Association, P.O. Box 50, Sliema Post Office, Sliema. Tel: 512368. President: Mr J P Galea, Secretary: Mr G J Bonello.

Mexico—Federacion Mexicana de Tenis AC., Durango No. 225-301, 06700 Mexico, D.F. Cable: Mextenis, Mexico City, Tel: (5) 514-37-59, Telex: 1761056 FMDTME. President: Mr L Lavalle, Secretary: Mr L Riefkohl.

Monaco—Federation Monegasque de Lawn-Tennis, 46 Rue Grimaldi, 98000 Monaco. Cable: Federation-Tennis-Monaco, Tel: (93) 30-01-02, Telex: CONG 469760 MC (mark: for LTA). President: Mr L Caravel, Secretary: Mr J C Riey.

Morocco—Federation Royale Marocaine de Tennis, Maison des Sports, Parc de la Ligue Arabe, Casablanca. Cable: Tenisfede, Maroc, Tel: 27-87-31 or 26-75-53, Telex: FRTENNIS 23745 M. President: Mr M M'Jid, Secretary: Mr M Moufid.

Netherlands—Koninklijke Nederlandse Lawn Tennis Bond, P.O. Box 107, 1200 AC Hilversum. Cable: Tennisbond, Hilversum, Tel: (35) 46941, Telex: 73250 LINE NL. President: Mr K T M Hehenkamp, Vice-President: Mr J F Steensma, Secretary: Mr Y Buruma.

New Zealand—New Zealand Lawn Tennis Association, P.O. Box 11541, Manners Street, Wellington. Cable: Tennis, Wellington, Tel: (41) 731 115. Executive President: Mr I D Wells, Executive Secretary: Mrs S A Reeve.

Nigeria—Nigeria Lawn Tennis Association, National Stadium, Syrulere, P.O. Box 145, Lagos. Cable: Tennis Natsports, Lagos, Tel: (1) 83 0649, Telex: 26559. President: Alhaji R A Adejumo, Secretary: Mr L A Ayorinde.

Norway—Norges Tennisforbund, Hauger Skolevei 1, 1351 Rud. Cable: Norsktennis, Oslo, Tel: (2) 134290, Telex: 78586 NIF N. President: Mr A Melander, Secretary: Mr T Kverneland.

Pakistan—Pakistan Tennis Federation, Rawalpindi Club, P.O. Box 16, The Mall, Rawalpindi. Cable: Paktennis, Rawalpindi, Cantt.Tel: (51) 64026, Telex: 5830 SAEED PK. President: Gen. R U Khan, Secretary: Mr M Pirzada.

Paraguay—Asociacion Paraguaya de Tenis, Colon 1054, Casilla de Correo 26, Asuncion. Tel: 43350, Telex: 362 PY HORIZONTE. President: Dr A V Ugarte Secretary: Mr J Martinez N, General Manager: Mr D L Llamosas.

Peru—Federacion Peruana de Tenis, Casilla 2243, Lima. Cable: Fepetennis, Lima, Tel: 24 99 79, Telex: 25650 PE PB HISHER. President: Ing Y Senno, Secretary: Mr A Pereda Pareja.

Philippines—Philippine Tennis Association, Rizal Memorial Sports Complex, Vito Cruz Street, Manila. Cable: Philta, Manila, Tel: (2) 58-35-35 or 86-46-81, Telex: 45967 FPTC PM or 64619 FPTC PN. President: Col. M B Barba, Secretary: Mr N R Reyes.

Poland—Polski Zwaizek Tenisowy, Ul. Marszalkowska 2, IIIrd Floor, 00-581 Warsaw. Cable: Poltenis, Warsaw, Tel: (22) 21 80 01 or 29 26 21, Telex: 816494 PAISP PL or 812466 COS PL. President: Mr R Garbaczewski, Hon. Secretary: Mr K Tarasiewiez, General Secretary: Mr P Dudzinski.

Portugal—Federacao Portuguesa de Tenis, Instalacoes Municipais de Tennis, Parque Florestal de Monsanto, 1300 Lisbon. Cable: Portugaltenis, Lisbon, Tel: (1) 648067, Telex: 13109 TENLIS P. President: Mr A Vaz Pinto, Secretary: Mr J M Dias.

Romania—Federatia Romana de Tenis, Str. Vasile Conta 16, 70139 Bucharest. Cable: Sportrom, Bucharest, Tel: (0) 11 97 87, Telex: 11180 SPORT R. President: Mr I Gheorghe, General Secretary: Ms F Mihai.
Saudi Arabia—Saudi Arabian Tennis & T.T. Federation, P.O. Box 4674, Riyadh 11412. Cable: Koratawla, Riyadh, Tel: (1) 4788145/7966, Telex: 204130 TENNIS SJ. President: Mr S Al-Jabhan, Secretary: Mr S Abdulaziz.
Senegal—Federation Senegalaise de Lawn Tennis, B.P. 510, Dakar. Tel: 22-44-67, Telex: 3159 SG CTDSENE. President: Mr Y Ndiaye, Secretary: Mr A Ndiaye.
Singapore—Singapore Lawn Tennis Association, Apt Blk 13 Dover Close East No 15-212, Singapore 0513, Tel: 4733533, Telex: MAPAL RS 37679 or MBL RS 23527. President: Dr O. L Boon, Secretary: Mr T Teo.
South Africa—The South African Tennis Union, P.O. Box 2211, Johannesburg 2000. Cable: Tennis, Johannesburg, Tel: (011) 402 3580, Telex: 425976 SA. President: Mr A de W Horak, Secretary/Treasurer: Mr G L Talbot.
Spain—Real Federacion Espanola de Tenis, Avda. Diagonal 618 3°D, 08021 Barcelona. Cable: Fedetenis, Barcelona, Tel: (3) 2005355 or 20108 44. President: Mr A P Niubo, Secretary: Mr T Garcia Balmaseda.
Sri Lanka—Sri Lanka Tennis Association, 45 Sir Marcus Fernando Mawatha, Colombo 7. Cable: Tennis, Colombo, Tel: (1) 91425, Telex: 22082 XPOINT CE or 22291 XPOINT CE. President: Mr E Perera, Secretary: Mr A T Madugalle.
Sudan—Sudan Lawn Tennis Association, P.O. Box 1553, Khartoum. Tel: 70081. President: Mr A Eltahir Bakr, Secretary: Mr M Ali Amer.
Sweden—Svenska Tennisforbundet, Lidingovagen 75, S 115 37 Stockholm. Cable: Svensktennis, Stockholm, Tel: (8) 679770, Telex: 12235 TENNIS S. President: Mr L Olander, Secretary General: Mr R Levin.
Switzerland—Schweizerischer Tennisverband, Talgut Zentrum 5, P.O. Box, 3063 Ittigen/Berne. Cable: Suissetennis, Bern, Tel: (031) 58 74 44, Telex: 911391 STV CH. President: Mr B Frischknecht, Director: Mr R Julita.
Syria Arab Republic—Syrian Arab Tennis Federation, P.O. Box 421, Damascus. Tel: 225026/34/52, Telex: HOTECH SY 411935. President: Dr S Al Jabi, Secretary: Mr M Hendi.
Thailand—The Lawn Tennis Association of Thailand, c/o Sports Promotion Organisation of Thailand, Hua Mark, Bangkok 10240. Cable: Thai Tennis, Bangkok. Tel: (2) 314 0808 or 314 6142, Telex: 20843 MIDASIA TH. President: Col S Amornwichet, Secretary: Capt B Phantawong.
Trinidad and Tobago—The Lawn Tennis Association of Trinidad and Tobago, c/o Trintoc, P.O. Box 601, Port-of-Spain, Trinidad.Cable: Lawntenna, Port-of-Spain, Tel: 62-32911. President: Mr V E Bruce, Secretary: Mr G A Matthew.
Tunisia—Federation Tunisienne de Tennis, Cite Sportive Bourguiba, El Menzah, 1004 Tunis. Tel: (1) 238 144, Telex: 14637 TOPMED TN. President: Mr M Farah, Secretary: Mr M Azzouz.
Turkey—Turkiye Tenis Federasyonu, Ulus Is Hani, Ankara. Cable: Tennis Sport, Ankara, Tel: (41) 12 41 50/261, Telex: 42251 TFF TR. President: Mr Y Das, Secretary: Mr Y Tenkin Kurat.
U.S.S.R—Lawn Tennis Federation of the U.S.S.R., Luzhnetskaya Naberezhnaya 8, Moscow 119270. Cable: Sportkomitet, Moscow, Tel: (095) 201 08 64, Telex: 411287 PRIZ SU. President: Mr B Volynov, Secretary General: Mr V Yanchuk.
U.S.A.—United States Tennis Association Incorporated, 12th Floor, 1212 Avenue of the Americas, New York N.Y. 10036. Cable: Ustennis, New York, Tel: (212) 302 3322, Telex: 424499 ULTA UI. President: Mr J Randolph Gregson, Executive Director: Mr D F Conway, Executive Secretary: Mr M J Burns.
Uruguay—Asociacion Uruguaya de Lawn Tennis, Calle Pablo De Maria 1065, Montevideo. Cable: Urutennis, Montevideo, Tel: (2) 4-63-63, Telex: CADE UY 22333. President: Mr C R Estrada, Secretary: Dr G Inda.
Venezuela—Federacion Venezolana de Tenis, Apartado 70539, Los Ruices, Caracas 1070-A. Cable: Fevetenis, Caracas, Tel: (2) 9792421/1487/0697, Telex: 28465 FVT VC. President: Mr A Plaza Rivas, Secretary: Mr G Barrera.
Yugoslavia—Tenis Savez Yugoslavije, Terazije 35, Belgrade. Cable: Tesaj, Belgrade, Tel: (11) 33 33 36, Telex: 12 595 SFKJ YU. President: Mr R Nikolic, Secretary: Mr Z Peric.
Zimbabwe—Tennis Association of Zimbabwe, P.O. Box 2346, Harare. Tel: (01) 32901, Telex: 2501 ZW LIQUOR. President: Mr I D F Godden, Secretary: Mrs C Greener.

(b) ASSOCIATE MEMBERS WITHOUT VOTING RIGHTS (37)

Afghanistan— Afghan Lawn Tennis Association, c/o National Olympic Committee of Afghanistan, National Stadium, Kabul. Cable: Olympic Kabul, Telex: 20579. President: Mr O Saraj, Secretary: Mr H Osman.
Bahamas—The Bahamas Lawn Tennis Association, P.O. Box N-10169, Nassau. Tel: (809) 326 1625 or 322 2694, Telex: 20307 OPSTAT. President: Mr P Phillips, Secretary: Mrs S Ryan.
Barbados—Barbados Lawn Tennis Association, P.O. Box 615c, Bridgetown. Tel: 427-5298. President: Mr N F Symmonds, Secretary: Mr B Hackett.
Benin—Federation Beninoise de Lawn Tennis, Club du Benin, B.P. 63, Akpakpa, Cotonous II. Cable: Lawn Tenning Box 516, Tel: 31 34 94. President: Mr G Ligan, Secretary: Mr C Martins.
Bermuda—Bermuda Lawn Tennis Association, P.O. Box 341, Hamilton 5. Cable: Ernsaudit, Bermuda, Tel: (29) 57272, Telex: 3680 ERNST BA. President: Mr W F Way, Secretary: Mrs G Butterfield.

Bhutan—Bhutan Tennis Federation, P.O. Box 103, Thimphu. Cable: Olympíc. President: Mr T Dorji, Secretary: Mr L Tsering.
Botswana—Botswana National L.T.A., P.O. Box 1174, Gaborone. Tel: 53029 or 51743, Telex: 2538 AUTOG BD. President: Dr J Letsunyane, Secretary: Mrs L Ranasinghe.
British Virgin Islands—British Virgin Islands Lawn Tennis Association, P.O. Box 201, Road Town, Tortola. Cable: Veritatem, Tortola, Tel: (809) 49 42616, Telex: 7918. President: Dr K Adamson, Secretary: Mr N Barton.
Brunei Darussalam—Brunei Darussalam Lawn Tennis Association, P.O. Box 1300, Bandar Seri Begawan. Telex: DCABWN BU 2267. President: Mr T R Butcher, Secretary: Mr A Ajmain.
Burma—Burma Tennis Federation, Aung San Memorial Stadium, Kandawgalay Post Office, Rangoon. Cable: Ubsped, Rangoon, Tel: 01-71731. President: Mr K K Gyi, Secretary: Mr A Thein.
Cayman Islands—Tennis Federation of the Cayman Islands, P.O. Box 1352, George Town, Grand Cayman , British West Indies. Tel: (1809 94) 92077, Telex: 4310 CORPSER CP. President: Mr D Price, Secretary: Mr G Barlow.
Congo—Federation Congolaise de Lawn-Tennis, B.P. 2092, Brazzaville.
Cook Islands—Cook Islands Tennis Association, P.O. Box 610, Rarotonga, Cook Islands. Tel: 22327, Telex: 62026 SSIRARO. President: Mr B R Baudinet, Secretary: Mr W Jon.
Costa Rica—Federacion Costarricense de Tenis, P.O. Box 326-1005, B° Mexico, San Jose. Cable: HOPEC, San Jose, Tel: 236133, Telex: 2101 HOPEC CR. President: Mr F Holtermann, Secretary, Mr R Mendieta.
Djibouti—Fédération Djiboutienne de Tennis, Rue Pierre-Pascal, B.P. 728, Djibouti. Cable: P.O. Box 728, Djibouti, Tel: 35 22 86. President: Mr H Houmed, Secretary General: Mme M A Farah.
Dominican Republic—Federacion Dominicana de Tennis, Club Deportive Naco, Calle Central, Ens Naco, Santo Domingo, Republic Dominicana. Tel: 565 48 36/685 8059, Telex: 3460418 BONELLY. President: Mr G Mejia, Secretary: Mr J Raveilo.
El Salvador—Federacion Salvadorena de Tenis, Apartado Postal (01) 110, San Salvador. Cable: Molino, San Salvador, Tel: (503) 23 38 92, Telex: 20542 MOLINO. President: Ing R Sanchez, Secretary: Ms P Rodriguez.
Ethiopia—Ethiopia Lawn Tennis Federation, P.O. Box 3241, Addis Ababa. Cable: Addis Ababa (c/o Sports Commission), Tel: (01) 156205, Telex: 21377 NESCO ET. President: Mr H Balcha. Secretary: Mr H Afework.
Fiji—Fiji Lawn Tennis Association, P.O. Box 313 B.A., Fiji Islands. Tel: 60870. President: Mr B K Reddy, Secretary: Mr P R Singh.
Ghana—Ghana Tennis Association, National Sports Council, P.O. Box 1272, Accra. Cable: Ghansport, Tel: 63924 or 63927. President: Mr E Annan, Secretary: Mr A K Ocloo.
Guatemala—Federacion Nacionale de Tenis, Palacio de Los Deportes Zona 4, Guatemala. Tel: (2) 31026. President: Dr J Mansilla, Secretary: Mr R Rivera.
Guinee Conakry—Federation Guineene de Tennis, Ministere de la Jeunesse et Sports, B.P. 262, Guinee Conakry. Tel: 44 19 62, Telex: 2102 MJ GUI. President: Mr M L Damba.
Guyana—Guyana Lawn Tennis Association, P.O. Box 10205, Georgetown. Cable: Lawntenna, Georgetown, Tel: 02-71195 (President), 02-67826 (Secretary), Telex: 2281 CALA GY. President: Mr T B E Richmond, Secretary: Dr G Muller.
Haiti—Federation Haitienne de Tennis, c/o Mr J Etienne, Box 1728, 1377 Rue Carlstroem, Port-au-Prince. Cable: Joetienne, Port-au-Prince, Tel: 5-0703 or 5-1377. President: Mr J Etienne, Secretary: Mr O Nadal.
Jordan—Jordan Tennis Federation, P.O. Box 35121, Amman. Cable: Tenfed, Amman, Tel: 962-6 662707, Telex: 22500 HILAL JO. Chairman: Dr M Al-Fawwaz, Secretary: Mr I Jarallah.
Korea, People's Democratic Republic—Tennis Association of the Democratic People's Republic of Korea, Munsin-Dong, Dongdaewon Dist., Pyongyang. Cable: Tennis, DPR Korea, Tel: 6-2386 or 6-3998, Telex: 5-472. President: Mr P Jung Yang, Secretary: Mr Li Won-Gun.
Malawi—Lawn Tennis Association of Malawi, P.O. Box 1417, Blantyre. Secretary: Mrs S Windsor.
Mali—Federation Malienne de Tennis, Ministere des Affairs Etrangeres, Koulouba, Mali. Tel: 225489/225633/225092. President: Mr A Nafo, Secretary: Mr A Traore.
Mauritius—Mauritius Lawn Tennis Association, Rose-Hill Club, Bruce Street, Rose-Hill. Cable: Tennis, Mauritius, Tel: 4-1666. President: Mr C Cure, Secretary: Mlle C de Maroussem.
MontserratMontserrat Tennis Association, P.O. Box 386, Plymouth, Montserrat, British West Indies. Tel: 4915363/5368. President: Mr L Arnold, Secretary: Miss E Fenton.
Mozambique—Federacao Mocambicana de Tenis, Caixa Postal 4351, Maputo. Tel: 27027, Telex: 6-597 SATCC MO. President: Mr P M Figueiredo, Secretary: Mr J Nhabangue.
Nepal—All Nepal Tennis Association, P.O. Box 2090, Dasarath Stadium, Kathmandu. Tel: 211732 or 215712, Telex: 2390 NSCNP. President: Mr S Singh, Secretary: Mr P K Shrestha.
Netherlands Antilles—Netherlands Antilles Tennis Association, P.O. Box 3360, Emmastad, Curacao. Tel: 44192. President: Mr Ing M R Paula, Secretary: Mr H Thomas.
Panama, Republic of—Comision Nacionale de Tennis de Panama, Apartado 6-6717, El Dorado, Panama. Tel: 600019 or 262785/60, Telex: 2534 INDE PG. President: Mr H Spalding, Secretary: Mr E Palomo.
Puerto Rico—Puerto Rico Tennis Association, Box 40456 — Minillas Station, Santurce, Puerto Rico 00940. Tel: 721-9112 or 721-1665, Telex: 3454212 (mark: Att. Mrs de la Rosa. President: Mr J Baldrich, Secretary: Mrs L de la Rosa.

Qatar—Qatar Tennis Federation, P.O. Box 4959, Doha, Qatar. Tel: 831788/831786, Telex: 4059 QTSF DH. President: H E Issa G Al Kawari, Secretary: Mr K Al Dafa.
San Marino—Federazione Sammarinese Tennis, Republic of San Marino 47031. Cable: Piazza M Tini n. 15-47031 DOGANA, Tel: 905303, Telex: 550885 SP RSMI. President: Mr A S Belluzzi, Secretary: Mr E Belluzzi.
Tanzania—Tanzania Lawn Tennis Association, P.O. Box 965, Dar es Salaam. Tel: (51) 23351, Telex: 41009. President: Mr A Fernandes, Secretary: Mr R Rugimbana.
Togo—Federation Togolaise de Lawn Tennis, B.P. 4632, Lome, Togo. Tel: 21456, Telex: 5015 CNOT TO. president: Mr A Kokou, Secretary: Mr G Tohonou.
United Arab Emirates—United Arab Emirates Tennis Association, P.O. Box 87, Dubai. Tel: (04) 434 989, Telex: 46347 FAGEN EM. President: Lt Col S Khalfan, Secretary: Mr N Madani.
Yemen—P.D.R. Yemen Tennis & Table Tennis Federation, P.O. Box 157, Aden. Cable: Madhrab, Aden, Tel: 53244 or 53639. President: Mr A Haithami Salem, Secretary: Mr Ibrahim Mohammed.
Zambia—Zambia Lawn Tennis Association, P.O. Box 36013, Lusaka. Tel: (01) 218212, Telex: ZA 45820. Chairman: Mr M S Mulenga, Acting Hon Secretary: Miss H Bright.

AFFILIATED REGIONAL ASSOCIATIONS

Confederacion Sudamericana de Tenis (COSAT), Complejo Nacional de Tenis, Calle A, Urb Santa Rosa de Lima, Caracas 1060, Venezuela. Cable: Fevetenis, Tel: (2) 979 0697, Telex: 28465 FVT VC. President: Mr A Plaza, Executive Secretary: Mr R Gomez.
European Tennis Association, Dornacherstrasse 250, CH-4018 Basle. Tel: (61) 50 76 75, Telex: 64571 EURTA CH. President: Dr H Grimm, Secretary: Dr M Ferralli.

THE SOCIETY OF LAWN TENNIS REFEREES

(Affiliated to The Lawn Tennis Association)

HONORARY MEMBERS

B J Austin(Pre 1979)—Flat 2, Carr Croft, Parish Ghyll Road, Ilkley LS29 9NE (0943 607448).
Mrs J Rowsell (Pre 1979)—Red-A—Ven, 388 Topsham Road, Countess Weir, Exeter 2EX 6HE (039 287 3184).

FULL MEMBERS

INTERNATIONAL. I. *GRAND PRIX

***Mrs J Angus** (1978)—The Manor, Water Stratford, Buckingham MK18 5DR (02804 7137).
***Mrs G H Clark** (1982)—8 Kings Stile, Middleton Cheney, Banbury, Oxon (0295 710645).
***Mrs J I Fyfe** (1983)—33 Princes Avenue, London W3 8LX (01-992 6508).
***Dr S H Gangji** (1983)—14 Wessex Gardens, London NW11 9RT (01 455 3646).
***T D Gathercole** (1977)—62 Westville Road, Thames Ditton, Surrey (01-398 0216).
Capt M B Gibson (Pre 1979)—Olde Denne, Warnham, Horsham, Sussex (0403 65589).
***C H Hess** (1977)—Flat A, 16 Crediton Hill, Hampstead, London NW6 1HP (01-794 6613).
***F W Hoyles** (Pre 1979)—Manor Hill Farm, Sutton St James, Spalding, Lincs PE12 0JB (094 585 225).
Mrs A S Jones (1985)—85 Westfield Road, Edgbaston, Birmingham B15 3JF (021 454 4964).
***M J Lugg** (1984)—17 Stanford Close, Laceby, Grimsby, South Humberside (0472 73678).
***A R Mills** (1976)—5 Daneswood Close, Weybridge, Surrey (0932 48403).
***J Moore** (Pre 1979)—Flat 6, Keswick Heights, Keswick Road, Putney SW15 (01-870 0388).
Mrs B M Seal (Pre 1979)—4 Glendene, 115 Victoria Drive, Wimbledon SW19 6PR (01-789 3339).
***Mrs J M Sexton** (1981)—Parkview, 24 Fife Road, East Sheen, London SW14 7EL (01 876 3695).
***J M Treleven** (1979)—LTA Offices, Barons Court, West Kensington, London W14 9EG (01 385 2366).

INTERNATIONAL MATCH. I (M).

E B Auger (Pre 1979)—'Pilkem,' 49 Lawrie Park Avenue, London SE26 6HA (01-778 6363).

NATIONAL. N. *GRAND PRIX

M E Absalom (1981)—51 Finchdean Road, Rowlands Castle, Hants PO9 6DA (070 541 2442).
J E Bone (Pre 1979)—Wyngarth, 9 Andover Road North, Winchester, Hampshire SO22 6NN (0962 881185).
J R Coates (Pre 1979)—164 Church Lane, Cantley, Doncaster DN4 6RY (0302 538342).
M R Cox (1981)—Mahe Woods, 225 Longdale Lane, Ravenshead, Nottingham NG15 9AH (0623 796860).
R Cushing (1981)—31 Balcombe Court, West Parade, Worthing, West Sussex BN13 3BG (0903 206557).
L F Dart (1983—71 Findon Road, Worthing BN14 0BB (0903 60208).
Mrs J C Davidson (1983)—2 Ettrick Grove, Edinburgh, Scotland EH10 5AW (031 229 1678).
Mrs B Davis (1979)—Park House, 8 Totteridge Common, London N20 (01-446 4620).
D G Fletcher (1983)—99 Addison Road, Caterham, Surrey (0883 48918).
Wing Cmdr G H Grime (1982)—Dental Centre, RAF Swinderby, Lincoln, Lincs LN6 9QE (052 286 421 ext 331).
A G Grosset (1979)—3a Abbotsford Crescent, Edinburgh, Scotland EH10 5DY (031 447 6460).
I Hine (1978)—10 Crescent Road, Felixstowe, Suffolk IP11 7PD (0394 283686).
D G Lock (Pre 1979)—Whitehouse Farm, The Broyle, Chichester, Sussex PO19 3PH (0243 783689).
R J Lumb (1983)—8 Hughes Close, Barton Park, Marlborough, Wilts SN8 1TN (0672 53746).
M C Martin (Pre 1979)—The Paddocks, Hungarton, Leicester LE7 9JR (053 750 230).
***N A McCallen** (1980)—144 Cemetery Road, Southport PR8 5EG (0704 38610).
P J Mornard (1976)—Slip Cottage, School Hill, Nacton, Ipswich, Suffolk IP10 0EH (047 388 640).
Miss J E Packwood (1984)—18c Milton Road, Bournemouth BH8 8LP (0202 23228).
I E Shaw (1983)—10 Rydal Avenue, Poulton le Fylde, Lancs FY6 7DJ (0253 891246).
Lt Col P B Webster (1982)—52 Castle Road, Salisbury, Wilts SP1 3RL (0793 782551) ext 2588).
I Wood (1979)—21 The Poplars, Gosforth, Newcastle-upon-Tyne NE3 4AE (091 285 5877).

REGIONAL R

T A Adamson (1985)—4 Eastmoor Court, Harpenden, Herts (05827 2189).
P H Asquith (1984)—White House Farm, Kirby Misperton, Malton YO17 0XR (065 386 218).
E E Bann (1981)—Camdean, 29 Briton Hill Road, Sanderstead, Surrey CR2 0JJ (01-657 1832).
T W Baron (1982)—8 Byron Street, Blackpool, Lancs FY4 1DE (0253 405264).
C P Bateman (1981)—100 Fotheringham Road, Bush Hill Park, Enfield, Middx EN1 1QE (01 366 6051).
M H Bateman (1983)—19 Luctons Avenue, Buckhurst Hill, Essex IG9 5SG ((01-504 5520).
G G Birchall (1985)—17 Arden Vale Road, Knowle, Solihull, W Midlands B93 9NS (056 45 79389).

G S Blake (Pre 1979)—33 Crabbe Street, Ipswich, Suffolk IP4 5HR (0473 712288 ext 107 office hours).
R L Blundell (1984)—2 Bishops Avenue, Northwood, Middlesex (01-868 4737 office hours).
D J Bone (1983)—9 Knights Templar Way, High Wycombe, Bucks HP11 1PX (0494 442547).
G R Bone (1983)—Harlu, 109 Church Road, Hanwell, London W7 3BJ (01-579 2169).
M J Boyle (1984)—101 Skipton Road, Ilkley, W Yorkshire LS29 9BJ (0943 608028).
Miss P A Brailsford (1981)—70 Virginia Road, Thornton Heath, Surrey (01-764 4883).
D P Brett (1979)—Clare Hill, Lea End Lane, Forhill, Worcs B38 9EE (0564 822482).
Mrs O Brown (1983)—10 Cavendish Road, Bristol BS9 4DZ (0272 623473).
W F G Brunsdon (1982)—65 Heol-Y-Gors, Whitchurch, Cardiff, South Glam CF4 1HG (0222 68241).
L A Bumford (1984)—15 High Moss, Ormskirk, Lancs L39 4TP (0695 73032).
A N Bunn (1982)—Meadfoot, Eggington Road, Wollaston, Stourbridge, West Midlands DY8 4QJ (03843 5930).
Mrs E M Chamberlain (1979)—Fox House, 7 The Knoll, Grendon, Northants (0933 664969).
R C Champion (1984)—29 The Grove, Burnham on Sea, Somerset TA8 2PA (0278 784955).
J A Cheetham (1982)—15 Park Crescent, Chatham, Kent ME4 6NR (0634 46369).
Mrs S A Clunie (1981)—Greystone Barn, Marldon, Paignton, South Devon TQ3 1SJ (0803 558446).
R C J Coburn (1982)—183 St Leonards Road, Horsham, Sussex RH13 6BD (0403 60854).
J R Cochrane, CBE (Pre 1979)—Filia Regis, Cheltenham Place, Park Gate, South Wirral L64 6QT (051 336 7503).
Mrs N Collier (1981)—24 Barley Way, Putnoe, Bedford MK41 8HY (0234 66140).
G T Collinson (1983)—14 Woodlands Road, Shotley Bridge, Consett, Co Durham DH8 0DE (0207 50 3247).
Mrs N G Constant (1981)—"Staithe House", 17 Pilgrims Way, Reigate, Surrey RH2 9LE (07372 45547).
M J Cooper (1985)—2 Wood Lane, Timperley, Altrincham, Cheshire WA15 7QB (061 980 6490).
R Cope-Lewis (1980)—27 Newburgh Place, Highworth, Swindon, Wilts SN6 7DH.
L W S Couldridge (1981)—2 Chapel Close, Corfe Mullen, Wimborne, Dorset BH21 3SH (0202 693652).
D Coyte (1982)—7 Blatchford Court, Hersham Road, Walton on Thames, Surrey (09322 28724).
N D Crown (1983)—21 Britten Close, Colchester Essex CO4 3UN (0206 867267).
W E Curtis (1971)—22 Longfield Road, Capel St Mary, Ipswich, Suffolk IP9 2XG (0473 311526).
J N Davey (1981)—12 Woodthorpe Avenue, Woodthorpe, Nottingham NG5 4FD (0602 262352).
P J Deakin (1981)—16 Empsons Hill, Dawlish, Devon EX7 9BE (0626 863942).
K L Dewick (1984)—55 Chessfield Park, Little Chalfont, Amersham, Bucks (02404 3818).
Mrs F A Edwards (1981)—4 Northfields Close, Lansdown, Bath, Avon BA1 5TE (0225 311926).
Dr J A Elliott (1985)—Beacon Hurst, Church Road, Crowborough, Sussex TN6 1BN (089 26 3526).
A G P Ellis (1981)—39 Newlands Crescent, Northowran, Halifax, West Yorkshire HX3 7HU (0422 202111).
G R S Evans (1984)—18 Oakwood Avenue, Woodlands Park, North Gosforth, Newcastle-upon-Tyne NE13 6QE (0632 363007).
C S Falconer (1979)—1 Exton Close, Lords Wood, Chatham, Kent ME5 8QN (0634 61331).
A G Farrant (1983)—15 Colne Road, Winchmore Hill, London N21 2JB (01-360 4646).
B C Fitch (1984)—1 Clock House, Glebe Court, Bishops Stortford, Herts CM23 5AD (0279 54013).
Mrs S G Fitch (1981)—1 Clock House, Glebe Court, Bishops Stortford, Herts CM23 5AD (0279 54013).
Mrs M E Ford (1985)—71 Valley Road, Rickmansworth, Herts WD3 4BL (0923 776880).
N Foreman (1982)—142 The Glade, Old Coulsdon, Surrey (07375 52517).
Capt R D Franks RN (Retd) (1984)—Swan House, Dartmouth, Devon TQ6 9RL (080 43 2511).
Mrs S Fulcher (1983)—Thurleston Lodge, Henley Road, Ipswich, Suffolk IP1 6TD (0473 51928).
A Fyfe (1984)—33 Princes Avenue, London W3 8LX (01-992 6508).
M Garden (1979)—3 Rubislaw Park Road, Aberdeen, Scotland AB1 8BX (0224) 322109).
Mrs J Gates (1982)—Grove End, Elm Grove, Berkhamsted, Herts HP4 1AE (04427 5589).
H George CMG OBE MA (1981)—c/o Churchill College, Cambridge CB3 0DS (0223 61200 ext 312).
R R H Gill (1983)—3 Ashburton Road, West Kirby, Wirral L48 4ER (051 625 7895).
J M W Grainger (1983)—55 Linden Way, Darras Hill, Ponteland, Newcastle-upon-Tyne (0632 844290).
P J Greatorex (1984)—20 Osberton Place, Sheffield S11 8XL (0742 680905).
J W D Greatrex (1980)—Crantock, 81 Cardiff Road, Dinas Powis, South Glamorgan CF6 4JT (0222 512320).
R C Green (1981)—63 Watford Road, King's Langley, Herts WD4 8DY (09277 64573).
C H Hall (1985)—10 Cavendish Drive, Waterlooville, Hants PO7 7PJ.
M E D Hare (1983)—12 Prenton Farm Road, Prenton, Birkenhead, Wirral (051 608 2247).
J Harrop (1981)—27 Cumnor Hill, Oxford OX2 9EY (0865 863470).
W J Hartland (1981)—20 Southcourt Road, Penylan, Cardiff CF2 7DA (0222 493205).
Mrs K N Harvey (1983)—Lickey House, 45 Twatling Road, Barnt Green, nr Birmingham (021 445 4840).
N K Haugh (1982)—4 Burdett Avenue, West Wimbledon, London SW20 0ST (01-946 8572).
M F Hayes (1981)—37 Ware Road, Hertford, Herts SG13 7EB (0992 551393).
B Hempsall (1983)—11 Coterel Crescent, Cantley, Doncaster, S Yorks DN4 6JY (0302 531912).

J M Henk (1984)—76 The Crescent, Belmont, Surrey SM2 7BS (01-643 2592).
D Hill (1977)—42 Oakwood Drive, Heaton, Bolton BL1 5EH (0204 42672).
R R Hillier (1984)—5 Northumberland Road, Redland, Bristol BS6 7AU (0272 40857).
Mrs G J Holden (1983)—58a Boroughbridge Road, Northallerton, North Yorkshire DL7 8BN (0609 70559).
C J Holt (1985)—4 Bewick Close, Snettisham, Kings Lynn, Norfolk PE31 7PJ (0485 41534).
Mrs G Hood (1980)—21 Eddington Close, Loose, Maidstone, Kent ME15 9XG (0622 41619).
D C Howie (Pre 1979)—89 Romway Road, Evington, Leicester LE5 5SE (0533 737702).
T R G Huggett (1983)—97 Lambs Lane, Rainham, Essex (040 27 55274).
Mrs M G Hughes (1984)—41 Woodlea Drive, Solihull, West Midlands B91 1PQ (021 705 5458).
W D Hughes (1976)—19 Western Gardens, Ealing, London W5 (01-992 4747).
J Hunting, (1983)—21 Roundhill Road, Leicester LE5 5RJ (0533 737260).
D Johnson (1984)—Greenways, 32 Shawfield Park, Bromley, Kent BR1 2NG (01 460 0978).
Mrs E R Jones (1982)—Rockcliffe, 7 Langland Bay Road, Swansea, West Glam (0792 68113).
L W Kelly (1985)—School House, Thenford, Banbury, Oxon OX17 2BX (0295 710445).
D Kilby (1985)—7 Grangefield Road, Shrewsbury, Shropshire (0743 66994).
T F Kinloch (1984)—27a Moray Place, Glasgow G41 2BL (041 423 3348).
K G Lea (1983)—6 Prenton Lane, Prenton, Birkenhead, Merseyside L42 9NX (051 608 3095).
P Lee (1984)—77 Pembroke Crescent, Hove, Sussex BN3 5DF (0273 777658).
D A Lewis (1984)—39 Garrison Lane, Felixstowe, Suffolk (0394 278059).
J Lightbody (1982)—42 Fairy Grove, Killay, Swansea, South Wales SA2 7BY (0792 202580).
A Little (1982)—Rockford, 41 The Oaks, Horsham Road, Beare Green, Dorking, Surrey (0306 711294).
G M Lloyd (Cmdr RN Retd) (1982)—Greystones, 2 Lan Park Road, Pontypridd, Mid Glamorgan CF37 2DH (0443 402904).
A J Lydiate (1984)—8 Henley Close, Neston, South Wirral L64 0SQ (051 336 4279).
T E Mabbitt (1982)—8 The Paddock, Middleton St George, Co Durham (0325 332008).
D W MacDermid (1985)—16 Stafford Street, Aberdeen AB2 3UX (0221 647179).
J R T Mayo (1983)—254 Sedlescombe Road North, St Leonards on Sea, East Sussex TN37 7JL (0424 752369).
J M McBrien (1980)—7 Wavertree Nook Road, Liverpool L15 7LE (051 722 0120).
I McDiarmid (1985)—'Heatherdale,' 12 Greenbank Crescent, Southampton SO1 7FQ (0703 766302).
J R McDonald (Pre 1979)—34 Manor Road, Cheam, Sutton, Surrey SM2 7AG (01-642 2929).
K J McDonald (1984)—67 Illingworth, St Leonards Hill, Windsor, Berks SL4 4UP (07535 69896).
B C Mead (1984)—Wickham Barn, 12 College Lane, Hurstpierpoint, Sussex BN6 9AG (0273 833161).
C Morris (1984)—27 Thackeray Drive, Vicars Cross, Chester, Cheshire CH3 5LP (0244 42546).
Mrs A Mutimer (1984)—Burewood House, Beech Road, Wroxham, Norfolk NR12 8TP (060 53 3382).
R W Needham (1985)—8 Ebnal Road, Shrewsbury SY2 6PW (0743 247555).
Mrs J D Newby (1983)—Verney Farm Cottage, Kimblewick, nr Aylesbury, Bucks HP17 8SX (029 661 2138).
Mrs A C Noakes (1984)—27a Bridge Street, Pinner, Middlesex (01-868 4737).
Mrs V F Nuttall (1982)—6 Ferry Road, Felixstowe, Suffolk IP11 9LY (039 42 4997).
T J Oakes (1984)—37 Seaforth Lodge, Barnes High Street, London SW13 (01-878 6174).
G J Oladipo (1985)—29 George Lansbury House, Progress Way, Wood Green, London N22 5PD.
J R Palmer (1985)—Forest Green, 22 Springfield Road, Parkstone, Dorset BH14 0LQ (0202 741550).
Mrs S J Pape (1982)—Ravensden Farm, Bedford Road, Rushden, Northants NN10 0SQ (093 34 56221).
Dr D H Paul (1985)—44 Parkfield Road, Cheadle Hulme, Cheshire SK8 6EX (061 485 1996).
Mrs M O Pescod (1984)—61 Brook Gardens, Emsworth, Hants PO10 7JY (024 34 71348).
S H Phillips (1985)—10 Witham Gardens, West Horndon, Brentwood, Essex CM13 3NH (0277 811640).
P Piggott (1985)—1 Thornton Way, Cambridge CB3 0NL (0223 276028).
G R D Porteous (1981)—'Kinross', 8 Church Meadow Lane, Lower Heswall, Wirral, Merseyside (051 342 1713).
A Prescott (1984)—10 Rosemary Avenue, Stockton Heath, Warrington, Cheshire WA4 2XA (0925 64069).
D W Purchon (1984)—64 Broomfield, Adel, Leeds LS16 7AD (0532 676054).
J R Ramsbottom (1983)—Woodlands, 26 Falcon Road, Bingley, W Yorkshire (0274 565218).
A Rattenbury (1984)—310a Neasdon Lane, Neasdon NW10.
K S Reynolds (1983)—8 Ewart Lane, Alfreton, Derbyshire DE5 7AU (0773 835916).
Miss S Rich (1982)—CULTC Fenner's, Gresham Road, Cambridge CB1 2EP (0223 357185).
F J Richardson (1981)—Barclays Bank, 94 Regent Street, Cambridge CB2 1DA (0223 311236).
D J Roberts (1983)—Evergreen Cottage, 1 Brockton, Much Wenlock, Shropshire TF13 6JR (074 636 675).
C M Robertson (1985)—49 Gordon Road, Edinburgh EH12 6LX (031 334 1901).
Mrs J A Robinson (1984)—Oldborough Barn, Loxley, nr Warwick, Warwickshire (0789 841760).
J J F Robinson (1985)—Temple Bar, 100 Bury Street, Stowmarket, Suffolk IP14 1HE (0449 612513).
N M A Roderick (1984)—11 Johns Road, Fareham, Hants (0329 237108).

Miss S M Rothwell (1984)—16 Blakes Avenue, New Malden, Surrey (01-942 5652).
K Sainty (1985)—30 Boulsworth Avenue, Haworth Park, Hull, N Humberside HU6 7DZ (0482 802376).
M J Sanderson (1983)—Slough Tennis Centre, PO Box 501, Salthill Park, Bath Road, Slough, Berks SL1 3TR (0753 38983).
T Scarlett (1981)—16 Martindale, East Sheen, London SW14 7AL (01 876 9593).
K Sefton (1985)—The Barn, Bakers Lane, Thorpe Satchville, Leics LE14 2DE (0664 840589).
Mrs E C Simmons (1984)—6 Stephenson Drive, East Grinstead, West Sussex RH19 4AP (0342 23098).
A M Smithers (1982)—66 Hartfield Road, Chessington, Surrey KT9 2PW (01-397 7005).
G Stone (1979)—17 Newton Road, Knowle, Solihull, West Midlands (05645 3445).
K R G Suckling (Pre 1979)—16 St Mary's Avenue, Alverstoke, Gosport, Hants PO12 2NB (07017 83764).
P B Teare (1985)—15 Barton Heys Road, Formby, Merseyside L37 2EY (070 48 72220).
G B Telfer (1983)—21 Briardene Crescent, Kenton Park, Newcastle upon Tyne NE3 4RX (0632 856251).
Mrs J A Thirlwall (1984)—Briar Bank, Walpole Avenue, Chipstead, Surrey CR3 3PP (07375 52556).
Mrs E M Thomson (1983)—Amaranth, Little Shurdington, Cheltenham, Glos GL51 5TX (0242 862439).
J A Tillin (1985)—7 Wood End Road, Harpenden, Herts AL5 3EE (05827 62523).
R E Timms (1983)—The Gables, 4 Monkhams Lane, Woodford Green, Essex IG8 0NL (01-504 4046).
Miss K Turton (1984)—'Bluehayes,' 27 Layters Avenue, Chalfont St Peter, Gerrards Cross, Bucks (0753 885491).
E J Udal (1979)—30 Warblington Road, Emsworth, Hants PO10 7HQ (02434 5266).
P J Warren (1983)—20 Heol Lewis, Rhiwbina, Cardiff, South Glam CF4 6QA (0222 67457).
N H Webb (1984)—Norvic, Ballinger Road, South Heath, Great Missenden, Bucks HP16 9QH (024 06 2438).
A de G Webster (1981)—Red Cottage, 8 Northrepps Road, Cromer, Norfolk (0263 512483).
T H Whitaker (1981)—13 St George's Road, Harrogate, North Yorkshire HG2 9BP (0423 503 493).
A V Wilding (1984)—Hooton House, Benty Heath Lane, Hooton, South Wirral (051 327 4493).
P J Willetts (1982)—4 The Copse, Beaconsfield, Bucks (04946 77656).
Mrs R B R Wilson (1984)—Dendrons, The Chase, Oxshott, Surrey KT22 0HR (Oxshott 2227).
R V Wilson (1985)—12 Diomed Drive, Gt Barton, Bury St Edmunds, Suffolk IP31 2TD (0284 87 455).
N A Woodcock MBE (Cmdr RN Retd) (1980)—Windy Willows, Earl Soham, Woodbridge, Suffolk IP13 7RU (072 882 429).
Mrs A Wortley (1985)—The School of Education, 26 University Road, Leicester LE1 7RF. (0533 551122).
I D W Wright (1984)—50 Tredegar Road, Wilmington, Dartford, Kent DA2 7AZ (0322 72200).

ASSOCIATE MEMBERS A

J O Alexander (1981)—1 Priory Road, Wilmslow, Cheshire SK9 5PS (0625 525071).
C R Applewhaite (1983)—LTA Offices, Barons Court, West Kensington W14 9EG (01 385 2366).
B A Blincoe (1981)—Lime Kiln Barn, Norwich Road, Stoke Holy Cross, Norwich, Norfolk NR14 8AB (05086 3603).
A P H Chalmers (1976)—Ingleside, Hook Heath Road, Woking, Surrey GU22 0DP (04862 21453).
T S Lees (1983)—20 Canterbury Road, Folkestone, Kent (0303 44063).
Miss S Livingston (1985)—Beaconsfield School of Lawn Tennis, Beaconsfield, Bucks HP9 2BY (049 46 4744).
R D Loughton (1986)—The LTA, Barons Court, West Kensington, London W14 9EG (01 385 2366, ext 241).
D J Mercer (1984)—Flat D, 142/144 Cromwell Road, Kensington London SW7 4EF (01-373 7984).
M C W Sertin (1980)—48 Cleaveland Road, Surbiton, Surrey (01-390 5208).
J A Southworth (1982)—East Lodge, Adlington Road, Wilmslow Park, Cheshire SK9 2BH (0625 523763).

TRAINEE MEMBERS T

J H Anderson (1985)—32 South Way, Seaford, East Sussex BN25 4JG (0323 891475).
G W Armstrong (1984)—233 Eastbourne Road, Polegate, East Sussex BN26 5DP (03212 6625).
Mrs L A Beesley (1985)—3 Passmore, Tinkers Bridge, Milton Keynes MK6 3DY (0908 678833).
J D Bryson (1984)—63 St Peters Close, Newbury Park, Ilford, Essex IG2 7QN (01-599 4798).
M P Burridge (1985)—58 The Crescent, Henleaze, Bristol BS9 4RR (0272 624314).
P Darbyshire (1984)—82 Stockport Road, Timperley, Altrincham, Cheshire WA15 7SN (061 904 0822).
D H M Davies (1985)—12 South Avenue, New Milton, Hants BH25 6BY (0425 613313).
Miss M M DesBois (1983)—53 Stanley Wooster Way, Colchester, Essex CO4 3XX (0206 862475).
J J Glaister (1985)—3 Oakhaven, Crawley, West Sussex RH10 6BX (0293 513248).
Mrs J Godman (1985)—"Thurlestone", 4 Old Malt Way, Horsell, Woking, Surrey GU21 4QD (048 62 61840).
Miss K A Grant (1984)—21 Thetford Road, Mildenhall, Suffolk IP28 7HX (0638 713765).
P Herke (1985)—Kabara, Thicket Grove, Maidenhead SL6 4LW (0628 27773).
L Hoffman (1985)—33a Grove Avenue, Muswell Hill, London N10 2AS (01 883 5115).
Mrs S Holland (1984)—3 Walmer Drive, Bramhall, Stockport SK7 3AT (061 439 2051).
R D Jones (1983)—23 Tregonwell Road, Minehead, Somerset TA24 5DU (0643 3061).

Miss J G Kimber (1985)—New Bois, Little Kingshill, Great Missenden, Bucks HP16 0DP (024 06 3895).
S Lampert (1985)—32 Hanmer Road, Simpson, Milton Keynes MK6 3AY (0908 679988).
D Luddy (1984)—Flat 2, 13 Greville Place, London NW6 5JE (01 624 8476).
B E Mardling (984)—6 Bloomsbury Court, Bath Road, Cranford, Middx TW5 9SX (01 759 0898).
M C Massey (1984)—12 Woodchester Road, Westbury-on-Trym, Bristol BS10 5EX (0272 506418).
M J Nevett (1985)—13 Alderdale Drive, High Lane, Stockport SK6 8BX (06632 2800).
J R Newton (1985)—Thornfield, 79 Taunton Road, Ashton-under-Lyne, Lancs OL7 9EB (061 330 4191).
G A Paxton (1984)—12 Charfield Road, Kingswood, Wotton-under-Edge, Glos GL12 8RL (0453 842484).
M K Rickman (1983)—188 Cavendish Avenue, Ealing W13 0JW (01 998 3930).
Mrs I P Taylor (1984)—The Niblick, 196 Cooden Sea Road, Bexhill-on-Sea, East Sussex TN39 4TH (04243 2881).
B L Wolfenden (1985)—38 Station Road, Collingham, Newark, Notts NG23 7RA (0636 892463).
K Womersley (1985)—7 Rosedale Avenue, Hartsheap, Liversedge, West Yorkshire WF15 8AU (0274 872251).
A M Wynne (1984)—"Dolanog", St Albans Road, Tanyfron, Wrexham, Clwyd LL11 5SY (0978 756246).
A Zarrabi (1985)—37 Rutland Court, Newchurch Road, Hove, Sussex (0273 726021).

OVERSEAS MEMBERS O

***R Howe** (Pre 1979)—c/o USTA, 51 E 42nd Street, New York, NY 10017, USA.
E L Otto (1979)—Lorenzstrasse 56, D-1000, Berlin 45, German Federal Republic (010 49 30 773 63 14).
G Sacco (1985)—Corso Del Popolo, No 99-30172 Venezia, Italy (041 98.67.92).

LAWN TENNIS ASSOCIATION REGISTER OF PROFESSIONAL COACHES 1986

LONDON AND SOUTH EAST

(London, Middlesex, Kent, Surrey, Sussex)

†**J Ackers (1968),** Downie Mount, Church Road, Hartley, Dartford, Kent DA2 8DW (014747-2706).

***R D Ambrose (1969),** 16 Seymour Gardens, Surbiton, Surrey (01-399 3006).

†**Miss M A Ballheimer (1979),** 3 Britten Close, Park Court, Off Wellgarth Road, London NW11 7HF (01-455 2688).

*†**J E Barrett (1969),** The Oaks, Coombe Hill Glade, Beverley Lane, Kingston-upon-Thames, Surrey KT2 7EF (01-949 1440).

†**E C Baxter (1984),** 26 Leigham Hall, Streatham High Road, Streatham SW16 1DN (01-769 5327).

N B Bedford (1972), 6 Braid Avenue, East Acton W3 7TU (01-743 7489).

†**C D Best (1979),** 11 Michell Close, Horsham, Sussex RH12 1JT (0403-56718).

R G Birchley, 2 Parolles Road, London N19 3RE (01-272 7808).

*†**W P Blake (1938),** The Cumberland LTC, 25 Alvanley Gardens NW6 1JD (01-435 6022).

*†**G R Bone (1973),** Harlu, 109 Church Road, Hanwell, London W7 3BJ (01-579 2169) and LTA South East Region, Lamerton House, 23A High Street, Ealing W5 5DF (01-840 4060).

†**Mrs J E Bone (1973),** Harlu, 109 Church Road, Hanwell, London W7 3BJ (01-579 2169).

†**Miss J V A Boothman (1974),** 27 Shirlock Road, London NW3 2HR (01-485 0186).

†**J A Brazier (1976),** 191 London Road, Ewell, Surrey KT17 2BT (01-393 5940).

†**I Brown (1984),** 12 Belvedere Road, Biggin Hill, Kent TN16 3HY (0959-75651).

E R Bulmer (1977), Midtrees, 12 Fox Close, Pyrford, Surrey GU22 8LP (Byfleet 47095).

†**Ms Angela Buxton (1968),** 16 Winnington Road, London N2 0UB (01-455 6216).

†**Mrs M P Carr (1960),** Malmains Cottage, Pluckley, Ashford, Kent TN27 0SD (023384-400).

†**D C Chambers (1985),** 1 The Archers, Moyses Farm, Fletching, E Sussex TN22 3SA (0825 790891).

†**Lt Col R J Christie RE (1981),** 38 Tilford Road, Farnham, Surrey (0252-724046).

***R N Collins (1953),** 4 Clarence Street, Richmond, Surrey.

A. C. Cooke (1968), c/o 18 Bernard Avenue, Northfield, London N13.

Terry Cooper (1981), 89 Coulsdon Road, Caterham, Surrey CR3 5NS (0883 45763).

†**K F Cowell (1964),** 53 Tilehurst Road, Wandsworth, London SW18 3EU (01-874 8513).

Mrs P M Cox (1973), 11 Portland Avenue, New Malden, Surrey KT3 6AX (01-942 0180).

*†**Miss A G Curtis (1947),** 9 Armstrong House, Manor Fields, Putney, London SW15 3NF (01-788 0284).

†**Miss L Mottram (1983),** 3 Coombe Hill Glade, Beverley Lane, Kingston, Surrey KT2 7EF (01-949 0591).

***H A Deadman (1958),** 'Wheathill', 60 Livesay Crescent, Worthing, Sussex BN14 8AT (0903-36825).

*†**Mrs M E R Dewhurst,** 21 Elm Park Lane, London SW3 6DD (01-352 4005).

H Dhiraj (1976), 36 Springdale Road, Stoke Newington, London N16 9NX (01-249 0017).

†**J Dhiraj (1974),** 94 Twyford House, Elwood Street, London N5 (01-226 7597).

†**Mrs B Diggens (1969),** 34 Withdean Road, Brighton, Sussex BN1 5BL (0273-506072).

†**P Diggens (1969),** 34 Withdean Road, Brighton, Sussex BN1 5BL (0273-506072).

P J C Douglas (1958), 'Craigalan', 1 Camphill Road, West Byfleet, Surrey KT14 6EH (09323-49038).

†**G Ellis (1948),** 123 Mackie Avenue, Patcham, Brighton, Sussex BN1 8SG (0273-554990).

D L K Faraker (1960), 66 Stone Road, Broadstairs, Kent CT10 1EB (0843-601030).

†**A Fine (1975),** 12 Betseman Walk, Yateley, Camberley, Surrey (0276-76400).

†**Mrs V Forrester (1979),** c/o Chichester Lawn Tennis & Squash Club, Oaklands Park, Chichester, West Sussex PO19 4AR (0243-785664/787269).

H Gershfield (1979), 18 Woodland Close, Kingsbury, London NW9 (01-204 8930).

†**J A W Hancock (1950),** 'Oakdene', 38 Crescent Road, Sidcup, Kent DA15 7HW (01-300 7643).

†**E Harari (1979),** 108 Squires Lane, London N3 2AD (01-346 7947).

†**F L Harbour (1974),** 16 Aylesford Avenue, Beckenham, Kent BR3 3SD (01-650 0900).

E C Harradence, 13 Herne Bay Road, Tankerton, Kent CT5 2LH (0227-273572).

†**D W Haynes (1947),** 'Tudorcroft', 104 Stonegrove, Edgware, Middlesex HA8 7UB (01-958 8088).

P Henesey-Smith (1981), 22 Thorpebank Road, London W12 0PQ (01-740 7293) and Campden Hill LTC, 9 Aubrey Walk, Campden Hill, London W8 (01-740 7293).

D R G Horwood (1983), 31 Tealing Drive, West Ewell, Epsom, Surrey KT19 0JS (01-330 2908).

†**P Hutchins (1984),** 6, Coombe Gardens, Wimbledon, London SW20 (01-385 2366).

†**C Iles (1968),** 12 Ratton Drive, Eastbourne, Sussex (0323-505809).

†**D H U James (1984),** 2 Model Cottages, Occupation Road, Ealing, London W13.

†**Major P R Jarvis-Cazaly (1958),** Hadrian House, Hurst Road, East Preston, West Sussex BN16 3AP (09062-3040).

†**A L Jonathan (1968),** The Jays, 27 Aultone Way, Sutton, Surrey SM1 3LD (01-641 1601).

†**A L Jones (1971),** 22 Old Park Ridings, Winchmore Hill, London N21 (01-360 0680).

J Key (1984), 8 Boileau Road, Barnes, London SW13 9BL (01-748 9841).

E King (1954), 23 Rivermount, Walton-on-Thames, Surrey KT12 2PR (0932-227207).

R G Lambert (1955), 31 Ulleswater Road, Southgate, London N14 7BL (01-886 6721).

R W I Lawie (1959), 91 Rattle Road, Westham, Pevensey, East Sussex BN24 5DH (0323-761155).

†**Ms C A Leatham (1981),** Flat 3, 34 Victoria Road, Kensington, London W8 5RG.

B C Lee (1978), 118 St. Lawrence Avenue, Worthing, Sussex BN14 7JL (0903-201993).

†**Miss F V Lovell (1968),** 7 High Beech, Eversley Park Road, Winchmore Hill, London N21 1NS (01-360 8623).

†**R W Mabberley (1964),** 11 Kingsdown Park, Tankerton, Whitstable, Kent (0227-272846).

†**Capt H T M McCue (1977),** "Perran Brae", Ridgeway, Horsell, Woking, Surrey GU21 4QR (04862-73256).

†**Mrs T McFadden (1952),** The Bungalow, Filching Polegate, Sussex, BN26 5QA (0323-3027).

†**Mrs J F McHugo (1969),** Tuckaway, Warren Drive, Kingswood, Surrey KT20 6PY (0737-832009).

*†**C. W. McKerrow,** 6 Thornton Road, Wimbledon SW19 4NE (01-588 2800 bus, 01-946 6195 pri).

†**G D Master (1980),** 10 Winterdown Gardens, West End, Esher, Surrey KT10 8NB (0273-65640), and Foxhills Country Club, Ottershaw, Surrey KT16 0EL (093287-2137).

†**Mrs E E Mercer (1966),** 16 The Close, Wonersh, Guildford, Surrey GU5 0PA (0483-893470).

†**A J Mottram (1962),** 3 Coombe Hill Glade, Kingston-upon-Thames, Surrey KT2 7EF (01-949 0591).

†**Miss L Mottram (1983),** 3 Coombe Hill Circle, Beverley Lane, Kingston, Surrey, KT2 7EF (01-949 0591).

D B Nicholls (1948), The Lawn Tennis School, Purley, Surrey CR2 3HE (01-660 8244/5).

Mrs A Noakes (1977), 27a Bridge Street, Pinner, Middlesex (01-868 4737).

†**B P Pembro (1967),** 130 Spur Road, Orpington, Kent BR6 0QW (66-31381).

***Mrs D J Peyton (1954),** 260 Kings Drive, Eastbourne BN21 2XD (0323-501946).

†**J R Pocock (1979),** West Worthing Club, Titnore Road, Goring-By-Sea, Worthing, W Sussex (Worthing 47270).

†**D Potter (1954),** Venns Cottage, Two Mile Ash, Southwater, W Sussex RH13 7LA (0403 731175).

†**Miss B Poucher (1984),** 96 Garlands Road, Redhill, Surrey RH1 6NZ (0737-61738).

†**M V Prowse (1973),** The Hurlingham Club, Fulham, London SW6 (01-736 8411).

†**B Rees (1980),** 12 Wharfedale Close, Allestree, Derby (0332-552428).

Miss J Rich (1982), 44 Millman Road, Queen's Park, London NW6 (01-969 6028).

†**M K Rickman (1982),** 188 Cavendish Avenue, Ealing, London W13 0JW (01-998 3930).

***Mrs J Roddick (1968),** Coney Warren Cottage, Golf Club Road, St. George's Hill, Weybridge, Surrey KT13 0NJ (Weybridge 43696).

†**D Ross (1973),** 139 Commercial Road, Paddock Wood, Kent TN12 6DS (089-283-2076).

†**R A Savage (1980),** Pleasant Rise Sports Centre, Pleasant Rise, Alfriston, Sussex BN26 5TN (0323-870560).

S A Sinclair (1973), 8B Tibberton Square, London N1 8SF (01-226 8547).

†**A Tony Smith (1958),** The Sussex School of Lawn Tennis, Farthings Cottage, Farthings Hill, Horsham, Sussex RH12 1TS (0403-65055).

***P E Smith (1946),** Battle Boarding Kennels, Marley Lane, Battle, Sussex TN33 0RB (04246-3276).

†**Miss D Stewart (1985),** 180 Heene Road, Worthing, Sussex BN11 4NX (0903 210251).

F N Still (1946), 80A Ashmore Road, Paddington, London W9 (01-969 8639).

†**A A Stonebridge (1960),** The Stonebridge Academy, 3 St. Normans Way, East Ewell, Surrey KT17 1QW (01-393 3722).

†**M R Tigg (1985),** 12 Whitehill Road, Crowborough, E Sussex TN6 1JB (Crowborough 5721).

Mrs M Tyler-Wilson (1980), 53 Copse Avenue, West Wickham, Kent BR4 9NN (01-777 0728).

Capt H S Uberoi (1958), Gun Farm Sports Centre, Blackboys, East Sussex TN22 5JZ (082582-240).

*†**D T Willson (1950),** 33 Gatesden Road, Fetcham, Leatherhead, Surrey KT22 9QW (0372-374543).

†**Miss J Woolley (1978),** "Kismet", Pearson Road, Torton Hill, Arundel, West Sussex BN18 6HP (0903-882100).

EAST

(Bedfordshire, Cambridgeshire, Essex, Hertfordshire, Norfolk and Suffolk)

†**J Banham (1983),** 6 Highfield Avenue, Harpenden, Herts AL5 5VA (05827-67638).

†**Mrs A C Barden (1971),** 1 Granville Gardens, Hoddeston, Herts EN11 9QB.

*†**B A Blincoe (1965),** Lime Kiln Barn, Norwich Road, Stoke Holy Cross, Norwich, Norfolk NR14 8AB (05086-3603).

†**Mrs C Blincoe (1974),** Lime Kiln Barn, Norwich Road, Stoke Holy Cross, Norwich, Norfolk NR14 8AB (05086-3603).

†**Miss S A Cartwright (1979),** St. Agnells Farm Cottage, Lybury Lane, Redbourn, St. Albans, Herts AL3 7JL (058285-2680).

†**E C W Cross (1950),** Tennis Director, The Hemingford School of Tennis Coaching, 16 Stepping Stones, Hemingford Grey, Huntingdon, Cambs (0480-62508).

*†**C H Dunkley (1980),** 100 Station Road, Blenham, Beds (0767-40090) and LTA East Region, Clearview Tennis Centre, Warley Hall Lane, Little Warley, Nr Brentwood, Essex CM13 3EN (0277-811323).

***Mrs S G Fitch (1964),** 1 Clock House, Glebe Court, Bishops Stortford, Herts CM23 5AD (0279-54013).

†**G Fogg (1984),** 25 Onslow Gardens, Ongar, Essex CM5 9BG (0277-362308).

Mrs P Forster (1979), 1 Comet Way, St Ives, Cambridgeshire.

Mrs L G Fulcher (1974), Merrileaves, Chattisham, Ipswich, Suffolk.

*†**D F Georgeson (1958),** The Georgeson Tennis Academy, 44 The Hill, Wheathampstead, Herts AL4 8PS (058-283-3820).

†**Mrs R Illingworth (1972),** 10 Lake Rise, Romford, Essex RM1 4DY (0708-43738).

†**P D Jehan (1981),** 26 Gravel Hill, Stoke Holy Cross, Norwich, Norfolk NR14 8LH (05086-3166).

K R Langford (1978), 28A Airthrie Road, Goodmayes, Essex (01-597 6292).

†**Miss E Locke (1981),** 6 Ainslie Wood Gardens, Chingford, London E4 9BN (01-524 1532).

M G Matthews (1977), 239 Buckhurst Way, Buckhurst Hill, Essex IG9 6JG (01-504 4354).

†**Mrs E Mercer (1966),** 16 The Close, Wonersh, Guildford, GU5 OPA (0453-893470).

†**R Moss (1984),** 4 Friern Walk, Wickford, Essex SS12 0HZ (03744-3597).

†**F E Ong (1966),** "Midgard", 37 Queens Road, Hethersett, Norwich, Norfolk NR9 3DA (0603-810532).

†**Miss S E Rich (1979),** Richmond Villa, 59 Richmond Road, Cambridge CB4 3PS (0223-314976).

H W A Ruffell (1973), Clipt Bushes, Cockfield, Bury St. Edmunds, Suffolk (0284-828262).

*†**H E Skeet,** 4 Fayerfield, Potters Bar, Herts (Potters Bar 57427).

M D Smith (1979), 14 The Street, Ingworth, Nr Aylsham, Norfolk NR11 6AE (Aylsham 732611).

†**N B D Smith (1981),** 88 Harvey Lane, Norwich, Norfolk NR7 0AQ (0603-39788).

†**P G Smith (1963),** Tennis Coaching International, Woodlands, East of England School of Tennis & Squash, Milton Ernest, Bedford MK44 1RF (02302-2914).

†**D Somers (1980),** c/o Mrs G M Somers, 4 Ashwood Road, Potters Bar, Herts EN6 2PQ (0707-59395).

†**M T J Sullivan (1983),** 6 Fyfield Close, West Horndon, Brentwood, Essex CM13 3NQ (0277-810636).

†**T A Sullivan (1976),** 6 Fyfield Close, West Horndon, Brentwood, Essex CM13 3NQ (0277-810636).

Mrs J L Thomas (1985), 18 Central Drive, St Albans, Herts AL4 0UR (0727 31847).

P D Thomson (1962), 75 Hunter Avenue, Shenfield, Essex CM15 8PE (0277-214844).

†**J F Vincent (1967),** 101 Ridge Lane, Watford, Herts WD1 3SX (0923-28601).

*†**J M Watson (1962),** 28 Moorhurst Avenue, Goffs Oak, Cheshunt, Waltham Cross, Herts EN7 5LE (0707-872207).

*†**A V Woodbridge (1964),** 52 Edinburgh Road, Newmarket, Suffolk CB8 0QD (0638-663621).

SOUTH

(Berkshire, Buckinghamshire, Hampshire & Isle of Wight, Oxfordshire, Channel Islands)

†**Mrs J Angus (1968),** The Manor, Water Stratford, Buckingham MK18 5DR (02804-7137).

†**S M Bailey-Kennedy (1981),** "Cobwebs", 67 Stratton Road, Princes Risborough, Bucks HP17 9AX (08444-7921).

Mrs B Barker (1968), 91 Brook Lane, Warsash, Southampton, Hants SO3 6FE (04895-2562).

A W J Beale (1965), 95 Norreys Road, Cumnor, Oxford OX2 9PU (0865-862324).

†**J S Beirne (1960),** The Racquet Centre, 96 High Road, Swaything, Southampton SO2 2HZ (0703 582577).

*†**D J Bone (1969),** 9 Knights Templar Way, High Wycombe, Bucks HP11 1PX (0494-442547).

†**Mr. W A Boyle (1972),** c/o Cranwell Cottage, Pitt, Winchester, SO22 5QW (Winchester 52920).

†**L Bradford (1950),** Thicket Meadows North, Newland Drive, Maidenhead, Berks SL6 4LL (0628-29744).

†**Miss J Caplan (1985),** 2 Victena Road, Fairoak, Nr Eastleigh, Hants SO5 7FX (0703 692317).

M Connelly (1983), Caesarean LTC, Grands Vaux, Jersey, Channel Islands (0534 22011).

Mrs J M Crosby (1971), Meadowcroft, 164 High Street, Wootton Bridge, Isle of Wight PO33 4LZ (0983-883726).

†**A Davidson (1984),** 55 Highbury Park, Warminster, Wiltshire BA12 9JE (0985-213540).

†**D E Emery (1976),** 98, Downlands Way, South Winston, Winchester, SO21 3H8 (0962 884438).

†**T J Ferrier (1979),** 2 Links Cottages, Tichborne Down, Alresford, Hants SO24 9PS (096273-4041).

†**C Haworth (1985),** 2 Station Road, Cippenham, Slough, Berks SL1 6JJ (06286 61589).

†**R Henderson (1983),** 103 High Street, Old Portsmouth, Hampshire PO1 2HJ (0705-820060).

†**Miss P Hird (1968),** Greenways, Playstreet Lane, Ryde, Isle of Wight PO33 3LQ (0983-6431).

†**Miss S Holt (1965),** The Racquet Centre, 96 High Road, Swaythling, Southampton SO2 2HZ (0703 582577).

†**Miss S J Huntingdon (1973),** 10 York Close, Amersham, Bucks HP7 9HE (0204-4183).

†**Mrs R H Lauder (1975),** "Hazel Grove", Tile Barn, Wootton Hill, Nr Newbury, Berkshire RG15 9UU (0635-253414).

†**B Littleford (1978),** 56 Quarrendon Road, Amersham, Bucks HP7 9EH (02403-21277).

†**J M C McCardle (1982),** 13 Rampart Row, Haslar Road, Gosport, Hants PO12 1HT (0705-52683).

†**Mrs H B Melhuish (1964),** "Arlanza Cottage", Crocker End, Nettlebed, Oxon RG9 5BL (0491-641181).

D G Orchard (1979), 24 Glenfield Close, Aylesbury, Bucks HP21 7NE (0296-86242).

†**Mrs A E Pankhurst (1968),** 47 Carlton Road, Caversham Heights, Reading, Berks (0734-484049).

B Rees (1970), 12, Wharfe Dale Close, Allestree, Derby (0332 55248).

†**Miss E A Riddell (1959),** 10 Fox Close, Hailey, Witney, Oxon OX8 5XL (0993-5893).

D M Russell (1964), 33 Carlton Road, Caversham, Reading, Berkshire (0734-476756).

*†**M J Sanderson (1971),** L.T.A. South Region, Regional Office, Slough Tennis Centre, P.O. Box 501, Salt Hill Park, Bath Road, Slough SL1 3TP (0753-38983).

†A Scholfield (1984), 12 Frank Lunnon Close, Bourne End, Bucks (06285-30239).
†R S C Sharp (1960), 31 Matlock Road, Caversham, Reading, Berks RG4 8BP (0734-474526).
*†G D Thompson (1966), The Brae, Old Dashwood Hill, Studley Green, High Wycombe, Bucks HP14 3XD (024026-2195).
Miss J A Timmis (1981), 42 Compton Road, Church Crookham, Fleet, Hampshire (02514-21826).
*†S V Villiers (1948), 33 Canberra Road, Christchurch, Hampshire BH23 2HN (0202-484341).
Mrs J E Wilcock (1979), Upper Farm Court, Upton Barns, Upton, Nr Aylesbury, Bucks (0296-748043).
†P J Willetts (1982), The Copse, Beaconsfield, Bucks (Beaconsfield 77656) and The Gerrards Cross LTC, Bull Lane, Gerrards Cross, Bucks (Gerrards Cross 884402).

SOUTH WEST

(Avon, Somerset, Devon, Cornwall, Dorset, Wiltshire)

Mrs B E Beatty (1959), Heckley Lodge, Ashwick, Oakhill, Bath BA3 5BE (0749-840231).
†**P C J Bendall (1974)**, Dune House, Crosslands, Pilning, Bristol BS12 3LG (04545-3220).
†**Mrs B Blackburn (1984)**, Rose Cottage, Burtle Road, E Huntspill, Highbridge, Somerset (0278-785974).
†**T A C Blackburn**, Rose Cottage, Burtle Road, E Huntspill, Highbridge, Somerset (0278-785974).
†**G Bradley (1950)**, 17 Knights Road, Runnymede Park, Bearwood, Bournemouth, Dorset BH11 9ST (0202-577328).
†**Major F H S D Brancker (1976)**, Marks Barn Cottage, Crewkerne, Somerset (0460-72389).
A L Burrow (1967), The Lookout, Causeway, Sidford, Devon.
****Mrs K M Cheetham (1974)**, Stonefield, South Park, Barnstaple, North Devon EX32 9DX (0271-42384).
†**Roy Cope-Lewis (1980)**, Clint Sports, 27 Newburgh Place, Highworth, Swindon, Wilts SN6 7DN (0793-763379).
†**Mr A Davidson (1984)**, 55 Highbury Park, Warminster, Wilts BA12 9JE (0985-213540).
†**R A S Dunster (1978)**, 12 Arlington, Southill, Weymouth, Dorset DT4 9SG (0305-771808 or 0305-69008).
†**M Evans (1948)**, 48A Branksome Wood Road, Bournemouth, Dorset BH4 9LA (0202-760466).
†**W E J Gordon (1954)**, 18 Vicarage Close, Marlborough, Wiltshire SN8 1AY (0672-52020).
R E Griffin (1962), 68 Hales Road, Cheltenham, Glos (0242-523445 pri, 521556 bus).
†**Miss V M Hillage (1979)**, 85 Napier Road, Upper Weston, Bath BA1 4LW (0225-331896).
†**D Kemp (1966)**, Burleigh Cottage, 1 Burleigh Lane, Street, Somerset BA16 0SH (0458-43993).
†**Mrs M Linklater (1959)**, Wellhams Mill, Tintinhull, Yeovil, Somerset BA22 8PB (0935-822331).
†**Miss S M Lovick (1963)**, 1 Highcliffe Court, Copse Road, Clevedon, Avon BS21 7QP (0272-875416).
†**J W S Mahoney (1969)**, "Videre", 1 Two Trees, Wadebridge, Cornwall PL27 7PF (09274-26951).
G Mudge (1962), Flat B1, Shirley Towers, Vale Hill Road, Torquay, Devon (0803-214738).
†**S J Newman (1981)**, High Trees, Upper Wanborough, Swindon, Wilts SN4 0DD (079379-424).
†**D E Pottow (1976)**, 8 Gogs Orchard, Wedmore, Somerset BS28 4BP (0934-712186).
†**R G Smith (1950)**, 14 Newbridge Gardens, Bath, Avon BA1 3LT (0225-318920).
†**J M Tucker (1977)**, John Tucker Tennis Services, 40 Lower Bristol Road, Weston-Super-Mare, Avon BS23 2PS (0934-22985).
†**J M Webster (1966)**, Tennisville Holidays, Sunny Banks Farm, Fletchers Bridge, Bodmin, Cornwall PL30 4AN (0208-5048).
†**Mrs E Workman (1963)**, 30 Redland Court Road, Redland, Bristol BS6 7EQ (0272-43181).

NORTH MIDLANDS

(Derbyshire, Leicestershire, Lincolnshire, Northamptonshire, Nottinghamshire)

†**Miss S Bennett (1985)**, Derwent Lodge, Derwent Drive, Baslow, Nr Bakewell, Derbyshire (024 688 3293).
†**R Boulton (1984)**, 27 Flaxpiece Road, Clay Cross, Chesterfield, Derbyshire S45 9HB (0246-864408).
†**A Broomhead (1979)**, 1A Ewart Lane, Alfreton, Derbyshire DE5 7AU (0773-836223).
R T F Burgess (1950), 111 Victoria Road, Mablethorpe, Lincs LN12 2AL (0521-72342).
†**S P Cloke (1974)**, 91 Newhaven Road, Evington, Leicester LE5 6JH (0533-418273).
Miss P Cummins (1985), 64 Yew Tree Crescent, Melton Mowbray, Leicestershire.
Mrs H M Fleming (1968), Crow Trees, Makeney Road, Duffield, Derby DE6 4BD (0332-840200).
D E Kirk (1967), The Doug Kirk School of Tennis, 23 Nurses Lane, Skellingthorpe, Lincoln LN6 5TT (0522-682685).
†**Jim Lee (1959)**, "Taiping", 12 Arno Vale Road, Woodthorpe, Nottingham NG5 4JJ (0602-268847).
†**J D Logan (1984)**, 45 Yew Tree Lane, Gedling, Nottingham NG4 4AN (0602-612633 pri, 624040 bus).
†**M Marshall (1982)**, Flat 1, 422 Woodborough Road, Nottingham (0602 604121).
†**Mrs C M Mathias (1971)**, Burnside, Wilson, Melbourne, Derbyshire (03316-2994).
†**K S Reynolds (1978)**, LTA North Midlands Region, Watchorn Tennis Club, Ewart Lane, Alfreton, Derbyshire DE5 7AU (0773-836717).
†**P Whitehead (1982)**, 9 Chestnut Avenue, Killamarsh, Nr Sheffield, Derbyshire S31 8HN (0742-470239).
*†**H Wightman**, 16a Springfield Road, Hinckley, Leics LE10 1AN (0455-632812).

WEST MIDLANDS

(West Midlands, Warwickshire, Staffordshire, Gloucestershire, Shropshire, Hereford and Worcester)

†**Mrs A Applewhaite (1958)**, Lyneal Mill Cottage, Lyneal, Nr Ellesmore, Shropshire SY12 0LE (094-875-391).

E A Beards (1969), The Thatch, Oaken Lane, Codsall, Wolverhampton WV8 2BD (09074-2888).

†**Mrs P. M. Bocquet (1960),** 21 Glencairn Court, London Road, Cheltenham, Glos. GL50 2NB (0242-524701/30562).

†**Mrs V A Brewer (1973),** 82 Pereira Road, Harborne, Birmingham B17 9JN (021-427-2929).

Mrs E Brown (1978), 53 Newbridge Crescent, Wolverhampton WV6 0LH (0902-758890).

†**P M Brown (1969),** 53 Newbridge Crescent, Wolverhampton WV6 0LH (0902-758890).

Mr M A Cook (1983), 19 Hillands Drive, Leckhampton, Cheltenham, Glos (0242-514281).

†**J J L Crooke (1959),** Fidelio, Oakfield Road, Shrewsbury, Shropshire SY3 8AA (0743-62460).

A Deadman (1978), Stone Cottage, Little Shurdington, Glos GL51 5TX (0242-862023).

Mrs G M Evans (1967), Hillview, Monkham Thorn, Wotton-under-Edge, Glos GL12 8AD (0453-842438).

†**B Fairclough (1969),** 112 Park Hall Road, Walsall, W Midlands WS5 3LZ (021-357-4972).

†**Mrs A Farr (1979),** The Royal Wolverhampton School, Penn Road, Wolverhampton WV3 0EG (0902-334117).

†**C J Foulkes (1980),** Deuce, 43 Blackberry Lane, Stoke Heath, Coventry CV2 3JQ (0203-83498).

†**Mrs B Goolden (1976),** Ashfield, Weston Lane, Oswestry, Shropshire SY11 2BQ (0691-652586).

†**Miss N M Hall (1979),** Monks Orchard, Whitbourne, Worcester WR6 5RB (0886-21207).

†**Mrs B Hilltout (1949),** North Farm Cottages, Shipton Oliffe, Nr Cheltenham, Glos (0242-820522).

†**M J Jacobs (1965),** Centre Court, 10 Cedar Avenue, Malvern Link WR14 2SG (068-45-2501).

†**Major A E Millman,** 127 Old Bath Road, Cheltenham, Glos GL53 7DH (0242-522898).

†**Mrs D J Poynder (1949),** The Poynder School of Tennis, 1 South Grove, 69 Abbey Road, Malvern, Worcs WR14 3HL (06845-4435).

†**Miss J C L Poynder (1969),** The Poynder School of Tennis, 1 South Grove, 69 Abbey Road, Malvern, Worcs WR14 3HL (06845-4435).

*†**D Roberts (1980),** LTA West Midlands Region Telford Racquet & Fitness Centre, St Quentin Gate, Telford, Shropshire TF3 4JH (0952-506997).

Mr R Routledge, 41 Park Avenue, Solihull, W Midlands.

NORTH EAST AND YORKSHIRE

(Cleveland, Co Durham, Northumberland, Tyne & Wear, Yorkshire and Humberside)

†**J Biggins (1969),** 168 Dore Road, Dore Village, Sheffield S17 3HA (0742-365677).

†**Mrs N Burden (1969),** 26 High Street, Scalby, Nr Scarborough, Yorkshire YO13 0PT (0723-362710).

†**J N Clark (1974),** 3 Brookside Cottages, Ashbrooke Road, Sunderland (0783-210473).

†**K A Goldsmith (1972),** 8 Spring Lane, Carlton, Barnsley, South Yorkshire S71 3EX (0226-722213).

†**P S Green (1966),** 10 Glenmount, Cottingley, Bingley, Yorks BD16 1QZ (0274-568641).

J B Howarth (1980), 199 Oakbrook Road, Sheffield S11 7EB (0742-305407).

†**Mrs R M Huntingdon (1963),** Rowan House, Back Lane, Heslington, York YO1 5EE (0904-413344).

†**S Ickringill (1982),** c/o Ilkley LTC, Stourton Road, Ilkley, West Yorkshire LS29 9SG (0943-601609).

†**T Mabbitt (1973),** c/o Millcourt Club, off Windmill Road, Flitwick, Beds (0525-714836).

†**D G Munro (1984),** c/o Chapel Allerton LTC, Wessley Avenue, Stainbeck Lane, Leeds 7 (0532-682862).

*†**Mrs S Pashby (1965),** 10 Ambrey Close, Hunbanby, Filey, North Yorkshire YO14 0LZ (0723-891377).

†**I A Smith (1983),** LTA North East Region, Hull YP1, Chanterlands Avenue, Hull HU5 4EF (0482-448430).

†**J R E Tucker (1949),** 3 Castle Close, Thornton Dale, Pickering, N Yorkshire YO18 7TW (0751-74520).

T Wilder (1947), 12 Hill Rise Market Weighton, York YO4 3JX (0696-72383).

J Willis (1982), 99 Cusworth Lane, Scawsby, Doncaster, Yorkshire DN5 8JN (0302-784466).

†**Mrs E R Wilson (1970),** High Court, 12 Layton Mount, Rawdon, Nr Leeds LS19 6PQ (0532-503776).

NORTH WEST

(Lancashire, Cheshire, Cumbria, Merseyside, Greater Manchester and Isle of Man)

*†**C R Applewhaite (1966),** Netherleigh, 68 Hill Top Avenue, Cheadle Hulme, Greater Manchester SK8 7J (061-486 9403).

†**Ms A Bailey-Moult (1976),** 14 Summerfield Place, Holly Road South, Wilmslow, Cheshire SK9 1NE (0625-533240).

†**M J Ballardie (1985),** 6 Kenilworth Road, Blundellsands, Liverpool L23 3AD (051 924 1606).

†**F T Bamford (1946),** 2 Crosender Road, Liverpool L23 3BB (051-924 4906).

†**F R Collins (1971),** "Tanglewood", 28 Beachcroft Road, Meols, Wirral L47 6BE (051-632 5633).

*†**R F Cowell (1977),** LTA North West Region, Regional Tennis Centre, Dairy House Lane, Bramhall, Cheshire SK7 1RW (061-439 9096).

†**Miss G Crossley (1963),** Storrs Haven, Windermere, Cumbria LA23 3LE (09962-5754).

M G Farrington (1970), 150 Hoghton Lane, Higher Walton, Preston PR5 4EH (0772-36866).

†**T C Francis (1971),** Whisp'ring Trees, Saltcotes Road, Lytham St Annes, Lancs FY8 4LJ (0253-734170 pri, 0253-739769 bus).

†**Mrs M S Knowles (1975),** "Springfield Court", 123, Regent Road, Lostock, Bolton BL6 4DK (0204 42309).

R McGuire (1977), Paddock Chase, Moor Lane, Wilsmow, Cheshire SK9 6DN (0625-531435).

†**H Malabar (1975),** 18 Handley Court, Riversdale Road, Grassendale, Liverpool L19 3QS (051-427 5445).

†**C H Marsland (1949),** 5 Lynton Road, Southport, Merseyside PR8 3AN (0704-68734).

†**K Riley (1964),** 26 Winchester Avenue, Bowerham, Lancaster LA1 4HX (0524-66738).

A A Simcox (1985), 29 Pike House Road, Eccleston, St Helens, Merseyside WA10 5JZ (0744 26991).

†**Peter Hugh Taylor (1979),** 18 Birch-Lea Close, Bury, Lancs BL9 9RZ.

†**R H Thomson (1977),** 9 Alstead Avenue, Hale, Cheshire WA15 8BS (061-980 3869).

†**G H Turner (1966),** 23 St Philips Street, Wilton, Blackburn, Lancs BB2 1HT (0254-677088).

†**I P Twist (1969),** Morecambe Sports Centre, Ian Twist School of Lawn Tennis, 4 Morecambe Street, Morecambe, Lancs LA4 5HE (0524-413903).

*†**F J Watson (1978),** 30 Brackley Road, Heaton Chapel, Stockport SK4 2RE (061-442 6130).

SCOTLAND

*†**J Bromley-Williams (1979),** 10 Hill Park Road, Wormit, Newport-on-Tay, Fife DD6 8PR (0382-541525).

T B Bruce (1983), 33 West Relugas Road, Edinburgh EH9 2PN (031-667 1215).

†**W J Moss (1959),** 148 Capelrig Road, Newton Mearns, Glasgow (041-639 4963).

†**K F Selbie (1974),** 2 Crossdykes, Kirkintilloch, Glasgow (041-776 6929).

Mrs J M Taylor (1969), Burngrains, Kemback Bridge, Cupar, Fife KY15 5TP (0334-53464).

†**I G Woodcraft (1963),** 30 Holly Road, Broughty Ferry, Dundee DD5 2LZ (0382-76482).

WALES

***Miss M Barrow (1966),** Butler's Cottage, Llanarth, Nr Raglan, Gwent NP5 1AU (0873-85295).

†**Mrs D P Brabner (1965),** Gliffaes Hotel, Cickehowell, Powys NP8 1RH (0874-730371).

†**D Carroll (1966),** Bron-Haul, 23 Gronant Road, Prestatyn, Clwyd, North Wales LL19 9DT.

R A Fish (1959), Nant Noddfa, Nebo, Caernarvon, Gwynedd, North Wales LL54 6RY (0286-881291).

†**V Ganz (1975),** 45 Summerland Lane, Newton, Swansea, West Glamorgan SA3 4RX (0792-66251).

*†**Miss V M Glasspool (1936),** Heol-y-Ffynnon, Llanarth, Raglan, Gwent NP5 2AU (0873-85-262).

A J Goold (1973), Fairlight, Croescade Lane, Llantwit, Fardre, Pontypridd, Mid-Glamorgan (0443-204762).

†**S D Jones,** 216 The Hawthorns, Cyncoed, Cardiff (0222 731007).

J Lightbody (1985), 42 Fairy Grove, Killay, Swansea, West Glamorgan (0792 22580).

†**Mrs P Loosemore (1979),** 7 Merevale, Dinas Powis, South Glamorgan (0222-514278).

†**M C Rowe (1968),** 27 Alleryn Close, Newport, Gwent NP7 5ED (0633-63120).

R G Wallace, 26 Radnor Road, Canton, Cardiff, South Glamorgan (0495-322447).

*†**P J Warren (1966),** 20 Heol Lewes, Rhiwbina, Cardiff, South Wales CF4 6QA (0222-627457).

OVERSEAS

Mr R Algate, Squash Rackets Clubs, Brusselsestraat 74A, Maastricht (043 216387).

Mrs G Algate Williams (1964), Herik 8, 6381 RJ Ubach-over-Worms, Limburg, The Netherlands (010-31-45-325601).

†**J M Blake (1979),** Box 30364, Lilongwe 3, Malawi (730036).

†**J Buyse (1984),** Brugstraat 37, Heusden-Zolder 3550, Belgium (32-11-425155).

†**M Cole (1974),** Biermannstrasse 4, 2800 Bremen 1, West Germany (010-49-421-210445).

†**C Dodman (1984),** PO Box 4184, Nicosia, Cyprus (021-50623).

†**J F M Easter (1974),** Hotel la Toc, Castries, St Lucia, West Indies (St Lucia 23081).

†**Mrs S Evans (1961),** 5116 Le Mans Drive, Apt E11, Indianapolis, Indiana 46205, USA (317-251-2564).

†**J G H Goodwin (1980),** PO Box 42607, Nairobi, Kenya (61356).

Ms A W Greenwell (1959), Tin-A-Branch, Andrews Road, Hout Bay, Capetown 7800 RSA (010-2721-709125).

P Hemingway, 214 E Ocean Avenue, Lantana, Florida 33462, USA.

M G James (1973), Rotkreuzstr 14A, Lustenau, Austria, A6890 (010-43-5577-48922 pri, 2046 bus).

†**Ms H Lennon (1982),** 35 Boyne Court, Harolds Cross, Dublin 12, Ireland (01-961479).

M Neighbour (1974), Collegestraat 52 bus 9, 2300 Turnhout, Belgium (010-32-14-425062).

†**P O'Farrell (1978),** 29 Home Farm Park, Dublin 9, Ireland (Dublin 377639).

†**Mrs B O'Rafferty (1973),** 288 Limetree Avenue, Portmarnock, Co Dublin, Ireland (Dublin 461749).

†**Miss M Phillips (1979),** Trelawny Beach Hotel, PO Box 54, Falmouth, Jamaica, West Indies (954-2450-8).

†**G Ramsden (1958),** 3 Theodosiou St, Flat 25, Nicosia 135, Cyprus.

†**F Robinson (1979),** The Racket Shop, PO Box 243, Jeddah, Saudi Arabia (010-966-2-6692020).

C Rothwell (1979), BP 55, Cabourg, France 14390 (010-33-31-24-65-02).

†**Mrs A Ruane,** 41 Lawrence Grove, Clontarf, Dublin 3, Ireland.

†**I Russell (1975),** Les Reves D'Or, C0009, Avenue Sidi Brahim, Grasse, France 06130 (93-70-14-41).

†**R E Stead (1980),** Meulenborg, Gartnerhuset, Bogebakken 5, 3000 Helsingor, Denmark (010-45-2-21-04-06).

E G Topham (1978), Nudelshalbach 100, 5630 Remscheid 11, West Germany (010-49-02191-26679).

†**S Tuff (1978),** 3, Templeburn Road, Raffrey, Crosgar, Co. Down, N.I. BT30 9NF, Ireland (0396 830417).

†**P Waroquiers (1981),** 14 Rue du Dr Timsit, 78100 Saint Germain-en-Laye, France (010-333-451-76-92).

†**Mrs E A Willis (1959),** 7 Lloyd George Road, Gisborne, New Zealand (Gisborne 88848).

*Not available for private coaching.
†Member of the PTCA.

LAWN TENNIS ASSOCIATION LIST OF ASSISTANT COACHES 1986

LONDON AND SOUTH EAST

(London, Middlesex, Kent, Surrey, Sussex)

Mrs D E Abdollahyan (1976), 3 Ravens Close, Bromley, Kent BR2 0EL (01-464 3971).

†**Mrs M Ackers (1974),** "Downie Mount", Church Road, Hartley, Nr Dartford, Kent DA3 8DW (04747-2706).

†**S Adams (1985),** London Indoor Tennis Club, Alfred Road, London W2 (01-624 9128).

†**Ms n Addison (1985),** 142f Shakespeare Road, Hanwell, London W7 1LX (01-567 2631).

Mrs C G E Akers (1977), Griggs Gate, Drungewick Lane, Loxwood, Billingshurst, W Sussex (0403-700385).

†**P Ambrose (1985), 11a Kelvin Grove, Hook, Chessington, Surrey KT9 1DP (01-397 1852).**

†**R Appleson (1978),** 45 Cyprus Avenue, London N3 1SS (01-349 1957).

J Arris (1967), 22 West Hill, Sanderstead, Surrey CR2 0SA (01-657 3080).

†**Miss P Atkinson (1983),** "Gastons", Amberley, Nr Arundel, W Sussex BN18 9NT (079-881-806).

†**A Austin (1982),** 19 Bidborough Ridge, Bidborough, Tunbridge Wells, Kent TN4 0UT (0892-29436).

Miss P Bailey (1980), 8B Harley Gardens, London SW10 (01-373 7691).

Miss J Bard (1969), 122 Pears Road, Hounslow, Middlesex TW3 1SJ (01-572 3526).

M S Barnham (1980), Elms Garage Cottage, Iden, Rye, E Sussex TN31 7PY (07978-259).

†**N A Basing (1985),** 46 Kyoto Court, Nyewood Lane, Bognor Regis, West Sussex (0243-867592).

P Beal (1977), 27 Little Woodcote Lane, Purley, Surrey CR2 3PZ (01-668 7584).

Miss M Beaumont (1983), Caenwood House, Ashtead Woods Road, Ashtead, Surrey KT21 2EN (037-22-75511).

Mrs S Beaveridge (1981), Springfields, Chalk Road, Ifold, Loxwood, Billingshurst, W Sussex RG14 0UD (0403-752450).

***J Belcher (1970),** Brown Tiles, 14A Mayfield Road, Weybridge, Surrey (Weybridge 51767).

J Bercow (1982), 105 Dollis Road, Mill Hill, London NW7 1JX (01-349 2716).

W W Birk (1967), 2 Tower View, Shirley, Croydon, Surrey CR0 7PU (01-654 7652).

Mrs S Bitel, 16 Marlborough Hill, London NW8 (01-586 0426).

†**Mrs A Blake (1977),** 51 Devon Road, Cheam, Surrey SM2 7PE (01-643 3699).

†**A Blatiak (1984),** Conifers, Grove Way, Esher, Surrey KT10 8HH (01-398 1860)

†**D J Bloxham (1985),** 22 Rothesay Avenue, Richmond, Surrey (01-876 1473).

†**R L Blundell (1985),** 27a Bridge Street, Pinner, Middlesex (01-868 4737).

†**Ms J Blyth-Lewis (1985),** "High Trees", 2 Woodville Close, Darby Green, Yateley, Surrey (Yateley 876112).

R J Blyth-Lewis (1973), "Springcourt", 1B Henwood Green Road, Pembury, Tunbridge Wells, Kent TN2 4LB (089282-3813).

†**P N P Bond (1984),** Studio Penthouse A, 117 Haverstock Hill, London NW3 4RS (01-722 7692).

E F Borchert (1973), Richmond House, 17 Marlow Copse, Walderslade, Chatham, Kent ME5 9DR (0634-67201).

P E Braam (1971), 57 Woodhill Park, Pembury, Kent TN2 4NP (089292-3262).

P Bradfield (1982), 36 Catherine Street, Rochester, Kent ME1 2JH (0634-811768).

C Bradnam (1983), 53 Broadfields Avenue, Winchmore Hill, London N21 1AG (01-360 7124).

Miss P A Brailsford (1975), 70 Virginia Road, Thornton Heath, Surrey (01-764 4883).

***Miss D A Brickell (1965),** 8 Bath Court, Droitwich Close, London SE26 6TW.

G F Bristow (1969), 56 Manton Road, London SE2 0JB (01-311 4958).

G Brown (1981), 59 Brittany Road, Worthing, W Sussex BN14 7DZ (0903-203785).

†**Mrs P M E Brown (1970),** 15 Lucas Close, Yateley, Camberley, Surrey GU17 7JD (Yateley 872186).

C D Burns (1971), 154 Harland Avenue, Sidcup, Kent DA15 7PA (01-300 2281).

***Miss W Burrows (1972),** Chelsea School Brighton Polytechnic, Gaudick Road, Eastbourne, E Sussex BN20 7SP (0323-21400).

R Burston (1964), 74 Reigate Road, Brighton BN1 5AG (0273-502501).

†**Miss F Candy (1977),** 10 Hollington Park Road, St Leonards-on-Sea, Sussex (0424-426235).

***Mrs A Carey (1982),** 15 Archer Way, Swanley, Kent BR8 7XR (0322-69806).

D C Chambers (1982),

†**G Charles (1971),** 9 Gledwood Drive, Hayes, Middlesex (01-561 5268).

†***Ms L Charles (1985),** c/o Lawn Tennis Association, Barons Court, West Kensington, London W14 9EG (01-385 2366).

F C Chesterton (1969), 13 Chichester Road, Sandgate, Folkestone, Kent CT20 3BN (0303-38597).

†**D P J Cianfarani (1980),** 107 Herne Hill, London SE24 9LY (01-733 3850).

A S Cohen (1982), 67 Templars Avenue, London NW11 0NU (01-455 5522).

Mrs J Cope (1978), Cobbins, Blackheath, Guildford, Surrey GU4 8RB (0483-893385).

***M Cox (1985),** "The Oaks", Ashtead Woods Road, Ashtead, Surrey KT21 2ER.

Miss P A Cox (1983), Cranbrook, Hawks Hill, Leatherhead, Surrey KT22 9DS (0372-372173).
Miss T Cox (1974), St Michael's Convent Grammar School, Nether Street, North Finchley N12 (01-446 2256).
R J Coy (1978), 8B Layfield Road, Hendon NW4 3UG (01-202 6718/9569).
***P Davey (1976),** "Lundy", 16 Fernhurst Gardens, Aldwick, W Sussex PO21 4AZ (02432-3436).
†Mrs J E Davies (1970), 36 Shrewsbury Lane, Shooters Hill, Woolwich, London SE18 3JF (01-856 0586).
Miss E A Dean (1982), 9 Merrow Woods, Guildford, Surrey GU1 2LQ (0483-68054).
P J Donegan (1980), 8 Crossway, Raynes Park, London SW20 9JA (01-540 6852).
***Mrs P Douglas (1972),** "Craigalan", 2 Camphill Road, West Byfleet, Surrey KT14 6EH (09323-49038).
R Drysdale (1985), 10 Finlay Street, London SW6 (01-736 5643).
A Dunne (1981), 244 Haverstock Hill, Hampstead, London NW3 (01-794 4997).
Mrs Y Durham (1977), "Windermere", 37 Martyns Way, Bexhill-on-Sea, E Sussex TN40 2SE (0424-210529).
J Earland (1972), 33 Pembroke Crescent, Hove, Sussex BN3 5DF (07917-3356).
Miss T Eaton (1981), 1 Keable Road, Wrecclesham, Farnham, Surrey (0252-710372).
***Mrs A Edwards (1977),** 9 St Helens Crescent, Hastings, E. Sussex.
***Ms C P Elliott (1985),** 30 Woodstock Drive, Ickenham, Uxbridge, Middlesex UB10 8EG (71-34999).
†Miss L K Espley (1985), 'Esperides', Kithurst Close, East Preston, Sussex BN16 2TQ (0903-783758).
M T Fallon (1977), "Rossway", 71 Bidborough Ridge, Bidborough, Tunbridge Wells, Kent TN4 0UU (0892-36554).
K M Farrant (1982), 38 Colesburg Road, Beckenham, Kent BR3 4HP (01-658 2029).
J P Fayle (1975), 15 Pepys Road, Raynes Park, London SW20 8NJ (01-947 9787).
D L Feaver (1975), 13 Old Gardens Close, Tunbridge Wells, Kent TN2 5ND (0892-31784).
Mrs B J Fentiman (1970), 4 Barnfield Close, Hastings, E Sussex TN34 1TS (0424-432854).
†L Ferdinand (1981), 19 Elm Park House, Fulham Road, London SW10 (01-794 8003).
M V Fermor (1973), Culls Farm, Dean Street, East Farleigh, Maidstone, Kent ME15 0PS (0622-26665).
†Ms H Fernandes (1985), Nether House, 24 Oakleigh Park South, Whetstone W20 9JU (446-1191/446-7801).
†Mrs P Fordyce (1985), 30 Tite Street, London SW3 4JA (01-352 7264).
Miss S Freeman (1977), 27 Shirlock Road, London NW3 2HR (01-485 0186).
†R N Froud (1985), 25 Buckhurst Road, frimley Green, Camberley, Surrey GU16 6LH (0252-835792).
Mrs M P George (1973), Rustlings Lyne Lane, Lyne, Chertsey, Surrey KT16 0AL (093287-3574).
†R P Ghosh (1979), 5 Sunningdale Avenue, Ruislip, Middlesex HA4 9SS (01-868 1065).
Mr M Gibb, 1 Holland House, 11 Sundridge Avenue, Bromley, Kent BR1 2PU (01-460 2503).
†P Glanville (1973), 41 Batemans Road, Woodingdean, Brighton, Sussex BN2 6RD (0273-31396).
Miss J Goodacre (1981), 56 Dartmouth Road, Hendon, London NW4 3HX (01-202 0740 pri, 01-580 3618 bus).
†J M Grantham (1985), 14 Brenchley Road, Sittingbourne, Kent ME10 4EG (0795 72317).
†J P Guillonnet (1983), 17 Devon Avenue, Twickenham, Middlesex TW2 6PN (01-898 7456).
I D Habens (1979), 48 Carden Avenue, Brighton BN1 4NE (0273-552824).
†J Hall, 91 Bullsmoor Lane, Enfield, Middx EN3 6TG (Lea Valley 763243).
R Hall (1980), 35 Gilkes Crescent, Dulwich Village, London SE21 7BP (01-693 2538).
Miss K E Halliwell (1981), 10 Lytham Close, St Leonards-on-Sea, E Sussex TN38 0XE (0424-436640).
H R Hanscombe (1969), 14A Wycliffe Road, Wimbledon, SW19 1ER (01-540 3937).
†Mrs C Harding (1980), 51 Falcon Way, Sunbury-on-Thames, Middlesex TW16 6JN (09327-65346).
Mrs C A Hardwick (1976), The Coppice, Godolphin Road, Weybridge, Surrey KT13 0PT (Weybridge 43514).
Mrs F Hargreaves (1982), Little Garth, Woodlands Road West, Virginia Water, Surrey GU25 4PL (09904-2121).
†W P Hartfree (1983), 20 Ely Close, New Malden, Surrey KT3 4LG (01-942 6212).
G S Haslehurst (1977), 195 Lawrence Street, Mill Hill, London NW7 4JH (01-959 4415).
†N K Haugh (1967), 4 Burdett Avenue, West Wimbledon, London SW20 0ST (01-946 8572).
L R Hilborne (1977), 13 The Old Convent, Moat Road, East Grinstead, Sussex RH18 3RS (0342-28038).
Mrs S Hodges (1973), 18 Blackwood Close, West Byfleet, Surrey KT14 6AF (Byfleet 44058).
†N D Hoffmann (1981), 16 Hodgson Gardens, Burpham, Guildford, Surrey GU4 7J (0483-572938).
D G Holt (1979), 17 Thornden, Cowfold, Nr Horsham, RH18 8AG (040386-366).
***E J Hooker (1971),** 13 Sandilands, Chipstead, Sevenoaks, Kent TN13 2SP (0732-459864).
J Horler (1979), 9 Hillersdon Avenue, Barnes, London SW13 0EG (01-876 4458).
†Mrs S L Hornsby (1977), 31 Woodmere Way, Park Langley, Beckenham, Kent BR3 2SJ (01-650 0323).
***H A S Howard (1970),** 7 Nash Drive, Redhill RH1 1LH (0737-62522).
†A R Howcroft (1977), Green Trees, 5 Quarry Hill, Sevenoaks, Kent TN15 0HH (0732-452872).
†Miss J Hughes (1983), 37 Vicarage Road, Eastbourne, E Sussex BN20 8AL (0323-30029).
T Hughesman (1985), 4 Rosedale, Astead, Surrey KT21 2JJ (03722-74261).
***Mrs P Hunt (1982),** 14 Cowley Street, London SW1 (01-222 7149).

†**Mrs D Hunter (1979),** Wild Pines, Godolphin Road, Weybridge, Surrey KT13 0PT (0932-51597).
Mrs A P Hutchins (1978), 30 Pennington Drive, Weybridge, Surrey KT13 9RU (0932-229887).
†**M H Jamal (1978),** 223 The Fairway, South Ruislip, Middlesex HA4 0SN (01-845 2865).
†**D James (1981),** 42 Stanley Grove, West Croydon, Surrey (01-689 6210).
Mrs P M Jenkins (1972), 10 Laurel Crescent, Woodham, Woking GU21 5SS (Byfleet 47612).
Miss S Johnson (1982), 78 Charles Rowan House, Margery Street, London WC1 (01-467 9796).
Miss W Johnson (1985), 73 Pevensey Road, Eastbourne, Sussex (0323-648497).
†**Miss L Jonas (1984),** 9 Elsa Court, Hayne Road, Beckenham, Kent BR3 4HY (01-658 1558).
Dr S M Jones (1979), The William Harvey Hospital, Kennington Road, Willesborough, Ashford, Kent TN24 0LZ.
†**D Kelly (1984),** 7A Belgrave Gardens, St John's Wood NW8 0QY (01-328 4163 pri, 01-212 3770 bus).
H S King (1965), 20B Elms Lane, Wembley HA0 2NN (01-904 2860).
P Klimek (1981), 9 Gander Close, Burgess Hill (04446-2337).
†**A Lahiffe (1985),** 4 Edward Road, Harrow, Middlesex HA2 6QB (01-427 0396 or 01-861 4691).
*†**Miss K I Laszlo (1978),** 58 West Close, Ashford, Middlesex TW15 3LN.
J Lee (1985), Shoot Up Hill, London NW2 3XJ (01-208 0874).
†**P Lee (1980),** Inter Tennis, 77 Pembroke Crescent, Hove, Sussex BN3 5DF (0273-721811).
T S Lees (1984), Folkestone Sports Centre, Radnor Park Avenue, Folkestone, Kent (0303-58222/3).
Miss J N F Leslie (1980), 72 Boxgrove Road, Guildford, Surrey GU1 1UD (0483-66990).
Mrs C Leverington (1976), 18 Oakfield Gardens, Dulwich Wood Avenue, London SE19 1HF (01-670 1414).
R J Levine (1982), 2 Beulah Close, Edgware, Middlesex HA8 8SP (01-958 7343).
A J Lewandowski (1984), 25 Western Gardens, Ealing Common, London W5 3RS (01-992 1420).
†**Miss D Lewis (1984),** 4 Baxendale, London N20 0EG (01-446 0030).
†**R A Lewis (1985),** 40a Stanwell Road, Ashford, Middx TW15 3ER (07842-43541).
***A N Liddiard (1969),** 274 Pickhurst Lane, West Wickham BR4 0HT (01-460 4659).
Mrs T Lister (1978), 63 Bathgate Road, Wimbledon SW19 5PQ (01-946 1647).
†**R M Loughton (1985),** 'Dawn', 47 London Road, Camberley, Surrey (0276-682207).
***D P Lowen (1967),** 82 Pitshanger Lane, Ealing W5 (01-998 0289).
H Lumb (1981), Hugh Lumb Tennis School, 19 Tenby Avenue, Kenton, Harrow, Middlesex HA3 8RU (01-907 9986).
H R Maconachie (1964), 27 Homefield Road, Warlingham, Surrey CR3 9HU (088-32-3268).
Mr & Mrs D Mailer (1974), 78 Queen Elizabeth's Drive, Southgate, London N14 6RD (01-886 4515).
M D Manton (1982), 51 Hendon Street, Kemptown, Brighton, Sussex BN2 7EG (0273-696688).
*†**Ms S Mappin (1985),** The Lawn Tennis Association, Barons Court, West Kensington W14 9EG (01-385 2366).
Mrs S Marsden (1974), 15 Cromer Villas Road, London SW18 1PH (01-870 2437).
†**A Marshall (1985),** 77 Ringford Road, Wandsworth SW18 (01-874 3556).
***M A Maynard (1968),** Redwood House, Clemsfold, Guildford Road, Broadbridge Heath, Horsham, W Sussex RH12 3PW (0403-790145).
†**J R T Mayo (1970),** Olympus Sports, 6A Arbuthnot House, Breeds Place, Hastings, E Sussex TN34 3AA (0424-428195).
Mr D J McBride, 277 Cannon Hill Lane, London SW20 9DB (01-542 2120).
†**J McGhie (1976),** 1A Lawrie Park Avenue, Sydenham, London SE26 6HA (01-778 0471).
†**D J Mercer (1973),** Flat D, 142/144 Cromwell Road, Kensington, London SW7 4EF (01-373 7984).
Miss G Metcalfe (1969), Thames Polytechnic, Oakfield Lane, Dartford, Kent DA1 2SZ (0322-21328 ext 249 bus).
G R Middleton (1974), Laurel Tree Cottage, 22 Linton Hill, Linton, Maidstone, Kent ME17 4AS (0622-45975).
†**R A Miles (1980),** 46 Morris Road, South Nutfield, Surrey RH1 5SA (073-782 2409).
I K Milligan (1979), 74 Old Dover Road, Blackheath, London SE3 (01-853 2879).
Miss C J Monro (1981), Bedgebury School, Bedgebury Park, Goudhurst, Kent TN17 2SH (0580-211221).
†**C Moore (1985),** 42d South Audley Street, Mayfair, London W1 (01-499 8492).
Miss H Moore (1982), 24 Oakhill Lodge, 15 Reedham Drive, Purley, Surrey (01-668 7738).
B R Morgan (1981), 1 Ashford Road, Brighton, E Sussex BN1 6LL (0273-550831).
D E Morley (1977), 1 Clayton Avenue, Hassocks, W Sussex BN6 8HB (07918-4310).
R T I Munro (1980), The Istana, Freezeland Lane, Bexhill, Sussex TN39 5JD (0424-219133).
†**V Munt (1974),** 39 Raffles Court, Kings Drive, Edgware, Middlesex HA8 8BJ (01-958 2378).
R J Mussell (1979), 4 Lexden, Portley Wood Road, Caterham, Surrey CR3 0BP (0883-44760).
A Orchard (1974), 28A Cavendish Avenue, Finchley N3 3QN (01-346 6005).
S Palfreyman (1981), 30B Upper Montagu Street, London W1 (01-258 0262).
†**M Parker (1974),** 35 Cranleigh Road, Merton Park, London SW19 3LX (01-542 2417).
Mrs S Pegler (1972), "Link" Coach to Deaf Players, 12 Hillside Walk, Haywards Heath, Sussex RH16 1NF (0444-455369).
*†**P L Peirce (1969),** 4 River Drive, River, Dover CT17 0LT (0304-825451).
†**D Perkins (1981),** 76A Whitehill Road, Gravesend, Kent DA12 5PF (0474-67558).
B J Perris (1978), 50 Elmstead Lane, Chislehurst, Kent BR7 5EQ (01-467 4566).

†**Miss W Peyto (1984),** 16 Charter Way, Southgate, London N14 4JT (01-886 7829).
†**Miss A J Pidgeon (1983),** 33 The Laurels, Homefield Road, Bromley, Kent BR1 3LA.
†**R W Plews (1985),** 37 Woolstone Road, Forest Hill, London SE23 2TR (01-699 5871).
Mrs J Porter (1975), Orchard House, 22 Birds Hill Road, Oxshott, Surrey KT22 0NJ (Oxshott 2043).
†**S C Porter (1985),** Bridge House, 10 Hillcrest Road, Hythe, Kent CT21 5EX (0303-65612).
†**S Poxon (1985),** 85 Winnington Road, Hampstead, London N2 (01-455 3355 or 01-458 1749).
Miss S Pullen (1981), 139A North View Road, Hornsea N8 7LR (01-341 3669).
†**Ms J Price (1985), 16 Essex Road, Westgate-On-Sea, Kent CT8 8AP ((0843-32962).**
S R Prideaux (1985), 14 Ratton Road, Eastbourne, E Sussex BN21 2LS (0323-28456).
†**R Rave (1985),** 61 Seafield Road, London N11 1AR (01-368 0454).
†**Mrs S M Record,** Edge O'Beyond, Golf Links, Hythe, Kent (0303-67734).
D Reid (1985), 35 Gladstone Park Gardens, Dollis Hill, London NW2 6LA (01-450 2938).
***G. Rhodes (1982),** 33 Moresby Avenue, Surbiton, Surrey KT5 9DT (01-399 5536).
P A Richmond (1980), Kenmare, Sheerwater Avenue, Woodham, Surrey (09323-47513).
†**N Roberts (1985),** 52 Doods Road, Reigate, Surrey RH2 0NW (07372-44215).
Miss A Robinson (1980), 46 Lancaster Mews, London W2 (01-723 6400).
Miss P J Robinson (1984), 4 Costons Court, Costons Lane, Greenford, Middlesex UB6 8RW (01-575 1311).
K Rolfe (1977), 66 Holly Avenue, Walton-on-Thames, Surrey KT12 3AU (Walton 223254).
Mrs M J Rowland (1977), Pine Copse, Woodland Drive, East Horsley, Surrey KT24 5AN (04865-3742).
Miss S Ryman (1980), 66 Burma Road, Newington Green, London N16 9BJ (01-249 8650).
†**W Sarama (1984),** 35 Birch Grove, Acton, London W3 9SP (01-992 2561).
P W Saunders (1978), 9 Clifford Court, Heathfield Road, London SW18 3JE (01-874 1206).
*†**N Sears (1985),** 57 Hawkenbury Way, Lewes, Sussex BN7 1LT (0273-478071).
J H Servent (1980), 7 St Mary's Avenue, Northwood, Middlesex HA6 3AY (09274-22827).
R Seymour-Lynn (1978), 95 Sudbury Avenue, North Wembley, Middlesex (01-904 2396 pri, 01-743 9822 bus).
Miss S Shepherd (1982), "Champery", Arford Road, Headley, Nr Bordon GU35 8BT (0428-713739).
M M Silver (1966), 64 Wentworth Road, Temple Fortune, London NW11 0RL (01-455 9621).
†**Mrs E Simmons (1979),** 6 Stephenson Drive, East Grinstead, Sussex RH19 4AP (0342-23098).
D Simms (1984), Brent Tennis, 18 South View Avenue, Neasdon NW2 (904-1244 ext 4229 bus, 452-6663 pri).
B T Simpson (1983), 21 Oldfield Gardens, Agates Lane, Ashtead, Surrey KT21 1AS (Ashtead 77924).
A A G Sims (1976), 28 Queen Anne Road, London E9 7AH (01-985 0737).
G W Smith (1965), 17 Roehampton Close, Roehampton Lane, London SW15 5LU (01-876 5477).
Ms B Snapes (1981), 1 Westfield Avenue, Barnes SW13 (01-878 8034).
Mrs S B Snook (1974), 47 Broadwater Rise, Tunbridge Wells, Kent TN2 5UD (0892-46252).
†**L Sones (1984),** 22 Silvester Road, Bexhill-on-Sea, E Sussex TN40 2AY (0424-223181).
*†**C M Sordyl (1985),** 9 East Close, London W5 3HE (01-997 7748).
G J Spriggs (1973), 1 Gunyah Court, Spencer Road, London W4 3SZ (01-995 3920).
†**W A Standing (1985),** 94 Old Street, London EC1V 9AY (01-253 5586).
K H Standish (1971), "Armston", Woodcote Drive, Purley, Surrey CR2 3PD (01-660 0994).
P Stent (1980), "White Cottage", Common Hill, West Chiltington, W Sussex RH20 2NL (07983-2790).
J R Stokes (1956), 51 Wicklands Avenue, Saltdean, Brighton BN2 8EQ (0273-35112).
Mrs S Talbot (1970), 1 Belmont Lane, Stanmore HA7 2PL (01-954 1575).
Ms E Taplin (1976), 133 High Street, Farnborough, Orpington, Kent BR6 7AZ (0689-61099).
Mrs J A Thirlwall (1977), Briar Bank, Walpole Avenue, Chipstead, Surrey CR3 3PP (07375-52556).
Mrs B Thomas (1979), Great Yew Cottage, River, nr Petworth, W Sussex GU28 9AY (07985-300).
P Thomas (1984), 91 Hamlet Gardens, London W6 (01-741 8330).
†**C Thorne (1980),** 167 Dennett Road, Croydon, Surrey CR0 3JH (01-684 8654).
R C Thorn (1980), 22 Heath Rise, Hayes, Bromley, Kent BR2 7PD (01-462 3219).
W Thursby (1984), 10 Blake Drive, Larkfield, Maidstone, Kent ME20 6UE (0732-848300).
Mrs M S Trevor (1981), 15 Calmont Road, Bromley, Kent BR1 4BY (01-466 6980).
Miss C Vigar (1979), 157 St James Road, Croydon, Surrey (01-683 1610).
N G Walden (1975), 3 The Gables, Banstead, Surrey SM7 2HD (Burgh Heath 55091).
***Mrs T Wantoch (1969),** The Tile House, 4 Hollymead Road, Chipstead, Surrey CR3 3LQ (Downland 54932).
M P Watson (1982), 71 Dupont Road, Raynes Park, London SW20 8SH (01-540 4674).
†**Mrs K Weatherup (1982),** 14 Croft Close, Lords Wood, Chatham, Kent ME5 8TT (0634-64511).
P E Weaver (1983), 20 Foresters Close, Wallington, Surrey SM6 9DL (01-647 8993).
†**Miss B M Weston (1975),** 75 Priory Road, South Park, Reigate, Surrey (07372-40519).
***Miss L Wheatcroft (1968),** 8 Shaftesbury Road, Brighton BN1 4NE (0273-689205).
Miss M Wheeler (1983), 32 Brabourne Rise, Beckenham, Kent BR3 2SG (01-650 9373).
†**A White (1985), 907 Frobisher House, Dolphin Square, London SW1 V3L (01-834 3800 ext 907).**
Miss J White (1977), 10 Peartree Close, Burgess Hill, W Sussex RH15 9PF (04446-5139).

W J Wilding (1965), 18 Britannia Way, Stanwell, Staines, Middlesex TW19 7HJ (Ashford 50793).
Mrs M Willitts (1975), 7 Rosecroft Walk, Pinner, Middlesex HA5 1LJ (01-866 4895).
***Mrs P C Willson (1952),** 33 Gatesden Road, Fetcham, Leatherhead, Surrey KT22 9QW (03723-74543).
F E Wilson (1973), Chantry, Sopers Lane, Steyning, W Sussex BN4 3PU (0903-812088).
Ms G Wilson (1985), Dendrons, the Chase, Oxshott, Surrey KT22 0MR (037-284 2227).
R K Wilson (1975), 79 Southway, Totteridge, London N20 (01-445 7433).
Miss S Wilson (1976), 83 Angel Road, Thames Ditton KT7 0BA (01-398 8176).
Miss E Wiltshire (1970), 104 Cardinal Avenue, Kingston-upon-Thames, KT2 5SA (01-549 7003).
Mrs V M Winn (1974), 8 Broadlands Court, Kew Gardens Road, Richmond, Surrey TW9 3HW (01-940 1062).
***D A Wise (1975),** 3 Craigholm, Shooters Hill, London SE18 3RR (01-856 1087).
L L Witton (1964), 37 Attleborough Court, Sydenham Hill, London SE23 3PL (01-693 8506).
Miss J Woodbridge (1977), 8 Avenue Road, Staines, Middlesex TW18 3AW (0784-56964).
†**J Woods (1977),** 9 Cliveden Road, Wimbledon SW19 (01-540 2908).
†**Ms W Wooldridge (1985),** Holland House, Jackmans Lane, Woking, Surrey G21 1QU (04862-24945).
P Worrall (1984), 29 Bycroft Road, Southall, Middlesex UB1 2XG (01-578 2840).
R W Wright (1981), 35 Garth Road, Childs Hill, London NW2 2BD (01-458 5337).
B Young (1980), Flat 6, 23 Queensboro' Terrace, Bayswater, London W2 (01-229 3051).
S L Zackon (1980), 99 Messina Avenue, London NW6 4LG (01-625 9480).

EAST

(Bedfordshire, Cambridgeshire, Essex, Hertfordshire, Norfolk, Suffolk)

†**J E Ager (1976),** 8 Post Mill Close, Grundisburgh, Woodbridge, Suffolk, IP13 6UU (047-335-541).
Mrs J S Allnutt (1980), 2 Cowper Road, Berkhamsted HP4 3DA (04427-73075).
K D Ames (1980), 9 East Avenue, Brundall, Norwich NR13 5PB (0603-714151).
R K Ames (1983), 9 East Avenue, Brundall, Norwich NR13 5PB (0603-714151).
K H Anderson (1983), 59 Bernwell Road, Chingford E4 6HX (01-524 2259).
Miss E Andrews (1981), 1 Denner Road, Chingford E4 7SQ (01-529 0532).
P Atherton (1969), 233 Lowestoft Road, Sorleston, Great Yarmouth NR31 6JH (0473-665400).
C G P Aylin (1983), 6 Redebourne Lane, Bury-Ramsey PE17 1PB (0487-815015).
Mrs C M Baker (1975), 18 Orchard Close, Watford, Herts WD1 3DU (0923-40178).
N. Baker (1985), 20 St James Gardens, Westcliffe-on-Sea, Essex SS0 0BU.
Mrs P Bashford (1978), 20 Normandie Way, Bures, Suffolk CO8 5BE (0787-227721).
J L Baxter (1963), "Portelet", 6 Grove Road, Boxmoor, Hemel Hempstead, Herts HP1 1NG (0422-3782).
Mrs J L Beckman (1974), 20 Mount Pleasant, Cockfosters, Barnet, Herts EN4 9HH (01-449 4681).
Mrs S Birchall (1977), 1 Eaton Road, St Albans, Herts AL1 4UD (0727-35039).
Mrs V Bonham (1981), 60 Anthony Drive, Norwich, Norfolk NR3 4EN (0603-414704).
A Boyle (1984), 123 Bradley Road, Luton, Bedfordshire LU4 8SW (0582-595834).
M R J Broad (1982), 9 Cambridge Road, St Albans, Herts AL1 5LH (0727-35551).
R H Brookes (1976), 13 Glebe Road, Sandy, Bedfordshire SG19 1LS (0767-80650).
†**Mrs S Bullerwell (1984),** Duncombe Heights, Renhold Road, Wilden, Bedfordshire (0234-771419).
C Burks (1984), 1A Exchange Buildings, High Street, Barnet, Herts EN5 5SY (01-449 8812).
†**C G R Byrnes (1985),** 8 Rowan Walk, Eastwood, Essex (0702-529706).
J E Carpenter (1978), 68 Minster Way, Hornchurch, Essex RM11 3TD (04024-46077).
Miss K L Cass (1981), Middlefield, Huntingdon Road, Cambridge CB3 0LH (0223-276234).
R N Castle (1967), 1 Leicester Close, Ipswich IP2 9EX (0473-687639).
Miss M Chapman (1975), 23 Kings Avenue, Watford, Herts WD1 7SB (Watford 34615).
†**P T Cosford (1982),** 1 Kingston Avenue, Stony Stratford, Milton Keynes MK11 (0908-562945).
T P Cosford (1984), 1 Kingston Avenue, Stony Stratford, Milton Keynes MK11 (0908-562945).
†**Mrs J F Cradduck (1976),** Fir Tree Cottage, 24A East Street, Rochford, Essex (0702-547425 pri, 219442 bus).
†**P H S Crawley (1979),** Garth House, Hertingfordbury, Herts SG14 2LG (0992-52963).
†**N D Crown (1984),** Winton Cottage, New Thorpe Avenue, Thorpe le Soken, Clacton-on-Sea, Essex CO16 0LR (0255-861872).
A Crowther (1982), 167a Hatfield Road, St Albans, Herts.
I Currie (0000), 10 Imperial Avenue, Westcliffe-on-Sea, Essex SS0 8NE (0702-345083).
P A Davies (1975), 13 Dalmeny Road, New Barnet, Herts EN5 1DE (01-449 0029).
Mrs J Dayer-Smith, Tower Cottage, Mill Lane, Weston, Nr. Hitchin, Herts.
†**Miss H Dixon (1983),** 76 Burges Road, Thorpe Bay, Essex SS1 3HU (0702-582592).
D J Donovan (1979), 3 Sorrel Close, Braiswick, Colchester, Essex (0206-852382).
P A Dorking (1981), 13 Tamar Square, Woodford Green, Essex IG8 0EA (01-505 9834).
†**Miss J M Dyer (1977),** 19 Fitzgilbert Road, Colchester, Essex CO2 7XB (0206-575239).
Miss J M Farebrother (1981), 11 Baynards Crescent, Frinton-on-Sea, Essex CO13 0QS (0255-77170).

*Miss J M Fennell (1968), Bedford College of Higher Education, 37 Lansdowne Road, Bedford MK40 2BZ (Bedford 51966).
†Mrs W Flack (1985), Home Farm, Culford, Bury St Edmunds, Suffolk IP28 6DS (028484-335).
†J E E Frew (1977), "Conesford", Litcham Road, Mileham, King's Lynn, Norfolk PE32 2PT (0328 701500).
†Mrs J Gates (1978), Grove End, Elm Grove, Berkhamsted, Herts HP4 1AE, (044-27-5589).
Ms C F George (1978), 32 Tyrone Road, Thorpe Bay, Essex SS1 3HF (0702-586286).
P Gilbertson (1970), 278 Gorleston Road, Lowestoft NR32 3AJ (0502-518610).
D R Glenister (1964), 6 St Michael's Crescent, Luton, Beds (Luton 23840 pri, Harpenden 61219 bus).
*J Gollifer (1985), 'Barima', The Green, Greater Bentley, Nr Colchester, Essex CO7 8PD (0206-250960).
D C Gould (1978), 11 Ian Road, Billericay, Essex CM12 0JX (02774-53192).
†R C Green (1980), 53 Roman Gardens, King's Langley WD4 8LP (09277-69970).
Wg Cdr R L Greenhall (1980), 15 Patteson Close, Cringleford, Norwich, Norfolk NR4 6XX (0603-501187).
R Greenham (1983), 218 Broadway, Peterborough, Cambs (0733-314585).
Mrs E S Guymer (1975), Mowhills House, 133 High Street, Harrold, Bedford MK43 7ED (0234-720448).
†Mrs P M Hall (1974), 67 Billy Lows Lane, Potters Bar, EN6 1UX (0707-58661).
†Mrs J M Harris (1974), Cavell House, Swardeston, Norwich NR14 8DZ (0508-78195).
Mrs M P Harrison (1981), 6 Burstead Road, Gt Shelford, Cambridge CB4 8EJ (0223-842312).
*M Haynes (1979), Bradfords Tennis Academy, 200 Buckhurst Way, Buckhurst Hill, Essex IG9 6HZ (01-505 0920).
N Henery (1982), 15 Norton Road, Loddon, Norwich NR14 6JN (0508-20293).
†P Hewing (1984), 15 Shakletons, Ongar, Essex (0277-363671).
J Hofstetter (1982), 2 Willenhall Avenue, New Barnet EN5 1JN (01-440 1741).
Mrs I Holmes (1975), "Bowerside", Tyndales Lane, Danbury, Essex CM3 4NA (024-541-6214).
†J N Hughes (1985), 54 Black Street, Martham, Great Yarmouth NR29 4PR (0693-740079).
Miss S Hughes (1983), 21 Bradmore Way, Brookmans Park, Hatfield, Herts AL9 7QY (0707-59349).
†J E Innocent (1985), 36 James Gardens, Westcliffe on Sea, Essex SS0 0PU (0702 344004).
S M Jacka (1978), 83 Gaywood Road, Kings Lynn, Norfolk PE30 2PU (0553-2937).
'I E Johnson (1985), 466 Mutton Lane, Potters Bar, herts EN6 3BB (0707-53830).
†R Keeling (1981), 97 Cuffley Hill, Goffs Oak, Herts EN7 5JT (0707-874570).
Mrs A Kent (1978), 27B Townsend Drive, St Albans AL3 5RF (0727-54113).
Mrs H U P Kerrison (1977), The White House, Haddiscoe, Norwich NR14 6PG (050-277-246).
Miss J Kidner (1979), The Cottage, Norwich Road, Denton, Harleston IP20 0BD (098-686-629).
†Mrs J Kirk (1983), 12 Warley Mount, Warley, Brentwood, Essex CM14 5EN (0277-220993).
Miss D G Lake (1979), Threxton House, Nr Watton, Thetford, Norfolk IP25 6LT (0953-881289).
S Lampert (1981), 32 Hanmer Road, Simpson, Milton Keynes MK6 3AY (0908-679988).
A Leach (1978), 54 Elm Road, Wisbech, Cambs PE13 2TB (0945 581302).
†E W Lewis (1984), "Cotswold", South Road, Chorley Wood, Herts WD3 5AS (09278-2566).
*W E Linford (1965), 3 Church Walk, St Neots, Huntingdon, Cambs PE19 1JH.
*Miss D Locke (1979), 6 Ainslie Wood Gardens, Chingford E4 (01-524 1532).
J A Lucas (1980), 27 Sycamore Way, Brantham, Nr Manningtree, Essex CO11 1TL (0206-395634).
†S Luck (1980), 4 Keats Close, Maldon, Essex CM9 6BD (0621-57858).
Mrs E A Macdonald (1978), 71 Green End Road, Cambridge CB4 1RS (0223-323000).
*Mrs P Mace (1981), 14 Blithe-Meadow Drive, Spronston, Norwich (0603-411190).
J S Martin (1984), "Woodbury", Fieldings Place, Graveley, Cambs PE18 9PN (0480-830917).
†S Meads (1983), 17 Homelands Grove, Ramsden Heath, Nr Billericay, Essex CM11 1NJ (0268-710748).
Miss R C Meadows (1978), 63 Warwick Street, Norwich, Norfolk NR2 3LD (0603-665437).
Ms H Moore (1985), 34 Cambridge Street, Cambridge.
Miss D Murray (1980), 34 Pasquier Road, Walthamstow E17 (01-527 3142).
†Miss M Napier (1982), Primrose Cottage, Lower End, Swaffham Prior, Cambridge CB5 0HT (0638-741867).
R Neal (1979), Chingford School of Tennis, British Legion Road, Off Whitehall Road, London E4 (01-527 3142).
A H Neilly (1977), 84 Trapstyle Road, Ware, Herts SG12 0BB (0920-67789).
C Nicholls (1980), 68 Alzey Gardens, Harpenden, Herts Al5 4SY (05827-64995).
†K R Palmer (1979), 5 Sandpipers, Rampart Terrace, Shoeburyness, Essex SS3 9AD (03708-2655).
†Miss J Poole (1977), 3A Maywin Drive, Hornchurch, Essex RM11 3ST (04024-77719).
Miss A Powell (1979), 8 Elgar Rise, Eaton, Norwich, Norfolk (0603-55150).
A J Pryke (1973), 11 Dales View, Washbrook, Ipswich IP8 3EX (0473-505).
†Ms A Quince (1985), 55 Top End, Renhold, Bedford MK41 0LS (0234-878704).
†R Rate (1979), 55 Halt Drive, Linford, Standford-le-Hope, Essex SS17 0RG (03752-77668).
†C Rees (1985), 31 Bradmore Way, Brookmans Park, Hatfield, Herts AL9 7QY (Potters Bar 56800).
*I R Richards (1950), Pen-y-Bryn, Martlesham, Woodbridge, Suffolk IP12 4SN (0473-622518).
'Mrs J A Rodgers (1977), Marles Farm, Epping Upland, Essex CM16 6PF (0378-73870).

†Mrs P Rogers (1977), "Pound Cottage", Dennington, Woodbridge, Suffolk (09275-696).
J L Rudd (1984), 1 Waltham Walk, Eye, Peterborough PE6 7XE (0733-222630).
†**M F Schools (1985),** 10 Helston Place, Abbots Langley, Watford, Herts WD5 0NB (0923 672759).
Miss F Simpson (1983), 112 Brookmans Avenue, Hatfield, Herts AL9 7QQ (0707-54958).
†**B Smart (1985), Marlow House, Bailey Street, Castle Acre, Norfolk PE32 2AG (07605 315).**
G Spowage (1980), 49 Pleasant Valley, Saffron Walden, Essex (0799-22991).
P J Stagg (1974), "Pemalbill", 20 Grenville Way, Thetford, Norfolk IP24 2JH (0842-3619).
†**Ms P F Stuart-Paul (1985),** 34 South Road, Brampton, Huntingdon, Cambs PE18 8PX (0480-57660).
J B Swan (1973), "Fen View", 26 Newark Road, Lowestoft, NR33 0LY (0502-63558).
†**L E Talbert (1969),** 23 Mentmore Road, Linslade, Leighton Buzzard, Beds LU7 7NY (0525-376772).
***N A Thompson (1975),** 1 Lovell Rise, Leigh-on-Sea, Essex SS9 5UB (0702-528835).
Miss L K Turner (1976), 15 Broadway Close, Woodford Green, Essex IG8 0HD (01-504 0832).
*†**P Villis-Pocock (1974),** 100 Batchwood Drive, St Albans, Herts (St Albans 61566).
†**P Vivian (1978),** 66 Warwick Road, Stratford, London E15 4LA (01-534 7487).
J Warren (1981), "Medfield", Tuttles Lane (West), Wymondham, Norfolk NR18 0JJ (0953-603853).
S Watts (1984), 16 Grange Lane, Kesgrave, Ipswich, Suffolk IP5 7QD (0473-622288).
A J Wickham (1981), "World of Sport", Grove Road, Norwich NR1 3RH (0603-27799/617657).
†**G S Woodgett (1978),** 6 Belmont Court, High Street, Newmarket, Suffolk CB8 9BP (0638-662712).
***G C Woodhouse (1982),** 9 Cardiff Road, Watford, Herts WD1 8DS (Watford 37714).
D Wright (1964), 131 Highlands Boulevard, Leigh-on-Sea, Essex SS9 3TH (0702-72619).
Miss S M Wright (1974), Northern House, The Drive, Sawbridgeworth, Herts CM21 9EP (0279-722141).
Wg Cdr M R Yule (1979), 14 Montagu Road, Brampton, Huntingdon, Cambs PE18 8QG (0480-57019 pri, 52151 ext 2515 bus).

SOUTH

(Berkshire, Buckinghamshire, Hampshire and Isle of Wight, Oxfordshire and Channel Islands)

Miss H M Anscomb (1977), Hightrees, Ashmansworth, Newbury RG15 9QH (0635-253079).
J R C Bothwick (1978), 25b Outram Road, Phoenix Court, Southsea, Portsmouth, Hants PO5 1QS (0705-754689).
Mrs P Bradford (1973), Thicket Meadows North, Newland Drive, Maidenhead, Berks SL6 4LL (0628-29744).
†**Ms C Brooks (1981),** 13 Bonhomie Court, Broadcommon Road, Hurst, Reading, Berks RG1 0RE (0734-340295).
Ms A M Brotherston (1985), 35 Goodrington Close, Banbury, Oxon OX16 0DB (0295-68087).
Miss S Caunter (1979), 6 Gladridge Close, Earley, Reading (0734-64469).
†**D Chapman (1985),** San Sebastian, Cupernham Lane, Romsey, Hampshire (0794-515642).
Mrs H Cheadle (1983), 22 Fairfield Road, Barton-on-Sea, New Milton, Hants BH25 7NL (0425-620578).
Miss P Church (1982), 33 Glen Road, Woolston, Southampton, Hants SO2 9EJ (0703-438079).
Mrs G Clark (1976), 8 Kings Stile, Middleton Cheney, Banbury, Oxon (0295-710645).
†**Lt Cdr R W Clarke RN (1968),** 74 Park Road, Chandlers Ford, Eastleigh, Hants SO5 1GN (04215-61838).
N J Clifford (1982), 1 Bear Close, Woodstock OX7 1JS (0993-812126).
***Ms M Clifton (1985),** c/o Bisham Abbey NSC, Nr Marlow, Bucks SL7 1RT (06284-74146).
J M Coe (1972), 3 Kipling Road, Hilsea, Portsmouth, Hants PO2 9NH (0705-644779).
*†**P J Cooper (1973),** Shene, Sedgmoor Road, Flackwell Heath, High Wycombe, Bucks HP10 9AU (06285-22562).
J H C Coulson (1982), Boyne House, Grove End, Beaconsfield, Bucks HP9 1PE (04946-2018/4744).
A Cox (1984), 23 Greenham Wood, Birch Hill, Bracknell, Berks (0344-482120).
Ms S Cronshaw (1985), Lower Farm, School Lane, Headbourne Worthy, Winchester, Hants (882394).
Miss A Dadds (1983), 7 Castle Street, Tichfield, Hants.
Anne R Elliot (1979), "The Swarthel", 52 Vanner Road, Witney, Oxon OX8 6PF (0993-4914).
R G J Ferrier (1971), 10 Tazewell Court, Bath Road, Reading, Berks RG1 6HQ (0734-594394).
Mrs J A Gauntlett (1982), "Windy Ridge", Portsdown Hill Road, Cosham, Portsmouth PO6 1BE (0705-371534).
D J Gill (1981), "Milnthorpe", Sleepers Hill, Winchester, Hants SO22 4NF (0962-56294).
†**J Godfrey (1985),** 1 Cutlers Lane, Stubbington, Hampshire PO14 2JN (0329-661486).
J Graveling (1979), 72 Birch Grove, Slough SL2 1EP (0753-78101).
K J Gundry (1976), 11 Kipling Road, Hilsea, Portsmouth, Hants PO2 9NA (0705-661837).
P Gunter (1984), "Fairhaven", Bedales School, Stead, Petersfield, Hants GU32 2DG (0730-64156).
S G Hall (1980), 8 Lautrec Way, Haydon Hill, Aylesbury HP19 3SG (0296-85367).
†**B J Herman (1985),** 6 Four Acre Coppice, Raven Meadow, Hook, Hampshire RG27 9NF (025672-3776).
R J Hilary (1972), 74 Alton Road, Fleet, Aldershot, Hants GU13 98HW (02514-5978).
†**Dr G O Hopkins (1983),** 27 Napoleon Avenue, Farnborough, Hants (0252-546588).
†**A Horwood (1985),** Glenfield, Boars Hill, Oxford OX1 5DL (0865-735370).
Mrs T Hurd (1981), 3 Spring Lane, Idbury, Oxon OX7 6RU (0993-830367).
K Ingram (1976), 69 Philip Drive, Flackwell Heath, High Wycombe, Bucks HP10 9JD (06284-25389).

C Jeynes (1980), Melmott End, Thepound, Cookham, Berks SL6 9QD (062-85-20241).
Mrs E C Jones (1984), 11 Silwood Close, Winchester, Hants SO22 6EN (0962-67207).
†**L W Kelly (1984),** School House, Thenford, Banbury, Oxon OX17 2BX (0295-710445).
Miss R Kermode (1984), Pendle Wood, Cothill, Abington, Oxon OX13 6QQ (0865-390518).
M Lambert (1982), 35 Carisbrooke Court, New Milton, Hants BH25 5US (0425-619951).
†**T F Le Tarouilly (1985),** L'Amandier, La Ville De La Croix, St Ouen, Jersey, Channel Islands (0534-81996).
Mrs S A Lee (1965), Bisham Abbey N.S.C., Nr Marlow, Bucks (06284-2818).
W Lilley (1968), 10 Coln Road, A.E.R.E. Harwell, Oxon OX11 0QA (0235-834233).
A J R Lines (1966), "Chalkrise", Newbury Road, Lambourn, Berks (0488-71744).
H Macbeth (1979), 5 Highdown Avenue, Emmer Green, Reading, Berks RG4 8QT (0734-476816).
Miss L Machin (1984), Prospect Farm, Monxton, Andover, Hants SP11 7DA (0264-710218).
†**M Makein (1963),** 23 Stapleton Close, Marlow, Bucks SL7 1TZ (06284-6208).
G G Martel (1985), Fleur De Lis, Retot Lane, Albecq Castel, Guernsey (0481-53009).
S C McEwan (1971), 3 Oakenbrow, Brighton Road, Sway, Lymington, Hants SO4 0DY (0590-683214).
†**I Morgan (1985),** Rosehill, Rue des Arbes, St Helier, Jersey (0534-61009).
Miss S Morgan (1984), 1 Rosedene Gardens, Fleet, Hants GU13 7AH (025-14-21346).
†**Major A S Moore (1983),** 6 The Crescent, Farnborough, Hants GU14 7AH (0252-543848).
P Morrish (1982), "Silverdale", Main Drive, Gerrards Cross, Bucks (0753-886833).
P Munton (1978), Battlefield Cottage, 31 Essex Street, Newbury, Berks (0635-41358).
S Partridge (1982), 1 Westfield Way, Wantage, Oxon OX12 7EW (02357-67097).
G Petrie (1981), 44 Thornbridge Road, Iver Heath, Bucks SLO 0QD (0753-651810).
*†**Miss D Phillips (1984),** 39 Hobb Lane, Hedge End, Southampton, Hants SO3 4GG (04892-5194).
†**R W Purkis, 137 Cavalier Road, Old Basing, Basingstoke, Hampshire RG24 0ET (0256-20836).**
M J S Reed (1983), Volleys, 5 Warren Drive, Abbotts Ann, Andover, Hants SP11 7DE (0264-710781).
Col B Reeves (1980), Kwetu, Thruxton, Andover, Hants SP11 8NF (026477-2563).
A B W Risman (1982), 11 Rasenswood Avenue, Crowthorne, Berks RG11 6AX (0344-772452).
B Robinson (1981), 18 Rickman Close, Woodley, Reading, Berks RG5 3LL (0734-662535).
I Robinson (1980), 3 Fosse Andre, St Peter Port, Guernsey (0481-28404).
Mrs J Robinson (1979), 3 Fosse Andre, St Peter Port, Guernsey (0481-28404).
D H Sanders (1970), 57 Woodstock Avenue, Horndean, Hants PO8 9TF (0705-594831).
†**N N Searles (1984),** 2 Princes Way, Shanklin, Isle of Wight PO37 7DY (0983-872779).
†**Miss E M Sherwood-Smith (1976),** 59 Belmont Road, Maidenhead, Berkshire SL6 6LF (Maidenhead 781201).
R Townsend (1966), 9 Daisy Lane, Locksheath, Southampton SO3 6RA (04895-4945).
G L M Tucker (1981), 132 Northern Road, Slough, Berks (Slough 32907).
†**Miss K Turton (1982),** 'Bluehayes', 27 Layters Avenue, Chalfont St Peter, Gerrards Cross, Bucks (0753-885491).
R W Vincent (1979), 16 Stocklands Way, Prestwood, Great Missenden, Bucks HP16 0SJ (02406-4537).
D L Waite (1980), Crofton House, 16 Monument Lane, Chalfont St Peter, Bucks SL9 0HT (02407-4810).
B M Walker (1968), 23 Golden Crescent, Everton, Nr Lymington, Hants SO4 0LN (0590-43665).
R J Wardle (1968), 55 Green Lane, Clanfield, Portsmouth, Hants PO8 0JX (0705-598379).
P Warr (1979), 18 Richmere Road, Didcot, Oxon OX11 8HT (0235-814057).
Mrs D Weatherill (1976), 9 Andrews Way, Marlow Bottom, Marlow, Bucks SL7 3QJ (06284-76103).
†**Miss C Whitehead (1980),** The Pines, 4 The Fairway, Lake, Sandown, Isle of Wight PO36 9EE (0983 404379).
†**Mrs M A Wicken (1977),** 35 Oaks Drive, St Leonards, Ringwood, Hants BH24 2QR (0202-873696).
†**P M Will (1978),** 10 Pirbright Road, Farnborough, Hants (0252-546121).
†**J L Woodward (1972),** 43 Rochester Avenue, Woodley, Reading, Berks (0734-695749).
J Wright (1965), Havant College, Havant, Hants (0705-483856).

SOUTH WEST

(Avon, Cornwall, Devon, Dorset, Gloucestershire, Somerset, Wiltshire)

†**Ms S Atkinson (1985),** 2 Cannons Close, Winterbourne, Bristol, Avon BS17 1PG (0454-775244).
R S Barber (1976), 8 Littledown Drive, Queens Park, Bournemouth BA7 7AQ (0202-484161).
A Barker (1972), 165 Southmead Road, Bristol BS10 5DW (0272-624016).
Miss A F Baughan (1981), 15 Tilting Road, Thornbury, Bristol BS12 1EP (0454-413155).
G N Baughan (1984), 15 Tilting Road, Thornbury, Bristol BS12 1EP (0454-413155).
†**T J Beaglehole (1983),** Flat 1, Rear of 128 High Street, Street, Somerset BA16 0AD.
D C Bendall (1972), 29 Priory Avenue, Westbury-on-Trym, Bristol BS9 4BZ (0272-623368).
J Bird (1978), Lowertown Farm, Camelford, Cornwall PL32 9QS (0840-213280).
†**D J Blackmore (1978),** 14 Viney Street, Taunton, Somerset TA1 3AY (0823-52838).
J Blair (1979), 68 Winchester Street, Taunton, Somerset TA1 1QF (0823-83141 ext 168).
R C Bond (1984), The Junipers, Old Totnes Road, Buckfastleigh, S Devon TQ11 0LR (03644-3493).

R. Booth (1985), c/o West Hants LTC, Roslin Road South, Bournemouth, Dorset (0202-526512).
F C Bowles (1980), The Post Office Stores, West Pennard, Nr Glastonbury, Somerset BA6 8NL (0458-32955).
P Bray (1976), 4 Manor Close, Stratton, Dorchester, Dorset DT2 9RY (0305-63766).
Miss M J Brehaut (1982), Pitwell House, Holywell Road, Edington, Bridgwater, Somerset TA7 9LB (0278-722282).
†**Mrs O Brown (1981),** 10 Cavendish Road, Bristol BS9 4DZ (0272-623473).
M P Burridge (1978), 58 The Crescent, Henleaze, Bristol BS9 4RR (0272-624314).
J R Cane (1968), 61 High Street, Wimborne, Dorset (0205-883104).
***Mrs E Canterbury (1965),** Staddlestones, Mount Pleasant, Pilton, Shepton Mallet, Somerset (074-989-448).
V G Carr (1966), 2 Willows Close, Frogmore, Kingsbridge, S Devon (054853-382).
Mrs P Carter (1980), 3 Kenton Mews, Henleaze, Bristol BS9 4LT (0272-629996).
†**Ms J Champion,** 29 The Grove, Burnham-on-Sea, Somerset TA8 2PA (0278-784955).
***P Charles (1984),** 25 Purn Road, Bleadon Hill, Weston-Super-Mare, Avon BS24 9JQ (0934-812719).
†**P Chadwick (1985),** 30 Winchester Walk, Merley, Wimborne, Dorset BH21 1SN (0202-886412).
R F Chitty (1980), 'The Ferns', 2 Pirton Lane, Churchdown, Nr Gloucester GL3 2RT (0452 857330).
Rev E A J Chivers (1971), 40 Calcott Road, Knowle, Bristol BS4 2HD (0272-777867).
†**R H B Clarke (1973),** 'Cromwell', Riversmeet, Appledore, Bideford, Devon EX39 1RE (02372-4417).
†**Miss S Cleeves (1984),** 9 Sandringham Road, Swindon, Wilts SN3 1HW (0793-22409).
Mrs K Coran (1983), 7 Bridge Street, Ipplepen, Devon (0803-813205).
Mr R Craddock, 'Furzebank', Verwood Road, Woodlands, Wimborne, Dorset BH21 6LJ (0202 825325).
†**M Crouch (1985),** 23 Lanmydrock View, Bodmin, Cornwall PL31 1BG (0208-3731).
†**R J Cruse (1985),** Croft Cottage, Abbotskerswell, Newton Abbot, Devon TQ12 5NS (0626-66026).
P D Davis (1976), 46 Bradford Close, Eggbuckland, Plymouth (0752-782586).
M Delacole (1984), 33 Knowlands, Highworth, Swindon SN6 7NB (0793-763357).
†**Ms E A Deuxberry (1985),** Glebe Cottage, West Knighton, Dorchester, Dorset DT2 8PG (0305-853643).
†**J A Doe (1985),** 186 Stoke Lane, Stoke Bishop, Bristol, Avon BS9 3RS (0272-681161).
P Duggan (1983), 6 St Johns Road, Christchurch, Dorset BH23 1LX (0202-473016).
Mrs C A Embury (1969), 14 Blackdown View, Sampford Peverell, Tiverton, Devon EX16 7BE (0884-820108).
Mrs B Entract (1981), York House, Prince of Wales Road, Dorchester, Dorset DT1 1QA (0305-64115).
Mrs V Ford (1981), 3 Sage Close, Portishead, Bristol BS20 8ET (0272-843495).
A G Ginn (1976), 5 Pill Way, Clevedon, Avon BS21 7UN (0272-874298).
†**C R Hold (1980),** 19 Shorelands Road, Barnstaple, N Devon EX31 3AA (0271-45879).
†**Miss J M Holland (1972),** Salisbury College of Technology, Southampton Road, Salisbury, Wilts (0722-23711 ext 230).
†**Mrs R A Horton (1978),** 11 Wain-A-Long Road, Salisbury, Wilts SP1 1LJ (0722-28469).
Mrs S M J Hurdle (1972), 57 Lacy Drive, Wimborne, Dorset BH21 1DG (0202-884633).
†**R Hurley (1983),** 111 Quemerford, Calne, Wiltshire SN11 8JU (0249-813959).
Mrs M Johnson (1972), Thame House, Queen Street, Colyton, Devon EX13 6JU (0297-52064).
P Jones (1978), 31 Bidbury Avenue, Stoke Lodge, Patchway, Bristol BS12 6DF (0454-614420).
G D Julian (1981), 3 Old Castle Road, Weymouth, Dorset DT4 8QB (03057-771504).
†**M R Keat (1985),** 56 Killerton Road, Bude, Cornwall EX23 8EW (0288-3721).
Miss A Latham (1979), 17 Pine Close, Street, Somerset.
Mrs J K Le Neve-Foster (1983), Clover Cottage, 126 Four Forks Lane, Spaxton, Bridgwater, Somerset TA5 1AB (0278-67-541).
R E A Louis (1965), 63 Douglas Avenue, Exmouth, Devon EX8 2HG (0395-274689).
Mrs P Luton-Lozach Meur (1965), Rowden Mill House, Stourton Caundle, Sturminster Newton, Dorset DT10 2JT (096-323-212).
Mrs B MacGregor (1976), 7 Woodstock Road, Weston-Super-Mare, Avon BS22 8AH (0934-416055).
Mrs S M Mann (1972), 9 Starbarn Road, Winterbourne, Avon BS17 1NU (0454-775814).
†**Mrs J E Manners (1983),** Coole's Farmhouse, Minety, Malmesbury, Wilts SN16 9QA (066-860-447).
Miss S Mitchell (1977), 7 Brook Cottages, Corston, Bath BA2 9BA (02217-2238).
†**Ms E Molton (1985),** 11 Queens Drive, Bishopston, Bristol BS7 8JQ (0272-422040).
*†**S J Partridge (1984),** 3 Henrietta Villas, Bath, Avon (0225-66596).
†**Ms C Pickering (1985),** 7 Mill Street, Puddletown, Dorchester, Dorset DT2 8SQ (0305-84724 or 0305-69008 (24 hrs).
†**Miss J A Pincombe (1978),** Alfords Villavin, Roborough, Winkleigh, N Devon EX19 8TF (08053-291).
Mrs J E Pink (1976), 'The Laurels', Fursehill, Wimborne, Dorset BH21 4HD (0202-889893).
J A Pocock (1974), 55 Oakley Hill, Wimborne, Dorset BH21 1QQ (0202-883984).
J Potts (1978), 28 Start Bay Park, Strete, Nr Dartmouth, South Devon TQ6 0RY.
J R Putman (1984), 8 Hollycroft Road, Higher Compton, Plymouth PL3 6PP (0752-779441).
G M Reid (1975), Taunton School, Taunton, Somerset TA2 6AD (0823-76081).
Flt Lt D Ross (1981), 1 Glendale Road, Durrington, Wilts SP4 8EP (0980-52897).
*†**J L Schofield (1975),** 72 Waveney Road, Keynsham, Bristol, Avon BS18 1RU (027-56-4826).

Mrs E P Scott (1981), 13 Hartington Park, Redland, Bristol BS6 7ES (0272-45882).
Mrs G Shell (1981), 7 Pyne Point, Clevedon, Avon (0272-872800).
G S Slade (1977), 19 Fairfield Road, Crediton, Devon (03632-2059).
D L Smart (1974), 'Valden', 17 The Perrings, Nailsea, Bristol BS19 2YD (0272-857866).
†**K A F Thomas (1955),** Quarry Farm, West Monkton, Taunton, Somerset TA2 8QZ (0823-412561).
J M Treleven (1977), 'Klosters', 17 Thornhill Way, Mannamead, Plymouth, Devon PL3 5NP (0752-265525).
Major J A Valdés-Scott (1985), Woodwalls, Corscombe, Dorchester, Dorset DT2 0NT (Corscombe 477).
†**A Ward (1984),** 61 Chestnut Springs, Lydiard Millicent, Swindon, Wilts SN5 9NB (0793-770759).
†**Mrs E J Weaver (1981),** The Cottage, Dunstone, Nr Yealmpton, Plymouth, Devon PL8 2EL (0752-881064).
†**P Weaver (1985),** 42 Newbarn Park Road, Taunton, Somerset TA1 4NF (0823-77011).
†**D J Whitehead (1984),** 142 Holford Road, Bridgwater, Somerset TA6 7PA (0278-57212).
***Mrs P Whiting (1967),** "Millbrook", Brook Street, Chipping Sodbury, Bristol BS17 6AZ (0454-318740).
M Withers (1984), Church Farm, Clutton, Bristol, Avon BS18 4SG (0761-52245).
Mrs S V Worsdale (1976), The Manor, Knole, Long Sutton, Somerset TA10 9JB (0458-24571).
Mrs J Young (1977), Ashleigh, Manor Road, Seaton, Devon EX12 2AQ (0297-20575).

NORTH MIDLANDS

(Derbyshire, Leicestershire, Lincolnshire, Northamptonshire, Nottinghamshire)

***S E Andrew MBE (1965),** 25 Matmore Gate, Spalding, Lincs PE11 2PN (0775-2763).
†**H R Bailey (1964),** 21 Field Close, Hilton, Derbyshire DE6 5GL (028-373-2273).
I J Bailey (1984), 18 Hall Close, Kettering, Northamptonshire NN15 7LQ (0536-81743).
Miss S A Baker (1984), 9 Oak Close, Duffield, Derby DE6 4HF (0332-841773).
Dr S G Baker (1966), 9 Oak Close, Duffield, Derby DE6 4HF (0332-841773).
S Barnes (1982), 36 Acres Road, Leicester Forest East, Leicester LE3 3HA (0533-392621).
Mrs A Baseley (1965), 93 Westcliffe Road, Ruskington, Sleaford, Lincs NG34 9AX (0526-832475).
***M F Batty (1969),** 72 Latimer Road, Cropston, Leicester LE7 7GN (0533-362237).
T W Blackburn (1977), 27 Kirby Lane, Kirby Muxloe, Leicester LE3 3JG (0533-393778).
†**M J Breslin (1985),** 39 Bushland Road, Northampton NN3 2NS (0604-408913).
†**D J C Burford (1978),** 31 St Mary's Road, Bingham, Notts NG13 8DX (0949-37357).
Mrs J Butterfield (1980), 8 Southernhay Road, Leicester LE2 3TJ (0533-703416).
†**Mrs H Byford (1977),** Kinchley House, Rothley, Leicester LE7 7SB (0533-302636).
*†**N J Clarke (1979),** 34 Ratby Road, Groby, Leicester (0533-311381).
Mrs A M Cloke (1972), 91 Newhaven Road, Evington, Leicester LE5 6JH (0533-418273).
†**C Cropper (1973),** Woodthorpe Village, Loughborough, Leics LE12 8UG (0509-261616).
***P G Cross (1960),** Westmount, 38 Wirksworth Road, Duffield, Derby DE6 4GZ (0332-840232).
†**J N Davey,** 12 Woodthorpe Avenue, Woodthorpe, Nottingham NG5 4FD (0602-262352).
Miss C M Davy (1980), 40 Littlemoor Crescent, Newbold, Chesterfield, Derbyshire S41 8QJ (0246-32590).
Mrs M E Dawson (1975), Dalby House, Dalby, Nr Spilsby, Lincs PE23 4PN (0790-52237).
†**Ms C Drury (1985),** "Top House", Kestral Rise, Eagle, Lincoln (0522-86545).
Miss K J Dyer (1981), 5 Blackthorn Lane, Oadby, (0533-715716).
†**Mrs S Fisher (1981),** 28 Elder Lane, Griffydam, Leics LE6 4HD (0530-222520).
E A Fox (1977), 14 Burton Close, Oadby Grange, Oadby, Leicester LE2 4SQ (0533-713291).
Miss D Frearson (1979), 20 Winterton Rise, Bestwood Park, Nottingham (0602-204997).
†**Mrs J D Gartshore (1978),** 64 Knighton Drive, Stoneygate, Leicester LE2 3HB (0533-709431).
†**Ms S C Gartshore (1985),** 64 Knighton Drive, Stoneygate, Leicester LE2 3HB (0533-709431).
***Mrs R A Gee (1979),** 2 Devonshire Close, Boughton, Northampton NN12 8RY (0604-842728).
A J Hall (1985), 44 Norman Road, Ripley, Derbyshire DE5 3GL (0773-49703).
G Harris (1984), 16 Craighill Road, Knighton, Leics LE2 3FA (0533-700332).
L Haydon (1981), Flat 5, 38 Queens Road, Leicester (0533-707022).
M Henry (1979), Ground School FTS, RAF Cranwell, Sleaford, Lincs NG34 8HB.
J D Hubbard (1952), 'Pinfold', Newton Harcourt, Leicester LE8 0FH (053759-2742).
K Janes (1965), 15 Springfield Road, Chellaston, Derby DE7 1SL (0332-700232).
R Joyner (1984), 6 North Road, West Bridgford, Nottingham NG2 7NH (0602-811259).
Miss V J Kemp, 30 Cottingham Drive, Moulton, Northants NN3 1LD.
A Littlewood (1965), 6 Dorchester Drive, Mansfield, Notts NG18 4QQ (0623-25204).
Mrs M Masson (1966), 82 Weaverthorpe Road, Woodthorpe, Nottingham NG5 4PT (0602-268470).
I Masters (1982), 104 Winchester Street Sherwood, Nottingham (0602-620606).
***F S Parker (1962),** 11 Frinton Avenue, Leicester LE5 6PN (0533-415387).
***Mrs P M Parker (1962),** 11 Frinton Avenue, Leicester LE5 6PN (0533-415387).
B Rees (1980), 12 Wharfedale Close, Allestree, Derby (0332-552428).
Mrs C A Robson (1979), 28 Greenways, Walton, Chesterfield S40 3HF (0246-74942).
B R Scott (1966), 158 Leicester Road, Oadby, Leicester LE2 4AA (0533-713116).
K Sefton (1969), 'The Barn', Bakers Lane, Thorpe Satchville, Leics LE14 2DE (0664-840589).

†**S Shelton (1985),** The Cottage, Porter's Lane, Findern, Derby DE6 6AJ (0283-703571).
†**N Smith (1973),** Crabtree Cottage, 26 Trevor Road, Hinckley, Leics LE10 1JD (0455-636486).
†**N R Smith (1974),** 45 London Road, Great Glen, Leicester LE8 0FL (053759-3427).
†**Mrs J Stokes (1980),** 10 Huntingdon Drive, The Park, Nottingham NG5 1BW (0602-418308).
***W D Swan (1978),** 4 St Crispin Road, Earls Barton, Northants NN6 0PL (0604-810122).
S C Taylor (1982), Farm Cottage, Silver Street, North Clifton, Newark, Notts (077785-410).
†**Mrs J A Walker (1978),** Mayfield, Main Road, Stickney, Boston, Lincs PE22 8EQ (0205-78-388).
†**Ms C Watson-Pegman (1985),** 159 Manthorpe Road, Grantham, Lincolnshire NG31 8DH (0476-63056).
P N White (1983), Hanby Grange, Hanby, Grantham, Lincs NG33 4MJ (047685-230).
W J White (1978), 3 Doudney Close, Stoney Stanton, Leics LE9 6TG (045527-2734).
†**Mrs L Whitehead (1980),** Whitehead School of Tennis, 9 Chestnut Avenue, Killamarsh, Nr Sheffield S31 8HN (0724-470239).
Miss A Wright (1980), 6 Tavistock Drive, Evington, Leicester LE5 5NT (0553-738102).
D A Wrigley (1983), 41 Casterton Road, Stamford, Lincs PE9 2UA (0780-64357).
†**I S Young (1985),** Launderdale, Church Brampton, Northampton NN6 8AX (0604-844029).

WEST MIDLANDS

(Hereford & Worcester, Shropshire, Staffordshire, Warwickshire, West Midlands and Gloucester)

†**Mrs P Allberry (1982),** Highfield Cottage, Somerford Road, Cirencester, Glos GL7 1TS (0285-3140).
†**Mrs C Aspinwall (1983),** Glebe Farm, Shipton Oliffe, Cheltenham, Glos GL54 4HZ (024-820239).
†**A N Beesley (1985),** 'Coaches', 4 Napleton Lane, Kempsey, Worcestershire (0905-820989).
M L Booth (1983), 11 Claverdon Drive, Little Aston Park, Sutton Coldfield, W Midlands B74 3AH (021-353 4157).
N L Brookshaw (1963), 57 Sandringham Road, Wolverhampton WV4 5SU (0902-342561).
M J Byrne (1975), 152 Lythwood Road, Bayston Hill, Shrewsbury, Shropshire SY3 0LW (0743-72-4361).
Miss V Cosier (1977), 16 Swift Close, Bromsgrove, Worcs B61 7BS (0527-35125).
Mrs K Davies (1975), West Farm, Enchmarsh, Church Stretton, Shropshire (06943-250).
M J Davis (1985), 46 Kittoe Road, Four Oaks, Sutton Coldfield, West Midlands B74 4SA (021-308 5702).
C J Dight (1974), 122 Coventry Road, Coleshill, Birmingham B46 3EH (0675-63829).
†**J W Dyas (1985),** 2 Acacia Close, Prestbury, Cheltenham, Glos GL52 3EQ (0242-575762).
C Elks (1976), 47 Three Oaks Road, Wythall, Worcs B47 6HG (0564-823390).
Mr G C J Ellis (1973), Rose Cottage, Farm Street, Fladbury, Pershore, Worcs WR10 2QD (0386-860181).
†**M J Erskine (1985),** 105 Streetbrook Road, Solihull, West Midlands B90 3PE (021-745 1554).
Miss E Evans (1971), 27 Rowantrees, Rednal, Birmingham B45 8DP (021-453 8266).
†**Anne Flower (1980),** Rothara, Leamington Road, Long Itchington, Nr Rugby, Warwicks (092-682-2747).
†**D Gadd (1985),** 5 Headingley Mount, Headingley, Leeds LDD 3EL (0532 740318).
Mrs A Gallimore (1974), 3 The Greenway, Colletts Green, Powick, Worcs WR2 4RZ (0905-830605).
Miss J Harris (1983), 5 Starbold Court, Starbold Crescent, Knowle, Solihull, W Midlands B93 9LB (05645-78134).
C Heath (1977), 26 Yew Tree Avenue, Lichfield, Staffs WS14 9UA (05432-55758).
†**Mrs A E S Howarth (1966),** Elmhurst, 130 Old Station Road, Hampton-in-Arden, Solihull, W Midlands B92 0HF (06755-2744).
L F Irving (1978), 60 New Road, Bromsgrove, Worcs B60 2JX (0527-74536).
B W Jowett (1975), 36 Dorridge Road, Dorridge, W Midlands B93 8BT (05645-4106).
S Key (1983), 8 Verstone Road, Shirley, Solihull, W Midlands B90 3LA (021-744 5908).
†**D Kilby (1985),** 7 Grangefields Road, Shrewsbury, Shropshire (0743-66994).
†**June Kup (1983),** Church View, Selattyn, Oswestry, Shropshire SY10 7DJ (0691-661498).
†**A R Laing (1985),** 32 Oakfield Park, Much Wenlock, Shropshire (0952-727218).
J Lomas (1968), 29 Lanesfield Park, Greenhill, Evesham, Worcs WR11 4NU (0386-47029).
†**J Lomasney (1968),** 1 Elm Farm Avenue, Marston Green, Birmingham B37 7AA (021-779 2479).
J Mellor (1981), 33 Berry Hill, Heonesford, Staffs WS12 5UJ.
Mrs P Marchant (1974), 169 Hatherley Road, Cheltenham, Glos GL51 6EP (0242-511471).
†**J Paish (1985),** 5 Maple Close, Shifnal, Shropshire TF11 8HA (0952-460015).
†**K Park (1977),** Hillfields, Fishpool, Kempley, Glos GL18 2BT (098-985-379).
†**R D Peach (1969),** Walsall School of Lawn Tennis, 59 Buchanan Road, Walsall, W Midlands WS4 2EW (0922-23638).
†**N F Pegg (1978),** 33A Fox Elms Road, Tuffley, Gloucester (0452-31589/25792).
M N Powell (1982), 44 Dell Road, Cotteridge, Birmingham B30 2MZ (021-458 5470).
T Pyatt (1981), 73 Longmore Road, Shirley, Solihull, W Midlands B90 3EF (021-744 5584).
A W Roberts (1976), Flat 12, 71 Reonal Mill Drive, Birmingham B45 8XZ (021-453 1186).
†**J Rothery (1985),** 9 Dovecote Close, Tettenhall, Wolverhampton WV6 8NA (0902-757422).
J B Royle (1980), 12 Baswich Lane, Stafford, Staffs ST17 0DB (0785-212597).
†**Mrs S Sadler,** Little Queenswood, Stone Drive, Colwall, Nr Malvern, Worcs WR13 6QL (0684-40047).

*†**H P Salt (1966),** 57 Duncroft Road, Yardley, Birmingham B26 2JA (021-783 2373).

†**W Skinner (1974),** 'Heathcroft', 15 Oakfield Avenue, Kingswinford, W Midlands DY6 8HJ (03841-274818).

*†**D C Slater (1976),** 69 Salford Close, Woodrow South, Redditch, Worcs B98 7UL.

Mrs C J Smallman (1980), 8 The Walmers, Aldridge, Walsall WS9 8QW (0922-57590).

K G Smith (1976), 10 Oak Avenue, Newport, Shropshire TF10 7EF (0952-811781).

W A Stapleforth (1966), 6 Overross Close, Ledbury Road, Ross-on-Wye, Herefordshire HR9 7BQ.

†**V Toplisek (1983),** 69 Princethorpe Way, Coventry CV3 2HG (0203-455748).

†**I Watson (1984),** 21 Odensil Green, Solihull, W Midlands B92 8NA (021-743 6298).

†**Mrs M E Weaver (1966),** Hillcrest, Aldsworth, Cheltenham, Glos GL54 3QX (045-14-381).

E Wood (1968), 2 Queens Park Road, Harborne, Birmingham B32 (021-427 4857).

NORTH EAST

(Cleveland, Co Durham, Northumberland, Tyne & Wear, Yorkshire and Humberside)

B K Anderson (1982), 70 Littledale, Pickering, N Yorks YO18 8PT (0751-72172).

E Angus (1969), 4 Edington Grove, Tynemouth, Tyne & Wear NE30 3QT (0632-579045).

Miss J E Attewell (1982), 50 Archery Rise, Durham DH1 4LA (0385-67298).

Miss L C Attewell (1982), 50 Archery Rise, Durham DH1 4LA (0385-67298).

†**G N Barlow (1985),** Kareith, Pump Lane, Kirklevington, Yarm, Cleveland TS15 9LQ (0642-78770).

†**S C Bowen (1980),** 43 Portal Crescent, Mirfield, W Yorks WF14 0JJ (0924-492006).

***Miss C Bowker (1967),** Flat D, 113 Trinity Street, Huddersfield, W Yorks (0484-41473).

†**P S Butcher (1984),** 3 Hallam Grange Road, Fulwood, Sheffield S10 4BH (0742-301712).

D R Butler (1982), 15 Lindisfarne Close, Morpeth, Northumberland NE6 1UG (0670-512206).

J R Butterfield (1966), 9 Cromwell Road, Scarborough, N Yorks YO11 2DR (0723-372385).

†**G Clarkson (1984),** 22 Highside Drive, Sunderland SR3 1UW (0783-285560).

I Colligon (1984), 15 Adelaide Road, Marton, Middlesbrough, Cleveland TS7 8NR (0642-314034).

G T Collinson (1970), 14 Woodlands Road, Shotley Bridge, Consett, Co Durham DH8 0DE (0207-503247).

***M Cooper (1974),** 10 Abbeydale Oval, Kirkstall, Leeds LS5 3RF (0532-587312).

R S Coulson (1979), 2 Sinclair Drive, North-Lodge, Chester-le-Street, Co Durham DH3 4BJ (0385-891007).

†**J J Crabb (1982),** Russett House, The Green, Upper Poppleton, York YO2 6DR (0904-798868).

C Dransfield (1982), 9 Emsworth Drive, Eaglescliffe, Cleveland TS16 0NR (0642-781724).

Mrs J Durban (1984), The North East Tennis Centre, Tees-side Airport, Middleton St George, Darlington, Co Durham (0325-333245).

G Durrans (1969), 64 Southfield Road, Waterloo, Huddersfield HD5 8RJ (0484-20009).

Mrs P J Durrans (1975), 64 Southfield Road, Waterloo, Huddersfield HD5 8RJ (0484-20009).

D Edwards (1984), 154 Askew Avenue, Hull, N Humberside HU4 6NS (0482-561398).

G R S Evans (1975), 18 Oakwood Avenue, Woodlands Park, North Gosforth, Newcastle-Upon-Tyne NE13 6QE (0632-363007).

A D Fletcher (1984), 12 Stirling Grove, Heslington Lane, York YO1 4HT (0904-36532).

J D G Furlong (1966), 40 Bawtry Road, Bessacarr, Doncaster, S Yorks DN4 7AA (0302-539967).

†**E J Furness (1985),** 14 Nelson Place, Burncross, Chapeltown, Sheffield S30 4WG (0742-469089).

†**Ms J A Gibson (1985),** 21 Mount Road, Stanley Wakefield, West Yorkshire WF3 4JQ (0924-822417).

J R Gledden (1983), 17 Brooklands Crescent, Fulwood, Sheffield S10 4GE (0742-305663).

J C Graham (1975), 1 Broadgate Crescent, Almondbury, Huddersfield HD5 8HT (0484-22819).

C G Hall (1984), 17 Crook Lane, Barnard Castle, Co Durham DL12 8JY (0833-38492).

R H Harland (1974), 7 Coniston, Vigo, Birtley, Chester-le-Street, Co Durham DH3 2LB (091-4103531).

†**B Harpin (1978),** 69 Sunnybank Road, Mirfield, W Yorks WF14 0NL (0924-493532).

G D Henderson (1985), 38 Newmin Way, Whickham, Tyne & Wear (091 4888954).

†**Mrs A Hill (1979),** 10 Totley Brook Road, Totley Rise, Sheffield S17 3QS (0742-352289).

†**J K Jarvis (1975),** 17 Cornmill Lane, Liversedge, W Yorks WF15 7DT (0924-402102).

***Mrs J E Kemp (1975),** Whiteley Wood Manor, Whiteley Woods, Sheffield S11 7TG (0742-303811).

†**G Kent (1969),** 'Riasgill', 22 Station Road, Grassington, Nr Skipton, N Yorks BD23 5NQ (0756-752207).

Mrs G Kitching (1974), The Grange, Great Ayton, Middlesbrough TS9 6PY (0642-722595).

B Layfield (1978), 36 Oakdene Close, Pudsey, W Yorks LS28 9LW (0532-574044).

Miss C Lievesley (1982), 33 Bruce Road, Sheffield S11 8QD (0742-686664).

M J Lugg (1976), 17 Stanford Close, Laceby, Grimsby, S Humberside DN37 7AG (0472-73678).

Miss J M Mallen (1967), 10 Maynard Road, Rotherham, S Yorks S60 3LP (0709-530113).

†**S McLoughlin (1981),** 4 Coach Road, Hove Edge, Brighouse, Yorkshire HD6 2LX (0484-712711).

***R P Metcalfe (1980),** 94 Beach Road, Tynemouth, North Shields NE30 2QP (0632-575298).

K Mewett (1970), 24 Hawthorn Gardens, Whitley Bay, Tyne & Wear NE26 3PQ (091-252 5888).

Miss J E Morton (1984), Low Meadows Farm, Lanchester, Co Durham DH7 0RE (0207-520503).

†**D J Newman (1982),** 12 Woodstock Close, Adel, Leeds LS16 8DL (0532-671979).

J M O'Kelly (1984), 49 Leylands Lane, Heaton, Bradford, W Yorks BD9 4PY (0274-46560).

†**Mrs J G Oldridge (1983),** 'Chestnuts', Elm Road, Waltham, S Humberside (0472-825146).
†**A A Price (1983),** 9 Birchitt Road, Bradway, Sheffield S17 4SN (0742-368055).
A Rattenbury (1981), 49 Main Street, Grenoside, Sheffield, S Yorks (0742-467563).
***D W Riley (1970),** 2 Shaws Park, Hexham, Northumberland NE46 3BJ (0434-603704).
T D Ross (1981), 2 Grasslees, Rickleton, Washington, Tyne & Wear NE38 9JA (091-4178253).
A Sidebottom (1972), 5 Longley Road, Almondbury, Huddersfield, HD5 8JL (0484-34044).
R C Stead (1972), Rockwood House, 14 Main Street, Embsay, Skipton, N Yorks BD23 6RE (0756-69755).
P Suddaby (1982), High Viewley Hill, West Street, Swinton, Malton, N Yorks YO17 0SP (0653-2507).
J B Thompson (1968), 10 Benfield Close, Shotley Bridge, Consett, Co Durham DH8 0RH (0207-505566).
R J Thomson (1983), 11 Cedarwood Grove, Tunstall, Sunderland, Tyne & Wear SR2 9EJ (0783-287635).
C P Trousdale (1983), Virginia Cottage, 13 First Row, Ashington, Northumberland NE63 8ND (0670-816454).
†**G B Tuffs (1979),** 18 Raylton Avenue, Marton-in-Cleveland, Middlesbrough TS7 8EF (0642-313501).
R Weedon (1982), Brookside East, Seaton Burn, Newcastle-Upon-Tyne NE13 6EY (0632-367580).
I Wilkinson (1982), 10 Middridge Lane, Shildon, Co Durham DL4 2BL (0388-773472).
***Mrs M Woodward (1968),** 22 Hollybush Green, Collingham, Nr Wetherby, Yorkshire LS22 5BG (0937-72050).
Mrs E J Wray (1982), 66 Cambridge Road, Linthorpe, Middlesbrough, Cleveland TS5 5HG (0642-819723).
***Miss A E Wright (1982),** 34 Granby Drive, Riddlesden, Keighley, W Yorks BD20 5AX (0535-603572).

NORTH WEST

(Cheshire, Cumbria, Greater Manchester, Lancashire, Merseyside and Isle of Man)

M Allan (1982), 166 Ack Lane East, Bramhall, Stockport SK7 2AA (061-439 1670).
D B Ashworth (1969), 591 Parrs Wood Road, East Didsbury, Manchester M20 0QS (061-445 4807).
†**L N Atkinson (1966),** 15 Prospect Road, Standish, Wigan, Lancs WN6 0TZ (0257-423924).
T W Baron (1972), 8 Byron Street, South Shore, Blackpool FY4 1DE (0253-405264).
P J Barton (1969), 103 Norville Road, Liverpool L14 3LX (051-228 7436).
A Boardman (1964), 'Birch Villa', 205 Droylsden Road, Brookdale Park, Newton Heath, Manchester M10 6NY (061-681 6938).
M Briscoe (1980), 41 Bellefield Avenue, Liverpool L12 1LR (051-228 0449).
A J Burgess (1976), 'Hazeldene', Top Road, Frodsham, Cheshire WA6 6SP (0928-33554).
J N Cadman (1972), 66 Hoole Road, Chester, Cheshire CH2 3NL (0244-25937).
R Carroll (1982), 6 Chatsworth Road, Eccles, Lancs M30 9DY (061-707 3621).
†**J Chadwick (1971),** 497 Devonshire Road, Blackpool FY2 0JR (0253-53356).
N A Chamberlain (1980), 72 Lostock View, Lostock Hall, Preston, Lancs PR5 5LS (0772-324173).
Mrs L A Collins (1978), 'Tanglewood', 28 Beachcroft Road, Meols, Wirral, Merseyside L47 6BE (051-632 5633).
Mrs V Cording (1975), 6 Langdale Road, Bramhall, Cheshire SK7 1DH (061-440 0265).
Mrs D M Cowley (1983), Fairfield, Ramsey, Isle of Man (0624-812247).
Mrs B Cross (1976), 10 Arnside Road, Oxton, Birkenhead, Merseyside L43 2JU (051-652 9842).
†**P Darbyshire (1976),** 82 Stockport Road, Timperley, Altrincham, Cheshire WA15 7SN (061-904 0822).
W Davies (1985), 55 Shaws Avenue, Southport, Merseyside PR8 4LD (0704 69805).
†**B Dixon (1985),** 'Ranmoor', Bonville Road, Altringham, Cheshire WA14 4QR (061-928 3844).
Mrs J A Farrington (1977), 150 Hoghton Lane, Higher Walton, Preston PR5 4EH (0772-36866).
Mrs U M Gribble (1965), 2 The Orchard, Victoria Road, Great Crosby, Liverpool L23 7XS (051-924 6498).
A Hamnett (1985), "Westlands", Portinscale, Keswick CA1 2RW, Cumbria (Keswick 72028).
G Hart (1971), 31 Welbeck Road, Bolton BL1 5LE (0204-46954).
S E Haywood (1969), 35 Lovelace Road, Liverpool L19 1QF (051-427 7150).
R Henwood (1971), 43 Larkhill Lane, Freshfield, Liverpool L37 1LU (07048-76616).
†**F A Jones (1971),** 26 Carroll Drive, Wistaston, Crewe, Cheshire CW2 8DH (0270-663926).
F Jordan (1980), 20 Catherine Road, Swinton, Manchester M27 3FX (061-793 9476).
G A P Lomax (1985), 258a Bury New Road, Whitefield, Manchester M25 6QN (061-766 2418).
†**R Lowe (1978),** 15 Mardale Crescent, Lymm, Cheshire (0925-75-4570).
J M McBrien (1968), 7 Wavertree Nook Road, Liverpool L15 7LE (051-722 0120).
Mrs C A Messenger (1971), 23 Croft Road, Stanwix, Carlisle, Cumbria CA3 9AQ (0228-36123).
R P Midgley (1983), 38 School Road, Heysham, Morecambe, Lancs LA3 2RG (0524-51768).
J R Newton (1967), Thornfield, 79 Taunton Road, Ashton-Under-Lyne, Lancs OL7 9EB (061-330 4191 pri, 061-665 1225 bus).
I H Nutter (1979), 44 Park Road, Worsley, Manchester M28 5DY (061-790 2632).
***J R Ormerod (1965),** 'The Longhouse', Hill Lane, Hurst Green, Blackburn, Lancs BB6 9QT (0254-86680).
D J G Paterson (1976), 6 Baslow Drive, Heald Green, Cheshire SK8 3HP (061-436 2667).
I A R Price (1963), 10 Prince Road, Higher Poynton, Cheshire SK12 1TW (0625-876476).
*†**S Riley (1982),** 353 Highfield Road, Blackpool, Lancs FY4 5AP (0253-63717).

F B Rowan (1983), Bootle Tennis Centre, Maguire Avenue, Bootle L20 9PQ (051-521 8099).

†**J H Schofield (1981),** Eastfield, 42 Chapman Road, Hoddlesden, Darwen, Lancs (0254-74403).

R Sladden (1984), The Vicarage, Lower Peover, Knutsford, Cheshire WA16 9PZ (056-581 2304).

I G Smith (1975), The Bungalow, Oliver Fold Farm, Engine Lane, Tyldesley, Manchester M29 8NA (0942-877507).

M J Sweetingham (1967), 13 Brookfield Cottages, Lymm, Cheshire WA13 0DH (0925-75-6364).

*__L M Thompson (1967),__ 20 The Barn, Vandyke Street, Rochdale, Lancs OL12 7QG (0706-40373).

†**G Weatherburn (1985),** 34 Thwaite Street, Barrow-in-Furness, Cumbria LA14 1AL (0229-38431).

D C Whittle (1981), 20 Nottingham Drive, Brownlow Way, Bolton BL1 3RY (0254-55101 ext 62).

Miss C M Williamson (1970), Morecambe Sports Centre, Ian Twist School of Lawn Tennis, 4 Morecambe Street, Morecambe, Lancs LA4 5HE (0524-413903).

J T T Yates (1964), 104 St Lukes Road, Blackpool, Lancs FY4 2EH (0253-42701).

SCOTLAND

S Reeve (1979), 11 Grosvenor Crescent, Edinburgh EH12 5EL (031-337 4640).

*__Mrs M Robinson (1968),__ 7 Carnegie Gardens, Aberdeen AB2 4AW (0224-33582).

WALES

†**W F G Brunsdon (1975),** 65 Heol-y-Gors, Whitchurch, Cardiff CF4 1HG (0222-628241).

P I Collier (1976), 25 Bettws y Coed Road, Cyncoed, Cardiff CF2 6PH (0222-751791).

G H Dimmock (1974), 50 Ridgeway Avenue, Newport, Gwent (0633-62800).

†**J Hicks,** North Wales School of Lawn Tennis, 23 Carlines Avenue, Ewloe, Deeside, Clwyd CH5 3RF (0244-535458).

Mrs S Hutchinson (1975), 8 Cae'r Gog Terrace, Aberystwyth, Dyfed (0970-611000).

D Jones (1964), 18 Station Terrace, Dowlais, Merthyr Tydfil, Mid-Glamorgan CF48 3PU (0685-71619).

G Jones (1971), 9 Heol yr Ysgol, Tondu, Bridgend, Mid-Glamorgan CF32 9EG (0656-720830).

*__P Lewis (1966),__ 10 St John's Crescent, Whitchurch, Cardiff CF4 7AF (0222-626869).

†**A Lightbody (1985),** 42 Fairy Grove, Killay, Swansea, West Glamorgan.

*__Captain G N McNamara (1974),__ Dennel Hill Farmhouse, Tidenham Chase, Chepstow, Gwent NP6 7JN (02912-5484).

Miss S J Mottershaw (1981), 20 Ffordd y Rhos, Trevddyn, Mold, Clwyd CH7 4NJ (0352-771252).

*†**Mrs J E Smith (1967),** Plas Emu, Pwllheli Road, Criccieth, Gwynedd LL52 (076671).

†**R J Walbyoff (1985),** 11 Waun Bant, Pontycymmer, Nr Bridgend, Mid Glamorgan, South Wales (0656 871584).

OVERSEAS

Miss E Beck (1981), 1 Dorpsstraat, Vossem-Tervuren 1981, Belgium (010-02-7678917).

J J Butler (1979), Apt 1D, 125 Ocean Parkway, Brooklyn, New York 10803, USA (010-718-438-3844).

†**P Crowe,** 7 Granville Park, Blackrock, Co Dublin, Ireland (0001-893673).

†**A Ferreira (1982),** 19 Glenelg Avenue, Pomono, Borrowdale, Harare, Zimbabwe (010-263-10-883382).

P Finn (1976), PO Box 125, Limassol, Cyprus (010-357-51-51292).

†**L Fudge,** Broicherdorf Str 67, 4044 Kaarst 1, W Germany.

G R Griffiths (1954), 69 Strand Road, Portsteward, Co Londonderry BT55 7LX (026583-3811).

P D L Harrison (1980), PO Box 42, Fourways, Transvaal, South Africa.

R P Hewitt (1981), Gloucester School, Hohne, B.F.P.O. 30 (010-49-5051-8789).

A Holmes (1983), Skidbacken 36 NB, 17245 Sundbyberg, Sweden (010-4608-292344).

Mrs C Hughes (1981), Box 24614, Nairobi, Kenya, (010-2542-891-972).

†**A Jarrett,** Al Nasr Leisureland, PO Box 2652 Dubai, United Arab Emirates.

N D Leapman (1983), Heuvelhof 7, 3078 Everberg, Belgium (010-02-759-3211).

Mrs J A Le Cesne Byrne (1982), 'Torytops', Ballinteer Road, Dundrum, Dublin 16 (0001-981859).

P R Norton (1976), Mooswaldstrasse 12, D-7801 Vorstetten, West Germany (010-49-7666-5605).

T Passby (1980), Rue de Cales, Lamanon, 13560 Senas, France (010-33-90-575028).

S Patel (1981), PO Box 30605, Lusaka, Zambia (010-260-1211549).

M Pedroletti (1984), Via R Mauri 8, 21013 Gallarate (VA), Italy (010-39-331-799193).

J Shanabrook (1984), Virgilio Sporting Club, Via Tito Lucrezio Caro 6, Naples, 80123, Italy (010-39-81-7695261).

M W Terry (1975), 25 Fifth Street, Hong Lok Yuen, Taipo, New Territories, Hong Kong (010-852-6530125).

J E Thomas (1981), Schierbroker Strasse 20A, 2875 Ganderlesee 2, West Germany (010-49-4221-50834).

†**C S Wells,** 38 Thuringer Strabe, 2870 Delmenhorst, W Germany.

*Not available for private coaching
†Associate Member of the PTCA.

RULES OF THE LAWN TENNIS ASSOCIATION

1. Name.
The Association shall be called "THE LAWN TENNIS ASSOCIATION".

2. Objects.
The Association shall be the governing body of the game of Lawn Tennis (hereinafter referred to as "the Game") in Great Britain, the Channel Islands and the Isle of Man and its objects shall be to advance and safeguard the interests of the Game and those of the Association and particularly:

(a) To employ the funds of the Association for the purposes and objects of the Association in such manner as shall be deemed to be in the best interests of the Game.
The funds or other property of the Association shall not be paid to or distributed among the Members of the Association, but shall be applied towards the furtherance of the Association's objects or for any charitable purpose.
In the event of dissolution, the funds remaining will be devoted to objects similar to those of the Association or to some charitable object.

(b) To invest any part of such funds as shall not be required immediately for the said purposes and objects, in such manner as may be considered advisable from time to time, and to charge all or any such investments to secure the repayment of any temporary advance of money made to the Association for such purposes and objects.

(c) To make, vary, alter, maintain and enforce Rules and Regulations for the control and governance of the Game in Great Britain.

(d) To uphold the following Rules and Regulations for the time being in force, namely: the Rules of Tennis, the Rules and Regulations for the International Tennis Team Championships (Davis Cup and Federation Cup).

(e) To enter and manage teams to represent Great Britain in international team competitions and to arrange and/or manage ties held in Great Britain.

(f) To make, maintain and publish Regulations relating to and for the management of Inter-County Championships, Tournaments and Club and other matches.

(g) To make, vary, alter, maintain, observe and carry into effect any agreement with The All England Lawn Tennis and Croquet Club and/or others for the joint promotion and management of "The Championships", which include the Official Lawn Tennis Championships on Grass Courts recognised by the International Tennis Federation.

(h) To control, sanction and where necessary promote television in all its aspects in regard to the Game in Great Britain and to permit Associations, Tournament Committees, Leagues, Clubs and other Organisations to arrange for the television of events taking place under their management or control, on such terms as the Association may from time to time determine.

(i) To make, vary, alter, maintain, observe and carry into effect agreements with the television authorities or others as may be required to carry out the objects set forth in clause (h) of this Rule.

(j) To take such steps as may be open to the Association to retain and/or acquire any copyright in the Game in Great Britain which the Law may provide in so far as television is concerned.

(k) To promote National Championships and competitions, and to regulate, arrange and manage all matches in connection therewith.

(l) To sanction the holding of Championships, Official Tournaments and public competitions in Great Britain, and to approve and regulate the dates and arrangements for the same.

(m) To promote the teaching of the Game and to encourage those recognised as Coaches and Teachers.

(n) To promote the training of Referees and Umpires.

(o) To decide all doubtful and disputed points in connection with the Game and the Rules and Regulations thereof.

(p) Generally to do all such acts, matters and things in connection with, or incidental to, the effective carrying out of any of the objects mentioned in the previous sub-clauses hereof.

3. Constitution.
The Association shall consist of the following affiliated organisations:

Directly Affiliated—

(a) The National Associations of Scotland and Wales.

(b) The County Associations of England (as defined in Rule 36).

(c) The Island Associations of the Channel Islands and the Isle of Man.

(d) The Lawn Tennis Associations of the Services (The Royal Navy, The Army and The Royal Air Force).

(e) The Oxford and Cambridge University Lawn Tennis Clubs.

(f) The All England Lawn Tennis and Croquet Club.
(g) The Civil Service Lawn Tennis Association.
(h) The British Schools Lawn Tennis Association.
(i) The International Lawn Tennis Club of Great Britain.
(j) The Veterans' Lawn Tennis Association of Great Britain.
(k) The British Tennis Umpires' Association.
(l) The British Women's Tennis Association.
(m) The Professional Tennis Coaches' Association.
(n) The Society of Lawn Tennis Referees.
(o) Non-Territorial Organisations representing at least 2,000 lawn tennis players or such lesser number as the Council may in individual cases decide.

Indirectly Affiliated

(p) The Clubs and other Organisations affiliated to the National, County and Island Associations shown in Rule 3(a), (b) and (c).

4. Associate Membership.
The Council may admit persons as Associate Members upon such terms and at such rates of subscription as it may from time to time think fit, provided that an Associate Member shall have no right to attend or vote at any General Meeting of the Association in that capacity. The liability of each Associate Member shall be limited to the amount of the annual subscription which he has or ought to have paid.

5. Council.
The Association's Council shall consist of a President, Deputy President, Vice-Presidents, an Honorary Treasurer or, if the Annual General Meeting shall so decide, two Joint Honorary Treasurers (hereinafter referred to as "the Honorary Treasurer(s)"), elected under Rules 16 and 18; a Deputy Honorary Treasurer, if appointed by the Council; a Secretary, appointed from time to time by the Board of Management; Councillors, elected under Rules 19 and 20; and Honorary Life Vice-Presidents and Honorary Life Councillors elected under Rules 17 and 21 but subject to the restrictions on voting rights contained in those Rules. 30 members entitled to vote shall form a quorum.

No person shall be eligible for election or re-election in any capacity except as Honorary Life Vice-President or Honorary Life Councillor at or after the Annual General Meeting in the calendar year in which (a) his 70th birthday falls; or (b) his 55th birthday falls unless he is already a member of the Council or the permission of the of Management Committee is obtained prior to the submission of the nomination. Application for such permission must reach the Secretary not later than 1st October.

No person shall represent more than one organisation or have more than one vote (except for the chairman's casting vote following an equality) upon the Council and any person accepting nomination to the Council who has any financial interest in the game must, before his election, state in writing to the Association all such interests. Failure to do so will lead to automatic disqualification from the Council membership. The Council has the right to veto such an election if, in its opinion, it is not in the best interests of the game.

6. Management.
The Council shall manage the Association and the Game in Great Britain through a Management Committee and other Committees in accordance with Rule 29.

7. Direct Affiliation.
Application for direct affiliation must be made to the Secretary, and the reception or rejection of such application shall be in the discretion of the Council, whose decision shall be final.

8. Liability for Taxation.
The rates of subscriptions, contributions and other levies payable to the Association under these Rules shall be deemed to include any taxation which may be payable thereon.

9. Financial Year and Accounts.
The financial year of the Association, in respect of which, inter alia, subscriptions and players' contributions shall be payable, shall close on the 30th day of September in each year, and a statement of the accounts for such year shall be prepared and completed by the Honorary Treasurer(s) as soon as possible thereafter.

10. Subscriptions of Directly Affiliated Organisations.
Directly affiliated organisations, excluding The All England Lawn Tennis and Croquet Club, shall pay an annual subscription due on the first day of May in each year, of an amount to be decided annually at the Annual General Meeting. In the case of National, County and Island Associations this shall be based on Membership as at the previous 30th September.

11. Players' Contributions:

(a) Each club affiliated under Rule 3(o) shall pay as part of its annual subscription to its National, County or Island Association an amount which shall include in respect of each playing member of whatever category, a "player's contribution". Of this player's contribution a proportion shall be for the benefit of the National, County or Island Association, which shall retain it when remitting the balance (if any) to and for the benefit of The Lawn Tennis Association; such remittance to be due on the 1st day of May in each year, based on membership figures at the previous 30th September or, in the case of a newly formed club or following a substantial change in membership resulting from a merging or splitting of clubs or like cause, on such basis as shall be authorised by the

Management Committee. The amount or scale of such players' contributions shall be decided annually in advance at the Annual General Meeting and the proportion for the benefit of each National, County or Island Association shall be decided by the Council.

(b) In the case of clubs in which it is not practicable to establish the number of members liable for payment, the contribution shall, subject to the approval of the Council, be calculated on the basis of 25 senior and 10 junior playing members per court or, in special cases, on such other basis as may be agreed by negotiation.

(c) For the purpose of Rules 19 and 37 a "unit" shall be the amount equivalent to the sum of the players' contributions payable by 20 senior and 10 junior members and this amount shall be used to derive the number of units attributable to each National, County or Island Association from the total gross sum of players' contributions (however composed) collected from its affiliated clubs. To the number of whole units so derived in any financial year one half unit shall be added in respect of each school affiliated for that year. The resultant total number of units shall be applicable throughout the next financial year thereafter but in the case of a newly affiliated National, County or Island Association or in the event of any change of county boundary under Rule 36 having taken place in the intervening period, appropriate adjustments shall be made by the Council for the Associations concerned.

12. Non-payment of Subscriptions.
Any affiliated organisation whose first subscription remains unpaid for one calendar month after the receipt of notice of affiliation, or whose annual subscription in any subsequent year remains unpaid by 31st August, shall cease to be eligible for grants and other advantages offered to affiliated organisations (including the right, if any, to elect representative(s) on the Council) or such of them as the Management Committee shall decide. If unpaid by 30th November such organisation shall, subject to any further period of grace that may be authorised by the Management Committee, cease to be affiliated, but without prejudice to its indebtedness. For the purposes of this Rule, "subscriptions" includes players' contributions.

13. Membership Returns.
Every National, County and Island Association shall, on application for affiliation and thereafter on or before the 15th day of January in each year, send to the Secretary a complete and certified list of the clubs and other organisations affiliated to it. Such lists shall differentiate between affiliations under Rules 38 and 39. Failure to make this return shall be deemed to be non-payment of a subscription under Rule 12.

Notice of every subsequent addition to such list (with a remittance for the additional subscription payable) and of any withdrawal therefrom shall also be sent forthwith to the Secretary by every such Association.

14. General Meetings:
(a) The Annual General Meeting of the Association shall be held during the first fifteen days of December to transact the following business: (i) to receive the Report of the Council and the Statement of Accounts for the past year duly audited, to elect the President, Deputy President, Honorary Treasurer(s) and Auditors for the ensuing year, to elect Vice-Presidents and Honorary Life Vice-Presidents and to confirm the election of Councillors by the directly affiliated organisations; (ii) to decide subscriptions, contributions and payments as required by Rules 10 and 11; and (iii) to consider motions of which due notice has been given.

(b) An Extraordinary General Meeting of the Association may be convened by the Council whenever it thinks fit, and shall be convened by the Secretary within six weeks after the receipt by him of a requisition in writing to that effect by three or more directly affiliated organisations, or 50 or more clubs affiliated to a National, County or Island Association. Every such requisition shall specify the business for which the meeting is to be convened, and no other business shall be transacted at such meeting.

(c) No business other than the formal adjournment of the meeting shall be transacted at any General Meeting unless a quorum is present, and such quorum shall consist of not less than 30 persons present and entitled to vote.

(d) Subject to the provisions of Rules 29(a) and 47 all business of a General Meeting shall be decided by a bare majority of the votes properly recorded at such meeting, but all business of an Extraordinary General Meeting being special shall be decided by a two-thirds majority of the votes properly recorded at such meeting.

(e) At a General Meeting every question or motion shall be decided by a show of hands, unless prior to such vote being taken or immediately thereafter a ballot is (a) directed by the Chairman, or (b) demanded by not less than six persons present and entitled to vote.

(f) Votes may be recorded by proxy if so directed by the Chairman or demanded by not less than six persons present and entitled to vote. Proxy votes shall be recorded by word of mouth unless a ballot has been decided upon. All proxies to be valid must be duly completed and lodged with the Secretary four clear days before the date of the General Meeting at which they are to be used.

(g) Where a decision by a bare majority only is required and there is an equality of votes, there shall be a second count, and if upon such second count there be again an equality of votes, the Chairman shall have a casting vote.

(h) A printed notice of every General Meeting, with a ticket of admission and form of proxy, shall be sent to the officers and members of the Council and Council Committees, to the secretaries of all directly affiliated organisations and to the secretaries of clubs affiliated to the National, County and Island Associations, 14 days at least prior to the date fixed for such meeting. Such notice shall specify the date, time and place of such meeting and the nature of the business to be transacted, and in case of an Annual General Meeting shall be accompanied by the Report, Statement of Accounts for the past year, and the names of persons nominated as officers and Councillors for the ensuing year. The accidental omission to give any such notice to any person entitled thereto, or the non-receipt thereof by him, shall not invalidate the proceedings at any General Meeting.

15. Voting at General Meetings

Every officer and other member of the Council or of a Council Committee shall be entitled to vote at all General Meetings.

16. Nominations and Motions.

(a) Candidates for the offices of President and Deputy President for the ensuing year may be nominated only by the Council. The current President may be nominated for re-election to that office but, otherwise, a candidate for office as President or as Deputy President must have already been nominated in accordance with these Rules for election as a member of the Council as Vice-President, Honorary Treasurer or Councillor or be an existing Vice-President not due to retire under Rule 18(d).

The President on election shall not hold office also as Vice-President, Honorary Treasurer or Councillor and if he would otherwise have occupied such other office, his election as President shall supersede this and create a vacancy in the other office. The like consideration shall not apply in the case of the Deputy President.

Candidates for the offices of Honorary Treasurer(s) and Auditors may be nominated by (a) the Council or (b) any two directly affiliated organisations.

(b) Every such nomination by directly affiliated organisations shall be in writing, and shall be sent so as to reach the Secretary on or before the 10th day of October in each year.

(c) The Council or any directly affiliated organisation or club may bring forward any motion at the Annual General Meeting provided, in the case of directly affiliated organisations and clubs, that due notice thereof is given to the Secretary on or before the 10th day of October in each year.

17. Honorary Life Vice-Presidents.

The distinction of Honorary Life Vice-President may be conferred for special services rendered in connection with the Game.

(a) The distinction shall be conferred only at a General Meeting.

(b) Candidates shall be nominated only by the Council.

(c) An Honorary Life Vice-President shall be entitled to all the rights and privileges of a member of the Council except that although entitled to attend and speak he shall not be entitled to propose or second a motion or to vote at a Council meeting unless elected as Honorary Life Vice-President prior to 1982 and he shall not be eligible for election or re-election to any office or position on the Council other than as a member of the Joint Finance Board. He may, however, attend, speak, propose or second a motion and vote at a General Meeting and he may be co-opted to a committee as an additional member.

18. Vice-Presidents.

(a) The number of Vice-Presidents shall not exceed 12.

(b) They shall be elected only at an Annual General Meeting.

(c) Candidates shall be nominated only by the Council.

(d) Not less than four Vice-Presidents shall vacate that office each year, including any who attain age 70 during the year, but those retiring shall be eligible for re-election subject to Rule 5.

(e) No person shall be eligible for the office of Vice-President who has not been a member of the Council for at least ten years.

(f) A Vice-President shall be entitled to all the rights and privileges of a member of the Council.

19. Councillors.

The representation (if any) on the Council to which directly affiliated organisations are entitled shall subject to Rule 12 be in accordance with the following scale:

(a) The National Associations of Scotland and Wales and the Island Associations of the Channel Islands the Isle of Man — These organisations shall be regarded as County Associations for the purposes of representation, except that subject to eligibility in accordance with Rule 5 the President of the Scottish L.T.A. shall be an additional representative.

(b) County Associations of England—County Associations having less than 25 units as defined in Rule 11(c) shall not be entitled to representation. Associations having not less than 25 but less than 150 units—one representative. Associations having not less than 150 but less than 400 units—two representatives. Associations having not less than 400 units—three representatives.

(c) The All England Lawn Tennis and Croquet Club and The British Schools Lawn Tennis Association — two representatives each.

(d) Each of the following organisations shall be entitled, on affiliation, to one representative: The Lawn Tennis Associations of The Royal Navy, The Army and The Royal Air Force; The Oxford University Lawn Tennis Club; The Cambridge University Lawn Tennis Club; the Civil Service Lawn Tennis Association; The International Lawn Tennis Club of Great Britain; The Veterans' Lawn Tennis Association of Great Britain; The British Tennis Umpires' Association; The British Women's Tennis Association; The Professional Tennis Coaches' Association; The Society of Lawn Tennis Referees.

20. Election of Councillors.

(a) Directly affiliated organisations entitled to representation on the Council shall elect their representatives from time to time in conformity with Rule 5 and in accordance with their own rules or in such manner as they may decide, and shall officially notify in writing the full names, addresses and dates of birth of their elected representatives, such notification to reach the Secretary on or before the 10th day of November in each year.

(b) The names of such elected representatives shall be submitted to the ensuing Annual General Meeting and their election formally confirmed, and thereupon every such representative shall be entitled to hold office subject to (e) of this Rule and to Rule 29(g) until the conclusion of the Annual General Meeting in the following year.

(c) For the purposes of such annual election, the representation to which a National, County or Island Association is entitled under Rule 19 shall be ascertained by reference to unit entitlement under Rule 11 (c) on the date of the Annual General Meeting at which the representatives are due to be elected.

(d) Any failure or omission by a directly affiliated organisation to comply with paragraph (a) of this Rule shall be dealt with in such manner as the Council may decide.

(e) Any casual vacancy may be filled or change of representative effected by the directly affiliated organisation affected thereby. Notice of such vacancy, and the name and address of the representative elected to fill such vacancy, shall be sent immediately to the Secretary who shall submit the name of the new Councillor for confirmation by the next Council meeting.

21. Honorary Life Councillors.
Anyone who, in the opinion of the Council, has rendered outstanding service to the Council and who has served as a Council member for at least 15 years may be elected by the Council to become an Honorary Life Councillor. An Honorary Life Councillor shall, on election, cease to be a representative under the provisions of Rules 19 and 20 but shall be entitled to all the rights and privileges of membership except that although entitled to attend and speak he shall not be entitled to propose or second a motion or to vote at a Council meeting unless elected as Honorary Life Councillor prior to 1982 and he shall not be eligible for election or re-election to any office or position on the Council other than as a member of the Joint Finance Board. He may, however, attend, speak, propose or second a motion and vote at a General Meeting and he may be co-opted to a committee as an additional member.

22. Retirement of Officers.
The President, Deputy President, Honorary Treasurer(s) and Auditors shall retire annually, but shall continue to hold office until the conclusion of the Annual General Meeting at which they retire, and shall be eligible for re-election subject, in the case of the President, Deputy President, and Honorary Treasurer(s), to Rules 5 and 16.
Any casual vacancy occurring in the aforesaid offices may be filled by the Council at its discretion.

23. Representation and Voting at General Meetings.
The directly affiliated organisations and clubs shown in Rule 3, whose subscriptions are not in arrears, shall each be entitled to send a representative with power of voting to all General Meetings.

24. Affiliation of Clubs and Other Organisations.
A club or other organisation shall be eligible for affiliation only to the Association of the County within the geographical area in which its headquarters or ground are situated, but a club or other organisation having headquarters in one County and its ground in another County, or having headquarters and/or grounds in two or more Counties shall, subject to the approval of the Council, elect to which of those Counties it shall become affiliated.

25. Resignation.
Any directly affiliated organisation desiring to withdraw from the Association must give notice in writing to the Secretary prior to the first day of March in any year, and in default will be liable to pay its subscription for that year.

26. Obligation of Members.
—On or before the 15th day of January in every year, each organisation directly affiliated under

Rule 3(a) - (n) shall send to the Secretary the names and addresses of its Secretary, Treasurer and Match Secretary and in the case of a National, County or Island Association shall send also the names and addresses of the Secretaries of its affliated clubs and other organisations. Every affiliated National, County and Island Association shall also send to the Secretary the name of every club and other organisation subsequently affiliated to it during the year, with the name and address of the Secretary of such club or other organisation (see Rule 13).

27. Council and Management Committee Meetings.

The Council and the Management Committee shall meet at such times and places as they may from time to time decide but a special meeting of the Council shall be convened by the Secretary within four weeks after the receipt by him of a requisition in writing to that effect by 15 or more members of the Council entitled to vote, specifying the business for which the meeting is to be convened. Additional business may be included at the discretion of the Management Committee. At least seven days prior to the date fixed for any Council meeting a notice, stating the business to be transacted, shall be sent by the Secretary to every person entitled to attend.

28. Travelling Expenses.

Every member of the Council or of a Committee attending a meeting officially convened for the purpose of transacting the business of the Association shall be entitled to be reimbursed out of the funds of the Association travelling and incidental expenses as may from time to time be approved by the Council.

29. Powers of Council and Management Committee.

— The Council shall draw up and maintain Standing Orders which inter alia shall (i) determine the composition or method of appointment of the Management Committee (which shall include the President, Deputy President, Honorary Treasurer(s) and Secretary and the voting members of which shall not exceed a total of fifteen); and (ii) define the delegation of duties to the Management Committee. Management Committee decisions shall be subject to the Council's overriding authority. The Council and the Management Committee shall have further power to establish and maintain office premises, to appoint staff and to delegate all or any of their powers to the governing bodies of the directly affiliated organisations, or to Committees or Sub-Committees formed in such manner as they may decide.

Subject to the above the Council and/or the Management Committee shall have power:

(a) To carry out the objects of the Association specified in Rule 2 excepting such of them as under these Rules or by resolution of a General Meeting, carried by a majority of at least two-thirds of the votes properly recorded at such meeting, can only be dealt with by the Association in General Meeting and to make, maintain and publish all necessary standing regulations and bye-laws in connection therewith.

(b) To appoint any two of its members to act on the committee of management of any official tournament or public competition in Great Britain.

(c) To prohibit the holding of unauthorised championships, tournaments and public competitions in Great Britain.

(d) To prohibit any act or practice by associations, clubs, committees, organisations or persons, which, in the opinion of the Council, is detrimental to the interests of the Game, and to deal with any association, club, committee, organisation or person disregarding such prohibition in such manner as it may think proper.

(e) To inflict penalties on such associations, clubs, committees, organisations and persons for any infringement of the Rules of the Game, or of the Rules and Regulations of the Association, or for conduct which, in the opinion of the Council, is detrimental to the interests of the Game.

(f) To consider and deal with all applications for direct affiliation and decide all questions as to the right to representation at General Meetings.

(g) To decide all questions of eligibility of persons nominated or elected as officers or other members of the Council, and to annul any election if through non-attendance or any other cause continuation as a member of the Council is not considered to be in the interests of the Association.

(h) To enlist by co-option for any special purpose the services of any person or persons not members of the Council.

30. Conditions Governing Players.

A player, when playing in events authorised by any association or an affiliated body, or when playing in events organised by bodies other than associations or their affiliated organisations:

(a) Shall accept the conditions of entry of the competition he has entered, including the conditions of any code of conduct adopted for that competition.

(b) Shall not enter or signify the intention to enter for more than one tournament, match or competition advertised to take place during the same period.

(c) Shall not contribute under his own name to the press, radio or television, in regard to and during the time of any tournament, match or competition, in which he is entered as or is a competitor, except with the general previous consent of the Association of the country concerned and under the direct control of the chairman of the committee or other authorised management of the event to which the contribution relates.

(d) Shall in no circumstances participate in the profit or gross receipts of a tournament, match, exhibition match or other competition.

(e) Shall not play with or against a person who is under suspension in events authorised by the International Tennis Federation or an association or affiliated body thereof.

(f) Shall not play for a declared bet or wager.

The Council and/or the Management Committee shall have full power to suspend in Great Britain any British player who fails to comply with the above conditions.

31. Non-playing Captains.
A non-playing Captain of a team shall be subject to all Rules governing players except in regard to sex or age.

32. Age Limit.

(a) In any tournament, match or competition in which there is a maximum age limit, only those who have not reached the maximum age limit on the 31st day of December preceding the date of any match or competition in which they are entered as competitors shall be eligible to compete, except that in the case of a school competition or a competition which is not due to be completed until the following year, the Council may authorise an alternative date.

(b) In any tournament, match or competition in which there is a minimum age limit, only those who have reached the minimum age limit on the 31st day of December preceding the date of any match or competition in which they are entered as competitors, shall be eligible to compete.

33. National Qualifications.

(a) The qualification of a player to represent Great Britain shall, subject to any regulations for a particular match or competition, be in accordance with Rule 39 of The International Tennis Federation, see Appendix 2. In the application of that rule the citizenship, where required, is British Citizenship in accordance with the British Nationality Act, 1981, and "Country", in connection with residence, refers to Great Britain, the Channel Islands and the Isle of Man.

(b) The qualification of a player to represent England, Scotland or Wales shall be in accordance with (a) above except that

  (i) "Country", in connection with residence, refers to England, Scotland or Wales respectively;

  (ii) The authority to decide any appeal for special treatment under paragraph (d) of I.T.F. Rule 39 shall be the Council of The Lawn Tennis Association, and

  (iii) Exercising a qualification for Great Britain does not affect a qualification to play for England, Scotland or Wales, nor vice-versa.

34. Area Qualifications.
For the purposes of this Rule, a competition, the entries for which are restricted to persons having a qualification for a County, Island or other area as provided by Rule 36, is hereinafter referred to as an "area competition".

A player being a British Citizen in accordance with the British Nationality Act, 1981 shall be qualified to represent an area in a match or to play in an area competition provided he shall not have exercised a qualification in respect of another area during the previous 12 months (six months in the case of Juniors) and:

(a) If his place of birth shall be in such area or if, in the event of a change of boundary having taken place, it shall have been in such area at the time of his birth and he shall have already exercised such birth qualification and no other; or

(b) If his place of permanent residence shall for at least one year immediately preceding the match or competition (six months in the case of Juniors) have been at a place (or places) which is in such area; or

(c) If at any time his place of permanent residence shall for a consecutive period of ten years have been at a place (or places) which is in such area; or

(d) If, being on the active list or serving in the Royal Navy, the Army or the Royal Air Force, he shall have resided at a place (or places) which is in such area for at least six months immediately preceding a match or competition or being the wife or child of a man on such active list or service she/he shall have so resided with husband or father; or

(e) If, being a woman, she elects at any time after marriage to adopt the residential qualifications of her husband or any other qualification he may be exercising for the time being, provided that before playing under any such qualification she gives notice in writing to the Secretary of The Lawn Tennis Association.

The above Clauses are subject to the following:

(i) War service or conscripted service under the orders of the government shall be held not to break any period of residential qualification.

(ii) Any player who has once played under a residential area qualification under paragraph (b) or (c) above may continue to do so until such time as he exercises any qualification in respect of another area when he shall forfeit all residential area qualifications previously exercised.

(iii) No player may represent more than one area in any one competition.

(iv) A player shall be deemed to have represented an area if he shall have been nominated to play in a match for that area and shall have accepted such nomination, and to have played in an area competition if his entry for the same shall have been accepted.

(v) Any person born abroad of British parentage shall, during the acquisition of a residential qualification for any area, be deemed to have the area birth qualification of his father.

(vi) Any person who, following a change of boundary or of the division or grouping of counties under these Rules, acquires a qualification for an area for which he was not qualified immediately prior to such change, shall subject to provision (iii) of this Rule be permitted to adopt and exercise such qualification (or, subject to the consent of the Association in writing, another qualification to which he is entitled) on the next occasion when he exercises an area qualification, notwithstanding that he may have exercised a different area qualification during the previous 12 months (six months in the case of Juniors); and in the event of his playing in one area competition while another area competition in which he has played is still in progress he shall be permitted until the end of the competition which started first to represent the one area in one competition and the other area in the other.

(vii)Residence at or in connection with an educational or training establishment does not of itself constitute a residential qualification.

35. Definition of and Eligibility for a Closed Championship.

(a) For the purpose of these Rules a Closed Championship or tournament is any tournament in which eligibility to compete is restricted by nationality, place of birth or residence, or membership of an association, club or other group not related to sex, age or standard of play.

(b) In a National Closed Championship of Great Britain a player shall be eligible to compete only if:

- (i) he has not competed in the 12 months preceding the event in a National Closed Championship of a Country other than those named in Rule 33 and
- (ii) he is qualified either under Rule 33 to represent a Country named therein or under Rule 34 to represent an area.

36. County Boundaries.

For the purposes of these Rules, the county boundaries of England shall be those which apply for the purposes of local government as defined from time to time by Act of Parliament, except as follows; for reasons of county size, communications or otherwise the Council shall authorise and define, and publish as an Appendix to these Rules, the division of any such counties and/or the grouping of any two or more of such counties or parts thereof, to operate as "County Associations" for the purposes of lawn tennis administration and area competitions. Corresponding arrangements for the regions of Scotland and the counties of Wales shall be under the control of the respective National Associations.

37. Apportionment of Grants.

The apportionment of any grant or other advantages offered by the Association to National, County or Island Associations shall be calculated on a unit basis in accordance with Rule 11(c), unless otherwise authorised by the Council.

38. Definition of a Club.

For the purpose of these Rules, a Club is:

(a) An organisation of not less than 20 persons, associated together for the purpose (either solely or inter alia) of playing lawn tennis, and managed by a committee in accordance with rules which shall be approved by the National, County or Island Association and if required, by the Council, and which shall provide:

- (i) For the holding of annual and other general meetings of the club;
- (ii) For the election by members of the club, either annually or at other stated periods, of their representatives on a committee of management provided that, where the ownership of the club is not vested in the members as a whole, such representation is not less than one-half of the committee; and
- (iii) For the election of officers and alteration of the rules of the club by members of the club in general meeting, or by the committee of management.

(b) A league or other organisation representing not less than 60 persons associated together for the sole purpose of playing Lawn Tennis in public parks and open spaces, and having rules approved by its National, County or Island Association and if required, by the Council.

39. Definition of other Affiliated Organisations.

For the purposes of these Rules, the expression "other organisation" includes (a) such educational establishments as are not affiliated as clubs; (b) tournament committees; and (c) schools. Such organisations shall not be entitled to exercise the rights conferred upon clubs by Rules 14, 16 and 23 nor shall they be liable for any players' contributions under Rule 11.

40. Definition of a Tournament Committee.

For the purposes of these rules a tournament committee is an organisation (other than an affiliated association or club) of not less than six persons associated together for the purpose of promoting and managing an official championship or tournament or public competition.

41. Open Championships and Tournaments.

For the purpose of these Rules an open tournament is any tournament at which cups, prizes or rewards are competed for by more than eight players (whether as individuals or as doubles partnerships) over a period of more than two days, with the following exceptions:

(a) Any tournament, the entries for which are restricted to full playing members of a particular club.
(b) Any tournament, the entries for which are restricted to persons having a fixed place of residence within a radius of 25 miles of the ground where the tournament is held.
(c) Any tournament promoted by an affiliated organisation, the entries for which are restricted to its own members, or to the members of its affiliated clubs, or, in the case of a National, County or Island Association, to persons having the relevant qualification.
(d) Any tournament which is not publicly advertised nor for which general or official invitations to play are issued, nor at which either gate money or its equivalent is taken.
(e) Any public competition as defined in Rule 43.

No open tournament shall be held on an affiliated ground in Great Britain, nor with the consent or assistance of an affiliated organisation, without the written sanction of the Council nor on dates other than those sanctioned. Such sanction, which shall confer the title of L.T.A. official championship or L.T.A. official tournament as the Council may decide, shall be granted only to affiliated organisations. No application for a new or revived official tournament nor for a change from the dates equivalent to those of the previous year shall be considered without reference to the directly affiliated organisation, if any, within whose area of jurisdiction such tournament is proposed to be held. Application must be made annually to the Council on a form to be obtained from the Secretary, and such form duly filled up must be returned to the Secretary on or before the first day of October (or whatever date is decided by the Council in the case of tournaments which are to be included in the I.T.F. Calendar) immediately preceding the date of the proposed tournament, accompanied by such fee as shall be fixed from time to time by the Council.

42. Association Fee at Tournaments.
Unless otherwise decided by the Council, at all official championships and tournaments in Great Britain, every competitor (other than those in junior events only) shall pay to the committee of such tournaments an Association Fee as decided by the Council and the amount of such fees shall be remitted by the committee to the Association within one calendar month after the first day of the holding of such tournament.

43. Public Competitions.
Any competition in which the matches are played over an extended period and/or at different places, shall be known as a public competition and shall require the sanction of the Council unless it comes within one of the exceptions set out in (a) to (d) of Rule 41. The Council shall decide from time to time the terms upon which such sanction shall be granted and the fees payable in connection therewith.

44. Exhibition Matches.
For the purpose of these Rules an exhibition match is any game of lawn tennis to which members of the public are admitted for a cash or other consideration, or which is broadcast on radio or television, or recorded on film or tape etc. for such purposes in the future, other than:
(a) An International Team match approved by the Association.
(b) An open tournament as defined in Rule 41 or a tournament comprised in the exceptions (a) to (e) of that rule.
(c) A public competition as defined in Rule 43.

It is not permitted to stage an exhibition match in Great Britain without the written permission of the Council (and, if required, of the International Tennis Federation).

45. Prohibition.
No tournament, match or competition shall be promoted by, or played on the courts of, an association, club, tournament committee or organisation directly or indirectly affiliated to the Association except with the consent and, if required, under the control of the Council.

46. Rules of the Game, etc.
The Rules of Tennis as adopted and amended from time to time by the International Tennis Federation and the Rules and Regulations of the Association, for the time being in force, and the decisions of the Council on all doubtful and disputed points arising in connection therewith, shall be binding on all affiliated organisations of Great Britain.

47. Alterations in Rules, etc.
No alteration of these Rules, nor of the terms of any agreement for the time being in force for the joint promotion and management of "The Championships" which include the Official Lawn Tennis Championships on grass courts referred to in Rule 2(g) shall be made except at a General Meeting, by a resolution carried by a majority of at least two-thirds of the votes properly recorded at the meeting. Any alterations so made shall take effect as and from the 1st day of January following, unless the meeting shall by the like majority otherwise decide.

48. Right of Appeal.
Any association, club or committee within the jurisdiction or under the control of any directly affiliated organisation or any person being a member of any such organisation, association, club or committee, being aggrieved by a decision or ruling of the governing body of such directly affiliated organisation, may apply to the Council for leave to appeal against such decision or ruling, and if such leave be granted, the appeal shall be heard at such place and time and in such manner as the Council shall direct. All out of pocket expenses incurred in connection with any such appeal shall be paid by such party or parties to the appeal and in such manner as the Council shall determine.

The decision of the Council shall be final and binding on all parties concerned and no party shall have the right to appeal against such decisions either to a court of law or otherwise. (See also Appendix 3).

49. Interpretation.
Except where otherwise stated, every reference in these Rules to the masculine includes the feminine gender and every reference to Great Britain includes the Channel Islands and the Isle of Man.

APPENDIX 1

GROUPING OF COUNTIES
(See L.T.A. Rule 36)

The following Counties of England are divided and/or grouped for all lawn tennis purposes as follows:

(a) Greater London—

Grouped with Essex; Boroughs of Barking, Havering, Newham, Redbridge, Waltham Forest;

Grouped with Kent: Boroughs of Bexley, Bromley, Greenwich, Lewisham;

Regarded as Middlesex: Cities of London, Westminster, Boroughs of Barnet, Brent, Camden, Ealing, Enfield, Hackney, Hammersmith, Haringey, Harrow, Hillingdon, Hounslow, Islington, Kensington and Chelsea, Richmond-upon-Thames north of the river, Tower Hamlets.

Grouped with Surrey: Boroughs of Croydon, Kingston-upon-Thames, Lambeth, Merton, Richmond-upon-Thames south of the river, Southwark, Sutton, Wandsworth.

(b) Cleveland, Durham, Northumberland, Tyne and Wear—

Tyne and Wear north of the River Tyne grouped with Northumberland; remainder of Tyne and Wear grouped with Cleveland and Durham.

(c) Humberside—

Districts of Cleethorpes, Glanford, Grimsby, Scunthorpe grouped with Lincolnshire; remainder grouped with the three Yorkshires.

(d) North, South and West Yorkshire—

Grouped together; see also (c) above.

(e) Greater Manchester, Merseyside—

The area north of the River Mersey and west of the River Tame grouped with Lancashire; remainder grouped with Cheshire.

(f) West Midlands—

The Metropolitan Districts of Dudley, Sandwell, Walsall, Wolverhampton grouped with Staffordshire; remainder grouped with Warwickshire.

(g) East Sussex, West Sussex—grouped together.

(h) Hampshire, Isle of Wight—grouped together.

APPENDIX 2

QUALIFICATION OF A PLAYER TO REPRESENT A COUNTRY
(I.T.F. Rule 39) — See L.T.A. Rule 33(a)

(a) A player shall be qualified to represent a country if he:

(i) is a citizen of that country, has a current valid passport for that country and has lived there for thirty-six consecutive months at some time; or

(ii) has been a permanent resident of that country for a period of thirty-six consecutive months immediately preceding the event. Residence in a country for educational purposes does not count towards a residential qualification.

A player who is qualified under (a) above to represent more than one country has the right to represent any of those countries but, having accepted nomination to represent one of those countries shall not thereafter be eligible to represent any other country, except as provided for in paragraph (b) below.

(b) When once a player has represented a country, he shall always be eligible to represent that country and shall represent no other subject to the following exceptions:

(i) If a player shall have represented a country and such a country is divided into two or more countries, he shall immediately be eligible to represent any one of those countries but, having done so, shall not thereafter be eligible to represent any other country.

(ii) If a player shall have represented a country and such a country shall be absorbed in whole in part by another country, he shall immediately be eligible to represent such other country but, having done so, he shall not thereafter be eligible to represent any other country.

(c) A player shall be deemed to have represented a country if he shall have been nominated and shall have accepted the nomination to play in any International Team Competition recognised by the Federation.

(d) A National Association may appeal to the Committee of Management to nominate a player who would not be eligible under the above Rules and the Committee of Management may agree the appeal if the full circumstances warrant an exception being made.

Note.—A player who represented a country under the Rules in force in 1982 or prior thereto, shall continue to be eligible to represent that country even if he is no longer qualified to do so under the amended terms of this Rule.

APPENDIX 3

PENALTIES AND APPEALS
(see L.T.A. Rule 48)

1. Infliction of Penalties.
Before arriving at any decision involving the infliction of a penalty under Rule 29 (e) the Council and/or Management Committee shall cause a notice, in writing, to be forwarded to the alleged offender stating the nature of the alleged offence and shall give the alleged offender an opportunity of being heard.

2. Procedure in Regard to Appeals (Rule 48 and Tournament Regulation 33).

(a) On receipt of an application for leave to appeal the Secretary shall refer the matter forthwith to the affiliated organisation concerned, except when such organisation is a party to the dispute, with a request that the matter be settled amicably if possible. Failing such settlement, the President shall select the Committee to which the application shall be referred, and the Secretary shall request every party affected by the application to furnish forthwith a statement of the facts relating to the complaint.

(b) The selected Committee shall consider the statements, correspond, if it so desires, with the parties concerned, and endeavour to arrange a friendly settlement of the matter.

(c) If the applicant declines to withdraw his application, the said Committee shall report to the Council and/or Management Committee whether, in its opinion, leave to appeal should be granted or refused.

(d) If leave to appeal is granted by the Council and/or Management Committee the President shall nominate as an Appeal Committee three members of the Council (naming one as Chairman), who are willing to serve, have taken no part in the preliminary enquiry, and have no personal interest in the matter or the County or area where the cause of the complaint arose, and the Appeal shall be heard by them at such place and time as they shall appoint.

(e) The Secretary shall give notice of the place and time fixed for the Appeal to the parties concerned.

(f) At the hearing, each member of the Appeal Committee shall be entitled to interrogate witnesses and one person representing each party concerned shall be permitted to conduct the case of that party and put questions to the witnesses. The Appeal Committee may direct, if it thinks proper, that a note shall be taken of the proceedings.

(g) The Appeal Committee shall decide the case on the evidence and in accordance with the Rules and Regulations of the Association, and shall report its decision to the Council and/or Management Committee which shall take such steps as it may think proper to enforce penalties and payment of expenses as shall have been adjudged by the Appeal Committee.

Note.—It is advisable that one member, at least, of each Appeal Committee should be a Magistrate, Barrister, Solicitor, or other person with experience in the holding of judicial investigations.

STANDING ORDERS FOR GENERAL MEETINGS

1. Chairman of Meeting.
The President of the Association shall take the Chair and in his absence the Deputy President. If the President and Deputy President are both absent, the meeting shall vote a Vice-President or other member of the Council to the Chair before proceeding to business.

2. Persons Eligible to Speak.
No person other than those attending a meeting with the right to vote shall be eligible to address the meeting without the consent of the Chairman.

3. Duration of Meeting.
It shall be competent for any person to move that the proceedings do terminate at a given hour, and, if the motion be seconded, it shall be put to the vote forthwith by a show of hands. Any subsequent motion to extend such time must be carried by the affirmative vote of not less than two thirds of the persons present and voting.

4. Time Limit for Speeches.
The speech of the proposer of a motion shall not exceed 15 minutes in length, and that of each subsequent speaker thereon 10 minutes, without the consent of the meeting. The consent shall be ascertained without debate and where such extension of time is allowed it shall not be for more than 5 minutes at a time.

5. Motions and Amendments.
Every motion and every amendment to a motion shall be proposed and seconded. All amendments to a motion must be submitted to the Chairman in writing and signed by the proposer. In the event of there being more than one amendment to any motion, the last amendment shall be the first voted upon, and if carried shall become a substantive motion. If an amendment is not carried, the amendment (if any) immediately preceding it shall be next voted upon, and if carried shall become a substantive motion. In the event of no amendment being carried the original motion shall be voted upon.

A motion or amendment of which due notice has been given may be proposed by any person present.

6. Conduct of Debate.
No person shall address the meeting more than once on any motion or amendment but if directed by the Chairman he or she may reply to questions or give further information. The proposer of an original motion may, however, speak for five minutes in reply. Except by leave of the Chair, the right of reply shall not extend to the proposer of an amendment which, having been carried, has become a substantive motion. After the reply, the question shall be put forthwith.

7. That the Question be now put.
It shall be competent for any person to move without debate at the close of the speech of any other person that the question be now put, and the motion, if seconded, shall, unless the Chairman rules otherwise, be put forthwith and decided by a show of hands.

8. Motion to Proceed to the Next Business.
It shall be competent for any person to move without debate at the close of the speech of any person that the meeting do proceed to the next business, and if the motion be seconded it shall be put forthwith and decided by a show of hands. When a motion is carried that the meeting do proceed to the next business, the question under discussion shall be considered as dropped. During the same debate a second motion that the meeting do proceed to the next business shall not be made within half an hour.

9. Counting of Votes.
If the recording of votes by proxy has been directed or demanded the Chairman shall first count the persons present voting for and against a motion or amendment. Proxy votes shall then be cast and when these have been checked and all the votes counted the Chairman shall announce the result to the meeting.

10. Motions Not Reached.
The motions not reached when the time arrives to close the meeting shall be adjourned.

11. Suspension of Standing Orders.
These Standing Orders may be suspended without previous notice if a motion to that effect be carried by the affirmative vote of not less than two-thirds of the persons present and voting.

12. Chairman's Decision.
The decision of the Chairman on any point shall be final, and any person disobeying the ruling of the Chair may be suspended by ordinary resolution of the meeting.

13. Alteration of Standing Orders.
No alteration to these Standing Orders shall be made except at a General Meeting by a resolution carried by a majority of at least two-thirds of the votes properly recorded at the meeting. Any alteration so made shall take effect immediately.

THE RULES OF TENNIS (APPROVED BY THE INTERNATIONAL TENNIS FEDERATION 1985)

RULES

THE SINGLES GAME

1. The Court

The Court shall be a rectangle 78 feet (23.77m.) long and 27 feet (8.23m.) wide.

It shall be divided across the middle by a net suspended from a cord or metal cable of a maximum diameter of one-third of an inch (0.8 cm.), the ends of which shall be attached to, or pass over, the tops of two posts, which shall be not more than 6 inches (15 cm.) square or 6 inches (15 cm.) in diameter. The centres of the posts shall be 3 feet (0.914 m.) outside the court on each side and the height of the posts shall be such that the top of the cord or metal cable shall be 3 feet 6 inches (1.07 m.) above the ground.

When a combined doubles (see Rule 34) and singles court with a doubles net is used for singles, the net must be supported to a height of 3 feet 6 inches (1.07 m.) by means of two posts, called "singles sticks" which shall be not more than 3 inches (7.5 cm.) square or 3 inches (7.5 cm.) in diameter. The centres of the singles sticks shall be 3 feet (0.914 m.) outside the singles court on each side.

The net shall be extended fully so that it fills completely the space between the two posts and shall be of sufficiently small mesh to prevent the ball passing through. The height of the net shall be 3 feet (0.914 m.) at the centre, where it shall be held down taut by a strap not more than 2 inches (5 cm.) wide and completely white in colour. There shall be a band covering the cord or metal cable and the top of the net for not less than 2 inches (5 cm.) nor more than 2½ inches (6.3 cm.) in depth on each side and completely white in colour. There shall be no advertisement on the net, strap, band or singles sticks. The lines bounding the ends and sides of the Court shall respectively be called the base lines and the side lines. On each side of the net, at a distance of 21 feet (6.40 m.) from it and parallel with it, shall be drawn the service lines. The space on each side of the net between the service line and the side lines shall be divided into two equal parts called the service courts by the centre service line, which must be 2 inches (5 cm.) in width, drawn half-way between, and parallel with, the side line. Each base line shall be bisected by an imaginary continuation of the centre service line to a line 4 inches (10 cm.) in length and 2 inches (5 cm.) in width called the "centre mark" drawn inside the Court, at right angles to and in contact with such base lines. All other lines shall be not less than 1 inch (2.5 cm.) nor more than 2 inches (5 cm.), in width, except the base line, which may be 4 inches (10 cm.) in width, and all measurements shall be made to the outside of the lines. All lines shall be of uniform colour. If advertising or any other material is placed at the back of the court, it may not contain white, or yellow, or any light colour.

If advertisements are placed on the chairs of the linesmen sitting at the back of the court, they may not contain white or yellow.

Note.—In the case of the International Tennis Championship (Davis Cup) or other Official Championships of the International Federation, there shall be a space behind each base line of not less than 21 feet (6.4 m.), and at the sides of not less than 12 feet (3.66 m.).

2. Permanent Fixtures

The permanent fixtures of the Court shall include not only the net, posts, singles sticks, cord or metal cable, strap and band, but also, where there are any such, the back and side stops, the stands, fixed or movable seats and chairs around the Court, and their occupants, all other fixtures around and above the Court, and the Umpire, Net-cord Judge, Footfault Judge, Linesmen and Ball Boys when in their respective places.

Note.—For the purpose of this Rule, the word "Umpire" comprehends the Umpire, the persons entitled to a seat on the Court, and all those persons designated to assist the Umpire in the conduct of a match.

3. The Ball

The ball shall have a uniform outer surface and shall be white or yellow in colour. If there are any seams they shall be stitchless. The ball shall be more than two and a half inches (6.35 cm.) and less than two and five eighths inches (6.67 cm.) in diameter, and more than two ounces (56.7 grams) and less than two and one sixteenth ounces (58.5 grams) in weight. The ball shall have a bound of more than 53 inches (135 cm.) and less than 58 inches (147 cm.) when dropped 100 inches (254 cm.) upon a concrete base. The ball shall have a forward deformation of more than .220 of an inch (.56 cm.) and less than .290 of an inch (.74 cm.) and a return deformation of more than .350 of an inch (.89 cm.) and less than .425 of an inch (1.08 cm.) at 18 lb. (8.165 kg.) load. The two deformation figures shall be the averages of three individual readings along three axes of the ball and no two individual readings shall differ by more than .030 of an inch (.08 cm.) in each case.

All tests for bound, size and deformation shall be made in accordance with the Regulations in the Appendix hereto.

4. The Racket

Rackets failing to comply with the following specifications are not approved for play under the Rules of Tennis:

(a) The hitting surface of the racket shall be flat and consist of a pattern of crossed strings connected to a frame and alternately interlaced or bonded where they cross; and the stringing pattern shall be generally uniform, and in particular not less dense in the centre than in any other area.

The strings shall be free of attached objects and protrusions other than those utilised solely and specifically to limit or prevent wear and tear or vibration, and which are reasonable in size and placement for such purposes.

(b) The frame of the racket shall not exceed 32 inches (81.28cm.) in overall length, including the handle and 12½ inches (31.75cm.) in overall width. The strung surface shall not exceed 15½ inches (39.37cm.) in overall length, and 11½ inches (29.21cm.) in overall width.

(c) The frame, including the handle, shall be free of attached objects and devices other than those utilised solely and specifically to limit or prevent wear or vibration, or to distribute weight. Any objects and devices must be reasonable in size and placement for such purposes.

(d) The frame, including the handle, and the strings, shall be free of any device which makes it possible to change materially the shape of the racket, or to change the weight distribution, during the playing of a point.

The International Tennis Federation shall rule on the question of whether any racket or prototype complies with the above specifications or is otherwise approved, or not approved, for play. Such ruling may be undertaken on its own initiative, or upon application by any party with a bona fide interest therein, including any player, equipment manufacturer or National Association or members thereof. Such rulings and applications shall be made in accordance with the applicable Review and Hearing Procedures of the International Tennis Federation, copies of which may be obtained from the office of the Secretary.

Case 1. Can there be more than one set of of strings on the hitting surface of a racket?

Decision. No. The rule clearly mentions a pattern, and not patterns, of crossed strings.

Case 2. Is the stringing pattern of a racket considered to be generally uniform and flat if the strings are of a different gauge?

Decision. No.

Case 3. Is the stringing pattern of a racket considered to be generally uniform and flat if the strings are on more than one plane?

Decision. No.

5. Server & Receiver

The players shall stand on opposite sides of the net; the player who first delivers the ball shall be called the Server, and the other the Receiver.

Case 1. Does a player, attempting a stroke, lose the point if he crosses an imaginary line in the extension of the net,

(a) before striking the ball,

(b) after striking the ball?

Decision. He does not lose the point in either case by crossing the imaginary line and provided he does not enter the lines bounding his opponent's Court (Rule 20(e)). In regard to hindrance, his opponent may ask for the decision of the Umpire under Rules 21 and 25.

Case 2. The Server claims that the Receiver must stand within the lines bounding his Court. Is this necessary?

Decision. No. The Receiver may stand wherever he pleases on his own side of the net.

6. Choice of Ends & Service

The choice of ends and the right to be Server or Receiver in the first game shall be decided by toss. The player winning the toss may choose or require his opponent to choose:

(a) The right to be Server or Receiver, in which case the other player shall choose the end; or

(b) The end, in which case the other player shall choose the right to be Server or Receiver.

7. The Service

The service shall be delivered in the following manner. Immediately before commencing to serve, the Server shall stand with both feet at rest behind (i.e. further from the net than) the base line, and within the imaginary continuations of the centre mark and side line. The Server shall then project the ball by hand into the air in any direction and before it hits the ground strike it with his racket, and the delivery shall be deemed to have been completed at the moment of the impact of the racket and the ball. A player with the use of only one arm may utilize his racket for the projection.

Case 1. May the server in a singles game take his stand behind the portion of the base line between the side lines of the Singles Court and the Doubles Court?

Decision. No.

Case 2. If a player, when serving, throws up two or more balls instead of one, does he lose that service?

Decision. No. A let should be called, but if the Umpire regards the action as deliberate he may take action under Rule 21.

8. Foot Fault

(a) The Server shall throughout the delivery of the Service:

  (i) Not change his position by walking or running. The Server shall not by slight movements of the feet which do not materially affect the location originally taken up by him, be deemed "to change his position by walking or running".

  (ii) Not touch, with either foot, any area other than that behind the base line within the imaginary extension of the centre mark and side lines.

(b) The word "foot" means the extremity of the leg below the ankle.

9. Delivery of Service

(a) In delivering the service, the Server shall stand alternately behind the right and left Courts beginning from the right in every game. If service from a wrong half of the Court occurs and is undetected, all play resulting from such wrong service or services shall stand, but the inaccuracy of station shall be corrected immediately it is discovered.

(b) The ball served shall pass over the net and hit the ground within the Service Court which is diagonally opposite, or upon any line bounding such Court, before the Receiver returns it.

10. Service Fault

The Service is a fault:

(a) If the Server commits any breach of Rules 7, 8 or 9;

(b) If he misses the ball in attempting to strike it;

(c) If the ball served touches a permanent fixture (other than the net, strap or band) before it hits the ground.

Case 1. After throwing a ball up preparatory to serving, the Server decides not to strike at it and catches it instead. Is it a fault?

Decision. No.

Case 2. In serving in a singles game played on a Doubles Court with doubles posts and singles sticks, the ball hits a singles stick and then hits the ground within the line of the correct Service Court. Is this a fault or a let?

Decision. In serving it is a fault, because the singles stick, the doubles post, and that portion of the net or band between them are permanent fixtures. (Rules 2 and 10, and note to Rule 24).

11. Second Service

After a fault (if it is the first fault) the Server shall serve again from behind the same half of the Court from which he served that fault, unless the service was from the wrong half, when, in accordance with Rule 9, the Server shall be entitled to one service only from behind the other half.

Case 1. A player serves from a wrong Court. He loses the point and then claims it was a fault because of his wrong station.

Decision. The point stands as played and the next service should be from the correct station according to the score.

Case 2. The point score being 15 all, the Server, by mistake, serves from the left-hand Court. He wins the point. He then serves again from the right-hand Court, delivering a fault. This mistake in station is then discovered. Is he entitled to the previous point? From which Court should he next serve?

Decision. The previous point stands. The next service should be from the left-hand Court, the score being 30/15, and the Server has served one fault.

12. When to Serve
The Server shall not serve until the Receiver is ready. If the latter attempts to return the service, he shall be deemed ready. If, however, the Receiver signifies that he is not ready, he may not claim a fault because the ball does not hit the ground within the limits fixed for the service.

13. The Let
In all cases where a let has to be called under the rules, or to provide for an interruption to play, it shall have the following interpretations:-

(a) When called solely in respect of a service that one service only shall be replayed.
(b) When called under any other circumstance, the point shall be replayed.

Case 1. A service is interrupted by some cause outside those defined in Rule 14. Should the service only be replayed?

Decision. No, the whole point must be replayed.

Case 2. If a ball in play becomes broken, should a let be called?

Decision. Yes.

14. The "Let" in Service
The service is a let:

(a) If the ball served touches the net, strap or band, and is otherwise good, or, after touching the net, strap or band, touches the Receiver or anything which he wears or carries before hitting the ground.
(b) If a service or a fault is delivered when the Receiver is not ready (see Rule 12).

In case of a let, that particular service shall not count, and the Server shall serve again, but a service let does not annul a previous fault.

15. Order of Service
At the end of the first game the Receiver shall become Server, and the Server Receiver; and so on alternately in all the subsequent games of a match. If a player serves out of turn, the player who ought to have served shall serve as soon as the mistake is discovered, but all points scored before such discovery shall be reckoned. If a game shall have been completed before such discovery, the order of service remains as altered. A fault served before such discovery shall not be reckoned.

16. When Players Change Ends
The players shall change ends at the end of the first, third and every subsequent alternate game of each set, and at the end of each set unless the total number of games in such set is even, in which case the change is not made until the end of the first game of the next set. If a mistake is made and the correct sequence is not followed the players must take up their correct station as soon as the discovery is made and follow their original sequence.

17. The Ball in Play
A ball is in play from the moment at which it is delivered in service. Unless a fault or a let is called it remains in play until the point is decided.

Case 1. A player fails to make a good return. No call is made and the ball remains in play. May his opponent later claim thé point after the rally has ended?

Decision. No. The point may not be claimed if the players continue to play after the error has been made, provided the opponent was not hindered.

18. Server Wins Point
The Server wins the point:

(a) If the ball served, not being a let under Rule 14, touches the Receiver or anything which he wears or carries, before it hits the ground;
(b) If the Receiver otherwise loses the point as provided by Rule 20.

19. Receiver Wins Point
The Receiver wins the point:

(a) If the Server serves two consecutive faults;
(b) If the Server otherwise loses the point as provided by Rule 20.

20. Player Loses Point
A player loses the point if:

(a) He fails, before the ball in play has hit the ground twice consecutively, to return it directly over the net (except as provided in Rule 24 (a) or (c)); or
(b) He returns the ball in play so that it hits the ground, a permanent fixture, or other object, outside any of the lines which bound his opponent's Court (except as provided in Rule 24(a) and (c)); or
(c) He volleys the ball and fails to make a good return even when standing outside the Court; or
(d) In playing the ball he deliberately carries or catches it on his racket or deliberately touches it with his racket more than once; or
(e) He or his racket (in his hand or otherwise) or anything which he wears or carries touches the net, posts, singles sticks, cord or metal cable, strap or band, or the ground within his opponent's Court at any time while the ball is in play; or
(f) He volleys the ball before it has passed the net; or
(g) The ball in play touches him or anything that he wears or carries, except his racket in his hand or hands; or
(h) He throws his racket at and hits the ball; or
(i) He deliberately and materially changes the shape of his racket during the playing of the point.

Case 1. In delivering a first service which falls outside the proper Court, the Server's racket slips out of his hand and flies into the net. Does he lose the point?

Decision. If his racket touches the net whilst the ball is in play, the Server loses the point (Rule 20 (e)).

Case 2. In serving, the racket flies from the

Server's hand and touches the net after the ball has touched the ground outside the proper court. Is this a fault or does the player lose the point?

Decision. This is a fault because the ball was out of play when the racket touched the net.

Case 3. A and B are playing against C and D. A is serving to D, C touches the net before the ball touches the ground. A fault is then called because the service falls outside the Service Court. Do C and D lose the point?

Decision. The call "fault" is an erroneous one. C and D had already lost the point before "fault" could be called, because C touched the net whilst the ball was in play (Rule 20 (e)).

Case 4. May a player jump over the net into his opponent's Court while the ball is in play and not suffer penalty?

Decision. No. He loses the point (Rule 20 (e)).

Case 5. A cuts the ball just over the net, and it returns to A's side. B, unable to reach the ball, throws his racket and hits the ball. Both racket and ball fall over the net on A's Court. A returns the ball outside of B's Court. Does B win or lose the point?

Decision. B loses the point (Rule 20 (e) and (h)).

Case 6. A player standing outside the service Court is struck by a service ball before it has touched the ground. Does he win or lose the point?

Decision. The player struck loses the point (Rule 20 (g)), except as provided under Rule 14 (a).

Case 7. A player standing outside the Court volleys the ball or catches it in his hand and claims the point because the ball was certainly going out of Court.

Decision. In no circumstances can he claim the point:

(i) If he catches the ball he loses the point under Rule 20 (g).

(ii) If he volleys it and makes a bad return he loses the point under Rule 20 (c).

(iii) If he volleys it and makes a good return, the rally continues.

21. Player Hinders Opponent

If a player commits any act which hinders his opponent in making a stroke, then, if this is deliberate, he shall lose the point or if involuntary, the point shall be replayed.

Case 1. Is a player liable to a penalty if in making a stroke he touches his opponent?

Decision. No, unless the Umpire deems it necessary to take action under Rule 21.

Case 2. When a ball bounds back over the net, the player concerned may reach over the net in order to play the ball. What is the ruling if the player is hindered from doing this by the opponent?

Decision. In accordance with Rule 21, the Umpire may either award the point to the player hindered, or order the point to be replayed. (See also Rule 25.).

Case 3. Does an involuntary double hit constitute an act which hinders an opponent within Rule 21?

Decision. No.

22. Ball Falls on Line

A ball falling on a line is regarded as falling in the Court bounded by that line.

23. Ball Touches Permanent Fixture

If the ball in play touches a permanent fixture (other than the net, posts, singles sticks, cord or metal cable, strap or band) after it has hit the ground, the player who struck it wins the point; if before it hits the ground, his opponent wins the point.

Case 1. A return hits the Umpire or his chair or stand. The player claims that the ball was going into Court.

Decision. He loses the point.

24. A Good Return

It is a good return:

(a) If the ball touches the net, posts, singles sticks, cord or metal cable, strap or band, provided that it passes over any of them and hits the ground within the Court; or

(b) If the ball, served or returned, hits the ground within the proper Court and rebounds or is blown back over the net, and the player whose turn it is to strike reaches over the net and plays the ball, provided that neither he nor any part of his clothes or racket touches the net, posts, singles sticks, cord or metal cable, strap or band or the ground within his opponent's Court, and that the stroke be otherwise good; or

(c) If the ball is returned outside the posts, or singles sticks, either above or below the level of the top of the net, even though it touches the post or singles sticks, provided that it hits the ground within the proper Court; or

(d) If a player's racket passes over the net after he has returned the ball, provided the ball passes the net before being played and is properly returned; or

(e) If a player succeeds in returning the ball, served or in play, which strikes a ball lying in the Court.

Note to Rule 24.—In a singles match, if, for the sake of convenience, a doubles Court is equipped with singles sticks for the purpose of a singles game, then the doubles posts and those portions of the net, cord or metal cable and the band outside such singles sticks shall at all times be permanent fixtures, and are not regarded as posts or parts of the net of a singles game.

A return that passes under the net cord between the singles stick and adjacent doubles post without touching either net cord, net or doubles post and falls within the area of play, is a good return.

Case 1. A ball going out of Court hits a net post or singles stick and falls within the lines of the opponent's Court. Is the stroke good?

Decision. If a service; no, under Rule 10 (c). If other than a service: yes, under Rule 24 (a).

Case 2. Is it a good return if a player returns the ball holding his racket in both hands?

Decision. Yes.

Case 3. The service, or ball in play, strikes a ball lying in the Court. Is the point won or lost thereby?

Decision. No. Play must continue. If it is not clear to the Umpire that the right ball is returned a let should be called.

Case 4. May a player use more than one racket at any time during play?

Decision. No; the whole implication of the Rules is singular.

Case 5. May a player request that a ball or balls lying in his opponent's Court be removed?

Decision. Yes, but not while a ball is in play.

25. Hindrance of a Player

In case a player is hindered in making a stroke by anything not within his control, except a permanent fixture of the Court, or except as provided for in Rule 21, a let shall be called.

Case 1. A spectator gets into the way of a player, who fails to return the ball. May the player then claim a let?

Decision. Yes, if in the Umpire's opinion he was obstructed by circumstances beyond his control, but not if due to permanent fixtures of the Court or the arrangements of the ground.

Case 2. A player is interfered with as in Case No. 1, and the Umpire calls a let. The Server had previously served a fault. Has he the right to two services?

Decision. Yes; as the ball is in play, the point, not merely the stroke, must be replayed as the Rule provides.

Case 3. May a player claim a let under Rule 25 because he thought his opponent was being hindered, and consequently did not expect the ball to be returned?

Decision. No.

Case 4. Is a stroke good when a ball in play hits another ball in the air?

Decision. A let should be called unless the other ball is in the air by the act of one of the players, in which case the Umpire will decide under Rule 21.

Case 5. If an Umpire or other judge erroneously calls "fault" or "out", and then corrects himself, which of the calls shall prevail?

Decision. A let must be called unless, in the opinion of the Umpire, neither player is hindered in his game, in which case the corrected call shall prevail.

Case 6. If the first ball served—a fault—rebounds, interfering with the Receiver at the time of the second service, may the Receiver claim a let?

Decision. Yes, But if he had an opportunity to remove the ball from the Court and negligently failed to do so, he may not claim a let.

Case 7. Is it a good stroke if the ball touches a stationary or moving object in the Court?

Decision. It is a good stroke unless the stationary object came into Court after the ball was put into play in which case a let must be called. If the ball in play strikes an object moving along or above the surface of the Court a let must be called.

Case 8. What is the ruling if the first service is a fault, the second service correct, and it becomes necessary to call a let either under the provision of Rule 25 or if the Umpire is unable to decide the point?

Decision. The fault shall be annulled and the whole point replayed.

26. Score in a Game

If a player wins his first point, the score is called 15 for that player; on winning his second point, the score is called 30 for that player; on winning his third point, the score is called 40 for that player, and the fourth point won by a player is scored game for that player except as below:

If both players have won three points, the score is called deuce; and the next point won by a player is scored advantage for that player. If the same player wins the next point, he wins the game; if the other player wins the next point the score is again called deuce; and so on, until a player wins the two points immediately following the score at deuce, when the game is scored for that player.

27. Score in a Set

(a) A player (or players) who first wins six games wins a set; except that he must win by a margin of two games over his opponent and where necessary a set shall be extended until this margin be achieved.

(b) The tie-break system of scoring may be adopted as an alternative to the advantage set system in paragraph (a) of this Rule provided the decision is announced in advance of the match.
In this case, the following Rules shall be effective:
The tie-break shall operate when the score reaches six games all in any set except in the third or fifth set of a three set or five set match respectively when an ordinary advantage set shall be played, unless otherwise decided and announced in advance of the match.

The following system shall be used in a tie-break game.

Singles

(i) A player who first wins seven points shall win the game and the set provided he leads by a margin of two points. If the score reaches six points all the game shall be extended until this margin has been achieved. Numerical scoring shall be used throughout the tie-break game.

(ii) The player whose turn it is to serve shall be the server for the first point. His opponent shall be the server for the second and third points and thereafter each player shall serve alternately for two consecutive points until the winner of the game and set has been decided.

(iii) From the first point, each service shall be delivered alternately from the right and left courts, beginning from the right court. If service from a wrong half of the court occurs and is undetected, all play resulting from such wrong service or services shall stand, but the inaccuracy of station shall be corrected immediately it is discovered.

(iv) Players shall change ends after every six points and at the conclusion of the tie-break game.

(v) The tie-break game shall count as one game for the ball change, except that, if the balls are due to be changed at the beginning of the tie-break, the change shall be delayed until the second game of the following set.

Doubles

In doubles the procedure for singles shall apply. The player whose turn it is to serve shall be the server for the first point. Thereafter each player shall serve in rotation for two points, in the same order as previously in that set, until the winners of the game and set have been decided.

Rotation of Service

The player (or pair in the case of doubles) who served first in the tie-break game shall receive service in the first game of the following set.

Case 1. At six all the tie-break is played, although it has been decided and announced in advance of the match that an advantage set will be played. Are the points already played counted?

Decision. If the error is discovered before the ball is put in play for the second point, the first point shall count but the error shall be corrected immediately. If the error is discovered after the ball is put in play for the second point the game shall continue as a tie-break game.

Case 2. At six all, an advantage game is played, although it has been decided and announced in advance of the match that a tie-break will be played. Are the points already played counted?

Decision. If the error is discovered before the ball is put in play for the second point, the first point shall be counted but the error shall be corrected immediately. If the error is discovered after the ball is put in play for the second point an advantage set shall be continued. If the score thereafter reaches eight games all or a higher even number, a tie-break shall be played.

Case 3. If during the tie-break in a doubles game a partner receives out of turn, shall the order of receiving remain as altered until the end of the game?

Decision. If only one point has been played, the order of receiving shall be corrected immediately, and the point already played shall be counted. If the error is discovered after the ball is put into play for the second point, the order of receiving shall remain as altered.

Case 4. If during a tie-break in a singles or doubles game, a player serves out of turn, shall the order of service remain as altered until the end of the game?

Decision. If only one point has been played, the order of service shall be corrected immediately and the point already played shall be counted. If the error is discovered after the ball is put in play for the second point, the order of service shall remain as altered.

28. Maximum Number of Sets

The maximum number of sets in a match shall be 5, or, where women take part, 3.

29. Role of Court Officials

In matches where an Umpire is appointed, his decision shall be final; but where a Referee is appointed, an appeal shall lie to him from the decision of an Umpire on a question of law, and in all such cases the decision of the Referee shall be final.

In matches where assistants to the Umpire are appointed (Linesmen, Netcord Judges, Foot-fault Judges) their decisions shall be final on questions of fact except that if in the opinion of an Umpire a clear mistake has been made he shall have the right to change the decision of an assistant or order a let to be played. When such an assistant is unable to give a decision he shall indicate this immediately to the Umpire who shall give a decision. When an Umpire is unable to give a decision on a question of fact he shall order a let to be played.

In Davis Cup matches or other team competitions where a Referee is on Court, any decision can be changed by the Referee, who may also instruct an Umpire to order a let to be played.

The Referee, in his discretion, may at any time postpone a match on account of darkness or the condition of the ground or the weather. In any case of postponement the previous score and previous occupancy of Courts shall hold good, unless the Referee and the players unanimously agree otherwise.

Case 1. The Umpire orders a let, but a player claims the point should not be replayed. May the Referee be requested to give a decision?

Decision. Yes. A question of tennis law, that is an issue relating to the application of specific facts, shall first be determined by the Umpire. However, if the Umpire is uncertain or if a player appeals from his determination, then the Referee shall be requested to give a decision, and his decision is final.

Case 2. A ball is called out, but a player claims that the ball was good. May the Referee give a ruling?

Decision. No. This is a question of fact, that is an issue relating to what actually occurred during a specific incident, and the decision of the on-court officials is therefore final.

Case 3. May an Umpire overrule a Linesman at the end of a rally, if in his opinion, a clear mistake has been made during the course of a rally?

Decision. No, unless in his opinion the opponent was hindered. Otherwise an Umpire may only overrule a Linesman if he does so immediately after the mistake has been made.

Case 4. A Linesman calls a ball out. The Umpire was unable to see clearly, although he thought the ball was in. May he overrule the Linesman?

Decision. No. An Umpire may only overrule if he considers that a call was incorrect beyond all reasonable doubt. He may only overrule a ball determined good by a Linesman if he has been able to see a space between the ball and the line; and he may only overrule a ball determined out, or a fault, by a Linesman if he has seen the ball hit the line, or fall inside the line.

Case 5. May a Linesman change his call after the Umpire has given the score?

Decision. Yes. If a Linesman realises he has made an error, he may make a correction provided he does so immediately.

Case 6. A player claims his return shot was good after a Linesman called "out". May the Umpire overrule the Linesman?

Decision. No. An Umpire may never overrule as a result of a protest or an appeal by a player.

30. Continuous Play & Rest Periods

Play shall be continuous from the first service until the match is concluded, in accordance with the following provisions:

(a) If the first service is a fault, the second service must be struck by the Server without delay.
The Receiver must play to the reasonable pace of the Server and must be ready to receive when the Server is ready to serve.
When changing ends a maximum of one minute thirty seconds shall elapse from the moment the ball goes out of play at the end of the game to the time the ball is struck for the first point of the next game.
The Umpire shall use his discretion when there is interference which makes it impossible for the Server to serve within that time.
The organisers of international circuits and team events recognised by the ITF may determine the time allowed between points, which shall not at any time exceed 30 seconds.

(b) Play shall never be suspended, delayed or interfered with for the purpose of enabling a player to recover his strength, breath, or physical condition. However, in the case of accidental injury, the Umpire may allow a one-time three minute suspension for that injury.
The organisers of international circuits and team events recognised by the ITF may extend the one-time suspension period from three minutes to five minutes.

(c) If, through circumstances outside the control of the player, his clothing, footwear or equipment (excluding racket) becomes out of adjustment in such a way that it is impossible or undesirable for him to play on, the Umpire may suspend play while the maladjustment is rectified.

(d) The Umpire may suspend or delay play at any time as may be necessary and appropriate.

(e) After the third set, or when women take part the second set, either player is entitled to a rest, which shall not exceed 10 minutes, or in countries situated between latitude 15 degrees north and latitude 15 degrees south, 45 minutes and furthermore, when necessitated by circumstances not within the control of the players, the Umpire may suspend play for such a period as he may consider necessary. If play is suspended and is not resumed until a later day the rest may be taken only after the third set (or when women take part the second set) of play on such a later day, completion of an unfinished set being counted as one set.
If play is suspended and is not resumed until 10 minutes have elapsed in the same day the rest may be taken only after three consecutive sets have been played without interruption (or when women take part two sets), completion of an unfinished set being counted as one set.
Any nation and/or committee organising a tournament, match or competition, other than the International Tennis Championships *Davis Cup* and Federation Cup), is at liberty to modify this provision or omit it from its regulations provided this is announced before the event commences.

(f) A tournament committee has the discretion to decide the time allowed for a warm-up period prior to a match but this may not exceed five minutes and must be announced before the event commences.

(g) When approved point penalty and non-accumulative point penalty systems are in operation, the Umpire shall make his decisions within the terms of those systems.

(h) Upon violation of the principle that play shall be continuous the Umpire may, after giving due warning, disqualify the offender.

31. Coaching

During the playing of a match in a team competition, a player may receive coaching from a captain who is sitting on the court only when he changes ends at the end of a game, but not when he changes ends during a tie-break game.
A player may not receive coaching during the playing of any other match.
The provisions of this Rule must be strictly construed. After due warning an offending player may be disqualified. When an approved point penalty system is in operation, the Umpire shall impose penalties according to that system.

Case 1. Should a warning be given, or the player be disqualified, if the coaching is given by signals in an unobtrusive manner?

Decision. The Umpire must take action as soon as he becomes aware that coaching is being given verbally or by signals. If the Umpire is unaware that coaching is being given a player may draw his attention to the fact that advice is being given.

Case 2. Can a player receive coaching during the ten minute rest in a five set match, or when play is interrupted and he leaves the court?

Decision. Yes. In these circumstances, when the player is not on the court, there is no restriction on coaching.

Note.—The word "coaching" includes any advice or instruction.

32. Changing Balls

In cases where balls are changed after a specified number of games, if the balls are not changed in the correct sequence the mistake shall be corrected when the player, or pair in the case of doubles, who should have served with the new balls is next due to serve. Thereafter the balls shall be changed so that the number of games between changes shall be that originally agreed.

THE DOUBLES GAME

33. The Doubles Game

The above Rules shall apply to the Doubles Game except as below.

34. The Doubles Court

For the Doubles Game, the Court shall be 36 feet (10.97 m.) in width, i.e. 4½ feet (1.37 m.) wider on each side than the Court for the Singles Game, and those portions of the singles side-lines which lie between the two service-lines shall be called the service side-lines. In other respects, the Court shall be similar to that described in Rule 1, but the portions of the singles side-lines between the base-line and service-line on each side of the net may be omitted if desired.

35 Order of Service in Doubles

The order of serving shall be decided at the beginning of each set as follows:

The pair who have to serve in the first game of each set shall decide which partner shall do so and the opposing pair shall decide similarly for the second game. The partner of the player who served in the first game shall serve in the third; the partner of the player who served in the second game shall serve in the fourth, and so on in the same order in all the subsequent games of a set.

Case 1. In doubles, one player does not appear in time to play, and his partner claims to be allowed to play single-handed against the opposing players. May he do so?

Decision. No.

36. Order of Receiving in Doubles

The order of receiving the service shall be decided at the beginning of each set as follows:

The pair who have to receive the service in the first game shall decide which partner shall receive the first service, and that partner shall continue to receive the first service in every odd game throughout that set. The opposing pair shall likewise decide which partner shall receive the first service in the second game and that partner shall continue to receive the first service in every even game throughout that set. Partners shall receive the service alternately throughout each game.

Case 1. Is it allowable in doubles for the Server's partner or the Receiver's partner to stand in a position that obstructs the view of the Receiver?

Decision. Yes. The Server's partner may take any position on his side of the net in or out of the Court that he wishes.

37. Service Out of Turn in Doubles

If a partner serves out of his turn, the partner who ought to have served shall serve as soon as the mistake is discovered, but all points scored, and any faults served before such discovery, shall be reckoned. If a game shall have been completed before such discovery, the order of service remains as altered.

38. Error in Order of Receiving in Doubles

If during a game the order of receiving the service is changed by the Receivers it shall remain as altered until the end of the game in which the mistake is discovered, but the partners shall resume their original order of receiving in the next game of that set in which they are Receivers of the service.

39. Service Fault in Doubles

The service is a fault as provided for by Rule 10, or if the ball touches the Server's partner or anything which he wears or carries; but if the ball served touches the partner of the Receiver, or anything which he wears or carries, not being a let under Rule 14 (a) before it hits the ground, the Server wins the point.

40. Playing the Ball in Doubles

The ball shall be struck alternately by one or other player of the opposing pairs, and if a player touches the ball in play with his racket in contravention of this Rule, his opponents win the point.

Note.—Except where otherwise stated, every reference in these Rules to the masculine includes the feminine gender.

APPENDIX

REGULATIONS FOR MAKING TESTS SPECIFIED IN RULE 3

(i) Unless otherwise specified all tests shall be made at a temperature of approximately 68° Fahrenheit (20° Centigrade) and a relative humidity of approximately 60 per cent. All balls should be removed from their container and kept at the recognised temperature and humidity for 24 hours prior to testing, and shall be at that temperature and humidity when the test is commenced.

(ii) Unless otherwise specified the limits are for a test conducted in an atmospheric pressure resulting in a barometric reading of approximately 30 inches (76 cm.).

(iii) Other standards may be fixed for localities where the average temperature, humidity or average barometric pressure at which the game is being played differ materially from 68° Fahrenheit (20° Centigrade), 60 per cent and 30 inches (76 cm.) respectively.
Applications for such adjusted standards may be made by any National Association to the International Tennis Federation and if approved shall be adopted for such localities.

(iv) In all tests for diameter a ring gauge shall be used consisting of a metal plate, preferably non-corrosives, of a uniform thickness of one-eighth of an inch (.32 cm.) in which there are two circular openings 2.575 inches (6.54 cm.) and 2.700 inches (6.86 cm.) in diameter respectively. The inner surface of the gauge shall have a convex profile with a radius of one-sixteenth of an inch (.16 cm). The ball shall not drop through the smaller opening by its own weight and shall drop through the larger opening by its own weight.

(v) In all tests for deformation conducted under Rule 3, the machine designed by Percy Herbert Stevens and patented in Great Britain under Patent No. 230250, together with the subsequent additions and improvements thereto, including the modifications required to take return deformations, shall be employed or such other machine which is approved by a National Association and gives equivalent readings to the Stevens machine.

(vi) Procedure for carrying out tests:

(a) Pre-compression. Before any ball is tested it shall be steadily compressed by approximately one inch (2.54 cm.), on each of three diameters at right angles to one another in succession; this process to be carried out three times (nine compressions in all). All tests to be completed within two hours of pre-compression.

(b) Bound test (as in Rule 3). Measurements are to be taken from the concrete base to the bottom of the ball.

(c) Size test (as in paragraph (iv) above).

(d) Weight test (as in Rule 3).

(e) Deformation test. The ball is placed in position on the modified Stevens machine so that neither platen of the machine is in contact with the cover seam. The contact weight is applied, the pointer and the mark brought level, and the dials set to zero. The test weight equivalent to 18 lb. (8.165 kg.) is placed on the beam and pressure applied by turning the wheel at a uniform speed so that five seconds elapse from the instant the beam leaves its seat until the pointer is brought level with the mark. When turning ceases the reading is recorded (forward deformation). The wheel is turned again until figure ten is reached on the scale (one inch (2.54 cm.) deformation). The wheel is then rotated in the opposite direction at a uniform speed (thus releasing pressure) until the beam pointer again coincides with the mark. After waiting ten seconds the pointer is adjusted to the mark if necessary. The reading is then recorded (return deformation). This procedure is repeated on each ball across the two diameters at right angles to the initial position and to each other.

PLAN OF THE COURTS

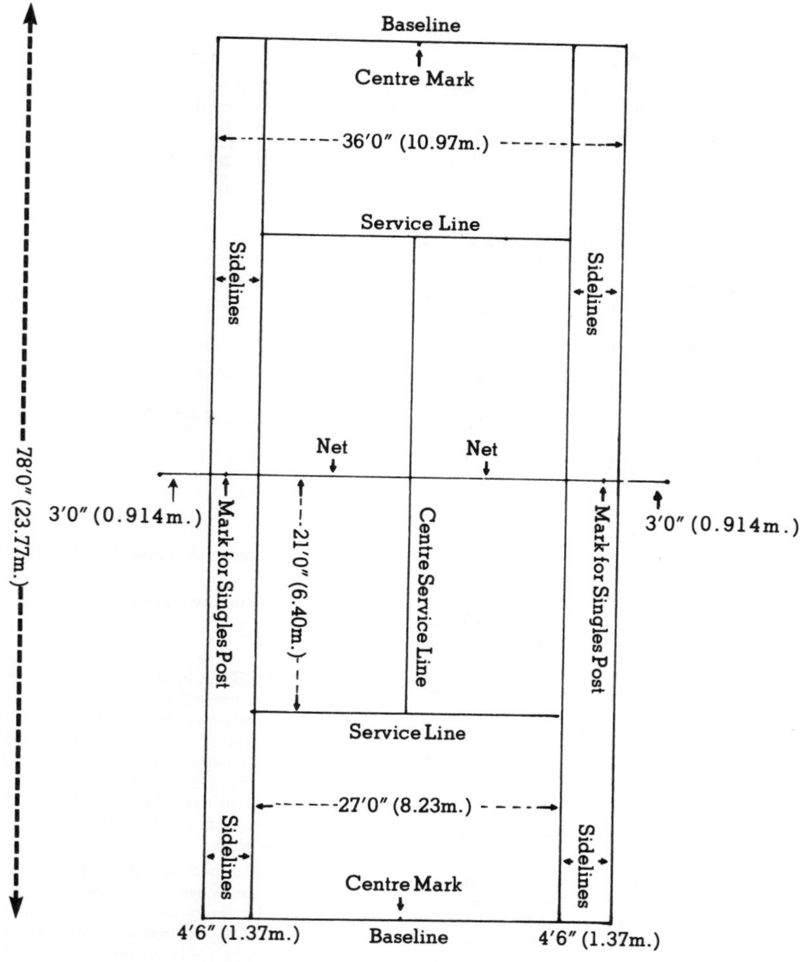

SUGGESTIONS ON HOW TO MARK OUT A COURT

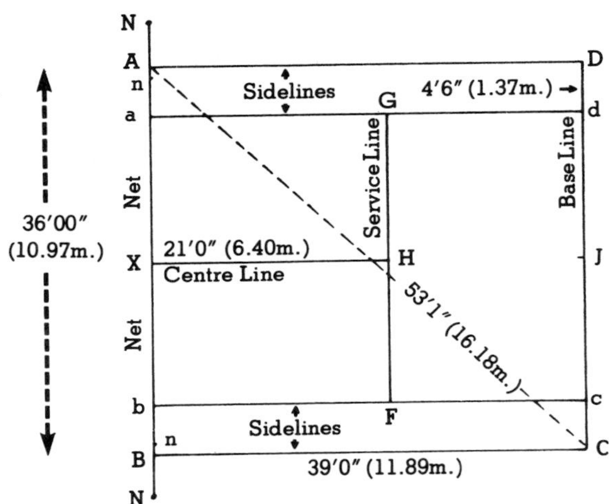

The following procedure is for the usual combined Doubles and Singles Court. (See note at foot for a Court for one purpose only.)

First select the position of the net; a straight line 42 feet (12.8 m.) long. Mark the centre (X on the diagram) and, measuring from there in each direction, mark:-

at 13'6" (4.11 m.) the points a, b, where the net crosses the inner side lines,

at 16'6" (5.03 m.) the positions of the singles posts (or sticks) (n, n),

at 18'0" (5.49 m.) the points A, B, where the net crosses the outer sidelines,

at 21' 0" (6.40 m.) the positions of the net posts (N, N) being the ends of the original 42'0" (12.8m.) line.

Insert pegs at A and B and attach to them the respective ends of two measuring tapes. On one, which will measure the diagonal of the half-court, take a length 53'1" (16.18 m.) and on the other (to measure the sideline) a length of 39'0" (11.89m.). Pull both taut so that at these distances they meet at a point C, which is one corner of the Court. Reverse the measurements to find the other corner D. As a check on this operation it is advisable at this stage to verify the length of the line CD which, being the base line, should be found to be 36'0" (10.97m.); and at the same time its centre J can be marked, and also the ends of the inner side lines (c,d), 4'6" (1.37 m.) from C and D.

The centre-line and service-line are now marked by means of the points F, H, G, which are measured 21'0" (6.40 m.) from the net down the lines bc, XJ, ad, respectively.

Identical procedure the other side of the net completes the Court.

Notes –

(i) If a Singles Court only is required, no lines are necessary outside the points a, b, c, d, but the Court can be measured out as above. Alternatively, the corners of the base-line (c, d) can be found if preferred by pegging the two tapes at a and b instead of at A and B, and by then using lengths of 47'5" (14.46 m.) and 39' 0" (11.89 m.). The net posts will be at n, n, and a 33'0" (10 m.) singles net should be used.

(ii) When a combined Doubles and Singles Court with a doubles net is used for singles, the net must be supported at the points n, n, to a height of 3 feet 6 inches (1.07 m.) by means of two posts, called "singles sticks", which shall be not more than 3 inches (7.5 cm.) square or 3 inches (7.5 cm.) in diameter. The centres of the singles sticks shall be 3 feet (0.91 m.) outside the singles court on each side.

To assist in the placing of these singles sticks it is desirable that the points n, n, should each be shown with a white dot when the court is marked.

OVERALL COURT DIMENSIONS AND LIGHTING REQUIREMENTS

The Rules lay down, for certain International and other Official Championships only, the minimum space required outside the court markings: these requirements are shown in column (a) of the table below.

For other purposes the dimensions are not formally laid down in the Rules but for general club and school use the LTA recommends that, if possible, the same minimum figures should be observed except that, if two or more adjacent courts are to have no canvas or netting barriers between them, the space between courts can be partially shared. The effect of this recommendation is shown in column (b). If however the space available makes it impossible to provide the dimensions shown in column (b), lawn tennis can be satisfactorily played on a court with the slightly smaller area in column (c). **Dimensions smaller than these are not considered satisfactory.**

Figures in bold type are mandatory; others are "recommended".

Figures in Column (a) are derived from Rules 1 and 34 of Tennis, published by the ITF; except in regard to height, which is from the 1974 General Meeting decision of the ITF, and Light Intensity which is from Rule 15 of the International Tennis Championship (Davis Cup) and is therefore mandatory only for that Event. The light intensity figures shown in brackets are a lower standard which may be used only with the approval of the Referee, as agreed at the I.T.F. General Meeting, 1979.

Standards of Play	(a) **International and National Official Championships**	(b) **County and Club Recommended**	(c) **Recreational**
Marked Out Playing Area			
Length	**78ft. 0in.** **23.77m.**	**78ft. 0in.** **23.77m.**	**78ft. 0in.** **23.77m.**
Width	**36ft. 0in.** **10.97m.**	**36ft. 0in.** **10.97m.**	**36ft. 0in.** **10.97m.**
Length of Net (Doubles) (Note 1)	**42ft. 0in.** **12.80m.**	**42ft. 0in.** **12.80m.**	**42ft. 0in.** **12.80m.**
Width of lines (White) included within above court size (Note 2)	**2in.** **5cm.**	**2in.** **5cm.**	**2in.** **5cm.**
Minimum Runback (ie Depth clear behind baseline, at each end) (Note 3)	**21ft. 0in.** **6.40m.**	21ft. 0in. 6.40m.	18ft. 0in. 5.49m.
Minimum Side-run (ie Width clear beside sideline, each side)	**12ft. 0in.** **3.66m.**	12ft. 0in. 3.66mm.	10ft. 0in. 3.05m.
Minimum Side-run between Courts not separately enclosed		14ft. 0in. 4.27m.	12ft. 0in. 3.66m.
Overall Minimum Size of Enclosure			
Length (Note 3)	**120ft. 0in.** **36.58m.**	120ft. 0in. 36.58m.	114ft.0in. 34.75m.
Width for One Enclosed Court	**60ft. 0in.** **18.29m.**	60ft. 0in. 18.29m.	56ft. 0in. 17.07m.
Width for Two Courts in One Enclosure		**110ft. 0in.** 35.53m.	**104ft.0in.** 31.70m.
Width added for each additional Court		50ft. 0in. 15.24m.	48ft. 0in. 14.63m.
For Indoor Courts			
Unobstructed Height over Net	35ft. 0in. 10.67m.	29ft. 6in. 9.00m.	26ft. 3in. 8.00m.
Unobstructed Height over end of Runback	14ft. 0in. 4.27m.		
For Artificial Lighting			
Minimum Light Intensity: Lumens per sq foot Lumens per sq metre (Lux)	 **46**(28) **500** (300)	 35 375	 25 270

Notes—

1. A Singles Net is 33ft. 0in. (10m) but it is acceptable and usual to use a Doubles Net for both Singles and Doubles, supporting it in the case of Singles by means of Singles Posts (Sticks) at the appropriate points 3ft. 0in. (.914m) outside the inner Sidelines.
2. For allowable variations in the width of some lines, see Rule 1 of Tennis. The lines are normally white: this includes multi-purpose sports areas marked for more than one sport, for which international convention allots white to tennis.
3. On Indoor Courts, or if the boundary is a wall or such that balls may otherwise rebound from it onto the Court, netting or canvas is placed 1ft 0in. (30cm) clear of the wall and the space required for this, at one or both ends, is extra to the dimensions shown in the Table.

REGULATIONS FOR THE MANAGEMENT OF LAWN TENNIS TOURNAMENTS

1. General Conditions.
The Rules of the Association, the Rules of Tennis and the Regulations hereinafter contained (so far as the same are applicable and not inconsistent with the Regulations governing any particular Competition) shall be observed in all Championships, Prize Competitions, Leagues and Tournaments (each of which is hereinafter referred to as "a Tournament") held in Great Britain.

2. Management Committee.
All details connected with any Tournament shall be settled by the Committee of the Club holding the Tournament, or by a Committee of Management especially appointed for the purpose, of whom two, or such larger number as the Committee may determine, shall form a quorum.

3. Prospectus.
A prospectus with an entry form shall be issued by the Committee of every Official Tournament, which prospectus shall specify the conditions of the Competition, and shall include the following particulars:

(a) That the Tournament is sanctioned by the Council of the L.T.A. and will be conducted under the present Rules of Tennis and the Rules and Regulations of the L.T.A.

(b) The names of the Committee, the Referee and Handicapper (See Regs. 8 and 22).

(c) The events, amount of entrance fees, and, where possible, the value of the prizes (Reg. 5) and the conditions relating to any challenge trophy (See Reg. 35 and Appendix E).

(d) The days and dates in full, and the hours of commencement of play.

(e) The date, time and place of the draw for the level events (See Reg. 18).

(f) The number and description (i.e., grass or otherwise) of the courts available for use (See Reg. 28).

(g) If the holding of an event is conditional on the size of the entry, the minimum number of such entries.

(h) Restrictions as to clothing to be worn (including footwear and accoutrements) and the extent of any advertising permitted thereon (See Reg. 30).

(i) That no complaint in connection with the Tournament can be entertained by the Committee unless made in writing and lodged with the Secretary of the Tournament within 48 hours of the occurrence of the cause of the same and no application for leave to appeal against any decision of the Committee can be entertained by the Council unless made in writing and lodged with the Secretary of the Association within ten days after the receipt of such decision by the complainant (see Regs. 32 and 33).

(j) That in the case of certain events competitors will not be required to attend before a stated time on a day or days mentioned.

(k) Details of any experimental rule or regulations authorised by the Council.

(l) The ball to be used, which must be one duly authorised by the Council (See Reg. 29).

(m) The place of receiving and the date and hour of closing entries.

(n) The location of the ground.

(o) The number and type of sets to be played in each match (See Reg. 23, and Nos. 27 and 28 of the Rules of Tennis.

(p) A tournament which wishes to restrict the number of entries in any of its events must state clearly the method of elimination to be used and, if applicable, the fact that entries will be closed when those numbers have been reached.

A copy of the prospectus and entry form when printed shall be sent forthwith to the Secretary of the L.T.A. and, in the case of a Tournament which is being held for the first time, a proof print of these documents shall be sent to such Secretary for approval by the Council prior to its issue to the public.

4. Medical Tests

(a) Any Competitor may be required to undergo any dope test approved by the L.T.A.

(b) If there is any question as to the eligibility of a competitor on grounds of sex, such competitor may be required to undergo any test approved by the L.T.A.

5. Prize Money and Payments to Competitors.

(a) The prize money as advertised in a prospectus or programme, or declared in advance by or to the Association, shall be paid out except to amateurs unless some restriction has been specified. Tennis players may only win prize money as divided and advertised in the prospectus or programme.

(b) Tournament organisers and sponsors shall be penalised if any unauthorised payments are made to players either directly or indirectly, and the responsibility for proving that no unauthorised payments have been made rests with them.

(c) Payments to amateurs. These must be in accordance with I.T.F. Rule 46.

Note.—"Amateur" refers to certain nationals from other countries.

6. Handicap Form.
The Handicap Entry Form set out in Appendix A shall be used at all Tournaments at which handicap events are held.

7. Tournament Accounts.
The Management Committee referred to in Regulation 2 shall keep separate accounts in respect of each tournament controlled by it, setting out full details of all receipts and expenditure relating to that tournament. Not later than three months from the closing date of any tournament a copy of such accounts shall be rendered to the Council, and, if demanded, all vouchers and other supporting documents shall be delivered to the Council for inspection within fourteen days of such demand. If required, full facilities shall be given to the Council or their nominees to investigate any matters arising out of such accounts.

8. Referee.
The Committee shall appoint as Referee some person approved by the Council. Such Referee shall have power, with the consent of the Committee, to appoint a substitute and shall, during the Tournament and any longer period which the Committee may decide, be ex-officio a member of the Committee.

A Referee or his deputy, when receiving directly or indirectly remuneration for his services, shall be ineligible to compete.

9. Umpires, Foot Fault Judges and Linesmen.
The Referee or such other member or members of the Committee as may be selected for the purpose, shall have power to appoint Umpires, Footfault Judges and Linesmen, and the Referee shall decide any point of law which an Umpire may profess himself unable to decide, or which may be referred to him on appeal from the decision of an Umpire. In all such cases the decision of the Referee shall be final.

10. Competitors.
All competitors shall sign an entry form. They shall pay their own entrance fees including, except in the case of junior events, the Association fee of fifty pence and must neither ask nor accept to be excused therefrom, but a player when officially selected to represent an association may receive his entrance fee from such association.
A player is specifically prohibited from entering or signifying intention to enter for more than one tournament, match or competition advertised to take place during the same period, except in the case of two events which overlap by not more than two days and then only with the prior written consent of the organisers of both events.

11. Guarantee of Acceptance.
A player whose entry has been accepted shall not withdraw except for reasons of health or bereavement or with the consent of the Organising Committee, and any so doing shall have his entry refused for future tournaments, matches, or competitions unless a written undertaking is given that such action will not recur. In no circumstances shall there be racial discrimination or political interference.

12. Powers of Committee.
The Committee shall help to keep order on the ground and shall consult and decide upon any question arising out of the competition, if summoned for that purpose by the Referee or by any two of their number; and if, when so convened, the misconduct of a competitor shall have been reported to them by a member of the Committee or an Umpire, they shall have power (after giving to the alleged offender particulars of the grounds of complaint and an opportunity of being heard) to disqualify him and further to order him off the ground if in their opinion his misconduct shall appear to justify such action.

13. Duties of Umpire.
It is the duty of an Umpire:

(a) To ascertain that the net is at the right height before the commencement of play, and to measure and adjust the net during play, if asked to do so, or if, in his opinion, its height has altered.

(b) To call the faults (subject to Regulation 14).

(c) To call the points when won, or when he is asked to call them, and to record them on the Umpire's scoring sheet.

(d) To call the games and the sets at the end of each, or when asked to call them, and to record them on the Umpire's scoring sheet.

(e) To direct the Competitors to change ends in accordance with No. 16 of the Rules of Tennis.

(f) To decide any doubtful or disputed point (subject to Regulation 14) and, if unable to do so, to have the point replayed.

(g) to decide all doubtful or disputed questions of law (subject to Regulation 15).

(h) In handicap matches to call the odds at the commencement of each game.

(i) To sign the Umpire's scoring sheets, and to deliver them at the conclusion of the match to such persons as the Committee may authorise to receive them.

Provided that no omission of any of the foregoing duties on the part of an Umpire shall of itself invalidate a game or match.

Note to Reg. 13.—At the end of each even game the score should be called thus: "Game to A. A (or B) leads by 5 games to 3 in the first set (or the games are 4 all in the first set)". At the end of each odd game the score in sets should be called thus:

"Game to A. A (or B) leads by 2 games to 1 and by 1 set to love (or A leads by 2 games to 1—first set to B)".

14. Duties of Foot Fault Judge and Linesman.

(a) It is the duty of a foot-fault judge to adjudicate on all breaches of No. 7 of the Rules of Tennis, and, should no foot-fault judge be present, this duty shall be discharged by the linesman appointed to the base-line.

(b) It is the duty of a linesman to call faults and decide points relating solely to the line for which he is appointed, and should a linesman not be present or being present declare himself unsighted, this duty shall be discharged by the Umpire.

15. Decision of Umpire.

The decision of an Umpire shall be final upon every question of fact, and any Competitor expressing disapproval of it, either by word or action, will render himself liable to be disqualified; but if an Umpire be in doubt as to a point of law, or if a Competitor appeals against his decision on such a point, the Umpire shall submit it to the Referee, whose decision shall be final.

16. Objection to Referee, Umpire, Foot Fault Judge or Linesman.

(a) The Committee shall have power to suspend the Referee, an Umpire or any other court official.

(b) The Referee shall have power to remove an Umpire or any other court official and to make any necessary replacement but shall report the circumstances to the Committee as soon as possible. The court official so removed shall be given the opportunity to state his case to the Committee, whose decision shall be final.

17. Code of Conduct.

The Association's Code of Conduct (See Appendix F) shall apply at all tournaments. The Code, as drawn up by the Council and revised from time to time at its discretion, specifying penalties for violations and making provision regarding their application, shall be published as an Appendix to these Regulations and shall also be printed in the programme of any tournament or prominently displayed at the ground.

18. Draw to be Public.

The date, time and place where the Draw for the various level events is to be made must be stated on the prospectus of every Tournament, and competitors shall have a right to be present at the draw.

19. Restricted Seeding of the Draw.

At any official Tournament in Great Britain, the draw in the level events may be arranged or "seeded". Unless the Council authorises special arrangements (which it shall not if the total prize money for the tournament exceeds £6,000) such seeding shall be subject to the following:

(a) With not less than 8 entries in an event 2 may be seeded.
With not less than 16 entries in an event 4 may be seeded.
With not less than 24 entries in an event 6 may be seeded.
With not less than 32 entries in an event 8 may be seeded.
With not less than 48 entries in an event 12 may be seeded.
With not less than 64 entries in an event 16 may be seeded.

(b) The entries to be seeded shall be selected by the Committee as being, in their opinion, the best in the event.

(c) The seeded entries shall be placed or drawn as set out below:

(i) Numbers 1 and 2 shall be placed at the top and bottom of the draw respectively.

(ii) Numbers 3 and 4 shall be drawn by lot, the first drawn to be placed at the top of the 2nd quarter of the draw, the other at the bottom of the third quarter.

(iii) Numbers 5 and 6, 7 and 8, 9 and 10, 11 and 12, 13 and 14, 15 and 16 (or as many of these as are permitted to be seeded in accordance with (a) above) shall be drawn by lot in these pairs, the first drawn in each case to be for the top half and the other for the bottom half of the draw.

(iv) Those of numbers of 5-8 which have been so drawn for the top half shall be placed, by lot, at the bottom of the 1st quarter or the bottom of the 2nd quarter of the draw; and those for the bottom half shall be placed, by lot, at the top of the 3rd quarter or the top of the 4th quarter.

(v) Those of numbers 9-16 which have been drawn for the top half shall be placed, by lot, at the bottom of the 1st eighth, top of the 2nd eighth, bottom of the 3rd eighth and top of the 4th eighth; and those for the bottom half shall be placed, by lot, at the bottom of the 5th eighth, top of the 6th eighth, bottom of the 7th eighth and top of the 8th eighth.

20. Method of Draw.

Unless otherwise authorised by the Council the procedure shall be as follows:

(a) **When the number of entries is a power of two:**
When the number of entries is 4, 8, 16, 32, 64 or any higher power of two, they shall meet in pairs, in accordance with the system shown by the diagram set out in Appendix B, Part I.

(b) **When the number of entries is not a power of two:**
When the number of entries is not a power of two there shall be byes in the first round, the number of such byes being equal to the difference between the number of entries and the next higher power of two.

The positions of the byes shall be in accordance with one or other of the following methods, viz:

Method No. 1. The byes shall be in two groups, respectively at the top and bottom of the draw, of equal size if the number of byes is even but otherwise with one more at the bottom than at the top. See Example in Appendix B, Part II; or

Method No. 2. As many seeded players as are within the number of byes shall be allotted byes (with priority if necessary in the order of seeding) and shall be placed in the draw in the positions required by Regulation 19. If further byes are required, or if there is no seeding, the bye positions shall be such that (including any which have been allotted to seeded players) they are spread as evenly as possible throughout the draw. See Example in Appendix B, Part II.

(c) Any seeded players having been already placed in the draw in the positions required by Regulation 19, the unseeded players shall be drawn by lot to fill the remaining places.

21. Division of Events into Classes or Sections.

(a) When the entries for any event at a Tournament exceed 32 in number the Committee may divide the event into classes and/or sections, with separate prizes for each class and/or section, subject to the condition that any title attached to the event shall be allocated to Class I, and that the prospectus of the Tournament announces that the Committee reserve the right to avail themselves of the provisions of this Regulation.

(b) In all events the entries to be included in Class I shall be selected by the Committee as being in their opinion the best in the event, but any competitor excluded from Class I in a level event shall be entitled to withdraw from the event prior to taking part in it, and upon such withdrawal his entrance fee shall be repaid.

(c) Any event may be divided into two sections, consisting of:

(i) Those who can play before a certain time, and

(ii) Those who can play only after that time, provided that the two sections are joined together without the above time restriction, either in the last eight or in the semi-final, and that the prospectus of the Tournament announces that the Committee reserves the right to avail themselves of the provisions of this Regulation.

(d) If a competitor enters specifically under a time restriction in accordance with Clause (c), he shall be entitled to withdraw from the event prior to taking part in it and to demand repayment of his entrance fee in the event of the Committee deciding before the draw not to avail itself of the provisions of this Regulation.

22. Handicapping.

In handicap matches the Competitors shall be handicapped by the Committee, or by a Handicapper appointed by the Committee and approved by the Council. Except as otherwise provided in these Regulations, no handicap allotted to a competitor shall be altered after a round has been played by such competitor, but a walk-over shall not for this purpose be considered a round played.

(a) **Received Odds.**—Odds are received in each group of six games of a set, in the first place, in the **earliest** possible **even** games; that is to say, a receiver of one-sixth receives a point in the second game of each group of six; a receiver of two-sixths, in the second and fourth games; a receiver of three-sixths, in the second, fourth and sixth games.

When the even games are exhausted, odds are then received in the **earliest** possible **odd** games; that is to say, a receiver of four-sixths, receives his points over and above a receiver of three-sixths, in the first game of each group of six, a receiver of five-sixths, in the first and third games.

The positions in which points are received are shown in the Table set out in Appendix C, Part 1.

(b) **Owed Odds.**—Odds are owed in each group of six games of a set, in the first place, in the **latest** possible **odd** games; that is to say, an ower of one-sixth owes a point in the fifth game of each group of six; an ower of two-sixths, in the fifth and third games; an ower of three-sixths in the fifth, third and first games.

When the odd games are exhausted, odds are then owed in the **latest** possible **even** games; that is to say, an ower of four-sixth owes his points, over and above an ower of three-sixths in the sixth game of each group of six; an ower of five-sixths, in the sixth and fourth games.

The positions in which points are owed are shown in the Table set out in Appendix C, Part II.

(c) **Handicap Table.**—Where the system of handicapping by sixths is used, handicaps shall be allotted on the basis of the table set out in Appendix D, Part I.

No competitor shall be allotted a handicap of over owe 50 or more than receive 40 and no competitor shall receive more than 30 from any opponent, but when a player is debarred by this Regulation from receiving his full handicap, his opponent shall give him, by way of owed odds, the additional points to which he is entitled up to a limit of owe 50. For this purpose two owed points shall be reckoned as the equivalent of one received point. The odds to be owed in such cases are set out in Appendix D, Part II.

(d) **Handicap Incorrectly Marked.**—If a handicap match is played at the wrong odds the match stands unless the referee or anyone acting on his behalf has marked the handicap incorrectly on the score sheet when putting the match into court. In the latter case the loser may claim to have the match replayed, unless the mistake in the odds has been in his favour, and provided that he makes his claim before the winner competes in the next round.

23. Playing of Advantage, Tie-break or Short Sets.
In all level events at official tournaments only advantage sets or tie-break sets (in accordance with Rule 27 of Tennis) shall be played. In handicap events at official tournaments advantage sets shall be played with the exception that, if weather conditions are adverse and only for the purpose of enabling the programme to be completed within the advertised time, the Committee may order the best of three short sets, or, alternatively, one advantage set. A short set is a set in which one or other of the players first wins six games.

24. Continuity of Play.
Play shall be continuous in accordance with the Rules of Tennis (No. 30). Sub-paragraph (e) of that Rule of shall not apply.

25. Postponement of Matches.
The Committee or the Referee may postpone any match or part of a match within the limits of the days sanctioned by the L.T.A. if, in their or his opinion, the state of the weather or of the light, or the condition of the ground, or other circumstances, render it advisable to do so.

26. Warm-up.
The warm-up must not exceed a maximum of five minutes, unless specially authorised otherwise by the Council. Only in the event of change of court or postponement of play to another day are players permitted a further warm-up of five minutes, but a warm-up of up to one minute is permitted on the resumption of play on the same day when there has been a stoppage and the players have left the court.

27. Local Competitions.
In cases where local competitions are played concurrently with open competitions, the latter must take precedence.

28. Surface of Courts.
At tournaments authorised to be held on grass courts the Committee may order any match or part of a match to be played on a surface other than grass, if the prospectus of the tournament contains a statement that a court or courts with other surface is or are available, and will be used if the condition of the grass courts shall, in the opinion of the Committee, render such course necessary.

29. Ball.
At official tournaments the ball used shall be one of those duly authorised by the Council of the Lawn Tennis Association as an "L.T.A. Official" ball. Any question arising during a match as to the use of new balls shall be referred to the Committee, whose decision shall be final.

30. Clothing.

(a) Footwear liable to damage the court shall not be permitted.

(b) Advertising on clothing shall be limited to:
  (i) the logo of the garment manufacturer and
  (ii) a total of two further logos.

No logo shall exceed 2 square inches (13 sq. cm.).

31. L.T.A. Official Pass.
Every officer and member of the Council shall be entitled to free admission to a Tournament and to a seat in a stand at such Tournament, if available, upon production of the official pass which shall be issued annually to such officers and councillors.

32. Complaints.
Any complaint connected with a Tournament must be made in writing to the Committee and delivered to the Secretary, or sent by post so as to reach him within 48 hours of the occurrence of the cause of the complaint. Before considering the complaint and arriving at any decision, the Committee shall forward to the alleged offender a notice, in writing, stating the grounds of complaint and giving him an opportunity of being heard. After considering the complaint, the Committee shall cause their decision to be delivered or sent by post to the complainant and the alleged offender within four days after the same shall have been made. Save as provided in Regulation 33 such decision shall be final and binding on all parties concerned and no party shall have the right to appeal against the same either to a court of law or otherwise.

33. Right of Appeal.
Any person dissatisfied with or aggrieved by a decision of the Committee may apply to the Council within ten days after the receipt of such decision for leave to appeal against the same, and the Council shall forthwith give notice of such application to the Committee, and if such leave be granted the appeal shall be heard at such place and time and in such manner as the Council shall direct. All out-of-pocket expenses incurred in connection with such appeal shall be paid by such party or parties to the appeal and in such manner as the Council shall determine.

The decision of the Council shall be final and binding on all parties concerned, and no party shall have the right to appeal against such decision either to a court of law or otherwise.

34. Programme.
A copy of the completed programme of, and a list of the value of the prizes awarded at, every Official Tournament shall be sent by the Committee to the

Secretary of the L.T.A. within fourteen days after the final day sanctioned for the holding of such Tournament.

35. Challenge Trophies.
Every Challenge Trophy offered for competition by an affiliated club, committee, or other organisation shall be subject to the terms and conditions set out in Appendix E.

36. Definitions.
Except where otherwise stated, every reference in these Regulations to the masculine includes the feminine gender, to Great Britain includes the Channel Islands and the Isle of Man, to a competitor or player includes a pair, and to an entry includes the entry of a single competitor or a pair.

LIST OF APPENDICES

A. HANDICAP FORM.

B. METHOD OF DRAW.
Part I—When the number of entries is a power of two.
Part II—When the number of entries is not a power of two.
—Method no. 1 and Method no. 2.

C. TABLES OF RECEIVED AND OWED ODDS.
Part I.—Received odds.
Part II.—Owed odds.

D. HANDICAPPING.
Part I.—Handicap Table.
Part II.—Table of Odds to be owed to players whose handicap on difference is more than Receive 30.

E. CHALLENGE TROPHIES.

F. L.T.A. CODE OF CONDUCT.

APPENDIX A (See Regulation 6)

Handicap Form

Important notice to all players entering for any handicap event.

All Competitors—**not** excepting those who are known to the Handicapper—entering for **any Handicap Event, must fill out** one of the two forms given below.

FORM A. For players who have previously competed in Official Tournaments.

1. The last two Official Tournaments in which I won a Handicap prize of **any description** were:

	Tournament	Month	Year	Singles Handicap Prize—1st, 2nd, etc.	
I	______	______	______	______	______
II	______	______	______	______	______

2. The last two Official Tournaments in which I have played were:

I	______	______	______	______
II	______	______	______	______

3. The last Official Tournament in which I was handicapped by Mr.* ______________

   was______________

4. I was allotted a Standard Handicap of ______ in 19 ______

5. I am now playing in the ______________ Tournament at ______________

   which my handicap was ______

   *Here insert **name of Handicapper** at Tournament.

FORM B.
For those who have never competed in an Official Tournament.

1. Your form as compared with that of some player who plays in Official Tournaments or alternatively has a Standard Handicap.

   (e.g.)______________ who played at the ______________ Tournament

   in 19______ can give me ______________ or can receive from me ______________
   (Strike out whichever is inapplicable)

   or

2. Your club handicap (if any), and the name and club handicap of the best player in your club.

   ____

   or

3. Any other definite information as to your form which will assist the handicapper.

   ____

Notes—

I Any Competitor winning a prize of any description after sending in this form must submit full details to the handicapper before playing in any handicap event at this tournament under penalty of disqualification.

II Competitors are strongly advised, in their own interests, and in fairness to other competitors, to give the handicapper as much definite information as possible as to their form. The only result of insufficient information is that they will be placed on a safe mark; and of incorrect information that they will be liable to disqualification.

APPENDIX B (See Regulation 20)

METHOD OF DRAW

PART I

When the number of entries is a power of two

Example for 8 entries

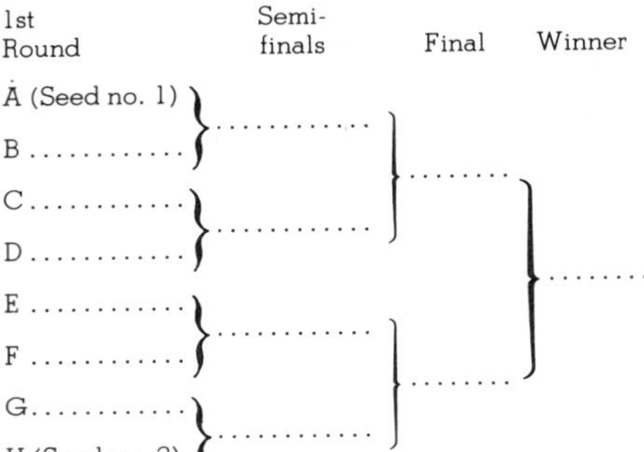

APPENDIX B (See Regulation 20) contd.

Method of Draw

PART II

When the number of entries is not a power of two

Examples for 23 entries

Next higher power of two is 32

Number of byes: 32 – 23 = 9

Number of seeds: 4 (the maximum for an entry of 23)

Method No. 1

The 9 byes are in groups of 4 at the top of the draw and 5 at the bottom of the draw.

The seeds are placed in accordance with Regulation 19 and the other players are drawn for the remaining positions.

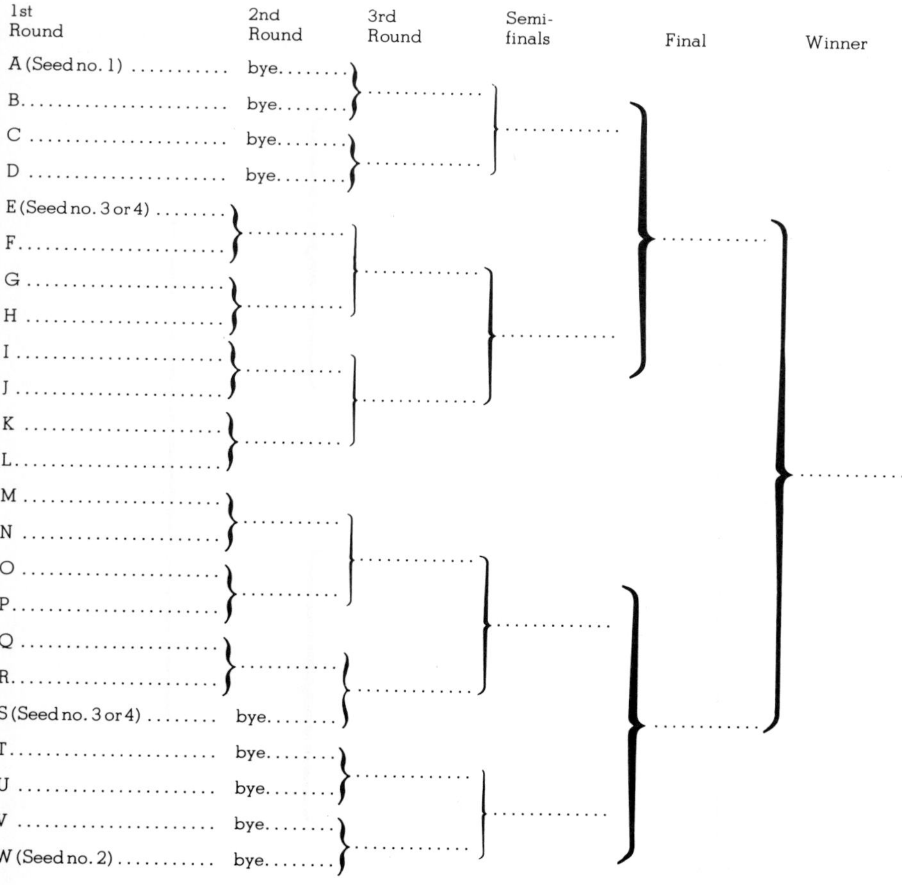

APPENDIX B (See Regulation 20) contd.

Method of Draw

PART II

When the number of entries is not a power of two

Examples for 23 entries contd.
Next higher power of two is 32
Number of byes: 32 – 23 = 9
Number of seeds: 4 (the maximum for an entry of 23)

Method No. 2
The 4 seeds, being fewer than the number of byes, are allotted byes and placed in accordance with Regulation 19. A further 5 byes are required and spaces for them are placed so that the 9 byes are spread as evenly as possible in the second round. The unseeded players are then drawn for the unfilled positions.

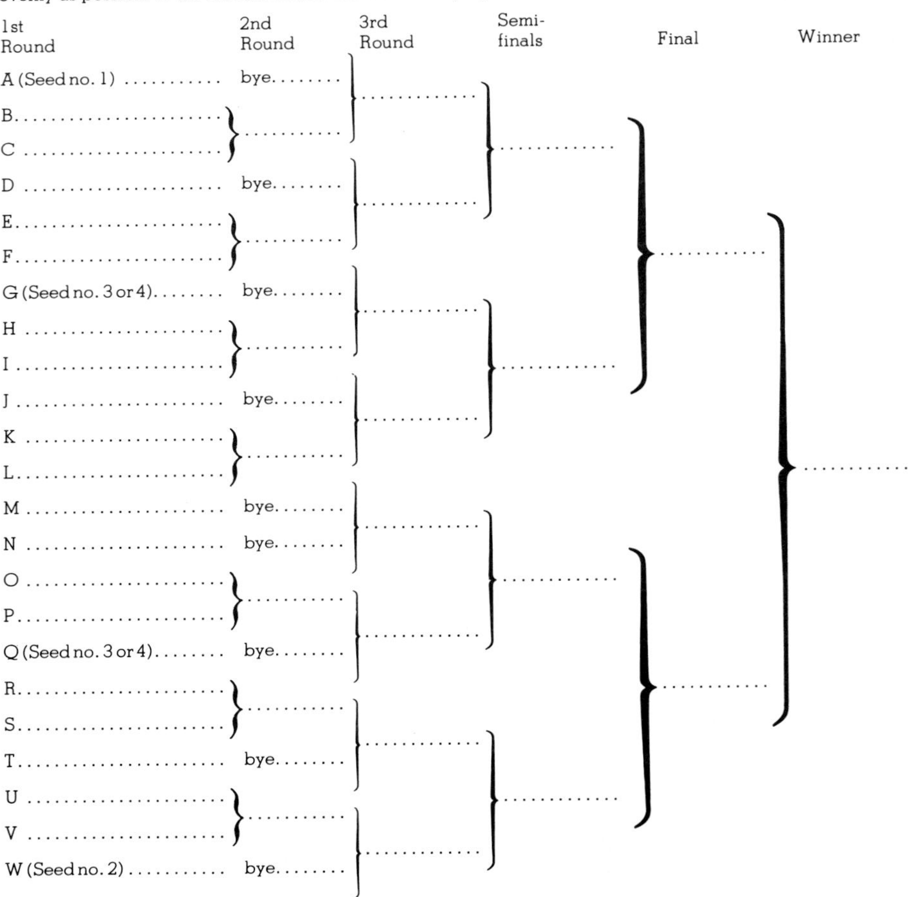

APPENDIX C

Part I

TABLE OF RECEIVED ODDS
(SEE REGULATION 22(a))

	1st Game	2nd Game	3rd Game	4th Game	5th Game	6th Game
1/6th of 15		15				
2/6th of 15		15		15		
3/6th of 15		15		15		15
4/6th of 15	15	15		15		15
5/6th of 15	15	15	15	15		15

Example.
A player receiving four-sixths of fifteen receives nothing in the third and fifth games, and fifteen in the first, second, fourth and sixth games, of a set.

Note.
The table is not carried beyond the sixth game, as in the next and every succeeding six games the odds recur in the same positions.

The above odds may be received in augmentation of the other received odds.
Fifteen is one point received at the beginning of every game of a set.
Thirty is two points received at the beginning of every game of a set.

Part II

TABLE OF OWED ODDS
(SEE REGULATION 22(b))

	1st Game	2nd Game	3rd Game	4th Game	5th Game	6th Game
1/6th of 15					15	
2/6th of 15			15		15	
3/6th of 15	15		15		15	
4/6th of 15	15		15		15	15
5/6th of 15	15		15	15	15	15

Example.
A player owing two-sixths of fifteen would owe fifteen in the third and fifth games, and nothing in the first, second, fourth and sixth games of a set.

Note.
The table is not carried beyond the sixth game, as in the next and every succeeding six games the odds recur in the same positions.

The above odds may be owed in augmentation of other owed odds.
Fifteen is one point owed at the beginning of every game of a set.
Thirty is two points owed at the beginning of every game of a set.
Forty is three points owed at the beginning of every game of a set.

APPENDIX D

(See Regulation 22(c))

Part 1

HANDICAP TABLE

Owe 50
,, 40.5
,, 40.4
,, 40.3
,, 40.2
,, 40.1
,, 40
,, 30.5
,, 30.4
,, 30.3
,, 30.2
,, 30.1
,, 30
,, 15.5
,, 15.4
,, 15.3
,, 15.2
,, 15.1
,, 15
,, .5
,, .4
,, .3
,, .2
,, .1
Scratch
Rec'd. .1
,, .2
,, .3
,, .4
,, .5
,, 15
,, 15.1
,, 15.2
,, 15.3
,, 15.4
,, 15.5
,, 30
,, 30.1
,, 30.2
,, 30.3
,, 30.4
,, 30.5
,, 40

(a) When two players who are handicapped to owe odds meet, the player who owes the smaller odds is put forward to scratch and shall meet the player who owes the larger at the difference between the face values of their odds.

(b) When two players who are handicapped to receive odds meet, the player in receipt of the smaller odds is put back to scratch and shall, subject to clause (c) hereof, meet the player in receipt of the larger odds at the difference between the face values of their odds.

(c) No competitor shall be allotted a handicap of over owe 50 or more than than receive 40 and no competitor shall receive more than 30 from any opponent, but when a player is debarred by this Regulation from receiving his full handicap his opponent shall give him, by way of owed odds, the additional points to which he is entitled up to a limit of owe 50. For this purpose two owed points shall be reckoned as the equivalent of one received point. The odds to be owed in such cases are set out in Part II.

Examples:

(i) A player whose handicap is Receive 30.5 drawn against a player whose handicap is Receive one-sixth shall receive 30 and be owed 15 and two-sixths.

(ii) The same player drawn against a player whose handicap is owe one-sixth shall receive 30 and be owed 15 and five sixths.

APPENDIX D—contd.

Part II

TABLE OF ODDS TO BE OWED TO PLAYERS WHOSE HANDICAP ON DIFFERENCE IS MORE THAN RECEIVE 30

A player whose handicap is as stated at top of columns shall receive 30 and in addition shall be owed the odds stated in each column opposite the handicap of his opponent.

Opponent	Rec. 40	Rec. 30.5	Rec. 30.4	Rec. 30.3	Rec. 30.2	Rec. 30.1
Owe 50	Owe 50	Owe 50	Owe 50	Owe 50	Owe 50	Owe 50
,, 40.5	,,	,,	,,	,,	,,	,,
,, 40.4	,,	,,	,,	,,	,,	,,
,, 40.3	,,	,,	,,	,,	,,	,, 40.5
,, 40.2	,,	,,	,,	,,	,,	,, 40.4
,, 40.1	,,	,,	,,	,,	,, 40.5	,, 40.3
,, 40	,,	,,	,,	,,	,, 40.4	,, 40.2
,, 30.5	,,	,,	,,	,, 40.5	,, 40.3	,, 40.1
,, 30.4	,,	,,	,,	,, 40.4	,, 40.2	,, 40
,, 30.3	,,	,,	,, 40.5	,, 40.3	,, 40.1	,, 30.5
,, 30.2	,,	,,	,, 40.4	,, 40.2	,, 40	,, 30.4
,, 30.1	,,	,, 40.5	,, 40.3	,, 40.1	,, 30.5	,, 30.3
,, 30	,,	,, 40.4	,, 40.2	,, 40	,, 30.4	,, 30.2
,, 15.5	,, 40.5	,, 40.3	,, 40.1	,, 30.5	,, 30.3	,, 30.1
,, 15.4	,, 40.4	,, 40.2	,, 40	,, 30.4	,, 30.2	,, 30
,, 15.3	,, 40.3	,, 40.1	,, 30.5	,, 30.3	,, 30.1	,, 15.5
,, 15.2	,, 40.2	,, 40	,, 30.4	,, 30.2	,, 30	,, 15.4
,, 15.1	,, 40.1	,, 30.5	,, 30.3	,, 30.1	,, 15.5	,, 15.3
,, 15	,, 40	,, 30.4	,, 30.2	,, 30	,, 15.4	,, 15.2
,, .5	,, 30.5	,, 30.3	,, 30.1	,, 15.5	,, 15.3	,, 15.1
,, .4	,, 30.4	,, 30.2	,, 30	,, 15.4	,, 15.2	,, 15
,, .3	,, 30.3	,, 30.1	,, 15.5	,, 15.3	,, 15.1	,, .5
,, .2	,, 30.2	,, 30	,, 15.4	,, 15.2	,, 15	,, .4
,, .1	,, 30.1	,, 15.5	,, 15.3	,, 15.1	,, .5	,, .3
Scratch	,, 30	,, 15.4	,, 15.2	,, 15	,, .4	,, .2
Receive						
,, .1	,, 15.4	,, 15.2	,, 15	,, .4	,, .2	—
,, .2	,, 15.2	,, 15	,, .4	,, .2	—	—
,, .3	,, 15	,, .4	,, .2	—	—	—
,, .4	,, .4	,, .2	—	—	—	—
,, .5	,, 2	—	—	—	—	—
,, 15	—	—	—	—	—	—

APPENDIX E (See Regulation 35)

CHALLENGE TROPHIES

1. A trophy may be either (a) perpetual or (b) offered on the condition that it becomes the absolute property of the winner (in the case of doubles with the same partner) if won three times consecutively or four times in all. No trophy may be removed from category (b) to category (a) without the consent of the Council which shall not normally be given unless the consent of the donor and winners during the previous seven years (if living) has been obtained.

2. A trophy which has been offered for competition and won shall be offered again at each successive similar tournament promoted by the same Club, Committee or other organisation until it has been won outright, and in no case shall the sequence of such tournaments be broken by more than two years.

3. A trophy, until won outright shall be insured by the Committee of Management against all risks, and immediately after the conclusion of the tournament may be handed over to the winner thereof upon his giving to the Committee of Management a receipt in writing therefor.

4. A trophy, until won outright, shall be returned by the holder to the Committee of Management so as to reach the secretary of the tournament not later than twelve calendar months after the date upon which it was won, or seven clear days at least before the date advertised for the commencement of the next successive tournament promoted by the same club, committee or other organisation, whichever date shall be the earlier.

5. If no win shall be scored or conceded in the final of any event to which a Trophy is attached, the winning of the Trophy shall be suspended for that year, but provided the holder shall have competed in the event and shall not have been defeated therein, any sequence of wins to which he may then be, or thereafter become, entitled shall be in no way affected by such suspension.

6. For the purposes of the conditions a Tournament shall be deemed to have been abandoned, if it shall not be held for three consecutive years, and any question or dispute as to whether a Tournament has or has not been abandoned shall be referred to the Council, whose decision shall be final and binding on all parties concerned.

7. If any question shall arise as to the ownership or custody for the time being of a Trophy offered for competition at a Tournament, such question shall be referred to the Council and the Trophy shall be handed over to the Council to be dealt with in such manner for the benefit of Lawn Tennis as the Council shall deem advisable.

8. Any dispute relating to a Trophy if not settled by the parties concerned, shall be referred to the Council, whose decision shall be final and binding, but the parties concerned shall have the right to appear in person before the Council or any Committee thereof appointed to enquire into the matter.

APPENDIX F (See Regulation 17)

THE L.T.A. CODE OF CONDUCT

(All references to the masculine include also the feminine gender)

Off Court

1. A player withdrawing from a tournament after the draw is made, or defaulting during a tournament except for illness, injury or personal emergency, is liable to disciplinary action by The Lawn Tennis Association.
2. Every competitor must sign the attendance sheet at the control table immediately on arrival each day and until he has done so will be assumed to be absent.
3. Every competitor shall present himself for play in acceptable tennis attire as laid down by the Tournament Committee and it is his responsibility to be so dressed and ready for play when his match is called. A competitor not ready to play within 15 minutes of his match being called is liable to be defaulted. The official clock shall be that designated by the Referee.
4. A competitor may not leave the ground without first ascertaining from the Referee when he is next required.

On Court

5. The warm-up period shall not exceed five minutes.
6. A player shall not waste time during a match. The maximum time for changing ends as laid down by Rule 30(a) of the Rules of Tennis is one minute thirty seconds. The maximum time between points (and between games with no change of ends) is thirty seconds unless a shorter time has been published in the Conditions of an Event. Violations of this Section shall be penalised in the first instance by a warning and in each subsequent instance by a one point penalty. A failure to play after being so ordered by an official shall be penalised in accordance with the Point Penalty schedule set forth in Section 10.
7. A player shall not use an audible obscenity nor make an obscene gesture during a match nor hit, kick or throw a racket, ball or other object in anger.
8. A player shall not receive coaching during a match, which includes audible or visible advice, except from his partner in a doubles match.
9. A player shall at all times conduct himself in a sportsmanlike manner with due regard to the authority of officials and the rights of opponents, spectators and others.
10. Violations of Section 7-9 of this Code in any one match shall be punishable in accordance with the following sequence of penalties:-

First Offence	warning
Second Offence	loss of one point
Third Offence	loss of one game (irrespective of number of points played in the game)
Fourth Offence	default

11. In tournaments where a full complement of qualified officials is not available for every match, the penalties in Sections 6 and 10 may be applied by the referee or, at the discretion of the committee and/or referee, by umpires and/or supervisors authorised for this purpose.
12. A player who, over a series of matches, persistently commits Code violations subject to the above penalty system or commits one or more acts particularly injurious to the tournament and/or the Game may be defaulted by the Referee and/or have further disciplinary action taken against him by The Lawn Tennis Association.
13. A player who leaves the court during play without the permission of the umpire (or, if there is no umpire, of the Referee) is liable to be defaulted.

General

14. A player shall at all times, both on and off court, conduct himself in a manner which reflects favourably on the Game and upon fellow players and failure to do so shall render the player liable to disciplinary action by The Lawn Tennis Association.

REGULATIONS FOR THE PRUDENTIAL COUNTY CUP (INTER-COUNTY LAWN TENNIS CHAMPIONSHIPS)

GENERAL REGULATIONS

Note: For the purpose of these Regulations "Great Britain" includes the Channel Islands and the Isle of Man and "railway fares" includes sea ferry fares.

1. The Championships shall be competed for annually as (a) a grass court and (b) winter championships. The President and the Honorary Treasurer of The Lawn Tennis Association shall be for all intents and purposes, the legal owners of any cups attached to the Championships in trust for the Association.

2. The management of the Championships shall be entrusted to a Committee nominated annually by the Council of the Lawn Tennis Association, with power to suspend or modify any of these Regulations to meet exceptional circumstances and to decide any question of eligibility, qualifications of competitors, interpretation of the Regulations or otherwise. The Committee's decision shall be final.

3. For the purpose of these Championships, which shall be area competitions subject to the Association's Rules 34 and 36, the following shall be regarded as Counties: East of Scotland, North of Scotland, South of Scotland, West of Scotland, North Wales, South Wales, Channel Islands, Isle of Man.

4. All Counties which competed in the grass court and/or winter championships respectively during the previous year shall be entered (subject to Regulation 29 (Grass)) for the competitions held during the following year unless notice of withdrawal is lodged with the secretary of The Lawn Tennis Association on or before the first day of October in the previous year.

5. A County which did not compete in the previous competition and now wishes to do so, shall give notice in writing to the secretary of The Lawn Tennis Association, on or before the first day of October in the previous year.

6. For the purposes of these Regulations, a rubber is the best of three sets, a match in doubles competitions is the best of nine rubbers, a match in singles competitions is the best of twelve rubbers, and a match in which both singles and doubles are played is the best of nine rubbers. In all rubbers the tie-break shall operate in the first and second sets only.

7. A Referee appointed in manner hereinafter provided shall decide any point of law which may be referred to him. He shall decide whether or not the match shall be stopped owing to the state of the courts, the state of the weather, darkness, or other unavoidable hindrance.

8. A County shall not be bound to play the same team throughout the Championships, but no change shall be made in the composition of the teams engaged in a match after the start of play. If a match is postponed before any play shall have taken place, or if a match is replayed (under Regulations 20 (Grass) or 45 or 53 (Winter)), the composition of the competing teams may be changed.

9. No player may represent more than one County in any competition.

10. When taking part in any inter-county event, players may only receive reimbursement either in whole or in part of expenses actually incurred.

SPECIAL REGULATIONS FOR THE GRASS COURT CHAMPIONSHIPS

11. The competing Counties shall be divided into groups of not more than six counties each (except group 7) and the grouping for the year 1986 shall be as follows:

MEN'S CHAMPIONSHIP

Group 1 Eastbourne (Sussex)
A Essex
B Kent
C Middlesex
D Somerset
E Buckinghamshire
F Yorkshire

Group 2 Cromer (Norfolk)
A Lancashire
B Lancashire
C Surrey
D Berkshire
E West of Scotland
F Leicestershire

Group 3 Southsea (Hampshire)
A Warwickshire
B Hertfordshire
C East of Scotland
D North Wales
E Avon
F Cheshire

Group 4 Hunstanton (Norfolk)
A Oxfordshire
B Nottinghamshire
C Sussex
D Hereford & Worcester
E South Wales
F Hampshire & I.O.W.

Group 5 Malvern (Hereford & Worcester)
A Gloucestershire
B Northamptonshire
C Dorset
D Norfolk
E Devon
F Lincolnshire

Group 6 Cambridge – Churchill (Cambridgeshire)
A Northumberland
B Staffordshire
C Wiltshire
D Bedfordshire
E Suffolk
F Cornwall

Group 7 Chiswick Civil Service (Middlesex)
A Cambridgeshire
B Durham & Cleveland
C North of Scotland
D South of Scotland
E Shropshire
F Channel Islands
G Cumbria
H Isle of Man

Note: The inclusion of 8 teams in Group 7 is an experimental arrangement for 1986 and the necessary modifications to Regulations 4, 11, 15, 16, 20, 25 and 29 will be notified to the Counties affected in 1986 and, if approved for continuation, incorporated herein for the 1987 printing.

PRUDENTIAL COUNTY CUP – GRASS COURT CHAMPIONSHIPS 1986

LADIES' CHAMPIONSHIP

Group 1 Eastbourne (Sussex)
A Surrey
B Essex
C Yorkshire
D Kent
E Sussex
F Devon

Group 2 Worthing (Sussex)
A Lancashire
B Warwickshire
C Norfolk
D Lincolnshire
E Avon
F Cheshire

Group 3 Cheltenham (Gloucestershire)
A Hampshire & I.O.W.
B Middlesex
C Nottinghamshire
D Buckinghamshire
E Derbyshire
F Leicestershire

Group 4 Exmouth (Devon)
A Berkshire
B Hereford & Worcester
C West of Scotland
D Bedfordshire
E Hertfordshire
F North Wales

Group 4 Exmouth (Devon)
A Berkshire
B Hereford & Worcester
C West of Scotland
D Bedfordshire
E Hertfordshire
F North Wales

Group 5 Poole (Dorset)
A Cambridgeshire
B Oxfordshire
C Somerset
D Staffordshire
E Cornwall
F Gloucestershire

Group 6 Cambridge – Christ's & Sidney Sussex (Cambridgeshire)
A Durham & Cleveland
B North of Scotland
C Suffolk
D East of Scotland
E Dorset
F Northumberland

Group 7 Felixstowe (Suffolk)
A Shropshire
B South Wales
C Northamptonshire
D Wiltshire
E South of Scotland
F Channel Islands
G Cumbria
H Isle of Man

See Note above concerning Regulations affecting Group 7.

12. The competition shall be played in a week to be selected each year by the Council, and each Group shall play in one place to be known as a "Centre".

13. The Council shall from time to time select the make or makes of ball to be used in the Competition.

14. A Referee or Referees shall be appointed for each Centre by the Committee.

15. Each competing County shall play one match against each other County in the same Group.

16. Before play is due to start on the first day each County Captain shall nominate in writing to the Referee not more than nine players who are eligible on that day in accordance with the Association's Rule 34. No other player may represent the County during the week except that if exceptional circumstances such as illness, injury or bereavement reduce the number of available nominated players to less than six for any County team, the Referee, who shall if possible consult the Chairman of the Committee, or failing him the Secretary, may authorise the nomination of the necessary number of substitutes for the remainder of the Championship.

17. Each County shall be represented in each match by a team of six players, who shall be arranged in pairs by their respective Captains, and each pair shall play against each pair of the opposing team one rubber. Not less than fifteen minutes before each match is due to start each County Captain shall nominate his team in pair order to the Referee, with whom the information shall remain confidential until the opposing team nomination has been received. Unless decided in advance and notified by the Committee the order of play for the first round shall be decided by lot; for the second round it shall be decided by lot which of the two available pairs some one pair of the opposing team shall meet; as soon as this shall have been done, the order of play for the remaining rubbers (two in the second round and three in the last) will be found to have been determined.

18. In no case shall any pair play more than one rubber on the same court on any one day without the unanimous consent of the Captains and the knowledge of the Referee. The order of the courts for the first round shall be decided by lot after the order of play shall have been fixed. As soon as this shall have been done, the order of the remaining courts (three in the second round and three in the last) will be found to have been determined.

19. If any player is absent when called upon to play by the Referee the opponents shall be entitled to two love sets but if in any rubber one or more player(s) is absent from each pair the rubber shall be void.

20. If a match in progress cannot be finished on any day it shall if possible be finished on the following day, when, in the morning only, it shall have priority over that day's programme. If no play takes place on any day at the Centre the programme for that day shall, unless otherwise mutually agreed by the competing teams, be played on the day immediately following the conclusion of the programme for the week as originally arranged by the Committee.

21. If the state of the weather shall prevent the competition being brought to a conclusion during the week the Committee shall decide the arrangements to be made for playing any matches which have not been completed.

22. The Referee may order any match or part of a match to be played on a surface other than grass turf, if the condition of the grass courts shall, in his opinion, render such course necessary, and subject thereto every match shall be played on grass turf.

23. The team which shall win the majority of the nine rubbers shall be declared the winner of the match and shall score one point. If under the terms of Regulation 19 less than nine rubbers shall have been completed the match shall be decided

(a) by the majority of rubbers won; or

(b) if there is equality of rubbers, by the majority of sets won; or

(c) if there is equality of rubbers and sets, by the majority of games won.

24. The County scoring the highest number of points in Group I shall be the Champion County for the year, and the County scoring the next highest number of points in Group I shall be runner-up County for the same year.

25. If two or more Counties in any Group shall score an equal number of points the order of precedence in the Group shall be determined by the majority of rubbers. Should the number of rubbers be equal the percentage of sets won to sets played shall decide; and should the number of rubbers and the percentage of sets won to sets played be equal the percentage of games won to games played shall decide.

26. The Council shall decide the allocation of any profits accruing at a Centre.

27. A sum equivalent to the second-class return railway fares from their ordinary place of residence in Great Britain to the Centre where they play of not more than eight persons of each competing team shall be paid by The Lawn Tennis Association to the Association of such County. (See Note preceding Regulation 1).

28. At the conclusion of each annual competition the Counties in each Group shall be placed by the Committee in order of precedence in accordance with the provisions of Regulations 24 and 25 hereof, and the same shall be published in the Official journal of the Association.

29. For each year the Committee shall rearrange the Counties in each Group in such manner that the Counties which were respectively first and second in the previous year in Group 2 and in each subsequent Group shall be placed in the Group immediately above the one in which they last competed and the Counties which were respectively last and last but one in the previous year in each Group (other than the lowest Group) shall be placed in the Group immediately below the one in which they last competed. The Counties which were last and last but one in the lowest Group shall be placed at the bottom of any waiting list of applicants.

30. The Committee may rearrange each year the number of Counties in all Groups, other than Groups 1 and 2, in such manner as they may deem necessary, and for the purpose of such arrangement may promote to a higher Group or relegate to a lower Group more than two Counties provided that in such promotion or relegation the order of precedence established by the previous competition is strictly maintained.

31. If any County shall enter for the Competition and fail to compete in it each County in its Group shall score one point, and in the event of any two or more Counties in the same Group entering and failing to compete the final order of their precedence in the Group as between each other shall be determined in such manner as the Committee may from time to time decide.

32. If it shall be found impracticable to complete all matches during a season the Committee shall decide the promotion and relegation of Counties under Regulations 29 and 30 hereof.

33. If any County which has not previously entered for the Competition or which, having previously entered, has dropped out of the Competition shall give due notice of its desire to compete, it shall be placed in the lowest Group or, if necessary, on a waiting list of applicants.

SPECIAL REGULATIONS FOR THE WINTER CHAMPIONSHIPS

34. In both the Men's and the Ladies' Championships the Committee shall, after the date fixed for the receipt of Entries (Regulations 4 and 5), set aside the eight Counties which reached the Quarter-Final stage in the Competition of the previous year, or such of them as may have entered, and then divide the remaining entries into two Divisions (Northern and Southern) each consisting of four appropriate Groups of Counties on a geographical basis (with liberty to sub-divide any Group into two sections), but so that there shall not be more than five Counties in any undivided Group nor more than four Counties in any section of a Group.

35. Men's Championship.—Each County shall be represented by a team of six players. Each Captain shall arrange his team strictly in order of merit, and shall convey this order in writing to the opposing Captain and to the Referee, prior to the commencement of play. A match shall consist of twelve singles, as follows:

Nos. 1 and 2 shall each play Nos. 1 and 2 of the opposing team.

Nos. 3 and 4 shall each play Nos. 3 and 4 of the opposing team.

Nos. 5 and 6 shall each play Nos. 5 and 6 of the opposing team.

In the first round No. 1 shall play No. 1 of the opposing team, No. 2 shall play No. 2 and so on.

In the second round the order of courts shall be decided by toss between the Captains of the teams, that is to say, players Nos. 1, 2, 5 and 6 of the team winning the toss and players 3 and 4 of the opposing team shall play on the courts on which they played in the first round.

Ladies' Championship.—Each County shall be represented by a team of six players. Each Captain shall arrange her team strictly in order of merit, both for singles and for doubles, and shall convey this order in writing to the opposing Captain and to the Referee, prior to the commencement of play. The six singles players may be paired for the doubles in any manner desired. A match shall consist of six singles and three doubles, as follows:

In the singles, No. 1 shall play No. 1 of the opposing team; No. 2 shall play No. 2 and so on.

In the doubles the first pair shall play the first pair, the second pair shall play the second pair, and the third pair shall play the third pair of the opposing team.

The singles shall be played before the doubles.

Subject to Regulation 45, each match shall be decided on the combined result of singles and doubles.

36. The time of cessation of play shall be fixed prior to the commencement of play by the Captains of the opposing teams, or by the Referee if they shall disagree. It shall be the duty of the Referee to stop play when the time arrives; provided, nevertheless, that the Referee may extend the time with the consent of the Captains of the opposing teams.

37. If any player is absent when called upon to play by the Referee the opponents shall be entitled to two love sets but if in any rubber one or more player(s) is absent on each side the rubber shall be void.

38. The Council shall from time to time select the make or makes of ball to be used in the Competition.

39. Subject to Regulation 52 every match shall be played on any hard court surface except the following which may only be used by mutual consent: (i) synthetic matting or carpets with or without sand impregnation; (ii) wood.

40. The Championships shall be played in four stages: (a) Preliminary, in which the non-exempted Counties will play off to produce four to go forward; (b) Intermediate, in which these successful Counties will each play a losing Quarter-Finalist of the previous year, producing four Counties to go forward; (c) Quarter-Final, in which these successful Counties will each play a winning Quarter-Finalist of the previous year; and (d) Semi-Final and Final. In the event of any County entitled to exemption from any stage not entering the Championship of any year or having lost a match in the previous year's Championship by default, or the Quarter-Finals of the previous year not having been completed, the Committee shall make adjustments to these arrangements as it thinks suitable.

For the Preliminary, Intermediate and Quarter-Final Stages:

41. The matches shall be managed and all necessary arrangements made by the County Associations concerned.

42. The choice of ground for each match shall be decided by the Committee by lot except that, unless otherwise arranged by mutual consent:

(a) When one County shall have had final choice of ground in a match with another County in any Stage of the competition during the three preceding competitions, the latter shall have choice of ground in its next match with the same County except that a County which concedes a walk-over to its opponent shall not have choice of ground against the same opponent on the occasion of their next meeting.

(b) When a match shall have been abandoned after the arrival of the visiting team owing to the state of the weather or of the light or the condition of the ground or have to be replayed under Regulation 45, the visiting team shall have choice of ground for the replay, and so on alternately.

43. A Referee shall be appointed for each match by mutual agreement of the competing Counties.

44. When gate money is taken in any match played, the proceeds after deduction of the incidental expenses, shall be divided between the two Counties competing.

45. (a) In the event of neither team having at the time of cessation of play won sufficient rubbers and/or sets and/or games to arrive at a definite result, then:

(i) In singles competitions, if the first round shall have been completed and the second round shall not have been completed, all rubbers, sets and games played in the second round shall be ignored and the match shall be decided on the one completed round.

(ii) In singles competitions, if the first round shall not have been completed, but one side shall have attained a winning position in that round, then the match shall be decided on the uncompleted first round.

(iii) In competitions consisting of both singles and doubles, if the round of singles shall have been completed and the round of doubles shall not have been completed, all rubbers, sets and games played in the doubles shall be ignored and the match shall be decided on the round of singles.

(iv) In competitions consisting of both singles and doubles, if the round of singles shall not have been completed, but one side shall have attained a winning position in the round of singles then the match shall be decided on that uncompleted round of singles.

(b) If no result shall have been thus achieved the Referee shall decide a date for replaying the match, subject to the right of appeal by either Captain to the Committee if notice in writing of such appeal is handed to the Referee or to the Captain of the opposing team at the ground. For such replay the previous scores shall be ignored and counties shall be entitled to alter the composition of their teams.

46. The Committee shall fix the date by which all matches shall be played. If in any match no result shall have been reached on or before the fixed date, the Committee shall have power either to scratch a County making the default, or to scratch both Counties and eliminate the match from the Competition.

47. The County Association winning any match shall be responsible for notice in writing of the result with the full score of all rubbers, sets and games won and lost, being sent to the Secretary of the Association within 48 hours of the conclusion of such match. The Committee shall be under no obligation to recognise the result of any match notice of which has not been sent in accordance with these regulations.

48. Any County intending to scratch shall give information of its intention to do so to the Captain or Secretary of the opposing County not less than three days before the date agreed upon for playing, and in default of so doing shall be reported to the Committee, who shall have power to take such action as they may consider right.

For the Preliminary Stage:

49. (a) Each County in an undivided Group shall play one match against every other County in the same Group. Each County in a section of a Group shall play one match against every other County in the same section.

(b) One point shall be scored for each match won, and the County securing the highest number of points shall be the winner of the Group or section.

(c) If two or more Counties tie for the first place with an equal number of points, the County winning the greatest number of rubbers shall be the winner. Should the number of rubbers be equal the percentage of sets won to sets played shall decide; and should the number of rubbers and percentage of sets won to sets played be equal, the percentage of games won to games played shall decide.

(d) Should a County give a walk-over to another County, the latter County shall receive the following:
In the Men's Championship—1 point, 12 rubbers, 24 sets and 144 games.
In the Ladies' Championship—1 point, 9 rubbers, 18 sets and 108 games.
The Committee shall, however, have power to ignore all the matches played by a County which does not fulfil all its engagements.

(e) The winners of the two sections in any Group shall play each other to decide the Group Winner. The eight Group winners shall then play a Group play-off to reduce their number to two in the Northern and two in the Southern Divisions.

For the Intermediate Stage:

50. (a) The winning County of each Preliminary Stage Group play-off shall meet an exempt County which was a losing Quarter-Finalist of the previous year.

(b) The Lawn Tennis Association shall be liable to a County Association for a sum equivalent to the second-class return railway fares of not more than seven members of each visiting team from their ordinary place of residence in Great Britain to the place of the meeting. (See Note preceding Regulation 1).

(c) The winning Counties shall pass into the Quarter-Final Stage where they shall meet the four exempted Counties which were winning Quarter-Finalists of the previous year.

For the Quarter-Final Stage:

51. (a) Each winning County in the Intermediate Stage shall be drawn against an exempted County.

(b) The winning Counties shall pass into the Semi-Final Stage.

(c) Regulation 50(b) shall apply.

For the Semi-Final and Final Stage:

52. (a) All arrangements shall be made by the Committee, who shall make the draw and appoint a Referee. The meeting shall extend over two days, on such ground and on such dates as the Committee shall decide.

(b) The matches in this stage may be played indoor or outdoor on any surface approved by the Committee.

(c) The Lawn Tennis Association shall be liable to a County Association for a sum equivalent to the second-class return railway fares of not more than eight members of each visiting team from their ordinary place of residence in Great Britain to the place of the meeting. (See Note preceding Regulation 1).

53. The Regulations for the Preliminary, Intermediate and Quarter-Final Stages which permit of a decision being attained on one round do not apply to the Semi-Final and Final Stage. If, owing to the condition of the courts, the state of the weather or other unavoidable hindrance a match in the semi-final cannot be played or completed on the first day, it shall be played or continued on the following day. If any play shall have taken place on the first day of the Meeting, the composition of the competing teams shall not be varied. In the event of a match in the semi-final being played or completed on the second day of the Meeting, the Referee shall decide, after consultation with the Captains, whether the Final is to be played that day. If in any match in the semi-final and/or final no result shall have been obtained during the two days of the Meeting, there shall be a replay, if possible on the same ground, on a date to be arranged by the Committee, and for such replay Counties shall be entitled to alter the composition of their teams.

REGULATIONS FOR THE PRUDENTIAL JUNIOR COUNTY CUP

(Inter-County Junior Lawn Tennis Championships)

1. The Prudential Junior County Cup shall be competed for annually on hard courts.
2. The Management shall be entrusted to a Committee nominated annually by the Council of The Lawn Tennis Association, with power to suspend or modify any of these Regulations to meet exceptional circumstances and decide any question of eligibility, qualifications of competitors, interpretation of the Regulations or otherwise. The Committee's decision shall be final.
3. For the purpose of these Championships, which shall be area competitions subject to the Association's Rules 34 and 36, the following shall be regarded as Counties: East of Scotland, North of Scotland, South of Scotland, West of Scotland, North Wales, South Wales, Channel Islands, Isle of Man.
4. All County teams which compete during any year shall be entered for the following year's Competition, unless notice of withdrawal is lodged with The Lawn Tennis Association on or before the first day of December. A County which did not compete in the previous competition and wishes to enter shall give notice in writing to the Secretary of The Lawn Tennis Association on or before the first day of December.
5. The Competition shall be played over a period of three days in groups of not more than four Counties and each group shall play at one place to be known as a "Centre". Each County shall play one match against each other County in the same group. The grouping for 1985 shall be as follows:

BOYS

Group 1
A Essex
B Surrey
C Middlesex
D Lancashire

Group 2
A Yorkshire
B Hertfordshire
C Devon
D South Wales

Group 3
A Kent
B Avon
C Buckinghamhire
D Hampshire & I.O.W.

Group 5
A Norfolk
B East of Scotland
C Cheshire
D Sussex

Group 5
A Nottinghamshire
B North Wales
C Dorset
D Staffordshire

Group 6
A Durham & Cleveland
B Gloucestershire
C Warwickshire
D Leicestershire

Group 7
A Cornwall
B Berkshire
C Lincolnshire
D West of Scotland

Group 8
A Derbyshire
B Suffolk
C Oxfordshire
D Cambridgeshire

Group 9
A Somerset
B Hereford & Worcester
C Shropshire
D North of Scotland

Group 10
A Wiltshire
B Bedfordshire
C Cumbria
D Northamptonshire

Group 11
A Northumberland
B Channel Islands
C South of Scotland
D Isle of Man

GIRLS

Group 1
A Essex
B Surrey
C Yorkshire
D Avon

Group 2
A Middlesex
B Devon
C Leicestershire
D Nottinghamshire

Group 3
A Kent
B Warwickshire
C Hampshire & I.O.W.
D Berkshire

Group 4
A Lancashire
B Cambridgeshire
C Sussex
D Lincolnshire

Group 5
A Cheshire
B Oxfordshire
C Norfolk
D Hertfordshire

Group 6
A Buckinghamshire
B North Wales
C Derbyshire
D Dorset

Group 7
A Hereford & Worcester
B East of Scotland
C Staffordshire
D Gloucestershire

Group 8
A South Wales
B Somerset
C Cornwall
D North of Scotland

Group 9
A West of Scotland
B Durham & Cleveland
C Wiltshire
D Northumberland

Group 10
A Bedfordshire
B Northamptonshire
C Suffolk
D Shropshire

Group 11
A South of Scotland
B Channel Islands
C Cumbria
D Isle of Man

Fixtures:
Monday 1st September: A v. C and B v. D
Tuesday 2nd September: A v. D and B v. C
Wednesday 3rd September: A v. B and C v. D

6. A Referee shall be appointed by each Centre and approved by the Committee.
7. The Committee shall select the make of ball to be used at each Centre.
8. All players must be under the age of eighteen years on 31st December of the previous year.
9. Each County shall be represented in each match by a team, with a minimum of six and a maximum of eight players.
10. Teams must be notified to The Lawn Tennis Association not later than 15th August.

Alterations may be made after this date provided that notification is received by The Lawn Tennis Association before the date on which the competition is due to commence.

11. The team nominations, in order of merit for singles, must be submitted to the Referee for approval, at least one hour before the commencement of play on the first day. This order must be maintained throughout the competition.

12. The teams must be nominated in order of merit for both singles and doubles on the appropriate scorecards. These must reach the Referee, in confidence, not later than 30 minutes before the start of each match. No substitution is permitted during the entire match.

13. Each match will consist of nine rubbers — six singles followed by three doubles; No. 1 shall play No. 1 of the opposing team, No. 2 shall play No. 2 and so on. All rubbers must be the best of three sets. The tie-break shall apply at six games all in the first two sets.

14. If any player is absent when called upon to play by the Referee, the opponent(s) shall be entitled to two love sets.

15. Team officials are not allowed on court during the matches and no advice by any person is permitted during play.

16. If a match in progress cannot be finished on the first and/or second day, it shall, if possible, be finished on the following day but the scheduled programme for the second and third days shall take priority over the playing of any unfinished match(es).

17. In the event of no play being possible on the first and second days, the result of the scheduled match on the third day will determine the final order in each group.

18. If no play is possble on all three days of the competition, the Committee shall decide the arrangements to be made to determine the final order in each group.

19. (i) If at the end of the third day there remain one or more matches in which a result has not been achieved but the round of singles has been completed or either team has won at least four singles rubbers, the match(es) shall be decided thereon.

(ii) The final order in each group in which all matches have been completed (or a result has been reached in accordance with (i) above) shall be determined by the number of matches won.

(iii) In a group to which (ii) above applies but there are teams with an equal number of matches won and in a group to which (ii) above does not apply, the positions shall be determined by:

(a) The percentage of rubbers won to rubbers completed or should this still fail to determine the order, then:

(b) The percentage of sets won to sets completed or should this still fail to determine the order, then:

(c) The percentage of games won to games completed or should this still leave two teams tied, then:

(d) The result of the match between them.

20. The winning team in each group (except Group 1) will be promoted to the group above and the bottom team in each group (except the last group) will be relegated to the group below for the following year's competition. The Committee shall however have power to re-arrange the groups if the number of teams entered differs from that of the previous year.

21. Any dispute arising between Counties shall be referred to the Referee, and any appeal against his decision to the Committee.

REGULATIONS FOR CLUB AND OTHER MATCHES

The following Regulations apply to the extent that a match is not subject to other specified Regulations.

1. The Rules of Tennis, and the Regulations for the Management of Lawn Tennis Tournaments, as far as applicable, shall be observed.

2. A Referee shall be appointed by mutual agreement: he shall have power to appoint umpires, and shall decide any point of law which an umpire may profess himself unable to decide, or which may be referred to him on appeal from the decision of an umpire, or in case an umpire be not employed by the players; he shall decide, if he be called upon to decide by the Captain of either side, whether or not the match shall be stopped owing to the state of the courts, the state of weather, darkness or other unavoidable hindrance.

3. The balls shall be selected by mutual agreement between the competing sides. In case of dispute, the ball to be used shall be decided by lot.

4. Provision for the payment for balls, and the division of gate money, if there be any, shall be made by mutual agreement.

5. For a short match, unless some other system of play be agreed upon:

(a) Each team shall consist of six players, who shall be arranged in pairs by their respective Captains, and each pair shall play against each pair of the opposing team the best of three sets using the tie-break system of scoring, except in a final set. The order of play for the first round shall be decided by lot. For the second round it shall be decided by lot which of the two available pairs some one pair of the opposing team shall meet; as soon as this shall have been done, the order of play for the remaining rubbers (two in the second round and three in the last) will be found to have been determined.

(b) In no case shall any pair play more than one rubber on the same court without the unanimous consent of the Captains and the knowledge of the Referee. The order of the Courts for the first round shall be decided by lot after the order of play shall have been fixed. As soon as this shall have been done, the order of the remaining courts (three in the second round and three in the last) will be found to have been determined.

(c) The time of cessation of play shall be fixed prior to commencement of play by the Captains of the opposing teams, or by the Referee if they shall disagree. It shall be the duty of the Referee to stop play when the time arrives; provided, nevertheless, that the Referee may extend the time with the consent of the Captains of the opposing teams.

(d) The team which shall win the majority of rubbers shall be declared the winner of the match; should the number of rubbers be equal, the majority of sets shall decide, and should the number of rubbers and sets be equal, the majority of games shall decide.

(e) If, at the time of cessation of play, neither team shall have won sufficient rubbers to arrive at a definite result on the above basis then in the event of the first two rounds having been completed, and the third round not having been completed, all rubbers, sets and games played in the third round shall be ignored and the match shall be decided on the two completed rounds.

6. For a long match unless some other system of play be agreed upon:

(a) In addition to the doubles arranged for in Regulation 6 hereof, six singles shall be played, and for the purposes of this Regulation the members of each team shall be arranged in order of merit by their respective Captains, and shall play each against each in these orders the best of three sets. The tie-break system of scoring shall be used, except in a final set. In the case of the Captain of either team disputing the order of merit of the opposing team, the decision of the Referee shall be final.

(b) Separate times for cessation of play in Singles and Doubles shall be fixed, prior to the commencement of play, by the Captains of the opposing teams, or by the Referee if they shall disagree. It shall be the duty of the Referee to stop play when the time arrives; provided, nevertheless, that the Referee may extend the times with the consent of the opposing teams.

(c) In Singles, if at the call of time less than four rubbers shall have been completed, the Captains by mutual agreement may decide upon a date for completing this portion of the match; should no agreement be come to, and should no other method of scoring be decided upon, this portion of the match shall be declared a draw; but in the event of four rubbers having been completed, sets and games in uncompleted rubbers shall not be taken into account.

(d) The match shall be decided by the combined results of Singles and Doubles, and provided that the requisite number of Singles and Doubles shall be played, the team which shall win the majority of rubbers shall be declared the winner of the match; Should the number of rubbers be equal, the majority of sets shall decide, and should the number of rubbers and sets be equal, the majority of games shall decide.

(e) The same teams shall represent their respective sides in both contests.

7. In both short and long matches the Captains of either side may concede rubbers, sets and/or games to the opposing sides for the purpose of completing any round and the Captains may mutually agree some alternative method to those set out in Regulations 5 and 6 for deciding the result of a match.

8. No change shall be made in the composition of the teams after the start of play, except in the case of illness or other unavoidable hindrance, and then only with the consent of the Captain of the opposing team. But when a match shall be postponed before any play shall have taken place, the composition of the competing teams may be changed.

9. Play in each rubber shall be continuous and without unnecessary delay on the part of the players from the first service until the rubber is concluded.

10. If any player be absent when he be called upon to play by the Referee, his opponent shall be entitled to two love sets.

11. A Captain who may wish to play a substitute, that is, a player who is not a bona-fide member of the County or Club in question, shall before the start of play declare the same to the Captain of the opposing team, who may require his withdrawal.

12. County areas and area qualifications shall be as defined in L.T.A. Rules 34 and 36.

13. The qualifications to play for a club shall be bona-fide membership of that Club of at least fourteen days' standing prior to a Match.

THE LAWN TENNIS ASSOCIATION CLUB MANUAL 1986

Edited and Compiled by Geoffrey Bluett
Bagenal Harvey Consultants

Sponsored by
The Prudential Assurance
Company Limited

CONTENTS

INTRODUCTION

It is perhaps an anomaly that although the vital role played by clubs was fully recognised, the constitution of the LTA did not include specifically a Clubs Committee until 1974 when information flowing from IBM's Club of the Year competition provided the ideal base on which to build.

The Committee thus formed, a blend of Councillors and non-Councillors, was a team of experienced club administrators who were well aware of clubs' need for guidance.

Details of their work will be found in the chapter "How the LTA Helps" but, not surprisingly, the first task was to produce the Club Manual—a book of reference—capable of advising any club committee, whatever its size or function.

Many ideas have been included which are designed to make life easier for those with club responsibilities and it is hoped that, in its new form as part of the Handbook, this section will be read for its general advice as well as for more specific purposes. It should also be borne in mind that where particular advice seems irrelevant to some, it will be extremely pertinent to others.

CLUB CONSTITUTIONS

MEMBERS' NON-PROFIT-MAKING CLUB

This is the most common constitution for the smaller lawn tennis club or any club not owning its freehold.

The Rules set out the constitution of a members' club and should be available for immediate adoption at the inaugural meeting of the club. Failing this, they are one of the most urgent tasks of the newly formed committee, who will then have to call an early General Meeting to adopt them. Subsequently they can be altered to meet changing needs, but only at a general meeting and in accordance with the provisions for alteration which they themselves must contain.

Simple specimen Rules are shown in the next section. For a composite club providing various sports, the Rules will need to be more complex but extension, according to the needs of the case, should not be difficult.

A "Members' Club" does not have a legal existence as an entity, i.e. separate from its members. It can therefore neither sue nor be sued, nor prosecuted, in the Courts in its own name but only through its Officers, and the same applies to the making of formal contracts. This, however, matters little as far as day-to-day business is concerned: landlords, banks, insurance companies, brewers and other traders will be happy to deal with officials of a club. There may, however, be difficulty in such major matters as the purchase or ownership of land, and there is at least a theoretical risk to the Officers (and indeed, strictly speaking, the members) in the event of their being sued for the club's debts, or for damages for injury (if not adequately covered by insurance), etc. In regard to the holding of investments, some Company or Stock Registrars will happily accept a club as a share or stock holder, while others prefer the appointment of trustees for this purpose, a procedure which has the advantage that changes of club officials do not then have to be notified to the Registrar.

MEMBERS' NON-PROFIT-MAKING CLUB, WITH TRUSTEES

One method of overcoming some of the difficulties of the preceding paragraph is to have Trustees who will hold property on behalf of the club. In the simplest case of holding an investment, if the club itself is not acceptable to the Registrar concerned, your bank may be willing to hold as Trustees with no more formality than a Committee resolution, duly minuted, requesting them to do so; but for anything more complex, such as land, individuals are more usual as trustees: a Trust Deed will be required and this must essentially be drawn up by a

Solicitor. Such a deed will appoint the first trustees and lay down the method of replacing them.

LIMITED COMPANY

If for the purpose of holding land or investments, issuing debentures etc., or limiting the liability of Officers, Committee and Members it is desired to obtain Corporate Status—and this is probably to be recommended at least for the larger clubs—this can best be achieved by Registration under the Companies Acts:

(a) Company Limited by Shares

Numerically of course the vast majority of Limited Companies are business ventures and the constitution which these follow is known as a Company Limited by Shares. Quite a few clubs—often ill-advisedly—have adopted this type of constitution and endeavoured, with mixed success, to adapt it to their own needs. This is possible although considerable redrafting of the standard provisions is required in order to ensure continued eligibility for the benefits of non-profit-making status, viz in regard to rate relief, taxation, government and other grants towards capital improvements, etc. It is necessary, for example, specifically to exclude any club member, shareholder, or other person from receiving any profit or dividend or even a share of the assets in the event of winding up. When this has been done, any purpose in having shareholders disappears but the club (company) remains saddled with them and with an unnecessarily cumbersome administrative procedure when a shareholder member dies or resigns from membership. Therefore (b) below is usually more suitable.

(b) Company Limited by Guarantee and not having a Share Capital

This is provided by the Companies Acts as the counterpart to the Company Limited by Shares, for cases where shareholders are not required and profits are not to be distributed. *It should therefore be regarded as the normal company constitution for a non-profit-making club* and *the Lawn Tennis Association would certainly recommend it in normal cases, when corporate status is sought.*

When registration has been decided upon it is imperative that a Solicitor's services be obtained to put it into effect. When he drafts the "Memorandum and Articles of Association" (which are the legal documents setting out the form of a company) he should be asked to bear in mind the need to retain non-profit-making status for the club (company) and therefore to ensure that, even in the event of winding up, no member, guarantor or other person can benefit from the proceeds.

LIMITED COMPANY COMBINED WITH MEMBERS' CLUB

Some clubs operate partly as a company and partly as a Members' Club. The company deals with the ownership of premises and major financial transactions while the Members' Club handles day-to-day matters. The reason for this is that a Limited Company, as such, may be too formal.

The principal objection is psychological: the members may not understand the arrangement and be suspicious that it is a device to deprive them of the right to run their own club their own way. Indeed regrettably this can sometimes happen, especially if the company directors are older members who may not be in full touch with current requirements.

If such an arrangement is made, it is suggested that there should be a careful watch, when the documents are being drawn up, to ensure that the running of the club does remain effectively in the hands of the current active membership.

PROPRIETARY CLUBS

This constitution comes halfway between a Members' Club and a Business. It has members, who pay a subscription, and is run outwardly along the general lines of an ordinary club: so much so, that visitors may not realise that it is not a Members' Club. There will be a Committee and Rules (if advantage is to be taken of a club registration for supplying liquor to members, rather than an Excise Licence) but the members' and indeed the Committee's powers are limited and in some matters, especially financial, the Proprietor retains control although this may not be for reasons of profit-making. For example, a business house club may operate under the proprietorship of the business organisation for whose staff it is set up, but may nevertheless be run on the most desirable club-like and non-profit-making lines.

The law relating to Proprietary Clubs is more complex than that relating to Members' Clubs and it is not appropriate to consider it in detail in this Manual.

CHARITABLE STATUS

The question is sometimes raised whether a sports club can obtain registration as a charity, thereby gaining additional advantages in taxation, rating etc. Legally sport is not of itself "charitable". Some individual clubs may, of course, be so, usually when they form a part of a larger charitable organisation such as a YMCA, but otherwise the general experience of clubs which have seriously investigated the matter is that, in order to qualify, they would have to impose upon themselves conditions which would be quite unacceptable in the running of a club.

Unless there is a change in the law, the LTA would have difficulty in recommending the general run of ordinary lawn tennis clubs to seek charitable status. Any which think that their own special circumstances might make them an exception should seek professional advice and, before proceeding far, should also make contact with the appropriate Government Departments which are: The Charity Commission, 14 Ryder Street, London, SW1Y 6AH (Tel: 01-214 6000); The Department of the Environment, Sport and Recreation Division, 17-19 Rochester Row, London, SW1P 1LH. (Tel: 01-212 3434.)

CLUB MANAGEMENT

THE COMMITTEE AND ITS WORK

There can be little doubt that the degree of success a club enjoys is directly related to the organising ability of its committee(s). Although structures vary widely, the diagram (see over) shows a good example, with the main committee consisting of 12 people: Chairman, Treasurer, Secretary and a representative from each area of activity—Planning, Finance, Ground, Tennis, House, Social, Bar, Catering and Juniors—i.e. the match captain or secretary for Tennis, perhaps one of the older juniors for the Juniors Committee and so on.

Whereas larger clubs will find their committees specialising more and more, creating the need for sub-committees, the small club will combine House with Ground, Finance with Planning and Bar with Catering, co-opting when necessary. (This, incidentally, is where small clubs often have an advantage for club spirit is never higher than when every member rallies to a common cause as the need arises). But whatever the size of membership, liaison between Committees or representatives is essential. It does not help the Table Tennis section, for example, to find the hall they use on a particular match night being prepared for a social. Such oversights should occur only once, if at all, before they are covered by your communications system.

The following analysis of Committees and their work should help clubs to assess their present structure.

The Main Committee

(a) Consists of club officers and one representative from each area of activity.

(b) Responsibilities include overall control of club affairs, committee and rules. A word immediately on delegation: where members of the main committee sit on other committees, the majority of them will be involved in many meetings. To ease the calls on their time, make sure as much responsibility as possible is delegated. The main committee should come together only to receive reports on Committee progress and to make major decisions e.g. if an extra court is recommended, that recommendation and the case for and against should be put by the Planning Committee. The final decision should be made by the main committee.

(c) Regarding personnel, although the prime requirement is enthusiasm, people with trade or professional experience have much to offer. Include them if at all possible. Further ideas for specific committees are to be found later in this chapter.

Finance Committee

(a) Consists of Hon. Treasurer, Subscriptions Secretary if any, another main committee member, a member of the Planning Committee plus others as appropriate.

(b) Responsibilities include reporting on the club's overall viability, accounts (and auditing), subscription levels, revenue-producing ideas, and the handling of grant and loan applications, costing of major enterprises, staff wages

Planning Committee

(a) Consists of main committee member, a representative of the Finance Committee plus others as appropriate.

(b) Responsibilities must include not only a short term but also a long term plan (say 5-10 years) for the club, major club improvements and new facilities. Obviously "Planning" and "Finance" must work closely together.

Tennis Committee

(a) Consists of Men's and Ladies' captains (and vice-captains if appropriate), Match Secretary, Club Coach, if any, and a representative (preferably a junior) from the Juniors Committee. One member will be on the main committee and another should be a delegate on the Ground Committee.

(b) Responsibilities: In larger clubs, work should be divided between the Match Sub-Committee and the Club Tennis Sub-Committee. Smaller clubs will combine the responsibilities shown here separately:

Match Sub-Committee:
Fixture calendar, selection of teams, entering of County and other club team competitions (probably through the Secretary and Treasurer), match fees and hospitality for visiting teams, organising court preparation through Ground Committee delegate and maintaining the supply of tennis balls.

Club Tennis Sub-Committee:
Club tournament, organising times of play for members, helping new members to integrate, coaching and playing-in tests, allocation of courts and collection of visitors' fees.

Ground Committee

(a) Consists of main committee member and at least one member from any Committee whose section uses the club's outdoor facilities e.g. Tennis, Bowls, Croquet etc., plus someone with a knowledge of the relevant court machinery if any. The Committee will number according to the size of the area involved and whether or not ground staff are employed.

(b) Responsibilities include care of the courts and club grounds, court and other equipment (including maintenance of machinery) and decisions on whether courts are fit for play, after consultation with the groundsman. Sometimes this committee will have difficulty finding personnel, which is unfortunate since clubs with an attractive appearance give a good impression to new members, visiting teams etc. A costly alternative is to employ a firm that specialises in landscaping—it might just be worthwhile.

House Committee

(a) Consists of main committee member plus enough members, again depending on the area involved, to maintain the pavilion and other buildings (groundsman's hut, squash courts etc.) in good condition.

(b) Responsibilities include all repairs and replacement of fixtures and fittings such as light bulbs, windows, heating appliances, furniture and soft furnishings, as well as decorations, the safety and soundness of the structure e.g. lagging of pipes and repairs to a roof leak, and equipment used for any of these purposes. (See under Fire Prevention and Security).

Social Committee

(a) Consists of main committee member and representatives from all sections of the club as well as delegates from the Bar, Catering and Juniors Committees. Anyone with enterprise and enthusiastic interest is an obvious candidate.

(b) Responsibilities include all the club's social activities such as dances, barbecues, rallies, parties, outings, jumble sales and so on. (Table Tennis and Bridge should be included unless catered for by separate sections). It is for this Committee to ensure the growth of the "non-playing members" section if this is required.

One idea worth considering is for each social project to be the responsibility of a different member of the Committee. This formula will help to promote variety through the year.

Bar Committee

(a) Often referred to by the Magistrates' Courts (Licensing Authority) as a "Wine Committee", it should consist of at least three members (exact number to be quoted in the Club's Rules—Chairman, Secretary and Treasurer will not suffice), one of whom is on the main committee —they must be elected by a general meeting.

(b) Responsibilities include arranging a rota system, ordering of stock, applying for an extension of opening hours on social occasions (probably through the Secretary) and the decoration and general appearance of the bar itself. It is advisable that one member of this Committee is a delegate on the Social Committee.

N.B. Reminders for renewal of bar registration are not usually sent—loss of bar facilities will result from failure to renew in time.

Catering Committee

(a) Consists of main committee member plus others appropriate to the size of membership and extent of the catering.

(b) Responsibilities include adequate provision of catering facilities for general and specific purposes, a rota system, match teas, equipment used in the kitchen and hygiene. It is advisable that one member of the Committee is a delegate on the Social Committee and another on the Match Sub-Committee.

Juniors Committee

(a) Consists of main committee member (ideally a junior), Club Coach if any, plus the most responsible juniors and, if possible, one or two parents. Juniors should hold a voting majority.

(b) Responsibilities include passing on to the main committee views and comments from the Juniors section, arranging junior socials, junior tournaments and the organisation and control of all other junior activities. Should any matter of junior discipline arise, it is best dealt with by this Committee. It should provide delegates to the Match and Club Tennis sub-committees and the Social Committee. The successful transition from junior to senior will depend to a great extent on the success of this Committee and the experience will stand the junior delegates and the club in good stead for the future.

Press and Public Relations Officer

Probably the most underestimated officer, his first duty is to write reports on matches and other items of club activity for the local newspapers and the Club Newsletter. Experience in this field is a great advantage for newspaper editors appreciate 'copy' typed clearly and concisely—the more professional the article, the less likely it is to be cut and altered. When an editor knows that he can 'trust' articles, the club will probably enjoy a more than satisfactory degree of coverage which effectively publicises the club and its activities at little cost, if any.

In return it is a good idea to make the newspapers' editors, photographers and correspondents welcome at the club at all times and particularly for socials and dances. If they can be involved, so much the better.

Other duties will include keeping members in touch with current and future plans and maintaining good relations with the club's neighbours.

It may serve the Club well if this office, with its necessary tact and diplomacy, were to be represented on the main committee particularly if explanations of policy are requested by members.

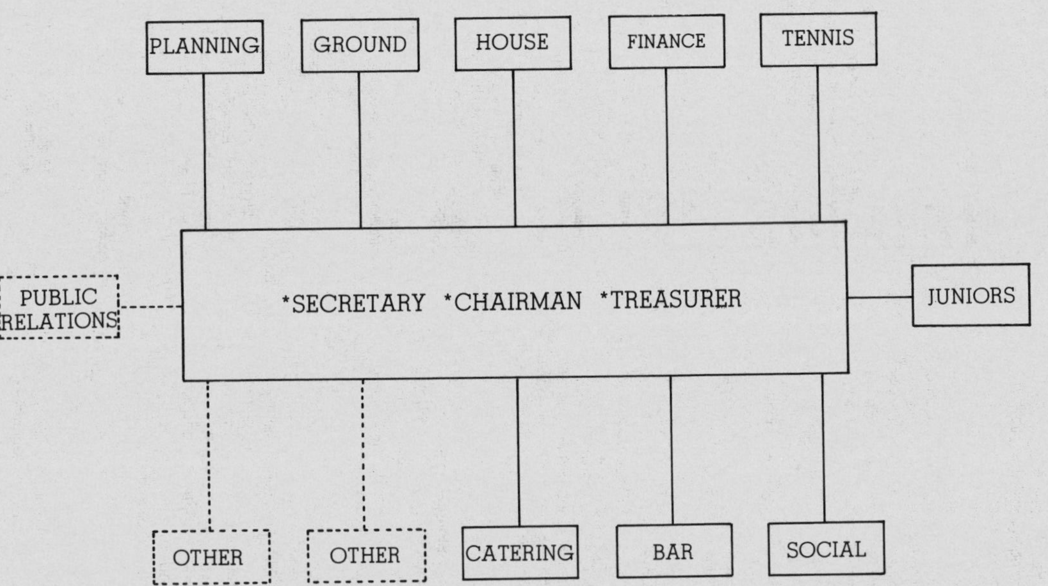

*Ex-officio members of all Committees

CHOOSING THE RIGHT PEOPLE

Having agreed your committee structure the next logical step is to allocate responsibilities. The principle behind this is that clubs should make an effort to select people for the various offices and avoid the risk of misdirected enthusiasm. Architects, accountants, solicitors or bank managers will easily be found areas in which to contribute and the following list shows some other obvious candidates for committee work.

Planning: Architect, solicitor, surveyor. The weighting here is not significant.
Finance: Accountant, bank manager, mortgage broker, insurance broker.
House: Builder (including carpenters, decorators, tilers, plasterers, electricians, engineers, plumbers).
Ground: Mechanic, gardener, farmer.
Publicity: Advertising agent, artist, journalist, signwriter, printer.
Social and Entertainment: Personnel officer, musician, representative, photographer, secretary, manager of local sports retailer, policeman.
Bar: Wine merchant, retail trader, accountant.
Catering: Baker, housewife, butcher, confectioner.
Juniors: Teacher, housewife, coach, policeman, not for discipline but because of their acknowledged work in youth clubs etc.

Accordingly, club secretaries should compile a list of members' trades and professions, adding new members as they join. It may prove invaluable.

There may well be other trades and professions whose advice would improve efficiency within the club. Although anyone involved in management will be a great asset, this is not to say that these are the only people; the basic requirement is enthusiasm, but this quality needs to be channelled in the right direction.

Paid Secretaries

One official who can be certain of a fair share of the work is the Club Secretary. He or she is likely to be the kingpin of most operations and is, therefore, a difficult person to replace (or even find in the first place).

Although an honorarium or salary does not guarantee loyalty, it should help in the search. Housewives, for instance, particularly those trained as Secretaries, might be ideal candidates.

The point is that this work has to be done. If that means paying someone and adding a little to the subscription, then do so. A backlog in this department is better not experienced!

CONDUCT OF MEETINGS

General

In most cases procedure at meetings is subject first to any requirements in the club's rules and secondly to the accepted procedure for meetings which has evolved over many years.

Chairmanship

Choose your Chairman with great care. His or her responsibilities are wide-ranging and few people, although they may aspire to the "honour", have the necessary qualities. The duties of the Chairman can be summarised as follows:

1. To welcome new members and put them at their ease.
2. To promote and guide discussion.
3. To get the business done.

These are the basic requirements of good chairmanship and it may help to expand them a little.

Try to avoid the practice of the most senior member of the committee becoming chairman automatically—the need is for the best person without too much regard for length of service.

The chairman must try to keep meetings relaxed and constructive however divisive the issue. He must give supporters of all shades of opinion a reasonable opportunity to express their views whilst endeavouring himself to maintain a neutral position. If in addition he can dissuade them from endless repetition of facts and arguments, he will earn the thanks of everyone at the meeting.

So that it is not necessary to vote on every proposal that is brought forward, a good chairman tries by discussion to obtain a consensus within the meeting. If this is possible everyone feels more committed to the decision than if there is a vote where some of those present must stand up and be counted against the proposal. Obviously this is not always possible but where a vote is necessary the chairman should ideally abstain unless a casting vote is needed to break a deadlock when he should generally veer towards "no change". A proposal is not carried unless it wins a majority and it is probably better to reconsider if it cannot do that without the help of the chairman's casting vote.

At a general meeting no decisions should be taken on any item not spelt out on the agenda. If under "Any Other Business" an attempt is made to push through a proposal not specifically referred to on the agenda, the chairman's duty is to defer the matter. This rule and practice is designed to ensure that if any major change affecting members is proposed the members should be given an opportunity to consider all aspects of the proposal before coming to the meeting—and to make a special journey to speak and vote if they wish.

At most club meetings the chairman will probably feel that he can, at the end of the formal business, allow some informal discussion of domestic affairs to give the committee guidance on the views of those present.

One technical point—if there is a specific motion before the meeting and an amendment to that motion is proposed and seconded it is necessary to vote on the amendment before voting on the main motion. If there is a second amendment the vote is on that first—always the last amendment properly proposed and seconded is the first to be voted on and so back in rotation. If any amendment is carried, there then has to be a vote on the original motion as amended.

A simple majority only is needed to pass an amendment whereas generally two-thirds is required to change, for example, a club rule.

Finally, never forget the third basic duty, to get the business done. The most brilliant and succinct businessman can become transformed at his club meetings and unless the chairman keeps the meeting moving the second item on the agenda may never be reached.

Notice of Meetings

Always try to give at least a fortnight's notice of meetings and indeed the date fixed for the A.G.M. should be notified to members much further ahead even than the issue of the formal agenda. This can be done by its inclusion in the club fixture list, by a notice in the club house and/or in any circulars issued to members during the season.

Agenda

A copy of the accounts is normally enclosed with the agenda for an A.G.M. although it is sufficient for these to be displayed in the club house for a reasonable period before the meeting. A footnote to the agenda should say so. (See also specimen Rule 12 under Rules and Regulations).

Minutes

It is usual at an A.G.M. to approve the minutes of the preceding one though this can be done at the first committee meeting after the general meeting when the proceedings would be fresher in mind. Time would also be saved at the next A.G.M. although the minutes must still be available to be read to the meeting if required.

Minutes should be concise—there is no need to name proposers or seconders of motions nor give voting figures. If they are principally confined to a record of decisions taken, as they should be, they meet all requirements and avoid subsequent arguments about who said exactly what twelve months ago.

Temporary Chairman

If at any duly convened meeting neither the President nor Chairman of the Club is present, members actually there choose their chairman for that meeting. The Club Secretary opens the meeting by inviting nominations and the Chair remains vacant until the choice is made.

Proxy Voting

For an ordinary club not subject to the Companies Acts, proxy voting is not allowed unless the rules specifically provide for it.

Plumping

Where there are more candidates than vacancies in a ballot to elect members of a committee, a group of members will sometimes get together to push one particular candidate at the expense of and without consideration for the balance and composition of the committee generally. They do this by voting only for that one candidate and deliberately not voting for as many candidates as there are vacancies. Whilst this is a system to be strongly discouraged, it is not illegal unless the Club Rules prescribe that a ballot paper will only be valid if it carries votes for the full number of vacancies to be filled.

Committee Meetings

Most of what has been said in this section applies to committee meetings just as to general meetings but these are normally conducted in a more informal atmosphere.

THE IMPORTANCE OF COMMUNICATIONS AND INVOLVEMENT

Reference has been made to the need to keep the outside world in touch with club news and events but the importance of communicating with members cannot be overstressed. Too many clubs to-day are struggling simply because not enough members are involved in the day to day running of socials, coaching and so on. This puts pressure on those who are prepared to do their share. It is perhaps a sign of our times that new members tend to expect payment of subscriptions to cover all the work which has to be done, and ideally this should be the case. However, it is not always possible, particularly where rival clubs in the neighbourhood are surviving happily with similar subscriptions and no paid secretariat.

In these instances clubs should try to make all members aware of the need for them to be involved in the running of the club—many hands make light work.

A priority should be some kind of regular newsletter, the cost of which should be allowed for within the subscriptions, so the following ideas may help to alleviate the more common problems which arise.

1. If large quantities are involved, enlist the services of someone having access to a magnetic card typewriter or addressing system. Members' addresses can be typed on to adhesive labels— several for each member. You can take batches of envelopes (minimum 120) for franking and despatch to the Post Office and you may be able to pay the total postage by cheque.
2. Don't forget to use these mailing shots for other items such as subscription reminders, fixture cards etc.
3. Where a number of enclosures are involved, use different coloured paper for anything special.

Most clubs have a noticeboard which, because it is either too small or too untidy, draws little attention. Team sheets, match results, newspaper cuttings and notices of socials need displaying according to their current importance. Anyone who has dressed a shop window or works with an advertising agency should know enough about displays to be able to change the character of the noticeboard so that it becomes the first priority of a visit to the club. One very simple idea is to use a swivelling arrow to point to anything new or special.

Finally, while most of the foregoing will help break down 'them and us' situations, these can still be a problem in clubs where good committee work is carried on too often behind closed doors. Certainly there are matters which demand privacy—staff salaries for example—but mostly the reverse is true, the more people knowing why a decision was made the better. There are two ways of dealing with this: either open some of the meetings to other club members or put a copy of the minutes on the noticeboard.

LAWN TENNIS CLUB RULES AND REGULATIONS

The specimen Rules and Regulations given below will serve as much as a check list for established clubs as a basis for new clubs. The main objects of the rules are:

(a) To enable Members to know their rights and the required discipline;

(b) To enable the Committee to enforce these without causing offence;

(c) To provide an adequate legal constitution for dealing with formal matters—leases or land purchase, licensing, taxation, rating relief, and so on. For some of these purposes the Rules will be subject to scrutiny by outside authorities and they must conform to certain requirements.

Although it is desirable to publish both the "Rules" and the "Regulations" in a single document, the difference between them should be realised when they are being drafted: the Rules cover the more formal aspects and can be altered only by the Members in general meeting, while the Regulations (occasionally but less appropriately referred to in some clubs as "Bye-laws") govern the day-to-day running of the Club and normally can be altered from time to time by the Committee.

The many different forms of clubs will require additional Rules and Regulations to cover their own range of activities but our starting point is a lawn tennis "members' club".

RULES as at ______________________________ 19___

1. Name and Objects

The Club, founded in 19___, shall be named "The___ Lawn Tennis Club and shall have for its objects the provision of lawn tennis, social and other facilities for its Members.

(The inclusion of the date founded is for identification in case there should be an earlier or later club taking the same name.)

2. Constitution

The Club is constituted by these Rules as a Non-profit-making Members' Club. In no circumstances during the continuance of the Club, nor at nor after its dissolution, shall any assets or surplus funds be distributed to any Member or other person nor to any organisation which is not itself either constituted as non-profit-making or a charity.

(Unless this is made clear, difficulties may arise over eligibility for rating relief, financial assistance for capital projects, and other benefits confined to non-profit-making clubs.)

3. Affiliation

The Club shall seek affiliation to The Lawn Tennis Association through the appropriate county lawn tennis association and shall adopt and conform to the Rules of these organisations in so far as they can apply.

4. Classes of Member and Subscription Rates

There shall be the following Classes of Member at the rates of subscription shown:

Class A Playing Member

Annual Subscription

£ ________

Reduction for payment by____________

£ ________

Etc. See 'Size of Membership and Restrictions'. Honorary Membership see Rule 6.

Notes to the Subscription Scale

(a) Every senior and junior Playing Member must, with the Club subscription, pay a Player's Contribution, which the Club passes on to the County LTA. The rates of contribution are decided annually at the A.G.M. of The Lawn Tennis Association.

(b) In the event of the Club being liable for Value Added (or any other) Tax on Members' subscriptions, the figures shown above shall be inclusive thereof (or exclusive as the case may be).

(c) The subscription year runs from______________to ______________________________

(d) For a subscription paid before the due date a reduction will be allowed as shown in the scale.

(e) A Member whose subscription is not paid by the due date will not be entitled to the privileges of membership until he has paid, and if not paid by ______________________ he will cease to be a Member (and any re-election will then be subject to the normal procedure).

(f) The subscription, and entrance fee if applicable, of a new Member shall be due on notification of election or within 14 days. Alternatively it may be paid with the membership application, in which case (i) it will be repaid if election to membership does not take place; (ii) at the discretion of the Honorary Secretary and one other Committee Member, the candidate may be allowed to use the Club pending the Committee's consideration of his application.

(g) For a new Member after the end of ________ the Committee may at their discretion accept a proportionately reduced subscription for the part-year. Likewise they may make a refund to a Member who becomes unable to use the Club for a substantial part of the year on account of injury, illness, or departure from the district.

(Notes:

(i) It is to be expected that most Members will take advantage of the reduction for early payment and the fixing of the scale should allow for this: the arrangement is found advantageous in speeding up payments and so reducing the work of collection.

(iii) There has been some tendency recently to show no subscription rates in the Rules but to provide instead that they will be fixed yearly at the annual general meeting, for the ensuing year. This is claimed to make it easier to keep up with inflation and can be regarded as a satisfactory alternative to the more usual arrangement envisaged by these draft Rules; but the further stage, occasionally encountered, of allowing the **Committee** *to fix the scale without reference to a general meeting, is* **not**, *in the view of the LTA, to be recommended.*

(iii) If an entrance fee is to be charged, this should be shown as an additional item in the subscription scale.)

5. Accountancy Year

Except for the purposes of subscriptions (see Rule 4, Note (c)), the Club's Financial Year shall run from 1st October to 30th September and the accounts submitted to the Annual General Meeting shall be prepared accordingly.

(While it is irksome that the subscription year may well differ from the accountancy year, any other arrangement involves the greater disadvantages of (i) holding the annual general meeting at an unsuitable time of year—see Note to Rule 12—or (ii) presenting accounts for a period long expired.)

6. Election of Members

Honorary Membership (other than temporary in accordance with Rule 10), including Honorary Life Membership, shall be strictly limited and at the discretion of the Committee, by way of reward for special services to the Club.

For the other classes of Membership provided in Rule 4, a candidate shall be proposed and seconded by Members aged 18 or over on a form to be provided for the purpose. Every application shall be posted on the Club noticeboard for at least seven days before being considered by the Committee, whose decision shall be by a simple majority and shall be final. The Committee shall have power to limit the numbers of Members in the respective Classes if they consider this necessary.

(Some Clubs, especially long-established ones, have an election procedure not based on a "simple majority" of the Committee but this is now not acceptable if the Club is to be eligible for financial assistance for capital projects.)

7. Resignation and Transfer between Classes

A Member wishing to withdraw from membership or to transfer to a Class at a lower rate of subscription shall notify the Honorary Secretary by ____________ in writing and otherwise shall be liable for the full subscription.

8. Suspension or Expulsion

The Committee shall have power to terminate or suspend the membership of any Member or to exclude any Member or Visitor whom it considers guilty of a breach of these Rules or of misconduct or offensive behaviour to any other Member, Visitor or Employee, whether on the Club's premises or elsewhere.

9. Injury, Loss of Property Etc.

Members or Visitors leaving unattended vehicles, rackets, clothing or other property at the Club do so at their own risk and the Club shall not be responsible for any loss, damage or injury resulting from this or any other cause.

10. Visitors and Temporary Members

Visitors may be introduced by the Honorary Secretary or other Member. Before a Visitor plays, the Member introducing him must make an appropriate entry in the Visitor's Book and pay the fee, which is

Monday to Friday **p per day
Saturday or Sunday **p per day

A Non-Playing Member may play, at the same fee as a Visitor, but neither a Visitor nor a Non-Playing Member may play more than three times in any year except with the special permission of the Committee.

Every member of a visiting match team shall be an Honorary Member for the day and every competitor in a tournament at the Club (and in the case of a competitor under age 18, his parent or guardian) shall be an Honorary Member for the period of the tournament.

Temporary Members, not permanently resident nor working within ______________________ miles of the Club, may be admitted at the discretion of the Honorary Secretary and one other Committee Member for a period not exceeding one calendar month, at the following fees:

One week: £**
Two weeks: £**
One month: £**

11. Management

The management of the Club shall be in the entire control of a Committee of ______________ members in addition to the Officers, who shall be ex-officio members of the Committee and shall be a Chairman, Vice-Chairman, Honorary Secretary, Honorary Treasurer, Men's and Ladies' Captains and/or Match Secretaries (but if more than one of these offices are held by a single person, no extra Committee vacancy shall be thereby created). All shall be elected for the year at the annual general meeting except that the elected Committee shall have power to fill any casual vacancy.

The Committee shall elect Members in accordance with Rule 6 and shall from time to time make and revise the Club's Regulations and shall have power to decide any matter unprovided for by these Rules and the current Regulations. They shall meet at least four times in every year and additionally as circumstances may require. The quorum at a Committee Meeting shall be ______________ and in the event of equality of voting the chairman shall have a second or casting vote.

The Committee may delegate any part of its duties (except the election of Members) to one or more sub-committees which may be composed of any Members of the Club, but any sub-committee to control a bar supplying intoxicating liquor shall be appointed in accordance with the Licensing requirements.

(The titles of Officers and the number of further Committee Members should be considered in the light of local circumstances. Some clubs include one or more of the following: Membership Secretary; Social Secretary; Juniors Secretary; but, of course, even if these are not formally provided for in the Rules, the Committee can appoint sub-committees for these special purposes, or others.)

12. General Meeting

An annual general meeting shall be held each year between 15th October and 30th November inclusive.

The Committee shall call an extraordinary general meeting at their discretion or within one month of receipt by the Honorary Secretary of a requisition signed by twenty Members or, if the total membership is less than 100, by one-fifth of the Members, stating the business proposed to be transacted.

Any Member wishing to propose a resolution at the annual general meeting must send a copy thereof to the Honorary Secretary before 1st October so that provision may be made on the Agenda. The Honorary Secretary shall send to every Member (other than Temporary Members) at least seven days' notice of any general meeting, together with a copy of the Agenda.

The business of the annual general meeting shall be the confirmation of the minutes of the previous annual general meeting and of any subsequent extraordinary general meetings, the consideration of the Committee's report and the Honorary Treasurer's Accounts for the year, the election of Officers and Committee for the ensuing year, the appointment of an Honorary Auditor, and any items of which notice has been given and details included in the Agenda.

The business of an extraordinary general meeting shall be in accordance with the requisition under which it was summoned and the Agenda issued. At any general meeting further business may be accepted at the discretion of the chairman provided that it does not call for an alteration of Rules, the winding up of the Club, the transfer of any of the Club's assets, the borrowing of money, or any expenditure not within the immediate financial resources of the Club.

Every Member (other than Temporary Members) shall be entitled to be present and to speak at any general meeting and, if aged 18 years or over, to vote thereat. In the event of an equality of votes, the chairman shall have a second or casting vote.

At any general meeting the quorum shall be__________ Members entitled to vote.

(It is important that the date laid down for the annual general meeting should be soon after the close of the summer season rather than at the start of the next. Otherwise, not only will the events of the previous summer have slipped from Members' memory, but the appointment of Officers will (if there are changes) involve the new ones in administering arrangements which they have not themselves had an opportunity of making—for example, a match secretary who is to operate the summer fixtures should have been concerned in making them during the winter. Also, any appointments made after December are likely to be too late for inclusion in the list of clubs in the LTA Handbook and any publications of the county LTA).

13. Rules and Regulations

A copy of these Rules and of the Regulations made by the Committee under Rule 11 shall be prominently displayed at all times on the Club noticeboard and all Members shall be deemed conversant therewith. The Rules shall not be altered except at a general meeting after due notice, and then only provided that two-thirds of those present and voting are in favour. The Regulations shall be made and periodically revised by the Committee.

(If the Club does not have premises where it can display the Rules and Regulations, the above wording must be altered accordingly but there must be some means incorporated whereby Members have no excuse for not knowing the Rules. Failing any other means of achieving this, they should be printed (or duplicated) and the Rule should say: ". . . . shall be issued to all Members on election." In the larger Clubs this is common practice in any event.)

14. Dissolution

The Club shall be dissolved on the passing of a resolution to that effect at a general meeting after due notice, by at least two-thirds of those present and voting. Such a meeting shall appoint a committee to wind up the affairs of the Club and shall give general directions as to the disposal of any assets, within the scope of Rule 2.

REGULATIONS as at____________________ 19___

Among the subjects to be covered may be:

1. Dates when summer season opens and closes.
2. Opening hours of courts, pavilion, and bar (if any).
3. Power of Committee to close courts to Members, for maintenance or for special reasons such as hire to local schools or other outside bodies.
4. Procedure for reserving courts or alternatively the prohibition of reserving courts. In framing this regulation the needs of club matches, club tournaments and players taking part in outside competitions where one player has to provide a court should be borne in mind.
5. Procedure for making up games, "club days", and the relinquishing of courts when others are waiting.
6. Any restrictions on particular classes of Member.
7. Procedure for drawing, safeguarding, and returning balls (if these are provided by the Club).
8. Dress, e.g. that it must be "predominantly white, except for track suits in bad weather" or that "recognised coloured tennis clothing may be worn". Also, unless the courts are all of a hard non-upkeep type, it should be required that shoes to be worn on court must be "rubber soled, without raised heels, spikes, studs, cleats, bars or deep ribbing".
9. Any restrictions on the admission of children, dogs, bicycles or perambulators to the ground, pavilion, bar, changing rooms, or to specified areas of these.
10. Any requirements of the "last to leave", e.g. lowering of nets, putting away balls, switching off lights and heating and checking water taps are turned off, locking up pavilion or ground.

SIZE OF MEMBERSHIP AND RESTRICTIONS

The size of membership that a club can happily manage depends on the percentage of "regulars" but one can reckon on an average of about 30 members per court. (This number may vary according to circumstances and number/type of courts.).

Assuming half hour periods in a four court club:

1st period	16 members would play
2nd period	32 members would have played
3rd period	48 members would have played
4th period	64 members would have played

Thus if one third of the 120 members arrive at the same time (which is unlikely) the maximum delay would be one hour—not unreasonable.

This is, of course, flexible and in the final reckoning one must assess how easy or difficult it is to "get on court".

One useful idea for expanding a small club is to vary the categories in which the memberships fall, perhaps making it more expensive to play at weekends or less expensive at less popular times.

One club introduced a "four-session membership" allowing play on one specific weekday evening plus Saturday morning and evening and Sunday evening. Other permutations could be worked out to suit.

The subject of restrictions on members, especially juniors, often creates acrimony. While everything should be done to allow as much playing time to juniors as possible, it is recognised that many will be lost to the game after leaving school because of university, marriage, professions and so on.

Another restriction area is the "playing-in test". Although it helps maintain a balance of standard within the club, it does on occasion prevent some people from playing and improving.

All of which leads to the conclusion that restrictions ought to be based on practical reasoning. For example a good standard junior playing in the first team should be welcome to play at any time whereas an adult beginner should be rationed for his good and the club's to certain times that include group coaching sessions. This way he or she will meet other players of a similar standard. If this principle is agreed, transfer to a higher grade membership would follow at the appropriate time.

Subscriptions should be fixed according to the restrictions on play, except where students, juniors and other non-wage earners are concerned. They, together with wives of members where applicable, should be subject to lower rates.

Ideally, then, no one should be turned away from any club on grounds of standard.

Here is a possible set of membership categories to compare with your own:

Category 1
Full Members. Seniors & selected Juniors
Unrestricted play

Category 2
Country Membership. Students & Members living & working outside 25 mile radius
Unrestricted play

Category 3
Midweek Members. Senior & Junior
Play any weekday before 6.30 p.m.

Category 4
Four Session. Senior & Junior Members (N.B. no beginners)
Play either two specified mid-week evenings or one specified midweek evening and Saturday morning plus weekend evenings.

Category 5
Senior Beginners
Play after 6.30 p.m. two specified weekdays and can attend all senior coaching courses.

Category 6
Junior Beginners
Play before 6.30 p.m. one week-day and Saturday morning and can attend all junior coaching courses.

N.B. Subscription should include coaching fees to avoid the 'paying on the night' problems.

The subscription rates would fall accordingly from Category 1 to Category 6 and some suggestions and advice on rates are given under Budgeting and Accounting.

The Classes referred to above are as a guide only. Those required by a particular Club will depend on many local factors—whether the Club is in a commuter area, or a holiday town, or an area with a university or with Forces establishments, etc. They must be thought out carefully.

SECURITY OF TENURE

It should be a fundamental requirement of a club that it safeguards the continued enjoyment of its land and facilities. The two usual methods of "securing the tenure" are (a) by owning the freehold or (b) by holding a long lease. But why is this important? Why must a club have security of tenure? The following are some of the reasons and although one or two may be obvious, one or two may not.

1. If a club has a lease for only a short period of time—perhaps three or four years—it is unreasonable and wasteful to ask the members to contribute money, perhaps to improve the courts or maintain the clubhouse, when someone else will have the benefit at the end of the lease—so there is no incentive to spend money when the security is only a few years. Incidentally, an LTA survey showed that many clubs had leases with less than five years to run; this is very worrying because in all their cases there must be some uncertainty as to whether they will be able to carry on much longer. A wise club will start negotiations for an extension of the lease or purchase of the freehold whilst there are a few years of the lease remaining. Independent advice on the most suitable type of professional advisor is available to any tennis club from: The Secretary, The Incorporated Society of Valuers and Auctioneers, 3 Cadogan Gate, London SW1X OAS. Tel.: 01-235 2282.
2. Various grants are available from Local Authorities and others to assist a club in making improvements either to courts or clubhouse—or perhaps to build something extra like squash courts—but these are very limited unless the club has either a lease with a considerable number of years to run or owns the freehold. (See also "Financing of Projects.")
3. If the club owns the freehold of its ground, it owns an asset which in normal times will steadily appreciate in value as land values generally increase. Furthermore, members will not have to face the problem of periodic and regular rent increases. As land values have risen over recent years, some clubs have taken the opportunity to sell part of their grounds to raise money for improvements. There have been instances when the proceeds from the sale of an entire club situated in a valuable residential area have, even after payment of any tax, enabled that club to build new and better facilities elsewhere on cheaper land.

Legislation on sale of land for redevelopment and particularly on taxation aspects is subject to constant review. The facts to be taken into account will vary from club to club and therefore each individual club would need comprehensive advice on the legal and taxation position before committing itself to any major project. What must not be overlooked is the possibility of obtaining the so-called "rollover relief" whereby the immediate tax liability on a capital or development gain can be indefinitely deferred to a large extent if the proceeds of the gain are reinvested. In the case of a club, the proceeds would have to be reinvested in new buildings—clubhouse, squash courts etc. for use by the Club. One cannot over-emphasize that this is a most complicated area of legislation and specialist advice must be obtained at the time when the club wants to make a move.

Statutory provisions affecting leasehold clubs

Even if your club is dependent on a lease, you may still be able to obtain protection from eviction when the lease runs out under the Landlord & Tenant Act 1954. But if this happens your club must consult a Solicitor the moment notice to quit is received, since time limits are laid down for counter-notices. The provisions for obtaining protection under the Act are complicated and it pays with this, as with many other things, to be properly advised by a professional from the very beginning.

As the law stands, a business lease or tenancy, which for this purpose includes the lease of a members' club such as a tennis club, can only be brought to an end by the landlord under the specific provisions of the Act, and there are ways set out in the Act whereby the tenant can apply to the Court for a new tenancy. The landlord has to give his notice not more than twelve and not less than six months before the end of the tenancy. The tenant (the club) can, if it wishes to continue to occupy the premises, then give notice within a further two months that it is not willing to give up possession of the premises at the end of the tenancy. If you fail to meet this deadline, you lose all rights under the Act.

If within another two months formal application is made to the Court, it can consider whether and on what terms to give the club a new tenancy, but the landlord may still be able to prevent the Court from giving a new tenancy if he can establish one of various specified grounds for wanting possession himself. These grounds include such things as failure by the tenant to repair or maintain the premises, failure to pay the rent as it becomes due, other substantial breaches of obligations under the current tenancy, the offer by the landlord to provide reasonable alternative premises, the landlord's intention to demolish or build on the whole or part of the premises, or his intention to occupy the premises for a business which he is to carry on himself or for his own benefit.

In other words, although there are occasions when the club can obtain an extension even though the term of the lease has run out, there are also many circumstances when it is the landlord who wins the day. (See also "Threatened Loss of Ground").

FINANCE

BUDGETING AND ACCOUNTING

Many clubs use professionally qualified members in the accounts department and the value of this cannot be over-emphasised. It is not a subject for the inexperienced no matter how large or small the club. Budgeting on the other hand is an area where ordinary commonsense will go far towards setting the club's finance on a sound footing.

The first problem to be tackled in the majority of clubs is the subscription rate. The total income from this source must cover *all regular* expenditure including maintenance of courts, clubhouse and essential equipment such as mowers, rollers, nets and so on. In fact one must go a stage further and put some of the club's regular income into a fund which can be available when major capital expenditure on courts or clubhouse etc. is required. These items are too often the subject of extra fund-raising activities and requests for loans and grants. *If this situation applies to your club, sooner or later there will be financial troubles particularly if you rely on social events to make up the deficit.* In all clubs there is a regular turnover in members and this, coupled with the fact that often the same members bear the brunt of the work, eventually leads to a feeling among them that it is someone else's turn. One year the shortfall of income over expenditure will not be recouped and unless the club is very lucky that situation will grow more serious during the following years. Suddenly the problem becomes of major importance.

The safest way to operate is by using "social" money for luxuries which the club can manage without in the difficult years of the cycle. This should make sense to the uninitiated but there are side issues which the following notes may help to alleviate:

1. Doubling your subscription overnight will not make you popular. In many, many cases however there is little alternative, so far behind are the general subscription rates in UK clubs. If such a decision is reached, do not forget to explain simply and concisely to members what these increases are intended to cover and why they are necessary.
2. Do not be put off by the rates of comparable clubs in the area but before making a major increase there may be a case for consultation with them. The County Secretary could possibly help.
3. Do not forget that every year bad financial management causes a number of clubs to face bankruptcy.

FINANCING OF PROJECTS

Most clubs at one time or another find it necessary to embark on a project involving expenditure which cannot be fully met from the club's own resources, whether it be, for example, the construction of additional courts, the reconstruction of the club-house, or the purchase of the freehold.

The first essential is careful planning, and full use should be made of any professional expertise among the club members. It must also be realised that even if a club cannot finance the whole cost of a project from its own resources it will need to raise a substantial proportion (normally a minimum of 25%) of the total cost by its own efforts to be eligible for assistance from the outside sources referred to below. A far-sighted club may have foreseen the need for the project and set aside a proportion of its income each year in a separate fund. Even if this has been done, when the project has been planned and competitive estimates have been obtained, the club will almost certainly decide that, in addition to whatever can be devoted to the project from club funds, it is necessary to embark on special fund-raising activities and perhaps to seek support from individual members in the form of interest-free loans or the issue of debentures. Outside sources of grant or loan assistance will be much more ready to help a club which has obviously made a substantial effort to help itself.

As soon as any plans for fund-raising within the club are in hand it should start exploring external sources of assistance, bearing in mind that they cannot all be approached simultaneously and the whole process is likely to take several months to complete. It is obviously in the club's interests to secure as much assistance as possible in the form of grant aid rather than loans which have to be repaid, in some cases with interest. Until 1972 the main source of grant aid for local sports clubs was central Government funds, administered first by the Department of Education and Science and then by the Department of the Environment. They in turn were advised by the Regional Sports Councils on the relative priorities of the applications which had been put forward in a given period in each region; such Government grants could sometimes be supplemented by grants from local authority funds. Then in 1972 the Sports Council was established in a new form as an independent body with executive powers, and since then it has administered the central funds available for sport which were previously controlled directly by the Government. Sports Council grants for local sports clubs are still available, but it now concentrates much of its grant aid on schemes designed to serve larger than local needs; the primary responsibility for grant-aiding local sports clubs now rests with the local authorities.

So the first sources which a club should approach are the relevant *local authorities,* i.e. the District (or Borough) Council and also the County Council. It may be best to address any initial enquiry to the Chief Executive of the authority, since applications for grant aid are not handled by the same officer or department in all authorities. It is difficult to generalise about what may be expected from local authorities, since their powers to make grants to local sports clubs are permissive and not mandatory and the extent to which they are prepared to exercise them in practice varies widely. In any event a club will not receive more than half the total cost of a project, at the very most, from local authority sources; but some District Councils regrettably give little or nothing, others will only assist club projects by way of loan rather than grant, and some County Councils will only assist projects of county-wide significance. It is, however, essential that clubs should put in applications both to their District Council and to their County Council even where there appears to be little hope of success, both because approval of assistance from other sources may be made conditional on the results of applications to the local authorities and also because it is important to make even the less generous local authorities aware of the needs in their areas. Clubs would be prudent to expect a delay of perhaps three to four months between their first submission of an application to a local authority and the notification of a decision (though a quicker notification may be expected in cases where for any reason there is no prospect of a grant).

The conditions which applicants for local authority grants are required to satisfy are likely to be broadly similar to those for Sports Council grants set out below, but may vary in detail from one authority to another. For example, in some cases the security of tenure condition is that the club must have at least 21 years unless the Council can be satisfied that there are special circumstances; and some District or Borough Councils require that in addition to membership being open to all at least half the members must live in their area.

As already indicated, the other source of grant aid to be considered is the *Sports Council,* who have in addition instituted a system of interest-free loans (repayable in ten equal half-yearly instalments over five years) to supplement their grant aid arrangements. Facilities relevant to tennis clubs which can be assisted by Sports Council grant and/or loan are

(a) Indoor sports facilities such as sports halls and their associated changing facilities.

(b) Outdoor sports facilities such as courts, floodlighting and their associated changing facilities.

(c) Purchase of land.

(d) Purchase of new major items of sports equipment with a total capital cost of more than £1,000, or of equipment which is an integral part of the development of a new facility.

(e) Provision of social accommodation to complement an existing sports facility (eligible only for loan).

Clubs planning a project which falls within one or more of the above categories should, in addition to applying to their local authorities, also contact the appropriate Regional Office of the Sports Council who, if the project is considered eligible for assistance, will advise on how to proceed and provide an application form (a list of the addresses of the Regional Offices is given at the end of this section). In February, June and October each year each Regional Council makes recommendations to the Sports Council on which of the applications received during the preceding four months are deserving of grant and/or loan assistance, and the amounts recommended in each case, if necessary taking account of relative priorities.

The maximum amount of Sports Council grant or loan is 50% of the approved cost of the project; if both grant and loan are offered the maximum of the combined total is 75%, and exceptionally a grant of up to 75% may be given for projects in areas of special need which will make a positive contribution to reducing social deprivation. In practice the assistance offered is normally at a very much lower rate than these maxima and is assessed for each project after taking account of the financial need and the resources available to the applicant. The minimum grant is £500 (minimum project cost £1,000). The minimum loan is £1,000 (minimum project cost £2,000) and the maximum loan is £10,000. Grant or loan for the purchase of property or sporting rights is based on the valuation of the District Valuer or the actual cost, whichever is lower. If a grant is also obtained from e.g. a local authority the total grant contribution from public funds is limited to 75% of the cost of the project.

Sports Council grants and loans to local sports clubs are subject to the following conditions:

(a) The club must not be constituted for profit for its members and there must be no provision for the distribution of assets to members or other persons during the club's existence or on its dissolution.

(b) There must be evidence of financial need.

(c) Membership of the club must be open to all (this means that there must be no discrimination against classes of persons e.g. on grounds of colour, religion or political persuasion; it does not preclude a club from rejecting an applicant who is considered unsuitable as an individual).

(d) The managing body of the club must be composed mainly of members, with all playing members eligible for election to the managing body.

(e) The club must normally have security of tenure on its facilities either by owning the freehold or by a lease for 28 years; in certain cases a lesser period will be accepted, but the maximum amount of grant and/or loan will be scaled down (to £15,000 if security of tenure is for 21 years, to £10,000 if for 14 years and to £5,000 if for 7 years).

(f) The club must not have committed itself to the project by purchase, contract or other binding agreement in advance of a written offer of a Sports Council grant or loan unless prior written consent has been obtained.

(g) The club must be able to meet at least 25% of the capital cost from its own or other non-Governmental sources.

(h) The club must be able to satisfy the Sports Council that it can meet the balance of the capital cost, the cost of maintaining the facility and the cost of any loan repayments.

(i) The facility must be adequately insured, the Sports Council must have the right of access and inspection of the facility, and the club's books and accounts must be made available to the Sports Council if required.

(j) (Applicable only to grants). The club's property must not be subject to a mortgage or loan exceeding 25% of the cost of the project, unless the body making the loan gives the Sports Council an undertaking guaranteeing continued use of the facility for sports purposes or repayment of the grant in the event of foreclosure.

(k) (Applicable only to grants). If the facility is disposed of or ceases to be used for sports purposes or if any of the other grant conditions are not met, the club will be required to repay to the Sports Council an appropriate proportion of the grant or of the market value of the facility.

(l) (Applicable only to loans). There must be no constitutional restriction on the club borrowing the amount of the loan, the club will be responsible for the Sports Council's legal costs and stamp duties, and the loan must be secured by personal guarantors (normally not more than 10) or by local authority guarantee.

(m) (Applicable only to loans). The Sports Council will be entitled to withhold payment of the loan or to require immediate repayment of any advances made if the loan is not applied to carrying out the project, or the project is not completed to their satisfaction, or the borrower disposes of an interest in the project, or the facility ceases to be used for the purpose for which the loan was given, or the borrower does not comply with the agreed method and terms of repayment.

(n) The Sports Council may make further conditions, which will be set out when the offer is made.

The information in the preceding paragraphs about assistance from the Sports Council and from local authorities applies only to England. Scotland and Wales have their own Sports Councils. Any Scottish or Welsh club seeking assistance for a project should contact the Scottish Sports Council or the Sports Council for Wales (addresses on next page) as well as approaching the appropriate local authorities. The Scottish Sports Council do not normally make grants to local sports clubs but they make interest-free loans up to a maximum of £10,000.

When a club has established how much it can obtain by way of grants and/or loans from the local authorities and/or the Sports Council, it may well find that this, together with the maximum which it can raise from its own resources, is insufficient to meet the total cost of the project. It will then need to explore possible sources of supplementary loan assistance. The first of these to be considered in the case of a tennis club (or a multi-sport club undertaking a project from which its tennis members will benefit) is the *Lawn Tennis Association's* club loans scheme (see the chapter on How The LTA Helps).

An application form can be obtained either direct from the LTA or from the secretary of the County LTA to which the club is affiliated; the completed form has to be returned via the county secretary since the LTA relies on the comments of the county association to help them in considering applications. Repayment of an LTA loan may be spread over not more than 5 years; loans are interest-free except in the case of loans to proprietary clubs, for which the rate of interest is currently 7%. Security is normally required in the form of personal guarantors for the full amount of the loan; in certain circumstances a first charge on the freehold or leasehold property of the club may be required. The maximum amount of loan is normally £7,500, but in exceptional cases a loan of up to £12,500 can be considered. A decision can usually be expected from the LTA within about a month of their receiving an application.

In addition the LTA set up in 1985 a separate Special Projects Fund designed to assist larger projects, particularly those for covered courts. The *maximum* amount of loan available from this fund is £50,000, repayable over 10 years. These loans currently carry interest of 5% per annum for members' clubs and 7% per annum for proprietary clubs and in view of the larger amounts involved an approved form of legal security (usually *not* guarantors) is required, but in other respects the conditions are very similar to those for the ordinary club loans scheme.

Although the possibility of assistance from the local authorities and the Sports Council should be explored before the LTA is approached for a loan under either of these schemes the secretary of the County LTA should be informed of the project at the earliest possible stage of planning. He can give helpful advice and is often invited to comment on applications made to the Sports Council.

Another source of loan assistance for sports club projects has been, in a number of counties, the *County Playing Fields Association* and, until fairly recently, the *National Playing Fields Association*. Many projects of affiliated clubs have in the past been financed partly by loans from the NPFA; these were normally repayable over 5 years, the rates of interest being 1% in the first year, 2% in the second, 3% in the third, 4% in the fourth and 5% in the fifth. In cases where a County PFA has run its own loan scheme, its conditions have generally been similar to those of the NPFA.

The NPFA has, however, accepted legal advice to the effect that as a charity it can only make loans to registered charities and it is now only making loans to bodies which can prove themselves registered as charities. Very few private sports clubs will be in a position to do this (see "Charitable Status" in the chapter on Club Constitutions).

On the other hand, a number of County PFA's still run schemes for making small loans to clubs. In any event it is advisable that the secretary of the County PFA, whose address (if not in the telephone directory) can be obtained either from the National Playing Fields Association, 25 Ovington Square, London, SW3 1LQ (tel. 01-584 6445) or from the County LTA, should also be informed of projects at an early stage. Even if a particular County PFA is not in a position to offer loans, its secretary may still be able to give advice and he sometimes plays a part in processing applications to the local authorities.

It will be seen that most projects of any size are likely to require support from several sources. For example, a club planning a scheme costing £18,000 might raise, say, £6,000 from its own resources (including any loans from members), a grant of £2,000 from the local authority, a grant of £2,500 and an interest-free loan of £2,500 from the Sports Council and a loan of £5,000 from the LTA.

SPORTS COUNCIL OFFICES

NORTHERN REGION

County Court Building, 9 Hallgarth Street, Durham, DH1 3PB. (Tel: Durham 49595).

Area

Cleveland, Cumbria, Durham, Northumberland, Tyne & Wear.

NORTH WEST REGION

Astley House, Quay Street, Manchester, M3 4AE. (Tel: 061-834 0338).

Area

Cheshire, Greater Manchester, Lancashire, Merseyside.

YORKSHIRE AND HUMBERSIDE REGION

Coronet House, Queen Street, Leeds, LS1 4PW. (Tel: Leeds 436443).

Area

Humberside, N. Yorkshire, S. Yorkshire, W. Yorkshire.

EAST MIDLANDS REGION

26 Musters Road, West Bridgford, Nottingham, NG2 7PL. (Tel: Nottingham 821887).

Area

Derbyshire, Leicestershire, Lincolnshire, Northamptonshire, Nottinghamshire.

WEST MIDLANDS REGION

Metropolitan House, 1 Hagley Road, Five Ways, Birmingham, B16 8TT. (Tel: 021-454 3808).

Area

Hereford & Worcester, Shropshire, Staffordshire, Warwickshire, West Midlands.

EASTERN REGION

26-28 Bromham Road, Bedford, MK40 2QD. (Tel: Bedford 45222).

Area

Bedfordshire, Cambridgeshire, Essex, Hertfordshire, Norfolk, Suffolk.

GREATER LONDON & SOUTH EAST REGION

PO Box 480, Crystal Palace National Sports Centre, Ledrington Road, London, SE19 2BQ. (Tel: 01-778 8600).

Area

Greater London, East Sussex, Kent, Surrey, West Sussex.

SOUTHERN REGION

Watlington House, Watlington Street, Reading, Berkshire, RG1 4RJ. (Tel: Reading 595616).

Area

Berkshire, Buckinghamshire, Hampshire, Isle of Wight, Oxfordshire.

SOUTH WESTERN REGION

Ashlands House, Ashlands, Crewkerne, Somerset, TA18 7LQ. (Tel: Crewkerne 73491).

Area

Avon, Cornwall, Devon, Dorset, Gloucestershire, Somerset, Wiltshire.

SCOTTISH SPORTS COUNCIL

1 St Colme Street, Edinburgh, EH3 6AA. (Tel: 031-225 8411).

SPORTS COUNCIL FOR WALES

National Sports Centre for Wales, Sophia Gardens, Cardiff, CF1 9SW. (Tel: Cardiff 397571).

OTHER FUND RAISING

This is an art which depends for the most part on a little enterprise and a good deal of hard work to be effective. There are no formulae which guarantee substantial rewards: one club will be more successful with one idea and less with another. The *only* essential ingredient is hard work. To list every variation on a fund-raising theme would be impracticable but the best ideas have been gathered together here in groups with a hint or two where appropriate.

Jumble or 'Nearly New' Sales

One eminently successful 'Nearly New' Sale organiser described the procedure as follows:

1. Rent an empty shop for a fortnight (ask an Estate Agent in your area).
2. Hire tables etc.
3. Print as many leaflets as possible giving details of when, where etc.
4. Select twelve "day leaders" who will each be responsible for
   - (a) circulating leaflets
   - (b) collecting goods through the year
   - (c) organising their helpers (8-10 per day)
   - (d) one day's selling
5. Arrange regular (at least daily) trips to the bank (if you are successful, you will not want to have too much cash on your hands).
6. Lower your prices towards the end of the fortnight.
7. Make your final day a 'Jumble Sale' to clear all remaining merchandise.

The result for one highly organised club—annual revenue well into a four-figure amount!

Fruit Machines

Still one of the most popular means of producing income in spite of the Licence Duty, they can be bought or rented. Clubs are strongly advised to shop around since this is a highly competitive industry and a number of different arrangements can be made. Look under "Amusement Machines" in Yellow Pages for fruit machines, bar billiards, T.V. Tennis and others.

The 1983 Licence Duty may deter clubs which cannot foresee substantial use of a machine but, in assessing its potential viability, bear in mind that there are differing rates of duty depending on the coinage value and that a 'summer only' licence is available at 55% of the annual fee. Machines installed temporarily for the occasion of a sporting event such as a tennis tournament, or a fete, dinner, dance, etc, run non-commercially, are exempt from Licence Duty.

Sponsored Walks, Marathons etc.

Basic requirement is an unending supply of friends and relations prepared to pay anything from 1p to 50p (depending on the choice of endurance) for every mile walked or run, every hour of tennis played non-stop, every ball struck over the net and in court in one rally, every 50 'skips' accomplished, every length of a pool swum, every circuit of a running track and so on. The revenue, of course, entirely relates to the numbers competing and their powers of persuasion!

Lotteries, Raffles etc.

The present law, the Lotteries & Amusements Act 1976, is complex and the need for guidance arises.

Many local authorities and specialist lottery ticket printers will be able to help.

The following notes will, in broad terms, introduce the Act which can be found in its entirety at public libraries or at book-sellers and HM Stationery Office.

"Small Lottery" (Section 3 of L & A Act 1976)

This is the raffle or tombola taking place at a social or sporting event. Registration is not required but there are the following restrictions:

- (i) No Money prizes; prizes bought out of the takings must not exceed £50 in total.
- (ii) Tickets may be sold only *at* the social or sporting event.

"Private Lottery" (Section 4 of L & A Act 1976)

Prizes may be in cash or in kind and there is no restriction on the size or frequency of lotteries, ticket prices, or prize values. Registration with the Local Authority is not required and the principal features and formalities are:

- (i) The promoter must be a club member authorised in writing (e.g. by a committee resolution duly recorded in the Minutes).
- (ii) The promoter's name and address and certain other items of specified information must be printed on the tickets.
- (iii) Tickets may be sold only to members of the club or society which organises the lottery and to which any proceeds will be devoted. It is not permitted for two or more clubs to promote such a lottery jointly, nor for a parent organisation (such as a County LTA, for example) to open its scheme to those who are not its own direct members, e.g. to members of affiliated clubs.
- (iv) Leaflets, tickets and notifications of prizes may not be sent through the post: publicity is restricted to word of mouth and to notices at the club's premises.
- (v) All tickets to be at the same price: no form of seller's commission is allowed.

"Society's Lottery" (Sections 5, 10-13 and Schedule 2 of L & A Act 1976)

This is the club lottery in which tickets can be sold to anyone over 16 years of age and literature, tickets and prize notifications may be sent through the post or sold through agents on a commission basis. Various formalities are involved, principally registration of the Club with the Local Authority (and with the Gaming Board for schemes over a certain size) and the submission of returns. Although this may sound formidable, it is not necessarily beyond the reach of larger clubs. There are restrictions relating to ticket prices, the frequency of lotteries, prize values, expenses allowed and so on. If the lottery is to be of the "instant" type now becoming popular, it is advisable to employ a printer specialising in this field.

The above three are now the *only types of lottery which are legal* for a club and the penalties for non-compliance *are severe*.

There is some pressure, however, especially following the Report of the Royal Commission on Gambling, for revision of this law but further change is unlikely in the near future.

"100 Club"

This scheme, with variations, is now very popular among clubs of all sizes. A few local enquiries will certainly provide details but a typical format is as follows: 100 people, who must be existing club members, pay £1.00 per month into a club account. Each participant is given a number and these numbers are drawn monthly for cash prizes. There are usually two prizes per month, one of say £20 and one say £10, with a further £50 or £100 every three months, as follows:

January/February/April/May
July/August/October/November
£20 plus **£10**

March/September/December
£50 plus **£20** plus **£10**

June
£100 plus **£20** plus **£10**

giving through the year a total of

1 at	£100 - £100	
3 at	£ 50 - £150	
12 at	£ 20 - £240	
12 at	£ 10 - £120	
Total prize money	**£610**	
Plus say	£ 60	administrative expenses
Total	**£670**	

Deducting this from gross income of £1,200 leaves a surplus of £530.

Although this appears straightforward, many clubs will find such a target demands a great deal of time and effort.

In brief, the operation is as follows:

1. Obtain a committee decision to operate the scheme and appoint an organiser: ensure that this is recorded in the Minutes.
2. Estimate the number of members likely to participate and calculate the prize structure.
3. Produce posters for the clubhouse and banker's order forms if required; in regard to these, bear in mind that bank charges may be incurred if too many banker's orders are involved, but that monthly collection in cash soon becomes a major chore which you can do without. *Annual payment is best of all.*
4. Canvass all club members to join and to persuade other members to do so.
5. Try and make the monthly draw at a club function, even if it is simply the most popular night over the bar, so that other members can join in. It all helps to advertise the scheme and bring in revenue.

The variations are obvious. If only 50 people can be confidently foreseen, you have a "50 Club" and so on. The prizes vary according to the amount you wish to make—about 50% of the takings is usual. As a precaution against failing to reach the planned membership or losing a significant number of members in mid-year, the advertised prize list should make provision for a reduced prize structure.

The 100 Club will as a rule fall into the "Private Lottery" category and its associated restrictions will apply.

Use of the Club Hall

Do remember that a pleasant clubroom is often ideal for hiring out to other associations or individuals for dances, meetings, parties, play schools and so on. In most cases, access to a bar will be a prerequisite but even without one a very worthwhile revenue can be built up. This has an additional merit in that it brings new people to the club some of whom may well come back as members.

Before hiring out, check (a) the Licensing Act requirements regarding signing people in as temporary members and their eligibility to pay for drinks, (b) your ability to meet Fire Regulations and (c) your insurance cover.

Club dances, barbecues and socials are reasonably straightforward operations whether run to raise funds or as a service to members. They are, of course, an important factor in helping to foster a good spirit and where a club does not have a suitable room within its grounds it is certainly worth arranging such events at another local venue on a regular basis.

As already stated, the idea of deriving income from club socials should be accepted as a principle. Tennis clubs without sound financial reserves *are at risk* now and may be more so in the future.

RATING ASSESSMENTS AND RELIEF

Under section 40 of the General Rate Act 1967, local authorities give mandatory relief from rates of at least 50% to registered charities and they have discretionary power to give additional rate relief to them and to certain other organisations including non-profit-making sports clubs. Where these latter provide facilities either wholly or partly from funds of members, the local authority is relieved of its responsibility of providing similar facilities for ratepayers and ought to recognise this financially.

This is the basic case to argue when applying for rating relief but it is no easy matter as many people have discovered. With few local authorities *offering* help, clubs face a long-drawn-out struggle in most cases although it may be worth the effort in the end.

One successful application was made by a number of London clubs who formed an association to take up the struggle. All sports clubs in the area that paid rates direct to the Council were involved and the association's representatives met the Council's Finance Committee. This eventually resulted in a 50% reduction (eighteen months were spent in negotiation).

An appeal can, of course, be made against the valuation on which the assessment is made although there is probably more often a plausible case to be made for relief rather than revaluation.

TAXES

The taxes which are most likely to affect the administration of a tennis club are Value Added Tax, Corporation Tax and taxes on Capital Gains; notes on these appear below. Capital Transfer Tax will not normally affect clubs. The laws relating to tax are complex and constantly changing; therefore a club contemplating action that might in any way affect the tax position should take professional advice *first.*

Value Added Tax

This is a tax on goods and services which is borne by the eventual consumer, the parties involved in production, distribution and supply acting as collecting agents in respect of the value "added" to the product or service whilst it is under their control. It is administered by the Customs and Excise.

Organisations (including clubs) with an annual turnover exceeding the VAT ceiling figure (currently £19,500 but subject to possible change in the 1986 Budget) must register for VAT. Where the turnover is less than the ceiling figure registration is voluntary and it is usually (but not necessarily) better *not* to register. The basis of operation of VAT is that it is collected from the recipient of the goods and services supplied; hence a club falling within the scope of VAT has to add VAT to its subscriptions, among other things. The club will, of course, have paid out VAT on taxable goods and services which it receives, of which one example is stationery.* It then deducts such tax (inputs) from the tax which it charges (outputs) and pays the balance to the Customs and Excise quarterly.

If a club is exempt from registration and does not register it does not need to charge VAT on its goods and services supplied (including subscriptions) but cannot reclaim the VAT inputs referred to above.(*) Not all supplies are subject to VAT. Where they are, the rates of tax and the services and goods to which they apply are subject to change by the Government and the lists are too complex to be printed here. Understandably there can be confusion and it is not uncommon for traders to charge VAT where they should not. Club officials must check that their club does not suffer excess VAT especially if it is not registered. Of particular interest to clubs hiring sports facilities is the fact that a formal agreement for a series of bookings of a sports ground or premises equipped for sports *to a club, school or similar body,* where the periods of hire making up the series of lets occur at regular and reasonably frequent intervals, may be regarded as a single VAT-exempt supply of a licence to occupy land. While each case will be decided on its own particular facts, the following guidelines will be applied in determining whether or not there is a licence to occupy:-

(a) There must be clear evidence of the existence of a formal arrangement, including a requirement that payment be made in full whether or not the option to hire is actually exercised on a particular occasion. Suitable evidence would be a formal agreement between the parties, an exchange of letters or an invoice issued in advance of the series but requiring payment (not necessarily in advance) for the whole of the series.

(b) The series must extend over the playing season for the sport or for at least three calendar months whichever is less and must consist of at least ten individual hire periods occurring not less frequently than once a fortnight except for breaks caused by school holidays.

(c) The formal arrangement must be such that the licensee is granted exclusive use of the sports facilities during each period of hire.

As far as tennis clubs are concerned, examples of common areas in which confusion arises are as follows:

1. The complex regulations governing VAT in the printing industry too often cause VAT to be wrongly charged. Examples of the many items which are zero-rated are as follows:

   Books and booklets; sports programmes and fixture lists provided that a portion for completion does not exceed one-quarter of the total area; printed letters ("form letters") provided that no more than the date, addressee and signature are left blank for manuscript completion; brochures, pamphlets, leaflets and notices (except that if a "notice" is larger than A4 size and printed on only one side of the paper, it may be classed as a "poster" which is taxable); journals and periodicals, including sporting newsletters, etc.

2. Although membership subscriptions are taxable to the extent that they pay for taxable benefits, the tax charged to members can be proportionately reduced if the benefits include any which are non-taxable. For example, the LTA Handbook is zero-rated and the relevant proportion of the subscription paid by our member clubs through county associations is untaxed to the extent that they provide these benefits.
3. Entry fees for sports competitions and tournaments, whether open or internal, are exempt provided that *either* (a) they are applied wholly to the provision of prizes *or* (b) the event is organised by a non-profit-making body established for purposes of sport or physical recreation.
4. Players' Contribution Scheme money collected by clubs from members and passed on through the county association to the LTA is inclusive of VAT in accordance with LTA Rule 7. Tax will be accounted for by the LTA.
5. The prices of Wimbledon tickets issued through clubs are inclusive of VAT, which is accounted for by The All England Lawn Tennis Club. Clubs are acting only as agents in the distribution and need not record the transactions for VAT purposes.
6. Repair and maintenance of courts by a contractor is taxable but the construction of new courts at a club is not. The criteria currently being followed by HM Customs and Excise are as follows:
   (a) The construction of a new tennis court is zero rated.
   (b) The addition of extra courts to an existing court would be zero rated.
   (c) The complete demolition of the whole of an existing court with subsequent reconstruction of a new court in its place would be zero rated. Floodlighting would also be zero rated if put in at the same time as a part of a new court.
   (d) The replacing of one playing surface by another even if it involves additional foundation material would be subject to VAT.
   (e) Work done in levelling or correcting subsidence would be subject to VAT.
   (f) Any repair or maintenance work would be subject to VAT.

It is well worth ensuring that VAT is not charged if it is not due. The amount at stake is 15% (or the current rate from time to time) of the cost of the project. Even if the club is VAT registered and so hopes to recover any VAT eventually, it will still have had to raise and pay out the full amount in the first place and effectively pay interest on it over a period of months or years.

If therefore an operation comes within the above criteria for zero-rating a club should ensure that any estimate, contract, or invoice stresses the nature of the work in a manner favourable to the above wording and should seek early confirmation from the contractor that he will be treating it as not subject to VAT. If necessary insist on reference to the VAT office, making sure that the contractor's letter stresses the relevant features of the work.

Although this will rarely if ever affect tennis clubs, tennis courts built within the grounds of a private residence are liable to VAT at the standard rate.

There are VAT offices in most sizeable towns and a supply of free literature on various aspects of the tax is obtainable from them. Of particular relevance are Notice No: 700 (General Guide), Notice No: 701 (Scope and Coverage), and Leaflet No: 701/5 (Clubs and Associations - Liability to VAT.).

Corporation Tax

Subject to the exceptions mentioned below Corporation Tax is chargeable on the operations of all organisations other than partnerships and individuals.

The exceptions most likely to affect tennis clubs are:

(a) Companies limited by guarantee or registered under the Industrial and Provident Societies Act pay no tax on the surpluses arising from the normal activities between the club itself and members, this being regarded as "mutual trading". The same considerations apply in the case of a non-incorporated members' club.
(b) Charitable bodies are completely exempt.

Common sources of club income on which Corporation Tax is payable are:

(a) Bank and other deposit interest (which is still receivable without deduction of income tax).
(b) Other interest (including that from building societies) but the tax payable is reduced by any Income Tax deducted or deemed to have been deducted.
(c) The profits of Official Tournaments and similar functions, the tax being calculated by reference to that proportion of the total gross income derived from non-members. *Where such cases exist it is important to ensure that every expense attributable to the tournament or other function is charged.*

Dividends from preference and ordinary shares are received net of Income Tax and do not suffer Corporation Tax.

Tax on Capital Gains Arising from Disposal of Land

The sale of part or all a club's land will probably bring about liability to taxation at the normal Capital Gains rate of 30 per cent. Where a club contemplates selling its land and particularly where it is proposed to replace the land by the purchase of other land, it is *essential* to obtain the advice of a competent solicitor or accountant *well in advance* of entering into any binding agreements.

INSURANCE

The LTA is concerned at the degree of under-insurance in many clubs particularly where wooden structures are involved. It is always difficult to insure old premises for an adequate replacement value and you are advised to seek expert advice if you think this problem may apply to your club. There are now in fact specific schemes for tennis clubs wishing to insure their new or existing facilities and details of these schemes can be obtained from the LTA. In general, however, insurance can be placed direct with an insurance company or be negotiated through an insurance broker: if the latter is used, he may place the business either with an insurance company—perhaps the one to which the club might have gone direct—or with Lloyd's Underwriters. If a broker is used, the club should insist on knowing at the outset who is to be the actual insurer and, whether dealing direct or through a broker, it should satisfy itself that the insurer is well established and of good repute.

While it is, of course, possible to effect some of the insurance with one insurer and some with another, and there may be different insurers whose rates are better for the different classes of insurance, it will nevertheless generally be best for a club to place all its insurance together. This not only reduces the complexity of the operation but it enormously simplifies procedure in the event of a claim which might be held to be marginally placed between one policy and another, and the improved goodwill is likely to outweigh a small saving of premium. (A possible exception to this general rule might be item 8 below, as it is not so closely linked to the more general insurances in items 1-7.) Here then are the areas that need to be covered if applicable:

1. Fire and Lightning

All property of the club, whether buildings, court equipment, maintenance equipment and furniture, bar and catering stock. Money can be included but is often the subject of a separate "All Risks" insurance. If the club only rents its building, the insurance of the building itself is probably the responsibility of the landlord, but if there is any doubt on the matter, this should be checked upon. Telephone equipment, even though rented, is the club's responsibility for insurance. Any other rented equipment, e.g. fruit machine, bar equipment, should be investigated as to responsibility for insurance. Consideration should also be given to extending the insurance to cover aircraft, explosion, flood, storm, riot and civil commotion, malicious damage, burst pipes and impact.

2. Theft arising from Forcible Entry

The items will be largely the same as for fire insurance but there may be minor variations.

3. Television

If hired, investigate responsibility for insurance; if club property, insure.

4. Silver Cups and other Trophies ("All Risks" Insurance)

Unless otherwise agreed it is normally accepted that the organisation running a competition is responsible for the insurance of the permanent trophy (if any). The holder from year to year is entitled to rely on this but it should be a strict condition of any competition that the trophy may not be taken out of Great Britain.

5. Employer's Liability

By law, liability to employees must be insured for an indemnity of not less than £2 million. A certificate (supplied by the insurers) must be displayed on the premises.

6. Public Liability

This indemnifies the club for accidental injury (including food poisoning) to members and the public (other than employees) and damage to their property for which the club is legally responsible. The liability of one member to another should also be included.

7. Motor

Motor mowers and other motorised equipment which are licensed to go on the road will, of course be insured in the ordinary way, but it is sometimes overlooked that even if they are not licensed or taken out of the club's premises it is still possible to have accidents with them inside the club.

8. Pension provision, life and sickness insurance for employees

This is of course supplementary to the State Schemes. It is a "fringe" benefit to aid recruitment and retention of employees. The sickness insurance can, for example, contribute to the wages of the regular groundsman while he is ill or recovering from injury, and at the same time allow you to pay the wages of relief staff without taxing the Club's resources.

BANKING

Every club should have at least one bank account. Generally, the ordinary operating account for day-to-day transactions will be a current account with one of the high street banks, although it is not impossible to run a small club's finances through an account in the National Savings Bank, Trustee Savings Bank, or National Giro, the first two of which give the advantage of paying interest.

A formal committee resolution, duly recorded in the Minute Book, is required before a bank account is opened and the bank selected will probably supply their required specimen wording.

This resolution must specify what signatures are to be required to operate the account: a common and usually satisfactory arrangement is "any two of the three officials Chairman, Honorary Treasurer, Honorary Secretary".

Do not overlook the possible advantage of operating more than one account; for example it may be beneficial to have an additional account, used exclusively for paying in subscription money which can earn interest before it has to be periodically transferred to top up the club's main account to meet day to day commitments.

INVESTMENTS

(a) Large Scale

Investment of any substantial scale is beyond the scope of this Manual, in view of the relatively small number of clubs which have sufficient resources to indulge in it. Suffice it to stress that it essentially requires the expert advice of a stockbroker or other professional adviser, and that there is no straight answer to the question "What is the best investment?"

(b) Medium Scale

Many clubs, however, may occasionally be able to make more modest investments, perhaps for specific purposes. For example, a club which very prudently sets aside each year a reserve for the periodic relaying of courts and other substantial repairs, renewals and improvements, will not keep this money in its current account but will invest it to earn interest or capital appreciation or both until required.

For these purposes, advice need not necessarily be at such a high level as in (a) above. But if a stockbroker, banker, chartered accountant, solicitor, investment adviser, senior employee of a pension fund or investment trust or the investment department of an insurance company is available in the club, his help should certainly be invoked.

(c) Small Scale Short Term

Covers earning interest for a few months between the date when subscriptions come in and the time when the money is needed for use—perhaps evenly spread over the year, for example, for payment of groundsmen's wages. This should be within the competence of the Honorary Treasurer, assisted if necessary by the Bank Manager, and may involve nothing more than "putting money on deposit" at the bank. (See also "Banking" above).

The following notes may be of use to those not versed in the subject:

National Savings Bank: (formerly Post Office Savings Bank). No bank charges. An ordinary account pays a low rate of interest without deduction of tax but interest is chargeable to Corporation Tax and must be declared annually. An investment account pays a much higher rate of interest but withdrawals require a month's notice.

Trustee Savings Bank. A very similar service to that of the National Savings Bank but has better cheque service and provided there is a branch in the vicinity, is probably more suited to a tennis club's needs.

Bank Deposit Account. Usually held in conjunction with a current account. Interest rates vary from time to time and are displayed at all branch banks. Withdrawals nominally at one week's notice but this is seldom insisted upon: subject to Corporation Tax.

The arrangement whereby from April 1985 bank interest payable to *individuals* is paid net of basic rate tax does not apply to clubs, which continue to be paid gross by the bank. Note the different arrangement for building society interest, below.

Building Society Account. These are becoming more similar to bank accounts. Various terms of notice, withdrawal and interest rates are available. Some societies may not offer clubs the complete range of accounts available to individuals.

The special tax arrangements for individuals are modified for sports and social clubs whose net interest received is liable to Corporation Tax on the grossed up equivalent. However, credit for the basic rate income tax, paid by the society, is given by set-off against the Corporation Tax so that usually no further tax will be due. The interest must nevertheless be declared annually.

Premium Savings Bonds. These cannot be held in the name of more than one person or in the name of a society, club etc., and although it may be that funds have been invested in Premium Bonds in the name of one of the officials of the Club, this is not recommended: officials may change, leave, or keep confused records. Such a contract is made solely with the named holder of the bonds and the Post Office has no responsibility towards a club or other organisation which may provide the funds for the purchase of bonds.

National Savings Certificates. These cannot normally be held by a club.

PAVILION FACILITIES

THE PAVILION

A pavilion, just like a house, reflects the attitudes of its occupants by its condition, furnishing and accommodation.

When the time comes (and for many that time is already past) to consider plans for a new pavilion, extension or major refurbishing, a difficult choice has often to be made between a structure which creates the right atmosphere and one which can be afforded.

The financial position of most clubs is such that replacing the old clubhouse is a major undertaking of almost frightening proportions. However, if having taken the advice given in other chapters, you decide to proceed, the first priority will be to agree the design. Before putting artistic pen to paper, make a list of the facilities required, in order of priority, bearing in mind the following:

1. Type of Construction

Traditional brick or stone will, of course, have a very much longer life than most prefabricated forms of buildings available although (a) construction time is longer and (b) it may also be more complicated due to the requirements of certain building regulations not applicable to prefabricated types. These latter are usually quoted without foundations or services which have to be accurately and properly costed when comparisons are made. Maintenance differences must also be assessed, e.g. timber cladding will require regular treatment whereas brick facing will not.

2. Design

A new pavilion will serve a club for at least 30 years—probably many more—and it is therefore advisable to give careful thought to this subject. These are a few points worth noting:

(a) Siting:
Reserve the best aspect (and sunshine) for the lounge and bar areas.

Keep service areas together for economy, i.e. shower and toilet facilities, kitchen and bar.

Avoid a long walk from the car park. (N.B. provision for parking within the club's grounds is now a pre-requisite of many Planning Authorities and in fact *a general preliminary consultation with the local Planning Department would be prudent).*

Consult with the gas, electricity, water and drainage authorities so that the services they provide are sufficient for your ultimate needs.

(b) Uses:
Try to allow for as many dual-purpose areas as possible. For example, a large hall will be better used if it has removable partitions to house table tennis, bridge, television, juniors, large and small social functions, meetings, and so on.

Plan ahead. Scheme the facilities that you will need during the next ten years so that they can be built, if necessary, in stages. This also means leaving room for expansion.

(c) Atmosphere:
The character of the clubhouse, both inside and out, generally dictates the atmosphere of the club as a whole and new buildings, because they are designed with economy in mind, tend towards the plain and uninteresting. If cost and space prohibit an attractive design, then give serious thought to other ways of introducing "welcoming" features such as window boxes, carpeting, table lamps, wall lights and subdued lighting generally, wallpapers, fireplace in the lounge/bar where people tend to gather or even an unusual feature like an aquarium.

(d) Implications:
Major building projects need management both during and after construction.

At least one member will have to be readily available for site consultation and discussions on proposed changes in specification whether you have engaged an architect or not. Again, plan ahead for any new house and social committee duties, extra cleaning services, rotas for a new bar, and extra running costs.

Do not expect that a new pavilion will pay for itself in the same way as, say, squash courts. If it is to be self-liquidating, you must look carefully at the revenue-producing ideas under "Fund Raising".

Having decided on your requirements, the next operation is to prepare a written brief for the architect or whoever is to obtain estimates and make sure that these are all based on the same specification so that the most competitive can be selected.

3. Costs

While the LTA feel it is important for clubs to plan in the knowledge of the likely cost, where that cost can vary considerably it is easy to mislead. Additionally, inflation in recent years has meant that our example of cost in previous editions has had to become more broad and therefore less appropriate across the country. Clubs will, in any case, obtain their own competitive quotations for work and this is now unfortunately the only safe guide.

THE BAR

Depending on whether your bar is new or already established, the implications that must be considered, if maximum revenue is to be gained, include:

1. The need for a duty rota or staff and **reliable** opening times.
2. The ordering and taking in of new stock (someone to be available during the day).
3. Extra security—this probably is the most valuable area of the club (see under "Security").
4. Accessibility for deliveries, storage space etc. When a new pavilion is being built the size of the bar must be related to the ultimate size of membership.

Clubs often find that breweries will give advice on siting, size, fittings, accessories and so on. Occasionally they have been persuaded to build a complete bar, help with fittings, give a low interest loan or even a grant depending on whether they think it would ultimately be worth their while. Care should be taken, however, not to become "tied" as, in the case of a club, this is not allowed by the Licensing Act.

CATERING

The Club kitchen is not easy to design because of the varying numbers of people that use it—on both sides of the counter. As under "Bar", a new kitchen will allow more to be considered at the planning stages but a refit may be almost as good in practice.

These are among the points to be remembered.

1. **Safety:**
   Make sure that all electrical appliances are properly earthed; that correctly rated fuses are fitted to plugs and in fuse boxes (if in doubt ask an electrician); and that frayed flex is competently and quickly renewed. Do not allow babies or young children into the kitchen and keep out anyone who does not need to be there. Hang towels *away* from cookers, gas water heaters, fires and so on. Oil heaters must be guarded and kept clear of people working. Club suppers often include chips and chip-pan fires are particularly common and highly dangerous. See the notes under "Fire Prevention" and the booklet "Danger from Fire". A first aid kit must be accessible at all times and provided the service areas (dressing rooms, kitchen and bar) are close, probably only one will be needed. It should include the following:

   6 Triangular Bandages
   Small collapsible splints
   Pair of scissors
   2 x ½oz. packets cotton wool
   Reel of zinc oxide strip plaster
   Reel of medicated strip plaster
   2 packets each gauze and lint
   Reel of Tubagrip
   Box of various plasters
   Antiseptic cream and liquid
   Anti-Histamine Cream

   Wound dressings:
   3 x No. 8
   3 x No. 9
   3 x No. 15
   3 x No. 16 (Eyes)
   3 x No. 7 (Fingers)
   Tubagauze with applicator
   Roller bandages:
   3 x 1", 3 x 2"
   and 3 x 3 safety pins

2. **Hygiene:**
   One member of the catering committee should be responsible for ensuring all kitchen equipment is as clean as one would expect to find at home. This is particularly important because in many clubs, kitchens are used only at week-ends. The "Environmental Health Officer" is liable to inspect any premises where food is prepared or stored. There is a leaflet available from local authority Health departments—"A Guide to Food Hygiene Regulations"—which explains many points in layman's language.

3. **Design:**
   Best left to an expert. Most manufacturers of kitchen units give advice on layout and there are various heights which, based on British Standards Institution recommendations, will be suitable to most people for storage, working tops, etc. A large catering area such as the sink, cooker, refrigerator and one or two working tops are kept in reasonable proximity to each other and to any serving hatch.

   The remainder of such a kitchen would be used for extra working tops and storage.

4. It is false economy for a club to buy inferior equipment, make sure saucepans have insulated handles and are designed for use with your particular type of cooker, i.e. gas or electric.

5. In these days, a properly cared for freezer might be a good investment. It will be useful when matches are cancelled and when socials are better or less well attended than planned.

STAFF

In cases where a club needs to hire additional help on a casual or part time basis, do take note of the tax situation which will certainly apply. For example, if a waitress is hire for a special function, she is obliged to sign a P46 form, which the club should complete and keep in its files for HM Inland

Revenue, as proof of the tax position i.e. the Club's non-liability. Clubs are strongly advised to contact their accountants/auditors for further information.

FIRE PREVENTION AND SECURITY

There can be few clubs that have not suffered as a result of a robbery, fire or both. A little thought (and a surprisingly small outlay) will, in most cases, prove worthwhile. Fortunately, expert advice is freely available.

Fire Prevention

No club that has experienced a fire on the premises would want to be at risk again and yet many clubs are still relatively unprepared.

The one essential step for every club to take is to call in the local Fire Prevention Officer. You will find him in the telephone directory under "Fire Brigade" or ring Fire Brigade headquarters and ask for advice from the Fire Prevention branch. The service is free, highly recommended and arranged to suit your convenience. He will be able to suggest precautionary measures that may one day save serious injury or even lives. Because all clubs are different, it is not advisable to give many guidelines save that:

1. Fires are caused in the main by
   (a) People
   (b) Cigarettes
   (c) Faulty wiring.
2. Keep doors shut when club is not in use.
3. Pull out plugs for television, electric fires etc. at least 20 minutes before leaving premises.
4. The FPO will advise on siting and quantities of extinguishers.
5. Keep handy the booklet "Danger from Fire", obtainable from the Central Office of Information and Her Majesty's Stationery Office, or probably from your FPO.

The FPO consulted for this article stressed that each club needs a visit to pinpoint possible dangers and the LTA advise clubs to make good use of this valuable service.

N.B. A club applying for registration under the Licensing Act is liable to inspection in regard to its fire risk and precautions.

Security

One could generalise that vandals and amateur burglars are the main culprits with which clubs should be concerned and just as in the previous articles the best advice is to contact the Crime Prevention Officer for your area. He can be contacted through your local police station (see under "Police" in the telephone directory) and his advice is, of course, unbiased. Like the FPO he will call to suite your convenience and send you a report with his recommendations.

As for general guidelines:

1. Do not lock internal doors (especially if they are fitted to an alarm system).
2. Lock outside doors and fasten windows—noise must then be made to gain entry. (British Standard 362) for locks on final exit door).
3. Where "grilles" are concerned, consider their effect in case of fire and remember "life before property".
4. Try to make one area as secure as possible (the bar in most cases) and keep valuable equipment there when not in use. This protected area may require an alarm system (which can be rented). This will dissuade the petty thief from even attempting an entry. The majority of such criminals are "opportunists" and will move on to somewhere more accessible. The CPO will advise on the pros and cons of alarms. (It has been known for a small red box with white lettering to be fitted to an exterior club wall to act as a deterrent—this is **not a substitute** for genuine security measures).
5. An insurance company, faced with many claims from one source, may well demand some extra precautions before continued cover can be agreed.

Lastly, do keep your local police station up-to-date with changes of keyholders (and deputy keyholders at holiday times).

COURTS AND EQUIPMENT

TENNIS COURT SURFACES

There are three basic forms of outdoor courts—grass, loose-surface and fixed-surface. Their respective merits are, in the main, related to weather conditions.

Grass courts, generally in play from May to September, are dependent on good drainage, failing which they become unplayable for several hours after heavy rain.

The loose & fixed surfaces categories are well covered by an official leaflet, the text of which reads as follows:

The Lawn Tennis Association has recognised the need to give advice to Clubs on the construction and resurfacing of tennis courts and now provides a Court Advisory Service. The need for such a service has been highlighted by the confusion of trade names and the vast range of court surfaces now on the market. In the past the main emphasis has been placed on 'outdoor' surfaces, but with the emergence of new covered court facilities, the LTA is now prepared to offer advice on carpets, and all such enquiries should be referred to the Technical Dept of the LTA. It must be clearly understood by Clubs seeking guidance from the LTA that the information given for a particular product cannot in any way be construed as a recommendation.

In general the majority of court surfaces on the market are of the porous variety, and in the British climate they are understandably the most popular. However, non-porous courts are available and references is made to these in the Appendix.

The overall situation is confused by court constructors using many trade names for basically similar surfaces. Whatever the proprietary names given to the various porous surfaces, they fall mainly into the following categories:

(1) The loose surface or red shale court as it is more commonly known.

(2) The bituminous macadam non-slide surface.

(3) The bituminous macadam semi-slide surface with a gritted or dusted top, usually known as the 'grey-green' type.

(4) The concrete surface.

(5) The polyurethane/crumb rubber surface.

(6) The synthetic matting surface.

(7) The non-porous surface.

(8) The carpet surface.

In describing each surface in more detail, it is necessary to avoid giving opinions other than in the most general terms. Players have their likes and dislikes when it comes to bounce, speed, spin, etc., and the ideal surface has yet to be developed. The brief notes outlined in the Appendix are offered as a guide and to help clubs/players sort out their requirements. Clubs are advised to shop around before deciding on an estimate. As in all walks of life there are the less reputable firms who are likely to submit the lowest tender, but without the protection of any guarantee covering the rectification of faults appearing after construction has been completed. The conditions attaching to all tenders should in any case be closely studied.

A club considering putting down a new court or resurfacing an old one should ask itself a number of questions before seeking competitive tenders. Some of the factors, not necessarily in the order of importance, to consider are as follows:

(1) Pattern of play.

(2) Player preference (to include ball bounce, speed, slide/non-slide, softness).

(3) Overall court dimensions, including run back when resurfacing (as laid down in the LTA Handbook).

(4) Court costs and life expectancy.

(5) Manufacturer's guarantees including rectification of subsequent faults.

(6) Arrangements for court maintenance.

(7) Porous or non-porous surface.

(8) Colouring of surface.

(9) Drying time after rain.

(10) Effect of frost and heat.

(11) Restrictions on use of court after laying, e.g. softening.

(12) Wear and tear on balls.

(13) If resurfacing, state of existing foundations.

(14) Spectator area.

(15) Future plans for installation of floodlighting.

(16) If non-porous, cost of drying aids.

(17) Money available whether from club sources or loans from LTA or grants/loans from Sports Council (see section on Financing of Projects for further details).

Any club contemplating investing money in a new court is advised to see and, where possible, play on the surfaces before making a final decision. The manufacturers will normally provide a list of clubs, schools, sports centres where they have installed their courts, and club committees are urged to visit these sites to inspect the court in question and discuss the merits of the particular surface with club members. Clubs are also advised to maintain a 'diary of events', so that should a dispute arise all the facts are available on paper. The diary should start from the moment the tenders are requested.

The cost of court construction or resurfacing varies widely, not only between the different types of surfaces and contractors but even for the same surface in different locations and under varying circumstances. Accordingly, costs have not been listed in this report because they could be misleading. After selecting the preferred surface, clubs are advised to seek competitive tenders. If on receipt of estimates there is doubt in the minds of the club committee as to the best course of action the LTA will be pleased to offer advice. As previously mentioned, such advice will be given in good faith and in the light of the facts made available; however, in so doing the LTA cannot accept legal liability. Initial enquiries should be addressed to the Technical Dept., LTA, Barons Court, West Kensington, LONDON W14 9EG — Telephone 01-385 2366.

Appendix

NOTES ON COURT SURFACES

The red shale court

1. A popular loose surface court constructed of crushed rock, gravel, shale or brick. The surface is comfortable to play on, drains well, but needs regular maintenance such as dragging, watering and rolling. Given the proper attention the red shale court has a long life. In spite of an impression to the contrary, supplies of shale would appear to be adequate for current and long-term needs.

The macadam non-slide surface

2. This widely-used court is based on a foundation of stone or ash with a cold bituminous macadam or bituminous coated limestone surface. These courts are hard-wearing and can have a long life. They need the minimum of upkeep and are ideal for club use. The texture of the surface varies between manufacturers but such courts are usually constructed with either a black or inherent dark red coloured surface: alternatively the surface may be sprayed in single or dual colours. These courts require a period to harden off before being brought into use and if laid in the winter will soften during hot weather in the following spring or summer whilst the volatile oils are weathering out of the surface. Play must not take place when the surface is soft. Recent developments in the construction of the above type of court have alleviated some of the softening problem. This is achieved by laying the bitumen as a hot mix and blending a rubber additive into the surface mixture. This method of construction also allows the surface to be colour coated immediately, and for this purpose a proprietary acrylic coating containing a non-slip agent is used but in overall performance the court is similar to the standard macadam.

The gritted bituminous surface

3. This court is similar to that described above except that with the loose surface one obtains a measure of slide. The amount of surface dressing varies with manufacturers from a light dust to a fairy heavy sprinkling of green or grey grit. On the other hand, one manufacturer mixes an alkyd resin into the surface to give a firm playing area: after being played on for some months the surface begins to shed its final dressing allowing a measure of slide. Whatever the finish they all have the same weathering problems as the macadam surface referred to above. They are not recommended for intensive club use because porosity can be lost in 3 to 5 years or less. However, they are suitable for the private user who could reasonably expect a life in excess of 10 years.

The concrete surface

4. On a foundation of broken stone is laid a 3 to 4 inch layer of no fines concrete: the result is a grit-free medium-fast surface which is instantly porous and can be spray painted. The problems with this type of court are usually caused by ground movement of one type or another resulting in the movement of the concrete sections.

The polyurethane/crumb rubber surface

5. The basic construction is similar to that used with the bituminous macadam surfaces referred to above: however, in this case the surface comprises a thin layer of crumb rubber bound with polyurethane. The cost of this binder, which is a petroleum-based product and thus relatively expensive, largely accounts for the high cost of this court.

The synthetic matting surface

6. This court comprises a perforated plastics matting that is simply laid on any hard, smooth, level, preferably porous base such as concrete or tarmacadam. The court is self-draining and allows play to resume immediately following rain, is easily maintained and has been well tested on the continent, where a number of similar surfaces are being marketed. Experience of this surface in the United Kingdom is limited.

The non-porous surface

7. The basic foundations are similar to those described above, but the surface contains a cushioned layer sealed with colour acrylic sealers. For draining purposes these courts are laid with a pronounced crossfall; even so, the use of drying aids will be necessary. These courts are expensive but they have a long life.

The carpet surface

8. A wide range of carpet surfaces are now available on the market. Until recently most of the qualities offered were more suitable for indoor rather than outdoor use. A popular development, however, is a polypropylene tufted carpet which is designed for outdoor play. The carpet is best laid on a porous macadam or concrete base and then partially filled with a specially graded sand. This surface, which is virtually all weather, requires the minimum of maintenance on a day-to-day basis but from time to time needs to be dragged with a brush to level the sand. The combination of a firm porous base and a carpet accounts for the high cost of this type of court. It should be noted that the raw materials used in the manufacture of the carpet are UV stabilised but are at present only guaranteed for five years. This is not to say there will be any deterioration of the fibres after this period but no carpets have been in use in the UK long enough to determine their life expectancy.

Note: The minimum acceptable size of a tennis court is 114′ × 56′ but, where space permits, a size of 120′ × 60′ is desirable.

For further information clubs should contact the Technical Dept. of the L.T.A. who will be able to advise on most matters including the most appropriate court manufacturers in their area.

ORIENTATION

An outdoor court should preferably be positioned with its length running as nearly as possible North South. This is so that when the sun is lowest it will be across the court and not in the face of the players.

This need not preclude the construction of a court in another direction if the available space leaves a club no alternative. It should however be followed in any large area being laid out as lawn tennis courts—it will certainly be expected by most players.

GRADIENT

It is normal for all outdoor courts to be laid on a slight gradient to facilitate drainage.

The direction of the gradient should be across the court. If the existing levels of a site are such that the provision of a cross-fall would involve unacceptable expenditure, a gradient running from end to end, or even diagonally is acceptable. (It is not an alternative for the two ends of the court to slope away from net to baselines. This is because the effect is the same as raising the height of the net).

Generally speaking, the maximum cross-fall for an international court size 120′ × 60′ is 6″ and the alternative fall in length would be 12″. If your court is smaller the fall should be less pro rata.

As with orientation, there can be exceptions—site levelling can be expensive—but contractors should advise you on the problem and the gradient they recommend in the circumstances. If in doubt contact the LTA for further advice.

COURT MAINTENANCE

One factor to consider when choosing a new court is the cost (in labour, materials and equipment) of maintenance.

All-weather courts such as those surfaced with coated macadam or no-fines concrete require little attention other than brushing, hosing and occasional attention to lines.

Loose surface courts (surfaced with shale, crushed brick or stone etc.) need much more attention if good playing conditions are to be maintained and grass courts are even more demanding of regular maintenance work. Circumstances (of standards, soils, surfacing etc.) vary at different clubs so that the guide which follows may need to be varied slightly or, indeed, augmented by expert advice from an appropriate source.

Loose Surface Courts

The construction of a good court of this type is shown below. Regular maintenance is essential to avoid deterioration with subsequent cost and trouble in major repairs.

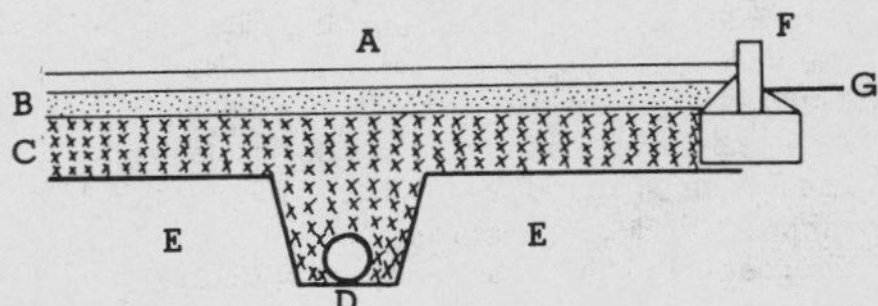

A. Surfacing material (depth as recommended by supplier—may be as little as ¾″ or as much as 1½″.)
B. 2″ blinding layer (⅛″-⅜″ hard gritty clinker ash)
C. 5″ permeable layer ⅜″-1″ predominantly single sized hard graded clinker or gravel.)

D. 3″ drain with invert 9″ below base level and covered with same material as in C.
E. Sub-soil base.
F. 6″ × 2″ concrete edging bedded on 8″ × 4″ concrete slab.
G. Ground level.

Equipment needed

Drag brush, 4′ to 6′ wide
Soft brush for tape cleaning
Lute
Rubber rake
Wire rake
Roller
Watering equipment
Miscellaneous (shovel, garden fork, barrow, etc.)

In the Spring. Spring restoration starts when weather conditions are suitable, possibly in the month of March, and a good start to the playing season is very important. After the winter (particularly a severe one) courts are rough looking and possibly some gritty material from below has worked to the surface.

The first step is to clean the surface by the best available means—brushing, light raking etc.—and remove from the site all the collected material. The raking also helps prepare the surface for top dressing.

Before top dressing is done any definite hollows which are visible should be made up after removing tapes where necessary. This may require light forking or heavy raking (of the surface material only) before making up with medium top dressing and rolling. For deep holes making up may have to be in two stages. In any case a final cover of fine top dressing is, of course, necessary.

Top dress whole courts. The top dressing material to use obviously depends on the kind of court and, frequently, two grades of top dressing are needed—medium and fine. Excess of either is to be avoided. First apply as evenly as possible (with a shovel expertly wielded!) a thin application of the medium dressing, say 5 to 6 cwt. per court. This should be carefully brushed with the drag brush in two directions, at right angles to each other. Follow up with careful rolling also in two directions.

Next apply fine top dressing, say 3 to 5 cwt. per court, as evenly as possible, preferably by dividing into two and spreading in transverse directions. Water in thoroughly and then, when the court has dried out sufficiently, finish off by brushing and rolling twice.

Note: Too much top dressing can be detrimental. If the layer of surfacing becomes too deep relative to its type this may result in poor drainage and/or early break up of the surface after a short dry spell. Similar results may also be caused by the use of inferior top dressing. In either case it may be worthwhile scraping off as necessary and restoring the surface afresh.

Maintenance during the summer

Brushing. Regular but careful use of the drag brush is advisable. Pull it steadily right across the courts and to the very edge where any rough material gathered can readily be picked up. Do not stop or turn within the body of a court. If courts become rather gritty, brushing from the net to the end of a court helps remove the grit. If the grittiness becomes very marked luting off may be necessary and this in turn may necessitate top dressing and/or rolling. (Note: grit not only interferes with play but also helps surface break-up when it is trodden in.)

Rolling. Regular rolling is required to maintain a good surface but the operation should preferably be carried out only when conditions are right, i.e. the courts clean and the moisture content suitable. If the courts are too wet, good results are not obtained and if the courts are too dry, disruption of the surface results. Work slowly and avoid marked twisting and turning of the roller.

If rolling is necessary when the courts are on the wet side so that top dressing sticks to the roller, then a weighted rolled-up sack tied over the top of the roller will wipe it clean as you roll.

Watering. Loose surface courts are described as "water-bound". Watering in dry weather is therefore, very important and a convenient watering system matched with the water supply and its pressure is, therefore, essential. A fixed watering system (as opposed to a portable sprinkler) is a great labour saver. Use it whenever the surface dries out; water in good time and water thoroughly; then, after the courts have drained, roll carefully.

Playing on a really dried out surface can soon cause the surface to break up.

Drying-up. Good courts should drain very freely but really heavy rain may cause temporary pools. If this happens shortly before an important event emergency action may be needed. If you can't borrow a drying roller use old blankets or similar. Soak them in the water and wring out into some receptacle. Do not drag the blankets or damage the surface in any way so that play can commence without the need for rolling.

In more difficult and less urgent circumstances spiking or forking may be necessary, great care being taken to minimise disturbance or damage in the surface layer. No matter how much care is taken, surface restoration is likely to prove necessary, i.e. brushing and rolling.

Repairs. Continued heavy play results in hollows at the base lines. These should be made up before they get too deep, using medium and fine top dressing appropriately, watering well in and rolling.

Care of tapes. Care of tapes is obviously important. They should always be cleaned before watering and rolling so as to avoid damage by grit. Use the right kind of brush carefully—not a garden or kitchen broom which will sweep top dressing from either side and leave the tapes proud, but a soft brush. When a tape is bulged by a player sliding into it, carefully level the surface and re-nail before doing normal brush and roll maintenance.

After a day's play. Lower the nets, brush the courts and clean the tapes. The courts will then be ready for play next day even after overnight rain. A churned up court will not.

Moss control. Good well-maintained and well-used courts seldom have a moss problem. If moss does occur treat with a proprietary moss killer and then, when the moss is dead, rake it out, lute the surface (working in a little top dressing if necessary) and roll.

Grass Courts

The requirement is for a smooth, fast surface giving a true bounce, with the ability to stand repeated heavy wear and preferably allow play even in wet weather.

The quality of a tennis court depends on the kind of grass, the strength of turf formation, the amount of fibrous growth at the surface, the success of root development, the physical nature of the soil and its degree of compaction, the fertility of the soil, drainage, management and all of these combined.

Equipment needed

Motor mower of suitable quality and size (this depends on number of courts).
Drag brush 4'-6' wide.
Aerating machine with solid or slit tines (hollow tines may be also be wanted).
Fertilizer distributor.
Mechanical scarifier.
Watering equipment.
Sprayer for application of weedkillers and fungicides.
Line marker.
Leafsweeper.
12' straight edge.
Small tools such as a turf iron and turf cutter (e.g. half moon), garden fork, spade, barrow.

End of season repairs. Work carried out immediately at the end of the playing season largely determines playing conditions for the following season. It should be tackled urgently and thoroughly on the following lines.

Determine which of any badly worn areas are to be renovated with seed and which are to be turfed. If play carries on until too late in the season then it may be too late for sowing grass seed and then all repairs will need to be done by turfing. Unless you have your own supply of turf, new turf deliveries should already have been organised.

Scarify the courts overall, preferably by suitable machine; sweep off dead grass and other debris, then mow.

Seeding. Hollow tining may be required on worn and compacted areas such as baselines and service areas prior to seed bed preparation. Prepare a firm but fine seed bed on areas to be sown, by light forking and raking, making up levels with suitable top soil. Sow grass seed at 1 oz./sq. yd. and lightly rake in—your seed merchant may be able to guide you on a suitable mixture to match existing turf.

Turfing

(a) Carefully cut and lift turf from the badly worn areas, i.e. hopefully no more than a small area at the base lines. Hand work to cut the turf to the right uniform thickness is both a skilled and a laborious operation so the hire of a mechanical turf cutter, with or without operator, is well worth while. It is usually most convenient to operate on a more or less rectangular area even though small amounts of good turf are removed.

    If you are using your own turf, the machine can be used to cut this to exactly the right size and uniform thickness, which may be 1¼" or 1½". As regards size, 12" squares are very convenient to handle and lay correctly but some people prefer 3' x 1'.

(b) Cultivate by forking to a shallow depth and break down the soil to a fine tilth without interfering with levels too much. Work in extra soil if required and firm up by treading carefully, taking 3" or 4" steps with pressure on the heels. The finished soil surface should be within 1¼" (or 1½") of turf surface level so that when the new turf is laid the finish is exactly true. A straight edge laid across the turf is essential. Rake into the soil fine bone meal at 1 oz./sq. yd. or a proprietary winter fertilizer at the supplier's recommended rate.

As far as possible lay turves in a pattern similar to that of bricks in a wall. Do not walk on the prepared bed; use planks placed on turf already laid. Check regularly with the straight edge and if unevenness appears adjust the soil below—do not beat down the turf.

On completion roll carefully and top dress with near-dry screened loam soil (3 to 4 lb./sq. yd.) well brushed into the joints by means of the drag brush.

Note: Depending on circumstances, the area from which the turf has been cut should be repaired by soiling up and sowing grass seed or, after some preparation, by turfing with imported turf which, while not good enough for direct introduction into the courts, can be worked upon for the future.

Avoiding the areas renovated by seed or turf, aerate, with solid or slit tines, the whole area of courts and surrounds. Aim to use a machine which gets as near as possible to a depth of 4" at fairly close centres.

Before growth ceases for the winter, top dress with near-dry screened loam when the surface is dry.

The loam should be spread as evenly as possible by a skilfully wielded shovel at a rate of 2-3 lb./sq. yd.. It should then be further dispersed and worked in thoroughly by drag brushing repeated in several directions. The main purpose of top dressing is to maintain and to improve surface smoothness. A dressing of good complete turf fertilizer at the end of August or the beginning of September will often be enough to last to the next spring but a proprietary winter fertilizer may be applied at a later date if necessary.

If worm casting is a problem then mild damp weather in October, when the worms are working near the surface, gives a good opportunity to apply wormkiller. Chlordane or carbaryl wormkillers are usually found efficient and lasting. Use carefully *(they are poisonous)* and strictly in accordance with supplier's instructions.

If the opportunity does not arise in the autumn, similar suitable conditions may occur in the spring.

During the autumn and even during the winter when the weather is mild, there can be appreciable grass growth which should be mown as necessary to prevent the grass getting too long (and thus giving the coarse grasses a better chance)—the mower should be set a little higher than it is during the playing season. A suitable bench setting of the mower might be ⅜" or even ½".

Nevertheless make sure your mower is overhauled in good time so as to be ready for the new season.

Spring and Summer. As growth recommences mowing should intensify, the first cut of ⅜"-½" being gradually reduced to the seasonal 5/16" about a fortnight or so before the season commences if possible.

Careful light scarification of the turf is beneficial fairly early in the spring and during the season further occasional light scarification or frequent brushing is desirable to maintain dense upright growth.

Follow this with a good spring and summer type complete fertilizer; spread very carefully to get it even and ensure a uniform response from the turf. Some fertilizers can be spread as bought but others may be better mixed with two or three times their weight of screened soil to give more bulk for spreading and to minimise scorch risk. In any case it is wise to divide the fertilizer into two and spread the halves in two directions at right angles—this whether the spreading is by hand or by distributor. Remember that even when spreading by distributor the results depend on the operator.

If no rain falls within 24 hours of fertilizer application it is wise to water in very carefully but thoroughly.

Careful rolling may give immediate benefit by firming and smoothing the surface—but this at a price. Compaction very much restricts soil permeability to water (i.e. interferes with drainage), reduces soil aeration and stunts root development and all these contribute to the production of poor turf courts with poor wear resistance. One good rolling with a 5-10 cwt. roller in several directions to firm up any winter upheaval before the rest of the season, should be sufficient use of the roller, the courts receiving enough rolling for the start of the season from the rollers on the mower.

For marking out see pages 432 to 435 or Rules Booklet. The courts must, of course, be accurately set out and marked with the aid of carefully placed and tightened strings. Once the original markings are made further lining is fairly easy since it follows the original lines. Care in selecting a good line marker is well worthwhile.

Mowing should be carried out with great regularity, boxing off the cuttings and putting them into a compost heap. During the main growing season mowing is required at least twice a week and it is an advantage to brush before mowing to lift up procumbent grass foliage and to disperse any worm casts.

Changing the direction of mowing occasionally helps the appearance and performance of all turf areas and avoids faults such as "washboarding".

Considerable skill is required to maintain sufficient soil moisture for grass growth (or survival) in dry weather without undue interference with the use of the courts. It is important to water quite early in a dry period, i.e. before the soil dries out and the grass goes brown. Watering in the evening is a good plan and if the water does not penetrate readily, shallow spiking (or pricking) beforehand may help. A fixed watering system (as opposed to portable sprinklers) is a great labour saver.

An occasional dressing of summer fertiliser is often beneficial and certainly a good complete summer fertilizer at the end of August or the beginning of September helps the surviving grass to recover from its summer pounding and see through the winter. Spreading etc, as above.

Broad-leaved weed control. Elimination of most broad-leaved weeds can be achieved very effectively through the correct use of a proprietary, broad spectrum, selective weedkiller sold for use on turf (i.e. one containing more than one chemical so that a wide range of weeds is attacked without damage to the grass). The weedkiller should be diluted with water and applied as a spray over the whole of an effected court strictly in accordance with maker's instructions. The work can be carried out any time in the growing season but late spring (shortly after the spring fertilizer application when growth is strong) is probably the best time. Pick a calm day (to reduce risk of drift on to neighbouring flower gardens and the like) when there seems likely to be 24 hours without rain. To allow absorption of the chemical do not mow for at least a day after treatment.

Spot treatment of individual weeds or weed patches by giving each a short spraying is possible but decidedly risky—damaged turf often results.

Grass weed control. There is no practical selective grass killer as yet. Unwanted grasses have to be controlled (or disguised) by scarification or alternatively they may be patched out.

Moss control. Moss in grass courts is commonly an indication that conditions are in some way unsatisfactory for grass which would otherwise keep out the moss. The best approach to moss control is to establish what the faulty conditions are (e.g. over-acidity, poverty or bad drainage) and correct them.

Sulphate of iron or dichlorophen treatments can be used but moss is likely to come back if the faulty conditions are not corrected. There are two main types of mercurised moss killer—those meant for winter application and those for use in the summer. Like selective weedkillers (though less risky) each can be used for treatment of individual areas but it is usually wise to treat a whole area. The winter-use products have little nitrogen fertilizer included and can be used at any time but particularly in autumn, winter and early spring. Those intended for use during the summer growing season typically contain a good deal of nitrogen fertilizer and should be used only during the growing season (they may then replace other intended fertilizer treatment). Particularly with the summer type, watering-in should be done if rain does not fall in the twenty-four hours after application. When the moss dries out some scarification is usually desirable to encourage the grass to grow through.

Disease control. Intensively maintained turf is subject to several fungal diseases, the most common of which are fusarium patch and red thread. Both may occur at any time of the year so a constant watch should be maintained. Fusarium is most prevalent in warm, damp weather in spring and autumn, often where excess of nitrogen fertilizer has been given. Red thread, on the other hand, is more prevalent in the summer and where there is a shortage of nitrogen.

Fusarium patch disease shows as yellow-brown patches of varying sizes up to about 12" diameter—in a bad attack the patches coalesce and considerable areas of turf can be badly damaged, sometimes very quickly, even overnight.

There are several turf fungicides on the market—either systemics or contact type—which are available for fusarium control and all can be used with success if maker's instructions are followed. Some are meant for dry application but most are meant for spray application—be sure you have the right nozzles on your sprayer. Repeated applications may be necessary.

Red thread disease usually shows as fairly widely spread small patches of rather bleached grass and close examination of the blades reveal pink needles which are outgrowths composed of fungal mycelium. Red thread is usually far less serious than fusarium and fungicide may not be required. Quite often a dressing of fertilizer providing quick acting nitrogen will cause the grass to outgrow the trouble. If direct treatment is considered necessary then use chlorothanil or iprodione.

Take care with poisons. *Chemicals used to curtail one form of life are seldom harmless to other forms of life!*

Take great care with moss killers, weedkillers, worm killers, fungicides etc. Read the label—follow the instructions—wear protective clothing as appropriate, especially gloves.

Soil tests and technical advice. Occasional laboratory tests of the soil can be useful—say every three years. Routine tests show whether or not the soil is over-acid (and so needing lime) and whether or not there are deficiencies in phosphate and potash. Lime should not be applied to turf unless soil tests indicate over-acidity and so prove it necessary since it encourages weeds, worms and fungal diseases. Deficiencies in phosphate and potash are unlikely on well maintained courts but, if present, they should be corrected. This is easily done by adjusting fertilizer treatment appropriately.

Some trade concerns offer an advisory service but there is also an independent organisation—The Sports Turf Research Institute at Bingley, West Yorkshire, BD16 1AU (tel. Bradford (0274) 565131). This exists for the benefit of sports turf users and is managed by a Board representing the controlling bodies of major sports, including The Lawn Tennis Association. It derives its funds mainly from the subscriptions of individual member clubs and advises such clubs on all technical matters relating to the construction and maintenance of tennis courts (especially but not exclusively grass) including disease identification and soil testing as well as full maintenance programmes etc.

The STRI advisory service is supported by nearly 50 years' experience and by a research programme aimed at finding tougher grasses, better drainage methods etc., all with a view to providing as economically as possible better and harder wearing playing surfaces for tennis and for other sports.

GROUND STAFF

Many clubs have a problem in finding suitable ground staff and the shortage tends to lead to more and more clubs converting to non-grass courts even though many players prefer grass.

The shortage of qualified groundsmen is not confined to tennis clubs and clearly reflects an inadequate supply of new entrants into the profession caused no doubt by a variety of factors including lack of training facilities and unattractive wage scales in the past.

In the short term, clubs can only advertise—in the local press and in "The Groundsman", the monthly magazine of the Institute of Groundsmanship, Wroughton Pavilion, Wroughton on the Green, Milton Keynes, MK6 3EA. (Tel. 0908 663600). Provision of a house is in practice a great attraction.

One possible way of easing the problem of adequate staffing is for two or three small clubs which are reasonably close together to share the cost and work of a groundsman. A difficulty to be solved in this set-up is making suitable arrangements to cover the circumstances of each club wanting courts prepared at the same time!

In the long term, clubs can help by supporting staff who want to attend courses which may involve day release etc. Some Local Authorities now run courses for groundsmen and they should be encouraged in their efforts. The Institute of Groundmanship organises courses and also has a scheme of qualifications obtained by examination (including practical).

The Sports Turf Research Institute runs intensive courses of one week's duration in the spring and autumn every year.

N.B. Please see note on page 28 concerning casual labour.

THE IMPORTANCE OF WINTER PLAY

The relative inclemency of our winters compared with say Australia and parts of America is often quoted as one of the reasons why Britain has not produced as many Wimbledon champions as other countries.

Good winter facilities are, of course, just as important for the many thousands of players who enjoy their tennis and want to be able to play in reasonable conditions throughout the year.

The Alternatives – Outdoor

As already stated in the section on "Courts" red shale cannot, in most cases, be considered as a serious contender because it is so easily put out of action by frost and snow. One is therefore faced with one of the varieties of all-weather court to which can be added a floodlighting system. Floodlights are at their best when the weather is still warm but daylight is too short for evening play. A pamphlet is available to clubs from the Technical Dept., LTA, giving some essential information on the subject.

There are a number of companies making floodlighting systems and these vary greatly in price. Clubs are advised to check with others having the facility and use their experiences before making a decision. You can, as many clubs testify, buy and install your own system.

If you decide to do-it-yourself you should not, under any circumstances, try to economise by cutting back on the amount of light recommended. You will find that darker areas on the court can be very distracting for even the more modest standard of play. Also, where a bank of courts is concerned avoid any system that involves the masts bearing the lamps being sited other than by the net or close to the back stop netting—they are at best distracting and at worst dangerous. However, before making too many plans, you are advised to discuss the project with the local electricity board.

The Alternatives – Indoor

There can be no doubt that the most enjoyable winter tennis is played indoors although the problems to be overcome before a club can join the elite who already have their own covered court are formidable.

Before even considering costs and types, you may find that the local authority will not grant planning permission. Accordingly, an exploratory meeting with the planning officer is the first move and you should discuss with him both methods of covering courts described below.

In the event of there being little or no chance of building either, ask whether his ruling holds for all sites in the area, and if not, which other tennis club (or other available land) would be likely to receive his blessing.

The point of the second enquiry is that if your club cannot obtain permission to build but has the means of finance and another club close by has a possible site, then there may be a case for dual ownership. It is at least worth considering as a two, three or even four club enterprise.

The choice of structures, determined by cost in most instances, is relatively simple. Since only a handful of clubs could raise in the region of £100,000 to build a single permanent i.e. brick-built or similar covered court and since the economics of such a venture are so daunting, it is not appropriate to go into the subject here. This is not to say that the LTA do not have a wealth of experience and advice to offer and *any organisation contemplating this major project should first write to the Technical Dept., giving details of the proposals.*

The main limitation on this type of structure chosen will be financial. The lower the budget the more likely the choice will be restricted to lighter weight structures of a temporary or short life nature. Structures vary from lightweight disposable to heavyweight permanent. Materials vary from 'bricks & mortar' to Carbon Fibre & Kenlar.

The main structure groupings are (i) unframed air-supported structures, (ii) unframed tented structures, (ii) frame tented, (iv) framed rigid cladding structures and (v) full permanent structures.

The following list covers those firms involved in 'lightweight structures' and clubs are advised not only to obtain detailed quotations but also to visit any existing installations for comparison. No LTA recognition is implied.

AIRHALLS

Air-Tech Industries Inc.,
85 Madison Circle Drive,
East Rutherford,
N.J. 07073
USA
(201) 460 9730

Bovan Ltd.,
Suite 3DD
3 Morpeth Terrace,
London.
SW1P 1EW
01-828 7918

Covair Structures Ltd.,
58 Main Street,
Barton in the Beans,
Nuneaton,
Warwickshire.
0455 619101

Air Structures Ltd.,
Station Road,
Hinckley,
Leicester,
LE10 1AP
0455 631326

Thomson Coverall Ltd.,
Fereneze Industrial Estate,
Barrhead,
Glasgow,
G78 1TR
041 881 8261

P.N. Structures Ltd.,
5 Vigo Street,
Piccadilly,
London,
W1X 1AH
01-734 2578

SLR (Sports) Ltd.,
21 Middlefield Road,
Cossington,
Leicester,
LE7 8UT
0509 813742

Clyde Canvas Goods & Structures Ltd.,
42 North Bar,
Banbury,
Oxon,
OX16 0TH
0295 61512

Indoor Tennis Systems,
Hayne Barn,
Saltwood,
Hythe,
Kent,
CT21 4QH
0303 65512

LIGHTWEIGHT STRUCTURES AND PERMANENT BUILDINGS

Air-Tech Industries Inc.,
85 Madison Circle Drive,
East Rutherford,
N.J. 07073,
USA
(201) 460 9730

Bovis Construction Ltd.,
Bovis House,
Northolt Road,
Harrow,
Middx.
HA2 0EE
01-422 3488

Bassett Enterprises,
22 Dukes Close,
North Weald,
Essex,
CM16 6DA
0378 823963

Spandrel Structures Ltd.,
Armadale Road,
Feltham,
Middx.
TW14 0LR
01-751 4464

Consolidated Building Services Ltd.,
Consolidated Buildings,
Ferry Road,
Cardiff,
CF1 7JL
0222 43698

Astron,
Keelawite Ltd.,
Birmingham Road,
Allesley,
Coventry.
0676 23459

Campbell Reith & Hill,
Hampton House,
62 Bramhall Lane South,
Bramhall,
Stockport,
SK7 2DU

P.N. Structures Ltd.,
5 Vigo Street,
Piccadilly,
London,
W1X 1AH.
01-734 2578

Tayfab Structures,
Taywood House,
345 Ruislip Road,
Southall,
Middx.
UB1 2QX
01-578 2366

Losch Retractable Roofs,
16 Burrowmoor Road,
March,
Cambridgeshire
PE15 9RP
03542 2670

Baco Contracts Ltd.,
Regal House,
London Road,
Twickenham,
TW1 3QA
01-892 4488

Clyde Canvas Goods & Structures Ltd.,
42 North Bar,
Banbury,
Oxon,
OX16 0TH
0295 61512

Pellikaan Building Co.,
Dr Hub van Doorneweg 95,
5026 RB Tilburg,
The Netherlands.
013 630055

Owen Brown & Sons Ltd.,
Bishop Meadow Road,
Loughborough,
Leicestershire
LE11 0RQ
0509 214334

Sprung Instant Structures Ltd.,
11 Langdon Avenue
Aylesbury
Bucks.
HP21 7UL
0296 85695

Clubs considering the installation of new courts with a view to floodlighting or covering them in the future would be wise to consider building-in cables or covered court foundations to avoid subsequent damage to adjacent courts.

Obviously, the economics of airhalls relate to the capital cost and the charge made to players but the experience of clubs that pioneered this idea in the U.K. suggests that a surplus can be realised given a reasonable degree of organisation. Reports from two clubs which have recently installed covered courts can be found on pages 50 to 52.

Note: There are local authority limitations on the number of people using these structures at any one time and their adoption as a 'social' facility may fall into this category. A check should be made with your local authority.

PLAYING EQUIPMENT

Since most of the equipment is bought by individual players, with cost determining the quality, only the subject of tennis balls may require some clarification.

The LTA keeps close control over ball standards by means of testing annually, and inspection of manufacturing processes in factories. The balls so recognised are classed as "Official" and marked accordingly. The Official balls for each year are shown in the LTA Annual Report, circulated to affiliated clubs at the beginning of December.

Manufacturers wishing to send balls for testing can do so and certificates would be given as appropriate. A fee is payable for this service.

The rules allow balls to be either white or yellow; no other colour is permitted. The yellow balls were introduced originally to suit certain indoor lighting conditions but whether even then they are better than white is arguable and a matter of personal choice in most cases. They are occasionally preferred outdoors on certain types of hard court which tend to discolour white balls more easily.

Non-pressurised balls, which can be kept from one year to the next—a great advantage—can also be submitted for testing. They rely for their bounce solely on the composition of the rubber as opposed to the internal pressure required by the more conventional ball.

Sports goods retailers usually allow discounts to affiliated clubs for quantities of three dozen minimum.

Used balls are available from The Championships at Wimbledon on application, at a very favourable price, through the county association, and also possibly from other national or local events such as tournaments, Prudential County Cup centres, etc.

Balls too worn for club use are usually welcomed and bought by local sports (or other) retailers, schools or professional coaches.

COURT EQUIPMENT

In general, the high costs of this equipment demand that care is taken in both selection and storage. Whilst details of availability and cost can be found and compared by sending for catalogues from the various court manufacturers or through your local sports retailer, there are a few points to be made on the main items of court equipment.

Storage

It is of paramount importance that all materials and machinery are kept in dry conditions. So many clubs pay little attention to sheds etc., particularly when pavilion maintenance seems a greater priority; this can be false economy since good playing surfaces depend to a large extent on the reliable condition of court maintenance equipment.

Surround Netting

Considering the required lifespan of this and the punishment that it must withstand, make sure that it is (a) of sufficient gauge, (b) well proofed against the weather and (c) that the size of the mesh prevents the ball from penetrating except under extreme pressure. It is difficult to be specific in these—far better to examine netting approved by other local clubs.

Nets

Again, wear and tear is a critical factor and in most cases it pays to shop around and buy the best quality. This applies especially to hard court nets where there is abrasion with the court's surface during play. Of course, the need to lower the nets and drape them when not in use cannot be stressed too highly. The life of nets will be prolonged if spares are kept in order that overhauling can be carried out *at the first sign of wear.*

Posts

When juniors are the prime users of the court, it is important that the winding mechanism, which can otherwise cause injury to prying fingers, is totally enclosed. Signs of rust must be treated without delay and an annual cost of paint is important. Do make sure that all posts are interchangeable. They should also be removed from their sockets periodically and greased.

Watering Systems

This has become a specialised field and clubs looking for a new or more efficient means of watering courts can write to any one of a number of companies for advice. (See below). When doing so, full details of your court layout, water outlet points and pressure should be given. The cost will vary according to whether you can manage with simple sprinklers or whether a more sophisticated method is needed such as overhead or pop-up systems. Consultation with your groundstaff would be important before making these enquiries. Among irrigation specialists that could advise are the following:

British and General Tube Co. Ltd.
Leigh Road,
Trading Estate,
Slough, Berks. SL1 4BA.
Tel. Slough 33404.

British Overhead Irrigation Ltd.
The Green,
Upper Halliford,
Shepperton, Middx.
Tel. Sunbury 88301.

RIS Cameron Irrigation Systems Ltd.,
Harwood Industrial Estate,
Littlehampton,
Sussex, BN17 7BA.
Tel. Littlehampton 3985.

Evenproducts Ltd.
Blayneys Lane,
Evesham,
Worcs. WR11 4TS.
Tel. Evesham 41212.

Farrow Division
Wright Rain Ltd.,
Horseshoe Road,
Spalding,
Lincs. PE11 3JA.
Tel. Spalding 3764.

Hazelock Ltd.,
Haddenham,
Aylesbury,
Bucks. HP17 8JD.
Tel. Haddenham 291881.

T. Parker & Son (Turf Management) Ltd.,
Worcester Park,
Surrey, KT4 7NF.
Tel. 01-337 7791.

Perrot Irrigation Ltd.,
38 High Street,
Rowhedge,
Colchester, CO5 7ET.
Tel. Colchester 867624

Toro Irrigation Ltd.,
Unit 7,
Millstream Trading Estate,
Ringwood, Hants, BH24 3SD.
Tel. Ringwood 6261.

Waternation Ltd.
Monument Way East,
Woking,
Surrey, GU21 5LY.
Tel. Woking 70303.

Court Covers

(This information may only apply to clubs holding a major annual tournament because of the cost and need for extra ground staff).

In addition to the usual covers which lie directly on the surface of the court, you can use a system similar in principle to airhalls. A polythene membrane is pulled across the court and inflated to lift it clear, limiting the formation of surface condensation and even allowing maintenance to be carried out. This is particularly important for grass courts.

Many clubs will consider such an item as a luxury but a club professional could take a different view.

COACHING AND PRACTICE

AVAILABILITY AND COST

The most accessible list of tennis coaches, region by region, appears earlier in this Handbook but the Professional Tennis Coaches' Association, which is an autonomous body, also produces and associate members. This can be obtained from the Secretary of the PTCA, Mrs. P. M. Bocquet, 21 Glencairn Court, Lansdown Road, Cheltenham, Gloucestershire, GL50 2NB.

Clubs should write to a selected coach giving details of the requirements, i.e. individual, group, weekly, monthly, school holiday courses and so on. Following this, the coach will probably meet you to discuss court allocation, times and cost.

The charge a professional makes will vary widely but, in general, individual coaching costs between £8 - £15 per hour. Group coaching is particularly recommended for beginners and the cost varies according to the numbers and courts involved. Every club should be able to offer some form of coaching, especially if a thriving junior section is sought.

ROLE OF THE COACH

Tennis coaches in this country have, in general, held a traditionally 'distant' position in Clubs, taking little or no part in the decision making processes of the Club or Clubs they attend. Tennis clubs throughout the country now have to compete with many other readily available pastimes and face an increasing need to modernise not only their physical premises but also their thinking and attitudes. The coach's business depends in much the same way as the Tennis Club upon people of all ages playing and enjoying the game of tennis. Having therefore the same objectives it is logical if not essential that the coach is given and accepts a more substantial involvement in the running of the Club to the benefit of the members, the Club and his or her own business.

Tennis coaches today are expected to do far more than teach the basic strokes and tactics of the game. They are being asked to attain new standards and will be subject to regular retraining. To varying degrees they should also be encouraged to become their Club's promoters, publicists, managers and organisers and have an involvement in the marketing of their sport.

It is therefore a logical step to see that your club coach has every opportunity to be substantially involved in the Club and the game in which he is a professional.

A Contract

A good coach can be a tremendous asset so ensure that the coach you appoint has the LTA qualification appropriate to the role required. Where a club has or intends to have a full time coach, it may be that a formal contract of employment is necessary. In this event, the club's solicitor should be involved.

In the majority of cases, however, a coach will need to have employment elsewhere and a letter from the club committee to the coach would probably be regarded as adequate. The LTA would not recommend verbal agreements as they must inevitably lead to misunderstandings, particularly where the committee's personnel may change.

The following points in respect of part-time coaches may help committees to cover the major issues:-

1. Is the coach to be an employee or self-employed? This is a very important decision both from the point of view of job security and tax. Also, who is to be the employer?
2. It is essential to have a proper job title and description setting out what the coach is, and is not, expected to do.
3. What charges the coach makes and the position regarding coaching of non-members will need to be agreed with the Committee.
4. The times when a coach has exclusive use of a court should be clearly stated (and shown on the club notice board).
5. Where a coach wishes to employ an assistant, the assistant should be qualified and approved by the committee.
6. The club should retain the right to allow other coaches to use the Club facilities.
7. Whether or not a coach has a shop on the club premises, the responsibility of both parties for insurance (including accidents, negligence and damage) should be established.
8. The agreement as a whole should be clearly recorded in the club minutes and should not be for a long term — a maximum of one year is suggested.

It must be appreciated that the important factor is to establish a beneficial working relationship between the coach, the club committees and the club members.

COACHING COURSES

Finally, of course, there are many club players who have taken coaching courses under the LTA

Training of Coaches Scheme and these members find themselves in great demand. If your club has members interested in becoming coaches they should apply to the Coaching Department, The Lawn Tennis Association, Barons Court, West Kensington, London W14 9EG.

The LTA organise courses for three grades of coach:

***LTA Elementary Tennis Teacher**

The Elementary Tennis Teachers Certificate courses are held regionally in addition to the National residential course and those passing are eligible to assist at LTA/Prudential Grass Roots Centres.

****LTA Assistant Coach**

After gaining the necessary experience ETTC holders may apply to attend an Assistant Coaches Award course. These also are held regionally in addition to National residential courses and are in two stages.

*****LTA Professional Coach**

Registration as an LTA Professional Coach is the final and highest award and candidates can apply to attend the Professional Registration course after they have the necessary experience.

PRACTICE WALLS

These take various forms; description and recommendations are listed below.

Materials

Wood boarding is not generally suitable on account of the noise, unless it is very solid and heavy, e.g. railway sleepers, but these are usually unacceptable because of unevenness. Stone or concrete blocks or brick, faced with cement, are best. A local builder or architect should be consulted on the need for buttressing and on the foundations, according to local conditions. **Minimum** thickness of the wall is the length of a brick at the base and the width of a brick at the top.

Dimensions

The desirable width is 9 yards (say 8m), i.e. the width of a singles court, but if this is not possible a minimum 6 yards (say 5.5m) i.e. half the width of a doubles court, will serve. The desirable height of a wall is 10 feet (say 3m), extended by means of wire netting to a total height of minimum 15 feet (say 4.5m). Even more is desirable for children's use, especially if the area behind is not accessible for recovery of balls.

Slope

Except for the most experienced players, for whom a vertical wall is acceptable, the face of the wall should lean backwards as this brings the ball back to a better length and promotes longer rallies. The suggested slope is 2 inches in every 3 feet of height (say, 1 : 20).

Markings

The net-line should be painted on the wall, preferably in the correct shape although a level 3 feet (.915m) will serve. If a full width wall is built, a singles court should be marked out on the ground in front. For a narrower wall, at least a baseline and service line should be provided. Possible refinements which have been advocated are an additional horizontal line on the wall at a height of six feet, to show when balls are being hit consistently high; and two round "targets" just above net height, at which services can be aimed. If the ground markings overlap or pass close to a proper court, they can be in a colour other than white to avoid confusion.

Siting

Unless indoors or within a complete "cage" of wire netting, the wall should be sited to facilitate recovery of balls which go over. In a residential area, noise should also be borne in mind. However, availability of space and ground surface will usually have to be the deciding factors. If the playing area is to be purpose laid, it should preferably be concrete or asphalt or non-attention hard court material. Economy can often be had by setting the wall in the surround netting of an existing hard court and indeed every club should have this type of practice wall even if there is no space for anything more.

Cost

It has been necessary to leave so many features undecided or subject to local considerations, e.g. foundations, availability of suitable local material and the extent of Do-it-Yourself labour, that no useful estimate of cost can be given.

Many coaches believe this type of practice wall is still the best because the uniform pace of the returning ball enables ground strokes and volleys to be "grooved". Footwork is helped in the same way and in these days of escalating costs its permanency is an important factor. It is recommended for all standards.

Wall Nets

Again recommended for all standards, the variable slope of the face enables a great variety of "returns" which also carry more pace than those from the well previously described. It can also be placed on an empty court either at the net or against the surround netting. However, it should be stored inside when not in use, particularly during bad weather, and although it is portable, two people are required. It is virtually silent. Available from sports goods retailers.

Variations and other forms of practice wall exist and will be available from sports goods retailers. Mention should perhaps be made of ball-firing machines which not only assist the beginner but also cater for the long and arduous practice required by aspiring champions. Such machines can deliver 50 or 60 balls at varying intervals and at velocities up to 90 miles an hour. They can be electrically operated or supplied with petrol motor and clutch.

HOW THE LTA HELPS

THROUGH THE COUNTIES

All tennis clubs and players derive benefit from The Lawn Tennis Association, the governing body of the game in Great Britain, without which there would be no uniformity of rules, equipment or courts, nor co-ordination of tournaments, club matches, etc.

The affiliation of a club to its County LTA (or in the case of Scottish or Welsh clubs to the Scottish or Welsh LTA) includes automatic affiliation to the LTA itself. Clubs pay a subscription to the County LTA, the amount of which differs from one county to another but usually relates to the size of the club. Also all club players pay an annual Player's Contribution which is collected by the clubs for the County Associations, which in turn pass the major proportion to the LTA; the rates for 1986 are £1.70 for each playing member aged 18 or over, 80p for each playing member under 18 and £50.50 per court (with the LTA's agreement only) for clubs where it is not practicable to establish the number of members liable. It is the County Associations that form the essential ink between individual clubs and the LTA and they can provide services to clubs which would be unmanageable on a national scale.

To many club members the most obvious of these is the competitive tennis provided by county inter club team competitions. At one time these were generally knock-out competitions, but nowadays they ae mostly run on a league basis, so that each club team has a programme of several matches with the incentive of promotion and relegation. There are usually summer and winter competitions, sometimes separate events for junior club teams (i.e. for players under a specified age), and in some counties, local leagues run by sub-associations serving a particular area.

Most counties also run individual singles and doubles events open to all members of their affiliated clubs and there may also be county closed championships restricted to those who hold a county qualification.

These events give club players opportunities to come to the notice of the county when teams for inter-county matches are being selected.

All County Associations are very active nowadays in junior development. Starting with the beginners, the county organisers play a key part in the LTA/Prudential Grass Roots coaching scheme, and a course at one of the centres under this scheme is an excellent way for children to learn the rudiments of the game before becoming junior members of a club. All counties run coaching and training schemes for the most promising juniors who are recommended by their clubs or who achieve good results in junior events in the county, and indeed a large proportion of the LTA grants to County Associations is earmarked for junior coaching. Then there are county junior championships open to all juniors who have a county qualification and, for the best of them, selection for the junior inter-county championships.

Most County Associations produce an annual handbook, which will normally contain among other things the association's rules and competition regulations and details of all affiliated clubs and their officials. Some also produce newsletters to keep club members in touch with what is going on in the county. There may also be an annual social event at which club members can meet county officials. Another responsibility is the distribution of Wimbledon tickets; a large county handles the distribution of many thousands of pounds worth of tickets to its clubs each year.

Finally, they should be prepared to deal with queries from clubs on a wide range of subjects, either giving advice or telling a club where expert help can be obtained and, in particular, should be able to advise clubs on questions of financial assistance for capital projects. They play an important part in assisting clubs to obtain loans under the LTA loans scheme (see "Financing of Projects".

This list of activities is by no means exhaustive, and the pattern may vary in detail from one county to another. But it should always be remembered that the efficiency of a County Association depends on the calibre of those who are elected by its member clubs to serve on its council. If your club can suggest improvements to the running of the County Association for the general benefit of the clubs, put them to the county and if possible nominate a candidate for membersip of the Association's council or committee.

If elected he (or she) will probably be expected to take an active part in the work and care should be taken to select a suitable candidate who has sufficient time available.

THE LTA ASSOCIATE MEMBERSHIP SCHEME

Launched at the LTA Conference in December 1982, this Scheme, although off to a slow start, now appears to be gaining momentum. The aims are twofold—to produce additional revenue for investment in British tennis at every level, and to promote a sense of mutual involvement in tennis throughout the country. Subscriptions are £10.00 per annum for seniors and £5.00 for juniors.

Benefits of membership are as follows:

1. A free copy of the quarterly newspaper 'Serve & Volley', sent to Members only.
2. A free copy of the Official LTA Handbook 'Tennis Great Britain' (cover price £5.95).
3. Each current Member is automatically included in a ballot for Wimbledon tickets, held on 1st May each year.
4. Discounted tickets for most major events held in Britain.
5. Insurance cover against injury whilst playing tennis which causes a subsequent loss of earnings.
6. Free admission to the LTA Volkswagen National Ratings (usual price £4), where this year nearly 200 tournaments will be held in 22 counties, and results will count towards a player's national rating.
7. Group membership offers which include the opportunity to purchase specially designed sweaters, ties and umbrellas, discounts on cars, life assurance, medical insurance, holidays and trips to the U.S. and French Open Championships.
8. The attractive plastic membership card itself.

Details are now available from your club secretary or from the Membership Secretary at the LTA to whom you should apply enclosing a stamped addressed envelope.

COUNTY AND CLUB COMMITTEE

In the introduction to this Manual, the background of this committee's formation is given. Following the changed structuring of the LTA at the end of 1981, the objectives of the Committee were amended slightly and are now:

1. To improve communications between Clubs and the LTA.
2. To advise Clubs generally.
3. To submit recommendations to the LTA Council on matters directly or indirectly relating to club administration and activities.
4. To co-operate with County Association as necessary and in consultation with them to maintain and increase the number of clubs affiliated to the LTA.

This Committee is also now responsible for the Club Loans Scheme and the Wimbledon ticket allocation to Counties.

Club Manual

Originally a separate production, the Manual was the first major undertaking of the committee. Now widely accepted by clubs large and small, it has become an integral part of the Handbook and will continue in this form, being updated as necessary each year.

Forums

Following the success of the Manual, the County and Club Committee looked at ways of developing further the system of communication between the LTA and its clubs. The many excellent County Associations transmit information from the LTA to their affiliated Clubs and most County Officials are well known in their areas. However, it could not be said that the same relationship existed between the LTA and many of the affiliated clubs. One important factor has always been that there are fewer opportunities for direct personal contact. The Committee recognised therefore the need for the governing body of the sport to leave its headquarters from time to time to meet club officials. To further this objective the Committee has already held a number of conferences for clubs in various parts of the country in order to invite open discussion on any subject that concerns the successful management of the game.

To date the venues have been Bramhall, Nottingham, Oxford, Leeds, Birmingham, Norwich, Sutton, Bristol, Newcastle, Exeter, Bedford, Bournemouth, Orpington, Boston, Draycott, Penrith, Upminster, Derby, Cheltenham, Nottingham (a second visit), Winchester, Tame Valley (Cheshire), Wolverhampton, Northampton, Malvern, St. Albans, Truro, Ipswich, Telford, Liverpool and Newcastle (a second visit).

The range of topics covered to date includes:

1. Subscriptions
2. Grants and loans
3. Juniors
4. Beginners
5. Court surfaces
6. Rating relief
7. Planning permission for a. floodlights; b. air halls
8. Use of school courts
9. Communication between members and management
10. Amalgamations
11. Playing-in tests

It is clear to the LTA that, judging by the requests from other areas, this scheme is proving its worth and will continue. For example, one particular subject which is causing concern among officials is the low subscription rate at many clubs, so low in fact as to seriously affect their future viability. Discussion on this point alone has in many respects justified the operation.

While this Committee is always available to help on a particular matter, there is nevertheless greater merit in talking in the presence of other clubs and the LTA recommend you to contact your County Secretary with a view to arranging a conference in your area.

CLUB LOANS SCHEME AND SPECIAL PROJECTS FUND

The LTA first instituted a scheme of loans to affiliated clubs on a small scale as long ago as 1928; of the few similar schemes run by other governing bodies, only that of the Rugby Football Union can claim such an early origin. The scheme has steadily expanded, and since 1955 the LTA has made loans totalling about £3 million to more than 1350 clubs; in other words, more than half the affiliated clubs have benefited. Two-thirds of this total has been advanced in the last five years, during which the amount available for lending has been very substantially increased. In 1985 alone £790,000 was advanced to 155 clubs.

In 1985 the LTA set up a separate Special Projects Fund designed to assist larger projects, particularly those for covered courts, and by September 1985 loans totalling £131,250 had been made from this fund.

Further details of these schemes are given under "Financing of Projects" but some extra points should be noted:

1. Clubs must first apply for assistance from the Local Authorities and the Sports Council. Approval of an LTA loan may be conditional on the results of such applications if they are not yet known.
2. A reasonable proportion of the total estimated cost of the project must be shown to have come from the club.
3. Details of the project, showing the various means of financing proposed, must be given.
4. The application must be accompanied by (a) copies of the last two years' accounts (and balance sheets at the end of those years if these are not included in the accounts), (b) an approximate up-to-date statement of funds if the most recent accounts are more than six months old, (c) a statement showing how repayment of the proposed loan is to be financed and (in the case of all-weather surfaces) how provision is to be made for replacing the new surface in due course and (d) a copy of the contractor's estimate if applicable.

LTA COURT ADVISORY SERVICE

The LTA continues to develop its services to clubs and in 1980 established this scheme to help clubs with problems such as improvements to existing courts, choice of new courts or replacement surfaces and disputes with court manufacturers. The Technical Department is responsible for co-ordinating information and advice, and requests for visits should be made directly through this Department.

Further details can now be found in the section 'Courts and Equipment'.

BOOKS AND FILMS

A list of approved books, films and videocassettes covering a wide range of tennis related activities is available from the LTA. Subjects include coaching, rules, the law, floodlighting, court maintenance as well as details of monthly and annual publications.

TOWN PLANNING MATTERS

Threatened Loss of Grounds
(See also "Security of Tenure")

Clubs on grounds rented from private landlords are most at risk. When leases expire landlords are likely to apply to develop the land more profitably for housing or other purposes.

On receiving a Notice of Intended Development your first object must be to persuade the Local Planning Authority to refuse the application. You should immediately consult a solicitor and seek the support of The Lawn Tennis Association, your County LTA, your Regional Council for Sport and Recreation and your County Playing Fields Association, as well as the owners and occupiers of adjacent land and property. Put your objections in writing to the Planning Officer, stressing the size of your senior and junior playing membership, the nearest comparable club facilities, the cost and difficulty of replacing the club on another site, the need to preserve existing sports grounds in an age of increasing leisure, and any other local factors. Lobby the Councillors on the Planning Committee, find out whether that Committee has the final decision or whether it merely recommends the Council to grant or refuse consent, and in the latter case lobby other Councillors as well.

If the application is refused the applicant can appeal to the Minister. You will be notified of the appeal and whether it is to be heard at a local enquiry or decided by written representations. In presenting your case to the Inspector who hears the appeal you may wish to employ a solicitor or town planning consultant. The LTA and the other bodies mentioned above can be asked to give evidence in person or submit letters of support. Those giving evidence at a hearing are liable to cross-examination.

It is encouraging to note that, where applications for planning permission to develop sites have been refused by local authorities, the appeals from the developers have in a number of cases been rejected.

One such case was an application in 1982 to develop the site of a club in North West England (4 hard courts) with town houses, flats and garages. The application was refused and the applicant appealed by written representations, but the Inspector dismissed the appeal.

The appellant contended that the appeal site was in an area allocated for housing. The Inspector considered that the Structure Plan showed it to be only in a mainly residential area, although it was allocated for residential use in the Town Map. He noted that in the Recreation section of the Structure Plan one of the main priorities was to resist further building on sports grounds and that such grounds should be protected in densely built-up areas, particularly if there was a shortage of land or an unsatisfied need for the activity. He deemed it wrong to approve development causing the loss of recreational space unless it was unused and unnecessary. There was no evidence that the need for homes in the area was so great as to override the objection. He also took into account the volume of representations from interested bodies and individuals and the fact that the cost of re-establishing the club elsewhere would be prohibitive.

Also in 1982 there was an application to develop a club in the South of England (4 grass and 2 shale courts) with two bungalows or alternatively one covered court. The site was zoned for Private Open Space (Sports Ground). The developers appealed against the Council's refusal of planning permission for both proposals and following a local hearing the Inspector dismissed the appeals.

The appellants contended that loss of the club would not have a damaging effect on local inhabitants as many of the members lived at a distance, and that in any case the provision of sports facilities was the Council's responsibility (this was also the view of the Planning Officer, who had recommended approval of the application).

The Inspector took into account over 100 letters and a petition with over 1000 signatures supporting the club's continued existence. With regard to the bungalow proposal he noted that while the area was heavily developed with housing there was a shortage of clubs and courts, and he considered it inappropriate to change the use to residential at the expense of the already deficient recreational facilities in the area. As to the covered court proposal, the existing club enabled over 100 reasonably local inhabitants to enjoy tennis at a cost they could afford, and the resultant loss of the club would mean that many members, especially the young, would be unable to continue such recreation. While a covered court would allow all-year play it was not intended as a commercial venture so that its use would be very restricted. He felt the intention of the zoning was for the land to be used for the benefit of the community at large and he did not consider that the proposed use, although of a sportive nature, was compatible with the current zoning.

In 1971 there was an application to develop the site of a club in Surrey (3 hard courts) with four houses. The area was allocated primarily for residential purposes in the approved Surrey Development Plan. The application was refused and the applicants appealed but the Inspector dismissed the appeal.

The appellants contended that the houses, for which there was a big demand, would complete the estate development begun in the 1930s, that the main body of objectors would not be affected by the proposal, that only club members could be affected by the loss of tennis and that they could be accommodated at other clubs in the area.

The Inspector found that there was a local deficiency of sports grounds and that the use of the site as a tennis club was compatible with the residential area and made a substantial contribution to the recreational and social life of the residents. While the site's value as building land to the applicants was considerable the overriding consideration was the more widespread communal benefit which the club use afforded. He noted the club's computation that on average about 17,000 member hours per annum were played, and he referred to the dismissal of similar appeals in respect of two other tennis clubs in the Home Counties.

Clubs threatened with development are strongly recommended to ask the LTA for copies of the letters issued by the Inspectors setting out in more detail the arguments in the three cases described.

Developments by Clubs

If your club is contemplating a development such as the purchase of land, a larger pavilion, additional courts, car parking or floodlighting, you should first check with your local Planning Authority whether planning permission is required and if so whether a fee is payable on lodging the application. If permission is required do not complete your purchase or start any works until you have a planning consent certificate. You can apply as a prospective purchaser, lessee or prospective lessee.

There may be local opposition to your proposal especially if it involves floodlighting, which often arouses fears among adjacent residents about a pool of light keeping children awake or noise from car doors at late hours. When applying, a stated willingness to accept a cessation of play at say 10 pm can be helpful.

If your proposal is refused the club can appeal to the Minister. You should then seek the verbal or written support of the LTA, your County LTA and your Regional Council for Sport and Recreation. You may wish to employ a solicitor or town planning consultant to conduct your case before the Inspector hearing the appeal. Your witnesses are subject to cross-examination.

Development Plans, Structure Plans, Town Maps, Village Maps, etc.

These are reviewed periodically by County and District Planning Authorities. An advertisement normally appears in your local paper under "Legal and Public Notices" or "Official Notices" setting out where documents can be inspected and the dates by which objections must be lodged. Bear in mind that a proposed change of land designation or the line of a new motorway or road can have a very serious effect on your ground.

THE PROBLEMS OF SMALLER CLUBS

Although nearly all clubs at one time or another face problems of falling membership, threatened loss of ground, rising costs or the need for new facilities and equipment etc., too often the club of few courts and perhaps 50 members has the greatest difficulty in fighting back. The secretary of one such club has strong and definitive views on the subject. He writes:

"Over-dramatisation is foreign to our national way of thinking. It is excusable only when it serves to highlight situations which require immediate consideration and action. Thus to begin this chapter, it must be said that the main problem facing the smaller tennis club is one of survival, be it in the short or long term. A generalisation of this nature will inevitably cause some clubs to react by saying that they are thriving and have no particular problems. Unhappily it is all too clear that under the present economic circumstances and depending upon their geographical location, large numbers of clubs with, say, five courts or less will become increasingly vulnerable to the ravages of inflation. Obviously those situated in suburban districts, where the availability and price of land are critical factors, have an even greater battle on their hands than clubs in country areas.

"The problem has its roots in the period immediately following the Second World War. Prior to 1939, the game had been enjoying great popularity with many clubs running successfully and new ones being established. The war years took their toll but only to a certain extent. Those who returned in many instances found that the club they had left had, contrary to their expectations, not closed down completely but had just been kept alive by the dedication and at times the ingenuity of a few older members. In the main, however, the courts and facilities had severely run down, if not actually fallen into decay. With the spirit of victory, coupled with the times of great austerity, the idea of getting the club started again appealed greatly to a limited number of post war players. An attitude of mind was present which regarded the old broken down pavilion, the chain-link netting renovated with chicken wire and the missing pieces of lead tape, part of a challenge which they were ready to accept. Undoubtedly for a time club spirit ran at a high level, whilst every endeavour was made to renovate, repair and even replace ageing equipment when supplies and money permitted. The low standard of facility being enjoyed at that time, however, lured the majority of committees into a trap. Subscriptions were kept at almost pre-war level and were allowed to remain so for a number of years. Effectively this set the pattern for the next two decades, resulting in what can only be described as a serious "under-pricing" of the sport.

"Another trap was the failure to realise that not enough people had returned to the game and even worse, that tennis, post-war, was not as popular at club level as it had been before. The quite disastrous situation came about that over this long period of resuscitation, most small clubs endeavoured to struggle back to viability (not prosperity), with memberships that were only half to two-thirds full, with subscription rates that would not have been adequate even if they had been enjoying full membership. Some fell by the wayside—a matter of great regret, as it is impossible to envisage their being replaced in the foreseeable future. Our concern now is to see that there are no further unnecessary casualties. Quite incredibly, recent surveys have shown that club committees are still allowing subscriptions to remain at a point where the total revenue from membership fees fails to cover the cost of running a club. They rely on the all too familiar round of socials, jumble sales and tombolas, together with marginal profits on catering and bar receipts, to balance the books. Little or no money is being put to reserve at a time that has seen the costs of pavilion repairs, court resurfacing and surround netting rising continually.

"It is apparent that there are varying attitudes to this potentially disastrous situation. There is on the one hand some evidence of apathy and helplessness, contrasted in a limited number of cases by signs of determination and enterprise. It would be wrong to be too critical of those club officials and committees who unfortunately fall into the first category. Frequently those responsible for the administration of their clubs are deserving of sympathy in that they have served for a long time and if they were given the opportunity, would like to stand down. They are, however, encountering new social attitudes and patterns which reveal that the average member has no wish to engage in organisation and shows no liking for taking any responsibility. They struggle on, therefore, usually doing more and more, sometimes achieving less and less. When challenging, particularly on the subject of delegation (a great and difficult art), their reply is usually philosophical and quite understandable. It is that they cannot interest anyone in sharing the load and if they do, it is usually carried out in a half-hearted fashion so that they are left with the feeling it would have been better and quicker to have done it themselves. This is a most dangerous attitude, because the more one is prepared to do as an amateur administrator, the more one will be allowed to do and the fewer will therefore be involved in the doing. Thus when the time comes for a long-serving club official to retire for whatever reason, there is a grave danger that the smaller club will go downhill and even eventually fold up. It must be realised that this is not an exaggeration, because the evidence has been too obvious to be ignored in recent years. The advice therefore to the club official who has been in office so long that he has come to regard the post, if not the club, as his own, is to put as much of his remaining energy as possible into persuading others to take their share of the workload and by so doing, engender a better club spirit and, hopefully with it, the realisation by the many of the difficulties with which the few have been contending. It should be remembered that apathy divides, whilst enthusiasm unites.

"On the other side of the coin, the prospect to the more energetic and enterprising committees must look discouraging. Faced, as undoubtedly they are or will be in the near future, with raising large sums of money for maintenance and improvement, they must see that grant aid will be increasingly difficult to obtain. The LTA, on the other hand, are doing all they can to assist progressive clubs with interest-free loans through their Club Loans Scheme, under which a steadily increasing amount is out on loan.

"The signs are clear and unmistakable. Existing club members must be made to realise that they are paying far too little for their tennis. The onus of communication must lie with the club secretary and treasurer, who should not be deterred by arguments concerning possible loss of membership or fear of competition from neighbouring clubs. Additionally, every possible effort should be made to achieve full membership. It is appreciated that this is particularly difficult in areas where there is a high density of clubs. The best remedy is to ensure that the club has as large a junior section as it is capable of handling and to give the more promising youngsters group and individual coaching in order to bring them to a reasonable standard at as early an age as possible and then to integrate them into the senior section of the club. Too often juniors reach the age of 15 or 16 and although still keen on the game have not reached a sufficiently high standard to make the transition to the senior section of the club, with the result that as juniors, they cannot be accorded the facility of weekend play. There is a tendency then for counter-attractions to take over and consequently they drift away from the sport. It is realised that small clubs may not be able to afford, or even obtain, the services of a coach, in which case it comes back again to the question of communicating to the club members the importance of giving up some of their own time for this purpose. It should also not be overlooked that there is a considerable potential membership available with the adult beginner. Some enterprising clubs have started to run mid-week evening coaching sessions, organised by their own members, with most encouraging results.

"Finally, a word of hope: tennis is enjoying a tremendous revival at club level in the United States. There is every hope that this pattern will be repeated over here. It is essential that all clubs should still be in existence when that boom time comes again!"

INTRODUCING COVERED COURTS

Although the number of covered tennis courts in Great Britain amounts to less than 200, there has been an increase in the number of clubs expressing an interest and, in some cases, installing covered courts. New materials, more competitive prices, the possible financial assistance from the LTA's Special Projects Fund, and a knowledge of the examples of good practice, have made this development more viable.

Below are reports from two clubs, Chapel Allerton Lawn Tennis and Squash Club in Yorkshire and Boston Lawn Tennis Club in Lincolnshire, which have approached their developments in different ways.

Chapel Allerton Lawn Tennis and Squash Club

Chapel Allerton Lawn Tennis Club celebrated its centenary in 1982, starting as a grass court club, developing 6 red shale in the 1920's, introducing floodlights in the 1950's and a squash section which ensured the survival of the club in the 1960's and 1970's.

By 1980 the club had reached the point where it could hardly generate enough income to cover costs and development had stagnated; management problems and maintenance problems dominated committee meetings. The tennis committee had toyed with dreams of indoor tennis in the late 1970's and this became a firm aim of a small number of members who decided as a development committee that this aim was essential to the future of the club.

The first scheme examined was a polythene 'tent', discounted on grounds of life, financing difficulties and maintenance. Improved airhalls were considered but capital cost and running costs were a problem and no permanent planning permission could be obtained. As the club held tenure of tennis courts only on an agricultural lease funding was a particular problem.

Protracted negotiations resulted in acquisition of the freehold of the tennis courts and the 'marriage' value of courts plus clubhouse, car park, squash courts, etc gave an equity foundation for the raising of commercial loans.

Planning permission was obtained for a timber framed structure with concrete ring beam foundation and reinforced PVC cladding. The frame and foundation had a long life and funding was theoretically possible. There remained the problem of confidence. Despite many doubters the club special general meeting approved the committee's recommendation to proceed if loans could be raised. Interest free loans were made by many members raising several thousand pounds 'up front' but this was insufficient to encourage our bankers. Applications for loans to local authorities produced refusals. The LTA offered a standard Club Loan of £3,000 repayable over a short period: unrealistic in view of our need for £200,000 over a long period. The indebtedness of the club had increased by £60,000 on acquiring the freehold and professional fees kept mounting up. The only prospect of financial help was the Sports Council and this proved to be the key to the realisation of the dream. Our application for grant was supported by the Yorkshire LTA and our prospects of assistance varied from nil to £10,000 according to fluctuations in the Government's plan for public spending.

We were ready to go so far as suppliers, planning authorities and members were concerned and the boost to the economy in early 1982 provided our opportunity. The Sports Council suddenly had an embarrasment of riches and as we were ready they offered £50,000 if we would start. Hopeful negotiations had been going on with the National Westminster Bank for some time and they gave a snap decision and we entered into contract for three indoor courts.

Construction delays were considerable—both main and ground works sub contractor proved to be financially unstable; the court foundation contractor was unable to meet the specification and the lighting system chosen proved to be a long way short of the required performance and reliability. Nevertheless, we became operational by November 1982 and our indoor tennis courts have become very popular achieving hours of usage which we never dreamed of and assisting in improving the financial viability of the club, also the atmosphere.

Membership fluctuates a lot but has risen from under 700 to nearly 1,000 in various categories. Since 1982 we have added two all-weather courts with LTA loan assistance and have ambitious plans to develop further. We feel that indoor tennis can hardly fail if added to a soundly established existing club.

Boston Lawn Tennis Club

Boston is a market town in South Lincolnshire with a population in the region of 25,000 and an additional rural catchment population of around 25,000.

Boston Lawn Tennis Club is the largest tennis club in the locality, and already in 1984 was attracting members from a radius of up to 20 miles or so. Its playing membership in 1984 was about 310 of whom approximately half were juniors or students. The Club stands in three acres of its own land and comprises six courts (grass), two blocks of two En-Tout-Cas Playdek courts (one pair about nine years old and the other pair about three years old) and a brick Clubhouse 20 years old. The annual subscription for an adult in 1984 was £25.00 (including LTA Players' Contribution). In 1984 two coaches were active in the club during the summer, one averaging 25-30 hours per week coaching, and the other 10-15 hours per week.

One of the two older all-weather courts has been floodlit since 1974. Because of the weather, use of the floodlit court averaged in the winter no more than 7-8 hours per week.

After investigating indoor facilities, the only type which we felt we could afford was the cheapest, manufactured by Covair Structures Ltd. Although their airhall is easily the cheapest available there were other advantages and some disadvantages:

Advantages

1. Cost. The cost of covering a pair of our Playdek courts with considerable help from the Community Aid Programme was just under £20,000.
2. Light from an inexpensive form of flood lighting is diffused through the bubble to provide a more even light with less glare than others.
3. The airhall protects the courts from their worst enemy — frost.
4. No lighting is necessary during daylight.

Disadvantages

1. The need to repair small holes in the membrane as necessary.
2. Limitation of use during heavy snow which would prevent the floodlighting from penetrating the membrane.
3. Condensation running down the inside of the bubble may form puddles round the edges.
4. The need to budget for the plastic membrane to be replaced.
5. Separate store for membrane and cables in summer.
6. Possible vulnerability to vandalism.

The airhall consists of a translucent plastic membrane (agricultural grade polyethylene) inflated by an electric fan and anchored to the ground by steel cables attached to the heavy concrete 'ring beam' surrounding the courts. The courts are entered by a revolving airtight door and are lit by a total of 16 × 1500 watt tungsten halogen floodlights on telegraph poles outside the courts.

Because of the technicalities of construction of the groundworks and the need for supervision of the Community Aid Programme (who undertook the shuttering, dismantling of the existing surround posts and netting, cleaning and re-painting, re-assembly and part renewal outside the ring beam, etc) it was decided to employ, through the architects, a site building manager.

The project included extending the floodlights to cover both courts, excavation around the perimeter of the courts to construct the ring beam, all electrical work including supply to the electric fans, re-erection of substantial perimeter netting to take account of security considerations and perimeter surface water drainage. All the labour for the project, apart from the final erection of the airhall itself was provided by the Community Aid Programme for no charge. This probably saved in the region of £2,000. The round-figure costs were as follows:

Concrete	£3,000
Electrical	3,000
Iron work and netting	2,000
Airhall (the price has since increased)	8,500
Sundries	1,000
VAT on all except airhall itself which was zero rated	1,000
Architects	1,000
	£19,500

We requested the manufacturer to make improvements on the specification of the previous airhalls which they had constructed, in particular extra height where it was needed for the effective playing of tennis.

The project was enthusiastically supported by the East Midlands Region of the Sports Council who made a grant of £5,000. We were very fortunate to receive a grant of £5,000 from Boston Borough Council who have also lent £5,000 interest free repayable by equal instalments over 10 years. The balance of the costs was contributed by the club.

We are budgeting on the plastic membrane of the airhall requiring to be replaced every three years or so, and the approximate cost of the plastic is likely to be £4,000. Our annual expenses therefore are £1,333 towards replacement of plastic, £500 loan repayment, approximately £300 cost of electricity for keeping the fan running for 32 weeks and ancillary expenses such as a small amount of heating to remove snow from the structure, groundsmans expenses, etc. Annual costs are therefore around £2,500 for a 32 week winter.

The result is that we can afford to make the cost of hiring the courts attractively cheap. Before 9 am and after 9 pm the courts are free, apart from floodlight costs. Also Saturday afternoons and Sunday mornings are free periods and unbookable, facilitating ordinary 'club play'. Between 4 pm and 6 pm on weekdays the maximum cost including floodlights, when necessary, is £1.50. At all other times the basic cost of a court is £1 per hour. In addition the floodlights cost £1.50 per hour per court. Accordingly the cost of a court varies depending on the time and the lighting conditions between nil and £2.50 per hour.

The annual subscription was not increased to help pay for the airhall; we decided that it should be paid for by those who use it through court fees and not by members regardless of whether they use the facility.

The project was completed on 20 November 1984 and since then the airhall has proved a total success. Each court has average usage of about 60 hours per week. There is a profit element in the floodlight charges and the net income of the airhall, after the electricity costs, has averaged approximately £110 per week. Over a 32 week winter period — late September to early May — this gives a net income of about £3,500, comfortably above expenses. The airhall is dismantled for the summer months. Dismantling and erection takes six people about six hours to complete.

The airhall project was a gamble because we had no precedents to follow and without the substantial grant aid we would not have dared take the chance. We expected that the coaches would make good use of the airhall, and of course we expected those people — a small percentage of our membership — who already played regularly in the winter to benefit. What we could not predict was the impact on club members who did not fall into either of these categories, namely the average adult club player. We are pleased to say that these members have responded enthusiastically, and about 60% of our members are now playing regular winter tennis.

Into the financial equation should be added the increased membership of the club. As the dominant club in a small town, we did not expect to attract many establised players from other clubs as would happen in a city. What is happening however is that we are attracting and maintaining beginners or near beginners and lapsed former players. Over 40 new members joined the club over the winter period 1984/5 at a time when normally one would expect only a handful.

This increase in members has continued; despite the poor summer of 1985 our membership increased from 310 to 365 and our subscription income rose by 35%. The gross financial turnover of the club doubled in the year.

Boston is only a small town, and yet because of readily available coaching and the airhall, the club is large by most standards and beginning to produce a steady stream of new players. Our message is that if planning considerations permit, clubs should not dismiss the idea of an airhall. If a club in a small town like ours can make it work, surely there must be hundreds throughout the UK which could do the same.

COMPETITIVE TENNIS

COMPETITIONS

Inter-Club

Few players fail to enjoy a spirit of rivalry during the season whether in the form of team or individual tournaments. This spirit has been kindled by the growth in recent years of National, County and other league competitions and the consequent reduction in numbers of inter-club 'friendlies'.

The LTA/Slazenger Club Championships (men's and ladies'), organised in two divisions in collaboration with the LTA, are the major national competitions on the scene, with two pairs representing each club. The number of entries has increased by leaps and bounds since their inception in 1972. Most league and knock-out competitions result in clubs meeting other clubs from their area, whereas these National Championships are divided into 16 regions only so that new encounters are more likely. The extra travelling involved has been enjoyed by many although a club, say, in Penzance will not meet a club in Fife until the later stages. However, despite the prizes and trophies, players compete with the honour of their club at stake and this factor is largely responsible for the numerous epic battles that take place. The entry of your club should be automatic whatever its standard.

Another competition, which supplements the LTA/Slazenger event, is the Silk Cut Championship for which each affiliated club may enter one team (two men and two ladies). The early rounds are played on a postal, knock-out basis and lead to eight area finals each consisting of four teams, culminating in a national final. There are some interesting conditions attached to entry, among them a requirement to be over 18 years of age and a disqualification for anyone who has either competed at The Championships, Wimbledon or represented their County in more than two matches of the Inter-County Championships within the last ten years. The latter point of course is designed to encourage all clubs to compete in the knowledge that they are on far more level terms with their rivals.

Another national inter-club competition is the En-tout-cas Winter League organised by the Lawn Tennis Foundation. Teams, consisting of two men and two ladies, play one men's doubles, one ladies' doubles and two mixed doubles, and the competition is intended for average club players: those who have represented their County in any Inter-County Championship match in the past five years are not eligible. The early stages of the competition are played at about 20 different centres in England, Scotland and Wales, at which a number of teams play each other on a league basis through the winter. The centre winners then take part in a knock-out competition in four areas, and the four area winners play each other in a final weekend.

The extensive involvement of the Counties in senior tennis has yet to spread, in the same degree, to the juniors although there are growing numbers of junior leagues being organised. If, therefore, your club's youngsters are still among those to be catered for, there are two options open to you—either bring local clubs in your area together and start a league (you should discuss this with your County Secretary) or arrange some friendlies, in this case leaving as much of the work as possible to the junior section.

Competition against other juniors is an essential part of young players' training so do make sure that your juniors play as many matches as possible.

Individual

The major event in the calendar is of course the Refuge Assurance National Closed Championships which run from Spring to Autumn each year. Comprising both singles and doubles, this event is run on a postal basis climaxing in Area and National Finals.

Mention should be made of outside tournaments, such as the 'Nestle', which provide excellent opportunities for young club players of all standards to develop match play. There are, of course, a great many LTA Official tournaments both senior and junior and current lists of these can be obtained from the LTA.

Clubs that hold these annual tournaments take great pride in their organisation and provide a valuable service to the tennis-playing community. Any club wishing to stage such an event should contact the LTA to obtain advice and details.

Club Tournament

This is the one competition which every club player should support. It is simple to stage once the entries are received and the draw sheets (which can easily be made rather than bought—they are expensive) are put on display. Full details of the method of conducting a draw can be found under "Regulations for the Management of Lawn Tennis Tournaments" earlier in the Handbook.

The only other points to be decided are: (a) duration—one or two weeks set aside or perhaps three weekends, (b) timing—avoidance of the holiday period, mid-July to mid-September, and (c) a suitable referee, whose main task will probably be to make sure competitors keep to the relevant dates by which matches should be played.

However, a helpful document which was produced for events up to international standards is reprinted here for your interest.

NOTES OF GUIDANCE FOR REFEREES OF LAWN TENNIS TOURNAMENTS

A. MAIN PRINCIPLES

1. References

These notes must be read in conjunction with:

"Rules of the Lawn Tennis Association".

"Regulations for the Management of Lawn Tennis Tournaments" (which includes as Appendix F the LTA Code of Conduct);

"Rules of Tennis";

all of which are printed elsewhere in this Handbook. It is imperative that a tournament referee should have this handbook by him at all times when he is officiating together with a copy of the tournament prospectus (entry form) and any special documents which may be relevant.

2. Eligibility and Method of Appointment of Referee

(a) On this matter generally, see Tournament Regulations 8 and 16.

(b) It is undesirable that a Referee should be competing in the tournament, although in the case of an Honorary Referee this is not prohibited, or that he should act as umpire or linesman. If, however, he does any of these things he must appoint a substitute Referee for the period for which he is on court. He should be available throughout all play in the tournament, or appoint a substitute for any period of unavoidable absence, where possible in writing.

3. Appointment of Handicapper

If there are handicap events it is usual for the Referee to be appointed Handicapper also, but this is not automatic.

4. Rules and Appeals

(a) As well as having the Rules handy for reference, the Referee must be fully conversant with them and be able to make quick accurate decisions and take full responsibility for his actions.

(b) Concerning complaints to the Tournament Committee and appeals to the LTA from a decision of the Tournament Committee, see Tournament Regulations 32 and 33.

5. Availability of Competitors

The Referee may excuse a player for a specified period and may scratch a player who has not been excused but is not ready to play when called upon to do so. In deciding how strict he should be in such decisions, the Referee should bear in mind not only the likely effect on completion or non-completion of the schedule, but also that leniency to an offending competitor may sometimes be harshness to an innocent opponent.

6. Darkness, weather conditions etc.

The Referee may postpone all play, or play on specific courts, on account of darkness or the conditions of weather or ground.

B. Procedures

7. Arithmetical aspects of Order of Play

Before planning his programme in even the most general terms it is MOST IMPORTANT that the Referee should "do his sums".

(a) In any knock-out event the number of matches is found simply by subtracting 1 from the number of competitors (or pairs). The first sum is to ascertain the total number of matches in all events of the tournament. This must then be compared with the number of days of the tournament multiplied by the number of courts multiplied by number of possible matches per day (perhaps 8, but depending on time of starting and time of year).

(b) These figures reveal whether it is theoretically possible to complete the tournament without finding extra courts or making other emergency arrangements and also indicate how much reserve of time is available to offset bad weather, and whether any adjustment of the originally declared time of starting is necessary, or abandonment of lunch break etc.

(c) The intended number of matches for each day should then be decided. This cannot be based on an equal number of matches each day because (i) some "getting ahead" is essential to cover possible bad weather and other eventualities and (ii) on the last two or three days fewer matches are available to go on court simultaneously—e.g. on the final day it is presumably intended to play only the finals, at least in the level events. It is best to calculate backwards from the end of the tournament on the lines of the following example (based on arbitrary figures):

Example of calculation of number of matches required each day.

No. of Events—15 (5 level, 5 handicap, 5 junior)
No. of entries in each event—24
No. of days—6
No. of courts—10
Play from 10 a.m. to 8 p.m., say 8 matches per court per day
No. of matches to be fitted in—345
Working backwards, allow
15 finals on Saturday
30 semi-finals on Friday
60 quarter-finals on Thursday leaving
240 matches for the first 3 days

345

Although these 240 matches for the first 3 days suggest at first sight 80 each day, provision for bad weather would make 100 a better target for the first day, with 80 the second and 60 the third day. (It may also be noted that the first day matches tend to be easier and therefore shorter matches than those which follow later, another reason for making the first day's target greater than the more theoretical figure).

(d) Daily throughout the week there will be a calculation on the same lines as above, to cover the outstanding matches and the remaining days of play.

(e) It is desirable to arrange that likely semi-finalists for the level singles are played early in their other events so that they are a round ahead. Also players who are in many events—possibly juniors who are good enough to go far in senior events as well, or handicap players who seem to have been under-handicapped—should be pushed on, or in the closing stages matches for which there are plenty of courts will be held up for unavailability of the players. It is therefore not good practice to aim at a neat regular appearance of the draw sheet at the end of each day's play, but rather to ensure ability to complete the tournament.

(f) A prominent note should be kept of any players who have been excused for certain periods.

8. Prospectus (Entry Form)

At an early stage of the preparations for a tournament, i.e. before the prospectus is printed, the Referee should be consulted and advise the Committee on the events to be included; on any limits to the numbers of entries acceptable for each event; on the maximum number of events which any one competitor may enter; and on any notes to be published regarding dates or times of starting various events or the times at which competitors must first present themselves at the ground.

9. Draw

The Referee should attend the draw if possible. If, however, he is prevented, e.g. because he is officiating at another tournament, he should maintain touch with the secretary with a view to assisting with the seeding (if any) and with the pairing of competitors entering doubles events with "partner wanted". He should be sent a copy of the draw at the earliest possible moment after it has been made, so that he can start work on his order of play for the first day and also watch for likely snags and possible errors or queries.

10. Handicapping

As far as possible this should be done before the draw is made and incorporated in the printing or writing out of the draw. Even so, decisions may have to be deferred on some competitors for whom insufficient information is available: perhaps, if they are in level events also, they can be assessed after they have played one of these.

11. Responsibility for Order of Play

The Referee's duties include deciding the Order of Play and ensuring that there are adequate arrangements for the allocation of courts and the despatch of the players to them at the right time, with umpire and linesmen, balls, ballboys, and score books (or such of these as are used in the tournament). On completion of the matches he receives the completed score books and records the results on his master copy of the draw. In all of this the Referee should have as much help as he needs from committee members, office staff (if available), and any representative of the ball supplier or sponsor who may be present: in the larger tournaments his requirement of such help will be considerable. On the score books for handicap events the Referee should himself write the handicaps of each player or pair and the combined handicap at which the match is to be played. It is very frustrating for players to arrive in response to a listing which merely shows, e.g. "All Event 3 at 2 p.m." or even as is sometimes seen "All handicap events 2 p.m.", when in all probability it is physically impossible for all such matches to be played together at that time. Perhaps even worse, some opponents may have leave of absence.

12. Publication of Order of Play

(a) If possible, a full order of play for the following day should be published in good time each evening, listing the matches by players' **names** on a 'followed by' basis.

(b) If one player is to appear more than once on a day's list, his matches should be spaced out so that his second opponent is not at risk of having a long wait for the previous match to finish.

(c) Singles should be given priority over doubles in level events, where possible.

13. Allocation of Courts

This is usually the responsibility of one or more Committee Members but in practice much help with this is given by the ball supplier's representative if he is present. He is usually experienced in the job as well as having the advantage of knowing by sight many of the visiting players. If no such representative is available, this is an important job which it is in the Referee's best interests to see capably filled, because any loss of time between matches means fewer matches played in the day and a programme behind time.

14. Umpires

Except in the largest tournaments, where the job may be taken over by a representative of the British Tennis Umpires' Association, and the smallest, where nowadays umpires may be largely dispensed with, a Committee Member or other assistant should be recruited to obtain umpires.

NOTES